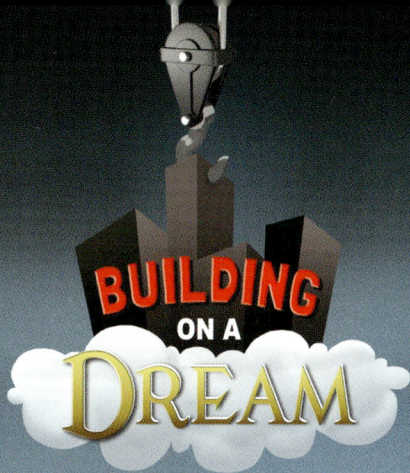

BUILDING ON A DREAM

THE LOUVRE

Nicole K. Orr

PURPLE TOAD
PUBLISHING

PURPLE TOAD
PUBLISHING

Printing   1   2   3   4   5   6   7   8   9

BUILDING ON A DREAM

Big Ben
The Burj Khalifa
The Eiffel Tower
The Empire State Building
Fallingwater
The Flatiron Building
The Golden Gate Bridge
The Great Wall of China
The International Space Station

The Leaning Tower of Pisa
The Louvre
The Space Needle
The Statue of Liberty
The Sydney Opera House
The Taj Mahal
The Trevi Fountain
The White House

Library of Congress Cataloging-in-Publication Data
Orr, Nicole, K.
   Building on a Dream: The Louvre / Written by Nicole K. Orr.
      p. cm.
Includes bibliographic references, glossary and index.
ISBN 9781624694394
1. The Louvre—Musée du Louvre—History—Juvenile Literature. 2. France—Paris—Art—Juvenile Literature. 3. France—18th Century—Kings and Rulers—Juvenile Literature. I. Series: Building on a Dream: The Louvre
   N2030.A64 2019
   708.4/361
Library of Congress Control Number: 2018944205

eBook ISBN: 9781624694387

ABOUT THE AUTHOR: Nicole K. Orr has been writing for as long as she's known how to hold a pen. She is the author of more than a dozen books by Purple Toad Publishing and has won National Novel Writing Month ten times. Orr lives in Portland, Oregon, and camps under the stars whenever she can. When she isn't writing, she's traveling the world or taking road-trips.

CONTENTS

Rue de Rivoli

Pavillon de Marsan

Tuileries Garden

Richelieu Entrance

Pyramid Entrance

Sully Entrance

Denon Entrance

Porte des Arts

Porte des Lions

Pavillon de Flore

La Seine

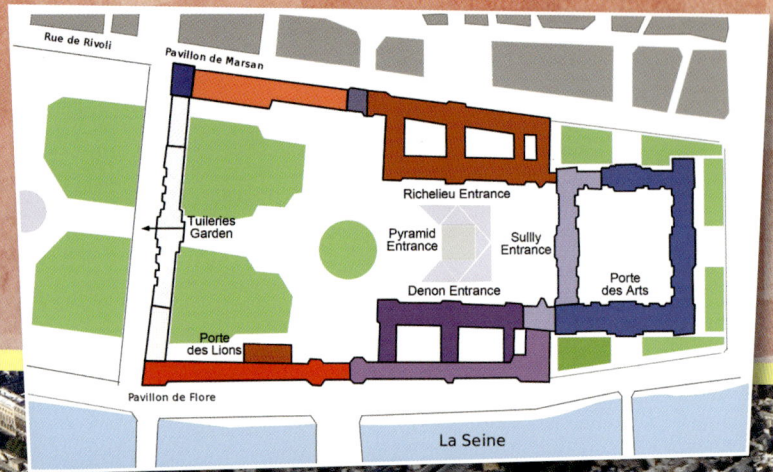

The Louvre Museum stretches along the Seine River. The glass pyramids are at the center of the museum's grounds.

The Phantom of the Louvre

The Louvre (LOOV-ruh) in Paris, France, is the largest museum in the world. It has more art, more rooms, and more to do than you could see in three months! If the Louvre could talk, what would it say? If you could rewind time and peek into history, who would you see walking through the grand hallways? The answers could include everything from ghosts to gnomes to the Louvre's very own Phantom.

The museum is huge. It has three wings: Richelieu Wing, Denon Wing, and Sully Wing. The Richelieu and Denon Wings stretch for more than two city blocks. They are connected at one end by the Sully Wing, which is built in a square around the Cour Carrée courtyard. Each of the Sully's four corridors is almost one city block long. On the opposite end of the grounds is the Tuileries [TWIL-er-eez] Garden.

The Louvre has five stories—but two of them are underground. Visitors have five entrances to choose from. Most tourists use the Louvre's striking glass pyramid entrance in the center of the grounds. First, they go down two stories. Then they take escalators up to one of the three wings. Those who use the Porte des Lions (Lions' Door) may have a shorter wait to get inside. This nearly hidden access point is near the Tuileries Garden, guarded by two lion statues. It is in the Denon Wing and is the closest entrance to the museum's most famous painting, Leonardo Da Vinci's *Mona Lisa.* A third entrance, Porte des Arts, goes straight into the Sully Wing from the street closest to the Seine (SAYN) River.

As a fortress, the Louvre was built to keep people out. It was completely different from the inviting complex of today.

Long before the Louvre was a museum, it was a fortress. Because of this, the building and grounds saw a lot of violence. Its dark history inspires superstition, and visitors claim they have seen strange things. Some tourists believed they saw spirits in the world's most famous paintings. There were those who saw a gnome in red clothing.

There were also reports of the Phantom of the Louvre. Also named Belphegor, the Phantom of the Louvre was a mummy brought back to life in a novel by French author Arthur Bernede. The story of a masked person sneaking around the Louvre was so popular, it was turned into a comic book, an animated TV series, and three movies.[1]

Very little of the original fortress is left, but this wall is an exception. It is the base of the fortress.

If you make a trip to Paris, you might find yourself in one of the spooky hallways of the Louvre. If you do, keep an ear and an eye out. You just might see a gnome dressed in red, hear a ghost whisper in your ear, or even meet the Phantom of the Louvre himself! One ghost you probably won't see wandering around is that of the architect. Despite a lot of research, the identity of the original architect is still a total mystery. All we know is that the project began with royalty.

As the halls wind around under stone arches, ornate stone columns appear like something straight out of a medieval dungeon.

A 19th-century painting by Jean-Baptiste Mauzaisse shows Philippe-Auguste watching as the Tour du Louvre (Louvre Tower) is raised in the year 1200.

From Soldiers to Kings

For many of the world's most famous buildings, one particular architect oversaw the entire project. This was not true of the Louvre. There were so many different people involved in designing the museum, building it, and adding on to it, it is impossible to give any one person more credit than another. The purpose of the structure, too, kept changing over the years.

The Louvre in 1190 did not house any art at all. Instead, it was a fortress, with walls 100 feet tall. At the center was a 98-foot-tall tower called the Grosse Tour. Circling the fortress were four moats. The fortress was where villagers would go for protection—and in 1190, protection was important. The King of France was afraid that Viking warriors were coming to Paris. Since he was especially worried that the Vikings would come by water, the king had a castle built where the fortress met the Seine River. While an attack never came, the King of France had begun what would one day become the foundation for the Louvre.[1]

Fortresses tended to be dirty and uncomfortable. In 1364, King Charles V ordered his architect Raymond du Temple to transform the fortress into a palace. To make the structure more beautiful, Temple put in fancy carved windows and a spiral staircase named the Grand Vis. These changes did make the fortress a nicer place to live, but in 1527, King Francis I decided it wasn't nice enough. He had the Grosse Tour torn down and gave his architect, Pierre Lescot, the job of making the

Pierre Lescot

building a true palace. While no one name can be said to be entirely responsible for the Louvre, Lescot's name comes the closest.

The palace Lescot helped create was built on top of the fortress that had already been there. The materials used in the foundation of the older structure ended up supporting the new one. The palace was built using the Italian Renaissance style, so decoration was very important.

During the many years that royalty lived in the Louvre Palace, a lot of changes were made. Kings and their families were picky about where they slept and would switch bedrooms often. New wings were constantly being added. Bedrooms were made larger. New buildings were added around the outside of the palace where the fortress' moats used to be. This time in the Louvre's history saw the fastest growth of the building.

The royal families eventually went to live elsewhere, and the Louvre was left empty until around 1564. That year, Queen Catherine de Medici ordered that a new building be placed near the Louvre. It was called the Tuileries Palace—a much more comfortable place than the Louvre.

Tuileries Palace was quieter—and cleaner—than the Louvre.

The Waterside Gallery (Galerie du Bord de l'Eau) is also called the Grande Galerie.

In 1572, King Henri IV approached the Louvre with a new set of goals. Instead of trying to make the Louvre fancier or larger, he decided to make the Tuileries Palace and the Louvre one structure. The first step was the completion of the Waterside Gallery. This passageway was 1,476 feet long from end to end. It allowed royalty to walk between the Tuileries and Louvre palaces without having to go outside.

The king wanted this hallway to be beautiful. He hired architects Louis Metezeau and Jacques II Androuet du Cerceau. He told them both to decorate the walkway, but to start at different ends. This would give the royal families two different architectural styles to enjoy. At this time, the King's Gallery was built as well.[2]

King Henri never walked this beautiful hallway. He was murdered in 1610.

In 1871, the Tuileries Palace was destroyed by fire. The burning of the palace would not be the last catastrophe the museum experienced. War was coming too.

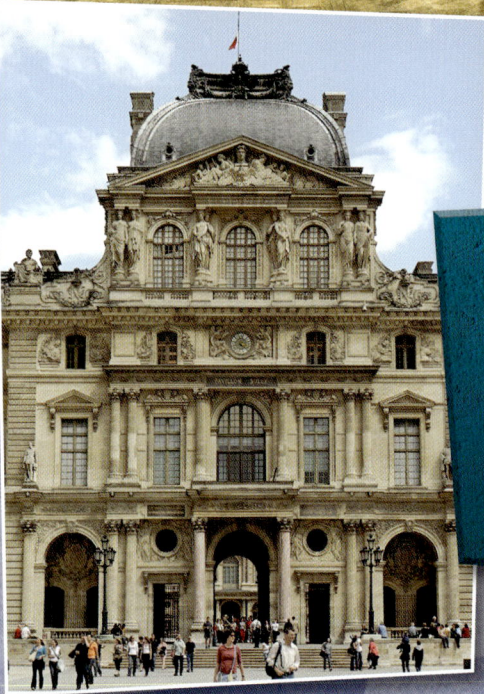

The Apollo Gallery (above) shines as brightly as the sun god the room is named after. The Sully Entrance (left) reflects the Italian Renaissance style of architecture.

Constantly Changing

Between 1624 and 1672, the Louvre was remodeled and added to almost constantly. One of the most significant additions was the Clock Pavilion in 1639. Also referred to as the Pavillion de Sully, the Clock Pavilion was added to the Sully Wing. Visitors could walk into the first floor of the Sully Wing and find themselves standing in what was once the moat of the old fortress. This wing also housed the oldest hall in the Louvre, the Hall of St. Louis.

The Apollo Gallery was finished in 1664. It was one long hallway with a domed ceiling and held expensive pieces such as the French crown jewels. More than 20 artists helped with the designs. Two of the more famous artists were Eugene Delacroix and Charles Le Brun. The second of these would later play an even bigger role in the museum's design.

Beginning in 1660, architect Louis Le Vau was made responsible for the Louvre's remodels and repairs. When Le Vau was asked to partner with another architect, he wasn't happy. Because of political differences, the partner, Jean-Baptiste Colbert, told Le Vau to stop all construction. He put together a *petit conseil* ("small council") in 1667 to help create a single vision for the project. On this team were Colbert, Le Vau, a scientist named Claude Perrault, and the official Chief Painter to the King, Charles Le Brun. Together, the four men came up with a new set of designs. Construction could finally continue.[1]

Eventually, the royal families decided that their royal power should be based out of Versailles. When they moved out of the Louvre in 1682, the grounds were mostly abandoned. The building remained empty for nearly one hundred years. In 1756, construction on the walls of the Cour Carrée began again. The walls of this central courtyard were finished and a roof was added.

The Louvre was not considered a museum in 1791, but it was considered a place to keep important pieces of art or advancements in science. It wasn't until 1793 that the building was opened to the general public. The word *museum* was not used, but that's exactly what it was. Just a few years later, the Louvre's name was changed. Emperor Napoleon Bonaparte I donated more artwork, most of which was won during his battles in Italy. In 1803, the Louvre was temporarily renamed the Musée Napoleon.[2]

A passageway looks out on the Cour Carrée. Natural light showcases the art and design of the Louvre, both inside and out.

The Arc de Triomphe du Carrousel was originally built as an entrance to Tuileries Palace. The arch survived the fire that destroyed the palace.

In 1806, Napoleon Bonaparte I had begun construction of the Arc de Triomphe du Carrousel. This arch honored the recent victories of his army. It was 75 feet wide, almost 23 feet deep, and 62 feet high. On top of the arch, four bronze horses pull a chariot. A statue of Bonaparte himself was supposed to be added but never was.

When Bonaparte left the Louvre, he took the statues with him as trophies. In order to preserve history, replacement statues were later provided. The Arc de Triomphe du Carrousel was completed in 1808 and placed at the historical axes. This was the spot where all the Louvre's buildings came together.[3]

Napoleon Bonaparte

Most of the Spanish and Italian artworks are kept in the Denon Wing.

Beginning in 1826, the Louvre went through many different owners, architects, and changes. More and more artwork arrived at the museum from all over the world. Pieces arrived from Egypt and Italy. Sections of the museum were given new themes, including Spanish, Medieval, and Renaissance.

Catastrophe struck in 1871 when the Paris Commune Revolt burned the Tuileries Palace. The Louvre wasn't damaged, but the Tuileries Palace could not be saved. Efforts were made to rebuild the palace, but in 1883, crews gave up.

More danger faced the Louvre between 1938 and 1945. World War II impacted Paris in a lot of ways, but one of the biggest was the need to protect artwork from Nazi soldiers. The war officially began September 3, 1939. More than 3,690 paintings were loaded into crates, then loaded onto trucks, ambulances, taxis, and even privately owned cars. Every piece of

Venus de Milo **was hidden in the countryside during World War II.**

German Field Marshal Gerd von Rundstedt (third from left) helped organize the Nazi occupation of the Louvre.

art was labeled yellow, green, or red as a way of marking its importance. These pieces were then transported to secret places in the French countryside.

Nazi soldiers took control of Paris, and in September 1940 they reopened the Louvre. Hardly anyone visited the museum because most of the rooms were empty. The Nazis then moved in artworks that they had stolen during the war. It wasn't until August 1944, when the war was over, that the Louvre's hidden artworks could go home again.[4] Most of the stolen artwork was eventually restored to their rightful owners.

Kings, queens, architects, and Nazi soldiers all came and went from the great museum. Each left their mark, making the building bigger, better, and more beautiful. In 1973, the Louvre finally belonged to Paris and its people as a public museum.

I.M. Pei took building the glass pyramid so seriously, he kept the fact he'd been offered the job a secret for four months! He wanted to be sure he was up to the task before he said yes.

Modern Touches

While tourism in the 1970s was great, the Louvre's ability to accommodate all the visitors was not. The entrances were too small. The many hallways were so complicated, people often got lost. No one, sometimes not even the employees of the Louvre, could remember exactly what was in each of the wings. Adding a new entrance would help solve these problems. The only decision that remained was choosing an architect. In 1983, Ieoh Ming Pei was given the responsibility.

At first, the people of Paris were upset. I.M. Pei was a Chinese-born American, and not French at all. Many locals also felt that the Louvre did not need any additions; it was lovely enough as it was. The people of Paris changed their opinions, both when they saw the finished entrance for themselves and when they saw how much the tourists liked it.

From the start, I.M. Pei took his job very seriously. The entrance had to lead from the ground down into the lower floors of the museum. He certainly did not want his masterpiece to look like a subway station. He wanted to create a beacon for the courtyard. Pei decided that to build something great, perhaps he should use something great for inspiration. He chose the Pyramid of Giza in Egypt. When he was finished, his structure would be the exact same proportions as the one in Egypt. At 116 feet wide and 70 feet high, this was just the first of five pyramids Pei would build. The way these structures were positioned would be very important. When the sun shone, the pyramids would

The rigging system that holds the pyramid together was created by Navtec rod rigging of Littleton, Massachusetts. The same technique was used in building yachts.

direct the light down into the museum below.[1]

The pyramids also needed to be beautiful. Pei designed the main pyramid with 675 diamond-shaped panes and 118 triangular panes. The glass was specially crafted to be as clear as possible. Instead of windows, visitors would see a jewel-like piece of art.[2]

Since the pyramids were made largely of glass, people feared they would break easily. To protect the panes from wind, structural glazing was used. This special sealant fused the glass panes to the aluminum and steel frame. When the wind blows, the frame handles the pressure instead of the glass. The entire pyramid required 95 tons of steel and 105 tons of aluminum. Aluminum was a good choice because it would make the pyramid stronger, but not heavier. To give it even more strength, 128 girders and 16 cables were used.[3]

In 1989, the new entrance was opened to the public. By this point, Pei had also added a few fountains and pools. These watery additions would make the pyramids look as if they were floating.

Pei contributed to the Louvre again in 1993. His American organization, Pei Cobb Freed and Partners, added a fifth pyramid to the museum. This pyramid could not be seen from the courtyard. It hangs upside down from the lower-floor ceiling and points to a tiny stone pyramid beneath it. To visit it, people have to enter the Carrousel

The inverted pyramid allows natural light to stream into the underground mall.

du Louvre, the museum's new shopping mall. From there, they can stand below the upside-down pyramid and look through it to the sky.[4]

In the end, the people of Paris and tourists were thrilled with the new pyramids. There was no one more pleased with the changes than I.M. Pei himself. Once the project was complete, he said, "I hope to do many more things, but never again will I have another opportunity like the Louvre."[5]

When visitors have finished admiring the inverted pyramid, they might want to find something to eat. There are more than 15 options, including full-service and fast-food restaurants, cafés, and smaller food stands. Other dining choices are Le Café Diane, located inside the Tuileries Garden, and the Angelina tea room, which serves hot chocolate so thick, you could eat it with a spoon.

The modern look and shopping area have proved a success. By 2002, after these additions, attendance at the Louvre had doubled. By 2017, the entrance, lobby, and shopping area had been improved to handle the Louvre's nearly 10 million visitors per year.

Mona Lisa is one of the most sought after paintings by thieves in the world. In 2009, a woman threw a mug of tea at the painting. Because of the protective glass, the mug shattered and the painting was unharmed.

Visiting the Grande Louvre

Architects come to the Louvre—also known as the Grande Louvre—to see a building unlike any other in the world. Artists come to see masterpieces made in every style there is. Lovers of music come to hear concerts in the museum's underground auditorium. Travelers come to stand in the spot where so many others have stood before: kings, queens, painters, Nazis, builders, and even thieves.

With 35,000 works of art organized into eight different departments, there is something for everyone at the Louvre. An astounding 650,000 square feet is dedicated just to gallery space. If you wanted to see absolutely everything there is to see, you'd have to walk over eight miles. It would also take more than three months—and that's if you spent only 30 seconds looking at each thing! Whether you're one of the 2,000 employees who run the Louvre each day or one of the millions of visitors each year, that's still a lot of walking.[1]

One of the paintings at this museum is so famous, even people who don't know much about art have heard its name. The *Mona Lisa* is considered one of the best-known pieces of art in the world. At 30 by 21 inches, it is also quite small. This painting is about the same size as the top of a school desk.[2]

The *Mona Lisa* is so popular, it was stolen from the Louvre in 1911. The people of Paris were so sad about this, they left flowers where the painting used to hang. A few years later, the painting was returned. The Louvre is now very protective of it. In fact, they keep it behind bulletproof glass at all times.

Security guards stay close to *Mona Lisa*.

Bulletproof glass is just one way that the Louvre's artworks are protected. The museum employs more than 1,000 security guards. Every hour, every day, and every year, there are guards in place throughout the building. High-tech cameras and alarms help the guards protect the tourists and the valuables they came to see.

After the *Mona Lisa*, the *Venus de Milo* is probably the most famous of the artworks in the Louvre. It is beautiful, even though it is missing several pieces. This

When *Venus de Milo* was found on an island, her arms were found with her. The people who discovered the statue thought the arms were too "rough" and left them behind.

statue was discovered on an island in Greece called Milo. Some people have said that it is based on a sea goddess. Others have said it must be a statue of Venus, the Roman goddess of love, beauty, and victory.[3]

The Cour Marly features *The Marly Horses* by Guillaume Coustou. These statues—of two horses and two men—are mounted on high pedestals. With great strength, these men attempt to hold back and calm down the fighting horses. The message behind the statue is thought to be the battle between people's human side and animal side.[4]

If you want something less serious, you could step into the Sully Wing and visit *The Cheat with the Ace of Diamonds*. Done by Georges de la Tour, this painting has so much action, you'll want to linger a few

The Cheat with the Ace of Diamonds has been on display in the Louvre since 1972.

The world actually has two Louvre Museums. Abu Dhabi, in the United Arab Emirates, opened its own Louvre in November 2017. Paris, however, is willing to let Abu Dhabi use the Louvre name for only 30 years and six months.

minutes. First, there are four people playing cards at a table. Second, two of the players are looking at each other as if sharing a secret. Third, the player on the left has cards hidden in his belt that will likely win him the game—if he isn't found out first![5]

There are a lot of famous buildings in the world. Most of them leave impressions on the people who visit them. The Louvre is different. This is true for the soldiers, kings, or artists of the past. It is also true for the architects, travelers, music lovers, and artists of today. No matter who you are or where you are from, a visit to the Louvre will leave you forever changed.

1190 King Philippe Auguste builds a fortress where the Louvre will one day be.

1364 King Charles V orders Raymond du Temple to turn the fortress into a palace.

1527 The fortress is torn down, but its foundation remains.

1546 King Francis I orders construction to begin on the Louvre Palace.

1564 Construction begins on the Tuileries Palace.

1595 The Waterside Gallery is built. It connects the Louvre Palace and the Tuileries Palace.

1639 The Clock Pavilion is added to the Louvre.

1667 Jean-Baptiste Colbert forms a council to help decide on designs for the Louvre.

1793 The Louvre opens to the public as a museum.

1808 Arc de Triomphe du Carrousel is completed.

1871 The Tuileries Palace burns down.

1911 The *Mona Lisa* is stolen from the Louvre. It is returned a few years later.

1939 World War II begins, launching one of the biggest evacuations of artworks in Europe's history.

1944 After the war, the artwork is moved back into the Louvre when the Seine risks flooding the museum.

1973 The Louvre becomes a public museum.

1989 I.M. Pei's Louvre Pyramid is finished.

2012 The Louvre is announced as the most-visited museum in the world for the year.

2016 The Louvre is temporarily closed and the artworks moved after massive flooding.

2017 The temporary Abu Dhabi Louvre opens to the public.

2018 In January, the museum closes and artworks are moved again as the Seine rises to risky flood levels.

Chapter 1

1. Nesselson, Lisa. "Belphegor: Phantom of the Louvre." *Variety*, April 4, 2001. http://variety.com/2001/film/reviews/belphegor-phantom-of-the-louvre-1200467990/

Chapter 2

1. Maranzani, Barbara. "6 Things You May Not Know About the Louvre." *History*, August, 2013. http://www.history.com/news/six-things-you-may-not-know-about-the-louvre

2. "History of the Louvre from Fortress to Palace Then to the Louvre Museum in Paris." EUTOURING, n.d. http://www.eutouring.com/history_louvre_fortress_palace.html

Chapter 3

1. Ranogajec, Paul A. "Claude Perrault, East Facade of the Louvre." Khan Academy, n.d. https://www.khanacademy.org/humanities/monarchy-enlightenment/baroque-art1/france/a/claude-perrault-east-facade-of-the-louvre

2. "History of the Louvre from Fortress to Palace then to the Louvre Museum in Paris." EUTOURING, n.d. http://www.eutouring.com/history_louvre_fortress_palace.html

3. "Arc de Triomphe du Carrousel in Paris." EUTOURING, n.d. http://www.eutouring.com/arc_de_triomphe_du_carrousel.html

4. "How France Hid the Louvre's Masterpieces During WWII." *Twistedsifter*, May 2013. http://twistedsifter.com/2013/05/louvre-and-mona-lisa-world-war-2/

Chapter 4

1. "The Louvre Pyramid: History, Architecture, and Legend." *Paris City Vision*, n.d. https://www.pariscityvision.com/en/paris/museums/louvre-museum/the-louvre-pyramid-history-architecture-legend

2. "Louvre Pyramid." *A View on Cities*, n.d. http://www.aviewoncities.com/paris/louvrepyramid.htm

3. Ibid.

4. Ibid.

5. "Le Grand Louvre: I.M. Pei's Fusion of Design and Technology." *Academic*, April 1992. http://www.academic.umn.edu/layon/portfolio2000/Writing/pei.html

Chapter 5

1. "10 Interesting Facts About the Louvre." *The List Love*, May 12, 2015. http://thelistlove.com/10-interesting-facts-about-the-louvre/

2. Puchko, Kristy. "14 Things You Didn't Know About the *Mona Lisa*." *Mental Floss*, April 1, 2015. http://mentalfloss.com/article/62280/14-things-you-didnt-know-about-mona-lisa

3. Alexander, Lisa. "Visiting the Louvre Museum: 15 Top Highlights, Tips, and Tours." *Planetware*, n.d. http://www.planetware.com/paris/louvre-f-p-l.htm

4. Ibid.

5. Ibid.

Works Consulted

"10 Interesting Facts About the Louvre." *The List Love.* May 12, 2015. http://thelistlove. com/10-interesting-facts-about-the-louvre/#

Clark, Josh. "How the Louvre Works." *How Stuff Works.* https://adventure.howstuffworks. com/destinations/landmarks/museums-tours/louvre1.htm

James, Rebecca. "These Secrets About the Louvre Museum Will Surprise You." *Architectural Digest.* April 26, 2017. https://www.architecturaldigest.com/story/secrets-you-never-knew-about-paris-louvre-museum

Maranzani, Barbara. "6 Things You May Not Know About the Louvre." *History.com.* August 9, 2013. http://www.history.com/news/six-things-you-may-not-know-about-the-louvre

Szalay, Jessie. "The Louvre Museum: Facts, Paintings, & Tickets." *Live Science.* May 10, 2013. https://www.livescience.com/31935-louvre-museum.html

Traub, Courtney. "A Short History of the Louvre: Intriguing Facts." *Trip Savvy.* May 15, 2015. https://www.tripsavvy.com/a-short-history-of-the-louvre-1618642

Books

Brown, Jeff, and Macky Pamintuan. *Flat Stanley's Worldwide Adventures: Framed in France.* New York: Harper Collins, 2014.

Delafosse, Claude, and Gallimard Jeunesse. *The Louvre.* Abingdon, Oxfordshire: Moonlight Publishing, 2012.

DiPucchio, Kelly, and Christian Robinson. *Antoinette.* New York: Atheneum Books, 2017.

Evans, Brooke DiGiovanni. *Are You an Art Sleuth? Look, Discover, Learn!* Beverly, MA: Rockport Publishers, 2016.

Foster, Jane. *Jane Foster's Cities: Paris.* New York: Little Bee Books, 2017.

McMenemy, Sarah. *The Louvre: A Three-Dimensional Expanding Museum Guide.* London: Walker Books, 2013.

On the Internet

History: Louvre
http://www.history.com/this-day-in-history/louvre-museum-opens

The Louvre Museum
http://www.louvre.fr/en

Time Out: Paris City Guide
https://www.timeout.com/paris/en/things-to-do/city-guide

architect (AR-kih-tekt)—A person who builds or designs things.

auditorium (aw-dih-TOR-ee-um)—A large hall or lecture room.

beacon (BEE-kun)—A bright light used as a signal to warn people or to help them find a location..

escalator (ES-kuh-lay-tur)—A set of moving stairs that carry people from one floor to another.

evacuation (ee-vak-yoo-AY-shun)—The complete removal of something's contents.

exhibit (ek-ZIH-bit)—A display of art or objects.

fortress (FOR-tres)—A well-protected building or town, usually enclosed by strong walls.

goddess (GOD-es)—A female god.

masterpiece (MAS-ter-pees)—A great artistic work.

moat (MOHT)—A body of water surrounding a building to protect it.

Nazi (NOT-zee)—A military follower of World War II German leader Adolf Hitler.

pedestal (PEH-des-tul)—A high platform.

political (poh-LIH-tih-kul)—Concerned with politics or government; relating to the interaction of powerful people.

proportion (proh-POR-shun)—Having the same relationship of the parts to the whole.

remodel (ree-MOD-ul)—To redo or update.

superstition (soo-per-STIH-shun)—Belief in magic, chance, ghosts, and other unexplainable events.

wing—A section or portion of a large building.

Index

Pearson Australia
(a division of Pearson Australia Group Pty Ltd)
707 Collins Street, Melbourne, Victoria 3008
PO Box 23360, Melbourne, Victoria 8012
www.pearson.com.au

Copyright © Pearson Australia 2019
(a division of Pearson Australia Group Pty Ltd)
First published 2019 by Pearson Australia
2022 2021 2020 2019
10 9 8 7 6 5 4 3

Lead Publisher: Misal Belvedere, Malcolm Parsons
Project Manager: Michelle Thomas
Production Editors: Casey McGrath, Virginia O'Brien
Lead Development Editor: Amy Sparkes
Development Editor: Haeyean Lee
Editor: David Meagher, Marta Veroni
Designer: Anne Donald
Rights & Permissions Editor: Samantha Russell-Tulip
Senior Publishing Services Analyst: Rob Curulli
Proofreaders: Sally McInnes, Jeanette Birtles
Indexer: Bruce Gillespie
Illustrator: DiacriTech
Printed in China

ISBN 978 1 4886 1928 1

Pearson Australia Group Pty Ltd   ABN 40 004 245 943

A catalogue record for this book is available from the National Library of Australia

Disclaimer

The selection of internet addresses (URLs) provided for this book was valid at the time of publication and was chosen as being appropriate for use as a secondary education research tool. However, due to the dynamic nature of the internet, some addresses may have changed, may have ceased to exist since publication, or may inadvertently link to sites with content that could be considered offensive or inappropriate. While the authors and publisher regret any inconvenience this may cause readers, no responsibility for any such changes or unforeseeable errors can be accepted by either the authors or the publisher.

Some of the images used in *Pearson Chemistry 12 New South Wales Student Book* might have associations with deceased Indigenous Australians. Please be aware that these images might cause sadness or distress in Aboriginal or Torres Strait Islander communities.

Practical activities

All practical activities, including the illustrations, are provided as a guide only and the accuracy of such information cannot be guaranteed. Teachers must assess the appropriateness of an activity and take into account the experience of their students and the facilities available. Additionally, all practical activities should be trialled before they are attempted with students and a risk assessment must be completed. All care should be taken whenever any practical activity is conducted: appropriate protective clothing should be worn, the correct equipment used, and the appropriate preparation and clean-up procedures followed. Although all practical activities have been written with safety in mind, Pearson Australia and the authors do not accept any responsibility for the information contained in or relating to the practical activities, and are not liable for any loss and/or injury arising from or sustained as a result of conducting any of the practical activities described in this book.

The Chemistry Education Association (CEA) was formed in 1977 by a group of teachers from secondary and tertiary institutions. It aims to promote the teaching of chemistry, particularly in secondary schools. The CEA has established a tradition of providing up-to-date text, electronic material and support resources for both students and teachers, and professional development opportunities for teachers.

PEARSON CHEMISTRY 12

NEW SOUTH WALES

Writing and development team

We are grateful to the following people for their time and expertise in contributing to the *Pearson Chemistry 12 New South Wales* project.

Drew Chan
President of the CEA and Teacher
Coordinating Author

Chris Commons
Educator
Author and Reviewer

Penny Commons
Educator
Author and Skills and Assessment Author

Emma Finlayson
Teacher
Author and Reviewer

Kathryn Hillier
Teacher and Lecturer
Author

Bob Hogendoorn
Science Consultant and Assessor
Author

Raphael Johns
Laboratory technician
Safety consultant

Louise Lennard
Teacher
Author

Mick Moylan
Chemistry Outreach Fellow
Author

Pat O'Shea
Teacher
Author

Jim Sturgiss
Science Consultant
Author

Paul Waldron
Teacher
Author

Erin Bruns
Teacher
Contributing Author

Warrick Clarke
Science Communicator
Contributing Author

Lanna Derry
Teacher
Contributing Author

Vicky Ellis
Teacher
Contributing Author

Elizabeth Freer
Teacher
Contributing Author

Simon Gooding
Teacher
Contributing Author

Elissa Huddart
Teacher
Contributing Author

Maria Porter
Teacher
Contributing Author

Geoff Quinton
President of ASTA and Teacher
Contributing Author

Bob Ross
Teacher
Contributing Author

Patrick Sanders
Teacher
Contributing Author

Robert Sanders
Education Consultant
Contributing Author

Reuben Bolt
Director of the Nura Gili Indigenous Programs Unit, UNSW
Reviewer

Sue Colman
Education consultant
Reviewer

Lyndon Smith
Curriculum developer
Reviewer

Trish Weekes
Science Literacy Consultant

Maria Woodbury
Teacher
Reviewer

Katrina Liston
Scientist
Answer checker

Brenden McDonnell
Teacher
Answer checker

Jamie Selby-Pham
Scientist
Answer checker

Sophie Selby-Pham
Scientist
Answer checker

Gregory White
Scientist
Answer checker

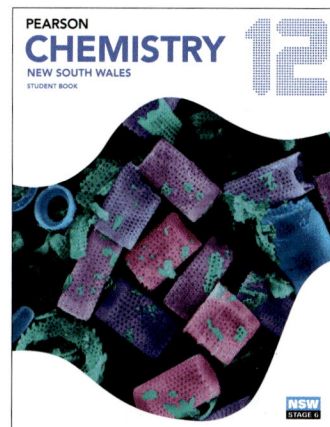

Contents

How to use this book

Pearson Chemistry 12 New South Wales

Pearson Chemistry 12 New South Wales has been written to fully align with the new Stage 6 syllabus for New South Wales Chemistry. The book covers Modules 5 to 8 in an easy-to-use resource. Explore how to use this book below.

Chapter opener

The chapter opening page links the syllabus to the chapter content. Key content addressed in the chapter is clearly listed.

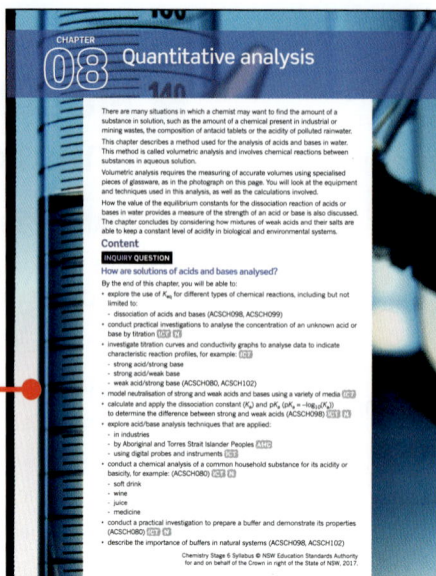

Section

Each chapter is clearly divided into manageable sections of work. Best-practice literacy and instructional design are combined with high-quality, relevant photos and illustrations to help students better understand the ideas or concepts being developed.

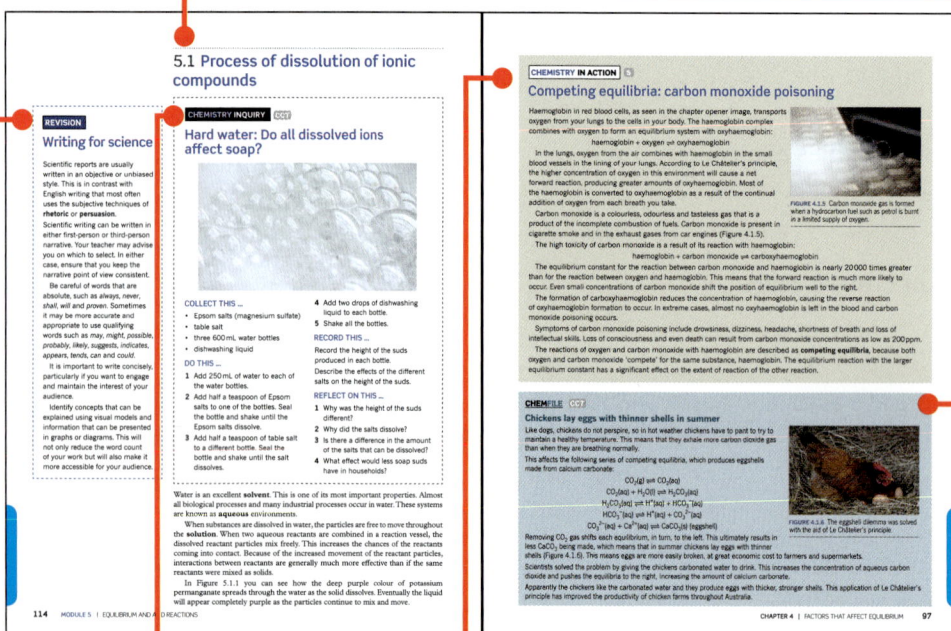

ChemFile

ChemFiles include a range of interesting and real-world examples to engage students.

Revision box

Revision boxes are used to remind students of vital concepts previously covered that are required for current learning.

Chemistry Inquiry

Chemistry Inquiry features are inquiry-based activities that assist students to discover concepts before learning about them. They encourage students to think about what happens in the world and how science can provide explanations.

Chemistry in Action

Chemistry in Action boxes place chemistry in an applied situation or a relevant context. They refer to the nature and practice of chemistry, its applications and associated issues, and the historical development of its concepts and ideas.

Worked examples

Worked examples are set out in steps that show thinking and working. This format greatly enhances student understanding by clearly linking underlying logic to the relevant calculations. Each Worked example is followed by a Try yourself activity. This mirror problem allows students to immediately test their understanding.

Highlight box

Highlight boxes focus students' attention on important information such as key definitions, formulae and summary points.

Additional content

Additional content includes material that goes beyond the core content of the syllabus. They are intended for students who wish to expand their depth of understanding in a particular area.

Section summary

Each section has a summary to help students consolidate the key points and concepts.

SkillBuilder

A SkillBuilder outlines a method or technique. They are instructive and self-contained. They step students through the skill to support science application.

Section review questions

Each section finishes with key questions to test students' understanding of and ability to recall the key concepts of the section.

How to use this book

Chapter review

Each chapter finishes with a list of key terms covered in the chapter and a set of questions to test students' ability to apply the knowledge gained from the chapter.

Module review

Each module finishes with a set of questions, including multiple choice and short answer. These assist students in drawing together their knowledge and understanding, and applying it to these types of questions.

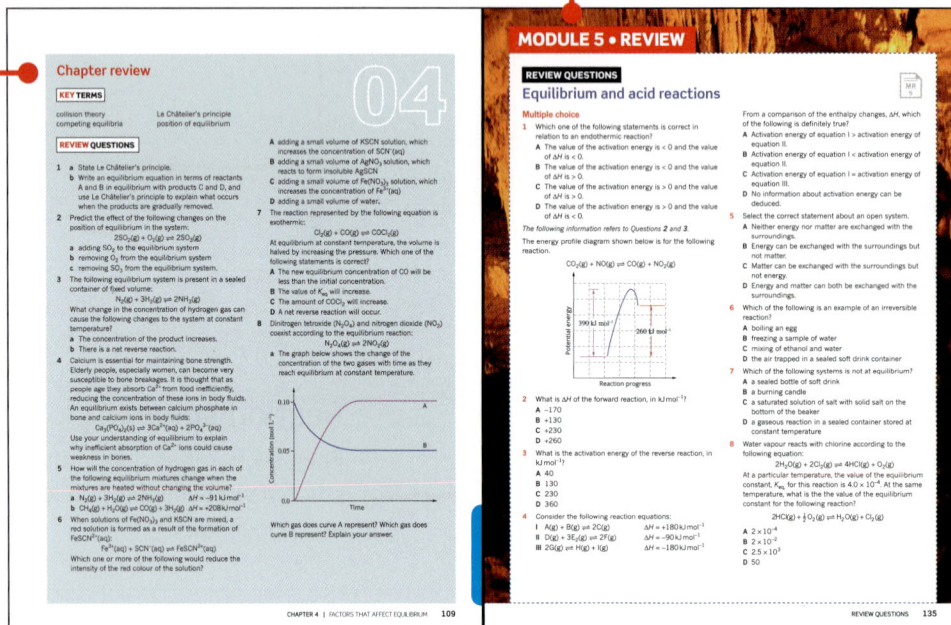

Icons

The NSW Stage 6 syllabus 'Learning across the curriculum' and 'General capabilities' content are addressed throughout the series and are identified using the following icons.

AHC A CC CCT DD EU ICT
IU L N PSC S WE

'Go to' icons are used to make important links to relevant content within the same Student Book.

GO TO ▶

This icon indicates when it is the best time to engage with a worksheet (WS), a practical activity (PA), a depth study (DS) or module review (MR) questions in *Pearson Chemistry 12 New South Wales Skills and Assessment* book.

This icon indicates the best time to engage with a practical activity on *Pearson Chemistry 12 New South Wales* Reader+.

Glossary

Key terms are shown in **bold** in sections and listed at the end of each chapter. A comprehensive glossary at the end of the book includes and defines all the key terms.

Answers

Numerical answers and key short response answers are included at the back of the book. Comprehensive answers and fully worked solutions for all section review questions, Worked example: Try yourself features, chapter review questions and module review questions are provided on *Pearson Chemistry 12 New South Wales* Reader+.

Pearson Chemistry 12 New South Wales

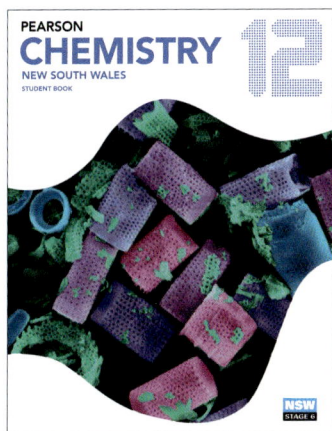

Student Book

Pearson Chemistry 12 New South Wales has been written to fully align with the new Stage 6 syllabus for New South Wales. The Student Book includes the very latest developments in, and applications of, chemistry and incorporates best-practice literacy and instructional design to ensure the content and concepts are fully accessible to all students.

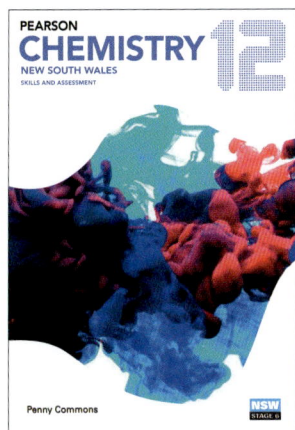

Skills and Assessment Book

Pearson Chemistry 12 New South Wales Skills and Assessment book gives students the edge in preparing for all forms of assessment. Key features include a toolkit, key knowledge summaries, worksheets, practical activities, suggested depth studies and module review questions. It provides guidance, assessment practice and opportunities for developing key skills.

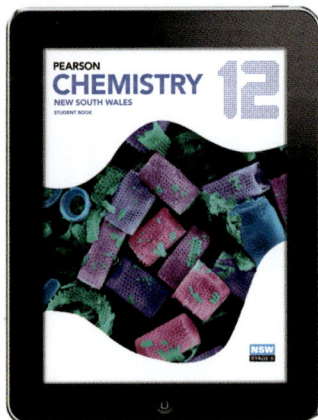

Reader+ the next generation eBook

Pearson Reader+ lets you use your Student Book online or offline on any device. Pearson Reader+ retains the look and integrity of the printed book. Practical activities, interactives and videos are available on Pearson Reader+, along with fully worked solutions for the Student Book questions.

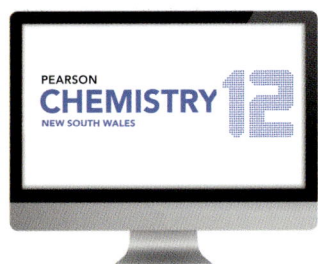

Teacher Support

Online teacher support for the series includes syllabus grids, a scope and sequence plan, and three practice exams per year level. Fully worked solutions to all Student Book questions are provided, as well as teacher notes for the chapter inquiry tasks. Skills and Assessment book resources include solutions to all worksheets, practical activities, depth studies and module review questions; teacher notes, safety notes, risk assessments and lab technician's checklists and recipes for all practical activities; and assessment rubrics and exemplar answers for the depth studies.

P Pearson

Access your digital resources at **pearsonplaces.com.au**
Browse and buy at **pearson.com.au**

01 Working scientifically

This chapter covers the skills needed to successfully plan and conduct investigations involving primary-sourced and secondary-sourced data.

1.1 Questioning and predicting describes how to develop, propose and evaluate inquiry questions and hypotheses. When creating a hypothesis, a consideration of the variables must be included.

1.2 Planning investigations outlines how to plan your investigation. You will learn to identify risks and to make sure all ethical concerns are considered. It is important to choose appropriate materials and technology to carry out your investigation. You will also need to confirm that your choice of variables allows for a reliable collection of data.

1.3 Conducting investigations is a guide to conducting scientific investigations. It describes ways to accurately collect and record data to reduce errors. Appropriate procedures need to be carried out when disposing of waste.

1.4 Processing data and information describes how to process your data appropriately. From an array of visual representation, you will learn how best to represent your information and how to identify trends and patterns in your data.

1.5 Analysing data and information explains how to analyse your results. It explains error and uncertainty and how to construct mathematical models to better understand the scientific principles of your research.

1.6 Problem solving is a guide to solving problems in a scientific manner. Using critical thinking, you will demonstrate an understanding of the scientific principles underlying the solution to your inquiry question.

1.7 Communicating explains how to communicate an investigation clearly and accurately using appropriate scientific language, nomenclature and scientific notation.

Outcomes

By the end of this chapter, you will be able to:

- develop and evaluate questions and hypotheses for scientific investigation (CH12-1)
- design and evaluate investigations in order to obtain primary and secondary data and information (CH12-2)
- conduct investigations to collect valid and reliable primary and secondary data and information (CH12-3)
- select and process appropriate qualitative and quantitative data and information using a range of appropriate media (CH12-4)
- analyse and evaluate primary and secondary data and information (CH12-5)
- solve scientific problems using primary and secondary data, critical thinking skills and scientific processes (CH12-6)
- communicate scientific understanding using suitable language and terminology for a specific audience or purpose (CH12-7)

Content

By the end of this chapter, you will be able to:

- develop and evaluate inquiry questions and hypotheses to identify a concept that can be investigated scientifically, involving primary and secondary data (ACSCH001, ACSCH061, ACSCH096) **L**
- modify questions and hypotheses to reflect new evidence **CCT**
- assess risks, consider ethical issues and select appropriate materials and technologies when designing and planning an investigation (ACSCH031, ACSCH097) **EU** **PSC**
- justify and evaluate the use of variables and experimental controls to ensure that a valid procedure is developed that allows for the reliable collection of data (ACSCH002)
- evaluate and modify an investigation in response to new evidence **CCT**
- employ and evaluate safe work practices and manage risks (ACSCH031) **PSC** **WE**
- use appropriate technologies to ensure and evaluate accuracy **ICT** **N**
- select and extract information from a wide range of reliable secondary sources and acknowledge them using an accepted referencing style **L**
- select qualitative and quantitative data and information and represent them using a range of formats, digital technologies and appropriate media (ACSCH004, ACSCH007, ACSCH064, ACSCH101) **L** **N**
- apply quantitative processes where appropriate **N**
- evaluate and improve the quality of data **CCT** **N**
- derive trends, patterns and relationships in data and information
- assess error, uncertainty and limitations in data (ACSCH004, ACSCH005, ACSCH033, ACSCH099) **CCT**
- assess the relevance, accuracy, validity and reliability of primary and secondary data and suggest improvements to investigations (ACSCH005) **CCT** **N**
- use modelling (including mathematical examples) to explain phenomena, make predictions and solve problems using evidence from primary and secondary sources (ACSCH006, ACSCH010) **CCT**
- use scientific evidence and critical thinking skills to solve problems **CCT**
- select and use suitable forms of digital, visual, written and/or oral communication **L** **N**
- select and apply appropriate scientific notations, nomenclature and scientific language to communicate in a variety of contexts (ACSCH008, ACSCH036, ACSCH067, ACSCH102) **L** **N**
- construct evidence-based arguments and engage in peer feedback to evaluate an argument or conclusion (ACSCH034, ACSCH036) **CC** **DD**

Chemistry Stage 6 Syllabus © NSW Education Standards Authority for and on behalf of the Crown in right of the State of NSW, 2017.

1.1 Questioning and predicting

Before starting your investigation, you need to understand the working scientifically skills essential to completing a meaningful scientific investigation. Working scientifically involves many dynamic and interrelated processes. These are:

- questioning and predicting
- planning investigations
- conducting investigations
- processing data and information
- analysing data and information
- problem solving
- communicating.

During this course you will choose and implement the processes appropriate to your investigation and use your knowledge and understanding of chemistry to draw and communicate conclusions and suggest areas for future research.

This section is a guide to some of the key steps that should be taken when first developing your inquiry questions and hypotheses.

REVISION

In Year 11 you learnt that scientific investigations are broken down into primary-sourced investigations (such as experiments in a lab, field work or designing a **model**) and secondary-sourced investigations (such as a **literature review**).

WHAT INITIATES AN INVESTIGATION?

Scientific investigations may be initiated simply out of curiosity about an unexpected or unexplained observation. They may also be initiated because there is a need to fill a knowledge gap, or because an advance in technology opens up a new area of investigation.

Whatever the reason, observation is a key process in all scientific investigations.

Observation

Observation includes using all your senses, as well as instruments that allow you to observe things that your senses cannot detect. For example, through careful observation using modern scientific equipment, you can learn a lot about the structure of organic compounds, including the presence of particular functional groups and how various compounds react.

The idea for a primary-sourced investigation comes from prior learning and observations. For example, ionic compounds containing the nitrate ion are highly soluble in water. This suggests the idea of investigating the solubility of other ions in water, which could result in new knowledge that could be applied to other areas, such as forming precipitates in gravimetric analysis.

How observations are interpreted depends on past experiences and knowledge. But to enquiring minds, observations will usually provoke further questions, such as those below.

- In various ionic compounds, which ions cause the compounds to be highly soluble?
- What ions have very low solubility in water?
- How does temperature affect solubility of a substance in water?

- What type of bonding exists between an ion and water molecules?
- What applications are there for the relative solubility of different substances in water?
- How does solubility affect the principles of chromatography?
- How can a supersaturated solution be prepared?
- Is the dissolution of an ionic compound in water endothermic or exothermic?

Many of these questions cannot be answered by observation alone, but they can be answered through scientific investigation. Many great discoveries have been made when a scientist has been busy investigating another problem. Good scientists have acute powers of observation and enquiring minds, and they make the most of these chance opportunities.

Advances in technology

Technology plays an important role in science. Atoms do not have sharply defined boundaries, so it is not possible to measure their radii directly. However, advances in technology have allowed scientists to measure the distance between the nuclei of atoms in molecules. For example, in a hydrogen molecule (H_2) the two nuclei are 64 picometres (pm) apart. The radius of each hydrogen atom is therefore assumed to be half that distance, which is 32 pm.

The opposite is also true. The development of new scientific theories, laws and models drives a need for new technologies, such as the development of atomic absorption spectroscopy, UV-visible spectroscopy, infra-red spectroscopy, nuclear magnetic resonance spectroscopy, mass spectrometry, gas chromatography, high-performance liquid chromatography and nanotechnology.

REVISION

Inquiry question, hypothesis and purpose

The inquiry question, purpose (aim) and hypothesis are linked. Each of these can be refined while the planning of the investigation continues.

An **inquiry question** defines what is being investigated. It is important that you can interpret what an inquiry question is asking you to do. Compile a list of topic ideas and start a literature review to formulate your inquiry question. Evaluate and refine your inquiry question once you have decided on a topic. Remember to consider the resources available to you when deciding on your inquiry question.

A **hypothesis** is a prediction that is based on evidence and prior knowledge. It often takes the form of a proposed relationship between two or more **variables** in a cause-and-effect relationship, such as: 'If x is true and this is tested, then y will occur.'

A good hypothesis should be a statement that includes the independent and dependent variables and is measurable and falsifiable. You may need to adjust your hypothesis as you conduct further research into your chosen topic.

The **purpose** (also known as the aim) is a statement describing in detail what will be investigated. The purpose includes the key steps required to test the hypothesis. Each purpose should directly relate to the variables in the hypothesis, and describe how each will be measured. An experiment or investigation determines the relationship between variables and measures the results.

There are three main categories of variables: **independent**, **dependent** and **controlled**. Variables are either **qualitative** (which includes **nominal** and **ordinal** **variables**) or **quantitative** (which includes **discrete** and **continuous variables**).

Reliable **primary** and **secondary sources** should be used when researching your topic and during your investigation.

PEER REVIEW

Peer review is a process in which other researchers who work in the same field review your work and provide feedback about your methodology and whether your conclusions are justified. Scientists are expected to publish their findings in peer-reviewed journals. Some examples of peer-reviewed chemistry journals are:

- *Australian Journal of Chemistry* (Figure 1.1.1)
- *Journal of the American Chemical Society*
- *Nature Chemistry*
- *Chemical Reviews*
- *Progress in Polymer Science*
- *Green Chemistry*
- *Nano Today.*

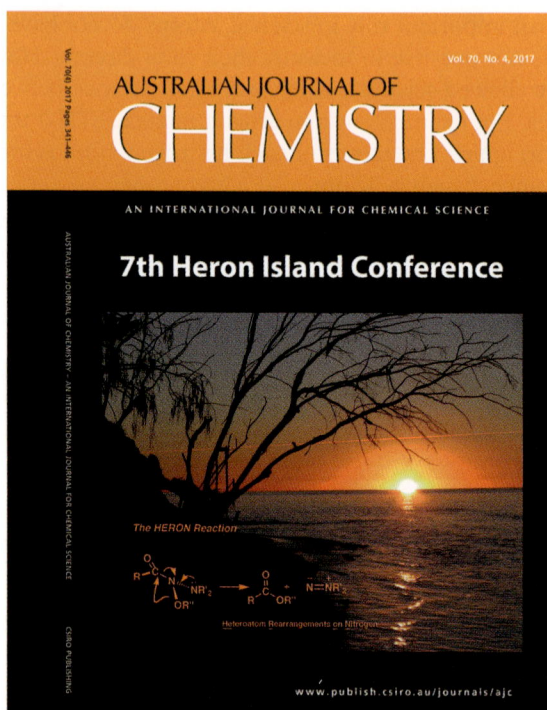

FIGURE 1.1.1 The *Australian Journal of Chemistry,* published by CSIRO, is Australia's leading chemistry journal.

Peer-reviewed journals have an editorial board consisting of experts in a particular field, who assess submitted papers and decide whether they are suitable for publication.

Your teacher may suggest that you conduct your investigations with one or more other students in your class, so that you can provide each other with constructive feedback about your inquiry question or hypothesis. There are many benefits from collaborating with others, including building on ideas and considering alternative perspectives. For example, the modern periodic table is the result of research originally conducted by many scientists in the 19th century.

When you are collaborating in a scientific investigation, you should consider the following questions:

- Is the inquiry question clear?
- Can the inquiry question be answered in the time available?
- Is the purpose of the investigation clear?
- If there is a hypothesis, is it written in a way that enables it to be falsifiable?
- Are the independent, dependent and controlled variables clearly defined?
- What are the strengths of the inquiry question?
- What are the weaknesses of the inquiry question?
- Do you have the time and resources to complete the proposed investigation?

The origin of the periodic table

The early forms of the periodic table were very different from the one we use today. Scientists had very limited information about some elements, and many elements had not been discovered. Several scientists suggested ways to organise the elements, and from their work and reworking of others' ideas we have arrived at the periodic table we use today.

In 1829, the German chemist Johann Dobereiner noticed that many of the known elements could be arranged in groups of three based on their chemical properties. He called these groups 'triads'. Within each of these triads, the properties of one element were intermediate between the other two elements. The intermediate relative atomic weight was almost exactly the average of the others.

Although Dobereiner's theory was limited because not all elements could be placed in triads, his work was remarkable, as he had fewer than 50 elements to work with at the time.

Three decades later, English chemist John Alexander Newlands noticed a pattern in the atomic weight of elements. His 'law of octaves' was published in 1865 and identified properties of new elements such as germanium. His law worked well for the lighter elements but not for the heavier elements, and it did not allow for the discovery of new elements.

Then in 1869, Dimitri Mendeleev published his periodic law, which was similar to Newlands' law of octaves, although they worked independently. This law led Mendeleev to develop a table of the elements that was the foundation of the table we use today (Figure 1.1.2).

Mendeleev is remembered because of his amazing ability to predict the characteristics of elements that had not yet been discovered. For example, when gallium was discovered in 1875, its atomic mass, density and melting point were very close to what Mendeleev predicted in 1871. His predictions proved to be a very powerful guide for future chemists and helped them to understand things not yet discovered.

The modern periodic table is an example of the importance of collaboration between scientific disciplines. Since the early 1900s, chemists and physicists have worked together to modify, expand and interpret the periodic table, and biologists use it constantly in developing ideas about how elements interact in biological systems and make life possible.

Group I Period	II	III	IV	V	VI	VII	VIII
1	H = 1							
2	Li = 7	Be = 9.4	B = 11	C = 12	N = 14	O = 16	F = 19	
3	Na = 23	Mg = 24	Al = 27.3	Si = 28	P = 31	S = 32	Cl = 35.5	
4	K = 39	Ca = 40	? = 44	Ti = 48	V = 51	Cr = 52	Mn = 55	Fe = 56 Co = 59 Ni = 59
5	Cu = 63	Zn = 65	? = 68	? = 72	As = 75	Se = 78	Br = 80	
6	Rb = 85	Sr = 87	?Yt = 88	Zr = 90	Nb = 94	Mo = 96	? = 100	Ru = 104 Rh = 104 Pd = 106
7	Ag = 108	Cd = 112	In = 113	Sn = 118	Sb = 122	Te = 125	J = 127	
8	Cs = 133	Ba = 137	?Di = 138	?Ce = 140				
9								
10			?Er = 178	?La = 180	Ta = 182	W = 184		Os = 195 Ir = 197 Pt = 198
11	Au = 199	Hg = 200	Tl = 204	Pb = 207	Bi = 208			
12				Th = 231		U = 240		

FIGURE 1.1.2 A representation of Mendeleev's periodic table, showing spaces left for undiscovered elements

1.1 Review

SUMMARY

- Before you begin your research it is important to conduct a literature review. By utilising data from primary and/or secondary sources, you will better understand the context of your investigation to create an informed inquiry question.
- The purpose (aim) of an investigation is a statement describing in detail what will be investigated.
- A hypothesis is a tentative explanation for an observation that is based on evidence and prior knowledge. A hypothesis must be testable and falsifiable and define a proposed relationship between two variables.

- Once an inquiry question has been chosen, stop to evaluate the question before progressing. The question may need further refinement or even further investigation before it is suitable as a basis for an achievable and worthwhile investigation.
- There are three categories of variables: independent, dependent and controlled.

KEY QUESTIONS

1 Distinguish between the terms inquiry question, hypothesis, and purpose of an investigation.

2 Which of the following could be an inquiry question?
   A What is the sodium content of baby foods?
   B The sodium content of baby food will be less than 100 mg per 100 g.
   C Babies need to have a low-sodium diet.
   D Sodium content can be measured using gravimetric analysis and atomic absorption spectroscopy.

3 In an experiment a student records the colour of precipitate formed when various solutions are mixed. What type of variable is 'colour'?

4 Which of the following is the most specific inquiry question?
   A What is the phosphate concentration of laundry detergent?
   B Is laundry detergent toxic?
   C What is the best brand of laundry detergent?
   D How much laundry detergent is needed to clean 5 kg of washing?

5 Which of the following inquiry questions is objective and specific?
   A How does temperature affect the pH of water?
   B Does temperature affect pH?
   C I think that Sydney drinking water should not be chlorinated.
   D Fluoride ions are added to Sydney's drinking water.

6 Select the best hypothesis from the options below. Give reasons for your choice.
   A The sodium content of food can be measured using gravimetric analysis.
   B The concentration of a substance in a solution can be expressed using various units, including molarity and parts per million.
   C If water is filtered through a domestic water purifier, the concentration of ions in the water will decrease.
   D Gravimetric analysis can be used to measure the pH of a solution.

1.2 Planning investigations

After you have formulated your hypothesis, defined the purpose of your investigation and determined your variables, you need to plan and design your investigation. Taking the time to carefully plan and design a practical investigation before beginning will help you to maintain a clear and concise focus throughout. Preparation is essential. This section is a guide to some of the key steps that should be taken when planning and designing a practical investigation.

CHOOSING AN APPROPRIATE TYPE OF INVESTIGATION

After you have drafted your inquiry question, purpose, hypothesis and variables, you need to choose an appropriate type of investigation. Examples of various investigations are listed in Table 1.2.1. When selecting the type of investigation you will use remember to consider how much time you have available, and whether you will need to work in a group or individually.

TABLE 1.2.1 Examples of different types of investigations

Type of data or activity	Type of investigation	Example
primary-sourced data	Design and conduct experiments.	Measure and reliably compare the enthalpy of combustion for a range of alcohols.
	Test a claim.	Measure the sodium content of food using various procedures such as gravimetric analysis or atomic absorption spectroscopy
	Test a device.	Test the efficiency of a portable water purification unit.
secondary-sourced data	Make a documentary or media report.	Investigate the concentration of lead in water passing through a commercial mixer tap, and contrast media reports with independent testing commissioned by the manufacturer of the tap.
	Conduct a literature review.	Research applications for precipitation titrations.
	Develop an evidence-based argument.	Use primary-sourced data of the concentration of lead in soil in Sydney households to propose strategies to avoid lead contamination in home-grown vegetables.
	Write a journal article.	Look at the style of a peer-reviewed journal and write literature review in that particular style.
	Write an essay on a historical or theoretical subject.	An essay on the work of a Nobel Prize winner in Chemistry. An essay on the history of polymer synthesis.
	Develop an environmental management plan.	To reduce phosphate concentration in waste water.
	Analyse a work of fiction or film for scientific relevance.	Book: *The Martian* by Andy Weir (2011) and / or Film: *The Martian*, director Ridley Scott (2015)
	Create a visual presentation.	Create a scientific poster.
	Investigate emerging technologies.	Investigate artificial leaf technology.
creating	Design and invent.	Build your own colorimeter.
	Create a working model.	Create a density column of compounds such as water, honey, methylated spirits, vegetable oil and food colouring, and use it to explain the concept of density and types of intermolecular bonding.
	Create a portfolio.	Compile a set of resources to answer an inquiry question.
fieldwork	Collecting samples or data for analysis.	Collecting water samples from streams to test for pollutants. Measuring the temperature and oxygen concentration in different parts of a pond.
data analysis	Primary- and secondary-sourced investigations.	Use original data to construct and analyse graphs or tables. Analyse data from a variety of sources.

Organising information

It is important to be able to organise the information that you collect in your investigation. This is particularly important if your investigation is an in-depth literature review. Table 1.2.2 shows how you might be able to summarise information from primary and secondary sources.

TABLE 1.2.2 Example of categories that help you to keep track of information as you conduct a literature review

Source of information	VegeSafe: A community science program measuring soil-metal contamination, evaluating risk and providing advice for safe gardening. *Environmental Pollution* volume 22, pages 557–566. http://www.sciencedirect.com/science/journal/02697491/222?sdc=1
Authors	Rouillon, M., Harvey, P.J., Kristensen, L.J., George, S.G., & Taylor, M.P.
Country / Region	Sydney, Australia
Year of publication	2017
Sample size	5200 samples from 1200 homes
Procedure	Free soil metal screening was offered to households. X-ray fluorescence spectrometry was used to analyse samples.
Summary of conclusions	40% of garden soil samples in Sydney exceeded the Australian health guideline of 300 mg of lead per kilogram of soil. Lead concentration of garden soil was higher where houses were painted prior to 1970. The highest lead levels in soils were found in the inner city area.
Key ideas	High lead levels in garden soils are a legacy of lead-based paints and fuels. The public is now better informed about garden lead levels, allowing them to make informed decisions about avoiding metal contamination in their vegetable gardens.

WRITING THE PROCEDURE

The procedure (also known as the method) of your investigation is a step-by-step description of how the hypothesis will be tested. Consider using a diagram of your equipment set-up such as the one shown in Figure 1.2.1.

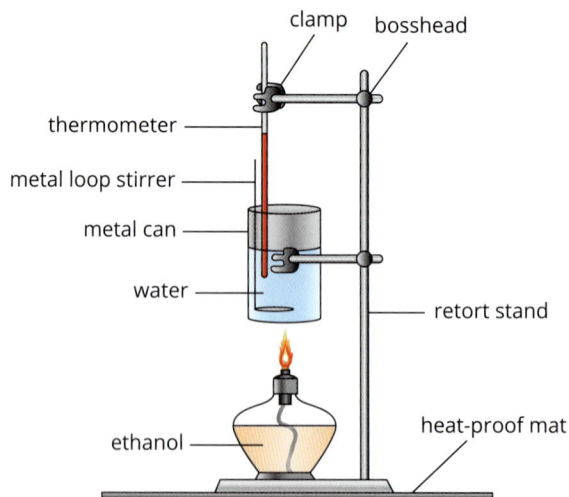

FIGURE 1.2.1 An equipment set up for determining the heat content of ethanol.

When you write the procedure, make sure it has the following elements so that it is a valid, reliable and accurate investigation.

Methodology elements

Validity refers to whether an experiment or investigation is in fact testing the set hypothesis and purpose. A valid investigation is one in which only one variable is changed at a time. To ensure validity, carefully determine the independent variable and how it will change, the dependent variable, and the controlled variables and how they will be maintained.

Reliability refers to the notion that the experiment can be repeated many times and the average of the results from all the repeated experiments will be consistent. This can be maintained by defining the control and ensuring there is sufficient replication of the experiment.

Accuracy is the ability to obtain the correct measurement. To obtain accurate results, you must minimise systematic errors.

Precision is the ability to consistently obtain the same measurement. To obtain precise results, you must minimise random errors.

In chemistry, it is important to know that the precision of glassware used in laboratory experiments varies. Table 1.2.3 shows the typical precision of some typical laboratory glassware.

TABLE 1.2.3 Typical measurement uncertainties for various laboratory glassware

Type of laboratory glassware	Typical precision
10 mL measuring cylinder	10 ± 0.1 mL
20 mL pipette	20 ± 0.03 mL
50 mL burette	50 ± 0.02 mL
250 mL volumetric (standard) flask	250 ± 0.3 mL

Build some testing into your investigation to confirm the accuracy and reliability of the equipment and your ability to read the information obtained. Reasonable steps to ensure the accuracy of the investigation include considering the unit in which the independent and dependent variables will be measured and the instrument that will be used to measure the variables.

Calibrate equipment before you begin to increase accuracy, and repeat the measurements to confirm them.

Describe the materials and procedure in appropriate detail. This should ensure that every measurement can be repeated and the same result will be obtained within reasonable margins of experimental error (less than 5% is reasonable). **Percentage uncertainty** (also known as percentage error) is a way to quantify the accuracy of a measurement. This is discussed further in Section 1.4.

Recording numerical data

When using measuring instruments, the number of significant figures (or digits) and decimal places you can use is determined by how precise your measurements are. See Section 1.4 for a discussion about how to identify and use an appropriate number of significant figures and decimal places.

Data analysis

Data analysis is part of the procedure. Consider how the data will be presented and analysed, such as in graphs so that trends can be seen, or in tables so that data can be compared. Preparing an empty table showing the data that needs to be obtained will help in planning the investigation.

The nature of the data being collected, such as whether the variables are qualitative or quantitative, influences the type of method or tool that you can use to analyse the data. The purpose and the hypothesis will also influence the choice of analysis tool.

It is a good idea to draft a table of results before you commence an experiment. A sample results table is shown in Table 1.2.4.

TABLE 1.2.4 Results table indicating the pH of three different mineral waters (X, Y and Z)

Brand of mineral water	Volume	Date tested	pH	Temperature (°C)
Brand X, 1 L	1 L	24 March 2018	5.5	22.3
Brand Y, 1 L	1 L	24 March 2018	6.0	22.3
Brand Z, 1 L	1 L	24 March 2018	5.8	22.3
Uncertainty of equipment	1 L	24 March 2018	±0.1	±0.1

TABLE 1.2.5 Types of variables and the ways in which they could be measured and used within an investigation.

State the inquiry question.	What is the pH of commercially available mineral waters?
List the independent variable. Is the variable quantitative or qualitative?	The independent variable is the brand of mineral water (qualitative).
List the dependent variable(s). What equipment will you use to measure these? What is the uncertainty of measurements?	The dependent variable is pH. A calibrated pH meter connected to a computer will be used to measure pH. The pH meter has an uncertainty of ±0.1 pH units.
List the controlled variable/s. What will you do to control these variables? What is the uncertainty of measurements?	The controlled variable is temperature. All mineral waters will be stored at room temperature until analysed. The temperature of each will be measured with an ethanol-filled glass thermometer. The uncertainty of the thermometer is ±0.1°C.

Sourcing appropriate materials and technology

When you are designing an investigation, you need to decide on the materials, technology and instrumentation that will be used. It is important to find the right balance between resources that are easily accessible and those which will give you accurate results. You will also need to consider any costs or risks associated with using the technology, how familiar you are with using it, and any limitations of the technology that might affect your investigation. As you move on to conducting the investigation, it is important to note the precision of your measuring equipment and how this will affect the accuracy and validity of your results. This is discussed in greater detail in Section 1.3.

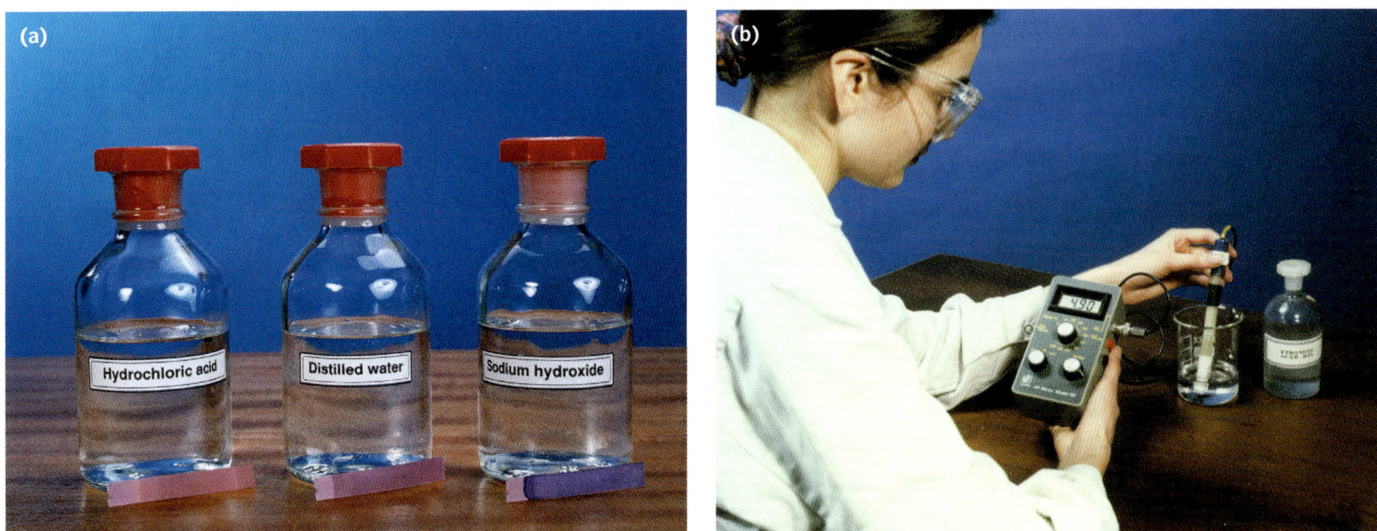

FIGURE 1.2.2 Determining whether a solution is acidic or basic can be qualitative or quantitative. (a) Litmus paper gives a qualitative observation indicating the nature of the solution. (If the paper turns purple, the solution is basic; If the paper turns pink, the solution is acidic). (b) A calibrated pH meter gives a quantitative measurement indicating the nature of the solution (pH < 7, the solution is acidic; pH > 7 the solution is basic at 25°C).

Data logging

A data logger is an instrument that measures a variable at set intervals and stores the data for later analysis. Ask your teacher whether data-logging equipment is available in your school. Some schools will have access to data loggers with probes for measuring a range of variables, such as pH, conductivity and temperature.

Modifying the procedure

The procedure may need modifying as the investigation is carried out. The following actions will help to identify any problems with the procedure and how to fix them:

• Record everything.
• Be prepared to make changes to the approach.
• Note any difficulties encountered and the ways they were overcome. What were the failures and successes? Every test carried out can contribute to the understanding of the investigation as a whole, no matter how much of a disaster it may appear at first.
• Don't panic. Go over the theory again, and talk to your teacher and other students. A different perspective can lead to a solution.

If the expected data is not obtained, don't worry. As long as the data can be critically evaluated, and you identify the limitations of the investigation and propose further investigations, the investigation is worthwhile.

COMPLYING WITH ETHICAL AND SAFETY GUIDELINES

Ethical considerations

Investigations involving animals or people may require an ethics approval. Your teacher will be able to advise you whether this applies to your research. When you are planning an investigation, identify all parts of the procedure that might involve ethical considerations, and evaluate their necessity. You may be able to change the methodology to reduce or eliminate any possible ethical issues.

GO TO ➤ Year 11 Section 1.2

Ethics and radiation

There are many different types of radiation, including electromagnetic radiation and alpha and beta particles released during the decay of radioactive nuclei. Some radiation occurs naturally; cosmic radiation and the decay of unstable radioisotopes in the Earth's crust are common examples. Alpha particles are the nuclei of helium atoms (charge +2) i.e. $^4_2$He. They cannot penetrate human skin, but they can damage living tissues if they are ingested or inhaled, or enter a wound. Beta particles are electrons, and gamma rays are very high energy electromagnetic radiation.

The decay of radioisotopes to produce different types of radiation can be represented by equations of balanced nuclear reactions. For example, the decay of naturally occurring uranium-238 produces thorium-234, an alpha particle and gamma radiation. This decay is represented by the following equation:

$$^{238}_{92}U \rightarrow \, ^{234}_{90}Th + \, ^4_2He + \gamma$$

The Greek letter γ is used to represent gamma radiation. Notice that when the decay produces alpha particles (helium nuclei), a new element is also formed.

The decay of radioisotope carbon-14 produce beta particles (electrons), as shown by the following equation:

$$^{14}_6C \rightarrow \, ^{14}_7N + \, ^0_{-1}e$$

The following applications of radiation can be useful to society:

- nuclear magnetic resonance, infra-red, atomic absorption and UV-visible spectroscopy in chemical analysis

- radiotherapy as a cancer treatment
- use of X-rays to detect broken bones and dental decay
- the production of energy from nuclear fission reactions in power plants.

However, radiation can be harmful to society:

- if nuclear weapons are used in war
- if nuclear waste contaminates water or food
- if a nuclear power station malfunctions and releases radiation into the environment
- if patients, medical practitioners, dentists or researchers are exposed to excessive doses of radiation.

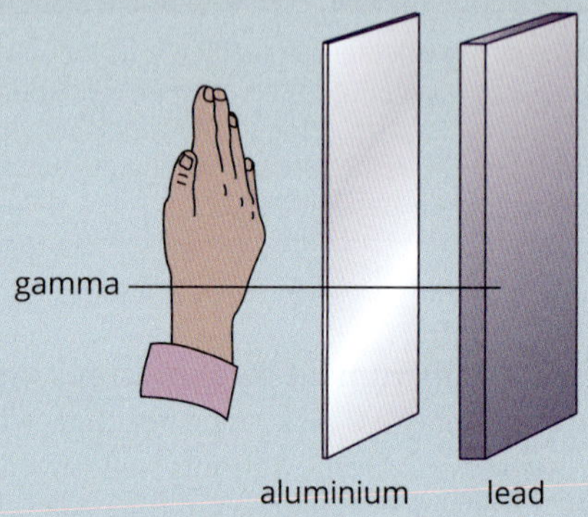

FIGURE 1.2.3 Gamma particles can pass easily through human tissues, and even through a sheet of aluminium.

REVISION

GO TO ➤ Year 11 Section 1.2

Risk assessments

Risk assessments help to identify, assess and control hazards. A risk assessment should be performed for any investigation, whether it is in the laboratory or outdoors. Always identify the risks and control them to keep everyone as safe as possible.

Ways to reduce risk are, in order from most effective to least effective, elimination, substitution, isolation, administrative control, and **personal protective equipment** (PPE). Special care must be taken to minimise the risks that come with working outdoors, such as wearing sunscreen, a hat, insect repellent, appropriate clothing, and gloves. Someone with first aid training should always be present, and any injuries or accidents must be immediately reported to your teacher or lab technician.

Chemical hazard codes

In 2017 the Globally Harmonized System of Classification and Labelling of Chemicals (GHS) was introduced in Australia for use in workplaces, including school laboratories. Pictograms indicating the types of hazards posed by chemicals are shown on containers and are included in safety data sheets. The more common pictograms denote chemicals that are explosive, flammable, oxidising, corrosive, toxic or under pressure, chemicals that can cause eye or respiratory problems, chemicals that are mutagenic or carcinogenic, and chemicals that become dangerous when wet (Figure 1.2.4a).

Vehicles and railway trucks carrying dangerous chemicals must display an appropriate HAZCHEM sign indicating the type of chemical and the hazard it poses (Figure 1.2.4b).

Safety data sheets

Each chemical substance has an accompanying document called a **safety data sheet (SDS)**. The SDS contains important safety and first aid information about each chemical you commonly use in the laboratory. If the products of a reaction are toxic or hazardous to the environment, you must pour your waste into a special container, not down the sink.

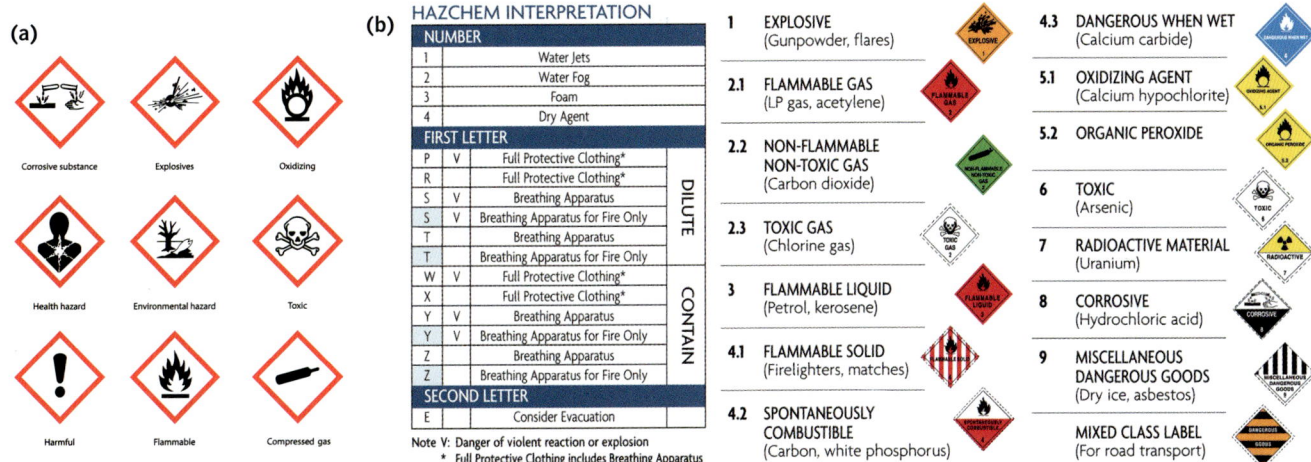

(a)

Corrosive substance | Explosives | Oxidizing
Health hazard | Environmental hazard | Toxic
Harmful | Flammable | Compressed gas

(b) HAZCHEM INTERPRETATION

NUMBER	
1	Water Jets
2	Water Fog
3	Foam
4	Dry Agent

FIRST LETTER			
P	V	Full Protective Clothing*	DILUTE
R		Full Protective Clothing*	DILUTE
S	V	Breathing Apparatus	DILUTE
S		Breathing Apparatus for Fire Only	DILUTE
T		Breathing Apparatus	DILUTE
T		Breathing Apparatus for Fire Only	DILUTE
W	V	Full Protective Clothing*	CONTAIN
X		Full Protective Clothing*	CONTAIN
Y	V	Breathing Apparatus	CONTAIN
Y		Breathing Apparatus for Fire Only	CONTAIN
Z		Breathing Apparatus	CONTAIN
Z		Breathing Apparatus for Fire Only	CONTAIN

SECOND LETTER	
E	Consider Evacuation

Note V: Danger of violent reaction or explosion
* Full Protective Clothing includes Breathing Apparatus

1 EXPLOSIVE (Gunpowder, flares)
2.1 FLAMMABLE GAS (LP gas, acetylene)
2.2 NON-FLAMMABLE NON-TOXIC GAS (Carbon dioxide)
2.3 TOXIC GAS (Chlorine gas)
3 FLAMMABLE LIQUID (Petrol, kerosene)
4.1 FLAMMABLE SOLID (Firelighters, matches)
4.2 SPONTANEOUSLY COMBUSTIBLE (Carbon, white phosphorus)
4.3 DANGEROUS WHEN WET (Calcium carbide)
5.1 OXIDIZING AGENT (Calcium hypochlorite)
5.2 ORGANIC PEROXIDE
6 TOXIC (Arsenic)
7 RADIOACTIVE MATERIAL (Uranium)
8 CORROSIVE (Hydrochloric acid)
9 MISCELLANEOUS DANGEROUS GOODS (Dry ice, asbestos)
MIXED CLASS LABEL (For road transport)

FIGURE 1.2.4 (a) Common GHS symbols for hazardous chemicals in the workplace, and (b) common HAZCHEM symbols for transporting dangerous goods

PEER REVIEW

Your teacher may suggest that you work with one or more other students in your class, so that you can provide each other with constructive feedback about your planning. The following are some questions that might be considered.

- Is the type of investigation appropriate and relevant to the inquiry question?
- Is the procedure written in easy-to-understand logical steps?
- Is the procedure valid and reliable?
- Has a thorough and complete risk assessment been undertaken prior to commencing the investigation?
- What are the strengths of the type of investigation and procedure?
- What questions do you have about the type of investigation and procedure?

1.2 Review

SUMMARY

- The procedure of your investigation is a step-by-step plan. When detailing the procedure, ensure it is a valid, reliable and accurate investigation.
- It is important to determine how many times the experiment needs to be repeated. Scientific investigations must have sufficient repetition to ensure that the results are reliable.
- Risk assessments must be carried out before conducting an investigation, to make sure that

the investigation will be safe. If elements of your investigation have too much risk, you will need to re-evaluate your design.

- It is important to choose appropriate equipment for your experiment that will give you accurate results.
- A risk assessment should be carried out for every investigation, and appropriate personal protective equipment (PPE) should be worn.

KEY QUESTIONS

1 Give the correct term (accurate, reliable or valid) that describes an experiment with each of the following conditions.
   a The experiment addresses the hypothesis and purpose.
   b The experiment is repeated and consistent results are obtained.
   c Appropriate equipment is chosen for the measurements required.

2 A student wants to determine the amount of suspended solids in water samples. Which of the following are potential sites for water sampling?
   A rivers
   B creeks
   C lakes
   D stormwater drains
   E beaches
   F all of the above

3 A student wants to collect water samples from a local stream. Which one or more of the following items of personal protective equipment should be included in the risk assessment for this work?
   A use of a fume cupboard
   B ear muffs
   C gloves
   D non-slip rubber boots

4 A journal article reported the materials and procedure used in order to conduct an experiment. The experiment was repeated three times, and all values were reported in the results section of the article. Repeating an experiment and reporting results supports:
   A precision
   B reliability
   C accuracy
   D systematic errors

5 You are conducting an experiment to determine the effect of water pH on the mass of mussels growing in the water. Identify:
   a the independent variable
   b the dependent variable
   c at least one controlled variable.

6 A student included the following diagram of the experimental set-up used in her investigation. Use the diagram to write clear instructions for the procedure.

Trial 1
The strong acid used was hydrochloric acid, HCl.
The equation for the reaction is as follows.

$$2HCl(aq) + CaCO_3(s) \rightarrow CaCl_2(aq) + CO_2(g) + H_2O(l)$$

- plug of cottonwool
- CO_2
- 100 mL 0.5 mol L^{-1} HCl
- 10 g marble chips
- digital scales

1.3 Conducting investigations

Once the planning and design of a practical investigation is complete, the next step is to undertake the investigation and record the results. As with the planning stages, there are key steps and skills to keep in mind to maintain high standards and minimise potential errors throughout the investigation (Figure 1.3.1).

This section focuses on the best methods of conducting a practical investigation, including systematically generating, recording and processing data.

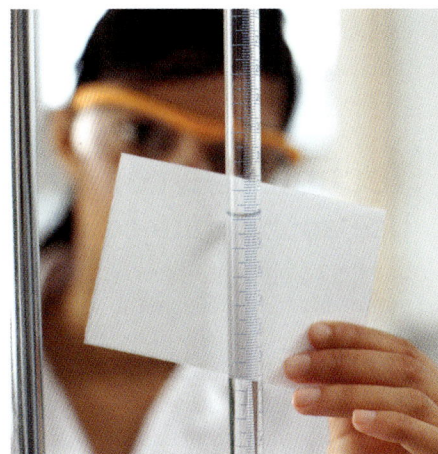

FIGURE 1.3.1 It is important to read the bottom of the meniscus at eye level in order to avoid parallax error. This student is showing how you can use a piece of white card (or a tile) to improve the contrast between the liquid and the scale.

REVISION

Collecting and recording data

For an investigation to be scientific, it must be objective and systematic. Always record all quantitative and qualitative data collected and the methods used to collect the data in your logbook. Also record any incident, feature or unexpected event that may have affected the quality or validity of the data. The recorded data is known as **raw data**. Usually this data needs to be processed in some manner before it can be presented.

Safe work practices

GO TO ➤ Year 11 Section 1.2

Always employ safe work practices while conducting your experiment. See Section 1.2 for information about how to conduct risk assessments.

You will also need to keep in mind safe procedures to follow when disposing of waste. Consult your teacher or visit education or government websites for information.

REVISION

GO TO ➤ Year 11 Section 1.3

Identifying errors

Errors can occur for a variety of reasons. Being aware of potential errors helps you to avoid or minimise them. Three types of errors that can occur in an experiment (Figure 1.3.2).

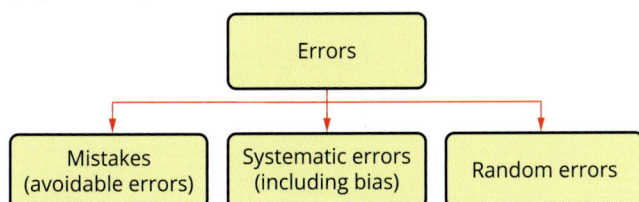

```
                    Errors
        ┌─────────────┼─────────────┐
   Mistakes     Systematic errors    Random errors
(avoidable errors)  (including bias)
```

FIGURE 1.3.2 Types of errors that can be made in an experiment

Mistakes are avoidable errors. A measurement that involves a mistake must be rejected and not included in any calculations, or averaged with other measurements of the same quantity.

A **systematic error** is an error that is consistent and will occur again if the investigation is repeated in the same way. Systematic errors are usually a result of instruments that are not calibrated correctly or procedures that are flawed. Whatever the cause, the resulting error is in the same direction for every measurement, so the average will be either too high or too low. Systematic errors result in bias. Examples of bias are shown in Figure 1.3.3.

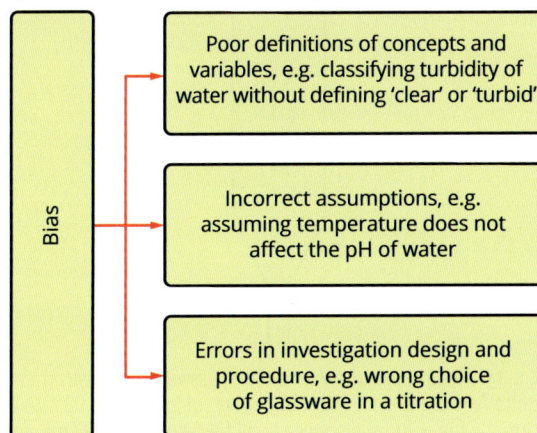

```
         ┌──► Poor definitions of concepts and
         │    variables, e.g. classifying turbidity of
         │    water without defining 'clear' or 'turbid'
         │
  Bias ──┼──► Incorrect assumptions, e.g.
         │    assuming temperature does not
         │    affect the pH of water
         │
         └──► Errors in investigation design and
              procedure, e.g. wrong choice
              of glassware in a titration
```

FIGURE 1.3.3 Types and examples of bias in an analysis of water quality

Random errors are unpredictable and follow no regular pattern. Measurements may be sometimes too large and sometimes too small. The effects of random errors can be reduced by taking several measurements and calculating an average.

Techniques to reduce error
Use appropriate equipment

Use the equipment that is best suited to the data that needs to be collected to validate the hypothesis. Determining the units of the data being collected and at what scale will help to select the correct equipment. Using the right unit and scale will ensure that measurements are more accurate and precise (with smaller systematic errors).

To minimise errors, check the precision of the equipment that you intend to use (Table 1.3.1). Pipettes, burettes and volumetric flasks have greater precision than a beaker when measuring volumes of solutions. However, you must still use the equipment correctly to reduce errors.

TABLE 1.3.1 Typical measurement precision of some water-testing equipment and glassware

Equipment	Typical precision
pH meter	±0.1
digital thermometer	±0.1°C
20 mL pipette	±0.03 mL
50 mL burette	±0.02 mL
100 mL beaker	±1 mL

Often glassware and equipment has information that indicates the measurement precision. Figure 1.3.4 shows where this can be found on a pipette.

25.00 mL ± 0.03 mL

FIGURE 1.3.4 Record the uncertainty for glassware and instruments. This pipette can dispense a volume (aliquot) of 25.00 ± 0.03 mL. When used correctly the volume dispensed will be between 24.97 mL and 25.03 mL.

USE CALIBRATED EQUIPMENT

Before carrying out the investigation, make sure the instruments or measuring devices are properly calibrated and are functioning correctly. Record the precision of glassware that you intend to use. If you are preparing a solution of known concentration you might have access to a volumetric flask, which has less uncertainty associated with measurements compared to a beaker.

USE EQUIPMENT CORRECTLY

Use the equipment properly. Ensure any necessary training on using the equipment has been done, and that you have had an opportunity to practise using the equipment before beginning the investigation. Improper use of equipment can result in inaccurate, imprecise data with large errors, and the validity of the data can be compromised.

Incorrectly reading instruments is a common mistake. Make sure all of the equipment needed in the investigation can be used correctly, and record the instructions in detail so they can be referred to if the data doesn't appear to be correct.

INCREASE SAMPLING SIZE

In general, the larger the sample taken for analysis, the more precise the measured values will be. However, if you are colecting samples outdoors you might be limited by the size of the container and number of containers you can transport back to to the laboratory.

REPEAT THE INVESTIGATION

As discussed in Section 1.2, reliability is ensured by repeating your experiment. Modifications to your procedure may be needed before repeating the investigation to ensure that all variables are being tested under the same conditions.

REFERENCING SECONDARY-SOURCED INFORMATION

While you are conducting your investigation, it is important to note any secondary-sourced data that you use, so that it can be included in your written report. This is discussed in detail in Section 1.7.

Your teacher may suggest that you work with another student in your class, so that you can provide each other with constructive feedback regarding your data collection. Consider the following questions:

- Is the data presented clearly in tables and / or graphs?
- Are all entries in the logbook dated?
- Are appropriate headings and units included?
- If anything unexpected occurred during data collection, was this recorded?
- What are the strengths of the data collected?
- What questions do you have about the data collected?

1.3 Review

SUMMARY

- During an investigation it is essential that you record the following in your logbook:
  - all quantitative and qualitative data collected
  - the procedure used to collect the data
  - any incident, feature or unexpected event that may have affected the quality or validity of the data.
- Mistakes are avoidable errors, and measurements affected by mistakes should be discarded.

- A systematic error is an error that is consistent and will occur again if the investigation is repeated in the same way. Systematic errors are usually a result of instruments that are not calibrated correctly or procedures that are flawed.
- Random errors are unpredictable and are usually small. A random error could be, for example, the result of a researcher reading the same result correctly one time and incorrectly another time.

KEY QUESTIONS

1 Where should observations and measurements be recorded?

2 Identify the type of error that is described in each scenario below, and how it could be avoided.
   a The electronic scale was not zeroed before the samples were weighed.
   b $1.0\,mol\,L^{-1}$ hydrochloric acid was used instead of $0.1\,mol\,L^{-1}$ hydrochloric acid.
   c One result was significantly lower than all the rest.
   d One student recorded a water sample as 'cloudy' while another student recorded it as 'very cloudy'.

3 During an investigation to determine the concentration of a solution, a student used a burette to measure out volumes (called titres). For the titres to be concordant (which means they are close enough to be acceptable) they must have a maximum range of 0.10 mL. The following titres were recorded in the investigation: 18.48 mL, 17.92 mL, 17.98 mL, 18.02 mL and 18.26 mL.
   a Identify the three concordant titres.
   b Calculate the average of the concordant titres.
   c What type of error does calculating the average of the concordant titres aim to reduce?

4 Identify whether each error is a mistake, a systematic error or a random error:
   a A pipette that should have dispensed volumes of $25.00 \pm 0.03\,mL$ actually dispensed volumes of $24.92 \pm 0.03\,mL$.
   b A student read the value on the dial of the voltmeter on an angle.
   c A sample of glucose powder was weighed three times. On the third weighing, a fluctuation in the power supply gave an unexpected value.

1.4 Processing data and information

Once you have conducted your investigation and collected data, you will need to find the best way of collating this. This section is a guide to the different forms of representation that will help you to better understand your data.

RECORDING AND PRESENTING QUANTITATIVE DATA

Raw data is unlikely to be used directly to test the hypothesis. However, raw data is essential to the investigation and plans for collecting the raw data should be made carefully. Consider the formulas or graphs that will be used to analyse the data at the end of the investigation. This will help to determine the type of raw data that needs to be collected in order to test the hypothesis.

Once you have determined the data that needs to be collected, prepare a table in which to record the data.

REVISION

GO TO ▶ SkillBuilder page 83

Significant figures

Significant figures are numbers that have meaning in relation to precision. A significant figure is an integer or a zero that follows an integer. A zero that does not have any integers before it is not significant. For example, the number 1.204 has 4 significant figures, and the number 0.00368 has 3 significant figures.

The number of significant figures in a measurement made using an instrument depends on the scale and precision of the instrument. When you record raw data and report processed data, you should only use the number of significant figures available from your equipment or observation. Using more or less significant figures can be misleading.

For example, Table 1.4.1 shows measurements of five samples taken using an electronic balance that is accurate to two decimal places. The data was entered into a spreadsheet to calculate the mean, which was displayed with 4 decimal places. You would record the **mean** as 5.69 g, not 5.6940 g, because two decimal places is the precision limit of the instrument. Recording 5.6940 g would be an example of false precision.

TABLE 1.4.1 An example of false precision in a data calculation

Sample	1	2	3	4	5	Mean
Mass (g)	5.67	5.75	5.62	5.71	5.72	5.6940

MULTIPLYING OR DIVIDING

In mathematical calculations, the basic rule is that answers should not be rounded off until the final calculation is done.

When values are multiplied or divided, the answer should have no more significant figures than the value with the least number of significant figures. For example, to calculate the amount, in mol, of a substance using concentration and volume, the formula is $n = c \times V$. If $c = 0.997$ mol L^{-1} (3 significant figures), and the volume is 21.62 mL (4 significant figures), the amount of substance, in mol, should be rounded off to the least number of significant figures in the data, which is 3. So $n = c \times V = 0.997 \times 0.02162 = 0.0216$ mol to 3 significant figures.

Although digital scales can measure to many more than two decimal places and calculators can give 12 figures, be sensible and follow the significant figure rules.

ADDING OR SUBTRACTING

When adding or subtracting measurements, report the calculated value to the least number of decimal places. For example, in a gravimetric analysis the following measurements were recorded:

- mass of watch glass and filter paper: 4.39201 g
- mass of watch glass, filter paper and dried precipitate: 4.53 g
- mass of precipitate: = 4.53 − 4.39201 = 0.13799 g = 0.14 g

The original answer of 0.13799 g is an example of false precision, because one value in the data was not measured to five decimal places. The final answer must be stated to the smallest number of decimal places seen in the data, which is 2 decimal places in the measurement 4.53 g.

Decimal places

As with significant figures, you must be careful to record your measurements to the precision of the equipment used. If the precision of a weighing balance is ±0.01 g, you should record your value only to the nearest 0.01 g, i.e. to 2 decimal places.

When adding or subtracting measurements, report the calculated value to the least number of decimal places used in the calculation. For example, in a pH analysis the following measurements were recorded:

Sample A: 4.93   Sample B: 5.04   Sample C: 4.82

The average of these results is:

$$\frac{4.93 + 4.99 + 4.82}{3} = 4.9133333\dot{3}$$

As the sample results are all to 2 decimal places this average also needs to be rounded to 2 decimal places, i.e. 4.91. It would be misleading to report the average to a greater number of decimal places.

> **ℹ** If a calculated statistic such as mean or uncertainty has more significant figures than the data, it is usual practice to round the value to one more significant figure than in the data.
>
> For example, for the data set [4, 5, 6, 6, 7, 7] the mean is 5.833, so this would conventionally be rounded to 5.8.
>
> The uncertainty is 5.833 − 4 = 1.833, so this would be rounded to 1.8.
>
> If you do round multiple values as in this example make sure you round to a consistent and appropriate number of significant figures.

ANALYSING AND PRESENTING DATA

The raw data that has been obtained needs to be presented in a way that is clear, concise and accurate.

There are a number of ways of presenting data, including tables, graphs, flow charts and diagrams. The best way of visualising the data depends on its nature. Try several formats before making a final decision, to create the best possible presentation.

REVISION

Presenting raw and processed data in tables

Tables organise data into rows and columns, and can vary in complexity according to the nature of the data. Tables can be used to organise raw or processed data, or to summarise results.

The simplest form of a table is a two-column format. In a two-column table, the first column should contain the independent variable and the second column should contain the dependent variable.

Tables should have a descriptive title, column headings (including any units), and numbers should be aligned on the position of the decimal point.

A table of processed data usually presents simple averages or mean values of data. However, a mean on its own does not provide an accurate picture of the results.

To report processed data more accurately, the **uncertainty** should be stated as well.

UNCERTAINTY

When there is a range of measurements of a particular value, the mean must be accompanied by the uncertainty for your results to be presented in a meaningful and accurate way. Uncertainty is defined as:

uncertainty = ±maximum difference from the mean

PERCENTAGE ERROR

Percentage error (also known as percentage uncertainty) is a way to quantify how accurate a measurement is. In order to calculate the percentage error of your data, divide the uncertainty by the measurement and multiply by 100. That is:

$$\text{percentage error} = \frac{\text{uncertainty}}{\text{measured value}} \times 100$$

OTHER DESCRIPTIVE STATISTICAL MEASURES

Other statistical measures that can be useful, depending on the data obtained, are:

- mode: the **mode** is the value that appears most often in a data set. This measure is useful to describe qualitative or discrete data
- median: the **median** is the 'middle' value of an ordered list of values. The median is used when the data range is spread (for example, because of the presence of unusual results), so that the mean is less representative of the data.

Table 1.4.2 is a guide to choosing the most appropriate measure of central tendency for a data set.

TABLE 1.4.2 The most appropriate measures of central tendency for different types the type of data.

Type of data	Mode	Median	Mean
nominal (qualitative)	yes	no	no
ordinal (qualitative)	yes	yes	possibly
discrete or continuous (quantitative)	yes	yes	yes

Graphs

It is important to choose an appropriate graph type to suit the data that you have collected. Table 1.4.3 summarises suitable graphs for discrete and continuous data.

TABLE 1.4.3 Suitable graph types for qualitative and quantitative data

<table>
<tr><th>Type of data</th><th>Appropriate type of graph</th><th colspan="2">Examples</th></tr>
<tr><td rowspan="2">discrete</td><td rowspan="2">bar graph (left), histogram (right) or pie chart (lower)</td><td>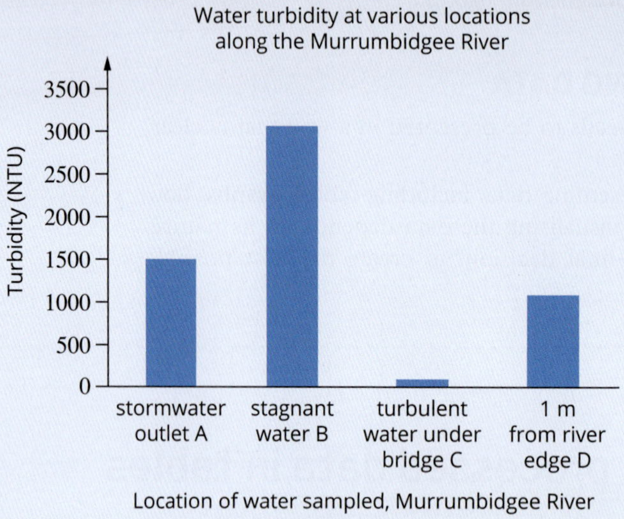
Water turbidity at various locations along the Murrumbidgee River
Turbidity (NTU)
3500
3000
2500
2000
1500
1000
500
0
stormwater outlet A
stagnant water B
turbulent water under bridge C
1 m from river edge D
Location of water sampled, Murrumbidgee River</td><td>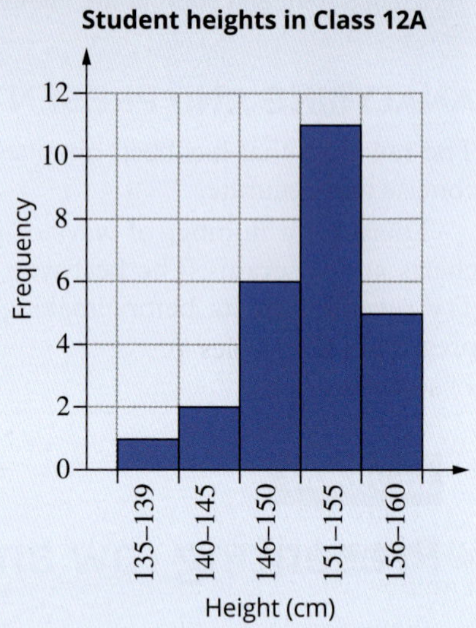
Student heights in Class 12A
Frequency
12
10
8
6
4
2
0
135–139
140–145
146–150
151–155
156–160
Height (cm)</td></tr>
<tr><td colspan="2">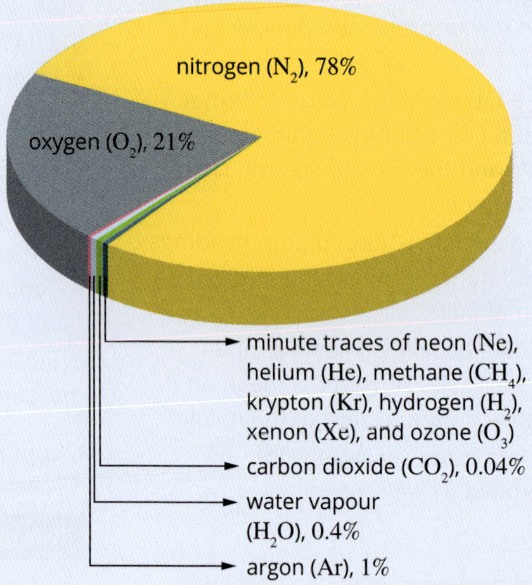
nitrogen (N2), 78%
oxygen (O2), 21%
minute traces of neon (Ne), helium (He), methane (CH4), krypton (Kr), hydrogen (H2), xenon (Xe), and ozone (O3)
carbon dioxide (CO2), 0.04%
water vapour (H2O), 0.4%
argon (Ar), 1%</td></tr>
</table>

Type of data	Appropriate type of graph	Examples
continuous	line graph or **scatter plot**, including a trend line	**Calibration curve of absorbance vs. concentration of sodium in standard solutions of sports drink**

In general, tables provide more detailed data than graphs, but it is easier to observe trends and patterns in data in graphical form than in tabular form.

Graphs are used when two variables are being considered and one variable is dependent on the other. The graph shows the relationship between the variables.

There are several types of graphs that can be used, including line graphs, **bar graphs** and pie charts. The best one to use will depend on the nature of the data and how you decide to analyse it.

General rules to follow when making a graph (Figure 1.4.1) include the following:

- Keep the graph simple and uncluttered.
- Use a descriptive title.
- Represent the independent variable on the x-axis and the dependent variable on the y-axis.
- Make axes lengths proportionate to the data.
- Clearly label axes with the variable and the unit in which it is measured.

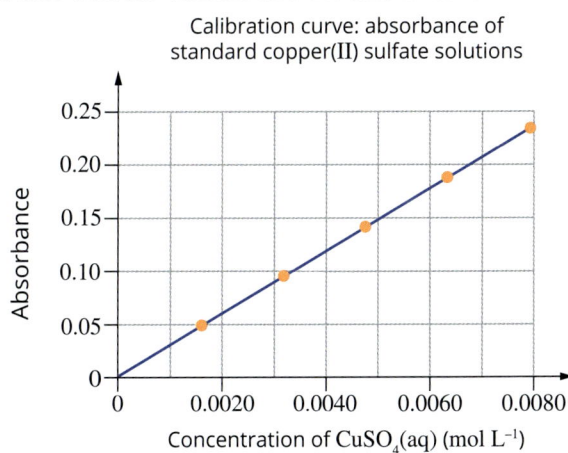

REVISION

Outliers

Sometimes a data point does not fit the overall **trend** and is clearly an error. This is called an **outlier**. An outlier is often caused by a mistake made in measuring or recording data, or from a random error in the measuring equipment. If there is an outlier, include it on the graph but ignore it when adding a **trend line**.

Calibration curve: absorbance of standard copper(II) sulfate solutions

FIGURE 1.4.1 A graph is a better way to show trends and patterns in data, compared to a table.

Distorting the truth

Poorly constructed graphs can alter your perception of the data. For example, Figure 1.4.2 shows two graphs that represent the same data, which are the test results of two groups of students. One group of students did not eat breakfast before doing the test and scored an average of 42 marks out of 50. The other group did eat breakfast and scored an average of 48 marks out of 50. One graph exaggerates the difference in marks between the two groups by using only a scale of 40 to 50 marks on the *y*-axis. It is important to make sure the graphs you create do not misrepresent your data in this way. You should also be wary of distorted data when interpreting graphs in other publications.

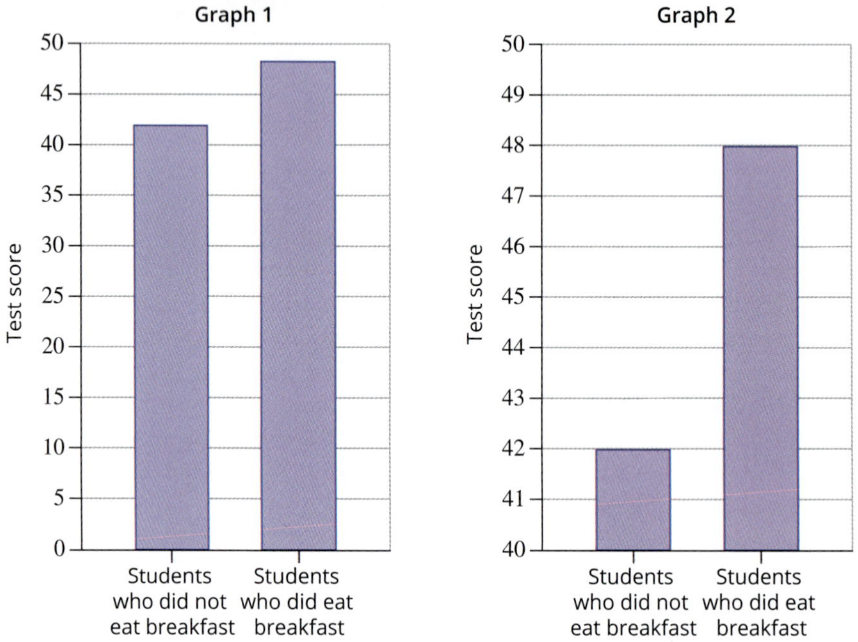

FIGURE 1.4.2 Graph 1 shows the difference in test scores between two groups of students out of the total 50 marks on the *y*-axis. Graph 2 shows the same difference but within only a narrow range of marks on the *y*-axis, which exaggerates the difference between the groups, making it appear larger than it really is.

PEER REVIEW

Your teacher may suggest that you partner with a student in your class, to provide each other with constructive feedback regarding the processing or your data. Consider the following:

- Is the processed data presented clearly in tables and / or graphs?
- Have any outliers been identified?
- Has the appropriate type of graph been selected to display the processed data?
- Are appropriate headings and units included?
- What are the strengths of the processed data collected?
- What questions do you have about the processed data collected?

1.4 Review

SUMMARY

- The number of significant figures or decimal places used for recording measurements depends on the precision of the instrument used. It is important to record data to the number of significant figures or decimal places available from the equipment or observation.
- Consider how the data will be presented and analysed. A wide range of analysis tools could be used. For example, tables organise data so that they can be compared, and graphs can show relationships and trends.
- The simplest form of a table is a two-column format in which the first column contains the independent variable and the second column contains the dependent variable.
- When there is a range of measurements of a particular value, the mean must be accompanied by a statement of the uncertainty for your results to be presented as a mean in an accurate way.
- General rules to follow when making a graph include the following:
  - Keep the graph simple and uncluttered.
  - Use a descriptive title.
  - Represent the independent variable on the x-axis and the dependent variable on the y-axis.
  - Make axes proportionate to the data.
  - Clearly label axes with both the variable and the unit in which it is measured.

KEY QUESTIONS

1 For the data set [21, 27, 19, 21, 24, 26, 22] determine:
  a the mean
  b the mode
  c the median.

2 a How many significant figures are there in the value 22.06 mL?
  b When multiplying or dividing, how many significant figures should be reported for the calculation?
  c When adding or subtracting, how many decimal places should be reported for the calculation?

3 a Which axis should be used to represent the dependent variable?
  b Which axis should be used to represent the independent variable?

4 A mass spectrum of an alcohol is shown below. What mass-to-charge ratio, m/z, is represented by the tallest peak?

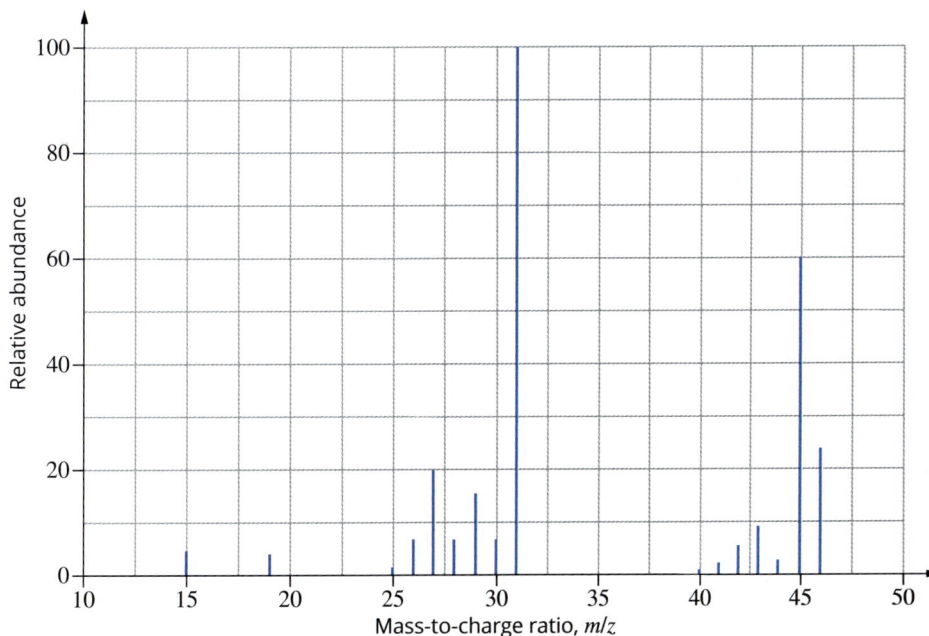

5 **a** Describe the trend in each of the following solubility curves.

b What conclusions can be drawn from this data?

Solubility curves of selected gases

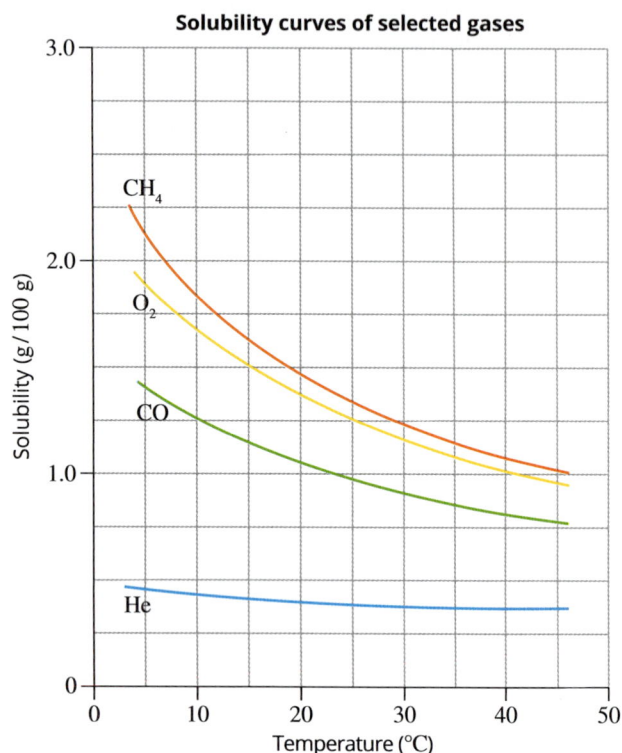

6 Standard sodium solutions were prepared and analysed using an atomic absorption spectrophotometer. Then a sodium solution of unknown concentration was inserted into the spectrophotometer under the same conditions. The following data were obtained.

Sodium concentration of solution (mg L^{-1})	Absorbance
0.00	0.000
0.50	0.034
1.00	0.068
1.50	0.103
2.00	0.140
2.50	0.175
3.00	0.242
3.50	0.247
4.00	0.280
4.50	0.315
5.00	0.352
unknown	0.155

a Plot the data on a scatter plot, using graph paper or a spreadsheet program.

b Define the term outlier, and describe what effect it could have on a line of best fit if left in the analysis.

c Identify any outliers in this set of data.

d Draw a trend line.

e Use your graph to determine the concentration of sodium of the unknown solution.

7 Describe at least four ways the graph below could be improved.

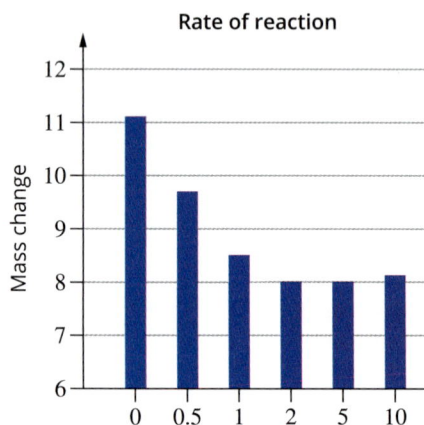

8 You are measuring the volumes of solutions in an experiment. Discuss the accuracy of your results if you are:

a using a 50 mL beaker

b using a 50 mL measuring cylinder

c using a 50 mL burette.

1.5 Analysing data and information

Now that the chosen topic has been thoroughly researched, the investigation has been conducted and data collected, it is time to draw it all together. You will now need to analyse your results to better understand the chemical processes behind them.

FIGURE 1.5.1 To discuss and conclude your investigation, use the raw and processed data.

FACTORS THAT CAN AFFECT THE INTERPRETATION, ANALYSIS AND UNDERSTANDING OF DATA

Correlation and causation

You need to be careful to distinguish between a correlation between two variables and a cause-and-effect relationship. For example, Figure 1.5.2 shows a direct correlation between the amount of cheese consumed per person in the USA and the number of people who died in the USA by becoming tangled in their bedsheets. However, we cannot assume that consumption of cheese increases the risk of death from entanglement in bedsheets. In other words, two sets of data might be correlated but have no relationship to each other; that is, there is no causation.

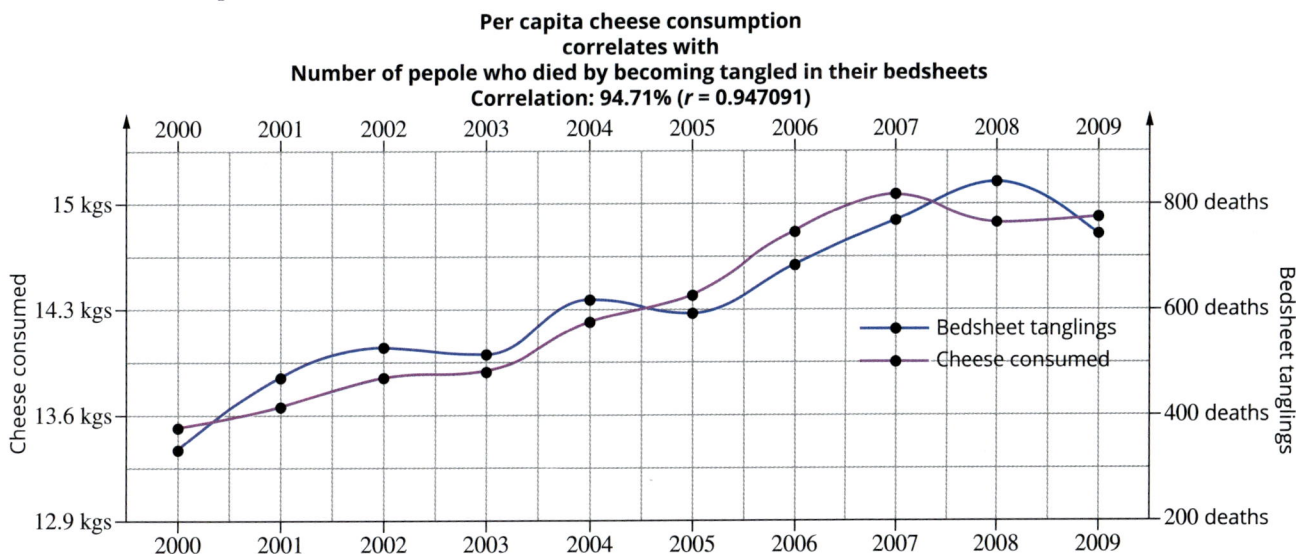

FIGURE 1.5.2 A correlation between two sets of data does not necessarily mean there is causation.

It is important to consider whether the relationship between data can be due to other factors. For example, the fact that sales of both ice-cream and sunscreen are greater in Sydney in February compared to July could be a consequence of the hotter weather, instead of any relationship between the sales of each product.

Evaluating the data

Some useful questions to consider when interpreting data include:

- Has the original question been answered?
- Do the results meet expectations? Do they make sense?
- What are the main conclusions? Are other interpretations possible?
- Is the supporting data of sufficient quality? How current is it? How was it collected?
- Can the results be supported statistically? (That is, are they statistically significant?)

REVISION   **GO TO ➤** Year 11 Section 1.5

Explaining results in the discussion

The key sections in the discussion of an investigation are:
- analysing and evaluating data
- evaluating the investigative procedure
- explaining the link between the investigation findings and the relevant chemical concepts.

Consider the message to be conveyed to the audience when writing the discussion. At the conclusion of the discussion, the audience must have a clear idea of the context, results and implications of the investigation.

Analysing and evaluating data

In the discussion, the findings of the investigation need to be analysed and interpreted.

- State whether a pattern, trend or relationship was observed between the independent and dependent variables. Describe what kind of pattern it was, and specify under what conditions it was observed.
- Were there discrepancies, deviations or anomalies in the data? If so, these should be acknowledged and explained.
- Identify any limitations in the data you have collected. Perhaps a larger sample or further variations in the independent variable would lead to a stronger conclusion.

Remember that unexpected results do not make an investigation a failure. However, the findings must be discussed and linked back to the hypothesis, purpose and procedure.

Describing more complex trends

You may find that you need to describe a more complex trend in data than a simple linear or exponential relationship. Figure 1.5.3 shows a titration curve of the pH change of a sodium hydroxide solution during the progress of titration with ethanoic acid. This trend shows a slow decrease in pH of the sodium hydroxide solution when up to 19 mL of ethanoic acid is added. Then a rapid drop in pH occurs when less than 1 mL of ethanoic acid is added, after the addition of 20 mL of ethanoic acid the pH slowly decreases from pH 6 to pH 5.

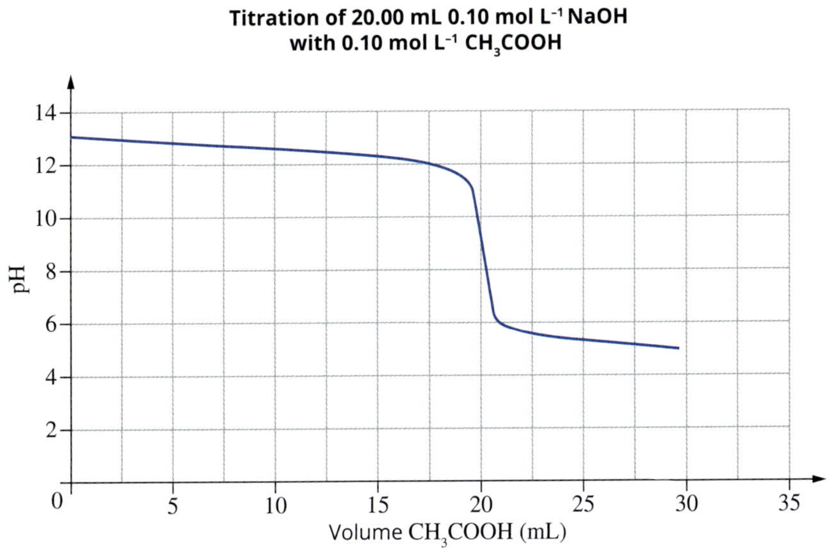

Titration of 20.00 mL 0.10 mol L⁻¹ NaOH with 0.10 mol L⁻¹ CH₃COOH

FIGURE 1.5.3 A titration curve showing the pH of a sodium hydroxide solution during titration with ethanoic acid

Reading information from a graph

An important skill is being able to extract information from a graph. Consider Figure 1.5.4, which shows the solubility curves of several compounds in water.

Solubility is a measure of the mass of solute that will dissolve in a solvent. The solubility of a solute depends on temperature. A solubility curve shows the relationship between the temperature of the solution and the maximum mass of solute that will dissolve in 100 g of water. The following example shows the steps required to determine the mass of sodium nitrate (the solute) that will dissolve in 100 g of water at 50°C.

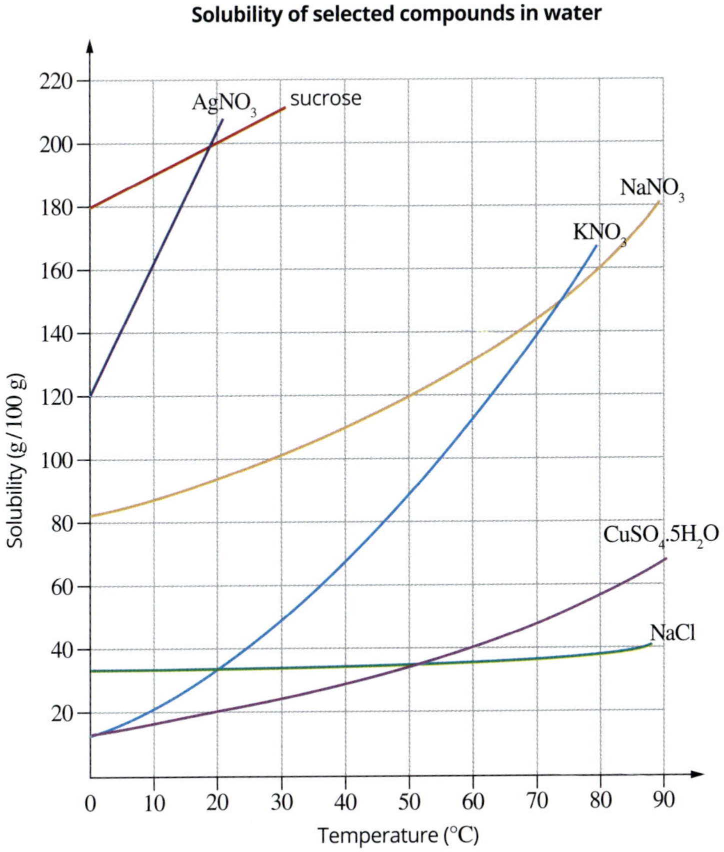

FIGURE 1.5.4 A line graph, showing continuous quantitative data.

Worked example 1.5.1

READING INFORMATION FROM A GRAPH

Using the graph below, determine the maximum mass of sodium nitrate ($NaNO_3$) that can be dissolved in 100 g of water at 50°C.

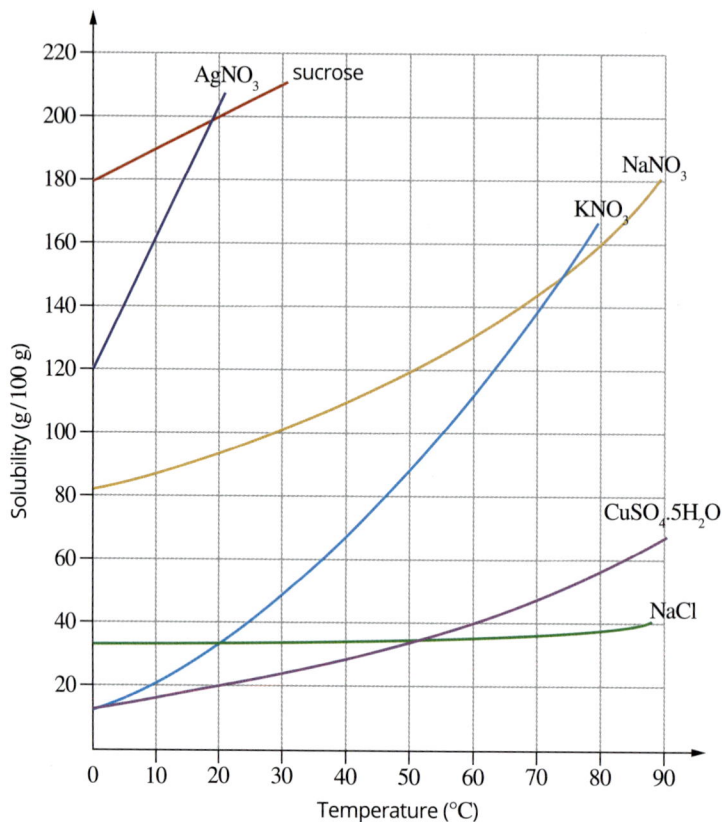

Thinking	Working
The solubility curve represents the maximum mass of solute that will dissolve in 100 g of water at a given temperature.	Draw a vertical line from 50°C on the x-axis to intersect with the solubility curve for $NaNO_3$.
Draw a vertical line from the required temperature on the x-axis to intersect with the solubility curve of the substance.	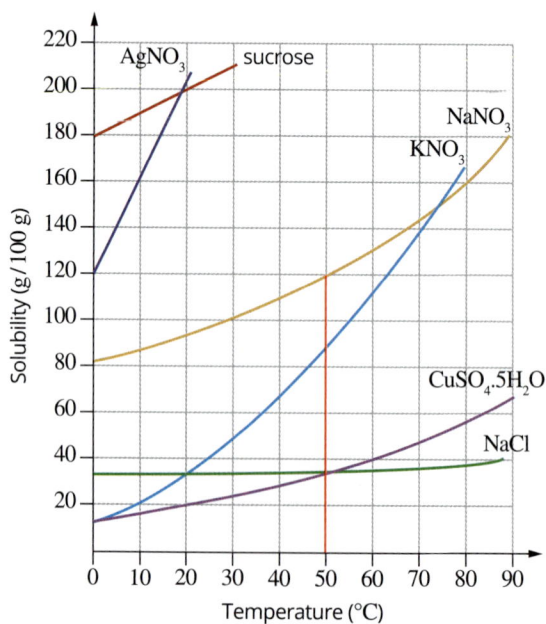

Draw a horizontal line from the intersection point of the solubility curve to the y-axis. The point on the y-axis represents the mass of dissolved substance per 100g of water.	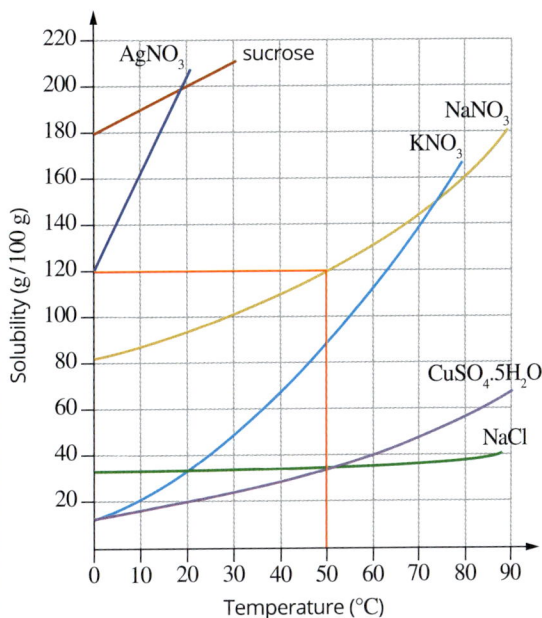
Read the solubility of the substance at the particular temperature from the graph	The horizontal line intersects the y-axis at 120g. Therefore the maximum mass of $NaNO_3$ that will dissolve in 100g of water at 50°C is 120g.

Worked example: Try yourself 1.5.1

READING INFORMATION FROM A GRAPH

Using the graph below, determine the maximum mass of potassium nitrate (KNO_3) that can be dissolved in 100g of water at 60°C.

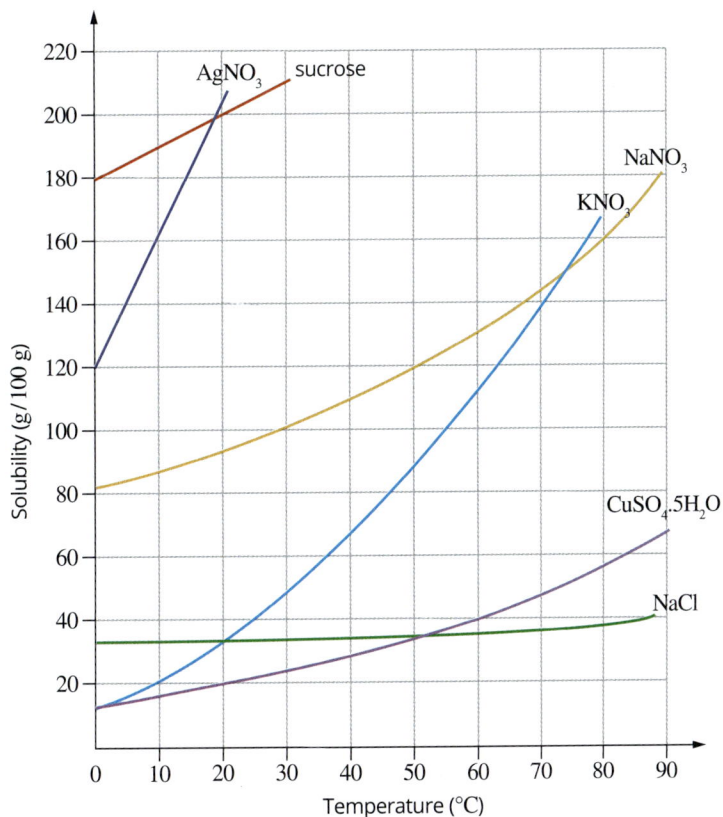

Evaluating the investigation

It is important to discuss the limitations of the investigation. Evaluate the procedure and identify any issues that could have affected the validity, accuracy, precision or reliability of the data. Sources of errors and uncertainty must also be stated in the discussion.

Once any limitations or problems in the methodology have been identified, recommend improvements that could be made if the investigation is repeated.

BIAS

Bias may occur in any part of the investigation, including sampling and measurements. Bias is a form of systematic error resulting from the researcher's personal preferences or motivations. There are many types of bias, including poor definitions of both concepts and variables, incorrect assumptions, and errors in the investigation design and procedure. Some biases cannot be eliminated, but they should at least be addressed in the discussion.

ACCURACY

In the discussion, evaluate the degree of accuracy and precision of the measurements for each variable of the hypothesis. Comment on the uncertainties obtained.

If it is relevant, compare the chosen procedure with any other procedure that might have been used, evaluating the advantages and disadvantages of the selected procedure and the effect on the results.

VALIDITY

Validity refers to whether an experiment or investigation is actually testing the set hypothesis and purpose. Factors influencing validity include:
- whether your experiment measures what it claims to measure (i.e. your experiment should test your hypothesis)
- whether the independent variable influenced the dependent variable in the way you thought it would (i.e. whether something observed in your experiment was the result of your experimental conditions, and not some other cause that you did not consider)
- the degree to which your findings can be generalised.

RELIABILITY

When discussing the results, indicate the range of the data obtained from replicates. Explain how the sample size was selected. Larger samples are usually more reliable, but time and resources might have been limited. Discuss whether the results of the investigation have been limited by the sample size.

The control group is important to the reliability of the investigation, because it helps to determine whether a variable that should have been controlled has been overlooked, and it could explain any unexpected results.

ERROR

Discuss any source of systematic or random error. When limitations of the procedure and results have been identified, suggest ways of improving the investigation.

CRITICALLY EVALUATING RESOURCES

Not all sources are **credible**. It is essential to critically evaluate the content and origin of each source. Questions you should always ask when evaluating a source include:
- Who created this information? What are the qualifications, **expertise**, **reputation** and **affiliation** of the author/s?
- Why was it written?
- Where was it published?
- When was it published?
- How often is the information referred to by other researchers?
- Are conclusions supported by data or evidence?
- What is implied?
- What is omitted?
- Are personal opinions or values presented?
- Does it objectively and accurately describe a scientific concept or **phenomenon**?
- How might other people understand or interpret this message differently from me?

When evaluating the validity or bias of websites, consider its domain extension. For example:

- .gov stands for a government organisation
- .edu stands for an educational organisation such as a school or university
- .org and .net can be used by an individual or organisation, but are often used by non-profit organisations
- .com and .biz stand for businesses.

When conducting a literature review, it can be useful to summarise your findings in a table, such as that shown in Table 1.5.2.

TABLE 1.5.2 A table can be used to help summarise information while researching. This example relates to techniques used by Indigenous Australians to remove toxins from food.

Type of bush food	Notes	Source	Reliability of source
bush tomato *Solanum centrale*	'The fruits were "probably the most important of all the Central Australian plant foods" (citing Latz 1995).' Purplish-green colour when unripe. Traditionally eaten raw when greenish-white to yellow-brown in colour. Dried on plant, then shaken from plant, rubbed into sand, followed by pounding or grinding into a paste with water, formed into balls or cakes (citing Peterson 1979).	Hegarty, M.P., Hegarty, E.E. & Wills, R. (2001). *Food Safety of Australian Plant Bushfoods*: Publication No 01/28, RIRDC, Barton, ACT.	Credible. Published by Rural Industries Research and Development Corporation (RIRDC), review article with credible primary sources.
Macadamia robusta (toxic type of macadamia nut)	Nuts treated by soaking and baking to remove toxins.	Hegarty, M.P., Hegarty, E.E. & Wills, R. (2001). *Food Safety of Australian Plant Bushfoods*: Publication No 01/28, RIRDC, Barton, ACT.	Credible. Published by Rural Industries Research and Development Corporation (RIRDC), review article with credible primary sources.
lemon-scented tea-tree	Toxins removed by grinding and baking.	Hegarty, M.P., Hegarty, E.E. & Wills, R. (2001). *Food Safety of Australian Plant Bushfoods*: Publication No 01/28, RIRDC, Barton, ACT.	Credible. Published by Rural Industries Research and Development Corporation (RIRDC), review article with credible primary sources.
cycad seed (*Macrozamia* species)		source: https://pubchem. ncbi.nlm.nih.gov/compound/ Macrozamin#section=Top	Credible government source.

PEER REVIEW

Your teacher may suggest that you work with another student in your class, so that you can provide each other with constructive feedback regarding the analysis of your data. Consider the following:

- Is the data accurately discussed?
- Have any limitations of the procedure or data collection been identified?
- Have any recommendations been made to improve the investigation if time permitted repeating the study?
- What are the strengths of the data analysis?
- What other questions do you have about the data analysis?

1.5 Review

SUMMARY

- After completing your investigation you must analyse and interpret your data. This is done in the discussion section of your investigation report.
  - State whether a pattern, trend or relationship was observed between the independent and dependent variables. Describe what kind of pattern it was and specify under what conditions it was observed.
  - If possible, create a mathematical model to describe your data.
  - Were there discrepancies, deviations or anomalies in the data? If so, these should be acknowledged and explained.
  - Identify any limitations in the data collected.

- It is important to discuss the limitations of your investigation procedure. Evaluate the procedure and identify any issues that could have affected the validity, accuracy, precision or reliability of the data. Sources of errors and uncertainty must also be stated in the discussion.
- When discussing the results, indicate the range of the data obtained from replicates. Explain how the sample size was selected. Discuss whether the results of the investigation were limited by the sample size.

KEY QUESTIONS

1 What types of graphs would be suitable for displaying discrete data?

2 Describe how the reaction rate changes over time based on information in the following graph:

3 Consider the solubility curve of potassium nitrate (KNO_3) shown in the graph below.

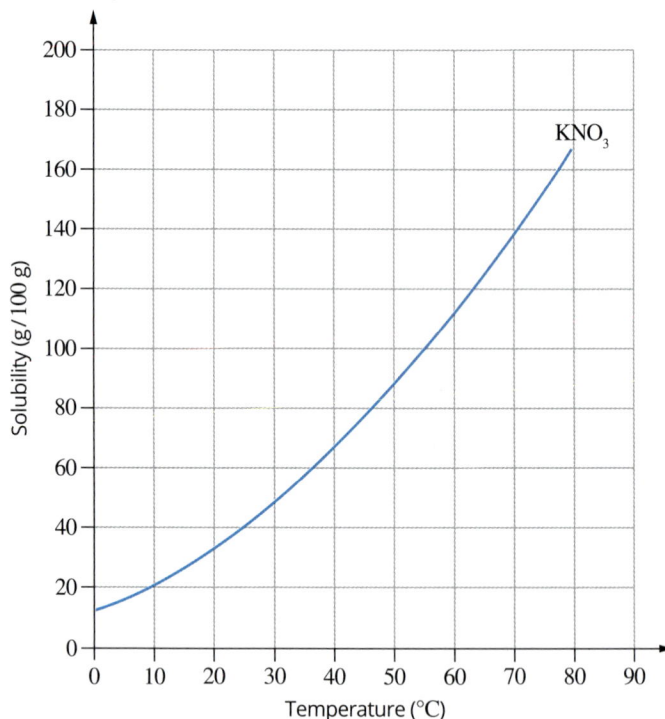

a What mass of potassium nitrate will dissolve in 500 g of water at 70°C?

b If 25 g of KNO_3 was added to 50 g of water at 70°C, how much more must be added until no more KNO_3 will dissolve?

c If 100 g of KNO_3 is added to 50 g of water at 40°C, what mass will remain undissolved?

4 List the features of a credible primary or secondary source.

1.6 Problem solving

Once you have analysed your results you can apply them to chemical concepts in order to evaluate your conclusions. In this section you will learn how analysing your investigation leads to a better understanding of the underlying scientific principles of your research.

MODELLING

Table 1.6.1 lists examples of investigations that could be used to explain phenomena, make predictions and solve problems.

TABLE 1.6.1 Examples of models that can be used in investigations

Type of investigation	Application	Example
Using mathematical modelling to make predictions.	Use a formula.	Calculate the pH, pOH, hydrogen ion (H^+) concentration and hydroxide ion (OH^-) concentration for a range of solutions.
Using molecular modelling to make predictions.	Use molecular modelling to explain intermolecular bonding.	Distinguish between the strength of intermolecular bonding including hydrogen bonding, dipole–dipole bonding and dispersion forces.
Using spectra to make predictions.	Use mass spectra, infra-red spectra and nuclear magnetic resonance spectra.	Draw the structure of an organic molecule.
Using computer modelling.	Use computer simulations in biochemistry.	Predict the tertiary structure of a protein from its primary structure.
Critiquing claims made by the media.	Compare emotive advertising with evidence-based claims, for example health claims on food packaging.	Evaluate the impact of societal and economic influences on the development of claims, including prediction of climate change and suggested remedies for health conditions.

LITERATURE REVIEW

Table 1.6.2 shows an example of how summarising information in a table can help you identify patterns in a literature review.

TABLE 1.6.2 An in-progress summary of information obtained through a literature review regarding the salinity of water and suitability for drinking

Source	Author and year of publication	Country/ Region	Sample size	Type	Key ideas	Credible?
'Will salt water quench the world's thirst'? *Scientific American,* volume 315, issue 5 https://www.scientificamerican.com/article/will-salt-water-quench-the-world-s-thirst/	Sabrina Stierwalt, 2016	USA	not applicable	review	Cost of desalination is reducing. Graphene could be used to filter water.	Yes. Author qualified scientist, credible science magazine.
'Aluminum-cycle ion exchange process for hardness removal: A new approach for sustainable softening' *Environmental Science and Technology* volume 50, issue 21, pages 11943–11950 DOI: 10.1021/acs.est.6b03021	Jinze Li et al., 2016		not applicable	primary source	Al^{3+} ions can be used to remove ions from water.	Yes. Primary source, credible authors, peer-reviewed journal, recent article.
'Methods used for the characterization of the chemical composition and biological activity of environmental waters throughout the United States, 2012–2014' U.S. Geological Survey Open-File Report 2017–1011	Romanok, K. et al.				Analytical results including major cations and anions at various sampling sites in USA – potential to compare with Australian data.	
'The role of water in Australia's uncertain future' http://www.bom.gov.au/water/	Amgad Elmahdi, Matthew Hardy				Link to Bureau of Meterology online database.	Yes. Qualified authors.

DISCUSSING RELEVANT CHEMICAL CONCEPTS

To make the investigation more meaningful, it should be explained in the context of current chemical ideas, concepts, theories and models. Within this context, explain the basis for the hypothesis.

Relating your findings to a chemical concept

During the analysing stage of your investigation (Section 1.5) you were able to find trends, patterns and mathematical models of your results. This is the framework in which to discuss whether the data supported or refuted the hypothesis. Ask questions such as:

- Was the hypothesis supported?
- Has the hypothesis been fully answered? (If not, give an explanation of why this is so and suggest what could be done to either improve or complement the investigation.)
- Do the results contradict the hypothesis? If so, why? (The explanation must be plausible and must be based on the results and previous evidence.)

Providing a theoretical context also enables comparison of the results with existing relevant research and knowledge. After identifying the major findings of the investigation, ask questions such as:

- How do the results fit with the literature?
- Do the results contradict the literature?
- Do the results fill a gap in the literature?
- Do the results lead to further questions?
- Can the results be extended to another situation?

Be sure to discuss the broader implications of the findings. Implications are the bigger picture. Outlining them for the audience is an important part of the investigation. Ask questions such as:

- Do the results contribute to or impact on the existing literature and knowledge of the topic?
- Are there any practical applications for the results?

DRAWING EVIDENCE-BASED CONCLUSIONS

Your conclusion links the collected evidence to the hypothesis and provides a justified response to the research question. Indicate whether the hypothesis was supported or refuted and the evidence on which this is based (that is, the results). Do not provide irrelevant information. Only refer to the specifics of the hypothesis and the research question, and do not make generalisations.

What type of evidence is needed to draw valid conclusions?

A valid conclusion can be drawn if:

- the procedure was designed to obtain data to answer the purpose and hypothesis
- only one independent variable was changed
- the dependent variable was measured or observed
- all other variables were controlled
- the experiment was replicated
- the procedure could be repeated by another person
- the data obtained was accurate and precise
- there were no significant limitations with the procedure and data obtained
- links were made between the data obtained and chemical theory.

Read the examples of weak and strong conclusions in Table 1.6.3 and Table 1.6.4 for the hypothesis and research question shown.

TABLE 1.6.3 Examples of weak and strong conclusions concerning a hypothesis

Hypothesis: An increase in the temperature of pond water will result in a decrease in the measured pH of the water sample.

Weak conclusion	Strong conclusion
The pH of water decreased as temperature increased.	When the temperature increased from 5°C to 40°C, the pH of the water decreased from 7.4 to 6.8.

TABLE 1.6.4 Examples of strong and weak conclusions in response to the inquiry question

Research question: Does temperature affect the pH of water?

Weak conclusion	Strong conclusion
The results show that temperature does affect the pH of water.	Analysis of the results on the effect of an increase in temperature of water from 5°C to 40°C showed an inverse relationship in which the pH of water decreased from 7.4 to 6.7. These results support the current knowledge that an increase in water temperature results in a decrease in its pH.

REVISION

Interpreting scientific and media texts

Sometimes you may be required to investigate claims and conclusions made by other sources, such as scientific and media texts. As discussed in Section 1.4, some sources are more credible than others. Once you have analysed the validity of the primary or secondary source, you will be able to follow the steps described above in evaluating their conclusions.

PEER REVIEW

Your teacher may suggest that you work with another student in your class, so that you can provide each other with constructive feedback regarding the analysis and interpretation of of your results. Consider the following:

- Are the findings accurately discussed in relation to relevant chemical concepts?
- Is the conclusion strong?
- Is the conclusion directed to the purpose, hypothesis and inquiry question?
- What are the strengths of the conclusion?
- What questions do you have about the conclusion?

1.6 Review

SUMMARY

- To make the investigation more meaningful, it should be explained in the context of current chemical ideas, concepts, theories and models. Within this context, explain the basis for the hypothesis.

- Indicate whether the hypothesis was supported or refuted and on what evidence this is based (that is, the results). Do not provide irrelevant information. Only refer to the specifics of the hypothesis and the research question and do not make generalisations.

KEY QUESTIONS

1 A student wants to select a wavelength at which a particular organic compound strongly absorbs ultra-violet light. The diagram below shows an absorption spectrum for the compound.

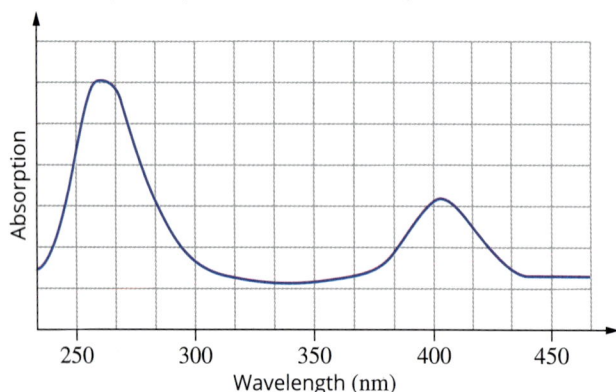

What wavelength should the student select?

A 260 nm   B 280 nm

C 400 nm   D 450 nm

2 A procedure was repeated five times. How should the following statement be rewritten?

In order to minimise the potential of random errors, many repeats of the procedure were conducted.

3 Most processed foods sold in Australia contain a nutrition information panel on the packaging. How could you test the manufacturer's claim about the sodium content of a processed food product?

4 A student summarised an organic reaction pathway to synthesise halothane (a general anaesthetic) as follows.

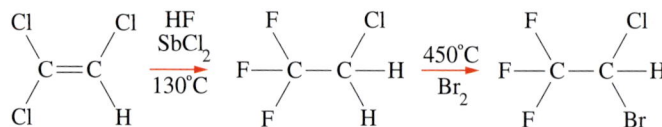

a What information is missing from the diagram?

b Write the molecular formula of:

  i the starting compound

  ii the intermediate compound

  iii halothane.

1.7 Communicating

The way you approach communicating your results will depend on the audience you want to reach. For example, if you are communicating with a general audience you may want to write a news article or blog post. These types of communication shouldn't use too much scientific language, because your audience probably does not have a science background.

Throughout this course you will need to present your research using appropriate scientific language and notation. There are many different presentation formats that are used such as posters, oral presentations and reports. This section covers the main characteristics of effective science communication and report writing, including objectivity, clarity, conciseness and coherence.

PRESENTING YOUR WORK

Your teacher will specify how you should present your work. Two common formats are a scientific report and a scientific poster.

First identify your audience. This might be your teacher, your peers or the general public. Then consider how you could use figures such as diagrams, graphs or flowcharts to aid communication, for example to show how equipment was set up, or to summarise an organic chemical pathway.

Scientific report

Scientific reports can be written to describe the findings of an experiment or a literature review. Your reports should include the following components, which may be used as headings:

- name (and lab partner name)
- date
- title
- introduction
  - summary of relevant background information
  - purpose
  - hypothesis
  - definition of independent, dependent and controlled variables
- materials
  - chemicals (including quantities and concentrations) and equipment
  - risk assessment (using safety data sheets)
- procedure
  - step-by-step instructions that the reader can follow to replicate the experiment if required
  - can include two-dimensional scientific diagrams
- results
  - summary data presented in tables or figures
  - all tables and figures are numbered and have an appropriate title
- discussion
  - brief explanation of the significance of the results
  - direct reference to data in tables and/or figures
  - links to relevant chemical theory
  - limitations of the research and proposed avenues for further research
- conclusion
  - summary of the research findings using evidence
  - relates to purpose and hypothesis
- references
  - formatted in a consistent style.

Scientific poster

Scientists often present their research at conferences in the form of a scientific poster. This is a summary of their research that includes visual support such as tables, diagrams, graphs and flowcharts (Figure 1.7.1).

Regardless of the style of the poster, it is a good idea to help readers find information easily by numbering tables and figures and referring to these in the text.

Is the order of the electrochemical series affected by half-cell solution concentration?
Louise Lennard
Heinemann Chemistry College
Unit 3 Chemistry 2017

Introduction

A galvanic cell can be constructed between two half-cells (Commons & Commons 2016). The electrochemical series can be used to predict whether a spontaneous redox reaction will occur between the strongest oxidising agent (oxidant) and strongest reducing agent (reductant). However, the table of standard reduction potentials published in the NESA Chemistry Data Book (Table 1) is based on reactions taking place under standard conditions (i.e. 25°C and using 1 M solutions in half-cells) (NESA 2017).

Table 1 Extracts of the table of standard reduction potentials (NESA, 2017)

Reaction	Standard electrode potential (E^0) in volts at 25°C
$Cu^{2+}(aq) + 2e^- \rightleftharpoons Cu(s)$	+0.34
$Pb^{2+}(aq) + 2e^- \rightleftharpoons Pb(s)$	−0.13
$Sn^{2+}(aq) + 2e^- \rightleftharpoons Sn(s)$	−0.14
$Ni^{2+}(aq) + 2e^- \rightleftharpoons Ni(s)$	−0.24
$Zn^{2+}(aq) + 2e^- \rightleftharpoons Zn(s)$	−0.76

Aim: To determine whether changing the concentration of the solutions in half-cells affects the recorded cell voltage and polarity of electrodes.
Hypothesis: If temperature affects cell potential, there will not be a difference in cell potential if the temperature is kept constant, and the concentration of half-cell solutions changes from 1 mol L⁻¹ to 2 mol L⁻¹ or 0.1 mol L⁻¹.
Alternate hypothesis: Changing the concentration of half-cell solutions will result in a measured difference in cell potential (compared to the NESA table of standard reduction potentials).

Methodology

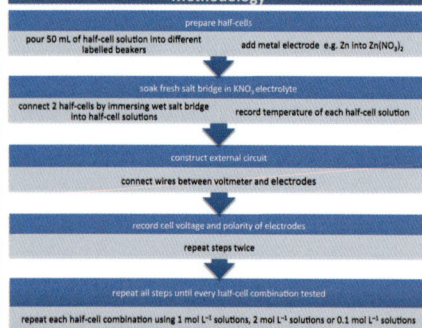

prepare half-cells

pour 50 mL of half-cell solution into different labelled beakers → add metal electrode e.g. Zn into $Zn(NO_3)_2$

soak fresh salt bridge in KNO_3 electrolyte

connect 2 half-cells by immersing wet salt bridge into half-cell solutions → record temperature of each half-cell solution

construct external circuit

connect wires between voltmeter and electrodes

record cell voltage and polarity of electrodes

repeat steps twice

repeat all steps until every half-cell combination tested

repeat each half-cell combination using 1 mol L⁻¹ solutions, 2 mol L⁻¹ solutions or 0.1 mol L⁻¹ solutions

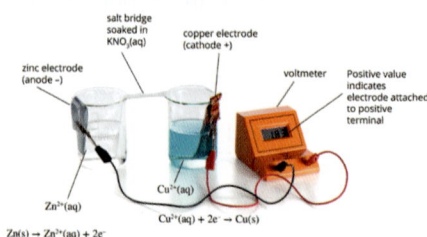

Figure 1 Example galvanic cell (Zn/Zn^{2+} and Cu^{2+}/Cu) under standard conditions, 25°C with 1 mol L⁻¹ solutions (Science Photo C024/3725RM)

Results

Table 2 Extracts of experimental data, average cell potential using 1.00 mol L⁻¹ half-cell solutions (from 3 values for each experiment)

Galvanic cell combination	Temperature of first half-cell (°C)	Temperature of other half-cell (°C)	Average cell potential (V)	Cathode
copper/zinc	22	22	1.05	copper
copper/lead	22	22	0.41	copper
copper/tin	22	22	0.40	copper
copper/nickel	22	22	0.50	copper
lead/zinc	22	22	0.61	lead
lead/tin	22	22	0.05	lead
lead/nickel	22	22	0.07	lead
nickel/zinc	22	22	0.41	nickel

Table 3 Comparison of the order of the table of standard reduction potentials under different conditions (differences highlighted)

Order of the table of standard reduction potentials (NESA 2017)	Table of standard reduction potentials derived from experiments using 1.00 mol L⁻¹ solutions	Table of standard reduction potentials derived from experiments using 2.00 mol L⁻¹ solutions	Table of standard reduction potentials derived from experiments using 0.010 mol L⁻¹ solutions
$Cu^{2+}(aq) + 2e^- \rightleftharpoons Cu(s)$	$Cu^{2+}(aq) + 2e^- \rightleftharpoons Cu(s)$	$Cu^{2+}(aq) + 2e^- \rightleftharpoons Cu(s)$	$Cu^{2+}(aq) + 2e^- \rightleftharpoons Cu(s)$
$Pb^{2+}(aq) + 2e^- \rightleftharpoons Pb(s)$	$Pb^{2+}(aq) + 2e^- \rightleftharpoons Pb(s)$	$Pb^{2+}(aq) + 2e^- \rightleftharpoons Pb(s)$	$Sn^{2+}(aq) + 2e^- \rightleftharpoons Sn(s)$
$Sn^{2+}(aq) + 2e^- \rightleftharpoons Sn(s)$	$Sn^{2+}(aq) + 2e^- \rightleftharpoons Sn(s)$	$Sn^{2+}(aq) + 2e^- \rightleftharpoons Sn(s)$	$Pb^{2+}(aq) + 2e^- \rightleftharpoons Pb(s)$
$Ni^{2+}(aq) + 2e^- \rightleftharpoons Ni(s)$	$Ni^{2+}(aq) + 2e^- \rightleftharpoons Ni(s)$	$Ni^{2+}(aq) + 2e^- \rightleftharpoons Ni(s)$	$Ni^{2+}(aq) + 2e^- \rightleftharpoons Ni(s)$
$Zn^{2+}(aq) + 2e^- \rightleftharpoons Zn(s)$	$Zn^{2+}(aq) + 2e^- \rightleftharpoons Zn(s)$	$Zn^{2+}(aq) + 2e^- \rightleftharpoons Zn(s)$	$Zn^{2+}(aq) + 2e^- \rightleftharpoons Zn(s)$

Discussion

Galvanic cells are rarely constructed under standard conditions (25°C and 1 mol L⁻¹ solutions). Consequently, the results of this investigation are important when trying to predict whether spontaneous redox reactions will occur, and identifying the strongest oxidising and reducing agents.

The cathode was identified as the electrode connected to the positive terminal of the voltmeter. Reduction always occurs at the cathode (Commons & Commons 2016). The order of the table of standard reduction potentials was determined by looking at each half-cell combination in turn.

The data in Table 2 shows the cell voltage recorded in each experiment. The largest cell potential measured was between the Cu/Cu^{2+} and Zn/Zn^{2+} half-cells, which supports the order of the table of standard reduction potentials published by NESA (2017). Individual cell voltages differed from NESA data, possibly due to the temperatures of half-cells not being controlled at 25°C, measured at 22°C. For example, the cell voltage for the zinc/copper galvanic cell was found to be 1.05 V (Table 2) in contrast to 1.10 V under standard conditions (NESA 2017).

The data in Table 3 shows that the order of the table of standard reduction potentials for experiments with half-cell cation concentrations at 2.00 mol L⁻¹ was the same as those measured at 1.00 mol L⁻¹. When 0.010 mol L⁻¹ solutions were used, the order of the lead and tin reduction equations was reversed when compared to the cell potentials published by NESA (NESA 2017). This could have been due to differences in temperature of the half-cells, or an effect of the concentration of solutions.

Further experiments should be conducted:
- maintaining the temperature at 25°C (e.g. by placing the half-cells in a water bath).
- repeating the experiments with different half-cell solutions (e.g. 0.001 mol L⁻¹, 0.00500 mol L⁻¹, 0.500 mol L⁻¹) would provide a useful comparison to determine whether a cause and effect relationship exists between half-cell concentration and the order of the table of standard reduction potentials.

Conclusion

There were measured differences in cell potential and electrode polarity at 22°C if the temperature was kept constant, when concentration of half-cell solutions changes from 1.00 mol L⁻¹ to 0.01 mol L⁻¹.

The results of this study suggest:
- that the concentration of half-cell solutions did at least partially affect the order of the table of standard reduction potentials when compared to data published by NESA (NESA 2017)

Further research:
- should be conducted using temperature data-logging equipment, with a higher degree of precision (the thermometers used to measure temperature were reliable only to the nearest 1°C)
- maintenance the half-cell concentration at 25°C by using a water bath should be trialled.

References:
Commons, P. & Commons, C. (2016) *Heinemann Chemistry 2*, 5th edition p. xx
NSW Education Standards Authority (2017) Chemistry formulae sheet, data sheet and periodic table.
http://syllabus.nesa.nsw.edu.au/assets/chemistry/files/chemistry-formulae-sheet-data-sheet-periodic-table-hsc-exams-2019.pdf

Acknowledgements:
Thanks to xx (e.g. lab technician) for organising the equipment.
Thanks to xx for direction.

FIGURE 1.7.1 An example of a scientific poster

Historical or theoretical essay

An essay contains the following elements or characteristics:
- There is a formal structure, including an introduction, body paragraphs and a conclusion.
- The introduction states the focus of the essay.
- Each paragraph makes a new point supported by evidence.
- Each paragraph has a link back to the previous paragraph.
- The concluding paragraph draws all of the information together but does not introduce any new information.
- Any illustrations are included in an appendix at the end of the essay.

Oral presentation

Consider the following elements when you prepare an oral presentation.
- The presentation must be engaging.
- Use cue cards but do not read directly from them.
- Look at the audience as you speak.
- Smile and appear confident (Figure 1.7.2).
- Try not to fidget.

Other types of presentation

There are many other ways to present your findings, such as:

- making a documentary or media report
- developing an evidence-based argument
- developing an environmental management plan
- analysing a work of fiction or film for scientific relevance
- creating a visual presentation.

Analysing relevant information

Scientific research should always be objective and neutral. Any premise presented must be supported with facts and evidence to allow the audience to make its own decision. Identify the evidence supporting or contradicting each point you want to make. It is also important to explain connections between ideas, concepts, theories and models. Figure 1.7.3 shows the questions you need to consider when writing your investigation report.

Once you have analysed your sources, annotate your outline, indicating where you will use evidence and what the source of that evidence is. Try to introduce only one idea per sentence and one theme per paragraph.

FIGURE 1.7.2 When you give an oral presentation, use body language to engage the audience. Make eye contact, look around the audience and smile.

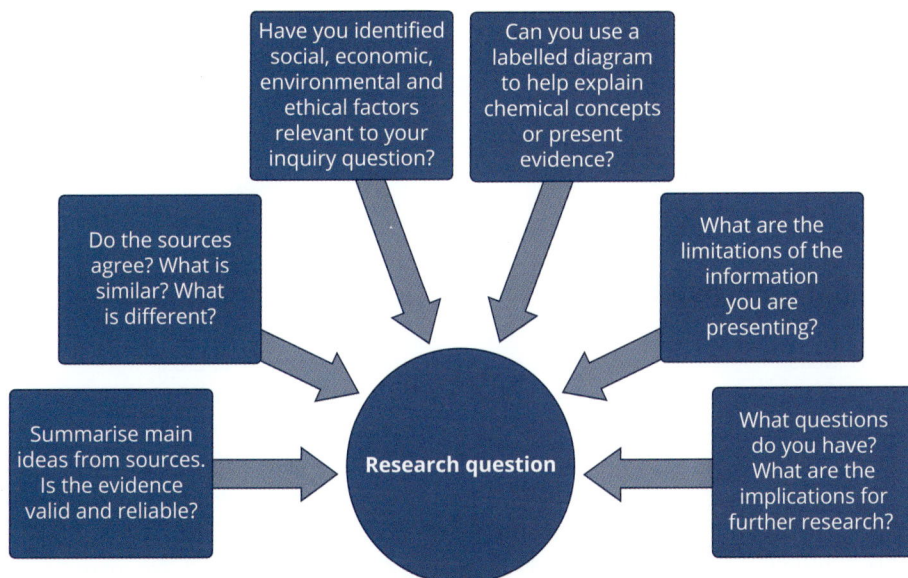

FIGURE 1.7.3 Discuss relevant information, ideas, concepts, implications and make sure your discussion is relevant to the question under investigation.

For example, in a report on 'Experimental research into biodegradability of plastics', the third paragraph might contain information from:

- Selke et al. (2015), who reported no significant degradation
- Chiellini et al. (2007), who reported a significant degradation.

A report should include an analysis and synthesis of your sources. The information from different sources needs to be explicitly connected, and it should be clear where sources agree and disagree. In this example, the final sentences could be:

Selke et al. (2015) reported that tests of plastic polymers treated with biodegradation additives resulted in no significant biodegradation after three years. This finding contrasts with that of Chiellini et al. (2007), who reported significant biodegradability of additive-treated polymers.

The different results can be explained by differences in the studies. The 2007 study tested degradation in natural river water, whereas the 2015 study tested degradation under ultraviolet light, aerobic soil burial and anaerobic aqueous conditions (Chiellini et al. 2007; Selke et al. 2015). As well as using different additives and different experimental techniques, Selke et al. (2015) used additive rates of 1–5% and tested polyethylene terephthalate (PET) as well as polyethylene, whereas Chiellini et al. (2007) used additive rates of 10–15% and tested only polyethylene.

Both studies were conducted under laboratory conditions, so they may not reflect what happens in the natural environment.

EDITING YOUR REPORT

Editing your report is an important part of the process. After editing your report, save new drafts with a different file name and always back up your files in another location.

Pretend you are reading your report for the first time when editing. Once you have completed a draft, it is a good idea to put it aside and return to it with 'fresh eyes' a day later. This will help you find areas that need further work and give you the opportunity to improve them. Look for content that is:

- ambiguous or unclear
- repetitive
- awkwardly phrased
- too long
- not relevant to your research question
- poorly structured
- lacking evidence
- lacking a reference (if it is another researcher's work).

Use a spellchecking tool (set to Australian English) to help you identify typographical errors. Also be wary of words that are commonly misused, for example:

- where/were
- their/they're/there
- affect/effect
- which/that.

REVISION

References and acknowledgements

All the quotations, documents, publications and ideas used in the investigation need to be acknowledged in the 'references and acknowledgments' section in order to avoid plagiarism and to ensure that authors are credited for their work. References and acknowledgements also give credibility to your work and allow readers to locate information sources should they wish to study it further.

The American Psychological Association (APA) academic referencing style is commonly used for reference lists. The following are examples of references for a journal article, a book and a website using this style:

- Selke, S., Auras, R., Nguyen, T.A., Aguirre, E.C., Cheruvathur, R., & Liu, Y. (2015). Evaluation of biodegradation—promoting additives for plastics. *Environmental Science & Technology*, 49(6), 3769–3777.
- Hanson, J.R. (2011). *Chemistry in the kitchen garden*. Cambridge, UK: Royal Society of Chemistry.
- Adamson, D. H. (2017). *Plastics*. Retrieved 26 February 2018 from http://www.worldbookonline.com/advanced/article?id=ar434080.

In-text citations

Each time you write about the findings of other people or organisations, you need to provide an in-text citation and provide full details of the source in a reference list. In the APA style, in-text citations include the first author's last name and date in brackets (author, date). List the full details in your list of references.

The following examples show two ways to write an in-text citation:

- Five pro-oxidant additives added to commonly manufactured polymers were tested, and none resulted in significant biodegradation after three years (Selke et al., 2015).
- Selke et al. (2015) tested five pro-oxidant additives added to commonly manufactured polymers, and reported that none resulted in significant biodegradation after three years.

There are many online guides to help you format your reference list and in-text citations. Some websites and journals suggest how to quote a source in a particular referencing style.

MEASUREMENT AND UNITS

Researchers in every area of chemistry attempt to quantify the phenomena they study. In practical demonstrations and investigations they generally make measurements and process those measurements in order to draw conclusions.

There are a number of standard ways of interpreting and analysing data from scientific investigations. There are also standard ways of writing chemical names and symbols, as well as numbers and units of measurement, which are set out in international standards. These are described in detail in the appendices at the end of this book.

GO TO > Appendix 1 page 545

GO TO > Appendix 2 page 546

REVISION

Conversion factors and prefixes

Conversion factors should be used carefully. You should be familiar with the conversion factors and the equivalent prefixes and their symbols shown in Table 1.7.1. The most common mistake made with conversion factors is multiplying rather than dividing. Note that the table gives all conversions as a multiplying factor.

Do not put spaces between prefixes and unit symbols. For example, write 35 mL, not 35 m L.

It is also important to use the correct case (upper or lower case) for prefix symbols. There is a huge difference between 1 mW and 1 MW.

TABLE 1.7.1 Common conversion factors and their prefixes and symbols

Multiplying factor	Scientific notation	Prefix	Symbol
1 000 000 000 000	10^{12}	tera	T
1 000 000 000	10^{9}	giga	G
1 000 000	10^{6}	mega	M
1000	10^{3}	kilo	k
0.01	10^{-2}	centi	c
0.001	10^{-3}	milli	m
0.000 001	10^{-6}	micro	μ
0.000 000 001	10^{-9}	nano	n
0.000 000 000 001	10^{-12}	pico	p

PEER REVIEW

Your teacher may suggest that you work with another student in your class, so that you can provide each other with constructive feedback regarding the presentation of your investigation.

Consider the following:

- Are the findings accurately communicated using chemical nomenclature?
- Is the presentation written towards the appropriate audience?
- Are tables, images, diagrams, graphs and flow-charts referenced in the text?
- Are appropriate in-text citations included for theoretical concepts and images not created by the student?
- Are all source citations and references listed in a consistent style?
- What are the strengths of the presentation?
- What questions do you have about the presentation?

REVISION

Correct use of unit symbols

Units and symbols used in science are standardised under the Système International d'Unités (SI). The correct use of SI units and symbols removes ambiguity, because they are recognised internationally.

The symbols for units, such as kg, s and m for kilograms, seconds and metres, are not abbreviations and should not be followed by a full stop unless they are at the end of a sentence. Symbols also never have a plural s. For example, 45 m is written for 45 metres, not 45 ms.

The product of two or more units is shown by separating the symbol for each unit by a space or a dot; for example, mol L^{-1} or mol.L^{-1}. The division or ratio of two or more units can be shown in fraction form, using negative indices or a slash; for example, mol L^{-1} or mol/L.

When symbols for units are used, the number value must be written as a numeral. For example, 30 g is correct, but thirty g is not.

Scientific notation

To make calculations easier and manage very large or small numbers, measurements are often written in scientific notation. Quantities are written as a number between 1 and 10 and then multiplied by an appropriate power of 10. For example, 12 037 would be written as 1.2037×10^{4}. You should be routinely using scientific notation to express numbers.

1.7 Review

SUMMARY

- The conclusion should include a summary of the main findings, a conclusion related to the issue being investigated, limitations of the research, implications and applications of the research, and potential future research.
- Scientific writing uses unbiased, objective, accurate, formal language. Scientific writing should also be concise and qualified.
- Illustrations can help to convey scientific concepts and processes efficiently.
- Ensure you edit your final report.
- SI units and symbols must be used when communicating your results.

KEY QUESTIONS

1 Which of the following statements is written in scientific style?
   A The results were okay...
   B The experiment took a long time...
   C The data in Figure 2 indicates...
   D The researchers felt...

2 Which one or more of the following statements is written in third-person narrative?
   A The researchers reported...
   B Samples were analysed using...
   C The experiment was repeated three times...
   D I reported...

3 a Write 235 000 in scientific notation.
   b Write 0.000 000 655 in scientific notation.
   c Explain why scientific notation is used.

4 Refer to Table 1.6.2 on page 35. If a student wanted to use the source listed in the first row, how should it be referenced using APA style?

Chapter review

KEY TERMS

accuracy
affiliation
bar graph
bias
continuous variable
controlled variable
credible
data analysis
dependent variable
discrete variable
expertise
hypothesis
independent variable

inquiry question
literature review
mean
median
mistake
mode
model
nominal variable
ordinal variable
outlier
percentage uncertainty
personal protective
  equipment (PPE)

persuasion
phenomenon
pie chart
precision
primary source
purpose
qualitative variable
quantitative variable
random error
raw data
reliability
reputation
rhetoric

safety data sheet (SDS)
scatter plot
secondary source
significant figures
systematic error
trend
trend line
uncertainty
validity
variable

REVIEW QUESTIONS

1 Which graph type from the following list would be best to use with each set of data listed here?
pie chart, scatter graph with trend line, bar graph, line graph

  a the levels of an organic compound detected in drinking water sampled at various locations

  b the pH of water sampled at the same time of day over a period of a month

  c a calibration curve showing absorbance of standard solutions of barium ions measured using atomic absorption spectroscopy

  d the proportion of specific pesticides detected in water.

2 Which one of the following would not provide a strong conclusion to a report?

  A The concluding paragraphs are relevant and provide supporting evidence.

  B The concluding paragraphs are written in emotive language.

  C The concluding paragraphs include reference to limitations of the research.

  D The concluding paragraphs include suggestions for further avenues of research.

3 Which of the following includes only secondary sources of information?

  A a periodic table, an article published in a science magazine, a science documentary, a practical report written by a Year 12 student

  B an article published in a peer-reviewed science journal, an article published in a science journal, a science documentary

  C a periodic table, a scientific article summarised on a science website, a science documentary, this Year 12 textbook

  D a science article summarised in a newspaper, an article published in a science journal, a science documentary, a practical report written by a Year 12 student

4 What is the correct in-text citation for the following source using APA style?
Zavabeti, A., Ou, J.Z., Carey, B.J., Syed, N., Orrell-Trigg, R., Mayes, E.L.H., Xu, C., Kaveei, O., O'Mullane, A.P., Kaner, R.B., Kalanter-Zadeh, K., & Daeneke, T. (2017), A liquid metal reaction environment for the room-temperature synthesis of atomically thin metal oxides. *Science* 358(6361), 332–335.

  A Zavabeti et al. (2017) used non-toxic gallium-based alloys in their experiment.

  B Zavabeti et al. used non-toxic gallium-based alloys in their experiment.[1]

  C Zavabeti et al. used non-toxic gallium-based alloys in their experiment (Zavabeti, A., Ou, J.Z., Carey, B.J., Syed, N., Orrell-Trigg, R., Mayes, E.L.H., Xu, C., Kaveei, O., O'Mullane, A.P., Kaner, R.B., Kalanter-Zadeh, K., & Daeneke, T. (2017), A liquid metal reaction environment for the room-temperature synthesis of atomically thin metal oxides. *Science* 358(6361), 332–335).

  D Zavabeti et al. (*Science* 358, 332–335, 2017) used non-toxic gallium-based alloys in their experiment.

5 Explain the meaning of the following terms:
purpose, hypothesis, variable

6 Consider the following research question:
'Is the concentration of copper ions in water sampled from the Hawkesbury River within acceptable limits?' For each of the following variables, state whether it is the independent, dependent or controlled variable.
a concentration of copper ions in water
b analytical technique, temperature of water sample, type of sampling container
c source and location of water.

7 Consider the following hypothesis:
'The lead concentration in waste water from a mine will be greater than the concentration in drinking water.' Name the independent, dependent and controlled variables for an experiment that tests this hypothesis.

8 List the independent and dependent variables in the following investigations.
a Determining the dissociation constant, K_a, for a number of organic acids.
b Comparing the relative solubility of ionic compounds in water at 50°C.
c Investigating the properties of organic chemical compounds in the alcohol homologous series, and explaining these differences in terms of bonding.

9 What is the meaning of each of the following GHS pictograms?

(a)

(b)

(c)

10 Convert 70.50 mL into L.

11 Define the following terms:
a mean
b mode
d median.

12 Six measurements of mass (in grams) of a compound were 16.05, 15.98, 16.80, 15.92, 16.20 and 17.01. What is the average and uncertainty of these values?

13 Which statistical measurement (mean, mode or median) is most affected by an outlier?

14 a Give examples of numbers with 2, 3, 4 and 5 significant figures.

b Summarise the rules for reporting a calculated value that involved multiplication or division.
c Summarise the rules for reporting a calculated value that involved addition or subtraction.

15 Identify whether each of the following is a mistake, a systematic error or a random error.
a A student uses an aluminium nitrate solution instead of a silver nitrate solution
b The reported measurements are above and below the true value.
c An electronic scale consistently reads 2 g more for each sample.

16 a Explain the terms 'accuracy' and 'precision'.
b When might an investigation be invalid?
c All investigations have limitations. Use an example to explain the meaning of 'limitations' of an investigation.

17 A scientist designed and completed an experiment to test the following hypothesis: 'Increasing the temperature of water results in a decrease in the pH of water.'

The discussion section of the scientist's report included comments on the reliability, validity, accuracy and precision of the investigation.

For each of the following sentences, state whether the information relates to the reliability, validity, accuracy, or precision of measurements.
a Three water samples from the same source were tested at each temperature.
b The temperature and pH of the water samples were recorded using data-logging equipment. The temperature of some of the water samples was measured using a glass thermometer.
c The data-logging equipment was calibrated for pH before measurements were taken.
d The data logger measured temperature to the nearest 0.1°C. The glass thermometer measured temperature to the nearest 1°C.

18 What is the purpose of referencing and acknowledging documents, ideas, images and quotations in your investigation?

19 A scientist designed and completed an experiment to test the following hypothesis:

'Increasing the temperature of water results in a decrease in the pH of water.'
a Write a possible purpose for this scientist's experiment.
b What would be the independent, dependent and controlled variables in this investigation?
c What kind of data would be collected? Would it be qualitative or quantitative?
d List the equipment that could be used and the type of precision expected for each item.
e What would you expect the graph of the results to look like if the scientist's hypothesis was correct?

20 Refer to Table 1.6.2 on page 35. Using the in-progress summary describe three similarities and two differences seen in the information that has been collected.

21 A student wants to test a claim made by a manufacturer on the package of a food or cosmetic. How might the student approach this type of investigation?

22 Refer to Figure 1.5.2 on page 27. Propose how a student might investigate whether there is a cause-and-effect relationship between per capita cheese consumption and death from being tangled in bedsheets.

23 List five advantages of seeking peer feedback on the various stages of an investigation.

24 Use the following solubility curves to determine:
   a the solubility of sodium nitrate ($NaNO_3$) at 60°C
   b the solubility of silver nitrate ($AgNO_3$) at 10°C
   c the maximum mass of potassium nitrate (KNO_3) that will dissolve in 100 g of water at 40°C
   d the maximum mass of hydrated copper sulfate ($CuSO_4 \cdot 5H_2O$) that will dissolve in 150 g of water at 60°C
   e the maximum mass of sodium nitrate ($NaNO_3$) that will dissolve in 83 g of water, at 50°C.

25 The following flowchart outlines the series of steps for the formation and combustion of two biofuels, ethanol and butan-1-ol. List the limitations of this flowchart.

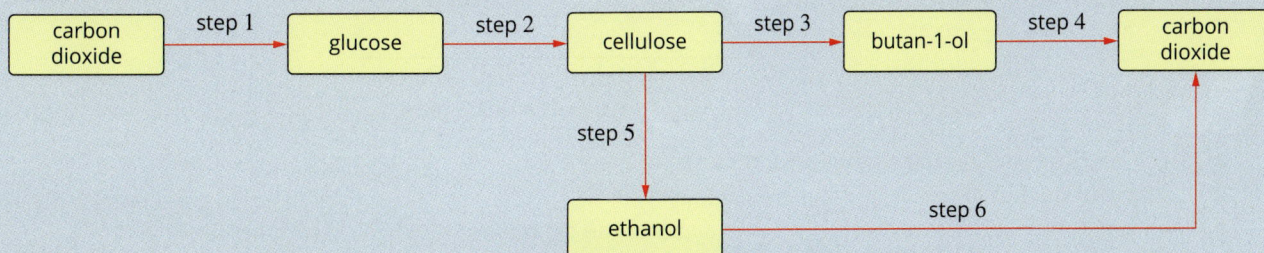

26 Compare the nutrition information panels of three different brands of breakfast cereal. Identify the cereal that has:
   a the highest concentration of sodium, in mg per 100 g
   b the lowest concentration of saturated fat, in g per 100 g
   c the highest concentration of sugars, in g per 100 g.
   Present your findings in a table.

27 Research the effect that increasing global temperatures are having on the acidity of seawater and coral bleaching in the Great Barrier Reef. Ensure that you include a list of references and acknowledgements for your sources. Present your research in digital form.

28 Two students conducted an experiment to determine the percentage composition of magnesium oxide. Some of their results are shown below.

The equation for the reaction is:

$$2Mg(s) + O_2(g) \rightarrow 2MgO(s)$$

Complete the following table of results.

Measurement	Value	Number of significant figures in measured or calculated value
Mass of crucible and lid (g)	41.893	
Mass of crucible, lid and magnesium ribbon (g)	42.633	
Mass of crucible, lid and magnesium oxide (g)	43.143	
Mass of magnesium (g)		
Mass of magnesium oxide (g)		
% of magnesium in magnesium oxide		
% of oxygen in magnesium oxide		

29 A student conducted an investigation to determine the percentage purity of a sample of impure magnesium sulfate ($MgSO_4$). She dissolved 15.02 g of the impure magnesium sulfate in distilled water and the solution was made up to 250.0 mL in a volumetric flask. Various volumes of 0.100 mol L^{-1} barium chloride solution ($BaCl_2$) were added to 25.00 mL aliquots of the magnesium sulfate solution. The sulfate ions were precipitated as barium sulfate ($BaSO_4$). The results were summarised in the following graph.

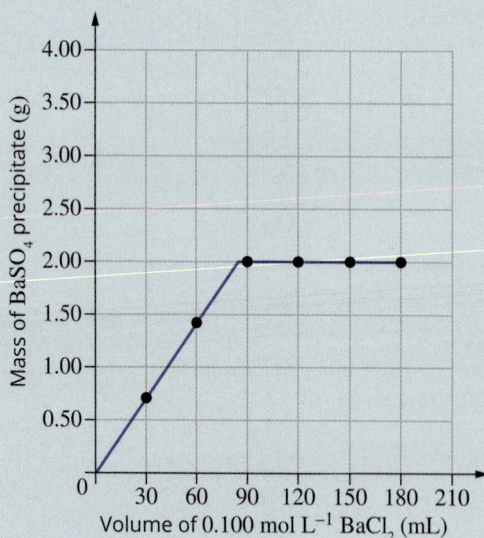

a Which reactant was in excess at the end of the experiment?

b Justify your answer to part **a**.

c If you could repeat this investigation, what changes to the procedure would you recommend? Why?

MODULE
5 Equilibrium and acid reactions

Chemical systems may be open or closed. They include physical changes and chemical reactions that can result in observable changes to a system. In this module you will study the effects of changes in temperature, concentration of chemicals and pressure on equilibrium systems, and consider that these can be predicted by applying Le Châtelier's principle. You will also analyse the quantitative relationship between products and reactants in equilibrium reactions to determine an equilibrium constant. From this calculation you will be able to predict the equilibrium position, favouring the formation of either products or reactants in a chemical reaction.

This module also allows you to understand that scientific knowledge enables scientists to offer valid explanations and make reliable predictions. You will make reliable predictions by comparing equilibrium calculations and equilibrium constants to determine whether a combination of two solutions will result in the formation of a precipitate.

Outcomes

By the end of this module, you will be able to:

- select and process appropriate qualitative and quantitative data and information using a range of appropriate media (CH12-4)
- analyse and evaluate primary and secondary data and information (CH12-5)
- solve scientific problems using primary and secondary data, critical thinking skills and scientific processes (CH12-6)
- communicate scientific understanding using suitable language and terminology for a specific audience or purpose (CH12-7)
- explain the characteristics of equilibrium systems, and the factors that affect these systems (CH12-12)

Chemistry Stage 6 Syllabus © NSW Education Standards Authority for and on behalf of the Crown in right of the State of NSW, 2017.

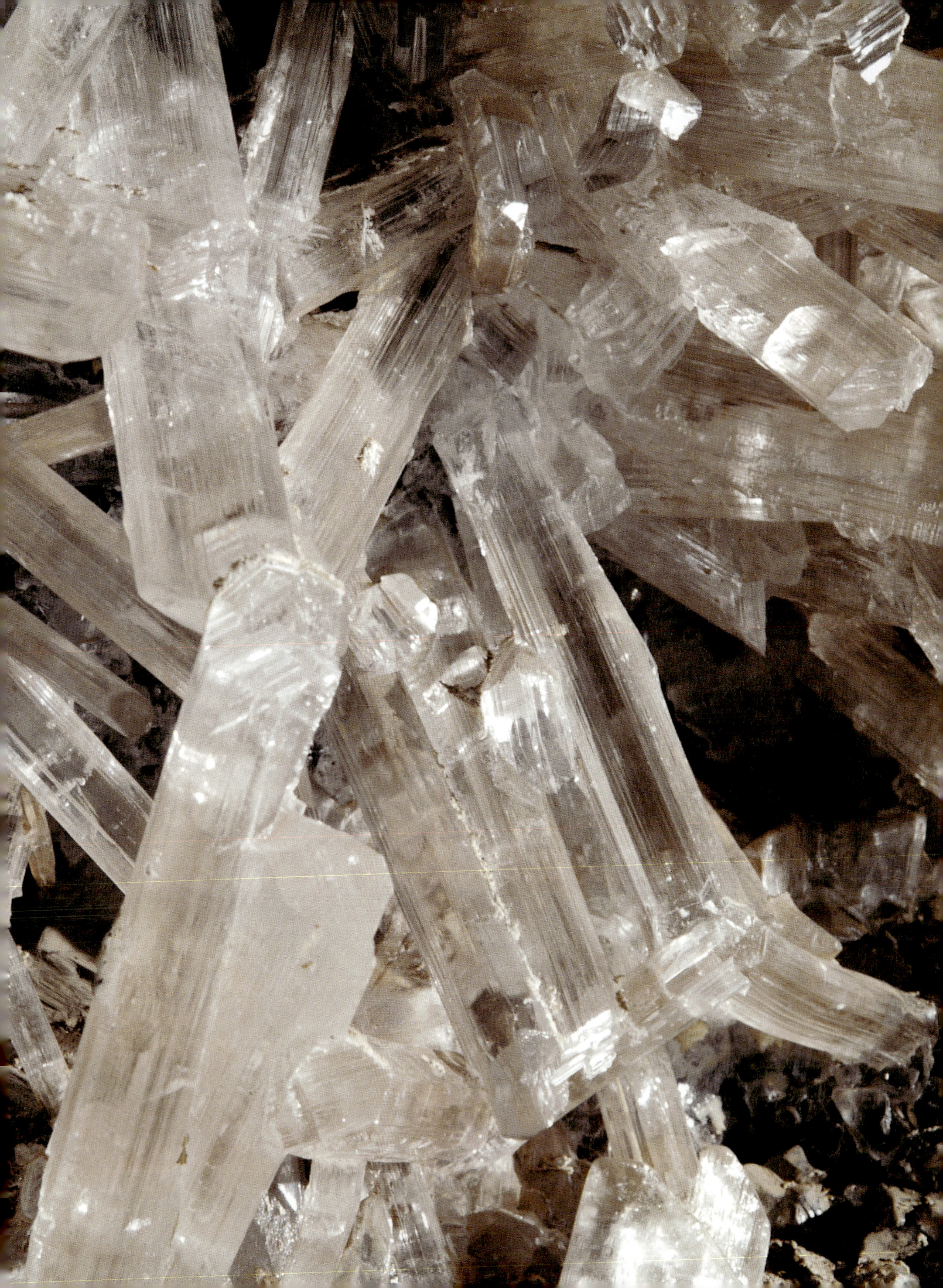

Static and dynamic equilibrium

In this chapter you will learn that some reactions can occur in both the forward and reverse directions. These reactions are called reversible reactions.

Reversible chemical systems are encountered in many everyday situations, including chemical manufacturing processes, the movement of ions within individual cells in your body and the reactions carbon dioxide undergoes in the environment.

This chapter also describes how some reversible reactions can reach a point where they appear to stop. At this point the concentrations of the reactants and products remain constant, even though there are still reactants remaining.

The fact that many reactions do not proceed to completion has serious consequences for the production of chemicals by industry. The presence of large amounts of unreacted starting materials in reaction mixtures is wasteful and costly. The profitability of an industry depends on the yield—the extent of conversion of reactants into products.

Content

INQUIRY QUESTION

What happens when chemical reactions do not go through to completion?

By the end of this chapter, you will be able to:

- conduct practical investigations to analyse the reversibility of chemical reactions, for example:
  - cobalt(II) chloride hydrated and dehydrated
  - iron(III) nitrate and potassium thiocyanate
  - burning magnesium
  - burning steel wool (ACSCH090) ICT
- model static and dynamic equilibrium and analyse the differences between open and closed systems (ACSCH079, ACSCH091)
- analyse examples of non-equilibrium systems in terms of the effect of entropy and enthalpy, for example:
  - combustion reactions
  - photosynthesis
- investigate the relationship between collision theory and reaction rate in order to analyse chemical equilibrium reactions (ACSCH070, ACSCH094) ICT

2.1 Chemical systems

In Year 11 you studied several topics that will form the basis for your understanding of chemical equilibrium in Chapters 2, 3 and 4. These topics are:

- exothermic and endothermic reactions
- rates of reaction
- entropy and free energy.

GO TO ➤ Year 11 Section 14.1

GO TO ➤ Year 11 Chapter 13

GO TO ➤ Year 11 Chapter 16

Exothermic and endothermic reactions

The substances involved in a chemical reaction can be thought of as a **system**, and everything else around this system (the rest of the universe) as the **surroundings**. Energy is conserved over the course of a chemical reaction. However, the total energy stored in the bonds of the reactant particles is different to the total energy stored in the bonds of the products. This means a chemical reaction will need to absorb energy from its surroundings (an **endothermic** reaction) or release energy to its surroundings (an **exothermic** reaction). Diagrams which show the energy changes that occur during the course of a chemical reaction are called **energy profile diagrams** (Figure 2.1.1).

The minimum amount of energy required before a reaction can proceed is called the **activation energy**. An activation energy barrier exists for both exothermic and endothermic reactions. If the activation energy for a reaction is very low, the chemical reaction may be initiated as soon as the reactants come into contact with each other because the reactants already have sufficient energy for a reaction to take place.

ENTHALPY AND THERMOCHEMICAL EQUATIONS

The **enthalpy change**, ΔH, of a chemical reaction is the heat (thermal) energy released or absorbed during the reaction. The enthalpy change can be expressed as:

$$\Delta H = H_p - H_r$$

where

H_p is the enthalpy of the products

H_r is the enthalpy of the reactants.

For an exothermic reaction ΔH is negative, and for an endothermic reaction ΔH is positive.

Thermochemical equations show the enthalpy change in a reaction by writing the ΔH value to the right of the chemical equation. Energy is usually measured in joules (J) or kilojoules (kJ) and the ΔH value has the units $J\,mol^{-1}$ or $kJ\,mol^{-1}$.

This means that the energy shown by the ΔH value corresponds to the mole amounts specified by the coefficients in the equation. Remember:

- When the coefficients are changed, the ΔH value changes by the same factor.
- When the reaction is reversed, the sign of the ΔH value is reversed.
- The states of matter must be shown in equations, because changes of state involve enthalpy changes.

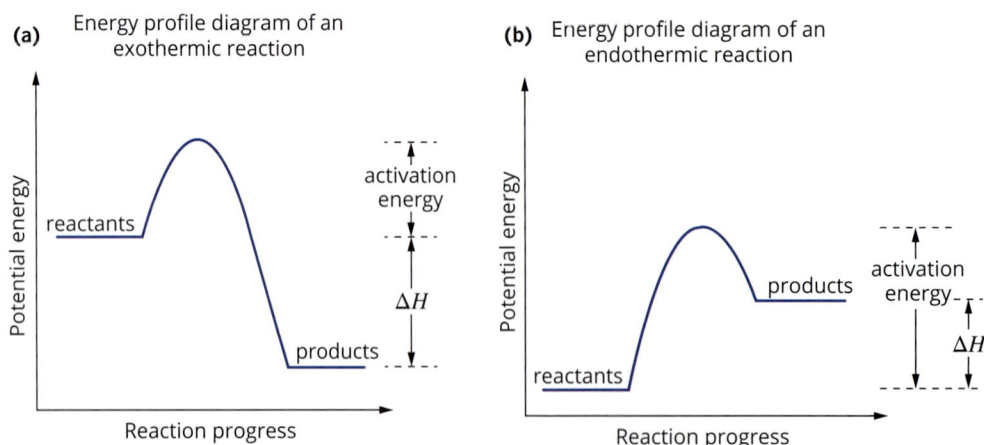

FIGURE 2.1.1 The characteristic shape of an energy profile diagram for (a) an exothermic reaction and (b) an endothermic reaction.

Rates of reaction

The rate of a chemical reaction can be determined by measuring the change in concentration of the reactants or products with time. As the reaction conditions change, the rate of reaction will change. The rate of a reaction can be increased by:

- increasing the concentration of solutions or pressure of gases
- increasing the surface area of a solid reactant
- increasing the temperature
- using a **catalyst**.

COLLISION THEORY

Chemical reactions occur when reactant particles collide, although not all collisions produce a reaction. These ideas form the basis of the **collision theory** of reaction rates. According to collision theory, the likelihood of a reaction occurring depends on:

- the frequency of collisions
- the orientation of the particles when they collide
- whether the energy of the particles during a collision is equal to, or greater than, the activation energy.

You can apply collision theory to understand why concentration, surface area, temperature and catalysts affect reaction rate.

Entropy and Gibbs free energy

Entropy, symbol S, is a measure of the number of possible arrangements of a system. It can be regarded as the degree of disorder or randomness in the system. In general, entropy increases ($\Delta S > 0$) when:

- the volume occupied by the particles in a system increases
- the number of particles in a system increases
- the temperature of a system increases
- a substance changes from solid to liquid to gas.

The **second law of thermodynamics** states that the overall entropy of the universe is increasing. This can be written mathematically as:

$$\Delta S_{system} + \Delta S_{surroundings} = \Delta S_{universe} > 0$$

Some chemical reactions involve an increase in entropy, whereas others involve a decrease in entropy. Chemical reactions involving a decrease in entropy ($\Delta S_{system} < 0$) can take place if the entropy of the surroundings increases ($\Delta S_{surroundings} > 0$) and the sum of the two entropies produces an increase in entropy for the universe overall.

A **spontaneous reaction** is one that occurs of its own accord, without outside intervention. A quantity called **Gibbs free energy** is used to determine if a reaction is spontaneous. The formula to calculate the change in Gibbs free energy, ΔG, is:

$$\Delta G = \Delta H - T\Delta S$$

At standard state conditions (298 K and 1 bar) this is written as:

$$\Delta G° = \Delta H° - T\Delta S°$$

- When $\Delta G < 0$ the reaction is spontaneous.
- When $\Delta G > 0$ the reaction is non-spontaneous.
- When $\Delta G = 0$ the reaction is at equilibrium.

Whether or not a reaction is spontaneous depends on the signs of ΔH and ΔS, and in some cases the relative values of ΔH and $T\Delta S$. For example, reactions that are exothermic (ΔH negative) and have an increase in entropy (ΔS positive) are always spontaneous. Reactions that are endothermic (ΔH positive) and have a decrease in entropy (ΔS negative) are never spontaneous.

Non-spontaneous reactions can occur, provided that the second law of thermodynamics is obeyed overall.

CHEMISTRY INQUIRY ⬛ CCT

Can you reverse the colour of a stain?

COLLECT THIS ...

- white cotton or linen cloth
- red wine (or red cabbage juice, made by boiling red cabbage in a small volume of water)
- vinegar
- sodium hydrogen carbonate (bicarbonate of soda) powder
- liquid soap
- camera

DO THIS ...

1 Spill a little red wine onto the white cloth.
2 Add a little vinegar to the spill and note the colour.
3 Then add a little sodium hydrogen carbonate to the spill and note the colour.
4 Repeat steps 1-3 using vinegar and then liquid soap instead of sodium hydrogen carbonate.

RECORD THIS ...

Record each colour change by taking a photo.
Describe what happened in each case.

REFLECT ON THIS ...

1 Can you change the colour of a red wine stain on a white cloth?
2 Why do you think this happened?
3 What properties of vinegar and sodium hydrogen carbonate cause the colour changes?
4 Can some chemical reactions be reversed?

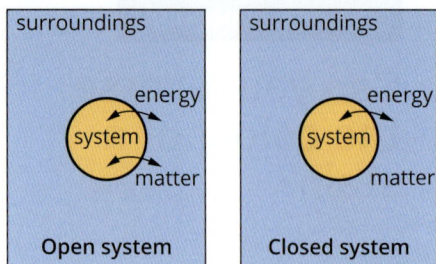

FIGURE 2.1.2 Open systems exchange energy and matter with the surroundings. Closed systems exchange only energy with the surroundings.

OPEN AND CLOSED SYSTEMS

A chemical reaction can be regarded as a system, with everything else around it (the rest of the universe) being the surroundings.

Figure 2.1.2 illustrates how you can distinguish between two different types of systems: **open systems** and **closed systems**.

The most common situation in everyday life is an open system. In an open system, matter and energy can be exchanged with the surroundings. In contrast, a closed system only exchanges energy with the surroundings.

Some everyday examples of open and closed systems are illustrated in Figure 2.1.3.

FIGURE 2.1.3 Everyday examples of open and closed systems. (a) A bushfire burning at Swan Bay in Port Stephens. This is an example of an open system. Carbon dioxide and water vapour produced by the burning trees are released into the atmosphere. (b) A submarine operating under water. The carefully monitored internal environment of the submarine can be regarded as a closed system.

IRREVERSIBLE AND REVERSIBLE SYSTEMS

You may have thought, as a younger student, that when chemical reactions occur, the reactants form products and these products cannot be converted back to the reactants. Such reactions, which occur only in one direction, are called non-reversible or **irreversible reactions**.

Baking a cake, like the one shown in Figure 2.1.4, involves several irreversible reactions. The reactions are complex, and include reactions that change the chemical structures of the proteins in flour and egg, as well as reactions between the proteins and sugars.

Combustion reactions such as the burning of methane are also irreversible:

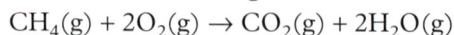

$$CH_4(g) + 2O_2(g) \rightarrow CO_2(g) + 2H_2O(g)$$

Once a fuel has burnt, the products, carbon dioxide and water, do not react with each other under normal conditions.

Other examples of irreversible reactions include the burning of magnesium or steel wool:

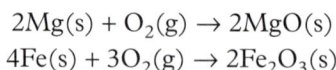

$$2Mg(s) + O_2(g) \rightarrow 2MgO(s)$$
$$4Fe(s) + 3O_2(g) \rightarrow 2Fe_2O_3(s)$$

However, other reactions are **reversible reactions** where the products, once formed, can react again, re-forming the reactants.

REVERSIBILITY OF PHYSICAL AND CHEMICAL CHANGES

Some examples of processes that are reversible are:
- the evaporation or condensation of water
- the formation of a **saturated** sugar solution
- the reaction between hydrated cobalt(II) chloride and dehydrated cobalt(II) chloride
- the reaction between iron(III) nitrate and potassium thiocyanate.

These four examples are described below.

FIGURE 2.1.4 Baking a cake involves a series of irreversible chemical reactions.

> ℹ️ Open systems exchange energy and matter with the surroundings.
>
> Closed systems only exchange energy with the surroundings.

Evaporation or condensation of water

You are familiar with the idea that a physical change, such as a change of state, can be reversed. The evaporation of water from lakes and rivers, leading to cloud formation and eventually rain, is an example of a physical change. Water can cycle between the different phases of solid, liquid and gas because each process is reversible.

The evaporation of water can be expressed by the equation:

$$H_2O(l) \rightarrow H_2O(g)$$

The condensation of water can be expressed by the equation:

$$H_2O(g) \rightarrow H_2O(l)$$

In chemistry, a double arrow ($\rightleftharpoons$) is used when writing a chemical equation to show a reversible process. In this way you can show the phase changes associated with the evaporation and condensation of water using a single equation:

$$H_2O(l) \rightleftharpoons H_2O(g)$$

As you can see in Figure 2.1.5, these changes of state can occur in either open or closed systems. In a closed system the water vapour cannot escape. In general, reversible reactions in a closed system eventually reach a point where the rates of the forward and reverse reactions are equal, and there will appear to be no further change. The system at this point is said to be in **equilibrium**.

However, although water in an open system can evaporate and condense, the rate of each process is not equal. Gaseous water molecules escape from the system into the atmosphere, so the rate of the reverse reaction (condensation) does not become equal to the rate of the forward reaction. Equilibrium is not achieved in an open system.

Saturated sugar solution

A saturated solution contains the maximum amount of solute dissolved in the solution. Consider a saturated solution of sugar in contact with undissolved sugar crystals at a constant temperature (Figure 2.1.6).

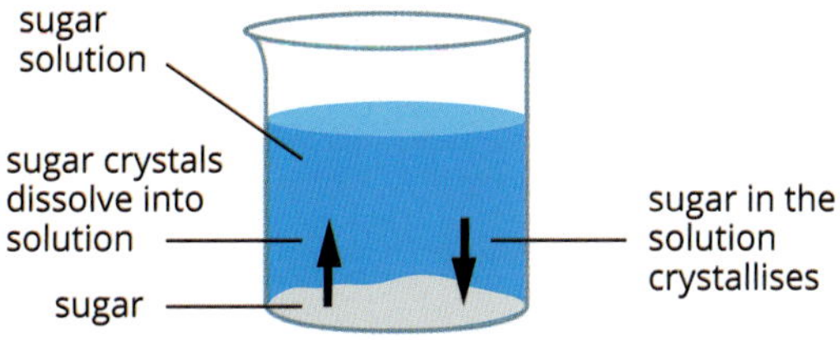

FIGURE 2.1.6 The processes occurring in a saturated sugar solution

The sugar molecules ($C_{12}H_{22}O_{11}$) are dissolving at the same rate at which they are crystallising, and the mass of sugar crystals is constant. The process is reversible and at equilibrium. It can be represented by the equation:

$$C_{12}H_{22}O_{11}(s) \rightleftharpoons C_{12}H_{22}O_{11}(aq)$$

Even though there is no lid on the beaker, this system involving solid and aqueous sugar can be regarded as a closed system. No gas is involved, so there is no loss of the reactant or product molecules to the surroundings.

Reaction of hydrated cobalt(II) chloride and dehydrated cobalt(II) chloride

Solid dehydrated cobalt(II) chloride is coloured blue. When it reacts with water, pink hydrated cobalt(II) chloride is produced. This is represented by the equation:

dehydrated cobalt(II) chloride + water $\rightleftharpoons$ hydrated cobalt(II) chloride

$$\underset{\text{blue}}{CoCl_2(s)} + 6H_2O(l) \rightleftharpoons \underset{\text{pink}}{CoCl_2 \cdot 6H_2O(s)}$$

As a result, paper impregnated with blue dehydrated cobalt(II) chloride can be used to detect the presence of water. The paper turns pink as hydrated cobalt(II) chloride is formed (Figure 2.1.7) but becomes blue again when heated as the water evaporates. Cobalt(II) chloride has been used as a humidity or moisture indicator in weather instruments.

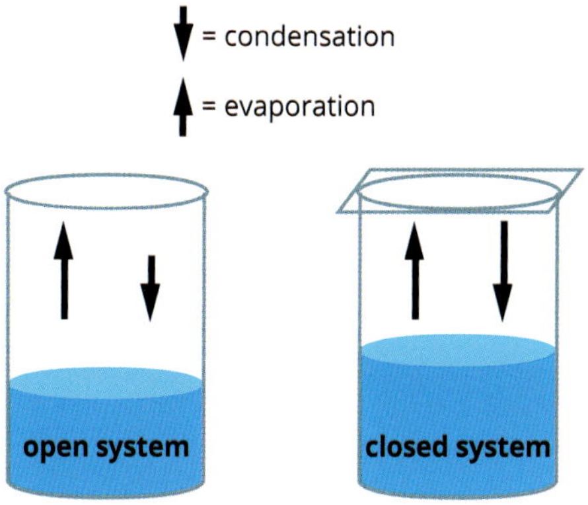

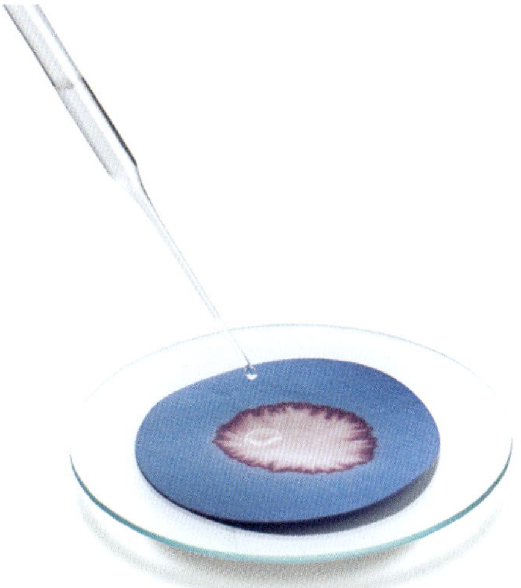

FIGURE 2.1.5 A physical change—the condensation and evaporation of water—in open and closed systems. In the open system, all the water may eventually evaporate.

> **i** Equilibrium is not achieved in an open system.
>
> Equilibrium is achieved in a closed system when the rates of the forward and reverse reactions are equal.

> **i** A forward reaction occurs when the reactants form the products.
>
> A reverse reaction occurs when the products re-form the reactants.

FIGURE 2.1.7 Blue dehydrated cobalt(II) chloride paper turns pink in the presence of water.

PA
5.2

The reaction between cobalt(II) chloride and water is a reversible chemical reaction. On heating, the hydrated form of cobalt(II) chloride reforms dehydrated cobalt(II) chloride and water.

Reaction of iron(III) nitrate and potassium thiocyanate

Solutions of iron(III) nitrate ($Fe(NO_3)_3$) are pale yellow and solutions of potassium thiocyanate (KSCN) are colourless. When these two solutions are mixed, they form the red-coloured complex ion, iron(III) thiocyanate ($FeSCN^{2+}$) (Figure 2.1.8). The reaction can be represented by the equation:

$$Fe^{3+}(aq) + SCN^-(aq) \rightleftharpoons FeSCN^{2+}(aq)$$

pale yellow   colourless   red

Like the other examples described above, this reaction is reversible and forms an equilibrium. You can carry out experiments in class using this reaction, and use the colour changes to learn more about the nature of a chemical equilibrium.

FIGURE 2.1.8 Pale yellow $Fe(NO_3)_3$ solution (left) and colourless KSCN solution (centre) produce a red $FeSCN^{2+}$ solution when mixed (right).

CHEMFILE CCT

Soft drink and equilibrium

In a sealed bottle of soft drink, CO_2 gas is in equilibrium with dissolved CO_2 according to the equation:

$$CO_2(g) \rightleftharpoons CO_2(aq)$$

The rate at which the gas dissolves in the solution is equal to the rate at which it leaves the solution to form a gas. To someone looking at the bottle, nothing appears to be happening.

When the cap is removed from the bottle, the pressure is reduced and carbon dioxide escapes to the atmosphere. The system changes from a closed system to an open system, and a net reverse reaction occurs as carbon dioxide comes out of solution. Bubbles of gas are observed when the bottle is opened.

This normally happens slowly, but when mints are added to a bottle of soft drink, the drink erupts violently, as you can see in Figure 2.1.9. The large surface area of the mints provides many sites for bubbles to form, increasing the rate of the reaction and quickly producing an eruption of soft drink from the bottle.

FIGURE 2.1.9 An erupting soft drink when mints have been added.

Limestone caves

An example of reversibility in nature is the formation of stalactites and stalagmites in limestone caves such as those in Jenolan in New South Wales (Figure 2.1.10).

The caves at Jenolan have been part of the cultural heritage of the Gundungurra people for tens of thousands of years. A Dreamtime creation story describes a struggle between two ancestral creator spirits: Gurangatch, an eel-like creature that was an incarnation of the ancestral rainbow serpent, and Mirrangan, a large native cat or quoll. The enormous struggle between the spirits created the countryside around the caves.

The main mineral in limestone caves is calcite ($CaCO_3$). Water saturated with carbon dioxide from the atmosphere drips through the roof of the cave, resulting in the following reaction:

$$CO_2(g) + H_2O(l) + CaCO_3(s) \rightarrow Ca^{2+}(aq) + 2HCO_3^-(aq)$$

As the water seeps through the rocks, it becomes saturated with Ca^{2+} ions and HCO_3^- ions. The water then evaporates and the reverse reaction produces stalactites from the ceiling of the cave:

$$Ca^{2+}(aq) + 2HCO_3^-(aq) \rightarrow CO_2(g) + H_2O(l) + CaCO_3(s)$$

Some of the solution drips onto the floor of the cave, where more deposits of $CaCO_3$ are produced, forming stalagmites. Stalactites and stalagmites grow in pairs and can produce beautiful columns (Figure 2.1.10 and the module opener image).

FIGURE 2.1.10 Stalactites and stalagmites in the Jenolan Caves in New South Wales. They consist of the mineral calcite.

EXPLAINING REVERSIBILITY

In Year 11 you learnt that energy profile diagrams like the one shown in Figure 2.1.11 can be used to represent the energy changes that occur during a chemical reaction. These diagrams can be used to show why reversible reactions can occur.

When particles collide, the energy associated with collisions can break bonds in the reacting particles, allowing them to rearrange to form new products. The energy required for a successful reaction to occur is known as the activation energy of the reaction.

You can see from the energy profile diagram that, once products form, if the product particles collide with energy equal to or greater than the activation energy of the reverse reaction, then it is possible to re-form the original reactants.

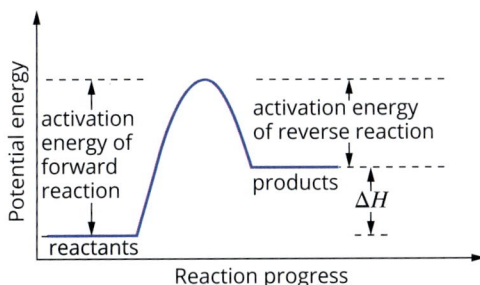

FIGURE 2.1.11 An energy profile diagram for an endothermic reaction, showing the activation energy required for both the forward reaction (formation of products) and reverse reaction (re-formation of reactants).

Note that if the forward reaction is endothermic then the reverse reaction is exothermic, and vice versa.

PA 5.1   PA 5.1

2.1 Review

SUMMARY

- In a closed system, only energy, not matter, is exchanged with the surroundings.
- In an open system, both matter and energy are exchanged between the system and the surroundings.
- A reversible reaction is a reaction in which the products can be converted back to the reactants.
- An irreversible reaction is a reaction in which the products cannot be converted back to the reactants.

- Reactions where the activation energies for the forward and reverse reactions are similar are likely to be reversible.
- Reversible reactions can reach a point where the rates of the forward and reverse reactions are equal. At this point equilibrium has been achieved.
- Equilibrium can be achieved in closed systems, but not in open systems.

KEY QUESTIONS

1 Which one of the following statements about a closed system is correct?

A A closed system must be completely sealed to stop reactants or products from escaping.

B In a closed system, the reactants and products cannot be exchanged with the surroundings.

C Energy cannot enter or leave a closed system.

D In a closed system, only products remain when the reaction is complete.

2 Select the correct terms from the list to complete the following paragraph about equilibrium. Some terms may be used more than once.

rates, processes, remains constant, increases, decreases, energy, matter, reversible, irreversible

Equilibrium occurs when there is a(n) _____ reaction in a closed system. _____ can be added to the system but _____ cannot be added or removed. At equilibrium, the _____ of the forward and reverse reactions are equal. The total mass of reactants and products present in the reaction _____.

3 Indicate whether each of the following processes occurs in an open system or a closed system, and explain your answers.

a A saturated solution of salt in a glass:
$$NaCl(s) \rightleftharpoons NaCl(aq)$$

b Solid $(NH_4)_2SO_4$ reacts with NaOH solution in a beaker:
$(NH_4)_2SO_4(s) + 2NaOH(aq) \rightarrow Na_2SO_4(aq) + 2NH_3(g) + 2H_2O(l)$

c A solution of CH_3COOH in a beaker dissociates:
$$CH_3COOH(aq) + H_2O(l) \rightleftharpoons CH_3COO^-(aq) + H_3O^+(aq)$$

d Toast burns.

4 The graph below shows the energy profile diagram for the following reaction:
$$CO_2(g) + NO(g) \rightarrow CO(g) + NO_2(g)$$
What is the activation energy for the reverse reaction, in $kJ\,mol^{-1}$?

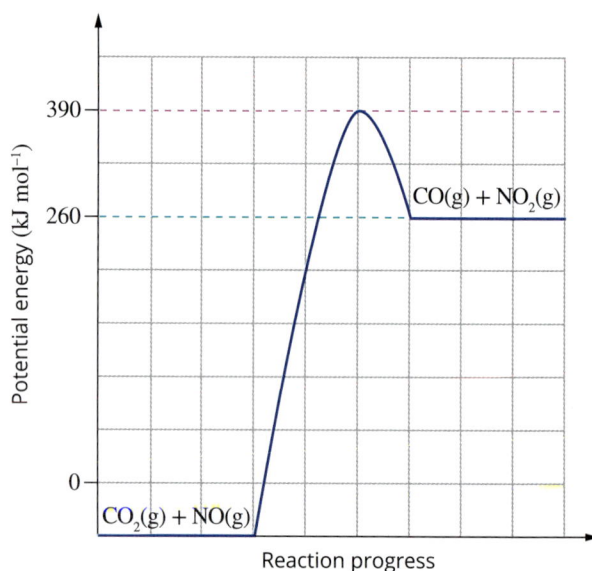

2.2 Dynamic equilibrium

In the previous section you learnt that reversible reactions can occur in both the forward and reverse directions. Some reversible reactions can reach a point where they appear to stop. At this point, the concentrations of the reactants and products remain constant, even though there are still reactants remaining and the reaction has not gone to completion.

The fact that many reactions do not proceed to completion has serious consequences for the production of chemicals by industry. The presence of large amounts of unreacted starting materials in reaction mixtures is wasteful and costly. The profitability of an industry depends on the **yield** of the reaction—the extent of conversion of reactants into products.

Although reactions appear to stop, they actually continue to proceed. If you could see what was occurring at the atomic scale, you would notice that as rapidly as the reactants are forming products, the products are re-forming reactants. This situation can be likened to the queue shown in Figure 2.2.1. Although the length of the queue may be constant, people at the front are continually leaving the queue and others are joining it at the back at the same rate.

In this section you will look more closely at how the particles in a chemical reaction behave as a reaction reaches an equilibrium.

FIGURE 2.2.1 A queue of constant length can be likened to a reaction that appears to have stopped, with people leaving the queue at one end at the same rate as others join it at the other end.

EQUILIBRIUM AND COLLISION THEORY

As you have seen, in reversible reactions the formation of products as a result of collisions between reactant particles is not the end of the process. Once some products are formed, collisions between product particles can result in the reactants being re-formed.

Consider the production of ammonia from hydrogen gas and nitrogen gas, known as the Haber process. The equation for the reaction can be written as:

$$N_2(g) + 3H_2(g) \rightleftharpoons 2NH_3(g)$$

Suppose you mix 1 mol of nitrogen gas and 3 mol of hydrogen gas in a sealed container. From the equation, you might expect that 2 mol of ammonia would eventually be formed. However, no matter how long you wait, the reaction seems to stop when much less than 2 mol of ammonia is present, as shown in Figure 2.2.2.

volume = 1 L
temperature = 400°C

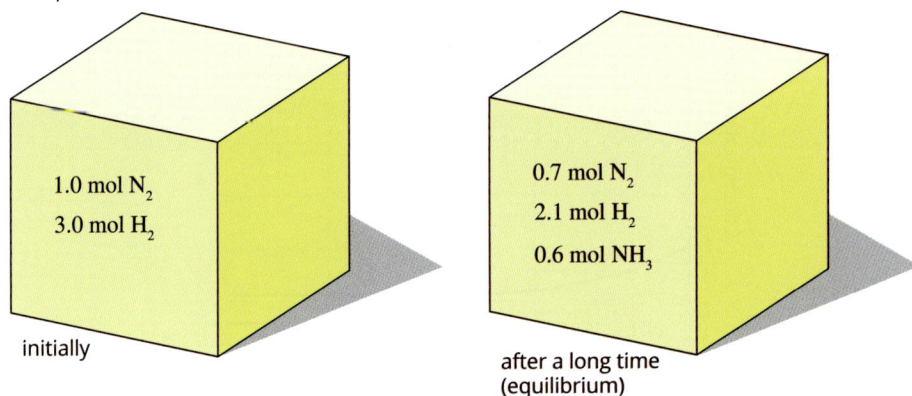

1.0 mol N_2
3.0 mol H_2

initially

0.7 mol N_2
2.1 mol H_2
0.6 mol NH_3

after a long time
(equilibrium)

FIGURE 2.2.2 When 1 mol of nitrogen and 3 mol of hydrogen are mixed, the reaction to form ammonia appears to stop before all the reactants are consumed.

The reaction vessel and its contents can be thought of as a closed system from which the reactants and products cannot escape. Reversible reactions in a closed system eventually reach a point where the rate of the forward reaction and the rate of the reverse reaction are equal.

> Reversible reactions can reach a state of equilibrium where the overall concentrations of reactants and products do not change over time.

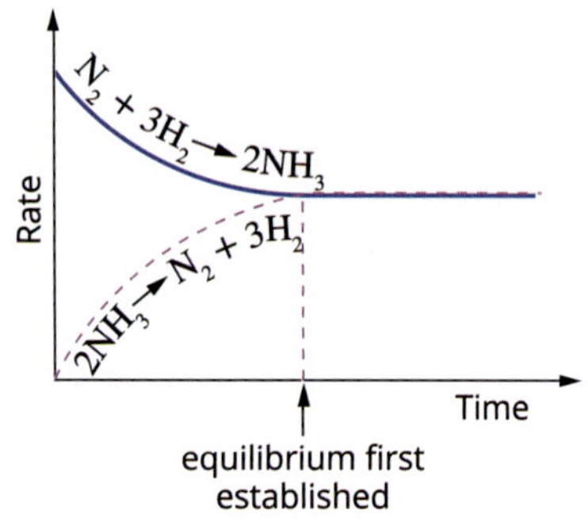

FIGURE 2.2.3 The variation of the rates of the forward and reverse reactions with time when nitrogen and hydrogen are mixed.

> Collision theory is a model that enables you to understand how reactions occur when particles collide.
>
> The rate of a reaction depends on the:
> - frequency of collisions
> - the orientation of the particles
> - whether the energy of the particles is greater than, or equal to, the activation energy.

> When considering graphs involving equilibrium systems, always check if the data is presented as a plot of concentration versus time or plot of reaction rate versus time.

At this point there appears to be no further change, and the system is at equilibrium. There still may be significant amounts of reactants in the system.

Because the reaction between nitrogen and hydrogen to form ammonia is a reversible reaction, it is best written using a double arrow:

$$N_2(g) + 3H_2(g) \rightleftharpoons 2NH_3(g)$$

The idea that processes can be reversed can be used to understand why this reaction reaches equilibrium. When nitrogen gas and hydrogen gas are mixed in a sealed container at a constant temperature, a sequence of events occurs that can be illustrated by a plot of reaction rate versus time like the one shown in Figure 2.2.3.

From this graph you can understand the following:

- Nitrogen and hydrogen gas molecules collide with each other and form ammonia in the forward reaction, $N_2(g) + 3H_2(g) \rightarrow 2NH_3(g)$. From collision theory, you can see that as the concentrations of nitrogen and hydrogen decrease during this reaction, the frequency of collisions between molecules decreases and therefore the rate of the production of ammonia also decreases.
- At the same time as ammonia is being formed, some ammonia molecules collide and decompose to re-form nitrogen and hydrogen in the reverse reaction, $2NH_3(g) \rightarrow N_2(g) + 3H_2(g)$.
- Eventually the forward and reverse reactions proceed at the same rate. When this situation is reached, ammonia is formed at exactly the same rate as it is breaking down. The concentrations of ammonia, nitrogen and hydrogen then remain constant. To an observer, the reaction now appears to have stopped with no observable change.

In a closed system at constant pressure and temperature, no further change will take place. The reaction has reached a point of balance—an equilibrium.

The concentration versus time graph in Figure 2.2.4 shows the changes in concentrations of the chemicals with time. As indicated by the coefficients of the equation for the reaction, for every mole of N_2 that reacts, three times as much H_2 reacts and twice as much NH_3 is produced. Equilibrium is established when there is no longer any change in any of the concentrations.

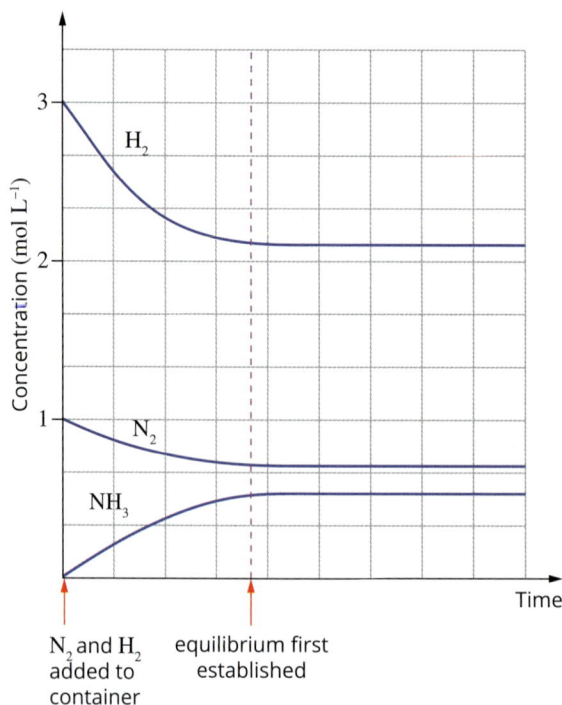

FIGURE 2.2.4 Changes in the concentrations of N_2, H_2 and NH_3 as a mixture of nitrogen and hydrogen gas reacts.

DYNAMIC STATE OF EQUILIBRIUM

A chemical equilibrium can be described as being in a dynamic state because the forward and reverse reactions have not ceased. Instead, they occur simultaneously at the same rate. During this **dynamic equilibrium**:

- the reaction is 'incomplete' and all of the substances (that is, the reactants and products) are present in the equilibrium mixture
- at the molecular level, bonds are constantly being broken and new bonds are being formed as the reactants and products continue to be converted from one to another.

The decomposition of dinitrogen tetroxide (N_2O_4) to nitrogen dioxide (NO_2) is an example of a reversible reaction that reaches a dynamic equilibrium. The progression of this reaction from pure N_2O_4 to the equilibrium mixture containing both N_2O_4 and NO_2 can be monitored through the changing colour of the gases in the reaction vessel. N_2O_4 is colourless and NO_2 is dark brown.

The reaction occurs according to the equation:

$$N_2O_4(g) \rightleftharpoons 2NO_2(g)$$

Figure 2.2.6 illustrates the observations made of a reaction vessel that is injected with some pure N_2O_4. As the forward reaction proceeds, the formation of a dark brown gas is observed. The depth of colour increases until equilibrium is reached, at which point there is no further change in the colour.

> **ⓘ** Dynamic equilibrium is reached by reversible physical or chemical processes taking place in a closed system.

FIGURE 2.2.6 The decomposition of dinitrogen tetroxide produces the brown gas nitrogen dioxide. As the concentration of nitrogen dioxide increases, the colour deepens until equilibrium is reached. At equilibrium (after 8 seconds), there is no further change in colour, regardless of how long the reaction is allowed to proceed.

Investigating dynamic equilibrium

Chemists can use radioactive **isotopes** to investigate systems in dynamic equilibrium. Radioactive isotopes behave chemically in the same way as non-radioactive atoms of the same element, but their presence and location can be determined easily with a radiation detector.

When solid sodium iodide (NaI) is added to water, it dissolves readily at first. As the concentration of dissolved sodium iodide increases, a saturated solution forms and no further solid dissolves. The concentrations of the Na^+ ions and I^- ions in solution remain constant and some solid NaI is always present on the bottom of the test tube.

When solid sodium iodide containing radioactive iodide ions is added to a saturated solution, the subsequent movement of these 'labelled' ions can be traced. Although solid sodium iodide is still observed in the bottom of the flask, the solution quickly becomes radioactive (Figure 2.2.7).

The radioactivity of the solution shows that some of the radioactive sodium iodide has dissolved. The concentrations of sodium ions and iodide ions remain constant, so particles that were not radioactive must have crystallised from the solution at the same rate that the radioactive solid was dissolving (Figure 2.2.8).

Even though nothing can be seen happening, there must be continual activity at the surface of the solid. The system is in dynamic equilibrium:

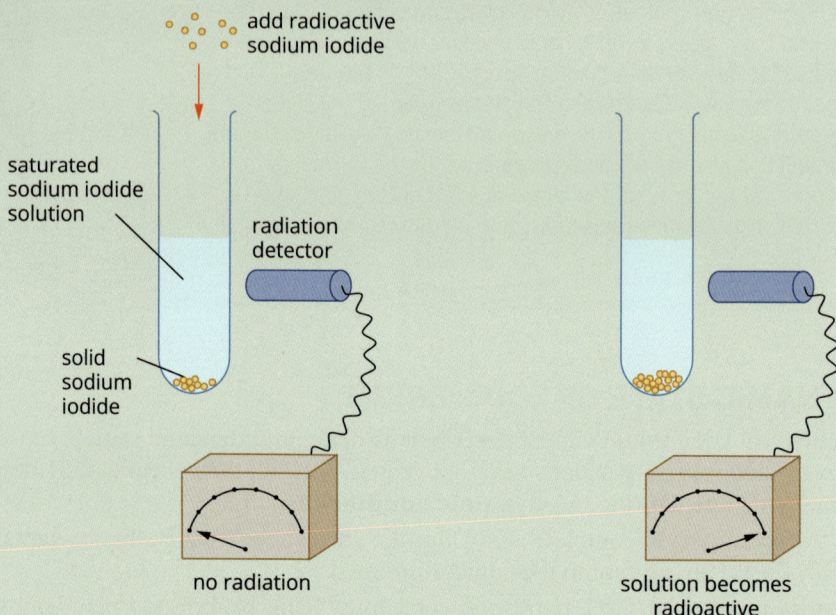

$$NaI(s) \rightleftharpoons NaI(aq)$$

FIGURE 2.2.7 This experiment shows that a dynamic equilibrium between the solid and the dissolved ions is present in a saturated solution.

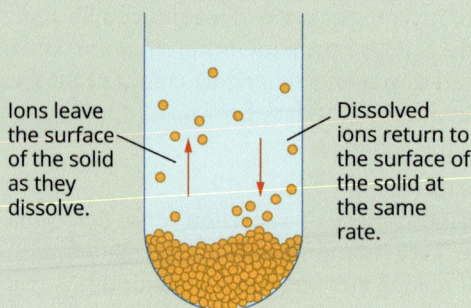

FIGURE 2.2.8 The cyclic dissolution and redeposition of ions in a saturated solution is an example of dynamic equilibrium.

Extent of reaction

You have seen that some reactions are reversible, but do all reactions that reach a dynamic equilibrium proceed to the same extent? This can be answered with a simple experiment.

Both hydrogen chloride (HCl) and ethanoic acid (CH_3COOH) react with water to form ions, according to the following equations:

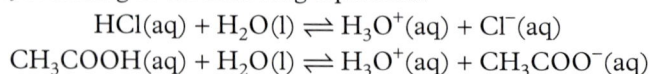

$$HCl(aq) + H_2O(l) \rightleftharpoons H_3O^+(aq) + Cl^-(aq)$$
$$CH_3COOH(aq) + H_2O(l) \rightleftharpoons H_3O^+(aq) + CH_3COO^-(aq)$$

Solutions of both chemicals conduct electricity because they contain mobile ions. The relative conductivity of the solutions is proportional to the number of free ions in the solution. By measuring the electrical conductivity of solutions of the same concentration, you can compare how much each compound dissociates in water.

Figure 2.2.9 shows the results obtained from such an experiment. You can see that when hydrogen chloride dissolves in water, the solution formed (hydrochloric acid) is a much better conductor than the ethanoic acid solution. Both solutions were formed by adding the same number of moles of acid molecules to identical volumes of water.

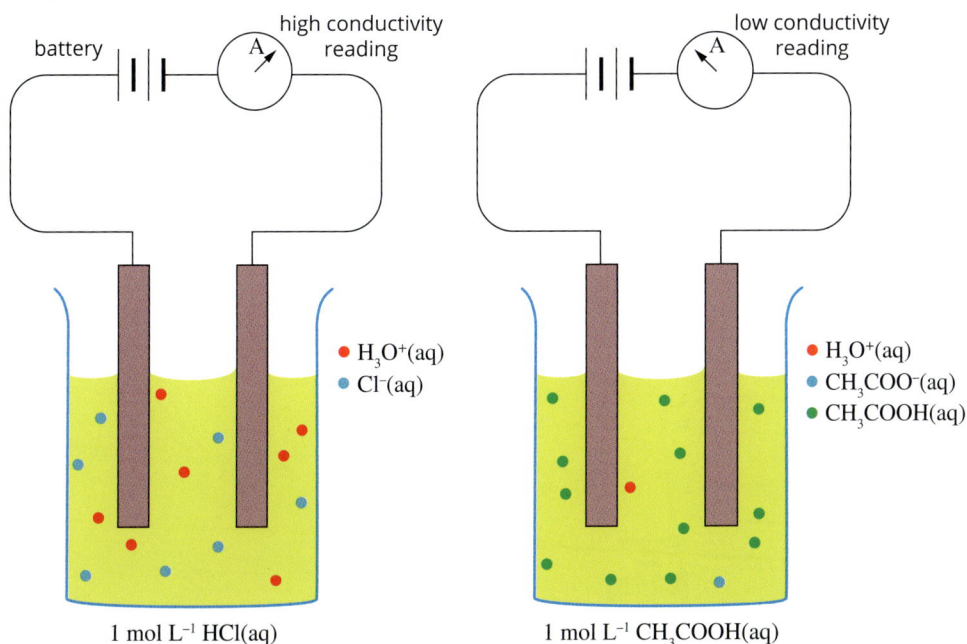

FIGURE 2.2.9 This experiment compares the electrical conductivity of $1\,mol\,L^{-1}$ solutions of hydrogen chloride and ethanoic acid.

Ethanoic acid is a weak acid and will therefore only partially dissociate in an aqueous solution. Hydrochloric acid is a strong acid that almost completely dissociates in aqueous solution. The concept of equilibrium allows us to better explain the idea of strong and weak acids by looking at the extent of the dissociation reaction. You will learn more about strong and weak acids in Chapter 7.

GO TO ➤ Section 7.1 page 162

The difference in conductivity observed in the experiment arises because these reactions occur to remarkably different extents. At equilibrium in a $1\,mol\,L^{-1}$ solution at 25°C, almost all the HCl molecules are dissociated, whereas only about 1% of the CH_3COOH molecules are dissociated. This demonstrates that different reactions proceed to different extents. The ratios of reactants to products are different for different equilibrium systems.

It is important to note that the **extent of reaction** describes how much product is formed when the system reaches equilibrium. However, the **rate of reaction** is a measure of the change in concentration of the reactants and products with time and is not directly related to the extent of reaction. The rates of reversible reactions range from very slow to very fast, and determine how long the reaction takes to reach equilibrium.

> ⓘ The extent of a reaction does not give any information about how fast a reaction will proceed. It only indicates how much product is formed once the system is at equilibrium.

STATIC EQUILIBRIUM

As you have seen above, there are many examples of reversible chemical reactions in a closed system that occur in both the forward and reverse directions and reach a dynamic equilibrium. In a dynamic equilibrium the concentrations of the reactants and products do not change over time, but at the atomic level the reactants are continually forming products and the products are continually forming reactants. The rate of the forward reaction is equal to the rate of the reverse reaction.

Figure 2.2.10a is an example of a dynamic equilibrium that does not involve a chemical reaction. In this example a tank is being filled with water as water simultaneously flows out of the tank at the same rate. The water level remains constant and an equilibrium occurs.

Figure 2.2.10b is a representation of a different type of equilibrium called a **static equilibrium**. All forces are in balance; there is no overall force and there is no movement.

> **ℹ** Static equilibrium occurs when the rates of the forward and reverse reactions are both almost zero.

Although the term static equilibrium is usually used in a mechanical sense and only rarely used in chemistry, it is sometimes applied to chemical reactions in which the rates of the forward and reverse reactions are almost zero. In these reactions there is no further conversion of reactions to products or products to reactants.

(a)   (b)

FIGURE 2.2.10 Two different types of equilibrium: (a) dynamic equilibrium and (b) static equilibrium

The conversion of graphite into diamond (Figure 2.2.11) can be regarded as a static equilibrium:

$$C(\text{graphite}) \rightleftharpoons C(\text{diamond})$$

(a)   (b)

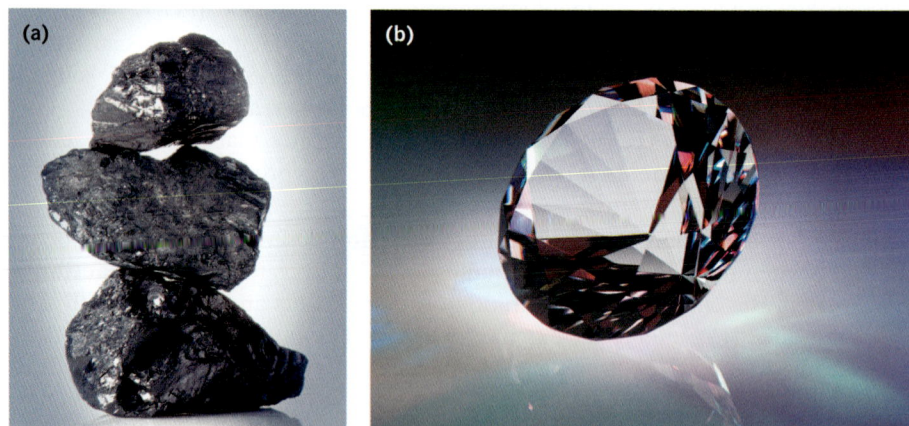

FIGURE 2.2.11 Allotropes of carbon: (a) graphite and (b) diamond

Between about 1 billion and 3.5 billion years ago, graphite was converted to diamond under intense heat and pressure in the Earth's mantle. Although in theory the reverse reaction to re-form graphite can occur, the diamond would have to be heated to above 2000°C because the activation energy of the reaction is very high. Under normal conditions it would take billions of years for diamond to become graphite, because the rate of the forward and reverse reactions is effectively zero.

Reactions that form a static equilibrium may be considered to be irreversible reactions. At the atomic level, the rates of the forward and reverse reactions are equal and are both almost zero.

Table 2.2.1 summaries the differences between dynamic and static equilibrium in chemical systems.

TABLE 2.2.1 Characteristics of static and dynamic equilibrium

Static equilibrium	Dynamic equilibrium
Rates of forward and reverse reactions are equal and almost zero.	Rates of forward and reverse reactions are equal and not zero.
There is no movement of reactant and product particles in either the forward or reverse direction.	Although concentrations do not change, there is an equal rate of reaction of reactants to form products, and vice versa.

WS 5.2

NON-EQUILIBRIUM SYSTEMS

Some systems are effectively irreversible and never reach an equilibrium state. These systems are called **non-equilibrium systems**.

Our understanding of non-equilibrium systems is incomplete and they are still being studied, especially in areas such as chemistry, medicine, finance, meteorology and drug design. Future research may help us to solve the complex, non-equilibrium systems involved in optimising the design of nanoparticles in new drugs, or understanding how epidemics spread, or predicting the likelihood of an extreme meteorological event. In chemistry, combustion reactions and photosynthesis are examples of non-equilibrium systems.

> **i** Non-equilibrium systems involve reactions that are effectively irreversible and never reach an equilibrium.

COMBUSTION

Combustion reactions are irreversible exothermic reactions. For example, the combustion of octane in petrol can be represented by the equation:

$$C_8H_{18}(g) + \frac{25}{2}O_2(g) \rightarrow 8CO_2(g) + 9H_2O(g) \qquad \Delta H = -5114\,\text{kJ mol}^{-1}$$

The products of this reaction, CO_2 and H_2O, are stable and do not react with each other to re-form octane and oxygen gas. Because the reaction is irreversible it cannot, in a closed system, reach equilibrium. Combustion reactions are therefore non-equilibrium systems.

The reaction involves an increase in entropy because the number of gas molecules in the system increases (13.5 reactant gas particles become 17 product gas particles). The value of $\Delta S°$ for the system is $+384\,\text{J mol}^{-1}\,\text{K}^{-1}$.

You can determine whether the combustion of octane is spontaneous at 100°C using the Gibbs free energy change formula:

$$\Delta H° = -5114\,\text{kJ mol}^{-1}$$
$$\Delta S° = +384\,\text{J mol}^{-1}\,\text{K}^{-1}$$
$$\Delta G° = \Delta H° - T\Delta S°$$
$$= -5114 - (373 \times 0.384) \text{ (T is in kelvin and $\Delta S°$ is converted to kJ mol}^{-1}\,\text{K}^{-1})$$
$$= -5257\,\text{kJ mol}^{-1}$$

Since ΔG is negative, this is a spontaneous reaction and does not need a continuing supply of energy to occur. Indeed, once the reaction commences, it continues to consume all the available octane or oxygen. The products of the reaction, carbon dioxide and water, never recombine to form octane and oxygen.

Combustion reactions are spontaneous non-equilibrium systems. The example of photosynthesis below shows you that the reactions involved in some non-equilibrium systems do not have to be spontaneous.

> **i** Entropy tends to increase (ΔS is positive) in reactions in which:
> - the number of particles increases
> - liquid or solid reactants become gaseous products.

Explosives: a blast of chemical energy

Explosives are used for road construction, tunnelling, demolition and mining (Figure 2.2.12). Explosions involve combustion reactions, in which chemical energy is transformed into large quantities of thermal energy very quickly. Although thermal energy is also released when fuels such as petrol and natural gas burn, the rate of combustion in these reactions is limited by the availability of oxygen gas to the fuel. In contrast, the compounds making up an explosive contain sufficient oxygen for a complete (or almost complete) reaction to occur very quickly.

Explosions are examples of irreversible spontaneous reactions that do not reach equilibrium. They are non-equilibrium systems.

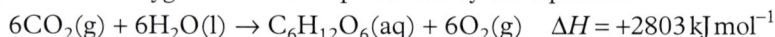

FIGURE 2.2.12 Controlled blasting in an open-cut mine. The explosive reaction is a non-equilibrium system.

PHOTOSYNTHESIS

GO TO ▶ Year 11 Section 15.3

Photosynthesis is an endothermic chemical process occurring in the cells of plants, algae and some bacteria. In this process, carbon dioxide and water are converted into glucose and oxygen. It can be represented by the equation:

$$6CO_2(g) + 6H_2O(l) \rightarrow C_6H_{12}O_6(aq) + 6O_2(g) \quad \Delta H = +2803\,kJ\,mol^{-1}$$

In the presence of chlorophyll, plants convert energy from light, via a series of many small steps, into chemical energy in the bonds of the products, glucose and oxygen. During many of these steps, heat energy is also produced and released to the surroundings, increasing the entropy of the surroundings ($\Delta S_{surroundings}$).

As a consequence of the steps involved in photosynthesis and the factors that affect them, the reaction is not reversible and cannot reach equilibrium. Photosynthesis overall is a non-equilibrium system.

Although there is the same number of gas molecules on each side of the equation, photosynthesis involves a decrease in entropy because there is a decrease in the number of particles in the system (12 reactant particles become 7 product particles) and the larger molecule of glucose has been formed from the smaller ones. The value of ΔS for the equation is $-212\,J\,mol^{-1}\,K^{-1}$.

Using the Gibbs free energy change formula, the sign and value of ΔG and therefore the spontaneity of this reaction can be determined. At 25°C:

$\Delta H° = +2803\,kJ\,mol^{-1}$

$\Delta S° = -212\,J\,mol^{-1}\,K^{-1}$

$\Delta G° = \Delta H° - T\Delta S°$

$\quad = +2803 - (298 \times -0.212)$ (T is in kelvin and $\Delta S°$ is converted to $kJ\,mol^{-1}\,K^{-1}$)

$\quad = +2803 + 63.18$

$\quad = +2866\,kJ\,mol^{-1}$

Since ΔG is positive, this is a non-spontaneous system that requires a continual supply of external energy for the reaction to occur.

So how can this reaction occur if it is non-spontaneous? Biological systems use spontaneous reactions to drive non-spontaneous reactions such as photosynthesis; the non-spontaneous reaction is coupled to spontaneous reactions so that the overall process is spontaneous. The energy released by the spontaneous reactions is used during the many small steps that occur in photosynthesis. Heat from the spontaneous reactions is also lost to the surroundings, with a subsequent increase in entropy.

This is an illustration of the second law of thermodynamics, which states that, over time, the entropy of the universe is increasing. The entropy of the universe is the sum of the changes in entropy of the system and the surroundings. The law may be expressed as:

$$\Delta S_{system} + \Delta S_{surroundings} = \Delta S_{universe} > 0$$

If the photosynthesis reaction is considered in isolation, the overall entropy of the universe would decrease, apparently in violation of the second law. However, when the entropy changes due to the spontaneous reactions that are coupled with and drive the photosynthesis reaction are taken into account, there is a net increase in the entropy of the universe, in accordance with the second law (Figure 2.2.13).

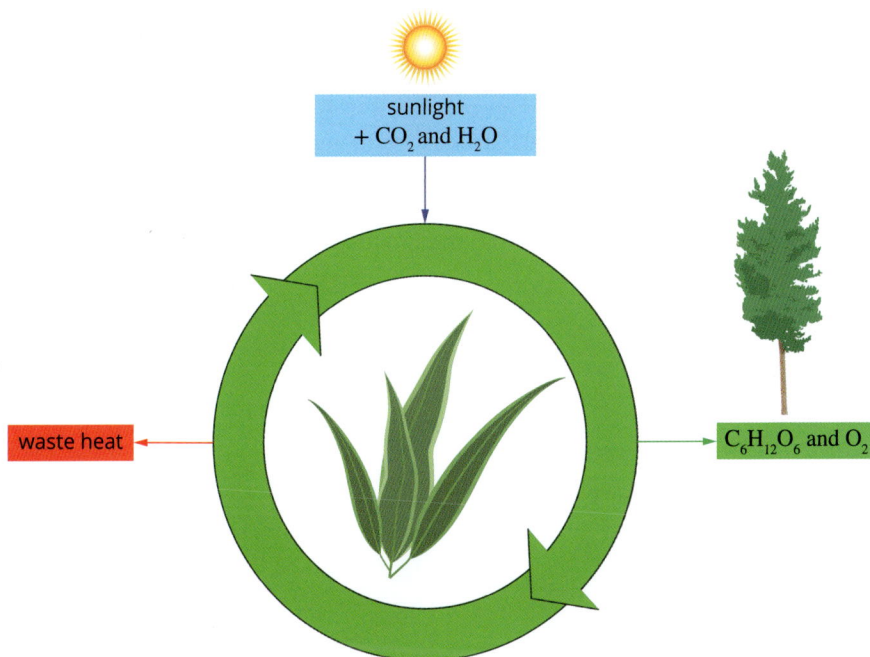

sunlight
+ CO_2 and H_2O

waste heat

$C_6H_{12}O_6$ and O_2

FIGURE 2.2.13 Photosynthesis is an endothermic, non-spontaneous, non-equilibrium system. The process is coupled with spontaneous reactions, resulting in a significant amount of heat being lost to the surroundings and an increase in the entropy of the universe overall.

2.2 Review

SUMMARY

- Reversible reactions can reach a state of equilibrium in which the overall concentrations of reactants and products do not change over time.
- At equilibrium, the rate of the forward reaction is equal to the rate of the reverse reaction. When there is continued conversion of reactants to products at equal rates, this is called a state of dynamic equilibrium.
- Different reactions proceed to different extents.
- The relative ratios of reactants to products when equilibrium is reached are different for different reactions.
- The extent of reaction indicates how much product is formed at equilibrium, whereas the rate of reaction is a measure of the change in concentration of the reactants and products with time.
- Static equilibrium occurs in chemical reactions when there is no further conversion of reactions to products or products to reactants and the rates of the forward and reverse reactions are almost zero.

- An irreversible reaction may be considered a non-equilibrium system if the products are stable and do not react to reform the reactants.
- The change in entropy of the universe is the sum of the changes in entropy of the system and the surroundings, and may be mathematically expressed as:

$$\Delta S_{system} + \Delta S_{surroundings} = \Delta S_{universe} > 0$$

- Combustion reactions are examples of non-equilibrium systems.
- The combination of an energy decrease ($\Delta H < 0$) and entropy increase ($\Delta S > 0$) means that combustion reactions are spontaneous reactions.
- Photosynthesis is a non-spontaneous, non-equilibrium process. It is driven by spontaneous reactions. Overall, the increase in the entropy of the universe caused by the spontaneous reactions in photosynthesis is greater than the decrease in entropy from the photosynthesis reaction.

KEY QUESTIONS

1 Which one of the following statements about the extent of reaction is true?

   A The extent of reaction indicates the rate of the reaction and the time taken to reach equilibrium.

   B The extent of reaction is the point when there are equal amounts of reactants and products.

   C The extent of reaction indicates how far the reaction has proceeded in the forward direction when equilibrium is achieved.

   D The extent of reaction indicates the rate of reaction and is the point when the rate of the forward reaction is equal to the rate of the reverse reaction.

2 Hydrogen gas is mixed with iodine gas in a sealed container. A reaction occurs according to the equation:

$$H_2(g) + I_2(g) \rightleftharpoons 2HI(g)$$

On the rate–time graph for this system shown on the right, label the lines for the forward and reverse reactions with the appropriate chemical equation. Also label the point when equilibrium is first established. Explain what the graph shows.

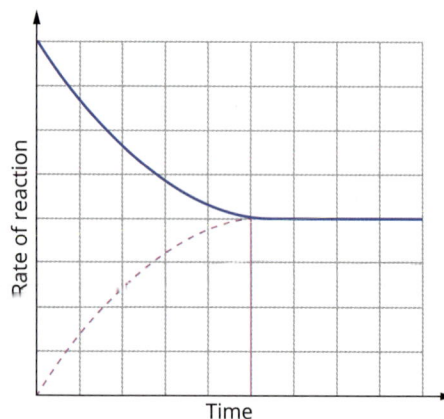

Rate of reaction vs Time graph

3 Fill in the blanks to complete the sentences about dynamic equilibrium.

In a(n) _____ system, as the concentrations of the reactants decreases, the rate of the forward reaction also _____. The collisions between these reactant molecules occur _____ frequently. Once some product starts to form, the _____ reaction occurs and the frequency of collisions between product molecules _____. At equilibrium, the rates of the forward and backward reactions are _____ and the concentrations of all species do not change.

4 The graph below shows the concentration versus time plot for the decomposition of dinitrogen tetroxide, which has the equation:

$$N_2O_4(g) \rightleftharpoons 2NO_2(g)$$

The reaction was performed at 100°C in a 1 L reaction vessel. N_2O_4 is a colourless gas and NO_2 is brown. Use the graph to answer the following questions.

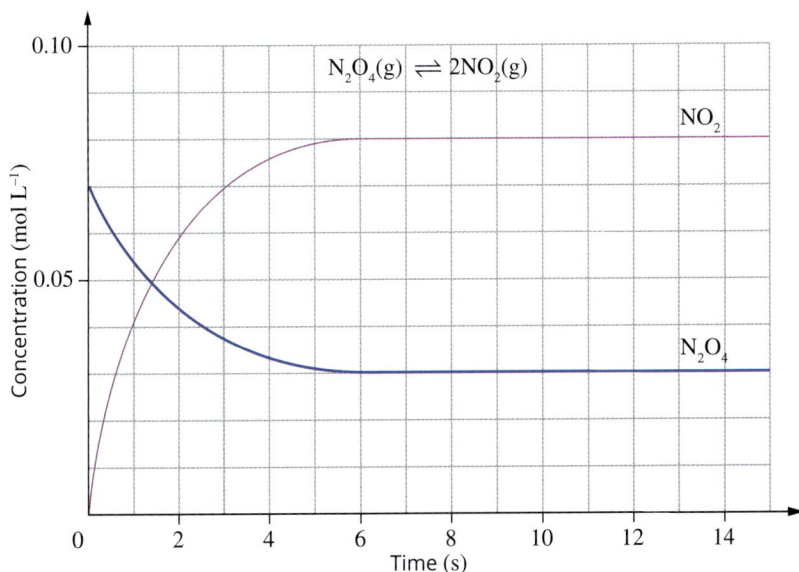

a What was the initial concentration of N_2O_4 in the flask?

b What was the initial concentration of NO_2 in the flask?

c What was the concentration of N_2O_4 at equilibrium?

d What was the concentration of NO_2 at equilibrium?

e Over the course of the reaction, how many moles of N_2O_4 decomposed?

f What do the horizontal regions of the graph indicate?

g How long did it take for equilibrium to be reached?

h A student studying this reaction records her observations over time. What will she observe as the reaction proceeds?

5 Which one of the following statements about photosynthesis is incorrect?

A Photosynthesis may be considered to be a non-equilibrium system overall.

B The change in entropy, ΔS, for photosynthesis is positive.

C Spontaneous reactions drive photosynthesis, increasing the entropy of the universe overall.

D The balanced equation for photosynthesis is:
$$6CO_2(g) + 6H_2O(l) \rightarrow C_6H_{12}O_6(aq) + 6O_2(g)$$

6 Consider the following data for the melting of ice, $H_2O(s) \rightarrow H_2O(l)$:

Heat of fusion, $\Delta H°_{fus} = +6.01\ kJ\,mol^{-1}$

Entropy of fusion, $\Delta S°_{fus} = +22.0\ J\,mol^{-1}\,K^{-1}$

a Determine the value of $\Delta G°$ for this process at 25°C.

b Is the melting of ice spontaneous at 25°C? Explain.

Chapter review

02

KEY TERMS

activation energy
catalyst
closed system
collision theory
dynamic equilibrium
endothermic
energy profile diagram
enthalpy change
entropy
equilibrium
exothermic

extent of reaction
Gibbs free energy
irreversible reaction
isotope
non-equilibrium system
non-spontaneous reaction
open system
rate of reaction
reversible reaction
saturated
second law of thermodynamics

spontaneous reaction
static equilibrium
surroundings
system
thermochemical equation

REVIEW QUESTIONS

1 Which one of the following statements about open systems is correct?
   A An open system can exchange matter and energy with the surroundings.
   B An open system can exchange nothing with the surroundings.
   C An open system can exchange only matter with the surroundings.
   D An open system can exchange only energy with the surroundings.

2 Which one of the following statements about the saturated sugar solution shown in Figure 2.1.6, page 55, is correct?
   A It is an example of a closed system which is non-reversible.
   B It is an example of an open system which is non-reversible.
   C It is an example of a closed system which is reversible.
   D It is an example of an open system which is reversible.

3 Which one of the following statements is not true for a reversible process?
   A A reversible process will not reach equilibrium in an open system.
   B A reversible process can reach equilibrium in a closed system.
   C Both chemical and physical changes can be reversible.
   D A reversible process only occurs when a chemical or physical change takes place in an open system.

4 Classify the following systems as open or closed and explain your reasoning.
   a a lit candle
   b a refrigerator with a door that is shut
   c a human being
   d a weather balloon

5 Determine whether each of the following statements are true or false. Use your understanding of systems and reversibility to explain your answer.
   a The burning of magnesium in air is a reversible physical change.
   b The system represented by the chemical equation $Fe^{3+}(aq) + SCN^-(aq) \rightleftharpoons FeSCN^{2+}(aq)$ is a reversible reaction.
   c Combustion of petrol provides energy to drive a car. The combustion process is an irreversible, open, exothermic system.
   d The evaporation of water from a river is a reversible equilibrium system.

6 Consider the following equilibrium:
$$H_2O(l) \rightleftharpoons H_2O(g)$$
   a Explain what is meant by the dynamic nature of equilibrium, and why wet clothes in a closed laundry bag do not dry.
   b When the laundry bag in part a is opened, the clothes begin to dry. Is this because of an equilibrium process? Explain your answer.

7 Suppose CO gas and Cl_2 gas are added to a sealed container at constant temperature. A reaction occurs according to the following equation:

$$CO(g) + Cl_2(g) \rightleftharpoons COCl_2(g)$$

Sort the following statements into the correct order to explain how equilibrium is established.

i Equilibrium has been reached and the concentrations of CO, Cl_2 and $COCl_2$ will now remain constant.

ii When the rates of the forward and reverse reactions become equal, $COCl_2$ is formed at the same rate as it is breaking down.

iii The forward reaction will occur as the concentrations of CO and Cl_2 decrease and the rate of the production of $COCl_2$ decreases.

iv As $COCl_2$ is formed, some $COCl_2$ molecules decompose to re-form CO and Cl_2.

8 Decide whether each of the following systems is at equilibrium, and explain your answer in each case.

a a salt crystal slowly dissolving in a beaker of water

b a saturated sugar solution with sugar remaining on the bottom of the cup

c an open bottle of perfume

d the combustion of a log of wood in a campfire

e an open bottle of sparkling mineral water

f an unopened bottle of sparkling mineral water.

9 Use collision theory to explain the shapes of the rate–time graph below for the reaction:

$$2SO_2(g) + O_2(g) \rightleftharpoons 2SO_3(g)$$

10 What is the difference between static and dynamic equilibrium? Give an example of each.

11 Why is combustion considered to be a non-equilibrium system?

12 Organising a pack of playing cards in order of number and suit is sometimes used as a way of introducing the concept of entropy. By considering the cards to be a system and the person doing the organising and the atmosphere to be the surroundings, explain how this example can be used to explain the second law of thermodynamics, which is expressed mathematically as:

$$\Delta S_{system} + \Delta S_{surroundings} = \Delta S_{universe} > 0$$

13 Airbags in cars are deployed within 30 milliseconds of an impact. The initial reaction that occurs is exothermic and can be represented as:

$$2NaN_3(s) \rightarrow 2Na(l) + 3N_2(g)$$

Can this reaction be considered a non-equilibrium system?

14 The biological process of respiration can be represented by the equation:

$$C_6H_{12}O_6(aq) + 6O_2(g) \rightarrow 6CO_2(g) + 6H_2O(l)$$

Given the following data for the reaction, calculate $\Delta G°$ and hence determine if respiration is a spontaneous process at 25°C.

$\Delta H° = -2803\,kJ\,mol^{-1}$

$\Delta S° = +212\,J\,mol^{-1}\,K^{-1}$

15 The laws of thermodynamics apply widely, from the reactions of atoms to the behaviour of galaxies. The processes that occur in photosynthesis have sometimes been compared with those that take place when a room is tidied. For each of these two systems (the photosynthesis reaction in one case and the objects in the room in the other), state whether:

a an increase or decrease in entropy occurs in the system, and give the sign of ΔS_{system}

b the system is spontaneous, and give the sign of ΔG

c the overall entropy of the universe ($\Delta S_{universe}$) increases or decreases when all processes that are occurring are taken into account.

16 Reflect on the Inquiry task on page 53. Red wine contains a pigment that can be represented by the formula HR_w. When hydroxide ions (OH^-) are added the pigment loses a proton and forms another pigment, R_w^-, and water, according to the equation:

$$HR_w(aq) + OH^-(aq) \rightarrow R_w^-(aq) + H_2O(l)$$

Liquid soap and solutions of sodium hydrogen carbonate are classified as bases and have relatively high concentrations of OH^- ions. Vinegar is classified as an acid and has a relatively high concentration of H^+ ions. H^+ ions react with OH^- ions to form water. (You will learn more about acids and bases in Chapter 6.)

a From your observations, what are the colours of HR_w and R_w^-?

b Write an equation for the reaction of R_w^- with H^+ ions.

c Explain why the formation of R_w^- from HR_w can be described as a reversible process.

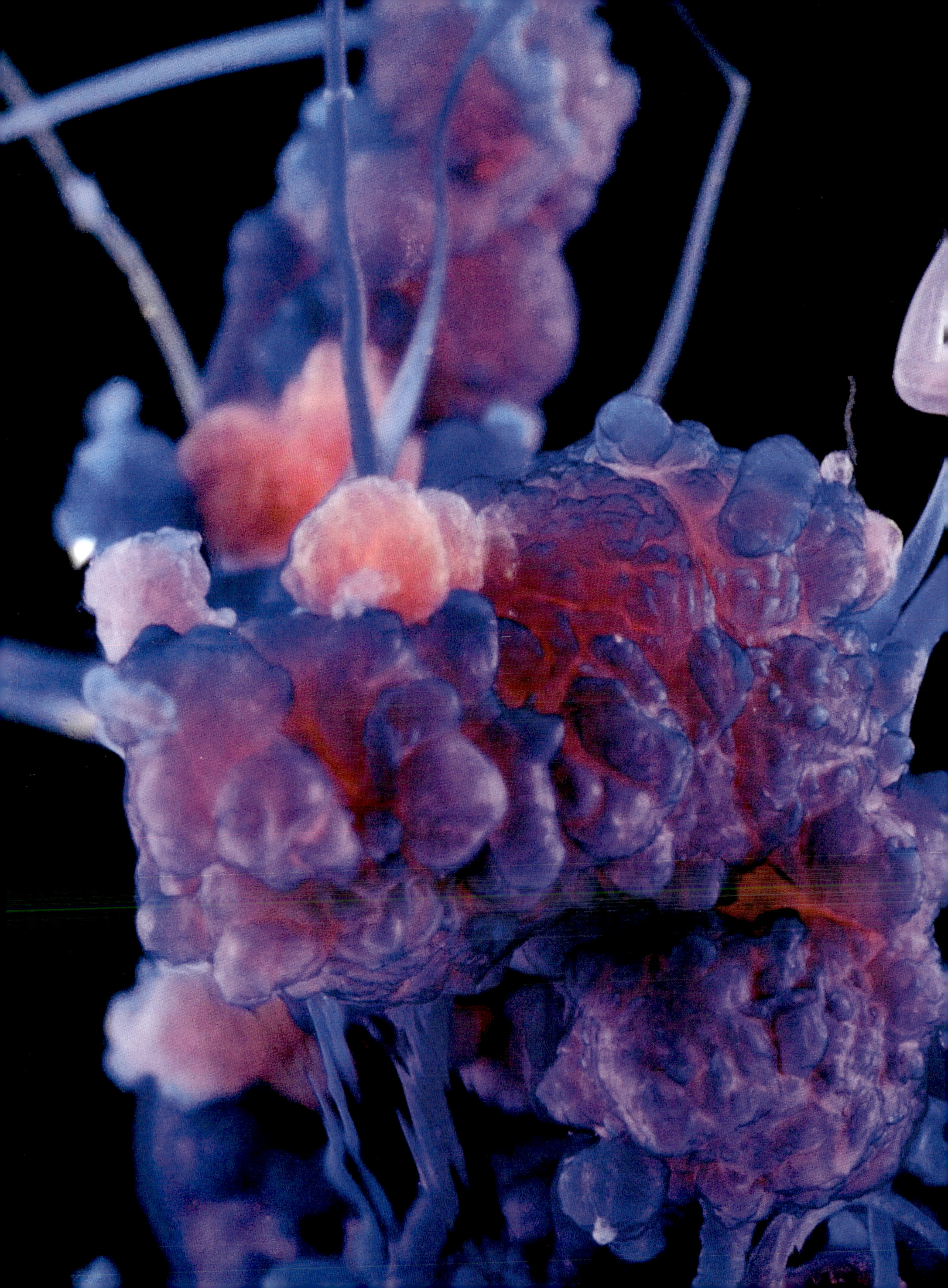

Calculating an equilibrium constant

The previous chapter introduced the concept of chemical equilibrium—some reactions in a closed system seem to stop before all the reactants are completely consumed. When a reaction is in chemical equilibrium, the rate at which the products are formed from the reactants is equal to the rate at which the reactants are formed from the products.

The quantitative nature of chemical equilibrium was first studied by chemists in the 19th century. They found that an equilibrium can be described in terms of a mathematical relationship called an equilibrium law.

This chapter introduces you to the equilibrium law and its use in determining the composition of a reaction mixture at equilibrium.

Content

INQUIRY QUESTION

How can the position of equilibrium be described and what does the equilibrium constant represent?

By the end of this chapter, you will be able to:

- deduce the equilibrium expression (in terms of K_{eq}) for homogeneous reactions occurring in solution (ACSCH079, ACSCH096) ICT N
- perform calculations to find the value of K_{eq} and concentrations of substances within an equilibrium system, and use these values to make predictions on the direction in which a reaction may proceed (ACSCH096) ICT N
- qualitatively analyse the effect of temperature on the value of K_{eq} (ACSCH093) ICT N
- conduct an investigation to determine K_{eq} of a chemical equilibrium system, for example:
  - K_{eq} of the iron(III) thiocyanate equilibrium (ACSCH096) ICT
- explore the use of K_{eq} for different types of chemical reactions, including but not limited to:
  - dissociation of ionic solutions (ACSCH098, ACSCH099)

3.1 The equilibrium law

In this section you will investigate the relationship between the quantities of reactants and the quantities of products present when a system reaches equilibrium. This relationship allows you to qualitatively predict the relative amounts of reactants and products in individual equilibrium systems.

REACTION QUOTIENT

Consider the equilibrium system involving the three gases, nitrogen, hydrogen and ammonia, that you were introduced to in Section 2.2:

$$N_2(g) + 3H_2(g) \rightleftharpoons 2NH_3(g)$$

An unlimited number of different equilibrium mixtures of the three gases can be prepared. Table 3.1.1 shows the concentrations of each of these gases in four different equilibrium mixtures at a constant temperature of 400°C. The value of the fraction $\frac{[NH_3]^2}{[N_2][H_2]^3}$ for each mixture is also given.

> **ℹ** The coefficients of the reactants and products in the chemical equation form the indices of the respective reactant and product concentrations used in the reaction quotient.

The fraction $\frac{[NH_3]^2}{[N_2][H_2]^3}$ is called the **reaction quotient** (Q) or **concentration fraction** of the mixture.

TABLE 3.1.1 Concentrations of reactants and products present in equilibrium mixtures

Equilibrium mixture (at 400°C)	$[N_2]$ (mol L^{-1})	$[H_2]$ (mol L^{-1})	$[NH_3]$ (mol L^{-1})	$\frac{[NH_3]^2}{[N_2][H_2]^3}$
1	0.25	0.75	0.074	0.052
2	0.25	0.65	0.089	0.052
3	0.0025	0.0055	4.6×10^{-6}	0.051
4	0.0011	0.0011	2.7×10^{-7}	0.051

As you can see from Table 3.1.1, the reaction quotient $\frac{[NH_3]^2}{[N_2][H_2]^3}$ has an almost constant value for each equilibrium mixture, regardless of the concentrations of each component.

While the reaction quotient can be calculated for any mixture of reactants and products at any time during a reaction, it is only when the mixture is at equilibrium that it gives a constant value. At equilibrium, the value of the reaction quotient is equal to the **equilibrium constant**, K_{eq}.

In general, for chemical reactions at equilibrium:
- different chemical reactions have different values of K_{eq}
- the size of K_{eq} indicates the proportions (relative amounts) of reactants and products in the equilibrium mixture
- for a particular reaction, K_{eq} is constant for all equilibrium mixtures at a fixed temperature.

THE EXPRESSION FOR THE EQUILIBRIUM LAW

By studying a large number of reversible systems such as the one between nitrogen, hydrogen and ammonia in the previous example, chemists have been able to develop the concept of the **equilibrium law**.

> **ℹ** K_{eq} is the equilibrium constant for a reaction. The value of K_{eq} is different for different reactions.

The equilibrium law states that:
- the equilibrium constant, K_{eq}, is the concentrations of products divided by the concentrations of reactants at equilibrium
- the index of each component concentration is the same as the coefficient for the substances in the balanced chemical equation.

For the general equation $aW + bX \rightleftharpoons cY + dZ$ at equilibrium at a particular temperature, the equilibrium expression can be written as:

$$K_{eq} = \frac{[Y]^c[Z]^d}{[W]^a[X]^b}$$

where K_{eq} is the equilibrium constant.

A useful way of remembering the equilibrium law is that K_{eq} can be represented as:

$$K_{eq} = \frac{[\text{products}]^{\text{coefficients}}}{[\text{reactants}]^{\text{coefficients}}}$$

Remember that if there is more than one product or reactant, you must multiply the terms.

> ℹ When you write an equilibrium expression, the concentrations of the products are always on the top of the expression (in the numerator).

The reaction quotient and the equilibrium law

An expression for the equilibrium constant, K_{eq}, can be written for any system at equilibrium. As you learnt above, a similar expression called a reaction quotient (Q) can be written for systems that are not necessarily at equilibrium. For example, for the reaction:

$$aA + bB \rightleftharpoons cC + dD$$

$$Q = \frac{[C]^c[D]^d}{[A]^a[B]^b}$$

Although a reaction quotient can be calculated for any mixture of reactants and products at any time during a reaction, it is only when the mixture is at equilibrium that the reaction quotient has a constant value. At equilibrium, the value of the reaction quotient is equal to the equilibrium constant, K_{eq}. If the reaction quotient, Q, is:
- smaller than K_{eq} then the system 'shifts to the right' to achieve equilibrium and more products are formed
- equal to K_{eq} then the system is at equilibrium
- greater than K_{eq} then the system 'shifts to the left' to achieve equilibrium and more reactants are formed.

The relationship between Q and K_{eq} is illustrated in Figure 3.1.1. By comparing the values of Q and K_{eq} for a reaction at a given temperature, it is possible to predict the direction in which a reaction will proceed in order to reach equilibrium.

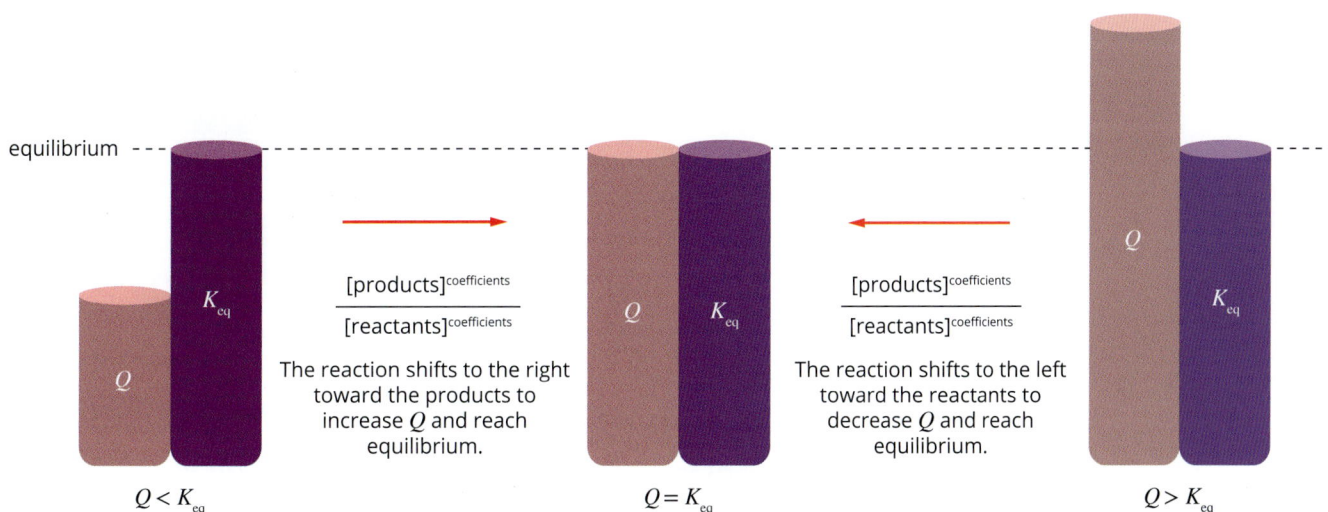

equilibrium

$\frac{[\text{products}]^{\text{coefficients}}}{[\text{reactants}]^{\text{coefficients}}}$

The reaction shifts to the right toward the products to increase Q and reach equilibrium.

$\frac{[\text{products}]^{\text{coefficients}}}{[\text{reactants}]^{\text{coefficients}}}$

The reaction shifts to the left toward the reactants to decrease Q and reach equilibrium.

$Q < K_{eq}$ $Q = K_{eq}$ $Q > K_{eq}$

FIGURE 3.1.1 $K_{eq} = Q$ for any reversible reaction at equilibrium, so comparing these two values for a reaction can indicate which way a reaction must progress to reach equilibrium.

Worked example 3.1.1

DETERMINING THE EXPRESSION FOR THE EQUILIBRIUM CONSTANT FOR AN EQUILIBRIUM SYSTEM

The decomposition of N_2O_4 is a reversible reaction that occurs according to the equation:

$$N_2O_4(g) \rightleftharpoons 2NO_2(g)$$

Write the expression for the equilibrium constant K_{eq}.

Thinking	Working
Identify the reactants and products. The reactants appear in the denominator of the expression, and the products appear in the numerator.	N_2O_4 is a reactant, so it appears in the denominator of the expression. NO$_2$ is a product, so it appears in the numerator of the expression.
Write the expression for K_{eq}. $$\frac{[products]^{coefficients}}{[reactants]^{coefficients}}$$ Remember that the index for each component concentration is the same as its coefficient in the balanced chemical equation.	$K_{eq} = \dfrac{[NO_2]^2}{[N_2O_4]}$

Worked example: Try yourself 3.1.1

DETERMINING THE EXPRESSION FOR THE EQUILIBRIUM CONSTANT FOR AN EQUILIBRIUM SYSTEM

Write the expression for K_{eq} for the reversible reaction:

$$2SO_2(g) + O_2(g) \rightleftharpoons 2SO_3(g)$$

CHEMFILE L

Equilibrium in the theatre

In Chapter 2 you saw that a yellow solution containing Fe^{3+} ions reacts with a colourless solution containing SCN^- ions to form an equilibrium with red $FeSCN^{2+}$ ions, according to the equation:

$$Fe^{3+}(aq) + SCN^-(aq) \rightleftharpoons FeSCN^{2+}(aq)$$

The equilibrium expression for this equation is:

$$K_{eq} = \frac{[FeSCN^{2+}]}{[Fe^{3+}][SCN^-]}$$

$$= 9 \times 10^2 \text{ at } 25°C$$

You will calculate the K_{eq} of this equilibrium system in a practical investigation this year. A substantial amount of the product $FeSCN^{2+}$ is present in an equilibrium mixture, so the mixture looks blood-red (Figure 3.1.2).

This equilibrium reaction has been used in theatrical productions to make fake blood. A layer of colourless SCN^- solution can be painted onto an actor's hand prior to the scene. If a plastic knife that has been previously dipped in pale yellow Fe^{3+} solution is used to make a fake cut across the hand, a blood-red 'cut' appears due to the production of red $FeSCN^{2+}$.

FIGURE 3.1.2 Making fake blood. An Fe^{3+} solution (left) is mixed with an SCN^- solution (centre) to produce a blood-red equilibrium mixture of Fe^{3+}, SCN^- and $FeSCN^{2+}$ (right).

HOMOGENEOUS AND HETEROGENEOUS EQUILIBRIA

The chemical reactions discussed so far have involved **homogeneous reactions**, in which all reactants and products are in the same phase. However, some equilibria involve **heterogeneous reactions**, in which reactants and products are in different phases.

The important feature of the equilibrium law for heterogeneous reactions is that the concentration of a pure solid or a pure liquid is assigned a value of 1. This is because these concentrations do not depend on how much of the pure substance is present.

Because the concentration of a solid in a heterogeneous system is considered to be constant, it is removed from the equilibrium expression. As a result, the expression for the equilibrium law of a heterogeneous system is often much simpler. For example, for the equation:

$$CaCO_3(s) \rightleftharpoons CaO(s) + CO_2(g)$$

the expression for the equilibrium constant is $K_{eq} = [CO_2]$.

Because CaO and $CaCO_3$ are both solids, they do not appear in the expression.

The dissolution of a solid to form an aqueous solution is another example of a heterogeneous equilibrium system. Ionic solids **dissociate** (break up) into ions when they dissolve in water. Consider the dissociation of solid lead(II) chloride ($PbCl_2$) into lead(II) and chloride ions in solution:

$$PbCl_2(s) \rightleftharpoons Pb^{2+}(aq) + 2Cl^-(aq)$$

Because the concentration of the solid lead(II) chloride is constant, it is assigned a value of 1 and does not appear in the expression for the equilibrium constant. This results in the expression:

$$K_{eq} = [Pb^{2+}][Cl^-]^2$$

You will learn more about how the solubility of an ionic substance is related to equilibrium in Chapter 5. The 'crystal gardens' shown in Figure 3.1.3 and the chapter opener image are heterogeneous systems involving ionic solids.

GO TO ➤ Section 5.2 page 121

Worked example 3.1.2

DETERMINING THE EXPRESSION FOR THE EQUILIBRIUM CONSTANT FOR A HETEROGENEOUS EQUILIBRIUM SYSTEM

Calcium sulfate is only slightly soluble in water. The equation for its dissolution can be written as:

$$CaSO_4(s) \rightleftharpoons Ca^{2+}(aq) + SO_4^{2-}(aq)$$

Write the expression for the equilibrium constant K_{eq}.

Thinking	Working
Identify the reactants and products. The reactants appear in the denominator of the expression, and the products appear in the numerator. The concentration of a pure solid or a pure liquid is assigned a value of 1.	$CaSO_4$ is a reactant. It is a pure solid so it will not appear in the equilibrium expression. Ca^{2+} and SO_4^{2-} are products so they appear in the numerator of the expression.
Write the expression for K_{eq}. $$\frac{[products]^{coefficients}}{[reactants]^{coefficients}}$$ Remember that the index of each component concentration is the same as its coefficient in the balanced chemical equation.	$$K_{eq} = [Ca^{2+}][SO_4^{2-}]$$

Worked example 3.1.2: Try yourself

DETERMINING THE EXPRESSION FOR THE EQUILIBRIUM CONSTANT FOR A HETEROGENEOUS EQUILIBRIUM SYSTEM

Lead(II) iodide is only slightly soluble in water. The equation for its dissolution can be written as:

$$PbI_2(s) \rightleftharpoons Pb^{2+}(aq) + 2I^-(aq)$$

Write the expression for the equilibrium constant K_{eq}.

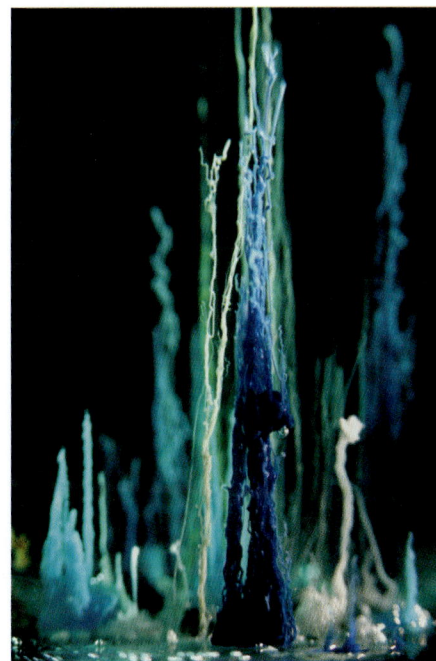

FIGURE 3.1.3 When small crystals of metal salts such as cobalt(II) chloride, copper(II) sulfate and nickel(II) sulfate are placed in a concentrated solution of sodium silicate, the metal ions react to form colourful crystals of insoluble metal silicates. As the metal salts continue to dissolve in the solution and more metal silicates form, the crystals grow upwards to form an attractive 'crystal garden'.

3.1 Review

SUMMARY

- The equilibrium constant, K_{eq}, is a constant for a particular chemical reaction at a particular temperature.
- The equilibrium expression for the equation:
$$aW + bX \rightleftharpoons cY + dZ$$
is:
$$K_{eq} = \frac{[Y]^c[Z]^d}{[W]^a[X]^b}$$
- A reaction quotient, Q, can be calculated for any stage of a chemical reaction. The reaction quotient has the same mathematical expression as the equilibrium constant.

- When a reaction system at a particular temperature has reached equilibrium, the reaction quotient is equal to the equilibrium constant.
- An expression for the equilibrium law can be written for both homogeneous and heterogeneous systems. For heterogeneous systems, the concentrations of a pure solid or a pure liquid are assigned a value of 1.

KEY QUESTIONS

1 Write an expression for the reaction quotient for the reaction of hydrogen and chlorine with the equation:
$$H_2(g) + Cl_2(g) \rightleftharpoons 2HCl(g)$$

2 At a particular temperature, the equilibrium constant for the reaction represented by the following equation is 0.667.
$$CO(g) + 3H_2(g) \rightleftharpoons CH_4(g) + H_2O(g)$$
At a specific point in the reaction, the reaction quotient is found to be 0.234. With reference to the concentration of the products, predict which way the reaction will shift in order to reach equilibrium.

3 Define the following terms:
  a homogeneous system
  b heterogeneous system
  c reaction quotient
  d equilibrium constant.

4 Consider the reaction represented by the equation:
$$Cu^{2+}(aq) + 4NH_3(aq) \rightleftharpoons [Cu(NH_3)_4]^{2+}(aq)$$
At 25°C the equilibrium constant is determined to be $K_{eq} = 0.46$. At a particular time during the reaction, the reaction quotient is 1.2.
Write an expression for the equilibrium constant for this reaction and predict what will happen to the system as it moves to equilibrium.

5 For each of the following reactions, write the correct expression for the equilibrium constant, K_{eq}.
  a $NH_4HS(s) \rightleftharpoons NH_3(g) + H_2S(g)$
  b $AgCl(s) \rightleftharpoons Ag^+(aq) + Cl^-(aq)$
  c $2Ag^+(aq) + CO_3^{2-}(aq) \rightleftharpoons Ag_2CO_3(s)$
  d $4HCl(g) + O_2(g) \rightleftharpoons 2H_2O(g) + 2Cl_2(g)$

3.2 Working with equilibrium constants

In Section 3.1, you learnt that an expression can be written for a chemical reaction at equilibrium. The mathematical expression for the equilibrium law is a fraction involving the concentrations of the reactants and products, which has a value equal to K_{eq}, the equilibrium constant for the reaction at equilibrium.

The value of the equilibrium constant indicates the extent of a reaction or how far a reaction will proceed towards the products. In this section you will learn how to interpret these values in terms of the relative amounts of reactants and products present at equilibrium.

You will also discover how temperature affects an equilibrium constant and what happens to the value of an equilibrium constant when an equation is reversed or the coefficients of the equation are changed.

DEPENDENCY OF AN EQUILIBRIUM CONSTANT ON THE EQUATION

The equilibrium law depends on the chemical equation used for a particular reaction. For example, the equilibrium between the gases N_2O_4 and NO_2 can be represented by several equations. For each equation below, the expression for the equilibrium constant K_{eq} is given.

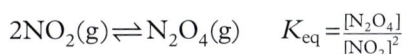

$$N_2O_4(g) \rightleftharpoons 2NO_2(g) \quad K_{eq} = \frac{[NO_2]^2}{[N_2O_4]}$$

$$2NO_2(g) \rightleftharpoons N_2O_4(g) \quad K_{eq} = \frac{[N_2O_4]}{[NO_2]^2}$$

$$2N_2O_4(g) \rightleftharpoons 4NO_2(g) \quad K_{eq} = \frac{[NO_2]^4}{[N_2O_4]^2}$$

$$\tfrac{1}{2}N_2O_4(g) \rightleftharpoons NO_2(g) \quad K_{eq} = \frac{[NO_2]}{[N_2O_4]^{\frac{1}{2}}}$$

You can see from these expressions that:
- if one equation is the reverse of another, the equilibrium constants are the inverse (or reciprocal) of each other
- if the coefficients of an equation are doubled, the value of K_{eq} is squared
- if the coefficients of an equation are halved, the value of K_{eq} is the square root of the original value of K_{eq}.

Therefore it is important to specify the equation when quoting an equilibrium constant.

> ℹ️ When comparing values of K_{eq}, it is important to know the equation associated with the equilibrium constant.

THE MEANING OF THE VALUE OF AN EQUILIBRIUM CONSTANT

The value of an equilibrium constant is based on the equilibrium concentrations of the products divided by the equilibrium concentrations of the reactants. It therefore indicates the extent of reaction at equilibrium (how far the forward reaction proceeds before equilibrium is established) and the **equilibrium yield** (the amount of products present at equilibrium).

The relationship between the value of K_{eq} and the relative proportions of reactants and products at equilibrium is shown in Table 3.2.1.

TABLE 3.2.1 The relationship between the value of K_{eq} and the extent of a reaction provides information on the relative amounts of reactants and products in the reaction mixture at equilibrium

Value of K_{eq}	Extent of reaction
Between about 10^{-4} and 10^4	The extent of reaction is significant. Appreciable concentrations of both reactants and products are present at equilibrium. e.g. $N_2(g) + 3H_2(g) \rightleftharpoons 2NH_3(g)$ $K_{eq} = 0.52$ at 400°C
Very large: $>10^4$	Almost complete reaction occurs. The concentrations of products are much higher than the concentrations of the reactants at equilibrium. e.g. $HCl(aq) + H_2O(l) \rightleftharpoons H_3O^+(aq) + Cl^-(aq)$ $K_{eq} = 10^7$ at 25°C
Very small: $<10^{-4}$	Negligible reaction occurs. The concentrations of reactants are considerably higher than the concentrations of products at equilibrium. e.g. $CH_3COOH(aq) + H_2O(l) \rightleftharpoons H_3O^+(aq) + CH_3COO^-(aq)$ $K_{eq} = 1.7 \times 10^{-5}$ at 25°C

When K_{eq} is very large, the numerator of the equilibrium expression must be large compared to the denominator, which means there is a large amount of products relative to the amount of reactants.

When K_{eq} is very small, the numerator of the equilibrium expression must be very small compared to the denominator, which means there is a large amount of reactants relative to the amount of products.

EFFECT OF TEMPERATURE ON AN EQUILIBRIUM CONSTANT

It has been shown experimentally that the value of the equilibrium constant, K_{eq}, for a particular reaction depends only on temperature. It is not affected by the addition of reactants or products, changes in pressure, or the use of catalysts.

The effect of a change in temperature on an equilibrium constant depends on whether the reaction is exothermic or endothermic:

- As temperature increases in an exothermic reaction, the value of K_{eq} decreases and so the amount of products present at equilibrium decreases.
- As temperature increases in an endothermic reaction, the value of K_{eq} increases and so the amount of products present at equilibrium increases.

Table 3.2.2 summarises the effect on K_{eq} when temperature increases. The opposite is true when temperature decreases.

> Only a change in temperature will change the value of K_{eq} for a given reaction.

PA
5.3

TABLE 3.2.2 The effect on the value of K_{eq} when the temperature of the system increases

ΔH	T	K_{eq}
exothermic (−)	increases	decreases
endothermic (+)	increases	increases

Because the value of K_{eq} depends on temperature, it is essential to specify the temperature at which an equilibrium constant has been measured.

Leuco dyes

Thermochromic materials are compounds that change colour when the temperature changes. Leuco dyes are a type of thermochromic material. The word leuco comes from the Greek leukos and means white or colourless.

Leuco dyes can switch between two differently coloured chemical forms, one of which is colourless. They are used in applications such as baby bottles, bath toys, T-shirts, mood rings and temperature indicators on packaging for microwave-heated foods. The dyes are usually applied to objects as micro-capsules that have the chemical sealed inside them.

Figure 3.2.1 shows the equilibrium involved between the colourless and coloured form of one leuco dye. The reaction is exothermic, so heating causes the reverse reaction to occur and the dye changes from its coloured form to its colourless form.

Some batteries have an indicator strip based on a leuco dye. A resistive strip on the side of the battery is coated with the dye. The resistance of the strip changes along its length and, when the strip heats up, the colour change of the dye shows the amount of current available from the battery.

Figure 3.2.2 shows a coffee mug that has a coating of a leuco dye. When hot water is poured into the mug, the dye absorbs the heat and becomes transparent, which changes the appearance of the mug.

FIGURE 3.2.2 The coating on this cup is temperature-sensitive, revealing the picture below it when hot water is added to the cup.

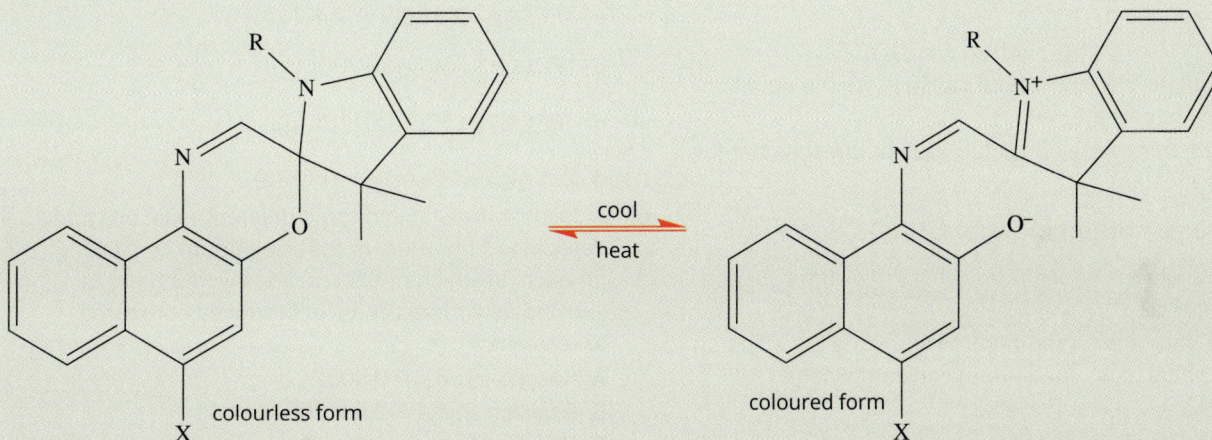

FIGURE 3.2.1 The equilibrium between two forms of a leuco dye

3.2 Review

SUMMARY

- The equilibrium constant, K_{eq}, for a reaction depends on the equation.
- The value of K_{eq} provides a measure of the extent of reaction and the relative concentrations of reactants and products at equilibrium.

Value of K_{eq}	Extent of reaction
Between about 10^{-4} and 10^4	Indicates significant reaction occurs
$>10^4$	Indicates an almost complete reaction occurs
$>10^{-4}$	Indicates negligible reaction occurs

- When an equation is reversed, the new equilibrium constant is the reciprocal, or inverse, of the original K_{eq}.
- When coefficients are doubled, K_{eq} is squared.
- As temperature increases, the value of K_{eq} increases for endothermic reactions and decreases for exothermic reactions.

KEY QUESTIONS

1. The equilibrium constant for the decomposition of ammonia is 100 at 255°C for the equation:
$$2NH_3(g) \rightleftharpoons N_2(g) + 3H_2(g)$$
   a. Write an expression for the equilibrium constant for the equation:
$$N_2(g) + 3H_2(g) \rightleftharpoons 2NH_3(g)$$
   b. Calculate the equilibrium constant for the equation given in part **a**.
   c. Write an expression for the equilibrium constant for the equation:
$$NH_3(g) \rightleftharpoons \tfrac{1}{2}N_2(g) + \tfrac{3}{2}H_2(g)$$
   d. Calculate the equilibrium constant for the equation in part **c**.
   e. Use your answers to parts **a–d** to state the effect on the value of an equilibrium constant when:
      i. the equation is reversed
      ii. the coefficients of the equation are halved.

2. Water reacts with chlorine according to the equation:
$$2H_2O(g) + 2Cl_2(g) \rightleftharpoons 4HCl(g) + O_2(g)$$
At a particular temperature, the value of the equilibrium constant for this reaction is determined to be 4.0×10^{-4}. Assuming no change in temperature, calculate the value for the equilibrium constant for the reactions represented by the following equations:
   a. $H_2O(g) + Cl_2(g) \rightleftharpoons 2HCl(g) + \tfrac{1}{2}O_2(g)$
   b. $2HCl(g) + \tfrac{1}{2}O_2(g) \rightleftharpoons H_2O(g) + Cl_2(g)$

3. For the chemical reaction: $PCl_5(g) \rightleftharpoons PCl_3(g) + Cl_2(g)$ the equilibrium constant is 1.70 at 250°C.
For each equation, calculate the value of K_{eq} at the same temperature.
   a. $4PCl_5(g) \rightleftharpoons 4PCl_3(g) + 4Cl_2(g)$
   b. $\tfrac{1}{2}PCl_3(g) + \tfrac{1}{2}Cl_2(g) \rightleftharpoons \tfrac{1}{2}PCl_5(g)$
   c. $\tfrac{1}{2}PCl_5(g) \rightleftharpoons \tfrac{1}{2}PCl_3(g) + \tfrac{1}{2}Cl_2(g)$
   d. $2PCl_3(g) + 2Cl_2(g) \rightleftharpoons 2PCl_5(g)$

4. A chemist investigated three different reactions and determined the value of the equilibrium constant for each. In which of the reactions would there be substantially more products produced compared to reactants?
   A Reaction 1: $K_{eq} = 0.0057$
   D Reaction 2: $K_{eq} = 2.5 \times 10^9$
   C Reaction 3: $K_{eq} = 3.1 \times 10^{-3}$

5. State whether the equilibrium constants for each of the following would be increased, decreased or unchanged by an increase in temperature:
   a. $2NH_3(g) \rightleftharpoons N_2(g) + 3H_2(g)$ $\Delta H = +91\,kJ\,mol^{-1}$
   b. $4HCl(g) + O_2(g) \rightleftharpoons 2H_2O(g) + 2Cl_2(g)$ $\Delta H = -113\,kJ\,mol^{-1}$
   c. $H_2(g) + CO_2(g) \rightleftharpoons H_2O(g) + CO(g)$ $\Delta H = +42\,kJ\,mol^{-1}$
   d. $2CO(g) + O_2(g) \rightleftharpoons 2CO_2(g)$ $\Delta H = -564\,kJ\,mol^{-1}$

3.3 Calculations involving equilibrium

In Section 3.1 you saw that, for a reversible reaction, an expression for an equilibrium constant K_{eq} can be written as a ratio of the molar concentrations of the products to the molar concentrations of the reactants. In this section you will learn how to determine equilibrium constants given molar concentrations. You will also learn how to calculate the concentration of a reactant or product using the equilibrium constant at a specified temperature.

SKILLBUILDER N

Identifying significant figures

In calculations it is important to note the number of significant figures that you use. The result of a calculation should be as accurate as possible, but it cannot be more accurate than the data or the measuring device used to calculate it. For example, if a set of scales that measures to the nearest gram shows that an object has a mass of 56 g, then the mass should be recorded as 56 g, not 56.0 g. This is because the actual value could be anything from 55.5 g to 56.5 g.

The value '56' has 2 significant figures. Recording it with 3 significant figures (e.g. 56.0 g or 55.8 g) would not be scientifically correct. If the mass of 56 g was used to calculate another value, it would also not be correct to give that value to more than 2 significant figures.

The number of significant figures required in an answer depends on what kind of calculation you are doing.

- If you are multiplying or dividing, use the smallest number of significant figures in the initial values.
- If you are adding or subtracting, use the smallest number of decimal places in the initial values.

Working out the number of significant figures

The following rules should be followed to avoid confusion in determining how many significant figures are in a number.

1. All non-zero digits are always significant. For example, 21.7 has 3 significant figures.
2. All zeroes between two non-zero digits are significant. For example, 3015 has 4 significant figures.
3. A zero to the right of a decimal point and following a non-zero digit is significant. For example, 0.5700 has 4 significant figures.
4. Any other zero is not significant, as it will be used only for locating decimal places. For example, 0.005 has just 1 significant figure.

CALCULATIONS INVOLVING THE EQUILIBRIUM CONSTANT AND CONCENTRATIONS

Calculating an equilibrium constant

An equilibrium constant can be calculated from the molar concentrations of reactants and products at equilibrium, as shown in Worked example 3.3.1.

Worked example 3.3.1

CALCULATING THE EQUILIBRIUM CONSTANT

A 2.00 L vessel contains a mixture of 0.0860 mol of H_2, 0.124 mol of I_2 and 0.716 mol of HI in equilibrium at 460°C according to the equation:

$$H_2(g) + I_2(g) \rightleftharpoons 2HI(g)$$

Calculate the value of the equilibrium constant, K_{eq}, at 460°C.

Thinking	Working
Find the molar concentrations for all species at equilibrium. Convert mol to mol L^{-1} using $c = \frac{n}{V}$.	Volume of vessel = 2.00 L $[H_2] = \frac{n(H_2)}{V}$ $= \frac{0.0860}{2.00}$ $= 0.0430 \, mol\,L^{-1}$ $[I_2] = \frac{n(I_2)}{V}$ $= \frac{0.124}{2.00}$ $= 0.0620 \, mol\,L^{-1}$ $[HI] = \frac{n(HI)}{V}$ $= \frac{0.716}{2.00}$ $= 0.358 \, mol\,L^{-1}$
Write the expression for K_{eq}.	$K_{eq} = \frac{[HI]^2}{[H_2][I_2]}$
Substitute values into the expression for K_{eq} to determine the value of K_{eq}.	$K_{eq} = \frac{0.358^2}{0.0430 \times 0.0620}$ $= 48.1$

Worked example: Try yourself 3.3.1

CALCULATING THE EQUILIBRIUM CONSTANT

A 3.00 L vessel contains a mixture of 0.120 mol of N_2O_4 and 0.500 mol of NO_2 in equilibrium at 460°C according to the equation:

$$N_2O_4(g) \rightleftharpoons 2NO_2(g)$$

Calculate the value of the equilibrium constant, K_{eq}, for the reaction at 460°C.

Calculating equilibrium concentrations

You can use the equilibrium constant for a reaction to determine the unknown molar equilibrium concentration of one of the species in the reaction, if you are given the molar equilibrium concentrations of the other species.

Worked example 3.3.2

CALCULATING AN EQUILIBRIUM CONCENTRATION

Consider the following reaction, which has an equilibrium constant of 0.400 at 250°C.

$$PCl_5(g) \rightleftharpoons PCl_3(g) + Cl_2(g)$$

An equilibrium mixture contains $0.0020 \, mol \, L^{-1}$ PCl_5 and $0.0010 \, mol \, L^{-1}$ PCl_3 at 250°C. What is the concentration of Cl_2 in this mixture?

Thinking	Working
Write the expression for K_{eq}.	$K_{eq} = \frac{[PCl_3][Cl_2]}{[PCl_5]}$
Substitute the known values into the expression for K_{eq}.	$0.400 = \frac{0.0010 \times [Cl_2]}{0.0020}$
Rearrange the expression to make the unknown the subject and calculate the concentration of this species.	$[Cl_2] = \frac{0.400 \times 0.0020}{0.0010}$ $= 0.80 \, mol \, L^{-1}$

Worked example: Try yourself 3.3.2

CALCULATING AN EQUILIBRIUM CONCENTRATION

Consider the following reaction, which has an equilibrium constant of 0.72 at 250°C.

$$N_2O_4(g) \rightleftharpoons 2NO_2(g)$$

An equilibrium mixture contains $0.040 \, mol \, L^{-1}$ N_2O_4 at 250°C. What is the concentration of NO_2 in this mixture?

Calculating an equilibrium constant using stoichiometry

For some calculations, stoichiometry is used to calculate the molar equilibrium concentrations of the reactants and products from the data provided. Once these are known, the equilibrium constant can then be calculated as you saw in Worked example 3.3.1.

A popular way to set out calculations of this type is with the use of a **reaction table** (also known as an ICE table). The reaction table shows the initial amounts of reactants and products, the changes that occur as the system reaches equilibrium and the final values at equilibrium, as Worked example 3.3.3 illustrates.

> **i** An ICE table (reaction table) sets up the steps for working out equilibrium calculations where the equilibrium concentration of one or more species is unknown. The first letter of each word corresponds to the information that is recorded in each row of the table: **I**nitial, **C**hange, **E**quilibrium.

Worked example 3.3.3

USING STOICHIOMETRY TO CALCULATE AN EQUILIBRIUM CONSTANT

An equilibrium is established between A and B at a specified temperature according to the following equation:

$$A(g) \rightleftharpoons 2B(g)$$

0.540 mol of A was placed in a 2.00 L vessel. When equilibrium was achieved, 0.280 mol of B was present. Calculate the value of the equilibrium constant at this temperature.

Thinking	Working
Construct a reaction table using each species in the balanced equation as the headings for the columns in the table. Insert three rows in the table labelled I (initial), C (change) and E (equilibrium): **Reactants $\rightleftharpoons$ Products** I C E Enter the data provided in the table. When a species is consumed, the change is negative; when a species is produced, the change is positive.	Initially, there is 0.540 mol of A(g) and 0 mol of the product B(g). Let x mol of A react; $2x$ mol of B is produced. At equilibrium, there is 0.280 mol of B(g). 		**A(g)** $\rightleftharpoons$ **2B(g)**	 |---|---|---
I	0.540 mol	0 mol
C	$-x$	$+2x$
E	$0.540 - x$	$2x = 0.280$ mol	
Using the coefficients from the equation, calculate the moles of all species at equilibrium.	Initially no B was present, so because 0.280 mol of B has been produced at equilibrium: $2x = 0.280$ mol $x = 0.140$ mol We can enter these values in the table: 		**A(g)** $\rightleftharpoons$ **2B(g)**	 |---|---|---
I	0.540 mol	0 mol
C	$x = -0.140$	$+2x = 0.280$
E	$0.540 - x$ $= 0.540 - 0.140$ $= 0.400$ mol	$2x = 0.280$ mol	
Using the volume of the vessel, calculate the equilibrium concentrations for all species at equilibrium. Use the formula $c = \frac{n}{V}$.	The volume of the vessel is 2.00 L. $[A] = \frac{n}{V}$ $= \frac{0.400}{2.00}$ $= 0.200$ mol L^{-1} $[B] = \frac{n}{V}$ $= \frac{0.280}{2.00}$ $= 0.140$ mol L^{-1}

Write the expression for K_{eq} and substitute the equilibrium concentrations. Calculate the equilibrium constant, K_{eq}.	$K_{eq} = \dfrac{[B]^2}{[A]}$ $= \dfrac{0.140^2}{0.200}$ $= 0.0980$

Worked example: Try yourself 3.3.3

USING STOICHIOMETRY TO CALCULATE AN EQUILIBRIUM CONSTANT

During one step in the synthesis of nitric acid, nitrogen dioxide (NO_2) is in equilibrium with dinitrogen tetroxide (N_2O_4) at 60°C.

$$N_2O_4(g) \rightleftharpoons 2NO_2(g)$$

0.350 mol of N_2O_4 was placed in a 2.00 L vessel. When equilibrium was achieved at 60°C, 0.120 mol of NO_2 was present. Calculate the value of the equilibrium constant at this temperature.

PA 5.4

PA 5.4

WS 5.3

CHEMISTRY IN ACTION L

Haemoglobin and oxygen

Haemoglobin is a large protein molecule that is the pigment in red blood cells (Figure 3.3.2). It is responsible for transporting oxygen from your lungs to the cells in the body. When you inhale, oxygen from the air combines with haemoglobin in the small blood vessels in the lining of the lungs to form oxyhaemoglobin.

haemoglobin + oxygen → oxyhaemoglobin

The reaction between haemoglobin and oxygen is a reversible chemical reaction. The oxyhaemoglobin is transported through the blood system to cells in the body, where oxygen is released:

oxyhaemoglobin → haemoglobin + oxygen

The oxygen is used by cells for respiration, to provide energy for the body.

The reaction can therefore be written as an equilibrium:

haemoglobin + oxygen ⇌ oxyhaemoglobin

Scientists use the principles you have learnt in this chapter to understand the operation of this vitally important biological process.

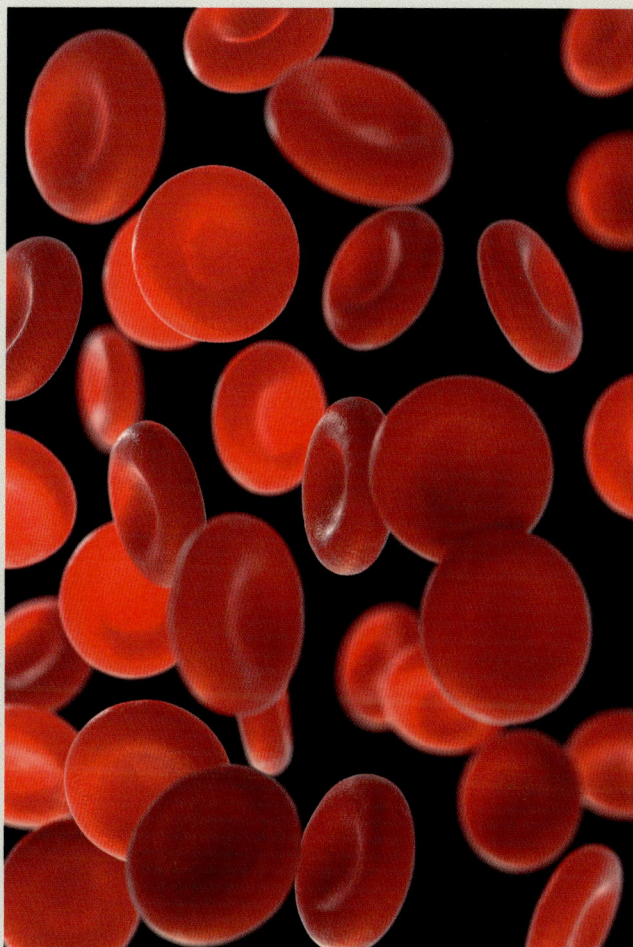

FIGURE 3.3.2 Red blood cells contain a pigment, haemoglobin, that transports oxygen from the lungs to other cells in the body.

3.3 Review

SUMMARY

- An equilibrium constant for a particular temperature can be calculated from the concentrations of the reactants and products at equilibrium and the expression for the equilibrium constant.
- The concentration of a reactant or product can be calculated if the concentrations of the other reactants and products and the equilibrium constant are known.
- Stoichiometry can be used to calculate equilibrium concentrations of reactants and products, and hence the value of the equilibrium constant, using a reaction (ICE) table.

KEY QUESTIONS

1. Calculate the equilibrium constant for the reaction represented by the equation $N_2O_4(g) \rightleftharpoons 2NO_2(g)$ if an equilibrium mixture in a 2.0 L container was found to consist of 0.80 mol of N_2O_4 and 0.40 mol of NO_2.

2. Phosgene is a poisonous gas that was used during World War I. It can be formed by the reaction of carbon monoxide with chlorine gas in an equilibrium reaction:
$$CO(g) + Cl_2(g) \rightleftharpoons COCl_2(g)$$
In an experiment, this reaction was allowed to proceed at 74°C until equilibrium was reached. The equilibrium concentrations of each species was determined and recorded as follows: $[CO] = 2.4 \times 10^{-2}\,mol\,L^{-1}$, $[Cl_2] = 0.108\,mol\,L^{-1}$ and $[COCl_2] = 0.28\,mol\,L^{-1}$. Calculate the equilibrium constant for the reaction at this temperature.

3. The following reaction was allowed to reach equilibrium at a temperature of 230°C:
$$2NO(g) + O_2(g) \rightleftharpoons 2NO_2(g)$$
The value of the equilibrium constant was determined to be 6.44×10^5.
If the equilibrium concentration of $[NO_2] = 15.5\,mol\,L^{-1}$ and $[NO] = 0.0542\,mol\,L^{-1}$, determine the concentration of O_2 in the equilibrium mixture.

4. 4.45 mol of PCl_3 and 5.50 mol of Cl_2 were mixed in a 2.00 L vessel. They reacted according to the equation:
$$PCl_3(g) + Cl_2(g) \rightleftharpoons PCl_5(g)$$
When equilibrium was reached, it was found that 0.35 mol of PCl_5 had been formed. Calculate the value of the equilibrium constant.

5. 5.89 mol of N_2 and 8.23 mol of H_2 were mixed in a 5.00 L vessel. They reacted according to the equation:
$$N_2(g) + 3H_2(g) \rightleftharpoons 2NH_3(g)$$
When equilibrium was reached, it was found that 0.48 mol of NH_3 had been formed. Calculate the value of the equilibrium constant.

6. The equilibrium constant for the following reaction is 48.8 at 455°C.
$$2HI(g) \rightleftharpoons H_2(g) + I_2(g)$$
   a. An equilibrium mixture in a 2.0 L vessel at 455°C contains 0.220 mol of H_2 and 0.110 mol of I_2. Calculate the concentration of HI in this mixture.
   b. Another mixture was prepared by placing 4.00 mol of HI in a 2.0 L vessel at 330°C. At equilibrium, 0.44 mol of H_2 and 0.44 mol of I_2 were present. Calculate the value of the equilibrium constant at this temperature.
   c. A third mixture consisted of 1.0 mol of HI, 0.24 mol of H_2 and 0.32 mol of I_2 in a 2.0 L container at 330°C. Decide whether the mixture is at equilibrium and, if not, predict the direction the reaction will shift to reach equilibrium.

Chapter review

KEY TERMS

concentration fraction
dissociate
equilibrium constant
equilibrium law

equilibrium yield
extent of reaction
heterogeneous reaction
homogeneous reaction

reaction quotient
reaction table

REVIEW QUESTIONS

1 Which one of the following is the expression for the equilibrium constant for the reaction shown?
$$2SO_2(g) + O_2(g) \rightleftharpoons 2SO_3(g)$$

A $\dfrac{[SO_3]}{[SO_2][O_2]}$

B $\dfrac{[SO_3]^2}{[SO_2]^2[O_2]}$

C $\dfrac{[SO_2]^2[O_2]}{[SO_3]^2}$

D $\dfrac{[SO_2][O_2]}{[SO_3]}$

2 Write the expression for K_{eq} for the following equilibrium system:
$$2Fe^{3+}(aq) + Sn^{2+}(aq) \rightleftharpoons 2Fe^{2+}(aq) + Sn^{4+}(aq)$$

3 Which one of the following equations has the expression for the equilibrium constant shown?
$$K_{eq} = \dfrac{[H_2]^2[CO]}{[CH_3OH]}$$

A $4H_2(g) + 2CO(g) \rightleftharpoons 2CH_3OH(g)$
B $2H_2(g) + CO(g) \rightleftharpoons CH_3OH(g)$
C $2CH_3OH(g) \rightleftharpoons 4H_2(g) + 2CO(g)$
D $CH_3OH(g) \rightleftharpoons 2H_2(g) + CO(g)$

4 Write balanced equations for the reactions with the following equilibrium constants. All reactants and products are in the gaseous state.

a $K_{eq} = \dfrac{[N_2][O_2]}{[NO]^2}$

b $K_{eq} = \dfrac{[H_2S]^2}{[S_2][H_2]^2}$

c $K_{eq} = \dfrac{[N_2O_4]^{\frac{1}{2}}}{[NO_2]}$

5 Write the expression for the equilibrium constant for each of the following chemical equations.
a $Cu^{2+}(aq) + CO_3{}^{2-}(aq) \rightleftharpoons CuCO_3(s)$
b $CuCO_3(s) \rightleftharpoons Cu^{2+}(aq) + CO_3{}^{2-}(aq)$
c $P_4(s) + 10Cl_2(g) \rightleftharpoons 4PCl_5(g)$
d $8PCl_5(g) \rightleftharpoons 2P_4(s) + 20Cl_2(g)$

6 Explain the difference between the reaction quotient (Q) and the equilibrium constant (K_{eq}).

7 The value of K_{eq} for the following reaction is 4.0 at 25°C.
$$C_2H_5OH(l) + CH_3COOH(l) \rightleftharpoons CH_3COOC_2H_5(l) + H_2O(l)$$

At time t the reaction quotient Q for a mixture of ethanol, water, ethyl ethanoate ($CH_3COOC_2H_5$) and ethanoic acid is 6.0. Assuming that the mixture is at 25°C, and referring to the values of K_{eq} and Q, describe what will happen to the concentration of ethyl ethanoate as the system reaches equilibrium.

8 Complete the following statements about the equilibrium constant, K_{eq}.
a If $K_{eq} = 0.0001$ for a particular reaction, at equilibrium the concentrations of products will be _____ the concentrations of reactants.
b For the reaction with the equation
$$2H_2(g) + 2NO(g) \rightleftharpoons 2H_2O(g) + N_2(g)$$
the expression for the equilibrium constant, K_{eq}, is _____.
c When the reaction quotient is smaller than K_{eq}, the reaction _____ to establish equilibrium.

9 The equilibrium constant for the following reaction at 25°C is 10^{-10}:
$$2Fe^{2+}(aq) + Sn^{4+}(aq) \rightleftharpoons 2Fe^{3+}(aq) + Sn^{2+}(aq)$$
a Explain whether a significant reaction would occur when solutions of tin(IV) chloride and iron(II) chloride are mixed.
b Determine the value of the equilibrium constant for the following reaction:
$$2Fe^{3+}(aq) + Sn^{2+}(aq) \rightleftharpoons 2Fe^{2+}(aq) + Sn^{4+}(aq)$$
c Explain whether a significant reaction would occur when solutions of tin(II) chloride and iron(III) chloride are mixed.

10 Consider the following equilibrium:
$$2BrCl(g) \rightleftharpoons Br_2(g) + Cl_2(g)$$
a Write the expression for K_{eq} for the equilibrium system.
b If the value of K_{eq} at 227°C for the expression in part a is 32, deduce the equilibrium constant for each of the following.
i $BrCl(g) \rightleftharpoons \frac{1}{2}Br_2(g) + \frac{1}{2}Cl_2(g)$
ii $Cl_2(g) + Br_2(g) \rightleftharpoons 2BrCl(g)$
iii $4BrCl(g) \rightleftharpoons 2Br_2(g) + 2Cl_2(g)$
iv $\frac{1}{2}Cl_2(g) + \frac{1}{2}Br_2(g) \rightleftharpoons BrCl(g)$

11 The reaction used to manufacture ammonia is represented by the equation:

$$N_2(g) + 3H_2(g) \rightleftharpoons 2NH_3(g)$$

The equilibrium constant for the reaction is 0.052 at 400°C.

A gas mixture contains 1.0 mol of N_2 gas, 1.0 mol of H_2 gas and 0.25 mol of NH_3 gas in a 1.0 L vessel at 400°C. Decide if the mixture is at equilibrium and, if it is not, predict the direction it will shift to reach equilibrium.

12 An equilibrium mixture contains 0.020 mol of H_2O gas, 0.030 mol H_2 gas, 0.040 mol CO gas and 0.050 mol of CO_2 gas in a 2.0 L container. The gases react according to the equation:

$$H_2(g) + CO_2(g) \rightleftharpoons H_2O(g) + CO(g)$$

Calculate the equilibrium constant at 900°C.

13 At a specified temperature the reaction between solutions of Sn^{2+} and Fe^{3+} reaches equilibrium according to the equation:

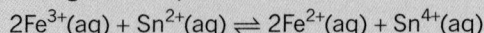

$$2Fe^{3+}(aq) + Sn^{2+}(aq) \rightleftharpoons 2Fe^{2+}(aq) + Sn^{4+}(aq)$$

The equilibrium concentrations are $[Fe^{3+}]$ = 0.30 mol L^{-1}, $[Fe^{2+}]$ = 0.40 mol L^{-1}, $[Sn^{4+}]$ = 0.20 mol L^{-1} and $[Sn^{2+}]$ = 0.10 mol L^{-1}.

Calculate the equilibrium constant at this temperature.

14 Acetone (C_3H_6O) is used to remove nail polish. It can be prepared from propan-2-ol (C_3H_8O) using a copper–zinc catalyst, according to the equation:

$$C_3H_8O(g) \rightleftharpoons C_3H_6O(g) + H_2(g)$$

If an equilibrium mixture of these gases consists of 0.018 mol of propan-2-ol, 0.082 mol of acetone and 0.082 mol of hydrogen in a 20 L vessel, calculate the value of the equilibrium constant.

15 Consider the equilibrium represented by the following equation:

$$PCl_5(g) \rightleftharpoons PCl_3(g) + Cl_2(g)$$

A 3.00 L vessel contained 6.00 mol of PCl_3, 4.50 mol of PCl_5 and 0.900 mol of Cl_2 at equilibrium at 250°C.

a Write an expression for the equilibrium constant for this reaction.

b Calculate the equilibrium constant for the reaction at 250°C.

c Another equilibrium mixture contains $[PCl_5]$ = 0.0020 mol L^{-1} and $[PCl_3]$ = 0.0010 mol L^{-1} at 250°C. What is the concentration of Cl_2 in this mixture?

d Determine the equilibrium constant at 250°C for the reaction:

$$PCl_3(g) + Cl_2(g) \rightleftharpoons PCl_5(g)$$

16 At one step during the synthesis of nitric acid, dinitrogen tetroxide is in equilibrium with nitrogen dioxide:

$$N_2O_4(g) \rightleftharpoons 2NO_2(g)$$

0.540 mol of N_2O_4 was placed in a 2.00 L vessel. When equilibrium was achieved, 0.280 mol of NO_2 was present. Calculate the value of the equilibrium constant at this temperature.

17 A mixture of 0.100 mol NO, 0.051 mol H_2 and 0.100 mol of H_2O were added to a reaction vessel with a volume of 1.0 L at 300°C. The reaction at equilibrium is given by the equation:

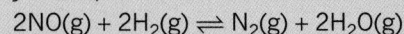

$$2NO(g) + 2H_2(g) \rightleftharpoons N_2(g) + 2H_2O(g)$$

After equilibrium was established, the concentration of NO was found to be 0.062. Determine the equilibrium constant K_{eq} for the reaction at 300°C.

18 Consider the following reaction:

$$A + 3B \rightleftharpoons 2C + D$$

An analysis of an equilibrium mixture in a 2.0 L container shows that 2.0 mol of A, 0.50 mol of B and 3.0 mol of D are present. If the equilibrium constant of the reaction is 0.024, calculate:

a the concentration of A, B and D at equilibrium

b the concentration of C in the equilibrium mixture

c the amount of C, in mol, in the equilibrium mixture.

19 The reaction used to manufacture ammonia is represented by:

$$N_2(g) + 3H_2(g) \rightleftharpoons 2NH_3(g)$$

The equilibrium constant for the reaction is 0.052 at 400°C.

Each of the following gas mixtures is contained in a 1.0 L vessel at 400°C. Decide if each mixture is in equilibrium. If not, predict the direction the reaction will shift in order to reach equilibrium.

a 0.20 mol of N_2, 0.20 mol of H_2, 0.20 mol of NH_3

b 0.050 mol of N_2 and 0.50 mol of H_2 only.

20 a The equilibrium constant is 0.67 at a particular temperature for the reaction:

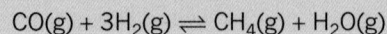

$$CO(g) + 3H_2(g) \rightleftharpoons CH_4(g) + H_2O(g)$$

A mixture of 0.100 mol L^{-1} CO, 0.200 mol L^{-1} H_2, 0.300 mol L^{-1} CH_4 and 0.400 mol L^{-1} H_2O is heated to this temperature. Predict whether the concentration of each of the following would increase, decrease, or not change.

i CO

ii H_2

iii CH_4

iv H_2O

b When the temperature of the reaction mixture in part **a** is increased by 10°C, the equilibrium constant for the reaction becomes 0.71. What conclusion can you make about the enthalpy change of this reaction?

21 Reflect on the Inquiry task on page 74. What type of system did you create? Use concepts from this chapter and Chapter 2 to justify your decision.

CHAPTER 04 Factors that affect equilibrium

An equilibrium is a state of balance. Two children sitting on a stationary see-saw is an example of a static equilibrium. All forces on the children are equal, and no movement occurs. On the other hand, although a dynamic chemical equilibrium might seem to involve no change in the concentrations of chemicals over time, at the atomic level the reactants are continually changing into products and the products are changing into reactants. Importantly, when a reaction is at equilibrium the rates of these two processes are equal.

In the previous two chapters you learnt that, when a reaction reaches equilibrium, a ratio based on the equilibrium concentrations of the reactants and products becomes equal to a constant value, called the equilibrium constant, K_{eq}.

This chapter continues the study of chemical equilibrium by examining how equilibria respond to various changes in external conditions. Some changes can cause a shift in the amounts of individual reactants and products that are present. You will learn the effect of several ways of changing an equilibrium, including:

- adding or removing a reactant or product
- changing the pressure of a gaseous equilibrium
- adding water to an aqueous equilibrium
- adding a catalyst
- changing the temperature.

Content

INQUIRY QUESTION

What factors affect equilibrium and how?

By the end of this chapter, you will be able to:

- investigate the effects of temperature, concentration, volume and/or pressure on a system at equilibrium and explain how Le Châtelier's principle can be used to predict such effects, for example:
  - heating cobalt(II) chloride hydrate
  - interaction between nitrogen dioxide and dinitrogen tetroxide
  - iron(III) thiocyanate and varying concentration of ions (ACSCH095)
- explain the overall observations about equilibrium in terms of the collision theory (ACSCH094)
- examine how activation energy and heat of reaction affect the position of equilibrium

Chemistry Stage 6 Syllabus © NSW Education Standards Authority for and on behalf of the Crown in right of the State of NSW, 2017.

4.1 Le Châtelier's principle

What is the effect on an equilibrium when more reactants are added?

COLLECT THIS...

- two large containers of different sizes
- 1 cup (250 mL) measuring scoop
- $\frac{1}{3}$ cup (80 mL) measuring scoop
- food dye (optional)
- waterproof marking pen
- tap water

DO THIS...

This activity is best undertaken in pairs.

Part A

1 Half fill the larger container with water. You can add food dye to the water to add interest. Do not put water in the smaller container.

2 Use the marking pen to label the container of water 'reactants' and the empty container 'products'.

3 Using the 1 cup measuring scoop, scoop water from the reactants container and place it in the products container.

4 At the same time, you or your partner should use the smaller measuring scoop to scoop any water in the smaller container and place it in the larger container (initially there is no water in the smaller container but this will soon change).

5 Repeat steps 3 and 4 until there is no further change in water levels in the two containers.

6 Use the marking pen to mark the water levels in each container.

Part B

Add more water to the 'reactants' container and repeat steps 3–5 in Part A.

RECORD THIS...

Compare the volumes of water in the two containers in Part A. Are they equal? If not, which container holds the most water?

For Part B, note how the volumes of water in the containers compare with the volumes in Part A.

REFLECT ON THIS...

1 Why does this activity represent a dynamic rather than static equilibrium?

2 Are the amounts of reactants and products necessarily equal in a dynamic equilibrium?

3 What is the effect of adding more reactants to an equilibrium system?

4 How could you modify this activity to show the effect on an equilibrium by adding (a) extra product, or (b) a catalyst?

In this section you will learn about some of the effects of changes on chemical systems at equilibrium. Your understanding of the underlying principles of chemical equilibrium will enable you to predict the impact of changes when a reactant or product is added or removed from an equilibrium system.

The effect of changes on a chemical equilibrium is very important to the chemical industry. Conditions must be carefully selected to ensure that optimum yields of products are obtained within a reasonable timeframe.

CHANGES TO AN EQUILIBRIUM SYSTEM

You have seen that different reactions proceed to different extents. As a consequence, the relative amounts of reactants and products differ from one reaction to another at equilibrium. The relative amounts of reactants and products at equilibrium is called the **position of equilibrium** and depends on reaction conditions.

For any equilibrium system, the position of equilibrium may be changed by:

* adding or removing a reactant or product
* changing the pressure by changing the volume (for an equilibrium involving gases)
* dilution (for an equilibrium in solution)
* changing the temperature.

Careful control of the reaction conditions allows chemists to maximise the equilibrium yield of a desired product by moving the position of equilibrium to the right (that is, increasing the amount of products formed).

> ℹ The position of equilibrium should not be confused with K_{eq}. The value of K_{eq} is changed only by a change in temperature.

LE CHÂTELIER'S PRINCIPLE

The effect of a change in conditions on an equilibrium system is summarised in a useful generalisation called **Le Châtelier's principle**.

> ℹ Le Châtelier's principle states that if an equilibrium system is subjected to a change, the system will adjust itself to partially oppose the effect of the change.

When a change occurs to an equilibrium system so that it is momentarily no longer at equilibrium, a net reaction occurs that partially counteracts the effect of the change. The system will establish a new equilibrium. As a result, the position of equilibrium will change. There may be an increase in the amount of either products or reactants, depending on the nature of the change.

By understanding Le Châtelier's principle, you can predict the effect of different changes on equilibrium systems.

Adding extra reactant or product

A sealed reaction vessel of hydrogen and nitrogen gases at a particular temperature will establish an equilibrium with ammonia gas, according to the equation:

$$N_2(g) + 3H_2(g) \rightleftharpoons 2NH_3(g)$$

At equilibrium, the rates of the forward and reverse reactions are equal. The concentrations of the three gases are constant. If extra nitrogen gas were added to the container without changing the volume or temperature, the mixture would momentarily not be in equilibrium. The system would then adjust to form a new equilibrium with different concentrations and partial pressures of N_2, H_2 and NH_3.

You can use Le Châtelier's principle to predict the change in the position of the equilibrium. The underlying basis for this prediction can be understood by applying the principles of collision theory and the rates of reactions.

CHEMFILE IU

Henri Le Châtelier

Henri Le Châtelier (Figure 4.1.1) was a French chemist and engineer. He is best known for developing the principle of chemical equilibrium, which is now named after him.

Le Châtelier acknowledged that the American scientist Josiah Gibbs had published mathematical explanations of thermodynamics linked to the Le Châtelier principle. Le Châtelier became a proponent of Gibbs's work and translated his major work into French for the benefit of other scientists.

Le Châtelier made an early attempt at synthesising ammonia from nitrogen and hydrogen, but an error in the design of the experiment resulted in an explosion that nearly killed one of his laboratory assistants. His work was used by Haber, who successfully synthesised ammonia in 1909. Le Châtelier also developed the oxyacetylene welding torch and the thermocouple for accurate temperature measurement.

FIGURE 4.1.1 Henri Le Châtelier (1850–1936)

> ℹ Collision theory is used to explain the different rates of chemical reactions. It states that, for a reaction to occur, the reactant particles must collide. A larger number of successful collisions in a specified time period results in a faster reaction rate.

Predicting the effect of a change using Le Châtelier's principle

The effect of adding the N_2 gas to the equilibrium may be predicted simply by applying Le Châtelier's principle. According to Le Châtelier's principle, if N_2 is added to an equilibrium system, the system will adjust to decrease the concentration of the added N_2, so a net forward reaction will occur.

It is important to note that, even though the concentration of N_2 gas decreases as the system moves to establish the new equilibrium, its final concentration is still higher than in the original equilibrium. Le Châtelier's principle states that the change is partially opposed. The system does not return to the initial equilibrium position following the change in conditions.

Explaining the effect of a change using collision theory and reaction rates

You can apply your knowledge of collision theory and reaction rates to understand the reasons for the effect of adding the extra N_2 gas. Because the concentration of N_2 molecules has increased, the rate of the forward reaction initially becomes greater than the rate of the reverse reaction. Then, as the concentration of N_2 and H_2 decreases and the concentration of NH_3 increases, the rate of the forward reaction decreases and the rate of the reverse reaction increases until they become equal again. A new equilibrium is formed.

The rate–time graph in Figure 4.1.2 shows the effects on the rate of the forward and reverse reactions as the composition of the mixture adjusts to form a new equilibrium.

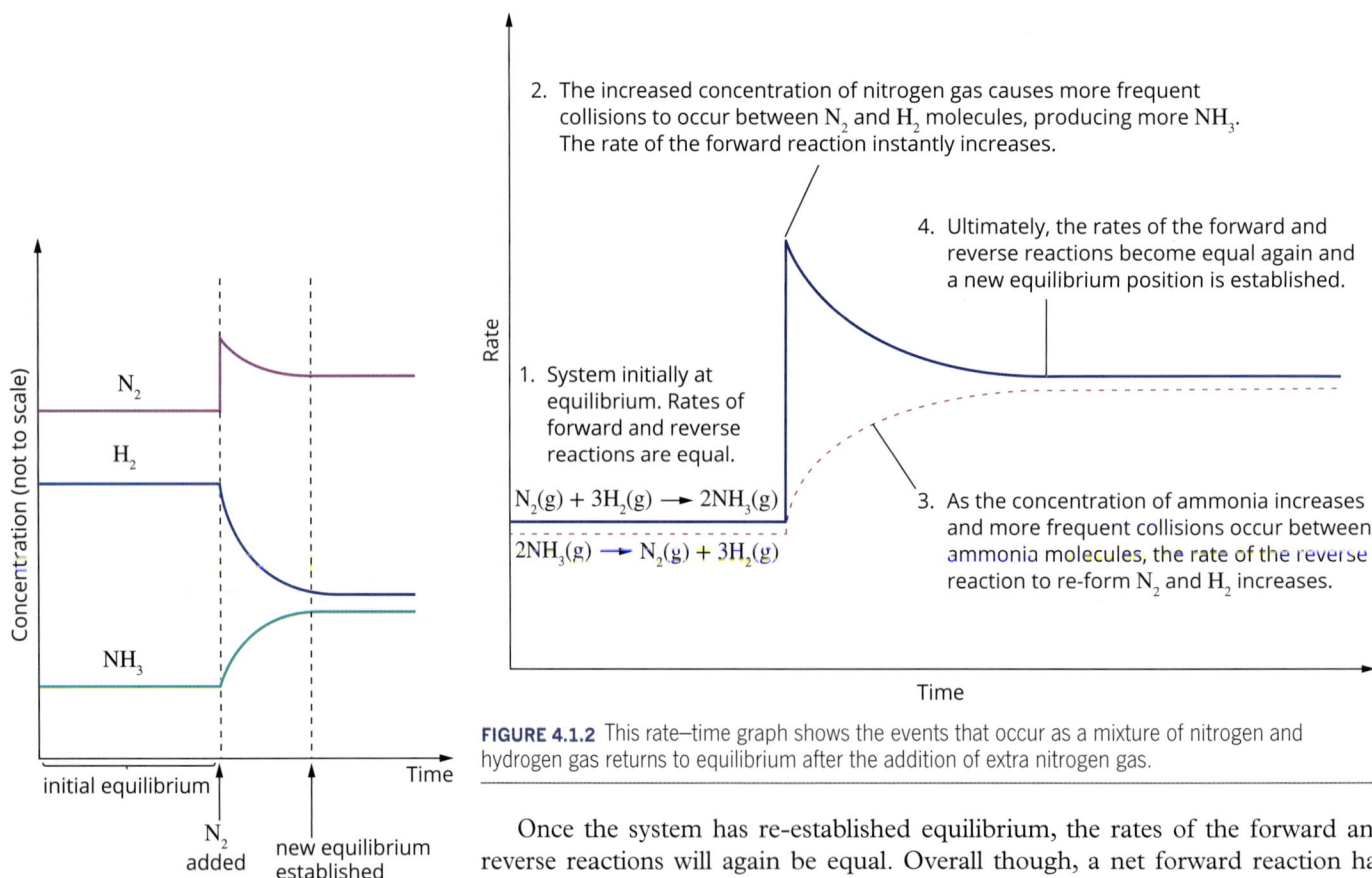

2. The increased concentration of nitrogen gas causes more frequent collisions to occur between N_2 and H_2 molecules, producing more NH_3. The rate of the forward reaction instantly increases.

4. Ultimately, the rates of the forward and reverse reactions become equal again and a new equilibrium position is established.

1. System initially at equilibrium. Rates of forward and reverse reactions are equal.

$$N_2(g) + 3H_2(g) \longrightarrow 2NH_3(g)$$

$$2NH_3(g) \longrightarrow N_2(g) + 3H_2(g)$$

3. As the concentration of ammonia increases and more frequent collisions occur between ammonia molecules, the rate of the reverse reaction to re-form N_2 and H_2 increases.

FIGURE 4.1.2 This rate–time graph shows the events that occur as a mixture of nitrogen and hydrogen gas returns to equilibrium after the addition of extra nitrogen gas.

FIGURE 4.1.3 Changes in concentrations that occur when additional nitrogen gas is added to the equilibrium for the reaction $N_2(g) + 3H_2(g) \rightleftharpoons 2NH_3(g)$. Note that the vertical axis of this graph shows the concentration, not rate of reaction.

Once the system has re-established equilibrium, the rates of the forward and reverse reactions will again be equal. Overall though, a net forward reaction has occurred, with an increase in the concentration of ammonia at equilibrium. The equilibrium position is said to have shifted to the right, because a net reaction to the right of the equation has taken place.

The changes occurring to the system can also be shown on a concentration–time graph. Figure 4.1.3 illustrates the effect on the system when N_2 gas is added as described.

Note that the value of K_{eq} for the equilibrium reaction remains unchanged as the temperature has not changed.

> ℹ️ Only temperature changes the value of K_{eq} for an equilibrium system.

If you follow the same reasoning as for N_2, you can see that adding extra amounts of the other reactant, H_2, to the system will also increase the concentration of NH_3 produced. However, the addition of more product, NH_3, would result in a net reverse reaction and the equilibrium position would shift to the left, which would reduce the concentration of NH_3 and increase the concentration of N_2 and H_2 (Figure 4.1.4).

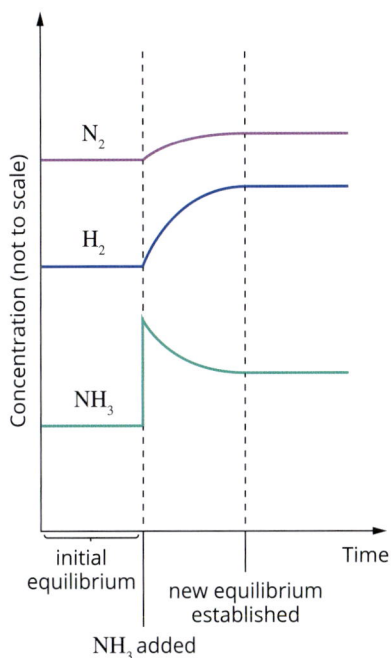

FIGURE 4.1.4 Changes in concentrations that occur when additional ammonia gas is added to the equilibrium for the reaction $N_2(g) + 3H_2(g) \rightleftharpoons 2NH_3(g)$. The reaction shifts to the left, forming more N_2 and H_2.

Although knowledge of collision theory and reaction rates can be used to determine the overall effect of changes on an equilibrium as was done above, applying Le Châtelier's principle is a simpler way of predicting these effects. Table 4.1.1 summarises how an equilibrium system acts to oppose the addition or removal of reactants and products.

TABLE 4.1.1 The general effects of a change to a system at equilibrium

Change to equilibrium	Effect
adding a reactant	• formation of more products—a net forward reaction • equilibrium position shifts to the right
removing a reactant	• formation of more reactants—a net reverse reaction • equilibrium position shifts to the left
adding a product	• formation of more reactants—a net reverse reaction • equilibrium position shifts to the left
removing a product	• formation of more products—a net forward reaction • equilibrium position shifts to the right

Predicting the effect of a change using the equilibrium law

The effect of adding more reactants or products can also be predicted using the equilibrium law. Consider again the equilibrium formed between nitrogen and hydrogen:

$$N_2(g) + 3H_2(g) \rightleftharpoons 2NH_3(g)$$

The expression for the equilibrium law for this reaction can be written as:

$$K_{eq} = \frac{[NH_3]^2}{[N_2][H_2]^3}$$

GO TO ➤ Section 3.1 page 74

If extra nitrogen is added, the concentration of N_2 is increased, so the reaction quotient Q is then less than the equilibrium constant K_{eq} and the mixture is no longer at equilibrium. As you saw in Chapter 3, when $Q < K_{eq}$ the reaction favours the formation of products (a net forward reaction). This increases the amount of products and decreases the amount of reactants, until the reaction quotient again becomes equal to K_{eq}.

Making predictions using the mathematical expression for the equilibrium law gives the same result as using the qualitative reasoning of Le Châtelier's principle, using collision theory to determine the effects of the change on the rates of the forward and reverse reactions.

Worked example 4.1.1 shows the use of collision theory to explain how an equilibrium system is affected by the addition of a reactant or product.

Worked example 4.1.1

USING COLLISION THEORY TO EXPLAIN THE EFFECT ON EQUILIBRIUM OF ADDING A REACTANT OR PRODUCT

In solution, $Co(H_2O)_6^{2+}$ ions form an equilibrium with $CoCl_4^{2-}(aq)$ ions, as shown by the equation:

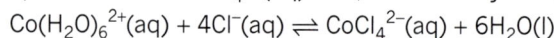

$$Co(H_2O)_6^{2+}(aq) + 4Cl^-(aq) \rightleftharpoons CoCl_4^{2-}(aq) + 6H_2O(l)$$

Use the concepts of rates of reaction and collision theory to predict the effect of the addition of Cl^- ions on the position of equilibrium.

Thinking	Working
Determine the initial effect of the change on the concentration of the particles.	Adding Cl^- ions increases the concentration of these ions.
Use collision theory to determine the initial effect on the rate of the forward (or reverse) reaction.	Collisions between $Co(H_2O)_6^{2+}$ ions and Cl^- ions become more frequent, increasing the rate of the forward reaction and reducing the concentration of $Co(H_2O)_6^{2+}$ and Cl^- ions.
Consider how the rates of the forward and reverse reactions change as the system reaches a new equilibrium.	As more product ions ($CoCl_4^{2-}$) are formed, the rate of the reverse reaction increases, until the rates of the forward and reverse reaction become equal and a new equilibrium is established.
Predict the overall effect of the change on the position of equilibrium.	A net forward reaction has occurred. The position of equilibrium has shifted to the right.

Worked example: Try yourself 4.1.1

USING COLLISION THEORY TO EXPLAIN THE EFFECT ON EQUILIBRIUM OF ADDING A REACTANT OR PRODUCT

Consider the equilibrium system represented by the following equation:

$$H_2(g) + CO_2(g) \rightleftharpoons H_2O(g) + CO(g)$$

Use the concepts of rates of reaction and collision theory to predict the effect of the addition of CO gas on the position of equilibrium.

Competing equilibria: carbon monoxide poisoning

Haemoglobin in red blood cells, as seen in the chapter opener image, transports oxygen from your lungs to the cells in your body. The haemoglobin complex combines with oxygen to form an equilibrium system with oxyhaemoglobin:

haemoglobin + oxygen $\rightleftharpoons$ oxyhaemoglobin

In the lungs, oxygen from the air combines with haemoglobin in the small blood vessels in the lining of your lungs. According to Le Châtelier's principle, the higher concentration of oxygen in this environment will cause a net forward reaction, producing greater amounts of oxyhaemoglobin. Most of the haemoglobin is converted to oxyhaemoglobin as a result of the continual addition of oxygen from each breath you take.

FIGURE 4.1.5 Carbon monoxide gas is formed when a hydrocarbon fuel such as petrol is burnt in a limited supply of oxygen.

Carbon monoxide is a colourless, odourless and tasteless gas that is a product of the incomplete combustion of fuels. Carbon monoxide is present in cigarette smoke and in the exhaust gases from car engines (Figure 4.1.5).

The high toxicity of carbon monoxide is a result of its reaction with haemoglobin:

haemoglobin + carbon monoxide $\rightleftharpoons$ carboxyhaemoglobin

The equilibrium constant for the reaction between carbon monoxide and haemoglobin is nearly 20 000 times greater than for the reaction between oxygen and haemoglobin. This means that the forward reaction is much more likely to occur. Even small concentrations of carbon monoxide shift the position of equilibrium well to the right.

The formation of carboxyhaemoglobin reduces the concentration of haemoglobin, causing the reverse reaction of oxyhaemoglobin formation to occur. In extreme cases, almost no oxyhaemoglobin is left in the blood and carbon monoxide poisoning occurs.

Symptoms of carbon monoxide poisoning include drowsiness, dizziness, headache, shortness of breath and loss of intellectual skills. Loss of consciousness and even death can result from carbon monoxide concentrations as low as 200 ppm.

The reactions of oxygen and carbon monoxide with haemoglobin are described as **competing equilibria**, because both oxygen and carbon monoxide 'compete' for the same substance, haemoglobin. The equilibrium reaction with the larger equilibrium constant has a significant effect on the extent of reaction of the other reaction.

Chickens lay eggs with thinner shells in summer

Like dogs, chickens do not perspire, so in hot weather chickens have to pant to try to maintain a healthy temperature. This means that they exhale more carbon dioxide gas than when they are breathing normally.

This affects the following series of competing equilibria, which produces eggshells made from calcium carbonate:

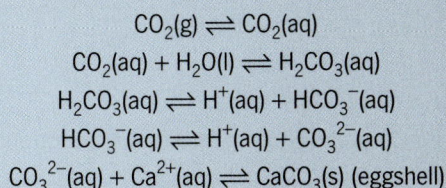

$$CO_2(g) \rightleftharpoons CO_2(aq)$$
$$CO_2(aq) + H_2O(l) \rightleftharpoons H_2CO_3(aq)$$
$$H_2CO_3(aq) \rightleftharpoons H^+(aq) + HCO_3^-(aq)$$
$$HCO_3^-(aq) \rightleftharpoons H^+(aq) + CO_3^{2-}(aq)$$
$$CO_3^{2-}(aq) + Ca^{2+}(aq) \rightleftharpoons CaCO_3(s) \text{ (eggshell)}$$

FIGURE 4.1.6 The eggshell dilemma was solved with the aid of Le Châtelier's principle.

Removing CO_2 gas shifts each equilibrium, in turn, to the left. This ultimately results in less $CaCO_3$ being made, which means that in summer chickens lay eggs with thinner shells (Figure 4.1.6). This means eggs are more easily broken, at great economic cost to farmers and supermarkets.

Scientists solved the problem by giving the chickens carbonated water to drink. This increases the concentration of aqueous carbon dioxide and pushes the equilibria to the right, increasing the amount of calcium carbonate.

Apparently the chickens like the carbonated water and they produce eggs with thicker, stronger shells. This application of Le Châtelier's principle has improved the productivity of chicken farms throughout Australia.

4.1 Review

SUMMARY

- Le Châtelier's principle states that if an equilibrium system is subjected to change, the system will adjust itself to partially oppose the change.
- The effect of a change on an equilibrium can be predicted from Le Châtelier's principle. The effects of changes can also be explained by the use of collision theory and the equilibrium law.
- The table below summarises the predicted effect of change on the position of equilibrium using Le Châtelier's principle and collision theory.

Change to system in equilibrium	Predicted effect on position of equilibrium	Collision theory explanation of effect of change on position of equilibrium
Adding extra reactant	Shifts to the right (net forward reaction)	Increased reactant concentration causes more frequent collisions, initially increasing the rate of the forward reaction. As reactants are consumed and more products form, the rate of the forward reaction decreases and the rate of the reverse reaction increases. A new equilibrium forms when the rates become equal. However, since the rate of the forward reaction was initially increased, this results in a net forward reaction.
Adding product	Shifts to the left (net reverse reaction)	Increased product concentration causes more frequent collisions, initially increasing the rate of the reverse reaction. As products are consumed and more reactants form, the rate of the reverse reaction decreases and the rate of the forward reaction increases. A new equilibrium forms when the rates become equal. However, since the rate of the reverse reaction was initially increased, this results in a net forward reaction.

KEY QUESTIONS

1 Use Le Châtelier's principle to predict the effect of adding more hydrogen gas to the following equilibria.
   a $H_2(g) + I_2(g) \rightleftharpoons 2HI(g)$
   b $2NH_3(g) \rightleftharpoons N_2(g) + 3H_2(g)$
   c $H_2(g) + CO_2(g) \rightleftharpoons H_2O(g) + CO(g)$

2 Use the concepts of rates of reaction and collision theory to explain the effect on the position of equilibrium by adding more hydrogen gas to the following systems.
   a $H_2(g) + I_2(g) \rightleftharpoons 2HI(g)$
   b $2NH_3(g) \rightleftharpoons N_2(g) + 3H_2(g)$

3 Predict the effect of the following changes on the position of each equilibrium.
   a Addition of SO_3 to the equilibrium:
$$2SO_2(g) + O_2(g) \rightleftharpoons 2SO_3(g)$$
   b Removal of CH_3COO^- from the equilibrium:
$$CH_3COOH(aq) + H_2O(l) \rightleftharpoons H_3O^+(aq) + CH_3COO^-(aq)$$

4 Consider the equilibrium:
$$Cu^{2+}(aq) + 4NH_3(aq) \rightleftharpoons Cu(NH_3)_4^{2+}(aq).$$
Which one of the following correctly describes a change that would cause an increase in the amount of $Cu(NH_3)_4^{2+}$ present?
   A $OH^-(aq)$ is added to react with Cu^{2+}, and the position of equilibrium shifts to the left.
   B More NH_3 is added, and the position of equilibrium shifts to the right.
   C $H^+(aq)$ is added to react with the NH_3, and the position of equilibrium shifts to the left.
   D None of the above reactions increase the amount $Cu(NH_3)_4^{2+}$.

4.2 Further applications of Le Châtelier's principle

Le Châtelier's principle can be used to understand how changes to chemical equilibria can affect numerous natural systems, as well as to optimise yields of reactions occurring in industrial processes.

For example, in the oceans, carbon dioxide gas is involved in equilibria that provide the carbonate ions needed for the growth of seashells, coral reefs and other marine organisms. Using Le Châtelier's principle, scientists predict that increasing levels of carbon dioxide in the atmosphere will affect the acidity of the Earth's oceans. This will put marine ecosystems and organisms at risk, including the cuttlefish in Figure 4.2.1, whose shell is made of calcium carbonate.

In this section you will continue your study of the effects of changes on chemical systems at equilibrium. Your understanding of chemical equilibrium, Le Châtelier's principle, collision theory and rates of reaction will enable you to predict the impact on an equilibrium system caused by a change in gas pressure, solution concentration or temperature, or by the addition of a catalyst.

FIGURE 4.2.1 Cuttlefish have an internal shell made of calcium carbonate. Cuttlefish and other marine animals could be affected by the increasing acidity of oceans.

CHANGING PRESSURE BY CHANGING VOLUME

The pressure of a gas is inversely proportional to the volume of its container. So the pressure of gases in an equilibrium mixture can be changed by increasing or decreasing the volume of the container while keeping the temperature constant.

GO TO ➤ Year 11 Chapter 9

Consider the effect of increasing the pressure on the equilibrium between sulfur dioxide gas, oxygen and sulfur trioxide gas for the following reaction:

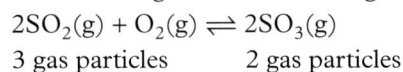

$$2SO_2(g) + O_2(g) \rightleftharpoons 2SO_3(g)$$
3 gas particles   2 gas particles

> ℹ️ Remember that gas pressure is a measure of the force per unit area, which is proportional to the frequency of collisions with the sides of the container. A change in the number of particles will change the pressure.

You can see that the forward reaction involves a reduction in the number of particles of gas from three to two. The formation of products would cause an overall reduction in pressure of the system. The reverse reaction involves an increase in the number of gas particles from two to three. So a net reverse reaction causes an overall increase in pressure of the system.

You saw in Section 4.1 that a change in the position of an equilibrium can be predicted by either applying Le Châtelier's principle or using an understanding of collision theory and the rates of reactions.

Predicting the effect of pressure change using Le Châtelier's principle

Le Châtelier's principle tells you that an equilibrium system will respond to an increase in pressure by adjusting to reduce the pressure. Therefore the position of equilibrium will move in the direction of the fewest gas particles.

Consider the reaction between sulfur dioxide gas and oxygen gas to form sulfur trioxide gas:

$$2SO_2(g) + O_2(g) \rightleftharpoons 2SO_3(g)$$

An increase in pressure will cause a net forward reaction to occur in order to reduce the overall pressure (three gaseous reactant particles become two gaseous product particles). The amount of SO_3 present at equilibrium will increase, as represented in Figure 4.2.2.

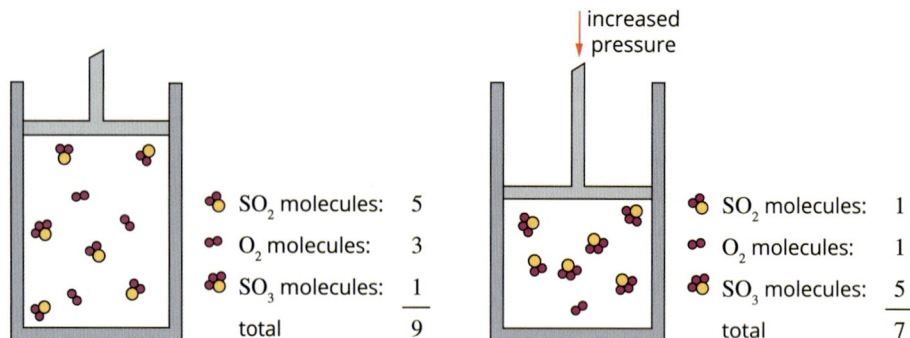

increased pressure

SO$_2$ molecules:	5
O$_2$ molecules:	3
SO$_3$ molecules:	1
total	9

SO$_2$ molecules:	1
O$_2$ molecules:	1
SO$_3$ molecules:	5
total	7

FIGURE 4.2.2 A representation of the effect of increased pressure on the equilibrium: $2SO_2(g) + O_2(g) \rightleftharpoons 2SO_3(g)$

An increase in pressure will favour the side of the reaction with the least number of particles.

The effect of the change can also be illustrated graphically (Figure 4.2.3). When the system is initially at equilibrium and there is an increase in pressure, the concentrations of all gases increase simultaneously.

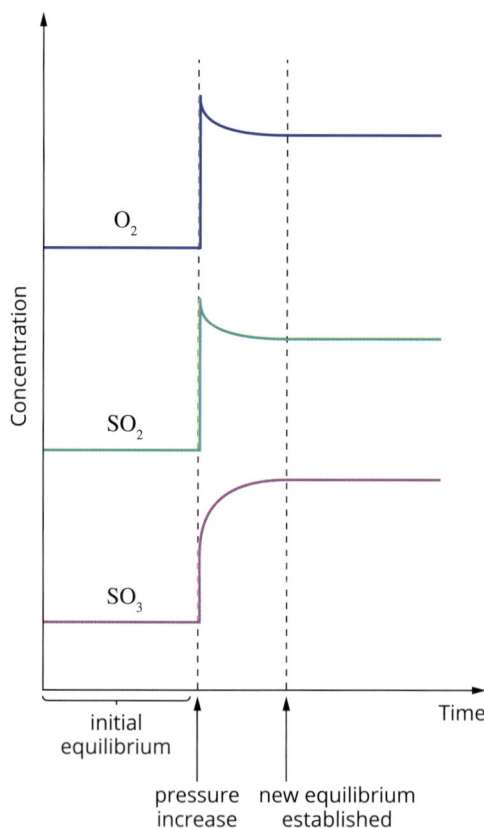

FIGURE 4.2.3 The effect of increased pressure on the equilibrium position for the reaction $2SO_2(g) + O_2(g) \rightleftharpoons 2SO_3(g)$

As the system adjusts, there is a gradual change in concentration of each of the species until the new equilibrium is established. At the new position of equilibrium the individual concentrations are different to those at the first equilibrium. However, the equilibrium constant, K_{eq}, has not changed. The ratio of products to reactants in the equilibrium law still equals K_{eq} at the new position of equilibrium.

Explaining the effect of pressure change using collision theory and rates of reaction

The effect of an increase in pressure on the equilibrium can also be understood using collision theory. Since the overall volume occupied by the gases has become smaller, the gas molecules are closer to each other and collisions between molecules become more frequent. The rate of the reaction involving the greater number of molecules (the forward reaction in this case) becomes greater than the rate of the reaction between the smaller number of molecules (the reverse reaction). Then, as more product is formed, the rate of the reverse reaction increases and the rate of the forward reaction decreases.

Eventually the rates of the forward and reverse reactions become equal and a new equilibrium is established. Since the forward reaction occurred to a greater extent initially, there has been a net forward reaction.

Pressure changes do not affect the equilibrium position of systems that are in the liquid or solid phases. Particles in these systems are too tightly packed for an increase in pressure to have a noticeable effect on volume. This means that there is negligible change in the concentration of the species involved and no effect on the concentration fraction (reaction quotient).

Further examples

The effect of changing the container volume, and therefore the pressure or concentration, depends on the relative number of particles on both sides of the equation.

When there are equal numbers of reactant and product particles, a change in pressure will not shift the position of equilibrium. This is the case for the reaction between hydrogen and iodine in the following equilibrium:

$$H_2(g) + I_2(g) \rightleftharpoons 2HI(g)$$
$$2 \text{ gas particles} \qquad 2 \text{ gas particles}$$

According to Le Châtelier's principle, it does not matter which way the system shifts; the number of particles in the container will remain constant (two particles of reactants and two particles of products). Therefore the system is unable to oppose the change applied and there is no net reaction.

In terms of collision theory, the volume decrease causes the rates of the forward and back reactions to be increased equally.

Worked example 4.2.1

USING LE CHÂTELIER'S PRINCIPLE TO DETERMINE THE SHIFT IN EQUILIBRIUM POSITION FOR A CHANGE IN VOLUME

Consider the equilibrium:

$$CH_4(g) + H_2O(g) \rightleftharpoons CO(g) + 3H_2(g)$$

Predict the shift in the equilibrium position and the effect on the amount of CO when the volume is halved at a constant temperature.

Thinking	Working
Determine the immediate effect of the change of volume on the pressure.	Halving the volume will double the pressure of all species at equilibrium.
The system will try to partially oppose the change in pressure by reducing or increasing the pressure of the system. (For a volume decrease, the system will shift in the direction of the fewest particles, and vice versa for a volume increase.) Decide how the equilibrium will respond.	There are 2 molecules of gas on the reactant side and 4 molecules of gas on the product side, so the system will shift to the left. This decreases the amounts of the products, including CO. The CO concentration will still be higher than it was at the initial equilibrium. The shift in the equilibrium position only partially compensates for the change.

USING LE CHÂTELIER'S PRINCIPLE TO DETERMINE THE SHIFT IN EQUILIBRIUM POSITION FOR A CHANGE IN VOLUME

Consider the equilibrium:

$$PCl_3(g) + Cl_2(g) \rightleftharpoons PCl_5(g)$$

Predict the shift in equilibrium position and the effect on the amount of Cl_2 when the volume is doubled at a constant temperature.

CHANGING PRESSURE BY ADDING AN INERT GAS

The total pressure of an equilibrium mixture of gases may also be changed, without changing the volume of the container, by adding an inert gas such as helium, neon or argon (Figure 4.2.4).

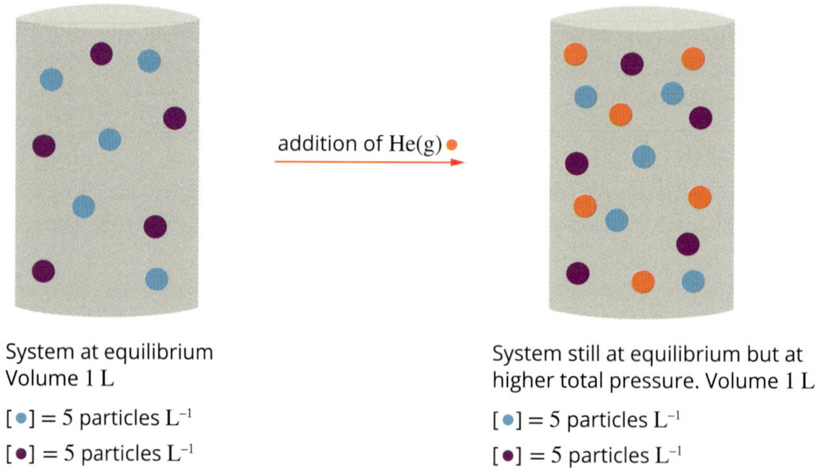

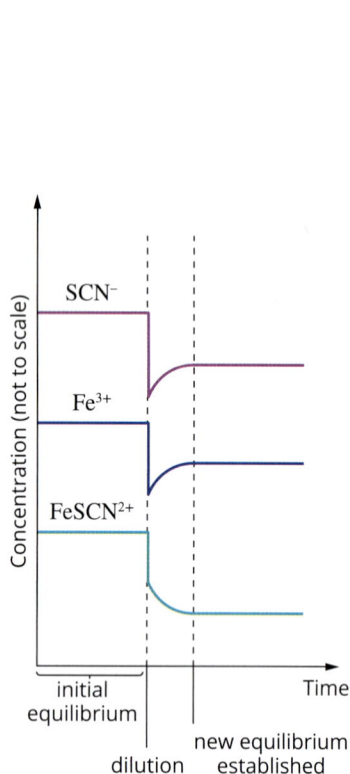

addition of He(g) •

System at equilibrium
Volume 1 L

[●] = 5 particles L^{-1}

[●] = 5 particles L^{-1}

System still at equilibrium but at higher total pressure. Volume 1 L

[●] = 5 particles L^{-1}

[●] = 5 particles L^{-1}

FIGURE 4.2.4 The equilibrium of a gaseous system is unaffected by the addition of an inert gas. The total pressure of the system increases without changes in concentrations of reactants or products, so there is no change to the reaction quotient.

Because the presence of the additional gas does not change any of the concentrations of the reactants and products, there is no effect on the position of equilibrium or the value of the equilibrium constant. Using collision theory, you can see that any collisions with inert gas molecules will not produce a reaction, so no net reaction occurs.

DILUTION

For an equilibrium in solution, the situation is similar to the one you saw with pressure and gases. The focus is on the number of particles per volume of solution. Dilution by adding water reduces the number of particles per volume. This results in a shift in the position of equilibrium towards the side that produces the greater number of dissolved particles. For example, consider the equilibrium system:

$$Fe^{3+}(aq) + SCN^-(aq) \rightleftharpoons FeSCN^{2+}(aq)$$

2 particles in solution   1 particle in solution

The addition of water immediately lowers the concentration of each species. In terms of Le Châtelier's principle, a net reverse reaction will then occur, increasing the total concentration of particles in solution.

Figure 4.2.5 shows the changes of concentrations that occur. Note that there is an instantaneous decrease in the concentration of all species at the time of dilution. (You will study this equilibrium between Fe^{3+}, SCN^- and $FeSCN^{2+}$ in more detail during your practical investigations in class.)

FIGURE 4.2.5 Effect of dilution on the equilibrium:
$Fe^{3+}(aq) + SCN^-(aq) \rightleftharpoons FeSCN^{2+}(aq)$
Although the equilibrium position shifts to the left, the concentrations of Fe^{3+} and SCN^- at the new equilibrium are lower than their concentrations before dilution, because the equilibrium shift only partially opposes the change.

ⓘ Dilution of an aqueous equilibrium system has no effect on the value of K_{eq} for the reaction.

CHANGING TEMPERATURE

In Section 3.2 you saw that the effect of a temperature change on an equilibrium reaction depends upon whether the reaction is exothermic or endothermic, as shown in Table 4.2.1.

> **ⓘ** Changing the temperature of an equilibrium in a closed system affects both the position of equilibrium and the value of the equilibrium constant.

The overall effect on the equilibrium position caused by a change in temperature can be predicted from Le Châtelier's principle and explained using collision theory and rates of reaction.

For example, consider the conversion of brown nitrogen dioxide gas (NO_2) to colourless dinitrogen tetroxide gas (N_2O_4). The reaction is exothermic, releasing energy to the environment. You could (but wouldn't usually) write an equation for the reaction that includes the energy released:

$$2NO_2(g) \rightleftharpoons N_2O_4(g) + \text{energy}$$

Increasing the temperature of the system increases the energy of the substances in the mixture. Applying Le Châtelier's principle, you can predict that the reaction can oppose an increase in energy by absorbing energy. Because the reverse reaction is endothermic, this favours a net reverse reaction. Figure 4.2.6 shows the gradual decrease in the concentration of N_2O_4 as the system moves to produce more reactant, NO_2. Note that with a change in temperature there is no instantaneous change in concentration.

Because the reactant and product of the system have different colours, you can monitor the change in this equilibrium visually. When a new equilibrium is attained, there is less dinitrogen tetroxide and more nitrogen dioxide present so the mixture appears a darker brown (Figure 4.2.7).

Heating an endothermic reaction causes the opposite result to occur. Applying Le Châtelier's principle, you can predict that the reaction opposes an increase in energy by absorbing energy, resulting in a net forward reaction. In summary:

- Increasing the temperature of an equilibrium mixture results in:
  - a net reverse reaction (fewer products) for exothermic reactions, and a decrease in K_{eq}
  - a net forward reaction (more products) for endothermic reactions, and an increase in K_{eq}.
- Decreasing the temperature has the opposite effect:
  - a net forward reaction (more products) for exothermic reactions, and an increase in K_{eq}
  - a net reverse reaction (fewer products) for endothermic reactions, and a decrease in K_{eq}.

The effect of temperature on equilibria can be explained by collision theory. When there is an increase in temperature, molecules move faster and there are more frequent and more energetic collisions. A larger number of molecules now have the necessary energy to overcome the activation energy barrier and undergo successful collisions.

At the higher temperature, the rates of both the forward and reverse reactions increase. One of these reactions is endothermic and the other is exothermic. Because the activation energy for the endothermic reaction is greater than for the exothermic reaction, the increased energy will mean there will be a greater proportion of molecules with the necessary energy to overcome the activation energy barrier for the endothermic reaction. The rate of this reaction will increase more than the rate of the exothermic reaction.

TABLE 4.2.1 The effect on the value of K_{eq} when the temperature of a system is increased

ΔH	T	K_{eq}
exothermic (–)	increase	decrease
endothermic (+)	increase	increase

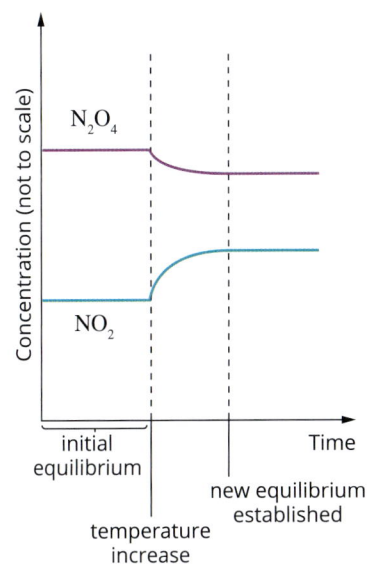

FIGURE 4.2.6 The effect of heating on the equilibrium $2NO_2(g) \rightleftharpoons N_2O_4(g)$.

FIGURE 4.2.7 Equilibrium mixtures of NO_2 and N_2O_4 in baths of hot water (left) and ice water (right). Heating the mixture favours the formation of brown NO_2 gas.

This can be seen from the graph in Figure 4.2.8, which shows the frequency distribution of molecules at different temperatures.

In the equilibrium between NO_2 and N_2O_4, the reverse reaction is endothermic and so there will be a net reverse reaction as the temperature increases. When the system re-establishes equilibrium at a higher temperature, the new equilibrium has a higher concentration of NO_2 and a lower concentration of N_2O_4.

Conversely, decreasing the temperature of the equilibrium results in a net reaction in the direction of the exothermic reaction and the new equilibrium has a lower concentration of NO_2 and a higher concentration of N_2O_4.

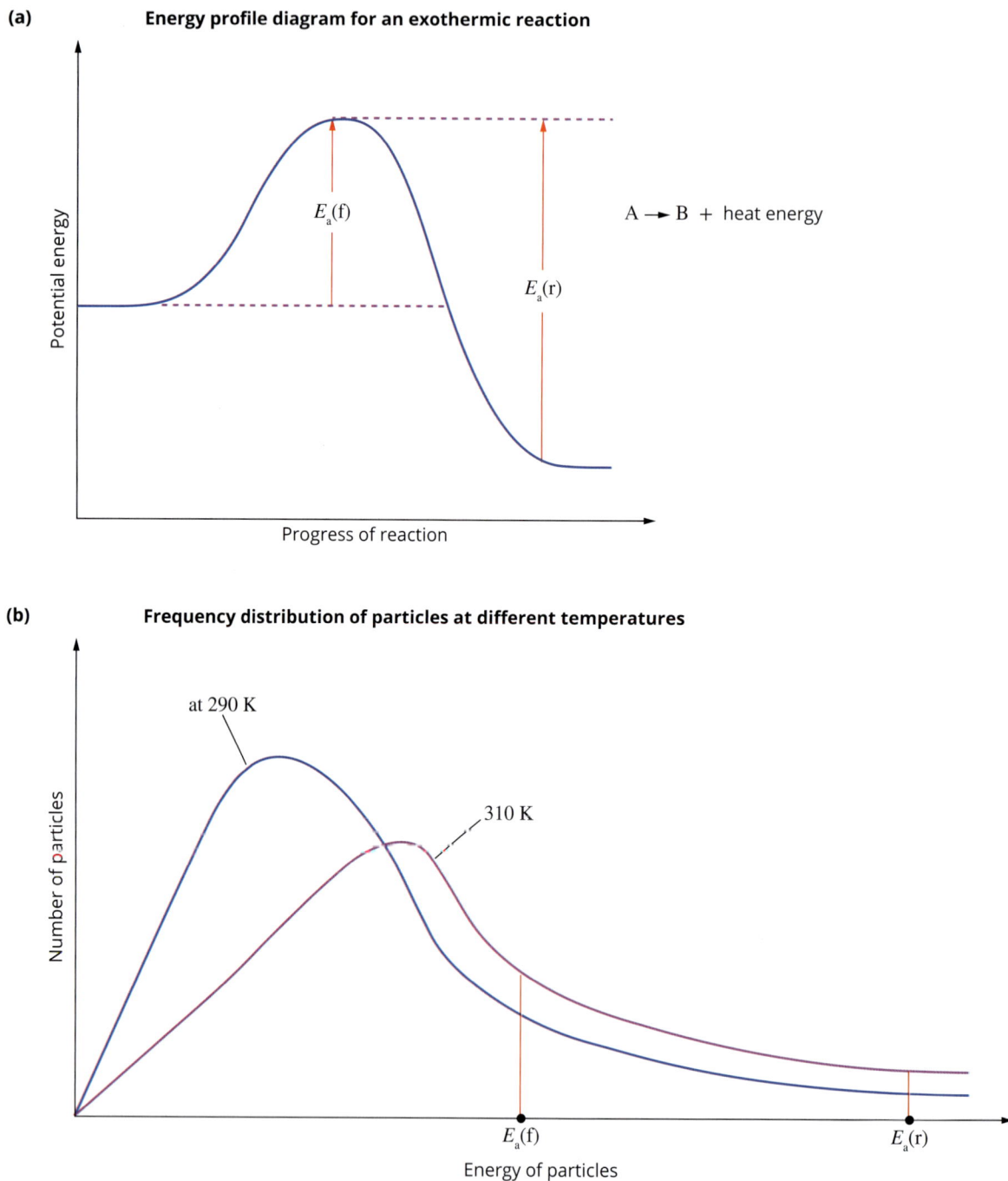

(a)

Energy profile diagram for an exothermic reaction

$E_a(f)$

$E_a(r)$

A $\longrightarrow$ B + heat energy

Potential energy

Progress of reaction

(b)

Frequency distribution of particles at different temperatures

at 290 K

310 K

Number of particles

$E_a(f)$

$E_a(r)$

Energy of particles

FIGURE 4.2.8 (a) Energy profile diagram for an exothermic reaction. The activation energy of the forward reaction, $E_a(f)$, is less than the activation energy of the reverse reaction, $E_a(r)$. (b) The frequency distribution of molecules at two different temperatures. At the higher temperature, a greater proportion of particles have the necessary energy to overcome the activation energy barrier for the endothermic reaction.

Worked example 4.2.2

USING COLLISION THEORY TO DETERMINE THE EFFECT OF TEMPERATURE ON AN EQUILIBRIUM SYSTEM

Consider the following reaction:

$$H_2(g) + CO_2(g) \rightleftharpoons CO(g) + H_2O(g)$$

Explain, using collision theory, the effect of an increase in temperature on the equilibrium state of this endothermic reaction.

Thinking	Working
Decide what effect the temperature change has on the initial rates of reaction. Remember that, for an equilibrium system, an increase in temperature increases the proportion of molecules with the necessary energy to overcome the activation energy barrier for the endothermic reaction to a greater extent than for the exothermic reaction, and so the endothermic reaction will be favoured.	With the temperature increase, all reactant and product molecules have more energy and move faster. Because the forward reaction is endothermic, its rate initially increases more than the rate of the reverse reaction.
Using collision theory, consider what happens to the rates of the forward and reverse reactions.	As H_2 and CO_2 react and the concentration of reactants decreases, the rate of the forward reaction decreases. As the concentration of CO and H_2O increases, the rate of the reverse reaction increases. Ultimately, the rates of the forward and reverse reactions become equal and a new equilibrium is established.
Determine the overall effect of the change on the equilibrium.	There is a net forward reaction, with higher concentrations of the products, CO and H_2O, and lower concentrations of the reactants, CO_2 and H_2.

Worked example: Try yourself 4.2.2

USING COLLISION THEORY TO DETERMINE THE EFFECT OF TEMPERATURE ON AN EQUILIBRIUM SYSTEM

Consider the following reaction:

$$CO_2(g) + 4H_2(g) \rightleftharpoons CH_4(g) + 2H_2O(g) \quad \Delta H = -165 \text{ kJ mol}^{-1}$$

Explain, using collision theory, the effect of an increase in temperature on the equilibrium state of this reaction.

CHEMFILE CCT

A chemical thermometer

When cobalt(II) chloride is dissolved in water it forms a pink solution because of the presence of $Co(H_2O)_6^{2+}$ ions. If cobalt(II) chloride is dissolved in hydrochloric acid, the $Co(H_2O)_6^{2+}$ ions form an equilibrium with Cl^- ions:

$$Co(H_2O)_6^{2+}(aq) + 4Cl^-(aq) \rightleftharpoons CoCl_4^{2-}(aq) + 6H_2O(l)$$
$$\text{pink} \qquad\qquad\qquad\qquad \text{blue}$$

The forward reaction is endothermic. If an equilibrium mixture that is pink at room temperature is heated, the position of equilibrium moves to the right and the solution becomes progressively more blue (Figure 4.2.9). Cooling the solution would then cause a net reverse reaction and the solution would return to the original pink colour as more $Co(H_2O)_6^{2+}$ is formed.

FIGURE 4.2.9 The effect of temperature changes on the position of equilibrium of an aqueous solution of cobalt(II) chloride. The forward reaction is endothermic, so a solution that is pink at room temperature (left) turns blue as the temperature increases and more $CoCl_4^{2-}$ is formed (right).

EFFECT OF A CATALYST ON EQUILIBRIUM

A catalyst lowers the activation energy of the forward and reverse reactions by the same amount. This can be seen in the energy profile diagram shown in Figure 4.2.10.

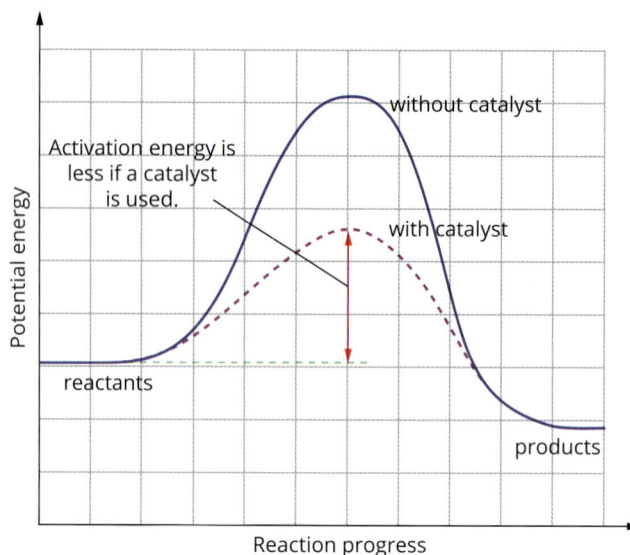

FIGURE 4.2.10 Energy changes in a catalysed and uncatalysed reaction

> **i** Lowering the activation energy of a reaction by adding a catalyst does not change the value of K_{eq} or the position of equilibrium of a system. It only affects how quickly equilibrium is attained.

The lower activation energy causes an increase in the number of effective collisions. As a result, there is an increase in the rate of both forward and reverse reactions. This occurs because more particles have energies greater than the activation energy barrier of the reaction.

A catalyst increases the rates of the forward and reverse reactions equally, so it will not change the relative concentrations of the reactants and products at equilibrium. Consequently the presence of a catalyst does not change the position of equilibrium or the value of the equilibrium constant, K_{eq}. A catalyst will, however, increase the rate at which a reaction proceeds towards equilibrium. It is for this reason that catalysts are used in many industrial and biological systems.

+ ADDITIONAL **N**

The relationship between K_{eq} and ΔH

The mathematical relationship between K_{eq} and ΔH was determined by Jacobus van't Hoff, a Dutch physical chemist who was awarded the first Nobel Prize in Chemistry in 1901. The relationship is known as the van't Hoff equation:

$$\ln\left(\frac{K_2}{K_1}\right) = \frac{-\Delta H^\circ}{R}\left(\frac{1}{T_2} - \frac{1}{T_1}\right)$$

where

K_1 and K_2 are the equilibrium constants at temperatures T_1 and T_2 respectively

ΔH° is the enthalpy change at standard conditions and R is the gas constant ($8.314\,J\,mol^{-1}\,K^{-1}$).

The equation can be used to calculate K_{eq} at any temperature once ΔH° and K_{eq} are known at a given temperature.

The equation shows that:

- as temperature increases, K_{eq} decreases for exothermic reactions (ΔH negative)
- as temperature increases, K_{eq} increases for endothermic reactions (ΔH positive)
- the magnitude of ΔH determines the size of the change in K_{eq} for a particular change of temperature.

Equilibria in a swimming pool

The water in swimming pools is used many times. Even though it is filtered, the water can quickly become contaminated with microscopic algae and bacteria. Some interesting chemistry involving chemical equilibria is involved in keeping swimming pools clean, clear and safe to swim in (Figure 4.2.11).

FIGURE 4.2.11 Chemical equilibria are responsible for keeping the water in backyard swimming pools hygienic and safe for swimmers.

Swimming pools are chlorinated to prevent the growth of harmful microorganisms. Chlorination produces hypochlorous acid (HOCl), which is a very efficient antibacterial agent and algicide.

Commercially available pool chlorine (Figure 4.2.12) consists of calcium hypochlorite ($Ca(OCl)_2$), which dissociates in water to release hypochlorite ions (OCl^-). The hypochlorite ions then react with hydronium ions in the water to form hypochlorous acid:

$$Ca(OCl)_2(s) \rightleftharpoons Ca^{2+}(aq) + 2OCl^-(aq)$$
$$OCl^-(aq) + H_3O^+(aq) \rightleftharpoons HOCl(aq) + H_2O(l)$$

FIGURE 4.2.12 Commercial pool chlorine is a source of hypochlorite ions (OCl^-), which form an equilibrium with H_3O^+ ions in water.

The H_3O^+ is available from the self-ionisation of water, another equilibrium reaction but this time between water molecules, forming H_3O^+ and OH^- ions:

$$H_2O(l) + H_2O(l) \rightleftharpoons H_3O^+(aq) + OH^-(aq)$$

The relative amounts of HOCl, OCl^- and H_3O^+ in a swimming pool need to be controlled carefully. This is done by monitoring the pH of the swimming pool and adding either more pool chlorine or more acid as needed to maintain a pH in the range 7.2–7.8. The pH value measures the concentration of H_3O^+ ions. Figure 4.2.13 shows the relationship between the three quantities.

As pH increases, the concentration of $H_3O^+(aq)$ decreases. Le Châtelier's principle predicts that the position of equilibrium will move to the left, consuming some of the HOCl. If the pH rises above about 7.8, the concentration of HOCl will be insufficient to control the growth of bacteria and algae.

On the other hand, as pH falls, the concentration of $H_3O^+(aq)$ increases. The position of equilibrium will move to the right and more HOCl will be formed. Although pH values below around 7.2 result in greater amounts of HOCl in the pool, if the pool is too acidic the water can irritate eyes and skin.

Maintaining a pool so that it is hygienic and comfortable for swimmers involves carefully maintaining an optimum position of equilibrium in the reaction mixture.

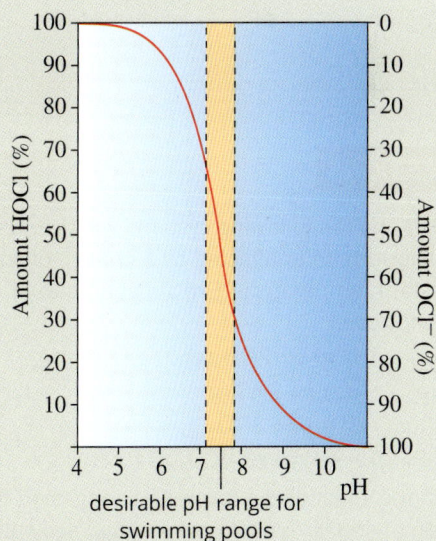

FIGURE 4.2.13 The effect of pH on the proportion of HOCl and OCl^- in water means that the position of the equilibrium can be monitored by changes in pH of the water.

4.2 Review

SUMMARY

- The effect of a change on an equilibrium can be predicted using Le Châtelier's principle and the equilibrium law (see table below).

- The effects of changes on an equilibrium can also be explained using collision theory and rates of reaction (see table below).

Change to system in equilibrium	Effect of change on equilibrium position	Collision theory explanation of effect of change on equilibrium position
Decreasing pressure by increasing volume (for gases)	shifts in the direction of the most particles	Less frequent collisions; the reaction that is less dependent on collisions (fewer particles reacting) occurs to a greater extent.
Increasing pressure by decreasing volume (for gases)	shifts in the direction of the fewest particles	More frequent collisions; the reaction that is more dependent on collisions (more particles reacting) occurs to a greater extent.
Adding an inert gas (container volume remains constant)	no change	No change in concentrations of the reacting gases, so no change to the rates of the forward and reverse reactions.
Adding water (dilution of solutions)	shifts in the direction of the most particles	Less frequent collisions; the reaction less dependent on collisions (fewer particles reacting) occurs to a greater extent.
Increasing the temperature for exothermic reactions	shifts to the left	All reactant and product molecules have more energy and move faster; increased temperature favours rate of an endothermic reaction; net reaction in direction of endothermic reaction, i.e. favouring the reverse direction.
Increasing the temperature for endothermic reactions	shifts to the right	All reactant and product molecules have more energy and move faster; increased temperature favours rate of an endothermic reaction; net reaction in direction of endothermic reaction, i.e. favouring the forward direction.
Decreasing the temperature for exothermic reactions	shifts to the right	All reactant and product molecules have less energy and move more slowly; decreased temperature favours rate of an exothermic reaction; net reaction in direction of exothermic reaction, i.e. favouring the forward direction.
Decreasing the temperature for endothermic reactions	shifts to the left	All reactant and product molecules have less energy and move more slowly; decreased temperature favours rate of an exothermic reaction; net reaction in direction of exothermic reaction, i.e. favouring the reverse direction.
Adding a catalyst	no change	Increases rates of forward and reverse reactions to the same extent; an equivalent change in the frequency of successful collisions in both directions; no net shift in the position of equilibrium.

KEY QUESTIONS

1. In which one the following systems will the position of equilibrium be unaffected by a change of volume at constant temperature? Explain your answer using collision theory.
   A $N_2(g) + 3H_2(g) \rightleftharpoons 2NH_3(g)$
   B $Cl_2(g) + H_2(g) \rightleftharpoons 2HCl(g)$
   C $2NO(g) + O_2(g) \rightleftharpoons 2NO_2(g)$
   D $2C_2H_6(g) + 7O_2(g) \rightleftharpoons 4CO_2(g) + 6H_2O(g)$

2. Predict the effect of the following changes on the position of equilibrium for the reaction shown:
   a halving the volume by doubling the pressure at equilibrium:
   $$N_2(g) + 3H_2(g) \rightleftharpoons 2NH_3(g)$$
   b increasing the pressure by reducing the volume at equilibrium:
   $$H_2(g) + I_2(g) \rightleftharpoons 2HI(g)$$

   c increasing the temperature at equilibrium for the endothermic reaction:
   $$N_2(g) + O_2(g) \rightleftharpoons 2NO(g)$$

3. For each of the reactions in Question **2**, explain the effect of the changes in terms of collision theory and rates of reaction.

4. An equilibrium mixture consists of the gases N_2O_4 and NO_2:
   $$N_2O_4(g) \rightleftharpoons 2NO_2(g)$$
   The volume of the container is increased without changing the temperature, and a new equilibrium is established. Predict how each of the following quantities would change at the new equilibrium compared with the initial equilibrium:
   a the concentration of NO_2
   b the mass of NO_2.

Chapter review

KEY TERMS

collision theory
competing equilibria

Le Châtelier's principle
position of equilibrium

REVIEW QUESTIONS

1 **a** State Le Châtelier's principle.
   b Write an equilibrium equation in terms of reactants A and B in equilibrium with products C and D, and use Le Châtelier's principle to explain what occurs when the products are gradually removed.

2 Predict the effect of the following changes on the position of equilibrium in the system:
$$2SO_2(g) + O_2(g) \rightleftharpoons 2SO_3(g)$$
   a adding SO_2 to the equilibrium system
   b removing O_2 from the equilibrium system
   c removing SO_3 from the equilibrium system.

3 The following equilibrium system is present in a sealed container of fixed volume:
$$N_2(g) + 3H_2(g) \rightleftharpoons 2NH_3(g)$$
   What change in the concentration of hydrogen gas can cause the following changes to the system at constant temperature?
   a The concentration of the product increases.
   b There is a net reverse reaction.

4 Calcium is essential for maintaining bone strength. Elderly people, especially women, can become very susceptible to bone breakages. It is thought that as people age they absorb Ca^{2+} from food inefficiently, reducing the concentration of these ions in body fluids. An equilibrium exists between calcium phosphate in bone and calcium ions in body fluids:
$$Ca_3(PO_4)_2(s) \rightleftharpoons 3Ca^{2+}(aq) + 2PO_4{}^{3-}(aq)$$
   Use your understanding of equilibrium to explain why inefficient absorption of Ca^{2+} ions could cause weakness in bones.

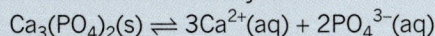

5 How will the concentration of hydrogen gas in each of the following equilibrium mixtures change when the mixtures are heated without changing the volume?
   a $N_2(g) + 3H_2(g) \rightleftharpoons 2NH_3(g)$ $\Delta H = -91\,kJ\,mol^{-1}$
   b $CH_4(g) + H_2O(g) \rightleftharpoons CO(g) + 3H_2(g)$ $\Delta H = +208\,kJ\,mol^{-1}$

6 When solutions of $Fe(NO_3)_3$ and KSCN are mixed, a red solution is formed as a result of the formation of $FeSCN^{2+}(aq)$:
$$Fe^{3+}(aq) + SCN^-(aq) \rightleftharpoons FeSCN^{2+}(aq)$$
   Which one or more of the following would reduce the intensity of the red colour of the solution?

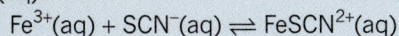

   A adding a small volume of KSCN solution, which increases the concentration of $SCN^-(aq)$
   B adding a small volume of $AgNO_3$ solution, which reacts to form insoluble AgSCN
   C adding a small volume of $Fe(NO_3)_3$ solution, which increases the concentration of $Fe^{3+}(aq)$
   D adding a small volume of water.

7 The reaction represented by the following equation is exothermic:
$$Cl_2(g) + CO(g) \rightleftharpoons COCl_2(g)$$
   At equilibrium at constant temperature, the volume is halved by increasing the pressure. Which one of the following statements is correct?
   A The new equilibrium concentration of CO will be less than the initial concentration.
   B The value of K_{eq} will increase.
   C The amount of $COCl_2$ will increase.
   D A net reverse reaction will occur.

8 Dinitrogen tetroxide (N_2O_4) and nitrogen dioxide (NO_2) coexist according to the equilibrium reaction:
$$N_2O_4(g) \rightleftharpoons 2NO_2(g)$$
   a The graph below shows the change of the concentration of the two gases with time as they reach equilibrium at constant temperature.

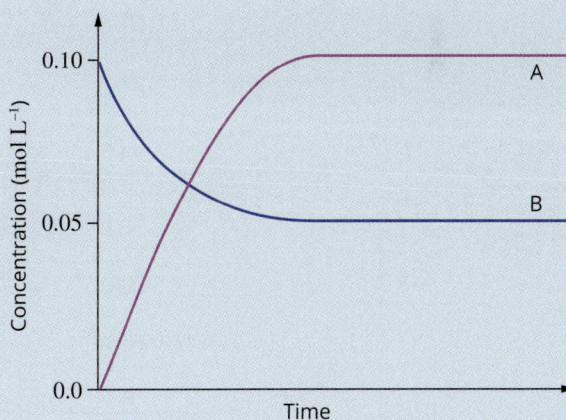

   Which gas does curve A represent? Which gas does curve B represent? Explain your answer.

b Which one of the following graphs correctly shows the effect on the concentrations of A and B when a catalyst is added? The dashed lines indicate their concentrations when the catalyst is added.

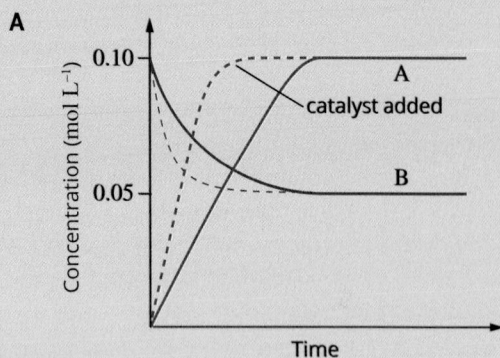

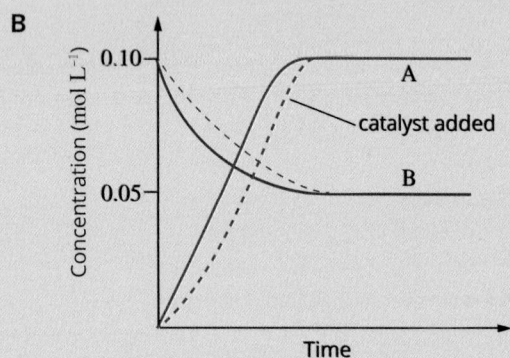

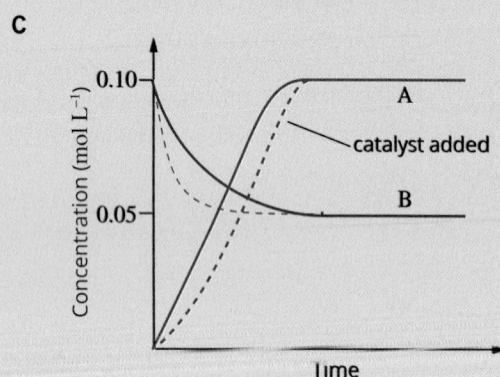

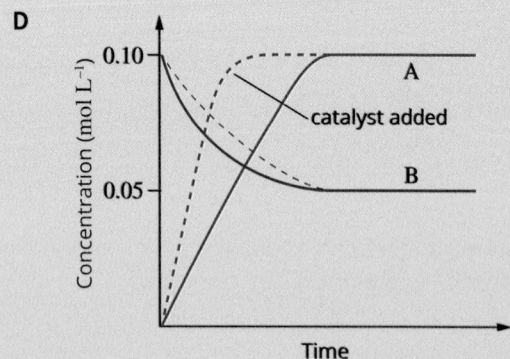

A

B

C

D

9 Which one of the following describes a change that would affect the value of the equilibrium constant, K_{eq}, of a gaseous equilibrium?
  A increasing the pressure by reducing the volume of the container
  B adding a catalyst
  C adding more reactants
  D increasing the temperature.

10 Consider the following equilibria:
  i $H_2(g) + CO_2(g) \rightleftharpoons H_2O(g) + CO(g)$ $\Delta H = +42\,kJ\,mol^{-1}$
  ii $N_2O_4(g) \rightleftharpoons 2NO_2(g)$ $\Delta H = +58\,kJ\,mol^{-1}$
  iii $H_2(g) + F_2(g) \rightleftharpoons 2HF(g)$ $\Delta H = -536\,kJ\,mol^{-1}$
  a How would you alter the temperature of each equilibrium mixture to produce a net forward reaction?
  b If it were possible, how would you alter the volume of each equilibrium mixture to produce a net forward reaction?

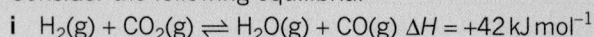

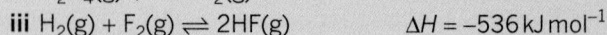

11 The following equations represent reactions that are important in industrial processes. Predict the effect on the position of equilibrium of each reaction mixture when it is compressed at constant temperature.
  a $C_3H_8O(g) \rightleftharpoons C_3H_6O(g) + H_2(g)$
  b $CO(g) + 2H_2(g) \rightleftharpoons CH_3OH(g)$
  c $N_2(g) + O_2(g) \rightleftharpoons 2NO(g)$

12 Which one of the following best describes the effect of adding a catalyst to a reversible reaction at equilibrium?
  A The equilibrium constant for the reaction, K_{eq}, increases.
  B The ΔH of the forward reaction decreases.
  C The activation energies of the forward and back reactions decrease.
  D The ΔH of the reverse reaction decreases.

13 Carbon monoxide is used as a fuel in many industries. It reacts according to the equation:
$$2CO(g) + O_2(g) \rightleftharpoons 2CO_2(g)$$
In a study of this exothermic reaction, an equilibrium system is established in a closed vessel of constant volume at 1000°C.
  a Predict what will happen to the position of equilibrium as a result of:
    i a decrease in temperature
    ii the addition of a catalyst
    iii the addition of more oxygen.
  b What will happen to the equilibrium constant as a result of each of the changes in part **a**?
  c Given that carbon monoxide can be used as a fuel, comment on the magnitude of the equilibrium constant for the reaction.

14 A step during nitric acid production is the oxidation of nitrogen oxide to nitrogen dioxide:

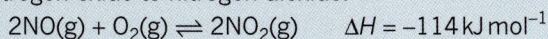

$$2NO(g) + O_2(g) \rightleftharpoons 2NO_2(g) \qquad \Delta H = -114\,kJ\,mol^{-1}$$

Nitrogen dioxide is a brown gas, and nitrogen oxide and oxygen are colourless. An equilibrium mixture was prepared in a 1 L container at 350°C. Copy the following table and, for each of the changes listed, indicate whether the reaction mixture would become darker or lighter. Explain your choice using Le Châtelier's principle and collision theory.

Change	Colour change (lighter or darker)	Explanation
a The temperature is increased to 450°C at constant volume.		
b The volume of the container is increased at constant temperature.		
c A catalyst is added at constant volume and temperature.		
d More oxygen is added at constant volume and temperature.		

15 The International Space Station uses waste hydrogen and the carbon dioxide released by astronauts during respiration to form water according to the reaction:

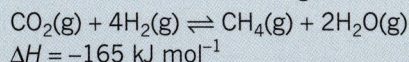

$$CO_2(g) + 4H_2(g) \rightleftharpoons CH_4(g) + 2H_2O(g)$$
$$\Delta H = -165 \text{ kJ mol}^{-1}$$

a How would you alter the temperature in order to produce a net forward reaction?

b How would you alter the volume in order to produce a net forward reaction?

16 Ethene gas is produced from ethane gas in an endothermic reaction represented by the equation:

$$C_2H_6(g) \rightleftharpoons C_2H_4(g) + H_2(g) \qquad \Delta H = +138\,kJ\,mol^{-1}$$

a State whether the following changes will result in the equilibrium percentage yield of ethene increasing, decreasing, or not changing.

   i The volume is reduced at constant temperature.

   ii More hydrogen gas is added at constant temperature and volume.

   iii The temperature is increased at constant volume.

   iv A catalyst is added.

   v Argon gas is added at constant temperature and volume.

b How will each of the changes in part **a** affect the rate at which the reaction proceeds towards equilibrium?

17 Methanol is manufactured for use as a fuel in racing cars. It can be made by reaction between carbon monoxide and hydrogen:

$$CO(g) + 2H_2(g) \rightleftharpoons CH_3OH(g) \qquad \Delta H = -103\,kJ\,mol^{-1}$$

As part of an investigation of this process, the concentration of a mixture of CO, H_2 and CH_3OH was monitored continuously. The mixture was initially at equilibrium at 400°C and constant volume. After 10 minutes, additional CO was added to the mixture, as shown in the figure below.

i Sketch a graph to show how concentrations would change as a consequence of the addition of CO.

ii Following the addition of the CO the mixture again reaches equilibrium. Sketch a second graph to show the effect on the concentrations if the temperature were then increased to 450°C.

18 A mixture of gaseous N_2, H_2 and NH_3 is initially at equilibrium in a sealed container:

$$N_2(g) + 3H_2(g) \rightleftharpoons 2NH_3(g)$$

The volume of the container is decreased at t_1. The rate-time graph below shows the changes in the rate of production of ammonia.

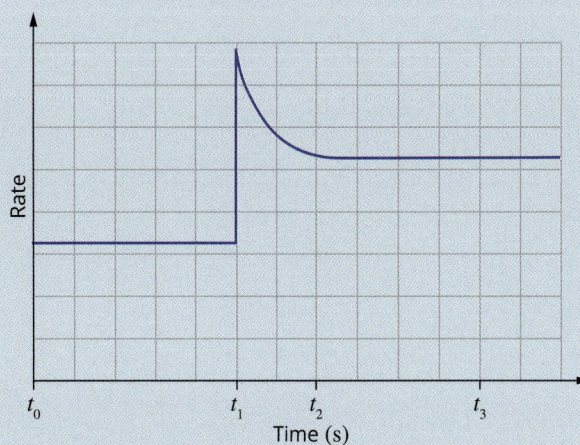

For each of the time intervals below, explain the shape of this graph in terms of collision theory and the factors that affect the rate of reaction.

a between t_0 and t_1

b at t_1

c between t_1 and t_2

19 Carbon disulfide gas (CS_2) is used in the manufacture of rayon. $CS_2(g)$ can be made in an endothermic gas-phase reaction between sulfur trioxide gas (SO_3) and carbon dioxide. Oxygen gas is also produced in the reaction.

a Write a balanced chemical equation for the reaction.

b Write an expression for the equilibrium constant of the reaction.

c An equilibrium mixture of these gases was made by mixing sulfur trioxide and carbon dioxide. The equilibrium mixture consisted of 0.028 mol of CS_2, 0.022 mol of SO_3, 0.014 mol of CO_2 and an unknown amount of O_2 in a 20 L vessel. Calculate:

  i the amount of O_2, in mol, present in the equilibrium mixture

  ii the value of the equilibrium constant at that temperature.

d Predict how each of the following changes to an equilibrium mixture would affect the yield of CS_2.

  i removing O_2 at constant total volume

  ii increasing the temperature

  iii adding a catalyst

  iv increasing the pressure by decreasing the volume of the reaction vessel at constant temperature

  v increasing the pressure by introducing argon gas into the reaction vessel at constant volume.

20 Sulfur dioxide gas and oxygen gas were mixed at 600°C to produce a gaseous equilibrium mixture:

$$2SO_2(g) + O_2(g) \rightleftharpoons 2SO_3(g)$$

A number of changes were then made, including the addition of a catalyst, resulting in the formation of new equilibrium mixtures. The graph below shows how the concentrations of the three gases changed.

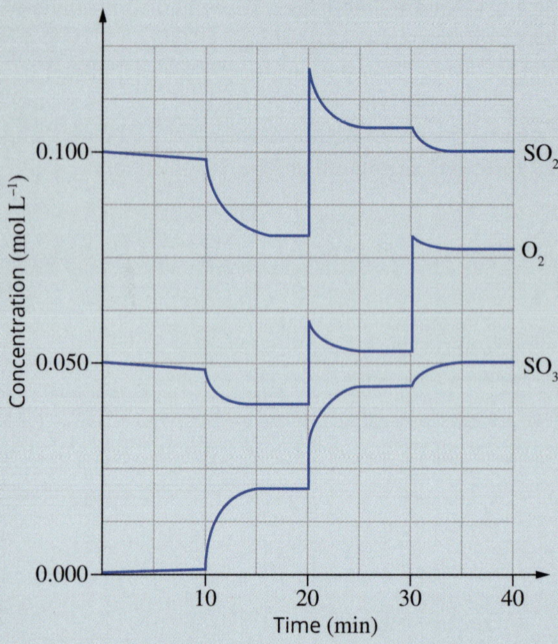

a Write an expression for the equilibrium constant, K_{eq}, of the reaction.

b During which time intervals was the reaction at equilibrium?

c Calculate the value of K_{eq} at 18 minutes.

d At what time was the catalyst added? Explain your reasoning.

e Calculate the value of K_{eq} at 25 minutes.

f What changes were made to the system at 20 minutes?

21 Reflect on the Inquiry activity on page 92. Explain your observations in terms of Le Châtelier's principle.

05 Solubility and equilibria

Think back to the last time you dissolved a solid in a liquid. One moment the solid has volume, shape and possibly colour; the next it is added to water and, with a little bit of stirring, it quickly seems to disappear.

Water is often described as the universal solvent because of the wide range of substances it can dissolve. However, some ionic substances are sparingly soluble in water, and an equilibrium is established between the undissolved solid and the ions in solution.

In this chapter, you will learn how to predict whether a compound is likely to be soluble, and relate the solubility of an ionic compound to its equilibrium constant.

Content

INQUIRY QUESTION

How does solubility relate to chemical equilibrium?

By the end of this chapter, you will be able to:

- describe and analyse the processes involved in the dissolution of ionic compounds in water
- investigate the use of solubility equilibria by Aboriginal and Torres Strait Islander peoples when removing toxicity from foods, for example: **AHC**
  - toxins in cycad fruit
- conduct an investigation to determine solubility rules, and predict and analyse the composition of substances when two ionic solutions are mixed, for example:
  - potassium chloride and silver nitrate
  - potassium iodide and lead nitrate
  - sodium sulfate and barium nitrate (ACSCH065)
- derive equilibrium expressions for saturated solutions in terms of K_{sp} and calculate the solubility of an ionic substance from its K_{sp} value **ICT** **N**
- predict the formation of a precipitate given the standard reference values for K_{sp}

Chemistry Stage 6 Syllabus © NSW Education Standards Authority for and on behalf of the Crown in right of the State of NSW, 2017.

5.1 Process of dissolution of ionic compounds

Water is an excellent **solvent**. This is one of its most important properties. Almost all biological processes and many industrial processes occur in water. These systems are known as **aqueous** environments.

When substances are dissolved in water, the particles are free to move throughout the **solution**. When two aqueous reactants are combined in a reaction vessel, the dissolved reactant particles mix freely. This increases the chances of the reactants coming into contact. Because of the increased movement of the reactant particles, interactions between reactants are generally much more effective than if the same reactants were mixed as solids.

In Figure 5.1.1 you can see how the deep purple colour of potassium permanganate spreads through the water as the solid dissolves. Eventually the liquid will appear completely purple as the particles continue to mix and move.

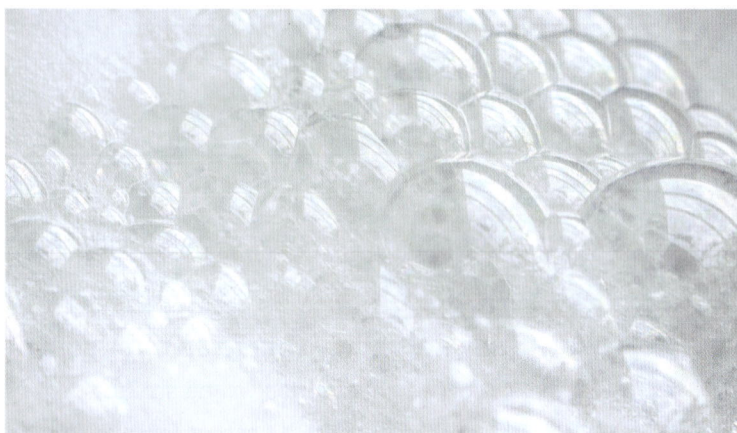

FIGURE 5.1.1 When solid potassium permanganate is added to water, it dissolves. The particles disperse into the solution and move around freely.

Although many ionic substances are readily soluble in water, like the Epsom salts seen at high magnification in the chapter opener image, some are not. This section looks at what happens when ionic substances dissolve in water, and reviews the solubility of ions in water.

GO TO ➤ Year 11 Chapter 14

REVISION

Dissolution of ionic substances in water

Water molecules are polar: the oxygen atom has a partial negative charge and the hydrogen atoms have a partial positive charge. When an ionic substance is added to water, the hydrogen atoms of the water molecules are attracted to the negatively charged ions and the oxygen atoms of the water molecules are attracted to the positively charged ions. The attraction between the water molecules and the ions is known as **ion–dipole attraction**. When these ion–dipole attractions are strong enough, the ions are removed from the ionic lattice and enter the solution. When an ion is surrounded by water molecules, it is said to be **hydrated.**

Figure 5.1.2 shows the hydration of sodium and chloride ions. Note the orientation of the water molecules: the hydrogen atoms of the water molecules (white) are oriented towards the negatively charged chloride ions (green), whereas the oxygen atoms of the water molecules (red) are oriented towards the sodium ions (yellow).

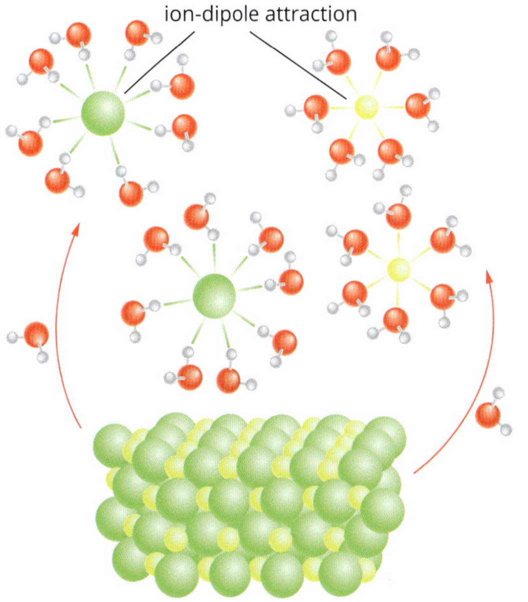

ion-dipole attraction

FIGURE 5.1.2 Ion–dipole attraction between the ions and adjacent water molecules to form hydrated sodium and chloride ions

DISSOLUTION OF AN IONIC COMPOUND IN WATER

Sports drinks are used by athletes to replace the electrolytes lost in sweat (Figure 5.1.3). The electrolytes are dissolved ionic substances such as sodium chloride and potassium phosphate.

Sodium chloride is a typical ionic compound that exists as a solid at room temperature. Figure 5.1.4 shows the arrangement of sodium cations (Na^+) and chloride anions (Cl^-) in a three-dimensional ionic lattice. The ions are held together by strong electrostatic forces between the positive and negative charges of the ions.

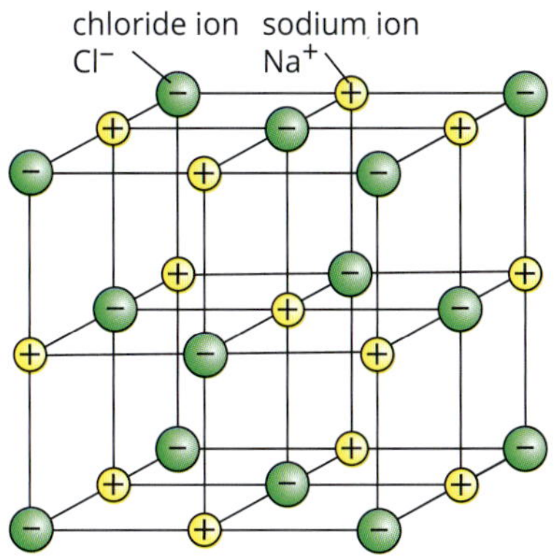

chloride ion   sodium ion
Cl^- Na^+

FIGURE 5.1.4 A representation of the crystal lattice of the ionic compound sodium chloride.

FIGURE 5.1.3 Sports drinks are used by athletes to replace water and dissolved ionic solutes.

The process of separating positive and negative ions from a solid ionic compound to form hydrated ions when an ionic compound dissolves in water is called **dissociation**.

Although the ionic bonds within the lattice are strong, the ions can be pulled away from the lattice by the interactions of many water molecules.

In summary, when sodium chloride dissolves in water:

- ionic bonds within the sodium chloride lattice are broken
- hydrogen bonds between water molecules are broken
- ion–dipole attractions form between ions and polar water molecules.

An equation can be written to represent the dissociation process:

$$NaCl(s) \xrightarrow{H_2O(l)} Na^+(aq) + Cl^-(aq)$$

Note that the formula of water sits above the arrow. This is because there is no direct reaction between the water and the sodium chloride. No chemical change occurs; only the state symbol for sodium chloride is altered from solid (s) to aqueous (aq), indicating it is now dissolved in water. (You may omit the H_2O from this equation if you wish.)

It is important to note that the dissociation of ionic compounds is simply freeing ions from the lattice so that they move freely throughout the solution. This is different from the ionisation of molecular compounds such as gaseous hydrogen chloride, where new ions are formed by the reaction of the molecule with water.

> **i** Ionic substances dissolve by dissociation. Ion–dipole attractions are formed between the ions and water molecules.

CHEMFILE PSC

Blood plasma

The human body is 66% water by weight. In biological organisms, water transports nutrients and soluble wastes, as well as essential reagents for chemical reactions to cells and tissues. The circulatory system of the body forms a transportation network (Figure 5.1.5). Essential nutrients, ions and molecules dissolved in water in the blood are carried to the organs, brain and tissues, and waste is carried away. This part of the blood is a component called plasma.

Plasma is a yellow substance that makes up over half of the blood volume in the body. Sodium chloride is present in blood plasma. Sodium and chloride ions play a vital role in many bodily functions, including regulating blood pressure and maintaining cell membrane potentials. Although plasma is more than 90% water, it can be used in the treatment of a range of conditions, including burns, haemophilia and immune disorders. Its medical versatility is due to the small amount of dissolved proteins that it contains, including coagulation factors, albumin and immunoglobulins. These proteins can be isolated from donated plasma and used in medical treatment. For instance, coagulation factors can be given to those who suffer from blood clotting conditions such as haemophilia.

Although blood plasma can be stored frozen for a year, it may take over one hundred donations to create one bag of plasma. It is for this reason that blood plasma donations are always needed.

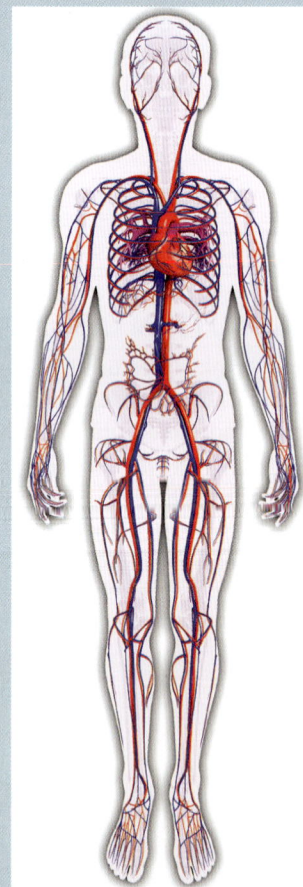

FIGURE 5.1.5 Plasma transports many substances, including dissolved salts, proteins, glucose and lipids around the body via the circulatory system.

Prussian blue and radiation poisoning

Prussia was a European state covering parts of modern Germany and Poland. In the early 18th century the first artificial dye was synthesised in Berlin, the Prussian capital. The deep blue pigment, chemically known as ferric ferrocyanide, with the formula $Fe_4[Fe(CN)_6]_3$, was used to colour the jackets of the Prussian army (Figure 5.1.6). For this reason the pigment has long been known as Prussian blue. Variations of Prussian blue are variously known as Turnbull's blue, bronze blue and Milori blue. Cyanide was first isolated from this pigment; its name comes from *kuanos*, the Greek word for dark blue.

Prussian blue also has a more surprising use: treating people with radiation sickness. In 1969 German pharmacologist Horst Heydlauf published an article in the *European Journal of Pharmacology* entitled 'Ferric-cyanoferrate (II): An effective antidote in thallium poisoning'. Heydlauf's breakthrough meant that thallium poisoning, once considered invariably fatal, could be treated. In Australia thallium was once sold as a rat poison called Thall-rat. Despite a string of thallium poisonings, Thall-rat was not banned until 1954, following several highly publicised cases of murder and attempted murder in NSW.

Prussian blue can also be used to treat caesium poisoning. In 1987 a cancer treatment device containing radioactive caesium was stolen from an abandoned hospital in Brazil and dismantled in the local community. As a result, 250 people were exposed to significant amounts of radiation. Prussian blue was used to treat these people, and as a result only four died from the effects of radiation exposure.

FIGURE 5.1.6 Prussian field marshal August Neidhart von Gneisenau (1760–1831). The deep blue of his jacket comes from Prussian blue dye.

INSOLUBLE IONIC COMPOUNDS

The solubility of a substance is a measure of how much of the substance will dissolve in a given amount of **solvent**. For example, sodium chloride is very soluble in water. A saline drip containing sodium chloride is often used during medical procedures to replenish body fluids in patients (Figure 5.1.7). However, many ionic substances are far less soluble.

FIGURE 5.1.7 A saline drip is a solution of sodium chloride.

Insoluble ionic compounds do not dissolve in water because the energy required to separate the ions from the lattice is greater than the energy released when the ions are hydrated.

Although substances are usually described as either soluble or insoluble, this is a generalisation. Substances that are described as insoluble tend to dissolve very slightly.

Definition of solubility

In chemistry, the term **solubility** has a specific meaning. It refers to the maximum amount of a **solute** (substance that is dissolved) that can be dissolved in a given quantity of a solvent (usually 100 g) at a certain temperature. Table 5.1.1 gives the solubility of some substances in 1 L of water at 25°C.

TABLE 5.1.1 Solubility of selected solutes at 25°C

Solute	Solubility in water (mol L^{-1})
sodium chloride	6.3
calcium hydroxide	0.016
calcium carbonate	6.0×10^{-6}

There are a number of ways that chemists describe the solubility of ionic substances. A simple version is as follows:

- When a substance is **soluble**, more than 0.1 mol of the substance will dissolve in 1 L of water.
- When a substance is **insoluble**, less than 0.01 mol of the substance will dissolve in 1 L of water.
- When a substance is **slightly soluble**, 0.01–0.1 mol of the substance will dissolve in 1 L of water.

Using this scale, sodium chloride is soluble, calcium carbonate is insoluble and calcium hydroxide is slightly soluble.

Solubility rules

Sometimes when two ionic solutions are mixed the ions interact to form a new substance with a lower solubility. This substance may be an insoluble solid, called a **precipitate.** To determine whether two ionic solutions will form a precipitate, you can either conduct an experiment or use the solubility rules.

Worked example 5.1.1 on page 120 shows you how to use the solubility rules to determine if two ionic solutions will form a precipitate.

SKILLBUILDER WE

Mixing solutions to form a precipitate

While this chapter explains how to use solubility rules to determine whether a precipitate is formed, you may want to confirm your working experimentally.

When mixing two solutions to form a precipitate, you need to remember the following points.

- Wear safety goggles. Your teacher or lab technician will tell you if you also need to wear gloves.
- Place the beaker you will be pouring the solutions into on a flat surface.
- Stand when pouring the solution.
- Slowly trickle the second solution down the inside of the beaker to form the best precipitate. If you add the solution quickly or do not trickle it down the inside of the beaker, the precipitate will trap bubbles and will not be as clear.
- Bring your eyes down to the beaker to observe the precipitate; never hold the beaker up to eye level.
- Ask your teacher or lab technician how to dispose of the remaining solutions and precipitate properly.

REVISION

GO TO ➤ Year 11 Chapter 10

In Year 11 you learnt the SNAAP rule that helps to remember which anions and cations never form precipitates:

- **S**odium (Na^+)
- **N**itrate (NO_3^-)
- **A**mmonium (NH_4^+)
- **A**cetate (CH_3COO^-)
- **P**otassium (K^+)

When you write ionic equations, these are regarded as **spectator ions**. For other ionic compounds you can refer to a **solubility table**. Tables 5.1.2 and 5.1.3 identify some combinations of ions that will form a precipitate, and to what extent they do this.

TABLE 5.1.2 Relative solubilities of soluble ionic compounds

Soluble in water ($>0.1\,mol\,L^{-1}$ at 25°C)	Exceptions: insoluble ($<0.1\,mol\,L^{-1}$ at 25°C)	Exceptions: slightly soluble ($0.01–0.1\,mol\,L^{-1}$ at 25°C)
most chlorides (Cl^-), bromides (Br^-) and iodides (I^-)	$AgCl$, $AgBr$, AgI, PbI_2	$PbCl_2$, $PbBr_2$
all nitrates (NO_3^-)	no exceptions	no exceptions
all ammonium (NH_4^+) salts	no exceptions	no exceptions
all sodium (Na^+) and potassium (K^-) salts	no exceptions	no exceptions
all acetates (CH_3COO^-)	no exceptions	no exceptions
most sulfates (SO_4^{2-})	$SrSO_4$, $BaSO_4$, $PbSO_4$	$CaSO_4$, Ag_2SO_4

TABLE 5.1.3 Relative solubilities of insoluble ionic compounds

Insoluble in water ($<0.1\,mol$ dissolves in 1 L at 25°C)	Exceptions: soluble ($>0.1\,mol$ dissolves in 1 L at 25°C)*	Exceptions: slightly soluble ($0.01–0.1\,mol$ dissolves in 1 L at 25°C)
most hydroxides (OH^-)	$NaOH$, KOH, $Ba(OH)_2$, NH_4OH, $AgOH$	$Ca(OH)_2$, $Sr(OH)_2$
most carbonates (CO_3^{2-})	Na_2CO_3, K_2CO_3, $(NH_4)_2CO_3$	no exceptions
most phosphates (PO_4^{3-})	Na_3PO_4, K_3PO_4, $(NH_4)_3PO_4$	no exceptions
most sulfides (S^{2-})	Na_2S, K_2S, $(NH_4)_2S$	no exceptions

* NH_4OH does not exist in significant amounts in an ammonia solution. Ammonium and hydroxide ions readily combine to form ammonia and water. AgOH readily decomposes to form a precipitate of silver oxide and water.

WS
5.5

Worked example 5.1.1

DETERMINING WHETHER A PRECIPITATE WILL FORM FROM TWO IONIC SOLUTIONS

Determine whether a precipitate will be formed when a solution of potassium chloride and a solution of silver nitrate are mixed. If so, identify the precipitate.

Thinking	Working
Identify the ions that are present in each ionic solution.	Potassium (K^+), chloride (Cl^-), silver (Ag^+) and nitrate (NO_3^-)
Identify any spectator ions.	Potassium (K^+) and nitrate (NO_3^-) never form precipitates.
Identify the remaining ions.	Chloride (Cl^-) and silver (Ag^+)
Use the solubility tables to determine if this combination of ions is insoluble.	Chloride (Cl^-) and silver (Ag^+) form an insoluble compound, so a precipitate of silver chloride will form.

Worked example: Try yourself 5.1.1

DETERMINING WHETHER A PRECIPITATE WILL FORM FROM TWO IONIC SOLUTIONS

Determine whether a precipitate will be formed when a solution of sodium hydroxide and a solution of barium acetate are mixed. If so, identify the precipitate.

5.1 Review

SUMMARY

- Many ionic substances are readily soluble in water.
- When ionic substances dissolve, ion–dipole attractions between the ions and water molecules cause the ionic lattice to dissociate. The ions are said to be hydrated.

- Ionic substances can be classified as soluble, slightly soluble or insoluble.
- The solubility rules are a guide to the solubility of substances.

KEY QUESTIONS

1 Sodium nitrate ($NaNO_3$) and calcium hydroxide ($Ca(OH)_2$) will dissociate when they dissolve in water. Write chemical equations to represent the dissolving process for each of these compounds.

2 Explain the process of the dissolution of potassium bromide.

3 Write the formulae for the ions produced when these compounds dissolve in water:
   a sodium carbonate
   b calcium nitrate
   c potassium bromide
   d iron(III) sulfate
   e copper(II) chloride

4 Which of the following substances would you expect to be soluble in water?
   A sodium sulfate
   B lead(II) carbonate

   C magnesium hydroxide
   D silver nitrate
   E iron(III) chloride
   F barium phosphate
   G ammonium chloride
   H potassium carbonate
   I silver sulfide
   J calcium acetate

5 Predict whether a precipitate will form when the following solutions are mixed. If a precipitate forms, state its chemical name.
   a silver nitrate and iron(III) chloride
   b potassium hydroxide and aluminium sulfate
   c copper(II) bromide and ammonium phosphate
   d sodium sulfate and zinc acetate
   e lead(II) nitrate and iron(II) iodide
   f magnesium iodide and calcium chloride.

5.2 Solubility of ionic compounds and equilibrium

Ionic substances classified as insoluble may still dissolve to some extent. For example, limestone ($CaCO_3$) is classified as insoluble in water. Limestone caves, such as those seen in Figure 5.2.1, are formed over a long period of time as $CaCO_3$ is dissolved and redeposited.

FIGURE 5.2.1 Stalactites and stalagmites form when limestone (calcium carbonate) dissolves over very long periods of time.

The solubility of ionic compounds in water depends on the difference in the energy required to separate the ions from the lattice, and the energy released when the ions are hydrated. This section investigates the relationship between solubility and chemical equilibrium.

SATURATED SOLUTIONS

In the previous section you saw that sodium chloride dissociates in water according to the following equation:

$$NaCl(s) \xrightarrow{H_2O(l)} Na^+(aq) + Cl^-(aq)$$

Sodium chloride is highly soluble in water, so if a small amount of solid is added to a large volume of water the dissociation can be considered to go to completion. Solutions of sodium chloride are usually **unsaturated solutions**: solutions that contain less than the maximum amount of solute that can be dissolved at a particular temperature. In fact, at 25°C up to 36 g of sodium chloride can be added to 100 g of water before the sodium chloride stops dissolving. At this point the solution would be a **saturated solution**: a solution that contains the maximum amount of solute that can be dissolved at a particular temperature.

Some ionic compounds are classified as insoluble. For example, silver chloride is considered to be insoluble in water. However, this is not strictly true: 0.002 g of silver chloride will dissolve in 100 g of water at 25°C. So it is more accurate to call insoluble compounds **sparingly soluble**. Because only very small amounts of sparingly soluble salts dissolve, they readily form saturated solutions. For example, any amount greater than 0.002 g of silver chloride in 100 g of water will form a saturated solution.

ℹ️ Unsaturated solutions are able to dissolve more solute. Saturated solutions are unable to dissolve any more solute at a particular temperature.

ℹ️ Sparingly soluble ionic compounds are those that only dissolve to a very small extent. Only very small amounts of these salts are needed to form a saturated solution.

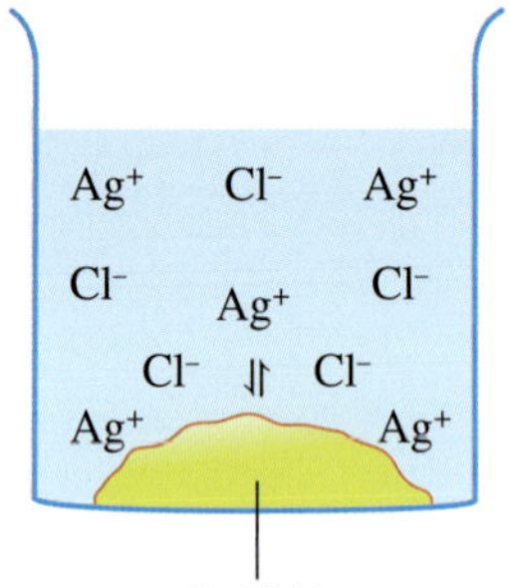

FIGURE 5.2.2 In a saturated solution of AgCl, the Ag^+ and Cl^- ions are breaking away from the ionic lattice at the same rate as they are returning to it. The system is in an equilibrium state.

GO TO ➤ Section 3.1 page 74

ⓘ In writing the equilibrium expression for a sparingly soluble salt, only the aqueous ions are included.

ⓘ The solubility product is the product of the concentration of ions in a saturated solution of a sparingly soluble salt.

ⓘ The ionic product equals K_{sp} only when a solution is saturated.

If 1 g of silver chloride crystals is added to 100 g of water, 0.002 g will dissolve and the remaining 0.998 g will remain as a solid. But if you could observe this on the atomic level, you would see that the shape of the ionic crystal lattice is constantly changing. Silver and chloride ions are continually breaking away from the lattice and returning to it. Because ions are leaving the lattice at the same rate that others are returning to it, the system is at equilibrium (Figure 5.2.2). This can be represented by an ionic equation:

$$AgCl(s) \rightleftharpoons Ag^+(aq) + Cl^-(aq)$$

Note that an equilibrium arrow is used. When a soluble substance dissolves it is assumed that the solid dissolves completely, so only the forward reaction occurs. But for sparingly soluble salts an equilibrium arrow shows that the rate of dissolution is the same as the rate of precipitation. The position of equilibrium lies very far to the left when sparingly soluble salts dissolve; although the rate of dissolution is the same as the rate of precipitation, most of the ions remain in the ionic lattice.

SOLUBILITY PRODUCT

In Chapter 3 you learnt to use the equilibrium constant K_{eq}. For the reaction:

$$aW + bX \rightleftharpoons cY + dZ$$

the equilibrium expression is:

$$K_{eq} = \frac{[Y]^c[Z]^d}{[W]^a[X]^b}$$

Equilibrium expressions for saturated solutions

The equation for the dissociation of silver chloride in water is:

$$AgCl(s) \rightleftharpoons Ag^+(aq) + Cl^-(aq)$$

The equilibrium expression for this reaction is therefore:

$$K_{eq} = \frac{[Ag^+][Cl^-]}{[AgCl]}$$

The reaction is heterogeneous: the silver ions and the chloride ions are aqueous and the silver chloride is solid. You will recall from Chapter 3 that, for heterogenous equilibria, the concentration of a pure liquid or solid is assigned the value of 1. Therefore the silver chloride can be removed from the equilibrium expression.

This gives the **solubility product**, K_{sp}:

$$K_{sp} = [Ag^+][Cl^-]$$

The product of the concentrations of the individual ions of a sparingly soluble salt present in a particular solution, whether it is saturated or not, is called the **ionic product**. For example, the ionic product of a silver chloride solution is represented by $[Ag^+][Cl^-]$. If the solution is saturated, the ionic product is equal to K_{sp}.

If a solution is unsaturated, all of the solid will dissolve and no equilibrium will be established between the solid and the aqueous ions.

Worked example 5.2.1

WRITING EQUILIBRIUM EXPRESSIONS IN TERMS OF K_{sp}

Write the equilibrium expression for a saturated solution of copper(II) hydroxide.

Thinking	Working
Check the solubility tables to determine if this combination of ions is insoluble.	Copper (Cu^{2+}) and hydroxide (OH^-) are insoluble.
Write a balanced ionic equation.	$Cu(OH)_2(s) \rightleftharpoons Cu^{2+}(aq) + 2OH^-(aq)$
Write the expression for K_{sp}.	$K_{sp} = [Cu^{2+}][OH^-]^2$

Worked example: Try yourself 5.2.1

WRITING EQUILIBRIUM EXPRESSIONS IN TERMS OF K_{sp}

Write the equilibrium expression for a saturated solution of silver carbonate.

Calculating the solubility of an ionic compound

Because the value of an equilibrium constant depends on temperature, K_{sp} values only apply to specific temperatures. Table 5.2.1 lists the values for a range of ionic compounds at 25°C.

TABLE 5.2.1 K_{sp} values for some common ionic substances at 25°C

Ionic substance	K_{sp} (at 25°C)
AgCl	1.77×10^{-10}
AgBr	5.35×10^{-13}
BaSO$_4$	1.08×10^{-10}
CaCO$_3$	3.36×10^{-9}
PbCl$_2$	1.70×10^{-5}
Fe(OH)$_2$	4.87×10^{-17}
Ca$_3$(PO$_4$)$_2$	2.07×10^{-29}
Fe(OH)$_3$	2.79×10^{-39}

CHEMFILE S

Solubility and coral formation

Although corals look like plants, they are actually invertebrate animals closely related to sea anemones. Corals take in carbonate and calcium ions from seawater, which they convert into calcium carbonate, depositing the precipitate as their exoskeleton. Coral reefs are formed when many thousands of corals are linked by calcium carbonate secreted by algae that live among them (Figure 5.2.3).

Increasing atmospheric CO_2 has caused the ocean to become more acidic. When pH decreases, it becomes harder for corals to get the calcium carbonate that they need to maintain their skeletons. If the acidity of the oceans reaches the level that some have forecasted, the calcium carbonate that holds reefs together could dissolve.

FIGURE 5.2.3 A clownfish among coral on the Great Barrier Reef. The reef is under threat from increasing acidity in the ocean.

Precipitation and the first photographs

Englishman William Henry Fox Talbot had many strings to his bow (Figure 5.2.4). He was a Member of Parliament, a mathematician and an astronomer. He also translated cuneiform tablets from the ancient city-state of Nineveh. However, it was his lack of talent in sketching that led him to invent the process that formed the foundation of modern photography.

While staying at Lake Como in Italy in 1833, Talbot was frustrated by his inability to reproduce sketches from nature faithfully and began to experiment with methods to assist him. By soaking a sheet in sodium chloride then brushing it with silver nitrate, a precipitate of silver chloride was formed on the surface. The sheet was then placed in a simple camera, called a camera obscura. Where light hit the sheet, the silver chloride would decompose, leaving dark silver metal behind. He further refined his method by 'fixing' the sheet, removing the silver. This reduced exposure times dramatically (Figure 5.2.5).

The daguerreotype was the other main form of early photography; however, it could only produce a single print. Talbot's method produced a negative, which could be used to generate many copies of an image. Although many modifications have since been made to Talbot's method, the fundamental aspects of it are still used in black-and-white film photography today.

FIGURE 5.2.5 The insolubility of silver salts made early photography possible. Talbot took this image of his third daughter, Matilda, in the 1840s.

FIGURE 5.2.4 A photograph of Talbot taken in the 1840s

MOLAR SOLUBILITY

The molar concentration of a salt in a saturated solution is called its **molar solubility**. If the molar solubility of a salt is known, it can be used to calculate K_{sp}.

> ℹ The molar solubility of a salt is the number of moles that will dissolve in water to form 1 L of saturated solution.
>
> The molar solubility of a sparingly soluble salt can also be regarded to be the number of moles that will dissolve per litre of water to form a saturated solution. Since the salt is sparingly soluble, there is negligible effect on the volume of water, so the volume of solution is essentially the same.

An ICE table (also called a reaction table) can be used to calculate the equilibrium concentration of ions and thus K_{sp}. You used ICE tables for homogeneous equilbria questions in Chapter 3, but ICE tables for the dissolution of sparingly soluble salts are slightly different: there are no concentrations entered for the solid, and the change in concentration for the aqueous ions is always positive.

GO TO ➤ Section 3.3 page 83

Worked example 5.2.2

CALCULATING K_{sp} FROM SOLUBILITY DATA

Silver chloride is a sparingly soluble salt. At a certain temperature, 1 L of water can dissolve 1.33×10^{-5} mol of AgCl. Calculate K_{sp} for silver chloride at this temperature.

Thinking	Working
Construct an ICE table using each species in the balanced equation as the headings for the columns in the table. Insert three rows in the table labelled I (initial), C (change) and E (equilibrium): <table><tr><td></td><td colspan="2">Reactants ⇌ Products</td></tr><tr><td>I</td><td></td><td></td></tr><tr><td>C</td><td></td><td></td></tr><tr><td>E</td><td></td><td></td></tr></table>	Initially, there is no Ag^+ or Cl^- present, so the initial amounts of both are zero. When the maximum amount of silver chloride that can dissolve in 1 L of water (1.33×10^{-5} mol) is added, 1.33×10^{-5} mol of Ag^+ ions and 1.33×10^{-5} mol of Cl^- ions enter the solution. Therefore, the amount of Ag^+ and Cl^- ions at equilibrium is 1.33×10^{-5} mol for both. <table><tr><td></td><td>AgCl(s) ⇌</td><td>Ag^+(aq) +</td><td>Cl^-(aq)</td></tr><tr><td>I</td><td></td><td>0</td><td>0</td></tr><tr><td>C</td><td></td><td>$+1.33 \times 10^{-5}$ mol</td><td>$+1.33 \times 10^{-5}$ mol</td></tr><tr><td>E</td><td></td><td>1.33×10^{-5} mol</td><td>1.33×10^{-5} mol</td></tr></table>
Write the expression for K_{sp} and substitute the equilibrium concentrations. Calculate the equilibrium constant, K_{sp}.	Since there is 1 L of solution: $[Ag^+] = 1.33 \times 10^{-5}$ mol L^{-1} $[Cl^-] = 1.33 \times 10^{-5}$ mol L^{-1} $K_{sp} = [Ag^+][Cl^-]$ $= (1.33 \times 10^{-5})(1.33 \times 10^{-5})$ $= 1.77 \times 10^{-10}$

Worked example: Try yourself 5.2.2

CALCULATING K_{sp} FROM SOLUBILITY DATA

Magnesium hydroxide is a white solid that is commonly used in antacids. At 25°C, 1 L of water can dissolve 1.12×10^{-4} mol of $Mg(OH)_2$. Calculate K_{sp} for magnesium hydroxide at this temperature.

When comparing the relative solubility of salts, K_{sp} cannot always be used, because different salts may produce different numbers of ions in solution. K_{sp} can only be used to compare the solubility of salts that produce the same number of ions.

Silver chloride (AgCl) and calcium sulfate ($CaSO_4$) both produce two ions when they dissociate, so you can compare their relative solubility by referring to their K_{sp} values. The salt with the smaller value of K_{sp} is the less soluble. The K_{sp} of silver chloride is 1.77×10^{-10}, smaller than the K_{sp} of 4.93×10^{-5} of calcium sulfate hence silver chloride is less soluble that calcium sulfate.

CHAPTER 5 | SOLUBILITY AND EQUILIBRIA **125**

However, to compare the relative solubility of salts that produce different numbers of ions in solution, the molar solubility needs to be calculated for each. For example, calcium sulfate ($CaSO_4$) produces two ions when it dissociates, and lead(II) chloride ($PbCl_2$) produces three ions when it dissociates. These salts have similar K_{sp} values but different molar solubilities, as shown in Table 5.2.2.

TABLE 5.2.2 K_{sp} (at 25°C) and molar solubility of calcium sulfate and lead(II) chloride

Ion	K_{sp} (at 25°C)	Molar solubility (mol L^{-1})
calcium sulfate	4.93×10^{-5}	7.02×10^{-3}
lead(II) chloride	1.70×10^{-5}	1.62×10^{-2}

Worked example 5.2.3

CALCULATING MOLAR SOLUBILITY FROM K_{sp}

Lead(II) chloride has a K_{sp} value of 1.70×10^{-5} at 25°C. Calculate the molar solubility of lead(II) chloride at this temperature.

Thinking	Working
Construct a reaction table using each species in the balanced equation as the headings for the columns in the table. Insert three rows in the table labelled I (initial), C (change) and E (equilibrium): 	Initially, there is no Pb^{2+} or Cl^- present. When the lead(II) chloride is added to water, lead(II) ions and chloride ions enter the water in a 1:2 ratio. This can be represented by s.

Reactants $\rightleftharpoons$ Products		
I		
C		
E		

$PbCl_2(s) \rightleftharpoons Pb^{2+}(aq) + 2Cl^-(aq)$		
I	0	0
C	$+s$	$+2s$
E	s	$2s$

Write the expression for K_{sp} and substitute s for the equilibrium concentrations. Calculate the molar solubility, including the correct units.	$K_{sp} = [Pb^{2+}][Cl^-]^2$ $1.70 \times 10^{-5} = (s)(2s)^2$ $1.70 \times 10^{-5} = 4s^3$ $4.25 \times 10^{-6} = s^3$ Take the cube root of both sides: $s = 1.62 \times 10^{-2}$ The molar solubility of lead(II) chloride is 1.62×10^{-2} mol L^{-1}

Worked example: Try yourself 5.2.3

CALCULATING MOLAR SOLUBILITY FROM K_{sp}

Zinc hydroxide has a K_{sp} value of 3.8×10^{-17} at 25°C. Calculate the molar solubility of zinc hydroxide at this temperature.

Predicting the formation of a precipitate

Earlier in this section you saw that the ionic product is the product of the concentration of ions of a sparingly soluble salt present in a solution. If the ionic product is equal to or greater than K_{sp} the solution is saturated, and a precipitate will form. If the ionic product is less than K_{sp} the solution is unsaturated, and no precipitate will form. This is summarised in Table 5.2.3.

TABLE 5.2.3 Predicting the formation of a precipitate by comparing ionic product and K_{sp}

Value of ionic product compared with K_{sp}	Saturated or unsaturated?	Precipitate formed?
ionic product < K_{sp}	unsaturated	no
ionic product > K_{sp}	saturated	yes

Therefore, by calculating the ionic product and comparing this value to K_{sp}, you can predict whether or not a precipitate will form.

Worked example 5.2.4

PREDICTING THE FORMATION OF A PRECIPITATE GIVEN K_{sp}

Barium sulfate has a K_{sp} value of 1.08×10^{-10} at 25°C. If 1.0×10^{-3} g of barium sulfate is added to 1 L of water at 25°C, predict whether a precipitate will form.

Thinking	Working
Calculate the concentrations for the ions at equilibrium. Use the formulae: $$n = \frac{m}{M} \text{ and } c = \frac{n}{V}$$	There is 1.0×10^{-3} g of barium sulfate. $$n(BaSO_4) = \frac{m}{M}$$ $$= \frac{1.0 \times 10^{-3}}{233.43}$$ $$= 4.3 \times 10^{-6} \text{ mol}$$ $$c = \frac{n}{V}$$ $$= \frac{4.3 \times 10^{-6}}{1}$$ $$= 4.3 \times 10^{-6} \text{ mol L}^{-1}$$
Calculate the ionic product.	Assume that each mole of barium sulfate ($BaSO_4$) dissociates to form 1 mol of barium ions and 1 mol of sulfate ions. Therefore, when 4.3×10^{-3} mol of barium sulfate is added to 1 L of water, 4.3×10^{-3} mol of barium ions and 4.3×10^{-3} mol of sulfate ions are formed. $$\text{ionic product} = \left[Ba^{2+}\right]\left[SO_4^{2-}\right]$$ $$= (4.3 \times 10^{-6})(4.3 \times 10^{-6})$$ $$= 1.8 \times 10^{-11}$$
Compare the ionic product to the value of K_{sp}.	The ionic product is 1.8×10^{-11}. This value is smaller than the K_{sp} value of 1.08×10^{-10} at 25°C. No precipitate will form.

Worked example: Try yourself 5.2.4

PREDICTING THE FORMATION OF A PRECIPITATE GIVEN K_{sp}

Calcium fluoride has a K_{sp} value of 3.2×10^{-11} at 25°C. If 1.0×10^{-3} g of calcium fluoride is added to 1 L of water at 25°C, predict whether a precipitate will form.

Sometimes chemists have to prepare a solution that contains more than one salt. In this case they can calculate whether any combination of ions is insoluble at a given concentration. If one combination of ions is insoluble, they can predict whether a precipitate will form by comparing the K_{sp} value of the salt to the ionic product.

Supersaturated solutions

It is possible for a solution to have an ionic product that is greater than K_{sp}. A supersaturated solution is an unstable solution that contains more dissolved solute than a saturated solution. If this type of solution is disturbed, some of the solute will separate from the solvent as a solid.

Figure 5.2.6 shows a supersaturated solution of sodium acetate. Supersaturated sodium acetate is prepared by cooling a saturated solution very carefully so that solid crystals do not form. Adding a small seed crystal to the supersaturated solution causes the solute to crystallise (form solid crystals) so that a saturated solution remains.

FIGURE 5.2.6 Crystals of sodium acetate form after a seed crystal is added to a supersaturated solution of the compound.

PA 5.5   PA 5.5

WS 5.6   WS 5.8

Worked example 5.2.5

PREDICTING THE FORMATION OF A PRECIPITATE WHEN SOLUTIONS ARE MIXED

20 mL of 0.10 mol L^{-1} silver acetate and 20 mL of 0.050 mol L^{-1} sodium chloride are mixed together. Predict whether a precipitate will form and, if so, identify the precipitate.

Thinking	Working
Identify the ions that are present in each solution, and determine whether any combination of these ions is insoluble.	Silver (Ag$^+$), acetate (CH$_3$COO$^-$), sodium (Na$^+$) and chloride (Cl$^-$) ions are present. Silver and chloride ions combine to form an insoluble compound, so they could form a precipitate.
Identify the value of K_{sp} for the compound that could form a precipitate.	The value of K_{sp} for silver chloride is 1.77×10^{-10}.
Calculate the concentration of the ions that would form the precipitate. The concentrations of the solutions and the final volume of the mixture are used to determine the concentration of these ions in the mixture. Use the formula: $$c_1V_1 = c_2V_2$$	$[Ag^+]_{mixture} = \frac{c_1V_1}{V_2}$ $= \frac{0.10 \times 0.020}{0.040}$ $= 0.050$ mol L^{-1} $[Cl^-]_{mixture} = \frac{c_1V_1}{V_2}$ $= \frac{0.050 \times 0.020}{0.040}$ $= 0.025$ mol L^{-1}
Calculate the ionic product for this salt.	ionic product $= [Ag^+][Cl^-]$ $= (0.050)(0.025)$ $= 1.3 \times 10^{-3}$
Compare this to the value of K_{sp} for the salt.	This is greater than the value of K_{sp} for silver chloride. A precipitate will form.

Worked example: Try yourself 5.2.5

PREDICTING THE FORMATION OF A PRECIPITATE WHEN SOLUTIONS ARE MIXED

5.0 mL of 0.010 mol L^{-1} barium chloride and 20 mL of 0.010 mol L^{-1} sodium sulfate are mixed together. Predict whether a precipitate will form, and, if so, identify the precipitate.

The common ion effect

In this chemistry course you have examined only the equilibria of salts dissolved in pure water. However, it is possible to dissolve salts into solutions that already contain dissolved ions. If the salt added and the existing solution have an ion in common, it is called a common ion. The **common ion effect** greatly decreases the solubility of ionic compounds, meaning that they are far less soluble in solutions with a common ion than they are in pure water. Consider the dissolution of AgCl:

$$AgCl(s) \rightleftharpoons Ag^+(aq) + Cl^-(aq)$$

If solid AgCl is added to a solution containing NaCl, then Le Châtelier's principle indicates that the position of equilibrium will shift to the left, because of the chloride ions that are already present from the dissolved NaCl. Therefore the solubility of silver chloride is reduced by the presence of the common ion.

If a sparingly soluble salt is added to a solution with a common ion, then it can be assumed that the concentration of the common ion comes entirely from the ions that are already present in the solution, and none from the sparingly soluble salt. This can greatly simplify calculations that involve a common ion.

> ⓘ The common ion effect greatly reduces the solubility of salts.

WS 5.7

Worked example 5.2.6

CALCULATING THE EFFECT OF A COMMON ION ON THE MOLAR SOLUBILITY OF AN IONIC COMPOUND

Lead(II) chloride has a K_{sp} value of 1.70×10^{-5} at 25°C. Calculate its molar solubility in a $0.20 \, mol \, L^{-1}$ solution of NaCl.

Thinking	Working
Construct a reaction table using each species in the balanced equation as the headings for the columns in the table. Insert three rows in the table labelled I (initial), C (change) and E (equilibrium): **Reactants ⇌ Products** I C E	Initially, there is no Pb^{2+} present and $0.20 \, mol \, L^{-1}$ of Cl^-. When the lead(II) chloride is added to water, lead(II) ions and chloride ions enter the water in a 1:2 ratio. This can be represented by s. For 1 L of solution: $PbCl_2(s) \rightleftharpoons Pb^{2+}(aq) + 2Cl^-(aq)$ I: 0 / 0.20 C: $+s$ / $+2s$ E: s / $0.20 + 2s$
Assume that the solute that is being added makes a negligible contribution of the common ion in the solution. Assume that all of the common ion comes from the solute already in solution.	Since the amount of chloride ions contributed from dissolving lead(II) chloride is so small, it can be assumed that all of the chloride ions come from the NaCl solution, hence this value is used for the equilibrium concentration of Cl^-. $PbCl_2(s) \rightleftharpoons Pb^{2+}(aq) + 2Cl^-(aq)$ I: 0 / 0.20 C: $+s$ / 0 E: s / 0.20
Write the expression for K_{sp} and substitute s for the equilibrium concentrations. Calculate the molar solubility, including the correct units.	$K_{sp} = [Pb^{2+}][Cl^-]^2$ $1.70 \times 10^{-5} = (s)(0.20)^2$ $s = \frac{1.70 \times 10^{-5}}{(0.20)^2}$ $= 4.3 \times 10^{-4} \, mol \, L^{-1}$ The molar solubility of lead(II) chloride in $0.20 \, mol \, L^{-1}$ NaCl is $4.3 \times 10^{-4} \, mol \, L^{-1}$. Note that this is lower than the molar solubility of lead(II) chloride in water calculated in Worked example 5.2.3 ($1.62 \times 10^{-2} \, mol \, L^{-1}$).

Worked example: Try yourself 5.2.6

CALCULATING THE EFFECT OF A COMMON ION ON THE MOLAR SOLUBILITY OF AN IONIC COMPOUND

Silver bromide has a K_{sp} value of 5.35×10^{-13} at 25°C. Calculate its solubility in a $0.50 \, mol \, L^{-1}$ solution of NaBr.

DETOXIFYING FOOD

In many parts of the world there are nutrient-rich plants that contain toxins in their seeds or fruits, and Australia is no different. However, the ingenuity of Aboriginal and Torres Strait Islander people has enabled them to detoxify these foods and render them edible.

Cycads

In Year 11 chemistry you were introduced to the techniques used by Indigenous Australians to detoxify the seeds of the cycad, which contain the toxin cycasin. The seeds are crushed to expose the inner kernel and increase the surface area, and then either soaked in water to leach out the water-soluble toxins, or fermented until they are no longer toxic.

Aboriginal people in New South Wales used two leaching methods to detoxify cycads. Briefly roasting the seeds and then leaching them in water for a short period of time yielded cycad seeds that, although free of poison, did not keep well and had to be eaten quickly. Leaching the fruit for longer periods meant that the seeds did not need prior roasting and lasted longer. Another technique is ageing, where seeds that have lain underneath the trees for some months are collected, or the seeds are dried and stored or buried for several months.

Bitter yam

The Tiwi islands, off the coast of the Northern Territory, are thought to have been inhabited for at least 15 000 years. The Tiwi people, in their relative isolation, have developed a unique culture. One of their principal ceremonies is the kulama, or yam ceremony. The bitter yam (*Dioscorea bulbifera*), shown in Figure 5.2.7, contains oxalates that would be toxic if consumed. In the Tiwi islands the kulama ceremony ritualises the detoxification of the yam.

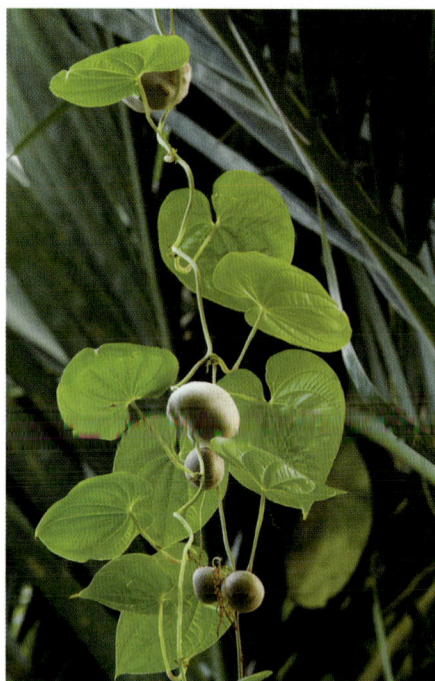

FIGURE 5.2.7 The bitter yam, *Dioscorea bulbifera*, occurs naturally in Africa and Asia, as well as northern Australia.

Tiwi creation stories explain how, in the creation time, a boobook owl man and barn owl woman performed the first kulama. The white-bellied sea-eagle joined the ceremony; according to the Tiwi creation story, it still wears its ceremonial head paint. The success of this kulama led the sea-eagle to conduct another kulama where bitter yam was prepared for the first time, demonstrating to the Tiwi how to prepare this otherwise toxic plant, and these processes have been followed ever since.

GO TO ▶ Year 11 Chapter 10

ℹ Cycad seeds are often mistaken for fruits because they have a fleshy outer layer, which is removed before they are prepared for eating.

CHEMFILE AHC

The Cicada Woman

In Arnhem land the Gunwinggu people also detoxify the bitter yam, which they call mangindjeg. According to their beliefs, the Cicada Woman, Ngalgindjeg-Ngalgindjeg, demonstrated the correct way to prepare mangindjeg to the Gunwinggu. She used the bone of a kangaroo to cut up the roots, which she roasted in an oven and then leached in water. Since then, the cicada's call tells the Gunwinggu that mangindjeg are ready to be dug up.

Towards the end of the wet season, a ring around the moon signals to the Tiwi that the moon man is performing kulama and that they, too, should begin. The yams are picked according to specific rules, with care being taken not to damage the roots. The yams are placed in running water to remove the oxalates by leaching. While this is taking place, an earth oven is prepared. When the oven is ready, the yams are roasted. The three days of the kulama ceremony feature singing, dancing and body painting. Such is the importance of kulama to the Tiwi that the ceremonial dance circle is a major feature of their art.

DS 5.1

WS 5.9   WS 5.10

CHEMISTRY IN ACTION   CCT   CC   L

The Marsh test

Arsenic has been used as a poison since the time of the Roman emperor Nero. Colourless, odourless and tasteless, arsenic could go undetected in food and drink. The symptoms of arsenic poisoning—cramps, vomiting and diarrhoea—could easily be mistaken for food poisoning. And because arsenic accumulates in the body, small doses could be given over long periods of time to slowly kill the victim.

In the 19th century arsenic was widely used in industry and homes. It was a component of Scheele's green, a pigment used in wallpaper, fabrics and food dyes. Powdered arsenic was available as a rat poison, meaning it was cheap and readily accessible, making it a poisoner's first choice.

In 1832 John Bodle was accused of poisoning his grandfather George with arsenic added to coffee grains. James Marsh was a chemist called upon by the prosecution to demonstrate that samples taken from George Bodle contained arsenic. He carried out the standard test of the day: adding hydrogen sulfide in the presence of hydrochloric acid. If a yellow precipitate formed, then the presence of arsenic would be confirmed.

The yellow precipitate, used as a pigment in Egypt and Asia in ancient times, is arsenic sulfide, also known as King's yellow or orpiment (Figure 5.2.9). It is a naturally occurring form of arsenic, and was called *zarnikh* by the Persians, from their word for gold. This became *arsenikon* in Greek, and led to the English name. The name *orpiment* is from the Latin for gold pigment.

Marsh carried out the test and the bright yellow precipitate appeared. However, in the time it took for the sample to get to court, it deteriorated and the colour faded. The defence were able to convince the jury that there was no arsenic present and Bodle was acquitted. Even worse for Marsh, Bodle later admitted his guilt, knowing that English law at the time meant that he could not be tried again. Frustrated, Marsh set about devising a better test.

The Marsh test for arsenic, as it is now known, was first used successfully in France in 1840 in the case of Madame Lafarge, who was convicted of poisoning of her husband. The test was used for more than 100 years (Figure 5.2.10). Today neutron bombardment can be used to detect minute amounts of arsenic.

FIGURE 5.2.9 Arsenic sulfide was used in ancient Egypt as a yellow pigment.

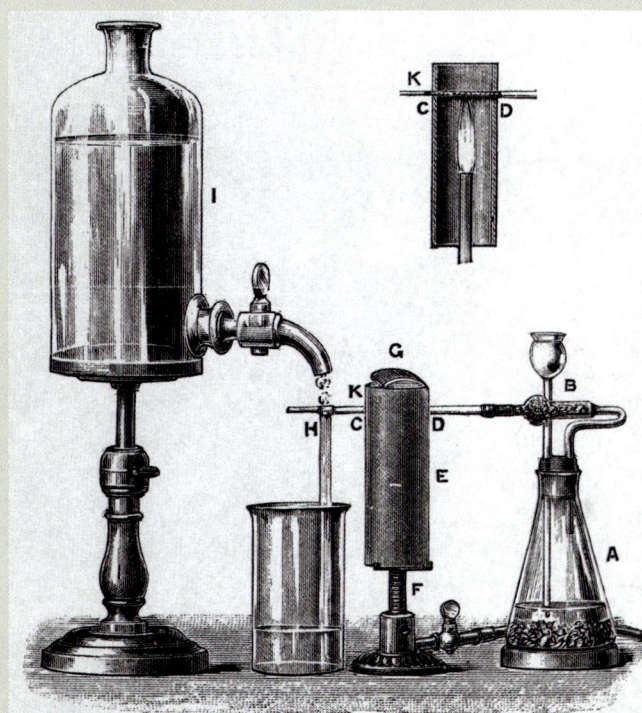

FIGURE 5.2.10 Arsenic detection apparatus used in the 19th century

5.2 Review

SUMMARY

- Salts that are considered insoluble do dissolve to a very small extent. These salts are best described as sparingly soluble.
- The solubility product, K_{sp}, is the product of the concentration of ions in a saturated solution of a sparingly soluble salt.
- The molar solubility of a salt is the number of moles that will dissolve per litre of water to form a saturated solution. Molar solubility can be used to calculate K_{sp} and vice versa.

- K_{sp} can be used to determine whether a precipitate will form.
- The common ion effect greatly reduces the solubility of salts.
- Aboriginal and Torres Strait Islander people use a range of methods to detoxify poisonous foods.

KEY QUESTIONS

1   Write equilibrium expressions for the dissolution of the following ionic compounds:
    a $CaSO_4$
    b $ZnCO_3$
    c PbI_2
    d $Fe(OH)_3$

2   The molar solubility of copper(II) hydroxide ($Cu(OH)_2$) was found to be $3.8 \times 10^{-7}\,mol\,L^{-1}$ at a certain temperature. Calculate the value of K_{sp} for $Cu(OH)_2$ at this temperature.

3   Calculate the molar solubility of strontium sulfate ($SrSO_4$) if its K_{sp} value at 25°C is 3.2×10^{-7}.

4   If 4.5 g of lead(II) bromide is added to a litre of water, will a precipitate form? The value of K_{sp} for $PbBr_2$ at 25°C is 6.60×10^{-6}.

5   Determine the molar solubility of silver chloride in a $0.15\,mol\,L^{-1}$ solution of NaCl.

6   State the toxin present in cycad seeds, and describe how Indigenous Australians detoxify the seeds.

Chapter review

KEY TERMS

aqueous
common ion effect
dissociation
hydrated
insoluble
ion–dipole attraction
ionic product

molar solubility
precipitate
saturated solution
slightly soluble
solubility
solubility product
solubility table

soluble
solute
solution
solvent
sparingly soluble
spectator ion
unsaturated solution

REVIEW QUESTIONS

1   a   What is the name given to the process that ionic solids undergo when dissolving in water?
    b   What ions will be produced when each of the following compounds is added to water?
        i $Cu(NO_3)_2$
        ii $ZnSO_4$
        iii $(NH_4)_3PO_4$

2   What ions would be produced when each of the following compounds is added to water?
    a   potassium carbonate
    b   lead(II) nitrate
    c   sodium hydroxide
    d   sodium sulfate
    e   magnesium chloride
    f   zinc nitrate
    g   potassium sulfide
    h   iron(III) nitrate.

3   Write equations to show the dissociation of the following compounds when they are added to water:
    a   magnesium acetate
    b   silver nitrate
    c   potassium bromide
    d   barium hydroxide
    e   sodium phosphate.

4   What type of attraction forms between ions and water molecules when an ionic compound dissociates in water?
    A   ionic bond
    B   ion–dipole attraction
    C   dispersion force
    D   dipole–dipole attraction

5   Briefly explain why the arrangement of water molecules around dissolved magnesium ions is different from that around dissolved chloride ions.

6   a   Write the formulae of three carbonate compounds that are soluble in water.
    b   Write the formulae of three carbonate compounds that are insoluble in water.

7   a   Write the formulae of three sulfate compounds that are soluble in water.
    b   Write the formulae of three sulfate compounds that are insoluble in water.

8   Using the information in Table 5.1.1 on page 118, calculate the mass of sodium chloride that can be added to 150 mL of water before it stops dissolving.

9   Use the solubility tables to identify the precipitate formed, if any, when the following solutions are mixed.
    a   silver acetate and potassium chloride
    b   sodium hydroxide and iron(II) chloride
    c   sodium iodide and lead(II) nitrate
    d   barium bromide and potassium nitrate.

10 a   Name the precipitate formed when aqueous solutions of the following compounds are mixed.
        i Na_2S and MgI_2
        ii K_2SO_4 and $Ba(NO_3)_2$
        iii $NaOH$ and $FeCl_3$
        iv NH_4Cl and $AgCH_3COO$
    b   Write a balanced chemical equation for each reaction.
    c   Write an ionic equation for the formation of each precipitate.

11 For each of the reactions in Question 10, identify the spectator ions.

12 Copy and complete the following table. Identify which reaction mixtures will produce precipitates and write their formulae.

	$MgSO_4$	KCl	NaOH	$AgNO_3$	$FeBr_2$
$Pb(CH_3COO)_2$					
K_2CO_3					
BaI_2					
Na_3PO_4					
NH_4S					

13 Species in which of the following states of matter are included in the equilibrium expression for a heterogeneous reaction?

A gases and pure liquids

B gases and pure solids

C aqueous solutions, gases and pure liquids

D aqueous solutions, gases and mixtures of liquids

14 Write ionic equations for the dissolution of the following compounds:

a $FeCl_2$ **b** $Al(OH)_3$

c Ag_2SO_4 **d** $Ba_3(PO_4)_2$

15 Write equilibrium expressions for the dissociation of the following compounds:

a $PbCl_2$ **b** $Zn(OH)_2$

c Ag_2CrO_4 **d** $BaSO_4$

16 For each of the pairs of salts listed, state which is the more soluble of the two.

a $BaSO_4$ ($K_{sp} = 1.08 \times 10^{-10}$) and $BaCO_3$ ($K_{sp} = 2.58 \times 10^{-9}$)

b $Zn(OH)_2$ ($K_{sp} = 3.8 \times 10^{-17}$) and $Fe(OH)_2$ ($K_{sp} = 4.87 \times 10^{-15}$)

c $PbCl_2$ ($K_{sp} = 1.70 \times 10^{-5}$) and PbI_2 ($K_{sp} = 9.8 \times 10^{-9}$)

17 Define the term 'molar solubility'.

18 Equations can be used to represent what occurs when ionic salts are added to water.

The equation for the dissolution of sodium chloride in water is:

$$NaCl(s) \xrightarrow{H_2O(l)} Na^+(aq) + Cl^-(aq)$$

The equation for silver chloride is:

$$AgCl(s) \rightleftharpoons Ag^+(aq) + Cl^-(aq)$$

Explain why an equilibrium arrow is used for the dissolution of silver chloride, but not for sodium chloride.

19 Explain why the change in concentration is always positive in an ICE table for the dissolution of sparingly soluble salts in water.

20 Calculate K_{sp} for the following substances:

a lead(II) bromide, given a molar solubility of 1.18×10^{-2} mol L^{-1} at 25°C

b barium sulfate, given a molar solubility of 1.04×10^{-5} mol L^{-1} at 25°C

c silver chromate (Ag_2CrO_4), given a molar solubility of 8.7×10^{-5} mol L^{-1} at 25°C.

21 Calculate the molar solubility of the following substances:

a zinc sulfide, given a K_{sp} of 2.0×10^{-25} at 25°C

b silver bromide, given a K_{sp} of 5.35×10^{-13} at 25°C

c silver sulfate given a K_{sp} of 1.20×10^{-5} at 25°C.

22 Explain why you cannot compare the K_{sp} values of silver cyanide (AgCN) and aluminium hydroxide ($Al(OH)_3$) to deduce their relative solubilities.

23 Calculate the masses of the following substances needed to form one litre of a saturated solution:

a lead(II) sulfate, given a K_{sp} of 2.53×10^{-8}

b silver sulfide, given a K_{sp} of 8.0×10^{-51}.

24 **a** Predict whether a precipitate will form in the following solutions:

    i 0.0010 g of silver carbonate is added to 100 mL of water. The K_{sp} of Ag_2CO_3 is 8.46×10^{-12} at 25°C.

    ii 0.20 g of copper(I) chloride is added to 1.0 L of water. The K_{sp} of CuCl is 1.9×10^{-7} at 25°C.

    iii 3.0×10^{-5} g of strontium chromate is added to 1.0 L of water. The K_{sp} of $SrCrO_4$ is 2.0×10^{-5} at 25°C.

b If a precipitate was not formed in the above solutions, calculate the total mass of salt that would need to be added to the water to form a saturated solution.

25 Predict whether a precipitate will form in the following instances:

a A 1.0 L solution contains 0.0030 mol L^{-1} NaI and 0.020 mol L^{-1} $Pb(NO_3)_2$

b A 1.0 L solution contains 0.0040 mol L^{-1} $(NH_4)_2CO_3$ and 3.0×10^{-5} mol L^{-1} $Mg(CH_3COO)_2$

c A 1.0 L solution contains 2.0×10^{-4} mol L^{-1} KCl and 5.0×10^{-6} mol L^{-1} $AgNO_3$.

26 Predict whether a precipitate will form if the following solutions are mixed:

a 10 mL of 0.0010 mol L^{-1} $AgCH_3COO$ and 10 mL of 0.0050 mol L^{-1} KBr

b 5.0 mL of 6.0×10^{-7} mol L^{-1} MgI_2 and 5.0 mL of 4.0×10^{-5} mol L^{-1} NaOH

c 20 mL of 1.0×10^{-4} mol L^{-1} $Pb(NO_3)_2$ and 5.0 mL of 0.020 mol L^{-1} $NaSO_4$.

27 Calculate the molar solubility of the following:

a lead(II) iodide in 0.050 mol L^{-1} potassium iodide solution (K_{sp} for lead(II) iodide is 9.8×10^{-9})

b iron(III) hydroxide in 0.020 mol L^{-1} sodium hydroxide solution (K_{sp} for iron(III) hydroxide is 2.79×10^{-39})

c zinc carbonate in 0.20 mol L^{-1} ammonium carbonate solution (K_{sp} for zinc carbonate is 1.4×10^{-11}).

28 **a** The value of K_{sp} for silver iodide is 8.52×10^{-17}. Calculate the molar solubility of silver iodide:

    i in pure water

    ii in 1.5 mol L^{-1} potassium iodide solution.

b Explain the difference in the calculated molar solubilities.

29 Explain how one food item was detoxified by Indigenous Australians.

30 Explain the purpose of crushing a cycad seed prior to leaching.

31 Reflect on the Inquiry activity on page 114. Using concepts from this chapter, explain why the dishwashing liquid did not produce suds in hard water.

REVIEW QUESTIONS

Equilibrium and acid reactions

Multiple choice

1   Which one of the following statements is correct in relation to an endothermic reaction?

A   The value of the activation energy is < 0 and the value of ΔH is < 0.

B   The value of the activation energy is < 0 and the value of ΔH is > 0.

C   The value of the activation energy is > 0 and the value of ΔH is > 0.

D   The value of the activation energy is > 0 and the value of ΔH is < 0.

The following information refers to Questions 2 and 3.

The energy profile diagram shown below is for the following reaction.

$$CO_2(g) + NO(g) \rightleftharpoons CO(g) + NO_2(g)$$

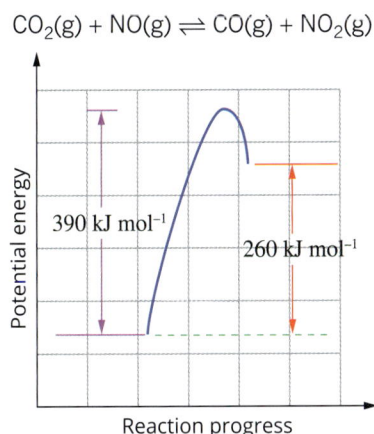

2   What is ΔH of the forward reaction, in $kJ\,mol^{-1}$?

A   −170

B   +130

C   +230

D   +260

3   What is the activation energy of the reverse reaction, in $kJ\,mol^{-1}$?

A   40

B   130

C   230

D   360

4   Consider the following reaction equations:

I $A(g) + B(g) \rightleftharpoons 2C(g)$ $\Delta H = +180\,kJ\,mol^{-1}$

II $D(g) + 3E_2(g) \rightleftharpoons 2F(g)$ $\Delta H = -90\,kJ\,mol^{-1}$

III $2G(g) \rightleftharpoons H(g) + I(g)$ $\Delta H = -180\,kJ\,mol^{-1}$

From a comparison of the enthalpy changes, ΔH, which of the following is definitely true?

A   Activation energy of equation I > activation energy of equation II.

B   Activation energy of equation I < activation energy of equation II.

C   Activation energy of equation I = activation energy of equation III.

D   No information about activation energy can be deduced.

5   Select the correct statement about an open system.

A   Neither energy nor matter are exchanged with the surroundings.

B   Energy can be exchanged with the surroundings but not matter.

C   Matter can be exchanged with the surroundings but not energy.

D   Energy and matter can both be exchanged with the surroundings.

6   Which of the following is an example of an irreversible reaction?

A   boiling an egg

B   freezing a sample of water

C   mixing of ethanol and water

D   the air trapped in a sealed soft drink container

7   Which of the following systems is not at equilibrium?

A   a sealed bottle of soft drink

B   a burning candle

C   a saturated solution of salt with solid salt on the bottom of the beaker

D   a gaseous reaction in a sealed container stored at constant temperature

8   Water vapour reacts with chlorine according to the following equation:

$$2H_2O(g) + 2Cl_2(g) \rightleftharpoons 4HCl(g) + O_2(g)$$

At a particular temperature, the value of the equilibrium constant, K_{eq}, for this reaction is 4.0×10^{-4}. At the same temperature, what is the the value of the equilibrium constant for the following reaction?

$$2HCl(g) + \tfrac{1}{2}O_2(g) \rightleftharpoons H_2O(g) + Cl_2(g)$$

A 2×10^{-4}

B 2×10^{-2}

C 2.5×10^3

D   50

9 Consider the following equation:
$$A + 3B \rightleftharpoons 2C + 4D$$
The correct expression for the equilibrium constant for this equation is:

A $\frac{[A][3B]^3}{[2C]^2[4D]^4}$

B $\frac{[C]^2[D]^4}{[A][B]^3}$

C $\frac{[A][B]^3}{[C]^2[D]^4}$

D $\frac{[2C][4D]}{[A][3B]}$

10 In which of the following reactions does increasing the concentration of W result in an initial increase the rate of the forward reaction?

I $2W + 2X \rightleftharpoons 2Y + Z$

II $X + W \rightleftharpoons Y + 2Z$

III $2X \rightleftharpoons 2W + Y$

A I and II only

B I and III only

C II and III only

D I, II and III

11 Examine the concentration-time diagram shown below.

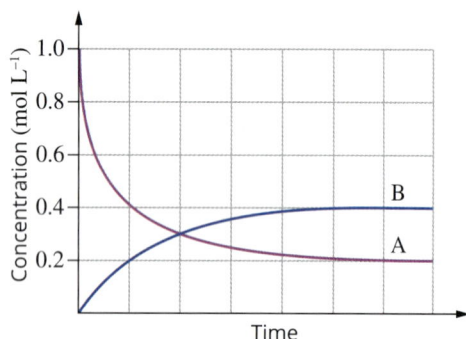

This graph could represent the concentrations of A and B in the reaction:

A $A \rightarrow B$

B $B \rightarrow A$

C $2A \rightarrow B$

D $A \rightarrow 2B$

12 In a sealed vessel, nitrogen monoxide, oxygen and nitrogen dioxide form the following equilibrium:
$$2NO(g) + O_2(g) \rightleftharpoons 2NO_2(g) \quad \Delta H = -114\,kJ\,mol^{-1}$$
Which one of the following sets of conditions is likely to lead to the highest yield of nitrogen dioxide gas?

A 200°C and 1 atm pressure

B 200°C and 2 atm pressure

C 300°C and 1 atm pressure

D 300°C and 2 atm pressure

13 A sample of NOCl is allowed to come to equilibrium according to the following equation:
$$2NOCl(g) \rightleftharpoons 2NO(g) + Cl_2(g)$$
The volume of the mixture is halved and the mixture is allowed to come to a new equilibrium, the temperature remaining constant. At the new equilibrium, which of the following is true concerning chlorine?

A Both the amount and concentration have decreased.

B The amount has increased and the concentration has decreased.

C The amount has decreased and the concentration has increased.

D Both the amount and concentration have increased.

14 The reaction between nitrogen monoxide and ozone is:
$$NO(g) + O_3(g) \rightleftharpoons NO_2(g) + O_2(g) \quad K_{eq} = 6 \times 10^{34} \text{ at } 25°C$$
Equal amounts of NO and O_3 are used. Which of the following statements cannot be inferred from the magnitude of the equilibrium constant?

A At equilibrium, $[NO_2][O_2] > [NO][O_3]$.

B The position of equilibrium of the reaction lies well to the right.

C The reaction has a low activation energy.

D Very little ozone will remain at equilibrium.

15 Carbon dioxide gas dissolves to a small extent in water, forming carbonic acid in an exothermic reaction.
$$CO_2(g) + H_2O(l) \rightleftharpoons H_2CO_3(aq) \quad \Delta H \text{ negative}$$
$$H_2CO_3(aq) + H_2O(l) \rightleftharpoons HCO_3^-(aq) + H_3O^+(aq)$$
This is the reaction involved in forming fizzy drinks. Which of the following strategies would not increase the amount of dissolved carbon dioxide?

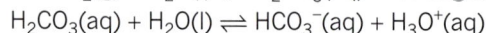

A increasing the amount of H_3O^+ in the solution

B decreasing the temperature of the solution

C increasing the concentration of carbon dioxide in the gas

D increasing the pressure of the carbon dioxide gas

16 When $(NH_4)_2SO_4$ powder is stirred into water, which of the following occurs?

A A precipitate is formed.

B N^{3-}, H^+ and SO_4^{2-} ions are released.

C NH_4^+ and SO_4^- ions are released.

D NH_4^+ and SO_4^{2-} ions are released.

17 A precipitate could be formed from the reaction between which of the following pairs of solutions?

A $Ba(NO_3)_2$ and NaCl

B $Ba(NO_3)_2$ and Na_2SO_4

C $NaNO_3$ and $BaCl_2$

D $BaCl_2$ and $Ba(NO_3)_2$

18 Which list contains only substances soluble in water?

A $ZnCO_3$, $BaSO_4$, KI

B $CaCO_3$, $AgCl$, KCH_3COO

C NH_4Cl, Na_3PO_4, KCH_3COO

D NH_4Cl, $AgCl$, $BaSO_4$

19 The molar solubility of Ag^+ ions in an AgBr solution at 25°C is 7.31×10^{-7} mol L^{-1}. What is the value of the solubility product constant for AgBr?

A 5.34×10^{-13}

B 7.31×10^{-7}

C 5.34×10^{-7}

D 8.44×10^{-4}

20 What is the equilibrium expression for the solubility product constant for $Ca_3(PO_4)_2$?

A $K_{sp} = [Ca_3(PO_4)_2]$

B $K_{sp} = [Ca^{2+}]^2[PO_4^{3-}]^2$

C $K_{sp} = [Ca^{2+}]^2[PO_4^{3-}]^3$

D $K_{sp} = [Ca^{2+}]^3[PO_4^{3-}]^2$

Short answer

1 An energy profile diagram is shown below.

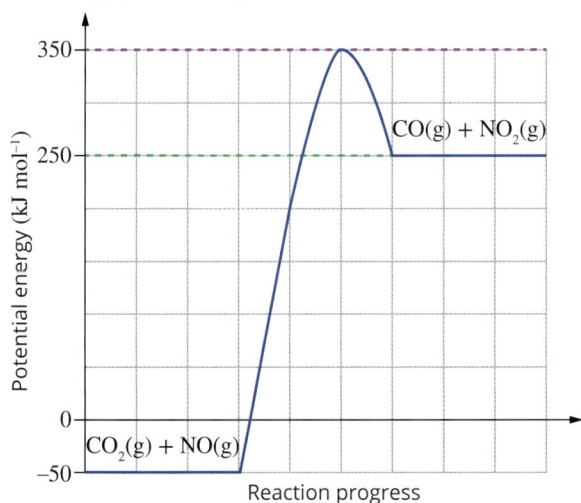

a Write a balanced equation for the reaction.

b What is the value of the activation energy for this reaction?

c What is the value of ΔH for this reaction?

d Is this reaction exothermic or endothermic?

2 Nitrogen and hydrogen gases can react to form ammonia. The equation is

$$N_2(g) + 3H_2(g) \rightleftharpoons 2NH_3(g)$$

a When 1 mol of nitrogen gas reacts with 4 mol of hydrogen gas,

  i will 2 mol of ammonia form?

  ii will all the nitrogen gas be gone when equilibrium is reached?

b A mixture of nitrogen and hydrogen gases is injected into an empty reactor and allowed to react until equilibrium is reached.

  i Has the reaction now stopped? Explain your answer.

  ii Will the amount of ammonia formed vary if the temperature is increased?

c If a sample of ammonia gas is injected into an empty reactor, will any reaction occur? Explain your answer.

3 Consider the following readily reversible gas–phase reaction.

$$W(g) + 2X(g) \rightleftharpoons Y(g) + Z(g)$$

The graph below shows the changes to the rates of the forward and reverse reactions when some additional reactant, W, is added to an equilibrium mixture of these gases at time T.

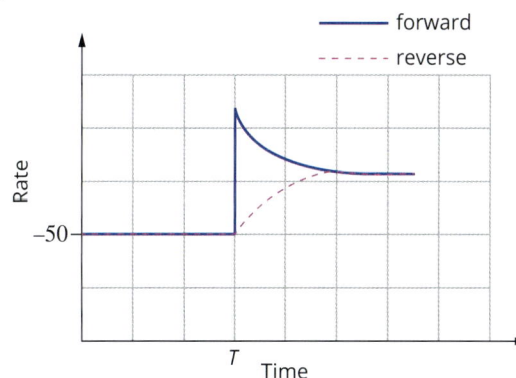

a Explain how this graph shows that the mixture was at equilibrium before time T.

b Use collision theory to account for the changes in the rates of the forward and reverse reactions from time T.

c The process was repeated several times, each time with a different change occurring at time T. Changes tested included:

- removing W from the mixture
- removing Y
- adding Y
- adding an inert gas (at constant volume)
- adding a catalyst
- increasing the volume of the container.

For each of the graphs below, select a change from this list that is consistent with the rate changes depicted. In each case, briefly justify your choice.

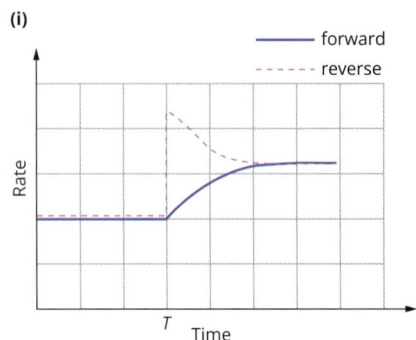

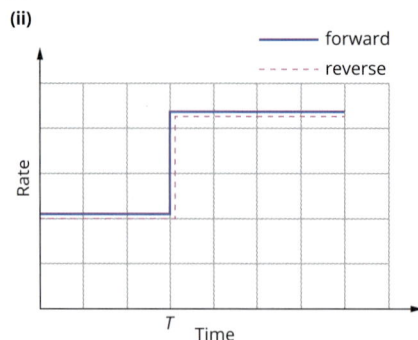

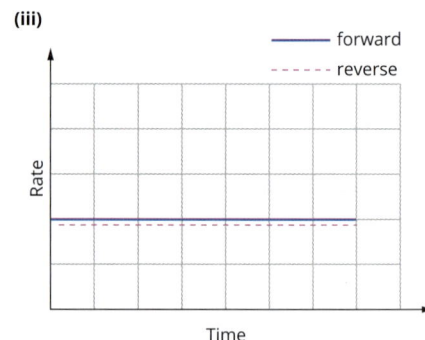

(i)

(ii)

(iii)

The graph below shows the rate changes after lowering the temperature at time T.

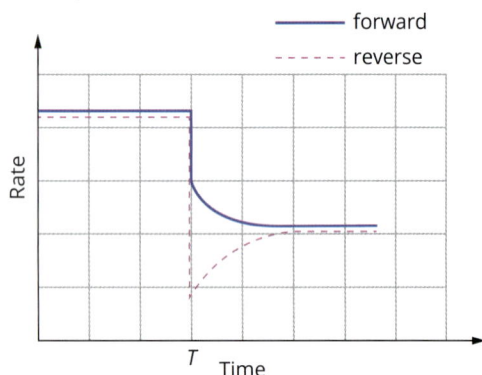

d Why does lowering the temperature cause an initial drop in both reaction rates?

e Considering the period during which the rates are unequal, in which direction does the equilibrium shift?

f Is the reaction exothermic or endothermic? Explain.

4 The gases dinitrogen tetroxide (N_2O_4) and nitrogen dioxide (NO_2) coexist according to the following equilibrium reaction.

$$N_2O_4(g) \rightleftharpoons 2NO_2(g)$$

A concentration–time graph for the system coming to equilibrium is shown below.

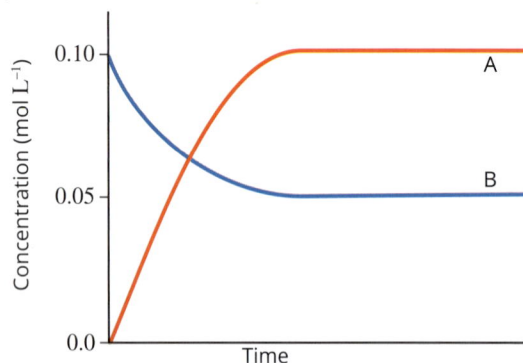

a Identify A and B.

b Write an expression for the equilibrium constant of the decomposition of N_2O_4.

c On the graph provided, sketch the line showing the effect on A if a catalyst had been present in the mixture from the beginning.

d Calculate K_{eq} for the reaction at equilibrium according to this concentration graph.

5 Carbon monoxide and iodine pentoxide react to form iodine and carbon dioxide in the equilibrium reaction.

$$5CO(g) + I_2O_5(s) \rightleftharpoons I_2(g) + 5CO_2(g) \quad \Delta H = -1175\,kJ\,mol^{-1}$$

Use your knowledge of Le Châtelier's principle to predict the effect (decrease, increase or no change) of the change (column 1) on the designated quantity (column 2). Assume that the change listed is the only one taking place (e.g. if I_2 is added, the volume and the temperature are kept constant).

	Change	Quantity	Increase/decrease/ no change
a	increase T	K_{eq}	
b	decrease T	amount of $I_2O_5(s)$	
c	add $I_2(g)$	K_{eq}	
d	add $CO_2(g)$	amount of $I_2(g)$	
e	double volume	amount of CO_2	
f	double volume	concentration of CO_2	
g	remove CO	amount of CO_2	
h	add catalyst	amount of $I_2(g)$	
i	add inert gas Ar	K_{eq}	

6 The reaction between hydrogen and iodine in the gaseous phase to produce hydrogen iodide is described by the following equation:

$$H_2(g) + I_2(g) \rightleftharpoons 2HI(g) \quad \Delta H \text{ negative}$$

The following diagram shows the change in concentration of gaseous hydrogen, iodine and hydrogen iodide as the equilibrium is reached and disturbed.

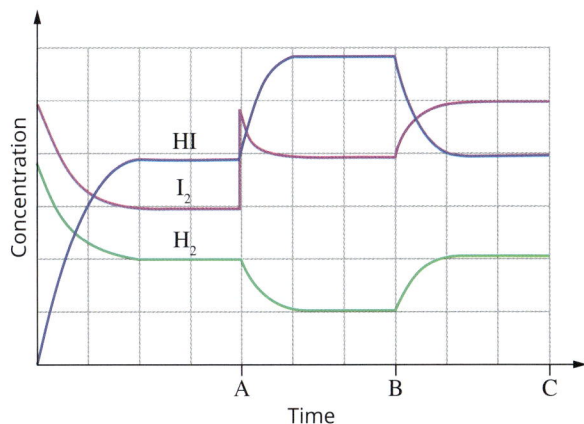

a At time A, a sudden change occurs to the system. What has happened?

b At time B, another change has occurred. What has happened?

c On the graph provided, mark an X on the time axis to indicate a point when the system is at equilibrium.

d Extend the graph past time C, until equilibrium is re-established, to show what would happen to the concentration of the gases if the volume of the reaction vessel was doubled. Assume the temperature remains constant.

7 Methanol is used as a fuel for some racing cars. The synthesis of methanol from methane involves two incomplete reactions:

Reaction 1: a reaction of methane with steam to yield carbon monoxide and hydrogen

Reaction 2: an exothermic reaction between carbon monoxide and hydrogen to produce methanol

a Write equations for the two reactions that are described.

b The reaction of carbon monoxide with hydrogen is performed at about 250°C and 100 atm pressure. Copper, zinc oxide and alumina are also present.

  i What is the likely function of the copper, zinc oxide and alumina in the reactor?

  ii How would the yield be affected if the reaction were performed at a higher temperature?

  iii State two advantages of using such a high pressure.

c Any process involving carbon monoxide presents hazards because of its toxicity, which arises because of its ability to bind very strongly to haemoglobin in competition with oxygen.

$$Hb_4 + 4CO \rightleftharpoons Hb_4(CO)_4$$
$$Hb_4 + 4O_2 \rightleftharpoons Hb_4(O_2)_4$$

i Referring to these competing equilibria, explain why exposure to carbon monoxide leads to decreased levels of oxyhaemoglobin ($Hb_4(O_2)_4$) in the blood.

ii Treatment for carbon monoxide poisoning often includes hyperbaric oxygen (pure oxygen at a pressure well above 1 atm). Explain how this helps remove $Hb_4(CO)_4$ from the blood.

d Another source of carbon monoxide is the incomplete combustion of many fuels. Write a balanced equation for the incomplete combustion of methanol to form carbon monoxide and water.

8 Write equilibrium expressions for saturated solutions of the following compounds.

a LiBr

b PbI_2

c $Cu_3(PO_4)_2$

9 Write the chemical formula for the precipitate formed when aqueous solutions of the following compounds are mixed.

a lead(II) nitrate and potassium chloride

b silver nitrate and sodium iodide

c barium nitrate and lithium sulfide

d nickel(II) nitrate and potassium hydroxide

10 Barium sulfate ($BaSO_4$) is considered insoluble in water.

a Calculate the value of K_{sp} at 25°C if the molar solubility is $1.04 \times 10^{-5}\,mol\,L^{-1}$.

b Predict whether a precipitate will form when 0.050 g of barium sulfate is added to 500 mL of water at 25°C.

11 The combustion reaction between methane and oxygen to form carbon dioxide and water is an example of a non-equilibrium system.

The reaction between methane gas and steam to form carbon monoxide and hydrogen gas does form an equilibrium system.

a i Write a balanced equation for the reaction between methane and oxygen.

  ii Write a balanced equation for the reaction between methane and steam.

b i If 5 mol of methane is reacted with excess oxygen, will any methane be present when the reaction is complete?

  ii If 5 mol of methane is reacted with excess steam, will any methane be present when the reaction is complete?

c i In a reaction 2 mol of methane is reacted with excess oxygen gas. What amount of carbon dioxide, in mol, is formed?

  ii In a reaction 2 mol of methane reacts with excess steam. Will the amount of carbon monoxide formed be greater than or less than 2 mol?

d i If 5 mol of methane is reacted with excess oxygen, does the amount of carbon dioxide formed depend upon the temperature?

  ii If 5 mol of methane is reacted with excess steam, does the amount of carbon monoxide formed depend upon the temperature?

e Determine the change in Gibbs free energy for the reaction between methane and oxygen gas at 100°C, assuming $\Delta H°$ and $\Delta S°$ do not change much with temperature. At 100°C:

$$\Delta H° = -890 \, \text{kJ mol}^{-1}$$
$$\Delta S° = +405.4 \, \text{J mol}^{-1} \, \text{K}^{-1}$$

12 The reaction between hydrogen chloride gas and oxygen is a reversible one:

$$4HCl(g) + O_2(g) \rightleftharpoons 2H_2O(g) + 2Cl_2(g) \quad \Delta H \text{ is negative}$$

Explain the impact upon

i the value of K_{eq}

ii the position of equilibrium

iii the concentration of HCl

iii the amount of HCl

when the following changes are made to the system at equilibrium.

a a decrease in temperature

b a decrease in volume

c the addition of extra oxygen gas.

13 The equation for the production of ammonia is

$$N_2(g) + 3H_2(g) \rightleftharpoons 2NH_3(g) \quad \Delta H \text{ is negative}$$

At 250°C, the numerical value of the equilibrium constant is 12.

a What is the value at 250°C of the equilibrium constant for the following equations?

  i $2NH_3(g) \rightleftharpoons N_2(g) + 3H_2(g)$

  ii $2N_2(g) + 6H_2(g) \rightleftharpoons 4NH_3(g)$

  iii $NH_3(g) \rightleftharpoons \frac{1}{2}N_2(g) + \frac{3}{2}H_2(g)$

b At the same temperature the equilibrium amounts of N_2 and NH_3 in a 10.0 L container are, respectively, 3.8 mol and 5.6 mol. Determine the amount of H_2 present, in mol, in the container.

c 2.6 mol of nitrogen gas and 4.4 mol of hydrogen gas are added to an empty 1.0 L reactor. At equilibrium the amount of nitrogen present is 2.2 mol. Determine the value of the equilibrium constant.

14 Ammonium carbonate ($(NH_4)_2CO_3$) is soluble in water.

a i Explain how you can predict that ammonium carbonate will be soluble.

  ii What ions are released when ammonium carbonate dissolves?

  iii Write an equation for the dissociation of ammonium carbonate.

b The dissociation of ammonium carbonate in water is endothermic. What happens to the temperature of water when solid ammonium carbonate is added to some water?

c When ammonium carbonate dissolves in water, name:

  i two types of bonding that are broken

  ii one type of bond that forms.

d A precipitate can form when solutions of ammonium carbonate and lead(II) nitrate are mixed together. Write a balanced chemical equation for the precipitation reaction that occurs.

15 Lead(II) iodide (PbI_2) is insoluble in water. A researcher finds that they can dissolve 1.3×10^{-3} mol of lead(II) iodide into 500 mL of water at 30°C.

a Calculate K_{sp} for lead(II) iodide at 30°C.

b The K_{sp} of lead(II) iodide at 25°C is 9.8×10^{-9}. Determine the molar solubility of lead(II) iodide at this temperature.

c If 0.0756 g of lead(II) iodide is added to 100 mL of water at 25°C, predict whether or not a precipitate will form.

d If 100 mL of 0.00170 mol L^{-1} lead(II) nitrate solution and 100 mL of 0.00240 mol L^{-1} potassium iodide solution are mixed together, predict whether or not a precipitate will form at 25°C.

e Calculate the molar solubility of lead(II) iodide in 0.10 mol L^{-1} solution of potassium iodide at 25°C.

f The solubility of which one of the following substances can be compared to that of lead(II) iodide using K_{sp} values?

MgO   Mg(OH)$_2$ Mg$_3$N$_2$

Acid/base reactions

In this module you will analyse how and why the definitions of both an acid and a base have changed over time, and how the current definitions characterise the many chemical reactions of acids. Acids react in particular ways with a variety of substances. These reactions follow a pattern that you will identify and explore in detail.

Acids and bases, and their reactions, are used extensively in everyday life and in biological systems. The chemistry of acids and bases is important in industrial, biological and environmental contexts. Therefore it is essential that the degree of acidity in these situations is monitored. By investigating the qualitative and quantitative properties of acids and bases, you will learn to appreciate the importance of factors such as pH and indicators.

Outcomes

By the end of this module, you will be able to:

- develop and evaluate questions and hypotheses for scientific investigation (CH12-1)
- design and evaluate investigations in order to obtain primary and secondary data and information (CH12-2)
- conduct investigations to collect valid and reliable primary and secondary data and information (CH12-3)
- analyse and evaluate primary and secondary data and information (CH12-5)
- describe, explain and quantitatively analyse acids and bases using contemporary models (CH12-13)

Properties of acids and bases

Acids and bases have important and diverse roles. They are common in homes and are used extensively in industry and agriculture. Acids and bases are also the reactants and products in many chemical reactions that take place in environmental and biological systems.

In this chapter you will study a theory that explains the properties of acids and bases and the characteristic reactions of acids and bases. You will learn to represent common reactions of acids and bases using ionic equations.

Content

INQUIRY QUESTION

What is an acid and what is a base?

By the end of this chapter, you will be able to:

- investigate the correct IUPAC nomenclature and properties of common inorganic acids and bases (ACSCH067)
- predict the products of acid reactions and write balanced equations to represent: ICT
  - acids and bases
  - acids and carbonates
  - acids and metals (ACSCH067)
- investigate applications of neutralisation reactions in everyday life and industrial processes
- conduct a practical investigation to measure the enthalpy of neutralisation (ACSCH093)
- explore the changes in definitions and models of an acid and a base over time to explain the limitations of each model, including but not limited to:
  - Arrhenius' theory
  - Brønsted–Lowry theory (ACSCH064, ACSCH067) ICT
- write ionic equations to represent the dissociation of acids and bases in water, conjugate acid/base pairs in solution and amphiprotic nature of some salts, for example:
  - sodium hydrogen carbonate
  - potassium dihydrogen phosphate

Chemistry Stage 6 Syllabus © NSW Education Standards Authority for and on behalf of the Crown in right of the State of NSW, 2017

6.1 Introducing acids and bases

CHEMISTRY INQUIRY S CCT

An environmentally friendly drain cleaner

COLLECT THIS...

- 60 g (¼ cup) sodium hydrogen carbonate (bicarbonate of soda) powder
- 250 mL (1 cup) vinegar
- 60 g (¼ cup) coarse salt
- tablespoon
- boiling water

DO THIS...

1 Using the spoon, sprinkle the sodium hydrogen carbonate into a drain, particularly around the edges of the underlying pipe. Residual water within the pipe should allow the sodium hydrogen carbonate to stick to the pipe.

2 Using the spoon, sprinkle the salt into the drain.

3 Pour the vinegar into the drain pipe. Be sure to go around the edges.

4 Wait 20 minutes.

5 Rinse the drain with about 1 cup of fresh boiling water.

RECORD THIS...

Describe what happened during the reaction of the sodium hydrogen carbonate and vinegar.

Research the ingredients of common drain cleaners.

REFLECT ON THIS...

1 What is the purpose of adding the coarse salt to the reaction?

2 Classify the vinegar and sodium hydrogen carbonate as either an acid or base.

3 With your understanding of reaction types, what are the expected products of this reaction?

4 Compare the ingredients of common drain cleaners. How is this reaction more environmentally friendly?

Acids and bases make up some of the household products in your kitchen and laundry (Figure 6.1.1). In this section you will be introduced to a theory that explains the chemical properties of acids and bases, helping you to explain their usefulness within the home and industry. You will also look at how the acidity of a solution can be measured, so that acid solutions can be defined as a strong or weak acid.

FIGURE 6.1.1 Some common household products that contain acids or bases

CHEMFILE IU

Saving the Nobel Prize gold medals

George de Hevesy (1885–1966) worked for the Niels Bohr Institute in Denmark during World War II. The Institute was looking after a number of valuable gold medals that had been awarded to recipients of the Nobel Prize.

When Germany invaded Denmark at the beginning of World War II, de Hevesy was concerned that the Germans would confiscate the gold medals. He dissolved the gold medals in aqua regia, which is a mixture of concentrated hydrochloric and nitric acid. Aqua regia is strong enough to dissolve gold, a metal known for its lack of chemical reactivity.

FIGURE 6.1.2 Recipients of the Nobel Prize are given a sum of money and a gold medal weighing about 175 g.

He hid the bottle containing the gold solution among the hundreds of other bottles on his laboratory shelves. The bottle was never found by the German occupiers and after the war de Hevesy retrieved the precious bottle and precipitated the gold out of solution. The gold was sent to the Nobel Foundation, who had the medals recast into duplicates of the originals and returned to their owners (Figure 6.1.2).

Between 1901 and 2017 the Nobel Prize in Chemistry has been awarded 109 times to 177 individuals, including de Hevesy in 1943 for his work on radioactive tracers. Frederick Sanger is the only double Nobel laureate in Chemistry: in 1958 for his work on the structure of proteins, especially that of insulin, and in 1980 for his fundamental studies on the biochemistry of nucleic acids, with particular regard to recombinant DNA.

Sir Fraser Stoddart, one of the recipients of the 2016 Nobel Prize in Chemistry for his contributions to the design and synthesis of molecular machines, commented that because of the rarity and unknowing nature of receiving the Nobel Prize, the dream of winning such a prize should not be the focus of a budding scientist. Instead, a focus on people, deep connections and an insatiable passion for the subject should inspire scientists.

ACIDS AND BASES

Acids are used in our homes, in agriculture and in industry. They also have important roles in our bodies. Table 6.1.1 gives the names, chemical formulae and uses of some common acids.

TABLE 6.1.1 Common acids and their everyday uses

Name	Formula	Uses
hydrochloric acid	HCl	present in stomach acid to help break down proteins; used as a cleaning agent for brickwork, and in the manufacture of a wide range of products
sulfuric acid	H_2SO_4	one of the most common chemicals manufactured; used in car batteries and in the manufacture of fertilisers, dyes and detergents
nitric acid	HNO_3	used in the manufacture of fertilisers, dyes and explosives
ethanoic acid (acetic acid)	CH_3COOH	found in vinegar; used as a preservative and in the manufacture of glues and plastics
carbonic acid	H_2CO_3	used to carbonate soft drinks and beer
phosphoric acid	H_3PO_4	used as a flavouring and in the manufacture of fertilisers and pharmaceutical products
citric acid	$C_6H_8O_7$	found in citrus fruits; used as a flavouring and preservative
ascorbic acid (vitamin C)	$C_6H_8O_6$	found in citrus fruits; used as a health supplement and as an antioxidant in food production

Many cleaning agents used in the home, such as washing powders and oven cleaners, contain **bases**. Solutions of ammonia are used as floor cleaners, and sodium hydroxide is the major active ingredient in oven cleaners. Bases are effective cleaners because they react with fats and oils to produce water-soluble soaps. A water-soluble base is called an **alkali**.

> ℹ️ Alkalis are bases that can dissolve in water. The solution is said to be alkaline, with a pH greater than 7.0. Calcium carbonate will react with acids, but it is not an alkali because it is insoluble in water.

Table 6.1.2 gives the names, chemical formulae and uses of some common bases.

TABLE 6.1.2 Common bases and their everyday uses

Name	Formula	Uses
Sodium hydroxide (caustic soda)	$NaOH$	drain and oven cleaners, soap-making, industrial applications
Ammonia	NH_3	household cleaners, fertilisers, explosives, plastics manufacture
Calcium hydroxide	$Ca(OH)_2$	cement and mortar, garden lime, food preparation
Magnesium hydroxide	$Mg(OH)_2$	antacids such as milk of magnesia, to treat indigestion
Sodium carbonate	Na_2CO_3	manufacture of washing powders, soaps, glass, paper

CHEMFILE WE

Handle strong bases with care

Bases feel slippery to the touch because they react with fats in our skin to produce soap. Strong bases should be handled with care. Oven cleaners contain about 4% of the strong base sodium hydroxide. A common name of sodium hydroxide is caustic soda.

Figure 6.1.3 shows the safety instructions on a can of oven cleaner.

FIGURE 6.1.3 Oven cleaners remove fatty deposits by reacting with them to form soaps. Note the safety instructions.

CHANGING IDEAS ABOUT THE NATURE OF ACIDS AND BASES

Over the years there have been many attempts to define acids and bases. At first, acids and bases were defined in terms of their observed properties such as their taste, effect on **indicators** and reactions with other substances.

For example, in the 17th century, British scientist Robert Boyle described the properties of acids in terms of taste, their action as solvents, and how they changed the colour of certain vegetable extracts (similar to red cabbage juice seen in Figure 6.1.4). He also noticed that alkalis could reverse the effect that acids had on these extracts.

FIGURE 6.1.4 Natural acid–base indicators are found in plants such as red cabbage. Red cabbage extract turns a different colour in (from left to right) concentrated acid, dilute acid, neutral solution, dilute base and concentrated base.

It was not until the late 18th century that attempts were made to define acids and bases on the basis of the nature of their constituent elements. Antoine Lavoisier, a French chemist, thought that acidic properties were due to the presence of oxygen. While this explanation applied to sulfuric acid (H_2SO_4), nitric acid (HNO_3) and phosphoric acid (H_3PO_4), it did not explain why hydrochloric acid (HCl) was an acid.

In about 1810, Humphrey Davy suggested that the acid properties of substances were associated with hydrogen and not oxygen. He came to this conclusion after producing hydrogen gas by reacting acids with metals. Davey also suggested that acids react with bases to form salts and water.

The Arrhenius theory of acids and bases

The ideas of Lavoisier and Davy were further developed by the Swedish scientist Svante Arrhenius. In 1887 the **Arrhenius theory** defined acids and bases as follows.

- Acids are substances that **dissociate** (break apart) and **ionise** (form ions) in water. They produce hydrogen ions (H^+).
- Bases dissociate in water to produce **hydroxide ions** (OH^-).

In 1923, Danish physical chemist Johannes Brønsted and English chemist Thomas Lowry were working independently on acids and bases. They each came up with the theory that now bears both of their names. The Brønsted–Lowry theory is more general than the one proposed by Arrhenius and provides an explanation for some observed acid–base behaviours that cannot be explained by the earlier theories.

THE BRØNSTED–LOWRY THEORY OF ACIDS AND BASES

According to the **Brønsted–Lowry theory**, a substance behaves as an acid when it donates a proton (H^+) to a base. A substance behaves as a base when it accepts a proton from an acid.

In summary:

- acids are **proton donors**
- bases are **proton acceptors**
- an **acid–base reaction** involves an exchange of protons from an acid to a base.

For example, hydrogen chloride (HCl) is a gaseous molecular compound that is very soluble in water. The molecules dissociate in water according to the following reaction:

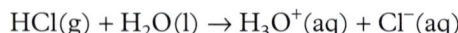

$$HCl(g) + H_2O(l) \rightarrow H_3O^+(aq) + Cl^-(aq)$$

In an aqueous solution of hydrogen chloride, nearly all the hydrogen chloride is present as ions—virtually no molecules of hydrogen chloride remain. This solution is known as hydrochloric acid.

In this reaction, each HCl molecule has donated a proton to a water molecule, forming the **hydronium ion**, $H_3O^+(aq)$. According to the Brønsted–Lowry theory, the HCl has acted as an acid. The water molecule has accepted a proton from the HCl molecule, so the water has acted as a base. This is outlined in Figure 6.1.5.

The hydronium ion can be represented as either $H_3O^+(aq)$ or $H^+(aq)$. The reaction of HCl(g) with water can be written as either:

$$HCl(g) + H_2O(l) \rightarrow H_3O^+(aq) + Cl^-(aq)$$

or

$$HCl(g) \rightarrow H^+(aq) + Cl^-(aq)$$

Writing the hydronium ion as $H^+(aq)$ in an equation makes it harder to see that a proton transfer has occurred. The hydronium ion is therefore usually written as $H_3O^+(aq)$ in this chapter.

The structural formulae of the hydronium ion and a water molecule are shown in Figure 6.1.6.

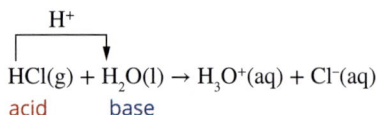

Advantages of the Brønsted–Lowry theory

Acid–base reactions are not restricted to aqueous solutions. A reaction between two gases can be an acid–base reaction. For example, the **salt** ammonium chloride can be formed by a reaction between:

- solutions of hydrochloric acid and ammonia:

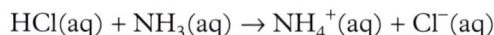

$$HCl(aq) + NH_3(aq) \rightarrow NH_4^+(aq) + Cl^-(aq)$$

- gaseous hydrogen chloride and gaseous ammonia:

$$HCl(g) + NH_3(g) \rightarrow NH_4Cl(s)$$

The Brønsted–Lowry theory classifies both of these reactions as acid–base reactions, because in each case the acid donates a proton to the base.

PROPERTIES OF ACIDS AND BASES

All acids have some properties in common. Bases also have common properties. The properties of acids and bases are summarised in Table 6.1.3.

$$\overset{\displaystyle H^+}{\overbrace{HCl(g)} + H_2O(l)} \rightarrow H_3O^+(aq) + Cl^-(aq)$$
acid   base

FIGURE 6.1.5 The reaction between hydrochloric acid and water is an example of an acid–base reaction, which involves a transfer of protons from an acid to a base.

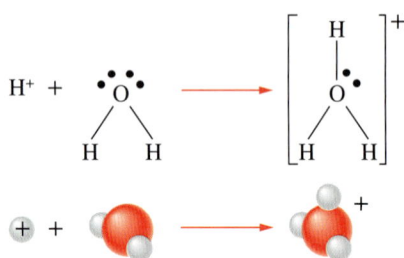

FIGURE 6.1.6 Formation of the hydronium ion

> **i** Remember that $H^+(aq)$ is often used interchangeably with $H_3O^+(aq)$ when discussing the nature of acids.

TABLE 6.1.3 Properties of acids and bases

Properties of acids	Properties of bases
• turn litmus indicator (purple litmus) red • tend to be corrosive • taste sour • react with bases • solutions have a pH below 7.0 • solutions conduct an electric current	• turn litmus indicator (purple litmus) blue • are caustic and feel slippery • taste bitter • react with acids • solutions have a pH above 7.0 • solutions conduct an electric current

CONJUGATE ACID–BASE PAIRS

A **conjugate acid–base pair** is two molecules or ions that differ by one proton (H^+). Consider the reactants and products when hydrochloric acid dissociates in water:

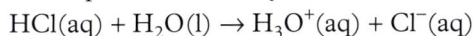

$$HCl(aq) + H_2O(l) \rightarrow H_3O^+(aq) + Cl^-(aq)$$

HCl and Cl^- differ by one proton, so they are a conjugate acid–base pair. Similarly, H_3O^+ and H_2O are also a conjugate acid–base pair. Because Cl^- is formed from HCl by the loss of a single proton, it is called the **conjugate base** of HCl. Similarly, HCl is the **conjugate acid** of Cl^-. Conjugate acid–base pairs are written in the format of acid/base; for example, HCl/Cl^-.

The relationship between acid–base conjugate pairs is represented in Figure 6.1.7.

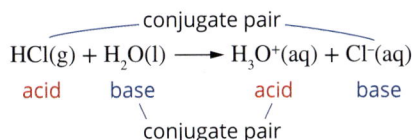

FIGURE 6.1.7 Conjugate acid–base pairs are formed when an acid donates a proton to a base.

In the reaction between NH_3 and H_2O shown in Figure 6.1.8, the conjugate acid–base pairs are NH_4^+/NH_3 and H_2O/OH^- because each acid differs from its corresponding base by one proton.

FIGURE 6.1.8 The reaction between ammonia and water, showing the conjugate acid–base pairs.

Figure 6.1.9 shows the formulae of some common acids and bases and their conjugates.

Acids ... donate a proton to form:

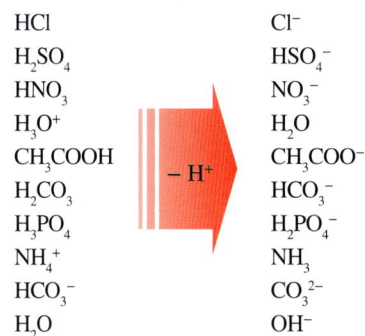

HCl	Cl^-
H_2SO_4	HSO_4^-
HNO_3	NO_3^-
H_3O^+	H_2O
CH_3COOH	CH_3COO^-
H_2CO_3	HCO_3^-
H_3PO_4	$H_2PO_4^-$
NH_4^+	NH_3
HCO_3^-	CO_3^{2-}
H_2O	OH^-

$-H^+$

Bases ... accept a proton to form:

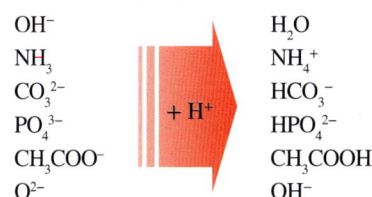

OH^-	H_2O
NH_3	NH_4^+
CO_3^{2-}	HCO_3^-
PO_4^{3-}	HPO_4^{2-}
CH_3COO^-	CH_3COOH
O^{2-}	OH^-

$+H^+$

FIGURE 6.1.9 Some common acid–base conjugate pairs.

AMPHIPROTIC SUBSTANCES

Some substances can either donate or accept protons, depending on the substance they are reacting with. This means they can behave as either an acid or a base. Such substances are called **amphiprotic**.

For example, in an aqueous solution of HCl, water gains a proton from HCl and therefore acts as a base.

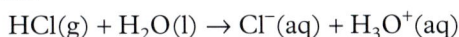

$$HCl(g) + H_2O(l) \rightarrow Cl^-(aq) + H_3O^+(aq)$$

However, in the reaction below, water donates a proton to NH_3 and therefore acts as an acid.

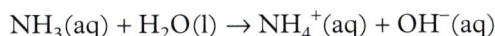

$$NH_3(aq) + H_2O(l) \rightarrow NH_4^+(aq) + OH^-(aq)$$

These reactions are represented in Figure 6.1.10.

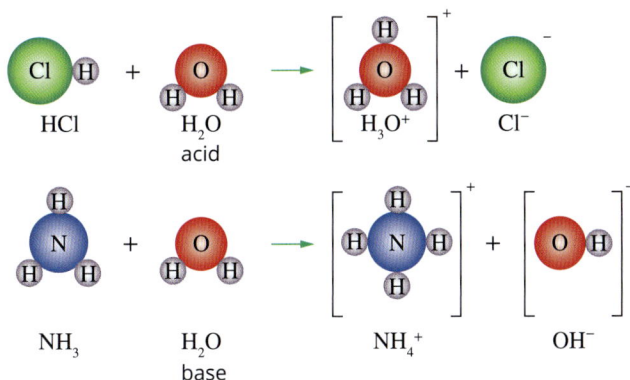

> ℹ️ When acids react with water, hydronium (H_3O^+) ions are produced. When bases react with water, hydroxide (OH^-) ions are produced.

FIGURE 6.1.10 The amphiprotic nature of water is demonstrated by its reactions with HCl and NH_3.

It is evident that water can act as either an acid or a base, depending on the **solute** present.

If the solute is a stronger acid than water, then water will react as a base. If the solute is a stronger base than water, then water will react as an acid.

Some common amphiprotic substances are listed in Figure 6.1.11.

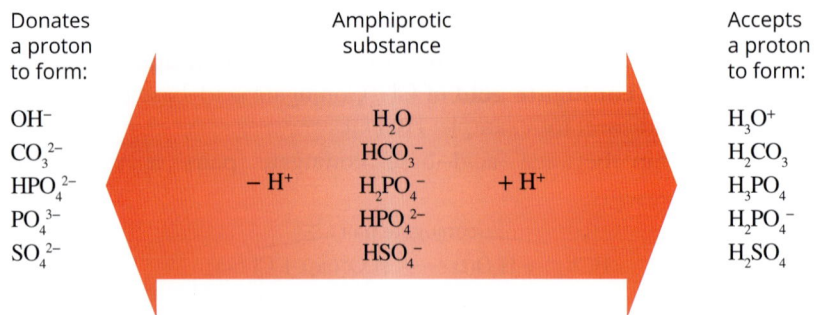

Donates a proton to form:	Amphiprotic substance	Accepts a proton to form:
OH^-	H_2O	H_3O^+
CO_3^{2-}	HCO_3^-	H_2CO_3
HPO_4^{2-} $-H^+$	$H_2PO_4^-$ $+H^+$	H_3PO_4
PO_4^{3-}	HPO_4^{2-}	$H_2PO_4^-$
SO_4^{2-}	HSO_4^-	H_2SO_4

FIGURE 6.1.11 Substances that are amphiprotic.

When an amphiprotic substance is placed in water, it reacts as both an acid and a base. For example, the hydrogen carbonate ion (HCO_3^-) reacts according to the equations:

$$HCO_3^-(aq) + H_2O(l) \rightleftharpoons CO_3^{2-}(aq) + H_3O^+(aq)$$
$$\text{acid} \qquad \text{base}$$

$$HCO_3^-(aq) + H_2O(l) \rightleftharpoons H_2CO_3(aq) + OH^-(aq)$$
$$\text{base} \qquad \text{acid}$$

Since HCO_3^- can act as both an acid and a base, it is amphiprotic.

Although both reactions are possible for all amphiprotic substances in water, generally one of these reactions dominates. The dominant reaction can be identified by measuring the pH (a measure of the amount of hydronium ion in solution) of the solution. (You will look more closely at pH in Chapter 7.)

GO TO ➤ Section 7.2 page 167

Salts that contain such ions are said to be amphiprotic in nature. Examples of these include sodium hydrogen carbonate ($NaHCO_3$) and potassium dihydrogen phosphate. The dihydrogen phosphate ion ($H_2PO_4^-$) reacts according to the following equations:

$$H_2PO_4^-(aq) + H_2O(l) \rightleftharpoons H_3PO_4(aq) + OH^-(aq)$$
$$\text{acid} \qquad \text{base}$$

$$H_2PO_4^-(aq) + H_2O(l) \rightleftharpoons HPO_4^{2-} + H_3O^+(aq)$$
$$\text{base} \qquad \text{acid}$$

MONOPROTIC ACIDS

Monoprotic acids can donate only one proton. These acids include hydrochloric acid (HCl), hydrofluoric acid (HF), nitric acid (HNO_3) and ethanoic acid (CH_3COOH).

Although ethanoic (acetic) acid contains four hydrogen atoms, each molecule can donate only one proton to produce an ethanoate (acetate) ion (CH_3COO^-), so ethanoic acid is monoprotic. Only the hydrogen that is part of the highly polar O−H bond is donated. This hydrogen is called the **acidic proton** (Figure 6.1.12).

POLYPROTIC ACIDS

Acids that can donate more than one proton from each molecule are called **polyprotic acids**. The number of hydrogen ions an acid can donate depends on the structure of the acid. Polyprotic acids do not donate all of their protons at once, but do so in steps when reacting with a base.

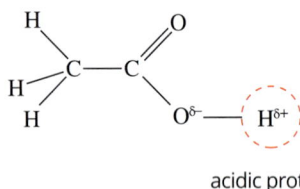

acidic proton

FIGURE 6.1.12 The structure of ethanoic acid. Each molecule can donate only one proton to a water molecule when ethanoic acid reacts with water.

Diprotic acids

Diprotic acids, such as sulfuric acid (H_2SO_4) and carbonic acid (H_2CO_3), can donate two protons. A diprotic acid, for example sulfuric acid, dissociates in two stages.

Stage 1:

$$H_2SO_4(l) + H_2O(l) \rightarrow HSO_4^-(aq) + H_3O^+(aq)$$

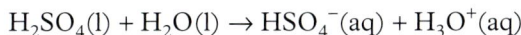

Sulfuric acid is described as a **strong acid** in water because it readily donates a proton, so this stage occurs almost to completion. Virtually no H_2SO_4 molecules are found in an aqueous solution.

Stage 2:

The HSO_4^- ion formed can also act as an acid. In a $1.0\,mol\,L^{-1}$ solution, only a small proportion of those ions reacts further to produce H_3O^+ ions and SO_4^{2-} ions.

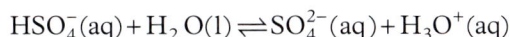

$$HSO_4^-(aq) + H_2O(l) \rightleftharpoons SO_4^{2-}(aq) + H_3O^+(aq)$$

HSO_4^- is described as a **weak acid** because it is only partially dissociated. A double (reversible) arrow indicates that an incomplete reaction occurs. (You will learn more about strong and weak acids later in this chapter.) Therefore a solution of sulfuric acid contains hydrogen ions, hydrogen sulfate ions and sulfate ions.

Triprotic acids

Triprotic acids can donate three protons. These include phosphoric acid (H_3PO_4) and boric acid (H_3BO_3). A triprotic acid, such as phosphoric acid, dissociates in three stages.

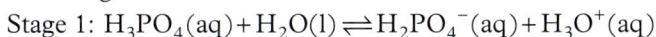

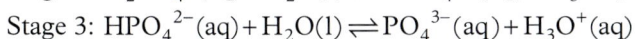

Stage 1: $H_3PO_4(aq) + H_2O(l) \rightleftharpoons H_2PO_4^-(aq) + H_3O^+(aq)$

Stage 2: $H_2PO_4^-(aq) + H_2O(l) \rightleftharpoons HPO_4^{2-}(aq) + H_3O^+(aq)$

Stage 3: $HPO_4^{2-}(aq) + H_2O(l) \rightleftharpoons PO_4^{3-}(aq) + H_3O^+(aq)$

Phosphoric acid is a weak acid in water, so in a $1.0\,mol\,L^{-1}$ solution only a small proportion of the protons is donated at each dissociation stage. The extent of the dissociation decreases progressively from stage 1 to stage 3. You will learn more about how the extent of dissociation is quantified in Chapter 8.

GO TO ➤ Section 8.5 page 220

NAMING ACIDS

To name a simple acid composed of hydrogen and another element, take the element's name and change the '-ide' ending to '-ic acid'. For example:

- hydrogen chloride becomes hydrochloric acid, and the anion is a chloride ion.

For acids that contain oxygen (oxyacids), the acid name often ends in '-ic acid'. The name of the anion of the acid often ends in '-ate'. For example:

- sulfuric acid (H_2SO_4) and the anion, sulfate (SO_4^{2-})
- nitric acid (HNO_3) and the anion, nitrate (NO_3^-)
- ethanoic acid (CH_3COOH) and the anion, ethanoate (CH_3COO^-).

For some oxyacids, the acid name ends in '-ous acid'. These oxyacids have fewer O atoms than the corresponding '-ic acid'. The anion name will end in '-ite'. For example:

- sulfurous acid (H_2SO_3) and the anion, sulfite (SO_3^{2-})
- nitrous acid (HNO_2) and the anion, nitrite (NO_2^-).

Lewis acids and bases

Not all acids are substances that can be easily defined by the donation of a proton. In the same year that the Brønsted–Lowry theory was published, Gilbert N. Lewis (of Lewis dot diagrams fame) defined an acid as being a substance that can accept a lone electron pair from another molecule. By contrast, Lewis bases are substances that donate a lone pair of electrons. Brønsted–Lowry bases are also Lewis bases because they donate a pair of electrons in order to accept a proton.

Lewis acids and bases are a diverse group of compounds. An example of a Lewis acid is boron trifluoride (BF_3). When it interacts with a Lewis base, such as ammonia (NH_3),

it accepts a pair of electrons from the nitrogen, which creates a bond with the ammonia molecule.

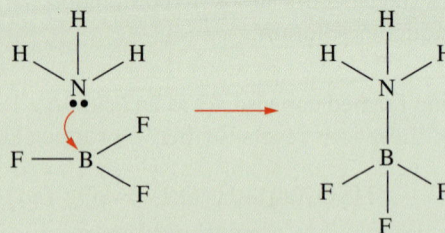

FIGURE 6.1.13 The lone-pair interaction between ammonia (NH_3) and boron trifluoride (BF_3)

6.1 Review

SUMMARY

- The Brønsted–Lowry model describes acid–base properties in terms of proton transfer. In this model, an acid is a proton donor and a base is a proton acceptor.
- When an acid donates a proton, it forms its conjugate base. When a base accepts a proton, it forms its conjugate acid.
- Conjugate acid–base pairs are molecules or ions that differ from each other by one proton (H^+).
- A proton or hydrogen ion in solution can be represented by the hydronium ion, $H_3O^+(aq)$, or simply as $H^+(aq)$.

- Amphiprotic substances can act as either acids or bases, depending on the substance with which they are reacting.
- A polyprotic acid can donate more than one proton to a base.
- The first dissociation of a diprotic acid occurs to a greater extent than the second dissociation. In a triprotic acid, the third dissociation occurs to the least extent.

KEY QUESTIONS

1   An acidic solution is formed when hydrogen bromide gas (HBr) is mixed with water (H_2O). Write an equation for this reaction.

2   In the following reaction, what are the two acid–base conjugate pairs?
$$H_2SO_4(l) + HNO_3(l) \rightarrow HSO_4^-(l) + H_2NO_3^+(l)$$

3   For each of the following equations, give the conjugate of the acid or base that is in bold.
   a $HF(aq) + \textbf{OH}^-\textbf{(aq)} \rightarrow H_2O(l) + F^-(aq)$
   b $HCOOH(aq) + \textbf{H}_2\textbf{O(l)} \rightarrow H_3O^+(aq) + HCOO^-(aq)$
   c $CH_3NH_2(aq) + HCl(aq) \rightarrow \textbf{CH}_3\textbf{NH}_3^+\textbf{(aq)} + Cl^-(aq)$

4   What is the conjugate acid of each of the following bases?
   a NH_3
   b CH_3COO^-

   c HPO_4^{2-}
   d CO_3^{2-}
   e O^{2-}

5   Show that the reaction between solutions of sodium hydroxide and hydrochloric acid is a Brønsted–Lowry acid–base reaction.

6   Write an equation to show each of the following acting as an acid and a base with water.
   a HCO_3^-
   b HPO_4^{2-}
   c HSO_4^-
   d H_2O

6.2 Reactions of acids and bases

Brønsted–Lowry acid–base reactions involve the exchange of a proton (H^+ ion), but there are other acid and base reactions that need to be considered to fully understand their properties and the products formed from such reactions.

In this section you will learn to use the patterns in the reactions of acids and bases to predict the products that are formed, calculate quantities of acids or bases required for neutralisation to occur, calculate the pH of the resultant solution when an acid or base is in excess after mixing, and develop an understanding of the enthalpy of neutralisation.

The general reaction types explored in this section include acids reacting with:
- metal hydroxides
- metal carbonates (including hydrogen carbonates)
- reactive metals.

ACIDS AND METAL HYDROXIDES

In the previous section you learnt that a Brønsted–Lowry acid is a proton donor and that a Brønsted–Lowry base is a proton acceptor. Bases that contain hydroxide ions will accept the protons from an acidic solution to form water. The metal cation and conjugate base anion of the acid thus become the salt.

This can be expressed generally as:

$$\text{acid} + \text{metal hydroxide} \rightarrow \text{salt} + \text{water}$$

For example, solutions of phosphoric acid and potassium hydroxide react to form a potassium phosphate salt and water. This can be represented by the full (or overall) equation:

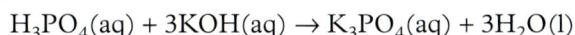

$$H_3PO_4(aq) + 3KOH(aq) \rightarrow K_3PO_4(aq) + 3H_2O(l)$$

Experimentally you can confirm the presence of the salt by evaporating the water, leaving the solid salt behind.

NEUTRALISATION REACTIONS

When a basic solution is added to an acidic solution, a reaction takes places that usually forms a salt and water. The solutions are said to have been **neutralised** when the concentrations of the hydronium and hydroxide ions within the mixture become equal.

Worked example 6.2.1

CALCULATING THE AMOUNT OF BASE NEEDED TO NEUTRALISE AN ACID

What volume of a $0.20\,mol\,L^{-1}$ solution of barium hydroxide ($Ba(OH)_2$) would be required to neutralise $150\,mL$ of a $0.15\,mol\,L^{-1}$ solution of nitric acid (HNO_3)?

Thinking	Working
Write the general reaction and identify the products.	acid + metal hydroxide → salt + water
	Products of this reaction are barium nitrate in solution and water.
Write a balanced chemical equation.	$2HNO_3(aq) + Ba(OH)_2\ (aq) \rightarrow Ba(NO_3)_2\ (aq) + 2H_2O(l)$
Calculate the amount, in mol, of known substance using the following relationship: $$n = c \times V$$	$n(HNO_3) = c \times V$ $= 0.150 \times 0.15$ $= 0.023\,mol$

Calculate the amount of substance, in mol, of the unknown chemical species using the mole ratio between known and unknown chemical species: $\text{mole ratio} = \frac{\text{coefficient of unknown chemical}}{\text{coefficient of known chemical}}$	$\frac{n(Ba(OH)_2)}{n(HNO_3)} = \frac{1}{2}$ $n(Ba(OH)_2) = \frac{1}{2} \times n(HNO_3)$ $\qquad\quad = \frac{1}{2} \times 0.023\,mol$ $\qquad\quad = 0.011\,mol$
Knowing the concentration, calculate the required volume for neutralisation using the following relationship: $V = \frac{n}{c}$	$V(Ba(OH)_2) = \frac{n}{c}$ $\qquad\quad = \frac{0.01125}{0.20}$ $\qquad\quad = 0.056\,L$ $\qquad\quad = 56\,mL$

Worked example: Try yourself 6.2.1

CALCULATING THE AMOUNT OF BASE NEEDED TO NEUTRALISE AN ACID

What volume of a $0.100\,mol\,L^{-1}$ solution of barium hydroxide ($Ba(OH)_2$) would be required to neutralise $75.0\,mL$ of a $0.0500\,mol\,L^{-1}$ solution of sulfuric acid (H_2SO_4)?

Enthalpy of neutralisation

Enthalpy of neutralisation is the thermal energy change in the reaction when an acid and a base react in stoichiometric proportions to make a salt and $1\,mol$ of water. It is represented by the symbol ΔH_{neut}.

The reaction is exothermic (ΔH is negative). In the reaction of strong acids with strong bases, the hydrogen and hydroxide ions that react to form water are already within solution.

The formation of $1\,mol$ of water releases $55.9\,kJ$ of energy.

The thermochemical equation thus can be represented as:

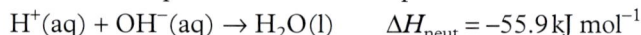

$$H^+(aq) + OH^-(aq) \rightarrow H_2O(l) \qquad \Delta H_{neut} = -55.9\,kJ\,mol^{-1}$$

Measuring the enthalpy of neutralisation using simple calorimetry

GO TO ➤ Year 11 Section 14.4

The enthalpy of neutralisation can be measuring using simple **calorimetry**. By measuring the temperature change of the salt solution formed, the energy released by the **neutralisation reaction** can be measuring using the formula:

$$q = m \times c \times \Delta T$$

where

q is the amount of energy released by the neutralisation reaction (in J)

m is the mass of the salt solution = the combined mass of the acid and base (in g)

c is the specific heat capacity of water ($4.18\,J\,g^{-1}\,K^{-1}$)

ΔT is the temperature change of the mixture of the acid and base (in K or °C).

A number of assumptions are made when determining the amount of energy released by the neutralisation reaction using this method:

- The salt solution formed from the reaction has the same specific heat capacity as that of water. This is a reasonable assumption because the salt solution is dilute, so it contains mostly water.
- All thermal energy released by the reaction is transferred to the salt solution. There is no energy loss.
- If the mass of the salt solution formed was not measured, it can be assumed that the salt solution has the same density as that of water, i.e. $1\,g\,mL^{-1}$. This is another reasonable assumption because the salt solution is dilute, so it contains mostly water.

Once the energy released by the neutralisation reaction has been determined, the enthalpy of neutralisation can be calculated by the following expression:

$$\Delta H_{neut} = \frac{q}{n(H_2O)}$$

where

ΔH_{neut} is the enthalpy of neutralisation (in $kJ\,mol^{-1}$)

q is the amount of energy released by the neutralisation reaction (in kJ)

$n(H_2O)$ is the amount of water produced by the neutralisation reaction (in mol).

PA 6.4   PA 6.4

Worked example 6.2.2

DETERMINING THE ENTHALPY OF NEUTRALISATION

50.0 mL of a diluted standard sodium hydroxide solution (NaOH) was added to neutralise 50.0 mL of a $2.0\,mol\,L^{-1}$ solution of ethanoic acid (CH_3COOH).

The temperature of the mixture rose from 22.0°C to a maximum temperature of 33.7°C.

Determine the enthalpy of neutralisation.

Thinking	Working
Write a balanced chemical equation for the reaction.	$NaOH(aq) + CH_3COOH(aq) \rightarrow NaCH_3COO(aq) + H_2O(l)$
Determine the amount, in mol, of acid using the expression: $$n = c \times V$$	$n(CH_3COOH) = c \times V$ $= 2.0 \times 0.0500$ $= 0.10\,mol$
Determine the temperature change of the mixture, ΔT.	$\Delta T = 33.7 - 22.0$ $= 11.7°C$
Determine the amount of energy released by the reaction using the formula: $$q = m \times c \times \Delta T$$ Assume the density of the mixture is $1\,g\,mL^{-1}$. Therefore the mass of the mixture is equivalent to the volume of the mixture.	$q = m \times c \times \Delta T$ $= 100.0 \times 4.18 \times 11.7$ $= 4.89 \times 10^3\,J$
Convert energy to kJ.	$\frac{4.89 \times 10^3}{1000}$ $= 4.89\,kJ$
Determine the amount of water, in mol, produced in the reaction, using the mole ratio with the limiting reactant.	$\frac{n(H_2O)}{n(CH_3COOH)} = \frac{1}{1}$ $n(H_2O) = n(CH_3COOH)$ $= 0.10\,mol$
Determine ΔH_{neut} using: $$\Delta H_{neut} = \frac{q}{n(H_2O)}$$ Because the temperature increased, the reaction was exothermic and hence ΔH_{neut} is negative.	$\Delta H_{neut} = \frac{q}{n(H_2O)}$ $= \frac{-4.89}{0.10}$ $= -49\,kJ\,mol^{-1}$

Worked example: Try yourself 6.2.2

DETERMINING THE ENTHALPY OF NEUTRALISATION

25.0 mL of a diluted standard barium hydroxide solution ($Ba(OH)_2$) was added to neutralise 50.0 mL of a $1.5\,mol\,L^{-1}$ solution of ethanoic acid (CH_3COOH).

The temperature of the solution rose from 21.3°C to a maximum temperature of 34.0°C.

Determine the enthalpy of neutralisation.

ACIDS AND METAL CARBONATES

Metal carbonates and metal hydrogen carbonates (bicarbonates) react with acids to form the same products. These products include a salt, carbon dioxide and water.

The general equation for the reaction between acids and metal carbonates is:

acid + metal carbonate → salt + water + carbon dioxide

For example, a solution of phosphoric acid reacting with sodium carbonate solution produces a solution of sodium phosphate, water and carbon dioxide gas. The reaction is represented by the equation:

$$2H_3PO_4(aq) + 3Na_2CO_3(s) \rightarrow 2Na_3PO_4(aq) + 3CO_2(g) + 3H_2O(l)$$

Similarly, the reaction between phosphoric acid and sodium hydrogen carbonate can be represented as:

$$H_3PO_4(aq) + 3NaHCO_3(s) \rightarrow Na_3PO_4(aq) + 3CO_2(g) + 3H_2O(l)$$

> **i** Spectator ions are ions that do not participate in a chemical reaction but are still present within the reaction mixture. Spectator ions are therefore not listed in a net ionic equation.

Worked example 6.2.3

WRITING IONIC EQUATIONS FOR REACTIONS BETWEEN ACIDS AND METAL CARBONATES

What products are formed when a dilute solution of hydrochloric acid is added to solid sodium carbonate? Write an ionic equation for this reaction.

Thinking	Working
Write the general reaction and identify the products.	acid + metal carbonate → salt + water + carbon dioxide The products of this reaction are sodium chloride in solution, water, and carbon dioxide gas.
Identify the reactants and products. Indicate the state of each.	Reactants: Hydrochloric acid is dissociated in solution, forming H^+(aq) and Cl^-(aq) ions. Sodium carbonate is an ionic solid, Na_2CO_3(s). Products: Sodium chloride is dissociated into Na^+(aq) and Cl^-(aq) ions. Water has the formula H_2O(l). Carbon dioxide has the formula CO_2(g).
Write the equation showing all reactants and products. (There is no need to balance the equation yet.)	H^+(aq) + Cl^-(aq) + Na_2CO_3(s) → Na^+(aq) + Cl^-(aq) + H_2O(l) + CO_2(g)
Identify the spectator ions.	Cl^-(aq)
Rewrite the net ionic equation, without the spectator ions.	H^+(aq) + Na_2CO_3(s) → Na^+(aq) + H_2O(l) + CO_2(g)
Balance the equation with respect to number of atoms of each element and charge.	$2H^+$(aq) + Na_2CO_3(s) → $2Na^+$(aq) + H_2O(l) + CO_2(g) Note that if hydronium ions are represented as H_3O^+(aq), rather than as H^+(aq), this reaction would be written as: $2H_3O^+$(aq) + Na_2CO_3(s) → $2Na^+$(aq) + $3H_2O$(l) + CO_2(g)

Worked example: Try yourself 6.2.3

WRITING IONIC EQUATIONS FOR REACTIONS BETWEEN ACIDS AND METAL CARBONATES

What products are formed when a solution of sulfuric acid is added to a solution of calcium hydrogen carbonate? Write an ionic equation for this reaction.

ACIDS AND REACTIVE METALS

When acids are added to reactive metals, bubbles of hydrogen gas are released and a salt is formed. Because there is no transfer of protons, it is not a Brønsted–Lowry acid–base reaction. Instead, it is a redox reaction. Copper, silver and gold do not react with acids because their respective ions are stronger oxidising agents than hydrogen ions so a spontaneous reaction does not occur.

The general equation for the reaction is:

$$\text{acid} + \text{reactive metal} \rightarrow \text{salt} + \text{hydrogen}$$

For example, the reaction between hydrochloric acid and magnesium metal can be represented by the chemical equation below.

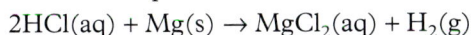

$$2HCl(aq) + Mg(s) \rightarrow MgCl_2(aq) + H_2(g)$$

PA
6.3

PA
6.3

Worked example 6.2.4

WRITING IONIC EQUATIONS FOR REACTIONS BETWEEN ACIDS AND REACTIVE METALS

Write an ionic equation for the reaction that occurs when hydrochloric acid is added to a sample of iron metal.

Thinking	Working
Write the general reaction and identify the products formed.	acid + reactive metal → salt + hydrogen Hydrogen gas and iron(II) chloride solution are produced.
Identify the reactants and products. Indicate the state of each.	Reactants: iron is a solid, Fe(s). Hydrochloric acid is dissociated, forming H^+(aq) and Cl^-(aq) ions. Products: hydrogen gas, H_2(g). Iron(II) chloride is dissociated into Fe^{2+}(aq) and Cl^-(aq) ions.
Write the equation showing all reactants and products. (There is no need to balance the equation yet.)	H^+(aq) + Cl^-(aq) + Fe(s) → Fe^{2+}(aq) + Cl^-(aq) + H_2(g)
Identify the spectator ions.	Cl^-(aq)
Rewrite the equation without the spectator ions. Balance the equation with respect to number of atoms of each element and charge.	$2H^+$(aq) + Fe(s) → Fe^{2+}(aq) + H_2(g)

Worked example: Try yourself 6.2.4

WRITING IONIC EQUATIONS FOR REACTIONS BETWEEN ACIDS AND REACTIVE METALS

Write an ionic equation for the reaction that occurs when aluminium is added to a solution of nitric acid.

6.2 Review

SUMMARY

- General equations for reactions involving acids and bases:
  - acid + metal hydroxide → salt + water
  - acid + metal carbonate → salt + water + carbon dioxide
  - acid + reactive metal → salt + hydrogen
- Neutralisation reactions involve balancing the hydronium and hydroxide ion concentrations by adding a base to an acid, or vice versa, in stoichiometric proportions to produce a salt and water.
- The enthalpy of neutralisation is the heat released per mol of water produced during a neutralisation reaction and is given the symbol ΔH_{neut} and has the unit $kJ\,mol^{-1}$.
- Neutralisation reactions are exothermic and as such ΔH_{neut} is negative.

KEY QUESTIONS

1 For the reactions between the following pairs of compounds, write:
  i the balanced chemical equation
  ii the balanced ionic equation.
  a magnesium and nitric acid
  b calcium and sulfuric acid
  c zinc and hydrochloric acid
  d aluminium and ethanoic acid.

2 Name the salt produced in each of the reactions in Question **1**.

3 For the reactions between the following pairs, write:
  i the balanced chemical equation
  ii the balanced ionic equation.
  a solid aluminium hydroxide and hydrofluoric acid
  b solid iron(II) hydroxide and nitric acid
  c solid zinc carbonate and ethanoic acid
  d solid tin(II) hydrogen carbonate and hydrochloric acid.

4 25.0 mL of a $1.00\,mol\,L^{-1}$ sodium hydroxide solution was completely neutralised by the addition of 12.5 mL of sulfuric acid. The temperature of the mixture rose from 19.5°C to 28.3°C. Assume the density of the mixture is $1\,g\,mL^{-1}$.
  a Write a balanced equation for the reaction between sulfuric acid and sodium hydroxide.
  b Calculate the amount of sodium hydroxide used in the neutralisation reaction.
  c Calculate the amount of energy released in the neutralisation reaction.
  d Calculate the amount of water, in mol, produced by the reaction.
  e Calculate the enthalpy of neutralisation, ΔH_{neut}.

5 Which one of the following best describes the species, apart from H_2O, that exist in an aqueous solution formed from the complete neutralisation of potassium hydroxide with nitric acid?
  A $K^+(aq)$ and $NO_3^-(aq)$
  B $K^+(aq)$, $OH^-(aq)$ and $H^+(aq)$
  C $K^+(aq)$, $NO_3^-(aq)$ and $H^+(aq)$
  D $K^+(aq)$, and $H^+(aq)$

Chapter review

KEY TERMS

acid
acid–base reaction
acidic proton
alkali
amphiprotic
Arrhenius theory
base
Brønsted–Lowry theory
calorimetry

conjugate acid
conjugate acid–base pair
conjugate base
diprotic acid
dissociate
dissociation
enthalpy of neutralisation
hydronium ion
hydroxide ion

indicator
ionise
monoprotic acid
neutralisation reaction
neutralise
polyprotic acid
proton acceptor
proton donor
salt

solute
solution
strong acid
triprotic acid
weak acid

REVIEW QUESTIONS

1 Identify the reactant that acts as an acid in each of the following reactions.

  a $NH_4^+(aq) + H_2O(l) \rightarrow NH_3(aq) + H_3O^+(aq)$

  b $NH_3(g) + HCl(g) \rightarrow NH_4Cl(s)$

  c $HCO_3^-(aq) + OH^-(aq) \rightarrow H_2O(l) + CO_3^{2-}(aq)$

  d $SO_4^{2-}(aq) + H_3O^+(aq) \rightarrow HSO_4^-(aq) + H_2O(l)$

  e $CO_3^{2-}(aq) + CH_3COOH(aq) \rightarrow HCO_3^-(aq) + CH_3COO^-(aq)$

2 Write balanced equations to show that in water:

  a PO_4^{3-} acts as a base

  b $H_2PO_4^-$ acts as an amphiprotic substance

  c H_2S acts as an acid.

3 Write the formula for the conjugate of:

  a the acid HCl

  b the base OH^-

  c the base O^{2-}

  d HSO_4^- when it acts as an acid.

4 Using suitable examples, distinguish between:

  a a diprotic and an amphiprotic substance

  b a strong and a weak acid.

5 Draw a structural formula of the monoprotic ethanoic acid molecule. Identify which proton is donated in an acid–base reaction.

6 Which of the following reactions are Brønsted–Lowry acid–base reactions?

  A $HCl(aq) + KOH(aq) \rightarrow KCl(aq) + H_2O(l)$

  B $2HNO_3(aq) + Mg(s) \rightarrow Mg(NO_3)_2(aq) + H_2(g)$

  C $AgNO_3(aq) + NaCl(aq) \rightarrow AgCl(s) + NaNO_3(aq)$

  D $CuO(s) + H_2SO_4(aq) \rightarrow CuSO_4(aq) + H_2O(l)$

7 Chromic acid (H_2CrO_4) is a diprotic acid.

  a Explain what is meant by a diprotic acid.

  b Write balanced chemical equations to represent the stages of dissociation for chromic acid.

8 In polyprotic acids, do the dissociation stages of removal of protons occur to a greater extent, a lesser extent, or the same extent? Explain.

9 Which of the following species is both diprotic and amphiprotic?

  A HCl

  B HSO_4^-

  C H_2SO_3

  D $H_2PO_4^-$

10 Complete and balance the following reactions:

  a $Fe(s) + 2HF(aq) \rightarrow$

  b $HClO_4(aq) + LiOH(aq) \rightarrow$

  c $HNO_3(aq) + KHCO_3(aq) \rightarrow$

  d $Li_2CO_3(aq) + 2CH_3COOH(aq) \rightarrow$

11 For each of the chemical equations in Question **10**, write the corresponding net ionic equation.

12 What volume of $0.0010\,mol\,L^{-1}$ potassium hydroxide solution would be required to neutralise 30.0 mL of a $0.0500\,mol\,L^{-1}$ hydrofluoric acid solution?

13 40.0 mL of a solution of $HClO_4$ was added to neutralise 40.0 mL of a $2.00\,mol\,L^{-1}$ solution of NaOH. The temperature of the mixture rose from 22.3°C to 35.2°C.

  a Write a balanced chemical equation for the reaction.

  b Calculate the enthalpy of neutralisation, ΔH_{neut}, for this reaction.

  c If the standard enthalpy of neutralisation for this reaction is $-57.3\,kJ\,mol^{-1}$, account for possible reasons why there might be a difference.

14 Hydrochloric acid is a key component in brick cleaner and sodium hydrogen carbonate is used in large quantities to neutralise acid spills.

  a Write a balanced chemical equation for the reaction between sodium hydrogen carbonate and hydrochloric acid.

  b What is the minimum mass of sodium hydrogen carbonate required to neutralise 2.00 L of a $12 \, mol \, L^{-1}$ solution of hydrochloric acid solution used to clean bricks?

15 Define what is meant by a spectator ion, and explain why spectator ions are not listed in net ionic equations.

16 a Write concise definitions for the following terms:

    i Brønsted–Lowry acid

    ii strong base

    iii molarity

    iv conjugate acid.

  b Explain, with the aid of equations, why HCO_3^- is classified as amphiprotic.

17 In the following reactions, identify the conjugate acid–base pairs:

  a $HCl(aq) + NaOH(aq) \rightarrow NaCl(aq) + H_2O(l)$

  b $HNO_3(aq) + NH_3(aq) \rightarrow NH_4NO_3(aq)$

  c $HCO_3^-(aq) + H_2O(l) \rightarrow CO_3^{2-}(aq) + H_3O^+(aq)$

18 Why can the hydrogen ion or proton (H^+) be represented by the hydronium ion (H_3O^+) when in solution?

19 Construct a concept map that demonstrates your understanding of the links between the following terms:

acid, base, proton, hydrogen ion, hydronium ion, conjugate

20 Reflect on the Inquiry activity on page 144. What type of reaction was demonstrated?

Using the Brønsted–Lowry theory

Most biological processes, particularly within the human body, exist in narrow limits, including the balance of acidic and basic components. Saliva is mildly acidic to begin the digestive process, and the stomach produces acid to further aid digestion and kill pathogens and unhelpful bacteria. A number of amino acids have acidic or basic side chains and are of great importance physiologically. Many acids and bases used in industry and in household applications are very strong, and can cause serious injury if they are mishandled or misused. It is important then to understand the nature of such acids and bases and quantify their strengths and applications.

In this chapter you will investigate the distinction between strong and weak acids, and concentrated and dilute acids. You will learn how to measure acidity and basicity, particularly with reference to their component concentrations and respective p-functions.

Content

INQUIRY QUESTION

What is the role of water in solutions of acids and bases?

By the end of this chapter, you will be able to:

- conduct an investigation to demonstrate the preparation and use of indicators as illustrators of the characteristics and properties of acids and bases and their reversible reactions (ACSCH101)
- conduct a practical investigation to measure the pH of a range of acids and bases
- calculate pH, pOH, hydrogen ion concentration ($[H^+]$) and hydroxide ion concentration ($[OH^-]$) for a range of solutions (ACSCH102) ICT N
- conduct an investigation to demonstrate the use of pH to indicate the differences between the strength of acids and bases (ACSCH102)
- construct models and/or animations to communicate the differences between strong, weak, concentrated and dilute acids and bases (ACSCH099) ICT
- calculate the pH of the resultant solution when solutions of acids and/or bases are diluted or mixed ICT N

Chemistry Stage 6 Syllabus © NSW Education Standards Authority for and on behalf of the Crown in right of the State of NSW, 2017.

7.1 Strength of acids and bases

CHEMISTRY INQUIRY `CCT`

Making an indicator from red cabbage

COLLECT THIS...

- lab coat
- disposable gloves
- safety glasses
- 3 large red cabbage leaves
- blender
- sieve
- 10 test tubes, 16 mm diameter
- white paper
- 250 mL distilled water
- 0.10 mol L^{-1} HCl solution
- 0.10 mol L^{-1} NaOH solution
- vinegar
- sodium hydrogen carbonate (bicarbonate of soda) powder
- lemon juice
- laundry detergent
- lemonade
- soluble aspirin (acetylsalicylic acid)
- cloudy ammonia

DO THIS...

1 Pour 1.0 L of distilled water into the blender.

2 Add three large red cabbage leaves.

3 Blend the water and cabbage leaves until the mixture appears smooth.

4 Using the sieve, strain off the liquid and keep the filtrate.

5 Half-fill each of the test tubes with the filtrate.

6 Set aside one test tube without adding any other solution to it. This will provide a reference for the colour of neutral solutions.

7 To one of the test tubes, add approximately 5.0 mL of 0.10 mol L^{-1} HCl solution and shake the tube gently to mix. This will provide a reference for the colour of acidic solutions.

8 To another test tube, add approximately 5.0 mL of 0.10 mol L^{-1} NaOH solution and shake the tube gently to mix. This will provide a reference for the colour of basic solutions.

9 To the remaining test tubes, add approximately 5.0 mL of the samples and shake each tube gently to mix. Dissolve any solid sample first in a small amount of distilled water before adding it to the indicator filtrate.

RECORD THIS...

Describe the colour change of each solution tested and determine by the colour whether the solution is acidic, basic or neutral compared with the reference test tube.

Present your results in a table.

REFLECT ON THIS...

1 Which substances are acidic?

2 Which substances are basic?

3 Were there any results that surprised you? Explain your response.

4 What is the purpose of the blender?

The acid solutions in the two beakers shown in Figure 7.1.1 are of equal **concentration**, yet the acid in the beaker on the left reacts more vigorously with zinc than the acid on the right. The acid on the left is described as a stronger acid than the one on the right.

FIGURE 7.1.1 Zinc reacts more vigorously with a strong acid (left) than with a weak acid (right). The acid solutions are of equal concentration and volume.

In Chapter 6 you learnt that the Brønsted–Lowry theory defines acids as proton donors, and bases as proton acceptors. In this section you will investigate the differences between:

GO TO ➤ Section 6.1 page 144

* strong and weak acids
* strong and weak bases.

ACID AND BASE STRENGTH

Experiments show that different acid solutions of the same concentration do not have the same pH (a measure of the concentration of hydronium ions in solution). (pH will be looked at more closely in Section 7.2.)

Some acids can donate a proton more readily than others. The Brønsted–Lowry theory defines the strength of an acid as its ability to donate protons to a base. The strength of a base is a measure of its ability to accept protons from an acid.

Since aqueous solutions of acids and bases are most commonly used, it is convenient to use an acid's tendency to donate a proton to water, or a base's tendency to accept a proton from water, as a measure of its strength.

Table 7.1.1 gives the names and chemical formulae of some strong and weak acids and bases.

TABLE 7.1.1 Examples of common strong and weak acids and bases

Strong acids	Weak acids	Strong bases	Weak bases
hydrochloric acid, HCl	ethanoic (acetic) acid, CH_3COOH	sodium hydroxide, NaOH	ammonia, NH_3
sulfuric acid, H_2SO_4	carbonic acid, H_2CO_3	potassium hydroxide, KOH	pyridine, C_5H_5N
nitric acid, HNO_3	phosphoric acid, H_3PO_4	calcium hydroxide, $Ca(OH)_2$	dimethylamine, $(CH_3)_2NH$

Strong acids

As you saw previously, hydrogen chloride gas (HCl) dissociates completely when it is bubbled through water; virtually no HCl molecules remain in the solution (Figure 7.1.2a). Similarly, pure HNO_3 and H_2SO_4 are covalent molecular compounds that also dissociate completely in water:

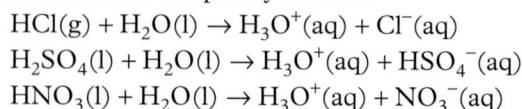

$$HCl(g) + H_2O(l) \rightarrow H_3O^+(aq) + Cl^-(aq)$$
$$H_2SO_4(l) + H_2O(l) \rightarrow H_3O^+(aq) + HSO_4^-(aq)$$
$$HNO_3(l) + H_2O(l) \rightarrow H_3O^+(aq) + NO_3^-(aq)$$

The single reaction arrow ($\rightarrow$) in each equation above indicates that the dissociation reaction is complete.

Acids that readily donate a proton are called **strong acids**. Strong acids donate protons easily. Therefore solutions of strong acids contain ions, with virtually no unreacted acid molecules remaining. Hydrochloric acid, sulfuric acid and nitric acid are the most common strong acids.

Weak acids

Vinegar is a solution of ethanoic (acetic) acid. Pure ethanoic acid is a polar covalent molecular compound that dissociates in water to produce hydrogen ions and ethanoate (acetate) ions. In a $1.0\,mol\,L^{-1}$ solution of ethanoic acid (CH_3COOH), only a small proportion of ethanoic acid molecules are dissociated at any one time (Figure 7.1.2b). A $1.0\,mol\,L^{-1}$ solution of ethanoic acid contains a high proportion of CH_3COOH molecules and only some hydronium ions and ethanoate ions. In a $1.0\,mol\,L^{-1}$ solution of ethanoic acid at 25°C, the concentrations of $CH_3COO^-(aq)$ and H_3O^+ are only about $0.004\,mol\,L^{-1}$.

The partial dissociation of a **weak acid** is shown in an equation using reversible (double) arrows:

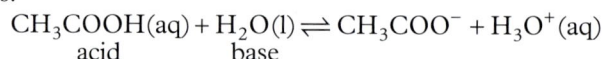

$$\underset{\text{acid}}{CH_3COOH(aq)} + H_2O(l) \rightleftharpoons \underset{\text{base}}{CH_3COO^-} + H_3O^+(aq)$$

Therefore ethanoic acid is described as a weak acid in water (Figure 7.1.2b).

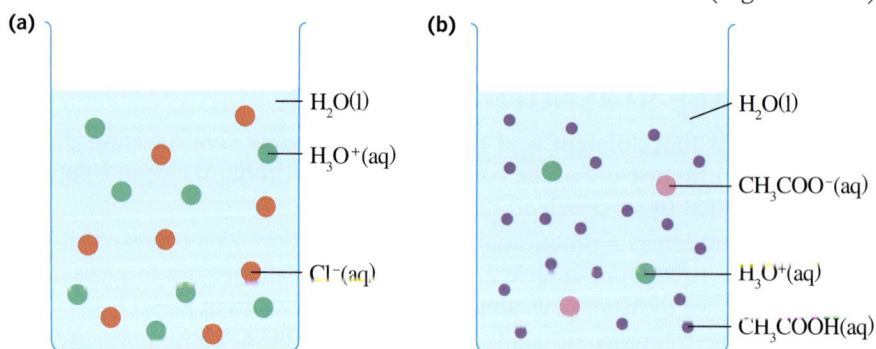

FIGURE 7.1.2 (a) In a $1.0\,mol\,L^{-1}$ solution of hydrochloric acid, the acid molecules are completely dissociated in water. (b) However, in a $1.0\,mol\,L^{-1}$ solution of ethanoic acid only a small proportion of the ethanoic acid molecules are dissociated.

Strong bases

The ionic compound sodium oxide (Na_2O) dissociates in water, releasing sodium ions (Na^+) and oxide ions (O^{2-}). The oxide ions react completely with the water, accepting a proton to form hydroxide ions (OH^-):

$$\underset{\text{base}}{O^{2-}(aq)} + \underset{\text{acid}}{H_2O(l)} \rightarrow 2OH^-(aq)$$

The oxide ion is an example of a **strong base**. Strong bases accept protons easily.

Sodium hydroxide (NaOH) is often referred to as a strong base. However, according to the Brønsted–Lowry definition of acids and bases, it is more correct to say that sodium hydroxide is an ionic compound that is a source of the strong base OH^-.

Weak bases

Ammonia is a covalent molecular compound that dissociates in water by accepting a proton. This dissociation can be represented by the equation:

$$\underset{\text{base}}{NH_3(aq)} + \underset{\text{acid}}{H_2O(l)} \rightleftharpoons NH_4^+(aq) + OH^-(aq)$$

Ammonia behaves as a base because it gains a proton. Water has donated a proton and so it behaves as an acid.

Only a small proportion of ammonia molecules are dissociated at any instant, so a $1.0\,\text{mol}\,L^{-1}$ solution of ammonia contains mostly ammonia molecules together with a smaller number of ammonium ions and hydroxide ions. This is shown by the double arrow in the equation. Ammonia is a **weak base** in water.

CHEMFILE Ⓝ

Super acids

Fluorosulfuric acid (HSO_3F) is one of the strongest acids known. It has a similar geometry to that of the sulfuric acid molecule (Figure 7.1.3). The highly electronegative fluorine atom causes the oxygen–hydrogen bond in fluorosulfuric acid to be more polarised than the oxygen–hydrogen bond in sulfuric acid. The acidic proton is easily transferred to a base.

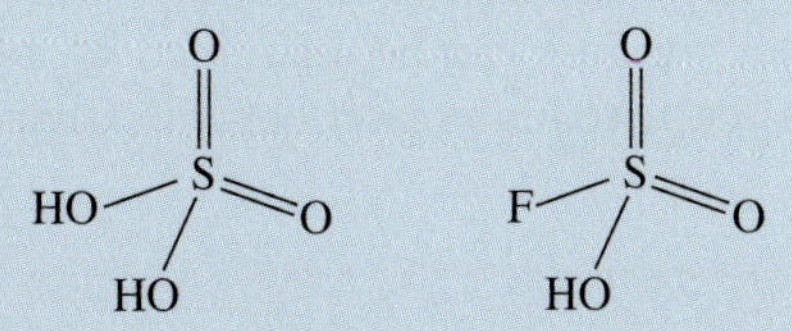

FIGURE 7.1.3 Structures of sulfuric acid (left) and fluorosulfuric acid (right) molecules

Fluorosulfuric acid is classified as a **super acid**. Super acids are acids that have an acidity greater than the acidity of pure sulfuric acid.

Super acids such as fluorosulfuric acid and triflic acid (CF_3SO_3H) are about 1000 times stronger than sulfuric acid. Carborane acid, $H(CHB_{11}Cl_{11})$, is 1 million times stronger than sulfuric acid. The strongest known super acid is fluoroantimonic acid (H_2FSbF_6), which is 10^{16} times stronger than pure sulfuric acid.

Super acids are used in the production of plastics and high-octane petrol, in coal gasification and in research.

Relative strength of conjugate acid–base pairs

GO TO ➤ Section 6.1 page 144

You will recall from Chapter 6 that conjugate acids and bases differ by one proton (H^+). In the reaction represented by the equation:

$$HF(aq) + OH^-(aq) \rightleftharpoons H_2O(l) + F^-(aq)$$

HF is the conjugate acid of F^- and OH^- is the conjugate base of H_2O. HF and F^- are a conjugate acid–base pair. H_2O and OH^- are another conjugate acid–base pair in this reaction.

The stronger an acid is, the weaker its conjugate base is. Similarly, the stronger a base is, the weaker its conjugate acid is. The relative strength of some conjugate acid–base pairs is shown in Figure 7.1.4.

Strength versus concentration

When referring to solutions of acids and bases, it is important not to confuse the terms 'strong' and 'weak' with 'concentrated' and 'dilute'. Concentrated and dilute describe the amount of acid or base dissolved in a given volume of solution. Hydrochloric acid is a strong acid because it readily donates protons. A **concentrated solution** of hydrochloric acid can be prepared by bubbling a large amount of hydrogen chloride into a given volume of water. By using only a small amount of hydrogen chloride, a dilute solution of hydrochloric acid would be produced.

Acid	Base
HCl	Cl$^-$
H$_2$SO$_4$	HSO$_4^-$
HNO$_3$	NO$_3^-$
H$_3$O$^+$	H$_2$O
HSO$_4^-$	SO$_4^{2-}$
H$_3$PO$_4$	H$_2$PO$_4^-$
HF	F$^-$
CH$_3$COOH	CH$_3$COO$^-$
H$_2$CO$_3$	HCO$_3^-$
H$_2$S	HS$^-$
H$_2$PO$_4^-$	HPO$_4^{2-}$
H$_2$O	OH$^-$
OH$^-$	O^{2-}

Increasing acid strength (strong → weak → negligible); *Increasing base strength (negligible → weak → strong)*

FIGURE 7.1.4 The relative strength of some conjugate acid–base pairs

However, in both cases, the hydrogen chloride is completely dissociated—it is a strong acid. Similarly a solution of ethanoic acid may be concentrated or dilute. However, as it is only partially dissociated, it is a weak acid (Figure 7.1.5).

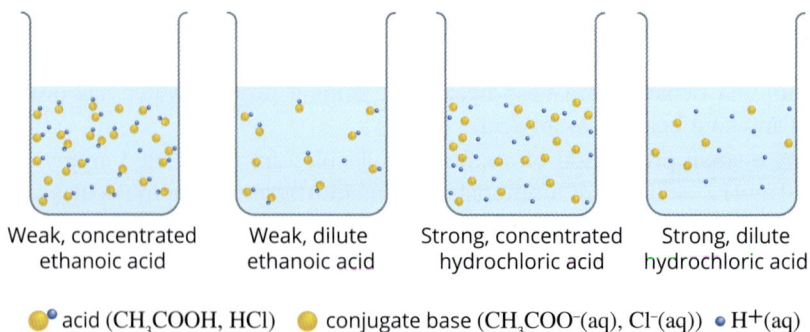

Weak, concentrated ethanoic acid   Weak, dilute ethanoic acid   Strong, concentrated hydrochloric acid   Strong, dilute hydrochloric acid

● acid (CH_3COOH, HCl)   ● conjugate base (CH_3COO^-(aq), Cl^-(aq))   • H^+(aq)

FIGURE 7.1.5 The concentration of ions in an acid solution depends on both the concentration and strength of the acid.

Terms such as 'weak' and 'strong' for acids and bases, and 'dilute' or 'concentrated' for solutions, are qualitative (or descriptive) terms. Solutions can be given accurate, quantitative descriptions by stating concentrations in $mol\,L^{-1}$ or $g\,L^{-1}$. The extent of dissociation of an acid or base can be quantified by measuring its **dissociation constant**. This will be discussed in greater detail in Chapter 8.

7.1 Review

SUMMARY

- A concentrated acid or base contains more moles of solute per litre of solution than a dilute acid or base.
- In the context of acids and bases, the terms 'strong' and 'weak' refer to the relative tendency to accept or donate protons.
  - A strong acid donates a proton more readily than a weak acid.

- A strong base accepts a proton more readily than a weak base.
- The stronger an acid is, the weaker is its conjugate base. The stronger a base is, the weaker is its conjugate acid.

KEY QUESTIONS

1 Write balanced equations to show that, in water:
  a $HClO_4$ is a strong acid
  b HCN is a weak acid
  c CH_3NH_2 is a weak base.

2 Write balanced equations for the three dissociation stages of arsenic acid (H_3AsO_4).

3 Which one of the following equations represents the reaction of a strong acid with water?
  A $HNO_3(aq) + H_2O(l) \rightarrow H_3O^+(aq) + NO_3^-(aq)$
  B $HF(aq) + H_2O(l) \rightleftharpoons H_3O^+(aq) + F^-(aq)$
  C $LiOH(s) \rightarrow Li^+(aq) + OH^-(aq)$
  D $NH_3(aq) + H_2O(l) \rightleftharpoons NH_4^+(aq) + OH^-(aq)$

4 Perchloric acid is a stronger acid than ethanoic acid. $1.0\,mol\,L^{-1}$ solutions of which acid would you expect to be a better conductor of electricity? Explain your answer.

7.2 Acidity and basicity of solutions

The Brønsted–Lowry theory defines an acid as a proton donor and a base as a proton acceptor. You have also seen that acids and bases can be classified as strong or weak, depending on how easily they donate or accept protons.

In this section, you will learn about the pH and pOH scales, which are a measure of acidity and basicity, respectively. You will also learn about the relationship between the concentration of hydronium and hydroxide ions in different solutions.

IONIC PRODUCT OF WATER

Water molecules can react with each other, as represented by the equation:

$$H_2O(l) + H_2O(l) \rightleftharpoons H_3O^+(aq) + OH^-(aq)$$

The production of the H_3O^+ ion and OH^- ion in this reaction is shown visually in Figure 7.2.1.

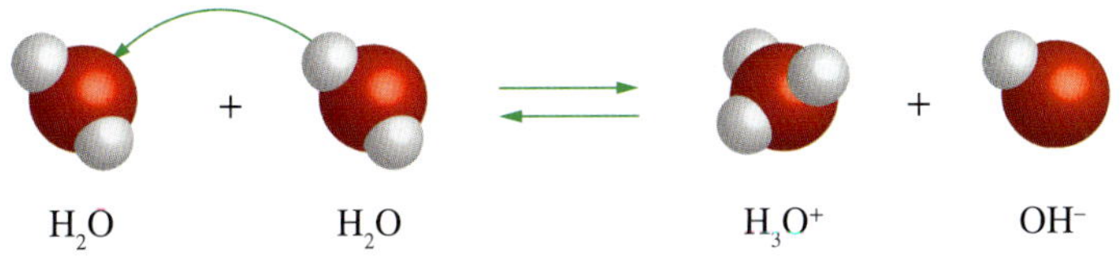

H₂O   H₂O   H₃O⁺   OH⁻

FIGURE 7.2.1 The ionisation of water molecules

Pure water undergoes this **self-ionisation** to a very small extent. In this reaction, water behaves as both a very weak acid and a very weak base, producing one hydronium ion (H_3O^+) for every one hydroxide ion (OH^-). Water therefore displays **amphiprotic** properties.

The concentration of hydronium and hydroxide ions is very low. In pure water at 25°C the H_3O^+ and OH^- concentrations are both $10^{-7}\,mol\,L^{-1}$. For each H_3O^+ ion present in a glass of water, there are 560 million H_2O molecules!

Experimental evidence shows that all aqueous solutions contain both H_3O^+ and OH^- ions, and that the product of their molar concentrations, $[H_3O^+][OH^-]$, is always 1.0×10^{-14} at 25°C. If either $[H_3O^+]$ or $[OH^-]$ in an aqueous solution increases, then the concentration of the other must decrease proportionally.

Remember that $[H_3O^+]$ represents the concentration of hydrogen ions and $[OH^-]$ represents the concentration of hydroxide ions. The expression $[H_3O^+][OH^-]$ is known as the **ionic product of water** and is represented by the symbol K_w:

$$K_w = [H_3O^+][OH^-] = 1.0 \times 10^{-14} \text{ at } 25°C$$

Acidic and basic solutions

In solutions of acidic substances, H_3O^+ ions are formed by reaction of the acid with water, as well as from self-ionisation of water. So the concentration of H_3O^+ ions will be greater than $10^{-7}\,mol\,L^{-1}$ at 25°C. Since the product $[H_3O^+][OH^-]$ remains constant, the concentration of OH^- ions in an **acidic solution** at this temperature must be less than $10^{-7}\,mol\,L^{-1}$.

The opposite is true for **basic solutions**. The concentration of OH^- ions in a basic solution is greater than $10^{-7}\,mol\,L^{-1}$ and the concentration of H_3O^+ ions is less than $10^{-7}\,mol\,L^{-1}$.

In summary, at 25°C:
- pure water and **neutral solutions**: $[H_3O^+] = [OH^-] = 10^{-7}\,mol\,L^{-1}$
- acidic solutions: $[H_3O^+] > 10^{-7}\,mol\,L^{-1}$ and $[OH^-] < 10^{-7}\,mol\,L^{-1}$
- basic solutions: $[H_3O^+] < 10^{-7}\,mol\,L^{-1}$ and $[OH^-] > 10^{-7}\,mol\,L^{-1}$.

The higher the concentration of H_3O^+ ions in a solution, the more acidic the solution is.

Conversely, the higher the concentration of OH^- ions in a solution, the more basic the solution is.

Square brackets [ ] are often used to represent molar concentration.

In acid–base chemistry, the terms 'dissociation' and 'ionisation' can be used interchangeably, and the ionic product is also called the ionisation constant.

Calculating the concentration of H_3O^+ in aqueous solutions

The expression for K_w can be used to determine the concentrations of hydronium and hydroxide ions in solution, knowing that the value of K_w in solutions at 25°C is 1.0×10^{-14}.

Worked example 7.2.1

CALCULATING THE CONCENTRATION OF HYDRONIUM AND HYDROXIDE IONS IN AN AQUEOUS SOLUTION

For a $0.10 \, mol \, L^{-1}$ HCl solution at 25°C, calculate the concentrations of H_3O^+ and OH^- ions.

Thinking	Working
Find the concentration of the hydronium (H_3O^+) ions.	HCl is a strong acid, so it will dissociate completely in solution. Each molecule of HCl donates one proton to water to form one H_3O^+ ion: $$HCl(aq) + H_2O(l) \rightarrow H_3O^+(aq) + Cl^-(aq)$$ Because HCl is completely dissociated in water, $0.10 \, mol \, L^{-1}$ HCl will produce a solution with a concentration of H_3O^+ ions of $0.10 \, mol \, L^{-1}$. $$[H_3O^+] = 0.10 \, mol \, L^{-1}$$
Use the expression for the ionisation constant of water to calculate the concentration of OH^- ions.	$$K_w = [H_3O^+][OH^-] = 1.0 \times 10^{-14}$$ $$[OH^-] = \frac{1.0 \times 10^{-14}}{[H_3O^+]}$$ $$= \frac{1.0 \times 10^{-14}}{0.10}$$ $$= 1.0 \times 10^{-13} \, mol \, L^{-1}$$

Worked example: Try yourself 7.2.1

CALCULATING THE CONCENTRATION OF HYDRONIUM AND HYDROXIDE IONS IN AN AQUEOUS SOLUTION

For a $5.6 \times 10^{-6} \, mol \, L^{-1}$ HNO_3 solution at 25°C, calculate the concentration of H_3O^+ and OH^- ions.

pH AND pOH: A CONVENIENT WAY TO MEASURE ACIDITY AND BASICITY

Definition of pH

The range of H_3O^+ concentrations in solutions is so great that a convenient scale, called the **pH scale**, has been developed to measure acidity. The pH scale was first proposed by the Danish scientist Sören Sörenson in 1909 as a way of expressing levels of acidity. The pH of a solution is defined as:

$$pH = -\log_{10}[H_3O^+]$$

Alternatively, this expression can be rearranged to give:

$$[H_3O^+] = 10^{-pH}$$

The pH scale eliminates the need to write cumbersome powers of 10 when we describe hydrogen ion concentration. It is part of a series of transformations known as **p-functions**. The use of pH greatly simplifies the measurement and calculation of acidity. Since the scale is based on the negative logarithm of the hydrogen ion concentration, the pH of a solution decreases as the concentration of hydrogen ions increases.

WS
6.2

Definition of pOH

The **pOH scale** is a measure of basicity, in the same way that the pH scale is a measure of acidity. The pOH of a solution is defined as:

$$pOH = -\log_{10}[OH^-]$$

Alternatively, this expression can be rearranged to give:

$$[OH^-] = 10^{-pOH}$$

At 25°C, the pOH and pH of a solution are linked according to the following relationship:

$$pH + pOH = 14$$

This means that the pOH scale is the reverse relationship of the pH scale. That is, as the pOH of a solution increases, the pH decreases.

pH and pOH of acidic and basic solutions

Figure 7.2.2 shows a pH meter, which can be used to measure the pH of a solution accurately.

Acidic, basic and neutral solutions can be defined in terms of their pH at 25°C.

- Neutral solutions have both the pH and pOH equal to 7.
- Acidic solutions have a pH less than 7 and a pOH greater than 7.
- Basic solutions have a pH greater than 7 and a pOH less than 7.

FIGURE 7.2.2 A pH meter is used to measure the acidity of a solution.

On the pH scale, the most acidic solutions have pH values slightly less than 0, and the most basic solutions have pH values of about 14. On the pOH scale, more basic solutions have a lower pOH. The pH and pOH values of some common substances are provided in Table 7.2.1.

TABLE 7.2.1 pH and pOH values of some common substances at 25°C

Solution	pH	pOH	$[H_3O^+]$ (mol L^{-1})	$[OH^-]$ (mol L^{-1})	$[H_3O^+][OH^-]$
1.0 mol L^{-1} HCl	0.0	14.0	1	10^{-14}	10^{-14}
lemon juice	3.0	11.0	10^{-3}	10^{-11}	10^{-14}
vinegar	4.0	10.0	10^{-4}	10^{-10}	10^{-14}
tomato juice	5.0	9.0	10^{-5}	10^{-9}	10^{-14}
rain water	6.0	8.0	10^{-6}	10^{-8}	10^{-14}
pure water	7.0	7.0	10^{-7}	10^{-7}	10^{-14}
seawater	8.0	6.0	10^{-8}	10^{-6}	10^{-14}
soap	9.0	5.0	10^{-9}	10^{-5}	10^{-14}
oven cleaner	13.0	1.0	10^{-13}	10^{-1}	10^{-14}
1.0 mol L^{-1} NaOH	14.0	0.0	10^{-14}	1	10^{-14}

WS
6.3

i A solution with a pH of 2 has 10 times the concentration of hydronium ions as one with a pH of 3.

A solution with a pH of 2 has one tenth the concentration of hydroxide ions as one with a pH of 3.

The reactions of acids and bases are important in a large variety of everyday applications, including biological functions. The high acidity of gastric juices is essential for protein digestion in the stomach. There is also a complex system of pH control in your blood, because even small deviations from the normal pH range of 7.35–7.45 for any length of time can lead to serious illness or death.

Indicators

One of the characteristic properties of acids and bases is their ability to change the colour of certain substances, called **indicators**. Many plant extracts are indicators, including litmus, a purple dye obtained from lichens. In the presence of acids, litmus turns red. Indicators can also be obtained from rose petals, blackberries, red cabbage and many other plants, although most commercial indicators are made from other substances. Some common indicators and their pH ranges are shown in Figure 7.2.3.

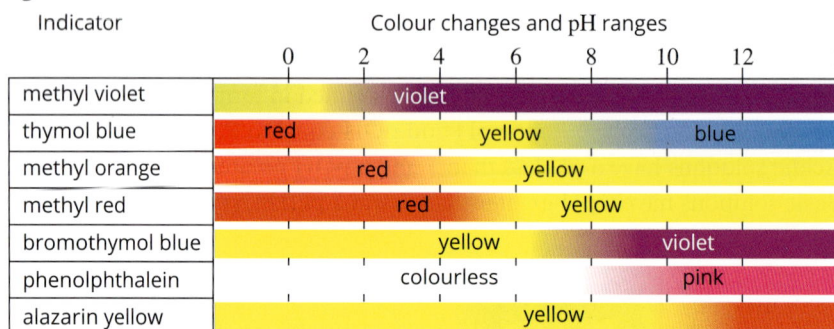

FIGURE 7.2.3 Common indicators and their pH ranges.

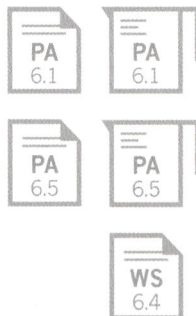

Indicators themselves are weak acids or weak bases. The conjugate acid form of the indicator is one colour and the conjugate base form is another colour. Indicators that undergo a single colour change are also used for many analyses.

Universal indicator

Universal indicator (Figure 7.2.4) is widely used to estimate the pH of a solution. It is a mixture of several indicators and changes through a range of colours, from red through yellow, green and blue, to violet. If a more accurate measurement of pH is needed, you can use a pH meter instead of universal indicator.

FIGURE 7.2.4 Universal indicator pH scale. When universal indicator is added to a solution, it changes colour depending on the solution's pH. The tubes contain solutions of pH 0 to 14 from left to right. The green tube (seventh from right) is neutral, pH 7.

Using litmus paper

Litmus paper is commonly used to test whether a substance is acidic or basic. Blue litmus paper will remain blue in the presence of a base, but will turn red in the presence of an acid (Figure 7.2.5). Red litmus paper will remain red in the presence of an acid, but will turn blue in the presence of a base (Figure 7.2.6). Purple litmus paper turns red in the presence of an acid, blue in the presence of a base, and remains purple if the substance is neutral.

Litmus paper does not tell you the pH value of a substance, but pH indicator papers can be used for this. Packets of pH inidcator papers include a colour chart that enables you to determine the pH of any substance (Figure 7.2.7).

FIGURE 7.2.5 Blue litmus paper turns red when exposed to the citric acid in an orange.

FIGURE 7.2.6 Red litmus paper turns blue when exposed to basic substances, such as wet alkaline soil.

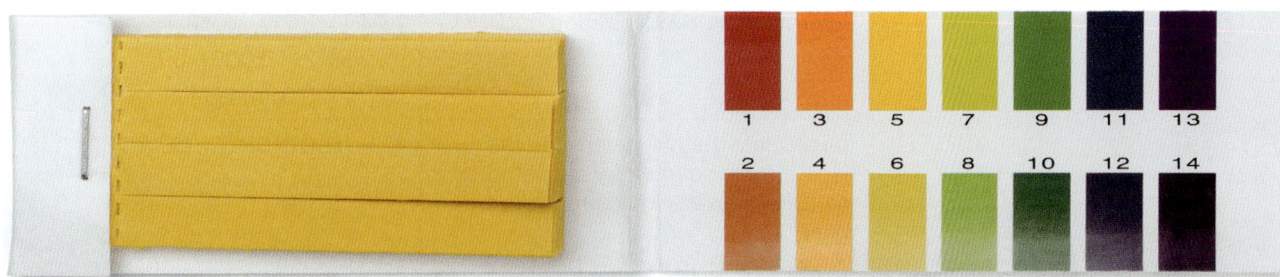

FIGURE 7.2.7 A packet of pH indicator papers with a colour chart.

Calculations involving pH and pOH

The pH of an aqueous solution can be calculated using the formula $pH = -\log_{10}[H_3O^+]$, and similarly $pOH = -\log_{10}[OH^-]$. Your scientific calculator has a logarithm function that will simplify pH and pOH calculations.

Worked example 7.2.2

CALCULATING THE pH AND pOH OF AN AQUEOUS SOLUTION FROM $[H_3O^+]$

Calculate the pH and pOH of a solution in which the concentration of $[H_3O^+]$ is $0.14\,mol\,L^{-1}$. Give your answer correct to 2 decimal places.

Thinking	Working
Write down the concentration of $[H_3O^+]$ ions in the solution.	$[H_3O^+] = 0.14\,mol\,L^{-1}$
Substitute the value of $[H_3O^+]$ into: $$pH = -\log_{10}[H_3O^+]$$ Use the logarithm function on your calculator to determine the answer (ensure to use log to the base 10 and not the natural logarithm, which may appear as *ln*).	$pH = -\log_{10}[H_3O^+]$ $= -\log_{10}(0.14)$ $= 0.85$
Calculate pOH from the relationship: $$pOH = 14 - pH$$	$pOH = 14 - pH$ $= 14 - 0.85$ $= 13.15$

Worked example: Try yourself 7.2.2

CALCULATING THE pH AND pOH OF AN AQUEOUS SOLUTION FROM $[H_3O^+]$

Calculate the pH and pOH of a solution in which the concentration of $[H_3O^+]$ is $6 \times 10^{-9}\,mol\,L^{-1}$. Give your answer correct to 2 significant figures.

Worked example 7.2.3

CALCULATING THE pH AND pOH IN A SOLUTION OF A BASE

What is the pH and pOH of a $0.005\,mol\,L^{-1}$ solution of $Ba(OH)_2$ at 25°C?

Thinking	Working
Write down the equation for the dissociation of $Ba(OH)_2$ in water.	In water, 1 mol of $Ba(OH)_2$ completely dissociates to release 2 mol of OH^- ions. $Ba(OH)_2(aq) \rightarrow Ba^{2+}(aq) + 2OH^-(aq)$
Determine the concentration of $[OH^-]$ ions.	$[OH^-] = 2 \times [Ba(OH)_2]$ $= 2 \times 0.005\,mol\,L^{-1}$ $= 0.01\,mol\,L^{-1}$
To calculate the pH, determine the $[H_3O^+]$ in the solution by substituting the $[OH^-]$ into the ionic product of water: $$K_w = [H_3O^+][OH^-] = 1.0 \times 10^{-14}$$	$K_w = [H_3O^+][OH^-] = 1.0 \times 10^{-14}$ $[H_3O^+] = \dfrac{K_w}{[OH^-]}$ $= \dfrac{1.0 \times 10^{-14}}{0.01}$ $= 1 \times 10^{-12}\,mol\,L^{-1}$
Substitute the value of $[H_3O^+]$ into: $$pH = -\log_{10}[H_3O^+]$$	$pH = -\log_{10}[H_3O^+]$ $= -\log_{10}(1 \times 10^{-12})$ $= 12.0$

Determine the pOH by using the pOH formula: $$pOH = -\log_{10}[OH^-]$$	$$pOH = -\log_{10}[OH^-]$$ $$= -\log_{10}(0.01)$$ $$= 2.0$$
Alternatively, calculate pH from the relationship: $$pH = 14 - pOH$$	$$pH = 14 - pOH$$ $$= 14 - 2.0$$ $$= 12.0$$

Worked example: Try yourself 7.2.3

CALCULATING pH AND pOH IN A SOLUTION OF A BASE

What is the pH and pOH of a $0.01 \, mol \, L^{-1}$ solution of $Ba(OH)_2$ at 25°C?

Worked example 7.2.4

CALCULATING pH AND pOH IN A SOLUTION WHERE THE SOLUTE MOLAR CONCENTRATION IS NOT GIVEN

Calculate the pH and pOH of a solution at 25°C that contains 1.0 g NaOH in 100 mL of solution.

Thinking	Working
Determine the number of moles of NaOH.	$$n(NaOH) = \frac{m}{M}$$ $$= \frac{1.0}{40.00}$$ $$= 0.025 \, mol$$
Write the equation for dissociation of NaOH.	$$NaOH(aq) \rightarrow Na^+(aq) + OH^-(aq)$$ NaOH is completely dissociated in water.
Determine the number of moles of OH^- based on the dissociation equation.	$$n(OH^-) = n(NaOH)$$ $$= 0.025 \, mol$$
Use the formula for determining concentration given number of moles and volume: $$c = \frac{n}{V}$$	$$n = 0.025 \, mol$$ $$V = 0.100 \, L$$ $$c = \frac{n}{V}$$ $$= \frac{0.025}{0.100}$$ $$= 0.25 \, mol \, L^{-1}$$
Determine the pOH by using the pOH formula: $$pOH = -\log_{10}[OH^-]$$	$$pOH = -\log_{10}(0.25)$$ $$= 0.60$$
Calculate pH from the relationship: $$pH = 14 - pOH$$	$$pH = 14 - pOH$$ $$= 14 - 0.60$$ $$= 13.40$$

Worked example: Try yourself 7.2.4

CALCULATING pH AND pOH IN A SOLUTION WHERE THE SOLUTE MOLAR CONCENTRATION IS NOT GIVEN

Calculate the pH and pOH of a solution at 25°C that contains 0.50 g KOH in 500 mL of solution.

Worked example 7.2.5

CALCULATING [H₃O⁺] AND [OH⁻] IN A SOLUTION OF A GIVEN pH

Calculate $[H_3O^+]$ and $[OH^-]$ in a solution of pH 5.0 at 25°C.

Thinking	Working
Decide which form of the relationship between pH and $[H_3O^+]$ should be used: $$pH = -\log_{10}[H_3O^+]$$ or $$[H_3O^+] = 10^{-pH}$$	As you have the pH and are calculating $[H_3O^+]$, use: $$[H_3O^+] = 10^{-pH}$$
Substitute the value of pH into the relationship expression and use a calculator to determine the answer.	$[H_3O^+] = 10^{-pH}$ $= 10^{-5.0}$ $= 1 \times 10^{-5}\,mol\,L^{-1}$
Determine the $[OH^-]$ in the solution by substituting the $[H_3O^+]$ into the ionic product of water: $$K_w = [H_3O^+][OH^-] = 1.0 \times 10^{-14}$$	$K_w = [H_3O^+][OH^-] = 1.0 \times 10^{-14}$ $[OH^-] = \dfrac{K_w}{[H_3O^+]}$ $= \dfrac{1.0 \times 10^{-14}}{1 \times 10^{-5}}$ $= 1 \times 10^{-9}\,mol\,L^{-1}$

Worked example: Try yourself 7.2.5

CALCULATING [H₃O⁺] AND [OH⁻] IN A SOLUTION OF A GIVEN pH

Calculate $[H_3O^+]$ and $[OH^-]$ in a solution of pH 10.4 at 25°C.

+ ADDITIONAL N

Effect of temperature on pH and pOH

At the start of this section the ionic product of water was defined as:

$$K_w = [H_3O^+][OH^-] = 1.0 \times 10^{-14} \text{ at } 25°C$$

You can use this relationship to calculate either $[H_3O^+]$ or $[OH^-]$ at 25°C in different solutions. But what happens if the temperature is not 25°C?

From experimental data it is known that the value of K_w increases as the temperature increases, as shown in Table 7.2.2.

In Chapter 4 it was noted that a change in temperature changes the value of the equilibrium constant, and that endothermic reactions are favoured at higher temperatures. The self-ionisation of water is an endothermic process. This means that the value of K_w will be larger at higher temperatures, and therefore the concentration of both the hydronium and hydroxide ions will be higher. This is why it is important that the temperature is given when the value of K_w is stated.

The pH and pOH of pure water are both 7.00 at 25°C. At other temperatures, even though the pH and pOH are not equal to 7.00, pure water can still be described as neutral because the concentrations of H_3O^+ and OH^- ions are equal. It is important to note, then, that as you move away from 25°C the pH + pOH = 14 relationship no longer applies.

TABLE 7.2.2 The effect of temperature on pH and pOH of pure water

Temperature (°C)	K_w	pH = pOH
0	1.1×10^{-15}	7.47
5	1.9×10^{-15}	7.37
15	4.5×10^{-15}	7.17
25	1.0×10^{-14}	7.00
35	2.1×10^{-14}	6.83
45	4.0×10^{-14}	6.70
55	7.3×10^{-14}	6.57

7.2 Review

SUMMARY

- Water self-ionises according to the equation:
$$H_2O(l) + H_2O(l) \rightleftharpoons H_3O^+(aq) + OH^-(aq)$$
- The ionic product for water is:
$$K_w = [H_3O^+][OH^-] = 1.0 \times 10^{-14} \text{ at } 25°C$$
- The concentration of H_3O^+ is measured using the pH scale:
$$pH = -\log_{10}[H_3O^+]$$
- The concentration of OH^- is measured using the pOH scale:
$$pOH = -\log_{10}[OH^-]$$

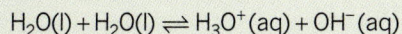

- At 25°C the pH and pOH of a neutral solution are both 7. The pH of an acidic solution is less than 7 and the pH of a basic solution is greater than 7. The pOH of a basic solution is less than 7 and the pOH of an acidic solution is greater than 7.
- The relationship between pH and pOH at 25°C can be expressed as:
$$pH + pOH = 14$$

KEY QUESTIONS

1 Calculate $[OH^-]$ at 25°C in an aqueous solution with $[H_3O^+] = 0.001 \text{ mol L}^{-1}$.

2 What is $[OH^-]$ in a solution at 25°C with $[H_3O^+] = 5.70 \times 10^{-9} \text{ mol L}^{-1}$?

3 Calculate $[H_3O^+]$ at 25°C in an aqueous solution in which $[OH^-] = 1.0 \times 10^{-5} \text{ mol L}^{-1}$.

4 What is the pH and pOH of a solution in which $[H_3O^+] = 0.01 \text{ mol L}^{-1}$?

5 Calculate the pH and pOH of a 0.001 mol L^{-1} solution of nitric acid (HNO_3).

6 The pH of water in a lake is 6.0. Calculate $[H_3O^+]$ and $[OH^-]$ in the lake.

7 Determine the pH and pOH of a 200 mL solution that contains 0.365 g of dissolved HCl.

7.3 Dilution of acids and bases

Although acids are frequently purchased as concentrated solutions, you will often need to use them in a more diluted form. For example, a bricklayer needs a 10% solution of hydrochloric acid to remove mortar splashes from bricks used to build a house. The brick-cleaning solution is prepared by diluting concentrated hydrochloric acid by a factor of 10.

In this section you will learn how to calculate the concentration and pH of acids and bases once they have been diluted.

CONCENTRATION OF ACIDS AND BASES

The concentration of acids and bases is usually expressed in units of $mol\,L^{-1}$. This is also referred to as molar concentration or **molarity**.

> **i** The unit for molarity can be written several ways: $mol\,L^{-1}$, mol/L and M are all acceptable forms. It is best to use only one of these options to be consistent.

REVISION   **GO TO ►** Year 11 Chapter 8

You will recall from Year 11 that the molar concentration of a solution, in $mol\,L^{-1}$, is given by the expression:

$$c = \frac{n}{V}$$

where

   c is the molar concentration in $mol\,L^{-1}$

   n is the amount of solute in mol

   V is the volume of the solution in L.

The most convenient way of preparing a solution of a dilute acid is by mixing concentrated acid with water, as shown in Figure 7.3.1. This is known as a **dilution**.

The amount of solute in a solution does not change when a solution is diluted; the volume of the solution increases and the concentration decreases. The change in concentration or volume can be calculated using the formula:

$$c_1 V_1 = c_2 V_2$$

where

   c_1 and V_1 are the initial concentration and volume

   c_2 and V_2 are the concentration and volume after dilution.

You can calculate the concentration of a dilute acid if you know the:

- volume of the concentrated solution
- concentration of the concentrated solution
- total volume of water added.

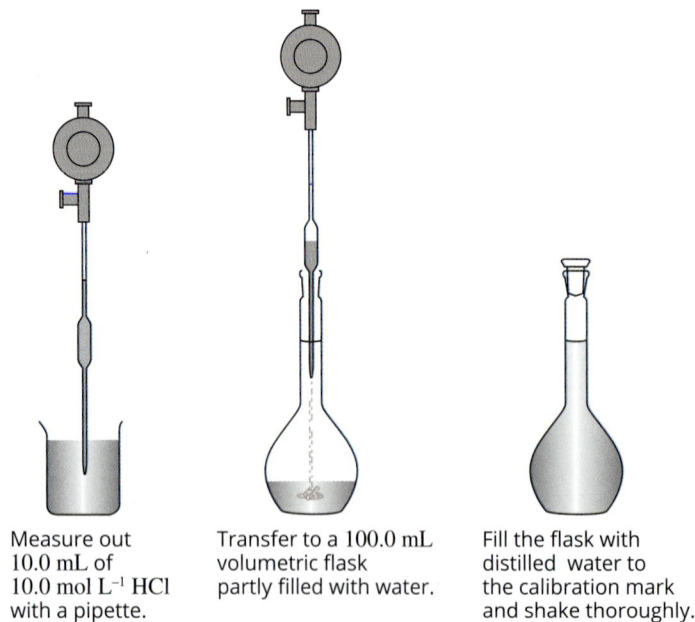

Measure out 10.0 mL of 10.0 mol L⁻¹ HCl with a pipette.

Transfer to a 100.0 mL volumetric flask partly filled with water.

Fill the flask with distilled water to the calibration mark and shake thoroughly.

FIGURE 7.3.1 Preparing a $1.00\,mol\,L^{-1}$ HCl solution by diluting a $10.0\,mol\,L^{-1}$ solution. Heat is released when a concentrated acid is mixed with water, so the volumetric flask is partly filled with water before the acid is added. (Extra safety precautions would be required for diluting concentrated sulfuric acid.)

The molar concentration of some concentrated acids are shown in Table 7.3.1.

TABLE 7.3.1 Molar concentrations of some concentrated acids

Concentrated acid (% by mass)	Formula	Molarity (mol L^{-1})
Ethanoic (acetic) acid (99.5%)	CH_3COOH	17
Hydrochloric acid (36%)	HCl	12
Nitric acid (70%)	HNO_3	16
Phosphoric acid (85%)	H_3PO_4	15
Sulfuric acid (98%)	H_2SO_4	18

You can prepare solutions of a base of a required concentration by:
- diluting a more concentrated solution, or
- dissolving a weighed amount of the base in a measured volume of water, as shown in Figure 7.3.2.

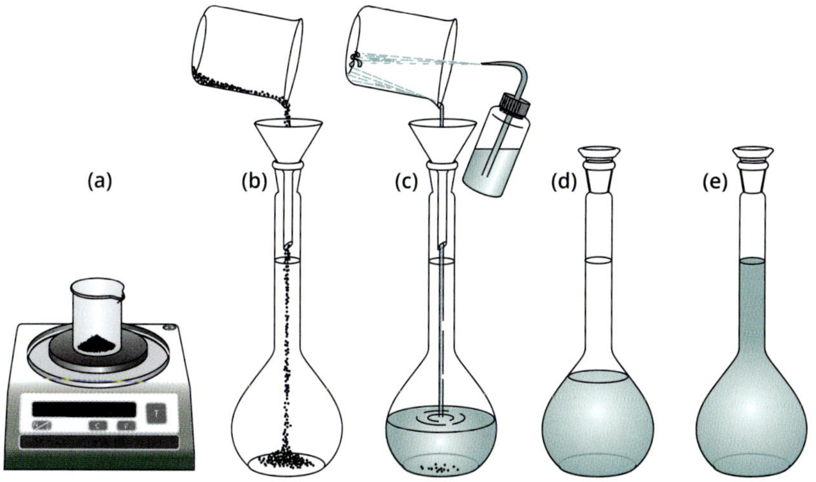

(a) Accurately weigh out a mass of the base.
(b) Transfer the base to a volumetric flask.
(c) Ensure complete transfer of the base by washing with water.
(d) Dissolve the base in water.
(e) Add water to make the solution up to the calibration mark and shake thoroughly.

FIGURE 7.3.2 Preparing a solution by dissolving a weighed amount of base in a measured volume of water.

Worked example 7.3.1

CALCULATING MOLAR CONCENTRATION AFTER DILUTION

Calculate the molar concentration of hydrochloric acid when 10.0 mL of water is added to 5.0 mL of 1.2 mol L^{-1} HCl.

Thinking	Working
The number of moles of solute does not change during a dilution. So $c_1V_1 = c_2V_2$, where c is the concentration in mol L^{-1} and V is the volume of the solution. (Each of the volume units must be the same, although not necessarily litres.)	$c_1V_1 = c_2V_2$
Identify given values for concentrations and volumes before and after dilution. Identify the unknown.	10.0 mL is added to 5.0 mL, so the final volume is 15.0 mL. (In practice, small volume changes can occur when solutions are mixed, however assume no volume changes occur.) $c_1 = 1.2$ mol L^{-1} $V_1 = 5.0$ mL $V_2 = 15.0$ mL You are required to calculate, c_2, the concentration after dilution.
Transpose the equation and substitute the known values into the equation to find the required value.	$c_2 = \frac{c_1 \times V_1}{V_2}$ $= \frac{1.2 \times 5.0}{15.0}$ $= 0.40$ mol L^{-1}

Worked example: Try yourself 7.3.1

CALCULATING MOLAR CONCENTRATION AFTER DILUTION

Calculate the molar concentration of nitric acid when 80.0 mL of water is added to 20.0 mL of 5.00 mol L^{-1} HNO$_3$.

Worked example 7.3.2

CALCULATING THE VOLUME OF WATER TO BE ADDED IN A DILUTION

How much water must be added to 30.0 mL of 2.50 mol L^{-1} HCl to dilute the solution to 1.00 mol L^{-1}?

Thinking	Working
The number of moles of solute does not change during a dilution. So $c_1V_1 = c_2V_2$, where c is the concentration in mol L^{-1} and V is the volume of the solution. (Each of the volume units must be the same, although not necessarily litres.)	$c_1V_1 = c_2V_2$
Identify given values for concentrations and volumes before and after dilution. Identify the unknown.	$c_1 = 2.50$ mol L^{-1} $V_1 = 30.0$ mL $c_2 = 1.00$ mol L^{-1} You are required to calculate V_2, the volume of the diluted solution.

Transpose the equation and substitute the known values into the equation to find the required value.	$V_2 = \frac{c_1 \times V_1}{c_2}$ $= \frac{2.50 \times 30.0}{1.00}$ $= 75.0\,\text{mL}$
The key word in the question is 'added', so you must calculate the volume of water to be added by finding the difference between the two volumes.	Volume of dilute solution = 75.0 mL Initial volume of acid = 30.0 mL So 75.0 − 30.0 = 45.0 mL of water must be added.

Worked example: Try yourself 7.3.2

CALCULATING THE VOLUME OF WATER TO BE ADDED IN A DILUTION

How much water must be added to 15.0 mL of 10.0 mol L^{-1} NaOH to dilute the solution to 2.00 mol L^{-1}?

PA 6.6   PA 6.6

EFFECT OF DILUTION ON THE pH OF STRONG ACIDS AND BASES

Consider a 0.1 mol L^{-1} solution of hydrochloric acid. Since pH = $-\log_{10}[H_3O^+]$, the pH of this solution is 1.0.

GO TO ➤ Section 7.2 page 167

If this 1.0 mL solution is diluted by a factor of 10 to 10.0 mL by the addition of 9.0 mL of water, the concentration of H_3O^+ ions decreases to 0.01 mol L^{-1} and the pH increases to 2.0. A further dilution by a factor of 10 to 100 mL will increase pH to 3.0. However, note that when acids are repeatedly diluted, the pH cannot increase above 7.

Similarly, the progressive dilution of a 0.10 mL NaOH solution will cause the pH to decrease until it reaches very close to 7.

You will now look at how to calculate the pH of solutions of strong acids and bases after dilution.

Worked example 7.3.3

CALCULATING THE pH OF A DILUTED ACID

5.0 mL of 0.010 mol L^{-1} HNO$_3$ is diluted to 100.0 mL. Calculate the pH of the diluted solution.

Thinking	Working
Identify given values for concentrations and volumes before and after dilution.	$c_1 = 0.010\,\text{mol L}^{-1}$ $V_1 = 5.0\,\text{mL}$ $V_2 = 100.0\,\text{mL}$ $c_2 = ?$
Calculate c_2, which is the concentration of H_3O^+ after dilution, by transposing the formula: $c_1V_1 = c_2V_2$	$c_2 = \frac{c_1 \times V_1}{V_2}$ $= \frac{0.010 \times 5.0}{100.0}$ $= 0.00050\,\text{mol L}^{-1}$
Calculate the pH using: pH = $-\log_{10}[H_3O^+]$	pH = $-\log_{10}[H_3O^+]$ $= -\log_{10}(0.00050)$ $= 3.30$

Worked example: Try yourself 7.3.3

CALCULATING THE pH OF A DILUTED ACID

10.0 mL of 0.10 mol L^{-1} HCl is diluted to 30.0 mL. Calculate the pH of the diluted solution.

Calculation of the pH of a base after dilution

The following steps show the sequence used to calculate the pH of a base after it has been diluted. Remember that pH is a measure of the hydronium ion concentration.

1 Calculate [OH$^-$] in the diluted solution.
2 Calculate pOH using pOH = $-\log_{10}$[OH$^-$].
3 Calculate the pH of the solution using pH = 14 − pOH.

Worked example 7.3.4

CALCULATING THE pH AND pOH OF A DILUTED BASE

10.0 mL of 0.1 mol L^{-1} NaOH is diluted to 100.0 mL. Calculate the pH and pOH of the diluted solution.

Thinking	Working
Identify given values for concentrations and volumes before and after dilution.	$c_1 = 0.1 \text{ mol L}^{-1}$ $V_1 = 10.0 \text{ mL}$ $V_2 = 100.0 \text{ mL}$ $c_2 = ?$
Calculate c_2, which is [OH$^-$] after dilution, by transposing the formula: $c_1V_1 = c_2V_2$	$c_2 = \frac{c_1 \times V_1}{V_2}$ $= \frac{0.1 \times 10.0}{100.0}$ $= 0.01 \text{ mol L}^{-1}$
Calculate the pOH using the expression: pOH = $-\log_{10}$[OH$^-$]	pOH = $-\log_{10}$[OH$^-$] $= -\log_{10}(0.01)$ $= 2.0$
Calculate the pH using the expression: pH = 14 − pOH	pH = 14 − pOH $= 14 − 2.0$ $= 12.0$

Worked example 7.3.4: Try yourself

CALCULATING THE pH AND pOH OF A DILUTED BASE

WS
6.5

15.0 mL of 0.02 mol L^{-1} KOH is diluted to 60.0 mL. Calculate the pH and pOH of the diluted solution.

Colourful chemistry

The flower colour of the popular garden plant *Hydrangea macrophylla* depends on the pH of the soil (Figure 7.3.3). In acidic soil hydrangeas are blue, but in alkaline (basic) soil they are pink. You can make the soil more acidic with garden sulfur, which has the added benefit of preventing rot fungi from germinating when handling cuttings of succulents. More alkaline conditions can be achieved by adding garden lime, which is mainly calcium carbonate ($CaCO_3$), a mild base. Garden lime has the added benefit of providing a source of calcium for plants.

FIGURE 7.3.3 The different colours displayed by these hydrangeas is caused by the acidity or basicity of the soil.

7.3 Review

SUMMARY

- The amount of an acid or base in solution does not change during a dilution. The volume of the solution increases and the concentration decreases.
- Solutions of acids or bases of a required concentration can be prepared by diluting more concentrated solutions, using the formula:

$$c_1V_1 = c_2V_2$$

where c_1 and V_1 are the initial concentration and volume, and c_2 and V_2 are the final concentration and volume after dilution.

- The pH increases when a solution of an acid is diluted.
- The pH of a diluted acid can be determined by calculating the concentration of hydronium ions in the diluted solution.

- The pH decreases when a solution of a base is diluted. The pH of a diluted base can be determined by:
  - calculating the concentration of hydroxide ions in the diluted base, and
  - using the ionic product of water to calculate the concentration of hydronium ions in the diluted base, or alternatively
  - calculating pOH based on the concentration of hydroxide ions in the diluted base, then converting to pH using the expression:

$$pH = 14 - pOH$$

KEY QUESTIONS

1 1.0 L of water is added to 3.0 L of 0.10 mol L^{-1} HCl. What is the concentration of the diluted acid?

2 How much water must be added to 10 mL of a 2.0 mol L^{-1} sulfuric acid solution to dilute it to 0.50 mol L^{-1}?

3 What volume of water must be added to dilute a 20.0 mL volume of 0.600 mol L^{-1} HCl to 0.100 mol L^{-1}?

4 Describe the effect on the pH of a monoprotic acid solution of pH 1.0 when it is diluted by a factor of 10.

5 Calculate the pH and pOH of the solution at 25°C that is formed by the dilution of a 20.0 mL solution of 0.100 mol L^{-1} NaOH to 50.0 mL.

6 For each of the solutions **a–e** (all at 25°C), calculate:
   i the concentration of H_3O^+ ions
   ii the concentration of OH^- ions
   iii the pH
   iv the pOH.
   a 0.001 mol L^{-1} HNO_3(aq)
   b 0.03 mol L^{-1} HCl(aq)
   c 0.01 mol L^{-1} NaOH(aq)
   d $10^{-4.5}$ mol L^{-1} HCl(aq)
   e 0.005 mol L^{-1} $Ba(OH)_2$(aq).

Chapter review

KEY TERMS

acidic solution
amphiprotic
basic solution
concentrated solution
concentration
dilution
dissociation constant

indicator
ionic product of water
molarity
neutral solution
p-function
pH scale
pOH scale

self-ionisation
strong acid
strong base
super acid
weak acid
weak base

REVIEW QUESTIONS

1 Write an equation to show that perchloric acid ($HClO_4$) acts as a strong acid in water.

2 Write an equation to show that hypochlorous acid ($HClO_3$) acts as a weak acid in water.

3 Write an equation to show that ammonia (NH_3) acts as a weak base in water.

4 Write a balanced ionic equation showing the $H_2PO_4^-$ ion acting as a weak base in water.

5 Write an equation to show that dimethylamine (($CH_3)_2NH$) acts as a weak base in water.

6 a Write an equation showing the dissociation of calcium hydroxide ($Ca(OH)_2$) in water.
   b Explain why calcium hydroxide acts as a strong base.

7 Calculate $[OH^-]$ at 25°C in aqueous solutions with $[H_3O^+]$ equal to:
   a $0.001\,mol\,L^{-1}$
   b $10^{-5}\,mol\,L^{-1}$
   c $5.7 \times 10^{-9}\,mol\,L^{-1}$
   d $3.4 \times 10^{-12}\,mol\,L^{-1}$
   e $6.5 \times 10^{-2}\,mol\,L^{-1}$
   f $2.23 \times 10^{-13}\,mol\,L^{-1}$

8 Calculate the pOH from the $[OH^-]$ values calculated in Question 7.

9 State the concentration of the following ions in solutions at 25°C, at each of the given pH values.
   i hydronium ions
   ii hydroxide ions.
   a pH 1
   b pH 3
   c pH 7
   d pH 11.7

10 The pH of human blood is tightly regulated so that it is between 7.35 and 7.45 at 37°C. What are the minimum and maximum concentrations of hydronium ions in blood within this pH range?

11 The pH of a cola drink is 3 and of black coffee is 5. How many more times acidic is the cola than black coffee?

12 Calculate the concentration of H_3O^+ and OH^- ions in solutions with the following pH values at 25°C:
   a 3.0
   b 10.0
   c 8.5
   d 5.8
   e 9.6
   f 13.5

13 The pH of a particular brand of tomato juice is 5.3 at 25°C. What is the concentration of hydroxide ions in this tomato juice?

14 A solution of hydrochloric acid has a pH of 2.0.
   a What is the molar concentration of hydrogen ions in this solution?
   b What amount of hydrogen ions, in mol, would be present in 500 mL of this solution?
   c What is the pOH of the hydrochloric acid solution?

15 Calculate the pH and pOH of each of the following mixtures at 25°C.
   a 10 mL of $0.025\,mol\,L^{-1}$ HCl is diluted to 50 mL of solution.
   b 20 mL of $0.0050\,mol\,L^{-1}$ KOH is diluted to 500 mL of solution.
   c 10 mL of $0.15\,mol\,L^{-1}$ HCl is diluted to 1.5 L of solution.

16 The molarity of concentrated sulfuric acid is $18.0\,mol\,L^{-1}$. What volume of concentrated sulfuric acid is required to prepare 1.00 L of $2.00\,mol\,L^{-1}$ H_2SO_4 solution?

17 When a 10.0 mL solution of hydrochloric acid was diluted, the pH changed from 2.00 to 4.00. What volume of water was added to the acid solution?

18 40.0 mL of $0.10\,mol\,L^{-1}$ HNO_3 is diluted to 500.0 mL. Will the pH increase or decrease?

19 A laboratory assistant forgot to label $0.10\,\mathrm{mol\,L^{-1}}$ solutions of sodium hydroxide (NaOH), hydrochloric acid (HCl), glucose ($C_6H_{12}O_6$), ammonia (NH_3) and ethanoic acid (CH_3COOH). In order to identify them, temporary labels A–E were placed on the bottles and the electrical conductivity and pH of each solution was measured. The results are shown in the table below. Identify each solution and briefly explain your reasoning.

Solution	Electrical conductivity	pH
A	poor	11
B	zero	7
C	good	13
D	good	1
E	poor	3

20 A standard laboratory usually dilutes concentrated stock solutions of acids or bases to make less concentrated solutions for use.

a Write an equation to represent the dissociation of sodium hydroxide in water.

b Is sodium hydroxide regarded as a strong or weak base? Explain your response.

c What mass of sodium hydroxide (NaOH) pellets would be needed to be added to a 500 mL volumetric flask in order to produce a $12\,\mathrm{mol\,L^{-1}}$ stock solution?

d i Calculate the volume of the stock solution required to make a 250.0 mL solution of $0.020\,\mathrm{mol\,L^{-1}}$ solution of NaOH.

ii Suggest a reason why it would not be suitable to make this dilution directly, and suggest an alternative method.

e What is the resultant pOH of the diluted solution?

f Hence calculate the pH of the diluted solution and the concentration of hydronium ions.

21 Reflect on the Inquiry task on page 162. You have been given two solutions, one contains a strong acid and the other contains a weak acid. Both acids are dilute and have the same concentration. How could you use the red cabbage indicator to tell the two solutions apart?

Quantitative analysis

There are many situations in which a chemist may want to find the amount of a substance in solution, such as the amount of a chemical present in industrial or mining wastes, the composition of antacid tablets or the acidity of polluted rainwater.

This chapter describes a method used for the analysis of acids and bases in water. This method is called volumetric analysis and involves chemical reactions between substances in aqueous solution.

Volumetric analysis requires the measuring of accurate volumes using specialised pieces of glassware, as in the photograph on this page. You will look at the equipment and techniques used in this analysis, as well as the calculations involved.

How the value of the equilibrium constants for the dissociation reaction of acids or bases in water provides a measure of the strength of an acid or base is also discussed. The chapter concludes by considering how mixtures of weak acids and their salts are able to keep a constant level of acidity in biological and environmental systems.

Content

INQUIRY QUESTION

How are solutions of acids and bases analysed?

By the end of this chapter, you will be able to:

- explore the use of K_{eq} for different types of chemical reactions, including but not limited to:
  - dissociation of acids and bases (ACSCH098, ACSCH099)
- conduct practical investigations to analyse the concentration of an unknown acid or base by titration [ICT] [N]
- investigate titration curves and conductivity graphs to analyse data to indicate characteristic reaction profiles, for example: [ICT]
  - strong acid/strong base
  - strong acid/weak base
  - weak acid/strong base (ACSCH080, ACSCH102)
- model neutralisation of strong and weak acids and bases using a variety of media [ICT]
- calculate and apply the dissociation constant (K_a) and pK_a (p$K_a = -\log_{10}(K_a)$) to determine the difference between strong and weak acids (ACSCH098) [ICT] [N]
- explore acid/base analysis techniques that are applied:
  - in industries
  - by Aboriginal and Torres Strait Islander Peoples [AHC]
  - using digital probes and instruments [ICT]
- conduct a chemical analysis of a common household substance for its acidity or basicity, for example: (ACSCH080) [ICT] [N]
  - soft drink
  - wine
  - juice
  - medicine
- conduct a practical investigation to prepare a buffer and demonstrate its properties (ACSCH080) [ICT] [N]
- describe the importance of buffers in natural systems (ACSCH098, ACSCH102)

Chemistry Stage 6 Syllabus © NSW Education Standards Authority for and on behalf of the Crown in right of the State of NSW, 2017.

8.1 Calculations involving acids and bases

How much acid is there in vinegar?

COLLECT THIS ...

- white vinegar
- sodium hydrogen carbonate (bicarbonate of soda) powder ($NaHCO_3$)
- tap water
- measuring jug
- laboratory scales
- 20 mL medicine cup
- oral medication syringe dispenser
- small beaker
- small plastic spoon
- safety glasses

DO THIS ...

1 Measure out 1 L of water using the measuring jug.
2 Use the scales to weigh out 20 g of $NaHCO_3$.
3 Dissolve the $NaHCO_3$ in the 200 mL of water.
4 Fill the dispensing syringe with 10 mL of the $NaHCO_3$ solution.
5 Use the medicine cup to measure out 20 mL of vinegar, and pour this into the beaker.
6 Add 5 mL of $NaHCO_3$ solution from the dispensing syringe and stir the mixture with the plastic spoon.
7 Add a further 5 mL of the $NaHCO_3$ solution to the vinegar, stir and note any effervescence.
8 Refill the syringe with 10 mL of the $NaHCO_3$ solution.
9 Continue adding 5 mL portions of $NaHCO_3$ solution until no more effervescence is observed.

RECORD THIS ...

Record the number of 5 mL portions of $NaHCO_3$ solution that were added to the vinegar. Present your results in a table.

Calculate the percentage of ethanoic acid in the sample of vinegar, given that 20 mL of the $NaHCO_3$ solution will react completely with 5.7 mL of a 1% ethanoic acid solution.

REFLECT ON THIS ...

1 How would the results change if only 10 mL of vinegar had been used?
2 How could you improve the design of this experiment so that it produces a more accurate result?
3 How could you experimentally measure the acid content of lemon juice or soft drinks?

GO TO ➤ | Section 6.2 page 153

In Chapter 6 you learnt how to predict the products of the reactions of acids with bases, carbonates or metals. In this section you will learn how to calculate how much product is produced and how much reactant is required in these reactions.

Being able to answer the 'how much' question has many useful applications, such as determining:

- how much lime should be added to soil to increase its pH
- how much calcium carbonate should be used to neutralise hazardous acidic wastes from an industrial plant or a mine site
- how much phosphoric acid is in a cola drink
- how much stomach acid can be neutralised by an antacid tablet.

You will use your knowledge of the reactions of acids, your ability to write balanced chemical equations, and your understanding of the mole concept and mole relationships to answer 'how much' questions like these. Chemical analysis that involves the measurements of mass, volume and concentration is called **quantitative analysis**. In this chapter you will learn about volumetric analysis, a quantitative technique that is used to determine the concentration of solutions containing acids or bases. Other quantitative techniques are outlined in Chapter 15.

Chemical analysis that identifies a substance or the components in a substance is referred to as **qualitative analysis**. Examples of the qualitative analysis of inorganic and organic compounds are discussed further in Chapters 15 and 16.

GO TO ➤ Section 15.1 page 408

GO TO ➤ Section 16.1 page 462

REACTING QUANTITIES OF ACIDS AND BASES

Calculations based on the reactions of acids usually involve determining the number of moles of a substance.

REVISION

You will recall that:

- the coefficients in a balanced chemical equation give the ratio in which substances react
- the amount of solid, in mol, can be calculated from the expression:

$n = \frac{m}{M}$

where

m is the mass in grams

M is the molar mass in $g\,mol^{-1}$

- the amount of solute, in mol, in a solution is given by:

$n = c \times V$

where

c is the concentration in $mol\,L^{-1}$

V is the volume in litres.

As you will see in the following worked examples, there are four main steps in solving calculation problems involving solutions of acids and bases:

1. Write a balanced equation for the reaction.
2. Calculate the amount, in mol, of the substance with known volume and concentration.
3. Use the mole ratio from the equation to calculate the amount, in mol, of the required substance.
4. Calculate the required volume or concentration.

The steps in a stoichiometric calculation are summarised in the flowchart in Figure 8.1.1.

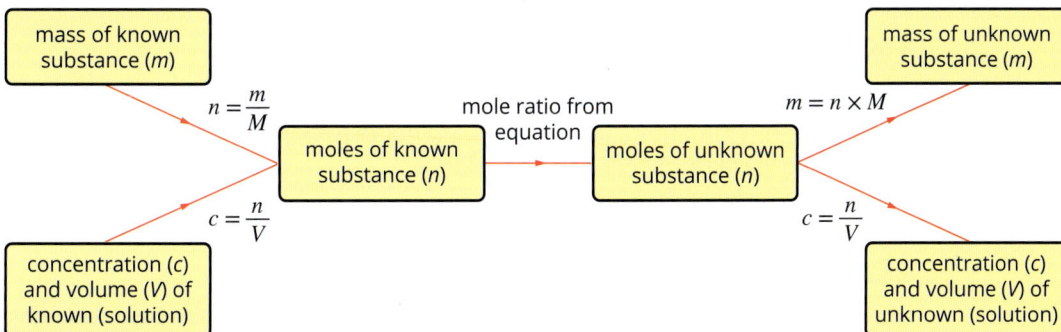

FIGURE 8.1.1 Flowchart for mass and solution calculations

ⓘ Use the balanced equation to determine the mole ratio of the known and unknown substances.

Worked example 8.1.1

A SOLUTION VOLUME–VOLUME CALCULATION

What volume of $0.100 \, mol \, L^{-1}$ sulfuric acid reacts completely with $17.8 \, mL$ of $0.150 \, mol \, L^{-1}$ potassium hydroxide solution?

Thinking	Working
Write a balanced full equation for the reaction.	$2KOH(aq) + H_2SO_4(aq) \rightarrow K_2SO_4(aq) + 2H_2O(l)$
Calculate the amount, in mol, of the substance with known volume and concentration.	The volume and concentration of potassium hydroxide solution are given, so use $n = c \times V$ (Remember that volume must be expressed in litres.) $n(KOH) = c \times V$ $\qquad = 0.150 \times 0.0178$ $\qquad = 2.67 \times 10^{-3} \, mol$
Use the mole ratio from the equation to calculate the amount, in mol, of the required substance.	The balanced equation shows that 1 mol of sulfuric acid reacts with 2 mol of potassium hydroxide. $\frac{n(H_2SO_4)}{n(KOH)} = \frac{1}{2}$ $n(H_2SO_4) = \frac{1}{2} \times n(KOH)$ $\qquad = 0.5 \times 2.67 \times 10^{-3}$ $\qquad = 1.34 \times 10^{-3} \, mol$
Calculate the volume or concentration required.	The volume of H_2SO_4 is found by rearranging and using $n = c \times V$. $V(H_2SO_4) = \frac{n}{c}$ $\qquad = \frac{0.00134}{0.100}$ $\qquad = 0.0134 \, L$ $\qquad = 13.4 \, mL$ So $13.4 \, mL$ of $0.100 \, mol \, L^{-1} \, H_2SO_4$ will react completely with $17.8 \, mL$ of $0.150 \, mol \, L^{-1}$ KOH solution.

Worked example: Try yourself 8.1.1

A SOLUTION VOLUME–VOLUME CALCULATION

What volume of $0.500 \, mol \, L^{-1}$ hydrochloric acid (HCl) reacts completely with $25.0 \, mL$ of $0.100 \, mol \, L^{-1}$ calcium hydroxide ($Ca(OH)_2$) solution? The salt formed in this acid–base reaction is calcium chloride.

STOICHIOMETRY PROBLEMS INVOLVING EXCESS REACTANTS

Reactants are not always mixed in stoichiometric amounts in acid–base reactions. There are occasions when one of the reactants, an acid or a base, is in excess. The following steps are used to determine the amount of product formed when either an acid or a base is in excess in a reaction mixture.

- Calculate the number of moles of each reactant.
- Determine which reactant is in excess and which is the limiting reactant.
- Use the amount of limiting reactant to work out the amount of product formed or the amount of reactant in excess.

GO TO ➤ Year 11 Section 7.5

ⓘ The limiting reactant is completely consumed in a chemical reaction.

Worked example 8.1.2

SOLUTION STOICHIOMETRY: A LIMITING REACTANT PROBLEM

20.0 mL of a 1.00 mol L^{-1} LiOH solution is added to 30.0 mL of a 0.500 mol L^{-1} HNO$_3$ solution. The equation for the reaction that occurs is:

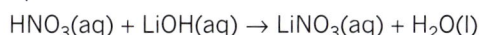

$$HNO_3(aq) + LiOH(aq) \rightarrow LiNO_3(aq) + H_2O(l)$$

a Which reactant is the limiting reactant?	
Thinking	**Working**
Calculate the number of moles of each of the reactants using $n = c \times V$.	$n(HNO_3) = 0.500 \times 0.0300$ $\quad\quad\quad\quad = 0.0150$ mol $n(LiOH) = 1.00 \times 0.0200$ $\quad\quad\quad\quad = 0.0200$ mol
Use the coefficients of the equation to find the limiting reactant.	The equation shows that 1 mol of HNO$_3$ reacts with 1 mol of LiOH. So the HNO$_3$ is the limiting reactant (it will be completely consumed).

b What mass of LiNO$_3$ will the reaction mixture contain when the reaction is complete?	
Thinking	**Working**
Find the mole ratio of the unknown substance to the limiting reactant from the equation coefficients: $\dfrac{\text{coefficient of unknown}}{\text{coefficient of limiting reactant}}$	From the equation coefficients: $\dfrac{n(LiNO_3)}{n(HNO_3)} = \dfrac{\text{coefficient of LiNO}_3}{\text{coefficient of HNO}_3} = \dfrac{1}{1} = 1$
Calculate the number of moles of the unknown substance using the limiting reactant: $n(\text{unknown}) = n(\text{limiting reactant}) \times$ mole ratio	$n(LiNO_3) = n(HNO_3) \times 1$ $\quad\quad\quad\quad = 0.0150 \times 1$ $\quad\quad\quad\quad = 0.0150$ mol
Calculate the mass of the unknown substance using: $n(\text{unknown}) = n(\text{limiting reactant}) \times$ molar mass	Molar mass of LiNO$_3$ = 68.95 g mol^{-1} $m(LiNO_3) = 0.0150 \times 68.95$ $\quad\quad\quad\quad = 1.03$ g

Worked example: Try yourself 8.1.2

SOLUTION STOICHIOMETRY: A LIMITING REACTANT PROBLEM

30.0 mL of a 0.100 mol L^{-1} H$_2$SO$_4$ solution is mixed with 40.0 mL of a 0.200 mol L^{-1} KOH solution. The equation for the reaction that occurs is:

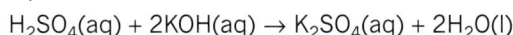

$$H_2SO_4(aq) + 2KOH(aq) \rightarrow K_2SO_4(aq) + 2H_2O(l)$$

a Which reactant is the limiting reactant?

b What will be the mass of K$_2$SO$_4$ produced by this reaction?

8.1 Review

SUMMARY

- Given the quantity of one of the reactants or products in a chemical reaction, the quantity of all other reactants and products can be predicted by working through the following steps.
  1. Write a balanced equation for the reaction.
  2. Calculate the amount, in mol, of the given substances.
  3. Use the mole ratios of reactants and products in the balanced chemical equation to calculate the amount, in mol, of the required substance.

4. Convert the amount, in mol, of the required substance to the quantity required in the question.
- In some chemical reactions, the reactants are not present in stoichiometric ratios. One reactant will be in excess and one will be the limiting reactant. The amount of the limiting reactant can be used to calculate the amount of product that forms, or the amount of excess reactant that remains unreacted.

KEY QUESTIONS

1. A $0.100\,mol\,L^{-1}$ H_2SO_4 solution is neutralised with $10.0\,mL$ of a solution of $0.300\,mol\,L^{-1}$ KOH.
   a Write a balanced equation for this reaction.
   b What volume of sulfuric acid was neutralised?

2. $15.0\,mL$ of a nitric acid solution is required to react completely with $10.0\,mL$ of a $0.100\,mol\,L^{-1}$ $Ca(OH)_2$ solution.
   a Write a balanced equation for this reaction.
   b What is the concentration of the nitric acid solution?

3. $10.0\,mL$ of a $0.200\,mol\,L^{-1}$ sulfuric acid solution is added to $16.0\,mL$ of a $0.100\,mol\,L^{-1}$ sodium carbonate solution. The equation for the reaction is:
$$Na_2CO_3(aq) + H_2SO_4(aq) \rightarrow Na_2SO_4(aq) + CO_2(g) + H_2O(l)$$
   a Calculate the amount, in mol, of H_2SO_4 in the acid solution.
   b Calculate the amount, in mol, of Na_2CO_3 in the sodium carbonate solution.
   c Identify the limiting reactant and excess reactant.
   d Calculate the amount, in mol, of excess reactant that remains unreacted.

4. $18.26\,mL$ of dilute nitric acid reacts completely with $20.00\,mL$ of $0.09927\,mol\,L^{-1}$ potassium hydroxide solution.
   a Write a balanced chemical equation for the reaction between nitric acid and potassium hydroxide.
   b Calculate the amount, in mol, of potassium hydroxide consumed in this reaction.
   c What amount, in mol, of nitric acid reacted with the potassium hydroxide in this reaction?
   d Calculate the concentration of the nitric acid.

8.2 Volumetric analysis

The pain caused by indigestion occurs when your stomach produces excessive quantities of acidic gastric juices. The protein-digesting enzyme pepsin in gastric secretions works best at a pH of 3. The pH of the stomach is maintained by hydrochloric acid contained in the gastric juice. Commercial antacids (Figure 8.2.1) contain bases such as magnesium hydroxide, sodium hydrogen carbonate and aluminium hydroxide to neutralise the acid secretions and relieve the discomfort.

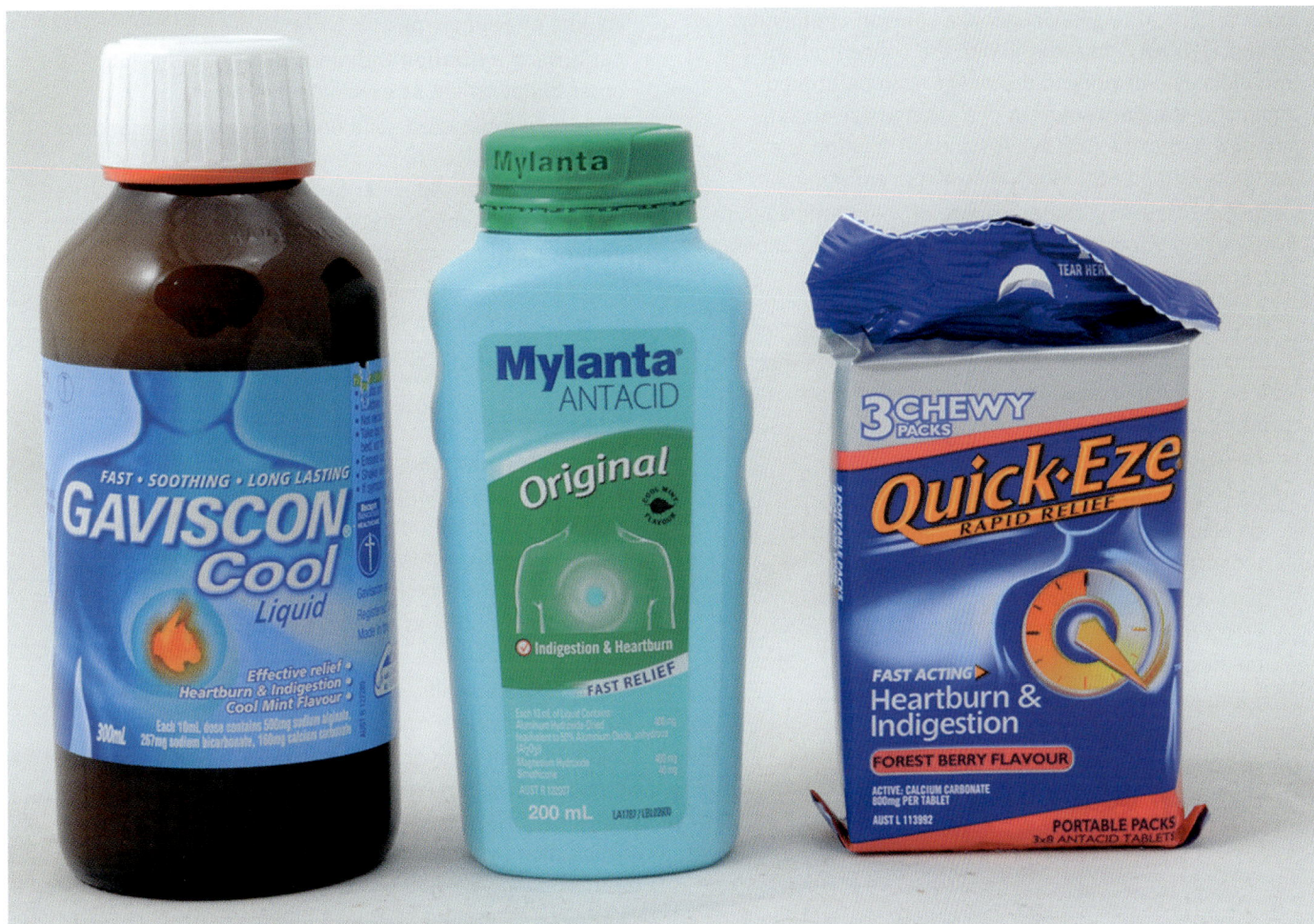

FIGURE 8.2.1 The effectiveness of antacids can be assessed using acid–base reactions.

To compare the effectiveness of antacids, you could design experiments to find out what volume of hydrochloric acid reacts with each brand. This would allow you to determine which antacid is best at neutralising the acidic secretions.

In this section you will learn about the experimental techniques that are used by chemists to perform such analyses involving acid–base reactions.

There are many situations in which a chemist may want to find the amount of a substance in solution. For example, they might want to determine the composition of antacid tablets, the acidity of liquid industrial wastes, or the acid content of fruit juices, soft drinks or wines.

This section describes a method used for the analysis of acids or bases in a solution. The method is called volumetric analysis and involves chemical reactions between acids and bases in aqueous solution.

GO TO ➤ Year 11 Section 8.4

REVISION

Standard solutions

Volumetric analysis can be used to determine the amount or **concentration** of a dissolved substance in a solution. For example, vinegar is a solution of ethanoic acid (CH_3COOH). In order to find the concentration of ethanoic acid in vinegar, the vinegar can be titrated against a **standard solution** of a strong base such as sodium hydroxide (NaOH). A standard solution is a solution with an accurately known concentration.

Before discussing the procedure of volumetric analysis further, it is important to recall how standard solutions are prepared.

PRIMARY STANDARDS

Substances that are so pure that the amount, in mol, can be calculated accurately from their mass are called **primary standards**. A primary standard should:

- be readily obtainable in a pure form
- have a known chemical formula
- be easy to store without deteriorating or reacting with the atmosphere
- have a high molar mass to minimise the effect of errors in weighing
- be inexpensive.

Examples of primary standards are:

- bases: **anhydrous** sodium carbonate (Na_2CO_3) and sodium borate ($Na_2B_4O_7 \cdot 10H_2O$)
- acids: hydrated oxalic acid ($H_2C_2O_4 \cdot H_2O$) and potassium hydrogen phthalate ($KH(C_8H_4O_4)$).

PREPARING STANDARD SOLUTIONS

Standard solutions are prepared by:

- dissolving an accurately measured mass of a primary standard in water to make an accurately measured volume of solution, or
- performing a **titration** with another standard solution in order to determine its exact concentration.

To prepare a standard solution from a primary standard, you need to dissolve an accurately known amount of the substance in deionised water to produce a known volume of solution. The steps in preparing a standard solution from a primary standard are outlined in Figure 8.2.2.

The molar concentration of the standard solution can then be found from the following formulas:

Amount in mol, $n = \dfrac{\text{mass of solute (in g)}}{\text{molar mass (in g mol}^{-1})} = \dfrac{m}{M}$

Concentration, $c = \dfrac{\text{amount of solute (in mol)}}{\text{volume of solution}} = \dfrac{n}{V} = \dfrac{m}{M \times V}$

In practice, making a standard solution directly from a primary standard is only possible for a few of the chemicals encountered in the laboratory. Many chemicals are impure because they decompose or react with chemicals in the atmosphere. For example:

- **strong bases**, such as sodium hydroxide (NaOH), absorb water and react with carbon dioxide in the air
- many hydrated salts, such as $Na_2CO_3 \cdot 10H_2O$, lose water to the atmosphere over time.

Solutions such as hydrochloric acid (HCl), sulfuric acid (H_2SO_4), sodium hydroxide (NaOH) and potassium hydroxide (KOH) must be **standardised** to determine their concentration by titration against a standard solution. Common standard solutions used contain sodium carbonate (Na_2CO_3) or potassium hydrogen phthalate ($KH(C_8H_4O_4)$). When a solution is standardised by titration with a primary standard, it is known as a **secondary standard**.

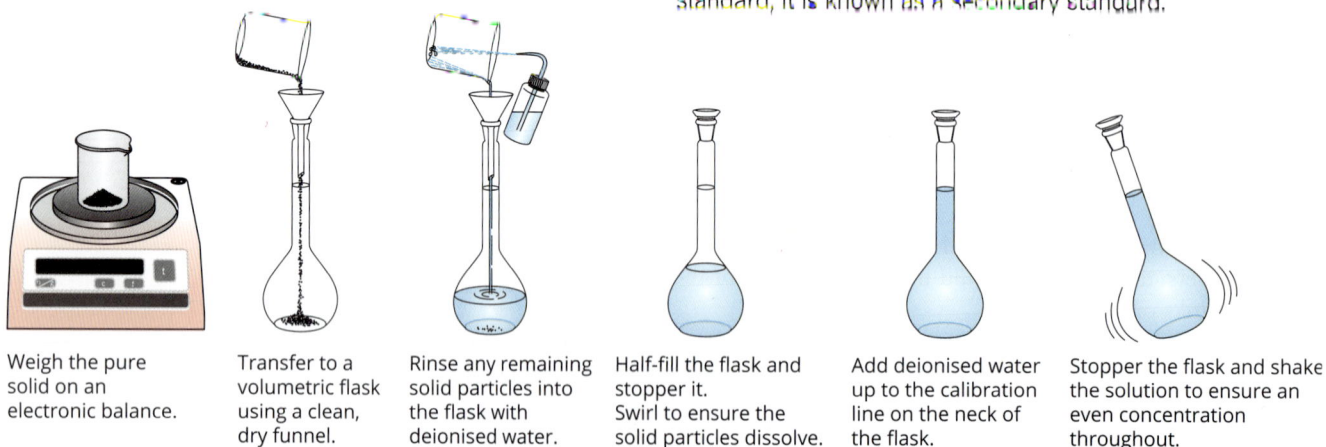

Weigh the pure solid on an electronic balance.

Transfer to a volumetric flask using a clean, dry funnel.

Rinse any remaining solid particles into the flask with deionised water.

Half-fill the flask and stopper it. Swirl to ensure the solid particles dissolve.

Add deionised water up to the calibration line on the neck of the flask.

Stopper the flask and shake the solution to ensure an even concentration throughout.

FIGURE 8.2.2 The steps taken to prepare a standard solution from a primary standard

Reading volume levels

Correctly reading the volume of a liquid in a flask is an important skill. The following steps will help you be as accurate as possible.

1 Ensure the flask is on a level surface.

2 Bring your eye level down to the surface of the liquid. This avoids **parallax error** (incorrectly reading a different volume due to the position of your eyes). Do not hold the flask up to your eye level as the liquid will not be level, and it is potentially hazardous.

3 Know what to read. Read the volume that is equal to the bottom of the meniscus (the concave curve of the surface of the liquid; Figure 8.2.3).

4 Hold up a piece of coloured card or tile to provide a contrasting background. This makes reading the volume easier.

FIGURE 8.2.3 This close-up view of the neck of a standard flask shows the bottom of the meniscus is level with the white graduation (measuring scale) line.

TITRATION

If you want to find the concentration of a solution of hydrochloric acid, you can perform a titration with sodium carbonate. Precisely calibrated glassware are used to carry out the analysis.

Volumetric equipment

Often the concentrations of acids and bases used in industry are unknown. The laboratory equipment shown in Table 8.2.1 is used to make precise measurements of mass and volume. These instruments, combined with calculations similar to those in the Section 8.1, allows scientists to determine unknown concentrations of acids and bases.

> **ⓘ** A titration is a form of volumetric analysis that is used to determine the concentration of an unknown solution.

Equipment	Visual reference	Use
Volumetric flask		A **volumetric flask** is used to prepare a standard solution; for example, a standard solution of sodium carbonate. An accurately weighed sample of sodium carbonate is placed in the flask and dissolved in deionised water to form a specific volume of solution.
Pipette		A **pipette** is used to accurately measure a specific volume of the solution of unknown concentration. This known volume, or **aliquot**, is then poured into a conical flask ready for analysis.
Burette		The standard solution is placed in a **burette**, which delivers accurately known, but variable, volumes of solution to the conical flask containing the acid or base. The volume of liquid delivered by a burette is called a **titre**.

Performing a titration

To determine the concentration of the acid, a standard solution of sodium carbonate is slowly added from a burette (titrated) to the acid solution in the conical flask until the reactants have just reacted completely in the mole ratio indicated by the balanced chemical equation (the **equivalence point**). These amounts are indicated by the coefficients in the equation for the reaction.

For the reaction between hydrochloric acid and sodium carbonate solution:

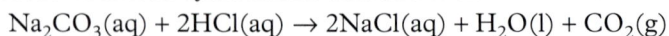

$$Na_2CO_3(aq) + 2HCl(aq) \rightarrow 2NaCl(aq) + H_2O(l) + CO_2(g)$$

The equivalence point occurs when exactly 2 mol of HCl has been added for each 1 mol of Na_2CO_3.

The reaction is complete when the equivalence point is reached. The number of moles of solute in the standard solution can be calculated from its concentration and volume. By using the mole ratio from the equation for the reaction, the number of moles of the solute in the solution of unknown concentration can be determined. The unknown solution concentration can then be calculated from the number of moles of solute and the volume of solution. In the example above, the concentration and volume of sodium carbonate (from the burette) required is now known, as is the volume of the aliquot of hydrochloric acid used. The concentration of the acid can now be calculated.

In an **acid–base titration**, an **indicator** that changes colour in the pH range of the equivalence point can be used to indicate when the acid and base have reacted completely. The **end point** is the point during the titration at which the indicator changes colour permanently. For an accurate analysis, the end point should be very close to the equivalence point.

The steps involved in an acid–base titration are as follows.

1 An aliquot of unknown concentration is measured using a pipette and transferred into a conical flask (Figure 8.2.4).

GO TO ➤ Section 7.2 page 167

ⓘ The equivalence point of a chemical reaction is when the reactants have both reacted completely. The end point is when the indicator has undergone a permanent colour change.

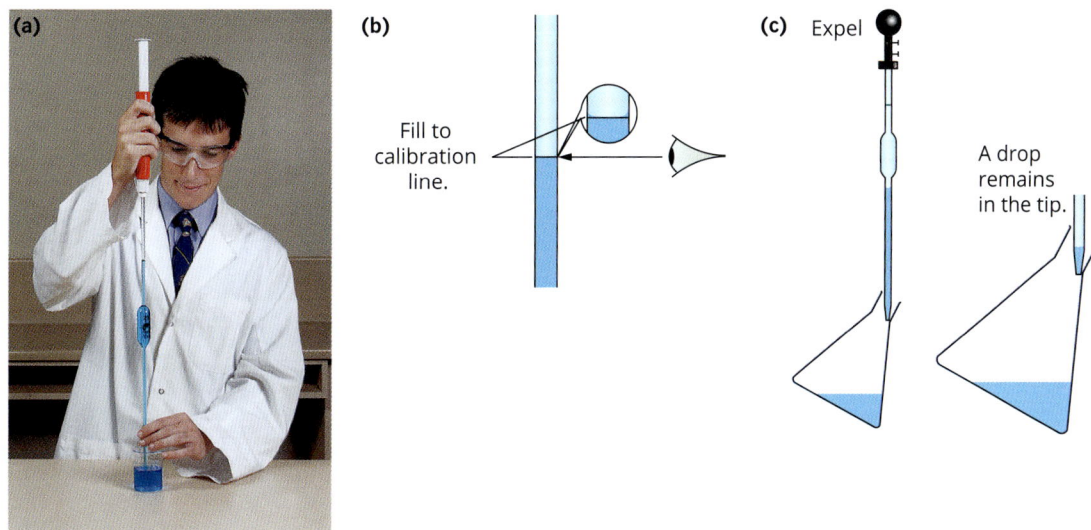

(a)

(b) Fill to calibration line.

(c) Expel

A drop remains in the tip.

FIGURE 8.2.4 Taking an aliquot of a solution using a pipette. (a, b) Fill the pipette with the solution up to the graduation line. (c) Expel the solution; the pipette is designed so that a drop remains in the tip after an aliquot has been delivered.

2 A few drops of an appropriate acid–base indicator are added so that a colour change signals the point at which the titration should stop.
3 The burette is filled with the standard solution, and the initial volume is noted.
4 The standard solution is dispensed slowly into the conical flask from the burette until the indicator changes colour permanently (Figure 8.2.5).

The volume of solution delivered by the burette is known as the titre. The titre is calculated by subtracting the initial burette reading from the final burette reading.

Rinsing of equipment used in a titration

To help ensure that there are no inaccuracies in your titration, you should rinse each piece of equipment with the correct solution. Pipettes and burettes should first be rinsed with water, then given a final rinsing with the solution being delivered. Volumetric flasks should be rinsed with water, because the flask will be filled with water. The conical flasks must only be rinsed with water. If the conical flask were to be rinsed with the solution that it is to be filled with, an unknown additional amount of that reactant would be introduced into the flask. This would lead to an inaccurate result in your titration. Table 8.2.2 summarises the rinsing needed for each piece of equipment in a titration.

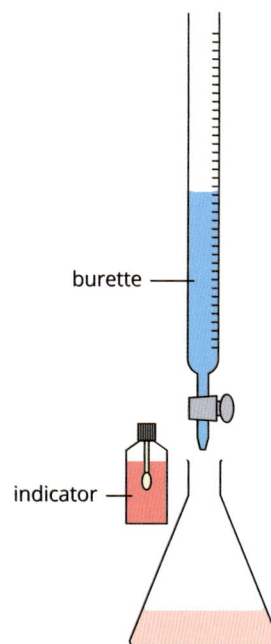

burette

indicator

FIGURE 8.2.5 Titration from the burette into the conical flask containing the aliquot of the unknown solution

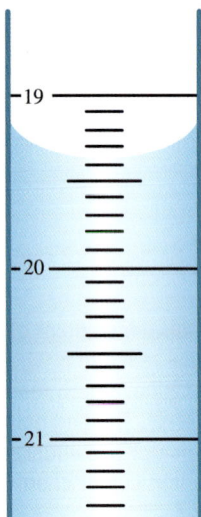

FIGURE 8.2.6 The burette is read from the bottom of the meniscus and the volume is estimated to the second decimal place. The volume measurement in this case is 19.38 mL.

> ℹ The volumes of concordant titres vary within a narrow range, usually within 0.10 mL from the lowest volume to the highest volume. The average of three concordant titres is used in calculations that use data obtained from volumetric analyses.

GO TO ➤ Section 8.3 page 203

TABLE 8.2.2 Summary of rinsing for each piece of equipment in a titration

Equipment	Solution for final rinsing
volumetric flask	water
pipette	the solution it will be filled with
burette	the solution it will be filled with
conical flask	water

Reading a burette scale

Burettes are usually calibrated in intervals of 0.10 mL. The volume of liquid in a burette is measured at the bottom of the meniscus of the liquid. The reading is estimated to the nearest 0.02 mL, as shown in Figure 8.2.6.

To minimise errors the titration is repeated several times and the **average titre** is found. Usually three **concordant titres** (titres that are within 0.10 mL from highest to lowest of each other) are used to find this average.

The volume of one single drop from a burette is about 0.05 mL, so taking the average of three results assumes that the results will be no more than one drop over or one drop under the accurate titre.

Consider the titration data represented in Table 8.2.3.

TABLE 8.2.3 Titration data collected over five trials

Reading	Titration number				
	1	2	3	4	5
Final burette reading (mL)	20.20	40.82	20.64	41.78	21.86
Initial burette reading (mL)	0.00	21.00	1.00	22.00	2.00
Titre (mL)	20.20	19.82	19.64	19.78	19.86

The first reading is a rough reading that gives an idea of the approximate end point. Titres 2, 4 and 5 are the concordant titres: they are within 0.10 mL from highest to lowest of each other. The difference between the highest and lowest readings is 19.86 − 19.78 = 0.08 mL, which is within the acceptable range for concordant results. The mean (average) of the concordant titres is:

$$\frac{19.82+19.78+19.86}{3}=19.82\,\text{mL}$$

Indicators

One of the characteristic properties of acids and bases is their ability to change the colour of certain chemicals called indicators. Some indicators, such as litmus, are extracted from fungi; others are synthetic. One such synthetic indicator is methyl orange, which is red in solutions of strong acids and yellow in solutions of bases.

Other common laboratory indicators include bromothymol blue and phenolphthalein. The colours of indicators are usually intense and highly visible, even at low concentrations of the indicator in solution. As Table 8.2.4 shows, different indicators change colour over different pH ranges. The choice of indicator for different types of titrations is discussed in more detail in Section 8.3.

TABLE 8.2.4 The pH ranges of a number of common acid–base indicators

Indicator	Colour of acid form	Colour of base form	pH range
methyl orange	red	yellow	3.1–4.4
bromothymol blue	yellow	blue	6.0–7.6
phenolphthalein	colourless	pink	8.3–10.0

Automated titrators

Automated titrators such as the one shown in Figure 8.2.7 are used in laboratories where a large number of titrations need to be carried out. During the titration, a pH or conductivity probe is lowered into a beaker containing the solution to be analysed. A sensor controls the addition of the **titrant** (the solution of known concentration being used in the titration) from an electronic burette. The sensor detects the equivalence point and a microcomputer calculates the volume of titrant added. The microcomputer calculates the concentration of analyte (the substance being measured) using the pH and/or conductivity data obtained.

Different formulae can be programmed into the microcomputer, depending on the nature of the substance being analysed and the titrant. The titrator shown in Figure 8.2.7 has an electronic burette that is refilled automatically. As the circular platform rotates, the next beaker containing a new sample to be analysed moves under the sensor.

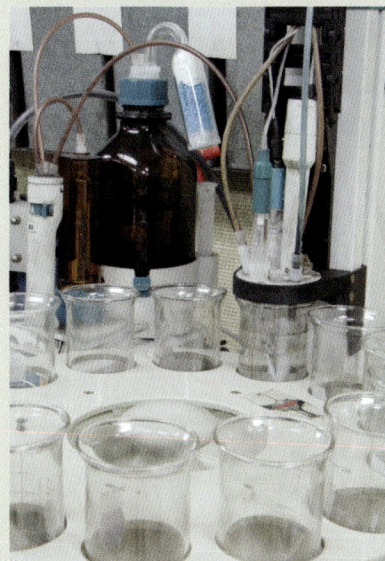

FIGURE 8.2.7 Automated titrators can rapidly analyse a large number of samples.

APPLICATIONS OF VOLUMETRIC ANALYSIS

Volumetric analysis is a basic technique used by analytic chemists in a wide range of industries including the food, mining, pharmaceutical, petrochemical and wine-making industries. The titration techniques outlined in this section are not restricted to acid–base reactions. Other chemical reactions such as redox and precipitation reactions are also used in volumetric analysis.

Analysis of the acid content of wine

Wine is a complex mixture of over a thousand chemicals, as illustrated in the diagram in Figure 8.2.8. It contains a mixture of acids, including tartaric, malic, citric and ethanoic acids. Some of these acids come from the grape juice used to make the wine, while others are produced during the fermentation process. These acids contribute to the taste of the wine and play a key role in the fermentation process. Acid–base titrations are used to determine the acid content of wine as part of the quality control process.

Amino acids
alanine
proline
glycine

Acids
tartaric acid
malic acid
lactic acid

Sugars
fructose
glucose

Other organic compounds
ethyl butyrate
isoamyl alcohol
limonene

Ethanol

FIGURE 8.2.8 This list of some of the compounds found in wine illustrates the complex nature of wine chemistry.

A common procedure used by wine chemists is to titrate an aliquot of the wine against a standardised solution of sodium hydroxide. The total acid content of wine is reported in terms of percentage of tartaric acid. Tartaric acid is the major acid found in wine, so when reporting acid content it is assumed for convenience that the total acid content is due only to tartaric acid.

Typically red wine has a total acid content about 0.6%, while the total acid content of white wine is between 0.7 to 0.8%.

Tartaric acid ($H_6C_4O_6$) is a diprotic acid and reacts with sodium hydroxide as follows:

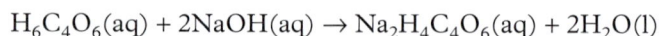

$$H_6C_4O_6(aq) + 2NaOH(aq) \rightarrow Na_2H_4C_4O_6(aq) + 2H_2O(l)$$

Analysis of the acid content of fruit juice and soft drink

Citric acid ($H_8C_6O_7$) is the major acid in fruit juices (Figure 8.2.9). It is also used to make lemonade and other soft drinks. Phosphoric acid (H_3PO_4) is added to some soft drinks to give them a 'zingy' taste.

FIGURE 8.2.9 The citric acid content of fruit juices can be determined by titration against a standardised solution of a base.

The acid content of fruit juices and soft drinks can be determined by titration against standardised solutions of a base such as sodium hydroxide. Both citric and phosphoric acids are triprotic and react with sodium hydroxide as shown in the following equations.

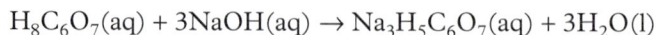

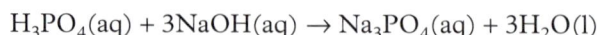

$$H_8C_6O_7(aq) + 3NaOH(aq) \rightarrow Na_3H_5C_6O_7(aq) + 3H_2O(l)$$

$$H_3PO_4(aq) + 3NaOH(aq) \rightarrow Na_3PO_4(aq) + 3H_2O(l)$$

Analysis of acids and bases used in medicines

The action of many medications depends upon their acidic or basic nature. Aspirin is a common pain killer (Figure 8.2.10).

Aspirin tablets contain 2-acetyloxybenzoic acid (also called acetylsalicylic acid) mixed with starch which acts as a binding agent. The amount of acetylsalicylic acid in a tablet can be determined by titration of a crushed tablet in water against standardised sodium hydroxide.

FIGURE 8.2.10 Volumetric analysis can be used to determine the amount of the active ingredient, 2-acetyloxybenzoic acid, in an aspirin tablet.

However, acetylsalicylic acid is not very soluble in water, which makes observing the titration end point difficult. A technique known as a back titration overcomes this problem. A crushed tablet is added to a measured excess volume of a standardised sodium hydroxide solution. The amount of excess sodium hydroxide is then determined by titration against a standardised hydrochloric acid solution. The amount of sodium hydroxide reacting with the acetylsalicylic acid is found by subtracting the amount of excess sodium hydroxide from the amount of sodium hydroxide initially added to the tablet. The amount of acetylsalicylic acid in the tablet can then be determined. Calculations involving back titrations are beyond the scope of this course.

The active ingredient in antacid tablets (Figure 8.2.11), used to treat gastric reflux, are bases such as aluminium hydroxide ($Al(OH)_3$), magnesium hydroxide ($Mg(OH)_2$), calcium carbonate ($CaCO_3$) and sodium hydrogen carbonate ($NaHCO_3$). With the exception of $NaHCO_3$, these compounds are insoluble in water and are best analysed using back titrations.

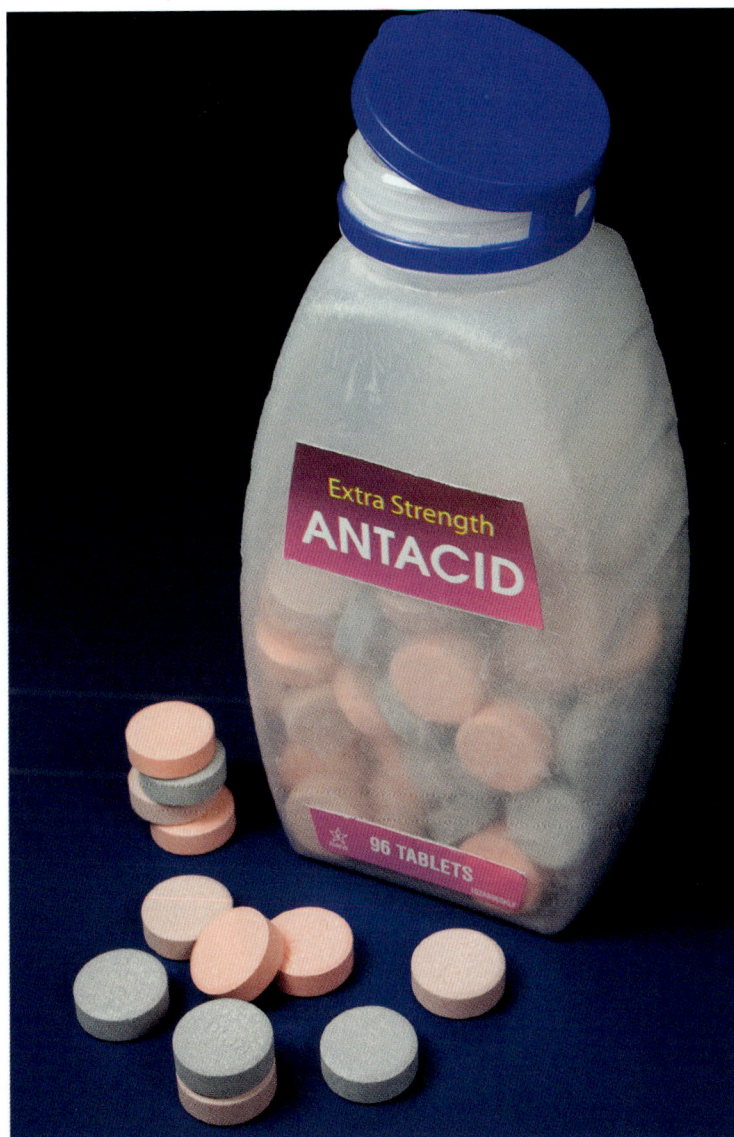

FIGURE 8.2.11 The bases in antacid medications can be determined by titration with a standardised solution of an acid.

Native Australian fruits

Native Australian fruits have been part of the diet of Indigenous Australian for tens of thousands of years. Fruits are eaten not only for their taste but also for their nutritional and medicinal values.

The taste of Australian fruits, as with introduced fruits, varies from sweet to sour depending on the relative amounts of sugars and acids in the fruit. Native Australian fruits such as the riberry (Figure 8.2.12) have a sweet taste because they contain a high proportion of sugars such as glucose, fructose and sucrose.

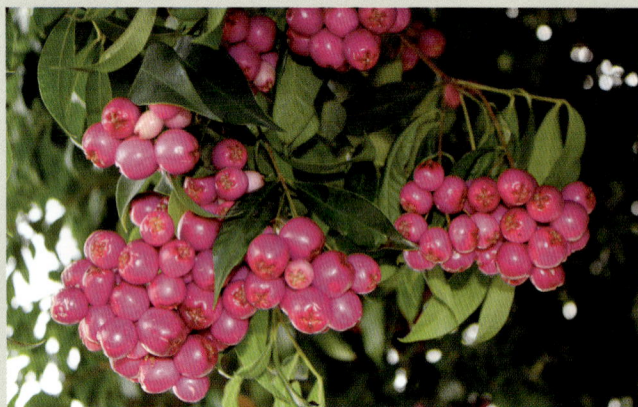

FIGURE 8.2.12 Riberries are valued by Indigenous peoples for their sweet taste, nutritional value and medicinal properties.

Fruits that contain a high proportion of acids, such as the Davidson plum (Figure 8.2.13a) and quandong (Figure 8.2.13b), have a sour or tart taste. Acids found in native and introduced fruits include citric acid, tartaric acid, malic acid and ascorbic acid (vitamin C). A quandong has twice the vitamin C content of an orange, while a Davidson plum has 100 times the vitamin C content of an orange. The quandong is also valued for its medicinal properties in the treatment of rheumatism and skin conditions, and is used as a laxative. It also plays an important role in the folklore and culture of many Indigenous groups.

One important group of chemicals found in fruits and vegetables are antioxidants, which may prevent the formation of free radicals associated with illnesses such as cancer, heart disease, diabetes and Alzheimer's disease. Free radicals are formed by some chemical reactions that occur naturally in the body. They are also produced when you are exposed to X-rays, air pollutants and cigarette smoke. Free radicals contain an unpaired electron and consequently are highly reactive, causing damage to biologically important molecules such as lipids (fats), proteins and nucleic acids (including DNA). Antioxidants such as vitamins C and E may disrupt the formation of these free radicals.

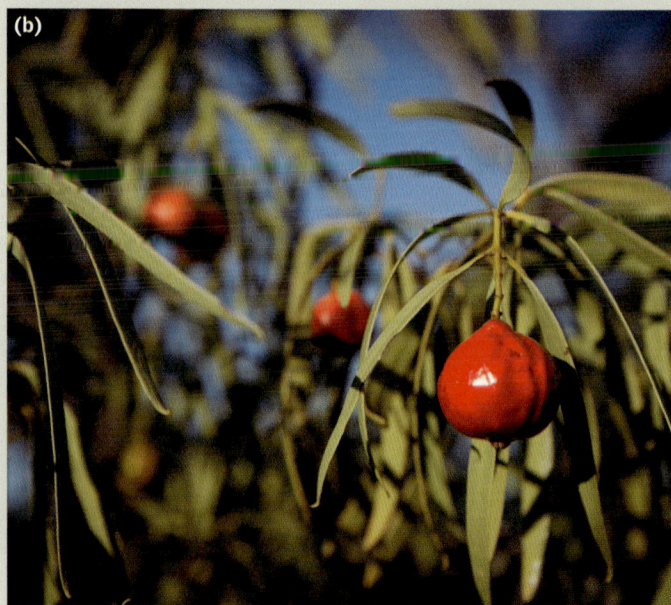

FIGURE 8.2.13 Native Australian fruits such as (a) the Davidson plum and (b) quandong have a tart or sour taste because of their high acid content. Both fruits have a higher vitamin C content than an orange.

Damage caused by free radicals may be somewhat prevented or reduced by eating fruits that are rich in antioxidants, such as berries, black plums and red grapes. Chemical analysis of Australian native fruits such as the Kakadu plum (Figure 8.2.14), Davidson plum and quandong has shown that these have significantly higher antioxidant levels than blueberries, which are considered to have the highest antioxidant content of the introduced fruits. The Kakadu plum has been recorded as having a vitamin C content as high as 7000 mg per 100 g of fruit, the highest of any known fruit. The Kakadu plum is also rich in other compounds that have antioxidant properties.

The acid content of fruits can be analysed using the volumetric techniques described in this chapter. Specific compounds in native Australian fruits that have antioxidant properties have been identified using such techniques such as high-performance liquid chromatography (HPLC) and liquid chromatography coupled with mass spectrometry (LC/MS).

The antioxidant content of some native Australian fruits and spices compared the antioxidant content of the introduced blueberry is shown in Figure 8.2.15.

FIGURE 8.2.14 The Kakadu plum has the highest recorded vitamin C concentration of any fruit. Vitamin C (ascorbic acid) is a significant antioxidant.

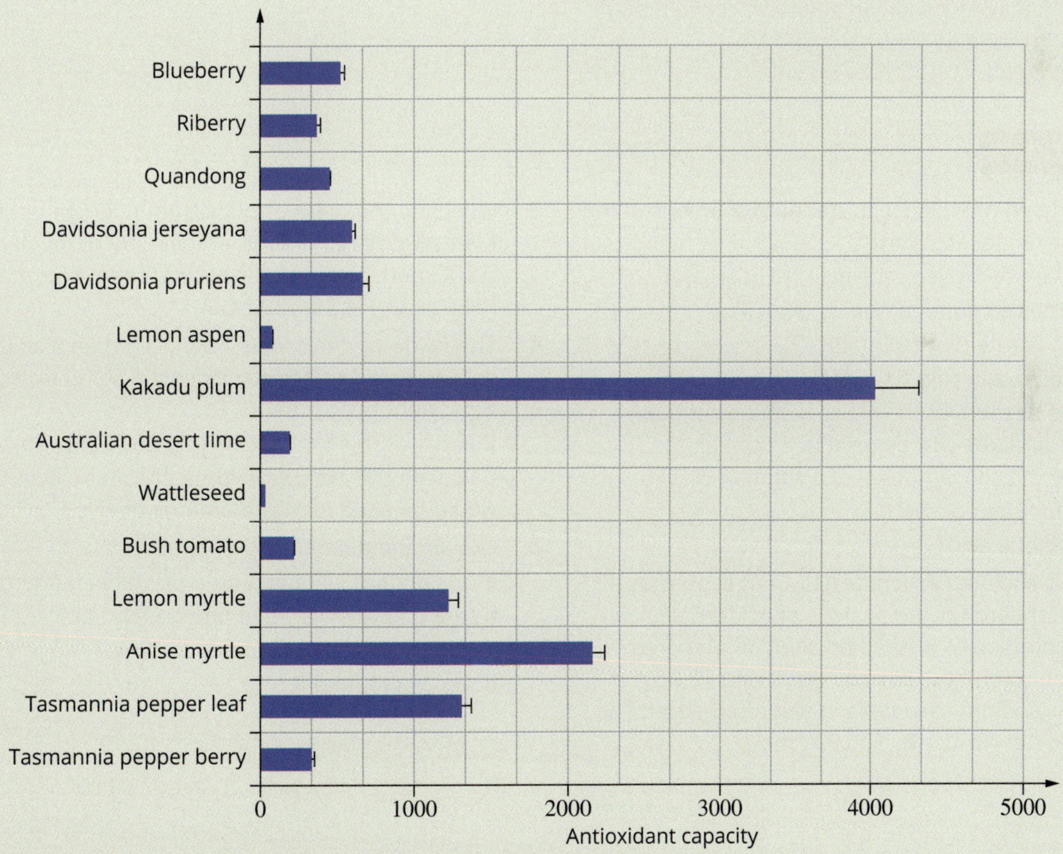

FIGURE 8.2.15 Average antioxidant capacity of some native Australian fruits, herbs and spices compared to the antioxidant capacity of the blueberry, an introduced fruit considered to be high in antioxidants.

8.2 Review

SUMMARY

- A standard solution is a solution with an accurately known concentration.
- A substance is suitable for use as a primary standard if it:
  - is readily obtainable in a pure form
  - has a known chemical formula
  - is easy to store without deteriorating or reacting with the atmosphere
  - has a high molar mass to minimise the effect of errors in weighing
  - is inexpensive.
- The concentration, in $mol\,L^{-1}$, of a prepared standard solution can be determined by measuring the mass of solid dissolved and the volume of solution prepared.
- Volumetric analysis is an analytical technique for determining the concentration of a solution by titrating it against a solution of known concentration (a standard solution) and volume.

- Volumetric flasks, pipettes and burettes are accurately calibrated pieces of laboratory glassware used in volumetric analysis.
- The point during a titration at which the reactants have just reacted completely in the mole ratio indicated by the balanced chemical equation is called the equivalence point.
- Three concordant titres are usually obtained during volumetric analysis. Concordant titres lie within a range of 0.10 mL.
- Titrations using automated equipment are used in the chemical, food and pharmaceutical industries to determine the concentrations of acids.
- Many fruits, including native Australian fruits, contain acids such as ascorbic acid (vitamin C) that have valuable nutritional properties.

KEY QUESTIONS

1 You have been provided with standard solutions of the following primary standards:
   A potassium hydrogen phthalate ($KH(C_8H_4O_4)$)
   B anhydrous sodium carbonate (Na_2CO_3)
   C sodium borate ($Na_2B_4O_7 \cdot 10H_2O$)
   D hydrated oxalic acid ($H_2C_2O_4 \cdot H_2O$)
   Which one or more of the above solutions of these primary standards can be used in a titration to determine the concentration of a solution of
   a potassium hydroxide?
   b hydrochloric acid?

2 Anhydrous sodium carbonate (Na_2CO_3) is used as a primary standard for the analysis of acids. Calculate the concentration of a standard solution prepared in a 50.00 mL volumetric flask by dissolving 13.25 g of anhydrous sodium carbonate in deionised water. The molar mass of Na_2CO_3 is $105.99\,g\,mol^{-1}$.

3 Calculate the mass of potassium hydrogen phthalate, $KH(C_8H_4O_4)$, required to prepare 100.0 mL of a $0.200\,mol\,L^{-1}$ standard solution. The molar mass of $KH(C_8H_4O_4)$ is $204.22\,g\,mol^{-1}$.

4 The following titres were obtained when a solution of sulfuric acid was titrated against a standard solution of potassium hydroxide.
   26.28 mL, 25.46 mL, 25.38 mL, 25.62 mL, 25.42 mL
   Calculate the average volume of sulfuric acid that would be used in the volumetric analysis calculations.

5 Explain the difference between:
   a a standard solution and a primary standard
   b the equivalence point and the end point
   c a burette and a pipette
   d an aliquot and a titre.

8.3 Titration and conductivity curves

TITRATION CURVES

The change in pH when a **strong acid** such as HCl is titrated against a strong base such as NaOH can be represented on a graph called a **titration curve** or **pH curve** (Figure 8.3.1).

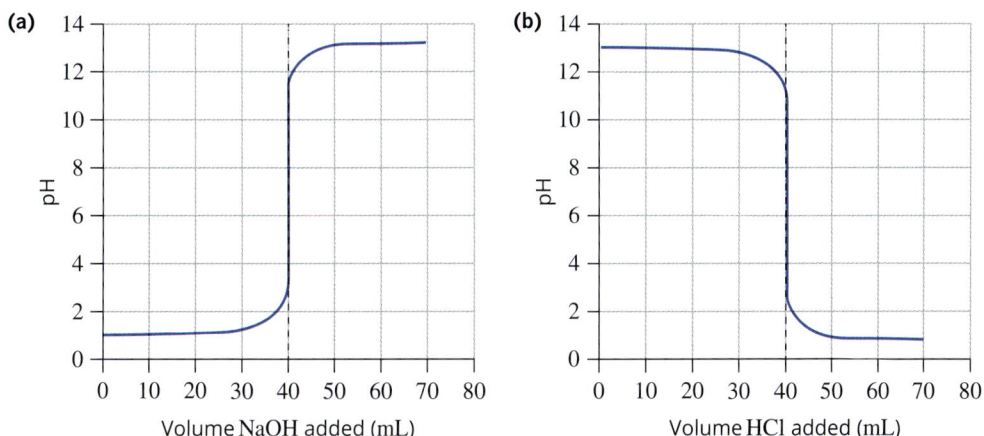

(a)

(b)

FIGURE 8.3.1 Titration curves for (a) the addition of a strong base to an aliquot of strong acid, and (b) the addition of a strong acid to an aliquot of a strong base.

The shape of a titration curve depends upon the combination of strong and weak acids and bases used in the titration.

The discussions of the titration curves that follow apply to the addition of acid from a burette to an aliquot of a base delivered by a pipette. The same principles apply when interpreting a titration curve for the addition of a base to an aliquot of an acid.

Titration of a strong acid with a strong base

The titration curve produced when $1\,mol\,L^{-1}$ HCl is added from a burette to an aliquot of $1\,mol\,L^{-1}$ NaOH is shown in Figure 8.3.2.

FIGURE 8.3.2 Titration curve for the addition of a strong acid to a strong base.

At the start of the titration, before any acid has been added, the pH of the NaOH solution is 14. As the HCl solution is added, OH^- ions react with H_3O^+ ions but there is little change in pH since the OH^- ions are in excess.

$$H_3O^+(aq) + OH^-(aq) \rightarrow 2H_2O(l)$$

or

$$HCl(aq) + NaOH(aq) \rightarrow NaCl(aq) + H_2O(l)$$

Near the equivalence point, the addition of a very small volume of HCl produces a large change in pH. In this titration the pH changes from 10 to 4 with just one drop of acid!

The equivalence point occurs at the midpoint of the vertical section of the graph. The volume of acid added at this point indicates the amount needed to completely react with the base according to the balanced equation. This volume is the titre that is recorded for the titration.

For a reaction between a strong acid and a strong base, the pH at the equivalence point is 7. Only water and Na^+ and Cl^- ions are present at the equivalence point, making the solution neutral.

As further HCl is added after the equivalence point, the solution contains an excess of H_3O^+ ions and the pH does not change significantly.

Titration of a strong acid with a weak base

The reaction between $1\,mol\,L^{-1}$ hydrochloric acid (a strong acid) and $1\,mol\,L^{-1}$ ammonia solution (a weak base) is presented by the following equation:

$$HCl(aq) + NH_3(aq) \rightarrow NH_4^+(aq) + Cl^-(aq)$$

The change in pH for the titration of HCl and NH_3 solution is shown in Figure 8.3.3.

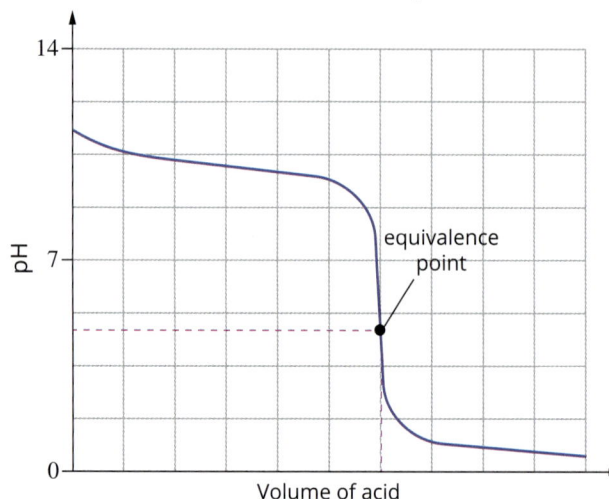

FIGURE 8.3.3 Titration curve for the addition of a strong acid to a weak base.

In comparison to the titration with NaOH, the pH of the ammonia solution before any acid is added is lower. Remember that ammonia is a weak base and is only partially dissociated:

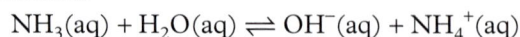

$$NH_3(aq) + H_2O(aq) \rightleftharpoons OH^-(aq) + NH_4^+(aq)$$

Initially there is a rapid drop in pH as the HCl reacts with OH^- ions. The reaction quickly generates sufficient NH_4^+ ions to form a buffer solution with unreacted NH_3. A buffer system counteracts any change in pH when an acid or base is added to it. The action of buffers is explained later in this chapter. Consequently the pH up to just before the equivalence point remains relatively unchanged.

GO TO ➤ Section 8.6 page 226

Close to the equivalence point, the addition of a small volume of HCl produces a drop in pH from 8 to 3. At the equivalence point the base has been neutralised by the acid. The solution contains H_2O as well as Cl^- and NH_4^+ ions. Ammonium ions (NH_4^+), the conjugate acid of the weak base, react with water to form hydronium ions (H_3O^+):

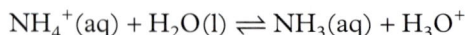

$$NH_4^+(aq) + H_2O(l) \rightleftharpoons NH_3(aq) + H_3O^+$$

This type of reaction is known as **hydrolysis**. The generation of H_3O^+ ions causes the pH at the equivalence point to drop below 7.

As further HCl is added after the equivalence point, the solution contains an excess of H_3O^+ ions and the pH does not change significantly.

Titration of a weak acid with a strong base

The reaction between $1\,mol\,L^{-1}$ ethanoic acid (a weak acid) and $1\,mol\,L^{-1}$ sodium hydroxide (a strong base) is presented by the following equation.

$$CH_3COOH(aq) + NaOH(aq) \rightarrow NaCH_3COO(aq) + H_2O(l)$$

The change in pH for the titration of CH_3COOH and NaOH solution is shown in Figure 8.3.4. The shape of the curve before the equivalence point is similar to that for the reaction of a strong acid with a strong base shown in Figure 8.3.2.

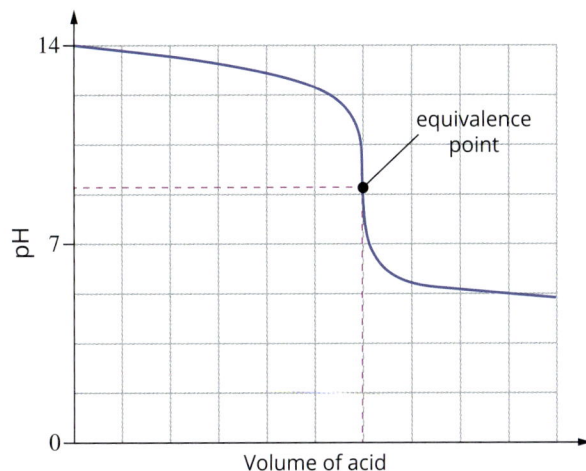

FIGURE 8.3.4 Titration curve for the addition of a weak acid to a strong base.

At the start of the titration, before any acid has been added, the pH of the NaOH solution is 14. As the CH_3COOH solution is added, OH^- ions react with H_3O^+ ions but there is little change in pH since the OH^- ions are in excess.

$$H_3O^+(aq) + OH^-(aq) \rightarrow 2H_2O(l)$$

or

$$CH_3COOH(aq) + NaOH(aq) \rightarrow NaCH_3COO(aq) + H_2O(l)$$

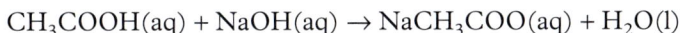

Near the equivalence point, the addition of a small volume of CH_3COOH produces a change in pH from 10 to 7.5.

At the equivalence point the solution contains H_2O, and Na^+ and CH_3COO^- ions. Ethanoate ions (CH_3COO^-), the conjugate base of the weak acid, react with water to produce OH^- ions.

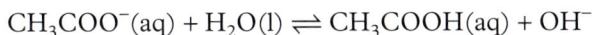

$$CH_3COO^-(aq) + H_2O(l) \rightleftharpoons CH_3COOH(aq) + OH^-$$

The generation of OH^- ions causes the pH at the equivalence point to rise above 7.

Titration of a weak acid with a weak base

The reaction between $1\,mol\,L^{-1}$ ethanoic acid (a weak acid) and $1\,mol\,L^{-1}$ ammonia solution (a weak base) is represented by the following equation:

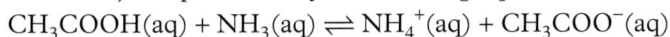

$$CH_3COOH(aq) + NH_3(aq) \rightleftharpoons NH_4^+(aq) + CH_3COO^-(aq)$$

The change in pH for the titration of CH_3COOH and NH_3 solution is shown in Figure 8.3.5.

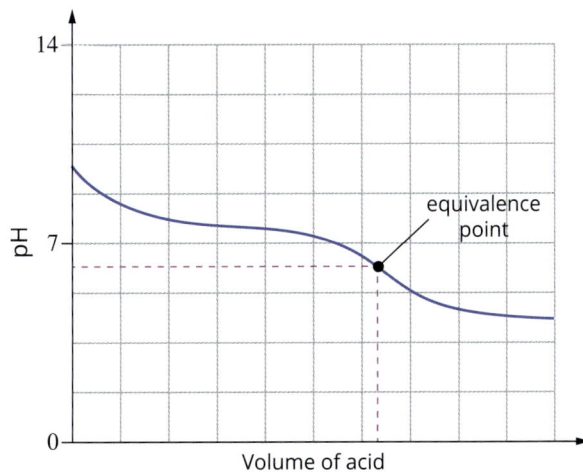

FIGURE 8.3.5 Titration curve for the addition of a weak acid to a weak base.

There is no clear change in pH at the equivalence point. The shape of the curve prior to the equivalence point is similar to the one for the strong acid – weak base pH curve. After the equivalence point the shape is similar to the shape of the weak acid – strong base curve shown in Figure 8.3.4.

SELECTING AN INDICATOR

During a volumetric analysis, the pH of the solution in the conical flask changes as the standard solution is delivered from the burette. The equivalence point occurs when the gradient of the titration curve is steepest (Figure 8.3.6).

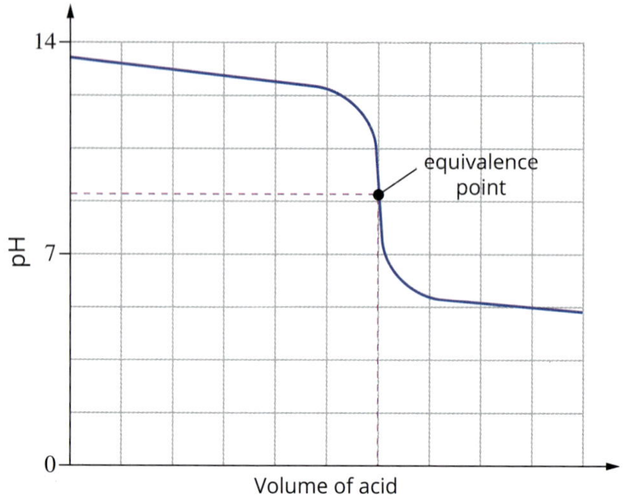

FIGURE 8.3.6 Change in pH during a titration between a strong base (sodium hydroxide solution) and a weak acid (ethanoic acid)

The equivalence point can be detected using an indicator. Indicators have different colours in acidic and basic solutions. The point during a titration when the indicator changes colour is known as the end point. It is important to select an indicator that changes colour during the steep section of the pH curve, so that the pH at the end point is near the pH at the equivalence point.

The colours of common acid–base indicators and the pH range over which they change colour are shown in Figure 8.3.7 and listed in Table 8.3.1.

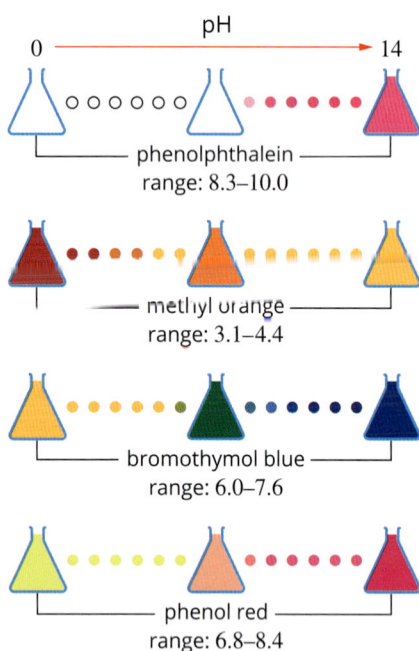

TABLE 8.3.1 The pH range of some common indicators

Indicator	Colour in acid solution	pH range	Colour in basic solution
phenolphthalein	colourless	8.3–10.0	pink
methyl violet	yellow	0.0–1.6	violet
methyl orange	red	3.1–4.4	yellow
methyl red	red	4.4–6.2	yellow
bromothymol blue	yellow	6.0–7.6	blue
phenol red	yellow	6.8–8.4	red/violet
alizarin yellow	yellow	10.0–12.0	red

For the titration of an aliquot of sodium hydroxide with hydrochloric acid, the pH changes from 10 to 4 near the equivalence point. By using an indicator that changes colour within this pH range, such as bromothymol blue which changes between pH 6.0 and 7.6, one drop will cause a colour change. This is referred to as a sharp end point. Therefore, knowing the pH range of an indicator is important for esuring a sharp end point. Other indicators, including phenolphthalein (pH range 8.3–10.0), could be used for this titration because they would also produce a sharp end point for this reaction.

FIGURE 8.3.7 To identify the equivalence point of a titration, you must use a suitable indicator. Although all of these indicators display different colours at low pH and high pH, the pH range in which they change is different.

Figure 8.3.8 compares the titration curves obtained when a strong acid is added to a strong base and when a strong acid is added to a weak base. Note that there is a sharp drop in pH in both graphs at the equivalence point. However, because this drop occurs over different pH ranges, the choice of indicator is important in detecting the equivalence point.

Phenolphthalein can be used successfully for the first titration because the volume of acid required to produce the colour change is very small. In the case of a titration of a weak base with a strong acid, the colour change occurs over a greater volume range. Methyl orange would be a better indicator in this case, because the volume of acid required to produce a colour change is very small.

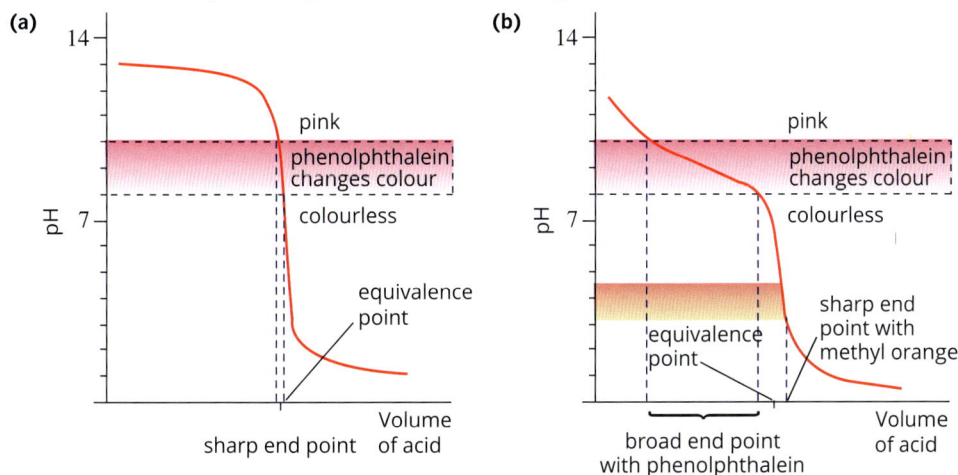

FIGURE 8.3.8 Titration curves, showing the pH during a titration of (a) a strong base with a strong acid, and (b) a weak base with a strong acid. Phenolphthalein, which changes colour in the pH range 8.3–10.0, gives a sharp end point in (a) but a broad end point in (b). Methyl orange, which changes colour between pH 3.2 and 4.4, would be a more suitable indicator for the second titration.

Commonly used indicators for different types of acid–base titrations are shown in Table 8.3.2. No indicator is suitable when a weak acid is titrated with a weak base, because there is no sharp change in pH at the end point.

TABLE 8.3.2 Indicators for different acid base titrations

Titration type	Typical pH change near the equivalence point	Commonly used indicator
strong acid – strong base	4–10	bromothymol blue or phenolphthalein or methyl orange
strong acid – weak base	3–7	methyl orange
weak acid – strong base	7–11	phenolphthalein

> ℹ️ For more accurate volumetric analyses, a pH meter attached to a data logger can be used instead of an indicator. Data from the meter is used to plot a titration curve, and the equivalence point can be identified from the steepest section of the curve.

WS
6.6

CONDUCTIVITY CURVES

When sodium hydroxide is added to a solution of hydrochloric acid, the H^+ ions are replaced by Na^+ ions. The concentration of H^+ ions decreases while the concentration of Na^+ ions increases as the added OH^- ions from the base are consumed by the H^+ ions from the acid.

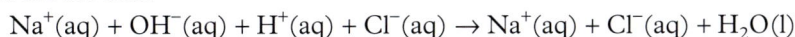

$$Na^+(aq) + OH^-(aq) + H^+(aq) + Cl^-(aq) \rightarrow Na^+(aq) + Cl^-(aq) + H_2O(l)$$

TABLE 8.3.3 Conductivities of some common cations and anions

Ion	Conductivity $(mS\,m^2\,mol^{-1})$
H^+	35.01
Na^+	5.01
NH_4^+	7.35
OH^-	19.92
Cl^-	7.64
CH_3COO^-	4.09

Since H^+ ions and OH^- ions move faster through solution than Na^+ and Cl^- ions, the ability of the solution to conduct an electric current decreases. The term **conductivity** is used to describe the ability of a solution to conduct an electric current. The molar conductivities of some common cations and anions are shown in Table 8.3.3.

The conductivity of a solution depends on:
- the identity of ions
- the charge of the ions
- the concentration of ions
- the mobility of the ions
- the temperature of the solution.

The change in conductivity during a titration is measured with a **conductivity meter** and is represented by a **conductivity curve**. The equivalence point of the titration is indicated by a sudden change in conductivity. A simple conductivity experiment is shown in Figure 8.3.9.

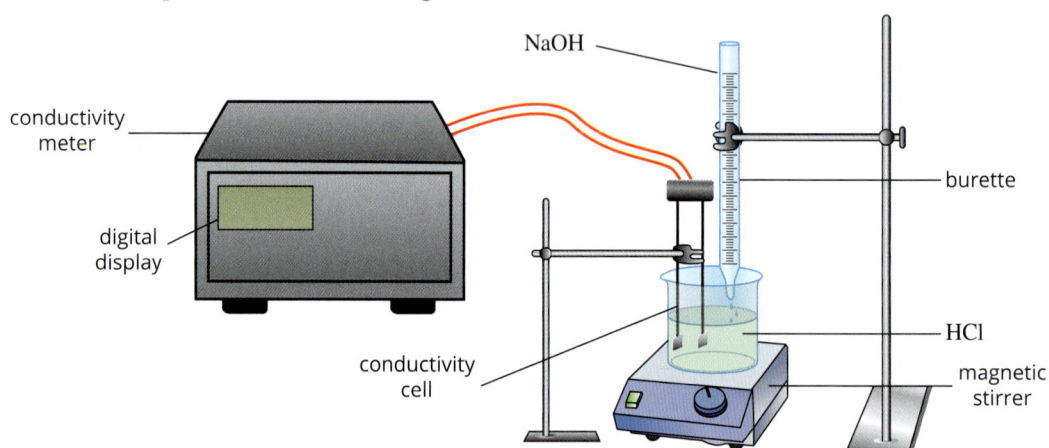

FIGURE 8.3.9 The change in conductivity during an acid–base titration is measured using a conductivity cell attached to a conductivity meter.

> ℹ The equivalence point in a conductivity titration is indicated by a sudden change in conductivity.

Conductivity curves for different titrations

Some typical conductivity curves for the various titrations of combinations of strong and weak acids and bases are described below. Each of the curves refers to the addition of a base to an acid. There is a sudden change in conductivity at the equivalence point.

Strong acid – strong base titration

The conductivity curve for the reaction between solutions of HCl and NaOH is shown in Figure 8.3.10. The main features are as follows:
- There is a high initial conductivity due to the presence of H^+ ions.
- Conductivity decreases as H^+ ions react with OH^- ions and are replaced by Na^+ ions, which have a lower conductivity.
- The equivalence point occurs at the point on the graph with the lowest conductivity.
- The solution at the equivalence point contains Na^+, Cl^- ions and H_2O molecules.
- Conductivity increases as more NaOH is added after the equivalence point, because of the presence of excess Na^+ and OH^- ions.

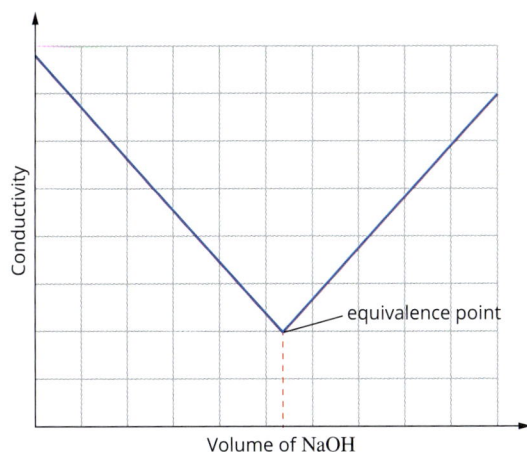

FIGURE 8.3.10 Conductivity curve for the titration for a strong acid (HCl) and a strong base (NaOH)

Strong acid – weak base titration

Figure 8.3.11 shows the conductivity curve for the titration of a strong acid (HCl) and a weak base (NH_3).

The main features of the curve are as follows:

- There is a high initial conductivity because of the high concentration of H^+ ions.
- Conductivity decreases as H^+ ions react with NH_3 molecules and are replaced by NH_4^+ ions, which have a lower conductivity.
- The equivalence point occurs at the point on the graph when the lowest conductivity is first reached, after which the conductivity remains constant.
- Conductivity does not change as more NH_3 solution is added after the equivalence point, because NH_3 is a weak base and is only dissociated to a very small extent.

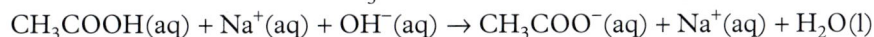

FIGURE 8.3.11 Conductivity curve for the titration of a strong acid (HCl) and a weak base (NH_3)

Weak acid – strong base titration

The conductivity curve for the titration of a weak acid (CH_3COOH) against a strong base (NaOH) is shown in Figure 8.3.12 on page 210.

The shape of the curve is influenced by a complex series of reactions. The main features are as follows:

- The initial conductivity is low because of the low concentration of H^+ ions from the partial dissociation of CH_3COOH.
- The conductivity increases as Na^+ ions are added and CH_3COOH molecules react with OH^- ions to form CH_3COO^- ions.

$$CH_3COOH(aq) + Na^+(aq) + OH^-(aq) \rightarrow CH_3COO^-(aq) + Na^+(aq) + H_2O(l)$$

- The solution at the equivalence point contains Na^+, CH_3COO^- ions and H_2O molecules.
- Conductivity increases as more NaOH is added after the equivalence point, because of the presence of excess Na^+ and OH^- ions.

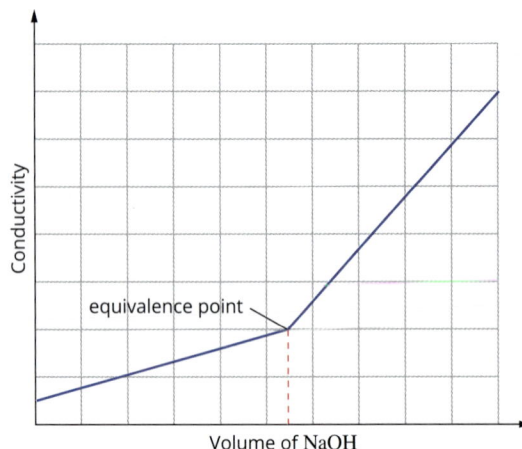

FIGURE 8.3.12 Conductivity curve for the titration of a weak acid (CH_3COOH) and a strong base (NaOH)

Weak acid – weak base titration

Figure 8.3.13 shows the conductivity curve for the titration of a weak acid (CH_3COOH) and a weak base (NH_3). The main features of the curve are as follows:
- The first part of the curve is similar to curve for the titration of a weak acid with a strong base.
- Conductivity increases prior to the equivalence point, because of the increasing concentrations of NH_4^+ and CH_3COO^- ions as NH_3 solution is added:
$$CH_3COOH(aq) + NH_3(aq) \rightleftharpoons NH_4^+(aq) + CH_3COO^-(aq)$$
- The equivalence point occurs at the point when the highest conductivity is first reached, after which the conductivity remains constant.
- Conductivity does not change as more NH_3 solution is added after the equivalence point, because NH_3 is a weak base and is only dissociated to a very small extent.

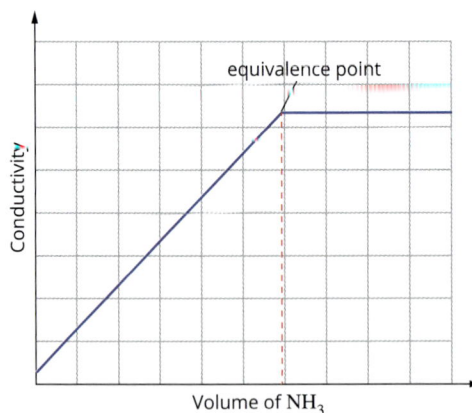

FIGURE 8.3.13 Conductivity curve for the titration for a weak acid (CH_3COOH) and a weak base (NH_3)

8.3 Review

SUMMARY

- The change in pH during a titration can be represented by a titration curve.
- The initial pH of the solution is indicated at the intersection of the curve and the pH axis.
- The equivalence point is the point in a titration when the reactants have reacted in the mole ratio shown by the reaction equation.
- The point in a titration when the indicator changes colour is called the end point.
- A sharp end point is one where the addition of one drop of titrant causes the indicator to change colour.
- The end point in an acid–base titration must be at or close to the equivalence point.
- The midpoint of the steep section of a titration curve represents the equivalence point.
- The pH at the equivalence point of titrations involving weak acid or bases is determined by the dissociation of conjugate weak acids or bases formed in the reaction.

- The features of various titration curves involving the addition of a strong/weak acid to a strong/weak base is summarised in the table below.

Acid–base strength	Typical pH before addition of acid	Typical pH at equivalence point
strong acid added to a strong base	13–14	7
strong acid added to a weak base	7–12	3–7
weak acid added to a strong base	13–14	7–11

- Conductivity curves record the change in conductivity during acid-base titrations.
- The equivalence point in a conductivity titration is indicated by a sudden change in conductivity.

KEY QUESTIONS

Use the information provided in the following titration curves to answer Question **1** to **5**.

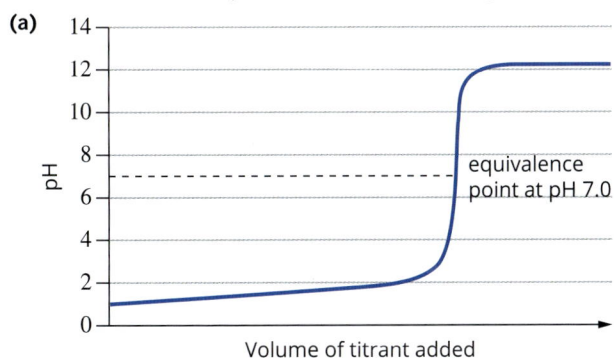

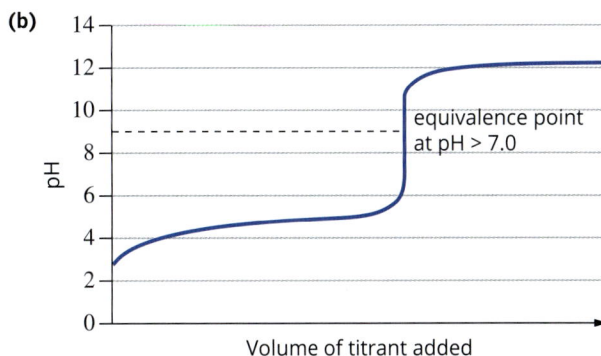

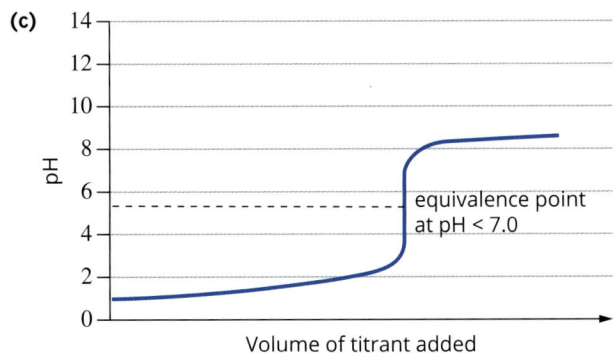

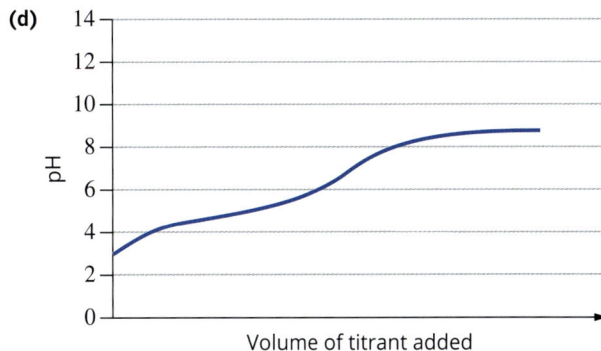

(a) equivalence point at pH 7.0

(b) equivalence point at pH > 7.0

(c) equivalence point at pH < 7.0

(d)

8.3 Review *continued*

1 Identify the combination of strong and weak acids and bases used to generate the four titration curves.

2 What is the concentration of the strong acid used in these titrations? (Assume the acid is monoprotic.)

3 What is the pH of the equivalence point for the titration shown in graph **a**?

4 Explain why the pH of the equivalence point in **c** is different to the equivalence point in **a**.

5 Why is it not possible to accurately determine the equivalence point from curve **d**?

6 From the information provided in the table below, select an indicator that would provide a sharp end point for each of the titrations represented by curves **a**, **b** and **c**.

Indicator	Colour in acid solution	pH range	Colour in basic solution
phenolphthalein	colourless	8.3–10.0	pink
methyl violet	yellow	0.0–1.6	violet
methyl orange	red	3.1–4.4	yellow
bromothymol blue	yellow	6.0–7.6	blue

7 What information is provided by the following titration and conductivity curves?

(a)

pH vs Volume of acid, 20.0 mL

(b)

Conductivity vs Volume of NaOH, 20.0 mL

8 Which one of the following curves represents the change in conductivity during the titration of a strong acid against a weak base (e.g. NH_3)?

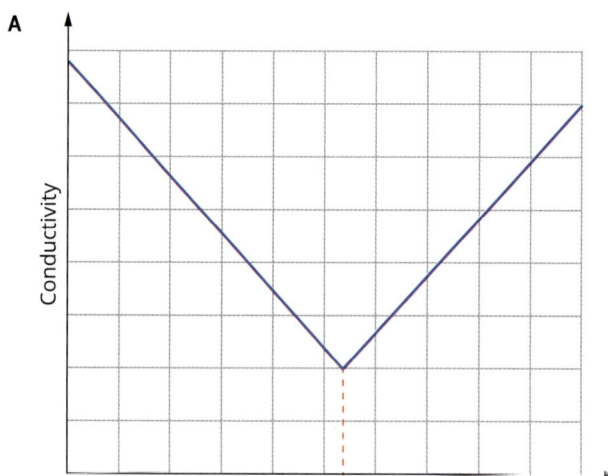

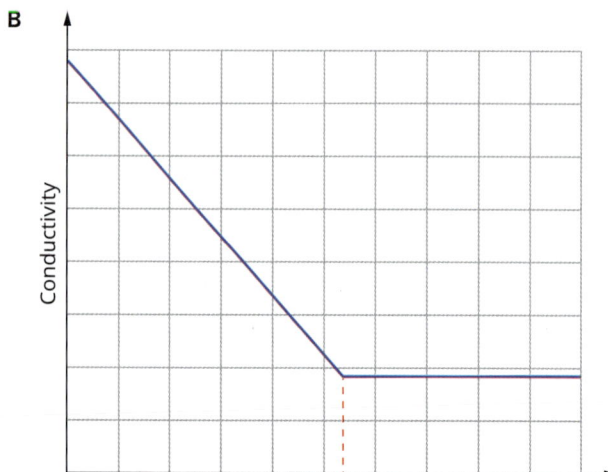

A

B

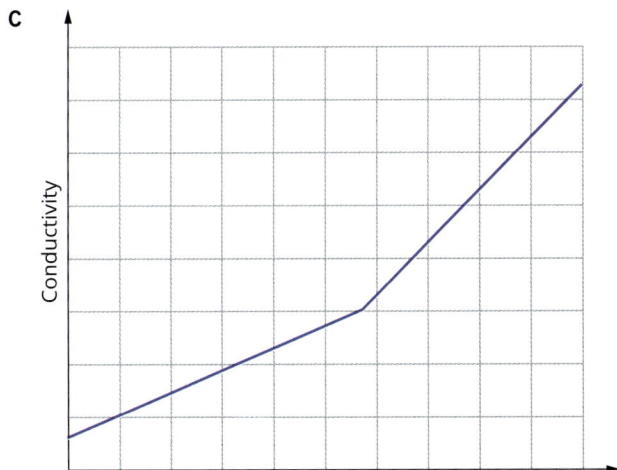

C

Conductivity

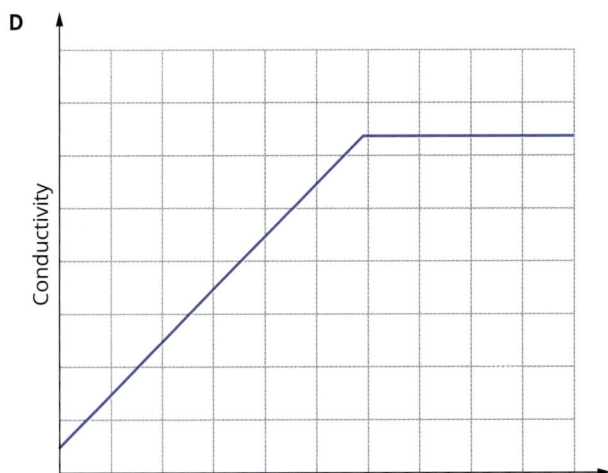

D

Conductivity

9   **a** Outline the difference between volumetric titration
        and conductivity titrations.
    b Describe two circumstances in which the use of
        a conductivity titration is preferable to using a
        volumetric titration using an indicator.

8.4 Calculations in volumetric analysis

In the previous section you learnt that volumetric analysis can be used to determine the amount of an unknown substance in solution by reacting it with a standard solution of known concentration.

This section shows you how to use data from a titration to calculate the concentration of the acid or base being analysed. You will also apply concepts of accuracy and precision in experimental work.

USING DATA FROM TITRATIONS

Simple titrations

Consider the data gained in an acid–base titration in which the concentration of a dilute solution of hydrochloric acid was determined by titration with a standard solution of sodium hydroxide (Table 8.4.1).

TABLE 8.4.1 Sample data obtained from a volumetric analysis

Volume of aliquot of HCl	25.00 mL
Concentration of standard NaOH solution	1.00 mol L^{-1}
Titre volumes of NaOH	25.05 mL, 22.10 mL, 22.00 mL, 22.05 mL

The concentration of hydrochloric acid is calculated by following a number of steps. These steps are summarised in the flowchart in Figure 8.4.1.

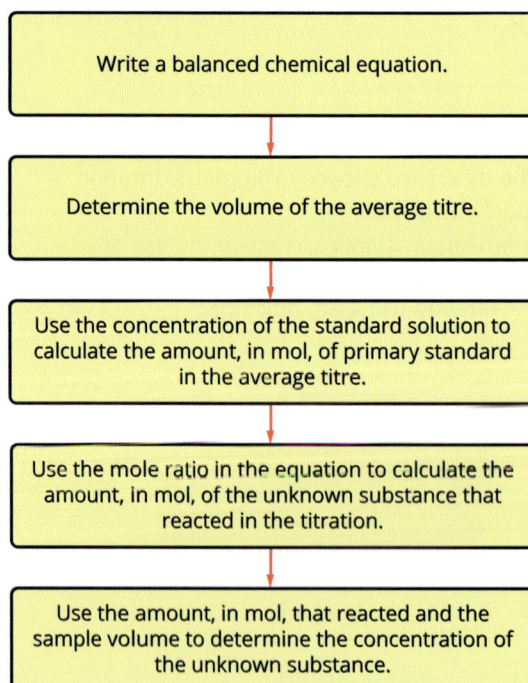

Write a balanced chemical equation.

Determine the volume of the average titre.

Use the concentration of the standard solution to calculate the amount, in mol, of primary standard in the average titre.

Use the mole ratio in the equation to calculate the amount, in mol, of the unknown substance that reacted in the titration.

Use the amount, in mol, that reacted and the sample volume to determine the concentration of the unknown substance.

FIGURE 8.4.1 Flowchart showing the steps in the calculation of the concentration of an unknown substance, using data from a titration in which the standard solution was in a burette

Worked example 8.4.1

CALCULATING CONCENTRATION USING A SIMPLE TITRATION

The concentration of hydrochloric acid was determined by titration with a standard solution of sodium hydroxide, as follows.

A 25.00 mL aliquot of HCl solution was titrated with a 1.00 mol L^{-1} solution of sodium hydroxide. Titres of 25.05 mL, 22.10 mL, 22.05 mL and 22.00 mL were required to reach the end point.

What is the concentration of the hydrochloric acid solution?

Thinking	Working
Write a balanced chemical equation for the reaction.	An acid is reacting with a metal hydroxide, or base, so the products will be a salt and water. $HCl(aq) + NaOH(aq) \rightarrow NaCl(aq) + H_2O(l)$
Discard any titre that is not concordant (i.e. not within a 0.10 mL range), then determine the volume of the average titre.	Discard the 25.05 mL titre because it is not concordant. $\text{average titre} = \dfrac{22.10 + 22.05 + 22.00}{3}$ $= 22.05 \text{ mL}$
Calculate the amount, in mol, of the standard solution that was required to reach the end point.	$n(NaOH) = c \times V$ $= 1.00 \times 0.02205$ $= 0.02205 \text{ mol}$
Use the mole ratio in the equation to calculate the amount, in mol, of the unknown substance that would have reacted with the given amount, in mol, of the standard solution.	$\text{mole ratio} = \dfrac{n(HCl)}{n(NaOH)} = \dfrac{1}{1}$ $n(HCl) = n(NaOH)$ $= 0.02205 \text{ mol}$
Determine the concentration of the unknown substance.	$c(HCl) = \dfrac{n}{V}$ $= \dfrac{0.02205}{0.02500}$ $= 0.882 \text{ mol L}^{-1}$

Worked example: Try yourself 8.4.1

CALCULATING CONCENTRATION USING A SIMPLE TITRATION

The concentration of a solution of barium hydroxide ($Ba(OH)_2$) was determined by titration with a standard solution of hydrochloric acid, as follows.

A 10.00 mL aliquot of $Ba(OH)_2$ solution was titrated with a 0.125 mol L^{-1} solution of HCl. Titres of 17.23 mL, 17.28 mL and 17.21 mL of HCl were required to reach the end point.

What is the concentration of the barium hydroxide solution?

Titrations that involve dilution

It is often necessary to dilute a solution before carrying out a titration, in order to obtain concentrations that are more convenient to use. For example, you might need to dilute the solution to make sure the titres are within the volume range of the burette.

Suppose you want to perform an acid–base titration to find the concentration of hydrochloric acid in a concrete cleaner. The concrete cleaner is so concentrated that it has to be accurately diluted before the titration. The following additional data needs to be recorded:

- the volume of the aliquot of undiluted concrete cleaner
- the volume of diluted solution that is prepared.

Sample data obtained from such a titration is shown in Table 8.4.2 on page 216.

TABLE 8.4.2 Data from a titration involving diluted concrete cleaner

Volume of undiluted concrete cleaner	25.00 mL
Volume of diluted concrete cleaner	250.0 mL
Volume of titre of diluted concrete cleaner	19.84 mL
Concentration of standard Na_2CO_3 solution	0.4480 mol L^{-1}
Volume of aliquot of Na_2CO_3 solution	20.00 mL

In this titration, 25.00 mL of concrete cleaner was diluted to 250.0 mL in a volumetric flask prior to taking a sample for titration. This means the **dilution factor** is 250.0 ÷ 25.00 = 10.00. The undiluted concrete cleaner will be 10.00 times more concentrated than the concentration of the aliquot. This must be taken into account in the calculations.

The steps required to calculate the concentration of undiluted concrete cleaner are summarised in the flowchart in Figure 8.4.2.

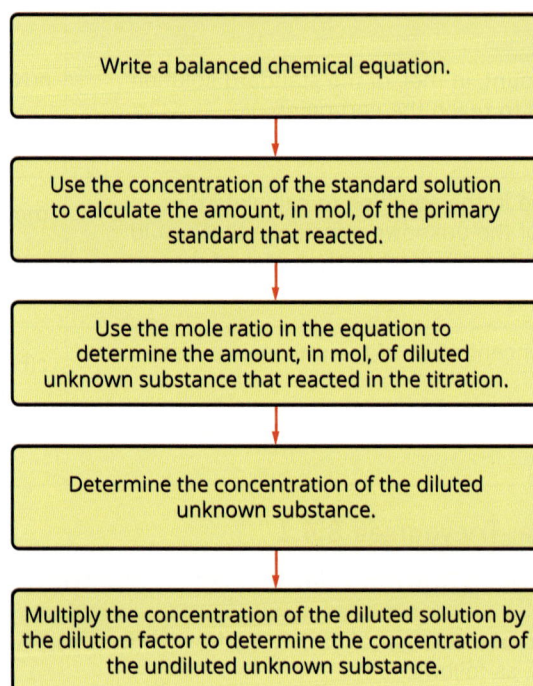

FIGURE 8.4.2 Flowchart showing the steps used in the calculation of the concentration of a substance that has been diluted for use in a titration

Worked example 8.4.2

TITRATION THAT INVOLVES DILUTION

A commercial concrete cleaner contains hydrochloric acid. A 25.00 mL volume of this cleaner was diluted to 250.0 mL in a volumetric flask.

A 20.00 mL aliquot of 0.4480 mol L^{-1} sodium carbonate solution was placed in a conical flask. Methyl orange indicator was added and the solution was titrated with the diluted cleaner. The indicator changed permanently from yellow to pink when 19.84 mL of the cleaner had been added.

Calculate the concentration of hydrochloric acid in the concrete cleaner.

Thinking	Working
Write a balanced chemical equation.	A dilute acid is reacting with a metal carbonate, so the products will be a salt, water and carbon dioxide gas. $2HCl(aq) + Na_2CO_3(aq) \rightarrow 2NaCl(aq) + H_2O(l) + CO_2(g)$
Using the concentration of the standard solution, calculate the amount, in mol, of the known substance that reacted in the titration. Remember that volumes must be expressed in litres.	$n(Na_2CO_3) = c \times V$ $\qquad = 0.4480 \times 0.02000$ $\qquad = 0.008960 \, mol$
Use the mole ratio in the equation to calculate the amount, in mol, of the diluted unknown solution that reacted in the titration.	$\dfrac{n(HCl)}{n(Na_2CO_3)} = \dfrac{2}{1} = 2$ $n(HCl) = 2 \times n(Na_2CO_3)$ $\qquad = 2 \times 0.008960$ $\qquad = 0.01792 \, mol$
Calculate the concentration of diluted unknown solution reacting in the titration.	$V(\text{diluted HCl}) = 0.01984 \, L$ $c(HCl) = \dfrac{n}{V}$ $\qquad = \dfrac{0.01792}{0.01984}$ $\qquad = 0.9032 \, mol \, L^{-1}$
Multiply by the dilution factor to determine the concentration of undiluted concrete cleaner.	dilution factor $= \dfrac{250.0}{25.00} = 10.00$ So undiluted $c(HCl) =$ diluted $c(HCl) \times 10.00$ $\qquad\qquad\qquad = 0.9032 \times 10.00$ $\qquad\qquad\qquad = 9.032 \, mol \, L^{-1}$

Worked example: Try yourself 8.4.2

TITRATION THAT INVOLVES DILUTION

A commercial concrete cleaner contains hydrochloric acid. A 10.00 mL volume of cleaner was diluted to 250.0 mL in a volumetric flask.

A 20.00 mL aliquot of 0.2406 mol L^{-1} sodium carbonate solution was placed in a conical flask. Methyl orange indicator was added and the solution was titrated with the diluted cleaner. The indicator changed permanently from yellow to pink when 18.68 mL of the cleaner had been added.

Calculate the concentration of hydrochloric acid in the concrete cleaner.

SOURCES OF ERRORS IN VOLUMETRIC ANALYSIS

The accuracy with which the volumes of aliquots and titres are measured in volumetric analysis depends on the calibration of the equipment used. There are always errors associated with measurements of quantities such as mass and volume made during experimental work.

These are some typical **uncertainties** associated with volumetric analysis:

- 20 mL pipette: ±0.03 mL
- 50 mL burette: ±0.02 mL for each reading
- 250 mL volumetric flask: ±0.3 mL
- 100 g capacity top loading balance: ±0.001 g
- 60 g capacity analytical balance: ±0.0001 g.
  Other graduated laboratory glassware provides less precise measures; for example:
- 50 mL measuring cylinder: ±0.3 mL
- 50 mL graduated beaker: ±5 mL.

Precision and accuracy

Every measurement in a quantitative analysis is subject to some form of error. Therefore a calculation that uses these measurements will produce a result in which the errors have accumulated.

If repeated measurements of the same quantity yield values that are in close agreement, then the measurement is said to be precise. For example, a titration is generally repeated until at least three titres are obtained that are within narrowly specified limits. These are called concordant titres. Repeated measurement of the titres increases the precision of the result and minimises errors that may have affected one titre more than others.

If the average of a set of measurements of a quantity is very close to the true or accepted value of the quantity, then the measurement is said to be accurate. It is possible for a result to be precise but inaccurate.

Methods used for accurate quantitative analysis should be designed to minimise errors. Where errors cannot be avoided, any discussion of results should refer to the level of inaccuracy that may have accumulated. This requires an understanding of the different types of errors.

GO TO ➤ Section 1.2 page 9

WS 6.7

GO TO ➤ Section 1.3 page 17

Types of errors made during titration

Mistakes

Mistakes are avoidable errors. Mistakes made during acid–base titrations could include:

- misreading the numbers on a scale
- mistakenly using a pipette of incorrect volume
- spilling a portion of a sample
- incorrect rinsing volumetric glassware.

The effects of incorrectly rinsing volumetric glassware are shown in Table 8.4.3.

TABLE 8.4.3 Rinsing glassware for volumetric analysis

Glassware	Correct	Incorrect
burettes pipettes	The final rinse should be with the acid or base they are to be filled with.	Rinsing with water only will dilute the acid or base solution.
volumetric flasks titration flasks (conical flasks)	Should only be rinsed with deionised water.	Rinsing with acidic or basic solutions will introduce unmeasured amounts of acids or bases into the flask, which can react and affect the results.

A measurement that involves a mistake must be rejected and not included in any calculations or averaged with other measurements of the same quantity. Mistakes are not generally referred to as errors.

Systematic errors

A **systematic error** produces a constant bias in a measurement that cannot be eliminated by repeating the measurement. Systematic errors that affect an acid–base titration could include:

- a faulty balance
- an inaccurately calibrated pipette
- using an unsuitable indicator
- reading the scale on a burette with a constant parallax error.

Whatever the cause, the resulting error is in the same direction for every measurement made with that particular equipment, and the average will be either higher or lower than the true value.

Systematic errors are eliminated or minimised by calibrating the apparatus and designing the procedure carefully. If a systematic error cannot be eliminated, an effort should be made to determine its size so that the error can be taken into account in calculations.

Random errors

Random errors follow no regular pattern. The measurement may be sometimes too large and sometimes too small. Random errors in volumetric analysis could be caused by:

- inherent uncertainty in the last value after the decimal place in the measurement of the mass of a primary standard on an analytical balance
- difficulty in judging where the meniscus sits on the line when measuring a volume using a pipette
- difficulty in judging the fraction between two scale markings on a burette.

The effects of random errors can be reduced by taking several measurements of the same quantity, then calculating an average. In volumetric analysis, taking the average of three concordant titres minimises random errors.

8.4 Review

SUMMARY

- The concentration of acidic or basic solutions can be determined by volumetric analysis.
- Dilution of the unknown solution is sometimes required to obtain manageable titre volumes.
- The mole ratio in a balanced chemical equation allows the amount, in mol, of a species in the equation to be calculated from the amount, in mol, of any other species.
- All quantitative measurements involve an error and have an uncertainty associated with them.
- Accuracy refers to how closely a measurement agrees with the true value.
- Precision refers to how closely a set of measurements are to each other.
- A systematic error produces a constant bias in a measurement that cannot be eliminated by repeating the measurement.
- A random error has an equal chance of being greater or lower than the true value.
- In volumetric analysis, random errors are minimised by averaging concordant measurements.

KEY QUESTIONS

1 A 20.00 mL aliquot of sulfuric acid solution is neutralised by the addition of 22.98 mL of 1.34 mol L^{-1} potassium hydroxide solution. The equation for the reaction is:

$$H_2SO_4(aq) + 2KOH(aq) \rightarrow K_2SO_4(aq) + 2H_2O(l)$$

Calculate the concentration of the sulfuric acid solution.

2 The concentration of ethanoic acid (CH_3COOH) in vinegar was determined by titration with a standardised solution of sodium hydroxide. A 25.00 mL aliquot of vinegar required 21.56 mL of 0.995 mol L^{-1} NaOH to reach the end point.

a Write an equation for the reaction between ethanoic acid and sodium hydroxide.

b Calculate the amount, in mol, of NaOH used in the titration.

c Calculate the amount, in mol, of ethanoic acid that reacted.

d Calculate the concentration of ethanoic acid in the vinegar.

3 A commercial concrete cleaner contains hydrochloric acid. A 25.00 mL volume of cleaner was diluted to 250.0 mL in a volumetric flask. A 25.00 mL aliquot of 0.5000 mol L^{-1} sodium carbonate solution was placed in a conical flask. Methyl orange indicator was added and the solution was titrated with the diluted cleaner. The indicator changed permanently from yellow to pink when 23.92 mL of the diluted cleaner had been added. The equation for the reaction is:

$$Na_2CO_3(aq) + 2HCl(aq) \rightarrow 2NaCl(aq) + CO_2(g) + 2H_2O(l)$$

Calculate the concentration of hydrochloric acid in the concrete cleaner.

4 The concentration of a solution of nitric acid (HNO_3) was determined by titration with a standardised solution of potassium hydroxide, using phenol red indicator. A 25.00 mL aliquot of nitric acid required 21.56 mL of 0.995 mol L^{-1} KOH to reach the end point.

a Write an equation for the reaction between nitric acid and potassium hydroxide.

b Calculate the amount, in mol, of KOH used in the titration.

c Calculate the amount, in mol, of nitric acid that reacted.

d Calculate the molar concentration of the nitric acid.

e Calculate the concentration of nitric acid in g L^{-1}.

5 20.00 mL aliquots of 0.386 mol L^{-1} sulfuric acid solution (H_2SO_4) were titrated against an ethanamine solution ($CH_3CH_2NH_2$) of unknown concentration. The equation for the reaction is:

$$2CH_3CH_2NH_2(aq) + H_2SO_4(aq) \rightarrow$$
$$(CH_3CH_2NH_3)_2SO_4(aq) + 2H_2O(l)$$

The average of three concordant titres was 21.02 mL. Calculate the molar concentration of the ethanamine solution.

6 Oxalic acid ($C_2H_2O_4$) is a diprotic acid. The concentration of an oxalic acid solution was determined by titration with a standard sodium hydroxide solution, using phenolphthalein indicator. A 20.00 mL aliquot of oxalic acid was titrated with a 1.25 mol L^{-1} solution of sodium hydroxide. Titres of 21.06, 21.00, 21.08 and 22.06 mL were required to reach the end point. Given that the end point occurred when both acidic protons on each oxalic acid molecule had reacted, calculate the molar concentration of the oxalic acid solution.

8.5 Dissociation constants

As you learnt in Section 7.1, acids with different strengths dissociate to different extents in water. Hydrochloric acid, for example, is a strong acid, so it completely dissociates in water according to the equation:

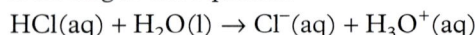

$$HCl(aq) + H_2O(l) \rightarrow Cl^-(aq) + H_3O^+(aq)$$

Terms such as 'strong acid' and 'weak acid' are qualitative and give only a limited indication of the extent of an acid's dissociation in water. A quantitative measure is needed to usefully express the strength of an acid and enable different acids to be compared.

MEASURING THE STRENGTH OF ACIDS

Consider the dissociation of ethanoic acid. This is a weak acid so it partially dissociates in water, according to the equation:

$$CH_3COOH(aq) + H_2O(l) \rightleftharpoons CH_3COO^-(aq) + H_3O^+(aq)$$

The expression for the equilibrium constant can be written as:

$$K_{eq} = \frac{[H_3O^+][CH_3COO^-]}{[CH_3COOH][H_2O]}$$

Since water is the solvent in aqueous solutions and its concentration is effectively constant, the equilibrium expression can be written as:

$$K_{eq}[H_2O] = \frac{[H_3O^+][CH_3COO^-]}{[CH_3COOH]} = K_a$$

The quantity K_a is known as the **acid dissociation constant** or acidity constant. The value of K_a for ethanoic acid is 1.7×10^{-5} at 25°C. The value is very small, indicating that in a solution of ethanoic acid the position of equilibrium favours the reactants and there is a relatively small amount of products.

Therefore, the acid dissociation constant is a way of measuring the strength of an acid. The greater the extent of dissociation, the greater the K_a value. For example, a strong acid like hydrochloric acid has a K_a value of 10^7 at 25°C.

Like all equilibrium constants, K_a is temperature dependent. K_a values are usually quoted for a temperature of 25°C.

An alternative way of representing acid strength is pK_a which is defined as:

$$pK_a = -\log_{10}(K_a)$$

This means that as acid strength increases, the pK_a value decreases.

The K_a and pK_a values of several common acids are given in Table 8.5.1.

TABLE 8.5.1 K_a and pK_a values of some common acids at 25°C

Acid	K_a	pK_a	Strong/weak acid
ethanoic acid	1.7×10^{-5}	4.76	weak
citric acid*	7.2×10^{-4}	3.14	weak
phosphoric acid*	7.1×10^{-3}	2.15	weak
nitric acid	20	−1.30	strong
hydrochloric acid	10^7	−7	strong
sulfuric acid*	10^9	−9	strong

*In the case of the polyprotic acids citric acid, phosphoric acid and sulfuric acid, the K_a value is for the loss of the first proton.

> **ⓘ** The acid dissociation constant can be used as a measure of an acid's strength. The stronger an acid, the larger its K_a value and the smaller its pK_a value.

CALCULATIONS INVOLVING ACIDITY CONSTANTS

Weak acids dissociate only to a limited extent, as evidenced by their low K_a values and high pK_a valucs. The general equation for the dissociation of a weak acid, HA, can be represented as:

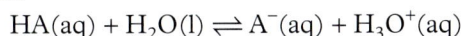

$$HA(aq) + H_2O(l) \rightleftharpoons A^-(aq) + H_3O^+(aq)$$

To simplify calculations involving acid dissociation constants, an assumption is made that the concentration of a weak acid at equilibrium is approximately the same as the initial concentration of the acid.

For example, if there is a $1.0\,mol\,L^{-1}$ solution of a weak acid HA for which $K_a = 1 \times 10^{-5}$, then at equilibrium $[HA] \approx 1.0\,mol\,L^{-1}$ (i.e. essentially unchanged). This assumption can be made because HA is a weak acid with a very small K_a, so it will dissociate only to a very small extent.

This assumption is valid if the initial concentration of the acid is significantly larger than the acid dissociation constant, K_a. In this example, the initial molar concentration is 10^5 times larger than K_a.

In calculations involving the dissociation of weak monoprotic acids, the following assumptions can be made:

- $[H_3O^+] = [A^-]$ (the only source of H_3O^+ is from the dissociation of the weak acid; self-ionisation of water does not contribute to $[H_3O^+]$)
- Equilibrium $[HA]$ = initial $[HA]$ (the concentration of HA does not change during the dissociation reaction).

The following Worked example shows how the acidity constant of a weak acid can be used to calculate:

- $pK_a = -\log_{10}(K_a)$
- $pH = -\log_{10}[H_3O^+]$
- the fraction of the acid that has dissociated, called the **percentage dissociation**:

$$\% \text{ dissociation} = \frac{[A^-]}{[HA]} \times 100$$

Worked example 8.5.1

CALCULATING THE pK_a, pH AND % DISSOCIATION OF A SOLUTION OF A WEAK ACID

The K_a for ethanoic acid (CH_3COOH) is 1.7×10^{-5}. For a $0.50\,mol\,L^{-1}$ ethanoic acid solution:

a calculate the pK_a	
Thinking	**Working**
Write the expression for the relationship between K_a and pK_a.	$pK_a = -\log_{10}(K_a)$
Substitute the value of K_a into the formula and calculate pK_a.	$pK_a = -\log_{10}(1.7 \times 10^{-5})$ $= 4.76$

b calculate the pH

Thinking	Working
Write the equation for the dissociation reaction.	$CH_3COOH(aq) + H_2O(l) \rightleftharpoons CH_3COO^-(aq) + H_3O^+(aq)$
Construct a reaction table, using each species in the balanced equation as the headings for the columns in the table. Insert three rows in the table labelled I (initial), C (change) and E (equilibrium): <table><tr><td></td><td colspan="2">**Reactants ⇌ Products**</td></tr><tr><td>**I**</td><td></td><td></td></tr><tr><td>**C**</td><td></td><td></td></tr><tr><td>**E**</td><td></td><td></td></tr></table>	Initially the weak acid has not dissociated, so its concentration is $0.50\,mol\,L^{-1}$. The initial concentrations of both CH_3COO^- and H_3O^+ are zero. As the acid dissociates, the CH_3COO^- and H_3O^+ ions are produced in a $1:1$ ratio. This can be represented by s. <table><tr><td></td><td colspan="3">$CH_3COOH(aq) + H_2O(l) \rightleftharpoons CH_3COO^-(aq) + H_3O^+(aq)$</td></tr><tr><td>**I**</td><td>0.50</td><td>0</td><td>0</td></tr><tr><td>**C**</td><td>$-s$</td><td>$+s$</td><td>$+s$</td></tr><tr><td>**E**</td><td>$0.50 - s$</td><td>s</td><td>s</td></tr></table>
Write an expression for K_a and substitute the equilibrium concentrations.	$$K_a = \frac{[CH_3COO^-][H_3O^+]}{[CH_3COOH]}$$ $$1.7 \times 10^{-5} = \frac{s^2}{0.50 - s}$$
What assumption can be made about the concentration of the weak undissociated acid at equilibrium?	Ethanoic acid is a weak acid with a very small K_a, so it will only dissociate to a very small extent. The concentration of ethanoic acid at equilibrium is therefore about the same as the initial concentration of ethanoic acid: $0.50 - s \approx 0.50$
Rewrite the expression for K_a, taking into account any assumptions made.	$$1.7 \times 10^{-5} = \frac{s^2}{0.50}$$
Solve for $s = [H_3O^+]$.	$s^2 = 1.7 \times 10^{-5} \times 0.50$ $s = [H_3O^+]$ $\quad = \sqrt{1.7 \times 10^{-5} \times 0.50}$ $\quad = 2.9 \times 10^{-3}\,mol\,L^{-1}$
Calculate the pH using: $$pH = -\log_{10}[H_3O^+]$$	$pH = -\log_{10}[2.9 \times 10^{-3}]$ $\quad = 2.54$

c calculate the percentage dissociation.

Thinking	Working
Write the expression for % dissociation of a weak acid.	$$\% \text{ dissociation} = \frac{[CH_3COO^-]}{[CH_3COOH]} \times 100$$
Determine the concentration of the conjugate base of the weak acid.	From the dissociation equation: $[CH_3COO^-] = [H_3O^+]$ $\quad\quad\quad\quad = 2.9 \times 10^{-3}\,mol\,L^{-1}$
Substitute the values for the concentration of the weak acid and its conjugate base into the formula and calculate the % dissociation.	$\% \text{ dissociation} = \frac{[CH_3COO^-]}{[CH_3COOH]} \times 100$ $\quad\quad\quad\quad = \frac{2.9 \times 10^{-3}}{0.50} \times 100$ $\quad\quad\quad\quad = 0.58\%$

Worked example: Try yourself 8.5.1

CALCULATING THE pK_a, pH AND % DISSOCIATION OF A SOLUTION OF A WEAK ACID

The K_a for hypochlorous acid (HOCl) is 3.0×10^{-8}. For a 0.10 mol L^{-1} HOCl solution:

a calculate the pK_a

b calculate the pH

c calculate the percentage dissociation.

Worked example 8.5.2

CALCULATING THE VALUE OF K_a FROM THE pH OF A SOLUTION OF A WEAK ACID

Calculate the K_a value for a 0.01 mol L^{-1} solution of methanoic acid (HCOOH) which has a pH of 2.9.

Thinking	Working
Write the equation for the dissociation reaction.	$HCOOH(aq) + H_2O(l) \rightleftharpoons HCOO^-(aq) + H_3O^+(aq)$
Determine [H$_3$O$^+$] at equilibrium using the formula: $[H_3O^+] = 10^{-pH}$	$[H_3O^+] = 10^{-pH}$ $= 10^{-2.9}$ $= 0.001$ mol L^{-1}
Construct a reaction table, using each species in the balanced equation as the headings for the columns in the table. Insert three rows in the table labelled I (initial), C (change) and E (equilibrium): 		**Reactants ⇌ Products**	
---	---	---
I		
C		
E				Initially, the weak acid has not dissociated, so its concentration is 0.01 mol L^{-1}. The initial concentrations of both HCOO$^-$ and H$_3$O$^+$ are zero. As the acid dissociates, the HCOO$^-$ and H$_3$O$^+$ ions are produced in a 1:1 ratio. This can be represented by s. |	$HCOOH(aq) + H_2O(l) \rightleftharpoons$	$HCOO^-(aq) +$	$H_3O^+(aq)$
---	---	---	---
I	0.01	0	0
C	$-s$	$+s$	$+s$
E	$0.01 - s$	s	s	
Using the coefficients from the equation, calculate the concentration of all species at equilibrium.	Initially no H$_3$O$^+$ was present. Since 0.001 mol L^{-1} is present at equilibrium: $s = 0.001$ mol L^{-1} So the table becomes: 		$HCOOH(aq) + H_2O(l) \rightleftharpoons$	$HCOO^-(aq) +$	$H_3O^+(aq)$
---	---	---	---
I	0.01	0	0
C	-0.001	$+0.001$	$+0.001$
E	$0.01 - 0.001 = 0.009$	0.001	0.001	
Write the expression for K_a and substitute the equilibrium concentrations. Calculate the K_a value.	$K_a = \dfrac{[HCOO^-][H_3O^+]}{[HCOOH]}$ $= \dfrac{0.001^2}{0.009}$ $= 2 \times 10^{-4}$

Worked example: Try yourself 8.5.2

CALCULATING VALUE OF K_a FROM THE pH OF A SOLUTION OF A WEAK ACID

> Calculate the K_a value for a 0.05 mol L^{-1} solution of propanoic acid (CH_3CH_2COOH) which has a pH of 3.09.

MEASURING THE STRENGTH OF BASES

> The stronger the base, the larger its K_b value and smaller its pK_b value.

Just as the strength of an acid is measured using the acid dissociation constant, the strength of a base can be measuring using the **base dissociation constant**, K_b.

The general equation for the dissociation of a weak base, A, can be represented as:

$$A^-(aq) + H_2O(l) \rightleftharpoons HA(aq) + OH^-(aq)$$

Based on this general equation, the expression for K_b is written as:

$$K_b = \frac{[HA][OH^-]}{[A^-]}$$

The strength of the base can also be represented using the p-function:

$$pK_b = -\log_{10}(K_b)$$

The K_b and pK_b values of several common bases are given in Table 8.5.2.

TABLE 8.5.2 K_b and pK_b values of several common weak bases at 25°C

Base	K_b	pK_b
ammonia (NH_3)	1.7×10^{-5}	4.76
ethanoate (CH_3COO^-)	5.8×10^{-10}	9.24
methanamine (CH_3NH_2)	4.4×10^{-4}	3.36

PA 6.7

8.5 Review

SUMMARY

- The equilibrium expression for the dissociation of a weak monoprotic acid in water:

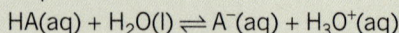

$$HA(aq) + H_2O(l) \rightleftharpoons A^-(aq) + H_3O^+(aq)$$

  is

$$K_a = \frac{[A^-][H_3O^+]}{[HA]}$$

- K_a is called the acid dissociation constant, or acidity constant.
- K_a is a measure of the strength of an acid. Strong acids have a higher K_a than weak acids.
- Acid strength can also be expressed in terms of pK_a, where p$K_a = -\log_{10}(K_a)$. Strong acids have a lower pK_a than weak acids.
- In calculations involving the dissociation of a weak monoprotic acid, HA, the following assumptions can be made:
  - $[H_3O^+] = [A^-]$
  - equilibrium [HA] = initial [HA]

- For the dissociation of a weak base in water, represented by the equation

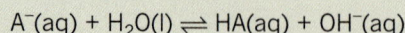

$$A^-(aq) + H_2O(l) \rightleftharpoons HA(aq) + OH^-(aq)$$

  the equilibrium expression is:

$$K_b = \frac{[HA][OH^-]}{[A^-]}$$

- K_b is called the base dissociation constant,
- K_b is a measure of the strength of a base. Strong bases have higher K_b than weak bases.
- Base strength can also be expressed in terms of pK_b where p$K_b = -\log_{10}(K_b)$. Strong bases have lower pK_b than weak bases.

1 Write the dissociation equations and the K_a expressions for the following acids.

   a NH_4^+

   b HCOOH

   c HCN(aq).

2 Identify the dissociation equation of the strongest acid.

   A $H_3PO_4(aq) + H_2O(l) \rightleftharpoons H_2PO_4^-(aq) + H_3O^+(aq)$

     $K_a = 7.1 \times 10^{-3}$

   B $H_2PO_4^-(aq) + H_2O(l) \rightleftharpoons HPO_4^{2-}(aq) + H_3O^+(aq)$

     $K_a = 6.3 \times 10^{-8}$

   C $HPO_4^{2-}(aq) + H_2O(l) \rightleftharpoons PO_4^{3-}(aq) + H_3O^+(aq)$

     $K_a = 4.2 \times 10^{-13}$

3 Complete the following table by inserting the missing K_a and pK_a values.

Acid	Formula	K_a	pK_a
nitrous acid	HNO_2	7.1×10^{-4}	
methanoic acid	HCOOH		3.74
hydrogen cyanide	HCN	6.2×10^{-10}	
hypochlorous acid	HOCl		7.52

4 Chloroethanoic acid ($CH_2ClCOOH$) is a weak monoprotic acid with a K_a of 1.3×10^{-3}. For a $1.0\,mol\,L^{-1}$ solution of chloroethanoic acid, calculate:

   a the pH

   b the percentage dissociation.

5 Ethanoic acid, with a K_a of 1.7×10^{-5}, is the principal acidic constituent in vinegar. A particular brand of vinegar is found to have a pH of 3.0. Calculate the concentration of ethanoic acid in the vinegar.

6 The pK_a of hydrofluoric acid is 3.17. Calculate the pH and percentage dissociation of a $0.5\,mol\,L^{-1}$ solution of hydrofluoric acid (HF).

7 Write the dissociation equations and the K_b expressions for the following bases.

   a NH_3

   b CH_3COO^-

   c CN^-

8.6 Buffers

Buffers are important in environmental and living systems, as well as in everyday life. In medicines, buffers are used to maintain the stability and effectiveness of the medicine. In food they preserve flavour and colour, and they are used during the fermentation of wine and in stages of textile dyeing. Buffers have a role in the maintenance and proper functioning of delicate chemical processes that can only occur within a narrow pH range. For example, there are buffer systems that ensure that the pH of blood is tightly maintained between pH 7.35 and pH 7.45.

In this section you will study what buffers are, how they are made, and how they work. You will also examine the application of buffers as dynamic equilibrium systems, and predict how they respond to pH changes according to Le Châtelier's principle.

WHAT IS A BUFFER?

Buffer solutions are able to resist a change in pH when small amounts of acid or base are added. This is important for processes that require stable and narrow pH ranges, such as maintaining the pH of a swimming pool (Figure 8.6.1).

You might have come across buffers around your house, particularly if you have a swimming pool, spa or aquarium.

Buffer solutions

A buffer consists of a weak **conjugate acid–base pair**. This means that a buffer could be:

- a weak acid and its conjugate base
- a weak base and its conjugate acid.

A **weak acid** donates hydrogen ions (protons) to a base to a limited extent. The acid's **conjugate base** contains one less hydrogen ion (proton) than the acid.

A **weak base** accepts hydrogen ions (protons) from acids to a limited extent. The base's **conjugate acid** contains one more hydrogen ion (proton) than the base.

The conjugate acid–base pair chosen for preparing a buffer helps determine the pH of the buffer. The pH ranges of some commonly used buffers are shown in Table 8.6.1.

FIGURE 8.6.1 It is desirable to maintain a pH of 7.2 to 7.8 in swimming pools to prevent irritation to the eyes, nose and skin. Buffers are added to pool water to maintain a comfortable pH range.

GO TO ➤ Section 6.1 page 144

TABLE 8.6.1 Some commonly used buffers

Weak acid	Conjugate base	Effective pH range
ethanoic acid (CH_3COOH)	ethanoate ion (CH_3COO^-)	3.5–5.5
dihydrogen phosphate ion ($H_2PO_4^-$)	hydrogen phospate ion (HPO_4^{2-})	6.2–8.2
hydrogen phosphate ion (HPO_4^{2-})	phosphate ion (PO_4^{3-})	11.3–13.3
carbonic acid (H_2CO_3)	hydrogen carbonate ion (HCO_3^-)	6.4–7.4
hydrogen carbonate ion (HCO_3^-)	carbonate ion (CO_3^{2-})	9.3–11.3
ammonium ion (NH_4^+)	ammonia (NH_3)	8.3–10.3

MAKING A BUFFER

A weak acid and its conjugate base gives an acidic buffer solution, while a weak base and its conjugate acid gives a basic buffer solution.

Acidic buffer solutions

An **acidic buffer solution** has a pH less than 7. Acidic buffers can be made from a weak acid and one of its salts. For example, a mixture of ethanoic acid and sodium ethanoate solution produces a CH_3COOH/CH_3COO^- buffer. If the solution contains **equimolar** concentrations of ethanoic acid and sodium ethanoate salt solution, it would produce a buffer solution of pH 4.76.

The ethanoic acid/sodium ethanoate buffer is prepared by dissolving approximately equal molar amounts of ethanoic acid (CH_3COOH) and sodium ethanoate ($NaCH_3COO$) in water.

The sodium ethanoate dissociates completely in water, producing sodium ions and ethanoate ions:

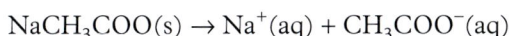

$$NaCH_3COO(s) \rightarrow Na^+(aq) + CH_3COO^-(aq)$$

At the same time only a small proportion of ethanoic acid molecules will dissociate, producing ethanoate (CH_3COO^-) and hydronium (H_3O^+) ions.

$$CH_3COOH(aq) + H_2O(l) \rightleftharpoons CH_3COO^- + H_3O^+$$

The resulting solution is an equilibrium mixture that contains H_3O^+ ions as well as a significant amount of both the weak acid CH_3COOH and its conjugate base CH_3COO^-. Sodium ions are spectator ions and are not involved in the equilibrium. The equation for the equilibrium system is:

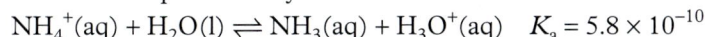

$$CH_3COOH(aq) + H_2O(l) \rightleftharpoons CH_3COO^-(aq) + H_3O^+(aq) \quad K_a = 1.7 \times 10^{-5}$$

This equilibrium system will resist a change in pH when a small amount of an acid or base is added.

Basic buffer solutions

A **basic buffer solution** has a pH greater than 7. Basic buffers can be made from a weak base and one of its salts. For example, a mixture of ammonia solution and ammonium chloride solution produces an NH_3/NH_4^+ buffer. If equal molar concentrations of weak base and its salt are mixed, the buffer solution will have a pH of 9.25.

An NH_3/NH_4^+ buffer can be prepared by dissolving approximately equal molar amounts of ammonia solution and an ammonium salt, such as ammonium chloride (NH_4Cl), in water.

The ammonium chloride dissociates completely in water, producing chloride ions and ammonium ions:

$$NH_4Cl(s) \rightarrow NH_4^+(aq) + Cl^-(aq)$$

At the same time only a small proportion of ammonia molecules will dissociate, producing hydroxide ions (OH^-) and ammonium (NH_4^+) ions:

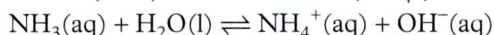

$$NH_3(aq) + H_2O(l) \rightleftharpoons NH_4^+(aq) + OH^-(aq)$$

The resulting solution is an equilibrium mixture of NH_3 molecules, OH^- ions and NH_4^+ ions. Chloride ions are spectator ions and are not involved in the equilibrium. The equation for the equilibrium system is:

$$NH_4^+(aq) + H_2O(l) \rightleftharpoons NH_3(aq) + H_3O^+(aq) \quad K_a = 5.8 \times 10^{-10}$$

The buffer solution contains a significant amount of both the weak base, NH_3, and its conjugate acid, NH_4^+. This equilibrium system can resist changes in pH when a small amount of an acid or base is added.

> **i** Buffer solutions can resist a change in pH when small amounts of acid or base are added.

> **i** A weak acid and its conjugate base gives an acidic buffer solution with a pH less than 7.

> **i** A weak base and its conjugate acid give a basic buffer solution of pH greater than 7.

HOW BUFFERS WORK

When 0.01 mol of hydrochloric acid is added to 1.0 L of water, the pH falls from 7.0 to 2.0, a drop of five pH units (Figure 8.6.2). This means that the hydronium ion concentration in the solution has increased 100 000 times.

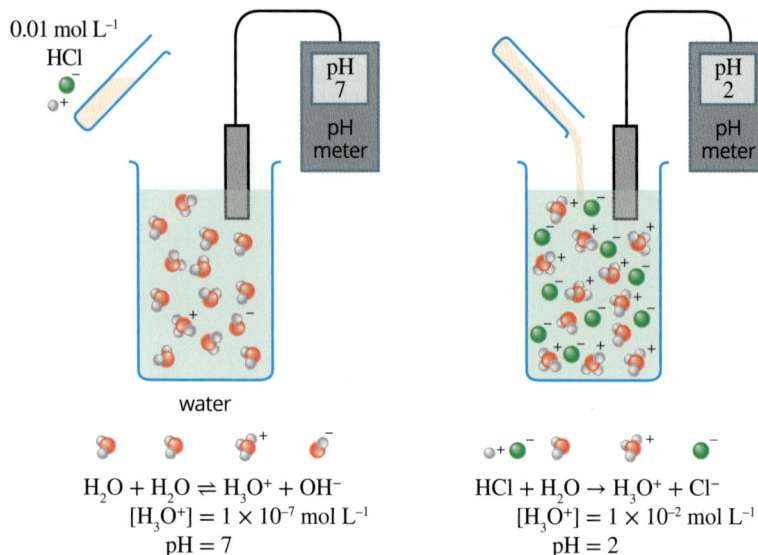

$$H_2O + H_2O \rightleftharpoons H_3O^+ + OH^-$$
$$[H_3O^+] = 1 \times 10^{-7} \text{ mol L}^{-1}$$
$$pH = 7$$

$$HCl + H_2O \rightarrow H_3O^+ + Cl^-$$
$$[H_3O^+] = 1 \times 10^{-2} \text{ mol L}^{-1}$$
$$pH = 2$$

FIGURE 8.6.2 A significant change in pH occurs when a small amount of hydrochloric acid is added to 1.0 L of water.

When the same amount of hydrochloric acid is added to a particular buffer solution initially at pH 7, the pH might drop to 6.9, a decrease of only 0.1 pH unit.

In this section you will investigate how buffers work to maintain a stable pH range.

Adding an acid to a buffer

If a small amount of a strong acid, such as HCl, is added to an ethanoic acid/ethanoate buffer (CH_3COOH/CH_3COO^-), the pH will decrease to a small extent, but not as much as if the buffer were not present. The extra H_3O^+ ions generated by the HCl disturb the existing equilibrium of the buffer solution.

$$CH_3COOH(aq) + H_2O(l) \rightleftharpoons CH_3COO^-(aq) + H_3O^+(aq)$$

GO TO ➤ Section 4.1 page 92

Le Châtelier's principle tells you that the system will respond to oppose the change and restore equilibrium. Therefore some of the additional H_3O^+ will react with CH_3COO^- ions present in the buffer. This produces more CH_3COOH molecules, decreasing the concentration of H_3O^+ ions in solution. The equilibrium in a buffer system is represented in Figure 8.6.3. Note that when acid is added, the conjugate base (A^-) combines with any H_3O^+ that is added to maintain a stable pH.

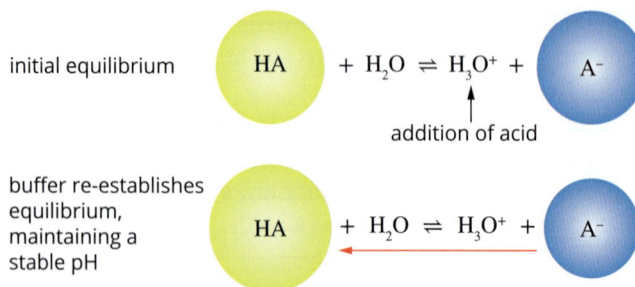

initial equilibrium   HA $+ H_2O \rightleftharpoons H_3O^+ +$ A^-

addition of acid

buffer re-establishes equilibrium, maintaining a stable pH   HA $+ H_2O \rightleftharpoons H_3O^+ +$ A^-

FIGURE 8.6.3 A constant pH is maintained by the equilibrium between a weak acid (HA) and its conjugate base (A^-) when acid is added, because A^-(aq) combines with the added H_3O^+.

Adding a base to a buffer

When a strong base is added to the CH_3COOH/CH_3COO^- buffer, the OH^- ions from the base react with CH_3COOH molecules in the buffer. This generates more CH_3COO^- ions and consumes most of the extra OH^- ions:

$$CH_3COOH(aq) + OH^-(aq) \rightleftharpoons CH_3COO^-(aq) + H_2O(l)$$

Note that when a base is added, the weak acid HA combines with any extra OH^- that is produced, minimising the effect on H_3O^+ concentration, thus maintaining a stable pH (Figure 8.6.4).

The overall effect of adding an acid or a base to a buffer solution on the final concentration of H_3O^+ or OH^- in the solution is small. Therefore the overall change in pH is also very small.

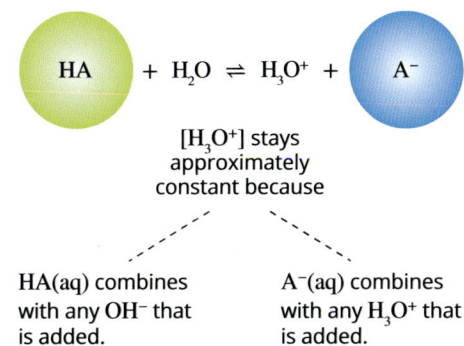

HA $+$ H$_2$O $\rightleftharpoons$ H$_3$O$^+$ $+$ A$^-$

[H$_3$O$^+$] stays approximately constant because

HA(aq) combines with any OH$^-$ that is added.

A$^-$(aq) combines with any H$_3$O$^+$ that is added.

FIGURE 8.6.4 A constant pH is maintained by the equilibrium between a weak acid (HA) and its conjugate base (A$^-$).

BUFFER CAPACITY

Buffer solutions have a working pH range and capacity that determines how much acid or base can be neutralised before the pH changes, and by how much the pH will change. It is the concentrations of the buffer, weak acid (HA) and its conjugate base (A$^-$) that influence how effective the buffer will be in resisting changes in pH. A buffer is most effective when more HA molecules and A$^-$ are available to react with and neutralise the effect of the addition of a strong acid or base.

If HCl is added to an ethanoic acid/ethanoate buffer, the H_3O^+ ions from the HCl will react with CH_3COO^- ions to form CH_3COOH. As more HCl is added, a new stage is reached where most of the CH_3COO^- ions have reacted. At this point, the buffer system is no longer effective. Additional H_3O^+ ions can no longer be removed by reaction with CH_3COO^- ions. From this point onwards, there will be a sharp decrease in pH as more HCl is added. Figure 8.6.5 on page 230 shows how the pH of a 1.0 L buffer solution (0.1 mol L^{-1} CH_3COOH and 0.1 mol L^{-1} CH_3COO^-) changes as HCl is added. A buffer can only resist changes in pH if some of each of its conjugate acid and base pair is present. If they are consumed (for example, by the addition of a large amount of strong acid or base), the solution is no longer a buffer.

Buffer capacity is a measure of the effectiveness of a buffer solution at resisting a change in pH when either a strong acid or a strong base is added.

Buffer capacity is greatest when:
- there is a high concentration of the weak acid and its conjugate base
- the concentrations of the acid and its conjugate base are equal.

An ethanoic acid/ethanoate buffer that has a high concentration of ethanoic acid can react with a greater amount of base. Similarly, a buffer that has a high concentration of the ethanoate ions can react with a greater amount of added acid (i.e. H_3O^+ ions).

> **i** The more A$^-$ and HA molecules available, the less of an effect adding a strong acid or base will have on the pH of a system.

> **i** Buffer capacity is a measure of the effectiveness of a buffer solution to resist a change in pH when either a strong acid or strong base is added.

Number of mol of HCl added	0	10^{-6}	10^{-5}	10^{-4}	10^{-3}	10^{-2}	10^{-1}	1.0
pH	4.74	4.7	4.7	4.7	4.7	4.6	2.7	0.05

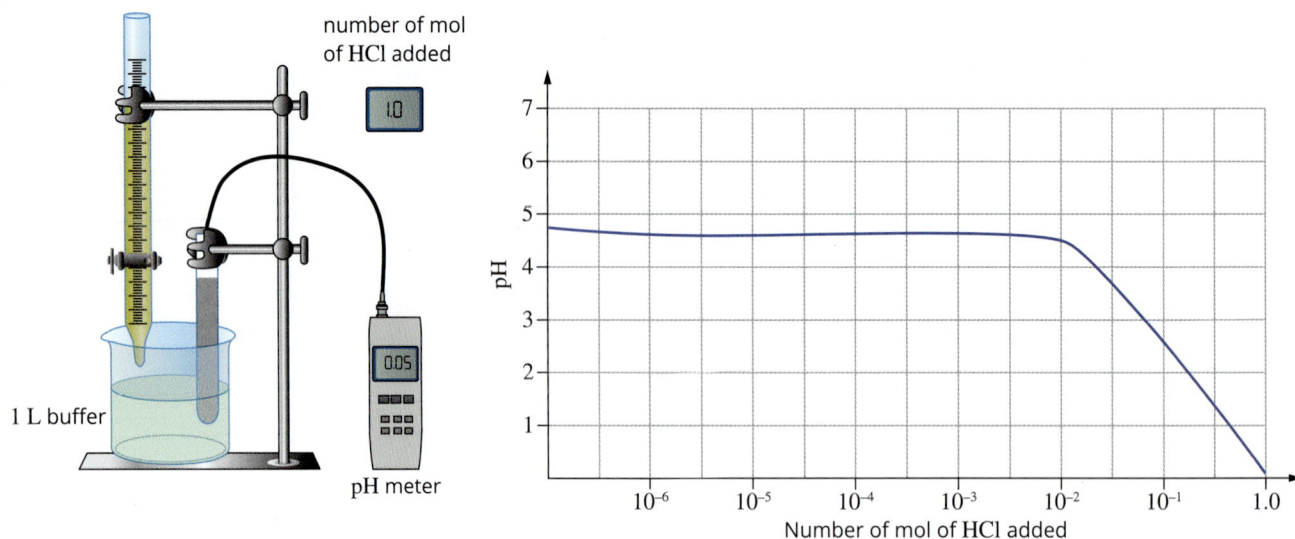

FIGURE 8.6.5 The change in pH of a 1.0 L buffer solution (0.1 mol L^{-1} CH$_3$COOH and 0.1 mol L^{-1} CH$_3$COO$^-$) when HCl is added

BUFFERS IN NATURAL SYSTEMS

Biological buffer systems

Many reactions that occur in the human body involve acid–base reactions. For example, respiration in cells produces carbon dioxide. The carbon dioxide dissolves and increases blood acidity according to the reaction:

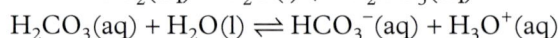

$$CO_2(aq) + H_2O(l) \rightleftharpoons H_2CO_3(aq)$$
$$H_2CO_3(aq) + H_2O(l) \rightleftharpoons HCO_3^-(aq) + H_3O^+(aq)$$

Buffers control the amount of H$_3$O$^+$ or OH$^-$ ions present in cells and tissues. Without buffers the pH of body fluids could fluctuate from extremely basic to extremely acidic, making it impossible for biological systems, including those that involve enzymes, to function. For example, blood is maintained within a narrow pH range of 7.35–7.45. Diseases such as pneumonia, emphysema and diabetes can cause the blood pH to drop to potentially lethal levels, a condition called acidosis. On the other hand, hyperventilation caused by rapid breathing increases pH and causes alkalosis (excessively basic blood). Figure 8.6.6 is a graphical representation of the effect of blood pH on the human body.

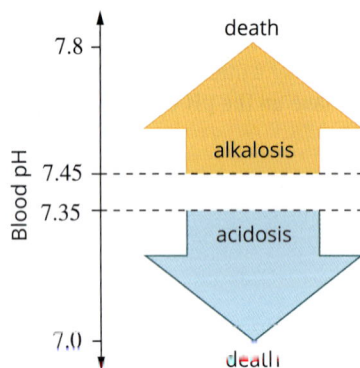

FIGURE 8.6.6 Physiological consequences of changes in blood pH in humans.

Carbonic acid buffer system

The presence of buffers maintains pH values within narrow limits in the body. The control of blood pH is achieved by different buffers. One important buffer is the carbonic acid buffer system consisting of carbonic acid (H$_2$CO$_3$) and the hydrogen carbonate ion (HCO$_3^-$):

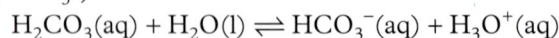

$$H_2CO_3(aq) + H_2O(l) \rightleftharpoons HCO_3^-(aq) + H_3O^+(aq)$$

The buffers in the blood act to reduce the effect of additional acid (H$_3$O$^+$). According to Le Châtelier's principle, the system responds to oppose the change and restore equilibrium, because some of the additional H$_3$O$^+$ will react with HCO$_3^-$ ions present in the buffer. This produces more H$_2$CO$_3$ molecules, decreasing the overall concentration of H$_3$O$^+$ ions in solution. If OH$^-$ ions are added they will react with H$_2$CO$_3$ molecules, minimising the effect on H$_3$O$^+$ ion concentration, thus maintaining the pH of the blood.

Phosphate buffer system

In the internal fluid of all cells another important buffer system is at work: the **phosphate buffer** system. This buffer system consists of dihydrogen phosphate ions ($H_2PO_4^-$) as a weak acid and hydrogen phosphate ions (HPO_4^{2-}) as the conjugate base of the weak acid. These two ions are in equilibrium with each other:

$$H_2PO_4^-(aq) + H_2O(l) \rightleftharpoons H_3O^+(aq) + HPO_4^{2-}(aq)$$

If additional H_3O^+ enters the cellular fluid, they are consumed in the reverse reaction. The HPO_4^{2-} reacts with the extra H_3O^+ and the position of equilibrium shifts to the left. If additional OH^- ions enter the cellular fluid, they react with $H_2PO_4^-$, minimising the effect on H_3O^+ ion concentration, so pH remains stable. Without the phosphate buffer in cell fluids, sharp changes in the pH would occur, bringing on cell death or causing proteins and cell structures to malfunction.

Environmental buffer systems

Soils

Soil is a complex system that contains:

- minerals such as sand, silt and clay derived from the underlying bedrock
- organic matter, microbes, invertebrates such as worms, and decaying plant and animal matter.
- air and water in the spaces between soil particles.

The food that we eat is ultimately dependent on the fertility of the soil in which plants grow. The pH of the soil is very important. Soil pH affects all soil chemistry and nutrient reactions. It is usually the first consideration when testing and evaluating a soil and when choosing a fertiliser to maximise crop yield.

Most plants perform best in slightly acidic soils at pH 6.0–7.0. Some plants, such as strawberries (Figure 8.6.7), blueberries and citrus grow better in more acidic soils (pH 4.0–6.5). Other plants, such as plums, sage and sunflowers grow better in a slightly basic (alkaline) soil (pH 7.0–7.5).

FIGURE 8.6.7 Strawberry plants grow best in more acidic soils at pH 4.0–6.5.

The uptake by plants of nutrients such as iron, nitrogen, phosphorus, potassium, sulfur, calcium and manganese is pH dependent. Small changes in a soil pH can have large effects on nutrient availability and plant health and growth (Figure 8.6.8).

FIGURE 8.6.8 A Camellia plant growing in soil with a high pH. If the pH of a soil is too high the plant cannot take up iron, which results in a decreased production of chlorophyll, making the leaf paler.

The pH of soils is naturally maintained by complex buffering systems involving carbonates, hydrogen carbonates and phosphates as well as organic acids.

Soil acidification, a decrease in soil pH, is a natural process that occurs very slowly as soil is weathered. Unfortunately this process is accelerated by agricultural practices such as the use of nitrogen fertilisers like ammonia. Microbes in the soil convert ammonia and ammonium ions to nitrate ions via a **nitrification** reaction that also produces hydrogen ions.

$$NH_4^+(aq) + 2O_2(g) \rightarrow NO_3^-(aq) + 2H^+(aq) + H_2O(l)$$

The chemical and biological properties of soil change as it becomes more acidic. One chemical change is an increase in the solubility of aluminum (Al) and manganese (Mn), which can be toxic to plants. The relationship between pH and aluminium concentration in the soil and the effect of aluminium on root growth are shown in Figure 8.6.9.

(a)

(b)

No lime
pH_{Ca}: 4.0
Aluminium:
15ppm

1 t/ha lime
pH_{Ca}: 5.1
Aluminium:
<2ppm

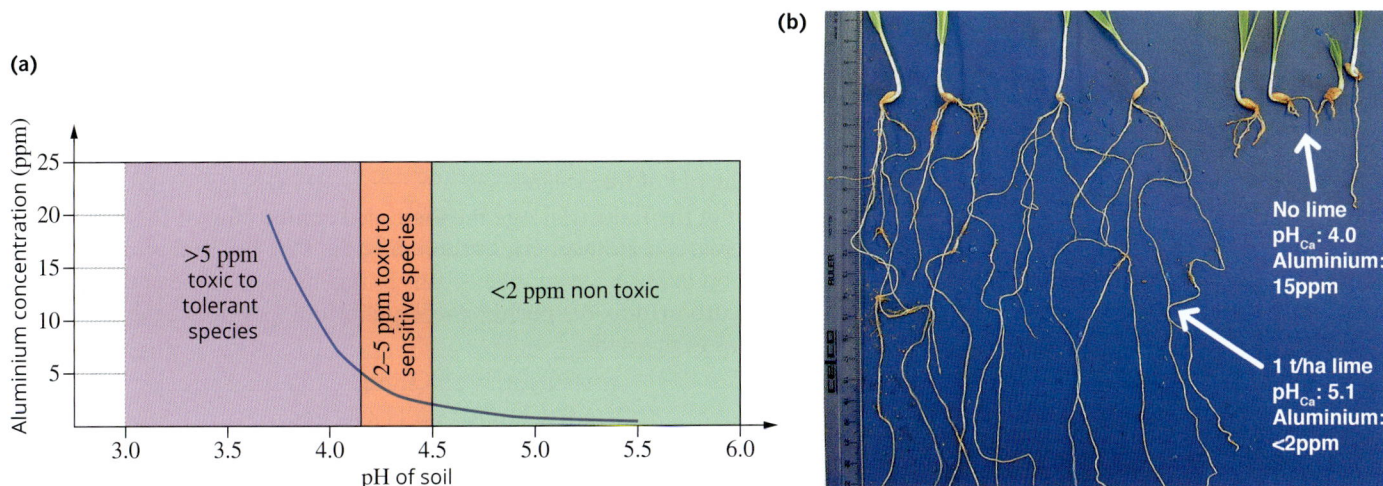

FIGURE 8.6.9 (a) The concentration of toxic aluminium in the soil is pH dependent. (b) The roots of plants grown in acidic soils are shortened due to increased levels of toxic aluminium.

When you measure the soil pH, you are measuring the concentration of hydrogen ions in the soil solution only. To counteract an increase in soil acidity, agricultural lime containing $CaCO_3$ or $MgCO_3$ can be added to the soil to neutralise hydrogen ions in the soil solution.

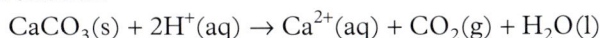

$$CaCO_3(s) + 2H^+(aq) \rightarrow Ca^{2+}(aq) + CO_2(g) + H_2O(l)$$

But hydrogen ions in soil are also adsorbed onto the surface of soil particles. To counter the loss of hydrogen ions from solution, hydrogen ions from the particle surfaces are released back into the soil solution. This buffering effect happens to maintain equilibrium and resist an increase in pH. Well-buffered soils are slower to acidify. But once they are acidic, it takes more agricultural lime to increase pH.

Ocean acidity: A stressed environmental buffer system

Before the start of the Industrial Age about 250 years ago, there was little variation in ocean acidity. The pH of the ocean was maintained by a complex buffer system (Figure 8.6.10).

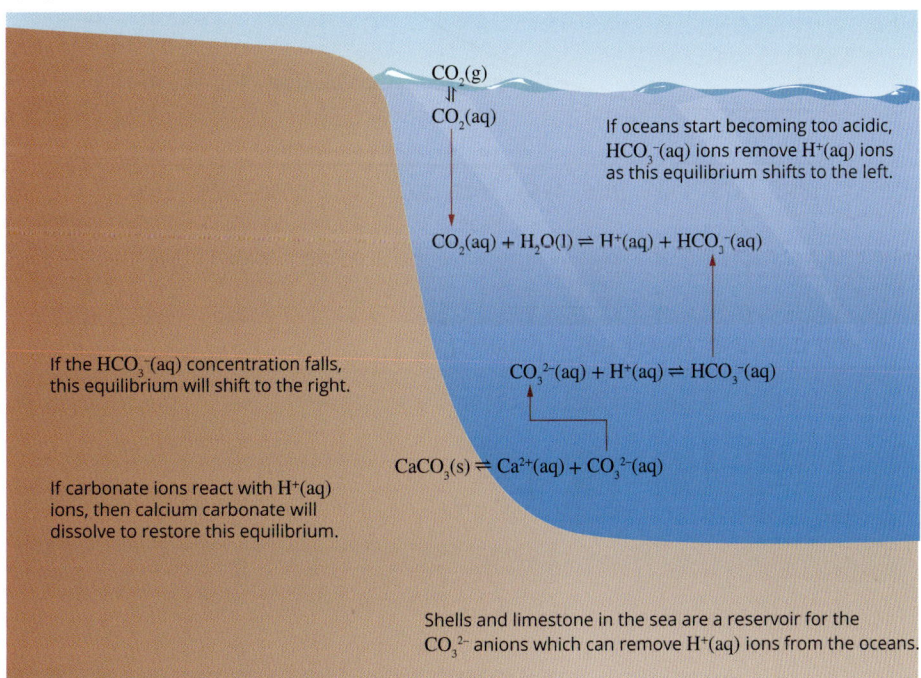

$CO_2(g)$
$CO_2(aq)$

If oceans start becoming too acidic, $HCO_3^-(aq)$ ions remove $H^+(aq)$ ions as this equilibrium shifts to the left.

$$CO_2(aq) + H_2O(l) \rightleftharpoons H^+(aq) + HCO_3^-(aq)$$

If the $HCO_3^-(aq)$ concentration falls, this equilibrium will shift to the right.

$$CO_3^{2-}(aq) + H^+(aq) \rightleftharpoons HCO_3^-(aq)$$

If carbonate ions react with $H^+(aq)$ ions, then calcium carbonate will dissolve to restore this equilibrium.

$$CaCO_3(s) \rightleftharpoons Ca^{2+}(aq) + CO_3^{2-}(aq)$$

Shells and limestone in the sea are a reservoir for the CO_3^{2-} anions which can remove $H^+(aq)$ ions from the oceans.

FIGURE 8.6.10 Ocean pH is buffered by a series of reactions.

The pH of the oceans is about 8. It is maintained at this level by a series of reactions, which are summarised in Figure 8.6.10 on page 233. A change in the equilibrium position of one reaction will cause a shift in the equilibrium position of others. The interaction between these reactions means that the oceans act as a giant buffer. Gradual changes over a period of thousands of years have not resulted in any great change to the pH of the oceans.

Since the start of the Industrial Age the increased combustion of fossil fuels has resulted in an increase in atmospheric carbon dioxide. This has lead to an increase in the concentration of H_3O^+ ions in the oceans as the increase in the concentration of atmospheric carbon dioxide pushes the equilibrium position of each of the following reactions to the right.

$$CO_2(g) \rightleftharpoons CO_2(aq)$$
$$CO_2(aq) + H_2O(l) \rightleftharpoons H_2CO_3(aq)$$
$$H_2CO_3(aq) + H_2O(l) \rightleftharpoons HCO_3^-(aq) + H_3O^+(aq)$$

This increase has happened too quickly for the buffer systems in the surface layers of the oceans to deal with. The result has been a decrease of 0.1 in ocean pH, representing a 30% increase in the concentration of H_3O^+ ions in the ocean.

With increasing levels of atmospheric carbon dioxide, the pH of the oceans is decreasing. The pattern of changes in ocean pH and dissolved carbon dioxide is shown in Figure 8.6.11.

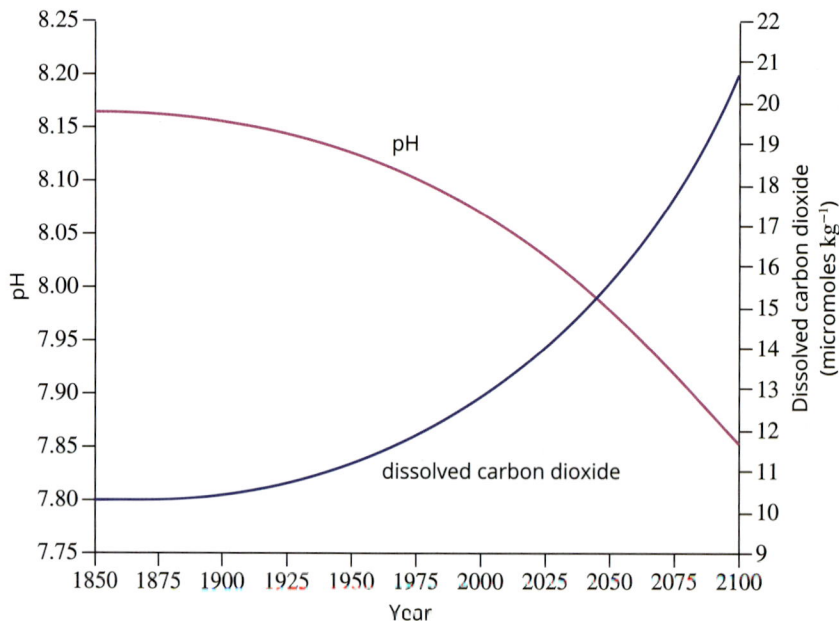

FIGURE 8.6.11 Historical (from 1850) and projected (to 2100) pH and dissolved CO_2 levels in the ocean

Environmental impact of increasing ocean acidity

Ocean acidity is a global issue affecting all oceans. Increasing acidity has a detrimental effect on cold ocean organisms such as plankton and krill (Figure 8.6.12) that are at the bottom of the food chain.

FIGURE 8.6.12 (a) Diatoms are single-celled algae that are an important component of plankton that forms the base of marine and freshwater food chains. (b) Krill feed on plankton and can be found in swarms kilometres wide. They are a major food source for many marine organisms, from small fish such as sardines to huge mammals such as whales.

Plankton such as diatoms are a food source for krill, which in turn are consumed by animals higher up in the food chain. An example of a food chain involving these organisms is shown in Figure 8.6.13.

Krill eggs will not hatch successfully if the water pH is too low. Therefore an increase in ocean acidity is predicted to have a harmful effect on the plankton and krill upon which other species depend for their survival. A collapse of the krill population coupled with ocean warming would have a disastrous effect on the ecosystem of the ocean.

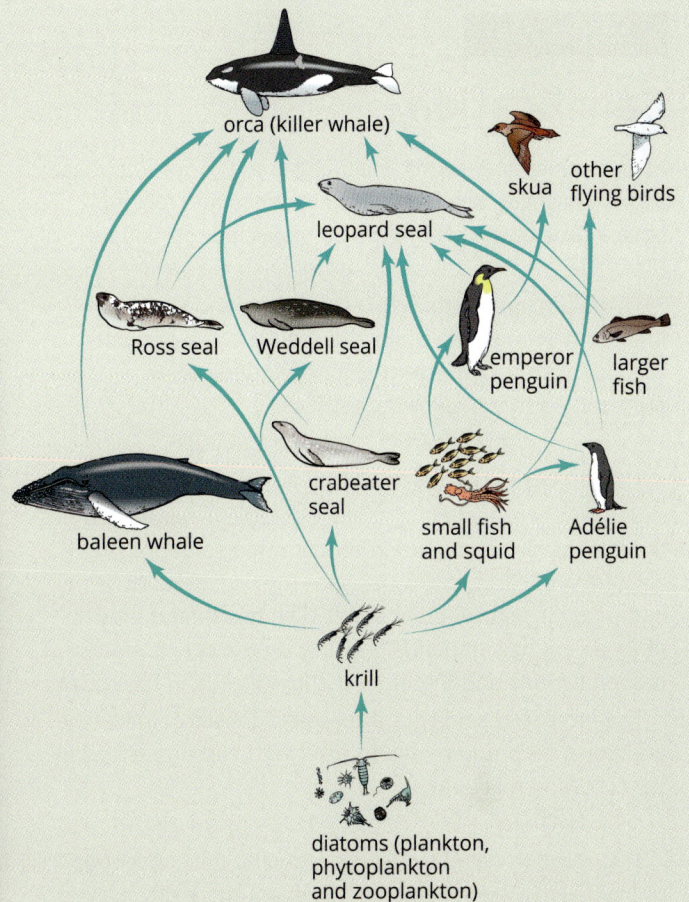

FIGURE 8.6.13 A food web showing the relationship between animals that live in Antarctic waters.

Impact of ocean acidity on humans

Increased ocean acidity is also predicted to have social and economic impacts, particularly for people in coastal communities. Some potential impacts are as follows.

- Food supplies: The oceans provide a diverse range of food sources for human consumption. Increased ocean acidity may affect stocks of fish, molluscs and crustaceans that are harvested and consumed by humans.
- Coastal protection: Coral reefs protect coasts from storms and erosion. The destruction of coral reefs could threaten coastal communities.
- Tourism: The colour and diversity of coral reefs make them popular tourist attractions. Their destruction would affect the economies of communities that rely on this tourism.

Calcification

Many aquatic organisms, including some corals and algae, as well as snails, shellfish, seastars, crabs and lobsters, have a protective covering made of calcium carbonate ($CaCO_3$).

These organisms absorb calcium ions and carbonate ions from seawater to build and maintain the calcium carbonate structure essential for their survival, as represented in the following reaction:

$$Ca^{2+}(aq) + CO_3^{2-}(aq) \rightleftharpoons CaCO_3(s)$$

This process is called calcification.

Calcium carbonate is virtually insoluble in water, and the oceans can be regarded as saturated solutions of calcium and carbonate ions. Once formed, calcium carbonate is usually quite stable. The health and growth of these animals depends critically on the concentration of carbonate ions and therefore carbon dioxide in the oceans.

The increased acidity of the oceans causes some of the additional hydronium ions to react with carbonate ions in the following reaction:

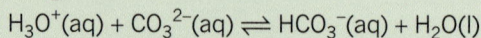

$$H_3O^+(aq) + CO_3^{2-}(aq) \rightleftharpoons HCO_3^-(aq) + H_2O(l)$$

This reaction has the effect of reducing the concentration of free CO_3^{2-} ions in seawater, making it more difficult for marine creatures to build or maintain their protective structures.

This process is called decalcification. It is estimated that the pH of the ocean will fall from 8.14 to 7.90 over the next 50 years, decreasing the rate and amount of calcification and putting coral reefs and other marine organisms at risk. Figure 8.6.14 shows the effect of decalcification on sea snails. The snail on the top has a healthy, glass-like shell with smooth edges.

The shell of the snail on the bottom has been affected by increased ocean acidity. Weak spots in the shell have an opaque, cloudy appearance and the shell edges are more ragged.

FIGURE 8.6.14 These tiny free-swimming sea snails are an important food source for other marine animals. The shell of the snail on the bottom is being dissolved by increasing ocean acidity

8.6 Review

SUMMARY

- Buffer solutions resist changes in pH when small amounts of acid or base are added.
- A buffer consists of a conjugate acid–base pair, with a weak base or weak acid.
- A weak acid and its conjugate base give an acidic buffer solution of pH less than 7.
- Acidic buffer solutions are usually made by mixing equal molar concentrations of a weak acid and one of its salts.
- A weak base and its conjugate acid give a basic buffer solution of pH greater than 7.
- Basic buffer solutions are usually made by mixing equal molar concentrations of a weak base and one of its salts.
- Le Châtelier's principle can be used to predict the change in the position of equilibrium of a buffer solution when an acid or a base is added.

- When an acid is added to a buffer solution, the conjugate base combines with any H_3O^+ that is added to maintain a stable pH.
- When a base is added to a buffer solution, the weak acid combines with any OH^- that is added to maintain a stable pH.
- Buffer capacity is a measure of the effectiveness of a buffer solution to resist a change in pH when either a strong acid or a strong base is added.
- Buffer capacity is greatest when:
  - there is a high concentration of the weak acid and its conjugate base
  - the concentrations of the acid and its conjugate base are equal.
- Buffers play an important part in maintaining pH in biological and environmental systems.

KEY QUESTIONS

1 Which one of the following substances could be used to maintain the pH range of water in an aquarium between 5.5 and 6.5?
   A a solution of a weak acid
   B a solution of a strong acid
   C a solution of a strong acid and its conjugate base
   D a solution of a weak acid and its conjugate base

2 Write the equilibrium equations for the following buffer systems:
   a ammonia / ammonium chloride buffer
   b hydrogen phosphate / phosphate buffer
   c hydrogen carbonate / carbonate buffer

3 Classify each of the three buffer solutions listed in Question **2** as either an acidic buffer or a basic buffer.

4 A small amount of sodium hydroxide solution is added to an ammonia / ammonium chloride buffer. Which one of the following statements is true?
   A The OH^- ions react with NH_4^+ ions and the pH decreases significantly.
   B The OH^- ions react with NH_3 molecules and the pH decreases significantly.
   C The OH^- ions react with NH_4^+ ions and the pH remains almost constant.
   D The OH^- ions react with NH_3 molecules and the pH remains almost constant.

5 The chemical equation that describes the CH_3COOH / CH_3COO^- buffer system is:
$CH_3COOH(aq) + H_2O(l) \rightleftharpoons CH_3COO^-(aq) + H_3O^+(aq)$
Describe how this buffer system reacts to the addition of a small amount of:
   a HCl
   b NaOH.

6 The compositions of four solutions, each containing 100 mL of a mixture of lactic acid (a weak acid) and sodium lactate (a weak base), are given below. Identify the solution with the greatest buffer capacity, and explain your choice.
   A $0.1 \, mol \, L^{-1}$ lactic acid and $0.1 \, mol \, L^{-1}$ sodium lactate
   B $0.1 \, mol \, L^{-1}$ lactic acid and $0.01 \, mol \, L^{-1}$ sodium lactate
   C $0.5 \, mol \, L^{-1}$ lactic acid and $0.5 \, mol \, L^{-1}$ sodium lactate
   D $0.05 \, mol \, L^{-1}$ lactic acid and $0.25 \, mol \, L^{-1}$ sodium lactate

7 The carbonic acid buffer involving the weak acid / weak conjugate base pair H_2CO_3 / HCO_3^- helps control the pH of blood.
   a Write the equation for the equilibrium that exists in the H_2CO_3 / HCO_3^- buffer.
   b Describe how the buffer works to stabilise the pH when acid is added.

8 Citric acid ($H_6C_8O_7$) is naturally found in some foods. Sodium citrate is added to these foods to control any change in acidity. Write the equation for the citric acid / sodium citrate buffer ($H_6C_8O_7 / H_5C_8O_7^-$).

Chapter review

08

08

KEY TERMS

accuracy
acid–base titration
acid dissociation constant
acidic buffer solution
aliquot
anhydrous
average titre
base dissociation constant
basic buffer solution
buffer capacity
buffer solution
burette
concentration
concordant titre

conductivity
conductivity curve
conductivity meter
conjugate acid
conjugate acid–base pair
conjugate base
dilution factor
end point
equimolar
equivalence point
hydrolysis
indicator
Le Châtelier's principle
mistake

nitrification
parallax error
percentage dissociation
pH curve
phosphate buffer
pipette
precision
primary standard
qualitative analysis
quantitative analysis
random error
standard solution
standardised
strong acid

strong base
systematic error
titrant
titration
titration curve
titre
uncertainty
volumetric analysis
volumetric flask
weak acid
weak base

REVIEW QUESTIONS

1   Sodium borate ($Na_2B_4O_7 \cdot 10H_2O$) is used as a primary standard in volumetric analysis. Some properties of $Na_2B_4O_7 \cdot 10H_2O$ are listed below. Which one of these properties is not important in its use as a primary standard?

   A It is highly soluble in water.
   B Its purity is greater than 99.5%.
   C It is a soft, white crystalline solid.
   D It has a molar mass of $381 \, g \, mol^{-1}$.

2   Calculate the concentration of a standard solution of hydrated oxalic acid ($H_2C_2O_4 \cdot 2H_2O$) prepared by dissolving 25.21 g of hydrated oxalic acid in 250.0 mL of deionised water.

3   Calculate the mass of Na_2CO_3 required to make a 500 mL standard solution of $0.100 \, mol \, L^{-1} \, Na_2CO_3$.

4   What volume of $0.200 \, mol \, L^{-1}$ KOH is required to react with 30.0 mL of $0.100 \, mol \, L^{-1} \, HNO_3$?

5   20.0 mL of a $1.00 \, mol \, L^{-1}$ solution of HCl reacts with 16.0 mL of a $1.00 \, mol \, L^{-1}$ of K_2CO_3 solution.

   a Calculate the amount, in mol, of HCl involved in the reaction.
   b Calculate the amount, in mol, of K_2CO_3 involved in the reaction.
   c Identify the reactant that is in excess.
   d By how much is this reactant in excess, in mol?

6   What volume of $0.100 \, mol \, L^{-1}$ of NaOH is required to react with 20.00 mL of $0.200 \, mol \, L^{-1}$ HCl?

7   15.0 mL of a $2.00 \, mol \, L^{-1}$ LiOH solution is added to 25.0 mL of a $0.400 \, mol \, L^{-1} \, HNO_3$ solution. The equation for the reaction that occurs is:
   $$HNO_3(aq) + LiOH(aq) \rightarrow LiNO_3(aq) + H_2O(l)$$
   a Which reactant is the limiting reactant?
   b What mass of $LiNO_3$ will the reaction mixture contain when the reaction is complete?

8   Explain the use of each of the following pieces of equipment during a titration:
   a burette
   b pipette
   c standard flask.

9   Why is it important to select an indicator with an end point close to the equivalence point for the reaction?

10   A standard solution of potassium carbonate is made by adding 1.227 g of K_2CO_3 to a 250.0 mL volumetric flask and filling to the mark with water. 20.00 mL aliquots are taken and titrated against a sulfuric acid solution, using methyl orange indicator. The average titre was 22.56 mL of sulfuric acid.
   a Write the equation for the reaction.
   b Calculate the concentration of the K_2CO_3 solution.
   c Calculate the concentration of the sulfuric acid solution.

11 A chemistry student is required to accurately determine the concentration of a solution of hydrochloric acid. First she makes up 250.0 mL of a standard solution of sodium carbonate. This solution contains 1.358 g of Na_2CO_3. She then takes a 20.00 mL aliquot of this standard solution and titrates it against the acid. An average titre of 20.24 mL of acid was required to reach the end point.

  a Write a balanced equation for the reaction involving the titration.

  b Calculate the concentration of the sodium carbonate solution.

  c Find the concentration of the acid as indicated by the student's results.

  d If sulfuric acid of the same concentration as the hydrochloric acid was used instead of the hydrochloric acid, what effect would this have had on the volume of acid required for the titration?

12 1.104 g of sodium carbonate (Na_2CO_3) is dissolved in water in a 250.0 mL volumetric flask. 20.00 mL aliquots of this solution were titrated with nitric acid. An average titre of 23.47 mL was found.

  a What is the concentration of the Na_2CO_3 solution?

  b What is the concentration of the nitric acid?

13 A $0.100\,mol\,L^{-1}$ solution of hypoiodous acid (HOI) has a pH of 5.80.

  a Write an equation for the dssociation of hypoiodous acid.

  b Write an expression for K_a for hypoiodous acid.

  c Calculate $[H_3O^+]$ in the solution.

  d Calculate K_a for hypoiodous acid.

14 A student investigating an equilibrium mixture produced by adding solid methanoic acid (HCOOH) to water finds that the pH of the solution is 2.40 and the concentration of HCOOH is $0.10\,mol\,L^{-1}$. Calculate the K_a of methanoic acid.

15 Benzoic acid is added in small amounts to some foods to act as a preservative. A $1.0\,mol\,L^{-1}$ solution of benzoic acid is 1.4% hydrolysed.

  a Calculate pK_a for benzoic acid.

  b What percentage of benzoic acid molecules will be hydrolysed in a $0.10\,mol\,L^{-1}$ solution?

16 A buffer consists of a weak conjugate acid–base pair. Complete the paragraph by filling in the blanks, using the words listed:

acid, base, less than, greater than

An acidic buffer is made from a weak _____ and its conjugate _____, producing a solution of pH _____ 7.

A basic buffer is made from a weak _____ and its conjugate _____, producing a solution of pH _____ 7.

17 The equilibrium concentrations in a solution of nitrous acid (HNO_2) are provided in the following table. Calculate the pK_a of nitrous acid.

Species	Equilibrium concentration ($mol\,L^{-1}$)
NO_2^-	8.4×10^{-3}
H_3O^+	8.4×10^{-3}
HNO_2	9.8×10^{-2}

18 The pK_a of hydrocyanic acid (HCN) is 9.21. Calculate the concentration of HCN, CN^- and H_3O^+ in a $0.10\,mol\,L^{-1}$ solution of hydrocyanic acid.

19 The acid dissociation constant of hydrobromic acid (HBr) is 1.0×10^9 and that of hypobromous acid (HOBr) is 2.4×10^{-9}.

Is it correct to assume that the pH of $0.10\,mol\,L^{-1}$ solutions of HBr and HOBr are the same? Justify your answer. Include appropriate calculations in your justification.

20 a Complete the following table by inserting the missing K_b and pK_b values.

Base	Formula	K_b	pK_b
butanoate	$CH_3(CH_2)_2COO^-$		9.18
fluoride	F^-	1.5×10^{-11}	
chlorate	ClO_3^-		6.47

  b Which of the bases is strongest? Explain your answer.

21 Separate solutions of perchloric acid ($HClO_4$) and hypochlorous acid (HClO) are provided. The volume and concentration of both solutions are the same. The acids dissociate in water according to the following equations. The acid dissociation constants are also provided.

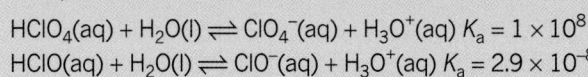

$HClO_4(aq) + H_2O(l) \rightleftharpoons ClO_4^-(aq) + H_3O^+(aq)$ $K_a = 1 \times 10^8$
$HClO(aq) + H_2O(l) \rightleftharpoons ClO^-(aq) + H_3O^+(aq)$ $K_a = 2.9 \times 10^{-8}$

Separate titration graphs are produced when both acids are titrated with $0.10\,L^{-1}$ sodium hydroxide solution.

  a Would you expect the volume of sodium hydroxide required to reach the equivalence point of perchloric acid to be greater than the volume required to reach the equivalence point of hypochlorous acid? Justify your answer.

  b Would you expect the pH at the equivalence point shown on the titration graphs to be the same for both acids? Justify your answer.

22 Which of the two pairs of substances could be used to make a buffer system? Explain your answer.

  A NaOH and H_2O

  B $NaCH_3COO$ and CH_3COOH

23 The phosphate buffer system is described by the chemical equation:

$$H_2PO_4^-(aq) + H_2O(l) \rightleftharpoons H_3O^+(aq) + HPO_4^{2-}(aq)$$

To predict the effect of adding H_3O^+ to the $H_2PO_4^-$/HPO_4^{2-} buffer system, complete the paragraph by filling in the blanks, using the words and species listed:

right, left, small, large, H_3O^+, $H_2PO_4^-$, HPO_4^{2-}, OH^-, H_2O

The addition of a small amount of HCl to the phosphate buffer system will disturb the equilibrium. As equilibrium is re-established, the added H_3O^+ reacts with _____. The position of the equilibrium in the equation given above shifts to the _____. Since the buffer contains a relatively large amount of HPO_4^{2-}, most of the added _____ is consumed and there is a _____ change in the concentration of H_3O^+.

When a small amount of base is added to the buffer system the OH^- reacts with _____. The excess OH^- is consumed without any large change in the concentration of _____.

24 Blood is buffered by the carbonic acid buffer, H_2CO_3/HCO_3^-. Write the equation for the buffer equilibrium. If the pH of blood increases, what happens to the concentrations of H_2CO_3, HCO_3^- and H^+?

25 The concentration of carbonic acid (H_2CO_3) in blood is 5% of the concentration of the hydrogen carbonate ion (HCO_3^-), yet the carbonic acid/hydrogen carbonate buffer can buffer the pH of blood against bases as well as acids. Explain why this is so.

26 The titration curve in in the graph below shows the change in pH as a solution of $0.10\,mol\,L^{-1}$ sodium hydroxide is added to a 20.00 mL solution of $0.10\,mol\,L^{-1}$ hydrochloric acid.

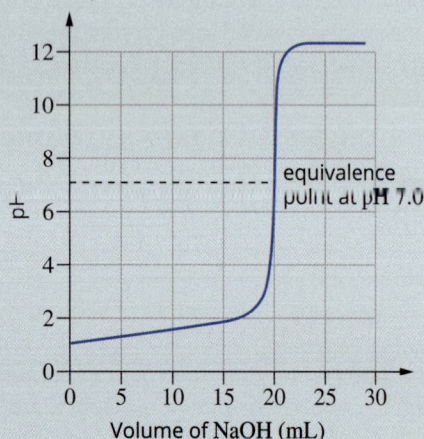

The titration is repeated using $0.20\,mol\,L^{-1}$ sodium hydroxide solution. Which one of the following statements about the second titration is correct?

A The equivalence point occurs when 10 mL of NaOH is added and the pH is then 7.

B The equivalence point occurs when 10 mL of NaOH is added and the pH is then greater than 7.

C The equivalence point occurs when 40 mL of NaOH is added and the pH is then 7.

D The equivalence point occurs when 40 mL of NaOH is added and the pH is then greater than 7.

27 The results for a conductivity titration are provided in the table below. In this titration the conductivity of the reaction mixture is measured when a $0.50\,mol\,L^{-1}$ sodium hydroxide solution is progressively added to 10.0 mL of a hydrochloric acid solution of unknown concentration.

Volume NaOH (mL)	Conductivity ($mS\,m^2\,mol^{-1}$)	Volume NaOH (mL)	Conductivity ($mS\,m^2\,mol^{-1}$)
0	30.0	10	11.67
1	27.5	11	12.50
2	25.0	12	13.33
3	22.5	13	14.17
4	20.0	14	15.00
5	17.5	15	15.83
6	15.0	16	16.67
7	12.5	17	17.50
8	10.0	18	18.33
9	10.8	19	19.17
		20	20.00

a Use the data provided to draw a conductivity graph.

b Calculate the concentration of the hydrochloric acid solution.

c Identify the factors that determine conductivity.

28 The change in conductivity when a $0.15\,mol\,L^{-1}$ solution of sodium hydroxide was added to 10.0 mL of a solution of methanoic acid (HCOOH) is provided below. The pK_a of methanoic acid is 3.74.

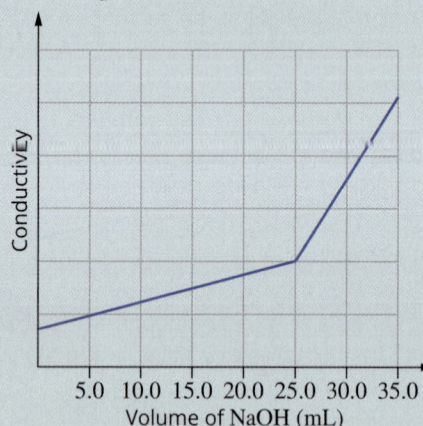

a Calculate the concentration of the methanoic acid solution.

b Prove an explanation for the shape of this graph.

29 The pH was measured when a 0.25 mol L^{-1} solution of sodium hydroxide was slowly added to 20.0 mL of nitrous acid (HNO$_2$) solution of unknown concentration.

Volume NaOH (mL)	pH	Volume NaOH (mL)	pH
0	6.1	10	7.9
1	6.4	11	8.0
2	6.7	12	8.2
3	7.0	13	8.4
4	7.1	14	8.7
5	7.3	15	10.3
6	7.4	16	11.8
7	7.5	17	12.1
8	7.6	18	12.2
9	7.7	19	12.4
		20	12.4

a Use the data provided to construct a titration curve.
b Calculate the concentration of the nitrous acid.

30 Identify what combination of strong and weak acids and bases is represented in each of the following titration curves.

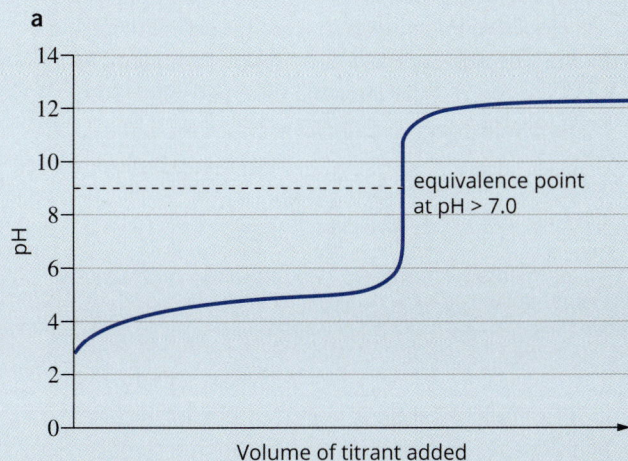

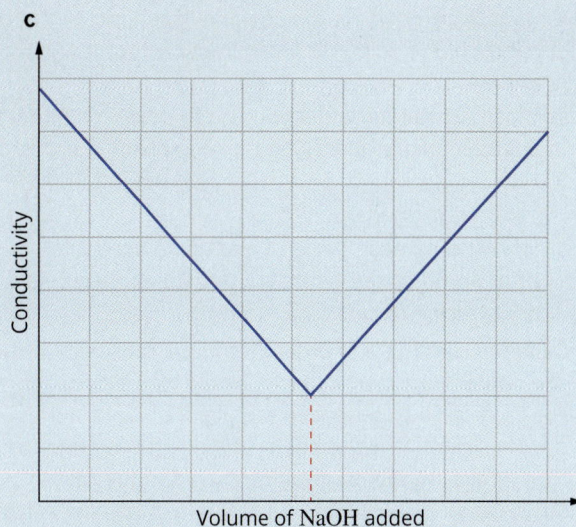

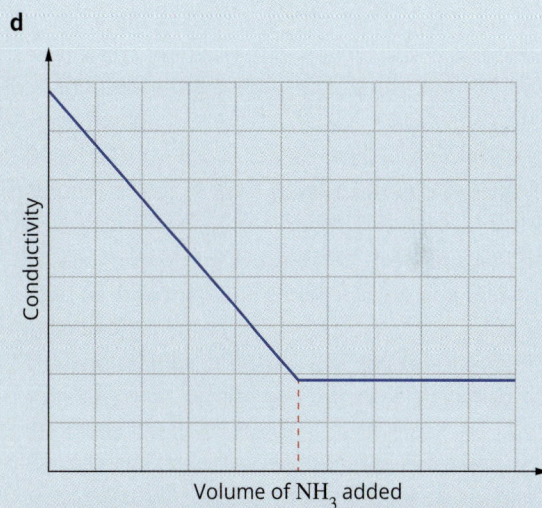

a

b

c

d

31 The concentration of ethanoic acid (CH$_3$COOH) in vinegar was determined by titrating vinegar against a 20.0 mL aliquot of 0.10 mol L^{-1} sodium hydroxide. The pH was measured throughout the titration. The titration curve is shown below.

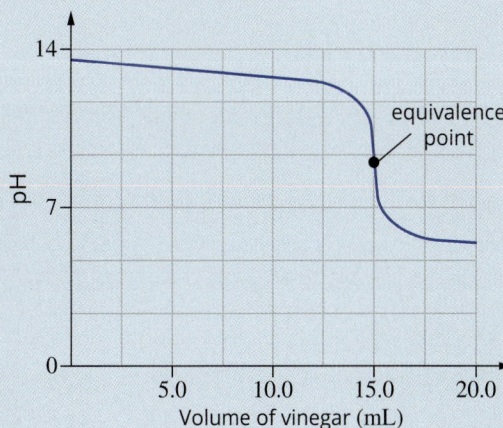

The equation for the reaction is:
CH$_3$COOH(aq) + NaOH(aq) → NaCH$_3$COO(aq) + H$_2$O(l)
Calculate the concentration of ethanoic acid in the vinegar.

32 A manufacturer wants to know the exact concentration of hydrochloric acid in the concrete cleaner it produces.

   a What substance would you use to make a standard solution for use in this titration? Explain your choice.

   b How would you prepare this standard solution for volumetric analysis?

   c How should each piece of glassware used in a titration be rinsed to ensure you obtain accurate and precise results?

33 Distance running and other strenuous muscle activity can cause a build-up of lactic acid in the blood. You may have experienced the effect of lactic acid accumulation as a wobbly feeling in your leg muscles. How would the build-up of lactic acid in the blood affect blood pH? Using Le Châtelier's principle explain how the blood buffer works to regulate this pH change.

34 Cardiac arrest occurs when the heart fails to effectively pump and circulate blood around the body. Cell reactions still continue.

   a Explain the effect of cardiac arrest on blood pH.

   b Doctors often injected sodium hydrogen carbonate solution ($NaHCO_3$) into the heart muscle. Explain how this injection counteracts the effect on blood pH from part a.

35 Citric acid ($H_6C_8O_7$) is a food additive that acts as a buffer and helps to preserve food.

   a Identify the conjugate base of citric acid.

   b Write an equilibrium equation for the citric acid buffer.

   c Citric acid is an acidic buffer. Explain this statement.

   d Describe how this buffer behaves to stabilise pH when an acid or a base is added.

36 Reflect on the Inquiry task on page 186. What type of analysis did you attempt? How could you improve your procedure to obtain a more accurate result?

REVIEW QUESTIONS

Acid/base reactions

MR 6

Multiple choice

1 Which one of the following solutions would have the highest pH?

A $1.0\,mol\,L^{-1}$ ethanoic acid

B $1.0\,mol\,L^{-1}$ hydrochloric acid

C $1.0\,mol\,L^{-1}$ sodium hydroxide

D $1.0\,mol\,L^{-1}$ ammonium chloride

2 Which one of the following represents a concentrated solution of a weak acid?

A $6.0\,mol\,L^{-1}$ CH_3COOH

B $0.01\,mol\,L^{-1}$ CH_3COOH

C $6.0\,mol\,L^{-1}$ HCl

D $0.01\,mol\,L^{-1}$ HCl

3 Which one of the following is the conjugate base of OH^-?

A H_2O

B O^{2-}

C H_3O^+

D NaOH

4 Which one of the following can act as either a Brønsted–Lowry acid or base in aqueous solutions?

A HS^-

B NH_4^+

C CO_3^{2-}

D CH_4

5 Which of the following acids can be classified as polyprotic in water?

CH_3COOH, H_2SO_3, NH_4^+

A CH_3COOH only

B H_2SO_3 only

C CH_3COOH and H_2SO_3 only

D all three acids

6 Consider the following statements, which compare $20.00\,mL$ of a $0.10\,mol\,L^{-1}$ solution of nitric acid with $20.00\,mL$ of a $0.10\,mol\,L^{-1}$ solution of ethanoic acid.

I Both solutions have the same strength.

II The pH of the nitric acid solution is higher.

III The electrical conductivity of the nitric acid solution is higher.

IV Both solutions require the same volume of $0.10\,mol\,L^{-1}$ NaOH for neutralisation.

Which two of the above statements are correct?

A I and II

B I and III

C II and IV

D III and IV

7 Beakers X and Y both contain nitric acid. The pH of the acid in beaker X is 3 whereas the pH of the acid in beaker Y is 1. From this information, what can be deduced about the concentration of hydrogen ions in beaker X?

A It is three times that in beaker Y.

B It is one-third of that in beaker Y.

C It is one hundred times that in beaker Y.

D It is one-hundredth of that in beaker Y.

8 A solution of NaOH has a pH of 13 at 25°C. What mass of sodium hydroxide is present in $500\,mL$ of this solution?

A $2.0 \times 10^{-12}\,g$

B $0.050\,g$

C $2.0\,g$

D $4.0\,g$

9 Since the mid 1700s the pH of the world's oceans has changed from 8.2 to 8.1. Which of the following substances is the main cause for this change?

A CO_2

B SO_2

C H_2SO_4

D $CaCO_3$

10 Which of the following represents a conjugate acid–base pair?

A NH_3/NH^{2-}

B NH_3/NH_2^-

C NH_4/NH_3^+

D NH_4^+/NH_3

11 The salt lithium sulfate could be formed from the neutralisation reaction between which two compounds?

A sodium sulfate and lithium sulfate

B sulfuric acid and lithium hydroxide

C lithium hydroxide and nitric acid

D sodium carbonate and lithium hydroxide

12 Which of the following is an example of a dilute solution of a strong acid?

A $2.0\,mol\,L^{-1}$ H_2SO_4

B $2.0\,mol\,L^{-1}$ CH_3COOH

C $0.001\,mol\,L^{-1}$ H_2SO_4

D $0.001\,mol\,L^{-1}$ CH_3COOH

13 Select the alternative that correctly describes a basic solution.

A $[H_3O^+] < 10^{-7}$ mol L^{-1}, pH > 7, pOH < 7
B $[H_3O^+] < 10^{-7}$ mol L^{-1}, pH < 7, pOH > 7
C $[H_3O^+] > 10^{-7}$ mol L^{-1}, pH > 7, pOH < 7
D $[H_3O^+] > 10^{-7}$ mol L^{-1}, pH < 7, pOH < 7

14 50 mL of 0.020 mol L^{-1} NaOH solution at 25°C is made up to 100 mL with de-ionised water. What is the pOH value of the diluted solution?

A 1.40
B 2.00
C 12.00
D 12.60

15 The following table shows the labels on four different solutions.

Solution	W	X	Y	Z
Label	pH = 4	pOH = 6	$[OH^-] = 10^{-2}$	$[H_3O^+] = 10^{-2}$

Arrange the solutions in order of least acidic to most acidic.

A Y W X Z
B Y Z W X
C Y X W Z
D Z W X Y

16 The expression for the acidity constant of a particular weak acid is

$$K_a = \frac{[H_3O^+][HCOO^-]}{[HCOOH]}$$

This expression is the acidity constant for which one of the following reactions?

A $H_3O^+(aq) + HCOO^-(aq) \rightleftharpoons HCOOH(aq) + H_2O(l)$
B $HCOOH(aq) \rightleftharpoons H_3O^+(aq) + HCOO^-(aq)$
C $HCOOH(aq) + H_2O(l) \rightarrow H_3O^+(aq) + HCOO^-(aq)$
D $HCOOH(aq) + H_2O(l) \rightleftharpoons H_3O^+(aq) + HCOO^-(aq)$

17 The equilibrium present in the ethanoic acid/ethanoate buffer is

$$CH_3COOH(aq) + H_2O(l) \rightleftharpoons CH_3COO^-(aq) + H_3O^+(aq)$$

When a small amount of NaOH is added to this system, which of the following will occur?

A The OH$^-$ ions will react with the CH_3COOH, producing more CH_3COO^- ions.
B The OH$^-$ ions will react with the water to form more H_3O^+ ions.
C The OH$^-$ ions will react with the CH_3COO^- ions to make CH_3COOH.
D The Na$^+$ ions will react with the CH_3COOH to form NaOH.

The following information relates to Questions 18 and 19.
The following acid–base titration curve shows the way pH changes when a base is added from a burette to a measured volume of acid. The concentration of both acid and base is 0.1 mol L^{-1}.

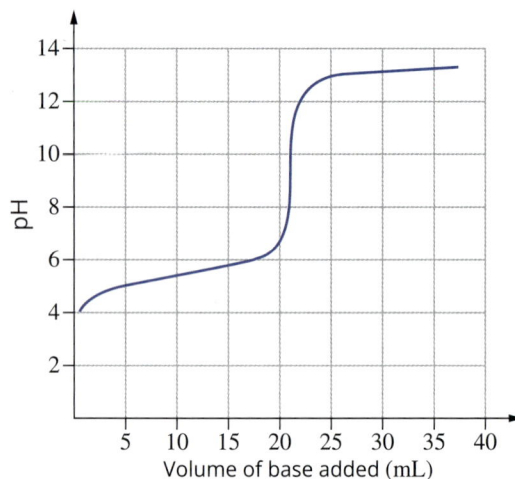

18 From the shape of the curve, what can be deduced about the relative strength of the acid and the base?

A The acid is weak and the base is strong.
B The acid is strong and the base is strong.
C The acid is weak and the base is weak.
D The acid is strong and the base is weak.

19 Which one or more of the following indicators could be used for this titration?

Indicator	pH range over which colour changes
methyl orange	3.1–4.4
methyl red	4.4–6.2
bromothymol blue	6.0–7.6
phenolphthalein	8.3–10.0

A methyl orange only
B bromothymol blue only
C phenolphthalein only
D methyl orange and methyl red only

20 A standard solution of HCl is titrated four times against some NaOH. The following titres are obtained: 21.05 mL, 20.75 mL, 20.65 mL, 20.75 mL.

The average titre is then calculated and used to determine the concentration of the NaOH. The correct value for the average titre is:

A 20.65 mL
B 20.72 mL
C 20.75 mL
D 20.80 mL

21 The self-ionisation of water is affected by temperature, as shown below.

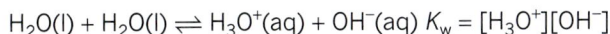

$$H_2O(l) + H_2O(l) \rightleftharpoons H_3O^+(aq) + OH^-(aq) \quad K_w = [H_3O^+][OH^-]$$

Temperature (°C)	Ionisation constant for water, K_w
5	1.9×10^{-15}
15	4.5×10^{-15}
25	1.0×10^{-14}
35	2.1×10^{-14}

What can be inferred from this data?

A The pH of pure water at 35°C is greater than 7.

B Self-ionisation of water is an exothermic reaction.

C Equilibrium for the reaction lies well to the left with mainly reactants present.

D In pure water at 15°C, $[OH^-]$ is lower than $[H_3O^+]$.

Short answer

1 5.00 g of NaOH is dissolved in 400 mL of water at 25°C. For the solution formed, determine the value of

a the NaOH concentration.

b $[OH^-]$

c $[H_3O^+]$

d pH

e pOH.

2 Write fully balanced chemical equations to represent each of the following reactions.

a Hydrochloric acid reacts with zinc powder.

b Dilute nitric acid reacts with a solution of calcium hydroxide.

c Dilute sulfuric acid reacts with a sodium carbonate solution.

d A piece of solid magnesium reacts with nitric acid.

3 a Define the term 'strong acid'.

b Give the formula of a substance that is polyprotic.

c HCO_3^- is an amphiprotic ion. Write chemical equations to show it acting in water as:

i a base

ii an acid.

d Give the formula of the conjugate acid of H_2O.

4 a Calculate the pH of each of the following at 25°C:

i 100 mL solution of 0.050 mol L^{-1} Ca(OH)$_2$

ii 400 mL solution of 0.125 mol L^{-1} nitric acid that has been diluted by the addition of 100 mL of water

iii 65.0 mL solution of hydrochloric acid that was prepared by dissolving 2.45 g of hydrogen chloride in water.

b Calculate the mass of HNO_3 present in 300 mL of nitric acid with a pH of 0.050.

5 An experiment was conducted to compare the conductivity of three solutions, A, B and C. Each solution had the same concentration. The results are shown in the table below.

	pH	Litmus paper test	Conductivity (relative units)
A	?	Turns blue litmus paper red	3
B	1.5	Turns blue litmus paper red	6
C	10.5	Turns red litmus paper blue	3

a Which solution (A, B or C) is most likely to be an aqueous sodium hydroxide solution? Give a reason for your choice.

b Which solution (A, B or C) contains the strongest acid? Explain your answer.

c Estimate the pH of solution A. Give a reason for your answer.

d Determine the hydrogen ion concentration in:

i solution B

ii solution C.

6 The pH of three different acids is given below.

Acid	Concentration in mol L^{-1}	pH
nitric acid (HNO$_3$)	0.010	2.0
propanoic acid (C$_2$H$_5$COOH)	0.010	3.4
sulfuric acid (H$_2$SO$_4$)	0.010	1.7

The three acids have the same concentration.

a Explain why propanoic acid has the highest pH of the three.

b Explain why sulfuric acid has the lowest pH of the three.

7 a A solution has a pH of 4. What is the concentration, in mol L^{-1}, of hydroxide ions in the solution at 25°C?

b 100 mL of hydrochloric acid of concentration 0.0100 mol L^{-1} is added to 100 mL of sodium hydroxide of concentration 0.0120 mol L^{-1}. Both solutions are at 25°C. Calculate the pH of the resultant solution.

8 Many household cleaners contain ammonia (NH$_3$) as the active ingredient. An acid–base titration was performed in order to determine the concentration of ammonia in a commercially available cleaner.

10.00 mL of the cleaner is diluted to 100.0 mL with water in a volumetric flask. 20.00 mL of this diluted cleaner solution is placed in a dry conical flask and titrated against 0.0950 mol L^{-1} hydrochloric acid using methyl orange as an indicator. The average of three concordant titres was 17.40 mL.

a Write an equation for the reaction between ammonia and hydrochloric acid.

b Calculate the molar concentration of ammonia in the cleaner.

c Calculate the mass, in grams, of ammonia in a 750 mL bottle of cleaner.

d Methyl orange is pink at pH lower than 3.1 and yellow at pH greater than 4.4. State the colour changes that would be observed in this titration.

e State whether each of the following changes to this titration procedure would lead to a higher, lower, or the same result for the concentration of ammonia in the cleaner. Give an explanation for your answer.

  i 20.00 mL of water was added to the 20.00 mL of diluted cleaner solution in the conical flask prior to titration.

  ii Phenolphthalein indicator was used instead of methyl orange. Phenolphthalein is colourless at pH less than 8.3 and pink at pH higher than 9.5.

  iii The conical flask was washed, then rinsed with the diluted cleaner solution before using it.

9 Succinic acid is one of the many acids present in wine. It is diprotic and has a molar mass of $118.1 \, \text{g mol}^{-1}$.

In order to find the solubility of succinic acid in water, 10 g of succinic acid was thoroughly mixed with 100 mL of water in a beaker. The beaker was allowed to stand overnight at a constant temperature of 25°C in order to saturate the solution.

The next day, it was noted that there was some undissolved succinic acid in the bottom of the beaker. 20.00 mL samples of the succinic acid solution were titrated against $0.790 \, \text{mol L}^{-1}$ NaOH using phenolphthalein indicator. The average of three concordant titres was 23.40 mL.

a Calculate the amount, in mol, of succinic acid in 20.00 mL of solution.

b Calculate the concentration of succinic acid solution in:

  i mol L^{-1}

  ii g L^{-1}

  iii %(w/v).

c The solubility of succinic acid at 25°C quoted in the literature is higher than that obtained in this experiment. Give a possible explanation for this difference.

10 Sulfuric acid is a strong diprotic acid.

  a **i** Write balanced equations to show the two stages in the dissociation of sulfuric acid in water.

  ii Select an example of an amphiprotic species from the two equations.

  iii Select an example of an acid–base conjugate pair from the above equations.

  iv List, in increasing order of concentration, the following species as they will exist in a $1.0 \, \text{mol L}^{-1}$ sulfuric acid solution:

    H_2SO_4 HSO_4^- SO_4^{2-}

b Sulfuric acid will react with zinc metal.

  i Write a balanced equation for the reaction.

  ii Write an ionic equation for the reaction.

  iii How does the pH of the solution change as the reaction proceeds?

c Sulfuric acid can react with solid K_2CO_3.

  i Write a balanced equation for the reaction.

  ii Write an ionic equation for the reaction.

  iii What would you observe as the reaction proceeds?

d Sulfuric acid (H_2SO_4) can be neutralised by a solution of lithium hydroxide (LiOH).

  i Write a balanced equation for the reaction.

  ii What amount of sulfuric acid, in mol, is required to neutralise 0.468 mol of LiOH?

11 50.0. mL of hydrochloric acid solution was added to neutralise 25.0 mL of $1.50 \, \text{mol L}^{-1}$ $Ba(OH)_2$ solution. During the reaction the temperature of the solution increased from 18.8°C to 31.6°C. Determine the enthalpy of neutralisation.

12 A buffer solution is created when a solution contains a significant concentration of both a weak acid and its conjugate base.

  a An example is the ammonium/ammonia buffer represented by the following equation:

$$NH_4^+(aq) + H_2O(l) \rightleftharpoons NH_3(aq) + H_3O^+(aq)$$

  i Identify the acid in the buffer system.

  ii Identify the base in this buffer system.

  iii Identify a substance that could be added to water to provide the acid for this buffer system.

b Describe how this buffer system reacts to the addition of a small amount of:

  i HCl

  ii NaOH.

c This buffer system can be prepared by reacting ammonia solution with hydrochloric acid. Write an equation for this reaction.

d Determine whether a buffer solution has been created in each of the following circumstances:

  i 50 mL of $1.0 \, \text{mol L}^{-1}$ ammonia solution is mixed with 50 mL of $1.0 \, \text{mol L}^{-1}$ hydrochloric acid.

  ii 100 mL of $1.0 \, \text{mol L}^{-1}$ ammonia solution is mixed with 50 mL of $1.0 \, \text{mol L}^{-1}$ hydrochloric acid.

  iii 50 mL of $1.0 \, \text{mol L}^{-1}$ ammonia solution is mixed with 100 mL of $1.0 \, \text{mol L}^{-1}$ hydrochloric acid.

13 A conductivity graph is shown below for the addition of $0.20\,mol\,L^{-1}$ KOH to a 20.0 mL solution of HCl.

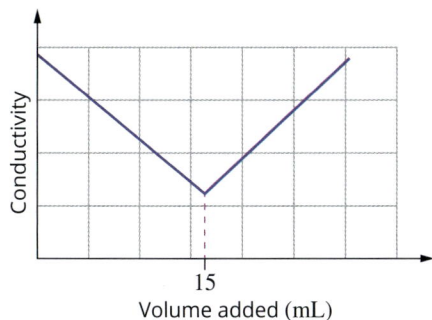

Volume added (mL)

a i Write a balanced equation for the reaction.
  ii Explain why the conductivity drops with the first additions of KOH.
  iii Explain why the conductivity increases with additions past the equivalence point.
  iv Use the information provided to determine the molar concentration of the HCl solution.
b A 25.0 mL sample of the same HCl solution used in part **a** is titrated against $0.20\,mol\,L^{-1}$ Na_2CO_3 solution. What value would you expect the titre to be?

14 Bromothymol blue is an acid–base indicator that changes from a yellow colour in an acid solution to blue in basic solutions. It is a weak acid with a K_a value of 10^{-7}.

Because it is a weak acid it will donate a proton when mixed with water. The formula of bromothymol blue is a complex one, so it is often given the symbol HIn, where In stands for indicator and the H is the proton that will be lost when it acts as weak acid.

a Complete the equation for the reaction of the weak acid bromothymol blue and water:
$HIn(aq) + H_2O(l) \rightleftharpoons$
b Two drops of bromothymol blue are added to a flask containing a dilute solution of NaOH.
  i What colour will the indicator be in this solution?
  ii Strong HCl is now added to the flask. Refer to the equation in part **a** to explain why the colour changes.
  iii Further NaOH is now added to the flask until the colour change is reversed. Explain why the second colour change occurs.
c i Use the equation in part **a** to write an expression for K_a for this reaction.
  ii At the end point the concentrations of the weak acid and its conjugate are about equal. Simplify your expression for K_a to determine the pH at which the colour change occurs.

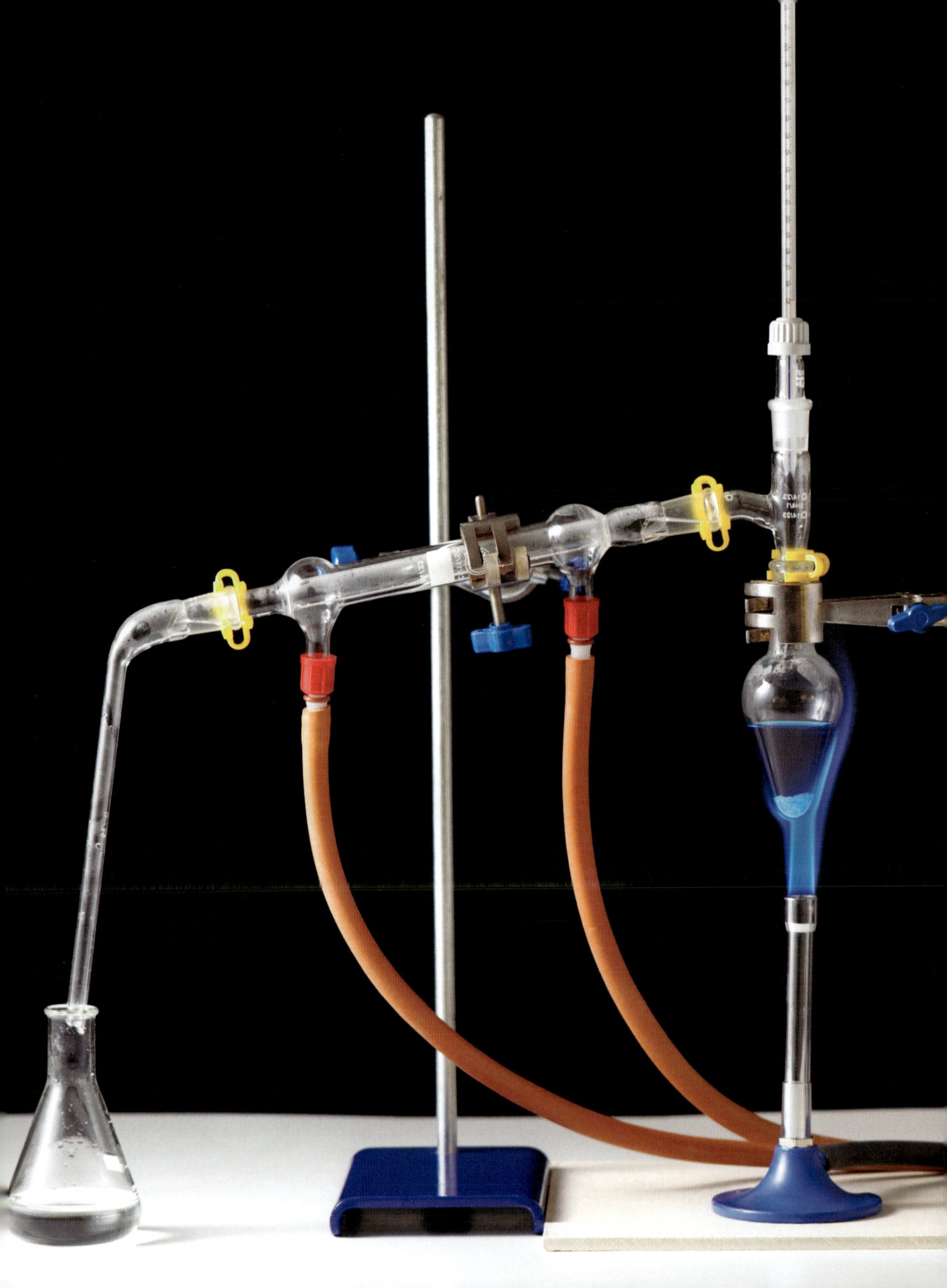

Organic chemistry

In this module you will focus on the principles and applications of chemical synthesis in the field of organic chemistry. Current and future applications of chemistry include techniques to synthesise new substances, including pharmaceuticals, fuels and polymers, to meet the needs of society.

Each class of organic compounds displays characteristic chemical properties and undergoes specific reactions based on the functional groups present. These reactions, including acid/base and oxidation reactions, are used to identify the class of an organic compound. You will investigate the many classes of organic compounds and their characteristic chemical reactions. By considering the primary, secondary and tertiary structures of organic materials, you will gain an understanding of the properties of materials, such as strength, density and biodegradability, and relate these to synthetic polymers.

Outcomes

By the end of this module, you will be able to:

- analyse and evaluate primary and secondary data and information (CH12-5)
- solve scientific problems using primary and secondary data, critical thinking skills and scientific processes (CH12-6)
- communicate scientific understanding using suitable language and terminology for a specific audience or purpose (CH12-7)
- analyse the structure of, and predict reactions involving, carbon compounds (CH12-14)

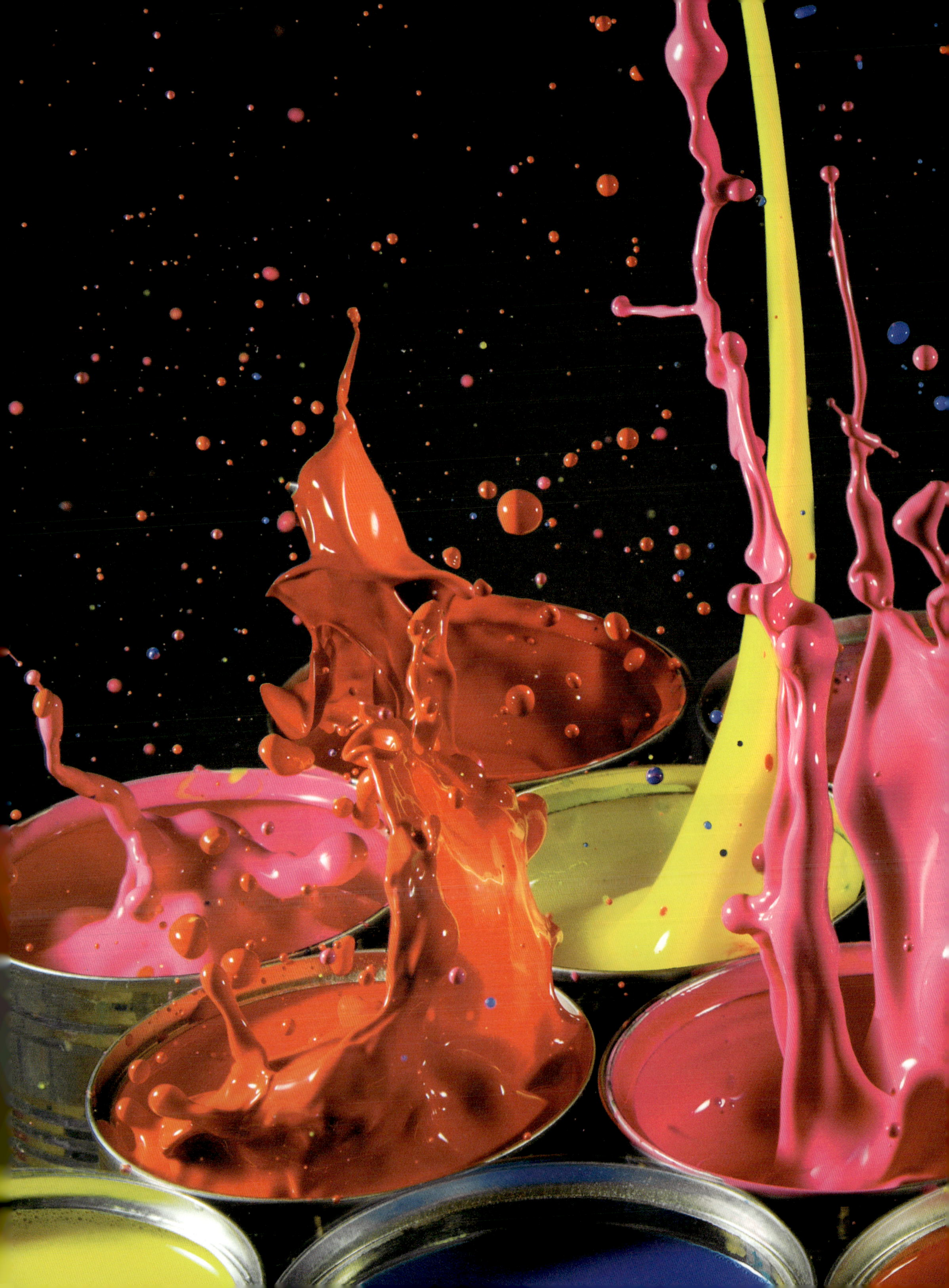

Structure and nomenclature of organic compounds

Scientists have recorded many millions of organic compounds, and more of these compounds are being discovered or synthesised all the time. Organic compounds exhibit an enormous range of properties, which allows chemists to develop materials for applications as diverse as fuels, fibres, plastics, detergents, dyes, paints, medicines, perfumes and insecticides. Organic compounds also form the basis of every cell in all living organisms.

This chapter looks at the groups, structures and names of a range of different organic compounds. It also looks at the element carbon and why such a vast range of organic compounds is possible.

Content

INQUIRY QUESTION

How do we systematically name organic chemical compounds?

By the end of this chapter, you will be able to:

- investigate the nomenclature of organic chemicals, up to C8, using IUPAC conventions, including simple methyl and ethyl branched chains, including: (ACSCH127) **ICT**
  - alkanes
  - alkenes
  - alkynes
  - alcohols (primary, secondary and tertiary)
  - aldehydes and ketones
  - carboxylic acids
  - amines and amides
  - halogenated organic compounds
- explore and distinguish the different types of structural isomers, including saturated and unsaturated hydrocarbons, including: (ACSCH035) **ICT**
  - chain isomers
  - position isomers
  - functional group isomers
- construct models, identify the functional group, and write structural and molecular formulae for homologous series of organic chemical compounds, up to C8 (ACSCH035) **ICT**
  - alkanes
  - alkenes
  - alkynes
- analyse the shape of molecules formed between carbon atoms when a single, double or triple bond is formed between them

Chemistry Stage 6 Syllabus © NSW Education Standards Authority for and on behalf of the Crown in right of the State of NSW, 2017.

9.1 Diversity of carbon compounds

WS 7.1

Carbon is an extremely versatile element. Because of the unique properties of the carbon atom, several million carbon compounds are known. The study of the chemistry of life on Earth is the study of carbon compounds. It was once thought that **organic molecules** (molecules containing carbon) could only be created by living organisms. However, in the 19th century chemists learned to synthesise these molecules in the laboratory. The pharmaceutical industry, textile industry and plastics industry produce a myriad of carbon-based compounds, many originating from petrochemicals. Figure 9.1.1 demonstrates some of the diversity of carbon compounds.

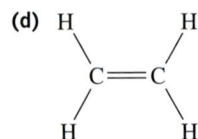

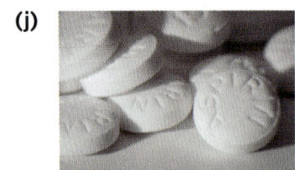

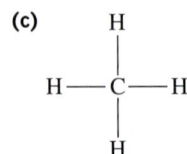

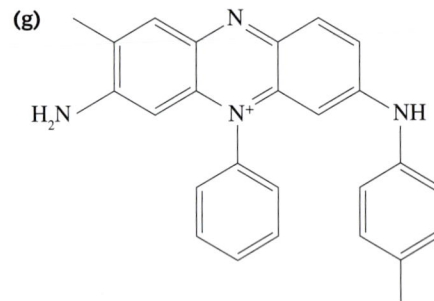

FIGURE 9.1.1 (a) Different types of organic molecules form the basis of all living systems, including the child, tomatoes, timber and plants in this photograph. (b) Methane is the gas used in most laboratory Bunsen burners and household gas stoves. (c) The structure of methane (CH_4). It is an organic molecule that contains one carbon atom with four single covalent bonds to four hydrogen atoms. (d) Carbon can form compounds that contain carbon–carbon double bonds. These compounds include ethene (C_2H_4). (e) Among other uses, ethene is used to make the polymers in these food storage containers. (f) Created by William Perkin in 1856 from coal tar, mauveine was the first synthetic dye. (g) Mauveine, also called aniline purple, is still used to dye textiles. (h) Carbon can form hydrocarbons that contain carbon–carbon triple bonds, such as ethyne (C_2H_2). (i) Ethyne (commonly called acetylene) is commonly used as the fuel in welding torches. (j) Aspirin (2-acetyloxybenzoic acid) was first synthesised in 1853.

CHEMISTRY INQUIRY

ICT CCT

Naming organic compounds systematically

COLLECT THIS ...

- a molecular modelling application

DO THIS ...

1 Open the molecular modelling application.
2 Create as many chain isomers of C_6H_{14} as possible.
3 Explore the 3D image by rotating it in space.
4 Choose different representations of the 3D models, including a space-filling model, and observe the differences.

RECORD THIS ...

1 Draw up the table below with as many rows as necessary, and present your results.

Name of C_6H_{14} chain isomer	Structural formula	3D image

Describe your understanding of chain isomerism.

REFLECT ON THIS ...

Describe one advantage and one disadvantage of the space-filling model.

Bush medicine and bush food

The Yaegl Aboriginal people from the north-east coastal region of New South Wales have long used local plants in their medicines. For example a paste made from the gum, stem and leaves of the local red ash or soap tree (*Alphitonia excelsa*) is known to cure infected skin sores (Figure 9.1.2).

Macquarie University scientists are working with the Yaegl community in the Clarence River valley in northern NSW. The scientists analysed the native red ash in their Sydney laboratories and found it contained high concentrations of anti-infection and anti-microbial organic compounds. They are now interested in analysing other traditional bush medicines to identify their properties and test how they can be administered safely and effectively.

Ferlin Laurie, a Yaegl elder, is eager to share his ancestral knowledge of the resources of the bush, including edible white apples and the berries of the pink-flowering coastal pigface plant. A high school program has been established, complete with a native bush food and medicine garden,

and a Yaegl bush medicine handbook has been produced. The Yaegl community is now looking to create a range of natural medicinal health and beauty products.

FIGURE 9.1.2 The medicinal properties of the red ash or soap tree have been studied by Macquarie University researchers.

BONDING IN CARBON COMPOUNDS

Carbon atoms contain six electrons—two electrons in the first shell and four in the second. The **electronic configuration** of a carbon atom can be written as 2,4 or $1s^22s^22p^2$. This configuration gives carbon some unique features.

- Each carbon atom has four valence electrons, which gives it a **valence number** of four. The valence number of an element is equal to the number of valence electrons in an atom of the element. All four of carbon's valence electrons are available for bonding with other atoms.
- A carbon atom can form four covalent bonds with up to four other carbon atoms, each of which in turn can bond with up to four other carbon atoms, potentially forming long, branched chains and even rings.
- A carbon atom can form four covalent bonds with up to four other non-metal atoms.
- Single, double or triple bonds can be formed between two carbon atoms. A molecule that contains only single carbon–carbon bonds is an **alkane**. It is classified as a **saturated** molecule. A molecule that contains one or more carbon-carbon double bonds is an **alkene**. A molecule that contains one or more carbon-carbon triple bonds is an **alkyne**. Alkenes and alkynes are classified as **unsaturated** molecules.

The wide variety of compounds formed by carbon is due to its ability to form strong covalent bonds with other carbon atoms and hydrogen atoms, and also covalent bonds with atoms of other elements such as oxygen, nitrogen, sulfur, phosphorus and halogens.

GO TO ➤ Year 11 Chapter 3

GO TO ➤ Year 11 Chapter 5

ⓘ Alkanes have single carbon bonds.

Alkenes have double carbon bonds.

Alkynes have triple carbon bonds.

ⓘ One way to remember which is which is to put the terms in alphabetical order: alkane, alkene, alkyne. This puts the number of carbon bonds in numerical order: 1, 2, 3.

HYDROCARBONS

Carbon is a very versatile atom because it can form four covalent bonds in different ways. For example:

- four single bonds with four other atoms (Figure 9.1.3a)
- one double bond and two single bonds with three other atoms (Figure 9.1.3b)
- one triple bond and one single bond with two other atoms (Figure 9.1.3c).

Hydrocarbons are formed solely from carbon and hydrogen. Despite consisting of only two types of atoms, there are an incredible number of hydrocarbon compounds with different structures.

(a)

$$H - \overset{\displaystyle H}{\underset{\displaystyle H}{\overset{|}{\underset{|}{C}}}} - H$$

(b)

$$\overset{H}{\diagdown}C = C\overset{\diagup H}{\diagdown H}$$
$$H \diagup \qquad \diagdown H$$

(c) H — C ≡ C — H

FIGURE 9.1.3 Methane (CH_4) contains one carbon atom with four single covalent bonds to four hydrogen atoms. (b) Carbon can form compounds that contain carbon–carbon double bonds, such as ethene (C_2H_4). (c) Carbon can form hydrocarbons that contain carbon–carbon triple bonds, such as ethyne (C_2H_2).

STABILITY OF CARBON BONDS WITH OTHER ELEMENTS

The covalent bonds between carbon and other atoms each have a **bond energy**. Bond energy is a measure of **bond strength** and is the amount of energy required to break the covalent bond. The higher the bond energy, the stronger the bond.

The bond energies of a number of covalent bonds are listed in Table 9.1.1. You can see that a carbon–carbon triple bond has a higher bond energy, so it is a stronger bond than a carbon–carbon single bond. You can also see that there is wide variation in the bond energies of single covalent bonds between carbon and other elements.

A single covalent bond between two carbon atoms (C–C) is very strong, particularly compared to covalent bonds between other atoms of the same type, such as O–O, Si–Si and P–P. This is one of the reasons why only carbon tends to form chain-like structures at the temperatures and pressures found on Earth, and why it is carbon upon which life is built.

TABLE 9.1.1 Bond energies of covalent bonds commonly found in organic molecules

Covalent bond	Bond energy ($kJ\,mol^{-1}$)
C≡C	839
C=C	614
C–C	346
C–F	492
C–H	414
C–O	358
C–Cl	324
C–N	286
C–S	289

REPRESENTING ORGANIC MOLECULES

Before exploring organic molecules further, you should revise the different ways that the formulae of molecules can be represented. The formulae used in this course are:

* molecular formulae
* structural formulae
* condensed structural formulae.

Molecular formulae

Molecular formulae such as C_2H_6O and $C_4H_8O_2$ indicate the number and type of atoms of each element present in a molecule. However, they do not indicate how the atoms are arranged.

Structural formulae

Structural formulae show the spatial location of atoms relative to one another in a molecule, as well as the number and location of covalent bonds. Non-bonding electrons (called lone pairs) are often omitted for convenience.

When four single bonds are formed around a carbon atom, the pairs of electrons in each bond act as a negatively charged cloud. **Valence shell electron pair repulsion (VSEPR) theory** says that these electron pairs repel each other and so the bonds are as far apart as possible, at an angle to each other of nearly 109.5°. The structure of methane (Figure 9.1.4) is described as a **tetrahedral** shape because the four single bonds are pointing to the corners of a tetrahedron.

Molecules consisting of long chains of carbon atoms joined by single bonds are often referred to as 'straight-chain' molecules. But because of the tetrahedral distribution of each carbon's bonds, the chain actually has a zig-zag shape (Figure 9.1.5a). Structural formulae showing a tetrahedral arrangement of bonds around carbon atoms can become complicated and difficult to interpret. To make the structure of these molecules clearer, the bonds are often drawn at right angles (Figure 9.1.5b).

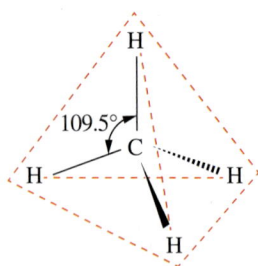

FIGURE 9.1.4 The structure of a molecule of methane (CH_4), showing the tetrahedral geometry (red lines). The solid wedge represents a bond coming out of the page, whereas the dashed wedge represents a bond going into the page.

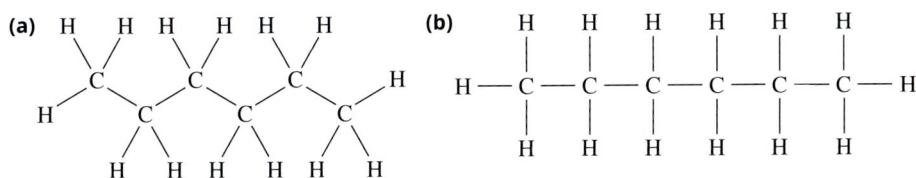

FIGURE 9.1.5 (a) The six carbon chain of hexane (C_6H_{14}). The tetrahedral arrangement of bonds around each carbon atom gives the chain a zig-zag shape. (b) The same chain drawn in a straight line for convenience.

Condensed structural formulae

A **condensed structural formula** is used to indicate the connections in the structure of a compound without showing the three-dimensional arrangement of atoms. The term 'condensed formula' is also used to describe this type of formula.

In a condensed structural formula, the carbon chain is represented on one line of text. The carbon atoms in the chain, and all the atoms attached to each of them, are listed in the order that they appear in the structural formula. Single bonds are not shown but double and triple carbon–carbon bonds are often shown. Groups of atoms that form branches in a molecule are written in parentheses after the carbon atom to which they are attached. Some examples of structural, condensed structural and molecular formulae are shown in Table 9.1.2.

TABLE 9.1.2 Examples of structural, condensed structural and molecular formulae

Structural formula and name	Condensed structural formula	Molecular formula
 butane	$CH_3CH_2CH_2CH_3$	C_4H_{10}
 but-1-ene	$CH_2{=}CHCH_2CH_3$	C_4H_8
 2-methylbutan-1-amine	$CH_3CH_2CH(CH_3)CH_2NH_2$	$C_5H_{13}N$

Three-dimensional space-filling models

Scientists are often interested in the shape and physical space a molecule occupies. Space-filling models, use spheres to represent atoms, and these are proportional to the size of the atom. The distances between atoms are kept to scale, and this creates a three-dimensional representation of the molecule.

Different colours represent atoms of different elements. Figure 9.1.6 compares the representation of propan-1-ol as a structural formula and as a space-filling model.

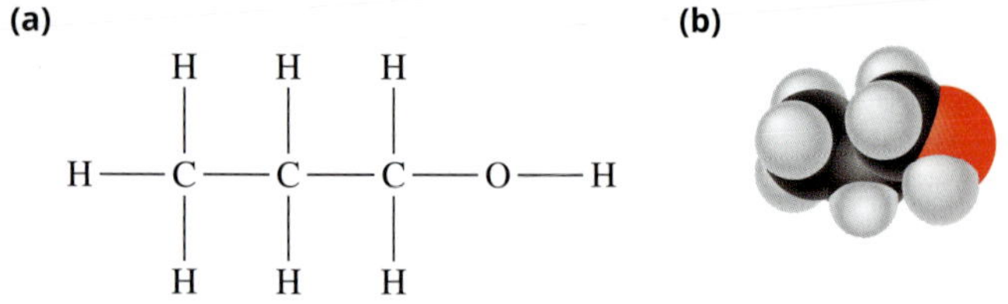

(a) **(b)**

FIGURE 9.1.6 Propan-1-ol (C_3H_5OH) depicted as (a) a structural formula, and (b) a space-filling model. In the space-filling model the carbon atoms are represented by black spheres, the hydrogen atoms by white spheres and the oxygen atom by the red sphere.

FUNCTIONAL GROUPS

A **functional group** is an atom, or group of atoms, which give the compound some characteristic chemical properties. Saturated hydrocarbons are very stable entities. Double-bond and triple-bond carbon atoms are functional groups because they are sites of chemical reactivity. Other functional groups are single atoms other than carbon or hydrogen such −Cl, −Br, or groups of atoms such as −OH (hydroxyl group) or −NH$_2$ (amino group). Functional groups are explored in detail later in this chapter.

GO TO ➤ Section 9.3 page 271

GO TO ➤ Section 9.4 page 278

ISOMERS

Isomers are molecules that contain the same number and type of atoms, but arranged in different ways. The existence of isomers is a major reason why there are so many different carbon compounds. Isomers of a compound have the same molecular formula but they can have different physical and chemical properties and so behave differently.

Isomers that have a different arrangement of atoms and different bonding patterns are called **structural isomers**. There are three main types of structural isomers:

- chain isomers
- position isomers
- functional group isomers.

Chain isomers

Chain isomers are a consequence of the branching that is possible in the carbon chains that form the backbone of any large organic molecule. Chain isomers of alkanes can contain more than one **alkyl group**; some molecules may also have more than one alkyl group attached to the same carbon atom. An alkyl group is a hydrocarbon branch group. The general formula for an alkyl group is C_nH_{2n+1}, where n represents an integer; for example, −CH$_3$ (methyl) and −CH$_2$CH$_3$ (ethyl). Alkyl groups are explored further in Section 9.2.

Hexane is an example of an alkane with no branches. It has the molecular formula C_6H_{14} and its structure is shown in Figure 9.1.7.

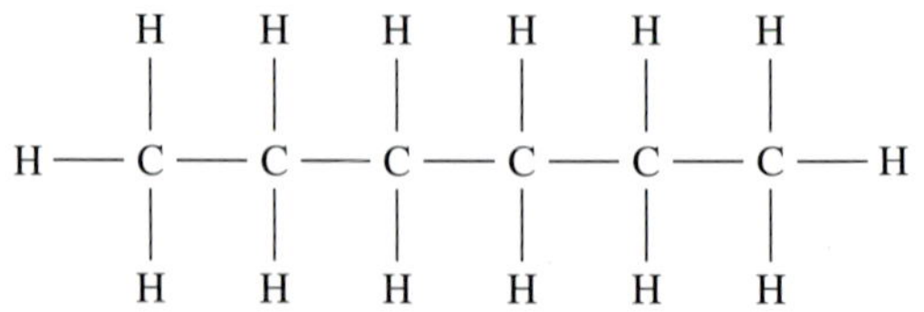

FIGURE 9.1.7 Hexane is a straight-chain hydrocarbon with single bonds that contains six carbon atoms and fourteen hydrogen atoms.

Three of the chain isomers of hexane are shown in Figure 9.1.8. Each isomer has a different name that represents its exact molecular structure. The naming system for chain isomers is described in Section 9.2.

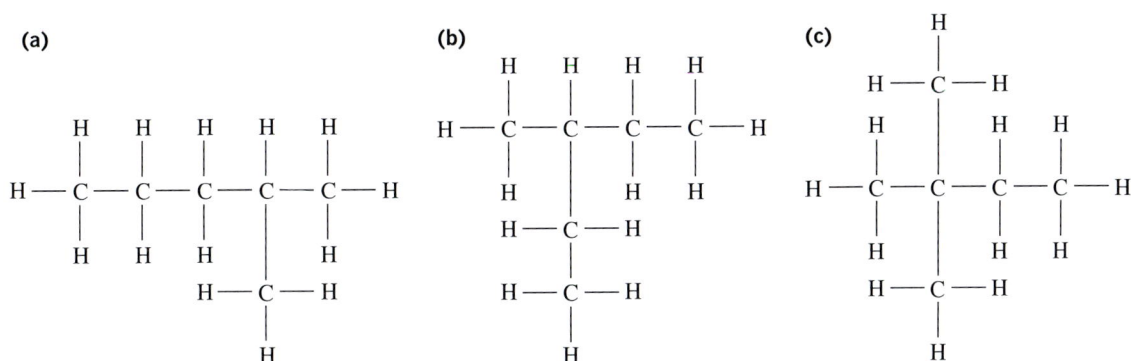

FIGURE 9.1.8 Three chain isomers of hexane: (a) 2-methylpentane, (b) 3-methylpentane, and (c) 2,2-dimethylbutane

Position isomers

Position isomers can exist for organic molecules that contain functional groups (you will learn more about different functional groups in the remaining sections of this chapter). They are molecules with the same carbon chain and functional group but with the functional group attached to a different location. For example, a number of position isomers can be drawn for the alcohol butanol, which has the molecular formula $C_4H_{10}O$ (Figure 9.1.9). Like chain isomers, each position isomer is given a different name.

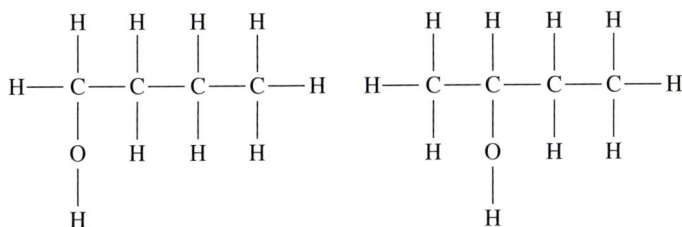

FIGURE 9.1.9 Two of the position isomers of butanol. The isomer on the left is butan-1-ol, and the one on the right is called butan-2-ol.

It is important to understand that alkenes and alkynes also contain functional groups, since they have double-bond or triple-bond carbon atoms. This means that position isomers can be formed when the multiple bond is located in different locations. Figure 9.1.10 shows the two position isomers of butene.

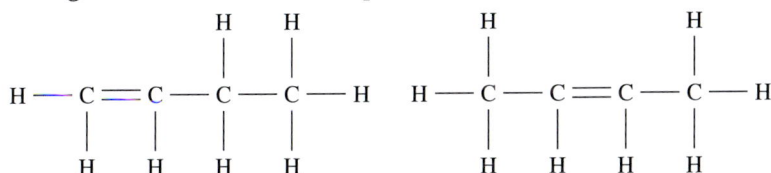

FIGURE 9.1.10 The two position isomers of butene: but-1-ene (left) and but-2-ene (right)

Position isomers only exist for molecules that contain a functional group and have a long enough carbon chain that different positions of the functional group are possible. When drawing position isomers, be careful that you do not just draw the same molecule from a different perspective. You can see that the two structural formulae of ethanol in Figure 9.1.11 do not represent position isomers.

FIGURE 9.1.11 Two representations of the structure of ethanol (C_2H_6O). These are not position isomers; if the first structure is flipped horizontally, it is identical to the second.

It is possible for structural isomers to form both position and chain isomers. Figure 9.1.12 shows two more isomers of butanol ($C_4H_{10}O$). They are chain isomers of the molecules shown in Figure 9.1.8, and position isomers of each other.

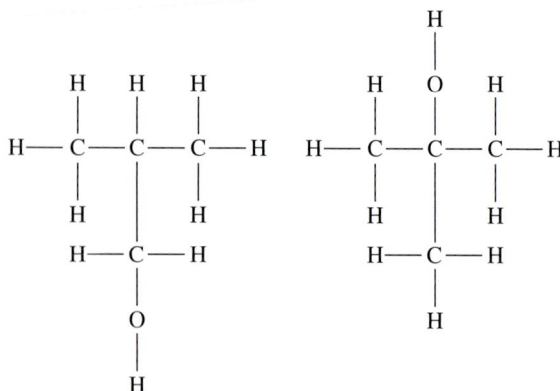

FIGURE 9.1.12 Two more isomers of butanol ($C_4H_{10}O$)

Functional group isomers

Functional group isomers will share the same molecular formula but will have different functional groups. Consequently, functional group isomers may have quite different chemical and physical properties.

Figure 9.1.13 shows that several functional group isomers are possible for the molecular formula C_3H_6O, including propanal and propanone. Propanal is a constituent of tobacco smoke, while propanone, commonly known as acetone, is a powerful organic solvent.

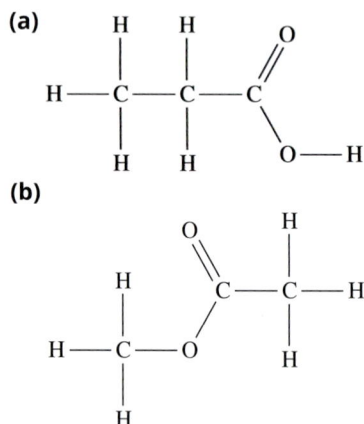

FIGURE 9.1.13 (a) Propanal, an aldehyde, and (b) propanone, a ketone

Figure 9.1.14 shows that for the molecular formula $C_3H_6O_2$, several structural isomers are possible, including propanoic acid and methyl ethanoate. Propanoic acid has a rather pungent smell and is a constituent of body odour. When reacted to form a salt, such as sodium propanoate, it is used as a food preservative. Methyl ethanoate is frequently used as a low-toxicity organic solvent.

FIGURE 9.1.14 (a) Propanoic acid, a carboxylic acid, and (b) methyl ethanoate, an ester

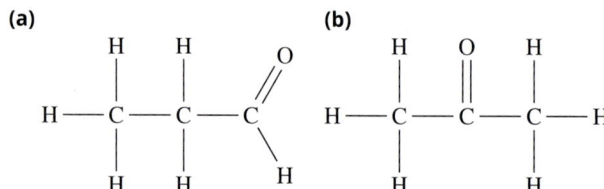

CHEMFILE IU

Organic chemistry and the vital force

These days, organic chemistry is the study of carbon compounds. However, this has not always been the case. Until the middle of the 19th century, chemists thought that the chemical make-up of plants and animals was uniquely organic. They thought that organic substances were the result of a 'vital force' possessed only by living things, so that only living organisms could produce organic substances such as fats, oils, sugars, esters and acids.

Then in 1828 German chemist Friedrich Wohler successfully synthesised organic urea from inorganic ammonium cyanate (Figure 9.1.15).

In 1860 French chemist Marcellin Berthelot published an authoritative book on organic chemistry outlining methods he had used to synthesise a variety of organic compounds including glycerol, organic acids and hydrocarbons. This was the end of the 'vital force' theory.

ammonium cyanate   urea

FIGURE 9.1.15 The first organic compound to be synthesised in the laboratory was urea.

Today the terms 'organic chemistry' and 'carbon chemistry' are used interchangeably. Inorganic chemistry usually refers to molecules that have no carbon atoms or do not have a biological origin.

Geometric isomers

Two atoms joined by a single bond can rotate freely around the single bond. You might think that the two models shown in Figure 9.1.16 show different molecules, but they are models of the same molecule because there is free rotation around the single bond. The first structure can rotate around the central single bond to the position seen on the right. Therefore these two structures are not isomers.

free rotation about this single bond

FIGURE 9.1.16 These two models represent the same molecule because the groups on either end can rotate around the single bond.

In contrast, geometric isomers can occur when there is restricted rotation somewhere in a molecule. Restricted rotation can occur about a carbon–carbon double bond or a ring.

Cis–trans isomers

Because of the way that the electrons are arranged in a double bond, groups attached to carbons on either side are unable to rotate freely. The models in Figure 9.1.17 represent two molecules that cannot be rotated to form the same structure because a double bond is present.

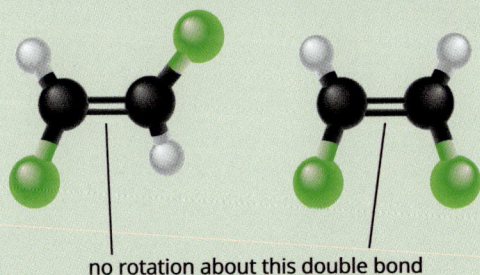

no rotation about this double bond

FIGURE 9.1.17 These two models represent different molecules because the groups on either end cannot rotate around the double bond.

Cis–trans isomers can occur in alkenes when there are two different groups attached to each carbon atom involved in the double bond. The different groups can be functional groups or hydrocarbon chains of different lengths. There are two possible arrangements: the groups can be on the same or opposite sides of the double bond. If the groups are on the same side, the isomer is called the *cis* isomer. If the groups are on opposite sides, the isomer is called the *trans* isomer. (IUPAC recommends using a different terminology, called *E–Z* notation, but the rules for this notation are more complex and beyond the scope of this course.)

In longer alkenes, the longest alkyl groups attached to the carbon atoms in the double bond are used to decide whether the molecule is a *cis* or *trans* isomer.

• In *cis* isomers, the longest alkyl groups on each carbon are on the same side of the double bond.

• In *trans* isomers, the longest alkyl groups on each carbon are on opposite sides of the double bond.

Figure 9.1.18 shows two isomers of but-2-ene, both with the condensed structural formula $CH_3CH=CHCH_3$. The two methyl groups are on the same side of the double bond in the *cis* isomer. The methyl groups are opposite each other in the *trans* isomer.

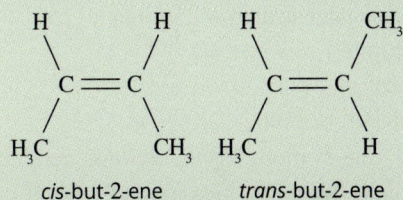

cis-but-2-ene   *trans*-but-2-ene

FIGURE 9.1.18 (a) *cis*-but-2-ene, and (b) *trans*-but-2-ene

9.1 Review

SUMMARY

- Carbon has a valence number of four.
- Carbon atoms form covalent bonds with each other and with other non-metallic atoms such as hydrogen, oxygen and nitrogen.
- Carbon atoms can form single, double or triple bonds with other carbon atoms.
- Bond strength is the amount of energy required to break a bond. The covalent bonds between carbon and other non-metal atoms have different bond strengths.
- The bonds with the highest strength also have the highest stability.

- Carbon compounds can have structural isomers with the same molecular formula. Structural isomers include chain isomers, position isomers and functional group isomers.
- Chain isomers have the same molecular formula but different branching of the carbon chain.
- Position isomers have the same molecular formula but at least one functional group is in a different position on the carbon chain.
- Functional group isomers have the same molecular formula but do not share the same functional groups.

KEY QUESTIONS

1 Which of the following bonds is the most stable?
   A C–S
   B C–F
   C C–Cl
   D C–O

2 Define the following terms:
   a structural formula
   b condensed structural formula
   c saturated
   d unsaturated
   e position isomer.

3 Which one or more of the following condensed structural formulae represent an alkane?
   A CH_3CH_3
   B $CH_3CHCHCH_3$
   C $CH_3CH_2CH_2CH_3$
   D $CH_3CH_2CHCH_2$

4 a What is the shortest alkane that can have chain isomers?
   b Draw structural formulae for all the chain isomers of this alkane.

5 Explain why carbon chains in alkanes are not straight, even though they are commonly drawn that way in structural formulae.

9.2 Hydrocarbons

The simplest organic molecules are the hydrocarbons. Although they only contain the elements carbon and hydrogen, the different ways their atoms can be arranged to form molecules results in an enormous diversity of compounds. Crude oil, the source of many hydrocarbons used in industry, contains a mixture of different hydrocarbons (Figure 9.2.1).

In this section you will learn about the molecules in the hydrocarbon families of alkanes, alkenes and alkynes. You will learn about their molecular, structural and condensed structural formulae, as well as some of their isomers and the ways they are named.

HOMOLOGOUS SERIES

The study of organic chemistry is simplified by grouping the millions of different molecules that exist into families called **homologous series**. Compounds that are members of the same homologous series have:

- similar structures
- similar chemical properties
- the same general formula
- a pattern to their physical properties.

Homologous series contain members that have increasingly longer chains. These chains grow by the addition of a $-CH_2$ unit to the previous member of the series. The hydrocarbons that you will focus on belong to three homologous series: the alkanes, the alkenes and the alkynes.

ALKANES

Alkanes are a homologous series of molecules that consist entirely of carbon and hydrogen atoms. They have the general formula C_nH_{2n+2}. The other distinguishing feature of alkanes is that their molecules contain only single bonds.

Alkanes are saturated molecules. A saturated molecule is one that contains only single bonds. The carbon atoms in alkanes are saturated because they cannot bond with any more atoms. When a molecule contains one or more carbon–carbon double or triple bonds, it is classified as unsaturated. An unsaturated molecule has the potential to bond with more atoms.

Naming simple alkanes

In the systematic name of simple 'straight-chain' alkanes, the prefix of the name refers to the number of carbon atoms in one molecule of the alkane. The prefixes used are listed in Table 9.2.1.

The names of all alkanes have the suffix (ending) '-ane' to indicate that the carbon–carbon bonds are all single bonds.

Combining the prefix and suffix, you can see that methane is an alkane that contains one carbon atom, ethane is an alkane that contains two carbon atoms and propane is an alkane that contains three carbon atoms, and each of the carbons have four bonds with different atoms (Figure 9.2.2).

FIGURE 9.2.2 Structural formulae of methane, ethane and propane

FIGURE 9.2.1 Crude oil is flammable because it contains a mixture of hydrocarbons.

> ℹ The names of alkanes end in '-ane', and they have the general formula C_nH_{2n+2}.

TABLE 9.2.1 Prefixes used to name molecules with between one and eight carbon atoms

Number of carbon atoms	Prefix
1	meth-
2	eth-
3	prop-
4	but-
5	pent-
6	hex-
7	hept-
8	oct-

Isomers of alkanes

Methane, ethane and propane are the smallest alkanes. There is only one possible arrangement for the carbon and hydrogen atoms in these small molecules. Once alkane molecules are above a certain size, their carbon and hydrogen atoms can be arranged in different ways, resulting in different structural isomers.

Butane (C_4H_{10}) has two structural isomers, as shown in Figure 9.2.3. One isomer has the carbon atoms in a chain, while the other has a branched arrangement.

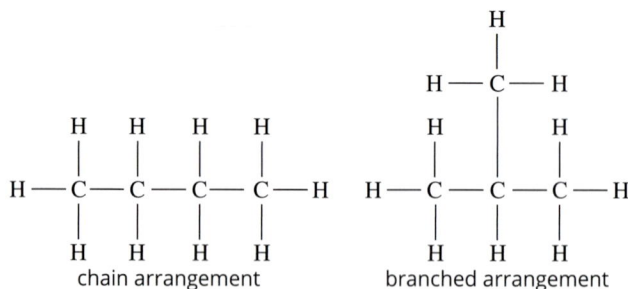

FIGURE 9.2.3 Structural isomers of butane (C_4H_{10})

Alkyl groups

Branched alkanes are named systematically to provide information about the number and size of branches on the molecule. Branches, also called **side chains**, can be thought of as alkane molecules that have lost a hydrogen atom. The side chain is called an alkyl group.

Alkyl groups are named in the following way:
- The prefix indicates the number of carbon atoms in the side chain.
- The suffix '-yl' is used.

Alkyl groups and the alkanes from which they are derived are shown in Table 9.2.2.

TABLE 9.2.2 Alkanes and their derivative alkyl groups

Alkane	Condensed structural formula	Alkyl group	Formula
methane	CH_4	methyl	$-CH_3$
ethane	CH_3CH_3	ethyl	$-CH_2CH_3$
propane	$CH_3CH_2CH_3$	propyl	$-CH_2CH_2CH_3$
butane	$CH_3(CH_2)_2CH_3$	butyl	$-CH_2(CH_2)_2CH_3$
pentane	$CH_3(CH_2)_3CH_3$	pentyl	$-CH_2(CH_2)_3CH_3$
hexane	$CH_3(CH_2)_4CH_3$	hexyl	$-CH_2(CH_2)_4CH_3$
heptane	$CH_3(CH_2)_5CH_3$	heptyl	$-CH_2(CH_2)_5CH_3$
octane	$CH_3(CH_2)_6CH_3$	octyl	$-CH_2(CH_2)_6CH_3$

Branched alkanes

The systematic naming of structural isomers of alkanes that contain branches requires the following steps as shown in Figure 9.2.4.

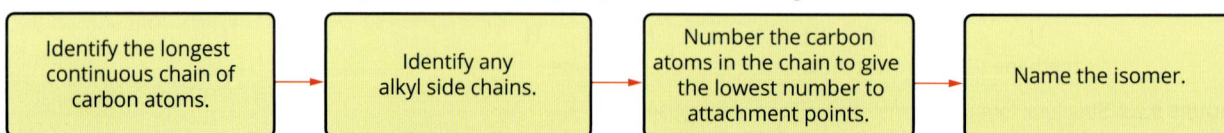

FIGURE 9.2.4 The steps used to name isomers of alkanes.

In the naming of an isomer, the following conventions are also used.

- Identify the parent name or **stem name** by finding the longest continuous chain of carbon atoms.
- Place the name of each alkyl group before the **parent molecule** name.
- If there is more than one type of alkyl group, list the groups in alphabetical order.
- If there is more than one of the same type of alkyl group, use the prefix 'di', 'tri' or 'tetra'.
- Specify the carbon atom to which each alkyl group is attached by a number before the alkyl group.
- Choose the direction of numbering to give the smallest possible number to each alkyl group.
- Do not include spaces in the name.
- Use hyphens to separate numbers from words.
- Use commas to separate numbers from other numbers.

An example of the naming of a branched isomer of C_6H_{14} is shown in Figure 9.2.5. The steps in naming this molecule are as follows.

1 There are five carbon atoms in the longest chain, so the parent name is pentane.
2 The only branch is a methyl group, $-CH_3$.
3 The methyl group is nearest to the right-hand end.
4 The methyl group is attached to the second carbon.
5 The name of the molecule is therefore 2-methylpentane.

> **i** Carefully check that you have identified the longest unbranched carbon chain. Sometimes the longest carbon chain is not drawn in a straight line.

FIGURE 9.2.5 The name of this alkane is 2-methylpentane.

Worked example 9.2.1

NAMING AN ISOMER OF AN ALKANE WITH MORE THAN ONE ALKYL BRANCH

Write the systematic name of the alkane with the following structure.

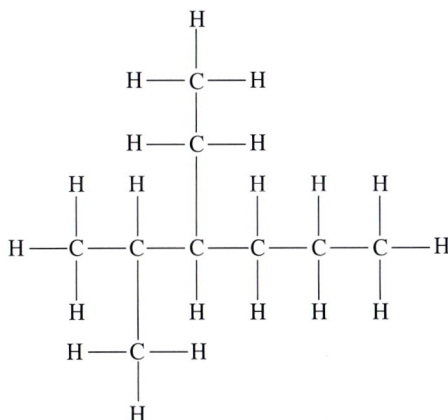

Thinking	Working
Identify the parent name by counting the longest continuous chain of carbon atoms.	longest continuous chain There are six carbon atoms in the longest continuous chain, so the parent name is hexane.
Identify any alkyl side chains by counting the number of carbon atoms in any branches.	ethyl group methyl group There is one carbon atom in the first alkyl group, so it is a methyl group. The second alkyl group has two carbon atoms, so it is an ethyl group.
Identify the number(s) of the carbon atom(s) to which any alkyl group is attached. Count from the end that will give the lowest possible number to the carbons the groups are attached to.	The alkyls are closest to the left-hand end. The methyl group is attached to carbon number 2 and the ethyl group is attached to carbon number 3.
Assemble the name of the isomer, listing alkyl groups in alphabetic order with the number of the carbon atom before each group.	The name of the isomer is 3-ethyl-2-methylhexane.

Worked example: Try yourself 9.2.1

NAMING AN ISOMER OF AN ALKANE WITH MORE THAN ONE ALKYL BRANCH

Write the systematic name of the molecule with the following structure.

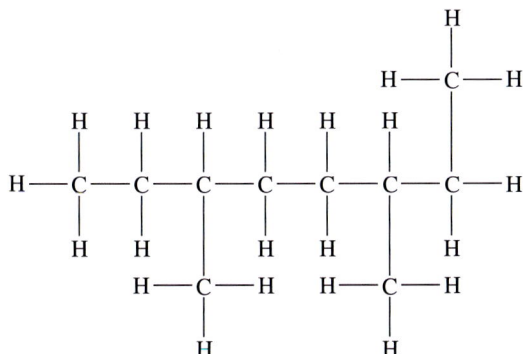

Cyclohexane

Cyclohexane is a hydrocarbon that is used as a solvent and in paint strippers, and to make other chemicals such as nylon. Figure 9.2.6 shows that the carbon atoms in the cyclohexane molecule form a ring. Molecules that form rings are known as cyclic molecules.

Although cyclohexane can be drawn as a hexagonal ring, it does not have this shape in reality. The ability of the carbon atoms to rotate to a limited extent around the single bonds means that the ring can take on different shapes. The most common arrangement (or conformation) is known as the chair conformation because it resembles the shape of a chair.

Like straight-chain hexane, cyclohexane is a saturated molecule that contains six carbon atoms. But because of the extra carbon–carbon bond that closes the ring structure there are two less hydrogen atoms, making the formula of cyclohexane C_6H_{12}, whereas hexane is C_6H_{14}. Cyclohexane is a member of the cycloalkane homologous series.

FIGURE 9.2.6 (a) The structural formula of cyclohexane (C_6H_{12}), and (b) a representation of the most common 'chair' conformation formed by the ring

ALKENES AND ALKYNES

Alkenes and alkynes are unsaturated hydrocarbons and contain at least one multiple carbon–carbon bond. Because this bond is shared by a pair of carbon atoms, all alkene and alkyne molecules must have two or more carbon atoms.

The homologous series of hydrocarbons that contains a carbon–carbon double bond is called the alkenes. The molecular, structural and condensed structural formulae of the first three members of the homologous series of alkenes are shown in Table 9.2.3. You can see that successive members differ by a –CH_2 unit. Alkenes have the general formula C_nH_{2n}.

Alkenes with four or more carbon atoms can have structural isomers, in which the location of the double bond changes.

> ℹ The names of alkenes end in '-ene', and they have the general formula C_nH_{2n}.

TABLE 9.2.3 Formulae of the first three members of the alkene homologous series. Butene is represented here by the isomer but-1-ene.

Name	Molecular formula	Structural formula	Condensed structural formula
ethene	C_2H_4		$CH_2{=}CH_2$
propene	C_3H_6		$CH_2{=}CHCH_3$
butene	C_4H_8		$CH_2{=}CHCH_2CH_3$

The homologous series of hydrocarbons that contain a carbon–carbon triple bond are called alkynes. They have the general formula C_nH_{2n-2}.

Just as with alkenes, alkynes with four or more carbon atoms have structural isomers. Representations of the first three members of the homologous series of alkynes are shown in Table 9.2.4.

ⓘ The name of an alkyne ends in '-yne' and alkynes have the general formula C_nH_{2n-2}.

TABLE 9.2.4 Formulae of the first three members of the alkyne homologous series. Butyne is represented here by the isomer but-1-yne

Name	Molecular formula	Structural formula	Condensed structural formula
Ethyne	C_2H_2	$H{-}C{\equiv}C{-}H$	$CH{\equiv}CH$
Propyne	C_3H_4		$CH{\equiv}CCH_3$
Butyne	C_4H_6		$CH{\equiv}CCH_2CH_3$

Naming alkenes

The rules for naming alkenes follow the rules used for alkanes, except for the following:

- Use the suffix '-ene' for the parent name.
- Number the carbon atoms from the end of the chain closest to the double bond.

- Specify the position of the double bond by the number of the lowest-numbered carbon atom in the double bond.
- Insert the number into the name immediately before '-ene'.

The flowchart in Figure 9.2.7 shows the steps involved in naming an alkene.

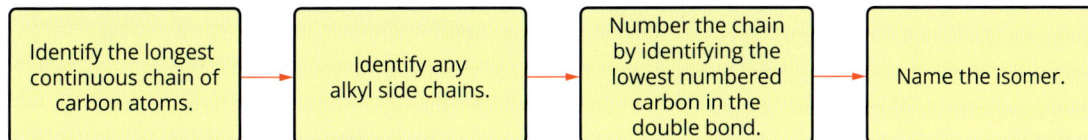

Identify the longest continuous chain of carbon atoms. → Identify any alkyl side chains. → Number the chain by identifying the lowest numbered carbon in the double bond. → Name the isomer.

FIGURE 9.2.7 The steps used to name alkenes

Worked example 9.2.2

NAMING AN ISOMER OF AN ALKENE

Write the systematic name of the following alkene.

Thinking	Working
Identify the parent name by counting the longest continuous chain of carbon atoms that contains the carbon–carbon double bond.	There are five carbon atoms in the longest continuous chain, so the parent name is pentene.
Identify any alkyl side chains by counting the number of carbon atoms in any branches.	There is one methyl group.

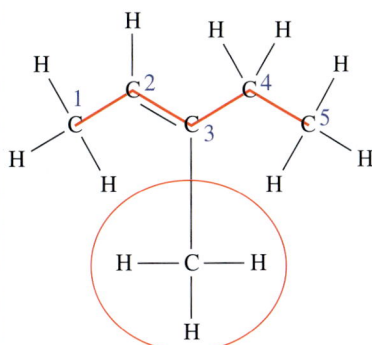

Number the chain from the end closest to the double bond and identify the lowest numbered carbon atom in the double bond.	
	The lowest numbered carbon atom in the double bond is 2, so the parent name becomes pent-2-ene.
Number any alkyl side chains using the numbers of the carbon atoms to which they are attached.	
	The methyl group is attached to the third carbon.
Name the isomer.	The name of the isomer is 3-methylpent-2-ene.

Worked example: Try yourself 9.2.2

NAMING AN ISOMER OF AN ALKENE

Write the systematic name of the following alkene.

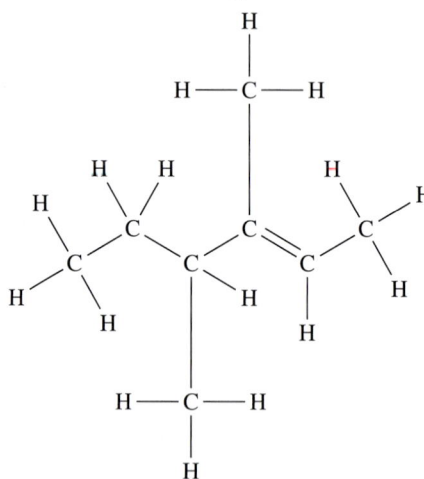

Naming alkynes

The rules for naming alkynes also follow the rules for alkanes and alkenes, except for the following:

- Use the suffix '-yne' for the parent name.
- Number the carbon atoms from the end of the chain closest to the triple bond.
- Specify the position of the triple bond by the number of the lowest-numbered carbon atom in the triple bond.
- Insert the number into the name immediately before '-yne'.

+ ADDITIONAL

Benzene

Benzene is an unsaturated cyclic hydrocarbon molecule. Its structure consists of six carbon atoms arranged in a ring. Three of the four outer-shell electrons from each carbon atom form normal covalent bonds, but the fourth electron is delocalised (shared) around all six carbons.

The structure of benzene, shown in Figure 9.2.8, is sometimes represented with alternating double and single bonds. Due to the shared nature of the delocalised electrons, it is more correct to describe each carbon as having one and a half bonds to each neighbour. For this reason, the bonds are often represented as a ring of normal single bonds with a circle inside the ring.

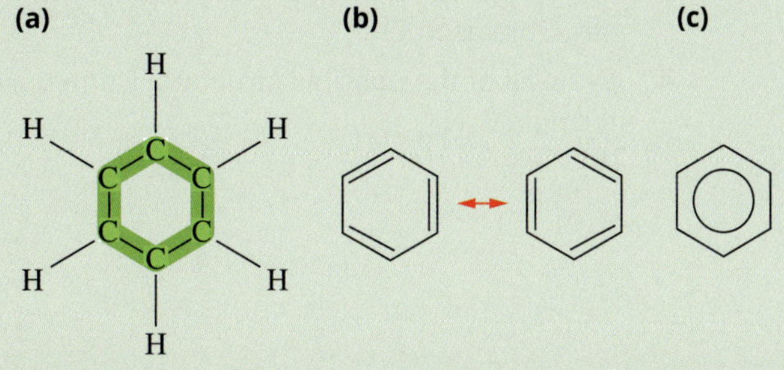

FIGURE 9.2.8 Representations of the molecular structure of benzene (C_6H_6), showing (a) the delocalised electrons in green, (b) a shorthand representation with alternating double and single bonds, and (c) the delocalised electrons represented as a circle inside the hexagon of carbon atoms.

9.2 Review

- Alkanes are the simplest hydrocarbons. Their molecules contain carbon and hydrogen atoms, and all bonds between atoms are single covalent bonds.
- Alkanes have the general formula C_nH_{2n+2}.
- Alkanes can have structural isomers.
- The naming of alkanes follows a set of rules.
- Alkenes are a homologous series of hydrocarbons that contain a carbon–carbon double bond.

- Alkenes have the general formula C_nH_{2n}.
- Alkynes are a homologous series of hydrocarbons that contain a carbon–carbon triple bond.
- Alkynes have the general formula C_nH_{2n-2}.
- The naming of alkenes and alkynes follows the same set of rules used for alkanes.

KEY QUESTIONS

1 Name the following molecules.

a
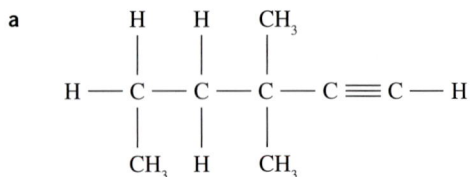

b
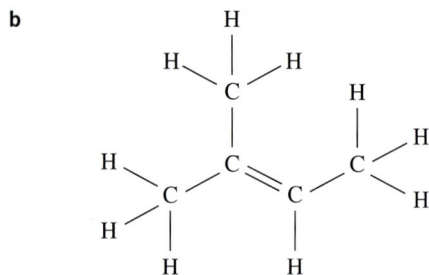

c
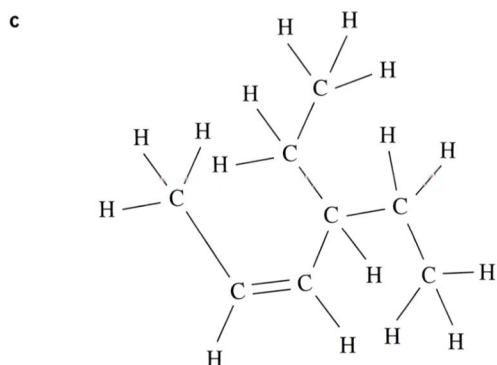

2 Draw the structure of each of the following hydrocarbons:
   a 2,3-dimethylpent-2-ene
   b 4-ethylhex-2-ene
   c 5-ethyl-2-methylhept-3-yne
   d 2,2-dimethyloct-3-yne.

3 Which two of the molecules in Question **2** are structural isomers?

4 Draw all of the possible structural isomers with the formula C_6H_{14}.

270   **MODULE 7** | ORGANIC CHEMISTRY

9.3 Functional groups—Part 1

Most organic compounds can be regarded as derivatives of hydrocarbons which have one or more hydrogen atoms replaced by other atoms or groups of atoms called a functional group.

The presence of a particular functional group in a molecule gives a substance certain physical and chemical properties. For example, vinegar and wine (Figure 9.3.1) both contain organic molecules based on ethane. The difference between their tastes and other properties is due to the different functional groups in each molecule.

In this section you will explore three classes of organic compounds:

- haloalkanes
- alcohols
- primary amines.

You will learn about the functional groups in each of these families of molecules, and how to name them.

> **i** A functional group is an atom, or group of atoms, which give the compound some characteristic chemical properties.

FIGURE 9.3.1 (a) Vinegar and (b) wine contain molecules with two carbon atoms. Vinegar contains ethanoic acid with a carboxyl functional group, and wine contains ethanol with a hydroxyl group.

HALOALKANES

Haloalkanes are derived from alkanes, in which one or more hydrogen atoms are replaced with **halogen** atoms.

Haloalkanes are used widely in industry as flame retardants, refrigerants, propellants, pesticides (Figure 9.3.2 on page 272), solvents and pharmaceuticals. Some haloalkanes are ozone-depleting chemicals, and their use has been phased out in many applications.

FIGURE 9.3.2 Bromomethane (CH_3Br) is a colourless, odourless, non-flammable gas that has been used as a pesticide. This photo shows a field covered in plastic sheeting to minimise loss of the pesticide from the soil.

The halogen elements are in group 17 of the periodic table. All halogen atoms have seven valence electrons, which means they can form a single covalent bond with carbon atoms. The halogen elements that commonly form **halo functional groups** in organic compounds are fluorine, chlorine, bromine and iodine. Table 9.3.1 shows the names, structures and uses of some haloalkanes.

TABLE 9.3.1 Names, structures and uses of some haloalkanes

Name	Structural formula	Condensed structural formula	Use
chloromethane		CH_3Cl	refrigerant
bromochlorodifluoromethane		$CBrClF_2$	fire extinguishers
iodoethane		CH_3CH_2I	production of chemicals
1-bromopropane		$CH_3CH_2CH_2Br$	industrial solvent

Naming haloalkanes

TABLE 9.3.2 Names of the haloalkane functional groups

Halogen	Functional group name
fluorine	fluoro
chlorine	chloro
bromine	bromo
iodine	iodo

The names of haloalkane functional groups are derived from the name of the halogen, as shown in Table 9.3.2.

The rules for naming haloalkanes follow the rules for naming alkanes (Table 9.3.3). In addition, the following conventions are applied:

- Place the name of the specific halo functional group at the start of the parent alkane's name.
- If position isomers are possible, use numbers to indicate the carbon to which the halo function group is attached.
- Number the carbons of the parent chain, beginning at the end closest to the first halo group or alkyl side chain.
- If there is more than one of the same type of halogen atom, use the prefix 'di', 'tri' or 'tetra'.
- If more than one type of halo functional group is present, list them in alphabetical order.

TABLE 9.3.3 Examples of haloalkanes and their names

Name	Condensed structural formula	Structural formula
bromomethane	CH_3Br	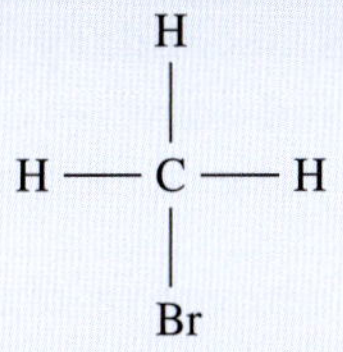
1,1-dichloroethane	CH_3CHCl_2	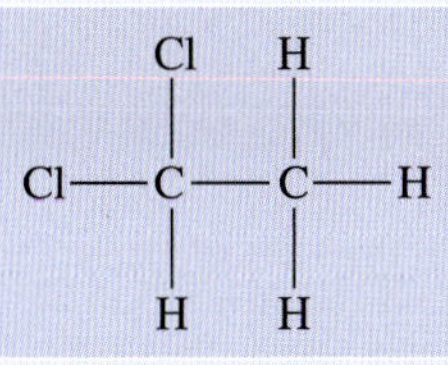
1-chlorobutane	$CH_3CH_2CH_2CH_2Cl$	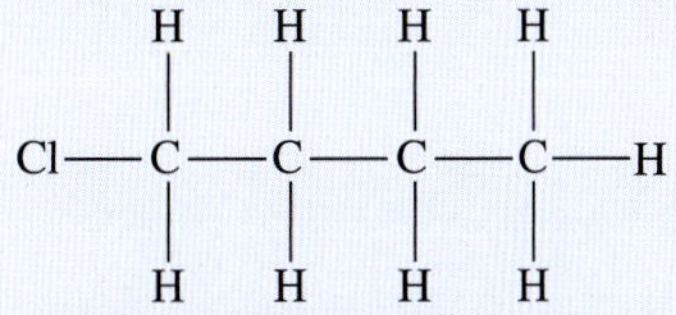
2-chloro-2-fluorobutane	$CH_3CClFCH_2CH_3$	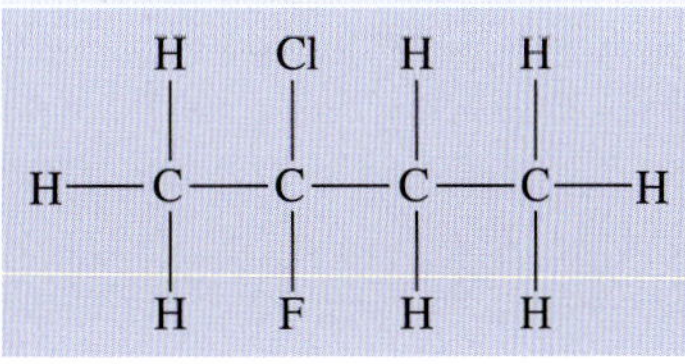

ALCOHOLS

Alcohols comprise a homologous series in which a **hydroxyl** (–OH) **functional group** is attached to a saturated carbon atom. A representation of the hydroxyl group is shown in Figure 9.3.3.

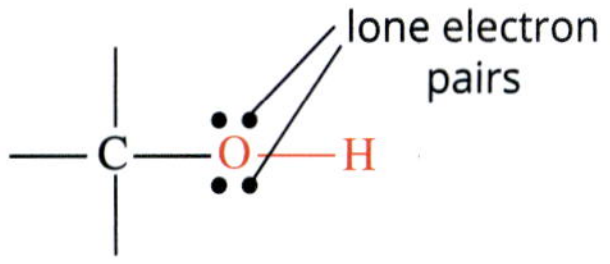

FIGURE 9.3.3 Alcohols contain the hydroxyl functional group, –OH (in red above). There are two pairs of non-bonding electrons on the oxygen.

Figure 9.3.4 shows the structural and condensed structural formulae of two alcohols. You can think of the hydroxyl group as taking the place of a hydrogen atom in an alkane.

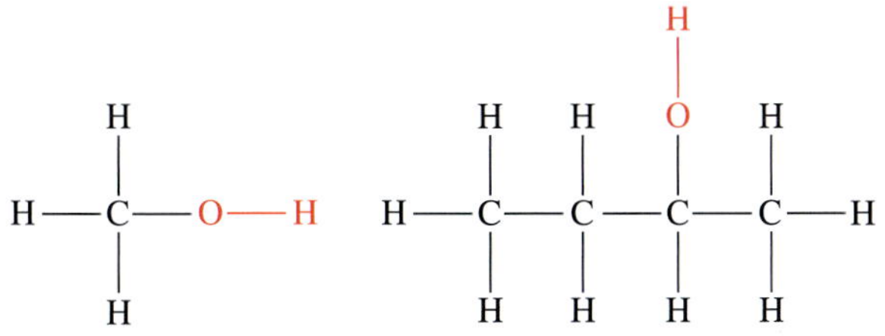

methanol
CH_3OH

butan-2-ol
$CH_3CH_2CHOHCH_3$

FIGURE 9.3.4 Structural and condensed structural formulae of two alcohols. Each contains the hydroxyl functional group (shown in red). Note that the non-bonding electron pairs on the oxygen atom are often omitted in structural formulae.

Types of alcohols

Alcohols are classified according to the number of alkyl groups attached to the carbon bonded to the hydroxyl group. The three different types of alcohols are **primary alcohols**, **secondary alcohols** and **tertiary alcohols**.

The definition and examples of each type are shown in Table 9.3.4. Alkyl groups are represented by the general symbol R.

TABLE 9.3.4 The three different types of alcohols. The hydroxyl group is shown in red.

Type of alcohol	Definition	General formula	Example
Primary	The carbon bonded to the –OH group is only bonded to one alkyl group.		
Secondary	The carbon bonded to the –OH group is also bonded to two alkyl groups.		
Tertiary	The carbon atom bonded to the –OH group is also bonded to three alkyl groups.		

Naming alcohols

Alcohol names follow the rules used for alkanes, except that the '-e' at the end of the parent alkane's name is replaced with the suffix '-ol'. The following rules also apply.

- Identify the parent name from the longest carbon chain containing the hydroxyl group.
- If position isomers are possible, a number is inserted before the '-ol' to indicate the carbon to which the hydroxyl functional group is attached.
- Number the carbon chain commencing at the end closest to the hydroxyl group. Table 9.3.5 shows some examples.

TABLE 9.3.5 Examples of naming alcohols. These three structures are all isomers of butanol ($C_4H_{10}O$).

Name	Condensed structural formula	Structural formula
butan-1-ol	$CH_3CH_2CH_2CH_2OH$	This is an example of a primary alcohol.
butan-2-ol	$CH_3CHOHCH_2CH_3$	This is an example of a secondary alcohol.
2-methylpropan-2-ol	$(CH_3)_3COH$	This is an example of a tertiary alcohol.

PRIMARY AMINES

Amines are a homologous series of organic compounds that contain the **amino functional group**. An amino functional group consists of one nitrogen atom covalently bonded to two hydrogen atoms as shown in Figure 9.3.5.

Amino functional groups with two hydrogens and one alkyl group are called **primary amines**. Unlike alcohols, amines are classified as primary, secondary or tertiary according to the number of alkyl groups attached to the nitrogen atom. Secondary and tertiary amines exist, but these compounds are not covered in this course. Some primary amines are shown in Figure 9.3.6.

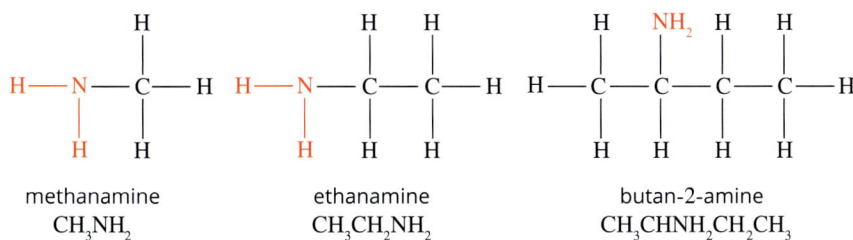

FIGURE 9.3.5 Primary amines contain the amino functional group, $-NH_2$ (shown in red). There are two non-bonding electrons on the nitrogen atom.

methanamine
CH_3NH_2

ethanamine
$CH_3CH_2NH_2$

butan-2-amine
$CH_3CHNH_2CH_2CH_3$

FIGURE 9.3.6 Structural and condensed structural formulae of three primary amines. The amino functional group is shown in red. Primary amines have one carbon atom bonded to the nitrogen atom.

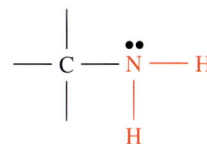

Amines, chocolate and happiness

An active ingredient in chocolate (Figure 9.3.7) is the primary amine 2-phenylethanamine. 2-phenylethanamine is also produced in the pleasure centres of the brain and has the effect of generating a general sense of wellbeing or happiness, as well as temporarily raising blood pressure and blood glucose levels.

Eating chocolate provides you with a boost of 2-phenylethanamine, so the reason eating chocolate might make you feel happy is partly due to organic chemistry!

However, it is important to limit your intake of chocolate, because it is high in sugar and fat. Eating too much increases your risk of weight gain, tooth decay, diabetes and heart disease. Enjoy your mood-boosting chocolate in moderation.

FIGURE 9.3.7 Chocolate contains an amine that makes humans feel happy.

Naming amines

Amines are named in a similar way to alcohols. The '-e' at the end of the parent alkane's name is replaced with the suffix '-amine'. If position isomers are possible, a number is inserted before '-amine' to indicate the carbon to which the amino functional group is attached. Table 9.3.6 shows two examples.

TABLE 9.3.6 Examples of naming amines

Name	Condensed formula	Structural formula
ethanamine	$CH_3CH_2NH_2$	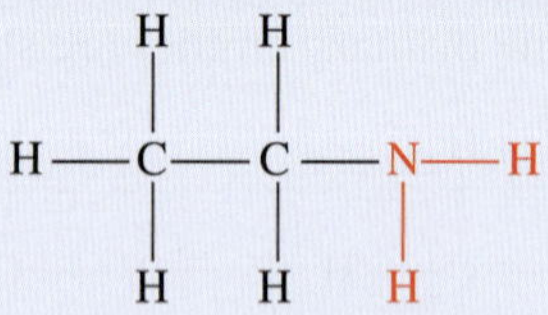
butan-2-amine	$CH_3CHNH_2CH_2CH_3$	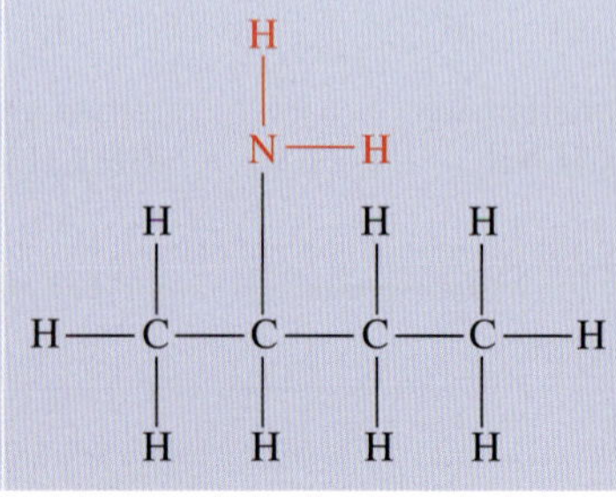

WS 7.4   WS 7.6

9.3 Review

SUMMARY

- Organic molecules containing functional groups include:
    - haloalkanes, which contain the halo groups –F, –Cl, –Br and –I
    - alcohols, which contain hydroxyl (–OH) groups
    - primary amines, which contain amino ($-NH_2$) functional groups.
- Haloalkanes, alcohols and primary amines can be regarded as being derived from alkanes. The name of the parent alkane is used as the basis for their names.

- Haloalkanes are named by adding the prefix for the halogen.
- Alcohols are named by replacing the '-e' at the end of the parent alkane with the suffix '-ol'.
- Primary amines are named by replacing the '-e' at the end of the parent alkane with the suffix '-amine'.
- When isomers exist, a number is used to specify the position of the functional group.

KEY QUESTIONS

1 Give the systematic name for this molecule.

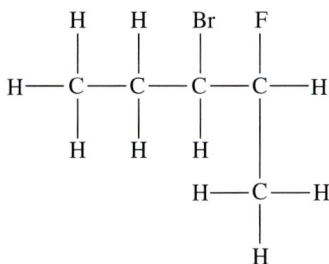

2 Write the condensed structural formula of 3-chloro-2-fluoro-2-iodohexane.

3 Draw the structure and then write the name of a tertiary alcohol with the molecular formula $C_5H_{12}O$.

4 Give the systematic names of:
a $CH_3CH_2CH_2Br$
b $(CH_3)_2CHCH_2CHClCH_3$
c $CH_3(CH_2)_3CH_2OH$
d $CH_3(CH_2)_3CHNH_2(CH_2)_2CH_3$

5 Explain why the names 1-chloroethane and propan-3-amine are not used.

9.4 Functional groups—Part 2

In this section you will look at five more classes of organic compounds:

- aldehydes
- ketones
- carboxylic acids
- primary amides
- esters.

The molecules in these classes are responsible for many natural fragrances, and are also found in essential oils and pheromones (Figure 9.4.1). Many are synthesised commercially to produce particular smells and flavourings.

ALDEHYDES AND KETONES

Molecules of aldehydes, ketones, carboxylic acids, amides and esters all contain a **carbonyl functional group,** as shown in Figure 9.4.2. A carbonyl functional group consists of a carbon atom connected to an oxygen atom by a double bond. All atoms bonded to the carbon atom are in one plane, and the angles between bonds are 120°.

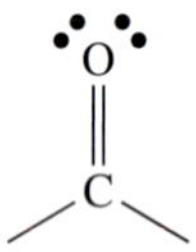

Aldehydes

In **aldehydes**, the carbonyl group is always at the end of the hydrocarbon chain. As shown in Table 9.4.1, the carbon atom of the carbonyl group is bonded to a hydrogen atom. The carbonyl functional group in an aldehyde is always written as –CHO at the end of the condensed structural formula.

The simplest aldehyde, methanal (HCHO) is commonly known as formaldehyde and is used to preserve biological specimens and embalming human remains. Table 9.4.1 lists the first three aldehydes. The suffix '-al' denotes an aldehyde.

FIGURE 9.4.1 Aldehydes, ketones and esters are common components of the fragrances used in perfumes.

FIGURE 9.4.2 The carbonyl functional group. The non-bonding pairs of electrons shown on the oxygen atom are not included in structural formulae.

TABLE 9.4.1 Formulae of the first three aldehydes

Name	Molecular formula	Structural formula	Condensed structural formula
methanal	CH_2O	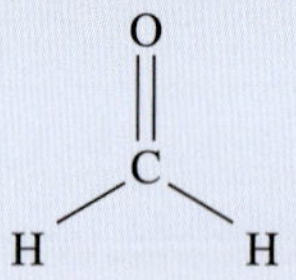	CH_2O
ethanal	C_2H_4O	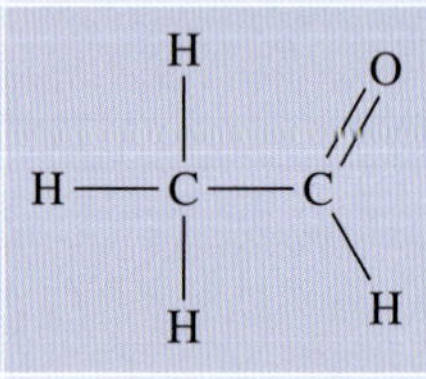	CH_3CHO
propanal	C_3H_6O	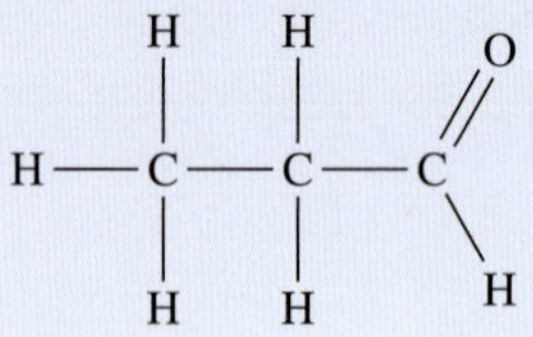	CH_3CH_2CHO

Ketones

In **ketones** the carbonyl carbon is attached to other carbon atoms. This means that the carbonyl group is never at the end of the molecule, as you can see in the examples in Table 9.4.2. In condensed structural formulae, the carbonyl functional group in a ketone is simply written as –CO–.

Propanone (CH_3COCH_3), the simplest ketone, is commonly called acetone. It is a useful polar organic solvent and is the main component of in nail polish remover and paint thinner. Table 9.4.2 lists the first three ketones. The suffix '-one' denotes a ketone.

TABLE 9.4.2 Formulae of the first three ketones

Name	Molecular formula	Structural formula	Condensed structural formula
propanone	C_3H_6O		CH_3COCH_3
butanone	C_4H_8O		$CH_3COCH_2CH_3$
pentan-2-one	$C_5H_{10}O$		$CH_3CO\ CH_2CH_2CH_3$

CARBOXYLIC ACIDS

Carboxylic acids comprise a homologous series of molecules that contain the carboxyl functional group. The carboxyl functional group (Figure 9.4.3) consists of a carbonyl group attached to a hydroxyl group.

The **carboxyl functional group** is represented in a condensed structural formula as −COOH and is always located at one end of a hydrocarbon chain. Figure 9.3.4 shows the structural and condensed structural formulae of three carboxylic acids.

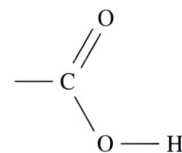

FIGURE 9.4.3 Structure of the carboxyl functional group.

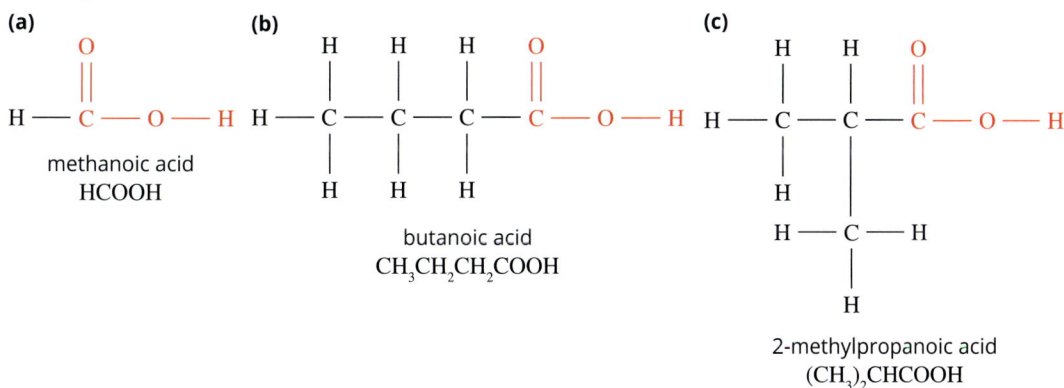

(a) methanoic acid HCOOH

(b) butanoic acid $CH_3CH_2CH_2COOH$

(c) 2-methylpropanoic acid $(CH_3)_2CHCOOH$

FIGURE 9.4.4 Structural and condensed structural formulae of three carboxylic acids. Each contains a carboxyl functional group shown in red. Note that molecules (b) and (c) are isomers with the molecular formula $C_4H_8O_2$.

Naming carboxylic acids

Carboxylic acid names also follow the rules used for alkanes, except that the '-e' at the end of the parent alkane's name is replaced with the suffix '-oic acid'. As the carboxyl group is always on the end of a chain, the carbon atom in the carboxyl group is always carbon number 1. Table 9.4.3 on page 280 shows three examples.

TABLE 9.4.3 Examples of naming carboxylic acids

Name	Condensed structural formula	Structural formula
ethanoic acid	CH_3COOH	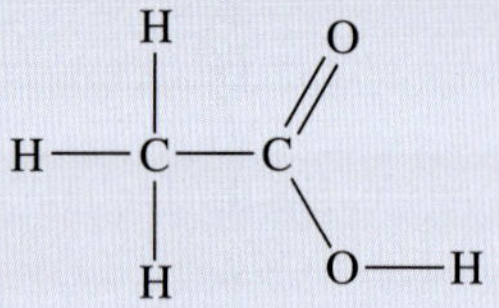
butanoic acid	$CH_3CH_2CH_2COOH$	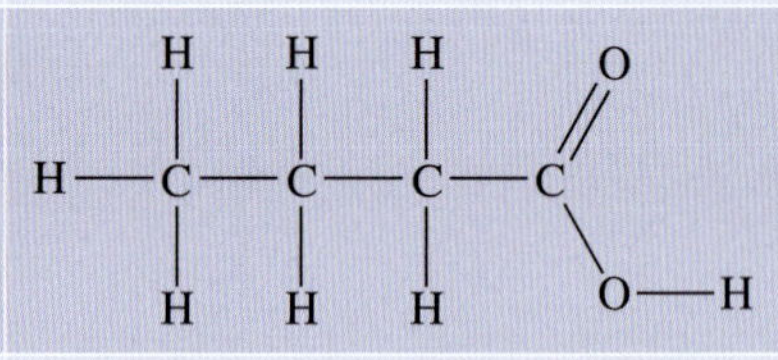
2-methylbutanoic acid	$CH_3CH_2CH(CH_3)COOH$	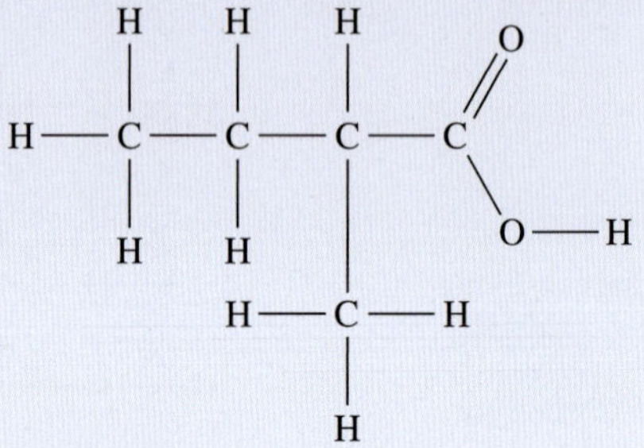

PRIMARY AMIDES

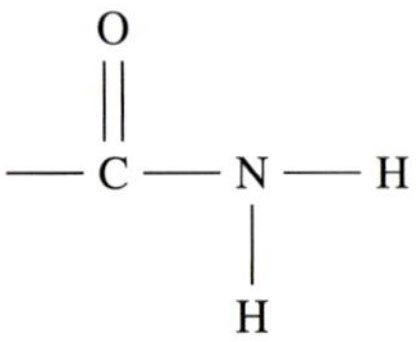

Primary amides contain a carbonyl functional group attached to an amino functional group. They are similar to carboxyl groups, except that the −OH is replaced with −NH_2 (Figure 9.4.5). Primary amides are named using the suffix '-amide'.

The nitrogen atom in primary amides is bonded to two hydrogen atoms. Secondary and tertiary **amides** exist, but these compounds are not covered in this course. The **amide functional group** is represented in a condensed structural formula as −$CONH_2$ and is always located at one end of a hydrocarbon chain. The structural and condensed structural formulae of the first three primary amides are shown in Table 9.4.4.

FIGURE 9.4.5 Structure of the amide functional group in a primary amide

TABLE 9.4.4 Formulae of the first three amides

Name	Molecular formula	Structural formula	Condensed structural formula
methanamide	CH_3NO	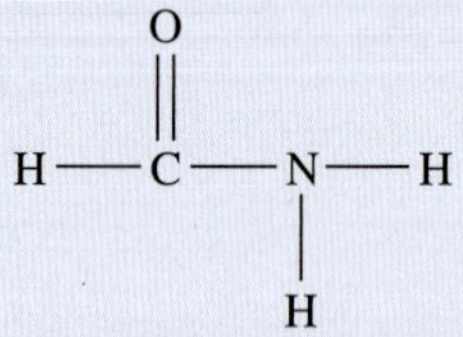	HCONH
ethanamide	C_2H_5NO	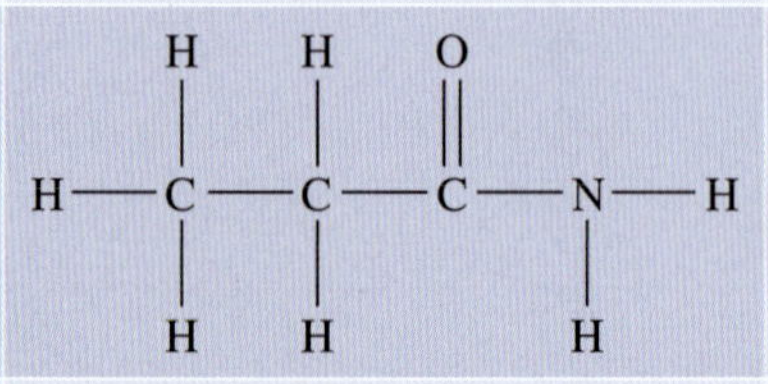	CH_3CONH_2
propanamide	C_3H_7NO	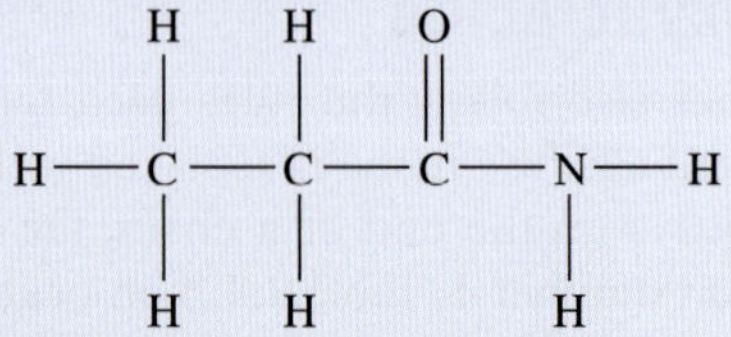	$CH_3CH_2CONH_2$

ESTERS

Esters are produced by the reaction of a carboxylic acid with an alcohol. The **ester functional group** (Figure 9.4.6) contains a carbonyl group attached to an oxygen linked to another carbon. It is similar to a carboxyl group, but the hydrogen of the −OH is replaced by an alkyl group. You will learn more about how esters are produced in Section 13.2.

Figure 9.4.7 shows the structural and condensed structural formulae of three esters. In condensed structural formulae the ester functional group is usually written as −COO−.

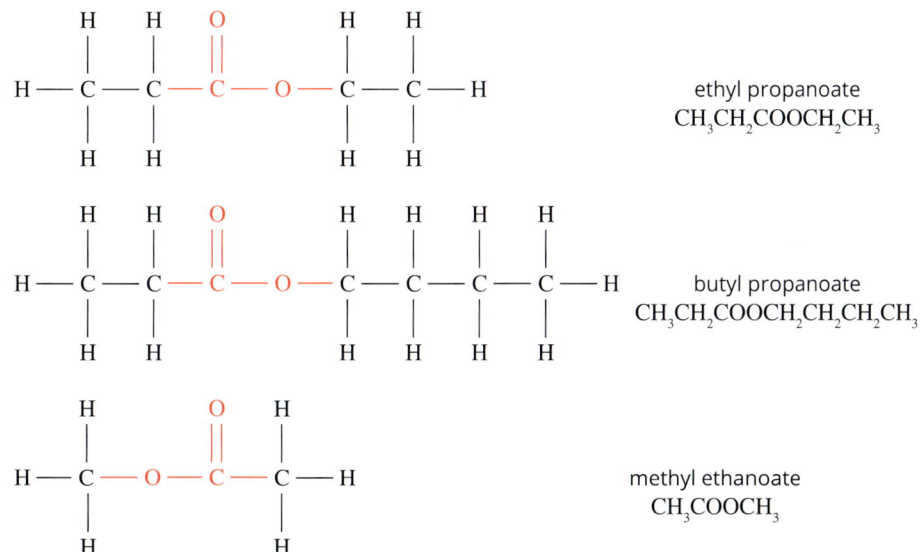

FIGURE 9.4.6 Structure of the ester functional group

ethyl propanoate
$CH_3CH_2COOCH_2CH_3$

butyl propanoate
$CH_3CH_2COOCH_2CH_2CH_2CH_3$

methyl ethanoate
CH_3COOCH_3

FIGURE 9.4.7 Structural and condensed structural formulae of three esters. Each contains the ester functional group shown in red.

Naming esters

The names of esters consist of two words. The name is built up from the names of the alcohol and carboxylic acid that reacted to form it. The first part is based on the number of carbon atoms in the chain attached to the singly bonded oxygen (−O−). The second part of the name is based on the number of carbon atoms in the chain containing the carbonyl group.

In the example in Figure 9.4.8, the chain attached to the single −O− contains one carbon atom, while the chain containing the carbonyl is three carbon atoms long.

methyl propanoate
$CH_3CH_2COOCH_3$

FIGURE 9.4.8 Esters are named using two words based on the number of carbon atoms in each of the two alkyl chains in the molecule.

The −O− section of an ester is derived from an alcohol and contributes the first word of the name. The name of the alcohol is adapted by changing the '-ol' suffix to '-yl'.

The section containing the carbonyl group is derived from a carboxylic acid and contributes the second word of the name. The name of the carboxylic acid is adapted by changing '-oic acid' to '-oate'.

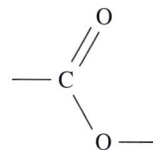

Using these rules, you can work out that the name of the ester shown in Figure 9.4.8 is methyl propanoate.

The names, condensed structural and structural formulae of some other esters are shown in Table 9.4.5, with the part of each molecule derived from an alcohol in red and the part of each molecule derived from the carboxylic acid in blue.

TABLE 9.4.5 The names, condensed structural and structural formulae of three esters

Name	Condensed structural formula	Structural formula
ethyl ethanoate	$CH_3COOCH_2CH_3$	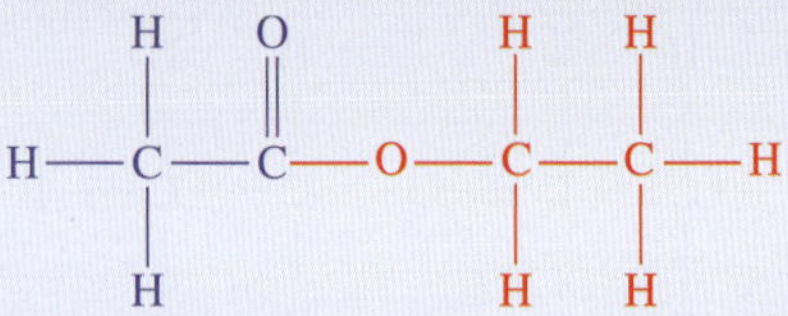
propyl propanoate	$CH_3CH_2COOCH_2CH_2CH_3$	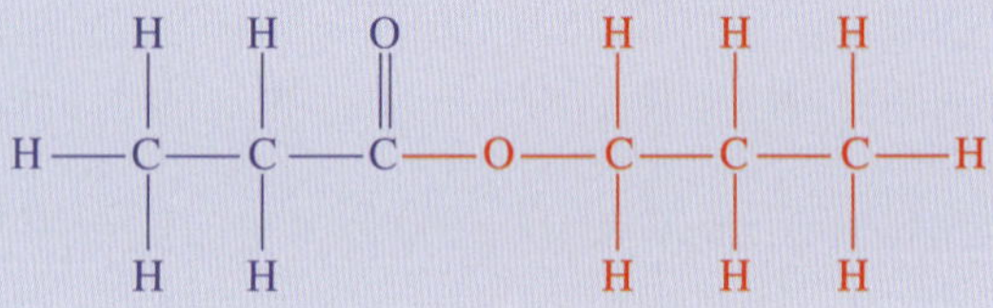
propyl ethanoate	$CH_3COOCH_2CH_2CH_3$	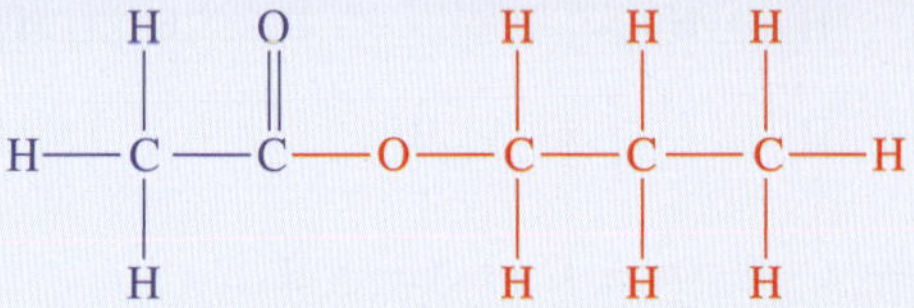

Esters, sweet flavours and strong aromas

Esters are responsible for some of the natural and synthetic flavours and smells found in ice creams, lollies, flowers and fruit (Figure 9.4.9). Table 9.4.6 lists the names of some esters with distinctive smells or flavours. These esters can be extracted from their natural sources, or artificially synthesised in a lab.

Your favourite perfume or cologne is likely to contain esters that are responsible for its distinctive and appealing odour.

FIGURE 9.4.9 Esters are responsible for many of the flavours and odours of fruit.

TABLE 9.4.6 Some sweet-smelling esters

Ester	Smell or flavour
pentyl propanoate	apricot
ethyl butanoate	pineapple
octyl ethanoate	orange
2-methylpropyl methanoate	raspberry
ethyl methanoate	rum
pentyl ethanoate	banana

9.4 Review

SUMMARY

- The carbonyl group (–CO–) is a component of a number of functional groups.
- Aldehydes and ketones are homologous series that contain a carbonyl group on its own.
- The carbonyl group is at the end of a hydrocarbon chain in aldehydes and within a hydrocarbon chain in ketones.
- Aldehydes are named using the suffix '-al'.
- Ketones are named using the suffix '-one'.
- Carboxylic acids are a homologous series of molecules that contain the carboxyl group (–COOH) at the end of a hydrocarbon chain.
- Carboxylic acids are named using the suffix '-oic acid'.

- Primary amides are a homologous series of molecules that contain the amide group (–$CONH_2$) at the end of the hydrocarbon chain.
- Primary amides are named using the suffix '-amide'.
- Esters are a homologous series of molecules that contain an ester group (–COO–) within the hydrocarbon chain.
- Esters have a two-word name.
  - The first part of the name comes from the section derived from an alcohol and the '-ol' suffix is changed to '-yl'.
  - The second part of the name is derived from the section that comes from a carboxylic acid and the suffix '-oic acid' is changed to '-oate'.

KEY QUESTIONS

1 What homologous series do each of the following molecules belong to?

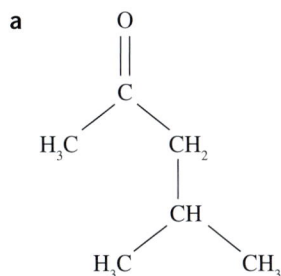

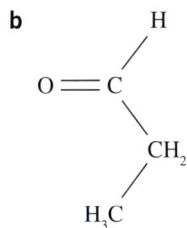

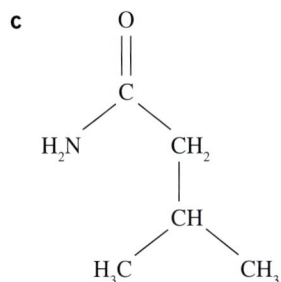

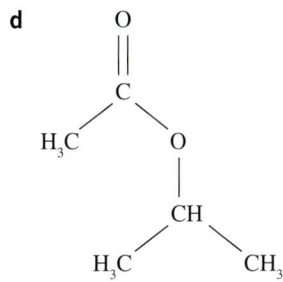

a

b

c

d

2 Write the systematic name for the following molecules.
  a $HCOOCH_3$
  b $HCOOH$
  c $CH_3CH_2CH_2COOCH_2CH_2CH_3$
  d CH_3COOCH_3
  e $CH_3(CH_2)_4COOCH_2CH_3$

3 Draw and name a carboxyl containing isomer of $HCOOCH_3$.

4 Write the systematic names for these molecules.

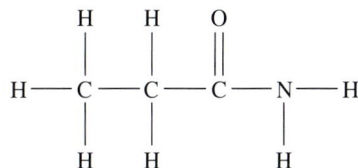

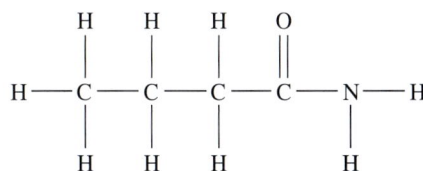

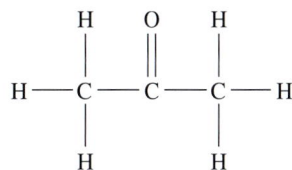

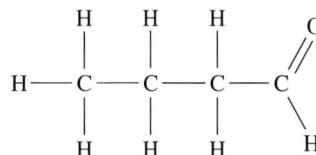

5 Draw the structure of these molecules:
  a pentan-2-one
  b propanal
  c ethanamide.

9.5 An overview of IUPAC organic nomenclature

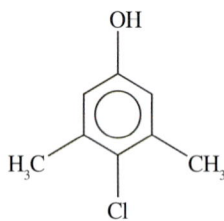

In the early 1960s the International Union of Pure and Applied Chemistry (IUPAC) endorsed a common naming system for carbon compounds. These rules are regularly updated and are used worldwide to enable organic chemists to communicate unambiguously with each other. The rules ensure that a carbon compound is given a unique name that provides useful information about its structure and distinguishes it from any isomers.

The rules specify the names for different parts of an organic molecule and may include both words and numbers to indicate locations of functional groups and alkyl branches (Figure 9.5.1).

This section summarises and extends your knowledge of the rules that you learnt in the previous sections for naming organic compounds. You will also learn how to name a range of organic molecules that contain two different functional groups.

IUPAC NOMENCLATURE

IUPAC nomenclature is the term used to describe the set of rules by which chemists can name a given compound. The rules can be used in reverse to derive a structure from the IUPAC name. IUPAC names of organic molecules can be short or very long, but, whether simple or complex, most IUPAC names follow the same basic pattern.

All organic molecules can be thought of as being derived from a hydrocarbon parent molecule, which provides the basis for the name of the molecule. Part of the IUPAC name reflects which alkane is the parent molecule.

The IUPAC name also indicates which functional groups are present in the molecule by adding a suffix to the end of the name or a prefix to the beginning of the name. The positions of functional groups are indicated by numbers. As an example, the meaning of each part of the name butan-2-ol, an alcohol, is shown in Figure 9.5.2 along with its structural formula.

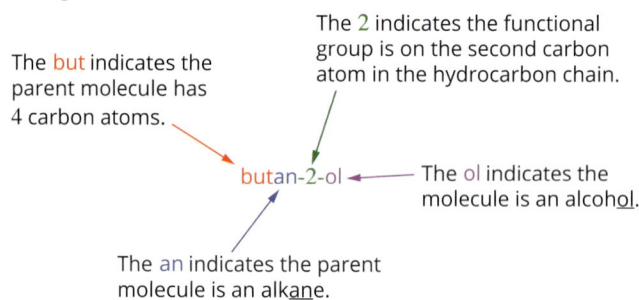

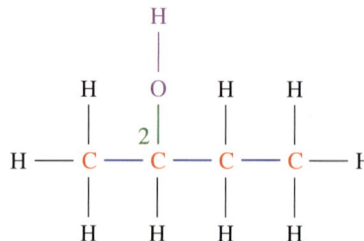

FIGURE 9.5.1 According to the IUPAC rules, the active ingredient in the antiseptic Dettol® has the name 4-chloro-3,5-dimethylphenol.

The **but** indicates the parent molecule has 4 carbon atoms.

The **2** indicates the functional group is on the second carbon atom in the hydrocarbon chain.

The **ol** indicates the molecule is an alcoh<u>ol</u>.

The **an** indicates the parent molecule is an alk<u>ane</u>.

butan-2-ol

FIGURE 9.5.2 The name and structural formula of butan-2-ol. The colours of each part of the name correspond with the section of the structure that it represents.

SUMMARY OF IUPAC RULES FOR NOMENCLATURE

The following conventions are used for naming organic molecules.

- There are no spaces in a name, apart from the two-word names of esters and carboxylic acids.
- The longest carbon chain is used to derive the parent name. The longest chain must include the functional group for alkenes, alkynes, alcohols, amines, aldehydes, ketones, carboxylic acids, primary amides and esters.
- The names and locations of branches and additional functional groups are added to this parent name.
- Numbers are used to identify the carbon atom that groups are attached to.
- Numbers and letters are separated by dashes.
- Numbers are separated from other numbers by commas.
- The names of branch alkyl groups are added before the parent name.
- If there is more than one type of functional group to be listed at the beginning of a name, they are listed in alphabetical order.
- If there is more than one of the same type of functional group, the prefixes 'di-', 'tri-' or 'tetra-' are used. Each group is still given a number to indicate its position on the carbon chain.

The presence of a particular functional group identifies the homologous series a molecule belongs to and changes the molecule's name, as shown in Table 9.5.1.

TABLE 9.5.1 The identity, functional groups and naming conventions of the homologous series.

Homologous series	Functional group name	Condensed structural formula	Naming convention
alkane	not applicable	not applicable	suffix -ane
alkene	carbon–carbon double bond	–C=C–	suffix -ene
alkyne	carbon–carbon triple bond	–C≡C–	suffix -yne
haloalkane	halo	–F, –Cl, –Br, –I	prefix fluoro-, chloro-, bromo-, iodo-
alcohol	hydroxyl	–OH	suffix -ol sometimes prefix hydroxy-
amine	amino	$–NH_2$	suffix -amine sometimes prefix amino-
carboxylic acid	carboxyl	–COOH	suffix -oic acid
ester	ester	–COO–	two-word name with suffixes -yl and -oate
aldehyde	carbonyl (aldehyde)	–CHO	suffix -al
ketone	carbonyl	–CO–	suffix -one
amide	amide	$–CONH_2$	suffix -amide

Naming organic molecules with a functional group and alkyl side chain

Organic molecules with functional groups can also have alkyl side chains. The names of alkyl groups are placed in alphabetical order in front of the parent name. The carbon chain is numbered from the end closest to the functional group to give the lowest possible number to the functional group.

This procedure is illustrated in Table 9.5.2 on page 286 with the naming of the structural isomers of an alcohol with the molecular formula $C_4H_{10}O$.

TABLE 9.5.2 Names of isomers of an alcohol with the molecular formula $C_4H_{10}O$

Structure	Name
	butan-1-ol
	butan-2-ol
	2-methylpropan-1-ol
	2-methylpropan-2-ol

Naming organic molecules with two functional groups

Many organic molecules have more than one functional group. If the functional groups are the same, a multiplier (di-, tri- etc.) can be used. If the molecule has different functional groups, you will need to know which one has the highest priority in order to work out what numbers and names to use.

IUPAC has designated a priority system for functional groups (Table 9.5.3). In an organic molecule with two functional groups, the following naming conventions are used.

- The functional group with the highest priority is assigned the lowest possible number and the suffix for this functional group is used in the name.
- The lower priority functional group is indicated by a prefix or alternative name.

TABLE 9.5.3 IUPAC functional group priorities

	Functional group	Suffix	Alternative name (when needed)
highest priority	carboxyl	-oic acid	–
	amide	-amide	carbamoyl-
	carbonyl (aldehyde)	-al	formyl-
	carbonyl (ketone)	-one	oxo-
	hydroxyl	-ol	hydroxy-
	amino	-amine	amino-
	alkene	-ene	-an- becomes -en-
	alkyne	-yne	-an- becomes -yn-
lowest priority	halo	–	halo-

This priority system is illustrated in Table 9.5.4 with the naming of molecules with two functional groups.

TABLE 9.5.4 Naming molecules with two functional groups

Structure	Name
	3-hydroxybutanoic acid
	2-aminoethanol
	5-chloropentan-2-ol

Worked example 9.5.1

NAMING AN ORGANIC MOLECULE WITH TWO FUNCTIONAL GROUPS

Name the following molecule according to IUPAC rules.

Thinking	Working
Identify the parent name by counting the longest continuous chain of carbon atoms.	There are four carbons in the longest chain, so the parent name is butane.
Identify the functional groups present.	The two functional groups present are hydroxyl and amino.
Determine which functional group has the higher priority and determine the prefixes and suffixes to use.	The hydroxyl group has the higher priority, so the molecule will end in -ol. The amino group has lower priority and so the prefix amino- will be used.
Number the carbon chain, giving the highest priority group the lowest number possible.	
Determine the number of the carbon each functional group is attached to.	The –OH is attached to carbon 2 and –NH_2 is attached to carbon 4.
Use the functional group names and carbon numbers to construct the full name.	The name of the molecule is 4-aminobutan-2-ol.

Worked example: Try yourself 9.5.1

NAMING AN ORGANIC MOLECULE WITH TWO FUNCTIONAL GROUPS

Name the following molecule according to IUPAC rules.

Trivial versus IUPAC systematic names

The 19th century was a golden age for chemistry. New and interesting organic compounds were being either isolated or synthesised at a prodigious rate.

In 1818, French chemist Michel Eugene Chevreul isolated an acid from rancid butter. It had the distinctive smell of human vomit and is also found in Parmesan cheese. He called it butyric acid from the Latin word for butter, *butyrum* (Figure 9.5.3).

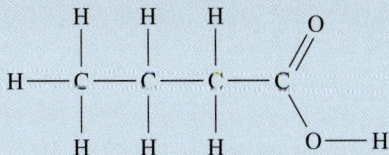

FIGURE 9.5.3 Butyric acid has the systematic name butanoic acid.

In 1863, German chemist Adolf von Baeyer synthesised a new compound from malonic acid and urea (Figure 9.5.4). As it was

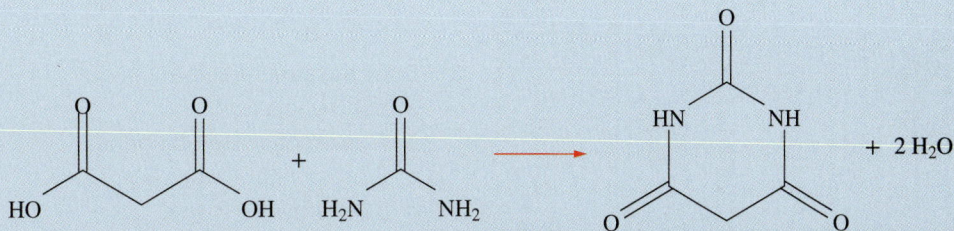

St Barbara's Day he named this new substance barbituric acid (2,4,6-trioxypyrimidine). At this time many scientists were naming compounds after astronomical bodies, mythological figures and saints.

In 1919, the International Union of Pure and Applied Chemistry (IUPAC) was formed. One of its aims was to standardise the plethora of non-systematic names that existed in organic chemistry. To this end, it publishes the *Nomenclature of Organic Chemistry* (informally called the Blue Book) as the authority on naming organic compounds. There is also an IUPAC nomenclature of inorganic chemistry.

Ideally, every possible organic compound should have a systematic name from which an unambiguous structural formula can be created.

Because systematic names can be tediously long, common names, also known as trivial names, are still in common use. See Table 9.5.5 for some examples.

FIGURE 9.5.4 Barbituric acid was first synthesised on St Barbara's Day (4 December).

TABLE 9.5.5 Trivial (common) names and IUPAC names for some organic compounds

Structural formula	Trivial name	IUPAC name
	wood alcohol	methanol
	acetone	propanone
	aspirin	2-acetyloxybenzoic acid

9.5 Review

SUMMARY

- IUPAC nomenclature is a set of rules for naming an organic compound.
- The naming of organic molecules follows a series of steps.
  - Identify the longest unbranched carbon chain to determine the parent name.
  - Name functional groups by prefixes or suffixes, depending on their priority.

- Number the longest carbon chain so that the carbon attached to the highest priority functional group has the lowest number.
- Insert numbers before each functional group.
- When multiples of a functional group are present, use a multiplier prefix (e.g. 'di').

KEY QUESTIONS

1 Draw the structural formula of the functional group of each of the following homologous series:
   a alkyne
   b carboxylic acid
   c aldehyde
   d primary amide
   e alcohol
   f ester.

2 Write the systematic name for the following molecules.

   a

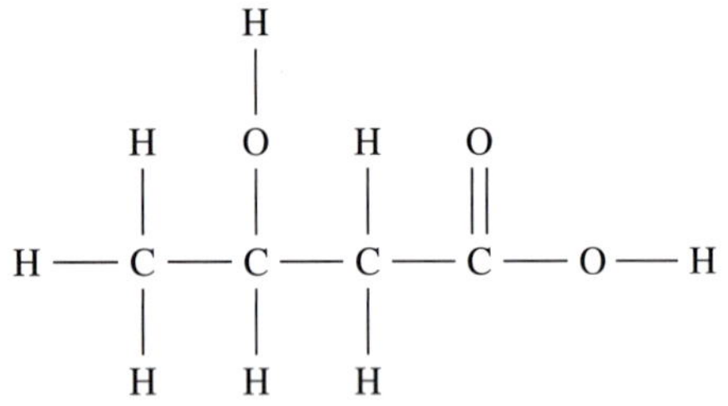

   b

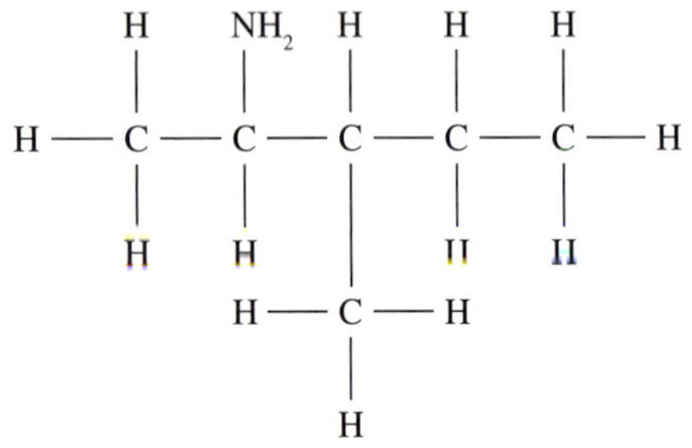

   c

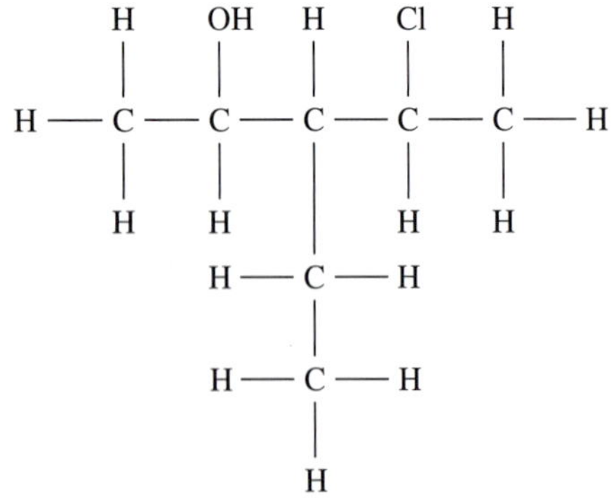

d

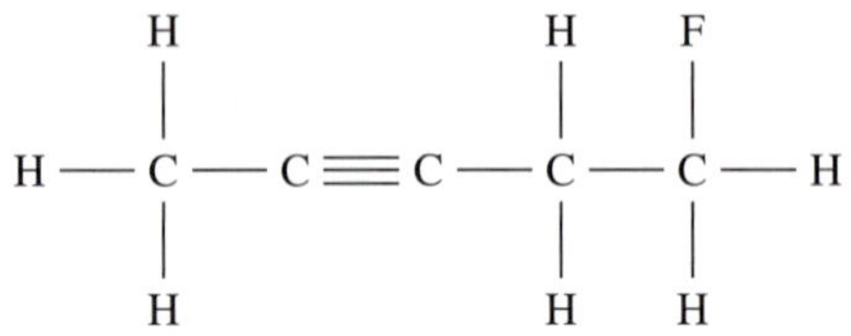

3 Draw the structural formula of:
   a but-3-ynoic acid
   b 4-chloropent-1-en-2-amine
   c 6-bromohept-4-en-2-ol
   d 3,4-diethylhex-3-ene.

4 a Write the condensed structural formulae based on the following incorrect names:
      i 3-aminoprop-1-ene
      ii 2-chloropentan-5-oic acid
      iii 1-ethyl-1-hydroxyprop-2-ene.
   b Give the correct IUPAC name for each organic compound in part a.

5 a Draw the structural formula of:
      i 2-bromopentan-3-one
      ii 3-hydroxybutanal
      ii 2-aminoethanoic acid.
   b Give the correct IUPAC name for each of the following compounds:
      i

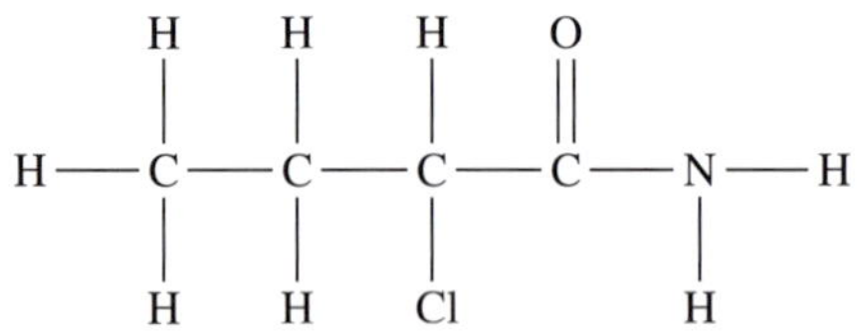

      ii

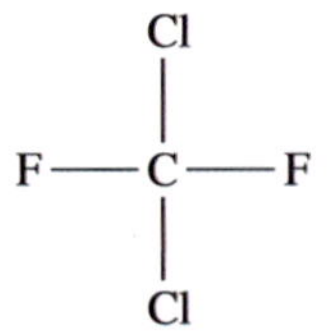

      iii

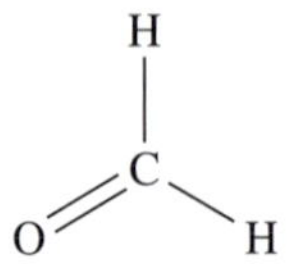

Chapter review

09

REVIEW QUESTIONS

1 The structural formula for 1-chloropentane is shown below. Draw and name all the possible position isomers of this alkane.

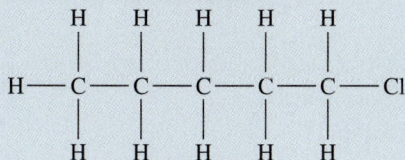

2 How is a chain isomer different from a position isomer?

3 How is a position isomer different from a functional group isomer?

4 Structures with the molecular formula C_4H_8 can be both chain isomers and position isomers. Write three condensed structural formulae of C_4H_8 to explain the relationship between position and chain isomers.

5 Give the IUPAC systematic name for each of the following compounds.

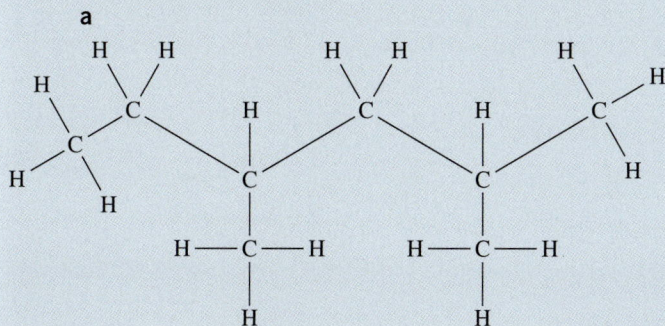

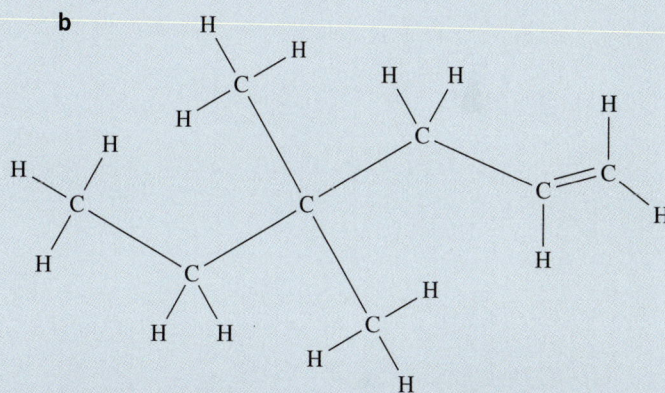

a

b

c

6 Draw the structural formulae of the following organic compounds.
   a propyl ethanoate
   b pent-2-ene
   c 2,2-dimethylpropane.

7 What is the molecular formula of:
   a an alkane with molar mass $72\,g\,mol^{-1}$?
   b an alkene with molar mass $84\,g\,mol^{-1}$?
   c an alkyne with molar mass $54\,g\,mol^{-1}$?
   d a hydrocarbon with molar mass $98\,g\,mol^{-1}$?

8 State how many isomers of pentane exist, and name them.

9 Explain why 2-ethylpentane is an incorrect name for the alkane, and give the correct name.

10 What types of isomers exist for pent-3-en-2-ol? Include the name and structural formula of one example for each type.

11 What elements are present in the following functional groups?
 a amino
 b chloro
 c hydroxyl.

12 Use propan-1-ol and propan-2-ol to explain the difference between a primary and secondary alcohol.

13 Determine the systematic name of each of the following compounds.
 a $CH_3CHNH_2CH_2OH$
 b $CH_3CHOH(CH_2)_5CH_2Cl$
 c $CH_3CH_2CH_2CH_2CHNH_2CHICH_3$

14 What is the structural difference between an aldehyde, a ketone, a carboxylic acid and an amide?

15 Why are carboxyl and primary amide groups only found at the end of a carbon chain?

16 State the IUPAC name of each of the following molecules.

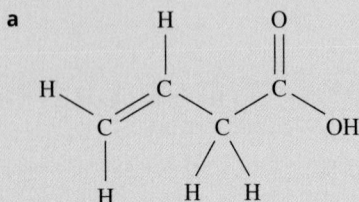

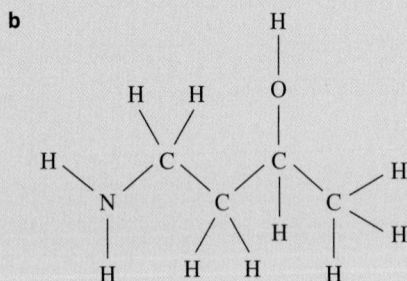

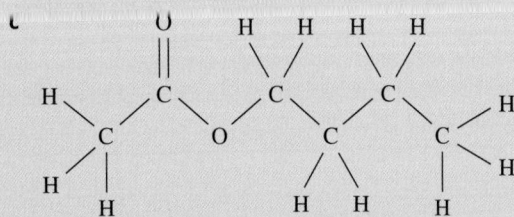

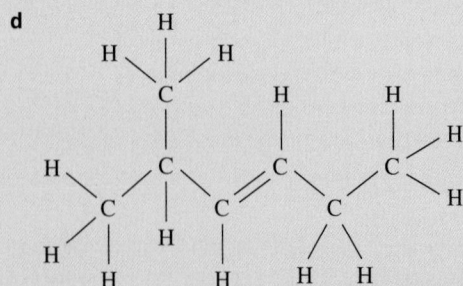

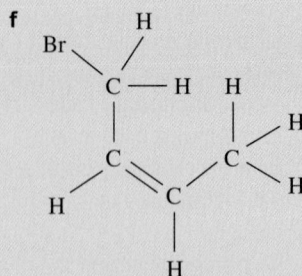

 a

 b

 c

 d

 e

 f

17 Draw the structure of:
 a heptyl propanoate
 b 4-iodo-3-methylpent-2-ene
 c oct-4-enoic acid
 d 3-methylbutan-1-amine
 e 3-hydroxy-2-methylbutanamide.

18 Write the condensed structural formulae of:
 a oct-3-ene
 b methyl hexanoate
 c 3-fluoropropan-1-ol
 d 4-hydroxybutanoic acid
 e 2,3-dimethylpentan-1-amine.

19 Convert the following structures to condensed structural formulae.

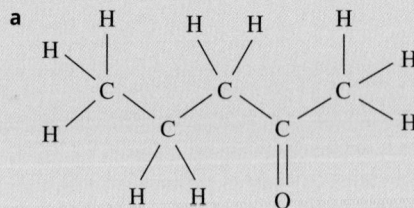

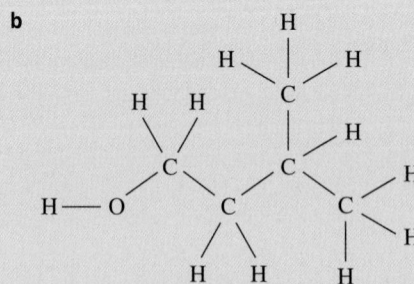

 a

 b

c

(structural formula with atoms: H, H, C, C, N, H, H, C, C, O, H)

d

(structural formula: H, H, C, C, Cl, H, C, C≡C, H, H, H)

e

(structural formula: H, H, C, C, O, C, H, C, H, H, H, O, H, H)

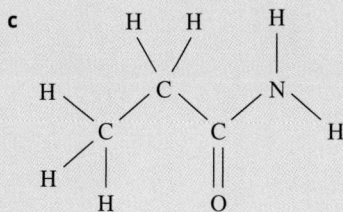

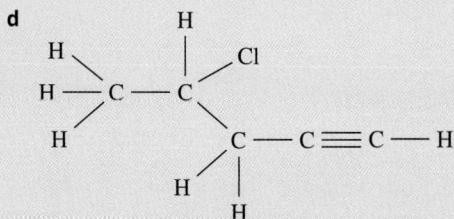

20 Determine the correct names of the organic compounds based on the following incorrect names:
a but-4-ene
b 2-hydroxyethan-1-amine
c 4-chlorohex-5-yne
d 2-chloro-3-ethylbutane
e 2,2-dimethylpent-4-ene
f 1-bromo-1,1-dipropylmethane.

21 The condensed structural formulae of some organic compounds are given below. For each compound, identify the homologous series to which it belongs and state its systematic name.
a $CH_3(CH_2)_5CH_2OH$
b $CH_3(CH_2)_2CHCl(CH_2)_2CH_3$
c $CH_3CHOH(CH_2)_3CH_3$
d $CH_3(CH_2)_3COOH$
e $CH_3CH_2CHNH_2CH_3$
f $(CH_3)_2CH(CH_2)_5CH_3$
g $(CH_3)_2C=CH_2$
h CH_3COCH_3
i CH_3CH_2CHO
j $CH_3(CH_2)_3CONH_2$

22 For each of the substances whose molecular formulae are given below, draw a structural formula of a molecule with this formula, and name the molecule you have drawn.
a $C_5H_{11}Cl$
b C_4H_8O
c $C_3H_6O_2$
d $C_4H_8O_2$
e $C_5H_{13}N$
f C_3H_7NO

23 Reflect on the Inquiry task on page 252. Return to your models and name them using the correct nomenclature.

10 Properties of hydrocarbons and haloalkanes

Life on Earth is often said to be carbon-based. This is because the structures of living things on Earth are based mainly on organic compounds. The growth and decay of living things involve a series of reactions in which these organic compounds are made, decomposed or changed from one form into another. There are many millions of different organic compounds.

By the end of this chapter, you will be able to describe some of the physical properties of the simplest organic compounds, namely alkanes, alkenes, alkynes and haloalkanes. Physical properties include boiling point, melting point and solubility in water and other solvents. You will see that members of different homologous groups of hydrocarbons exhibit quite similar chemical behaviours, and there are recognisable patterns. You will also gain an appreciation of the important relationship between organic compounds and humans. Specifically, you will see that our relationship to our environment and our health is closely tied to our use of organic compounds.

Content

INQUIRY QUESTION

How can hydrocarbons be classified based on their structure and reactivity?

By the end of this chapter, you will be able to:

- construct models, identify the functional group, and write structural and molecular formulae for homologous series of organic chemical compounds, up to C8 (ACSCH035) **ICT**
  - alkanes
  - alkenes
  - alkynes
- conduct an investigation to compare the properties of organic chemical compounds within a homologous series, and explain these differences in terms of bonding (ACSCH035)
- explain the properties within and between the homologous series of alkanes with reference to the intermolecular and intramolecular bonding present **ICT**
- describe the procedures required to safely handle and dispose of organic substances (ACSCH075) **ICT**
- examine the environmental, economic and sociocultural implications of obtaining and using hydrocarbons from the Earth

10.1 Boiling points, melting points and solubilities of organic compounds

What happens when oil mixes with water?

COLLECT THIS...

- vegetable oil
- water
- camera
- funnel
- empty soft drink bottle

DO THIS...

1 Using the funnel, pour the oil into the soft drink bottle to a height of about 1 cm.
2 Predict what will happen when you add water to the bottle.
3 Add water to the bottle until it is one-third full.
4 Leave the bottle to stand on a bench.
5 Record your observations.
6 Screw the cap firmly onto the bottle and shake the bottle vigorously for 30 seconds.
7 Place the bottle on the bench for 5 minutes.
8 Film or record your observations after step 7.

RECORD THIS...

Draw a table to record your results.

Description of experiment	Prediction	Observations
Mixing oil and water in bottle before shaking.		
Shaking oil and water mixture in bottle: initially.		
Shaking oil and water mixture in bottle: after 5 minutes.		

REFLECT ON THIS...

Explain the meaning of your observations.

What could you do next time to improve your experiment?

FIGURE 10.1.1 Propane gas is the fuel used in most Australian barbecues.

The physical properties of hydrocarbons are determined largely by the intermolecular forces and the size and shape of the molecules. These properties follow patterns that can be mapped neatly to the number of carbon atoms in the molecules. (You can see the CH_4 structure of methane in the chapter opener image.) Generally, hydrocarbons have low boiling and melting points. For example, the low boiling point of propane makes it a safe and useful fuel for barbecues (Figure 10.1.1).

At room temperature alkanes are either colourless gases (methane to butane) or colourless liquids (pentane to heptadecane). Hydrocarbon chains with more than 18 carbon atoms are colourless solids at room temperature, and have a wax-like consistency.

In this section you will discover patterns in the physical properties of the hydrocarbons and haloalkanes. You will see that the properties of haloalkanes are similar to hydrocarbons but differ because they contain polar bonds.

PHYSICAL PROPERTIES OF ALKANES, ALKENES, ALKYNES AND HALOALKANES

Boiling points of alkanes

Table 10.1.1 lists the boiling points of the first six alkanes from methane to hexane. The boiling points increase as the size of the alkane molecule increases.

Because alkane molecules are non-polar, the only intermolecular forces of attraction between them are weak **dispersion forces**. As the length of the carbon chain increases, the overall forces of attraction between molecules also increase (Figure 10.1.2).

The strength of dispersion forces between molecules increases because of the increased strength of temporary dipoles within the molecules. Because the boiling point of a molecular substance is determined by the strength of the intermolecular forces, boiling point increases as alkane chain length increases.

TABLE 10.1.1 Boiling points of the first six alkanes

Alkane	Molecular formula	Boiling point (°C)
methane	CH_4	−162
ethane	C_2H_6	−89
propane	C_3H_8	−45
butane	C_4H_{10}	−0.5
pentane	C_5H_{12}	36
hexane	C_6H_{14}	69

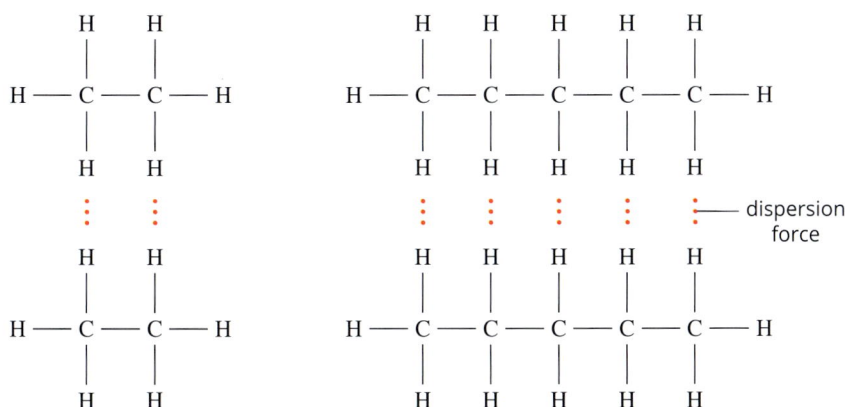

FIGURE 10.1.2 Dispersion forces are the strongest forces between alkane molecules. As molecules become longer, the dispersion forces become stronger.

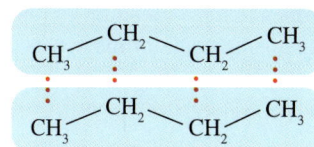

butane
• less compact molecule
• molecules are closer
• boiling point −0.5°C

methylpropane
• more compact molecule
• molecules are further apart
• boiling point −11.7°C

FIGURE 10.1.3 Molecular shape affects boiling point. Dispersion forces between butane molecules are stronger than those between 2-methylpropane molecules because butane molecules are less compact and can come closer together.

Molecular shape also influences the strength of dispersion forces and, therefore, boiling points. Straight-chain alkanes are able to fit together more closely and tend to have higher boiling points than their corresponding branched-chain **isomers**, which are unable to come as closely together in the bulk substance.

Figure 10.1.3 shows how the shapes of butane and its branched isomer 2-methylpropane (also known as isobutane) influence the strength of the dispersion forces between the molecules. Butane ($CH_3CH_2CH_2CH_3$) boils at −0.5°C, whereas 2-methylpropane ((CH_3)$_3CH$) boils at −11.7°C. Although both molecules have the same molecular formula of C_4H_{10}, molecules of $CH_3CH_2CH_2CH_3$ have a greater surface area and can fit more closely together, allowing more contact between the molecules and forming stronger dispersion forces.

ⓘ The strength of dispersion forces between molecules depends on the size and shape of the molecules.

Boiling points of alkenes, alkynes and haloalkanes

> The addition of polar functional groups to a hydrocarbon increases the boiling point for molecules of a similar size when compared to purely non-polar families.

Alkenes and alkynes, like alkanes, are non-polar hydrocarbons. Their molecules are also non-polar, so the forces of attraction between them are only weak dispersion forces. Members of these homologous series have relatively low boiling points similar to those observed for the alkanes with the same number of carbon atoms (Table 10.1.2).

As with alkanes, the boiling points of alkenes and alkynes increase with molecular size as the strength of dispersion forces between molecules increases.

TABLE 10.1.2 Boiling points of molecules containing four carbons in different functional groups

Compound	Boiling point (°C)
butane (C_4H_{10})	−0.5
but-1-ene (C_4H_8)	−6.3
but-1-yne (C_4H_6)	−8.1
1-chlorobutane (C_4H_9Cl)	78

Haloalkanes contain bonds that are quite polar. For example, chloromethane is a member of the haloalkane homologous series and contains a polar carbon–chlorine bond, as shown in Figure 10.1.4. Like all alkanes, chloromethane has weak dispersion forces between molecules. However, the presence of the carbon–chlorine dipole allows **dipole–dipole attractions** to also occur. Because dipole–dipole attractions are stronger than dispersion forces, the boiling points of haloalkanes are generally higher than those of hydrocarbons with a similar number of carbon atoms, as seen in Table 10.1.2.

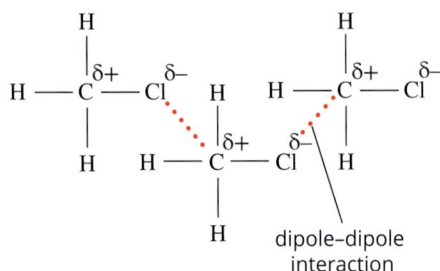

FIGURE 10.1.4 The carbon–chlorine bond in chloromethane is polar because the chlorine atom is more electronegative than the carbon atom. The presence of this permanent dipole produces dipole–dipole attractions between chloromethane molecules.

Melting points of alkanes

Melting points are affected by the same factors as boiling points, namely strength of dispersion forces and the size and shape of the molecule.

Melting points of hydrocarbons follow the same general pattern as boiling points, with a few exceptions. Melting points of straight-chain hydrocarbons increase as the number of carbon atoms increase. However, there are deviations in this trend, relating to whether the molecules have an even or odd number of carbon atoms. Chains with even numbers of carbon atoms pack slightly more efficiently in the solid state than chains with odd numbers. The more efficient packing requires more energy to melt the compound. This makes the graph of melting point versus carbon chain length have more of a step-like curve than the graph for boiling point versus carbon chain length (Figure 10.1.5).

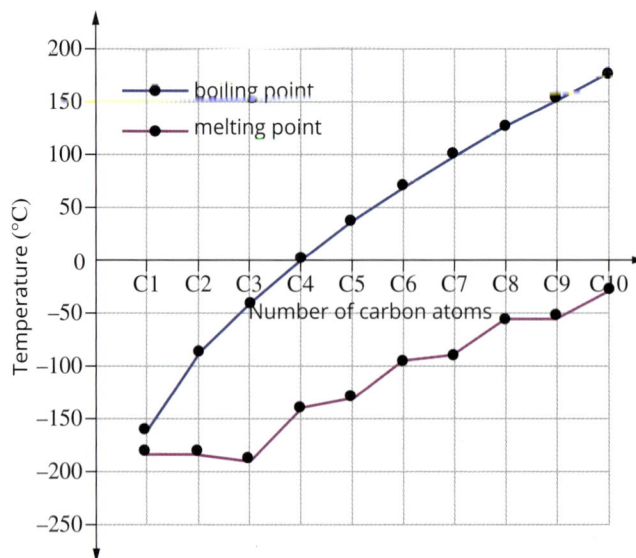

FIGURE 10.1.5 Boiling and melting points for alkanes from C1 to C10

Melting points of alkenes, alkynes and haloalkanes

The melting points of alkenes, alkynes and haloalkanes follow a similar pattern to that of alkanes. That is, as the length of the carbon chain increases, the melting point increases. The alkenes ethene, propene and butene are all gases at room temperature, alkenes with five to fourteen carbons are liquids, and longer-chained molecules are solid.

Alkynes follow the same general trend for melting points seen in alkanes and alkenes; that is, the melting point increases with carbon chain length. As with alkenes, this trend can be understood in terms of strength of dispersion forces and the shape of the molecule. The position of the triple bond can greatly affect melting points as the shape of the molecule changes. For example the melting points of the structural isomers but-1-yne and but-2-yne are −122°C and −24°C respectively, a difference of nearly 100°C.

Haloalkanes have higher melting points than the corresponding hydrocarbons. Again, this can be explained in terms of stronger dipole-dipole forces between haloalkane molecules. These intermolecular forces are caused by the presence of polar halogen-carbon bonds, which make the molecules more polar.

Solubility in water

The non-polar nature of alkanes, alkenes and alkynes makes them insoluble in water. You will recall from Year 11 chemistry that water molecules are polar and held together by strong **hydrogen bonds** (Figure 10.1.6). The weak dispersion forces between water molecules and hydrocarbon molecules are not strong enough to overcome the strong attraction between water molecules so the two substances remain separate and do not mix.

For example, when hexane is added to water it forms a layer on top of the water, because hexane is less dense than water and the two liquids cannot dissolve in each other. Liquids that do not mix are said to be **immiscible**.

As a result of the polar halogen–carbon bond in haloalkanes, haloalkanes are slightly more soluble than hydrocarbons in water. However, the solubility is still very low because the overall influence of the dipole–dipole interaction is small. The influence of the **halogen** decreases as the length of the carbon chain increases. Many haloalkanes are denser than water, so unlike hydrocarbons they settle to form a layer on the bottom when added to water.

Crude oil is a mixture of many different compounds. Most of these compounds are hydrocarbons of varying lengths. While there are some alkenes in crude oil, many of the hydrocarbons are alkanes. Because alkanes are generally less dense than water, when crude oil spills occur at sea the oil floats on the surface, forming a thick, insoluble layer. As the oil layer is moved by the waves of the sea, the oil can spread over many hundreds of square kilometres. This oil layer can have disastrous consequences for marine and bird life. Oil that reaches the shore, like the oil spill shown in Figure 10.1.7, has drastic effects on beaches and wildlife.

GO TO ➤ Year 11 Chapter 5

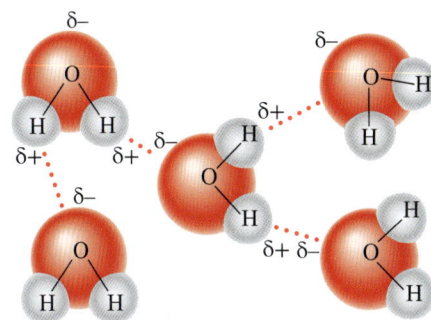

FIGURE 10.1.6 Water molecules are held to each other by strong hydrogen bonds.

FIGURE 10.1.7 Oil spills at sea can contaminate shorelines and are very difficult to clean because the oil is not soluble in water. Other non-polar solvents or physical methods are required to disperse or remove the oil.

Solubility in organic solvents

Alkanes mix with other non-polar liquids such as those that contain alkenes or symmetrical haloalkanes. This is because the forces of attraction between molecules of these liquids are also weak dispersion forces and are similar in strength to the alkane–alkane forces of attraction. Therefore, these liquids are **miscible**; that is, they are soluble in each other.

Many commercial cleaning agents contain non-polar liquids that are useful for removing oil stains. White spirit is a mixture of alkanes and other hydrocarbons obtained by the refining of crude oil. It is a useful cleaning agent because it can dissolve other non-polar liquids, such as oils and greases. It is used as a solvent in aerosols and in the home as a degreasing solvent. White spirit is also used for cleaning paintbrushes and as a general cleaning agent (Figure 10.1.8).

FIGURE 10.1.8 White spirit contains a mixture of alkanes. It is a useful solvent for other non-polar liquids.

A non-polar haloalkene

Tetrachlorethene is a solvent commonly used by commercial dry cleaners in Australia. It is also known as perchloroethene or 'perc'. This compound is a haloalkene, as seen by the structure shown in Figure 10.1.9. The molecule contains polar carbon–chlorine bonds, but the molecule is symmetrical, so the dipoles cancel each other. This makes the overall molecule non-polar. The non-polar liquid can dissolve oil and grease from fabrics without the use of water or detergents. An advantage that tetrachloroethene has over hydrocarbon solvents is that it is also non-flammable.

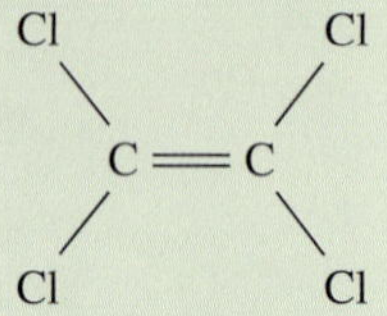

FIGURE 10.1.9 Tetrachlorethene is symmetrical and therefore non-polar. It is commonly used as a solvent in the dry-cleaning industry.

10.1 Review

SUMMARY

- The boiling points of organic molecules are determined by intermolecular forces. Dispersion forces are always present and there may also be dipole–dipole attractions or hydrogen bonds.
- The strength of dispersion forces between alkane molecules depends on the size and shape of the molecules.
- The only forces of attraction between molecules of the alkane, alkene and alkyne homologous series are dispersion forces. Molecules of haloalkanes are attracted to each other by dipole–dipole attractions, as well as by dispersion forces.

- The solubility of organic molecules in water is determined by the way the molecules of the organic compound interact with the molecules of water. This is affected by the polarity of functional groups and the length of the non-polar hydrocarbon chains of the organic molecules.
- Alkanes, alkenes and alkynes are insoluble in water, and haloalkanes are only slightly soluble in water.
- Alkanes, alkenes and alkynes are soluble in non-polar organic solvents.

KEY QUESTIONS

1 Complete the following paragraph by filling in the gaps with the appropriate words.
   Butane is a member of the _____ homologous series. The forces of attraction holding butane molecules to each other are _____. As the chain length of alkanes increases, the boiling point _____. Alkanes are _____ in water. This is because the forces of attraction between water molecules and alkane molecules are _____ than the _____ between water molecules.

2 Arrange the following compounds in increasing order of boiling point. Provide reasons for your answer.
   $CH_3CH_2CH_2CH_3$ $CH_3CH(CH_3)CH_3$
   $CH_3CH_2CH_2CH_2CH_2CH_2CH_2CH_3$
   $CH_3CH_2CH_2CH_2CH_2CH(CH_3)CH_3$

3 Arrange the following compounds in increasing order of boiling point.
   $CH_3CH_2CH_2CH_3$ $CH_3CH_2CH_2CH_2Cl$ $CHCH$
   CH_3CHCH_2

4 Identify each of the following pairs of compounds as either miscible or immiscible:
   a hexane and hex-2-yne
   b pentane and pent-1-ene
   c pent-1-yne and water
   d 3-bromobutane and 3-chloropentane.

10.2 Impacts of uses of organic substances

Organic substances are everywhere. They are in every cell of our bodies and are found throughout nature. Most of our food and many of our medicines are organic substances. Most of the energy used by modern societies comes from the combustion of organic substances. Humans have been using organic substances over their entire history, and over the past 150 years have become very good at manipulating natural organic substances through reaction pathways to make products for specific needs.

This section looks briefly at the need for organic substances in modern societies, specifically the use of hydrocarbons as fuels, and also questions the implications of that need. It also looks at ways to safely dispose of organic substances.

THE NEED FOR ORGANIC SUBSTANCES

Organic substances are no longer derived solely from nature. Chemists have become highly sophisticated in their ability to synthesise organic compounds. This has led to a great many new compounds such as flavourings, colourings, polymers, dyes, medicines, pesticides and plastics. Often laboratory-synthesised compounds are based on natural products or created to fit to known chemical receptors in organisms. Our modern life has been shaped by the synthesis of compounds such as Salvarsan (arsphenamine), which was synthesised in 1910 as a remedy for syphilis, and cyclosporine, which was isolated from fungi in the late 1970s and used as a powerful immunosuppressant, especially in transplant surgery.

As you will see in Chapter 11, alkenes are the starting materials for many plastics, a class of chemicals that have drastically transformed our world and are used in millions of products, including furniture, clothing, packaging, household appliances and cars (Figure 10.2.2).

FIGURE 10.2.2 Examples of items containing organic substances

CHEMFILE L IU

Origins of organic chemistry

Until the 1700s, chemistry (or alchemy as it was known then) was a single field of knowledge, concerned with all compounds. Alchemists attempted to change matter into a different type of matter, famously including attempts to turn cheap metals into gold. As they explored the nature of matter, alchemists started to notice unexplainable differences between compounds derived from living sources and those derived from minerals.

Compounds from plants and animals were generally difficult to isolate and purify. They were also found to be unstable and to decompose readily. This was the beginning of the differentiation between organic and inorganic chemistry. The term 'organic chemistry' was introduced by the chemist Jöns Jacob Berzelius, who believed that a wide range of carbon compounds only occurred in living systems. This terminology was a move away from the more medieval 'alchemy' to the more modern and scientific 'chemistry'.

FIGURE 10.2.1 Swedish chemist Jöns Jacob Berzelius, who coined the phrase 'organic chemistry' in 1806

The importance of basic organic chemistry to drug development

Pharmaceuticals are usually developed to fit a biological target and are themselves based on biologically active molecules. A great majority of medicinal chemists (those who make pharmaceuticals) originally trained as organic chemists, and started their training with a course similar to the one covered in this textbook. The analytical and problem-solving skills inherent to organic chemistry are central to drug development. Building organic molecules is like piecing together a puzzle, working out what fits where, but with the added complication that it must be done in a specific order. The skill and ingenuity of organic chemists allows them to find reaction pathways to synthesise organic substances that can be used as pharmaceuticals.

Some recent examples of compounds that highlight the contribution of organic chemists to extending and saving the lives of patients are ledipasvir, imatinib (Figure 10.2.3), azidothymidine and linezolid, which are used for treating hepatitis C, leukaemia, HIV/AIDS and bacterial infections, respectively. Each molecule was first synthesised on a very small scale in a laboratory before having the process scaled up to a safe, reliable and cost-effective level by process chemists.

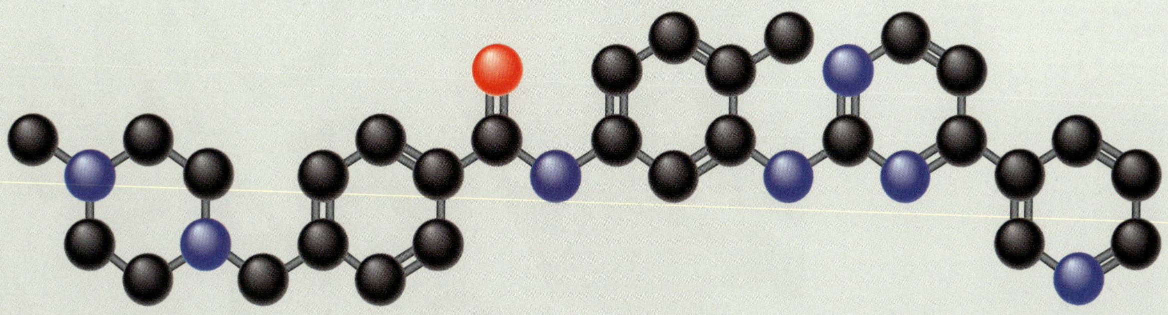

FIGURE 10.2.3 A model of imatinib, a drug first synthesised by organic chemists and used since 2001 for leukaemia chemotherapy. It is considered to be a modern 'miracle drug' because after therapy with the drug almost 80% of patients are still alive at 10 years after treatment.

ENVIRONMENTAL, ECONOMIC AND SOCIOCULTURAL IMPLICATIONS OF OBTAINING AND USING HYDROCARBONS

The most significant reaction that hydrocarbons, especially alkanes, undergo is **combustion**. Humans have been burning hydrocarbon fuels since the means of making fire was discovered hundreds of thousands of years ago. The first fuel sources to be exploited were the most abundant and accessible ones: wood, and later peat. These were burnt for cooking, baking, smelting and warmth. Having the ability to cook food and produce heat meant that humans were able to expand their food sources and migrate to colder regions of the world. Burning fuels also provided the energy for making new materials.

During the Industrial Revolution, coal (a hydrocarbon fuel) began to replace wood as the main source of energy in Europe and North America. Oil and coal gas were later added to the mix of fuels, and in the 1960s natural gas began to replace coal gas. Coal, oil and natural gas are preferred over wood and peat because they have a higher energy density than wood. This is a result of geological actions on these fuels as they were formed over millions of years. These hydrocarbons are called **fossil fuels** because they were made from the fossilised remains of plants and animals.

The past 250 years have seen the use of hydrocarbons for fuel increase nearly 800-fold. Much of this increase happened during the 20th century. Having access to energy-dense fuels has had enormous consequences for human development in the economic, social and environmental spheres.

FIGURE 10.2.4 A pile of coal. In the 19th century Australia was one of the wealthiest per capita regions of the world because of its rich supply of mineral resources, including coal.

The positive economic development realised by humans in the last few centuries has also led to positive social consequences. However, in the past few decades there has been an increasing realisation that there are negative social consequences and very negative environmental consequences. Smog, acid rain, the destruction of natural ecosystems and climate change are all due to the increased burning of hydrocarbons.

Over the past couple of decades, countries have worked independently and collectively to try to combat these environmental consequences. It is interesting that one of the strategies to reduce hydrocarbon burning is to use the ancient technologies of wind and water power. Other strategies include harnessing the Sun's energy using photovoltaic (solar) panels to make electricity and, on the personal level, by simply using less electricity.

FIGURE 10.2.5 In the first decades of the 21st century, many Australians have increasingly begun to believe that this country should use less coal and more renewable energy sources. Large protests have been organised to promote this message.

SAFE HANDLING AND DISPOSAL OF ORGANIC SUBSTANCES

As this section has shown, organic substances are integral to the lives of humans. However, some organic substances can be harmful to living things, including humans. Many hydrocarbons are flammable and need to be handled with special care. This is why they need to be safely handled and disposed of when working in the laboratory. The appropriate methods for handling and disposing of a chemical are indicated on its Safety Data Sheet. New South Wales has adopted the Globally Harmonized System of Classification and Labelling of Chemicals, and these international standards must be incorporated in all labels for chemicals produced after 1 January 2017. In your practical sessions your teacher or laboratory technician will tell you how to dispose of the chemicals you use. Most laboratories will collect and dispose of organic substances separately from other chemicals.

PA 7.1   PA 7.1

The role of a school laboratory technician

Many schools in NSW employ a laboratory technician whose job is to support the science teachers in running safe experiments and practical exercises (Figure 10.2.6). The laboratory technician may be a science teacher or someone who has a science degree. It is their job to make sure that the school follows the appropriate standards for the safe storage and handling of chemicals. To complete their work, laboratory technicians use many online resources. There are some subscription-based websites such as RiskAssess and Chemwatch that provide up-to-date news on safety, Safety Data Sheets, experimental methods, computer-generated risk assessment for experiments and labels for bottles of chemicals. The Australian Science Teachers Association hosts a website called Science ASSIST for science teachers and technicians. Some of the resources on this site can be accessed by students too.

Laboratory technicians are generally given specific training in how to do their jobs because there is so much to know about the standards. They also have their own associations in Australia, including the Association of Science Education Technicians NSW. The association provides a forum for technicians to share ideas and gain information. If you need help with an experiment, your school's laboratory technician could be a rich source of knowledge.

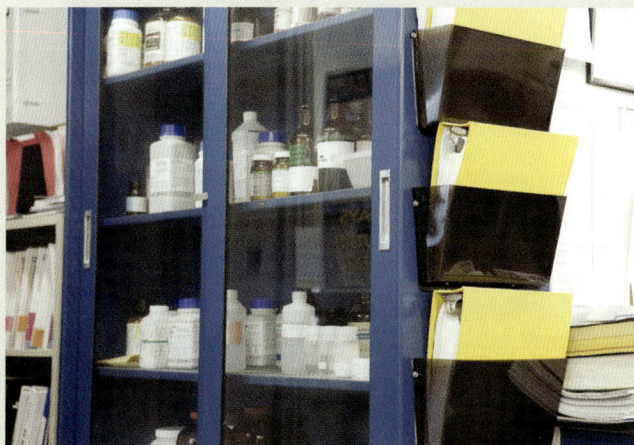

FIGURE 10.2.6 A chemical store cabinet, with the relevant Safety Data Sheets in yellow binders. These sheets tell you how to handle and dispose of the chemicals you use at school.

10.2 Review

SUMMARY

- Organic substances are everywhere in our world.
- Humans have become very good at manipulating organic substances to make new products such as plastics and pharmaceuticals.
- In the last 200 years hydrocarbons derived from fossil fuels have been the predominant source of energy.
- Burning fossils fuels has had both positive and negative economic, social and environmental effects.
- Organic substances need to be disposed of with care because they can harm organisms and environments.

KEY QUESTIONS

1 Name the three main fossil fuels used today.
2 Why are organic chemists required in the pharmaceutical industry?
3 When working in the laboratory, where would you find information about disposing of organic substances?
4 With respect to chemical safety, what system did New South Wales adopt at the beginning of 2017?

Chapter review

KEY TERMS

combustion
dipole–dipole attraction
dispersion force
fossil fuel

haloalkane
halogen
hydrogen bond
immiscible

isomer
miscible

REVIEW QUESTIONS

1   Describe the intermolecular forces that exist between the molecules in liquid and solid alkanes.

2   Complete the following table of the properties of hydrocarbons.

Property	Hydrocarbon
intramolecular bond type	
intermolecular bond type	
melting point, high or low?	
boiling point, high or low?	
solubility in water	
solubility in organic solvents	

3   Complete this table about alkanes.

Name	Formula	Condensed structural formula	Physical state at room temperature
methane	CH_4		gas
ethane		CH_3CH_3	gas
propane	C_3H_8		
butane			gas
pentane		$CH_3CH_2CH_2CH_2CH_3$	liquid
hexane	C_6H_{14}		

4   The parent hydrocarbon of an organic molecule is the basic hydrocarbon with the same backbone of carbon atoms, but without any substitutions of hydrogen atoms. For example, hexane (C_6H_{14}) is the parent hydrocarbon of 1-iodohexane ($C_6H_{13}I$). Why are the boiling points of haloalkanes higher than those of the parent hydrocarbon of comparable molecular mass?

5   The following table gives the relative molecular masses and boiling points of 2-methylpropane, butane, methyl methanoate and propan-1-ol. Explain why the boiling points differ even though the compounds have similar molar masses.

Compound	Molar mass ($g\,mol^{-1}$)	Boiling point (°C)
2-methylpropane	58	−11.17
butane	58	−0.5
methyl methanoate	60	32.0
propan-1-ol	60	97.0

6   Explain why, when comparing the effect of functional groups on the boiling points of different homologous series, it is important to compare molecules with a similar molar mass.

7   Consider the following compounds:
$CH_3CH(CH_3)CH(CH_3)CH_2CH_3$
$CH_3(CH_2)_5CH_3$
$CH_3CH(CH_3)CH_2CH_2CH_2CH_3$

a   Place the compounds in order of increasing boiling point.

b   Would the compounds be more soluble in water or in octane? Explain your answer.

8   Describe the different types of bonding that would be found in a sample of liquid octane.

9   Explain why hydrocarbons are generally insoluble in water.

10 Consider the following compounds:
CH_3Cl
CH_3CH_2Cl
$CH_3CH_2CH_2Cl$
Which would you expect to be the most soluble in water? Explain your answer.

11 What are some of the negative environmental effects caused by the combustion of fossil fuels?

12 Describe what will happen when oct-1-ene is added to the following substances:

a   water

b   7-methyloct-1-yne.

13 Why does burning coal, oil or natural gas produce more energy than burning wood?

14 How do laboratory technicians use the internet in their work?

15 Refer to the figure below. This is a page from the Science Assist Chemical Management Handbook. Use the information on this page to determine:
   a the physical description of hexane
   b how to dispose of a small quantity of hexane
   c what the first aid treatment is for inhalation of hexane.

Science ASSIST
Chemical
Summary

hexane
n-hexane
DANGER

Formula C_6H_{14}
CAS No.   110-54-3
User Group 11-12

DESCRIPTION
Clear, colourless, volatile liquid with a petrol-like odour. Less dense than water.

SOLUBILITY
Practically insoluble in water. Soluble in ethanol, diethyl ether and petroleum ether. Immiscible with methanol.

Solubility in water 10 mg/L (20°C)

PHYSICAL DATA

Molar mass	86.18
Melting point	-95°C
Boiling point	69°C
Specific gravity	0.66 (20°C)
Flammability	Highly flammable

REGULATORY INFORMATION

ADG Class	3
Packing Group	II
UN Number	1208
Poisons Schedule	S5
Security	-

HAZARD STATEMENTS
H225 Highly flammable liquid and vapour
H315 Causes skin irritation
H361 Suspected of damaging fertility or the unborn child
H336 May cause drowsiness or dizziness
H373 May cause damage to organs through prolonged or repeated exposure
H304 May be fatal if swallowed and enters airways
H411 Toxic to aquatic life with long lasting effects

SAFE HANDLING
Maintain safe laboratory work practices. Wash hands before breaks and at the end of work.
Wear PPE: safety glasses, closed shoes, lab coat, gloves (nitrile). Exposure may cause irritation to the skin, eyes and respiratory tract. Ingestion or inhalation may cause CNS depression, headache, drowsiness and dizziness. Repeated skin contact may have a degreasing effect. There is a risk of aspiration into the lungs if ingested.
Handle only in an operating fume cupboard or well-ventilated area. Avoid inhaling vapour or mist. Avoid contact with skin, eyes and clothing. Avoid prolonged or repeated exposure. Handle away from heat and other sources of ignition.
There is potential for the vapour to collect in low-lying, confined areas. The vapour can form explosive mixtures with air and can travel to an ignition source and flash back.

STORAGE
Store in a tightly closed container in a cool, dry, well-ventilated place away from heat and light. Ensure container is kept upright to prevent leakage. Store away from heat and any sources of ignition.
Store away from oxidising agents and halogens.
Store with flammable liquids in an AS compliant cabinet.

APPLICATIONS
Senior chemistry: comparing properties of saturated and unsaturated hydrocarbons; solvent for extracting halogens from aqueous solution, in thin-layer chromatography, in the preparation of nylon; a component of synthetic 'crude oil'.

SPILLS
Wear PPE. Remove all sources of ignition. Ensure good ventilation.
Small spill: Absorb with paper towel. Place paper towel in an operating fume cupboard and allow the solvent to evaporate. Dispose of paper towel as general waste.
Large spill: Cover spill with non-combustible absorbent material such as vermiculite, bentonite (clay cat litter) and/or sand and scoop up with a non-sparking tool. Place material into a suitable labelled container and store for collection.
Ventilate spill area and allow the solvent to evaporate. Wash any contaminated clothing before reuse.

WASTE DISPOSAL
Hexane is toxic for aquatic life. Avoid release to the environment. Do not dispose of down the sink.
Small quantity: Place in a shallow vessel in an operating fume cupboard and allow the solvent to evaporate.
Large quantity: Store in a suitable labelled container such as for non-halogenated organic liquid waste and arrange for collection by a licenced waste disposal contractor.
The bottle may be hazardous when empty due to residual vapour or liquid. Do not expose the empty bottle to heat, open flames or other sources of ignition.

FIRST AID
IF IN EYES: Rinse cautiously with water for several minutes. Remove contact lenses, if present and easy to do. Continue rinsing. If eye irritation persists: Get medical advice/attention.
IF SWALLOWED: Rinse mouth. Do NOT induce vomiting. Immediately call a POISONS CENTRE or doctor.
IF ON SKIN: Remove immediately all contaminated clothing and wash before reuse. Wash skin with plenty of soap and water. If skin irritation occurs: Get medical advice/attention.
IF INHALED: Move patient to fresh air and keep at rest in a position comfortable for breathing. Get medical advice/attention if you feel unwell.

POISONS CENTRE: 13 11 26

DISCLAIMER This chemical summary is not a safety data sheet (SDS). It is intended to provide generic information for this chemical. The manufacturer's SDS should be consulted for information specific to the chemical used.

VERSION
8 Dec 2016

---

16 Reflect on the Inquiry activity on page 296. What group of substances did the vegetable oil represent, and why was vegetable oil chosen?

11 Products of reactions involving hydrocarbons

Hydrocarbons are molecules that contain only carbon and hydrogen. They are the simplest class of organic compounds. Organic compounds that contain other elements are considered to be derivatives of hydrocarbons.

These simple molecules are vitally important to humans. Throughout history they have provided warmth and cooking fuel through the burning of charcoal or wood. The industrial production of many chemicals also involves organic reactions starting with hydrocarbons. These include the manufacture of paints, plastics, pharmaceuticals and even some foods.

By the end of this chapter, you will be able to describe some specific chemical reactions involving alkanes and alkenes, including combustion, hydrogenation, substitution, addition and hydration reactions.

You will learn that the functional groups of compounds are usually involved in chemical reactions and, as a result, members of a homologous series usually undergo similar reactions because they have the same functional group.

Content

INQUIRY QUESTION

What are the products of reactions of hydrocarbons and how do they react?

By the end of this chapter, you will be able to:

- investigate, write equations and construct models to represent the reactions of unsaturated hydrocarbons when added to a range of chemicals, including but not limited to:
  - hydrogen (H_2)
  - halogens (X_2)
  - hydrogen halides (HX)
  - water (H_2O) (ACSCH136) ICT
- investigate, write equations and construct models to represent the reactions of saturated hydrocarbons when substituted with halogens

11.1 Chemical properties of hydrocarbons

Do different fats and oils have different properties?

COLLECT THIS …

- margarine
- butter
- vegetable oil
- dairy blend (combination of margarine and butter)
- 4 slices of bread
- 4 knives or spatulas
- refrigerator

DO THIS …

1 Place the margarine, butter, oil and dairy blend in a refrigerator overnight.

2 Observe the appearance of the different fats and oil when you take them out of the refrigerator.

3 Predict what will happen when you try to spread the margarine onto a piece of bread.

4 While it is still cold, spread some margarine onto a slice of bread with a knife.

5 Repeat steps 2 and 3 for the butter, oil and dairy blend.

RECORD THIS …

Draw up the following tables to record your predictions and results.

Record your observations of the different fats and oils after refrigeration in Table 1.

Record your predictions and observations about spreading the different fats and oils onto bread in Table 2.

Describe what happened by recording your observations.

TABLE 1 Observations of the fats and oil after refrigeration

Fat or oil	Observation
margarine	
vegetable oil	
butter	
dairy blend	

TABLE 2 Predictions and observations about spreading the fats and oil on bread

Fat or oil	Prediction	Observation
margarine		
vegetable oil		
butter		
dairy blend		

REFLECT ON THIS …

Explain the meaning of your observations.

FIGURE 11.1.1 Vegetable oils are organic compounds that can be converted to margarine by reacting them with hydrogen gas.

The properties and reactions of an organic compound are determined largely by the functional groups in the compound. Compounds that have the same functional group are called a homologous series, and the members of that series typically undergo reactions of the same type.

For example, alkenes are a homologous series of compounds that contain a carbon–carbon double bond. Vegetable oils are liquids that contain molecules with one or more carbon–carbon double bonds. Vegetable oils react with hydrogen gas to form semisolid substances that have a consistency suitable for spreading on bread. These semisolid products (for example, margarine) are an alternative to **saturated** fats such as butter (Figure 11.1.1).

Chemists who are involved in the synthesis of organic compounds are often required to prepare complex molecules from simpler materials. These chemists must have a detailed knowledge of the reactions of functional groups in order to devise a way to produce the desired product.

In this section you will learn about some of the typical reactions that alkanes and alkenes undergo and the reaction conditions required.

REACTIONS OF ALKANES

Combustion of alkanes in air

Although alkanes are fairly stable compounds and undergo only a few chemical reactions, they do burn readily in air in an exothermic reaction. As discussed in Chapter 10, alkanes are very good fuels.

GO TO ➤ Section 10.1 page 296

Common fuels such as petrol, diesel and kerosene all contain mixtures of alkanes with other hydrocarbon molecules. The main component of natural gas is methane (CH_4), the simplest alkane.

Burning hydrocarbon fuels in excess oxygen results in complete combustion, producing carbon dioxide and water vapour. The equation for the complete combustion of methane in air is:

$$CH_4(g) + 2O_2(g) \rightarrow CO_2(g) + 2H_2O(g)$$

Octane is a major component of petrol. The reaction for the complete combustion of octane is:

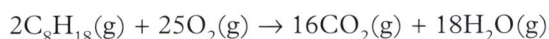

$$2C_8H_{18}(g) + 25O_2(g) \rightarrow 16CO_2(g) + 18H_2O(g)$$

CHEMFILE S

Burning ice

Large amounts of methane gas are stored around the world, trapped as solid methane hydrate. Methane hydrate looks very similar to ice, but there is one main difference: it can burn. The burning ice is a result of the methane gas being released from the crystal structure of the ice as it melts (Figure 11.1.2).

Large deposits of methane hydrate are trapped in the Arctic regions of the Earth and deep in the oceans, where low temperatures and high pressures trap methane. This methane is produced by the anaerobic decomposition of organic material by bacteria. The lattice structure of methane hydrate is shown in Figure 11.1.3.

FIGURE 11.1.3 The lattice structure of methane hydrate. Methane molecules are trapped inside the hexagonal structure.

FIGURE 11.1.2 The combustion of methane hydrate looks like burning ice. As the solid melts, methane gas is released, providing the fuel for the combustion reaction.

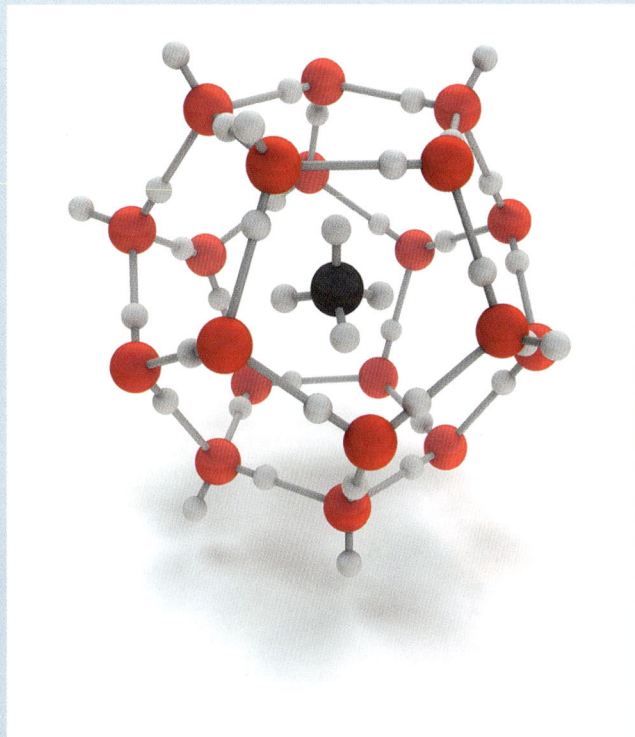

Oil companies have known of the existence of methane hydrate as far back as the 1930s. However, it is only now, with growing concerns over dwindling fossil fuel supplies and global warming, that countries are endeavouring to find a way to safely use these large fuel sources.

One fear is that rising temperatures will cause the deposits of methane hydrate to melt, releasing large amounts of methane into the oceans and atmosphere. Methane is a major contributor to the enhanced greenhouse effect, so a release of vast amounts of methane is likely to accelerate the effects of global climate change.

Substitution reactions of alkanes

A **substitution reaction** occurs when an atom or functional group in a molecule is replaced or 'substituted' by another atom or group.

Alkanes are saturated hydrocarbons and undergo substitution reactions with halogens, such as chlorine and bromine, to produce haloalkanes. At room temperature and in the dark, a reaction vessel containing a mixture of an alkane such as methane and chlorine gas will not react. In order for the substitution reaction to occur, the reaction must be initiated by ultraviolet (UV) light.

The reaction between methane and chlorine in the presence of UV light is given by the equation:

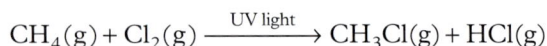

$$CH_4(g) + Cl_2(g) \xrightarrow{\text{UV light}} CH_3Cl(g) + HCl(g)$$

For each molecule of chlorine gas (Cl_2) that reacts, a hydrogen atom on the alkane is replaced by a chlorine atom.

Chloromethane (CH_3Cl) is called the substitution product of this reaction. As the reaction proceeds, the chloromethane product may continue to react with another chlorine molecule. If this occurs, the di-substituted product dichloromethane (CH_2Cl_2) is produced.

If enough chlorine is available, further reactions can result in all four hydrogen atoms of the original methane molecule being substituted by chlorine atoms (Figure 11.1.4). The different substituted products have different boiling points, so they can be separated from one another by fractional distillation.

> **ℹ** Substitution reactions of alkanes using excess chlorine gas can result in a mixture of chloroalkane products with varying levels of substitution.

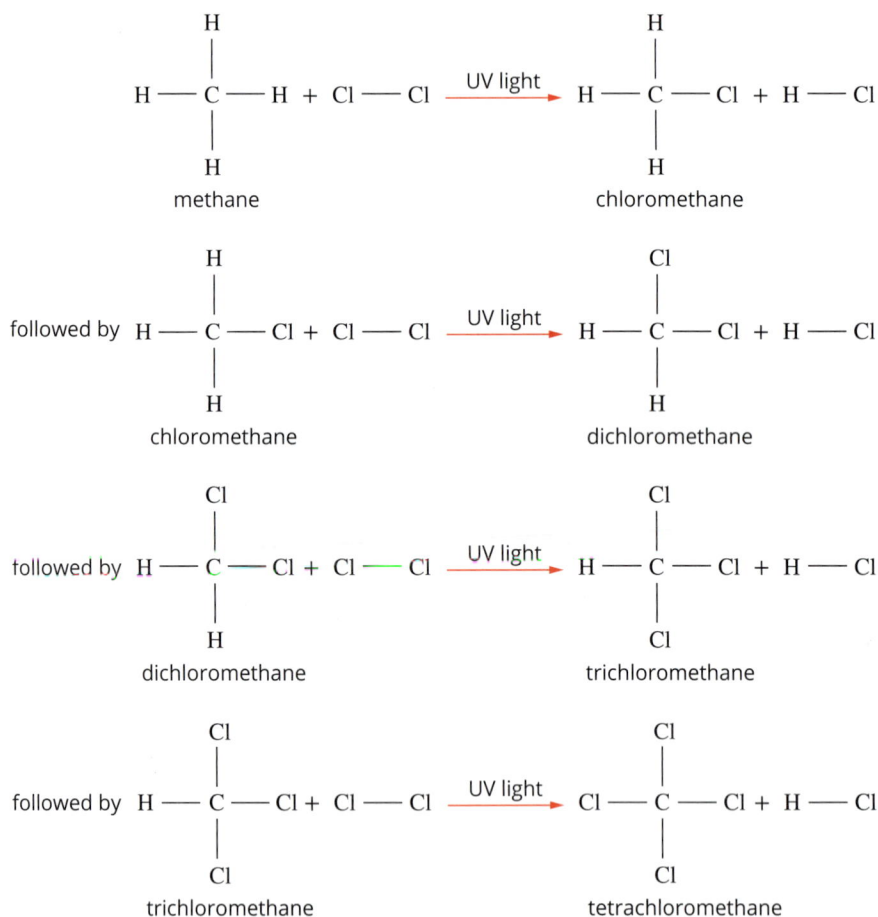

FIGURE 11.1.4 Substitution reactions between methane and chlorine

REACTIONS OF ALKENES

Alkenes are unsaturated, meaning that they contain a double carbon bond. The double bond makes alkenes more reactive than alkanes.

Combustion of alkenes in air

You have seen that alkanes are rather unreactive, but they are good fuels and burn in oxygen to produce carbon dioxide and water. Alkenes also burn in an excess of oxygen to produce carbon dioxide and water. The equation for the combustion of ethene is:

$$C_2H_4(g) + 3O_2(g) \rightarrow 2CO_2(g) + 2H_2O(g)$$

Addition reactions of alkenes

The double carbon–carbon covalent bond in alkenes has a significant effect on the chemical properties of its homologous series. Alkenes generally react more readily and with more chemicals than alkanes, which have only single carbon–carbon bonds. The reactions of alkenes usually involve the addition of a small molecule to the double bond of the alkene. These reactions are called **addition reactions**.

During addition reactions:

- two reactant molecules combine to form one product molecule
- the carbon–carbon double bond becomes a single bond
- an unsaturated compound becomes saturated
- the atoms of the small molecule adding to the alkene are 'added across the double bond', so that one atom or group from the molecule forms a bond to each of the carbon atoms in the double bond (Figure 11.1.5).

FIGURE 11.1.5 The reaction between ethene and hydrogen bromide. This is an example of an addition reaction between an alkene and a hydrogen halide.

When ethene reacts with hydrogen bromide, an addition reaction occurs and bromoethane is the only product. During this reaction the hydrogen atom from the HBr molecule forms a covalent bond to one carbon atom in the double bond of ethene, and the bromine atom forms a bond to the other carbon atom. All the atoms in the reactants end up in the final product.

Alkenes can undergo four different types of addition reactions:

- reaction with hydrogen
- reaction with halogens
- reaction with hydrogen halides
- reaction with water.

Reaction of alkenes with hydrogen

Alkenes react with hydrogen gas in the presence of a metal catalyst such as nickel to form alkanes. This reaction is known as a **hydrogenation reaction** and forms a saturated alkane. The reaction shown in Figure 11.1.6 is hydrogenation of ethene with hydrogen gas to produce ethane.

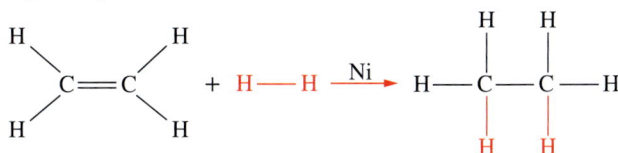

FIGURE 11.1.6 Addition reaction of ethene with hydrogen to form the corresponding saturated alkane, ethane.

Reaction of alkenes with halogens

Figure 11.1.7 shows the reaction of ethene with bromine to form 1,2-dibromoethane. The halogen adds across the double bond of the molecule, so in the product there is one bromine atom attached to each carbon atom.

This reaction proceeds at room temperature without a catalyst. Other halogens such as Cl_2 and I_2 also undergo addition reactions with alkenes to form the corresponding di-substituted haloalkanes.

FIGURE 11.1.7 Addition reaction of ethene with bromine.

Bromine is often used as a test for the presence of a carbon–carbon double bond because of the ease and speed with which it reacts with an alkene. The orange colour of the bromine quickly disappears when it is mixed with an alkene (Figure 11.1.8).

Reactions of alkenes with hydrogen halides

Hydrogen halides are chemical molecules that contain one hydrogen atom and one halogen atom, such as hydrogen chloride (HCl).

The alkene but-2-ene reacts with hydrogen chloride, a hydrogen halide, in an addition reaction. Figure 11.1.9 shows the reaction of but-2-ene with hydrogen chloride to produce a single product, 2-chlorobutane. In this reaction, a hydrogen atom is added to one of the carbon atoms in the carbon–carbon double bond, and a halogen atom is added to the other carbon atom.

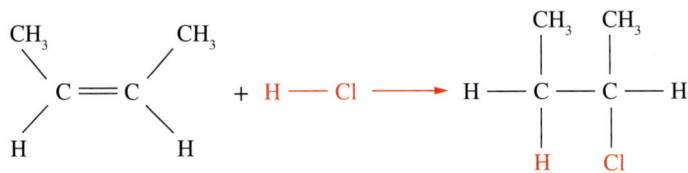

FIGURE 11.1.9 The addition reaction of but-2-ene with hydrogen chloride produces 2-chlorobutane.

However, as Figure 11.1.10 shows, when you react hydrogen chloride and but-1-ene, two products are possible.

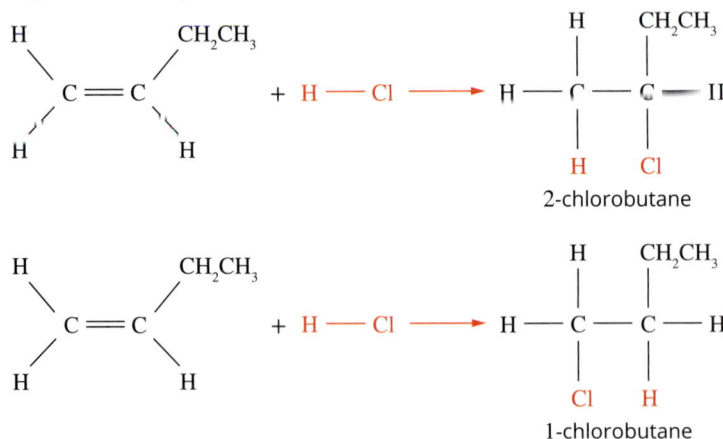

FIGURE 11.1.10 Addition reaction of but-1-ene with hydrogen chloride. Two isomers are possible as products.

FIGURE 11.1.8 (a) When an alkene is added to aqueous bromine, the alkene reacts with the coloured bromine and the solution loses colour. (b) When an alkane is added to aqueous bromine, no addition reaction occurs, so the colour does not change.

The addition reaction can produce two isomers. In one product the hydrogen atom from the hydrogen chloride molecule has been added to the carbon atom in the carbon–carbon double bond at the end of the but-1-ene molecule (C1). In the other product the hydrogen atom has been added to a carbon atom at the other end of the carbon–carbon double bond (C2).

When an asymmetrical alkene such as but-1-ene reacts with an asymmetrical reactant, two isomers are produced. More of one isomer is usually produced than the other. The reasons for this are beyond the scope of this course and are not discussed here.

Reaction of alkenes with water

Alkenes react with water under specific conditions to form the corresponding alcohol. For example, ethanol can be produced by an addition reaction of ethene and water, using a catalyst to increase the rate of the reaction. Figure 11.1.11 shows the addition reaction of steam and ethene, using a sulfuric acid (H_2SO_4) or phosphoric acid (H_3PO_4) catalyst. This reaction is used extensively in industry for the production of ethanol.

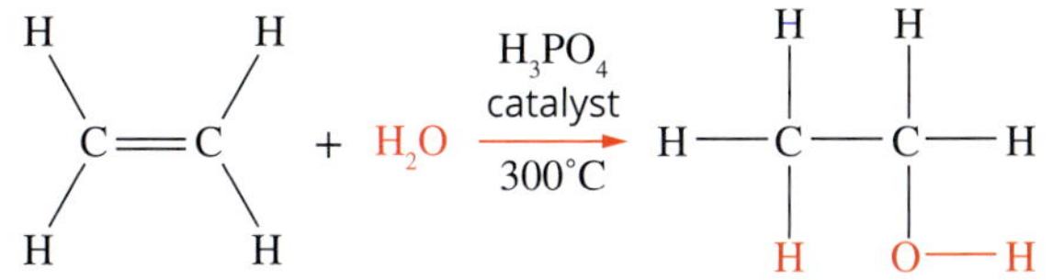

FIGURE 11.1.11 Addition reaction of ethene with water in the presence of a phosphoric acid catalyst.

The reaction is carried out at 300°C. The gaseous reactants are passed over a solid bed of the catalyst and gaseous ethanol is formed.

The reaction of ethene with steam is often described as a **hydration reaction**. In the addition reaction, water is 'added' across the double bond. The reaction is used for the commercial manufacture of ethanol because it is a one-step process that uses little energy, apart from initial heating. The heterogeneous nature of the reaction system means it is easy for manufacturers to remove the product from the reaction mixture, leaving the catalyst intact.

Just like the reaction with hydrogen halides, the reaction of asymmetric alkenes with water produces two isomers as possible products. For example, the reaction of propene with water in the presence of dilute sulfuric acid produces both propan-1-ol and propan-2-ol (Figure 11.1.12). More of one isomer will be produced, however, the reason for this is beyond the scope of this course.

> ℹ️ Reactions that involve water as a reactant are called hydration reactions.

propan-2-ol

propan-1-ol

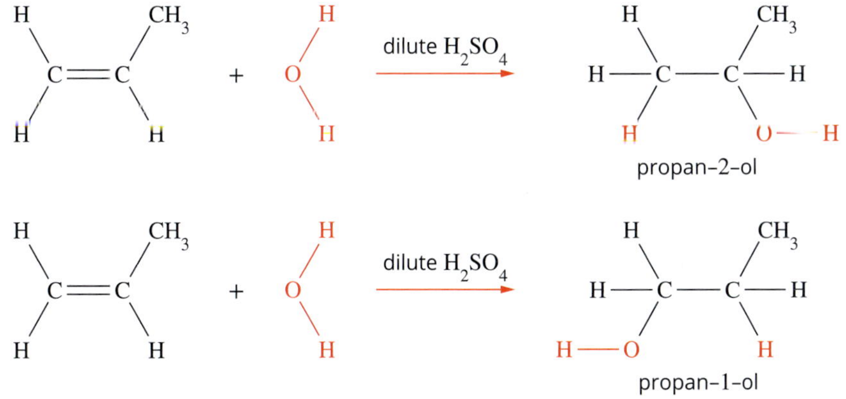

FIGURE 11.1.12 The addition reaction of propene with water. Two isomers are possible as products.

11.1 Review

SUMMARY

- Alkanes are generally unreactive, but they can undergo substitution reactions with halogens in the presence of ultraviolet light to produce haloalkanes.
- Alkanes and alkenes burn in the presence of oxygen to produce carbon dioxide and water.
- Alkenes are unsaturated hydrocarbons. They undergo addition reactions to produce saturated compounds.

- Alkenes undergo addition reactions with:
  - hydrogen and a metal catalyst to produce alkanes
  - halogens to produce dihaloalkanes
  - hydrogen halides to produce haloalkanes
  - water and acid catalyst to produce alcohols.

KEY QUESTIONS

1   Write balanced equations to represent the formation of all possible products of the reactions of chlorine with methane.

2   Name the products formed when ethene reacts with:
   a   hydrogen chloride
   b   chlorine
   c   water
   d   hydrogen.

3   Use structural formulae to write equations and name the products for the reactions of:
   a   but-1-ene with chlorine
   b   but-2-ene with hydrogen bromide.

4   Name the alkenes that could be hydrated to obtain these alcohols.
   a $CH_3CH_2CHOHCH_3$
   b $CH_3CH(CH_3)CH_2OH$
   c $CH_3CH_2CHOHCH_2CH_3$

Chapter review

KEY TERMS

addition reaction
hydration reaction
hydrogen halide

hydrogenation reaction
saturated
substitution reaction

REVIEW QUESTIONS

1   Complete this table about the different types of reactions of alkenes.

Reactants	Type of reaction	Product
alkene and hydrogen		
alkene and hydrogen bromide		
alkene and water (with a catalyst)		
alkene and bromine		

2   Give the structural formulae of the products of the following reaction.

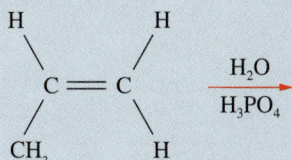

3   Write a balanced chemical equation for the reaction between:
   a   butane and chlorine
   b   ethane and oxygen.

4   Using condensed structural formulae, write a balanced chemical equation for each reaction:
   a   substitution reaction of between butane and chlorine
   b   complete combustion of pentane
   c   incomplete combustion of propene producing carbon monoxide.

5   How can an alkene be converted into an alkane?

6   Remembering what you learnt about periodicity in Year 11 chemistry, which halogen would you expect to be most reactive with alkenes? Explain your answer.

7   Name a substance that could be used to distinguish ethane from ethene. What happens when this substance is added to ethane and ethene?

8   What is needed in the substitution reaction of ethane and chlorine?
   A   platinum catalyst
   B   ultraviolet light
   C   high temperature
   D   hydrogen chloride

9   When hydrocarbons such as alkanes burn in air, what type of reaction is this?
   A   thermal decomposition
   B   thermal transformation
   C   combustion
   D   hydrogenation

10 Write an equation using structural formulae for the reaction between hex-3-ene and water. Do not forgot to include the reaction conditions required for this reaction.

11 a   Which alkene reacts in an addition reaction to produce 2,3-dichlorobutane?
    b   What other reactant is required for this reaction?

12 Name the products for the reactions of propene with:
    a H_2/Ni
    b   HBr
    c Br_2.

13 Write balanced chemical equations for the following reactions. (You do not need to include symbols for the states.)
    a   complete combustion of octane
    b   but-2-ene and hydrogen chloride
    c   pent-1-ene with bromine solution
    d   pentane with bromine solution.

14 What is the name of the reaction that produces hexane from hex-1-ene?
    A   substitution
    B   addition of chlorine
    C   hydrogenation
    D   hydration

15 a   When ethene undergoes a chemical reaction with water in the presence of acid and at a high temperature, what is the name of the product?
    b   Write a balanced chemical equation for this reaction.

16 Reflect on the Inquiry task on page 310. Using concepts you have learnt in this chapter, explain why there was variation in the spreadability of the substances.

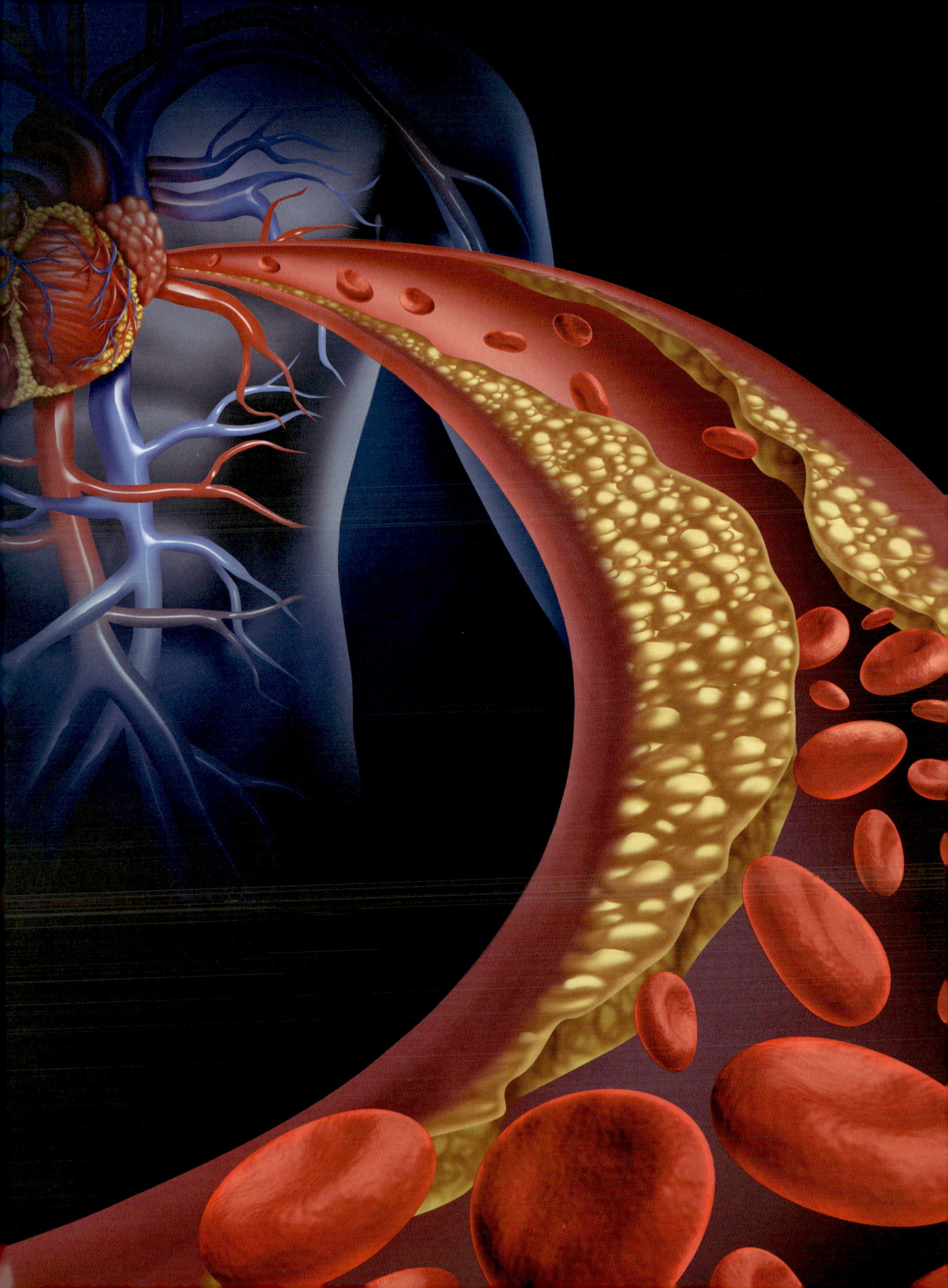

Humans have been making ethanol for thousands of years. It is one of the earliest uses of biotechnology, where the action of a microorganism is harnessed to make more complex molecules. This technology is probably more than 9000 years old.

The group of organic molecules known as alcohols is far more diverse than just ethanol, and includes many substances that are important in biology, industry and wider society. For example, cholesterol is an essential component of animal cells that helps them maintain their shape and flexibility, but at high levels it can restrict arteries, as seen in this chapter opener image. The molecule consists of a medium length hydrocarbon chain, a series of rings and a single –OH group that is essential for arranging the molecules in cell membranes.

In this chapter you will investigate simple and more complex alcohols and examine their structures, intermolecular forces and properties. You will examine the reactions for preparing alcohols and the way that alcohols react with some other molecules.

Content

INQUIRY QUESTION

How can alcohols be produced and what are their properties?

By the end of this chapter, you will be able to:

- investigate the structural formulae, properties and functional group including:
  - primary
  - secondary
  - tertiary alcohols ICT
- explain the properties within and between the homologous series of alcohols with reference to the intermolecular and intramolecular bonding present ICT
- conduct a practical investigation to measure and reliably compare the enthalpy of combustion for a range of alcohols ICT N
- write equations, state conditions and predict products to represent the reactions of alcohols, including but not limited to: (ACSCH128, ACSCH136)
  - combustion
  - dehydration
  - substitution with HX
  - oxidation
- investigate the production of alcohols, including:
  - substitution reactions of halogenated organic compounds
  - fermentation
- investigate the products of the oxidation of primary and secondary alcohols
- compare and contrast fuels from organic sources to biofuels, including ethanol ICT

Chemistry Stage 6 Syllabus © NSW Education Standards Authority for and on behalf of the Crown in right of the State of NSW, 2017.

12.1 Physical and chemical properties of alcohols

Some properties of ethanol

COLLECT THIS ...

- methylated spirits
- vinegar
- water
- vegetable oil
- sucrose (table sugar)
- long wooden skewer
- clear plastic disposable cups
- disposable spoons
- old ceramic plate
- matches
- face shield

DO THIS ...

Part A

1 Half fill each cup with methylated spirits.
2 To the first cup, add water to near the top of the cup, and mix with a spoon.
3 Record your observations.
4 Take a fresh cup and spoon and repeat steps 2–3 but, instead add vinegar to the methylated spirits.
5 Repeat step 4, but instead add vegetable oil to the methylated spirits.
6 Repeat step 4, but instead add 2 teaspoons of sucrose to the methylated spirits.

Part B

1 Pour 5 mL of methylated spirits onto a ceramic plate outside.
2 Put on the face shield.
3 Very carefully, light one end of a long wooden skewer with a match.
4 Hold the unlit end of the wooden skewer and carefully hold the lit end near the methylated spirits.
5 Record your observations.

RECORD THIS ...

Draw up a table to record your results.

Description of experiment	Prediction	Observations
Part A		
Methylated spirits mixed with water		
Methylated spirits mixed with vinegar		
Methylated spirits mixed with vegetable oil		
Methylated spirits mixed with sucrose		
Part B		
Methylated spirits with naked flame		

Describe what happened by recording your observations.

REFLECT ON THIS ...

1 Explain the meaning of your observations.
2 What could you do next time to improve your experiment?

PHYSICAL PROPERTIES OF ALCOHOLS

In this section you will consider the physical properties of alcohols, including trends in boiling point and solubility. Differences in chemical properties will be discussed in Section 12.2.

Boiling points

The boiling points of **alcohols** are considerably higher than the parent **alkane** because of the presence of **hydrogen bonds** between alcohol molecules. In contrast, the only type of forces between non-polar alkane molecules are much weaker **dispersion forces**. For example, the boiling point of methanol is more than 200°C higher than the boiling point of methane.

> ℹ️ Hydrogen bonds in alcohols give them higher boiling points than alkanes of a similar molar mass.

Oxygen is a more **electronegative** atom than hydrogen, so the oxygen–hydrogen bond in the hydroxyl functional group is a **polar bond**. Figure 12.1.1 shows how hydrogen bonding occurs between the partially charged hydrogen atom in the –OH group on one alcohol molecule and a non-bonding electron pair on the oxygen atom of a neighbouring alcohol molecule. The presence of the hydrogen bonds results in the higher boiling points observed.

Effect of chain length on boiling point

The hydrogen bonding between molecules gives all alcohols relatively high boiling points. As the length of the **hydrocarbon** chain increases from one member of the homologous series to the next, the dispersion forces between these gradually larger molecules also increase. So the boiling points of alcohols increase as molar mass increases, as shown in Table 12.1.1. This trend is discussed in detail in Chapter 13 in the context of other homologous series.

FIGURE 12.1.1 The red dotted line shows the hydrogen bond between molecules such as ethanol that contain the polar hydroxyl functional group.

> ℹ The boiling point of alcohols increases as molar mass increases.

TABLE 12.1.1 Boiling points of some alcohols

Alcohol	Number of carbons in chain	Boiling point (°C)
methanol	1	65
pentan-1-ol	5	138
octan-1-ol	8	195

The three-dimensional structure of molecules can also affect the boiling point of a compound. In the case of alcohols, in addition to the impact of branching on reducing the strength of dispersion forces between molecules, the position of the hydroxyl within the molecule affects hydrogen bonding. Figure 12.1.2 shows molecular models for three **isomers** of butanol: butan-1-ol, butan-2-ol and 2-methylpropan-2-ol. These isomers are examples of **primary**, **secondary** and **tertiary alcohols**, respectively.

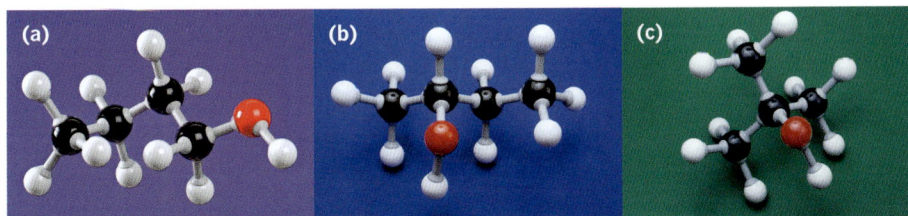

GO TO ➤ Section 9.3 page 271

FIGURE 12.1.2 Molecular models of the three isomers of butanol: (a) butan-1-ol, (b) butan-2-ol, (c) 2-methylpropan-2-ol.

You can see from the models that the hydroxyl group becomes increasingly 'crowded' moving from the primary alcohol through to the secondary and tertiary alcohol isomers. The presence of the alkyl groups further restricts a molecule's ability to form hydrogen bonds with other molecules. For this reason the boiling points of these alcohols decrease in the sequence from primary to secondary to tertiary alcohol, as seen in Table 12.1.2.

> ℹ Secondary and tertiary alcohols have lower boiling points than primary alcohols because hydrogen bonding is weaker in secondary and tertiary alcohols.

TABLE 12.1.2 The boiling point of primary, secondary and tertiary alcohols with the formula C_4H_9OH

Alcohol	Type of alcohol	Boiling point (°C)
butan-1-ol	primary	118
butan-2-ol	secondary	100
2-methylpropan-2-ol	tertiary	82

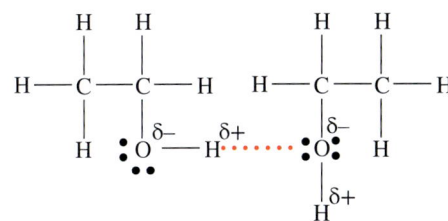

Solubility

As with all substituted hydrocarbons, the solubility of an alcohol depends on the strength of intermolecular interactions between the solute and the solvent. The common generalisation is that 'like dissolves like'.

Solubility in water

Alcohols containing molecules with short hydrocarbon chains (1–3 carbon atoms long) dissolve well in water because hydrogen bonds form between the partially positive hydrogen atom of the hydroxyl group and the lone-pair electrons of an adjacent water molecule (Figure 12.1.3). There is also attraction between the partially positive hydrogen within the water molecules and the lone-pair electrons on the alcohol molecules. This is how ethanol dissolves in water in alcoholic drinks such as beer and wine.

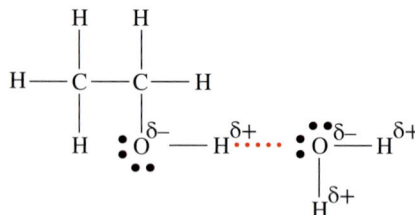

FIGURE 12.1.3 Hydrogen bonding between ethanol and water molecules.

Solubility and chain length

The graph in Figure 12.1.4 shows the solubility of three alcohols. The solubility of alcohols in water decreases with increasing length of the hydrocarbon chain.

> ℹ The solubility of alcohols in water decreases as the hydrocarbon chain of the molecule becomes longer.

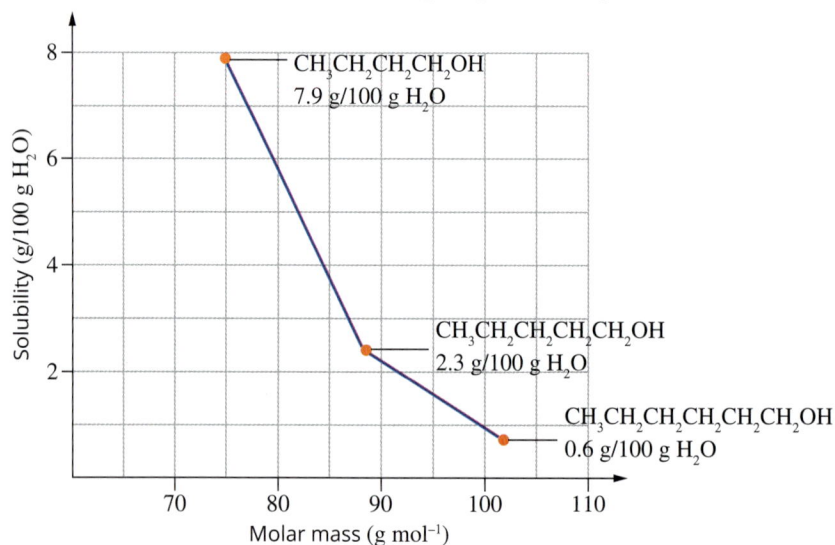

$CH_3CH_2CH_2CH_2OH$
7.9 g/100 g H_2O

$CH_3CH_2CH_2CH_2CH_2OH$
2.3 g/100 g H_2O

$CH_3CH_2CH_2CH_2CH_2CH_2OH$
0.6 g/100 g H_2O

FIGURE 12.1.4 The solubility of alcohols in water decreases with increasing hydrocarbon chain length.

> ℹ The solubility of alcohols in organic solvents increases as the hydrocarbon chain of their molecules becomes longer.

The longer hydrocarbon chains disrupt the hydrogen bonds between water molecules. While the hydroxyl group of an alcohol can form hydrogen bonds with water molecules, the hydrocarbon chain cannot. Only dispersion forces occur between the hydrocarbon chain and water molecules, which are not as strong as hydrogen bonds. As the chain length increases, the non-polar nature of the molecule also increases and the alcohol becomes less soluble.

Solubility in organic solvents

In contrast to their solubility in water, alcohols become more soluble in organic solvents as their molecules become larger. This is because organic solvents, such as hexane, benzene and toluene, are non-polar. Only relatively non-polar alcohols with long hydrocarbon chains dissolve well in non-polar solvents.

Small alcohols such as ethanol, which are very soluble in water, do not dissolve well in non-polar solvents. The dispersion forces between their hydrocarbon chains and the solvent molecules are not strong enough to disrupt the hydrogen bonds that hold the alcohol molecules together. Therefore the alcohol molecules do not separate and disperse throughout the solvent. Many of the more complex alcohols such as cholesterol (Figure 12.1.5) are very soluble in animal fats and have important biological roles.

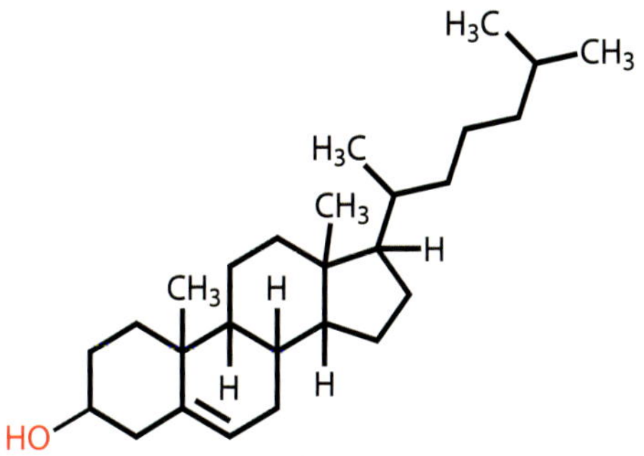

FIGURE 12.1.5 The alcohol functional group (in red) of cholesterol helps position this molecule in cell membranes.

+ ADDITIONAL

Nutrition: soluble vitamins

Vitamins are organic compounds that are required in the diet for the body to function properly. Vitamins also help to prevent specific diseases. For example, a deficiency of vitamin C leads to scurvy, and a deficiency of vitamin K can lead to uncontrolled bleeding.

The solubility of vitamins is important because vitamins need to be transported and stored in the body. Water-soluble vitamins are likely to be found in the aqueous environment of the blood. Fat-soluble vitamins are found in fatty tissues.

The differences in solubility relate to the number of functional groups in the molecule that can form hydrogen bonds with water. The more of these groups there are in a vitamin molecule, the higher its solubility in water. One such group is the hydroxyl group (–OH). Figure 12.1.6 contrasts the number of hydroxyl groups on a water-soluble vitamin with those on a fat-soluble vitamin.

The solubility of vitamins has implications for humans. For example, water-soluble vitamins:

- are excreted by the body if not used, so they must be consumed as a regular part of the diet
- should not be taken in large, irregular doses because the extra amounts are not stored
- are removed from foods if they are cooked in water.

By contrast, fat-soluble vitamins can be stored in fatty tissue in the body for long periods of time. For example, an adult can store several years' supply of vitamin A. If the diet is deficient in vitamin A, these reserves are mobilised. However, a person taking excessive quantities of vitamin supplements is in danger of overdosing on fat-soluble vitamins, because the body does not easily dispose of them.

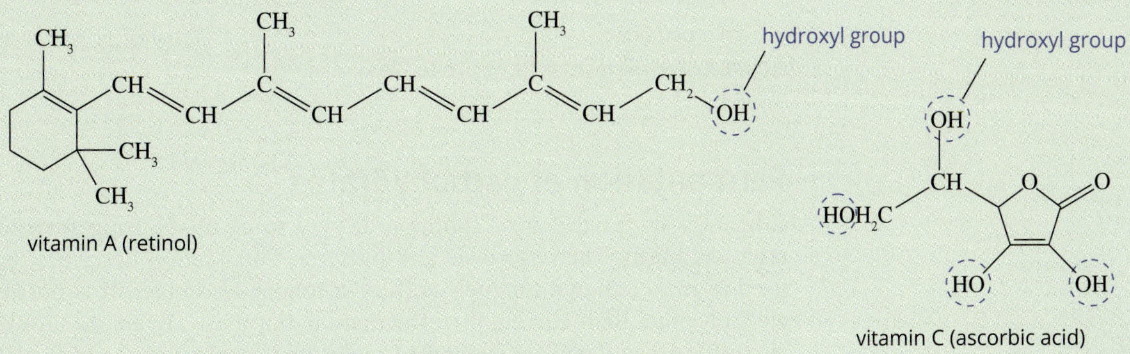

FIGURE 12.1.6 Chemical structures of vitamins A and C. The hydroxyl groups are circled. Vitamin A is fat-soluble and vitamin C is water-soluble.

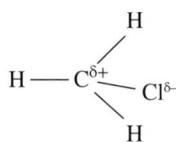

FIGURE 12.1.7 Structural formula of chloromethane. The electronegativity of carbon is 2.6 and that of chlorine is 3.2. This large difference in electronegativity results in a polar carbon–chlorine bond.

PRODUCTION OF ALCOHOLS

Substitution reactions of haloalkanes

A **substitution reaction** occurs when an atom or functional group in a molecule is replaced or 'substituted' by another atom or group.

In a molecule of chloromethane, the carbon–chlorine bond is polar because of the large electronegativity difference between chlorine and carbon. The carbon atom in the bond carries a partial positive charge and the more electronegative chlorine atom carries a partial negative charge (Figure 12.1.7).

As a consequence of the highly polarised bond between carbon and chlorine, the partial positive charge on the carbon atom can be 'attacked' by a negatively charged species, such as a hydroxide ion from aqueous sodium hydroxide. The organic product formed is methanol (Figure 12.1.8). Because the chlorine atom of the chloroalkane has been replaced by a hydroxyl group, this is a substitution reaction.

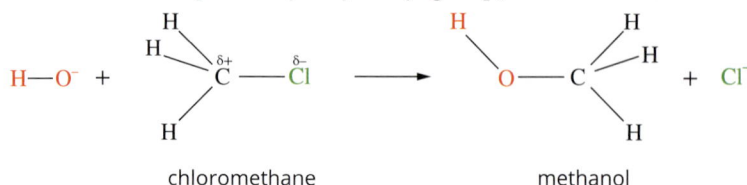

chloromethane   methanol

FIGURE 12.1.8 A chloromethane molecule reacts with a hydroxide ion to form methanol via a substitution reaction.

Chemists write the general unbalanced equation for a chloroalkane reacting with hydroxide ions in shorthand form as:

$$RCl \xrightarrow{\text{OH}^-} ROH$$

For all general equations, R represents an alkyl group. In general equations, it is standard that only the organic product is shown. It is important to remember that a chloride ion (Cl^-) is generated as part of this substitution reaction.

It is also possible for **haloalkanes** to undergo substitution reactions with water to form alcohols. This reaction occurs much more slowly and requires a **catalyst**. In the reaction shown in Figure 12.1.9, ethanol is produced by a substitution reaction between chloroethane and water.

> ⓘ The reaction of a haloalkane with hydroxide ion or water produces an alcohol. The reaction with water requires a catalyst for it to occur at a reasonable rate.

chloroethane   ethanol

FIGURE 12.1.9 The reaction between chloroethane and water is a slower reaction and requires the use of a catalyst.

Fermentation of carbohydrates

Ethanol is by far the most common alcohol to be made using **fermentation** by microorganisms such as yeasts and bacteria. This section describes the processes used to make ethanol for fuels and for alcoholic beverages. It is possible to make alcohols other than ethanol by fermentation, but these are almost always produced alongside ethanol and are generally undesirable byproducts. In particular, methanol is far more toxic to humans than ethanol, so methanol concentrations in drinks are very carefully controlled.

There are many different processes used in fermentation, and these vary depending on:

- the available starting material
- the strain or mixture of yeasts or bacteria used
- the fermentation temperature

- traditional steps and ingredients (especially for beverages)
- whether the process is sealed or open to the atmosphere
- the purification process (if any)
- the intended use of the product.

Fermentation reactions can be incredibly complex, involving hundreds of possible reactants and products; the pathways and final results are different depending on the availability of oxygen. In one of the simplest and most important reactions, a simple carbohydrate, glucose ($C_6H_{12}O_6$), is broken down to form ethanol and carbon dioxide. The reaction is:

$$C_6H_{12}O_6(aq) \rightarrow 2CH_3CH_2OH(aq) + 2CO_2(g)$$

Glucose (Figure 12.1.10) is a monosaccharide, which is a class of organic molecules that contain carbon, hydrogen and oxygen, almost always with the general formula $C_n(H_2O)_n$. Monosaccharides are often referred to as simple sugars or simple carbohydrates. These can reversibly react with each other to become the building blocks of much longer molecules called polysaccharides or complex carbohydrates, as shown in Figure 12.1.11. Polysaccharides are a type of natural polymer. You will investigate polymers in Chapter 14.

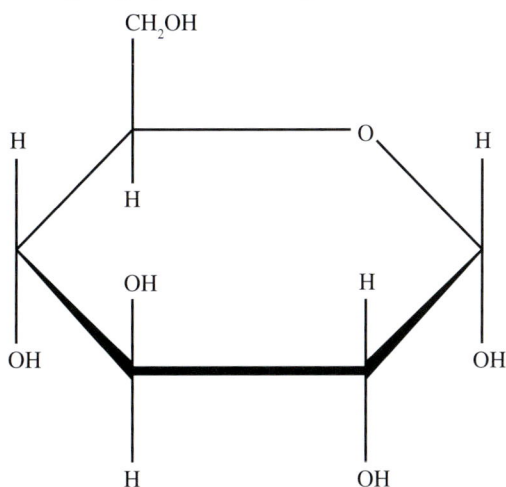

FIGURE 12.1.10 The structural formula of glucose, showing its cyclic structure

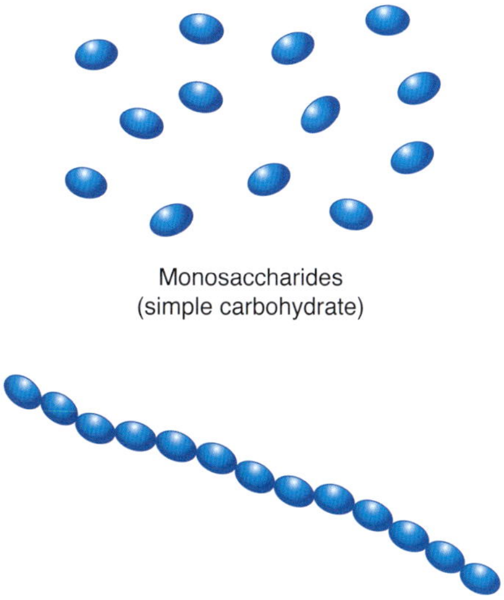

> **i** Yeasts and bacteria make alcohols by fermenting carbohydrates. Ethanol is the most common alcohol produced in fermentation reactions.

Monosaccharides (simple carbohydrate)

These are joined together to form a polysaccharide (complex carbohydrate)

FIGURE 12.1.11 Monosaccharides react with each other to form a long chain polymer molecule called a polysaccharide.

Fermentation starts with plant material that contains monosaccharides or polysaccharides. Wine is made from grapes that have high concentrations of monosaccharides (Figure 12.1.12), while other ethanol-containing drinks are made from grains or starchy vegetables such as potatoes that contain large amounts of polysaccharides. In Australia, ethanol for fuel is made mostly from polysaccharide-rich waste material from sugar production and grain refining (12.1.13).

FIGURE 12.1.12 Grapes growing on a vineyard near Cessnock, NSW

FIGURE 12.1.13 Waste from sugar cane crops is used to make ethanol for fuel in Australia.

The fermentation conditions must be carefully controlled to obtain the intended products. The temperature is held constant, generally between 15 and 35°C. A catalyst might be necessary to speed up the conversion from complex carbohydrates to simple carbohydrates, but fermentation reactions may take days or months to complete.

Even with this care, a pure sample of ethanol is never the product of a fermentation reaction. Yeast and bacteria cannot survive in ethanol concentrations above about 15%, so the fermentation process stops when the concentration reaches this level. These microorganisms also produce many byproducts during the reactions to give a fermentation product that is a mixture of ethanol and other alcohols along with water, aldehydes, ketones and carboxylic acids.

This mixture can be carefully separated by filtration and **distillation** to increase the ethanol concentration. A diagram of a laboratory distillation apparatus is shown in Figure 12.1.14. This separates the mixture according to the boiling points of the components. As the mixture is heated, ethanol, which has a lower boiling point (78°C) evaporates from the mixture, is cooled in the condenser, and collected, while components with higher boiling points remain in the heated flask. Aqueous solutions of ethanol are very difficult to purify to 100% ethanol by distillation, and the process is often repeated several times to obtain higher concentrations of ethanol for fuels.

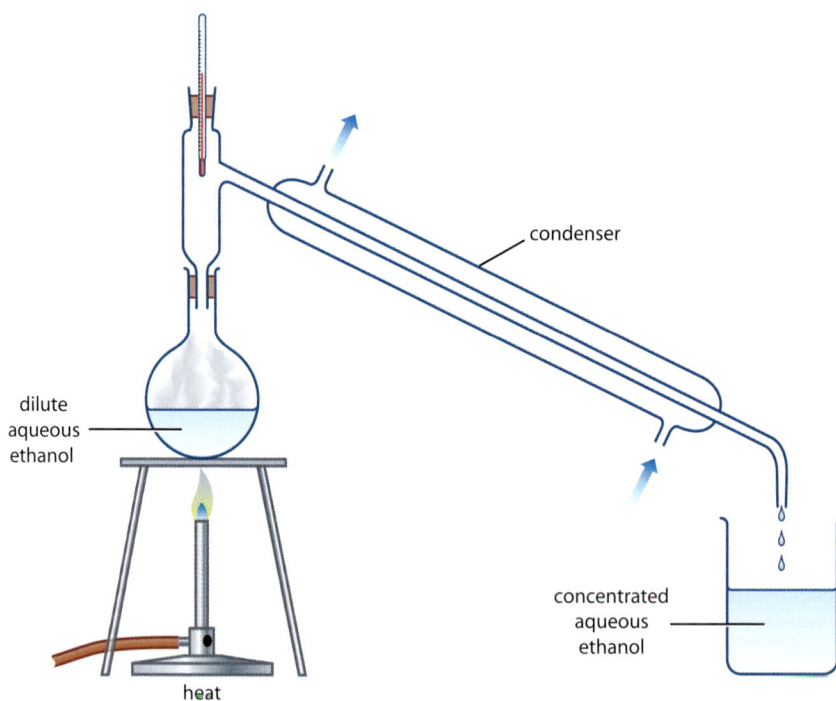

FIGURE 12.1.14 Laboratory apparatus for distilling the products of fermentation

REACTIONS OF ALCOHOLS

Ethanol is the most widely used alcohol in society, and the vast majority of ethanol that is produced worldwide is used as automotive fuel. You may have seen E10 fuel being sold at your local service station. The E10 classification indicates that the petrol contains 10% ethanol. In Brazil the use of ethanol fuels is widespread, with the percentage of ethanol being a minimum of 20–25% (Figure 12.1.15). Some cars have been developed to run on 100% ethanol.

The presence of the hydroxyl functional group means ethanol has very different properties in comparison to ethene and chloroethane. These properties make it useful for a variety of applications. Ethanol is a highly water-soluble liquid at room temperature. It is widely used as a solvent in cosmetics and pharmaceuticals, as well as being the active ingredient in alcoholic drinks such as wine, beer and spirits.

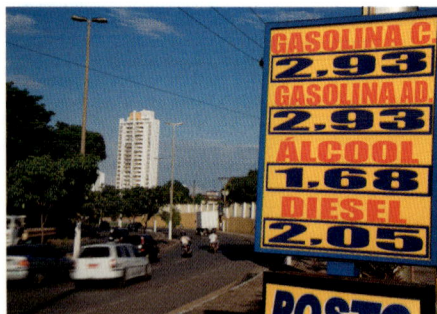

FIGURE 12.1.15 Ethanol (*álcool*) is used as a fuel in Brazil and is cheaper than petrol (*gasolina*), although petrol delivers lower fuel consumption.

When consumed, ethanol acts as a depressant on the human body, slowing reactions and responses. Excess ethanol consumption also blocks the production of antidiuretic hormones, increasing urination and resulting in dehydration.

Here you will examine some of the common reactions that alcohols undergo.

Combustion of alcohols

Like alkanes and alkenes, alcohols burn readily in air to form carbon dioxide and water as products. The equation for the complete combustion of ethanol is:

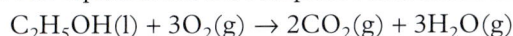

$$C_2H_5OH(l) + 3O_2(g) \rightarrow 2CO_2(g) + 3H_2O(g)$$

This is a highly exothermic reaction, which is why ethanol can be used as a fuel. On a smaller scale, methylated spirits, which contains about 95% ethanol mixed with other chemicals, is used as a fuel for camping stoves. Some cooking techniques even make use of the burning of alcohol for drama and flavour. Figure 12.1.16 shows how the ethanol in brandy can burn as it is added to enhance the flavour of a Christmas pudding.

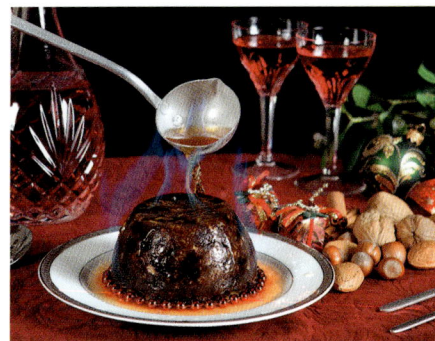

FIGURE 12.1.16 Burning brandy is sometimes poured over a Christmas pudding. Brandy can contain as much as 40% ethanol.

GO TO ➤ Year 11 Chapter 14

REVISION

Enthalpy of combustion

You will remember from Year 11 that the exchange of heat energy between the system and its surroundings under constant pressure is referred to as the **enthalpy change**, or **heat of reaction**, and is given the symbol ΔH. The enthalpy of combustion of a fuel is defined as the enthalpy change that occurs when a specified amount of the fuel burns completely in oxygen.

When a combustion reaction takes place, chemical energy is converted to thermal energy. You can use the thermal energy released by a specific quantity of fuel as it undergoes combustion to heat a measured volume of water. If you measure the temperature change of the water, it can be used to determine the approximate amount of energy released by the fuel. The temperature change is related to the heat energy absorbed by the fuel, using the equation for specific heat capacity:

$$q = m \times c \times \Delta T$$

where

q is the amount of heat energy in joules (J)

m is the mass in grams (g)

c is the specific heat capacity in $J\,g^{-1}\,K^{-1}$

ΔT is the temperature change in K.

An experimental arrangement for estimating the enthalpy of combustion of a liquid fuel, such as ethanol, is shown in Figure 12.1.17. Figure 12.1.18 summarises the steps followed in this experiment.

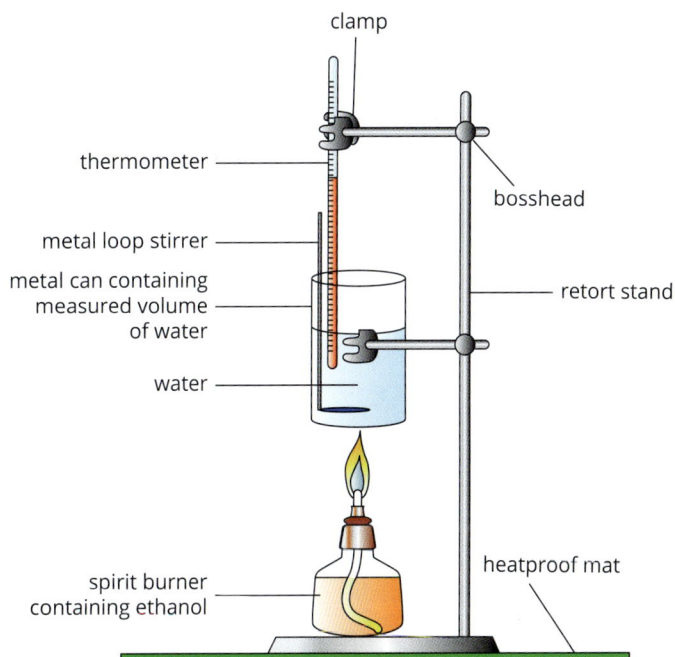

FIGURE 12.1.17 Apparatus for measuring the enthalpy of combustion of a liquid fuel. A metal can containing a measured volume of water is held above the wick of a spirit burner.

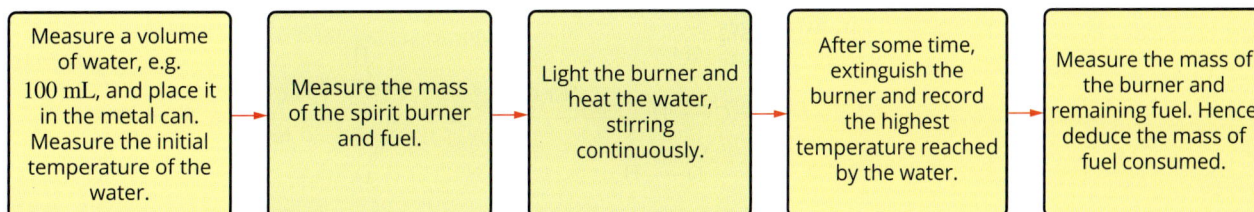

Measure a volume of water, e.g. 100 mL, and place it in the metal can. Measure the initial temperature of the water.	Measure the mass of the spirit burner and fuel.	Light the burner and heat the water, stirring continuously.	After some time, extinguish the burner and record the highest temperature reached by the water.	Measure the mass of the burner and remaining fuel. Hence deduce the mass of fuel consumed.

FIGURE 12.1.18 Flowchart of the steps followed when using the specific heat capacity of water to determine the enthalpy of combustion of a fuel

GO TO ➤ Year 11 Chapter 14

Three key pieces of information collected during the procedure shown in Figure 12.1.17 are:

- the mass of water (because the density of water is $1\,g\,mL^{-1}$, the volume of water in mL is equal to its mass in g)
- the change in temperature of the water
- the mass of fuel consumed.

This data can be used to determine the enthalpy of combustion of the fuel.

When performing these calculations, it is assumed that all of the energy released by the combustion of the fuel is used to heat the water. In reality, some of the energy heats the metal can as well as being lost to the surroundings. For this reason, measurements of enthalpies of combustion made in this way only give approximate values. More accurate measurements are obtained using bomb calorimetry, which was discussed in Year 11.

Oxidation of alcohols

The combustion of alcohols and other fuels can be classified as a type of oxidation–reduction (redox) reaction. Alcohols can also be oxidised by strong inorganic oxidising agents such as acidified solutions of potassium dichromate ($K_2Cr_2O_7$) and potassium permanganate ($KMnO_4$). The products of these oxidation reactions depend on the type of alcohol involved.

Recall that alcohols can be classified as primary, secondary or tertiary depending on the position of the hydroxyl group within the molecule.

- Primary alcohols are alcohols in which the −OH group is bonded to a carbon that is attached to only one alkyl group. These alcohols first oxidise to form aldehydes and then further oxidation forms the corresponding carboxylic acids.
- Secondary alcohols are alcohols in which the −OH group is bonded to a carbon that is bonded to two alkyl groups. These alcohols oxidise to form ketones.
- Tertiary alcohols are alcohols in which the −OH group is bonded to a carbon that is bonded to three alkyl groups. These alcohols are resistant to oxidation by inorganic oxidising agents and do not normally react.

You can see in Figure 12.1.19 how the different isomers of butanol can be classified as primary, secondary or tertiary alcohols. Chemists often use the symbols 1°, 2° and 3° as a shorthand way of indicating whether an alcohol is primary, secondary or tertiary, respectively.

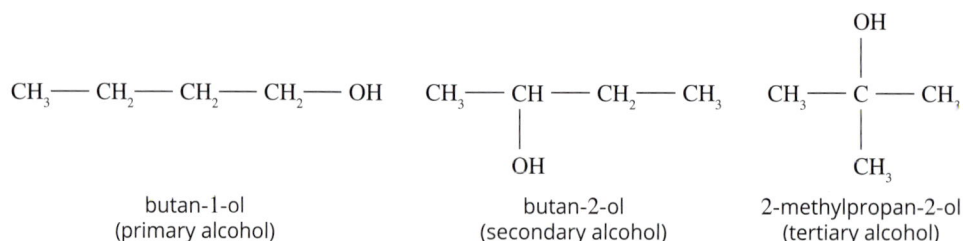

$$CH_3—CH_2—CH_2—CH_2—OH \qquad CH_3—CH—CH_2—CH_3 \qquad CH_3—C—CH_3$$

butan-1-ol
(primary alcohol)

butan-2-ol
(secondary alcohol)

2-methylpropan-2-ol
(tertiary alcohol)

FIGURE 12.1.19 Structures of some primary, secondary and tertiary alcohols with the formula C_4H_9OH.

Oxidation of primary alcohols

Figure 12.1.20 shows how a primary alcohol can be oxidised to a carboxylic acid in two stages.

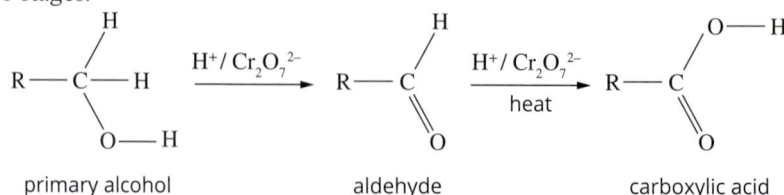

primary alcohol

aldehyde

carboxylic acid

FIGURE 12.1.20 General equation for the oxidation of a primary alcohol

In the first stage, the primary alcohol is oxidised to an aldehyde. In the second stage, further heating of the reaction mixture in the presence of the oxidising agent oxidises the aldehyde to a carboxylic acid.

The example in Figure 12.1.21 shows that propan-1-ol is oxidised first to propanal (an aldehyde) and then to propanoic acid (a carboxylic acid).

FIGURE 12.1.21 Equations for the oxidation of the primary alcohol propan-1-ol

If the desired product is an aldehyde rather than a carboxylic acid, milder conditions (lower temperatures and shorter reaction times) must be used and the aldehyde can be distilled from the reaction mixture as it is formed so that it is not oxidised further. Higher temperatures and longer reaction times favour the formation of the carboxylic acid over the aldehyde.

> ℹ️ Aldehydes are produced as an intermediate in the oxidation of a primary alcohol to a carboxylic acid. If an aldehyde is the desired product, it can be distilled off as it forms to prevent further oxidation.

Oxidation of secondary alcohols

When secondary alcohols are oxidised the corresponding ketones are produced. Figure 12.1.22 gives the general equation for the oxidation of secondary alcohols to ketones.

Figure 12.1.23 gives the equation for the production of the ketone propanone by the oxidation of the secondary alcohol propan-2-ol.

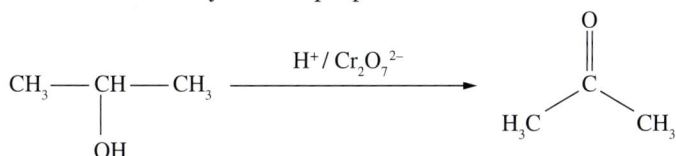

FIGURE 12.1.22 The general equation for the oxidation of a secondary alcohol. The R groups in the structures represent different alkyl groups.

FIGURE 12.1.23 The secondary alcohol propan-2-ol can be oxidised to propanone.

> ℹ️ Secondary alcohols are oxidised to produce ketones.

Tertiary alcohols and oxidising agents

Tertiary alcohols are resistant to reaction with solutions of acidified potassium dichromate ($K_2Cr_2O_7$) or potassium permanganate ($KMnO_4$).

During the oxidation of alcohols, there is an increase in the number of C–O bonds and a simultaneous decrease (at the same carbon atom) in the number of C–H bonds. In tertiary alcohols, the carbon attached to the hydroxyl group does not have a C–H bond to break, so oxidation cannot occur at that carbon atom.

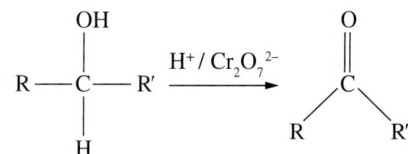

> ℹ️ Tertiary alcohols are not normally oxidised by heating in the presence of a strong oxidant such as acidified dichromate or acidified permanganate.

Table 12.1.3 summarises the reactions of primary, secondary and tertiary alcohols with an acidified solution containing dichromate or permanganate ions.

TABLE 12.1.3 Summary of the oxidation reactions of primary, secondary and tertiary alcohols with acidified dichromate solution or acidified permanganate solution

Type of alcohol	Products
Primary (1°)	Mild conditions produce aldehydes. Higher temperatures and longer reaction times produce carboxylic acids.
Secondary (2°)	Ketones
Tertiary (3°)	No products because tertiary alcohols are resistant to oxidation by these oxidising agents.

Dehydration of alcohols

The **dehydration reaction** is so named because water is formed as a product. Dehydration of an alcohol generates this water by removing the –OH functional group and a hydrogen atom from an adjacent carbon. The result is the formation of an alkene, as shown in Figure 12.1.24.

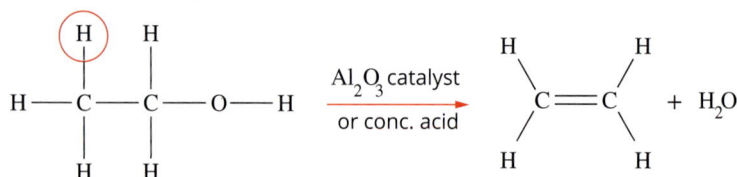

FIGURE 12.1.24 The reaction scheme for dehydrating ethanol to form ethane and water. A hydrogen atom from the carbon adjacent to the –OH group (such as the one circled) is removed along with the –OH group.

> **Dehydration of an alcohol produces an alkene and water.**

The dehydration reaction occurs quickly and at room temperature with tertiary alcohols but requires high temperatures with primary or secondary alcohols. The reaction is simple to perform on a small scale with an aluminium oxide (Al_2O_3) catalyst. The apparatus for this reaction is shown in Figure 12.1.25. The dehydration reaction can also be achieved in the presence of concentrated sulfuric acid (H_2SO_4) or phosphoric acid (H_3PO_4).

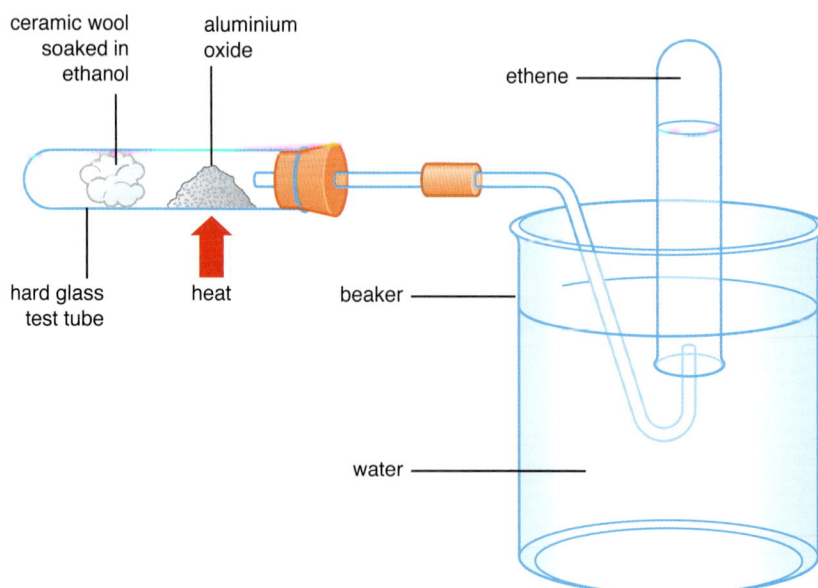

FIGURE 12.1.25 Producing ethene on a small scale from ethanol using an Al_2O_3 catalyst

Reaction of alcohols with hydrogen halides

Alcohols undergo a substitution reaction in the presence of a **hydrogen halide** (HX), where X = F, Cl, Br or I, to form an alkyl halide and water. The reaction is shown in Figure 12.1.26.

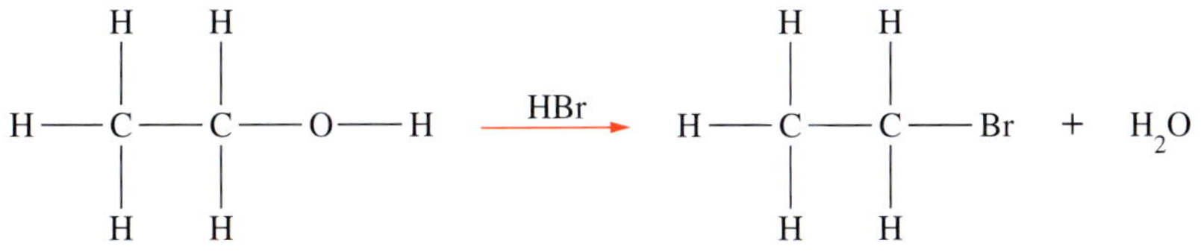

FIGURE 12.1.26 The reaction of ethanol with hydrobromic acid to form bromoethane.

The trend in reactivity is the same as for the dehydration reactions above, where primary alcohols are slowest and tertiary alcohols are quickest. Hydrogen halide reactivity increases down the halogen group, so HF is slowest to react and HI is the fastest.

12.1 Review

SUMMARY

- Molecules of alcohols contain hydroxyl functional groups that can form hydrogen bonds with other molecules. The strength of these hydrogen bonds causes alcohols to have boiling points that are relatively high compared to the parent alkanes.
- The solubility of an alcohol in water is determined by the way the alcohol molecules interact with the molecules of water. This is affected by the polarity of functional groups and the length of the non-polar hydrocarbon chains of the alcohol molecules.
- The smaller hydrocarbon chain alcohols are soluble in water. Solubility rapidly decreases as the chain length increases.
- The solubility of alcohols in non-polar organic solvents increases as the chain length increases.
- Alcohols may be formed by reacting haloalkanes with hydroxide ions or with water in the presence of a catalyst.
- Carbohydrates are fermented and distilled to make ethanol and other alcohols. These are often separated by distillation.

- Alcohols combust to form water and carbon dioxide. It is possible to measure the enthalpy of combustion using simple laboratory apparatus.
- Alcohols react with oxidising agents such as acidified solutions of dichromate ions and permanganate ions in different ways.
  - Primary alcohols are oxidised first to aldehydes, which may be oxidised further to carboxylic acids.
  - Secondary alcohols are oxidised to ketones.
  - Tertiary alcohols are resistant to oxidation by these oxidising agents.
- Alcohols can be dehydrated in the presence of strong concentrated acid or an aluminium oxide catalyst to form an alkene and water. Tertiary alcohols react quickest. Primary alcohols react slowly and require heating.
- Reacting an alcohol with a hydrogen halide produces a haloalkane.

12.1 Review *continued*

1   Arrange the following compounds in increasing order of boiling point. Provide reasons for your answer.
    $CH_3CH_2CH_2OH$ $CH_3CHOHCH_3$ $CH_3CH_2CH_2CH_2CH_2CH_2CH_2OH$ $CH_3CH_2CH_2CH_2OHCH_3CH_3CH_3$

2   Propan-1-ol is miscible with hexane but methanol is not. Explain why this is the case.

3   Identify each of the following alcohols as primary, secondary or tertiary.

a

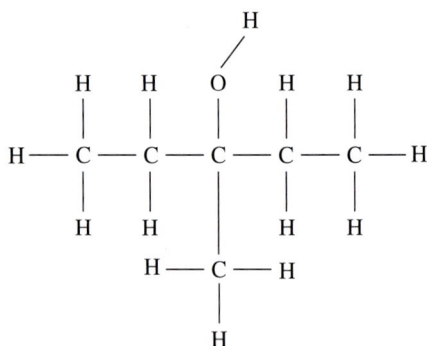

b

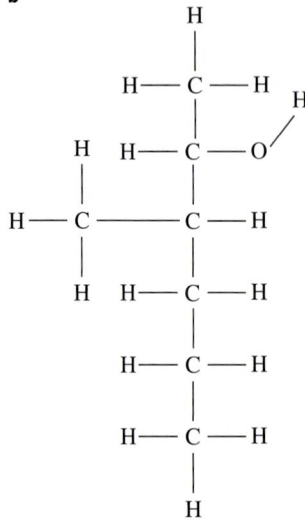

c

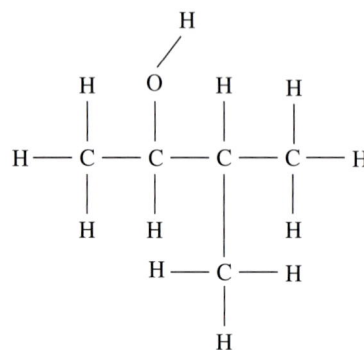

4   Pentan-3-ol, 2-methylbutan-2-ol and pentan-1-ol are all isomers of $C_5H_{12}O$.
    a   Write an equation for the complete combustion of $C_5H_{12}O$.
    b   Identify each isomer as a primary, secondary or tertiary alcohol.
    c   For each isomer, write the equation (using structural formulae) for all the reactions that would occur if each alcohol was heated with acidified potassium permanganate solution.
    d   The heat of combustion of pentan-1-ol is $-3324\,kJ\,mol^{-1}$. Determine the amount, in mol, of pentan-1-ol, which has to be burnt in order to heat 500 g of water from 20.0°C to boiling. Assume all the heat released is used to heat the water.

5   Name the organic products formed when each of the following pairs of compounds react.
    a   2-chlorobutane and aqueous sodium hydroxide
    b   2-bromopentane and water in the presence of a catalyst
    c   1-bromobutane and aqueous sodium hydroxide.

6   Write unbalanced chemical equations for the production of:
    a   methanol from chloromethane
    b   propan-1-ol from 1-chloropropane.

7   Why are the products of fermentation distilled before being used as a fuel?

12.2 Fossil fuels and biofuels

In this section, you will learn how fuels are used to meet global energy needs and gain an appreciation of the chemistry that underpins decisions about the use of fuels. Combustion reactions are used to release useful heat energy from the chemical energy stored in fuels. You will explore how fuels vary in terms of the energy that they produce when they are burnt.

You will consider the environmental impact of using different types of fuels, including their carbon emissions as well as the other pollutants they release into the atmosphere. Current research into the production of renewable fuels and the potential for reducing the harmful impact of fossil fuels will also be discussed.

TYPES OF FUELS

Fuels provide you with energy. They are substances that have chemical energy stored within them. All chemical bonds contain stored energy. What makes a fuel special is that this stored chemical energy can be released relatively easily.

Sugar is an example of a common fuel (Figure 12.2.1). A cube of table sugar (sucrose) can provide your body with 82 kilojoules of energy. This is about 1% of your daily energy needs. If sucrose is burnt, this energy is released as heat. The **combustion** of 1 kilogram of sucrose releases enough energy to melt more than 5 kilograms of ice and then boil all the liquid water produced.

Although sugars provide energy for your body, you do not heat your home, power cars or produce electricity by burning sugar. A range of other fuels such as wood, coal, oil, natural gas, LPG, ethanol and petrol are used for these energy needs (Figure 12.2.2).

In this section you will explore the range and sources of fuels that are used for transportation.

Although this chapter will focus on fuels with stored chemical energy, the term 'fuel' is also applied to sources of nuclear energy, such as uranium.

The use of fuels by society can be considered from a number of points of view, including:
- a local level (e.g. the type of petrol used in your car)
- a national level (e.g. whether Australia's use of energy resources is sustainable)
- a global level (e.g. whether the use of fossil fuels (coal, oil and natural gas) is contributing to the enhanced greenhouse effect).

These are not separate issues. Choices made locally have regional and global effects. The decisions of global and national governments affect which fuels are used, as well as how they are used.

FOSSIL FUELS

For a fuel to be **sustainable**, the starting material must be produced at least as quickly as it is consumed, and it must be possible for the environment to absorb or process all of the wastes produced by making and using the fuel. Fossil fuels are not sustainable under either of these criteria. The rate of consumption is far greater than the rate of production, and the build-up of atmospheric CO_2 from burning fossil fuels makes a large contribution to global climate change.

Fossil fuels—coal, oil and natural gas—are **non-renewable** fuels because they form in the environment over very long time periods but are used very quickly. Since reserves of fossil fuels are limited and they are consumed at unsustainable rates, they will eventually be exhausted or have to be replaced with **renewable** alternatives. Fuels that are renewable or sustainable are discussed later in this section.

FIGURE 12.2.1 Sugars such as sucrose are fuels for your body.

FIGURE 12.2.2 Petrol is just one type of fuel that is used each day to meet our energy needs.

> ⓘ Fossil fuels are neither sustainable nor renewable fuels.

Forming crude oil

The main deposits of crude oil were formed from small marine animals (zooplankton) and plants (phytoplankton) that lived up to 1 billion years ago. Some crude oil deposits are estimated to be even older, as much as 3–4 billion years old. If a deposit of crude oil was trapped beneath a layer of impermeable rock, then a layer of natural gas would also form.

The first commercial deposits of crude oil were discovered at the end of the 19th century in the United States. Today, the largest crude oil deposits are in Russia, Iran, Iraq and Saudi Arabia. The oldest deposits found so far are in Venezuela, where the oil is estimated to be almost 4 billion years old. However, only about 10% of the oil discovered is profitable to extract.

Permeable rocks contain tiny spaces through which liquid substances can move. Crude oil has a lower density than water, so oil migrates upwards through permeable rocks over time. Large deposits of oil are formed when portions of this migrating oil become trapped under impermeable rocks. To extract the crude oil, drilling into the impermeable rock has to take place (Figure 12.2.3). In most cases, the oil flows up by itself under high pressure that has gradually built up from when the oil was formed. As the extraction continues, the overall pressure drops and the remaining deposit is extracted using pumps or by injecting gases into the oil wells.

Global supply of crude oil is finite, and the consumption of crude oil damages the environment. Recognising that the way that this resource is used is not sustainable, many companies and countries are making preparations to move away from its use as a fuel. France and the UK have announced they will ban the sale of petrol cars by 2040, and Volvo will stop making cars powered only by petrol by 2019.

FIGURE 12.2.3 A drill operating during oil and gas exploration.

Formation of fossil fuels

Coal, oil and natural gas were formed from ancient plants, animals and microorganisms. Buried under tonnes of mud, sand and rock, this once biological material has undergone complex changes to become the fossil fuels used by societies today. The organic matter still retains some of the chemical energy the plants originally accumulated by carrying out **photosynthesis**. Chemical energy in fossil fuels can be considered to be trapped solar energy.

> ⓘ Fossil fuels formed from the decomposed remains of organisms that were alive millions or billions of years ago.

Fuels from crude oil

Australia's relatively small oil reserves are likely to be exhausted later this century. Australia already imports over 90% of the crude oil it uses. The importation of large amounts of oil has a significant impact on Australia's economy.

Crude oil is a mixture of hydrocarbon molecules that are mostly members of the **homologous series** of alkanes. Crude oil itself is of no use as a fuel, but it contains many useful compounds.

> ⓘ Petrol, diesel, natural gas, bitumen and some lubricants are extracted from crude oil by fractional distillation.

The hydrocarbons in crude oil are separated by **fractional distillation**, which uses heat and a fractionating column to separate a mixture into a number of different parts or fractions (Figure 12.2.4). Each fraction consists of alkanes within a specific mass range. Lighter alkanes condense in the cooler regions near the top of the tower, and heavier alkanes condense in the hotter areas near the bottom. For example, the petrol fraction that boils (and condenses) between 100°C and 250°C consists of alkanes containing 8–12 carbon atoms; that is, C_8H_{18} to $C_{12}H_{26}$.

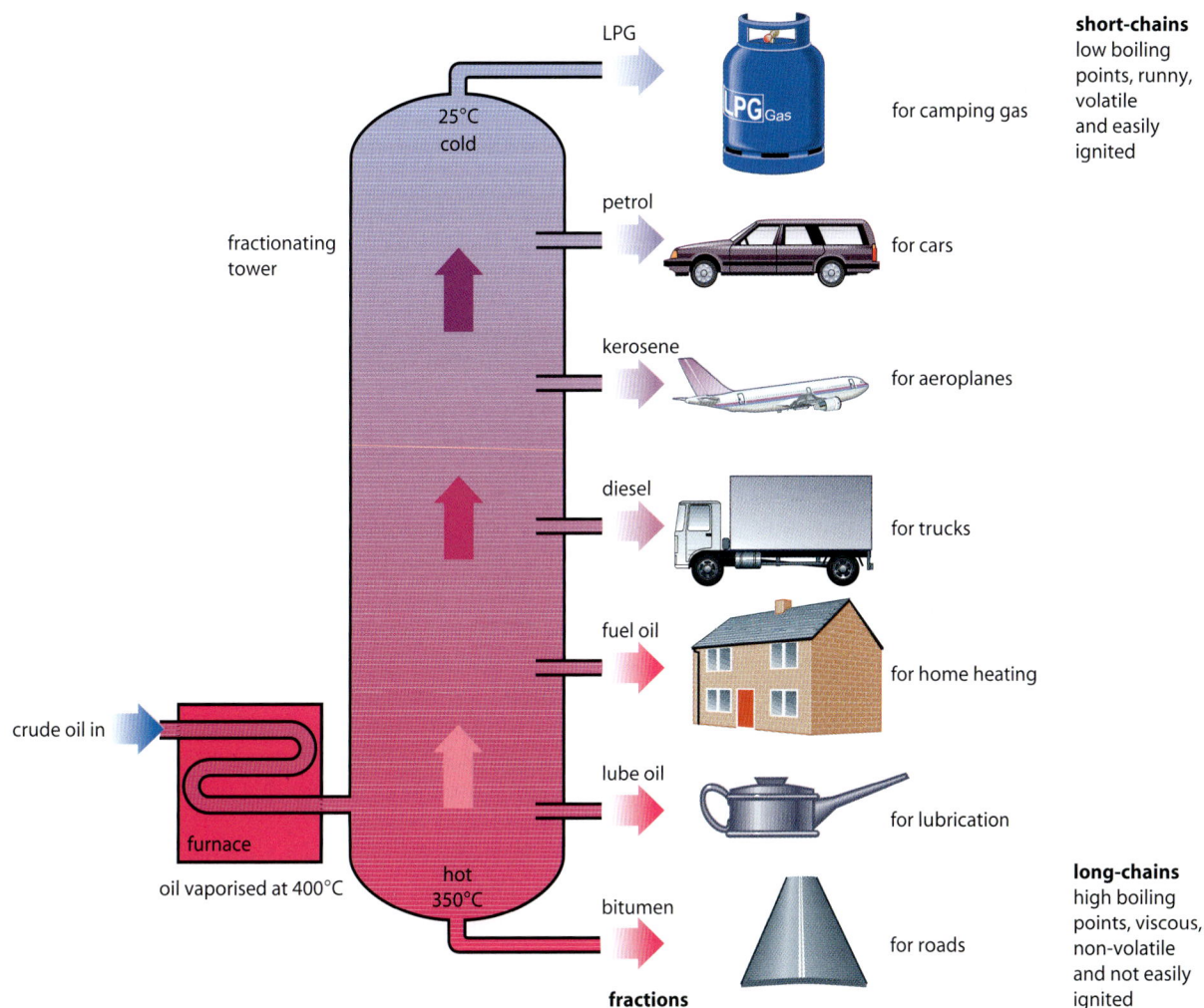

FIGURE 12.2.4 Many products can be separated from crude oil using fractional distillation.

Petrol and petrodiesel

Petrol is a mixture of hydrocarbons, with a key component being octane (C_8H_{18}). Another major transport fuel is **petrodiesel**, which consists mostly of alkanes ranging from $C_{10}H_{22}$ to $C_{15}H_{32}$. The combustion of these two fuels powers most of Australia's 18.8 million motor vehicles.

Natural gas

Natural gas is another fossil fuel found in deposits in the Earth's crust. It is composed mainly of methane (CH_4) but includes small amounts of other hydrocarbons such as ethane (C_2H_6) and propane (C_3H_8). Water, sulfur, carbon dioxide and nitrogen may also be present in natural gas.

Natural gas can be found:

- in gas reservoirs trapped between layers of rocks
- as a component of petroleum deposits
- in coal deposits where it is bonded to the surface of the coal.
- trapped in shale rock, where it is referred to as **shale gas**.

Coal seams usually contain water and the pressure of the water can keep the gas adsorbed to the coal surface. This type of natural gas is known as **coal seam gas** or CSG. It is a major component of the energy supplies of Queensland.

Shale gas is mined commercially in the USA, Canada, China and Argentina.

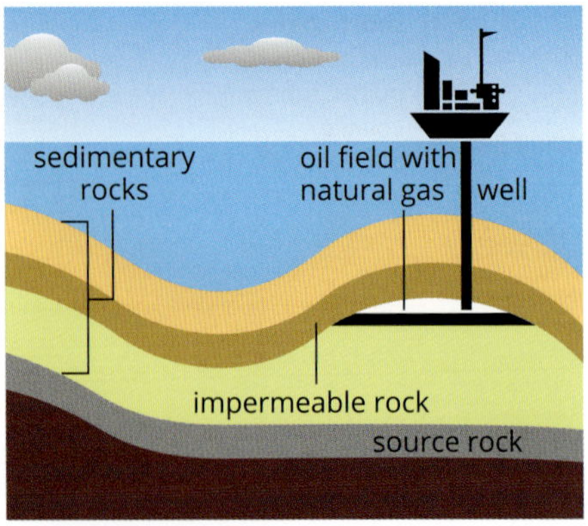

Natural gas is accessed by drilling as with crude oil; drilling causes the natural gas to flow to the surface (Figure 12.2.5).

Liquefied petroleum gas

Propane and butane gases can be separated from natural gas by fractional distillation. Propane and butane become liquids under pressure and are sold as **liquefied petroleum gas** (LPG). LPG is used as a fuel in cars and in home gas bottles such as those in Figure 12.2.6. The natural gas remaining after the removal of propane and butane is used widely as a fuel for home heating and cooking.

> ℹ Natural gas is a mixture of alkanes with four or fewer carbons that have low boiling points. Liquid petroleum gas (LPG) contains butane and propane extracted from natural gas.

BIOFUELS

Governments and industry are exploring alternatives to fossil fuels in order to meet our future energy needs and limit the impact of fossil fuels on the environment. Ideally, new sources of energy will be renewable and sustainable. Renewable energy is energy that can be obtained from natural resources that can be constantly replenished.

Biofuels (or **biochemical fuels**) are fuels derived from plant materials such as grains (maize, wheat, barley or sorghum), sugar cane and vegetable waste, and vegetable oils such as canola (Figure 12.2.7). The three main biofuels are biogas, bioethanol and biodiesel. They can be used alone or blended with fossil fuels such as petrol and diesel.

As well as being renewable, biofuels are predicted to have less impact on the environment than fossil fuels. The plant materials used in the generation of biofuels are produced by photosynthesis, which removes carbon dioxide from the atmosphere and produces glucose ($C_6H_{12}O_6$) in the following reaction:

$$6CO_2(g) + 6H_2O(l) \rightarrow C_6H_{12}O_6(aq) + 6O_2(g)$$

The plants convert the glucose into cellulose and starch. Although carbon dioxide is released back into the atmosphere when the biofuel is burnt, the net impact is less than for fossil fuels if the fuel is made from sustainable sources.

Biodiesel

Biodiesel is a mixture of esters with long hydrocarbon chains. These esters are produced by a chemical reaction between vegetable oils or animal fats and an alcohol, most commonly methanol (CH_3OH). This reaction is explored in detail in Chapter 13 and is very similar to the process used in making soap.

The usual raw material for the production of biodiesel is vegetable oil from sources such as soybeans, canola or palm oil. Recycled vegetable oil or animal fats can also be used. The structure of a typical biodiesel molecule is shown in Figure 12.2.8.

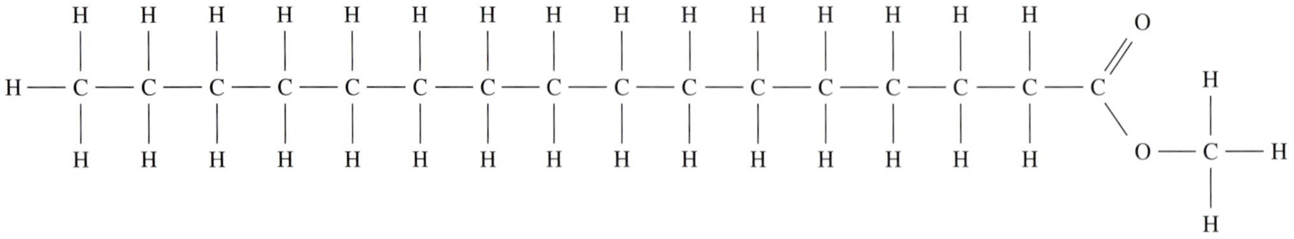

FIGURE 12.2.5 Natural gas deposits are often found trapped above crude oil. Once a well is sunk into the deposit, the natural gas flows to the surface.

FIGURE 12.2.6 Liquid petroleum gas bottles

FIGURE 12.2.7 A field of canola. Canola oil can be a source of the raw materials for the production of biodiesel.

GO TO ➤ Section 13.1 page 350

FIGURE 12.2.8 Structural formula of a typical biodiesel molecule

Palm oil plantations: Renewable versus sustainable

Palm oil is a very common ingredient in food and cosmetics, but it is also turned into biodiesel. It has a particularly high concentration of long hydrocarbon chain carboxylic acids that are used in producing this fuel. One of the acids, $CH_3(CH_2)_{14}COOH$, which has the non-IUPAC name palmitic acid because it was first discovered in palm oil, is a major component of the refined oil.

To judge the sustainability of a fuel, it is important to consider its sources. All biodiesel produced from palm oil is renewable, but almost none of it is sustainable. The oil is renewable because it comes from the fruit of the African oil palm, *Elaeis guineensis* (Figure 12.2.9). The tree is fast-growing and high-yielding, producing 40 kg of oil from each tree every year. The fruit is very hard, red when ripe and around the size of a large plum, and about 30% of the fruit is extractable oil. The fruit grows in bunches that can weigh 30 kg each (Figure 12.2.10).

About 85% of the world's supply of palm oil is grown in Malaysia and Indonesia, and much of this is not grown sustainably. Oil palm trees require large amounts of rainfall and fertiliser for their growth, and almost all areas where oil palm trees currently grow are cleared tropical rainforests. In 2015 an area twice the size of the Sydney metropolitan area was cleared from Indonesia's forests, and much of this land clearing was for agricultural purposes including oil palm plantations. Land clearing is a significant contributor to global CO_2 emissions and to habitat loss. Indonesian and Malaysian forests are hotbeds for biodiversity and home to many species that are found nowhere else, including the endangered orangutan (Figure 12.2.11).

A small but growing number of vehicles are powered by biodiesel from sources that are renewable and sustainable. For example, the biodiesel used by all trucks owned by the City of Sydney is made from recycled cooking oil from fish and chip shops.

FIGURE 12.2.9 Part of a plantation of oil palm trees

FIGURE 12.2.11 An adult and young orangutan. These apes are only found in small parts of Malaysia and Indonesia.

FIGURE 12.2.10 Ripe red fruit growing on an oil palm tree

Bioethanol

Bioethanol is produced from the fermentation of carbohydrates, commonly sourced from crops such as sugar cane. However, sugar cane is also needed for sugar production, so there are limits to the amounts of bioethanol that can be produced in this way. Instead, researchers are trialling less valuable and highly sustainable sources of sugar and starch for bioethanol production.

The Manildra plant at Nowra in New South Wales, shown in Figure 12.2.12, is one of Australia's largest ethanol refineries. At this plant, flour and starch are produced from wheat and sold for use in food manufacture. The waste that remains still contains high levels of starch, which is converted to ethanol.

FIGURE 12.2.12 Ethanol refinery in the Manildra plant at Nowra, New South Wales

Biogas

Biogas is gas that is released in the breakdown of organic waste by anaerobic bacteria. These bacteria decompose the complex molecules contained in substances such as carbohydrates and proteins into the simple molecular compounds carbon dioxide and methane. A digester (Figure 12.2.13) is a large tank filled with the anaerobic bacteria that digest (consume) the complex molecules to form biogas.

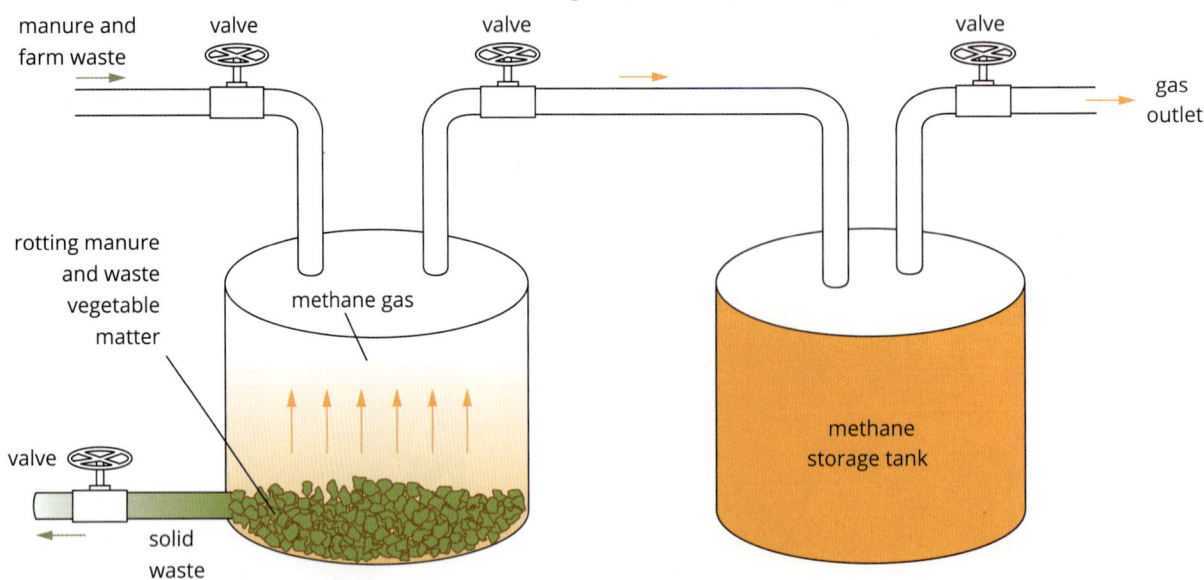

FIGURE 12.2.13 A digester is used in the production of biogas

A range of materials, including rotting rubbish (such as that seen in Figure 12.2.14) and decomposing plant material, can be used to produce biogas.

Biogas consists mainly of methane and carbon dioxide. Biogas can be used for heating and to power homes and farms. There are more than 7 million biogas generators in China. Biogas generators are particularly suited to farms, as the waste from a biogas generator makes a rich fertiliser.

FIGURE 12.2.14 Pipes buried in this rubbish tip collect biogas.

In the future, it is likely more energy will be obtained from biogas generated at sewage works, chicken farms, piggeries and food-processing plants. Your local rubbish tip also has the potential to supply biogas. The gas can be used directly for small-scale heating or to generate electricity.

USING FOSSIL FUELS AND BIOFUELS

Fuels contain stored chemical energy that can be harnessed to perform useful functions. The heat energy released when fuels are burnt provides heat for warmth and cooking, as well as generating electrical energy and mechanical energy for transport and other uses.

In this section you will look at the different fuels used to power vehicles and compare the environmental impact of these fuels.

Fuel for transport

Crude oil is the source of most of the fuels, such as LPG, petrol, kerosene and petrodiesel used for transport. However, because of global concerns about the greenhouse gas emissions from fossil fuels, there is great interest in the production of renewable biofuels such as bioethanol and biodiesel.

Petrol

Petrol is the main transport fuel used to power motor vehicles. Its main component is octane, and the equation for its combustion is:

$$2C_8H_{18}(l) + 25O_2(g) \rightarrow 16CO_2(g) + 18H_2O(l)$$

The combustion of 1 mole of octane releases 5450 kJ of energy, equivalent to $47.8\,kJ\,g^{-1}$.

> **Petrol** is a mixture that contains many components, including octane.

Petrodiesel

Petrodiesel is the other main transport fuel used to power motor vehicles. Since petrodiesel is a mixture of hydrocarbons, no one chemical equation can be used to represent its combustion. The known value for the **energy content** of petrodiesel is $48\,kJ\,g^{-1}$, which is very similar to that of petrol.

Liquefied petroleum gas

Liquefied petroleum gas (LPG) can also be used in vehicles. Most of the vehicles that use LPG as a fuel have a standard petrol engine with a fuel tank and fuel injection system modified to suit a gaseous fuel. The equation for the combustion of propane, a major component of LPG, is:

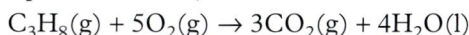

$$C_3H_8(g) + 5O_2(g) \rightarrow 3CO_2(g) + 4H_2O(l)$$

The combustion of 1 mole of propane releases 2220 kJ of energy, equivalent to 50.5 kJ g^{-1}.

In Australia LPG is a significantly cheaper fuel than petrol, yet its popularity is still limited. Some of the reasons for this are as follows:

- Most new vehicles are designed to run only on petrol, so the owner has to pay around $2500 to $4500 for a conversion.
- The LPG fuel tank takes up boot space.
- There are fears that LPG cylinders might explode if the vehicle crashes.
- The prices of fuels fluctuate, so often it is difficult to do meaningful price comparisons.

Biodiesel

Biodiesel can be used as a straight replacement for petrodiesel in motor vehicles. Because biodiesel molecules are esters with long hydrocarbon chains, biodiesel does have slightly different properties compared with petrodiesel; in particular, it has a higher melting point and viscosity, and is susceptible to absorption of moisture. Because of these factors, biodiesel for use in motor vehicles is usually blended with petrodiesel.

Bioethanol

Ethanol can be blended with petrol for use in motor vehicles. Australian government regulations limit the proportion of ethanol in petrol to 10%. This petrol blend is labelled E10 and sold at most Australian service stations. The presence of ethanol reduces the emissions of particulates and gases such as oxides of nitrogen, but higher levels of ethanol can damage engines, especially in older vehicles.

The equation for the combustion of ethanol is:

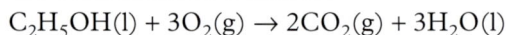

$$C_2H_5OH(l) + 3O_2(g) \rightarrow 2CO_2(g) + 3H_2O(l)$$

The combustion of 1 mole of ethanol releases 1367 kJ of energy, equivalent to 29.7 kJ g^{-1}. As Table 12.2.1 shows, the energy content of ethanol is about 62% that of petrol, so a larger mass of ethanol is required to provide the same amount of energy. At a simple level, the lower energy content of ethanol can be regarded as the result of the carbon atoms in an ethanol molecule being partly oxidised ('partly burnt'). This is because of the presence of oxygen in the ethanol molecule.

TABLE 12.2.1 Energy content and energy density of vehicle fuels

Fuel	Energy content (kJ g^{-1})
methane	56
propane (LPG component)	51
butane (LPG component)	50
octane (petrol fraction)	48
petrodiesel	48
biodiesel	41
ethanol	30

ENVIRONMENTAL IMPACT OF FUELS

A discussion of the environmental impact of fuels needs to consider both the impact of emissions from the combustion of the fuel, and the impact on the environment of obtaining the fuel in the first place.

Carbon dioxide emissions from fuel combustion

Because large quantities of fuel are burnt every day to meet society's energy needs, the level of carbon dioxide production is high. This is a concern because carbon dioxide is a **greenhouse gas**.

Energy from the Sun heats the surface of the Earth. The Earth in turn radiates energy back towards space, but greenhouse gases in the atmosphere absorb and re-radiate the energy in a process known as the **greenhouse effect**. The higher the concentration of greenhouse gas, the more energy is trapped (Figure 12.2.15).

The greenhouse effect occurs naturally because of the gases present in the atmosphere. However, the increasing levels of greenhouse gases produced by our use of fossil fuels are causing global warming and triggering consequential shifts in weather patterns and climate. This is referred to as the **enhanced greenhouse effect**.

Methane, water vapour, nitrogen oxides and ozone are also greenhouse gases. Methane is 21 times more effective at trapping heat than carbon dioxide.

> **i** The greenhouse effect is caused by heat being trapped in the Earth's atmosphere by greenhouse gases, which causes an increase in temperatures at the Earth's surface. As the amount of greenhouse gases in the Earth's atmosphere increases due to human activities, more heat is trapped, which is predicted to cause global changes in climate.

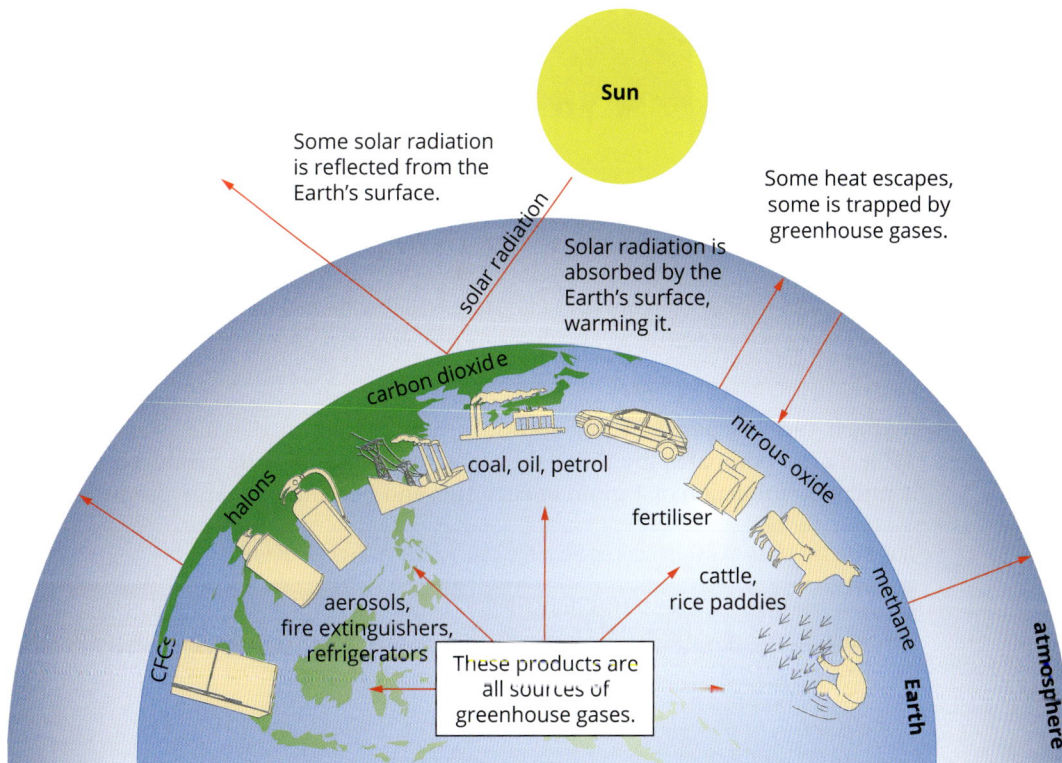

FIGURE 12.2.15 The greenhouse effect. Greenhouse gases help to maintain the temperature at the Earth's surface. Increased quantities of these gases as a result of human activities create an enhanced greenhouse effect.

Figure 12.2.16 on page 342 shows the warming of the Earth's atmosphere and scientific predictions of an increasing greenhouse effect. Many countries are choosing alternatives to fossil fuels to address these fears.

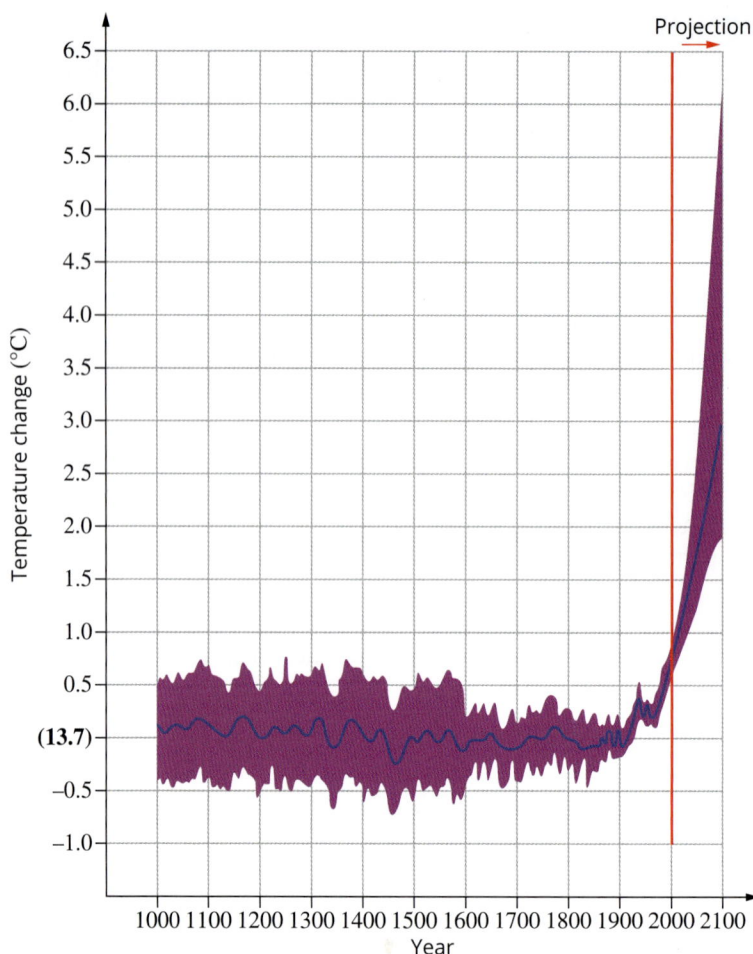

FIGURE 12.2.16 Change in the average surface temperature of the Earth from the year 1000 projected to 2100. Estimates of future temperature increases vary, depending on what assumptions are made.

Each fuel discussed in this section produces carbon dioxide when it burns. Table 12.2.2 compares the theoretical mass of carbon dioxide produced from the complete combustion of 1 gram of each fuel and per unit of energy produced.

TABLE 12.2.2 Mass of CO_2 produced from the combustion of 1 gram of fuel

Fuel	Mass of CO_2 (g) emitted per gram of fuel	Mass of CO_2 (g) per megajoule of energy produced (approx.)
coal	3.7	93
natural gas	2.8	56
LPG	3.0	65
petrol	3.1	73
ethanol	1.9	72

Bioethanol is a renewable fuel derived from plants. Although carbon dioxide is produced when bioethanol burns, carbon dioxide is also absorbed by the plants as they grow. For this reason the widespread use of bioethanol should lead to a net reduction in the levels of carbon dioxide emitted.

However, bioethanol is not **carbon neutral**. This is because energy is required, and emissions are produced, in the growing, transport and refining of the fuel. And although a relatively low mass of carbon dioxide is emitted per gram of fuel burnt, because bioethanol produces much less energy than the same mass or volume of petrol, a similar mass of carbon dioxide is emitted to produce the same quantity of energy.

Impact of sourcing the fuel

All fuels have to be extracted or synthesised, and the environmental impact of sourcing a fuel needs to be considered. Table 12.2.3 shows some of the sources of the fuels described in this chapter.

TABLE 12.2.3 Sources of fuels

Fuel source	Notes
Biogas collected under domes from a sewage plant	Biogas is often collected from sewage farms and rubbish tips. The gas collection minimises emissions associated with these sites. Because methane is much more effective as a greenhouse gas than carbon dioxide, it is better to collect the methane in biogas and combust it to produce carbon dioxide than to release it directly to the atmosphere.
An oil rig	Oil rigs, once in place, can operate with low impact on the environment, but the issues created when a spill or explosion occurs can be significant.
Harvesting a wheat crop for bioethanol production	Bioethanol is produced from crops. Growing crops requires energy expenditure and the use of resources such as water and fertiliser. Intensive farming can lead to land degradation and erosion. These are larger issues if crops are grown solely to produce ethanol, but of less concern if waste from food crops is used as a raw material, which is mostly the case in Australia. Diverting crops from fuel production could also drive up the cost of food produced from those crops.

Renewability

Fossil fuels are a non-renewable source of energy. It took millions of years for their formation in the Earth's crust, so the likelihood of new deposits forming cannot be considered. The reserves of each fossil fuel are summarised below.

- Crude oil—reserves are more limited than those of coal and availability is likely to decline in coming decades.
- Natural gas—deposits are likely to be exhausted over the coming decades but reserves of coal seam gas and shale gas could potentially provide natural gas into the next century. Concerns over fracking—the extraction of gas by injecting water under high pressure into rocks so as to break them open, releasing the gas—need to be resolved if natural gas is to be sourced from these reserves.

Biofuels are renewable and some aspects of our current production levels are sustainable. However, biofuels produce only a small percentage of Australia's fuel needs.

If biofuel production were to increase significantly, we could need to grow crops specifically for this purpose. This would present a number of issues, including land degradation, clearing of forest and bushland, and ensuring food supplies are maintained.

WS
7.7

12.2 Review

SUMMARY

- A fuel is a substance with stored energy that can be released relatively easily for use as heat or power.
- A fuel is non-renewable if it cannot be replenished at the rate at which it is consumed. Fossil fuels such as coal, oil and natural gas are non-renewable.
- Fossil fuels are produced over millions of years by the breakdown of biomass at high temperatures and pressures underground. Australia has large reserves of coal and natural gas.
- A fuel is renewable if it can be replenished at the rate at which it is consumed. Biofuels such as biogas, bioethanol and biodiesel are renewable.
- Bioethanol can be produced by fermentation of starches and sugars.
- Biodiesel is produced in a reaction between a vegetable oil or an animal fat and a small alcohol molecule such as methanol.
- Biogas is formed by the anaerobic breakdown of organic waste.
- Some of the non-renewable and renewable fuels in use in Australia are listed in the table below.

Non-renewable fuels	Renewable fuels
coal oil liquefied petroleum gas (LPG) natural gas coal seam gas (CSG)	bioethanol biogas biodiesel

- Fuels such as petrol, diesel, natural gas, biodiesel, biogas and bioethanol undergo combustion reactions in excess oxygen to form carbon dioxide and water.
- The combustion reactions of fuels are used to power vehicles.
- Petrol engines can use petrol or petrol blended with ethanol. Engines can also be modified to run on LPG.
- Petrol produces more energy per gram than LPG or bioethanol. However, bioethanol and LPG produce less carbon dioxide and particulates in emissions.
- Biodiesel is a renewable alternative to petrodiesel.
- Biofuels offer several environmental advantages. In particular, CO_2 is absorbed during the growth of crops used in their production, the resource is renewable, and they can be produced from material that would have otherwise been wasted.
- A shift to large-scale production of biofuels could place a strain on resources and available farmland.

- The table below compares the advantages and disadvantages of some fuels.

Fuel	Advantages	Disadvantages
natural gas	• more efficient than coal for electricity production • easy to transport through pipes • relatively high energy content	• non-renewable • limited reserves • polluting but less than coal and petrol
biogas	• renewable • made from waste • reduces waste disposal • low running costs • CO_2 absorbed during photosynthesis often sustainable	• low energy content • supply of waste raw materials limited
petrol	• high energy content • ease of transport	• non-renewable • polluting but less than coal • limited reserves
LPG	• low cost • easily separated from natural gas • relatively high energy content; fewer particulates produced than petrol	• non-renewable • polluting but less than petrol
bioethanol	• renewable • can be made from waste • CO_2 absorbed during photosynthesis • burns smoothly • fewer particulates produced than petrol	• limited supply of raw materials from which to produce it • lower energy content than petrol • may require use of farmland otherwise used for food production

1   What is the difference between a renewable and non-renewable fuel?

2   What factors must be considered to determine whether a fuel is sustainable or unsustainable?

3   Give an example of a renewable fuel source and a non-renewable fuel source used in Australia.

4   Wood from forests is a renewable resource that supplied global energy needs for thousands of years.
    a   Why is wood no longer sustainable as the major energy source for today's society?
    b   Is it possible for a resource to be both non-renewable and sustainable? Explain.

5   Explain why is it necessary to process crude oil by fractional distillation.

6   Classify each of the following as an advantage or a disadvantage of the use of bioethanol compared to petrol as an energy source.
    a   There is less CO_2 produced overall.
    b   it has a lower energy content ($kJ\,g^{-1}$).
    c   It can be produced from waste products.
    d   It is produced from a renewable resource.
    e   A greater amount of CO_2 is emitted by vehicles for each kilometre travelled.

Chapter review

KEY TERMS

alcohol
alkane
biochemical fuel
biodiesel
bioethanol
biofuel
biogas
carbon neutral
catalyst
coal seam gas
combustion
dehydration reaction

dispersion force
distillation
electronegative
energy content
enhanced greenhouse
 effect
enthalpy change
fermentation
fossil fuel
fractional distillation
fuel
greenhouse effect

greenhouse gas
haloalkane
heat of reaction
homologous series
hydrocarbon
hydrogen bond
hydrogen halide
isomer
liquefied petroleum gas
natural gas
non-renewable
petrodiesel

photosynthesis
polar bond
primary alcohol
renewable
secondary alcohol
shale gas
substitution reaction
sustainable
tertiary alcohol

REVIEW QUESTIONS

1 Which of the following is the main reason that propan-1-ol has a higher boiling point than propane?
   A Propan-1-ol has stronger dispersion forces than propane.
   B Propan-1-ol has a lower molar mass than propane.
   C The boiling points are difficult to measure because propane is so flammable.
   D Propan-1-ol is able to form intermolecular hydrogen bonds between molecules but propane is not.

2 Consider the following compounds:
   $CH_3CH(CH_3)CH(CH_3)CH_2CH_2OH$, $CH_3(CH_2)_5CH_2OH$,
   $CH_3CH(CH_3)CH_2CH_2CH_2CH_2OH$.
   a Place the compounds in order of increasing boiling point.
   b Would the compounds have a greater solubility in water or in hexane? Explain your answer.

3 Name the products of the following reactions:
   a bromoethane + sodium hydroxide
   b 1-iodopentane + heat, water and a catalyst
   c 2-chlorohexane + potassium hydroxide

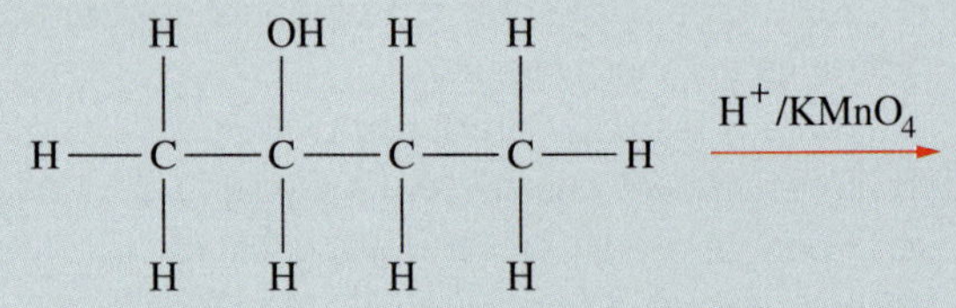

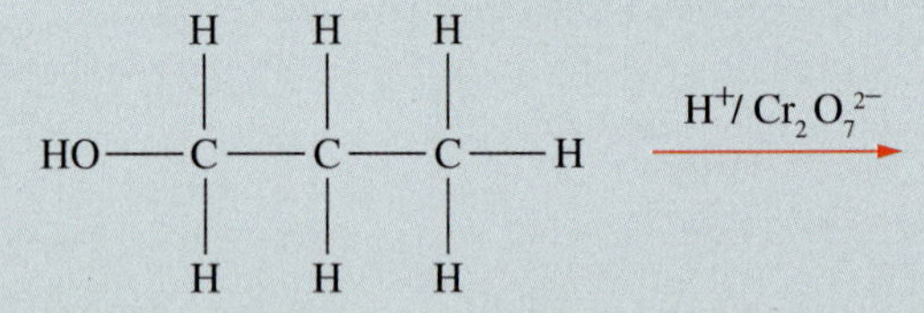

4 a Give one reason why fermentation reactions often produce multiple products.
   b What are some advantages and disadvantages of making alcohols by fermentation rather than by a substitution reaction with a haloalkane?

5 State the name of the functional group that will be formed in reactions of the following types of alcohols with acidified potassium permanganate solution. If there is more than one possible product, state both names:
   a primary alcohol
   b secondary alcohol
   c tertiary alcohol.

6 Draw the structural formulas of the products of the following reactions.

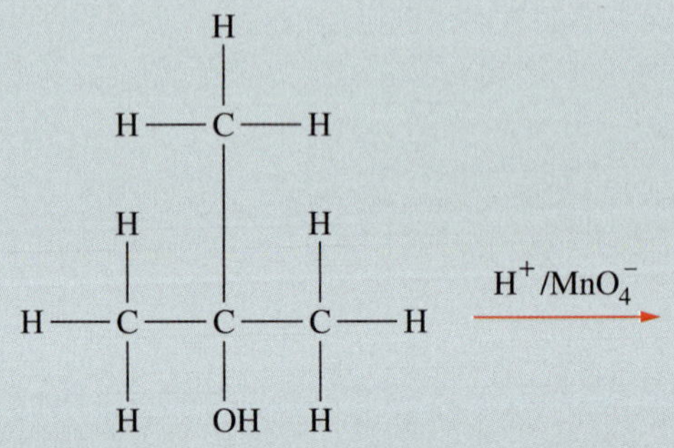

7 Identify the product that will be formed from the reaction of:
   a 2-methylhexan-2-ol heated with acidified potassium permanganate
   b ethanol boiled with acidified potassium permanganate, with a long heating time
   c pentan-3-ol heated with $H^+/Cr_2O_7^{2-}$
   d butan-1-ol reacted with $H^+/Cr_2O_7^{2-}$ using mild heat; the product is distilled off as it forms.

8 Write unbalanced chemical equations for the production of:
   a propene from propan-1-ol
   b butan-1-ol from 1-chlorobutane
   c 1-bromopropane from propan-1-ol.

9 Write fully balanced equations for the combustion reactions of:

    a pentan-1-ol   **b** propan-2-ol.

10 Raoul is working with his classmates and using the experimental apparatus shown in Figure 12.1.17 on page 327 to measure the enthalpy of combustion of 2-methylbutan-2-ol. In the experiment, 100.0 g of water increases in temperature from 22.72°C to 77.04°C and 0.793 g of 2-methylbutan-2-ol is used. The specific heat capacity of water is $4.18\,J\,g^{-1}\,K^{-1}$.

    a According to these results, what is the enthalpy of combustion of 2-methylbutan-2-ol?

    b What are the likely sources of experimental error in Raoul's experiment?

11 The world has become very dependent on the products of the petrochemical industry, but the raw materials of crude oil and natural gas are likely to be almost exhausted by 2100. Assuming that current production remains unchanged and no alternative sources are available, suggest the impact of the lack of raw materials on our lifestyle.

12 Fossil fuels formed from organisms that lived around:

    A 1000 years ago   **B** 100 000 years ago

    C 10 million years ago   **D** 1000 million years ago

13 Crude oil is a complex mixture. How are the components of this mixture separated for use as fuels?

14 Why are fossil fuels considered to be non-renewable?

15 What types of vegetable oils is biodiesel commonly sourced from?

16 Which of the following is the most likely component of petrodiesel?

    A propene   **B** C_3H_8 **C** $C_{11}H_{24}$ **D** $C_{16}H_{24}O_2$

17 What are some important factors to consider when classifying a fuel as sustainable?

18 Biogas, petrol and bioethanol are used to power vehicles.

    a List the currently used fuels in order of their energy content per gram (from highest to lowest). You may need to refer to Table 12.2.1 on page 340.

    b The emissions of carbon dioxide per gram from the combustion of bioethanol are less than that from octane (petrol). However, a car using bioethanol produces more carbon dioxide when driving the same distance as a car using octane. Which one of the following could be the best explanation for this difference?

        A Bioethanol is more efficient than octane.

        B The energy content of bioethanol is less than that of octane.

        C The temperature of the engine favours the combustion of octane.

        D More energy transformations are required in the combustion of bioethanol.

19 Explain why bioethanol is sometimes described as a 'carbon neutral' fuel. Use chemical equations for photosynthesis, fermentation and combustion to support your answer.

20 Trials are being conducted to source biodiesel from algae grown in the warm water of a power station cooling pond. The water is warm and carbon dioxide emitted from the power station can be trapped and bubbled through the water to enhance the growth of the algae. Classify the following as advantages or disadvantages of large-scale production of biodiesel from algae.

    a It is a renewable resource.

    b There is less reliance on fossil fuels.

    c It has a lower energy content than petrodiesel.

    d It produces lower overall CO_2 emissions than petrodiesel.

    e Oil can be 'harvested' many times per year.

    f It reduces the overall CO_2 emissions from coal-fired power stations.

21 a Explain what 'E10 petrol' means.

    b How does the introduction of E10 help with the potential shortage of crude oil?

22 Conduct some research using the internet to discover some of the consequences of global warming. Give one example each of the effect on:

    a the polar ice caps   **b** changing weather patterns

    c crop production   **d** extinction of species.

23 Ethanol is produced industrially by reacting ethene with water using a phosphoric acid catalyst at 300°C:

$$C_2H_4(g) + H_2O(g) \rightarrow CH_3CH_2OH(g)$$

    a Explain why this ethanol is not a biofuel.

    b Describe how biofuel ethanol could be produced.

24 Conduct some research on the internet to find out which nations are the 10 largest consumers of energy. Ensure you record the source of your data.

25 The 2015 Paris Agreement was an international response to global warming in which all nations were asked to commit to keeping the global average temperature rise to below 2°C, through reductions in greenhouse gas emissions.

    a What impact would adopting the Paris Agreement have on Australia?

    b Discuss the role that biofuels could play in helping Australia meet its target for reducing greenhouse gas emissions.

26 Reflect on the Inquiry task on page 320. Using concepts from this chapter explain why the ethanol did not dissolve in the vegetable oil.

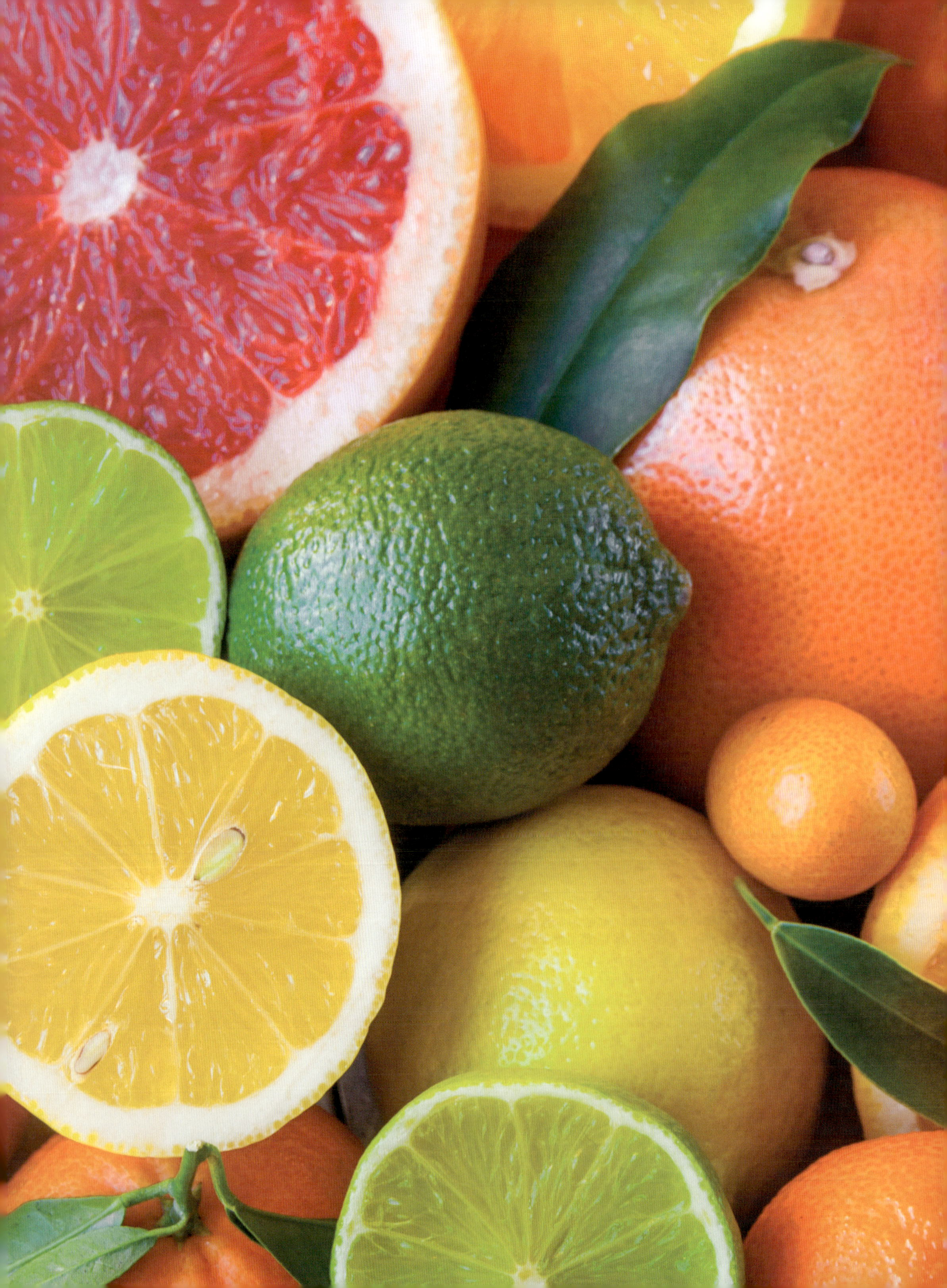

13 Reactions of organic acids and bases

The most common organic acid or base in most peoples' lives is ethanoic acid, which is found in vinegar. Vinegar is typical of many organic acids. It is soluble in water, has a distinctive smell that spreads through a room because it is volatile, has a sharp taste and is an important part of many other foods. Other very common carboxylic acids, such as citric acid in oranges and lemons and ascorbic acid (vitamin C) have important health or medical properties.

Your body is held together by other molecules that are discussed in this chapter. For example, amides can be formed from carboxylic acids. Amides form the core structure of proteins, which are the basis of skin, hair, muscle and many other vital parts of your body.

This chapter shows how some organic acids and bases, and molecules derived from them, interact with each other through some of the forces that have already been discussed in Chapters 10, 11 and 12. You will look closely at their structures and examine ways they react and change.

Content

INQUIRY QUESTION

What are the properties of organic acids and bases?

By the end of this chapter, you will be able to:

- investigate the structural formulae, properties and functional group including:
  - primary, secondary and tertiary alcohols ICT
  - aldehydes and ketones (ACSCH127) ICT
  - amines and amides
  - carboxylic acids
- explain the properties within and between the homologous series of carboxylic acids, amines and amides with reference to the intermolecular and intramolecular bonding present ICT
- investigate the production, in a school laboratory, of simple esters
- investigate the differences between an organic acid and organic base
- investigate the structure and action of soaps and detergents
- draft and construct flowcharts to show reaction pathways for chemical synthesis, including those that involve more than one step ICT

13.1 Physical properties of organic acids and bases

Acids and bases in foods

COLLECT THIS ...

- vinegar
- sodium hydrogen carbonate (bicarbonate of soda) powder
- 2 beakers or glass tumblers
- teaspoon
- detergent
- sherbet lolly

DO THIS ...

Part A

1 Predict what will happen when vinegar and sodium hydrogen carbonate are mixed.

2 Put 2 teaspoons of sodium hydrogen carbonate into a beaker.

3 Put the beaker in the laboratory sink.

4 Pour vinegar over the top of the sodium hydrogen carbonate.

5 Predict what will happen when vinegar and sodium hydrogen carbonate are mixed in the presence of a detergent.

6 Put a squirt of detergent into a clean beaker and repeat steps 2, 3 and 4.

Part B

1 Predict what will happen when you eat a sherbet lolly.

2 Put the sherbet lolly into your mouth (do this outside the lab).

3 Record your observations as the lolly dissolves.

4 List the ingredients of the sherbet lolly.

RECORD THIS ...

Part A

Draw up the following table.

Experiment	Prediction	Observations
Mixing sodium bicarbonate and vinegar		
Dissolving a sherbet lolly		

Record your predictions and observations.

REFLECT ON THIS ...

1 Explain the meaning of your observations.

2 What could you do next time to improve your experiment?

In this section you will consider the physical properties of amines, amides, carboxylic acids, aldehydes and ketones, such as boiling point and solubility. Differences in chemical properties will be discussed in Section 13.2.

PHYSICAL PROPERTIES OF AMINES, AMIDES AND CARBOXYLIC ACIDS

Compounds from the three homologous series — **amines**, **amides** and **carboxylic acids**—will be considered together because their molecules contain functional groups that can form hydrogen bonds. The ability of molecules to form **hydrogen bonds** has a significant effect on their properties.

Boiling points

Hydrogen bonds are the strongest of the intermolecular forces and, as a result, molecules that can form hydrogen bonds generally exhibit higher boiling points. You can see from Table 13.1.1 that alcohols, carboxylic acids, amines and amides have higher boiling points than alkanes of similar molecular mass. The intermolecular forces in **aldehydes** and **ketones** are **dipole–dipole** attractions, and these molecules have boiling points that lie between the values for alkanes and those for the strongly hydrogen-bonded alcohols, carboxylic acids, amines and amides.

TABLE 13.1.1 Comparison of boiling points of compounds with different functional groups based on molecular mass

Homologous series	Compound	Formula	Molar mass (g mol^{-1})	Boiling point (°C)
alkane	butane	C_4H_{10}	58	−1
alcohol	propan-1-ol	C_3H_7OH	60	97
carboxylic acid	ethanoic acid	CH_3COOH	60	118
amine	propan-1-amine	$C_3H_7NH_2$	59	49
amide	ethanamide	CH_3CONH_2	59	210
aldehyde	propanal	C_2H_5CHO	58	49
ketone	propanone	CH_3COCH_3	58	56

> ℹ️ Carboxylic acids, amines and amides have relatively high boiling points due to hydrogen bonds between molecules.

Boiling points of amines and amides

The presence of highly **polar** nitrogen–hydrogen covalent bonds in amine and amide molecules means that these molecules form hydrogen bonds. The formation of hydrogen bonds between amine and amide molecules is illustrated in Figure 13.1.1. The strength of the hydrogen bonding between molecules explains the relatively high boiling points of these molecules when compared to hydrocarbon molecules of similar size.

In amines the hydrogen bond forms between the non-bonding pair of electrons on the **electronegative** nitrogen atom and the partially positive hydrogen atom on another amine molecule. Amines have lower boiling points than alcohols because intermolecular forces between amine molecules are weaker than those between alcohol molecules. This is because the difference in electronegativity between carbon and nitrogen in an amine is less than the difference between carbon and oxygen in an alcohol. As a result, the hydrogen bond formed via the N–H bond is less polar than the hydrogen bond formed via the O–H bond.

Amides have much higher boiling points than their related amines because they have more atoms that can donate or accept hydrogen bonds. As a result, strong hydrogen bonds form between the non-bonding electron pairs on the oxygen atom of one molecule and the partially positive hydrogen atom on a neighbouring molecule.

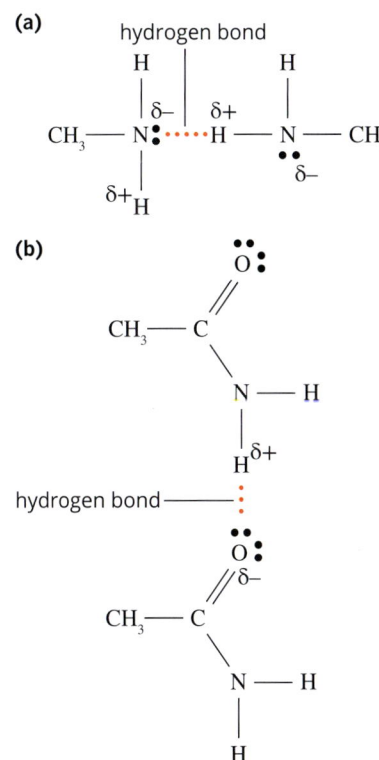

FIGURE 13.1.1 Hydrogen bonding between (a) amine molecules, and (b) amide molecules

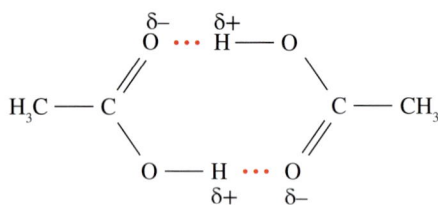

FIGURE 13.1.2 Hydrogen bonding between two ethanoic acid molecules results in the formation of a dimer.

Boiling points of carboxylic acids

Hydrogen bonding also has a marked effect on the boiling points of carboxylic acids. Figure 13.1.2 shows how two molecules of a carboxylic acid in the liquid state can form **dimers** in which two hydrogen bonds occur between the molecules.

The dimer produced is a stable species with a molar mass that is double that of a single carboxylic acid molecule. The increase in size that results from the formation of the dimer increases the strength of the **dispersion forces** between one dimer and its neighbours. The stronger dispersion forces and the hydrogen bonds between molecules result in the higher boiling point observed for carboxylic acids when compared to most other organic molecules of similar size.

CHEMISTRY IN ACTION ICT CCT

Citric acid

Citric acid is present in all organisms that consume oxygen, and it plays an important role in the release of stored energy in almost all living things. It is found in particularly high concentrations in citrus fruits, comprising around 8% of the dry weight of lemons and limes. It is partly responsible for the sour taste in many other foods, including dark chocolate.

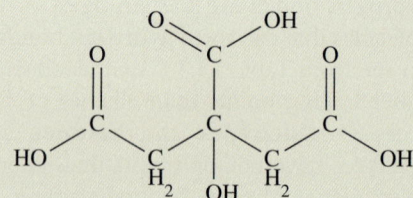

FIGURE 13.1.3 Citric acid, showing its three carboxyl functional groups

If you look at the ingredients of processed foods, it will not take you long to find something that has citric acid in it. This is to make the food taste more sour. It is also a very useful preservative because its acidity hinders the growth of bacteria. You will find citric acid sometimes listed in the ingredients as food acid 330.

Because it has four –OH groups, as shown in Figure 13.1.3, citric acid is able to form multiple intermolecular hydrogen bonds. As a result it has unusual physical properties for a molecule containing only six carbon atoms, melting at 153°C and boiling at 310°C.

GO TO ➤ Section 12.1 page 320

ℹ️ The boiling point of amines and carboxylic acids increases as the chain length grows. The trend is more complex for amides.

Effect of chain length on boiling point

The boiling points of amines and carboxylic acids increase as molar mass increases, for the same reasons as seen with alcohols in Chapter 12. The strong hydrogen bonds are complemented by dispersion forces that increase in strength as the hydrocarbon chain portion of the molecule grows larger. So an amine or carboxylic acid with a higher molar mass will have a higher boiling point, as shown in Figure 13.1.4.

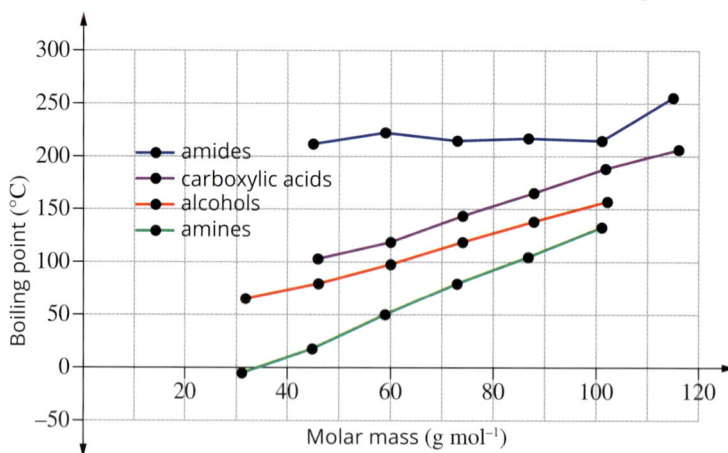

FIGURE 13.1.4 The nearly linear relationship between boiling point and molar mass for the alcohol, amine and carboxylic acid homologous series. Boiling points for all the amides are high, but the relationship is not linear because the intermolecular hydrogen bonding is complicated and extensive.

Amides do not share the neat relationship between chain length and boiling point that is seen in alcohols, amines and carboxylic acids, because the hydrogen bonding between amide molecules is more complex. The type of hydrogen bonding seen in amides, between N–H and O=C, is extremely important in biological chemistry.

It is responsible for around half of the connections between the double strands of DNA and is a significant reason why most proteins have their shape. In the solid state, amides often form the hydrogen-bonded 'ladders' or 'double chains' shown in Figure 13.1.5 and there is evidence that these arrangements also exist in liquid amides.

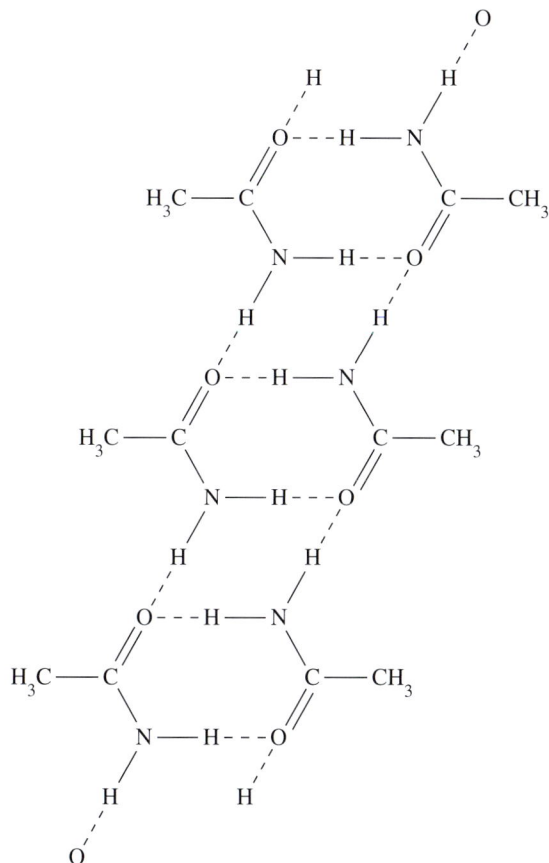

FIGURE 13.1.5 Amides often form extensive hydrogen-bonded networks such as this ladder that exists in solid ethanamide. The extensive arrangement of hydrogen bonds produces a complex, non-linear relationship between hydrocarbon chain length and boiling point in amides.

CHEMFILE ICT L

What's that smell? Stinky amines

Have you ever noticed an awful smell at the beach a few days after a storm? The odour of rotting fish is the odour of amines with short hydrocarbon chains. They are formed when amino acids from protein molecules in the fish are broken down in the environment, and the way that this awful smell persists is a consequence of the chemical properties of amines.

Short-chain amines have weaker intermolecular forces between molecules than alcohols, carboxylic acids or amides so they evaporate into the air more easily once they are formed, and this makes the smell spread quickly. They are also highly soluble in the aqueous environment of your nasal passages, so the stench lingers for a particularly long time in your nose.

Some particularly vile smelling (and toxic) amines have very descriptive common names. Putrescine (butane-1,5-diamine) smells putrid. Cadaverine (pentane-1,5-diamine) has the smell of dead organisms (cadavers). Both of these molecules (Figure 13.1.6) are ingredients of very bad breath. Food hygienists and forensic scientists sometimes monitor concentrations of these molecules during investigations, because they can be used to discover rancid food or determine a time of death.

FIGURE 13.1.6 (a) The smell of dead fish is a mixture of amines with small hydrocarbon chains; (b) putrescine (butane-1,4-diamine) and (c) cadaverine (pentane-1,5-diamine) are two particularly rancid-smelling amines.

Solubility

Solubility in water

Small amines, amides and carboxylic acids dissolve completely in water, but the solubility decreases as the hydrocarbon chain becomes longer. The solubility occurs because of the way that water forms hydrogen bonds with the polar nitrogen-containing and oxygen-containing functional groups in these molecules.

When amines interact with water molecules (Figure 13.1.7), hydrogen bonds can form between the lone-pair electrons of the nitrogen and the partially positive hydrogen of an adjacent water molecule, or between the hydrogen of an amine group and an oxygen of an adjacent water molecule.

Small amide and carboxylic acid molecules are also soluble in water. When carboxylic acids dissolve in water, hydrogen bonding occurs between water molecules and both the C=O group and the –OH group, making these compounds more soluble than alcohols in water (Figure 13.1.8). Hydrogen bonding between water and amides is very similar to that in carboxylic acids, with hydrogen bonds between the water molecules and the C=O group and both of the hydrogens in the –NH_2 group.

Solubility and chain length

As the hydrocarbon chain becomes longer, amides, carboxylic acids and amines become considerably less soluble in water and more soluble in organic solvents.

The functional groups in amides, amines and carboxylic acids are highly polar and can form hydrogen bonds with water molecules and with other polar, hydrogen bonding solvents, such as ethanol. Long hydrocarbon chains interrupt these hydrogen bonds and decrease the ability for the molecules to remain in aqueous solution. The hydrocarbon chain can only form dispersion forces with water molecules, which are not sufficient to allow these molecules to dissolve in water.

Solubility in organic solvents

Small amides, amines and carboxylic acids are insoluble in non-polar organic solvents, but the solubility increases as the hydrocarbon chain becomes longer. This is the same trend as seen in alcohols in Chapter 12. The short-chain amides, amines and carboxylic acids do not dissolve because the hydrogen bonding attraction between, for example, two small amide molecules is far stronger than the dispersion forces between molecules of an organic solvent and the small hydrocarbon chains of the amide molecules.

Less polar amides, amines and carboxylic acids with longer hydrocarbon chains are soluble in organic solvents.

PHYSICAL PROPERTIES OF ALDEHYDES AND KETONES

Aldehydes and ketones can be considered together because they are composed of molecules that are held together by dipole–dipole attractions. Their molecules cannot form hydrogen bonds with each other because they do not have a hydrogen atom bonded to an oxygen atom or a nitrogen atom.

Boiling points

Aldehydes and ketones contain a carbon–oxygen double bond. Oxygen is much more electronegative than carbon, so the carbon–oxygen double bond is polar. This means that molecules of aldehydes and ketones contain a permanent dipole, which can form dipole–dipole attractions with nearby molecules. The dipole–dipole interactions that arise between ketone molecules are shown in Figure 13.1.9.

> **i** The solubility of amines, amides and carboxylic acids in water decreases as the chain becomes longer.

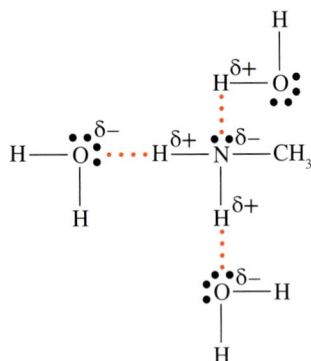

FIGURE 13.1.7 Hydrogen bonding between water molecules and an amine molecule

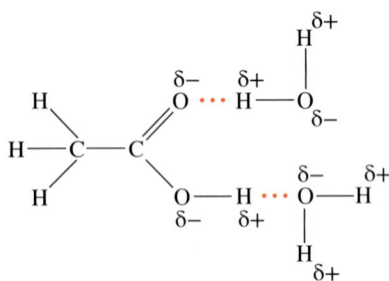

FIGURE 13.1.8 A small carboxylic acid molecule, such as ethanoic acid, is soluble in water because of hydrogen bonding between the carboxyl functional group and water molecules. Hydrogen bonding between water and amides is very similar.

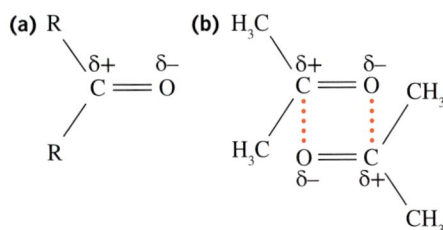

FIGURE 13.1.9 (a) A carbonyl bond is polar. (b) Dipole–dipole attractions between ketone molecules.

The strength of these dipole–dipole attractions between molecules gives aldehydes and ketones higher boiling points than similar-sized alkanes. However, their boiling points are not as high as similar-sized alcohols because dipole–dipole forces are not as strong as hydrogen bonds.

A comparison of the boiling points of a member of each of these homologous series with that of an alkane is shown in Table 13.1.2.

ℹ Aldehydes and ketones have lower boiling points than carboxylic acids or amides because the intermolecular forces between aldehyde and ketone molecules are weaker.

TABLE 13.1.2 Comparison of boiling points of organic molecules of similar molar mass from different homologous series

Homologous series	Condensed structural formula	Molar mass ($g\,mol^{-1}$)	Boiling point (°C)
alkane	$CH_3CH_2CH_2CH_3$	58	–0.5
alcohol	$CH_3CH_2CH_2OH$	60	97
aldehyde	CH_3CH_2CHO	58	48
ketone	CH_3COCH_3	58	56

Effect of chain length on boiling point

As the hydrocarbon chain lengths of aldehydes and ketones increase, their boiling points increase because the strength of the dispersion forces between molecules also increases. This trend is similar to that observed for alcohols and other compounds described earlier.

Solubility

Solubility in water

Molecules of aldehydes and ketones cannot form hydrogen bonds with each other. However, Figure 13.1.10 shows how a hydrogen bond can form between a lone pair of electrons on the oxygen atom of the carbonyl group and the partially positive hydrogen atoms in water molecules. The strength of this interaction is enough to make small aldehydes and ketones quite soluble in water.

As with other soluble organic compounds such as alcohols, when the non-polar hydrocarbon chain length of aldehydes and ketones increases, their solubility in water decreases.

Solubility in organic solvents

As the non-polar hydrocarbon chain length of aldehydes and ketones increases, they become more soluble in non-polar solvents. This is the opposite of the trend for their solubility in water, and occurs for the same reasons as the trend for amines, amides and carboxylic acids outlined on page 354.

ℹ Short chain aldehydes and ketones are soluble in water. The solubility decreases as the chain becomes longer.

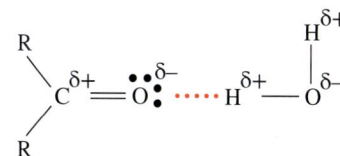

FIGURE 13.1.10 Hydrogen bond formed between the negatively charged electron pair on the oxygen atom in a carbonyl group and the positively charged hydrogen atom in a water molecule.

13.1 Review

SUMMARY

- The boiling points of organic molecules are determined by the strength of intermolecular forces between molecules. Dispersion forces are always present, and there may also be dipole–dipole attractions or hydrogen bonds.
- Molecules of carboxylic acids, amines and amides contain functional groups that can form hydrogen bonds with other molecules.
- Molecules of aldehydes and ketones have polar carbonyl functional groups and they are attracted to each other by dipole–dipole attractions.
- Comparing molecules of similar size in different homologous series, it is generally true that their boiling points increase in the order: alkanes, alkenes and alkynes < aldehydes and ketones < alcohols, carboxylic acids, amines and amides.

- The solubility of organic compounds in water is determined by the way the molecules of the organic compound interact with the molecules of water. This is affected by the polarity of functional groups and the length of the non-polar hydrocarbon chains of the organic molecules.
- The smaller members of the aldehyde, ketone, amine, amide and carboxylic acid homologous series are generally soluble in water. Solubility rapidly decreases as the chain length increases.
- The solubility of aldehydes, ketones, amines, carboxylic acids and amides in non-polar organic solvents increases as the chain length increases.

KEY QUESTIONS

1 Arrange the following compounds in increasing order of boiling point. Provide reasons for your answer.
$CH_3CH_2CH_2NH_2$, CH_3CH_2COOH, $CH_3CH_2CONH_2$, $CH_3CH_2CH_2OH$, $CH_3CH_2CH_2CH_3$

2 Arrange the following compounds in increasing order of boiling point. Provide reasons for your answer.
$CH_3CH_2CH_2CH_2NH_2$, CH_3NH_2, $CH_3CH_2NH_2$, $CH_3CH_2CH_2NH_2$, $CH_3CH_2CH_2CH_2CH_2CH_2CH_2NH_2$

3 Which three of the following molecules are most likely to be soluble in hexane?
ethanoic acid, octanoic acid, octan-2-one, ethanamide, methanamine, heptan-1-amine.

4 If an amine and an amide have the same hydrocarbon chain length, explain why the amide will have a much higher boiling point than the amine.

5 Which of the following molecules is likely to have the highest boiling point: octan-1-ol, octan-2-one or octanal?

13.2 Chemical properties of organic acids and bases

The acidic –COOH functional group, the neutral –$CONH_2$ group and the basic –NH_2 group support life. These functional groups are essential to the structure and function of proteins, the way that energy is stored and transferred through the body, the way that metal ions like iron and calcium are used in organisms, and the taste and properties of much of our food. Understanding the properties and reactivity of these functional groups is essential in many areas of biological chemistry and is very important in pharmaceutical chemistry. This section contains an overview of the acidic chemistry and **substitution reactions** of carboxylic acids, the acidic and basic chemistry of amides and the basic chemistry of amines.

REACTIONS OF CARBOXYLIC ACIDS

Molecules that contain carboxylic acids are common in the natural world and are present in most plants. Solutions of carboxylic acids taste sour. The sour taste of vinegar, lemons, yoghurt, rhubarb and most unripe fruits is due to the presence of carboxylic acids.

When fruits and berries like the blackberries in Figure 13.2.1 ripen, complex reactions take place. These include the conversion of carboxylic acids to other compounds. In some of these reactions, carboxylic acids react with alcohol molecules to produce **esters**. Esters give many fruits their characteristic aromas and tastes.

Dissociation in water

You will remember from Chapter 7 that ethanoic acid is a weak acid and only dissociates to a small extent in water to form hydronium ions. Other carboxylic acids react with water in a similar way.

The reaction of a carboxylic acid with water is a reversible process, so the equation for dissociation is written using equilibrium arrows. The equation for the dissociation of ethanoic acid in water is:

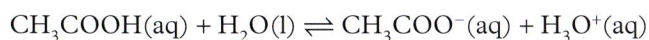

$$CH_3COOH(aq) + H_2O(l) \rightleftharpoons CH_3COO^-(aq) + H_3O^+(aq)$$

In contrast to the weakly acidic behaviour of carboxylic acids, amines behave as bases in water.

Reactions of carboxylic acids with alcohols

Reactions that involve the combination of two reactants and the production of a small molecule, such as water, are called **condensation reactions**. Esters are made by a condensation reaction between a carboxylic acid and an alcohol. A condensation reaction in which an ester is formed is also known as an **esterification reaction**.

For example, the ester ethyl ethanoate can be produced by gently heating a mixture of ethanol and pure ethanoic acid, with a trace amount of sulfuric acid added as a catalyst. As well as the desired ester, water is a product.

The general equation for the esterification reaction involving a carboxylic acid and an alcohol is shown in Figure 13.2.2. Two examples of esterification reactions are also shown.

In the esterification reaction, it is the hydrogen atom from the hydroxyl group of the alcohol and the –OH group from the carboxylic acid that combine to form water, which is the molecule eliminated in this condensation reaction.

As you learnt in Chapter 9, the first part an ester's name is derived from the name of the alcohol from which it was made. The second part of the name is derived from the name of the carboxylic acid from which it was made. Therefore the name of the ester formed from methanol (an alcohol) and propanoic acid (a carboxylic acid) is methyl propananoate.

FIGURE 13.2.1 The ripening of blackberries involves many chemical reactions, including the conversion of carboxylic acids to esters.

GO TO ➤ Section 7.1 page 162

ℹ Carboxylic acids can undergo condensation reactions with alcohols to form esters.

GO TO ➤ Section 9.4 page 278

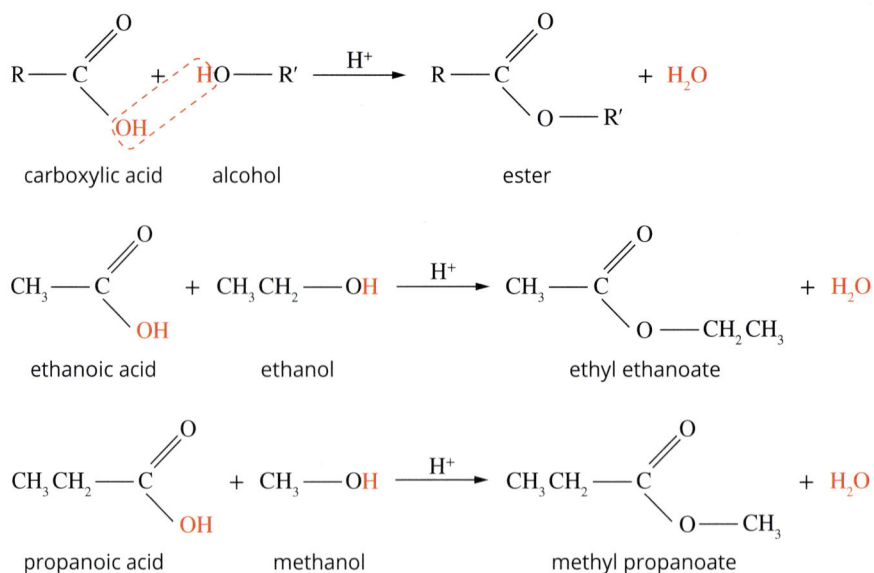

FIGURE 13.2.2 Esterification reactions occur when alcohols are heated with carboxylic acids in the presence of sulfuric acid, which acts as a catalyst. The top reaction shows the general equation for esterification. Two specific examples are also shown: ethanoic acid with ethanol, and propanoic acid with methanol.

CHEMFILE ICT IU

Aspirin, an ester derived from a herbal remedy

Pharmaceutical products are often developed from substances found in plants that have been used as a traditional medicine. For example, the origin of the mild painkiller aspirin is a naturally occurring substance called salicin that is present in the leaves and bark of willow trees and in the herb meadowsweet.

Extracts from willow and other salicin-rich plants were used in ancient Egypt and other regions. The Greek physician Hippocrates recommended the use of an infusion of willow leaves and bark to assist in childbirth and relieve other aches and pains (Figure 13.2.3). It was not until 1829 that the active ingredient, salicin, was identified and isolated.

It is now known that the body converts salicin to 2-hydroxybenzoic acid (also called salicylic acid), and that this is the active substance that helps to reduce fever and acts as a painkiller. Although 2-hydroxybenzoic acid was synthesised and sold as a painkiller and anti-inflammatory, it was hard to ingest and caused stomach irritation.

By the 1890s a number of chemists had synthesised 2-acetyloxybenzoic acid (also called acetylsalicylic acid), but the product was unstable and its pharmaceutical properties were untested. In 1897 Felix Hoffmann, working for the Bayer company in Germany, developed a superior synthesis method and persuaded Bayer to undertake clinical trials. The success of these trials led Bayer to develop and market the compound under the name Aspirin. Aspirin is much gentler on the mouth and stomach than salicylic acid, and became the primary drug of choice for pain relief until the 1950s.

The preparation of aspirin is a relatively simple process. It has one main step, in which the hydroxyl functional group of a salicylic acid molecule reacts with the carboxylic acid functional group of an ethanoic acid molecule in a condensation reaction, as shown in Figure 13.2.4. The product, aspirin, has properties that are quite different from those of either of the two reactant molecules.

Although this reaction can be carried out easily in a laboratory, the yield is quite low. A more complex reaction is used to produce aspirin on an industrial scale.

FIGURE 13.2.3 Around 3000–1500 BCE willow was used as a medicine by ancient civilisations such as the Sumerians and Egyptians. In Greece in about 400 BCE, Hippocrates administered willow-leaf tea to people suffering pain.

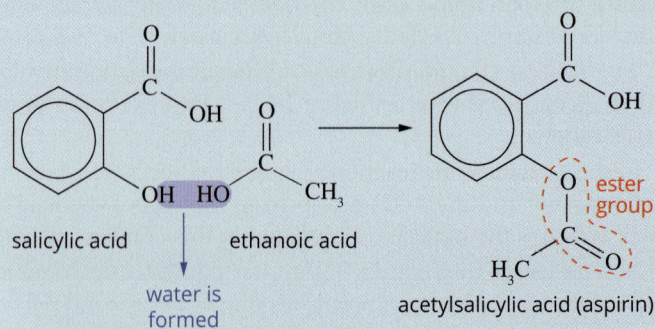

FIGURE 13.2.4 Aspirin can be made from 2-hydroxybenzoic acid and ethanoic acid. The process involves a reaction between hydroxyl and carboxyl functional groups to form an ester.

Reactions of carboxylic acids to form amides

Primary amides ($RCONH_2$) can be prepared by the reaction of a carboxylic acid with ammonia. Figure 13.2.5 shows the production of ethanamide from ethanoic acid and ammonia. The reaction is a condensation reaction similar to the one between a carboxylic acid and an alcohol to form an ester. A water molecule is produced during the reaction.

> ⓘ Amides are formed when carboxylic acids react with amines.

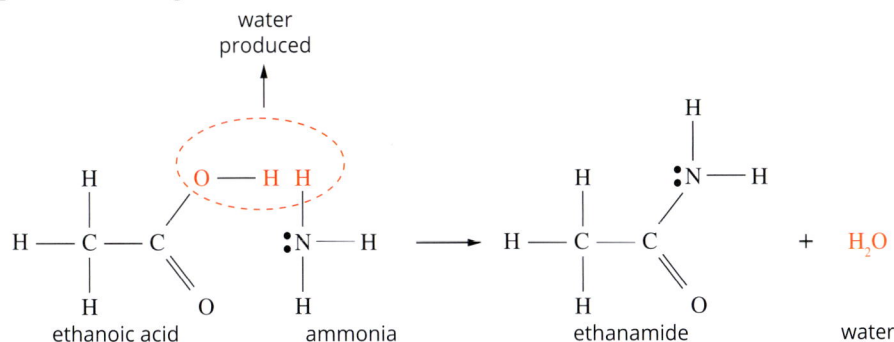

FIGURE 13.2.5 The reaction of ethanoic acid with ammonia to produce the primary amide ethanamide. Note the formation of the amide functional group, $RCONH_2$.

Secondary amides have the general formula $RCONHR'$, where R and R' represent alkyl groups. Secondary amides are formed when carboxylic acids react with primary amines. An amide link is formed in this reaction.

You can see in Figure 13.2.6 that the formation of a secondary amide is also a condensation reaction that produces a water molecule. The hydrogen of the primary amine is lost and combines with the –OH from the carboxylic acid. A new covalent bond is formed between the carbon of the carboxylic acid and the nitrogen of the primary amine.

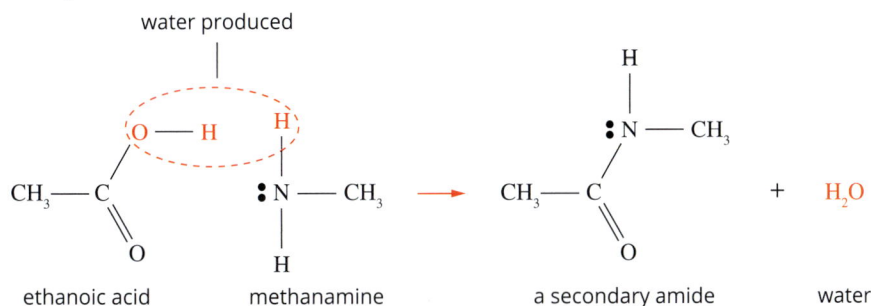

FIGURE 13.2.6 Formation of a secondary amide—reaction of ethanoic acid and methylamine to form the secondary amide N-methylethanamide.

REACTIONS OF AMINES AND AMIDES

For molecules that look similar, amides and amines have chemical behaviours that are very different from each other. Amides are very stable in aqueous solutions, participate in very few substitution reactions, and have extremely limited acid–base behaviour. The structure of all proteins contains very large numbers of amide bonds, and the unreactive nature of these bonds makes a large contribution to the stability of proteins. In contrast, amines are far more reactive than amides, are important in many substitution reactions, and have a comprehensive acid–base chemistry.

> ⓘ Amines are weak bases. For practical purposes, amides can be considered to be neither acids nor bases.

electron density drawn away from nitrogen

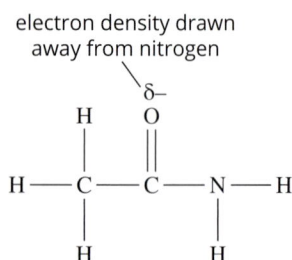

FIGURE 13.2.7 The presence of the highly electronegative oxygen draws electron density away from the nitrogen atom, making it less basic.

Dissociation in water

Ethanamine is a weak base and reacts to a small extent with water to form the ethanammonium and hydroxide ions. The equation for this dissociation reaction is:

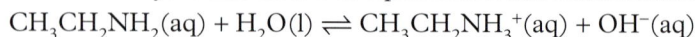

$$CH_3CH_2NH_2(aq) + H_2O(l) \rightleftharpoons CH_3CH_2NH_3^+(aq) + OH^-(aq)$$

Other simple amines react in the same way. The equilibrium arrow indicates that the reaction is reversible, but this equilibrium lies to the left. In contrast, ethanamide and other amides are essentially unreactive as either acids or bases.

The process of gaining H^+ in amines is assisted by the electronegativity of the nitrogen atom because it draws electron density away from the rest of the molecule. This extra electron density stabilises the positive charge when the amine acts as a base and accepts H^+. In amides the drawing of electron density occurs in the opposite direction. The presence of the highly electronegative oxygen atom in the C=O group pulls electron density away from the nitrogen atom, which makes it more difficult to gain a proton and hold a positive charge (Figure 13.2.7).

STRUCTURE AND ACTION OF SOAPS AND DETERGENTS

Humans have been making and using soap for thousands of years, and some of the first users of natural **surfactants** were Indigenous Australians. Many Australian plants contain molecules that have a soapy action, and commercial soaps made by Aboriginal businesses incorporate these traditional ingredients.

CHEMFILE AHC

Ngarinyman soap made with traditional bush plants

A group of Ngarinyman women from the community of Yarralin, about 400 km south-west of Katherine in the Northern Territory, are making bush soaps that contain traditional medicinal plants. The soap is called Ngarinyman, which is also the local language of the community.

A shrub that the Ngarinyman call manyinyi (scientific name *Blumea axillaris*) is a traditional cure for coughs and colds, reducing fevers and repairing dry or itchy skin. The active ingredients from manyinyi are extracted from the plant and added to the soap.

Another traditional soap comes from *Alphitonia excelsa*, commonly called the red ash or soap tree (Figure 13.2.8). Crushing the leaves of this tree releases surfactant molecules that can produce a lather in your hands and remove dirt.

FIGURE 13.2.8 The red ash or soap tree, *Alphitonia excelsa*

Making soap

Soaps are made by a process that has been essentially unchanged over the last 2000 years, in which animal or vegetable fats are boiled with a strong base, usually sodium hydroxide. Animal fats used for soap include tallow, lard and fish oil. Vegetable fats include palm, soybean, groundnut, coconut, canola and olive oils. The fats and oils contain large multi-ester molecules called triglycerides (Figure 13.2.9).

FIGURE 13.2.9 A triglyceride molecule. The long hydrocarbon chains commonly contain 12–18 carbons.

When heated with sodium hydroxide, the triglyceride breaks up to form sodium salts of carboxylic acids and a molecule that is commonly called glycerol but has the systematic name propan-1,2,3-triol. This process is called **saponification** (Figure 13.2.10) and is an example of a **hydrolysis** reaction. It is the reverse reaction of esterification, which you saw earlier in this section.

> ℹ Natural soaps are made by boiling animal or vegetable fats in sodium or potassium hydroxide solutions. This process hydrolyses the fats.

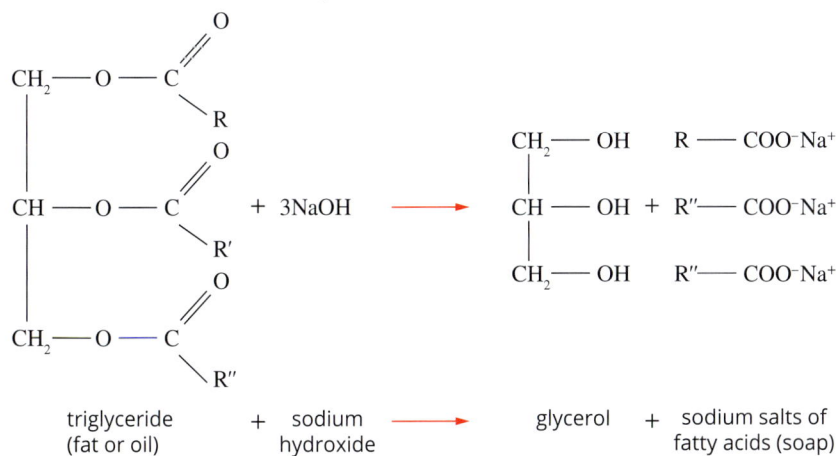

| triglyceride (fat or oil) | + | sodium hydroxide | → | glycerol | + | sodium salts of fatty acids (soap) |

FIGURE 13.2.10 Saponification is the reaction between a triglyceride and hot sodium hydroxide to form glycerol and sodium salts of long-chain carboxylic acids.

The most common carboxylic acid formed from the saponification of beef fat is sodium stearate. The stearate ion (Figure 13.2.11) has a long hydrocarbon 'tail' and a negatively charged carboxylate ion 'head'. The products of saponification reactions that start with other fats or oils are carboxylic acids with hydrocarbon chains that have lengths and shapes that vary according to the fat or oil that is used. These may also contain double bonds. The typical length of a tail is 12–18 carbons.

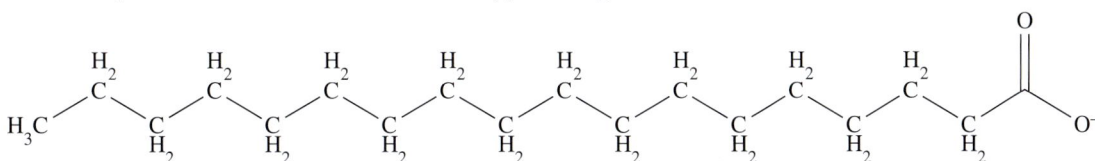

FIGURE 13.2.11 The stearate ion is a major soap molecule produced from animal fat.

The chain length and cation influences the properties of the soap that is made. Longer hydrocarbon chains with sodium salts produce very hard bars of soap, while shorter chains and potassium salts produce semi-solid and liquid soaps.

The action of soap

The soap ion in Figure 13.2.12 contains a long hydrophobic tail and a hydrophilic charged head. The term for this class of molecule is a surfactant, a name derived from its behaviour as a *surf*ace-*acti*ve agent. When a small amount of soap dissolves in water, the anions accumulate at the surface with their hydrophilic heads in the water and their hydrophobic tails out of the water. The surface tension of the water is reduced as this occurs.

At higher concentrations the soap molecules cluster together in the liquid as shown in Figure 13.2.12, with the hydrophobic tails grouping inwards away from the polar water molecules. The hydrophilic heads are facing outwards and surrounded by the water molecules. These clusters are called **micelles** and contain between 40 and 100 surfactant ions.

> ℹ Soaps allow droplets of fat and oil to mix with water by surrounding them in a structure called a micelle.

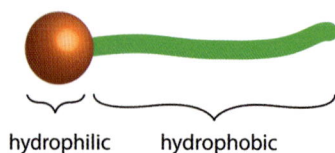

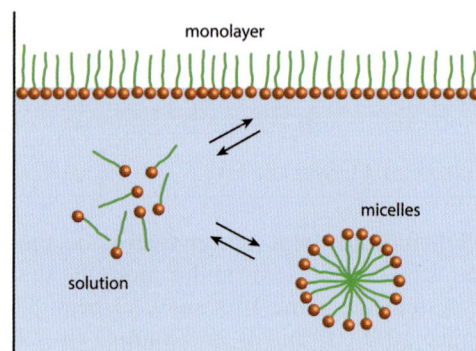

FIGURE 13.2.12 Low concentrations of surfactants are oriented with their hydrophilic heads in water and their tails pointing up at an aqueous surface. At higher concentrations they form micelles.

> ℹ Detergents are now used more widely than soaps because they do not form a scum (precipitate) with soluble ionic salts in water, such as calcium and magnesium salts. Detergents have a similar structure to soap and behave in a similar way, but they are made from petroleum products.

When soapy water comes in contact with oil or grease, a series of events happen:

- The non-polar tails of the soap molecules adsorb onto the grease. The charged heads of the surfactant form a layer around the grease, giving it a hydrophobic surface.
- The water penetrates between the grease and the surface below it, causing a grease droplet to form.
- The grease droplet is held in solution and attracted to the water molecules by the anions on the droplet's surface.

This arrangement of tiny grease particles trapped inside micelles dispersed in water forms a type of mixture called an **emulsion**, with the soap acting as an emulsifier. This arrangement is depicted in Figure 13.2.13.

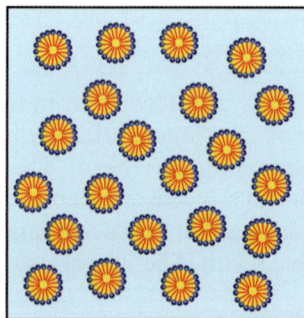

FIGURE 13.2.13 An emulsion with surfactant molecules arranged in micelles that are surrounding oil droplets.

13.2 Review

SUMMARY

- Carboxylic acids can react with alcohols in the presence of an acid catalyst to produce esters.
- Carboxylic acids react with ammonia and amines to form amides.
- Carboxylic acids partially dissociate in water, acting as acids.
- Amines react with water to a small extent, acting as bases.
- For practical purposes, amides can be considered to be neither acids nor bases.
- Surfactant molecules can be made from the salts of carboxylic acids that have long hydrocarbon chains.
- Surfactant molecules surround droplets of oil and grease to form clusters called micelles.

KEY QUESTIONS

1   Draw the structural formula of the organic product formed in the reaction between:
    a   ammonia and propanoic acid
    b   ethanol and propanoic acid, using concentrated sulfuric acid as a catalyst
    c   butanoic acid and ethanamide.

2   Write balanced chemical equations for the dissociation of the following substances in water.
    a   pentanoic acid
    b   propan-1-amine
    c   butanamide.

3   a   In general terms, explain the reaction conditions needed to make the following molecule undergo a saponification reaction.

$$H_2C-O-\overset{\overset{\displaystyle O}{\|}}{C}-CH_2CH_2CH_2CH=CHCH_2CH_2CH=CHCH_2CH_2CH_2CH_3$$

$$HC-O-\overset{\overset{\displaystyle O}{\|}}{C}-CH_2CH_2CH_2CH=CHCH_2CH_2CH=CHCH_2CH_2CH_2CH_3$$

$$H_2C-O-\overset{\overset{\displaystyle O}{\|}}{C}-CH_2CH_2CH_2CH=CHCH_2CH_2CH=CHCH_2CH_2CH_2CH_3$$

    b   Draw the condensed structural formulae of the products of the saponification of this molecule.

4   Why are stearate ions (pictured in Figure 13.2.11 on page 361) more stable in aqueous solution as part of a micelle rather than outside a micelle?

5   Once an oil droplet is part of a micelle, why does the oil droplet remain in the micelle when in water?

13.3 Organic reaction pathways

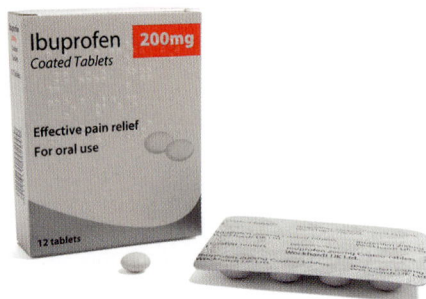

Organic chemists are highly skilled at developing compounds that have exactly the right properties needed for a particular purpose. These may be new pharmaceuticals, polymers or nanomaterials. Once the desired compound has been identified, chemists must devise a way to make it. Chemists have to design an efficient method for converting readily available starting materials—often alkanes or alkenes—into the more complex product they want.

Modern chemists are also interested in devising environmentally friendly synthetic routes. These pathways are designed to minimise waste, use 'greener' solvents, require less energy, and help to conserve the world's resources. The preparation of ibuprofen (Figure 13.3.1), a commonly used analgesic, is an example. Figure 13.3.2 illustrates two pathways for the preparation of ibuprofen, one more efficient than the other.

In this section, you will learn how to devise reaction pathways for the synthesis of some simple organic compounds by utilising the reactions you have learnt about in Chapters 11 and 12.

FIGURE 13.3.1 Ibuprofen is an analgesic (pain reliever) found in many commercially available products.

FIGURE 13.3.2 Two alternative reaction pathways for the production of ibuprofen. The green pathway is more efficient than the brown one. In the green pathway, fewer reactants are needed and a higher proportion of atoms in the reactants are present in the final product. This means that there is less waste in the green pathway.

SIMPLE REACTION PATHWAYS

Figure 13.3.3 shows chemical reaction pathways that can be used to form some compounds based on ethane and ethene. A **reaction pathway** is a series of one or more steps, or reactions, that can be used to convert a reactant containing certain functional groups to a desired product with different functional groups. Pathways for other alkanes can be constructed using the same inorganic reactants and reaction conditions.

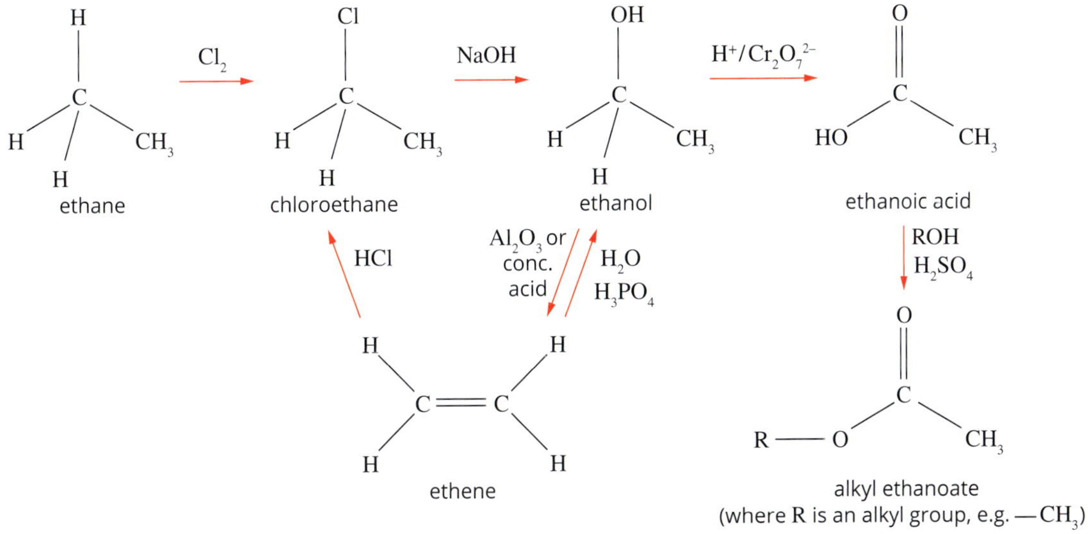

FIGURE 13.3.3 Some reaction pathways based on ethane and ethene. The same reaction conditions can be used to develop pathways for other members of the alkane and alkene homologous series.

CHEMFILE IU WE

Building the impossible

American chemist Robert Burns Woodward (Figure 13.3.4) was awarded the Nobel Prize in Chemistry in 1965 for his synthesis of complex organic molecules. Woodward devised synthetic procedures for the production of complex natural products that many considered to be impossible to replicate in the laboratory. His methodical approach resulted in the development of a number of rules that are now used by modern organic chemists to plan and predict how reactions will occur, in order to devise sequential pathways like the ones you will investigate in this chapter.

By the time he was awarded the Nobel Prize, Woodward had successfully proposed and conducted the synthesis of large complex molecules such as quinine, cholesterol, cortisone, lysergic acid (LSD), strychnine, reserpine and chlorophyll. His work on the total synthesis of vitamin B_{12} is considered to be the most complex. As you can see in Figure 13.3.5 on page 366, vitamin B_{12} is a large molecule. The synthesis required 69 steps and took more than 12 years to develop with the combined efforts of over 100 people from all around the world.

The discoveries that were made during the synthesis of vitamin B_{12} have contributed greatly to the field of organic chemistry and were recognised with another Nobel Prize in 1981. The prize was awarded to Roald Hoffmann, who worked closely with Woodward on the synthesis, and Kenichi Fukui, who had devised an alternative approach with a similar result to Hoffman and Woodward. Woodward was not named on the 1981 Nobel Prize because he had died in 1979, and Nobel Prizes are not awarded posthumously.

FIGURE 13.3.4 Robert Burns Woodward (1917–1979) synthesised complex organic molecules.

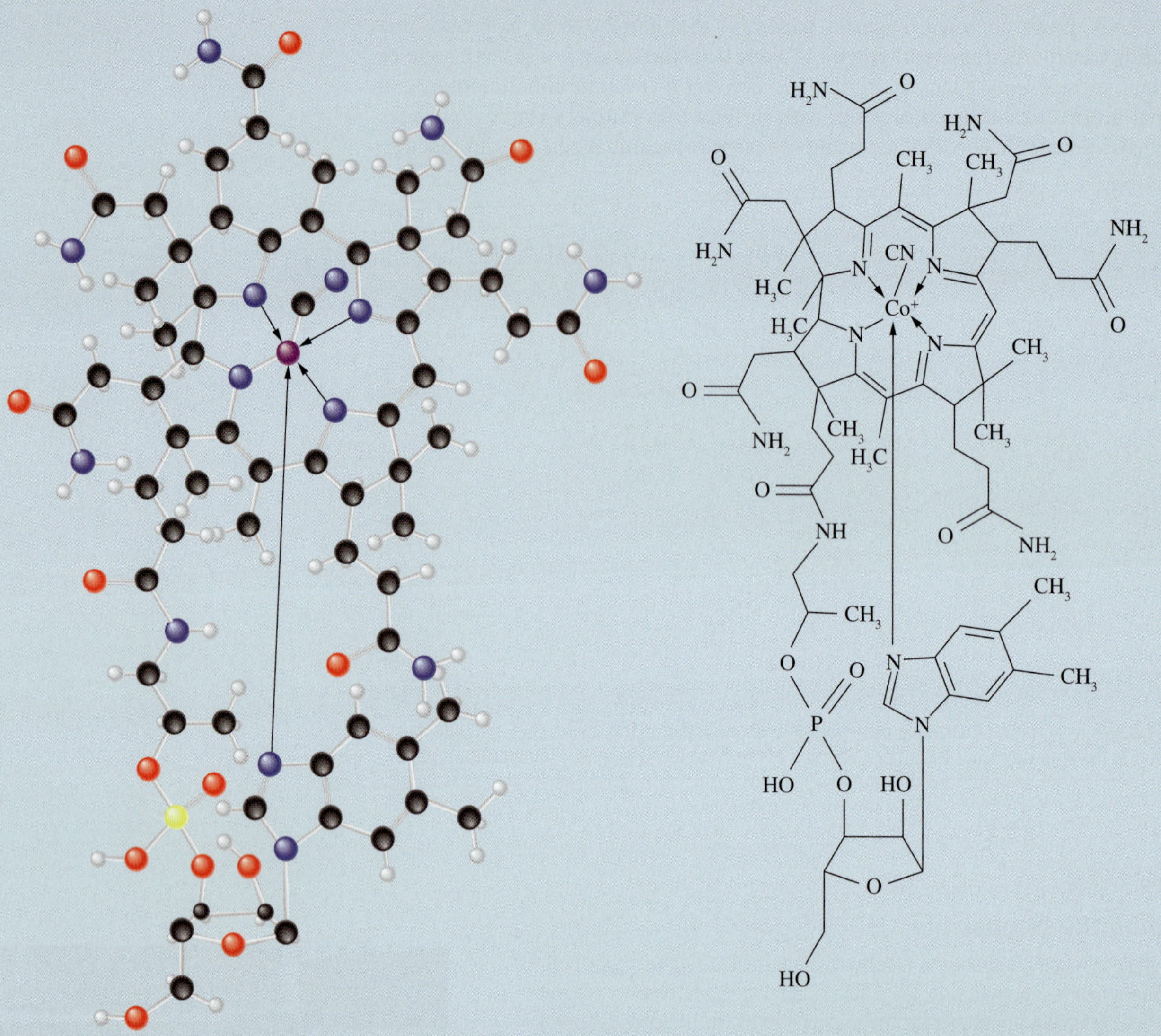

FIGURE 13.3.5 The structure of vitamin B₁₂. The manipulation of the functional groups and reaction conditions required to synthesise this large molecule from small starting materials takes 69 steps.

MORE COMPLEX REACTION PATHWAYS

Suppose you wanted to form ethyl propanoate using only alkanes or alkenes as starting materials. A close look at the structure of the compound shown in Figure 13.3.6 will show you that it is an ester produced by the condensation reaction between propanoic acid and ethanol, so each of these compounds must be prepared first as described below.

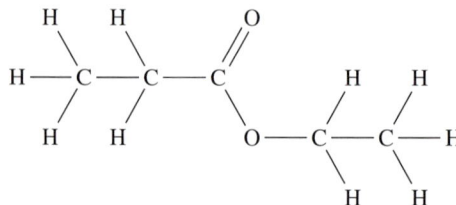

FIGURE 13.3.6 The structure of ethyl propanoate

Making ethanol

Ethanol is an alcohol containing two carbon atoms. It can be synthesised from ethene in two ways: in one step by the direct addition reaction with water, or in two steps via the intermediate product chloroethane. In this case the best option is the more direct route, the addition reaction with water. Figure 13.3.7 shows both possible pathways for the production of ethanol from ethene. You can see in each pathway that the inorganic reactant is placed above the arrow for each step.

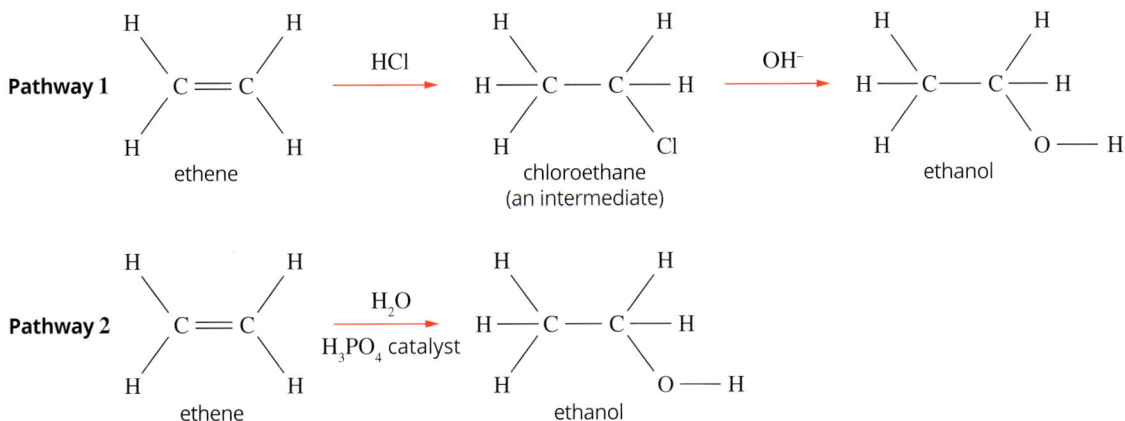

FIGURE 13.3.7 Synthetic pathways for making ethanol from ethene

Making propanoic acid

Propanoic acid is a carboxylic acid containing three carbon atoms. It can be prepared by the pathway shown in Figure 13.3.8. If you work backwards from propanoic acid, you can see that it can be formed from the oxidation of the primary alcohol propan-1-ol. This in turn can be formed by the reaction of 1-chloropropane with sodium hydroxide.

You will recall that 1-chloropropane can be prepared by reacting propane with chlorine. In this way you can devise the sequence of reactions that will produce a particular product. The pathway shown for the preparation of propanoic acid would produce several products, which can be separated by fractional distillation.

FIGURE 13.3.8 Synthesis of propanoic acid from propene

Making ethyl propanoate

Having synthesised ethanol and propanoic acid, you can now prepare the ester, ethyl propanoate, using a condensation reaction, as shown in Figure 13.3.9.

FIGURE 13.3.9 The formation of ethyl propanoate from the condensation reaction of ethanol and propanoic acid

The full reaction pathway for the preparation of ethyl propanoate from ethene and propane via ethanol and propanoic acid is summarised in Figure 13.3.10.

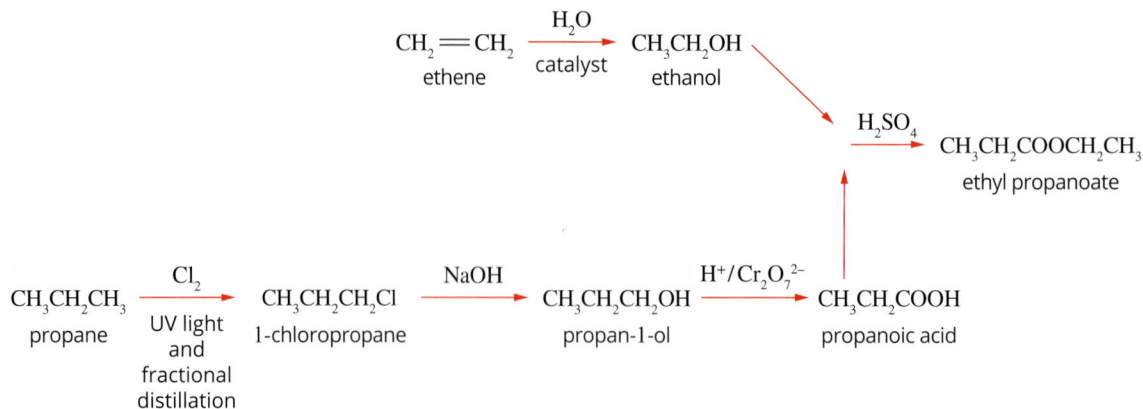

FIGURE 13.3.10 Reaction pathway for the preparation of ethyl propanoate

A reaction pathway summarises the reactions required to produce a product from simple starting materials.

The desired ester product can be separated from the reaction mixture and purified by fractional distillation. In Chapter 16 you will learn how to verify the identity of the product by instrumental analysis techniques such as infrared and nuclear magnetic resonance spectroscopy and mass spectrometry.

A summary of the reaction pathways described in Chapters 10–13 is shown in Figure 13.3.11.

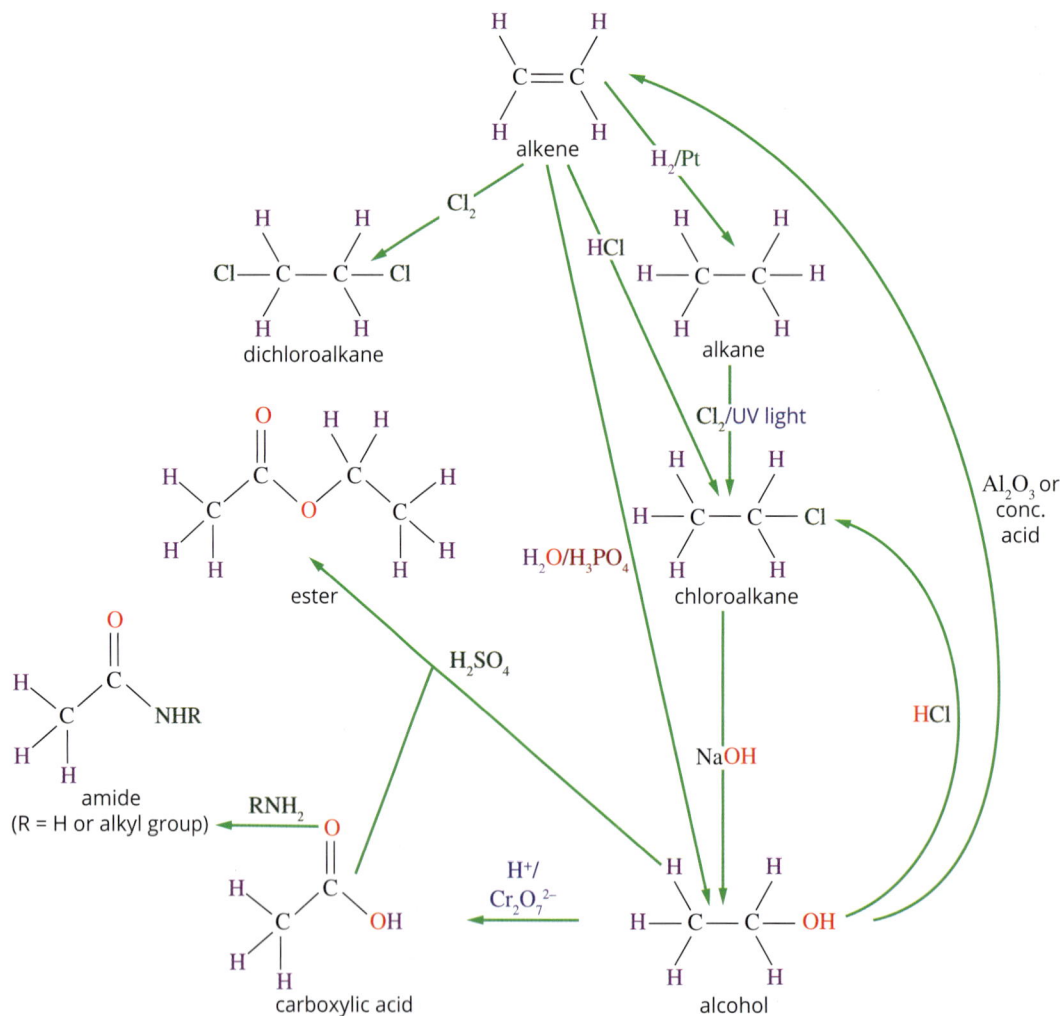

FIGURE 13.3.11 Synthetic pathways for the production of a variety of functional groups from an alkene starting product

Other considerations in devising a synthesis

When planning a reaction pathway, there are a number of considerations in addition to simply identifying a possible reaction sequence. As you will recall from Chapter 4, the position of equilibrium of a reaction can have a considerable impact on the overall yield.

GO TO ➤ Section 4.1 page 92

The principles of green chemistry must also be considered in terms of the solvents required and the by-products that are formed. You will learn more about green chemistry in Chapter 17. The flowchart in Figure 13.3.12 shows some of the stages in the planning process.

GO TO ➤ Section 17.1 page 518

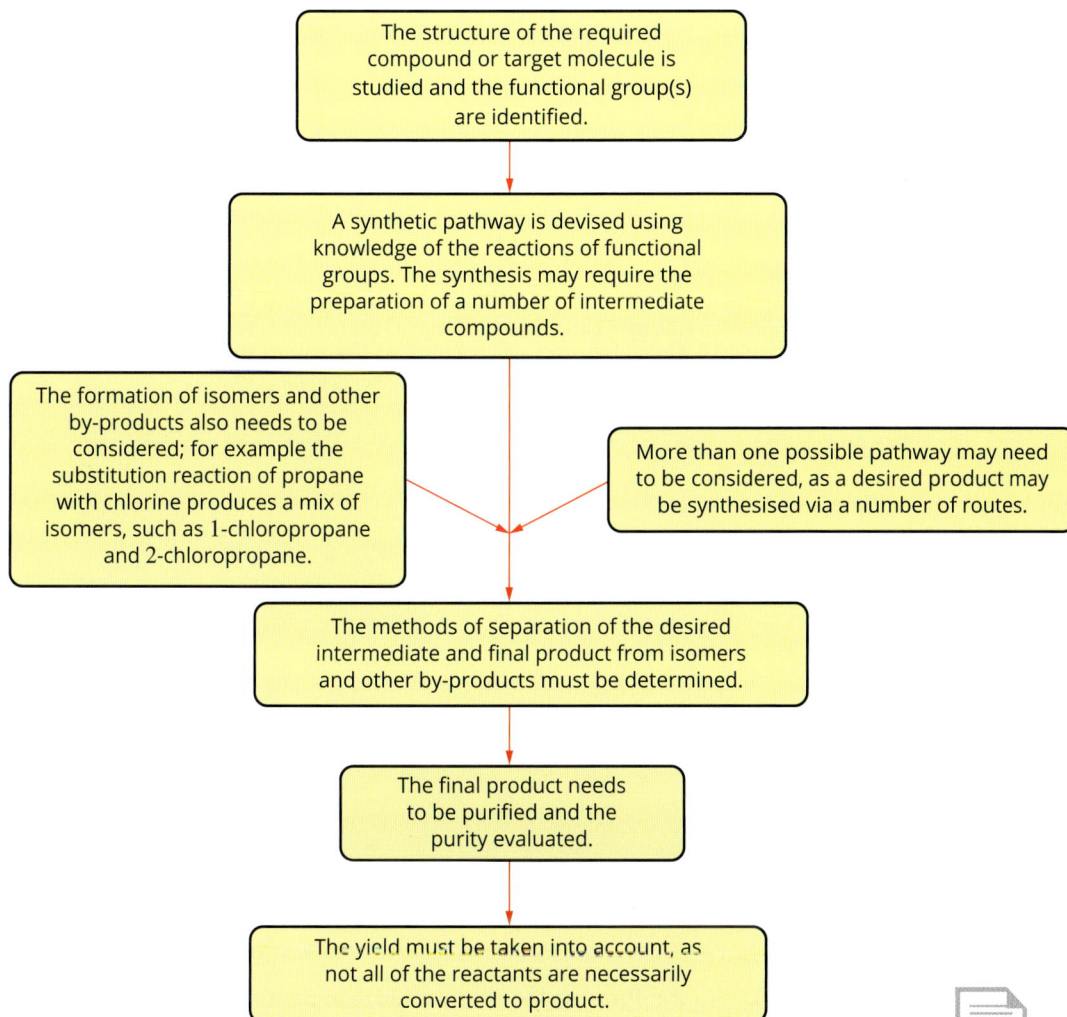

The structure of the required compound or target molecule is studied and the functional group(s) are identified.

A synthetic pathway is devised using knowledge of the reactions of functional groups. The synthesis may require the preparation of a number of intermediate compounds.

The formation of isomers and other by-products also needs to be considered; for example the substitution reaction of propane with chlorine produces a mix of isomers, such as 1-chloropropane and 2-chloropropane.

More than one possible pathway may need to be considered, as a desired product may be synthesised via a number of routes.

The methods of separation of the desired intermediate and final product from isomers and other by-products must be determined.

The final product needs to be purified and the purity evaluated.

The yield must be taken into account, as not all of the reactants are necessarily converted to product.

FIGURE 13.3.12 Steps in the design of a synthetic pathway of an organic compound.

WS
7.5

Retrosynthesis

Retrosynthesis is an important step in the design of a synthetic pathway. It is the act of looking at a target molecule and working backwards to imagine the basic chemical pieces that can be assembled to make it.

Breaking bonds

Retrosynthesis involves looking at a molecule and identifying the bonds that are most likely to be formed in a synthesis. These are generally not carbon-carbon bonds; they are more likely to be between carbon and other atoms.

Breaking up the target into fragments

To design a retrosynthesis for an amide, such as the one shown in Figure 13.3.13a, start by looking at the bonds in the main chain that are between carbon and non-carbon atoms. Draw red lines through these bonds to give the fragments shown in Figure 13.3.13b. The fragments are

not real molecules but they can be assembled from simple starting materials.

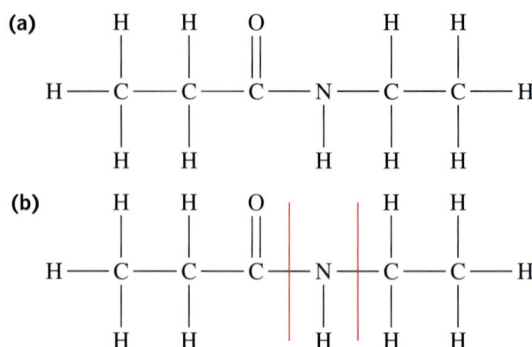

FIGURE 13.3.13 To start designing the retrosynthesis of the amide (a), draw red lines through the bonds in the main chain between carbon and non-carbon atoms to give the fragments in (b).

13.3 Review

SUMMARY

- A reaction pathway is a sequence of reactions that is used to convert a reactant into a product.
- Reaction pathways can be constructed using the organic reactions studied in this and previous chapters.
- Reaction pathways indicate the reaction conditions and reagents required for each step.

KEY QUESTIONS

1 Devise reaction pathways for the following reactions:
  a ethanamine from ethene
  b butan-1-ol from butane
  c pentanoic acid from 1-chloropentane.

2 Propose the shortest reaction pathway that will synthesise:
  a methanoic acid from methane
  b ethanol from ethene
  c propyl methanoate from propane and methane.

3 Pentanamide can be made from 1-chloropentane in the following reaction pathway:
  1-chloropentane → compound A → compound B → pentanamide
  a Identify compound A.
  b Name the chemical required to convert 1-chloropentane to compound A.
  c Identify compound B.
  d Name the chemicals and the reaction conditions used to convert compound A to compound B.
  e Name the compound that reacts with compound B to produce pentanamide.

4 Describe a reaction pathway for synthesising butyl ethanoate from appropriate alkane or alkene starting materials.

Chapter review

KEY TERMS

aldehyde
amide
amine
carboxylic acid
condensation reaction
dimer

dipole–dipole attraction
dispersion force
electronegative
emulsion
ester
esterification reaction

hydrogen bond
hydrolysis
ketone
micelle
polar
reaction pathway

saponification
substitution reaction
surfactant

REVIEW QUESTIONS

1 The table below gives the molar masses and boiling points of butane, methyl methanoate, propan-1-ol and ethanamide. Explain why the boiling points differ even though the compounds have similar molar masses.

Compound	Molar mass $(g\,mol^{-1})$	Boiling point (°C)
butane	58.12	−0.5
methyl methanoate	60.05	32.0
propan-1-ol	60.09	97.0
ethanamide	59.07	221.2

2 Explain why, when comparing the effect of functional groups on the boiling points of different homologous series, it is important to compare molecules with a similar molar mass.

3 Consider the following compounds:
$CH_3(CH_2)_6CHO$, $CH_3(CH_2)_5COOH$, CH_3CHO, CH_3COOH
   a Arrange the compounds in order of increasing boiling point.
   b Which two of these compounds would have a greater solubility in hexane? Explain your answer.

4 a Draw the structure of the dimer formed by butanoic acid molecules as they hydrogen bond together. Use Figure 13.1.2 on page 352 as a guide.
   b Draw part of the ladder formed by butanamide molecules as they hydrogen bond to each other. Use Figure 13.1.5 on page 353 as an example.
   c Why does butanamide have a higher boiling point than butanoic acid?

5 Methyl ethanoate has a high solubility in water because it is able to form hydrogen bonds with water molecules. Draw an arrangement of hydrogen bonds between water and methyl ethanoate.

6 Complete the following reactions:

   a

   b

   c

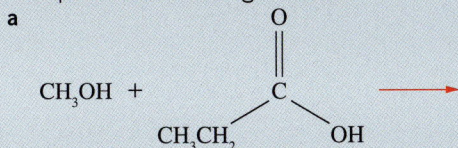

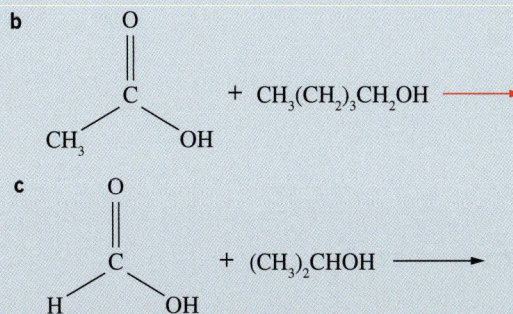

7 Write the names of the carboxylic acid and any other reagents that are needed to make:
   a ethyl propanoate
   b propanamide
   c butanamide
   d methyl methanoate.

8 Draw the structural formula of the product that is formed from the reaction of:
   a ethanoic acid and ammonia
   b methanamine and methanoic acid
   c butanoic acid, 2-methylpropan-1-ol and an acid catalyst.

9 Write the condensed structural formulae for the products of the dissociation of the following compounds in water:
   a butanamine
   b butanamide.

10 Explain why amines are better bases than amides with reference to the structures of these molecules.

11 Soap made from palm oil consists mainly of $CH_3(CH_2)_{14}COONa$, which is commonly called sodium palmate.
   a Identify the hydrophobic and hydrophilic sections of this molecule.
   b When sodium palmate is acting as a soap, which end of the molecule is likely to be in the centre of the micelle?

12 Briefly explain the action of soap in washing an oil stain from clothes. Include all of the following words in your explanation:
surfactant, hydrophobic, hydrophilic, emulsion, micelle

13 Soap made from coconut oil contains the surfactant molecule $C_{12}H_{23}O_2Na$, which is commonly called sodium laurate.

a Propose a condensed structural formula for sodium laurate.

b Draw the structural formula of a triglyceride that could be hydrolysed to produce sodium laurate.

14 Which of the following surfactant molecules would be most suitable for use in shampoo? Explain your answer.

A $CH_3(CH_2)_{14}COONa$

B $CH_3(CH_2)_2CH{=}CHCH_2CH{=}CHCH_2COONa$

C $CH_3(CH_2)_6COOK$

D $CH_3(CH_2)_{14}COOK$

15 Complete the flowchart of organic reactions by providing the correct reagents or products as required.

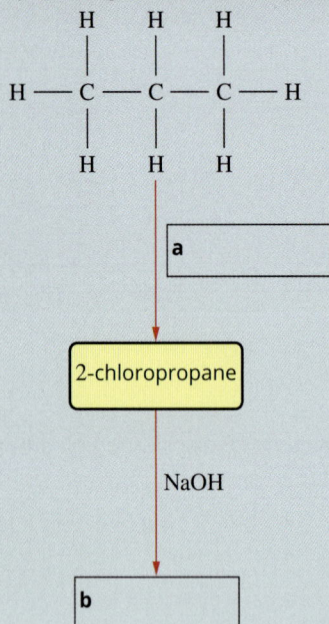

16 Write chemical pathways in the form of a flowchart (like the one in Question **15**) to describe the preparation of propanoic acid from an:

a alkane

b alkene.

17 Write a reaction pathway for the synthesis of:

a ethyl propanoate from ethene and 1-chloropropane

b ethyl ethanoate from an alkane.

18 a Write unbalanced equations for the production of:

i chloroethane from ethane

ii ethanol from ethene

iii ethanol from chloroethane

iv ethanoic acid from ethanol.

b Classifiy each of the reactions in part **a** as an addition, a substitution or an oxidation.

19 The reaction pathway shown below leads to the organic compound G (*N*-propylethanamide).

a Complete the pathway by filling in the boxes with the structural formulae of the appropriate compound for A–E.

b Describe a chemical test that could be carried out to distinguish between compounds A and D in the pathway.

c Which of the compounds B and F would be expected to have a greater water solubility? Explain your answer.

N-propylethanamide

20 Reflect on the Inquiry activity on page 350. What type of reaction has occurred between the bicarbonate of soda and vinegar? How do you know?

14 Polymers

Polymers, commonly called plastics, offer an almost limitless variety of properties, enabling them to be used for many different purposes.

In this chapter you will learn about the formation of polymers. The characteristics of the molecules used to make these very large molecules will be considered, as will the unique properties of the different polymers they form.

Starting with the most widely used synthetic polymer, polyethene, you will learn how the properties of polymers can be modified for different applications.

You will then examine the relative merits and disadvantages of the widespread use of polymers.

Content

INQUIRY QUESTION

What are the properties and uses of polymers?

By the end of this chapter, you will be able to:

- model and compare the structure, properties and uses of addition polymers of ethylene and related monomers, for example:
  - polyethylene (PE) `ICT`
  - polyvinyl chloride (PVC) `ICT`
  - polystyrene (PS) `ICT`
  - polytetrafluoroethylene (PTFE) (ACSCH136) `ICT`
- model and compare the structure, properties and uses of condensation polymers, for example:
  - nylon
  - polyesters

Chemistry Stage 6 Syllabus © NSW Education Standards Authority
for and on behalf of the Crown in right of the State of NSW, 2017.

14.1 Addition polymers

Can a plastic be made from milk?

COLLECT THIS...

- white vinegar
- full cream milk
- thermometer
- beaker or saucepan
- strainer
- hotplate
- gloves

DO THIS...

1 Pour 100 mL of milk into a beaker or saucepan.
2 Heat the milk slowly on the hotplate until it is around 50°C.
3 Remove the beaker or saucepan from the hotplate.
4 Add about 10 mL of vinegar to the milk.
5 Stir the mixture.
6 Clumps will form. Pour the thin liquid through a strainer to separate the lumps from the liquid.
7 Put on the gloves. Using your hand, squeeze the liquid from the lumps, then roll them into a ball.
8 Leave the ball to dry over the next few days.

RECORD THIS...

Describe the product formed and the liquid that was separated from the solid.

REFLECT ON THIS...

1 Would this product be of any use?
2 Does this experiment relate to an aspect of the dairy industry?
3 Would it matter what type of milk you used?

Polymers are often referred to by the general term **plastics**. You can probably identify many items that are made of polymers. Polymers are used in the construction of many different objects because they are cheap, versatile and easy to manufacture.

Many products such as combs, pen casings and rulers do not require special properties. They do not have to withstand high temperatures or highly corrosive environments. These products can be made from cheap, lightweight polymer materials.

Figure 14.1.1 shows a range of familiar polymers. The polymers that make up these objects are selected for their strength, flexibility or other properties. In this chapter you will learn about very sophisticated polymers that have been developed for specific performance properties.

POLYMER STRUCTURE

Polymers are covalent molecular substances composed of many small molecules all joined together. The word is made up of two parts, which come from Greek: *poly* (many), and *meros* (part). They are formed by joining together thousands of smaller molecules, called **monomers** (*mono* means 'one'), through a process called **polymerisation**, as shown in Figure 14.1.2.

FIGURE 14.1.1 (a) The polymer used to make the toy soccer players in this game was selected for its strength and how easy it is to mould. (b) The polymer bank notes used in Australia are strong and flexible. (c) The polymers in the helmet, gloves and bottle are similar, but differences in processing have given them very different properties.

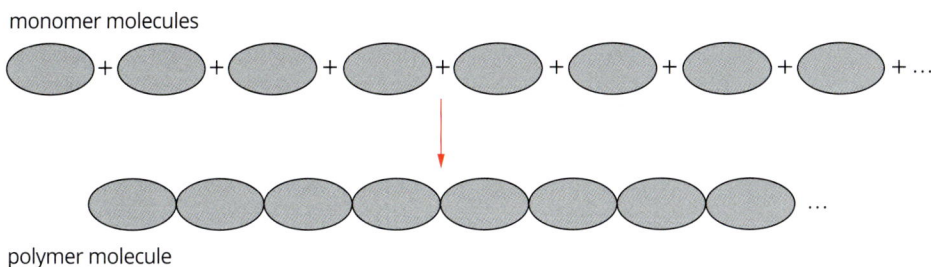

FIGURE 14.1.2 Monomers join to each other to form polymers.

Plastics and polymers

The word 'plastic' is frequently used to describe many items such as cling wrap and detergent bottles. For chemists the word 'plastic' describes a property of a material, not the material itself. A substance is described as being plastic if it can be moulded into different shapes readily. This is because the material from which it is made is a plastic material.

Figure 14.1.3 shows two examples of objects made from polymers. The polymer used to make the basket has plastic properties because upon heating, the polymer would melt, allowing it to be reshaped. However, the saucepan handle is hard and brittle and will not melt when heated.

FIGURE 14.1.3 A plastic basket has plastic properties, whereas a polymer frying pan handle does not.

ADDITION POLYMERISATION

You saw in Chapter 11 that addition reactions involve the reaction of an alkene with another molecule. All of the atoms of both molecules are present in the final molecule. Under some conditions alkenes can also undergo an addition reaction with themselves to produce long chains. The reaction of the monomer ethene with itself to form polyethene, shown in Figure 14.1.4, is an example of the **addition polymerisation** process. Several thousand ethene monomers usually react to make one molecule of polyethene.

> **ⓘ** The older, non-IUPAC names ethylene and polyethylene are often used for ethene and polyethene, and 'ethylene' is often used instead of 'ethene' in the names of other ethylene-based polymers.

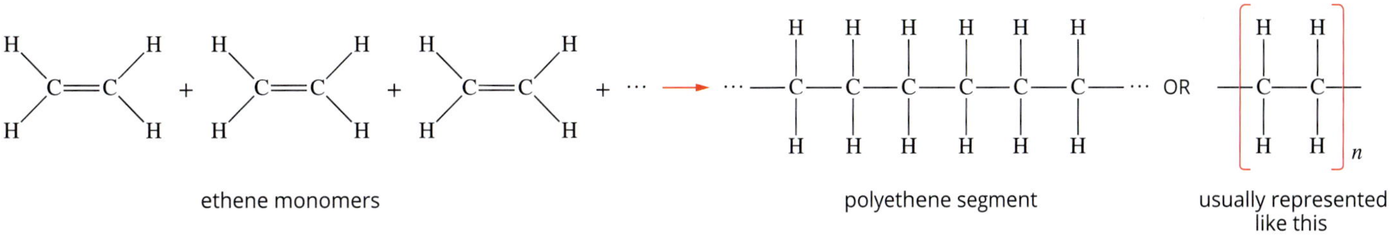

FIGURE 14.1.4 Thousands of ethene monomers join together to make one chain of polyethene. The standard notation shown simplifies the drawing of such a large chain.

Large square brackets and the subscript n are used to simplify the drawing of long polymer molecules. The value of n may vary within each polymer molecule, but the average molecular chain formed might contain as many as 20 000 carbon atoms. Polymers really are very large molecules!

Since all the atoms of the monomers are present in an **addition polymer**, the empirical formula of the monomer is the same as that of the polymer. Figure 14.1.5 shows an alternative representation of a polyethene chain segment, called a ball-and-stick model.

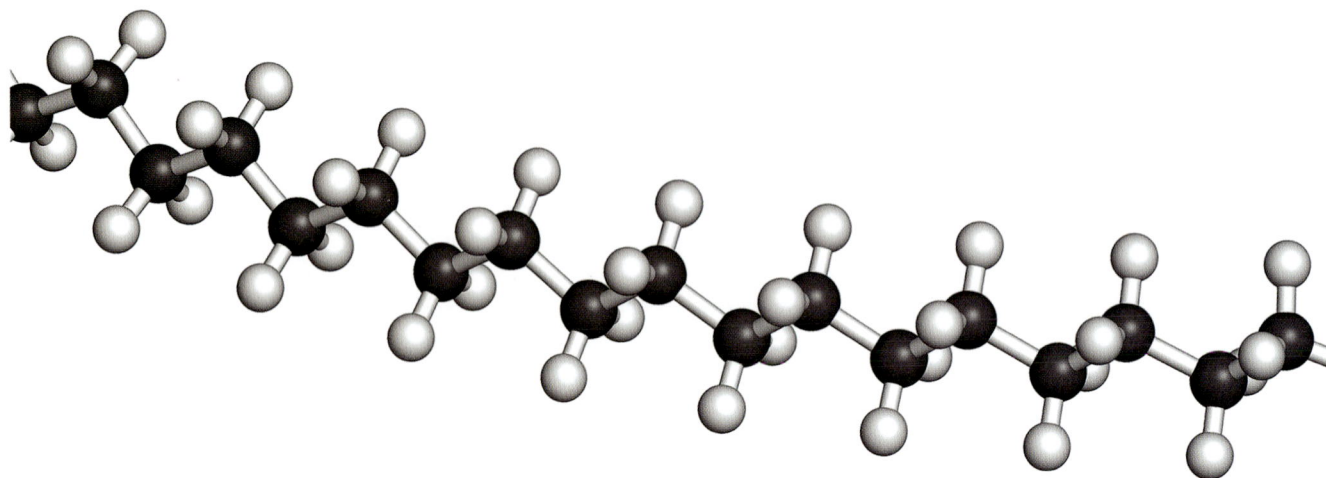

FIGURE 14.1.5 A ball-and-stick representation of a segment of polyethene

The name of a polymer formed through addition polymerisation will often include the monomer that was used to make it. The names of three common addition polymers and their monomers are listed in Table 14.1.1.

TABLE 14.1.1 Monomer and polymer names

Monomer	Polymer
ethene	polyethene
propene	polypropene
tetrafluoroethene	polytetrafluoroethene

Ethene is an **unsaturated** molecule because it contains a carbon–carbon double bond. When ethene polymerises, the double bonds break and new covalent bonds are formed between carbon atoms on nearby monomers. The polyethene formed does not contain any double bonds.

History of polymers

Wool, cellulose, rubber and proteins are naturally occurring polymers. However, most commercial polymers are synthetic and it is only in the last 100 years or so that their use has become widespread. Processed balls of natural rubber were being used for games in Central America more than 3500 years ago. These balls were made from latex (the sap of rubber trees) heated over a smoky fire until solid rubber formed.

American Charles Goodyear introduced large-scale production of rubber in 1839 when he developed the process of **vulcanisation**. This involved heating the rubber with a small amount of sulfur. Goodyear is still a famous name in tyres.

The first completely synthetic polymer was released in 1909 by Leo Baekeland, a Belgian-born American chemist. He reacted phenol and formaldehyde to form a hard material that he called Bakelite®. Bakelite continues to be used to make a small range of items, including billiard balls and saucepan handles. Table 14.1.2 shows a number of significant milestones in the history of polymers.

TABLE 14.1.2 Timeline for the development of some important polymers

Year	Polymer	Significance and examples of use
1869	cellulose nitrate (celluloid)	used in household goods, musical instruments, photographic film, table-tennis balls
1907	phenol formaldehyde resin	used in jewellery, household goods, electrical equipment, billiard balls, saucepan handles, circuit boards; e.g. Bakelite, Paxolin®
1927	nylon	nylon stockings created a shopping frenzy in the USA in 1940; used in clothing, parachutes, kitchen utensils, toothbrushes, fishing lines, guitar strings, seatbelts
1927	polyvinyl chloride (PVC)	low flammability and low electrical conductivity; used in drink bottles, toys, credit cards, water pipes, medical equipment, vehicle interiors
1931	polystyrene	first commercial production by IG Farben; used in disposable household products, plastic model kits, laboratory containers, insulation, packaging
1933	polymethyl methacrylate	transparency and shatter-resistance enabled it to be used instead of glass in aircraft and many other applications; e.g. Perspex®, Plexiglas®
1937	polyurethane	invented in Germany by Otto Bayer; first used to replace rubber; widely used in furnishings, insulation, packaging, sealants, engineering components
1938	polytetrafluoroethene (PTFE)	extremely difficult to handle due to its lack of 'stickiness'; used in cookware, fabrics, wiper blades, nail polish, industrial coatings; e.g. Teflon®, Fluon®
1951	polypropylene	second-most used polymer in the world; used in ropes, carpets, laboratory equipment, thermal clothing, banknotes
1972	polyparaphenylene terephthalamide	very strong and lightweight polymer; inflammable; e.g. Kevlar®, Twaron®
1980	polyacetylene	conductive polymer; no current commercial uses, but led to the development of other important materials
1990	polylactic acid (PLA)	biodegradable polymer; used in medical implants, packaging, disposable bags, 3D printing

The two contrasting photos of cyclists in Figure 14.1.6 highlight the rapid developments made by the polymer industry over the last 100 years. Not only have the materials that the bicycles are made from changed completely, but so has the attire of the cyclists. However, in both cases their clothing is made of polymers.

FIGURE 14.1.6 (a) Cyclists racing on metal bicycles in London around 1920. (b) Spanish cyclist Daniel Navarro pedals during Le Tour de France in 2013.

Polymer properties

GO TO ➤ Section 10.1 page 296

The length of polymer molecules gives them many of their useful properties. Polyethene is essentially an extremely long alkane. You know from Chapter 10 that the melting point of substances increases as the size of their molecules increases. The weak dispersion forces between the long polymer chains (as shown in Figure 14.1.7) are sufficiently strong to cause polyethene to be a solid at room temperature.

FIGURE 14.1.7 Dispersion forces between its molecules are sufficiently strong to make polyethene a solid at room temperature.

There are thousands of different polymers, many with specialised properties. However, in general polymers are:

- lightweight
- non-conductors of electricity
- durable
- versatile
- acid-resistant
- flammable.

Low-density polyethene

The earliest method of producing polyethene involved high temperatures (around 300°C) and extremely high pressures. Under these harsh conditions the polymer is formed too rapidly for the molecules to be neat and symmetrical. Figure 14.1.8 shows that the product contains many small chains, called branches, that divide off from the main polymer.

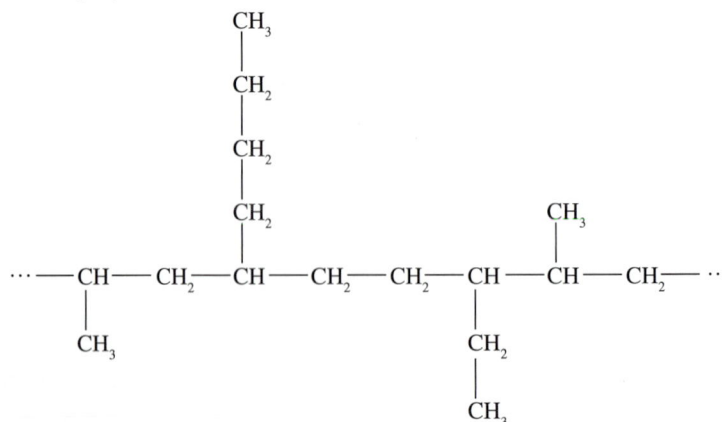

FIGURE 14.1.8 Polyethene made under high pressure and at high temperatures has short branches off the main chain.

The presence of these branches affects the properties of the polymer, because the molecules cannot pack closely together. The dispersion forces between molecules are weaker when the molecules are farther apart. The arrangement of the polymer molecules can be described as disordered or non-crystalline. This form of polyethene is known as **low-density polyethene** or LDPE. Its structure and properties are described in Figure 14.1.9.

The discovery of polyethene

The first practical method for the synthesis of polyethene was discovered by accident in 1933 in the laboratory of ICI in Cheshire, England, when some oxygen was accidently introduced into a container of ethene. The oxygen initiated the polymerisation reaction between the ethene molecules.

'When it first happened, it was a fluke,' recalled Frank Bebbington, a young laboratory assistant who was involved in the discovery. He assembled a reaction vessel to produce the polymer, only to watch the pressure slowly fall. 'We thought there was a small leak in the system. I felt embarrassed,' he said.

His colleagues went to lunch and he continued to top up the reaction vessel with more ethene. After they returned, the vessel was opened and they found that they had indeed made the new plastic. It took until 1938 for ICI to develop the industrial process that allowed them to produce their first commercial batch of polyethene.

Commercial use of the polymer flourished during World War II, when it was used to make replacements for much heavier components in planes and ships. It was also used for domestic products; Figure 14.1.10 depicts Earl Tupper showing off some of his first polyethene Tupperware containers.

FIGURE 14.1.10 Earl Tupper founded his own company, Tupperware, in 1945.

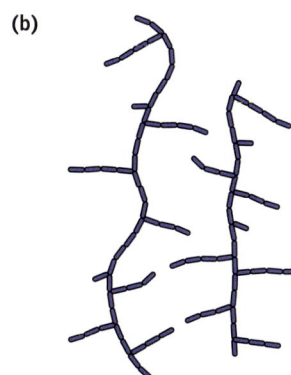

FIGURE 14.1.9 (a) A bottle made from low-density polyethene (LDPE). (b) The branched structure of LDPE.

High-density polyethene

A low-pressure method of producing polyethene was developed by Union Carbide in the late 1960s. Highly specialised transition metal catalysts, known as **Ziegler–Natta catalysts**, are used to avoid the need for high pressures. The polymer molecules are produced under much milder conditions and there are very few branches.

The lack of branches allows the molecules to pack together tightly, increasing the density and the hardness of the polymer formed. The arrangement of the polymer molecules is more ordered, resulting in crystalline sections. This form of polyethene is known as **high-density polyethene** or HDPE. Its properties and uses are summarised in Figure 14.1.11.

(a)

(b)

chains can pack more tightly than in LDPE

polyethene chains

FIGURE 14.1.11 Properties and structure of high-density polyethene (HDPE). (a) A bottle made from HDPE. (b) The structure of HDPE.

POLYMER VARIATIONS

One of the strengths of polymers is their versatility. The polymer used for household garbage bags is soft and tears easily. The polymer used in bullet-proof vests is extremely tough. Yet both products are made from polyethene. The properties of a particular polymer can be varied significantly if the degree of branching or the molecule length is altered.

Crystallinity

If the polymer chains have few branches, as is the case with HDPE, the molecules can sometimes line up in a regular arrangement, creating **crystalline regions** (Figure 14.1.12). This regular arrangement brings the polymer chains closer together. The intermolecular forces between the closely packed chains are stronger, and the presence of crystalline regions strengthens the material overall. Crystalline regions in a polymer prevent the transmission of light through the material, making it appear cloudy or opaque.

On the other hand, an **amorphous region** will form where the polymer chains are randomly tangled and unable to pack very closely. The polymer chains shown in Figure 14.1.13 are amorphous because they have no orderly arrangement.

In some polymer materials the entire solid is amorphous. Amorphous polymers are usually more flexible and weaker, and are often transparent. Polyethene chains formed under high-pressure reaction conditions have a high degree of branching. These longer, more frequent and random branches prevent the polymer molecules from forming extensive crystalline regions. Increasing the percentage crystallinity of a material makes it stronger and less flexible. This also makes the material less transparent because the crystalline regions scatter light.

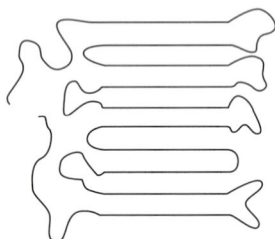

FIGURE 14.1.12 A crystalline region of a polymer material forms where the polymer chains are arranged in an ordered fashion.

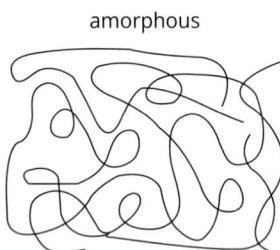

amorphous

FIGURE 14.1.13 An amorphous region forms when polymer chains are disordered.

Chain length

Ultra-high molecular weight polyethene (UHMWPE) consists of extremely long polymer molecules. As a consequence, dispersion forces between chains are much stronger than in shorter chains of polyethene. Because of this strength, UHMWPE is such a tough polymer that it can be used to make artificial hip joints, safety helmets and even bulletproof vests (Figure 14.1.14).

OTHER ADDITION POLYMERS

Many applications require polymers with more specialised properties than polyethene. For example, low flammability is essential for electrical wiring, and a baby's bottle needs a polymer with a higher melting point. One way to improve the properties of polyethene is to replace one or more of the hydrogen atoms on the monomer with more electronegative atoms or with a larger group of atoms.

As shown in Figure 14.1.15, when a chlorine atom replaces a hydrogen atom in ethene, the polymer polyvinyl chloride (PVC) is formed.

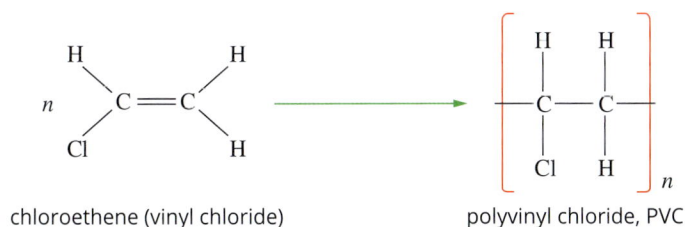

FIGURE 14.1.14 The toughness of a bulletproof vest is a result of the extremely long molecules of the polyethene used in its production.

chloroethene (vinyl chloride)   polyvinyl chloride, PVC

FIGURE 14.1.15 Polyvinyl chloride is made from the monomer chloroethene.

The chlorine atoms introduce dipoles into the long molecules (Figure 14.1.16). This increases the strength of the forces between polymer molecules, which leads to a higher melting point. PVC offers other advantages over polyethene: it has a low electrical conductivity and a low flammability. A PVC item burning in a flame will not continue to burn when it is removed from the flame. PVC is used in products such as conveyor belts, cordial bottles, water pipes and the covering of electrical wiring.

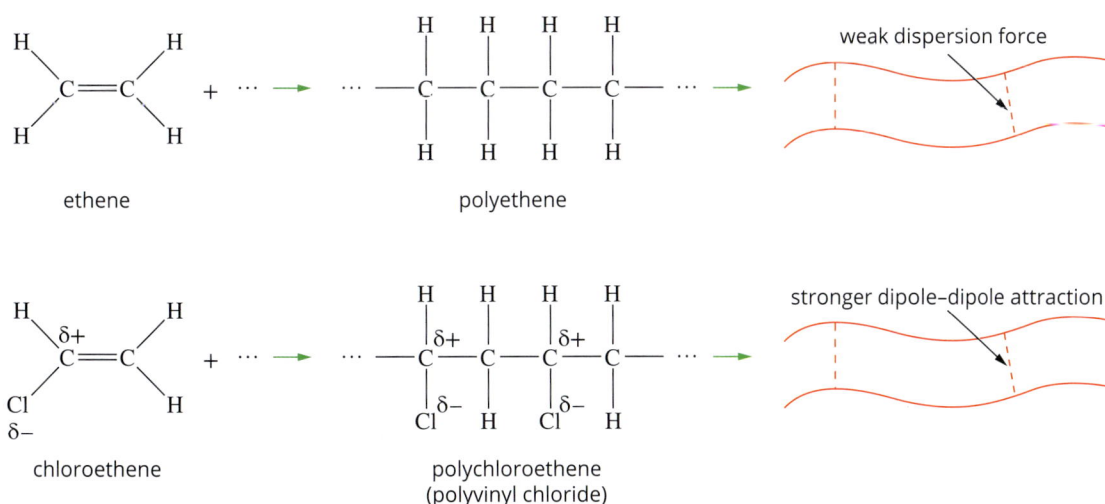

ethene   polyethene   weak dispersion force

chloroethene   polychloroethene (polyvinyl chloride)   stronger dipole–dipole attraction

FIGURE 14.1.16 The dipoles in PVC molecules lead to strong forces of attraction between chains.

Plasticisers

Plasticisers are small molecules that can be added to polymers during their manufacture. The polymer molecules are forced slightly further apart, weakening the forces between the chains and making the material softer and more flexible.

Because of the polar carbon–chlorine bond in polyvinyl chloride (PVC), the polymer chains are held together strongly by dipole–dipole attractions. Pure PVC is quite rigid at room temperature.

When a plasticiser is introduced between the chains, the chains can slide past each other, making the polymer softer and more flexible. By varying the amount of plasticiser used, PVC can

be produced with a wide range of flexibilities. You can see the difference between the packing of PVC polymer chains with and without plasticiser in Figure 14.1.17. Diisononyl phthalate is a plasticiser that is used to make PVC into vinyl floor coverings.

Although the use of plasticisers has increased the versatility of PVC, it does come at a cost. Plasticised PVC is very difficult to recycle. When the polymer is heated to remould it, the plasticiser decomposes to form compounds that can damage the structure of the polymer itself. For this reason PVC recycling is usually limited to unplasticised PVC, referred to as uPVC.

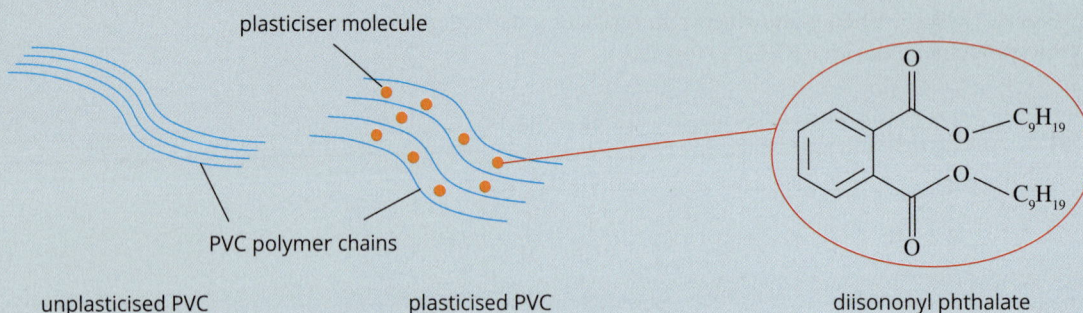

FIGURE 14.1.17 The presence of a plasticiser between the polymer chains weakens the attractive forces.

Polystyrene

The side group in a styrene monomer is a flat ring of six carbon atoms, often called a benzene ring, as shown in Figure 14.1.18.

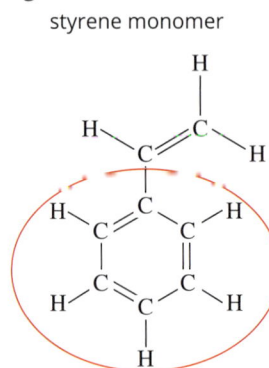

FIGURE 14.1.18 The chemical structure of the styrene monomer, showing the bulky side group circled in red

Styrene polymerises as shown in Figure 14.1.19: benzene rings are covalently bonded to every second carbon atom in the polymer chain. This causes polystyrene to be a hard but quite brittle plastic with a low density. It is used to make food containers, picnic sets, refrigerator parts, and CD and DVD cases.

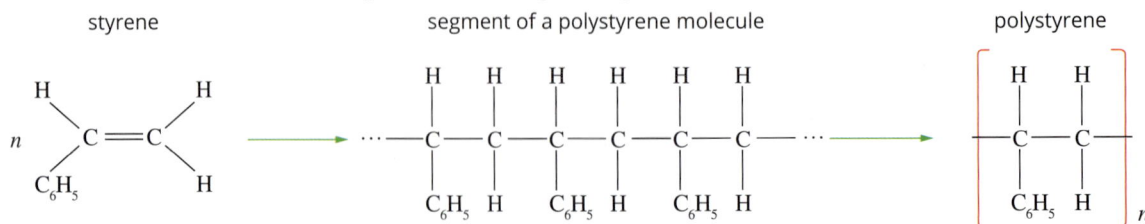

FIGURE 14.1.19 The polymerisation of styrene to form polystyrene

Polystyrene foam

Polystyrene is commonly manufactured as a **foam**. Foamed polymers are formed by blowing a gas through melted polymer materials. Foaming can drastically change the physical properties of a polymer material, as shown by the two examples of polystyrene in Figure 14.1.20.

Polystyrene foam is produced by introducing pentane into melted polystyrene beads. The beads swell up to produce the lightweight, insulating, shock-absorbing foam that is commonly used for take-away hot drink containers, bean bag beans, packaging materials and safety helmet linings.

Once polystyrene has been converted to a foam, it is difficult to recycle. Increasing awareness of polystyrene's environmental impact has resulted in it being replaced by alternatives such as paper, cardboard and biodegradable plastics.

FIGURE 14.1.20 The model plane is made from rigid polystyrene, while the white base is expanded polystyrene foam.

Polytetrafluoroethene

Tetrafluoroethene ($CF_2=CF_2$) (Figure 14.1.21) is formed when all of the hydrogen atoms in ethene are replaced by highly electronegative fluorine atoms. Molecules of tetrafluoroethene react with themselves to form the polymer polytetrafluoroethene, also known as Teflon.

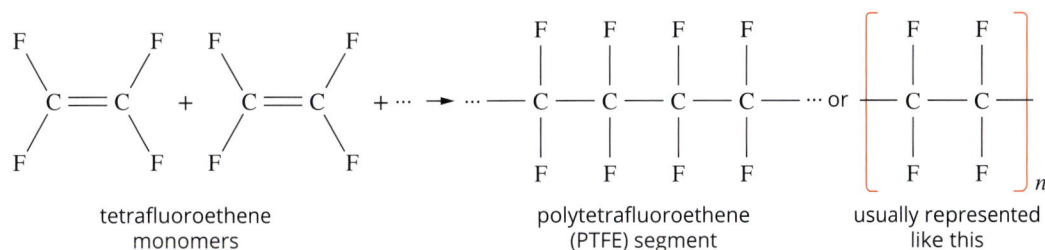

FIGURE 14.1.21 Tetrafluoroethene monomers react together to form polytetrafluoroethene (PTFE).

Polytetrafluoroethene has quite exceptional properties that are very different from those of polyethene. It can be used to make non-stick frying pans, medical implants, gears and clothing. The electronegative fluorine atoms reduce the strength of intermolecular bonds with other substances. The properties of polytetrafluoroethene are summarised in Table 14.1.3.

TABLE 14.1.3 A summary of the properties of tetrafluoroethene

Property	Description
non-stick	Repels all other substances, both hydrophobic (oil, fat) and hydrophilic (water).
heat-resistant	The melting point is 335°C and the upper operating temperature for this polymer is 260°C.
chemical-resistant	Extremely resistant to all known chemicals. It is not attacked by strong acids or bases and is inert towards all organic solvents.
good mechanical properties	Strong and durable, but not as hard as PVC.
low friction coefficient	Slippery to the touch. The friction coefficient between two pieces of Teflon is very low.
flame-resistant	Non-flammable.

There are thousands of commercial addition polymers. Table 14.1.4 shows a number of other polymers that may be familiar to you. Each of these polymers offers a unique property or properties that make it of commercial interest.

TABLE 14.1.4 Commercial addition polymers

Monomer	Polymer	Properties	Examples of application
propene 	polypropene (polypropylene)	durable, cheap	artificial grass, dishwasher-safe plastic, ice-cream containers, rope
tetrafluoroethene 	polytetrafluoroethene (PTFE, e.g. Teflon)	non-stick, high melting point	frying pan and iron coatings, plumber's tape, waterproof fabrics
dichloroethene 	polyvinylidene chloride (PVDC)	sticks to itself, transparent, stretchy	food wrap
propenenitrile 	polypropenenitrile (acrylic)	strong, able to form fibres	acrylic fibres, fabrics
phenylethene (styrene) 	polyphenylethene (polystyrene)	hard, brittle, low melting point	toys, packaging, expanded foams
methylcyanoacrylate 	polymethylcyanoacrylate	polymerises on contact with water	super glue
methyl 2-methylpropenoate 	polymethyl methacrylate (e.g. Perspex)	transparent, strong	shatter-proof glass substitute

Teflon—a wonder material

American polymer company DuPont first manufactured Teflon in 1938. It was used during World War II to coat valves and other equipment used in isolating uranium for the first atomic bomb. After the war its uses spread to plumbing tape, non-stick cookware and artificial hips and vocal chords as manufacturers sought to take advantage of its heat resistance and low coefficient of friction. The chemistry itself is neutral but the way it is used, for warfare or peacetime products, depends on people.

The non-stick nature of Teflon has the disadvantage of making it difficult to apply to a surface such as a clothes iron. The metal surface has to be sand-blasted and the Teflon applied in several layers, starting with a type of primer.

Another innovative application of Teflon is in Gore-Tex® (Figure 14.1.22), a fabric that 'breathes'. Rain cannot penetrate Gore-Tex, but water vapour from sweat can escape through it. For this reason it is used in high-quality trekking rainwear and boots.

Despite the popularity of non-stick cookware, there are concerns about its safety. The USA has banned the use of perfluorooctanic acid in the manufacture of Teflon to help limit its toxicity. It is also suggested not to overheat pans or saucepans containing Teflon.

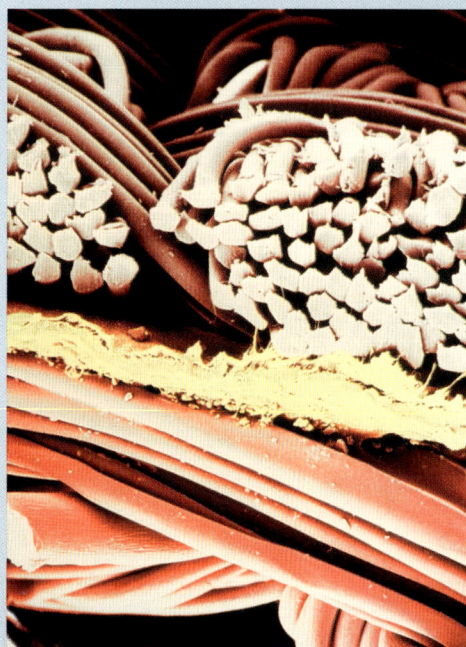

outer fabric

Teflon film

inner lining

FIGURE 14.1.22 Scanning electron micrograph of Gore-Tex fabric. The yellow layer is Teflon. The spaces in this layer are small enough to prevent water passing through but large enough to allow water vapour to pass through.

14.1 Review

SUMMARY

- Polymers are long molecules formed by the reaction of thousands of monomer units.
- Addition polymers are formed from the reactions of monomers containing carbon–carbon double bonds.
- In general, polymers are durable and have relatively low densities. They are non-conductors of electricity and have relatively low melting points.
- The most common polymer used is polyethene. It can be manufactured in two different ways to make two different products: high-density polyethene (HDPE) and low-density polyethene (LDPE).
- The percentage crystallinity of a polymer is a measure of the relative amounts of crystalline (ordered) regions and amorphous (disordered) regions in the material.
- No polymer is entirely crystalline. Some are entirely amorphous, but most are a combination of both.

- Factors that affect the physical properties of polymers include the:
  - polymer chain length
  - extent of branching of polymer chains, e.g. LDPE and HDPE
  - arrangement of side groups in the polymer chain
  - inclusion of additives such as plasticisers within the polymer.
- Polymers can be designed for a particular purpose by selecting suitable monomers, reaction conditions and additives.
- Polyvinyl chloride (PVC), polytetrafluoroethene (Teflon) and polystyrene are three examples of commonly used addition polymers. The properties of these polymers are superior to those of polyethene due to the substitution of hydrogen atoms with more electronegative elements or more complex groups of atoms.

14.1 Review *continued*

1 Many substances are composed of very long molecules, but not all of these substances are polymers. Which of the following is an essential feature of a polymer?
   A The molecule must be over 100 atoms long.
   B The chain in the molecule must consist of carbon atoms.
   C The molecule must be made from a smaller repeating unit.
   D The chain must contain carbon-to-carbon double bonds.

2 Which of the following molecule(s) could be used to form a polymer?

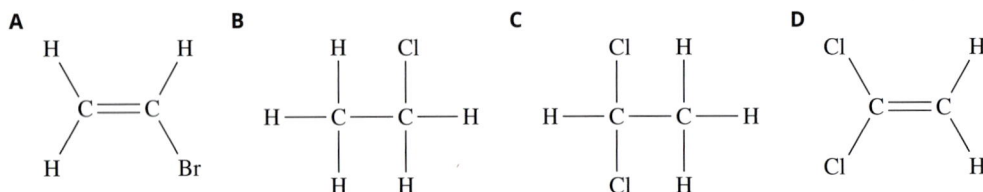

A
H   H
 \ /
  C=C
 / \
H   Br

B
    H   Cl
    | |
H—C—C—H
    | |
    H   H

C
   Cl H
    | |
H—C—C—H
    | |
    Cl H

D
Cl   H
 \   /
  C=C
 /   \
Cl   H

3 State the empirical formula of each of the following monomers.
   a ethene
   b propene
   c phenylethene
   d chloroethene.

4 What would be the molecular formula for a molecule made from an addition reaction of:
   a three propene monomer units?
   b six vinyl chloride monomer units?
   c 65 ethene monomer units?

5 How many repeating units does the following polymer segment contain?

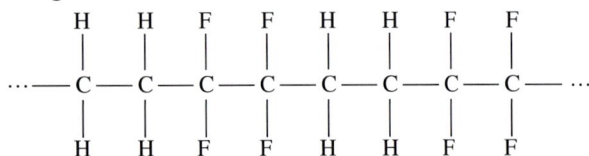

```
    H   H   F   F   H   H   F   F
    |   |   |   |   |   |   |   |
···—C—C—C—C—C—C—C—C—···
    |   |   |   |   |   |   |   |
    H   H   F   F   H   H   F   F
```

6 Explain why a molecule containing 18 repeating units from the monomer phenylethene would not be considered a polymer.

7 a In terms of their structures, explain the difference in properties between HDPE and LDPE.
   b Which of these two forms would be a suitable material for:
      i   a soft, flexible plastic wrap?
      ii a 2 L drink container?
      iii wrapping material for frozen food?

8 Refer to Table 14.1.4 on page 384 and draw diagrams to represent the formation of:
   a polypropylene
   b Teflon
   c polypropylenenitrile.

14.2 Condensation polymerisation

Addition polymerisation is limited to the use of unsaturated monomers. To obtain an even broader range of polymers, chemists use a second technique, known as **condensation polymerisation**. For condensation polymerisation to occur, the monomers must have two functional groups, one on each end of the monomer. These functional groups react chemically with the functional groups on neighbouring monomers, creating a different functional group in the process. The reaction links the monomers into long polymer chains, as shown in Figure 14.2.1.

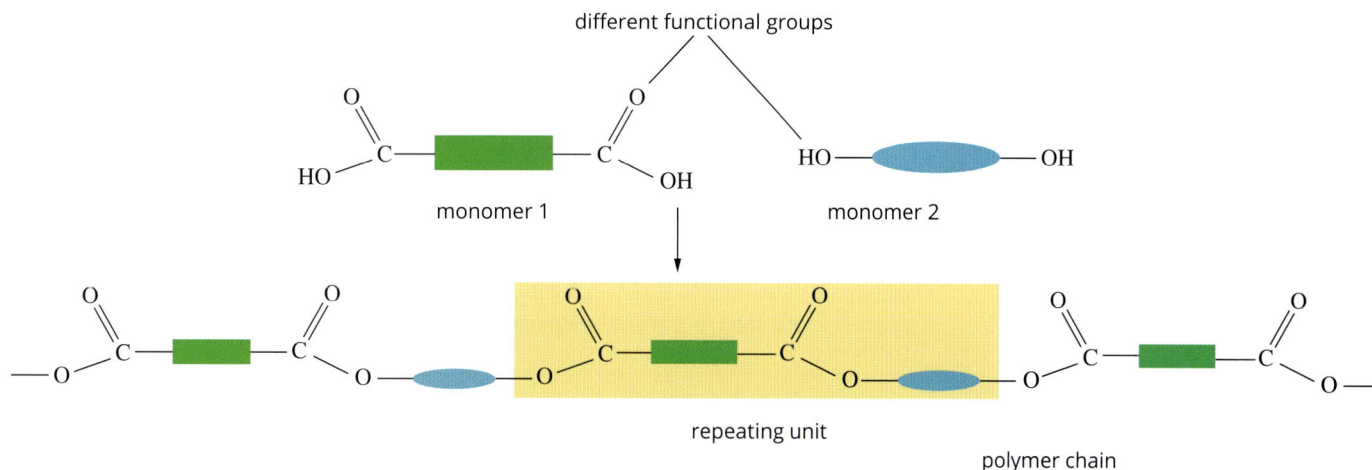

FIGURE 14.2.1 Condensation reactions require that the monomers have functional groups at each end of the molecule. These functional groups react together to form the polymer chain. As a result, an additional product is formed (in this case it is H_2O).

Another feature of condensation reactions is that small molecules are also produced during the reaction. In the two types of **condensation polymers** that will be examined in detail (polyamides and polyesters), a molecule of water (H_2O) is produced during each reaction between the two functional groups of the monomers.

The differences between addition and condensation polymers are summarised in Table 14.2.1.

TABLE 14.2.1 Comparison of addition and condensation polymers

Addition polymers	Condensation polymers
Monomers must be unsaturated, containing a double or triple carbon–carbon bond.	Monomers must contain two functional groups that can react with those on neighbouring molecules.
No by-products are produced during the reaction.	Small molecules, often water, are produced during the reaction.
The polymer backbone is a long C–C chain.	The polymer backbone contains functional groups; for example, amides or esters.

POLYESTERS

The term 'polyester' is often used for various synthetic clothing materials. However, in chemistry **polyesters** are a class of polymers that are formed through the process of condensation polymerisation. Polyesters are formed by combining monomers that contain carboxylic acid and hydroxyl functional groups. They are typically formed by reacting a dicarboxylic acid monomer with a diol monomer.

> **ⓘ** Polyesters are typically formed by combining a dicarboxylic acid monomer with a diol monomer in a condensation polymerisation reaction. Water molecules are also produced during the polymerisation reaction.

Polyethene terephthalate (PET)

The polymer most often used to make polyester fabric is polyethene terephthalate (PET or PETE). PET is synthesised by reacting benzene-1,4-dioic acid monomers with ethane-1,2-diol monomers, as shown in Figure 14.2.2. The monomers used for PET look very complex, but the key feature is the functional groups on both ends of the monomers.

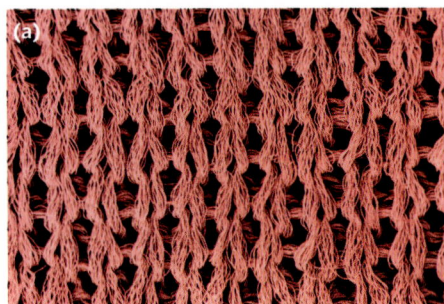

FIGURE 14.2.2 Polyethene terephthalate (PET) is formed when benzene-1,4-dioic acid reacts with ethane-1,2-diol. The PET is linked by ester groups, which is why it is part of the polyester family of polymers.

In addition to being used in fabrics, PET has a range of uses including recyclable drink bottles and food packaging (Figure 14.2.3). PET is a strong material because the ester groups are polar, so that there are dipole–dipole attractions between polymer chains.

(a)

(b)

(c)

FIGURE 14.2.3 Polyethene terephthalate (PET) has many uses. (a) A scanning electron micrograph showing knitted polyester fibres used in clothing. (b) PET is commonly used to make plastic bottles. (c) The recycling code for bottles and other items made of PET is 1.

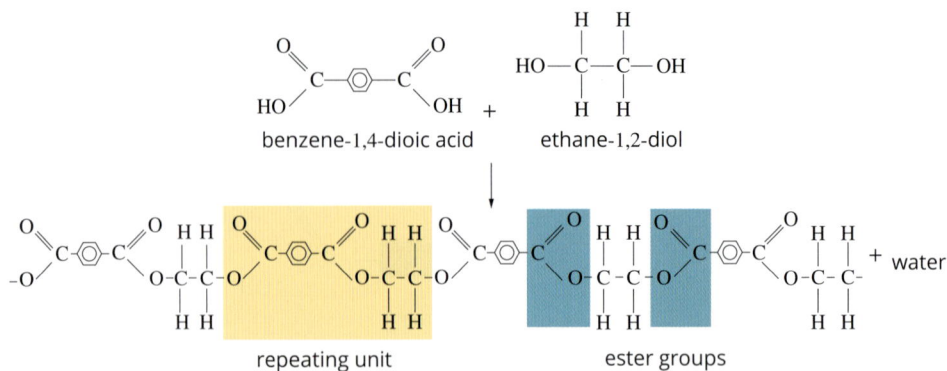

CHEMFILE S

Bisphenol A (BPA)

Bisphenol A (BPA) is an organic compound containing two hydroxyl functional groups, as shown in Figure 14.2.4.

BPA is often used to produce condensation polymers. It can be combined with a dicarboxylic acid molecule to produce a polyester. More commonly, it is combined with phosgene ($COCl_2$) to produce polycarbonate plastic. In this condensation reaction, HCl is released rather than H_2O. Polycarbonate plastic is used to produce water bottles, sports equipment, medical devices, CDs and DVDs and the lining of water pipes.

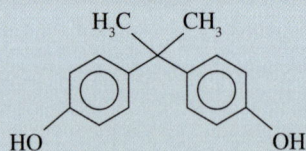

FIGURE 14.2.4 Bisphenol A (BPA) undergoes condensation polymerisation.

There have been health concerns about the use of BPA in recent years. In particular, its use in baby bottles has been questioned because it has been shown to mimic the action of the hormone oestrogen. The US Food and Drug Administration and the European Food Safety Authority have concluded that BPA poses no risk to consumers of any age, and Food Standards Australia New Zealand found no detectable BPA in infant formula prepared in a range of baby bottles. Even so, many drink bottles and other products used in the food industry are now labelled 'BPA free', largely because of consumer preference rather than any recognised health risk.

NYLON

You will have seen that when a molecule containing an amine functional group reacts with a molecule containing a carboxyl group, an amide bond can form. If a monomer containing an amine group on each end reacts with a monomer with a carboxyl group on each end, a **polyamide** can form (Figure 14.2.5).

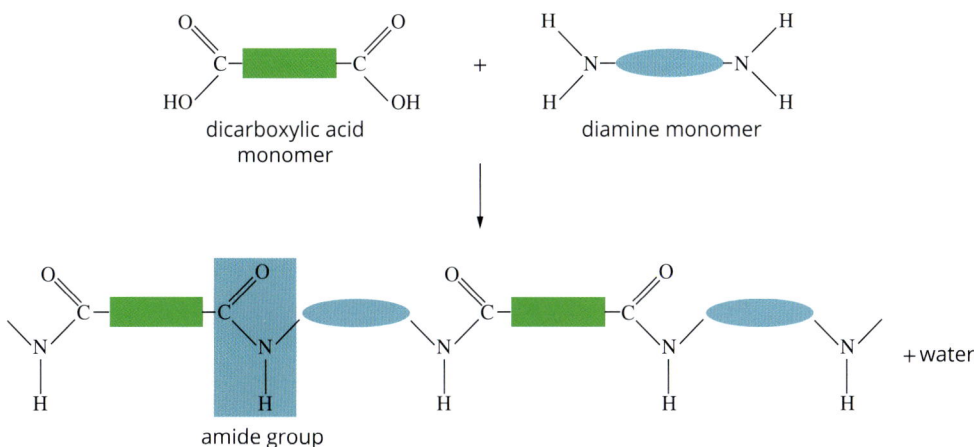

FIGURE 14.2.5 Dicarboxylic acid and diamine monomers undergo a condensation polymerisation reaction to produce a polyamide and water.

The term 'nylon' refers to a group of polyamides in which the monomers are linear carbon chains. A common example is nylon-6,6, which is so named because the dicarboxylic acid monomer has a chain of six carbons and the diamine monomer also has a chain of six carbon atoms, as shown in Figure 14.2.6.

FIGURE 14.2.6 Nylon-6,6 is a polyamide formed when hexanedioic acid reacts with hexane-1,6-diamine. Water is also produced.

Nylon can be easily drawn into fibres that have a high tensile strength. These fibres are used to produce strong, lightweight materials for clothes (Figure 14.2.7), parachutes, ropes, fishing line and even guitar strings. However, nylon can also be used to make hard, rigid plastics that can be used in pipes and machinery.

> ℹ️ Nylon is typically formed by combining a dicarboxylic acid monomer with a diamine monomer in a condensation polymerisation reaction. Water is also produced during the condensation reaction.

FIGURE 14.2.7 The strength of nylon fibres makes them suitable for stockings.

It is not essential to have two different monomers to make nylon or polyester. A form of nylon, nylon 6, can be made from the monomer shown in Figure 14.2.8, where the different functional groups are on opposite ends of the same monomer.

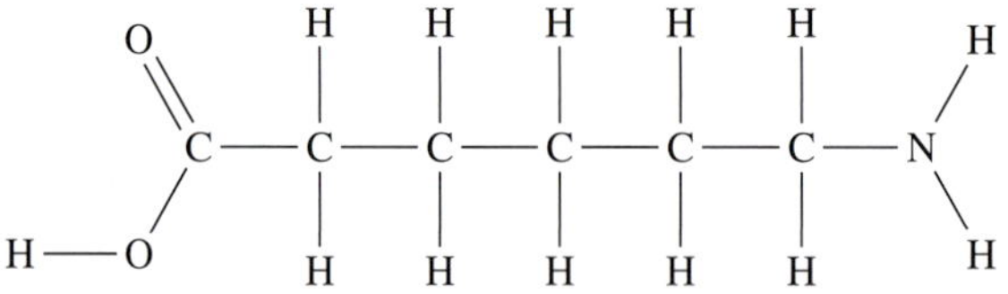

FIGURE 14.2.8 This monomer can be used to manufacture nylon. The functional group on the end of one monomer reacts with the other functional group on the end of a neighbouring monomer.

CHEMISTRY IN ACTION WE

Manufacturing nylon in the school laboratory

An interesting way to manufacture nylon in a school laboratory involves the following steps:

1 Prepare a 5%(v/v) solution of sebacoyl chloride in water.
2 Add 20 mL of this solution to a beaker or petri dish.
3 Prepare a 5%(v/v) solution of hexane-1,6-diamine in hexane.
4 Add 20 mL of this solution carefully to the same beaker or petri dish so that this solution sits on top of the sebacoyl chloride solution.

Where the two solutions come into contact, polymerisation occurs. Use tweezers to draw the nylon from the interface between the two liquids. As you draw the nylon out, further monomers come in contact, forming more polymer. In this way a long thread of nylon can be drawn from the solution (Figure 14.2.9). This process is known as **interfacial polymerisation** because the reaction occurs at the interface between the two solutions. A key to the process is the use of hexane and water, two liquids that do not mix.

FIGURE 14.2.9 Nylon forms at the interface between the two monomers.

THERMOPLASTIC AND THERMOSETTING POLYMERS

Polymers can be classified into two groups on the basis of their behaviour when heated:

- thermoplastic polymers
- thermosetting (or thermoset) polymers.

Thermoplastic polymers soften when heated, which means they can be remoulded or recycled. Polymers are only thermoplastic if the bonds between the long polymer chains are hydrogen bonds, dipole–dipole attractions or weak dispersion forces (Figure 14.2.10). When heated, the molecules in thermoplastic materials have enough energy to overcome these intermolecular forces and become free to move and slip past one another. If the polymer can be remoulded, then it can probably be recycled easily, a desirable property in modern society.

Thermosetting polymers decompose or burn when heated. They do not soften because the bonds between the chains are very strong (Figure 14.2.11). If the temperature becomes high enough to break the covalent bonds, the breaks may be at any point, causing the polymer to decompose. It is difficult to recycle thermosetting polymers as they cannot be remoulded into new shapes.

Covalent bonds between polymer molecules are called **cross-links**. Cross-links limit movement between the polymer molecules and make the polymer rigid, hard and heat resistant. Thermosetting polymers are used to make items such as saucepan handles, bowling balls and shatterproof crockery.

An example of a thermoset polymer is shown in Figure 14.2.12. The polymer is a condensation polymer formed from the reaction between phenol and methanal (formaldehyde). Note the covalent bond between neighbouring chains. This is the cross-link. It is a strong covalent bond. The high temperatures required to break this bond will also break the covalent bonds joining the monomers together.

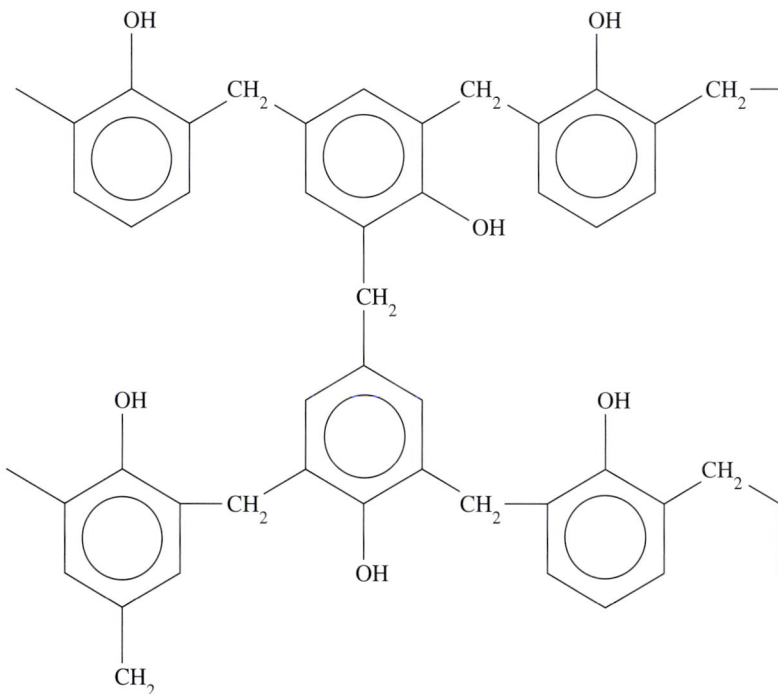

polymer chain

Heat causes the molecules to move enough to overcome the weak forces between molecules in adjacent chains.

FIGURE 14.2.10 A thermoplastic polymer has weak bonds between the chains.

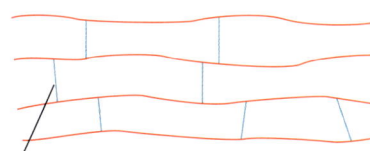

The heat required to break the cross-links is also sufficient to break the bonds within the molecules themselves.

FIGURE 14.2.11 A thermosetting polymer has strong covalent bonds between the chains.

FIGURE 14.2.12 Phenol formaldehyde can be manufactured with cross-links between chains.

Elastomers are an interesting class of polymers that are formed when only occasional cross-links are present. The chains in these polymers can still move past each other when stretched but the cross-links return the chains to their original positions once the force causing the stretching is released. Elastic bands and other rubber items are made of elastomers. The cross-links stop elastomers from completely melting when heated and make recycling difficult. For example, the sulfur cross-links in the polymer in car tyres (Figure 14.2.13) make the tyres non-recyclable.

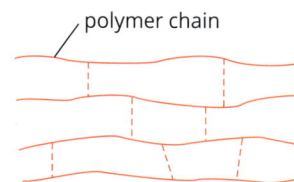

| PA 7.5 | PA 7.5 |
| WS 7.9 | WS 7.10 |

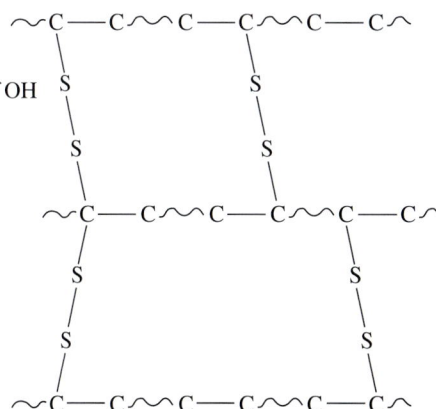

FIGURE 14.2.13 The elastomer chains in rubber car tyres are cross-linked by sulfur atoms.

Polymer waste

Plastics are durable, chemically resistant and lightweight. These properties make plastics very useful, but they also have a serious environmental impact. Australians consume more than 1.5 million tonnes (1.5 billion kilograms) of polymer materials every year, which includes many different plastics. The disposal of the waste polymer material is a serious issue in our society.

Two approaches to reducing polymer waste are the use of either recyclable polymers or **biodegradable** polymers such as polyvinyl alcohol (Figure 14.2.14). Biodegradable polymers will break down into harmless products when left exposed to rain and soil. The polarity of the −OH bonds in polyvinyl alcohol make it soluble in water.

If a polymer does not degrade quickly, the alternative is to recycle it. A numbering scale is used to identify plastics for recycling (Figure 14.2.15). All households should be guided by this chart when deciding which plastic items to recycle.

Not all polymers are readily recyclable or biodegradable. For example, plasticised PVC is difficult to recycle and is not biodegradable, leading to concerns about its use. At present only about 12% of polymer waste generated in Australia is recycled; the remainder is disposed of in landfill or ends up in waterways and oceans.

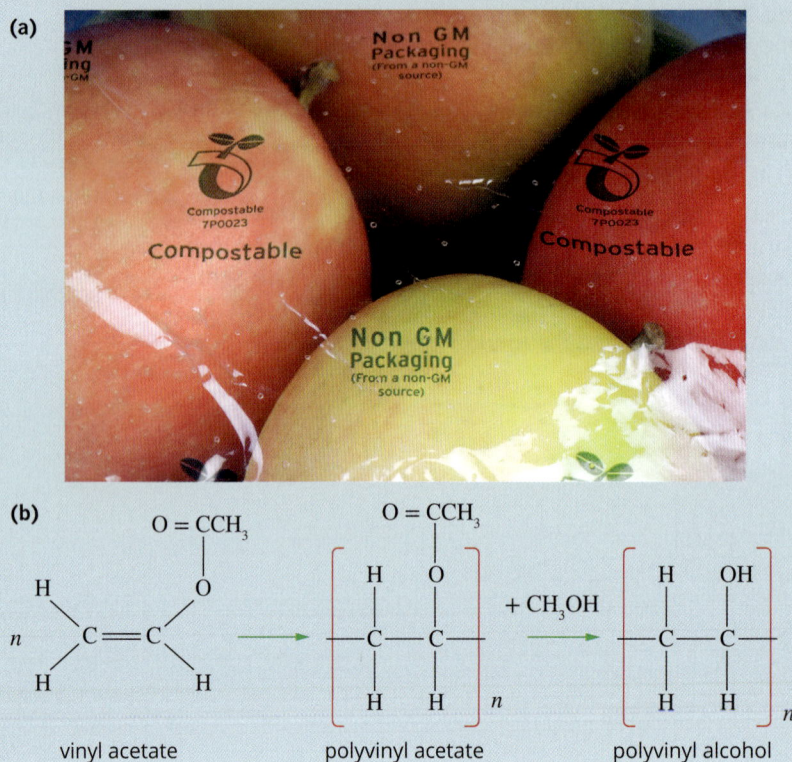

(a)

(b)

FIGURE 14.2.14 (a) Apples packaged in biodegradable plastic. (b) Polymerisation of vinyl acetate produces polyvinyl acetate, which is then reacted with an alcohol to produce polyvinyl alcohol.

	PETE	HDPE	PVC	LDPE	PP	PS	OTHER
	polyethene terephthalate	high-density polyethene	polyvinyl chloride	low-density polyethene	polypropene	polystyrene	includes polycarbonates, ABS, Teflon, various copolymers, nylon and other condensation polymers
	bottles for soft drinks, water, shampoo, take-away food containers	garbage bins, fuel tanks, hard hats, banners, water pipes, food storage containers	plastic wrap, cordial bottles, electrical wire covers, water pipes, floor tiles	plastic wrap, squeeze bottles, plastic tubing, shopping bags	rope, clothing, ice-cream containers, flip-top bottle lids	yoghurt containers, fridge shelves, drink cups, insulating beads, packaging	

FIGURE 14.2.15 International number code used to identify recyclable plastics.

14.2 Review

SUMMARY

- Condensation polymers can be formed when there are functional groups on both ends of the monomers.
- A small molecule, often water, is also produced when condensation polymers form.
- The reaction between monomers with carboxylic acid groups and hydroxyl groups will form a polyester.
- The reaction between monomers with carboxylic acid groups and amine groups will form a polyamide.
- Condensation polymers are often harder and stronger than addition polymers.
- A polymer is thermoplastic if it will soften when heated, allowing it to be reshaped. A thermoplastic polymer can be recycled by melting it, then moulding it into a new shape. Thermoplastic materials have no strong bonds between polymer chains.
- Some polymers have covalent bonds, or cross-links, between polymer chains. Such thermosetting materials do not melt and they cannot be reshaped. If they cannot be reshaped, recycling is limited.
- Elastomers are polymers with special cross-links that allow them to stretch.
- Because most polymers are made from non-renewable resources and are not biodegradable, they pose an environmental problem.

KEY QUESTIONS

1 Select the alternative that is a correct statement about condensation polymers.
   A Condensation polymers do not contain any double bonds.
   B All condensation polymers contain cross-links between the chains.
   C All condensation polymers have higher melting points than addition polymers.
   D The functional groups in a condensation polymer differ from the functional groups in the monomers used.

2 The molecule shown could be used to form a condensation polymer.

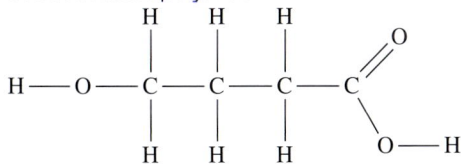

   a Draw a segment of the polymer that could be formed from this molecule (your segment needs to contain 12 carbon atoms).
   b What small molecule is produced in the polymerisation reaction?
   c Which category of condensation polymer will this polymer belong to?

3 Which one or more of the following molecules could act as monomers for condensation polymerisation reactions?

   A

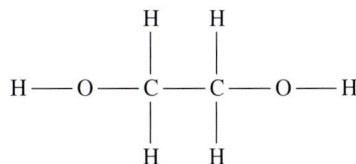

   B

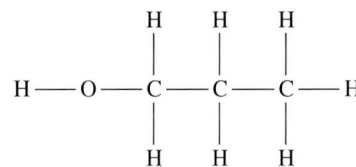

   C

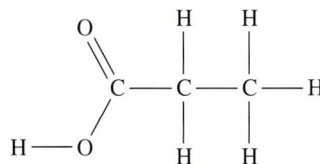

   D

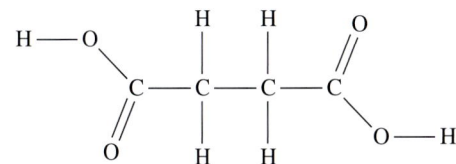

4 A segment of a condensation polymer (Kevlar) is shown. Kevlar can be used in bulletproof vests.

a Draw the two monomers this polymer is formed from.

b What are some of the properties Kevlar will exhibit?

c Give reasons for the strong bonding between molecules of Kevlar.

5 a List two features addition polymers and condensation polymers have in common.

b List two differences between addition polymers and condensation polymers.

6 Rank the following types of bonding between polymer chains in order of increasing strength:

dipole–dipole attractions, covalent bonds, dispersion forces

7 The polymer used inside a particular non-stick frying pan can be recycled but the polymer used as a handle cannot.

a Explain how the structure of the two polymers differs if one is recyclable and the other is not.

b What properties are important in the choice of the polymer used to coat the frying pan?

c What properties are important in the choice of the polymer used to form the frying pan handle?

Chapter review

KEY TERMS

addition polymer
addition polymerisation
amorphous region
biodegradable
condensation polymer
condensation
  polymerisation
cross-link
crystalline region

elastomer
foam
high-density polyethene
interfacial polymerisation
low-density polyethene
monomer
plastic
plasticiser
polyamide

polyester
polymer
polymerisation
thermoplastic
thermosetting
unsaturated
vulcanisation
Ziegler–Natta catalyst

REVIEW QUESTIONS

1 Select the statement about addition polymers that is correct.

 A All addition polymers contain double bonds in their chains.

 B All addition polymers have a recycle code to enable them to be sorted and reused.

 C A polymer that contains a greater amount of crystalline than amorphous regions is harder.

 D The molecules in a polymer sample are the same length.

2 A polymer can be formed from the monomer shown.

$$\begin{array}{c} H \qquad\qquad H \\ \backslash \qquad\quad / \\ C = C \\ / \qquad\quad \backslash \\ H \qquad\qquad F \end{array}$$

 a Draw a segment of this polymer containing three repeating monomer units.

 b Explain why the melting point of this polymer is likely to be significantly greater than that of polyethene.

3 A segment of a PVC polymer is shown here.

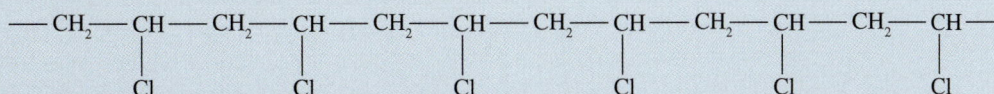

$$—CH_2—CH—CH_2—CH—CH_2—CH—CH_2—CH—CH_2—CH—CH_2—CH—$$
$$\qquad\quad | \qquad\qquad | \qquad\qquad | \qquad\qquad | \qquad\qquad | \qquad\qquad |$$
$$\qquad\quad Cl \qquad\quad Cl \qquad\quad Cl \qquad\quad Cl \qquad\quad Cl \qquad\quad Cl$$

 a Draw the structure of the monomer used to make PVC.

 b How many repeating monomer units are shown in the section of polymer?

 c What is the strongest type of bonding between PVC polymer chains?

4 Define the following terms:

 a monomer

 b thermoplastic

 c thermosetting

 d cross-link

 e plasticiser.

5 State whether each of the following statements about polymers is true or false.

 a Each chain in a polymer is the same length.

 b The chains in thermoplastic polymers are held together only by dipole–dipole attractions.

 c HDPE has no branches.

 d The properties of a polymer are different from the properties of the monomer it consists of.

6 Which of the following molecules can act as monomers in addition polymerisation?

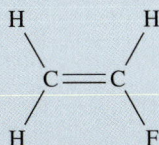

 A propene

 B propane

 C chloroethene

 D $CH_2=CHF$

7 Ethene (C_2H_4) is the smallest alkene.

 a Why is it described as unsaturated?

 b Draw the structural formula of ethene.

 c Could ethane (C_2H_6) act as a monomer? Explain your answer.

8 Use polyethene as an example to explain the following terms.
   a addition polymerisation
   b unsaturated and saturated
   c empirical formula

9 Draw a section of the polymer made from each of these monomers in an addition polymerisation process.

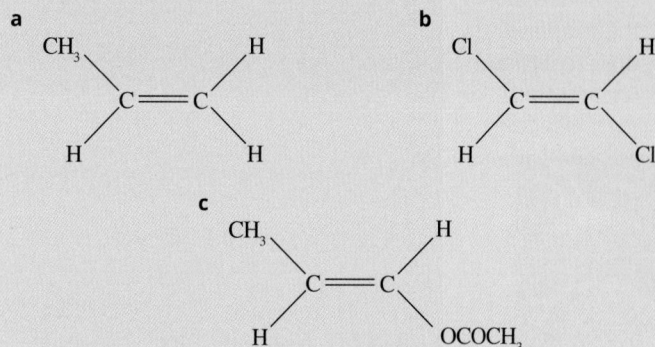

a

CH$_3$, H
C=C
H, H

b

Cl, H
C=C
H, Cl

c

CH$_3$, H
C=C
H, OCOCH$_3$

10 Identify the strongest type of intermolecular force present between polymer molecules produced from the following monomers:
   a ethene ($CH_2=CH_2$)
   b vinyl chloride ($CH_2=CHCl$)
   c styrene ($CH_2=CHC_6H_5$)
   d propene ($CH_2=CHCH_3$)
   e acrylonitrile ($CH_2=CHCN$)

11 The following side groups are found in different polymers. Sort the groups from smallest to bulkiest.
   –F (in Teflon), –NC$_{12}$H$_8$ (in polyvinyl carbazole), –H (in polyethene), –C$_6$H$_5$ (in polystyrene), –Cl (in polyvinyl chloride)

12 Select the correct word in each comparison of LDPE to HDPE. Compared to HDPE, LDPE:
   a will have more/fewer branches
   b will have more/fewer crystalline regions
   c will have a greater/lower density
   d will have a lower/higher melting point
   e will be less/more brittle.

13 Which one of the following pairs of compounds could form a condensation polymer?
   A ethene and a dicarboxylic acid
   B two diol molecules
   C a diamine and a dicarboxylic acid
   D a diol and a diamine

14 Classify each of the following polymers as a polyester or a polyamide.

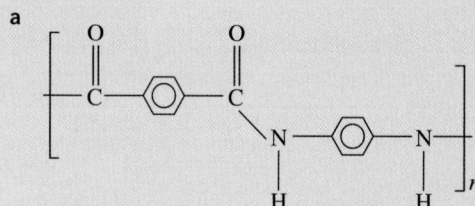

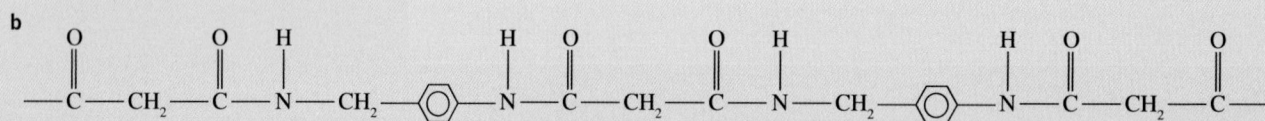

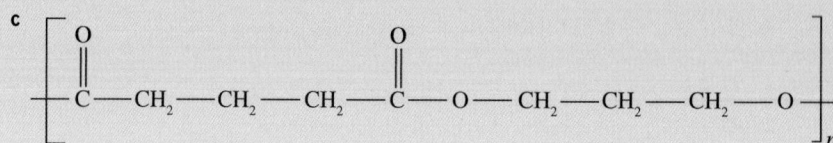

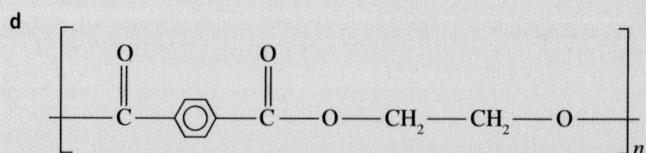

a

b

c

d

15 Draw the monomers that make up the following polymer.

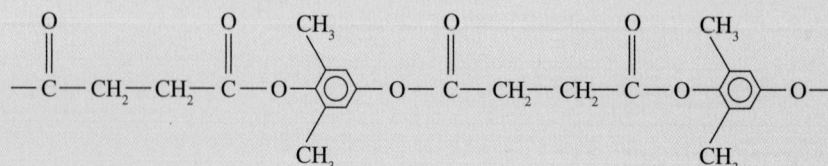

16 Draw the polymer that would be formed from each of the following pairs of reactants.

a

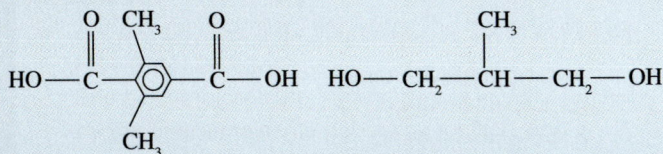

b

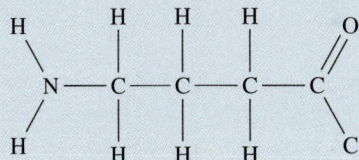

17 50 diamine monomers combine with 50 dicarboxylic acid monomers.
   a Which functional group joins these monomers?
   b How many molecules of water are produced?

18 In the name of nylon-6,6 the first 6 refers to the number of carbons in the diamine. The second 6 refers to the number of carbons in the dicarboxylic chain. Given this information, draw the structure of nylon-4,6.

19 The polymer chains of a certain material can be cross-linked to varying extents.
   a Sketch the polymer chains when there is:
      i no cross-linking
      ii a little cross-linking
      iii a lot of cross-linking.
   b Use diagrams to show the effect of stretching each of these materials.

20 How does the strength of the interchain bonding differ between thermosetting and thermoplastic polymers?

21 Why do thermosetting polymers decompose rather than melt when heated strongly?

22 Would a thermoplastic or thermosetting polymer be the most suitable material for the following purposes?
   a handle of a kettle
   b squeezable container for shampoo
   c knob of a saucepan lid
   d shopping bag
   e rope.

23 Elastic bands, golf balls and saucepan handles are made from polymers with some cross-linking.
   a Which material has the greatest degree of cross-linking?
   b Describe the properties of the material you chose in part **a** to support your answer.

24 Polymer chemists investigated the properties of polymers by increasing the length of chains in a controlled way. They identified the effect that this had on the relative molecular mass, melting point, strength of inter-chain forces and electrical conductivity. What would you expect the results for each property test to have been?

25 The backbone of a particular polymer consists of carbon atoms only. The melting point is relatively high compared to other polymers. The monomer used to make the polymer was most likely
   A fluoroethene
   B fluoroethane
   C propene
   D hexane-1,6-diamine

26 The monomer shown can be used to form a polymer.

   a What small molecule will be produced?
   b If 5000 monomers combine, how many small molecules are formed?
   c Name the type of bond connecting the monomers.
   d Draw the repeating unit of the polymer.

27 Reflect on the Inquiry activity on page 374. Would it be practical to produce polymers from milk?

REVIEW QUESTIONS

Organic chemistry

Multiple choice

1 Which of the following molecules is a functional group isomer of pentanoic acid?

A pentan-1-ol

B butanoic acid

C ethyl propanoate

D 2-methylbutanoic acid

2 What are the IUPAC names for the following three molecules?

A propanal, methyl ethanoate, propan-1-amine

B propanoic acid, propanone and propan-1-amine

C propanoic acid, propanone and propanamide

D propanal, propanone and propanamide

3 What is produced by the reaction between propan-1-ol and hydrogen iodide (HI)?

A 1-iodopropane only

B 1-iodopropane and water

C 1-iodopropane and hydrogen gas

D propane and water

4 In which of the following homologous series does the smallest molecule contain two carbon atoms?

A alkanes

B alcohols

C alkenes

D carboxylic acids

5 What is the systematic name for $CH_3CH_2CH_2CH(CH_3)_2$?

A 1,1-dimethylbutane

B 2-methylpentane

C 2-methylpentene

D propyldimethylmethane

6 Which of the following compounds would be expected to have the lowest boiling point?

A $CH_3CH_2CH_2OH$

B $CH_3CH_2CH_2CH_3$

C $CH_3CH_2CH_2Cl$

D $CH_3CH_2CH_3$

7 Which of the following statements are true of the homologous series of primary alcohols?

I The members differ by one CH_2 unit.

II They are all strong bases.

III They can be oxidised to form carboxylic acids.

A I and II

B II and III

C I and III

D I, II and III

8 What is the product formed by the reaction of CH_2CH_2 with Br_2?

A CH_2BrCH_2Br

B $CH=CHBr$

C CH_3CH_2Br

D $CHBrCHBr$

9 Consider the following reaction pathway:

ethene $\xrightarrow{\text{step 1}}$ chloroethane $\xrightarrow{\text{step 2}}$ ethanol

$\xrightarrow{\text{step 3}}$ ethanoic acid

What reactions occur in steps 1, 2 and 3 of this pathway?

A substitution, addition, hydrolysis

B chlorination, substitution, addition

C addition, substitution, oxidation

D addition, reduction, hydrolysis

10 When ethanol is heated under reflux with an acidified solution of potassium dichromate, what is the formula of the final product?

A $CH_3CH_2CH_2OH$

B CH_3COOCH_3

C CH_3COOH

D $CH_3CH_2CH_3$

11 The ester methyl ethanoate could be made by reacting together which of the following?

A CH_3CH_2OH and CH_3COOH

B CH_3CH_2OH and $HCOOH$

C CH_3OH and CH_3CH_2COOH

D CH_3OH and CH_3COOH

12 Which of the structures shown does not have a IUPAC name that ends with '-ol'?

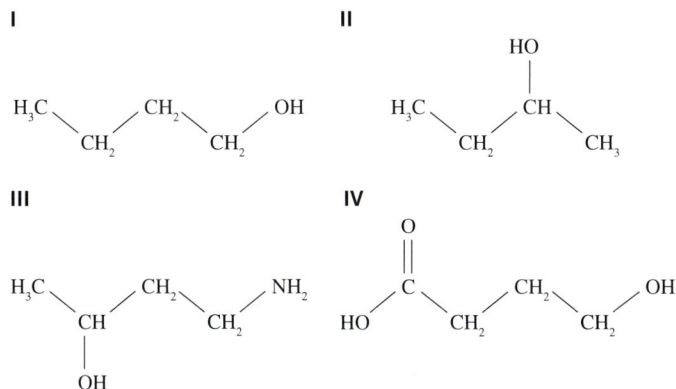

I

H_3C—CH_2—CH_2—CH_2—OH

II

H_3C—CH_2—CH(OH)—CH_3

HO on the CH

III

H_3C—CH(OH)—CH_2—CH_2—NH_2

IV

HO—C(=O)—CH_2—CH_2—CH_2—OH

A II and III

B III only

C IV only

D III and IV

13 Consider the following equation for the reaction of methanol with acidified potassium dichromate.

$2K_2Cr_2O_7(aq) + 3CH_3OH(aq) + 8H_2SO_4(aq) \rightarrow$
$2Cr_2(SO_4)_3(aq) + 3HCOOH(aq) + 2K_2SO_4(aq)$

Which statement about this reaction is not true?

A Dichromate ions have been reduced.

B Methanol has been oxidised.

C Hydrogen ions have been reduced.

D Sulfate ions have not been oxidised or reduced.

14 What hydrocarbon has the formula C_3H_8?

A propane

B prop-1-ane

C prop-1-ene

D propene

15 What is the name of the first member of the alkyne family?

A methyne

B methene

C ethyne

D ethene

16 Which one of the following is not a member of the alkyne homologous series?

A C_2H_2

B C_3H_8

C C_6H_{10}

D $C_{10}H_{18}$

17 How many different alkenes are there with the molecular formula C_4H_8?

A 1

B 2

C 3

D 4

18 Which one of the following alternatives lists the compounds in order of increasing boiling points?

A ethane, propane, ethanol, propan-1-ol

B ethane, ethanol, propane, propan-1-ol

C ethanol, propan-1-ol, ethane, propane

D ethanol, ethane, propan-1-ol, propane

19 Polyethenol (also called polyvinyl alcohol or PVA) is a polymer often used as a water-soluble film in packaging. The monomer used to form polyethenol is shown below.

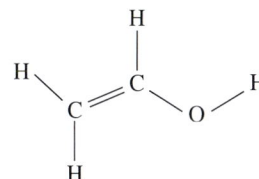

Which one of the following structures shows a possible segment of the polymer?

A

B

C

D

20 Polyethene is a polymer that has a wide range of uses. It can be produced as a high-density product (HDPE) or a low-density form (LDPE) that is softer and more flexible. Compared to LDPE, HDPE has:

A a higher softening temperature due to a greater degree of branching of the polymer chain

B a higher softening temperature due to a smaller degree of branching of the polymer chain

C a lower softening temperature due to a greater degree of branching of the polymer chain

D a lower softening temperature due to a smaller degree of branching of the polymer chain.

Short answer

1 For each of the following structures, write:
  i the molecular formula
  ii the condensed structural formula.

a

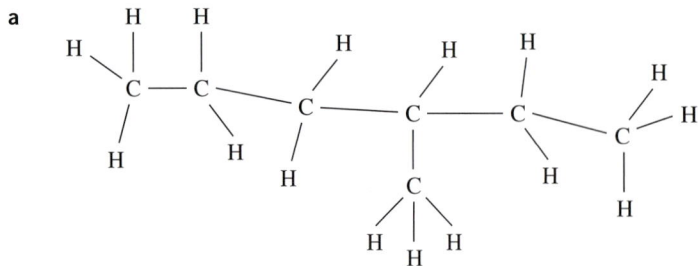

b

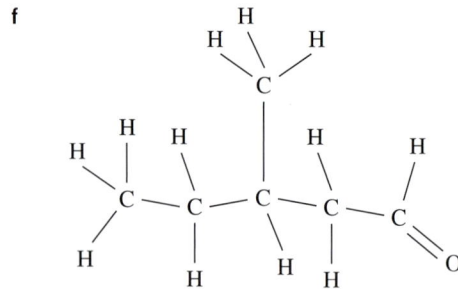

c

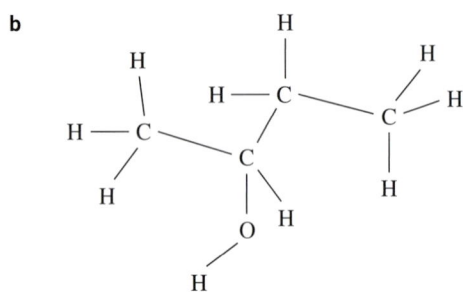

d

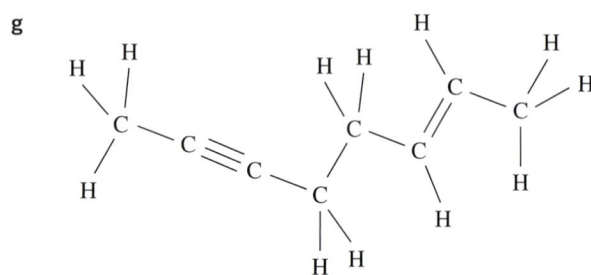

e

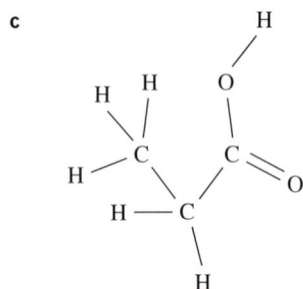

f

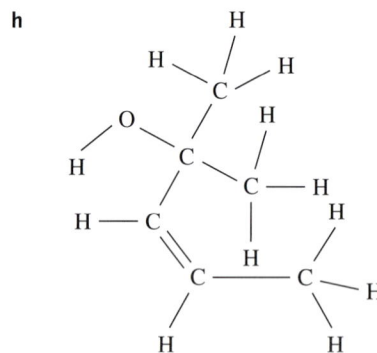

g

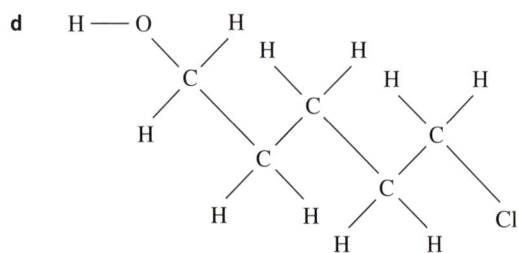

h

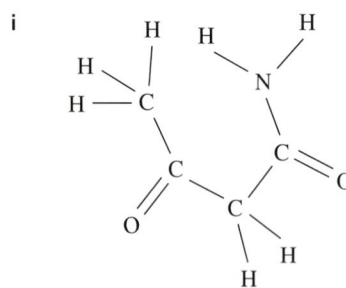

i

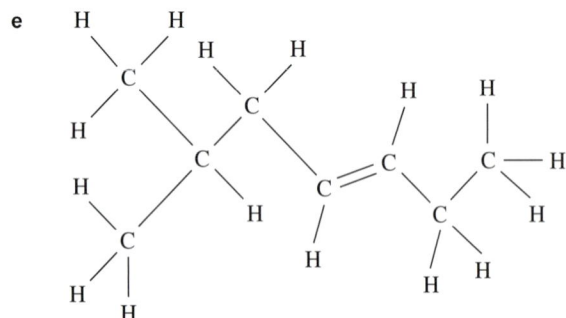

2 Draw the structural formula for each of the following, showing all bonds.

a $CH_3(CH_2)_3CH_3$
b $CH_2CHCH_2CHOHCH_3$
c $CH_2ClCH_2COCH_3$
d $CH_3(CH_2)_2CONH_2$
e $(CH_3)_2CHCHCH_2$
f $CH_3CH_2COH(CH_3)_2$
g $CH_3OCOCH_2CH_3$
h 4-ethylheptanoic acid
i 1-bromopropan-1-ol
j 4-methylpent-2-ene
k 1-iodobutan-2-amine
l 3-aminohexan-2-ol.

3 Give appropriate reagents/conditions to effect the conversion of:

a butan-2-ol to butanone
b 1-chloropropane to propan-1-ol
c pent-2-ene to pentan-3-ol and pentan-2-ol
d propan-1-ol to propanoic acid
e cyclohexene to cyclohexane.

4 Write out synthetic pathways/sequences, showing all organic intermediates and the reagents/conditions used, to prepare:

a propanoic acid from propane
b methyl ethanoate from methane and ethene
c propene from propane via propan-2-ol.

5 Write balanced chemical equations (excluding states) for the following reactions:

a acid–base reaction between propanoic acid and sodium hydrogen carbonate ($NaHCO_3$)
b oxidation of propan-1-ol to propanoic acid under acidic conditions (redox half-equation)
c condensation reaction between ethanol and propanoic acid to form ethyl propanoate
d acid–base reaction between ethanamine and propanoic acid
e complete combustion of propanoic acid.

6 State the name of each of the following compounds.

a $CH_3C{\equiv}CCH_3$
b $CH_3CH_2CH_2CH_2CH_2CH_2CH_3$
c

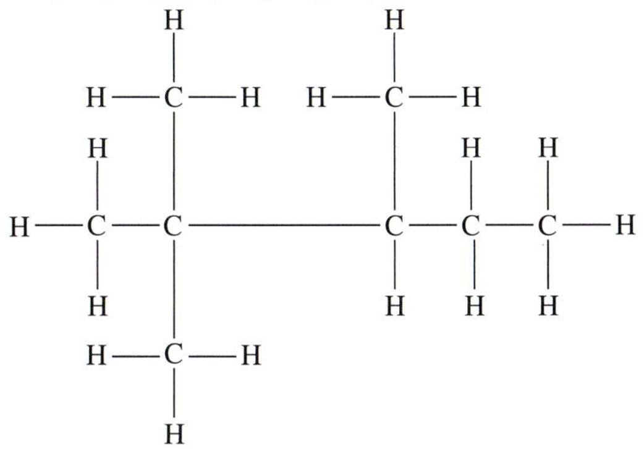

d

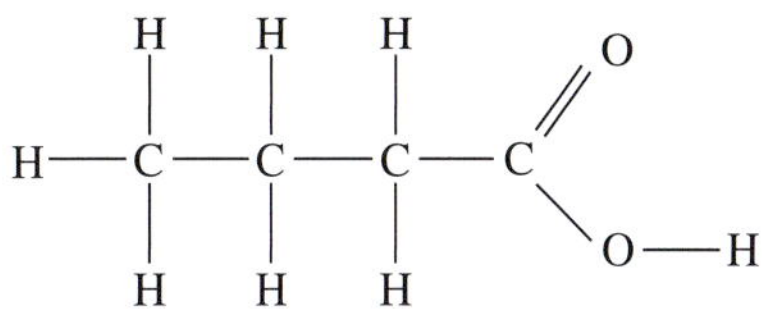

e CH_3CHCH_2OH with CH_3

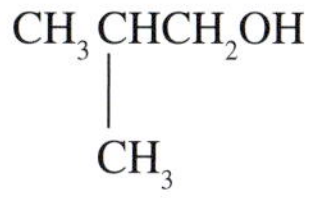

7 Draw the structural formula of each of the following compounds:

a hex-1-ene
b propanoic acid
c ethyl propanoate
d 2-methylpropan-2-ol
e pent-2-yne.

8 Give a condensed structural formula for each of the following compounds:

a hexanoic acid
b 4-ethyl-2,2-dimethylheptane
c butan-2-ol
d propyne
e 2,4-dimethylhex-1-ene.

9 Polymers are very large covalent molecular substances.

a The following is a representation of a section of an addition polymer.

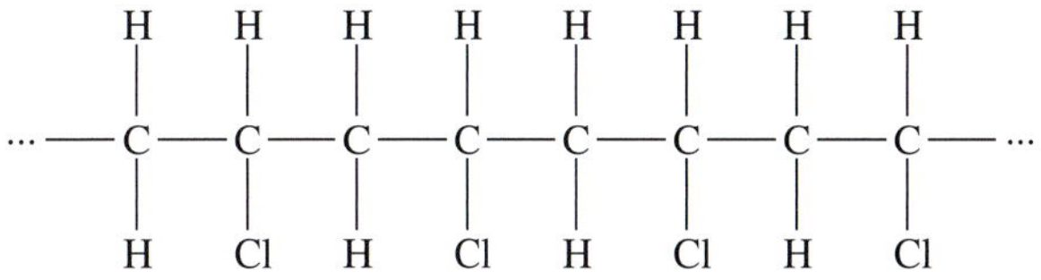

Draw the structure of the monomer from which this polymer was formed.

b A small section of a thermosetting polymer is heated over a flame.

  i Describe what observations you would expect to make.

  ii Describe the structure of thermosetting polymers and use this to explain your answer to part **i**.

10 Using a suitable example where possible, clearly explain the difference between the following pairs of terms:

a a monomer and a polymer
b a thermoplastic polymer and a thermosetting polymer
c a branched polymer and a cross-linked polymer
d crystalline and non-crystalline regions of a polymer.

11 Isomers are molecules with the same molecular formula but different arrangements of the atoms or functional groups. There are, however, different categories of isomers.

a i Hexane has several isomers. Draw and name three of these isomers.

  ii Use your answer to part **i** to explain what a chain isomer is.

  iii Will the physical properties of these isomers differ? Explain your answer.

b **i** Pentanol has several position isomers. Draw and name three of these isomers.

   ii Use your answer to part **i** to explain what a position isomer is.

   iii Use the reaction of pentanol isomers with $K_2Cr_2O_7$ in acid conditions to illustrate that the reactions of position isomers can lead to very different products.

c **i** Several carboxylic acids and esters exist with the molecular formula $C_4H_8O_2$. Draw and name two of these isomers.

   ii Use your answer to part **i** to explain what a functional group isomer is.

12 Complete the table for each of the molecules shown.

Molecule	Functional groups present	Correct IUPAC name
H_3C–CH_2–CH_2–CH_2–$CH(OH)$–CH_2–CH_3		
H_3C–$CH(F)$–CH_2–$C(=O)$–OH		
H_2C=$C(H)$–$C(H)(CH_2)$–CH_3 (pentene with H substituents)		
H_3C–CH_2–$CH(CH_2CH_3)$–$CH(NH_2)$–CH_2–CH_3		
H_3C–$CH(OH)$–CH_2–NH_2		
H_3C–$CH(OH)$–CH_2–$CH(Cl)$–CH_3		
HO–$C(=O)$–CH_2–CH_2–CH_2–$CH(OH)$–CH_2–CH_3		

Molecule	Functional groups present	Correct IUPAC name
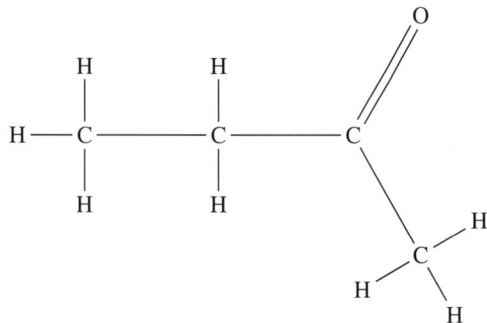		
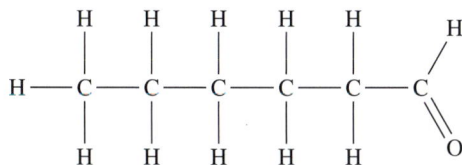		

13 For each of the following molecules, give the IUPAC name and a condensed structural formula, and suggest compounds that could be reacted together to produce the molecule.

(a)

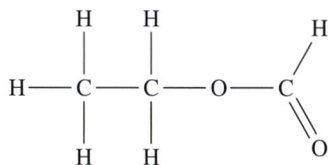

(b)

(c)

(d)

14 Complete and balance the following equations involving organic acids and bases.

a $CH_3CH_2COOH(l) + H_2O(l) \rightarrow$

b $CH_3CH_2CH_2NH_2(l) + H_2O(l) \rightarrow$

c $CH_3CH_2COOH(l) + CH_3CH_2CH_2NH_2(l) \rightarrow$

d $CH_3CH_2COOH(l) + CH_3CH_2CH_2OH(l) \rightarrow$

e $CH_3(CH_2)_{17}COOH(aq) + NaOH(aq) \rightarrow$

15 a i Draw a segment of the polymer that can be formed from the monomer $CH_2=CCl_2$.

ii What type of polymerisation forms this polymer?

iii A very branched form of this polymer is produced when the monomer is heated. However, the use of a catalyst can produce a linear form of the polymer. Compare the likely properties of the linear version with the likely properties of the branched version.

iv This polymer can be recycled or remoulded into a new product. Explain why.

b i Draw a segment of the polymer that can be formed from the monomer $H_2NCH_2CH_2CH_2CH_2CH_2COOH$.

ii What type of polymerisation forms this polymer?

iii Explain why the melting point of this polymer is relatively high.

Applying chemical ideas

The identification and analysis of chemicals is of immense importance in scientific research, medicine, environmental management, quality control, mining and many other fields.

In this module, you will investigate a range of methods used to identify and measure quantities of chemicals. You will investigate and process data involving the identification and quantification of ions present in aqueous solutions. This is particularly important because of the impact of poor water quality on human health and the environment. You will be able to deduce or confirm the structure and identity of organic compounds by interpreting data from qualitative tests of chemical reactivity, and by determining structural information using infrared spectroscopy, proton and carbon-13 nuclear magnetic resonance spectroscopy and mass spectrometry.

Outcomes

By the end of this module, you will be able to:

- develop and evaluate questions and hypotheses for scientific investigation (CH12-1)
- design and evaluate investigations in order to obtain primary and secondary data and information (CH12-2)
- conduct investigations to collect valid and reliable primary and secondary data and information (CH12-3)
- select and process appropriate qualitative and quantitative data and information using a range of appropriate media (CH12-4)
- communicate scientific understanding using suitable language and terminology for a specific audience or purpose (CH12-7)
- describe and evaluate chemical systems used to design and analyse chemical processes (CH12-15)

Chemistry Stage 6 Syllabus © NSW Education Standards Authority for and on behalf of the Crown in right of the State of NSW, 2017.

Water is a very good solvent for a wide variety of polar molecules and ionic salts. As a result of this property, all water systems contain some dissolved salts. Their presence can be attributed to a number of factors, such as natural processes, pollution, farming and industrial activities.

In this chapter you will examine the ways in which salts can enter the water system. You will also look at a number of methods used to test water samples for the presence of metal contaminants and other ions.

Content

INQUIRY QUESTION

How are the ions present in the environment identified and measured?

By the end of this chapter, you will be able to:

- analyse the need for monitoring the environment **S** **EU** **ICT**
- conduct qualitative investigations – using flame tests, precipitation and complexation reactions as appropriate – to test for the presence in aqueous solution of the following ions: **ICT** **N**
  - cations: barium (Ba^{2+}), calcium (Ca^{2+}), magnesium (Mg^{2+}), lead(II) (Pb^{2+}), silver ion (Ag^+), copper(II) (Cu^{2+}), iron(II) (Fe^{2+}), iron(III) (Fe^{3+})
  - anions: chloride (Cl^-), bromide (Br^-), iodide (I^-), hydroxide (OH^-), acetate (CH_3COO^-), carbonate (CO_3^{2-}), sulfate (SO_4^{2-}), phosphate (PO_4^{3-})
- conduct investigations and/or process data involving:
  - gravimetric analysis
  - precipitation titrations
- conduct investigations and/or process data to determine the concentration of coloured species and/or metal ions in aqueous solution, including but not limited to, the use of:
  - colourimetry
  - ultraviolet visible spectrophotometry
  - atomic absorption spectroscopy

Chemistry Stage 6 Syllabus © NSW Education Standards Authority for and on behalf of the Crown in right of the State of NSW, 2017.

15.1 The source of salts in the environment

CHEMISTRY INQUIRY CCT

Is it easy to tell one white solid from another?

COLLECT THIS ...

- sugar
- table salt
- plain flour
- sodium hydrogen carbonate (bicarbonate of soda)
- white vinegar
- clear plastic cups
- beaker
- hotplate
- plastic teaspoons

DO THIS ...

1 Half-fill 4 plastic cups with water. Add half a teaspoon of each solid (flour, sugar, salt, bicarbonate of soda) to a plastic cup and stir.

2 Place half a teaspoon of each solid on a large plate. Add a few drops of vinegar to each solid.

3 Place half a teaspoon of each solid at different points on the base of a large beaker. Heat gently until one of the solids shows a noticeable change.

RECORD THIS ...

Describe the result of each test on each of the four solids.

Summarise your results in a table.

Observation	Sugar	Salt	Flour	NaHCO$_3$
Soluble?				
Reaction with acid?				
Low melting point decomposition temperature?				

REFLECT ON THIS ...

1 Do all white solids have the same properties?

2 Are all solids soluble?

3 If each solid was ground to a fine powder, would you be able to test them to identify which solid is which?

4 If you had a chemistry laboratory at your disposal, what other tests could you have performed?

THE IMPORTANCE OF WATER

Water is found on Earth in three states (gas, liquid and solid) and it readily changes from one state into another. The **water cycle** involves the continuous movement of water between the land, oceans, streams and atmosphere (Figure 15.1.1). Solar energy is the primary source of energy for the cycle.

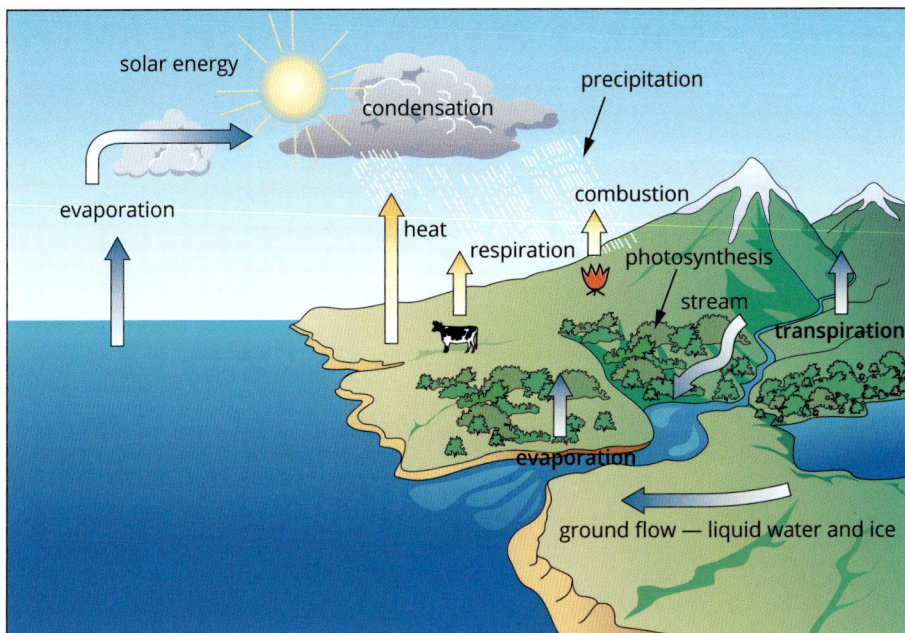

FIGURE 15.1.1 The water cycle illustrates how water is moved around the Earth through evaporation, condensation and precipitation.

The water cycle involves three main processes:
- Heat from the Sun causes water to evaporate from the oceans, lakes and streams.
- Water vapour is transported in the atmosphere until it condenses to form clouds.
- The water droplets combine to form rain, or occasionally ice crystals in hail or snow, and fall to the ground.

Human activities such as the combustion of fossil and biofuels, which produces steam, also contribute to the water cycle.

In Australia we expect clean drinking water to come out of the taps in our homes. To ensure that high-quality drinking water is available in towns and cities, protected water catchments and large infrastructure such as dams and pipelines are required. However, in some parts of inland Australia, and in some other countries in the Asia–Pacific region, water comes from sources other than protected catchments. In some cases water is taken directly from rivers and lakes that may be subject to contamination from run-off from farms and urban areas. Drinking water may also be obtained from **groundwater**, which is often referred to as **bore water** in Australia, or collected from roof run-off and stored in tanks. Water from these sources may need a more complex purification process than is needed for water from protected catchments.

SOURCES OF SALTS IN WATER

Figure 15.1.3 on page 410 shows a dry section of Lake Eyre, a very large inland salt lake in South Australia. On the rare occasions when the lake contains water, the salt concentration in the water is very high. When the lake dries up, the salts are deposited on the lake bed. The high concentration of salts in the water in Lake Eyre is an extreme example of **salinity**.

CHEMFILE S

Great Artesian Basin

The Great Artesian Basin is located within Australia (Figure 15.1.2). It has the following key features:

- It is the largest **artesian basin** in the world.
- It covers an area of over 1 700 000 square kilometres, which is nearly a quarter of the Australian continent.
- In some places the basin is up to 3000 m deep.
- The temperature of the water in the basin may be anywhere from 30°C to 100°C.
- It provides a reliable source of groundwater for a very large part of inland Australia.

Traditionally, the water could be readily accessed as it flowed to the surface under natural pressure. However, in the last century, government bodies have set up initiatives to try to limit access to stores of water within the basin.

FIGURE 15.1.2 The Great Artesian Basin provides water for livestock and the human population for a large area of inland Australia.

Sodium chloride (NaCl) is referred to as salt, but in the context of soil and water supplies the term 'salt' refers to any ionic compounds present. In this chapter you will examine ways in which these salts come to be in the water system. The sources of the salts found in water can be naturally occurring minerals and heavy metals, as well as human activities.

FIGURE 15.1.3 Lake Eyre is Australia's lowest natural point, at approximately 15 metres below sea level. Salt deposits on the dry bed are a result of the extreme salinity in this region.

Salts from minerals

Salts are naturally present in the water system. As part of the water cycle, water runs through soil and rocks, dissolving solid **mineral** deposits and transporting these salts into lakes, rivers, creeks and other bodies of water. Much of inland Australia was once submerged under the ocean, so the presence of salt in Lake Eyre should not be a surprise.

The region near Jenolan, west of the Blue Mountains, was also submerged under the ocean millions of years ago. During that time the remains of marine organisms containing calcium carbonate ($CaCO_3$) accumulated there. These layers of calcium carbonate deposits eventually formed limestone. The spectacular caves throughout the region are a result of underground rivers cutting through limestone rock. Figure 15.1.4 shows some of the formations that are the result of the dissolving and redepositing of limestone by rainwater over time as it passes through the caves.

There are many other regions in New South Wales with high mineral concentrations, including:

- Broken Hill: The area around Broken Hill has high concentrations of many different ores such as lead sulfide, zinc sulfide and silver oxide. Mining commenced in Broken Hill around 1884 and is still a large-scale industry in that region today.
- Orange: Newcrest Mining Limited operates commercial gold and copper mines near Orange, taking advantage of the high concentrations of both of these metals.
- Nyngan: The world's first scandium-only mining operation is at Nyngan, 500 km north-west of Sydney, tapping into deposits with a high concentration of scandia (scandium(III) oxide, Sc_2O_3) ore in that region.

FIGURE 15.1.4 The action of water dissolving and redepositing minerals has led to these limestone formations and caves.

Hard water

Hard water is a term used to describe water that requires a lot of soap to obtain a lather or froth. **Hardness** in water is caused by the presence of some metal ions, mainly calcium and magnesium. These metal ions are due mainly to the presence of dissolved minerals and interfere with the washing action of soaps and some detergents (Figure 15.1.5).

Hard water also causes deposits to form on the inside of kettles and water pipes. These deposits can lead to the eventual blocking of the pipes.

Salts from human activity

Human activities such as mining, agriculture, sewage treatment and domestic drainage can increase salt levels in water. In most cases the addition of these salts is considered a form of pollution. In many countries, governments monitor and regulate the levels of dissolved salts and other contaminants in waterways.

Climate uncertainty in Australia has led to the construction of several desalination plants for producing clean drinking water (Figure 15.1.6), but these plants also return concentrated salt solutions to the ocean.

FIGURE 15.1.5 Metal ions such as Ca^{2+} and Mg^{2+} in hard water react with ions in the soap to form a precipitate that reduces the lathering ability of soaps and detergents.

FIGURE 15.1.6 Desalination plants take in seawater and remove the salts and other impurities. The salts are then returned to the ocean in a concentrated form.

Mining

Mining industries can use large volumes of water to process the materials they are extracting. Some of this water, still containing various ions, may be discharged back into local waterways.

Agriculture

Most farms use fertilisers such as ammonium nitrate (NH_4NO_3), ammonium sulfate ((NH_4)$_2$$SO_4$) and superphosphate ($Ca(H_2PO_4)_2$) to improve the yield of crops. When it rains, some of this fertiliser dissolves and may be transported in run-off and contribute to the build-up of nutrients in streams and lakes.

Domestic sources

Until recently, most detergents contained softening agents made from phosphate compounds. As a result, the discharge from washing machines and sinks added metal cations and anions such as phosphate to the water system. Phosphate is a nutrient for plants and can cause to excessive algal growth in waterways, known as algal blooms (Figure 15.1.7). The growth of algal blooms caused by excess nutrients leads to a significant problem known as **eutrophication**.

Sewage treatment plants

All cities have treatment plants to process effluent (sewage) and grey water (other waste water). Although this water is treated to remove harmful contaminants, the water discharged from the treatment plants may contain a variety of ions similar to those from domestic sources.

> **ⓘ** There are many different ways in which human activity contributes to the salt content of waterways. This increase in salt content can have harmful effects on the environment.

FIGURE 15.1.7 Eutrophication caused by algal blooms can result from high concentrations of phosphate in the water.

Heavy metal salts

Definitions of **heavy metals** vary, but they are usually described as metals with a high density that have a toxic effect on living organisms. Cadmium, lead, chromium, copper and mercury all fit this description of heavy metals. Some metalloids, including arsenic, are also commonly included in lists of heavy metals because of their high toxicity.

Heavy metals occur naturally within the Earth's crust. Their salts can dissolve into groundwater and surface water, and so make their way into drinking water supplies. The concentrations of heavy metals from these natural sources are usually very low. However, heavy metals are often used in industry, and various human activities can result in elevated levels of heavy metals in the environment.

Heavy metal ions are released into the environment in two main ways:
- Directly through human activity. For example, heavy metal compounds can be released directly into waterways through waste from industries such as metal processing and mining. Other potential sources of contamination from heavy metals include leachate from landfill sites and agricultural run-off.
- Indirectly through combustion of fuels and wastes containing heavy metals, which can release the ions into the atmosphere where they can interact with water molecules. Rain can then take the dissolved salts into soils, rivers and groundwater.

CHEMISTRY IN ACTION EU

Lasting impact of heavy metals

The levels of heavy metals in waterways are closely monitored, because even amounts as small as 24.8 ppm (24.8 mg L^{-1}) can be deadly. The wide-ranging and long-term effects of heavy metal poisoning were shown clearly in Japan in the 1950s. A factory in the small fishing village of Minamata had been discharging wastes containing methyl mercury into the local bay. Because mercury compounds are not biodegradable, toxic mercury compounds built up in the aquatic organisms living in the bay. The main diet of the people of Minamata consisted of seafood caught in the contaminated bay.

The first indication of a problem was the erratic behaviour of the local cats, which were seen 'dancing' down the streets before collapsing and dying.

Neurological symptoms were also seen in the local population, with many residents suffering irreversible brain and organ damage. Many people died as a result of the high levels of mercury they unknowingly ingested. Originally referred to as 'Minamata disease', the neurological effects were eventually determined to be the direct result of mercury poisoning. The Minamata area residents still struggle with highly toxic levels of mercury to this day. The accumulated mercury levels in the people also led to the development of a number of congenital disorders in children born to parents suffering from Minamata disease. Figure 15.1.8 shows a young boy receiving physiotherapy to treat the effects of mercury poisoning.

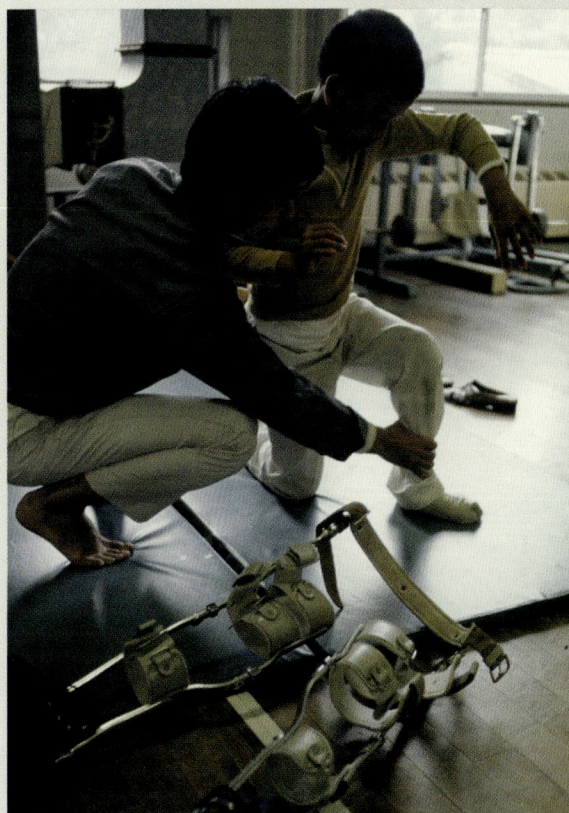

FIGURE 15.1.8 A young boy in Japan receives physiotherapy for the ravaging effects of mercury poisoning.

15.1 Review

SUMMARY

- It is important to maintain high-quality water systems for domestic and commercial purposes.
- Water supplies contain salts, either from natural sources or as the result of human activities. Natural salts are present in all areas of Australia, but they are particularly high where there are concentrated mineral deposits or where limestone is the predominant rock type.
- Pollution resulting from human activity is a source of salts in our water supplies. Activities include run-off from farms and cities, and the release of chemicals from industries and mines.

- Heavy metals are metals with a high density, such as lead and mercury, which have a toxic effect on living things. Heavy metals are present in nature, but processes in some industries add to the levels of these metals in water supplies.
- In some regions of Australia the high mineral level in water leads to the water being described as 'hard'. This means it contains high levels of metal ions such as Ca^{2+} and Mg^{2+}. Soaps do not function effectively in hard water, and precipitates formed by reactions between metal ions and soap ions can cause pipes to become blocked.

KEY QUESTIONS

1 The main mineral present in high concentrations in regions where underground caves are found is
   A $CaCO_3$
   B $NaCl$
   C Na_2CO_3
   D $HgCl_2$

2 Define the term 'heavy metal' and give one example.

3 List the ways in which toxic heavy metals can make their way into waterways.

4 a List one example of a salt used in agriculture.
   b Explain how agricultural activity can lead to an increase in salts in streams and lakes.

5 a Explain how hard water differs from normal water.
   b List two examples of ions found in hard water.
   c Why is hard water a problem?

15.2 Qualitative techniques for detecting salts

In the previous section you learnt about different ways salts enter the water system. There are many situations where it is important to know what salts are present and in what concentration. Typical examples include:

- domestic water supplies—These are sampled regularly for traces of heavy metals or for levels of other metals.
- water used on irrigated farms—If the salt level of a water supply is too high, the salts in the water can kill the crops the farmer is trying to grow.
- food processors—Care needs to be taken to ensure water supplies are not introducing contaminants into processed foods.
- pathology testing—Medical laboratories require very pure water to prevent interference from salts and other impurities.

A knowledge of the properties or characteristic reactions of metals or salts can often be used in analysis. Figure 15.2.1a shows a range of salt solutions. The characteristic colours of solutions can be used to identify the salts present. Figure 15.2.1b shows a bright yellow **precipitate** forming when two clear liquids are mixed. A chemist can determine the presence of either iodide or lead ions from this observation. In this section you will look at some of the methods used to identify the salts present in a sample. This procedure, known as **qualitative** analysis, is used to identify salts but not their concentrations.

GO TO ➤ | SkillBuilder page 118

> ℹ Qualitative analysis is the identification of a substance or the components of a mixture.

FIGURE 15.2.1 (a) Many salt solutions have unique colours. (b) The formation of a precipitate and its colour can help identify which salts are present.

Flame tests

Everyone is familiar with the colourful effects that are created in fireworks displays. Small quantities of different metal compounds are incorporated into the firework powders to produce different colours when they burn. For example, strontium compounds produce an eye-catching scarlet, and sodium compounds produce yellow (Figure 15.2.2). If you have spilt table salt into the flame of a gas stove, you might have noticed this same yellow colour in the flame.

FIGURE 15.2.2 Metal compounds incorporated into fireworks are responsible for the colours in this display.

Chemists use the fact that some metals produce particular colours when they are heated as a convenient and simple method of analysis. The metallic elements present in a compound can often be determined simply by inserting a sample of the compound into a non-luminous Bunsen burner flame, as shown in Figure 15.2.3a.

Each metal ion produces a characteristic colour. This means that the metal in an unknown sample can be identified by comparing the flame colour with the known characteristic colours produced by metals. Some examples of the flame colours produced by metals are shown in Figure 15.2.3b.

It is important to note that only a small number of metals produce characteristic colours in a flame test. And although the exact colour produced by each metal is unique, simple flame tests can result in a level of uncertainty when trying to decide between different shades of similar colours such as scarlet (strontium), crimson (lithium) and red (calcium).

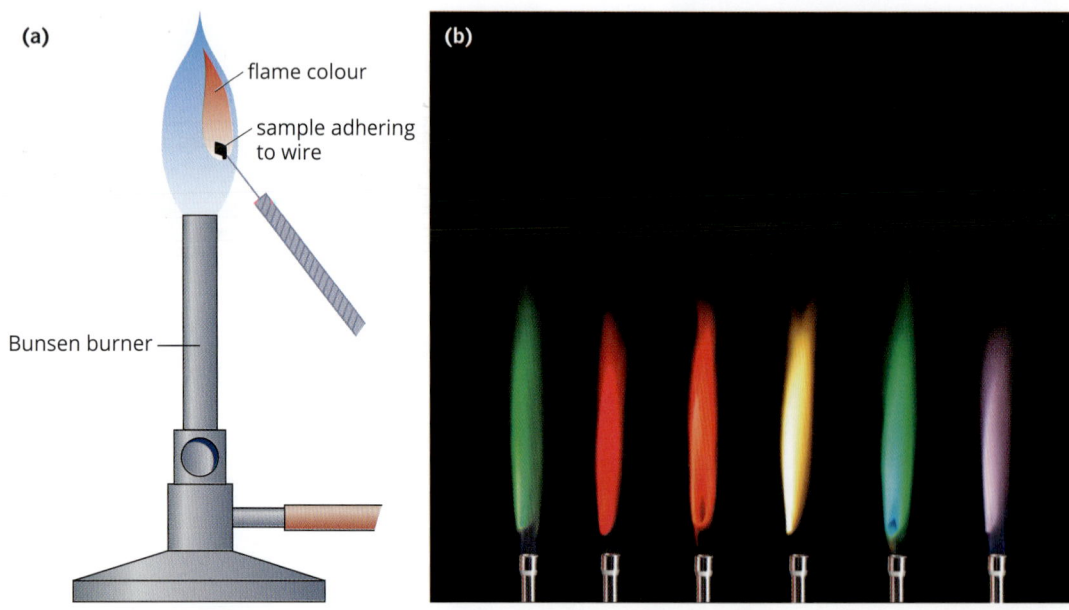

(a)
flame colour
sample adhering to wire
Bunsen burner

(b)

FIGURE 15.2.3 (a) Performing a flame test. A moist wire has been dipped in the sample and then placed in the flame. A fine spray of solution from a spray bottle could be used instead. (b) The colour of the flame is determined by the different metal compounds present and can be used to identify these metals. You can use Table 15.2.1 to identify the metal ions in these samples.

PRECIPITATION

You saw in Chapter 5 that a precipitate sometimes forms when two solutions are mixed. Solubility tables or the SNAAP guide can then be used to predict what that precipitate might be. In this chapter you will use your knowledge of **precipitation reactions** to help identify the ions present in a solution. Two examples of how this process can work are shown below.

GO TO ➤ Section 5.1 page 114

- Example 1. Testing to see if a water filter removes sodium chloride (NaCl) effectively. Most chloride salts are soluble, but silver chloride (AgCl) is not. If a few drops of silver nitrate ($AgNO_3$) solution are added to a sample of filtered water, a white precipitate would indicate that the filter did not remove all the chloride ions (Figure 15.2.4). The balanced chemical equation for the reaction occurring is:

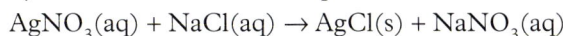

$$AgNO_3(aq) + NaCl(aq) \rightarrow AgCl(s) + NaNO_3(aq)$$

- Example 2. Detecting the presence of the heavy metal cobalt (Co) in water. Co^{2+} ions will form a precipitate with SO_4^{2-} ions. The precipitate has a characteristic royal blue colour. If Na_2SO_4 is added to the water sample and a precipitate forms, Co^{2+} ions might be present. The colour of the precipitate could confirm that it is in fact Co^{2+} ions causing the precipitate (Figure 15.2.5).

The two examples above demonstrate that a knowledge of solubility or precipitate colours can be used for qualitative analysis of the ions present. The colours of some common precipitates are listed in Table 15.2.2. The colours of precipitates are not predictable, but generally:

- main group metals form white precipitates
- transition metals are more likely to form coloured solutions and precipitates
- the colour of the precipitate will vary with the oxidation state of the ion.

Figure 15.2.6 shows the distinctive colours formed from the addition of NaOH to a series of transition metals.

TABLE 15.2.1 Characteristic flame colours of some metal ions

Metal	Flame colour
sodium	yellow
strontium	scarlet
copper	green
barium	yellow–green
lithium	crimson
calcium	red
potassium	lilac

FIGURE 15.2.4 If a cloudy, white precipitate forms when $AgNO_3$ is added to water, Cl^- ions might be present in the water.

TABLE 15.2.2 Colours of common precipitates

Cation	Solution colour	Anion SO_4^{2-}	Anion OH^-	Anion CO_3^{2-}
Ca^{2+}	colourless	white	white	white
Ag^+	colourless	white	brown	yellow
Fe^{2+}	pale green	no precipitate	green	green
Fe^{3+}	orange brown	no precipitate	brown	brown
Cu^{2+}	blue	no precipitate	blue	green

FIGURE 15.2.6 The precipitates formed from the addition of NaOH to solutions containing Fe^{2+}, Fe^{3+}, Cu^{2+} and Ni^{2+} respectively.

FIGURE 15.2.5 A royal blue precipitate will form when SO_4^{2-} ions are added to a solution containing Co^{2+} ions.

Detecting metals using precipitation

Worked example 15.2.1 shows how a knowledge of precipitates can be used to confirm the presence of a particular metal ion.

Worked example 15.2.1

IDENTIFYING THE PRESENCE OF A PARTICULAR METAL ION USING A PRECIPITATION REACTION

How can a precipitation reaction be used to confirm the presence of Cu^{2+} ions in a pale blue solution?

Thinking	Working
Use solubility tables to select a compound containing Cu^{2+} ions that is insoluble.	$Cu(OH)_2$ will be insoluble.
Use the solubility tables to select a soluble substance that contains the necessary anion to form the insoluble copper compound.	NaOH can be used to provide the OH^- ions.
Write an ionic equation for the reaction occurring.	$Cu^{2+}(aq) + 2OH^-(aq) \rightarrow Cu(OH)_2(s)$
What do you know about the appearance of the precipitate?	$Cu(OH)_2$ is blue. The formation of a blue solid indicates Cu^{2+} ions were present.

Worked example: Try yourself 15.2.1

IDENTIFYING THE PRESENCE OF A PARTICULAR METAL ION USING A PRECIPITATION REACTION.

How can a precipitation reaction be used to confirm the presence of Ca^{2+} ions in a colourless solution?

Worked example 15.2.1 uses a precipitation reaction to confirm the presence of copper(II) ions in a solution. If the solution was actually $CuSO_4$ it would also be possible to use another precipitation reaction to confirm that SO_4^{2-} ions were the anions present. The addition of $Ba(NO_3)_2$ solution will lead to the formation of a white precipitate of $BaSO_4$, indicating that SO_4^{2-} ions were present.

Identifying cations

Precipitation reactions are used in the examples above to confirm the presence of a specific ion. A more sequential approach is required if you do not know which metal ion might be present. The flowchart shown in Figure 15.2.7 can be used for the identification of an unknown cation. This process is usually successful if there is only one type of cation present.

The cation flowchart is based upon the testing of each solution with hydrochloric acid (HCl), then with ammonia solution (NH_3). If the addition of HCl leads to a precipitate it is likely that Pb^{2+} or Ag^+ ions are present. These ions produce precipitates of different colours when ammonia is added to them. If the original HCl added did not form a precipitate, the addition of ammonia is still helpful for distinguishing between other possible metal ions. The chemistry of the reactions that lead to the precipitates and colour changes is covered later in this section.

Unknown cation
$NH_4^+, Ag^+, Ba^{2+}, Ca^{2+}, Pb^{2+}, Cu^{2+}, Al^{3+}, Fe^{2+}, Fe^{3+}$

Test 1:
add dilute HCl

forms white precipitate   no precipitate

Ag^+, Pb^{2+}

$NH_4^+, Ba^{2+}, Ca^{2+}, Cu^{2+}, Al^{3+}, Fe^{2+}, Fe^{3+}$

Test 2:
add dilute NH_3
to a second sample

Test 2:
add dilute NH_3
to a second sample

no precipitate

forms brown precipitate that dissolves on addition of excess NH_3

forms white precipitate

forms white precipitate that dissolves on addition of excess NH_3

forms pale green precipitate

forms brown precipitate

forms blue precipitate that dissolves on addition of excess NH_3 to form a deep blue solution

NH_4^+, Ba^{2+}, Ca^{2+}

Test 3:
flame test on a third sample

Ag^+ Pb^{2+} Al^{3+} Fe^{2+} Fe^{3+} Cu^{2+}

no colour   red flame   yellow-green flame

NH_4^+ Ca^{2+} Ba^{2+}

Test 4:
add dilute NaOH to a fourth sample

smell of ammonia

NH_4^+

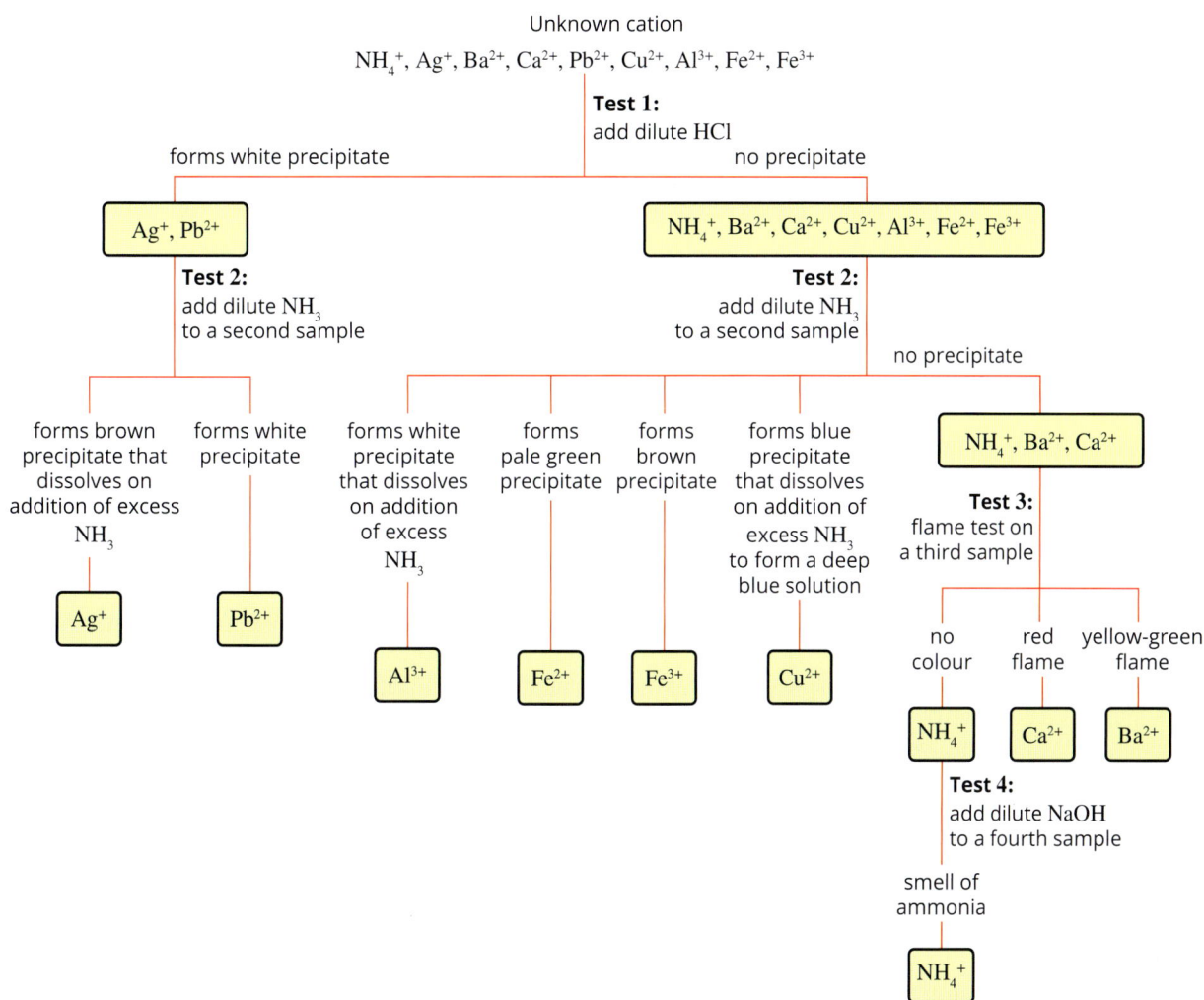

FIGURE 15.2.7 Flowchart for identifying unknown cations in a solution

If a solution of $CuSO_4$ is tested, the addition of HCl will not produce a precipitate but the addition of excess ammonia will eventually lead to the formation of the deep blue solution shown in Figure 15.2.8.

Worked example 15.2.2

IDENTIFYING THE PRESENCE OF AN UNKNOWN METAL ION

HCl added to a solution causes no change but the addition of NH_3 leads to a brown precipitate. Identify the metal ion present.

Thinking	Working
What does the response to HCl tell you about the metal ion present?	The ion is not Pb^{2+} or Ag^+.
What does the response to NH_3 tell you about the metal ion?	The colour matches that of a precipitate produced when NH_3 is added to Fe^{3+}.
Identify the metal ion present.	Fe^{3+}

Worked example: Try yourself 15.2.2

IDENTIFYING THE PRESENCE OF AN UNKNOWN METAL ION.

HCl added to a solution causes no change, nor does the addition of NH_3. A flame test produces a red flame. Identify the metal ion present.

FIGURE 15.2.8 When ammonia is added to the blue $CuSO_4$ solution on the right, a deep blue solution is formed.

Identifying anions

Systematic precipitation can be equally effective at identifying the anions present in a solution. Figure 15.2.9 provides a flowchart for this process. This time each solution is tested firstly with silver nitrate solution $(AgNO_3)$, then, depending upon the response to $AgNO_3$, with either nitric acid (HNO_3) or barium chloride solution $(BaCl_2)$. The flowchart may appear daunting at first but actually requires only two tests for each sample.

Note that in Test 1 only a very small amount of $AgNO_3$ solution should be added to the unknown solution. $AgSO_4$ is sparingly soluble. If the unknown solution contains SO_4^{2-}, the addition of too much $AgNO_3$ solution will result in the formation of a white $AgSO_4$ precipitate.

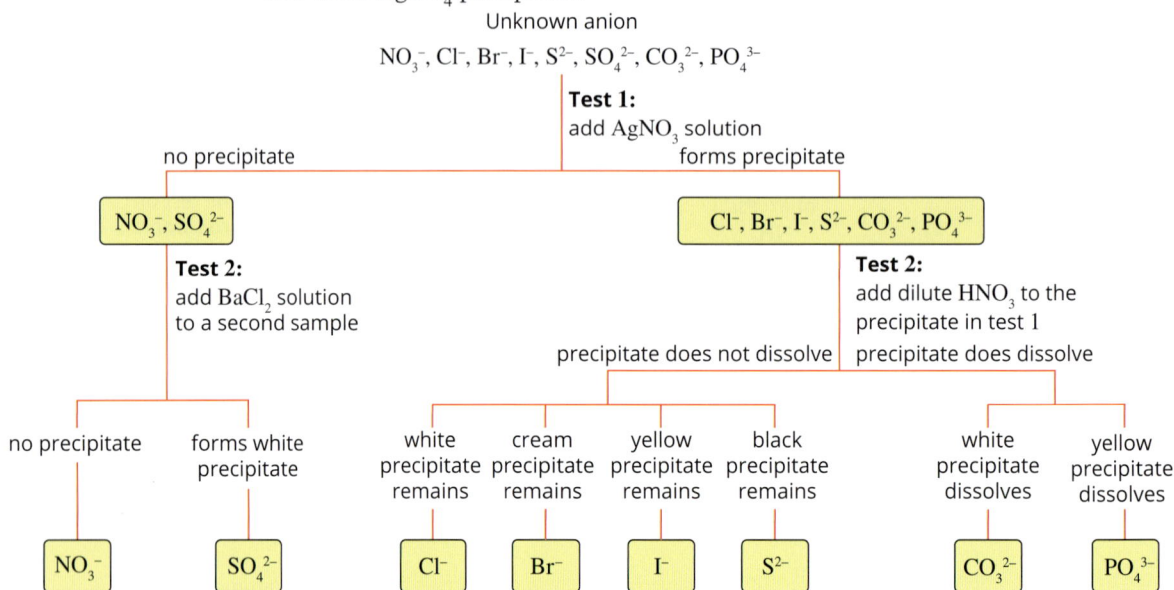

FIGURE 15.2.9 Flowchart for identifying unknown anions in a solution

The following two examples demonstrate the use of this flowchart.

- Example 1: $AgNO_3$ is added to a solution and no reaction occurs. $BaCl_2$ is added to a second sample of the solution and no precipitate forms.
  The lack of reaction with $AgNO_3$ indicates that the anion is either NO_3^- or SO_4^{2-}. The lack of reaction with $BaCl_2$ identifies the anion as (NO_3^-).
- Example 2: $AgNO_3$ is added to a solution and a white precipitate forms. When HNO_3 is added to the precipitate from the first test, a black precipitate forms.
  The reaction with $AgNO_3$ eliminates NO_3^- and SO_4^{2-}. The black precipitate formed when HNO_3 is added identifies the ions as sulfide ions (S^{2-}).

COMPLEXATION

Many of the coloured precipitates referred to so far in this chapter are examples of **metal complexes**. Transition metal ions are characteristically small and highly charged. The high charge density results in an ability to strongly attract anions or small polar molecules, forming a **complex ion**. The anions or small polar molecules are called **ligands.** The process of ligands forming an ion or compound around a metal ion is referred to as **complexation**.

Figure 15.2.10 illustrates the metal complex formed between cobalt(II) ions and ammonia molecules. Six ammonia molecules act as ligands and orient themselves around the positively charged cobalt(II) ion. Each ammonia molecule is orientated so that a bond is formed between the lone pair of electrons on the nitrogen atom and the positively charged cobalt(II) ion.

The cobalt and ammonia complex is represented as $[Co(NH_3)_6]^{2+}$, where square brackets indicate a metal complex. In this case the complex has a charge of +2 because ammonia molecules have no net charge. The net charge of the complex is shown outside the square brackets. The complexation reaction can be shown as

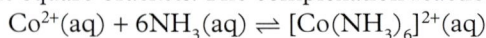

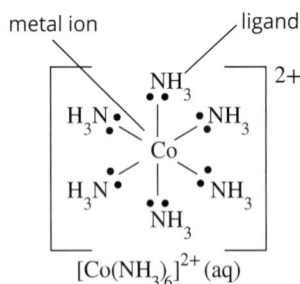

$$Co^{2+}(aq) + 6NH_3(aq) \rightleftharpoons [Co(NH_3)_6]^{2+}(aq)$$

FIGURE 15.2.10 The ammonia molecules bond with the Co^{2+} ions forming a metal complex.

The expression Co^{2+}(aq) assumes the presence of water acting as a ligand. The above reaction can be shown as:

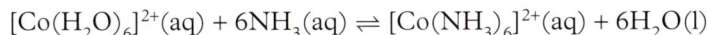

$$[Co(H_2O)_6]^{2+}(aq) + 6NH_3(aq) \rightleftharpoons [Co(NH_3)_6]^{2+}(aq) + 6H_2O(l)$$

Figure 15.2.11 shows other examples of metal complexes. The number of ligands that can fit around a metal ion depends upon factors such as ion size, charge and ligand shape.

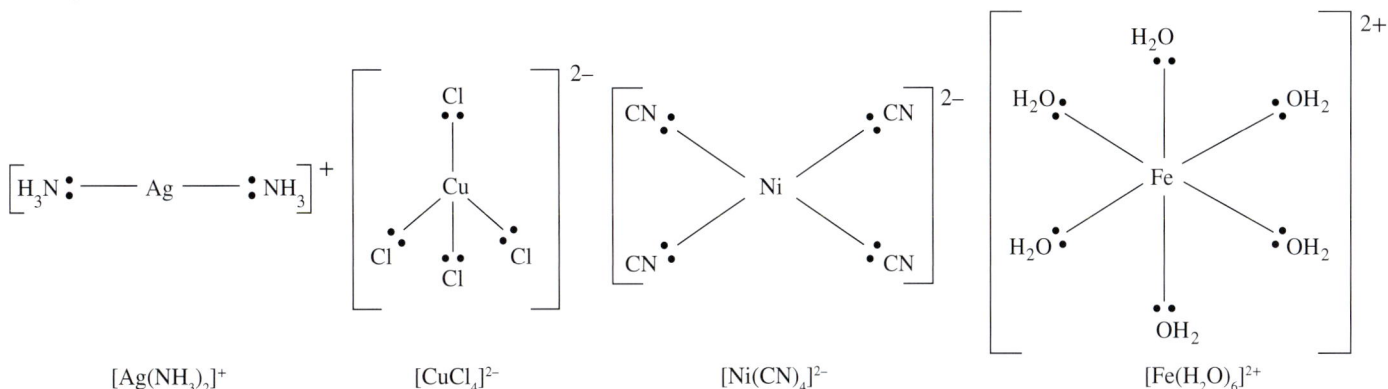

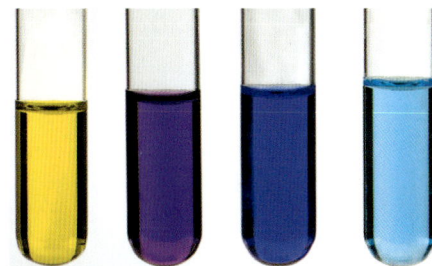

FIGURE 15.2.11 Four examples of metal complexes.

The transition metal ions shown in Figure 15.2.11 are Ag^+, Cu^{2+}, Ni^{2+} and Fe^{2+}. The ligands are a mixture of polar molecules, NH_3 and H_2O, and anions, CN^- and Cl^-. Anions will cause the complex ion to have an overall charge that is different to that of the transition metal ion, but uncharged molecules will not. Note that the oxidation state of the transition metal ion is unchanged in the complex ion.

Metal complexation reactions

You are more familiar with metal complexes than you might think, since water is a ligand. If you stir a spatula of solid blue copper(II) sulfate into a small volume of water, the characteristic blue colour is due to the complex formed between Cu^{2+} ions and water molecules.

When transition metal ions dissolve in water, metal complexes form between the ions and water molecules. When other ligands are added to the solution, a ligand exchange reaction occurs. The equation for the formation of the $[CuCl_4]^{2-}$ complex ion is:

$$[Cu(H_2O)_6]^{2+}(aq) + 4Cl^-(aq) \rightleftharpoons [CuCl_4]^{2-}(aq) + 6H_2O(l)$$

Concentrated HCl solution is used as a source of Cl^- ions. Most ligand exchange reactions are reversible.

If NH_3 solution is used instead of HCl, the complex ion formed is $[Cu(NH_3)_4(H_2O)_2]^{2+}$. The equation this time is:

$$[Cu(H_2O)_6]^{2+}(aq) + 4NH_3(aq) \rightleftharpoons [Cu(NH_3)_4(H_2O)_2]^{2+}(aq) + 4H_2O(l)$$

Each complex has its own characteristic colour, as shown in Figure 15.2.12, and it is this characteristic colour that can be used to identify the metal present.

Detecting metals using complexation

Knowing that different complex ions have characteristic colours should allow you to determine the transition metal ion and ligands that are present. Table 15.2.3 provides a more detailed key to metal ions and the colours of their complexes.

Various deductions can be made from Table 15.2.3. For example:
- A purple solution might contain Cr^{3+} ions.
- To test if a solution contains Cr^{3+} ions, add some ammonia solution and look for a purple precipitate.
- To test if a yellowish solution contains Fe^{3+} ions, add some NaOH and look for a brown precipitate.
- Several transition metals produce blue solutions but it is often possible to distinguish between the shades of blue produced.
- Aluminium forms white precipitates because it is not a transition metal.

FIGURE 15.2.12 The solutions shown contain copper complex ions. The ligands are, from left to right, Cl^- ions, ethane-1,2-diamine molecules, NH_3 molecules and H_2O molecules.

WS 8.2

TABLE 15.2.3 Colours of common metal ion complexes

	Fe^{2+}	Fe^{3+}	Co^{2+}	Cu^{2+}	Ni^{2+}	Al^{3+}	Cr^{3+}
Hydrated ion	$[Fe(H_2O)_6]^{2+}$ pale green solution	$[Fe(H_2O)_6]^{3+}$ yellow/brown solution	$[Co(H_2O)_6]^{2+}$ pink solution	$[Cu(H_2O)_6]^{2+}$ blue solution	$[Ni(H_2O)_6]^{2+}$ green solution	$[Al(H_2O)_6]^{3+}$ colourless solution	$[Cr(H_2O)_6]^{3+}$ green solution
OH⁻, dilute	$[Fe(H_2O)_4(OH)_2]$ dark green precipitate	$[Fe(H_2O)_3(OH)_3]$ brown precipitate	$[Co(H_2O)_4(OH)_2]$ blue/green precipitate	$[Cu(H_2O)_4(OH)_2]$ blue precipitate	$[Ni(H_2O)_4(OH)_2]$ green precipitate	$[Al(H_2O)_3(OH)_3]$ white precipitate	$[Cr(H_2O)_3(OH)_3]$ green precipitate
OH⁻, concentrated	$[Fe(H_2O)_4(OH)_2]$ dark green precipitate	$[Fe(H_2O)_3(OH)_3]$ brown precipitate	$[Co(H_2O)_4(OH)_2]$ blue/green precipitate	$[Cu(H_2O)_4(OH)_2]$ blue precipitate	$[Ni(H_2O)_4(OH)_2]$ green precipitate	$[Al(OH)_4]^-$ colourless solution	$[Cr(OH)_6]^{3-}$ green solution
NH₃, dilute	$[Fe(H_2O)_4(OH)_2]$ dark green precipitate	$[Fe(H_2O)_3(OH)_3]$ brown precipitate	$[Co(H_2O)_4(OH)_2]$ blue/green precipitate	$[Cu(H_2O)_4(OH)_2]$ blue precipitate	$[Ni(H_2O)_4(OH)_2]$ green precipitate	$[Al(H_2O)_3(OH)_3]$ white precipitate	$[Cr(H_2O)_3(OH)_3]$ green precipitate
NH₃, concentrated	$[Fe(H_2O)_4(OH)_2]$ dark green precipitate	$[Fe(H_2O)_3(OH)_3]$ brown precipitate	$[Co(NH_3)_6]^{2+}$ straw ccloured solution	$[Cu(NH_3)_4(H_2O)_2]^{2+}$ deep blue solution	$[Ni(NH_3)_6]^{2+}$ blue solution	$[Al(H_2O)_3(OH)_3]$ white precipitate	$[Cr(NH_3)_6]^{3+}$ purple solution
CO₃²⁻	$FeCO_3$ dark green precipitate	$[Fe(H_2O)_3(OH)_3]$ brown precipitate + bubbles	$CoCO_3$ pink precipitate	$CuCO_3$ blue/green precipitate	$NiCO_3$ green precipitate	$[Al(H_2O)_3(OH)_3]$ white precipitate + bubbles	$[Cr(H_2O)_3(OH)_3]$ green precipitate + bubbles

15.2 Review

SUMMARY

- Several qualitative tests can be conducted to identify metal ions in solution.
- Flame tests are performed by inserting a sample into a non-luminous Bunsen burner flame.
- Flame tests can be used to detect the presence of a small number of metallic elements in a compound.
- The accuracy of flame tests is hampered by the difficulty of detecting small differences in colours.
- The identity of a metal ion can be confirmed with precipitation reactions.
- Solubility tables are required to determine the relative solubility of salts.
- A flowchart can be used to systematically test a solution to identify the metal ion present.
- The high charge density of transition metal ions allows them to form metal complexes with anions or small polar molecules.
- The characteristic colours of metal complexes can be used to identify the metal ions in a salt.

KEY QUESTIONS

1 Which of the following is an example of qualitative analysis?
   A Finding the amount of salt in peanut butter.
   B Detecting the presence of arsenic in a water supply.
   C Measuring the fat content in milk.
   D Finding the NaOH concentration in oven cleaner.

2 Use Table 15.2.1 on page 417 to list the colour of the flame you would expect when each salt is inserted into a non-luminous Bunsen burner flame.

Compound	Flame colour
strontium chloride	
strontium carbonate	
copper chloride	
potassium sulfate	
sodium nitrate	

3 a Explain how the following data from a flame test can be used to prove that it is the metal ion that is responsible for the flame colour a salt produces: barium sulfate (green), potassium sulfate (lilac), barium chloride (green)
   b List three factors that limit the widespread use of flame tests for identifying metals in compounds.

4 Some brands of salt contain low percentages of sodium iodide (NaI). If a few drops of $Pb(NO_3)_2$ are added to a salt solution, a yellow precipitate will form if iodide ions are present.
   a What is the chemical formula of the precipitate formed?
   b Write an ionic equation for the reaction occurring when the precipitate is formed.

5 To test for the presence of Cu^{2+} ions in water, NaOH can be added to a sample.
   a What is the chemical formula of the precipitate formed?
   b How can a knowledge of precipitate colours help to confirm that the metal ions are in fact Cu^{2+}?
   c Write an ionic equation for the reaction occurring when the precipitate is formed.

6 HCl solution is added to a solution containing metal ions. A white precipitate forms. When ammonia is added to a different sample of the same solution, a brown precipitate forms. Refer to Figure 15.2.7 on page 419 to answer the following questions.
   a What can you learn from the reaction with HCl solution?
   b What can you learn from the reaction with ammonia?

7 Cobalt(II) ions (Co^{2+}) can form a complex ion with four chloride ions (Cl^-).
   What is the chemical formula and charge of this complex ion?

8 Use the complex ion shown to answer the following questions.

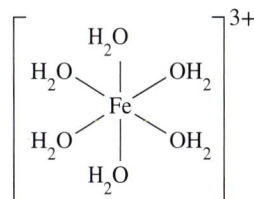

$$\left[\begin{array}{c} H_2O \\ H_2O \diagdown \diagup OH_2 \\ Fe \\ H_2O \diagup \diagdown OH_2 \\ H_2O \end{array} \right]^{3+}$$

   a What is the metal ion in this complex?
   b What is the ligand?
   c Explain why the ligand is orientated the way it is shown in the diagram.

15.3 Gravimetric analysis of a salt

i Gravimetric analysis can be used to determine the amount of a particular salt present in a solution.

As you saw in the previous section, you can use precipitation reactions to identify the ions present in solutions, but this test is only qualitative. However, if you then filter and dry the precipitate, you can extend the analysis to make it **quantitative**. The mass of precipitate can be used to determine the mass or concentration of the ions in solution. This is an example of **gravimetric analysis**.

The beaker in Figure 15.3.1 contains a colourless mercury(II) acetate solution. Because water is present, it is not obvious what mass of mercury is in the solution. The addition of sodium iodide leads to the precipitation of mercury(II) iodide. The mass of mercury can then be determined from the mass of the precipitate once it is dried.

The aim of forming a precipitate is to separate one of the ions of the salt being analysed from other ions present in solution.

For example, the concentration of barium ions in a solution containing both barium and sodium ions can be determined by adding sodium sulfate solution (Figure 15.3.2). The sodium ions remain in solution but a precipitate of barium sulfate is formed, which can be separated from the solution and dried. The mass of the precipitate can then be used to calculate the barium ion concentration in the initial solution.

FIGURE 15.3.1 When colourless aqueous solutions of mercury(II) acetate and sodium iodide are mixed, they produce a red precipitate, mercury(II) iodide. The mass of the precipitate from this reaction can be used to determine the amount of mercury present in the original sample.

Finding the concentration of Ba^{2+} ions in solution.

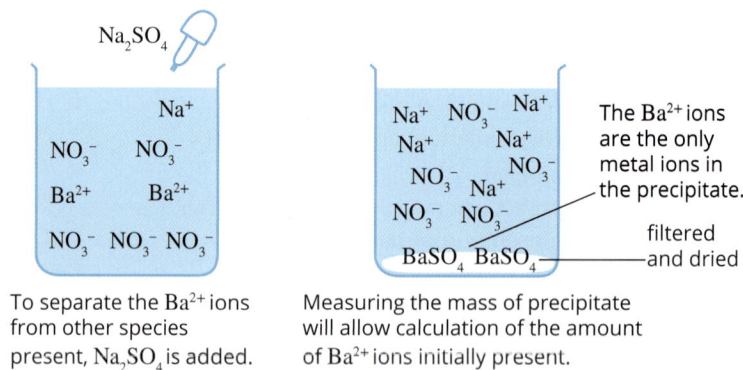

To separate the Ba^{2+} ions from other species present, Na_2SO_4 is added.

Measuring the mass of precipitate will allow calculation of the amount of Ba^{2+} ions initially present.

The Ba^{2+} ions are the only metal ions in the precipitate.

filtered and dried

FIGURE 15.3.2 The principle of gravimetric analysis. Ba^{2+} ions in a solution are separated from Na^+ ions and NO_3^- ions by precipitation. The precipitate is then collected and dried so that the initial mass of Ba^{2+} can be determined using stoichiometry.

MASS–MASS STOICHIOMETRY

Calculating the mass of a salt in solution from a precipitation reaction

GO TO ➤ Year 11 Chapter 6

Stoichiometry can be combined with your knowledge of precipitation reactions to find the amount of a salt in a solution.

There are several steps involved in calculating the mass of a salt in a water sample, based on the mass of a precipitate produced in a precipitation reaction.

1. Write a balanced equation for the reaction.
2. Calculate the number of moles of the precipitate from its mass, using the formula: $n = \frac{m}{M}$
3. Use the mole ratios in the equation to calculate the number of moles of the salt in solution.
4. Calculate the mass of the salt using $m = n \times M$.

Figure 15.3.3 shows a flowchart that summarises this process. Worked example 15.3.1 will help you to understand these steps.

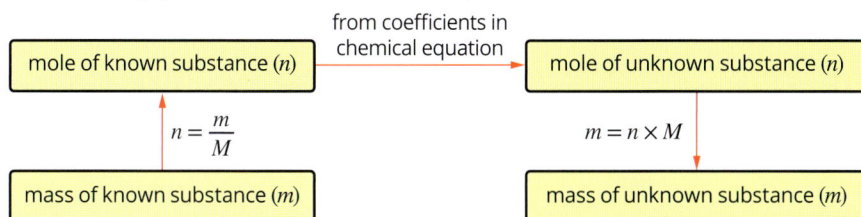

FIGURE 15.3.3 A flowchart for mass–mass stoichiometric calculations is helpful when trying to solve these problems.

Worked example 15.3.1

CALCULATING MASS–MASS STOICHIOMETRIC PROBLEMS

When solutions of potassium iodide and lead(II) nitrate are mixed, a precipitate of lead(II) iodide (molar mass 461.0 g) is formed. Calculate the mass of potassium iodide present in solution if a mass of 1.46 g of lead(II) iodide is precipitated.

Thinking	Working
Write a balanced equation for the reaction.	$2KI(aq) + Pb(NO_3)_2(aq) \rightarrow PbI_2(s) + 2KNO_3(aq)$
Calculate the number of moles of the known substance (the precipitate): $$n = \frac{mass\ (m)}{molar\ mass\ (M)}$$	$n(PbI_2) = \frac{1.46}{461.0}$ $= 0.00317\,mol$
Calculate the mole ratio: $$mole\ ratio = \frac{coefficient\ of\ unknown}{coefficient\ of\ known}$$	$mole\ ratio = \frac{coefficient\ of\ KI}{coefficient\ of\ PbI_2}$ $= \frac{2}{1}$ $= 2$
Calculate the number of moles of the unknown substance: $$n(unknown) = n(known) \times mole\ ratio$$	$n(KI) = 0.00317 \times 2$ $= 0.00633\,mol$
Calculate the mass of the unknown substance: $$m = n(unknown) \times molar\ mass$$	$m(KI) = 0.00633 \times 166.0$ $= 1.05\,g$

Worked example: Try yourself 15.3.1

CALCULATING MASS–MASS STOICHIOMETRIC PROBLEMS

A reaction between solutions of sodium sulfate and barium nitrate produces a precipitate of barium sulfate (molar mass 233.39 g) with a mass of 2.440 g. Calculate the mass of sodium sulfate required to produce this precipitate.

Gravimetric analysis can be used to determine the salt content of a number of samples, as long as a suitable precipitating agent can be found. Regardless of the salt being tested for, the steps in the process remain the same. Figure 15.3.4 shows the typical laboratory steps in a gravimetric analysis.

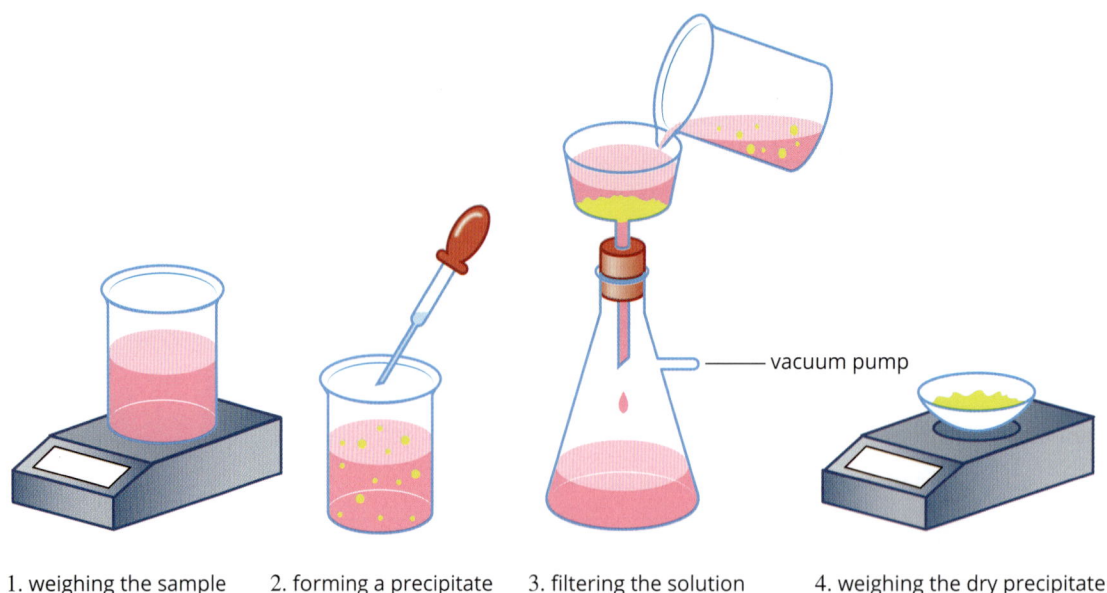

FIGURE 15.3.4 Laboratory procedure for gravimetric analysis.

1. weighing the sample   2. forming a precipitate   3. filtering the solution   4. weighing the dry precipitate

The steps in this process are listed below.

1. Prepare your sample solution (this includes dissolving a solid sample if required).
2. Add the precipitation solution in sufficient (excess) amounts to cause complete precipitation of the ion being analysed.
3. Collect the precipitate by filtration and wash it carefully to ensure that no soluble components are trapped in it.
4. Dry the precipitate carefully to ensure that the mass obtained is not higher than it should be. The precipitate is usually heated, cooled and weighed repeatedly until its mass is constant. This ensures that all water has been removed.

Note that the precipitate must be stable when heated. The number of moles of the precipitate cannot be calculated accurately if decomposition occurs and the precipitate is not a pure compound.

Uses of gravimetric analysis

Gravimetric analysis is one of the techniques used by chemists to analyse the amount or concentration of a substance. It is inexpensive and can be used for a range of common inorganic substances.

Because of its versatility and the relative ease with which it is conducted, gravimetric analysis has been used for analysis in a variety of industries. Gravimetric analysis can be used to determine the salt content of foods, the sulfur content of ores and the level of impurities in water. Since the introduction of modern instruments, gravimetric analysis has been largely replaced by faster, automated techniques. However, it is still used to check the accuracy of analytical instruments.

Gravimetric analysis is not appropriate for the analysis of all salts. For example, it is not suitable for salts such as sodium nitrate for which all compounds of both the anion and the cation are soluble.

ℹ️ In a gravimetric analysis, the filtrate obtained after filtering the precipitate is often tested with additional precipitating agent to ensure that all of the ions of interest have been precipitated from the sample.

ℹ️ Only salts that can form a stable precipitate are suitable for gravimetric analysis.

Figure 15.3.5 shows a simplified version of the steps in a gravimetric analysis to determine the amount of sulfur in a sample of iron sulfide (also called fool's gold). You should note that gravimetric analysis is not always a direct technique. The **analyte** being tested may be first subjected to a chemical reaction to convert it to a form suitable for precipitation. For example, this occurs in the analysis of iron sulfide in which the sulfide ions are converted to sulfate ions as part of the procedure.

FIGURE 15.3.5 Analysis of sulfur in iron sulfide ore by gravimetric analysis. (a) A sample of ore, (b) crushed, (c) dissolved in concentrated nitric acid to convert the sulfide ions to sulfate ions, (d) precipitated as barium sulfate.

Worked example 15.3.2

USING GRAVIMETRIC ANALYSIS

The silver chloride precipitate collected from a 7.802 g sample of peanut butter has a mass of 0.112 g. What is the percentage of sodium chloride (molar mass 143.32 g) in the peanut butter, assuming all chloride ions are present as sodium chloride?

Thinking	Working
Write a balanced equation for the precipitation reaction.	$NaCl(aq) + AgNO_3(aq) \rightarrow AgCl(s) + NaNO_3(aq)$
Calculate the number of moles of precipitate using: $$n = \frac{m}{M}$$	$n(AgCl) = \frac{m}{M}$ $= \frac{0.112}{143.32}$ $= 0.000781 \, mol$
Use the balanced equation to find the mole ratio of the known and unknown substances. The known substance is the one you know the mass of; the unknown substance is the one whose mass you are required to calculate.	$mole \ ratio = \frac{coefficient \ of \ NaCl}{coefficient \ of \ AgCl}$ $= \frac{1}{1}$
Calculate the number of moles of unknown substance.	$n(NaCl) = n(AgCl) = 0.000781 \, mol$
Calculate the mass of unknown substance in the sample.	$m(NaCl) = n \times M$ $= 0.000781 \times 58.44$ $= 0.0457 \, g$
Calculate the percentage mass of the unknown substance in the 7.802 g of sample.	$\%NaCl = \frac{0.0457}{7.802} \times 100$ $= 0.586\%$

Worked example: Try yourself 15.3.2

USING GRAVIMETRIC ANALYSIS

Water discharged from a mining plant contains silver ions present as silver nitrate ($AgNO_3$). Excess potassium chromate (K_2CrO_4) solution is added to a 50.0 g sample of the water to precipitate the silver as silver chromate (Ag_2CrO_4). The precipitate is heated to remove any water, producing 1.32 g of silver chromate.

Calculate the percentage mass of silver in the water sample. (The molar mass of Ag_2CrO_4 is 331.74 g mol^{-1}.)

PRECIPITATION TITRATIONS

Rather than filtering and drying a precipitate to weigh it, some precipitation reactions lend themselves to quantitative analysis through a titration. Two very different types of precipitation titration are possible.

Precipitation titration with colour change

When NaCl is added to a solution containing Ag^+, a precipitate forms. The ionic equation for this reaction is:

$$Ag^+(aq) + Cl^-(aq) \rightarrow AgCl(s)$$

This reaction can be analysed quantitatively as follows:

- A solution containing Ag^+ ions can be added to a burette (Figure 15.3.6).
- Aliquots of a solution of NaCl of known concentration are added to a conical flask.
- A few drops of yellow potassium chromate (K_2CrO_4) are added to the flask as an indicator. When all the Cl^- ions have precipitated (the equivalence point), the excess Ag^+ in solution will react with the chromate ions, forming a reddish brown precipitate of Ag_2CrO_4. The ionic equation for this reaction is:

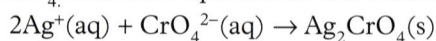

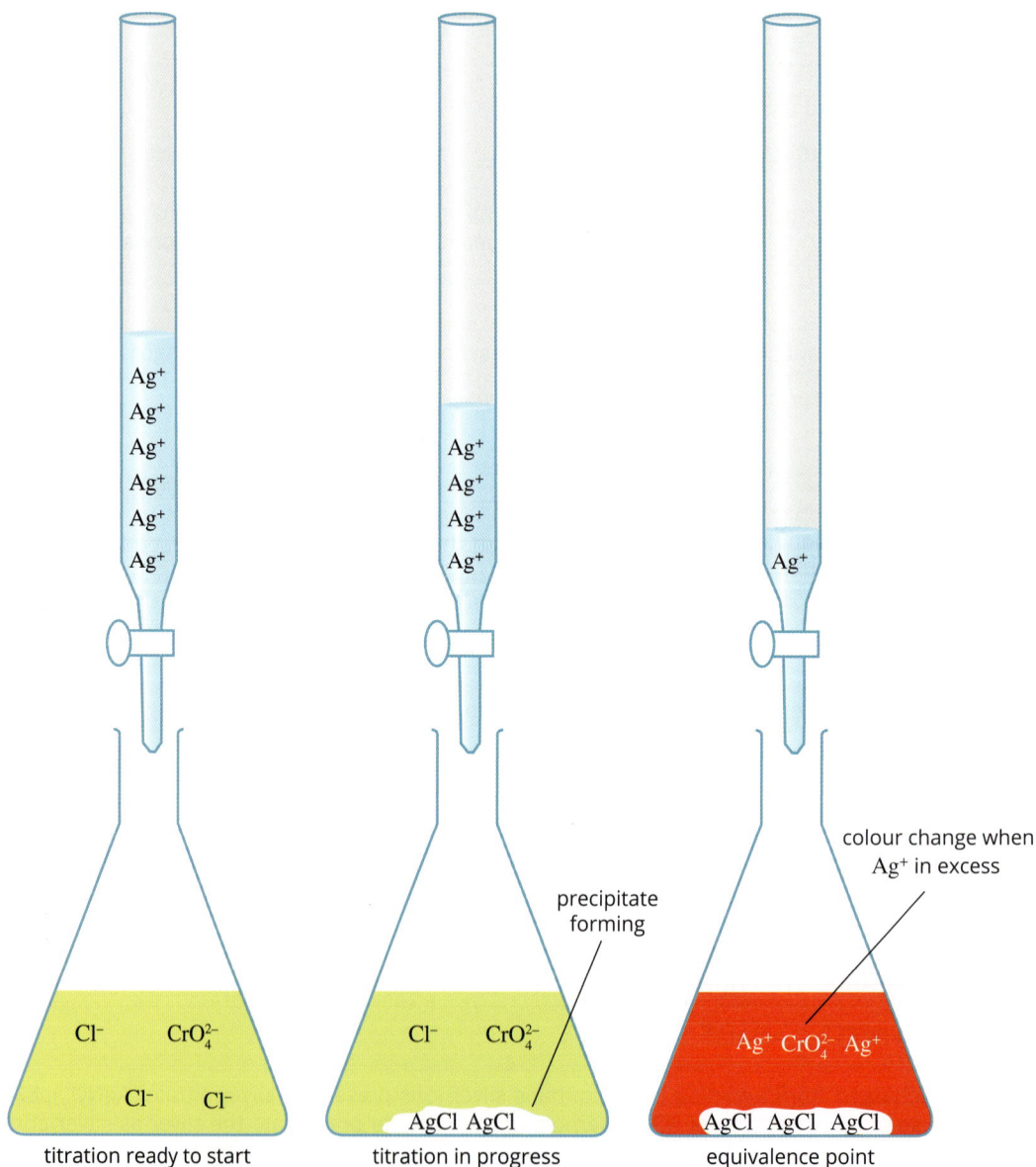

$$2Ag^+(aq) + CrO_4^{2-}(aq) \rightarrow Ag_2CrO_4(s)$$

FIGURE 15.3.6 As the titration proceeds, more precipitate is formed. Once the equivalence point is reached, Ag_2CrO_4 can now form, producing a reddish colour.

- A titration is conducted until a colour change to reddish brown is evident.
- The mean titre is used to calculate the concentration of the Ag^+ ions.

The aim of a titration is to find the **equivalence point**. The equivalence point is the point at which the two reactants are present in the mole ratio of the equation. It is the point where you can finally calculate the number of moles of the solution of unknown concentration. For the reaction above, the equation is:

$$Ag^+(aq) + Cl^-(aq) \rightarrow AgCl(s)$$

Therefore, at the equivalence point $n(Ag^+) = n(Cl^-)$.

Worked example 15.3.3

USING A PRECIPITATION TITRATION TO DETERMINE THE CONCENTRATION OF METAL IONS IN A SAMPLE

The concentration of Ag^+ ions in a solution was determined by a precipitation titration with 20.00 mL aliquots of a 0.100 mol L^{-1} solution of NaCl. K_2CrO_4 was used as an indicator for the titration.

The mean titre of Ag^+ solution was 31.20 mL. What was the molar concentration of silver ions?

Thinking	Working
Write an ionic equation for the precipitation reaction.	$Ag^+(aq) + Cl^-(aq) \rightarrow AgCl(s)$
Calculate the amount of NaCl, in mol, in the aliquot.	$n(NaCl) = c \times V$ $= 0.100 \times 0.02000$ $= 0.00200 \, mol$
Use the balanced equation to calculate the amount of Ag^+ ions, in mol, that reacted.	$n(Ag^+) = n(Cl^-) = n(NaCl)$ $= 0.00200 \, mol$
Determine the concentration of Ag^+ ions in the solution.	$c(Ag^+) = \frac{n}{V}$ $= \frac{0.00200}{0.03120}$ $= 0.0641 \, mol \, L^{-1}$

Worked example: Try yourself 15.3.3

USING A PRECIPITATION TITRATION TO DETERMINE THE CONCENTRATION OF METAL IONS IN A SAMPLE

The concentration of Zn^{2+} ions in a solution was determined by a precipitation titration with 15.00 mL aliquots of a 0.100 mol L^{-1} solution of NaOH. A few drops of ferric cyanide ($Fe(CN)_6^{3-}$) containing indicator were added to the NaOH.

The mean titre of Zn^{2+} solution required was 23.40 mL. What was the molar concentration of zinc ions?

PA 8.2   PA 8.2

PA 8.3   PA 8.3

Accurate results can be obtained using this process, but there are not a lot of metals with suitable colour changes, so it is not a common procedure.

Conductometric titrations

An alternative way of judging the equivalence point of a precipitation titration is to monitor the **electrical conductivity** of the solutions involved. Often the electrical conductivity is lowest when the concentration of excess ions is lowest (which is at the equivalence point). This type of titration is called a **conductometric titration**. (You were introduced to this type of titration in Chapter 8.)

GO TO ► Section 8.3 page 203

A conductometric titration can be used to determine the concentration of Ba^{2+} ions in a solution. The procedure is as follows:

- The solution containing Ba^{2+} is added to a burette.
- An aliquot of sodium sulfate solution of known concentration is added to a beaker below the burette.
- Two electrodes are placed in the beaker and connected to a power supply and conductivity meter (Figure 15.3.7).
- As the Ba^{2+} ions are added from the burette, a precipitate of $BaSO_4$ forms. The ionic equation for the reaction is:

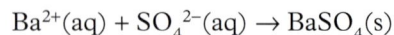

$$Ba^{2+}(aq) + SO_4^{2-}(aq) \rightarrow BaSO_4(s)$$

- The conductivity of the solution is measured after each addition from the burette.

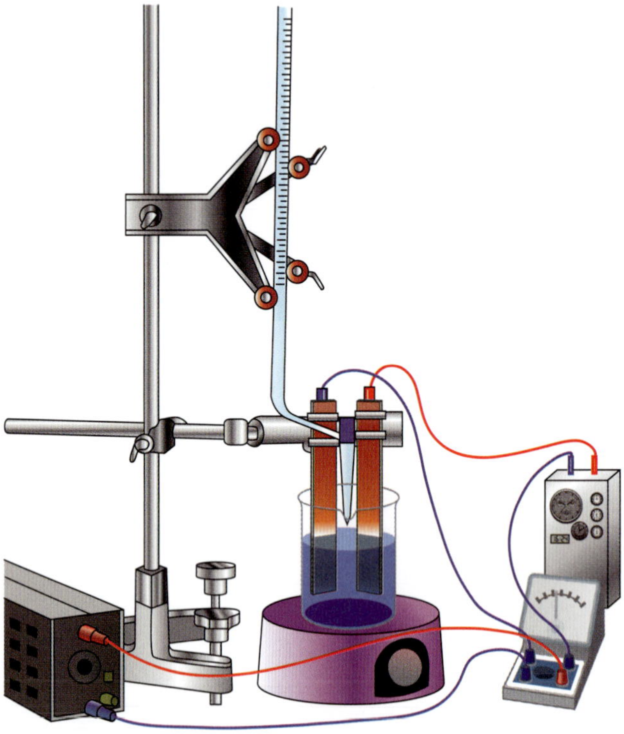

FIGURE 15.3.7 A conductometric titration requires a power supply, conductivity meter and electrodes in a circuit under the burette.

The change in conductivity that occurs during the titration depends upon the anions present in the Ba^{2+} solution. If the barium solution is barium acetate, the equation occurring is effectively

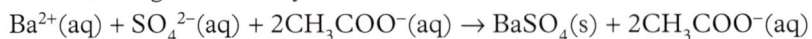

$$Ba^{2+}(aq) + SO_4^{2-}(aq) + 2CH_3COO^-(aq) \rightarrow BaSO_4(s) + 2CH_3COO^-(aq)$$

As Ba^{2+} ions are added to the beaker, SO_4^{2-} ions precipitate from the solution as $BaSO_4$. The total number of ions in solution is dropping so the conductivity also drops. The added ethanoate ions have little impact on conductivity. They are bulky ions that cannot easily flow through the solution so they do not add much to the conductivity. Therefore the conductivity of the solution drops as the equivalence point approaches (Figure 15.3.8).

$Ac^- = CH_3COO^-$

conductivity

conductivity lower

conductivity higher

Ac⁻Ac⁻
Ba²⁺
Ac⁻Ac⁻
Ba²⁺
Ac⁻Ac⁻
Ba²⁺
Ac⁻Ac⁻
Ba²⁺

Ac⁻Ac⁻
Ba²⁺
Ac⁻Ac⁻
Ba²⁺
Ac⁻Ac⁻
Ba²⁺

+ − + − + −

$Na^+ \longrightarrow$
$Na^+ \longrightarrow$
$Na^+ \longrightarrow$
$\longleftarrow SO_4^{2-}$
$\longleftarrow SO_4^{2-}\ Na^+ \longrightarrow$

Ac^-
$Na^+ \longrightarrow$
$Na^+ \longrightarrow$
Ac^-
$Na^+ \longrightarrow$
$\longleftarrow SO_4^{2-}$
$Na^+ \longrightarrow$
$BaSO_4$

$Ac^-\ \ Ac^-$
$Ac^-\ Na^+ \longrightarrow$
$Ac^-\ Ba^{2+} \longrightarrow$
$Na^+ \longrightarrow$
$Ac^-\ Ac^-\ Ac^-$
$Ac^-\ Na^+ \longrightarrow$
Ba^{2+}
$Na^+ \longrightarrow$
$BaSO_4\ \ BaSO_4$

titration ready to start   titration in progress   equivalence point

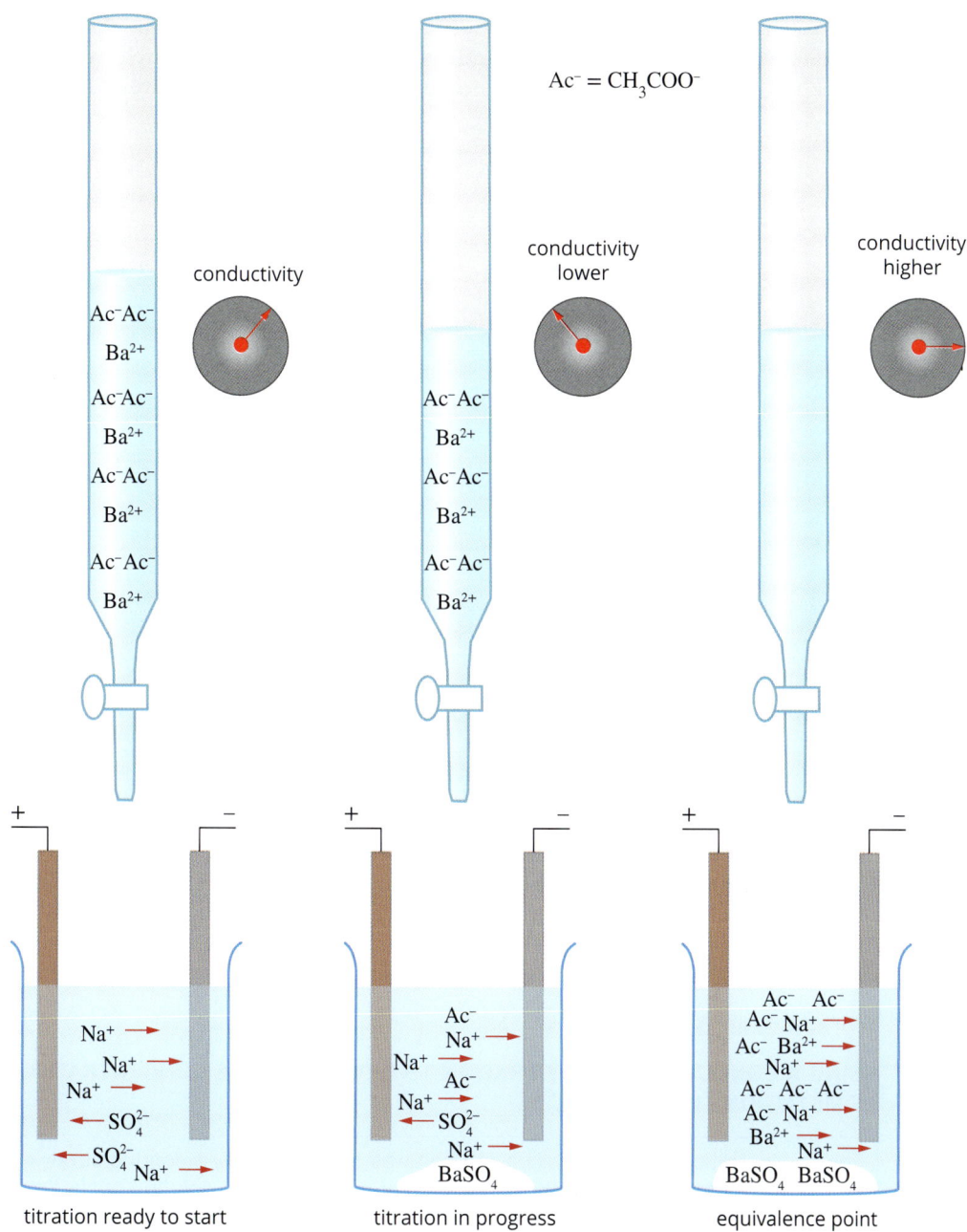

FIGURE 15.3.8 As the titration proceeds, the conductivity initially drops due to the precipitation of ions. After the equivalence point the conductivity rises as the concentrations of ions increases.

Once the equivalence point has been passed, each time extra Ba^{2+} ions are added the conductivity will increase. A graph of the titration will look like the one shown in Figure 15.3.9a on page 432. The unit for electrical conductivity is microsiemens per centimetre ($mS\,cm^{-1}$). The graph shows the equivalence point is occurring when the titre is 6.00 mL. This value can be used to determine the concentration of the Ba^{2+} ions.

If the barium solution was $BaCl_2$ instead of barium acetate, the equation for the reaction would be:

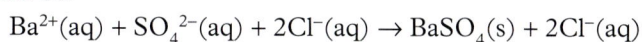

$$Ba^{2+}(aq) + SO_4^{2-}(aq) + 2Cl^-(aq) \rightarrow BaSO_4(s) + 2Cl^-(aq)$$

Unlike acetate ions, Cl^- ions increase the conductivity of the solution. As $BaSO_4$ precipitates, the Cl^- ions compensate and the conductivity in the beaker changes very little. The graph of conductivity versus volume added is shown in Figure 15.3.9b.

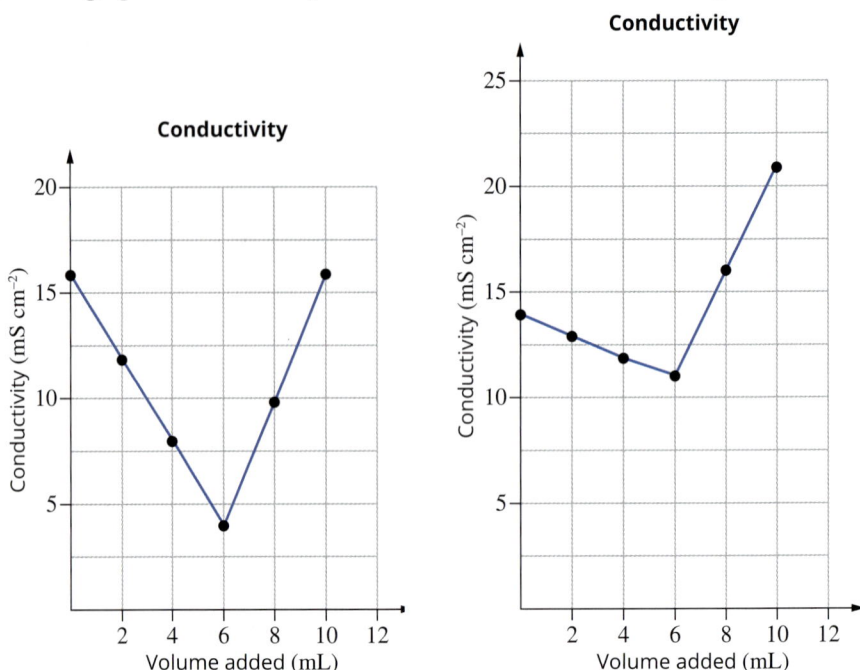

FIGURE 15.3.9 (a) Conductivity graph for a titration of a barium acetate solution. (b) Conductivity graph for a titration of a barium chloride solution.

An interesting aspect of a conductometric titration is that you do not have to work carefully around the equivalence point. In theory you need only two conductivity readings before the equivalence point to draw a straight line, and two points after the equivalence point. Titrations should be conducted at 25°C, because conductivity varies with temperature.

Worked example 15.3.4

USING A CONDUCTOMETRIC TITRATION TO DETERMINE THE CONCENTRATION OF METAL IONS IN A SAMPLE

The concentration of Pb^{2+} ions in a solution was determined by a conductometric precipitation titration with 20.00 mL aliquots of a $0.100 \, mol \, L^{-1}$ solution of NaCl.

The mean titre of Pb^{2+} solution required was 14.80 mL. What was the molar concentration of lead(II) ions?

Thinking	Working
Write an ionic equation for the precipitation reaction.	$Pb^{2+}(aq) + 2Cl^-(aq) \rightarrow PbCl_2(s)$
Calculate the amount of NaCl, in mol, in the aliquot.	$n(NaCl) = c \times V$ $= 0.100 \times 0.02000$ $= 0.00200 \, mol$
Use the balanced equation to calculate the amount of Pb^{2+} ions, in mol, that reacted.	$n(Pb^{2+}) = \frac{1}{2} \times n(Cl^-) = \frac{1}{2} \times n(NaCl)$ $= 0.5 \times 0.00200$ $= 0.00100 \, mol$
Determine the concentration of Pb^{2+} ions in the solution.	$c(Pb^{2+}) = \frac{n}{V}$ $= \frac{0.00100}{0.01480}$ $= 6.76 \times 10^{-2} \, mol \, L^{-1}$

Worked example: Try yourself 15.3.4

USING A CONDUCTOMETRIC TITRATION TO DETERMINE THE CONCENTRATION OF METAL IONS IN A SAMPLE

The concentration of Ag^+ ions in a solution was determined by a conductometric precipitation titration with 20.00 mL aliquots of a 0.0500 mol L^{-1} solution of NaCl.

The mean titre of Ag^+ solution required was 11.60 mL. What was the molar concentration of silver ions?

15.3 Review

SUMMARY

- A balanced equation shows the ratio of the amount, amounts, in mol, of reactants used and products formed in the reaction.
- Given the quantity of one of the reactants or products of a chemical reaction, such as in a precipitation reaction, the quantity of all other reactants and products can be predicted by working through the following steps:
  1. Write a balanced equation for the reaction.
  2. Calculate the amount, in mol, of the given substance.
  3. Use the mole ratios of reactants and products in the balanced equation to calculate the amount, in mol, of the required substance.
  4. Use the appropriate formula to determine the required quantities:

$$m = n \times M$$
$$c = \frac{n}{V}$$

- Precipitation reactions can be used to determine the amount of a salt in a solution of a sample. This process is known as gravimetric analysis.
- In gravimetric analysis:
  - the precipitation solution is added in sufficient (excess) amounts to cause complete precipitation of the ion being analysed

- the precipitate is filtered and dried until its mass is constant, to ensure that all water is removed
- the mass of precipitate is used to calculate the amount, in mol, of the original salt in solution, and hence the composition of the sample can be found.
- Gravimetric analysis can be used to determine the amount of salt in food, impurities such as sulfur in ores, or the level of impurities in water.
- Titrations involving precipitation reactions can be used to determine the concentration of a metal ion in solution.
- The equivalence point in a precipitation titration can sometimes be determined by a colour change when the metal ion is in excess.
- An alternative form of precipitation titration is a conductometric titration, in which the equivalence point is determined from the conductivity of the products of the reaction. The equivalence point is often the point where the minimum conductivity is recorded.

KEY QUESTIONS

1. Which one of the following reactions is most likely to be part of a gravimetric analysis?
   - **A** $HCl(aq) + NaOH(aq) \rightarrow NaCl(aq) + H_2O(l)$
   - **B** $2Na(s) + Cl_2(g) \rightarrow 2NaCl(s)$
   - **C** $AgNO_3(aq) + LiBr(aq) \rightarrow AgBr(s) + LiNO_3(aq)$
   - **D** $2HCl(aq) + Na_2CO_3(aq) \rightarrow 2NaCl(aq) + CO_2(g) + H_2O(l)$

2. State whether each of the following statements is true or false.
   - **a** All salts can be analysed by gravimetric analysis.
   - **b** A precipitate should be washed before it is dried.
   - **c** A poorly dried precipitate will lead to a result that is too high.
   - **d** Precipitates should be dried at high temperatures to ensure that all water is removed.
   - **e** A precipitate needs to be stable when heated.
   - **f** The electrical conductivity of the solution will change as a precipitate forms.
   - **g** A colour change occurs each time the equivalence point is reached in a precipitation titration.

3 There are a number of points during a gravimetric analysis where poor practice can affect the overall result. Match each of the poor practices listed below with its likely impact on the result.

Poor practice	Impact
Precipitate is not dried to constant mass.	The mass of the precipitate is too high because of the presence of impurities.
Precipitate is not washed with deionised water.	The composition of the precipitate is not known.
Precipitate is left on the sides of the flask.	The mass of the precipitate is too high because of the presence of water.
Precipitate decomposes when heated.	The precipitate is pure but its measured mass is lower than it should be.

4 The sodium chloride concentration in a solution used as eye drops is determined by adding a solution that causes the precipitation of the chloride ions as silver chloride.

a Suggest a solution containing an ionic compound that could be added to cause the precipitation of the chloride ions as silver chloride.

b Write a balanced chemical equation for the formation of the precipitate.

c Determine the required mole ratio for this reaction.

5 A 5.64 g precipitate of calcium phosphate is obtained when a solution of sodium phosphate is added to a solution of calcium nitrate. The equation for the reaction is:

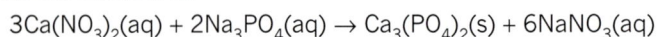

$$3Ca(NO_3)_2(aq) + 2Na_3PO_4(aq) \rightarrow Ca_3(PO_4)_2(s) + 6NaNO_3(aq)$$

What mass of calcium nitrate was required to produce this precipitate?

6 The mass of aluminium nitrate in a solution is determined by adding sodium carbonate solution to precipitate the aluminium as aluminium carbonate. The equation for the reaction occurring is:

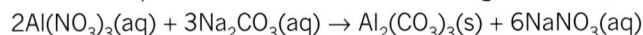

$$2Al(NO_3)_3(aq) + 3Na_2CO_3(aq) \rightarrow Al_2(CO_3)_3(s) + 6NaNO_3(aq)$$

In a particular reaction, 4.68 g of precipitate is obtained.

a Calculate the moles of aluminium carbonate produced.

b Determine the required mole ratio for the reaction.

c Calculate the mass of aluminium nitrate that reacted.

7 The reaction between mercury(II) acetate and sodium iodide is represented by the following equation.

$$Hg(CH_3COO)_2(aq) + 2NaI(aq) \rightarrow HgI_2(s) + 2NaCH_3COO(aq)$$

A precipitate of mass 4.82 g is formed when sodium iodide is added to a solution of mercury(II) acetate.
$M(Hg(CH_3COO)_2) = 318.70 \, g \, mol^{-1}$; $M(HgI_2) = 454.39 \, g \, mol^{-1}$

Calculate the mass of mercury(II) acetate that reacted to produce this precipitate.

8 A conductometric titration is conducted to determine the concentration of a lead(II) nitrate ($Pb(NO_3)_2$) solution. A burette is filled with the lead(II) nitrate solution. A 20.00 mL aliquot of KI solution is added to a beaker which is placed under the burette.

a Write a balanced chemical equation for the reaction occurring.

b How will the number of mole of Pb^{2+} ions compare to the number of mole of K^+ ions at the equivalence point?

c When the titration starts, the electrical conductivity drops. Explain why.

15.4 Determining salt concentration by colorimetry and UV–visible spectroscopy

In Section 15.3, you learnt how knowledge of precipitation reactions combined with stoichiometry can be used to determine the concentrations of salt solutions in the laboratory. Gravimetric analysis, like a titration (volumetric analysis) is a traditional form of chemical analysis that is relatively cheap and easy to perform. However, modern chemists have a range of chemical instruments at their disposal that can provide alternative methods of analysis. These methods are often faster and more accurate than traditional forms of analysis.

This section looks at how instruments called **colorimeters** and **ultraviolet–visible spectrometers** (also called UV–visible spectrometers) can be used to determine the concentration of a salt in solution. These instruments measure the interaction of light with a solution to determine the concentration of the solution. The intensity of the colour of a solution provides an indication of its concentration. Your eye can detect some differences in colour, but the instruments studied in this section can measure colour intensity accurately and use this to determine concentration.

SPECTROSCOPY

Light is a form of energy and is a type of **electromagnetic radiation**. Other forms of electromagnetic radiation are radio waves and X-rays. Visible light is only a small part of the range of different forms of electromagnetic radiation. The spread of the different types of radiation arranged according to their relative energies and wavelengths is referred to as the **electromagnetic spectrum** (Figure 15.4.1).

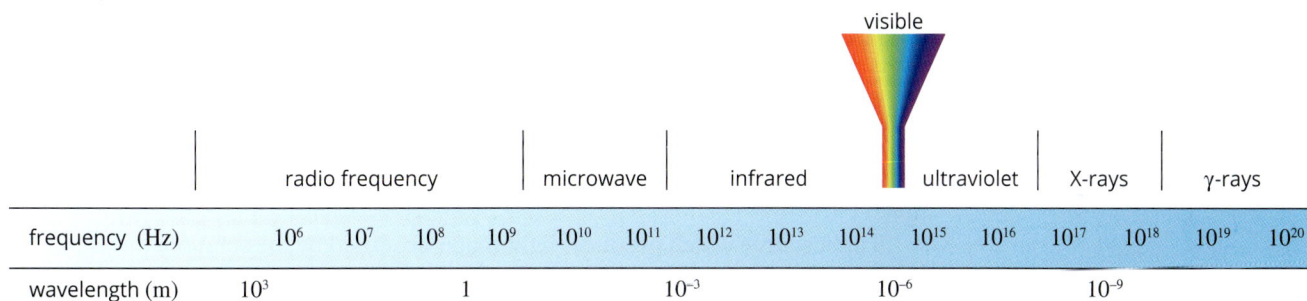

FIGURE 15.4.1 Visible light is only a small part of the electromagnetic spectrum. The spectroscopic techniques detailed in this chapter use radiation within the visible spectrum.

Electromagnetic radiation such as visible light can interact with atoms, and the nature of this interaction depends upon the energy of the electromagnetic radiation. In this section you will learn about an analytical technique called **spectroscopy**, which uses visible light and other parts of the electromagnetic spectrum to provide information about various materials. The spectroscopic techniques that you will look at in this section will specifically deal with light within the visible region of the electromagnetic spectrum.

When a substance absorbs visible light, it appears to be coloured. The colour observed is not the same as the colour of the light absorbed. The colour you see is caused by reflected or transmitted light. For example, plant leaves are green because their chlorophyll absorbs light in the purple and red ranges of the spectrum. Chlorophyll does not absorb light in the green region of the spectrum, so this is reflected and is the colour you see.

The observed colour and the absorbed colour are referred to as **complementary colours**.

> ℹ The visible region of light corresponds to wavelengths between 400 and 700 nm on the electromagnetic spectrum.

Colorimeters and UV–visible spectrometers are instruments used to determine the concentration of solutions by measuring their **absorbance** in the ultraviolet and visible region of the spectrum. The more concentrated the solution, the more radiation it will absorb. Figure 15.4.2 shows solutions of potassium permanganate ($KMnO_4$) at two different concentrations. The solutions appear purple because they absorb light in the yellow–green region of the electromagnetic spectrum (about 570 nm) and transmit the remaining violet light. The more concentrated solution absorbs more radiation.

light absorbed: yellow-green (570 nm)
light transmitted: violet

FIGURE 15.4.2 (a) Two solutions of potassium permanganate ($KMnO_4$); the darker solution has a higher concentration so it absorbs more light. (b) This solution has a violet colour because it absorbs yellow and green light.

> The colour of a substance is the colour of the light reflected from its surface (for opaque objects) or transmitted through it (for transparent objects and solutions).

COLORIMETRY

Colorimetry involves measuring the intensity of colour in a sample solution. Samples are often treated with a chemical compound in order to produce a coloured complex that can be analysed by colorimetry.

The construction of a colorimeter is shown in Figure 15.4.3. It consists of four main parts:

- a light source which produces light that is absorbed by the solution; this is passed through a filter to select a particular colour of light required for the analysis
- a transparent cell to hold the sample
- an electronic detector to measure the intensity of light that passes through the cell
- a recorder or electronic display that shows how much light was absorbed by the sample.

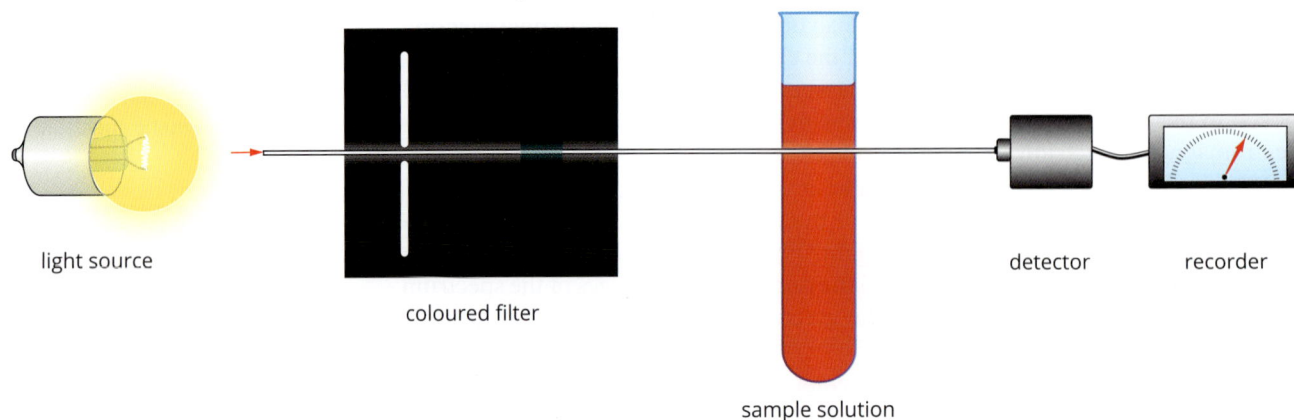

light source

coloured filter

sample solution

detector

recorder

FIGURE 15.4.3 The components of a colorimeter. Light of a suitable colour is passed through a sample. The recorder displays the amount of light absorbed by the sample.

The purpose of the filter is to select light of an appropriate colour that will be strongly absorbed by the sample. For example, since a chlorophyll solution absorbs strongly in the purple regions of the visible spectrum, a purple filter would be a good choice for chlorophyll analysis. The higher the concentration of chlorophyll, the higher the absorption of the purple light will be.

Table 15.4.1 shows the relationship between the colour of a solution and the selection of a filter for use in a colorimeter. Remember that the colour absorbed by the sample is the complementary colour to the colour you observe.

TABLE 15.4.1 Colours of visible light and the complementary colours that are absorbed

Wavelength (nm)	Colour absorbed (colour of filter)	Colour observed
380–420	violet	green-yellow
420–440	violet-blue	yellow
440–470	blue	orange
470–500	blue-green	red
500–520	green	purple
520–550	yellow-green	violet
550–580	yellow	violet-blue
580–620	orange	blue
620–680	red	blue-green
680–780	purple	green

A handy way to remember complementary colours is to write the initials of the main colours in order of their decreasing wavelengths, as ROYGBV (red, orange, yellow, green, blue and violet), and then to write the initials again of the complementary colours directly below, this time starting from green.

R O Y G B V
G B V R O Y

Calibration curves

To determine the concentration of a substance in a solution using colorimetry, a series of **standard solutions** (solutions of accurately known concentrations) of the substance are prepared, and their absorbances are then measured.

GO TO ➤ Year 11 Section 8.4

For example, if you wished to determine the concentration of nickel(II) sulfate, you would create a series of nickel(II) sulfate solutions of varying concentrations. Depending on the amount of nickel(II) sulfate you suspected to be in your sample, a suitable range of concentrations might be from $0.1\,mol\,L^{-1}$ to $0.5\,mol\,L^{-1}$. Once your standard solutions are prepared, you can measure their absorbance at the selected wavelength. Table 15.4.2 shows a series of data typical for the absorbances of standard solutions of nickel(II) sulfate.

TABLE 15.4.2 Absorbance of standard solutions of nickel(II) sulfate

Nickel(II) sulfate concentration ($mol\,L^{-1}$)	Absorbance
0.10	0.18
0.20	0.34
0.30	0.49
0.40	0.66
0.50	0.81

You can then construct a **calibration curve** from the data. A calibration curve is a plot of the absorbances of the standards against their concentration. Figure 15.4.4 shows the calibration curve created from the nickel(II) sulfate data in Table 15.4.2.

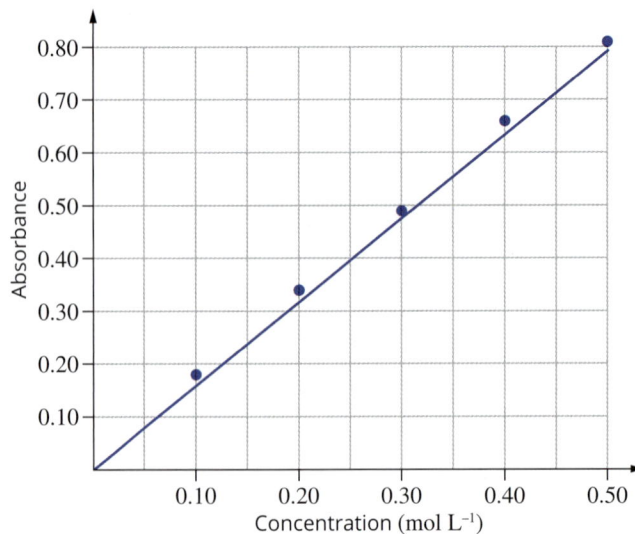

FIGURE 15.4.4 Calibration curve for nickel(II) sulfate.

If the absorbance of a solution of unknown concentration is now measured, the value can be used to determine the concentration from the calibration curve.

Figure 15.4.5 outlines the procedure that is followed when analysing a solution using colorimetry.

> ℹ️ A calibration curve is constructed by measuring the absorbance of a series of solutions with accurately known concentrations and then plotting the results on a graph of absorbance versus concentration.

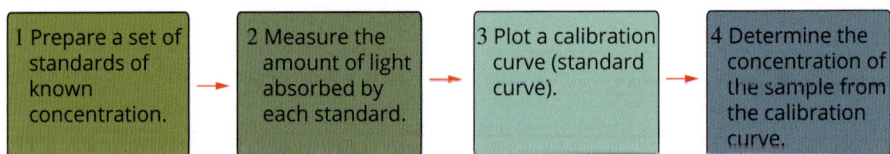

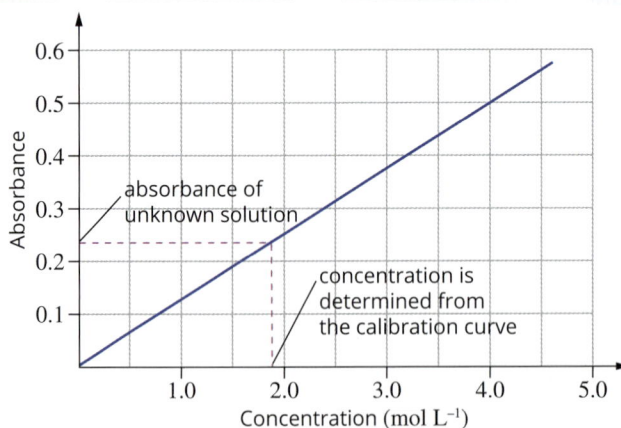

| 1 Prepare a set of standards of known concentration. | → | 2 Measure the amount of light absorbed by each standard. | → | 3 Plot a calibration curve (standard curve). | → | 4 Determine the concentration of the sample from the calibration curve. |

FIGURE 15.4.5 Procedure for the determination of concentration using a colorimeter.

Worked example 15.4.1

USING A CALIBRATION CURVE

The concentration of iron in dam water is determined by colorimetry. The absorbances of a series of standard solutions and a sample of dam water are shown in the table below. Determine the concentration of iron in the sample.

Concentration of Fe^{2+} ($mg\,mL^{-1}$)	Absorbance
4.0	0.16
8.0	0.31
12.0	0.47
16.0	0.63
sample	0.38

Thinking	Working
Construct a calibration curve from the data above. Concentration will be on the horizontal axis.	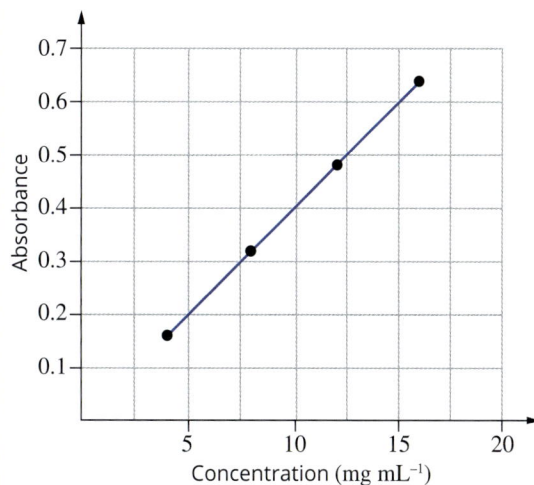
Mark where the absorbance of the sample lies on the calibration curve by tracing a horizontal line to the curve.	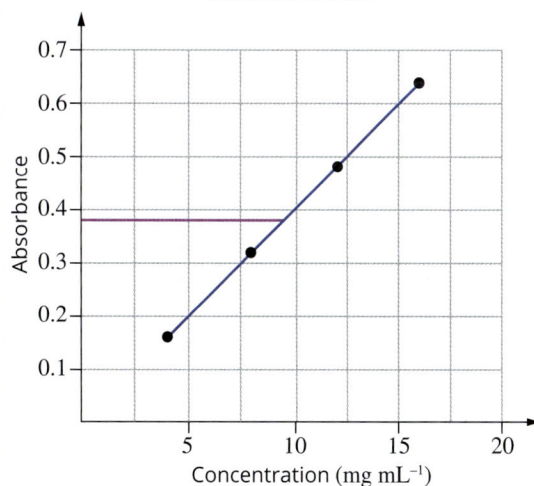 Plot the absorbance value of the unknown solution.

Draw a vertical line from the calibration curve to the horizontal axis.	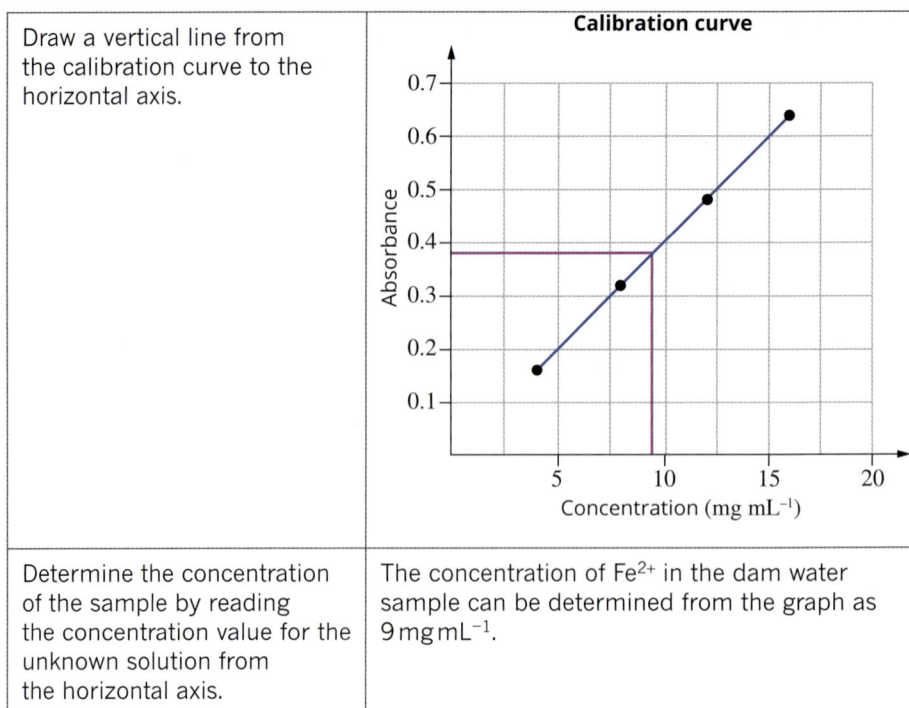 **Calibration curve**
Determine the concentration of the sample by reading the concentration value for the unknown solution from the horizontal axis.	The concentration of Fe^{2+} in the dam water sample can be determined from the graph as $9\,mg\,mL^{-1}$.

Worked example: Try yourself 15.4.1

USING A CALIBRATION CURVE

Determine the lead level in a solution using the following colorimetry data.

Concentration of Pb^{2+} ($mg\,mL^{-1}$)	Absorbance
2.5	0.18
5.0	0.35
7.5	0.51
10.0	0.68
sample	0.60

UV-VISIBLE SPECTROSCOPY

> UV–visible spectroscopy is also known as UV–visible spectrophotometry.

A colorimeter is simple and inexpensive, but its accuracy is limited. A UV–visible spectrometer, such as the one shown in Figure 15.4.6, is a more sophisticated instrument. A UV–visible spectrometer uses a **monochromator** rather than a filter to select light of an exact wavelength to be used in the analysis.

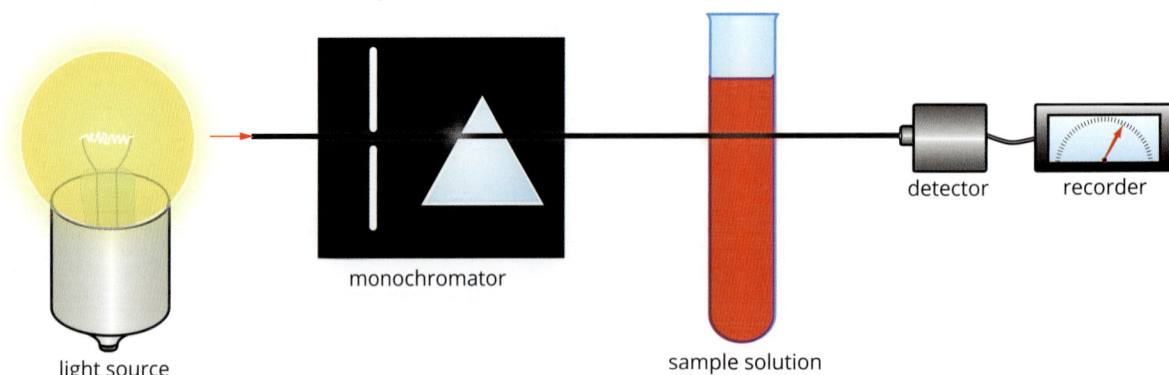

light source — monochromator — sample solution — detector — recorder

FIGURE 15.4.6 Diagram of the components of a UV–visible spectrometer. A monochromator is used to allow selection of specific wavelengths for the analysis of samples.

When a UV–visible spectrometer is used, the solution to be tested can first be scanned across multiple wavelengths to select the best wavelength to use. Scanning involves varying the wavelength of light used and checking the absorbance of the sample. Figure 15.4.7 shows an example of a scan for a solution of the green plant pigment chlorophyll.

FIGURE 15.4.7 Scan of a green chlorophyll solution showing absorbance maxima at around 450 and 660 nm.

The scan shows strong absorbance at wavelengths around 430 and 660 nm, which correspond to purple and red light respectively. The measurements of absorbance for the standard solution and sample would be conducted at one of these two wavelengths. In practice, the wavelength at which other compounds in the solution do not absorb strongly would be chosen.

> ℹ️ In UV–visible spectroscopy, the best wavelength for analysis of a sample is where maximum absorbance occurs without interference from other components in the sample. This is not always at the wavelength at which the sample absorbs most strongly.

CHEMFILE ICT

The Beer–Lambert law

You have learnt that the concentration of a particular species in solution can be measured in a spectrometer. In a spectrometer the sample is placed into a transparent cell, then light of a particular colour or wavelength is passed through it. Figure 15.4.8 shows that the intensity of the light emerging from a sample cell is lower than it was before entering the cell. This is because the solution absorbs some of the light. The original intensity of the light is referred to as I_0, and the intensity after absorption is labelled I.

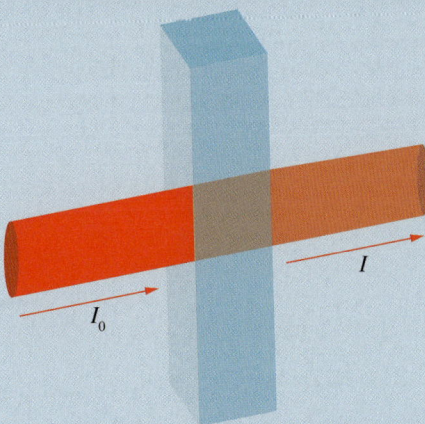

FIGURE 15.4.8 When light is passed through a solution in a sample cell, some of that light is absorbed. The absorption of light lowers the intensity of the light emerging from the cell.

The amount of light absorbed depends on:

- the substance itself: the amount of light absorbed depends on the species present, as does the most suitable wavelength of light to use
- the concentration of the sample: at higher concentrations, more light is absorbed
- the length of the sample cell: the longer the sample cell, the greater the absorption.

  These factors are illustrated in Figure 15.4.9.

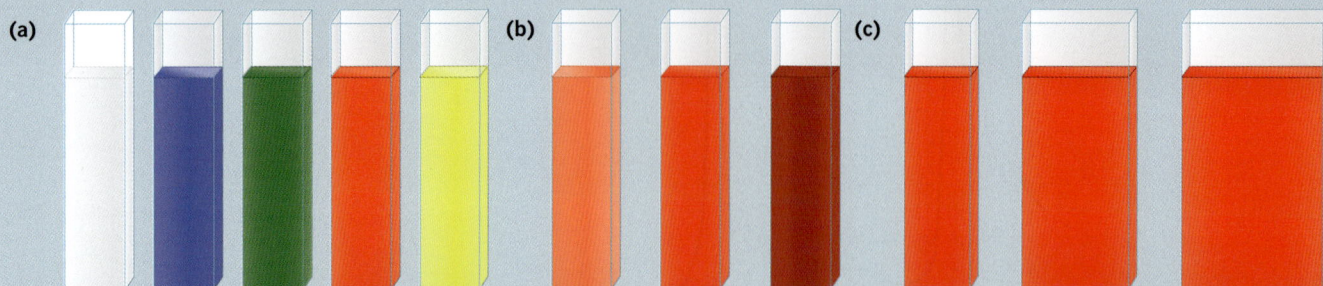

FIGURE 15.4.9 (a) The different substances in each solution will affect the amount of light absorbed and the wavelengths of light absorbed. (b) As the concentration of the solution increases, the absorption will increase. (c) The absorption of light will increase if the light has to travel further through the solution.

The **Beer–Lambert law** is a mathematical relationship that connects the amount of light absorbed to the factors previously identified. The two forms of the relationship are:

$$A = \varepsilon l c$$

$$A = \log_{10} \frac{I_0}{I}$$

where

A is the absorbance

ε is the molar absorption coefficient in $cm^{-1}\,mol^{-1}\,L$

l is the sample cell length in cm

c is the molar concentration in $mol\,L^{-1}$

I_0 is the intensity of light entering sample cell

I is the intensity of light exiting sample cell.

August Beer and Johann Lambert were both German scientists, but they did not work together or at the same time. They researched different aspects of this relationship.

The expression $A = \varepsilon l c$ states that absorbance depends on (is directly proportional to) the sample cell length and the solution concentration. For a particular species, the value of the **molar absorption coefficient** or **molar absorptivity**, ε (the Greek letter epsilon), will be a constant. The molar absorption coefficient is a measure of the absorbance under standard conditions, i.e. light travelling through 1 cm of a 1 mol L^{-1} solution.

In the second form of the Beer–Lambert law, the expression $A = \log_{10} \frac{I_0}{I}$ states that absorbance is measured in a spectrometer by comparing the intensity of the light entering the sample cell to the intensity of light exiting the cell.

One of the most common uses of UV–visible spectroscopy is testing solutions of the same substance but with differing concentration (Figure 15.4.10). In this case, the value of ε is constant as each solution contains the same substance, and the value of l is constant as the same sample cell is used for each test. So the Beer–Lambert law can be simplified to:

$$A = kc$$

where

k is a constant

c is the solution concentration.

The calibration curve is linear, so it can be used to the determine the concentration of a solution by measuring the absorbance.

Concentration	Absorbance
0.1	0.12
0.2	0.24
0.3	0.36
0.4	0.48

FIGURE 15.4.10 The Beer–Lambert equation in use. The absorbance increases linearly as the concentration increases.

Metal complexes

Solutions containing Fe^{2+} ions do not absorb very strongly in the ultraviolet or visible part of the spectrum. If the Fe^{2+} ions are oxidised to Fe^{3+}, then potassium thiocyanate (KSCN) is added to the solution, a bright red solution forms, as seen in Figure 15.4.11. This highly coloured red solution can be analysed using either a colorimeter or UV–visible spectrometer.

The reaction shown in Figure 15.4.11 can be represented by the equation:

$$Fe^{3+}(aq) + SCN^-(aq) \rightarrow FeSCN^{2+}(aq)$$

$FeSCN^{2+}$ is an example of a metal complex, a topic covered in Section 15.2. Transition metals in particular can form complexes, such as $FeSCN^{2+}$, many of which are brightly coloured and suited to analysis with a colorimeter or UV–visible spectrometer.

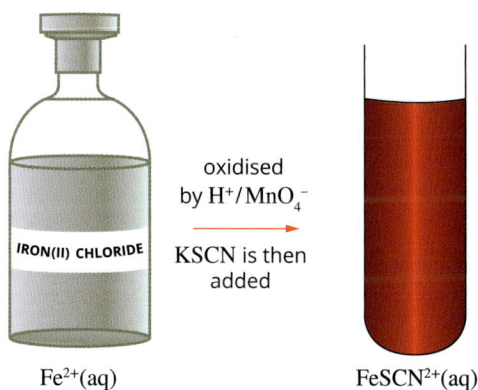

> **i** Some metal ions may need to be converted into highly coloured metal complexes to be analysed using UV–visible spectroscopy or colorimetry.

oxidised by H^+/MnO_4^-

KSCN is then added

IRON(II) CHLORIDE

$Fe^{2+}(aq)$ $FeSCN^{2+}(aq)$

FIGURE 15.4.11 A solution containing $Fe^{2+}(aq)$ is oxidised to form $Fe^{3+}(aq)$ ions. When KSCN is added, a blood-red solution of $FeSCN^{2+}(aq)$ ions forms.

The analysis of a sample using colorimetry or UV–visible spectroscopy can be summarised in the following steps.

1. If the metal ion to be analysed is not strongly coloured, a metal complex may need to be formed.
2. Select the wavelength or filter to be used for the analysis. This will correspond to the wavelength of light absorbed most strongly by the sample.
3. Measure the absorbance of a series of standard solutions of accurately known concentration at the selected wavelength.

4. Plot a calibration curve of absorbance (vertical axis) versus concentration (horizontal axis) for the standard solutions.

5. Measure the absorbance of the sample solution and determine the concentration from reading the corresponding value from the calibration curve.

6. Account for any dilutions that may have been carried out during your sample preparation to calculate the final concentration.

Uses of colorimetry and UV–visible spectroscopy

Colorimeters and UV–visible spectrometers are used in many and varied fields. These instruments can determine the concentrations of lead in urine, blood sugar levels, cholesterol levels, levels of haemoglobin in blood and phosphates in water. Portable colorimeters, such as the one shown in Figure 15.4.12a, are now available to make on-site testing easier.

Some other examples of the use of colorimetry or UV–visible spectroscopy are:

- measuring chromium levels in a workplace: a worker carries a pump and PVC filter unit for a set period of time. The pump samples the air around the worker, and solids in the air are collected on the filter paper. Chromium can be extracted from the filter paper and converted to yellow chromate ions (CrO_4^{2-}) before analysis.

- determining phosphate levels in waterways: phosphate ions can be harmful to the environment as they cause eutrophication. Ammonium molybdate and tin(II) chloride can be added to water samples containing phosphates, forming a dark-blue complex called molybdenum blue, which can then be used for spectroscopic analysis.

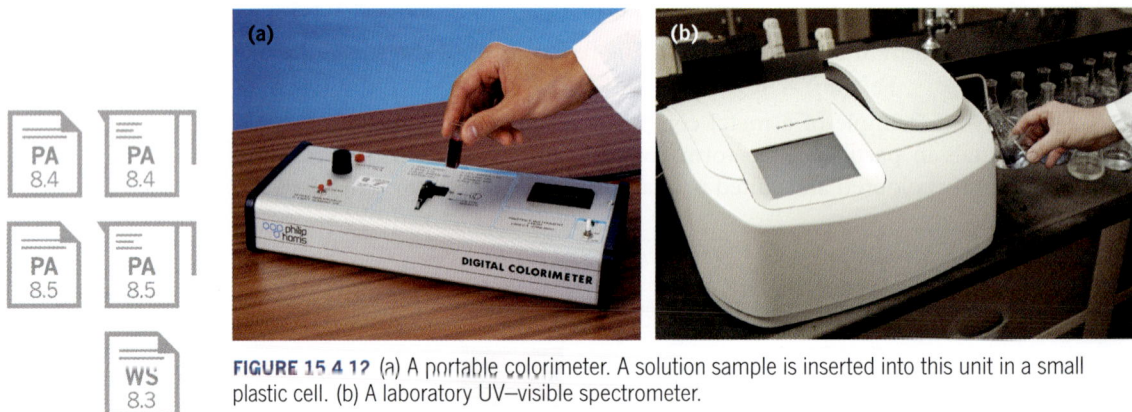

FIGURE 15.4.12 (a) A portable colorimeter. A solution sample is inserted into this unit in a small plastic cell. (b) A laboratory UV–visible spectrometer.

15.4 Review

SUMMARY

- Gravimetric analysis is cheap and simple to perform but has been largely replaced by faster instrumental methods.
- Radiation from each part of the electromagnetic spectrum can be described in terms of its frequency, wavelength and energy. Different colours of light have different frequencies, wavelengths and energies.
- Some solutions containing metal ions absorb light in the visible and ultraviolet regions of the spectrum. Colorimeters and UV–visible spectrometers can be used to determine the concentration of metal ions in these solutions.
- A metal complex consists of a metal ion bonded to molecules or anions. The solutions of many metal complexes are coloured so are suited to analysis by colorimetry or UV–visible spectroscopy.
- The amount of light absorbed by a solution is related to the concentration of the solution.
- Calibration curves are prepared by measuring the absorbance of a series of standard solutions of known concentration. The absorbance readings are then plotted against concentration. The concentration of a solution can be determined by plotting its absorbance on the calibration curve and reading off the corresponding concentration.
- A colorimeter uses a filter to select the colour of light to be used. The light chosen for the analysis should be complementary to the observed colour of the solution.
- A UV–visible spectrometer uses a monochromator in place of a filter. This allows a specific wavelength to be chosen.
- A scan across a range of wavelengths is used to determine the wavelength that offers the best absorbance for a particular solution.
- A UV–visible spectrometer can usually provide more accurate results than a colorimeter. Both instruments offer a means of determining the concentration of salts in a solution.

KEY QUESTIONS

1. Two samples of copper(II) sulfate solution with concentrations of $0.080\,mol\,L^{-1}$ and $0.30\,mol\,L^{-1}$ were analysed using a spectrometer.
   a. Which sample would allow the most amount of light to pass through to the detector?
   b. Which sample would show the strongest absorption of light?

2. Why would red light rather than blue light be used in a colorimeter to measure the concentration of a blue-coloured copper(II) sulfate solution?

3. The absorption spectrum of a commercial dye is shown in the graph below. The colour chart under the graph shows the colour of each region of the spectrum. What colour is the dye?

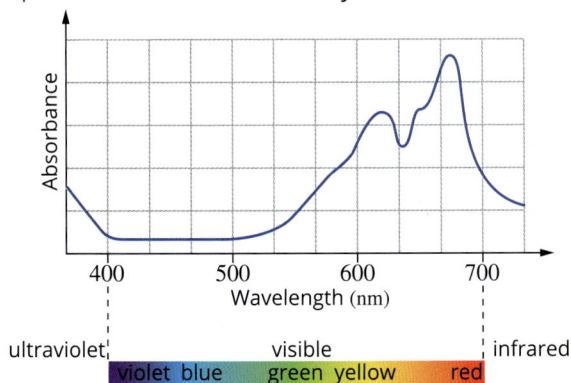

4. A colorimeter is used to analyse the concentration of iron(II) ions (Fe^{2+}) in the water in a tank. The calibration curve in graph below is obtained from measuring the absorbance of a series of standards.

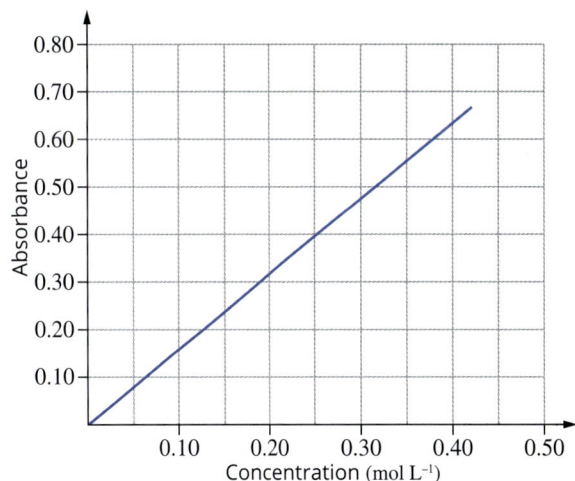

The iron solution is diluted from 5 mL to 20 mL before its absorbance is measured to be 0.24.
   a. What is the concentration of Fe^{2+}, in $mol\,L^{-1}$, of the solution analysed in the colorimeter?
   b. What is the concentration of Fe^{2+} in the original tank water sample?

c Fe^{2+} ions are generally too pale to be analysed by spectrometry directly. Outline the process for preparing Fe^{2+} ions for analysis through the formation of a metal complex.

5 What are the complementary colours to the observed colours of the following solutions?

Solution colour	Complementary colour
green	
purple	
orange	
green–yellow	
blue–green	

6 The concentration of copper(II) ions in industrial waste water was analysed by colorimetry. The absorbance values from a series of standards and the waste water are provided below.

Concentration (mg L^{-1})	Absorbance
50	0.12
100	0.23
150	0.36
200	0.48
250	0.58
Waste water sample	0.42

a Use the values provided to construct a calibration curve for the analysis of Cu^{2+}.

b Using the calibration curve you created in part **a**, determine the concentration of copper(II) ions in the waste water.

7 Potassium dichromate forms an orange-coloured solution. Describe how you would use colorimetry to determine the concentration of potassium dichromate in a solution.

8 The absorption spectrum of chlorophyll is shown in Figure 15.4.7 on page 441.

a At what wavelengths is there maximum absorbance of light?

b What wavelength would you select if you were required to determine the concentration of chlorophyll in a leaf extract using UV–visible spectroscopy? Provide an explanation for your answer. Assume that no other compounds in the leaf extract absorb strongly at the chosen wavelength.

15.5 Determining concentration by atomic absorption spectroscopy

In Section 15.2 you learnt that many metals emit light of a characteristic colour when placed in a flame. This knowledge can be harnessed to help identify the metal ions present in a sample. In this section you will examine how the emission and absorption of light by metals can be used to determine the concentration, not just the identity, of salts in solution.

REVISION

GO TO ➤ | Year 11 Chapter 3

Light emission by atoms

You will recall from Year 11 that electrons are arranged into different energy levels in atoms. Electrons in energy levels close to the nucleus have the lowest energies and experience the strongest attraction to the nucleus. When placed in a flame, an electron can jump up to a higher energy level if it absorbs energy that corresponds exactly to the difference in energy between the lower energy level and the higher energy level (Figure 15.5.1).

Atoms with electrons in higher energy levels are unstable, so the **excited electrons** quickly return to lower energy levels. Figure 15.5.2 shows that the energy absorbed by the electrons is emitted as light as they return to a lower energy level. When electrons are located in the lowest energy shells possible, this is known as the **ground state**.

Some of the energy emitted from the transitions of electrons falls within the region of the electromagnetic spectrum corresponding to visible light. This emitted light is what you observe as the coloured flame in a flame test. The different colours observed correspond to specific wavelengths of light.

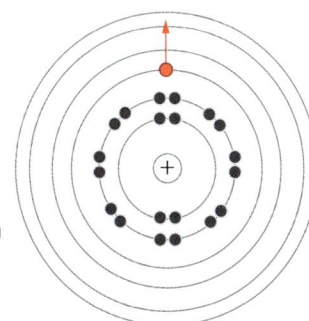

FIGURE 15.5.1 Energy from a flame can promote an electron in an atom to a higher energy level.

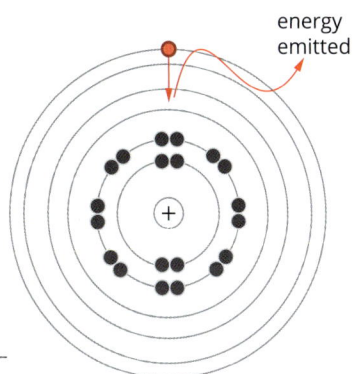

energy emitted

FIGURE 15.5.2 An excited electron quickly returns |to a lower energy level, emitting electromagnetic energy in the form of light of a particular wavelength.

ATOMIC EMISSION SPECTROSCOPY

Flame tests provide only limited information about the likely elements present in a sample. As mentioned previously, only a few elements give a coloured flame in a Bunsen burner, and the colours of some are similar. In impure samples, a faint colour may be masked by a stronger one.

Atomic emission spectroscopy (AES) requires an atomic emission spectrometer, which can determine the metal ions present in a sample (Figure 15.5.3). By also making two changes to the flame test technique, the reliability and usefulness of flame colour identification can be greatly improved.

GO TO ➤ | Year 11 Chapter 3

- Using a hotter flame ensures that sufficient energy is available to excite electrons in a wider range of elements.
- Passing the light through a prism separates the different energies in the light emitted by a heated sample into a series of coloured lines called a **line spectrum** or an **emission spectrum**.

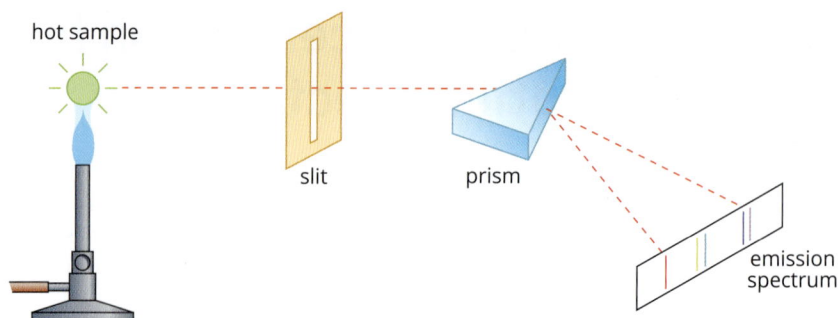

FIGURE 15.5.3 Essential components of an atomic emission spectrometer. The prism splits the emitted light into each of the component wavelengths, creating a line spectrum that is unique to the sample being tested.

When the light emitted from an excited atom is viewed through a spectrometer, it is much easier to see how the colour produced is unique. Because each element has a different number of protons in the nucleus and a unique electron configuration, the energy transitions that the electrons undergo as they move from the ground state to an excited state are also unique. So no two elements have exactly the same energy levels, and a spectrum is characteristic of a particular element. It may be used as a 'fingerprint' to identify the elements present in a substance. The emission spectra of calcium, sodium, mercury and cadmium are shown in Figure 15.5.4 as examples. You can see how the spectra consist of distinct lines corresponding to the different colours emitted by the atoms.

FIGURE 15.5.4 The emission spectra of (a) calcium, (b) sodium, (c) mercury, and (d) cadmium. The spectral lines are indicative of the different energies of light emitted in the visible region.

ATOMIC ABSORPTION SPECTROSCOPY

In the early 1950s, the Australian scientist Alan Walsh was working on the measurement of small concentrations of metals at the CSIRO. During this time he developed the technique of **atomic absorption spectroscopy** (AAS), which is now used widely for detecting the presence of most metals and determining their concentration.

How do we know what stars are made of?

The light produced by stars can be viewed through a spectroscope to produce what is known as an absorption spectrum. Unlike an emission spectrum, an absorption spectrum of an element contains dark lines against a coloured background that correspond to wavelengths of light that are absorbed (Figure 15.5.5). The position of the absorption lines in an element's absorption spectrum match the position of emission lines observed in an element's emission spectrum. This is because the energy required to excite an electron into a higher energy level is equal to the energy that is emitted when the electron returns to a lower energy level.

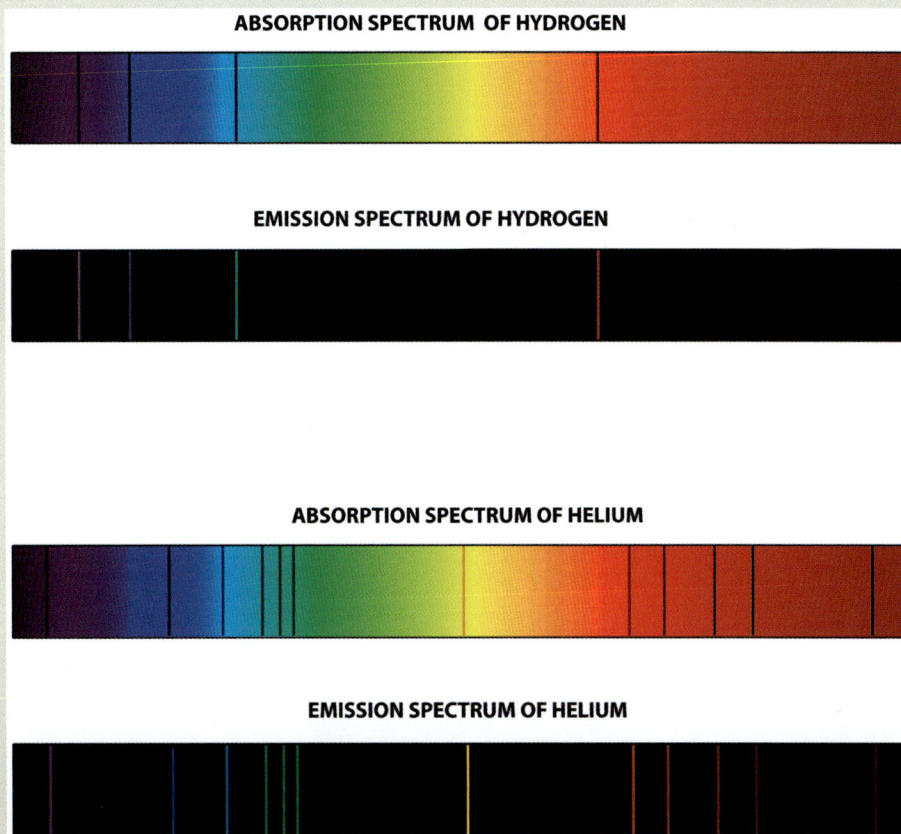

ABSORPTION SPECTRUM OF HYDROGEN

EMISSION SPECTRUM OF HYDROGEN

ABSORPTION SPECTRUM OF HELIUM

EMISSION SPECTRUM OF HELIUM

FIGURE 15.5.5 The absorption and emission spectra for hydrogen and helium. Notice how the absorption lines match up with the emission lines.

The Hubble space telescope, which is responsible for many of the well-known images of our universe, is equipped with a spectrograph. This allows astronomers to analyse the absorption spectra of stars and determine what they are made of.

The brightest star in our night sky is Sirius, a binary white star in the constellation Canis Major, approximately 6.8 light-years away from Earth. Figure 15.5.6 on page 450 shows Sirius as seen in the southern sky and its corresponding absorption spectrum. The dark lines in the spectrum are absorption lines that correspond to the wavelengths of light absorbed by elements present in the outer gas layers of the star.

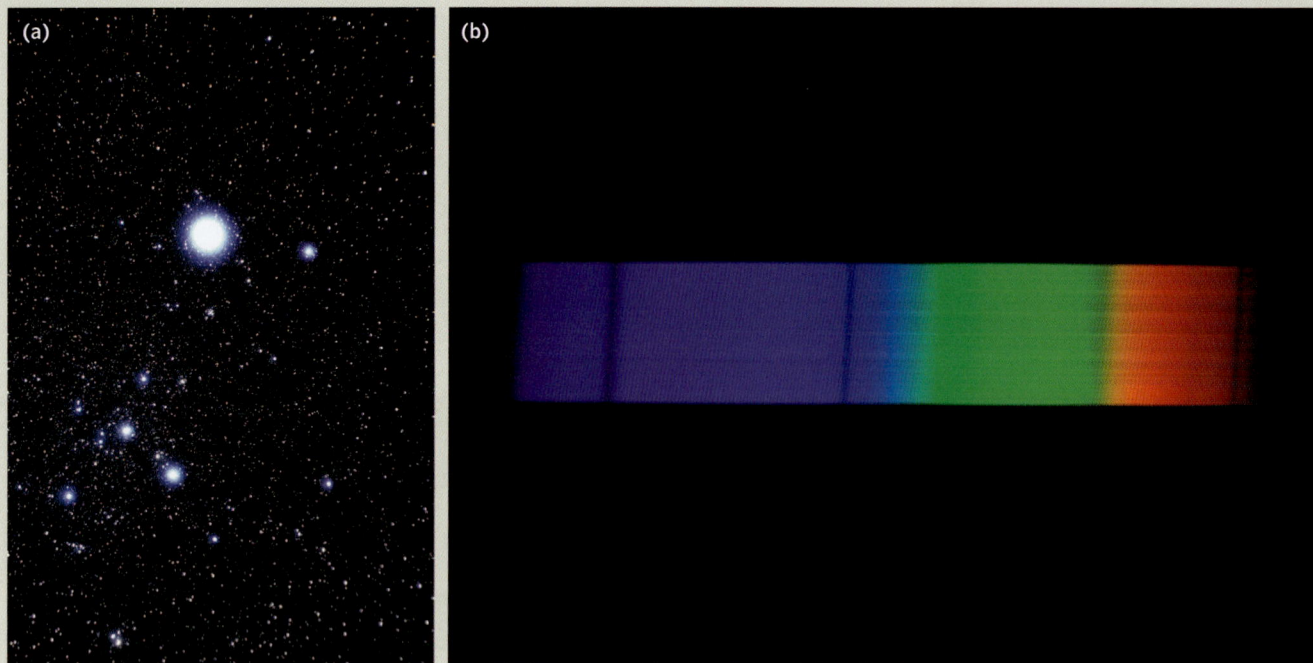

FIGURE 15.5.6 (a) The star Sirius, in the constellation Canis Major, as seen in the southern sky. (b) The absorption spectrum obtained from the light emitted by Sirius can be used to determine the elements in the star.

Comparing the spectrum obtained for a star with the spectra of known elements allows astronomers to identify the elements in the star.

Figure 15.5.7 shows the absorption spectra of 13 different stars. Each of these contains the characteristic lines representative of the absorption spectrum of hydrogen (the major component of most stars). The remaining dark lines correlate to other elements that are present in the outer layers of the star; these include calcium, sodium and iron, to name a few.

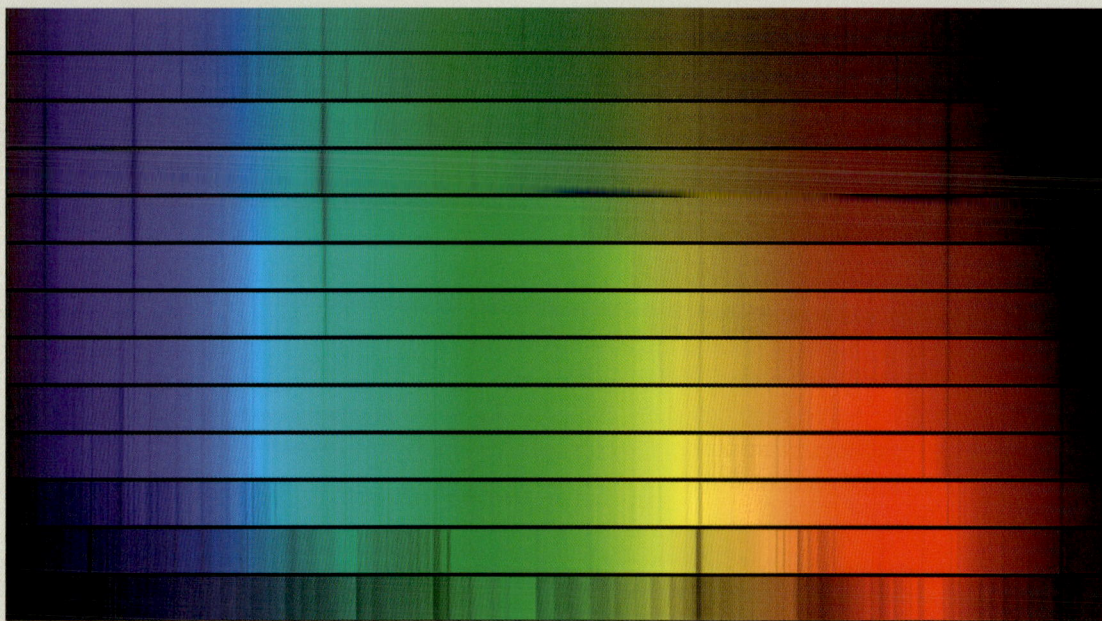

FIGURE 15.5.7 The absorption spectra of 13 different stars. Astronomers collated the spectral data from the observable stars in the universe and classified them according to 13 types. Each of these spectra shows distinct absorption lines corresponding to the absorption pattern for hydrogen.

Astronomers have created a classification system for the stars in our universe based on their absorption spectra. Spectral information is one of the most powerful tools we have for investigating the stars that exist light-years away from Earth.

How AAS works

Alan Walsh's breakthrough was to recognise that atoms will absorb light if the energy of the light is exactly equal to the energy required to promote an electron from its ground state energy level to a higher energy level. As every element absorbs light of different energies (and hence different wavelengths), the amount of light absorbed by a sample at a specific wavelength can be used to determine the concentration of that element.

Figure 15.5.8 gives a simplified depiction of how an atomic absorption spectrometer works.

> **i** Unlike emission spectroscopy, AAS measures the amount of light absorbed by the sample.

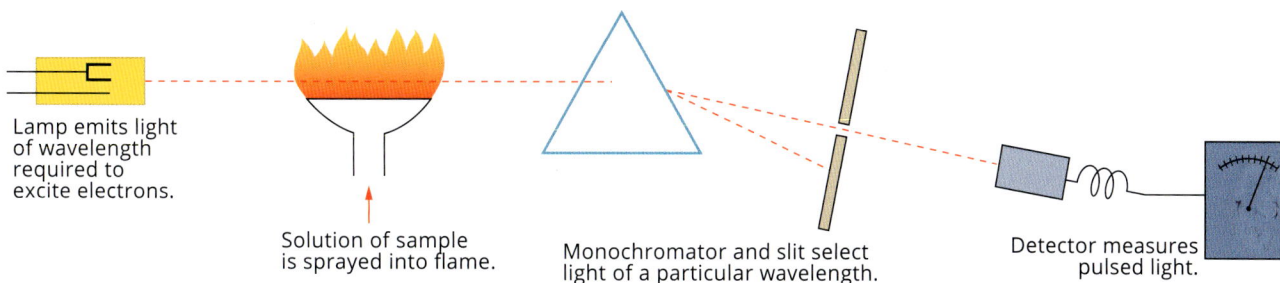

Lamp emits light of wavelength required to excite electrons.

Solution of sample is sprayed into flame.

Monochromator and slit select light of a particular wavelength.

Detector measures pulsed light.

FIGURE 15.5.8 Schematic diagram of the inner workings of an atomic absorption spectrometer.

The light absorbed at a specific wavelength by a sample can be determined by the following process.

1. A hollow-cathode lamp emits different wavelengths of light that are absorbed by the metal being analysed. The lamp must be made with a filament of the metal being analysed.
2. A solution of a sample is sprayed into the flame to create an atomic vapour.
3. A monochromator is used to select a wavelength of light for analysis.
4. A detector measures the amount of light that reaches it, and a computer determines the amount of light that has been absorbed by the sample.

Calibration curves

Atomic absorption spectroscopy can be used to simply detect the presence of most metals; however, it is more often used to determine the concentration of a metal in a sample. The absorbance measured for a sample can be related to the concentration of the metal being analysed by using a calibration curve.

To construct a calibration curve, you must first create a series of standard solutions of the metal ion, and then measure their absorbance by AAS. A calibration curve is then constructed by plotting the concentrations of the standard solutions against the absorbance of each solution, as shown in Figure 15.5.9.

> **i** As the concentration of the metal in the sample increases, the amount of light absorbed by the sample increases.

Because the amount of light that is absorbed by the sample is proportional to the amount of metal present, the relationship between concentration and absorbance is a linear one.

Once constructed, the calibration curve can be used to determine the concentration of the metal being analysed in the unknown sample. The absorbance of the unknown sample is measured and the corresponding concentration value can be read from the graph.

In Year 11 you learnt that there are many different units for concentration. For simplicity, concentration will be measured in $mg\,L^{-1}$ in the following examples, but it is important to always check the concentration unit specified on the horizontal axis of the calibration curve when answering questions involving AAS. In the example in the calibration curve, the unit $mg\,L^{-1}$ refers to the mass of metal (in mg) in every litre of the solution being analysed.

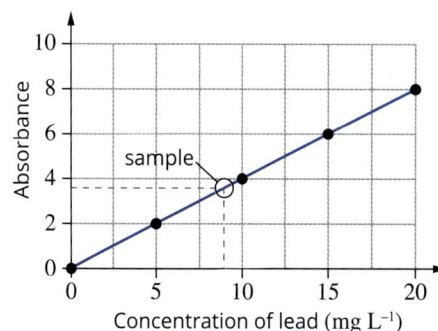

FIGURE 15.5.9 The AAS calibration curve that shows the relationship between the absorbance of light and the concentration of lead in a sample.

GO TO ➤ Year 11 Chapter 11

Worked example 15.5.1

USING A CALIBRATION CURVE TO DETERMINE CONCENTRATION

Determine the concentration of mercury in a sample given the data in the following table.

Concentration of mercury (mg mL^{-1})	Absorbance
1.0	0.026
2.0	0.053
3.0	0.078
4.0	0.105
sample	0.036

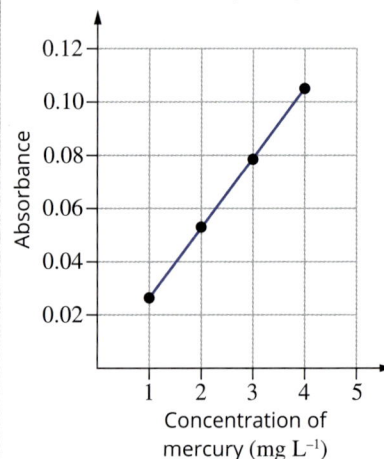

Thinking	Working
Construct a calibration curve using concentrations of the standard solutions and their absorbance.	
Mark where the absorbance of the sample lies on the calibration curve. This can be done by finding the absorbance of the sample on the vertical axis and moving horizontally right until you reach the calibration curve and marking that point.	

Determine the concentration of the sample by reading off the graph on the horizontal axis at the point where the sample's absorbance lies on the calibration curve.	**AAS calibration curve for mercury analysis**

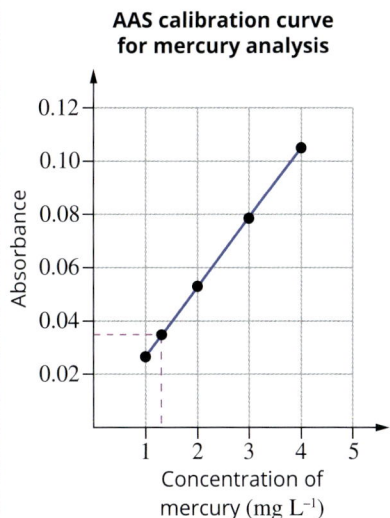

The sample's absorbance is 0.036.

The concentration of mercury for the sample can be read off the graph as $1.2\,mg\,L^{-1}$.

Worked example: Try yourself 15.5.1

USING A CALIBRATION CURVE TO DETERMINE CONCENTRATION

Determine the concentration of sodium in a sample, given the data in the following table.

Concentration of sodium (mg mL^{-1})	Absorbance
20	0.041
40	0.080
60	0.121
80	0.159
Sample	0.104

AAS today

Approximately 60 years after Alan Walsh developed atomic absorption spectroscopy, the technique is still used by many modern-day chemists. It is a very good tool for analysing the concentration of metals in a wide variety of samples, including water, urine, blood, soil, fish and other foods. AAS is capable of detecting 68 different metallic elements, and is sensitive enough to detect metals at concentrations of less than $1\,mg\,L^{-1}$. Figure 15.5.10 shows an analytical chemist using an atomic absorption spectrometer to analyse the concentration of potassium in a sample.

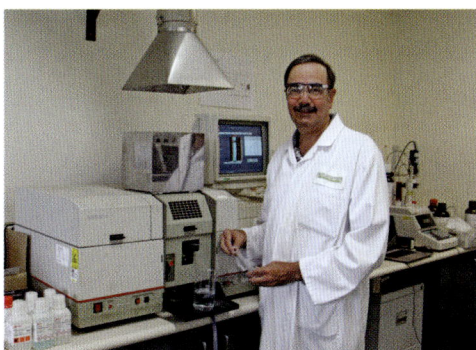

> **i** AAS is a very sensitive technique for the detection of metals, but it can only be used to detect one element at a time.

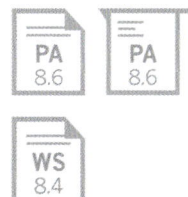

PA 8.6   PA 8.6

WS 8.4

FIGURE 15.5.10 An analytical chemist uses AAS to determine the concentration of metals in food samples.

ICP–AES analysis

Even with the use of very hot flames (a mixture of oxygen and ethyne gas gives the hottest flame, up to 3100°C), many elements cannot be analysed by AAS or give a poor response.

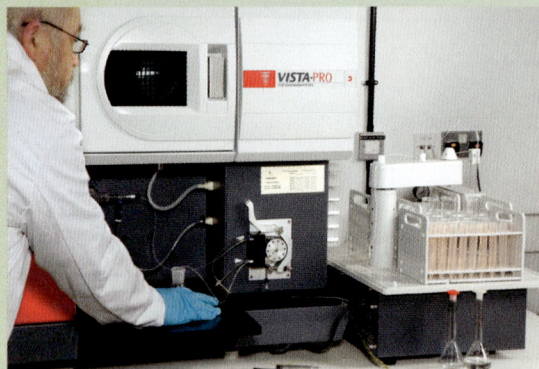

FIGURE 15.5.11 An inductively coupled plasma (ICP) analyser.

Modern instruments, such as that shown in Figure 15.5.11, can analyse most elements by using an energy source called inductively coupled plasma (ICP) in combination with atomic emission spectroscopy (AES). Instead of a flame to excite the atoms, the ICP generates very high temperatures of up to 10 000°C to create a plasma, a state of matter consisting of charged particles. At these temperatures virtually all the atoms in the sample are excited and are able to emit electromagnetic radiation as an emission spectrum as they return to their ground state.

There are several advantages in using ICP–AES rather than AAS:

- It can be used to identify most elements.
- It is suitable for almost all concentrations.
- It can rapidly identify many elements present in a sample at the same time, as the emission spectrum is resolved by comparison with a computerised database of spectral lines (analysis of 70 elements together takes just two minutes), whereas AAS can determine only one element at a time.

15.5 Review

SUMMARY

- An atom in which the electrons are in their lowest possible energy state is said to be in its ground state.
- When an element is heated, electrons may absorb energy and move into higher energy levels (shells). The atom is described as being excited.
- When the electrons move back to lower energy levels, they emit electromagnetic radiation, such as light, with specific energies; each element emits light with a unique set of energies called an emission spectrum.

- Emission spectra are unique for each element and represent each of the energy transitions within that element as a series of coloured lines.
- Atomic absorption spectroscopy (AAS) is based on the ability of electrons to absorb energy as they move between energy levels.
- AAS can be used to accurately determine the concentration of most metals in samples of water and other substances.
- The AAS technique involves the construction of a calibration curve to relate the concentration of the metal to the absorbance measured.

KEY QUESTIONS

1. Select words from the following list to complete the sentences below. Not all of the words provided are required.

   protons, higher, transition, electrons, lower, let out, emit, excited, absorb

   When a sample containing copper is heated in the flame of a Bunsen burner, the flame turns a green colour. This is because the _____ in the copper atoms absorb energy and move to _____ energy levels and then _____ light that corresponds to a green colour as they return to _____ energy levels.

2. Explain what an emission spectrum is.

3. Match each component of an AAS with its corresponding description.

Component	Description
flame	selects a specific wavelength of light
hollow-cathode lamp	measures the amount of light
computer	produces light with wavelengths that are absorbed by the metal being analysed
monochromator	where the sample is sprayed and light is absorbed
detector	converts the amount of light detected into the amount of light absorbed by the sample

4. Which one of the following best describes the elements that can be analysed by AAS?

   A all elements
   B all metal elements
   C most metal elements
   D most non-metal elements

5. a Plot a calibration curve using the absorbance readings of the standard solutions containing potassium given below.

Concentration of potassium ($mg\,L^{-1}$)	Absorbance
0.0	0.01
2.0	0.08
4.0	0.15
6.0	0.21

   b Use the calibration curve you created in part **a** to determine the concentration of potassium, in $mg\,L^{-1}$, in a sample solution that gives an absorbance of 0.17.

6. State whether each of the following statements is true or false.

   a An emission spectrum is caused by electrons returning from an excited state.
   b An absorption spectrum is caused by electrons returning from an excited state.
   c The same lamp can be used in atomic absorption spectroscopy for a range of metals.
   d Calibration curves can be used with atomic absorption spectroscopy.
   e The units of concentration used in atomic absorption spectroscopy must be $mg\,L^{-1}$.

7. Most calibration curves are straight lines with a positive gradient. What is the significance of this fact?

Chapter review

KEY TERMS

absorbance
analyte
artesian basin
atomic absorption
  spectroscopy
atomic emission
  spectroscopy
Beer–Lambert law
bore water
calibration curve
colorimeter
complementary colours
complex ion

complexation
conductometric titration
electrical conductivity
electromagnetic radiation
electromagnetic spectrum
emission spectrum
equivalence point
eutrophication
excited electron
gravimetric analysis
ground state
groundwater
hard water

hardness
heavy metal
ligand
line spectrum
metal complex
mineral
molar absorption
  coefficient
molar absorptivity
monochromator
precipitate
precipitation reaction
qualitative

quantitative
salinity
spectroscopy
standard solution
stoichiometry
UV–visible
  spectrometer
water cycle

REVIEW QUESTIONS

1 Maintaining fresh supplies of water is a major concern in society. Mercury, phosphate and ammonium ions all contribute to the salts present in waterways. The concentration of these ions is monitored and controlled.

  a Human activity can increase the concentration of these ions in water. Provide three examples of human activities that lead to the increase in the amount of salts in waterways.

  b How can heavy metal ions, such as mercury, be removed from water samples?

2 Mineral levels differ across New South Wales. List two examples of regions where levels of a particular mineral are higher than average.

3 A student wishing to detect the presence of Ag^+ ions in water adds a solution of NaBr to the water sample. A light yellow precipitate forms.

  a If Ag^+ ions are present, what will the chemical formula of the precipitate be?

  b Write an ionic equation for the reaction occurring.

  c Is this test conclusive? Explain your answer.

4 Figure 15.2.3a on page 416 shows a flame test being performed.

  a What colour would the flame be if copper were present in the sample?

  b Before performing the test, it is necessary to heat the wire strongly for several minutes. Why?

  c Why would copper wire be unsuitable for use in flame tests?

  d Why are flame tests not used for qualitative analysis by modern chemists?

5 The following figure shows a compound that can form when concentrated HCl is added to a copper(II) sulfate solution.

$$\left[\begin{array}{c} Cl \\ Cl - Cu - Cl \\ Cl \end{array} \right]^{2-}$$

  a What name is given to compounds such as the one shown?

  b What is the ligand present?

  c Complete the equation for the formation of this compound:

$$Cu^{2+}(aq) + \underline{\hspace{2cm}} \rightleftharpoons \underline{\hspace{2cm}}$$

  d Explain how the formation of this compound could be used in qualitative analysis.

6 HCl solution is added to a solution containing a metal ion. There is no reaction. When excess ammonia is added, a white precipitate forms. Deduce the likely identity of the metal ion.

7 For each amount given, calculate the amounts, in mol, of the other reactants and products required for a complete reaction according to the following equation:

$3Ca(NO_3)_2(aq) + 2Na_3PO_4(aq) \rightarrow Ca_3(PO_4)_2(s) + 6NaNO_3(aq)$

$Ca(NO_3)_2$	Na_3PO_4	$Ca_3(PO_4)_2$	$NaNO_3$
27 mol			
	0.48 mol		
		0.18 mol	
			2.4 mol

8 A student is given solutions of lead(II) nitrate, copper(II) chloride and barium hydroxide.

   a Name the precipitates that could be formed by mixing together pairs of these solutions. You may need to refer to a solubility table.

   b Write full and ionic equations for each of these reactions.

9 The silver content of a silver alloy is determined by dissolving a sample in nitric acid and precipitating the silver ions as silver chloride. A precipitate of 0.169 g is obtained from a sample with a mass of 0.693 g. Find the percentage by mass of silver in the alloy.

10 A chemist determined the salt content of a sausage roll by precipitating chloride ions as silver chloride. If an 8.45 g sample of sausage roll yielded 0.636 g of precipitate, calculate the percentage by mass of salt in the food. Assume that all the chloride is present as sodium chloride.

11 Water pollution can result from phosphate added to washing powders to improve the stability of their suds. The phosphorus in a 2.0 g sample of washing powder is precipitated as $Mg_2P_2O_7$. The precipitate weighs 0.085 g. What is the percentage by mass of phosphorus in the washing powder?

12 The barium concentration in a solution can be determined by precipitating the barium ions from the solution as barium sulfate and measuring the mass of the precipitate. The result obtained in a particular experiment is higher than it should be. What are some experimental errors that could lead to a high result?

13 A solution is tested for its salinity (NaCl) level. A 20.00 mL aliquot is added to a flask and a few drops of K_2CrO_4 added as an indicator. A solution of 0.084 mol L^{-1} AgNO$_3$ is added to a burette and a titration conducted. The titre obtained is 14.20 mL.

   a Write an ionic equation for the precipitation reaction occurring.

   b Write an ionic equation for the reaction that will act as an indicator for this titration.

   c Use the titre obtained to calculate the salt concentration in the sample.

14 A solution containing barium ions is added to a burette. A 20.00 mL aliquot of 0.14 mol L^{-1} sulfuric acid is added to a beaker under the burette. Electrodes are added to the beaker to allow the conductivity of the beaker contents to be recorded. The conductivity graph obtained during the titration is shown below.

   a Write an ionic equation for the reaction occurring in the beaker.

   b Explain why the conductivity drops initially.

   c Explain why the conductivity rises after the equivalence point.

   d Explain why it is not important to add solution drop by drop near the equivalence point.

   e Calculate the concentration of the barium ions.

15 Label the parts of the diagram of a UV–visible spectrometer in the diagram below.

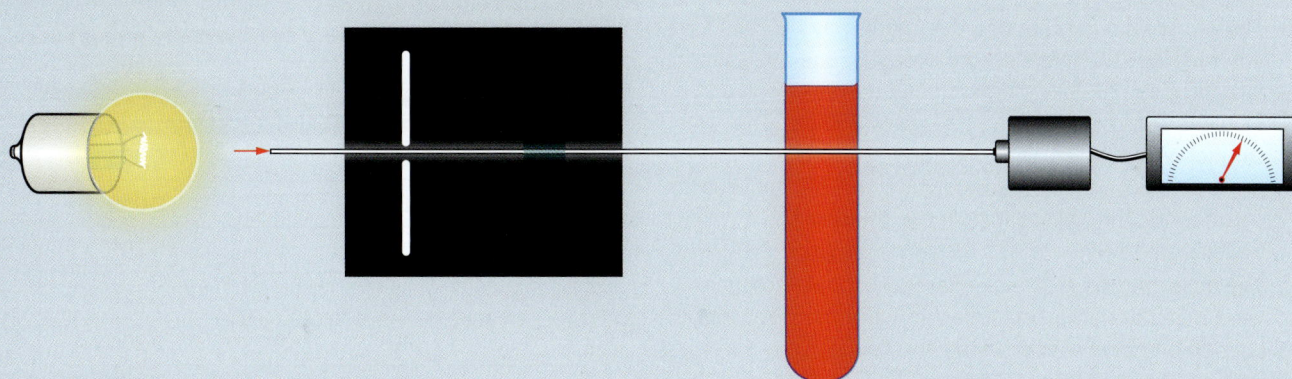

16 A scan of a copper(II) sulfate solution in a UV–visible spectrometer produces the spectrum shown in the graph below.

  a The scan shows the strongest absorption at what wavelength?

  b What colour of light is the solution absorbing?

  c What colour would you observe the solution to be?

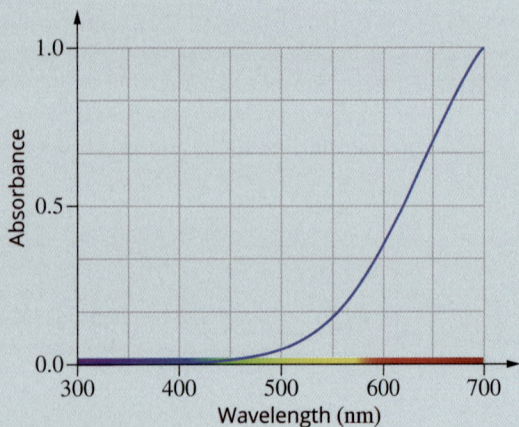

17 Match each component of a UV–visible spectrometer or colorimeter with its function.

Component	Function
detector	selects a range of wavelengths of light
filter	provides ultraviolet and visible light of all wavelengths
light source	transparent container that holds the sample
monochromator	measures the intensity of light
sample cell	displays the absorbance measurement
recorder	allows selection of light of a particular wavelength

18 The phosphate content of a detergent may be analysed by UV–visible spectroscopy. In one analysis, a 0.250 g sample of detergent powder was dissolved in water and the solution made up to 250 mL. The solution was treated to convert any phosphate present to a blue-coloured molybdenum phosphorus compound. The absorbance of the solution at a wavelength of 600 nm was measured as 0.17. The absorbances of five standard phosphate solutions were measured in a similar fashion and the following calibration curve was obtained.

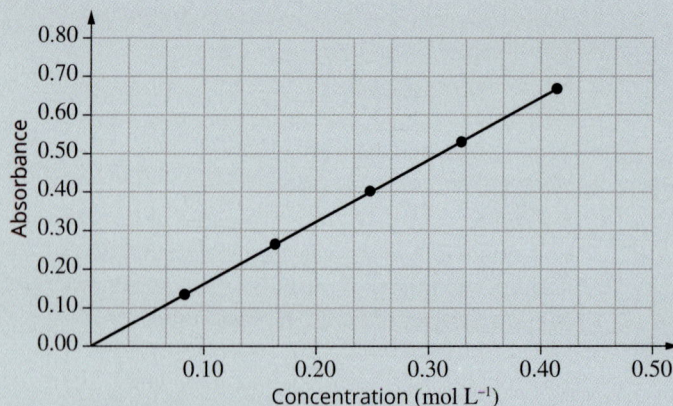

  a What is the concentration of phosphorus in the 250 mL detergent solution?

  b Determine the percentage by mass of phosphorus in the detergent powder.

  c Why was a wavelength of 600 nm selected for this analysis?

19 Decide if each of the following statements is true or false.

  a All visible light has the same wavelength.

  b A blue solution does not absorb orange light.

  c A purple solution will absorb green light.

  d All green solutions absorb the same quantity of purple light.

20 Why does an emission spectrum contain a number of lines of different colours?

21 The basis of the operation of an AAS instrument is that metal atoms can absorb light of certain energies. Where in the instrument does that absorption occur?

22 Compare the analytical techniques of AAS and UV–visible spectroscopy. In what way are they:

  a similar?

  b different?

23 The absorbances of a set of solutions of known concentrations of lead were measured by AAS and are recorded in the table below.

Concentration of lead (mg L^{-1})	Absorbance
0	0.008
10	0.059
20	0.107
30	0.155
40	0.206

  a Draw a calibration curve using this data.

  b From the calibration curve, determine the concentration, in mg L^{-1}, of lead in a sample solution that gives an absorbance of 0.135.

24 Match each analytical technique with a feature of the technique.

Technique	Feature
conductometric titration	The mass of a precipitate is used to determine the concentration of a salt.
atomic emission spectroscopy	A monochromator selects light of an exact wavelength that is strongly absorbed by the sample.
colorimetry	Conductivity is measured while one solution is added to another.
UV–visible spectrometry	A filter is used to select a range of wavelengths of visible light.
gravimetric analysis	A sample is injected into a flame.

25 A solution contains an equal number of moles of aluminium sulfate and sodium sulfate. Barium nitrate is added to precipitate all the sulfate ions as barium sulfate. The mass of barium sulfate (molar mass 233.39 g) obtained is 3.76 g.

  a Complete the equations for the two precipitation reactions occurring:

$$Al_2(SO_4)_3(aq) + 3Ba(NO_3)_2(aq) \rightarrow$$
$$Na_2SO_4(aq) + Ba(NO_3)_2(aq) \rightarrow$$

  b Calculate the number of moles of sulfate ions in the solution.

  c Calculate the number of moles of moles of sulfate provided by the aluminium sulfate and the number of moles of sulfate provided by the sodium sulfate.

26 Gravimetric analysis can be used to determine the mass of Fe^{2+} in a solution. The iron(II) ions can be precipitated from solution by adding a solution of NaOH. The precipitate is filtered, washed and heated until it forms iron(III) oxide.

  a What is the chemical formula of iron(III) oxide?

  b How many moles of iron were present in the solution if 2.4 mol of iron(III) oxide is formed?

  c Will the presence of sodium ions in the solution interfere with the analysis?

27 The Fe^{2+} concentration in a water sample can be determined by colorimetry. The Fe^{2+} ions are first converted to Fe^{3+} ions. Then a solution of SCN^- ions is added to produce a deep red solution.

  a What colour filter should be used for this analysis?

  b What will be the mole ratio for the number of moles of Fe^{3+} determined and the number of moles of Fe^{2+} in the original solution?

  c What steps must be conducted in order to determine the concentration of Fe^{2+} in the sample?

  d What type of lamp would be used to analyse a sample from the Fe^{2+} solution using atomic absorption spectroscopy (AAS)?

28 A solution is thought to contain $CuSO_4$.

  a Outline how you could use precipitation reactions to confirm the presence of Cu^{2+} ions.

  b Outline how you could use precipitation reactions to confirm the presence of SO_4^{2-} ions.

  c What colour flame will this solution produce in a Bunsen burner?

  d What type of lamp would be required to test this solution using atomic absorption spectroscopy?

  e This solution could be titrated against NaOH solution, and the conductivity monitored. Write an ionic equation for the reaction occurring.

  f This solution can form the metal complex $[CuCl_4]^{2-}$ when mixed with HCl solution. Write an equation for this reaction.

29 Reflect on the Inquiry activity on page 408. Using the concepts covered in this chapter, propose an experiment that would distinguish between salt and sugar, other than by melting point.

16 Analysis of organic substances

In previous chapters you were introduced to chemical methods of analysis such as volumetric analysis and gravimetric analysis. You were also introduced to instrumental methods of analysis such as atomic absorption spectroscopy. These methods are based on the chemical and physical properties of substances, and help analytical chemists to determine how much of a substance is present in a sample.

The properties of substances can also be used to determine their identity. Analytical chemists combine their knowledge of the properties of chemicals with instrumental methods to identify and quantify substances. Analytical instruments coupled with computers are fast and accurate and are able to detect and identify very small amounts of complex substances.

There are millions of known organic compounds, with new ones being discovered every day. Chemists use chemical and instrumental techniques to identify these. In this chapter, you will learn about some chemical tests that are used to identify categories of organic compounds. You will also learn about three instrumental techniques used to determine the structure of organic compounds—infrared spectroscopy, nuclear magnetic resonance spectroscopy and mass spectrometry. You will also investigate how data from a combination of these techniques can be interpreted to identify an organic compound and determine its structure.

Content

INQUIRY QUESTION

How is information about the reactivity and structure of organic compounds obtained?

By the end of this chapter, you will be able to:

- conduct qualitative investigations to test for the presence in organic molecules of the following functional groups:
  - carbon–carbon double bonds
  - hydroxyl groups
  - carboxylic acids (ACSCH130)
- investigate the processes used to analyse the structure of simple organic compounds addressed in the course, including but not limited to:
  - proton and carbon-13 NMR
  - mass spectroscopy (ACSCH19)
  - infrared spectroscopy (ACSCH130)

16.1 Chemical tests for functional groups

CHEMISTRY INQUIRY N ICT CCT

Steel ball bearing mass spectrometer

Does the path of a steel ball moving through a magnetic field depend on its mass?

COLLECT THIS ...

- magnet
- rigid sheet of clear plastic
- cardboard
- 3 or 4 steel balls of different sizes
- glass marble
- 4 small wooden or plastic blocks of equal size
- 1 large wooden or plastic block
- water-soluble markers of different colours

DO THIS ...

1 Place the sheet of clear plastic on the four small blocks.
2 Place the magnet underneath the plastic platform.
3 Make a ramp by folding the cardboard into a V shape, and place this on the large block next to the sheet of plastic.
4 Roll the smallest steel ball down the ramp onto the sheet of plastic. If the ball is captured by the magnet you will need to increase its speed by raising the high end of the ramp.
5 Place a mark on the ramp to indicate the release point for the steel ball.
6 Roll the glass marble down the ramp from the release point, and mark where it drops off the platform on the plastic sheet.
7 Demagnetise the largest steel ball by dropping it onto a hard surface.
8 Roll the steel ball down the ramp and mark the point where it falls off the platform.
9 Repeat step 8 several times with the same ball.
10 Repeat steps 7, 8 and 9 with the other steel balls.

RECORD THIS ...

Mark the curved trajectory of each of the steel balls from the point each left the ramp to the point each dropped off the platform on the plastic sheet. Calculate the radius of the curved trajectories of each of the steel balls. (Assume that the trajectories are circular.)

REFLECT ON THIS ...

1 What is the purpose of rolling a glass marble through the magnetic field?
2 Why was it necessary to release the ball from the same point on the ramp?
3 Why is it necessary to demagnetise the steel balls before each trial?
4 Is there a relationship between the radius and the mass of the steel ball?
5 How could you improve the design of this experiment so that it produces a more accurate result?

There are millions of known organic compounds. When chemists analyse organic compounds, they carry out chemical tests to identify any functional groups that might be present. In this section you will investigate chemical tests that are used to identify the presence of carbon–carbon double bonds and hydroxyl and carboxylic acid functional groups.

TESTING FOR THE PRESENCE OF A CARBON–CARBON DOUBLE BOND

You will recall from Chapter 9 that carbon–carbon double bonds are found in the group of compounds called alkenes. The structure of some alkenes are shown in Figure 16.1.1.

GO TO ➤ Section 9.1 page 252

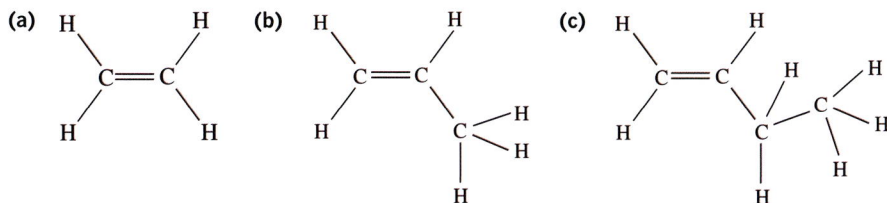

FIGURE 16.1.1 The structural formula of some common alkenes: (a) ethene, (b) propene and (c) but-1-ene

The presence of a carbon–carbon double bond can be detected using bromine water, which is a mixture of bromine (Br$_2$) and water. Bromine dissolved in an organic solvent such as hexane can also be used. Bromine has a characteristic orange-red colour which becomes clear when it is added to an alkene as shown in Figure 16.1.2.

This reaction is an example of an addition reaction in which the carbon–carbon double bond is broken and a bromine atom is added to each of the carbon atoms in the carbon–carbon double bond.

FIGURE 16.1.2 Bromine changes colour when it reacts with an alkene.

The reaction of ethene (C$_2$H$_4$) with bromine to form 1,2-dibromoethane (CH$_2$BrCH$_2$Br) is shown in Figure 16.1.3.

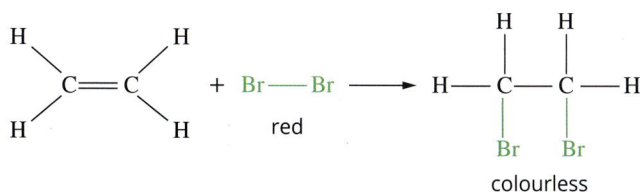

FIGURE 16.1.3 The addition reaction of ethene with bromine can be used as a test for the presence of carbon–carbon double bonds.

These tests do not distinguish between alkene isomers such as the butene isomers shown in Figure 16.1.4. The spectroscopic techniques that can be used to distinguish between specific isomers are discussed in other sections of this chapter.

ℹ The bromine test is used to detect the presence of a carbon–carbon double bond.

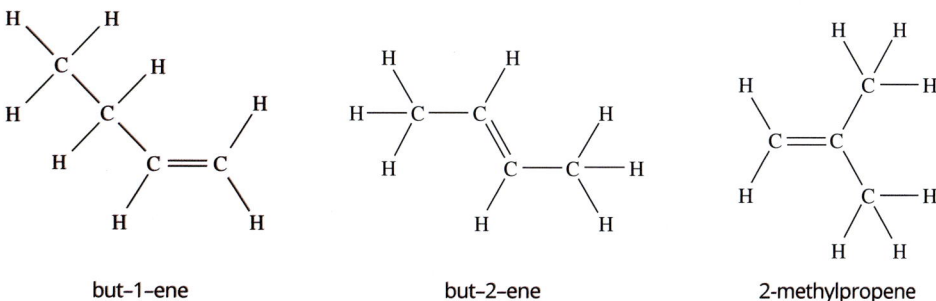

FIGURE 16.1.4 The bromine test does not distinguish between the butene isomers.

GO TO ➤ Section 9.4 page 278

FIGURE 16.1.5 There is vigorous effervescence when solid sodium hydrogen carbonate is added to a carboxylic acid.

GO TO ➤ Section 12.1 page 320

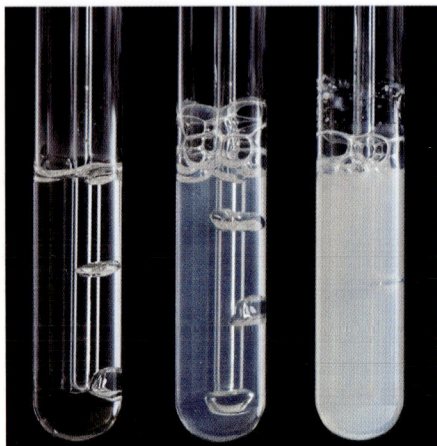

FIGURE 16.1.6 When carbon dioxide is bubbled through limewater, the limewater turns cloudy.

TESTS FOR THE PRESENCE OF THE CARBOYXL FUNCTIONAL GROUP

Carboxylic acids are weak acids that contain the carboxyl (–COOH) **functional group**. A characteristic property of acids is their reaction with carbonate salts. This property is used to test for the presence of the carboxyl functional group.

When sodium hydrogen carbonate is added to a carboxylic acid such as a solution of ethanoic acid, a bubbling or effervescence is observed as carbon dioxide gas is produced (Figure 16.1.5).

$$CH_3COOH(aq) + NaHCO_3(s) \rightarrow NaCH_3COO(aq) + CO_2(g) + H_2O(l)$$

The presence of carbon dioxide can be confirmed using the limewater test. Limewater turns cloudy when carbon dioxide is bubbled through it (Figure 16.1.6).

Other reactions of carboxylic acids can also be used as a chemical test for the presence of carboxylic acids; for example, reactions with indicators and esterification reactions with alcohols. Each combination of an organic acid and alcohol produces an ester that has a characteristic fruity odour.

> ℹ Reactions with carbonates, indicators and alcohols can be used to detect the carboxyl functional group (–COOH).

The carbonate and indicator tests can be used to detect both inorganic and organic acids. The esterification reaction occurs between an organic acid and an alcohol in the presence of concentrated sulfuric acid.

TESTS FOR THE PRESENCE OF THE HYDROXYL FUNCTIONAL GROUP

The chemistry of alcohols was discussed in Chapter 12. You will recall that alcohols have the hydroxyl (–OH) functional group.

The presence of the hydroxyl functional group can be detected by reacting a dry sample with a small piece of metallic sodium. Sodium methoxide ($NaCH_3O$) and hydrogen gas (H_2) are produced in this reaction (Figure 16.1.7).

$$CH_3OH(l) + Na(s) \rightarrow NaCH_3O(l) + H_2(g)$$

The alcohol must not contain any water, because sodium metal reacts violently with water.

FIGURE 16.1.7 Hydrogen bubbles rise gently to the surface when sodium metal reacts with an alcohol. The rate of reaction between alcohols and sodium metal is slower than the rate of reaction between sodium and water.

You will recall from Chapter 9 that some alcohols can exist as isomers. For example, there are four different alcohols that have the molecular formula $C_4H_{10}O$. These isomers are classified as primary, secondary or tertiary alcohols, depending on the position of the hydroxyl group within the molecule (Figure 16.1.8).

GO TO ► Section 9.3 page 271

ⓘ The sodium test is used to detect the presence of the hydroxyl functional group in alcohols.

$$CH_3—CH_2—CH_2—CH_2—OH$$
butan-1-ol
(a primary alcohol)

$$CH_3—CH—CH_2—OH$$
$$|$$
$$CH_3$$
2-methylpropan-1-ol
(a primary alcohol)

$$CH_3—CH_2——CH—CH_3$$ with OH above
butan-2-ol
(a secondary alcohol)

$$CH_3——C——CH_3$$ with OH above and CH_3 below
2-methylpropan-2-ol
(a tertiary alcohol)

FIGURE 16.1.8 Although the molecular formula of each these alcohols is $C_4H_{10}O$ their structural formulae are different.

Chemical tests to distinguish between primary, secondary and tertiary alcohols

Chemical tests can also be conducted to determine whether an alcohol is a primary, secondary or tertiary alcohol. As you discovered in Chapter 12, primary and secondary alcohols can be oxidised by solutions of either acidified potassium dichromate or acidified potassium permanganate.

A primary alcohol is first oxidised to an aldehyde. The aldehyde is further oxidised to a carboxylic acid if excess oxidising agent is used (Figure 16.1.9). Secondary alcohols are oxidised to ketones (Figure 16.1.10). Tertiary alcohols are not oxidised by acidified dichromate or permanganate solutions.

$$CH_3CH_2CH_2CH_2OH \xrightarrow{\text{acidified oxidising agent}} CH_3CH_2CH_2CHO \xrightarrow{\text{acidified oxidising agent}} CH_3CH_2CH_2COOH$$
butan-1-ol   butanal   butanoic acid

FIGURE 16.1.9 Equations for the oxidation of butan-1-ol, a primary alcohol

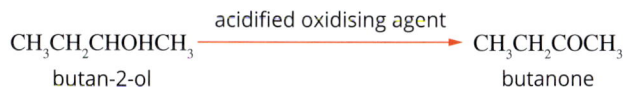

$$CH_3CH_2CHOHCH_3 \xrightarrow{\text{acidified oxidising agent}} CH_3CH_2COCH_3$$
butan-2-ol   butanone

FIGURE 16.1.10 The secondary alcohol butan-2-ol is oxidised to butanone in the presence of an acidified oxidising agent.

These strong oxidising agents are both highly coloured due to the presence of the transition metal elements chromium (Cr) and manganese (Mn). A solution of dichromate ions in water is orange. When this acidified dichromate solution is used to oxidise a primary or secondary alcohol, the dichromate is reduced to the chromium ion (Cr^{3+}), which is green. This colour change from orange to green can be used as a qualitative test to indicate that oxidation of an organic compound has taken place. The colour changes observed for the reaction of primary, secondary and tertiary alcohols with potassium dichromate are shown in Figure 16.1.11.

FIGURE 16.1.11 Solutions of the primary alcohol propan-1-ol and secondary alcohol propan-2-ol with acidified potassium dichromate change from orange to green on heating. Tertiary alcohols such as 2-methylpropan-2-ol will not react under these conditions, so no colour change is observed.

A solution of acidified potassium permanganate reagent is a deep purple colour. When this solution reacts with primary or secondary alcohols, the permanganate ion (MnO_4^-) is reduced to Mn^{2+}, which is colourless. Tertiary alcohols do not react so there is no change in the colour of the solution (Figure 16.1.12).

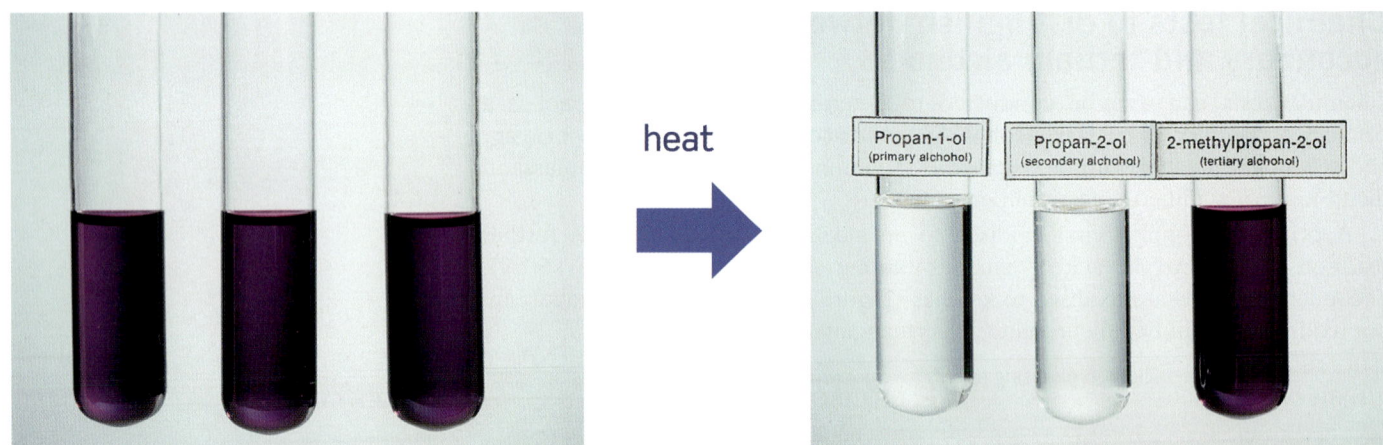

FIGURE 16.1.12 The strong oxidising agent potassium permanganate is deep purple in colour. On reaction with primary and secondary alcohols, the colour changes from purple to colourless. The tertiary alcohol is resistant to oxidation under these conditions and does not react, so the solution does not change colour.

The different rate of reaction between alcohols and solutions of zinc chloride in concentrated hydrochloric acid can alternatively be used to determine if an alcohol is a primary, secondary or tertiary alcohol. This is a substitution reaction resulting in the formation of an alkyl chloride. The alkyl chloride forms a separate layer in the test-tube as it is insoluble in water.

Tertiary alcohols will react immediately with the $ZnCl_2/HCl$ mixture. The reaction with a secondary alcohol may take up to 1 hour. Primary alcohols do not react with the $ZnCl_2/HCl$ mixture at all (Figure 16.1.13).

The results of the various tests for alcohols are summarised in Table 16.1.1.

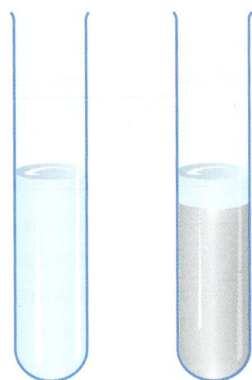

FIGURE 16.1.13 Primary alcohols (left) do not react with a $ZnCl_2/HCl$ mixture. Secondary alcohols (right) react slowly while tertiary alcohols react quickly. Both secondary and tertiary alcohols form a cloudy layer at the bottom of the test-tube.

ⓘ The acidified dichromate or permanganate test and the zinc chloride/concentrated hydrochloric acid test are used to distinguish between primary, secondary and tertiary alcohols.

TABLE 16.1.1 Results of tests for alcohols

Alcohol	Reaction with:			
	Na metal	$H^+/Cr_2O_7^{2-}$ solution	H^+/MnO_4^- solution	$ZnCl_2/HCl$ mixture
primary	production of hydrogen gas	colour change from orange to green	colour change from purple to colourless	no reaction
secondary	production of hydrogen gas	colour change from orange to green	colour change from purple to colourless	slow reaction; formation of a separate layer
tertiary	production of hydrogen gas	no reaction	no reaction	fast reaction; formation of a separate layer

PA 8.7   PA 8.7

16.1 Review

SUMMARY

- The characteristic reactions of different classes of organic compounds can be used to determine the class to which a compound belongs.
- Bromine water or bromine dissolved in hexane changes from orange-red to colourless when mixed with a compound that has a carbon–carbon double bond.
- Carboxylic acids react with carbonate or hydrogen carbonate salts, producing carbon dioxide gas. They change the colour of indicators and react with alcohols to form esters with fruity odours.
- Alcohols react with metallic sodium, producing hydrogen gas.
- When primary and secondary alcohols react with acidified dichromate solution, the colour changes from orange to green. Tertiary alcohols do not react

with acidified dichromate solution. Similarly, when primary and secondary alcohols react with acidified permanganate solution, the colour changes from purple to colourless. Tertiary alcohols do not react with acidified permanganate solution.
- Primary alcohols do not react with a mixture of zinc chloride in concentrated hydrochloric acid.
- Secondary alcohols react slowly with a mixture of zinc chloride in concentrated hydrochloric acid. The reaction product forms a separate layer at the bottom of the test-tube.
- Tertiary alcohols react quickly with a mixture of zinc chloride in concentrated hydrochloric acid. The reaction product forms a separate layer at the bottom of the test-tube.

KEY QUESTIONS

1 Describe how you could test if a compound is a carboxylic acid. What results would confirm that the substance being tested is a carboxylic acid?

2 How would you confirm that an unidentified liquid is an alkene?

3 An unknown liquid is thought to be an alcohol.
   a How could you test for the presence of the hydroxyl functional group?
   b Describe how you could determine if the alcohol is a primary, secondary or tertiary alcohol.

4 Bromine water became colourless when mixed with an organic liquid. Bubbles of gas were observed when the same compound was mixed with a solution of sodium hydrogen carbonate. Which functional group or groups are present in the compound? Justify your answer.

16.2 Infrared spectroscopy

INTERACTION OF ELECTROMAGNETIC RADIATION WITH MATTER

All types of spectroscopy use electromagnetic radiation to discover information about materials found around you. Electromagnetic radiation interacts with atoms and molecules. The nature of this interaction depends upon the energy of the radiation. Different types of spectroscopy utilise the effects electromagnetic radiation has on atoms and molecules to provide information about their structure.

The **electromagnetic spectrum** represented in Figure 16.2.1 is divided into different regions of radiation, with different frequencies, wavelengths and energies. Ultraviolet light has short wavelengths with high frequency and energy, while radio waves have long wavelengths and low frequency and energy.

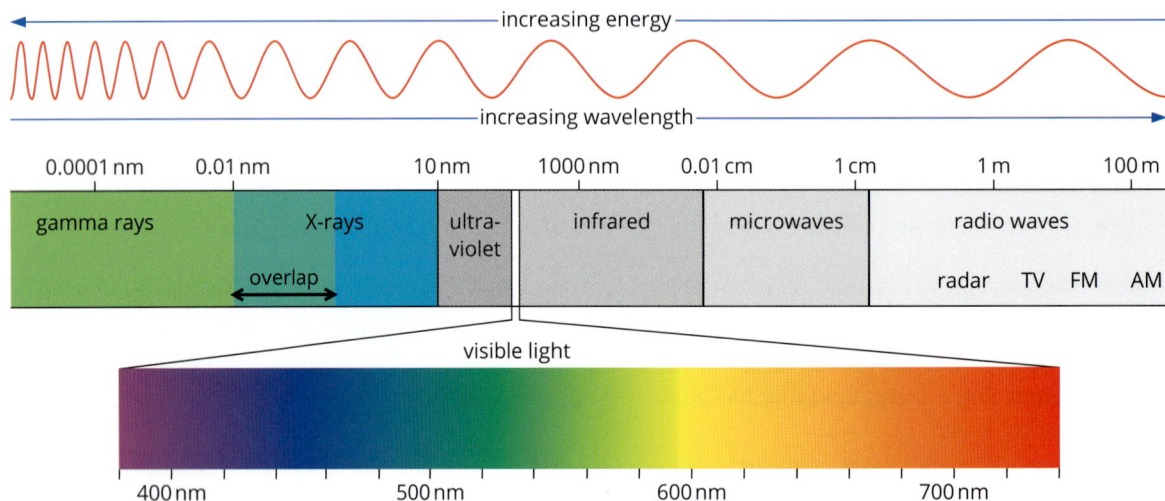

FIGURE 16.2.1 The electromagnetic spectrum, showing the energies, wavelengths and frequencies of the different regions

GO TO ➤ Section 15.5 page 447

Atoms and molecules have different types of energy. The water molecule in Figure 16.2.2 shows four different types of energy in order of increasing energy.

When you studied atomic absorbance spectroscopy in Chapter 15 you learned how electrons in an atom can absorb fixed amounts of energy and move to higher energy levels. In a similar way, molecules can also absorb energy and move to higher electronic, vibrational, rotational and translational energy levels.

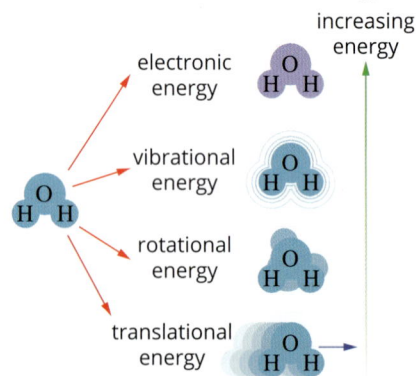

FIGURE 16.2.2 A water molecule has different types of energy.

The measurement of these energy transitions forms the basis of the spectroscopic techniques studied in this course. The electromagnetic radiation associated with some spectroscopic techniques are summarised in Table 16.2.1.

TABLE 16.2.1 Spectroscopic techniques and the regions of the electromagnetic spectrum they use

Spectroscopic technique	Region of the electromagnetic spectrum used	Type of energy level transition
nuclear magnetic resonance (NMR) spectroscopy	radio waves	nuclear spin states—makes the nuclear spin states flip in an applied magnetic field
infrared (IR) spectroscopy	infrared	vibrations of bonds in molecules—makes the bonds bend and stretch
colorimetry, ultraviolet–visible (UV–visible) spectroscopy and atomic absorption spectroscopy (AAS)	visible and ultraviolet	valence electrons in molecules and atoms—makes outer-shell electrons jump to higher energy levels

GO TO ➤ Section 15.4 page 435

GO TO ➤ Section 15.5 page 447

These spectroscopic techniques use the facts that:

- atoms and molecules absorb and emit electromagnetic radiation of specific energies
- atoms and molecules undergo a change when they absorb electromagnetic radiation
- different parts of the electromagnetic spectrum affect atoms or molecules in different ways.

Colorimetry, atomic absorption spectroscopy and UV–visible spectroscopy were covered in Chapter 15. In this and the following sections, you will study the principles of infrared and nuclear magnetic resonance spectroscopy and learn to interpret the respective spectra.

APPLICATIONS OF INFRARED SPECTROSCOPY

Infrared (IR) spectroscopy is a powerful analytical tool that can be applied to the analysis of many organic and inorganic compounds.

IR spectroscopy can be used to analyse solids, liquids and gases. IR spectroscopy is used as a quality control tool in industries such as pharmaceuticals, agriculture, food processing (Figure 16.2.3), paints and drug analysis (Figure 16.2.4). Researchers also combine IR spectroscopy with other techniques to study biological molecules. The technique is used to analyse blood and urine samples and is also used to determine the level of atmospheric pollutants.

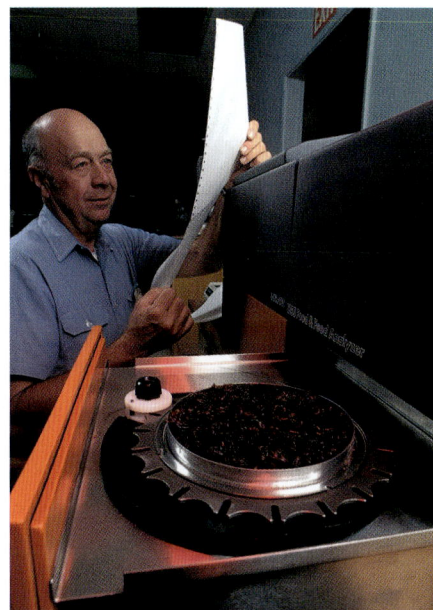

FIGURE 16.2.3 A food chemist uses an infrared spectrometer to evaluate the quality of raisins.

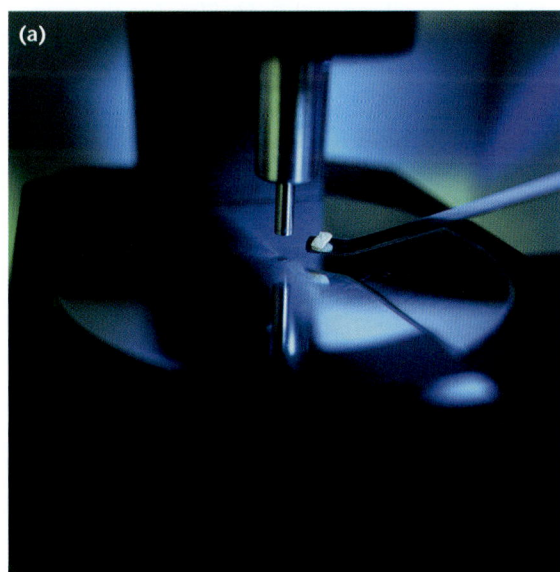

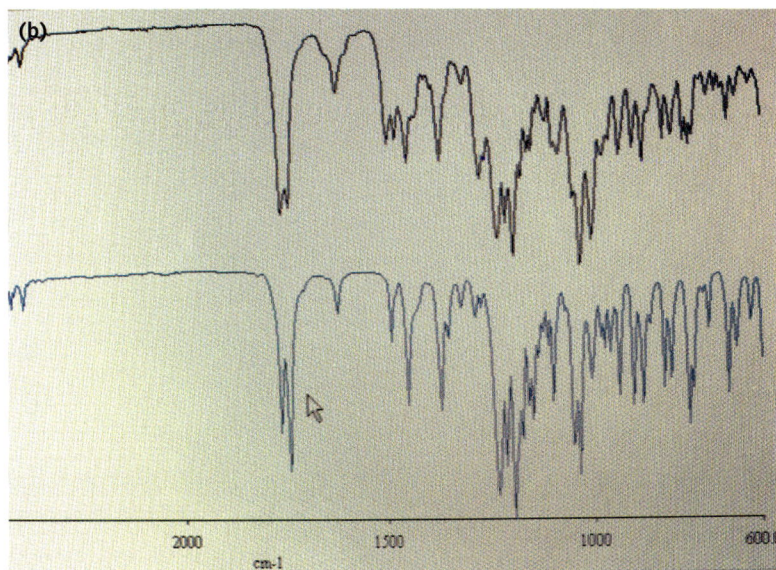

FIGURE 16.2.4 (a) Obtaining the infrared spectrum of a suspected illegal drug. (b) The spectrum of the substance (black) closely matches that of a heroin sample (blue), indicating that the substance contains the illegal drug.

IR spectroscopy is particularly useful because it can give you information about the functional groups present in an organic molecule. This information helps to clarify its structure.

PRINCIPLES OF INFRARED SPECTROSCOPY

IR radiation has a lower energy and a longer wavelength than visible and ultraviolet radiation. The energy from IR radiation is not enough to promote electrons to very high energy levels, but it is enough to change the vibration of the bonds in molecules.

Covalent bonds can be compared to springs that can undergo specific amounts of bending or stretching. The atoms in a molecule can change position because of bending or stretching of the bonds, as shown in Figure 16.2.5, so that the molecule vibrates.

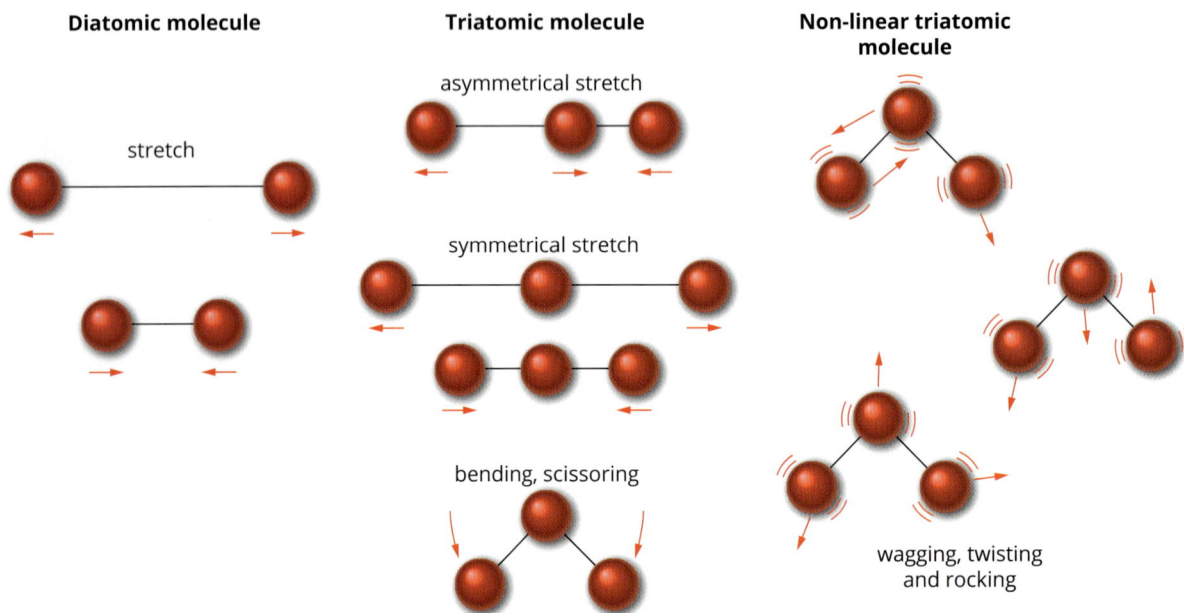

Diatomic molecule　　　**Triatomic molecule**　　　**Non-linear triatomic molecule**

stretch

asymmetrical stretch

symmetrical stretch

bending, scissoring

wagging, twisting and rocking

FIGURE 16.2.5 Stretching and bending motions in diatomic and triatomic molecules

IR spectroscopy exploits the ability of molecules to bend and stretch. Molecules are only able to occupy discrete **vibrational energy levels** (Figure 16.2.6). The amount of energy required to move from one vibrational energy level to the next is the same as the amount of energy contained in electromagnetic radiation from the IR region.

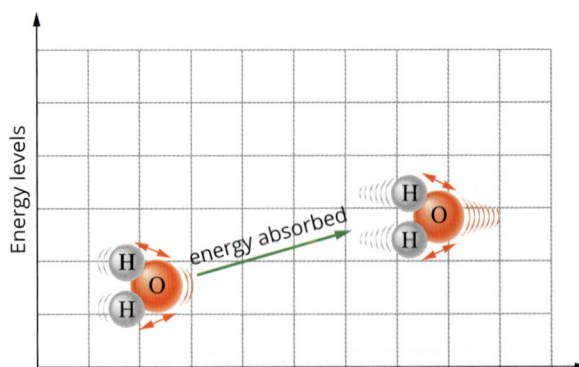

Energy levels

energy absorbed

FIGURE 16.2.6 A molecule can absorb energy and move to a higher vibrational energy level.

IR spectroscopy is a powerful analytical technique because almost all molecules absorb IR radiation. For a molecule to absorb IR radiation, the bending or stretching vibrations must change the overall **dipole** of the molecule.

When molecules absorb infrared radiation, the stretching or bending vibrations of the bonds become more energetic.

The frequency of vibration of the bond between two identical atoms depends on the strength of the bond, as shown in Table 16.2.2. The C−C bond is weaker and absorbs infrared radiation of a lower frequency than that absorbed by the C≡C bond. It is important to realise that the frequency of a vibration is directly proportional to the energy of the vibration. Note that in IR spectroscopy the frequency is expressed as the **wavenumber**, or waves per unit distance, and has the unit cm^{-1}.

TABLE 16.2.2 Bond energy, representing strength of the bond, compared to the wavenumber of infrared light absorbed. The energy of vibration decreases down the table.

Bond	Bond energy (kJ mol^{-1})	Typical absorption wavenumber (cm^{-1})
C≡C	839	2100–2250
C=C	614	1620–1680
C−C	346	750–1100

TABLE 16.2.3 Atomic mass affects the wavenumber of infrared light absorbed. The energy of vibration decreases down the table.

Bond	Typical absorption wavenumber (cm^{-1})
C−H	2850–3300
C−C	750–1100
C−O	1000–1300
C−Cl	600–800
C−Br	500–750

The mass of the atoms attached to a bond also affects the frequency of the IR radiation that will be absorbed. Atoms with higher masses absorb lower frequency radiation. Table 16.2.3 compares the energy absorbed when atoms of different masses are bonded to carbon with a single bond.

Infrared spectroscopy instrumentation

Figure 16.2.7 shows the main components of a simple IR spectrophotometer. These include:

- a source of IR radiation
- a sample and reference cell or disc made of NaCl, KBr or similar; glass and plastic cannot be used as they absorb IR radiation and so are opaque to IR radiation
- a wavelength selector (monochromator)
- an IR detector
- a computer and digital IR spectra data base.

The IR radiation from the source is split into two beams and passed separately through the sample cell and a reference cell. The reference cell is used to discount the effect of the material of the sample cell, the solvent, and any interference from water or carbon dioxide in the atmosphere.

The difference in **transmittance**, or transmitted radiation, between the sample and reference cell is due to the absorption of certain frequencies by the molecules of the sample. These absorptions result in changes in the vibrational energy in the molecule under examination. The signals from the detector are transmitted to a computer which interprets the data and presents this as a graph or spectrum. The information can be compared to the IR information of tens of thousands of compounds stored on large digital data bases enabling the **analyte**, or substance under investigation, to be identified since every substance has a unique IR spectrum.

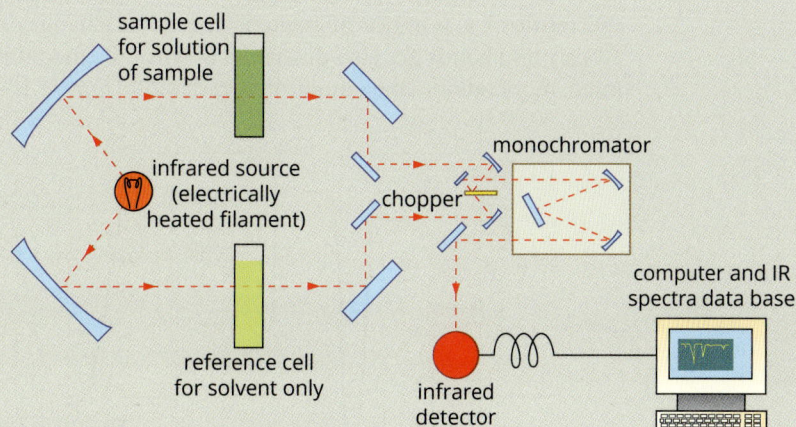

FIGURE 16.2.7 Essential features of a simple IR spectrophotometer

INTERPRETATION OF INFRARED SPECTRA

Features of an infrared spectrum

The frequency of the electromagnetic radiation in IR spectroscopy is usually expressed as wavenumber. The wavenumber is the number of waves per centimetre (cm^{-1}) and is inversely proportional to wavelength. A bond that vibrates at a higher frequency absorbs IR radiation with a higher wavenumber and greater energy than a bond that vibrates at a lower frequency.

The horizontal axis of an IR spectrum shows the wavenumber and the highest wavenumber is usually shown on the left. This axis often has two scales to ensure that all features are visible. For example, in the infrared spectrum of 2-methylpropan-2-ol shown in Figure 16.2.8 the scale starts with intervals of $1000\,cm^{-1}$, then changes to intervals of $500\,cm^{-1}$ in the region below $2000\,cm^{-1}$.

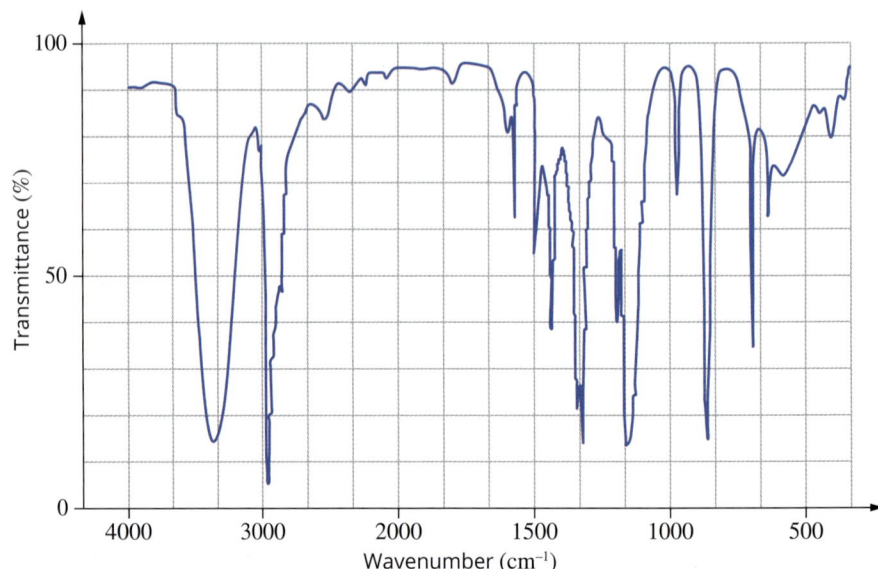

FIGURE 16.2.8 The infrared spectrum of 2-methylpropan-2-ol

The vertical axis of an IR spectrum shows the percentage transmittance. The baseline of the spectrum is where all of the IR radiation (100%) passes through the sample. Where the molecule absorbs IR radiation, the spectrum dips down to a lower transmittance. These **absorption bands** appear as inverted peaks in the spectrum.

Different terms can be used to describe absorption bands in IR spectra. Narrow absorption bands span only a few wavenumbers. This usually means that the peak corresponds to one specific type of molecular vibration. Broader bands may be the result of a number of related vibrational changes that have similar energies. Absorption bands are also described as 'strong', 'medium' or 'weak' if they absorb a large, moderate or small amount of radiation (Figure 16.2.9).

> ℹ The baseline of an infrared spectrum is at the top of the graph, where 100% of the radiation passes through the sample.

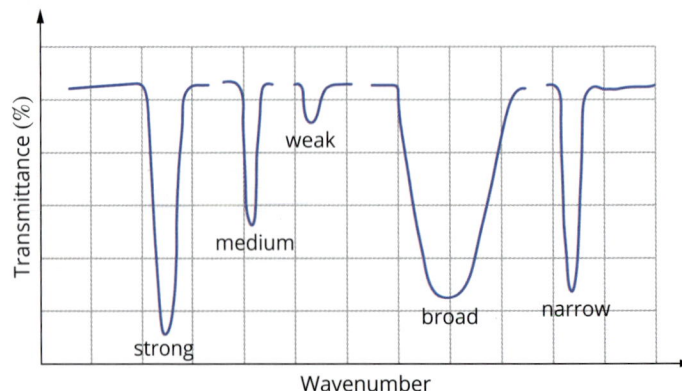

FIGURE 16.2.9 Descriptions used for different shapes and strengths of infrared absorption bands

Absorption bands above about $1400\ cm^{-1}$ are used to identify functional groups, because this region coincides with the energy associated with the characteristic stretching vibrations of the atoms in these groups. The region below $1400\ cm^{-1}$ is called the **fingerprint region** because absorption bands of this frequency tend to be unique to each compound. If a known compound and an unknown compound have the same absorption spectrum below $1400\ cm^{-1}$, they are almost certainly the same.

Interpreting infrared spectra

Each type of bond absorbs IR radiation over a typical range of wavenumbers. For example, it takes energy in the $2850–3300\ cm^{-1}$ region to stretch a C–H bond and energy in the $750–1100\ cm^{-1}$ region to stretch a C–C bond. The characteristic regions of absorption for different bonds in an IR spectrum are shown Figure 16.2.10.

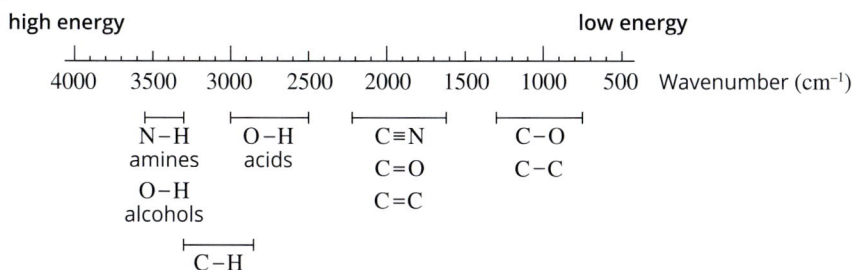

FIGURE 16.2.10 Typical regions for absorption bands from different bonds in the infrared spectrum

When chemists look at the IR spectrum of an unidentified organic compound, they often refer to tables and charts showing the wavenumbers at which the main functional groups absorb. This can give broad clues to the bond types and functional groups present in the molecule. For positive identification, the entire spectrum of an unidentified compound can be compared to a digital data base of spectra, often containing tens of thousands of spectra of known compounds.

The characteristic range for IR absorptions of common functional groups are summarised in Table 16.2.4.

TABLE 16.2.4 Infrared absorption data for some common functional groups

Bond	Wavenumber (cm^{-1})
C–Cl	700–800
C–C	750–1100
C–O	1000–1300
C=C	1620–1680
C=O	1680–1750
C≡N	2220–2260
O–H (acids)	2500–3000 (very broad)
C–H	2850–3300
O–H (alcohols)	3230–3550 (broad)
N–H (amines)	3300–3500

IR spectroscopy can be useful for distinguishing between very similar compounds. Consider the molecules propanoic acid and methyl ethanoate. These two compounds are isomers with the molecular formula $C_3H_6O_2$.

(a)

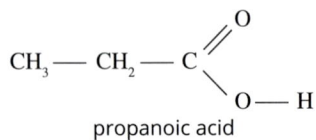

propanoic acid

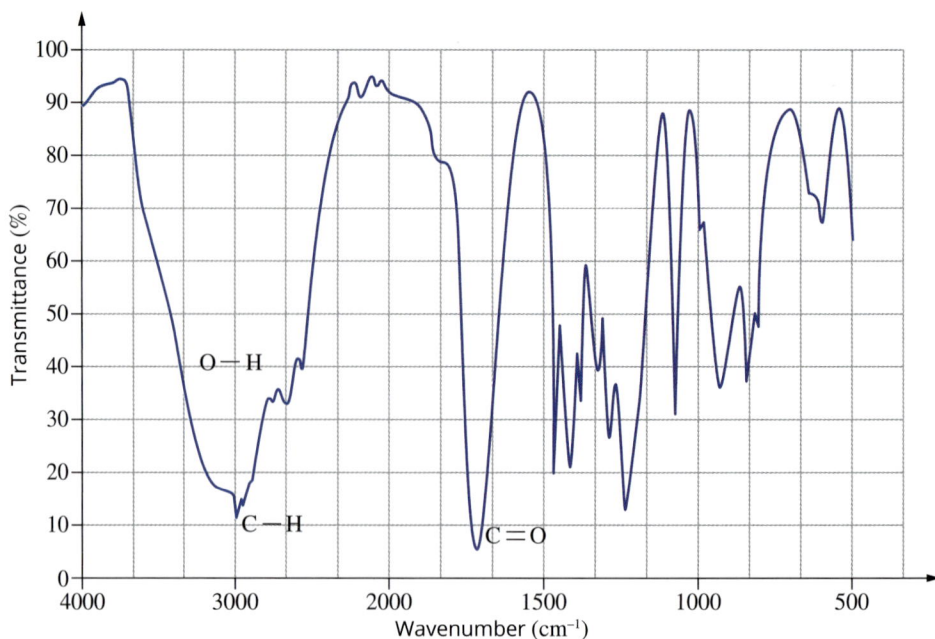

(b)

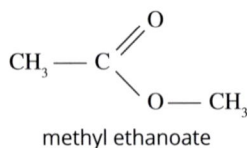

methyl ethanoate

FIGURE 16.2.11 Infrared spectra of (a) propanoic acid and (b) methyl ethanoate

The infrared spectra of these compounds (Figure 16.2.11) have some features in common and some differences. Both spectra have an absorption band at about $1700\,cm^{-1}$ due to the stretching of the carbonyl (C=O) bond. In methyl ethanoate, the narrow absorption band at around $3000\,cm^{-1}$ is due to the C–H bonds. In propanoic acid, the broad absorption band from $2700\,cm^{-1}$ to $3600\,cm^{-1}$ is due to the O–H bond in its carboxyl group. This very broad absorption band partly masks the absorption due to C–H bonds that are also present in this spectrum.

Using the data in Table 16.2.4 (page 473), you can identify the bonds that are likely to be present in an unidentified compound from their characteristic absorption bands. This information allows you to determine which of the main functional groups are present. The IR spectrum can also be used to prove that a functional group is not present, helping you to narrow down the possible structure of the compound.

> **ℹ** Different types of covalent bonds absorb IR radiation within a characteristic range of frequencies (wavenumbers), allowing the functional groups in an organic compound to be identified.

Worked example 16.2.1

INTERPRETING THE INFRARED SPECTRUM OF AN UNIDENTIFIED COMPOUND

Use the following infrared spectrum of an unidentified compound to identify the functional groups present. The molecular formula of the compound is $C_2H_4O_2$. You will need to refer to the IR absorption data in Table 16.2.4 (page 473).

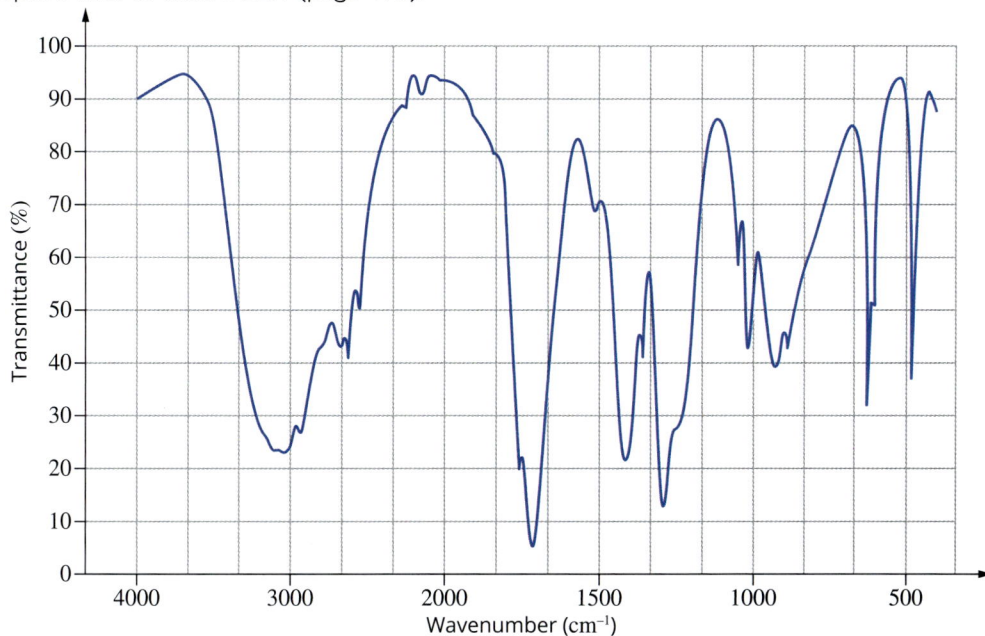

Thinking	Working
Identify the absorption bands that correspond to the absorption bands of bonds in the IR absorption data table.	There is a strong, narrow band at approximately $1700\,cm^{-1}$, which corresponds to the absorption by a carbonyl group (C=O).
	The strong, broad band centered at about $3000\,cm^{-1}$ corresponds to the absorption by the O–H bond of a carboxylic acid.
Identify the functional group or groups that are present.	The spectrum shows absorption bands corresponding to the presence of C=O and carboxylic acid O–H bonds.
	This suggests the presence of a carboxyl functional group (–COOH).
	From the molecular formula, it can be concluded that the compound is ethanoic acid (CH_3COOH).

INTERPRETING THE INFRARED SPECTRUM OF AN UNKNOWN COMPOUND

Use the infrared spectrum of an unidentified compound to identify the functional groups present. The molecular formula of the compound is C_3H_6O. You will need to refer to the IR absorption data in Table 16.2.4 (page 473).

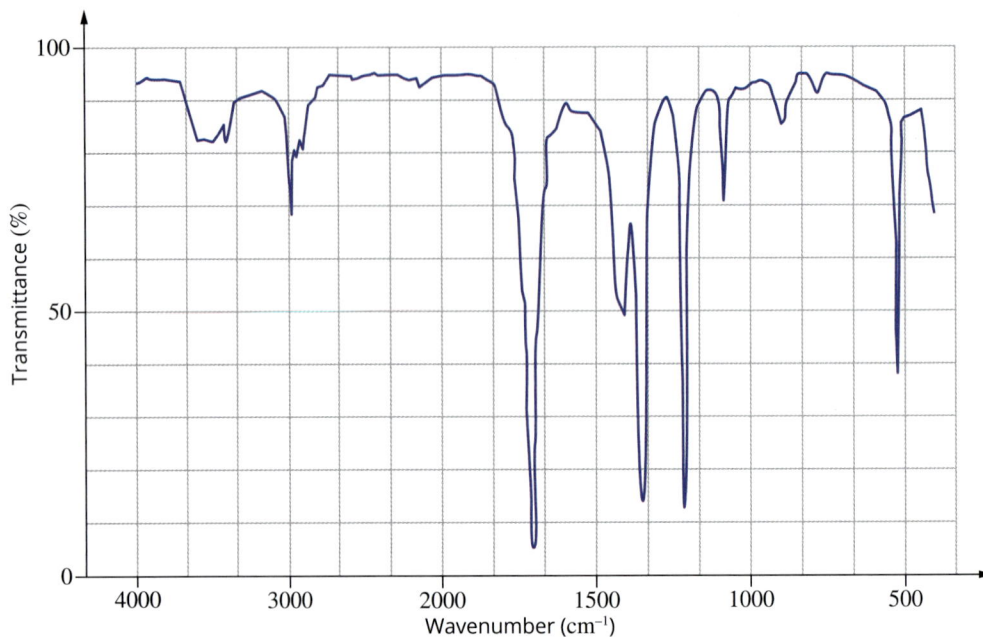

INFRARED SPECTROSCOPY AND QUANTITATIVE ANALYSIS

In Chapter 15 you saw that UV–visible spectroscopy can be used to determine the concentration of a solution by comparing its **absorbance** at a specific wavelength to the absorbance of solutions of known concentrations. In a similar way, the amount of light absorbed by a particular bond in an IR spectrum is directly related to the amount of the compound being tested. This means IR spectroscopy can be used for **quantitative** analysis. Measurements of the concentrations of toxic gases in the atmosphere, such as sulfur dioxide and hydrogen cyanide, are often carried out by infrared spectroscopy.

In practice, a molecule can be analysed in this way if its spectrum contains a strong sharp peak. As with other spectroscopic techniques, a **calibration curve** is constructed by using standards of known concentration. The concentration of the sample is found by comparison with the calibration curve. Unfortunately, the correlation of absorbance to concentration is not always reliable because the calibration curves obtained from IR absorbances are often significantly curved rather than linear.

WS
8.5

Infrared spectroscopy and breath tests

If a roadside breath test (Figure 16.2.12) indicates that a driver is over the legally allowed blood alcohol limit, the driver must undergo a second test. In the second test the driver breathes into the cell of an IR spectrophotometer. The absorption bands due to C–O, O–H and C–H bonds are measured to determine the ethanol concentration.

If the reading is above the legal limit, or the driver is unable to provide a breath test, a blood or urine sample may be taken for testing by other analytical methods.

There has been a significant drop in the road toll since the introduction of breath testing. There is a general acknowledgement in the community that it is unacceptable to drive while over the blood alcohol limit.

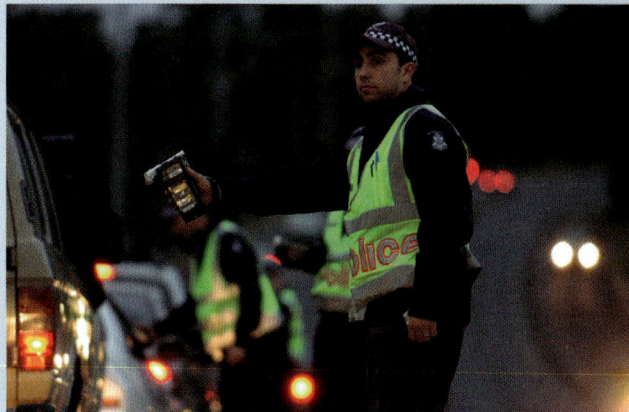

FIGURE 16.2.12 A police officer conducting a roadside breath test.

16.2 Review

SUMMARY

- Matter interacts with electromagnetic radiation in different ways depending on the energy of the radiation.
- Molecules have discrete vibrational energy levels. The absorption of IR radiation causes molecules to move to higher vibrational energy levels.
- Different types of covalent bonds absorb IR radiation within a characteristic range of frequencies (wavenumbers), allowing the functional groups in an organic compound to be identified.

- Each compound has a unique absorbance pattern in the fingerprint region of the IR spectrum and this can be used to identify the compound.
- IR spectroscopy can also be used in quantitative analysis.

KEY QUESTIONS

1   What kind of energy level transition is caused by the absorption of:
    a   infrared radiation?
    b   ultraviolet radiation?
    c   visible radiation?

2   Refer to Figure 16.2.1 (page 468). What parts of the electromagnetic spectrum does radiation with the following wavelengths belong to?
    a $0.94\,cm$
    b $3.5 \times 10^3\,nm$
    c $1.2 \times 10^2\,m$
    d $3.3 \times 10^{-4}\,nm$

3   What are the wavenumber ranges of the absorption bands that you would expect to see from the following functional groups? Use the data provided in Table 16.2.4 and Figure 16.2.10 on page 473 to help you answer this question.
    a   hydroxyl
    b   amide
    c   amine
    d   carboxyl
    e   ester
    f   carbonyl.

4   The absorption bands due to C–O and C–C bonds are often of little help when determining the structure of an unidentified compound, but are valuable in the confirmation of the identity of a known compound. Why is this so?

5   Identify the type of bonds causing the major absorption bands above the fingerprint region (above 1400 cm^{-1}) in the following spectra.

a

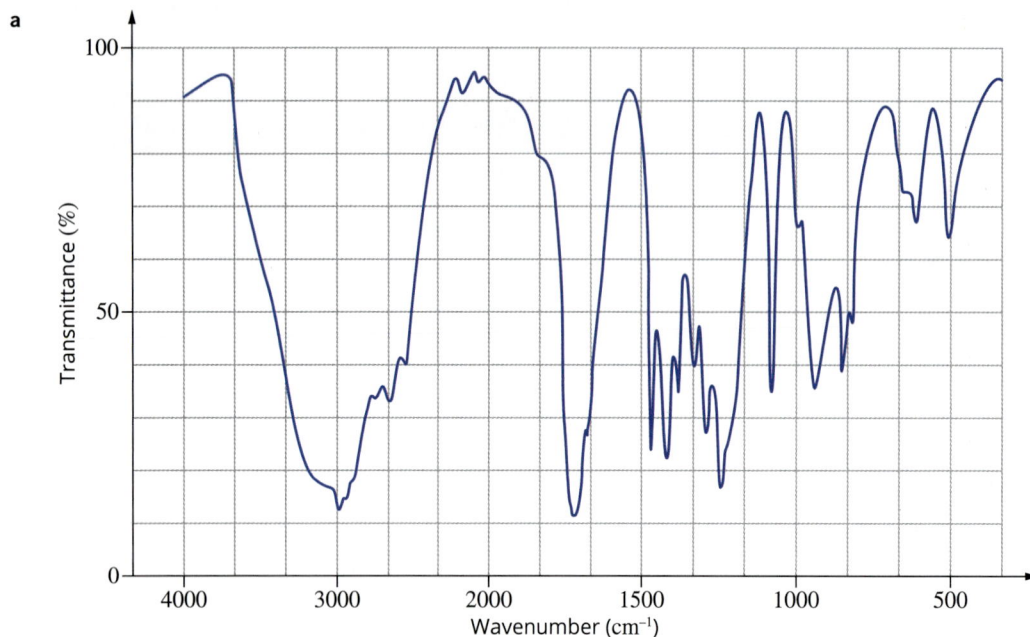

b

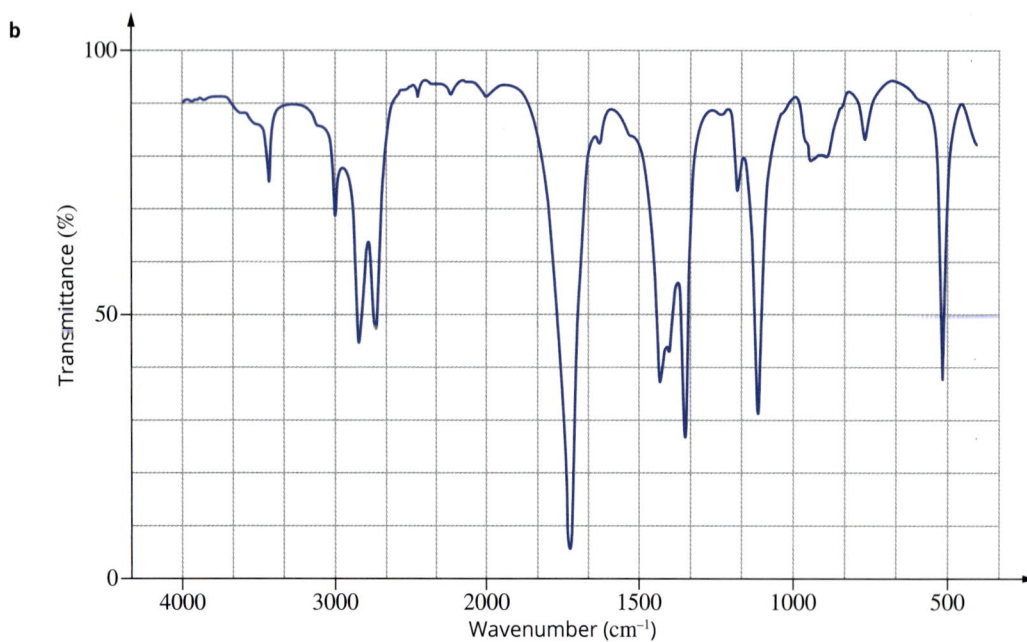

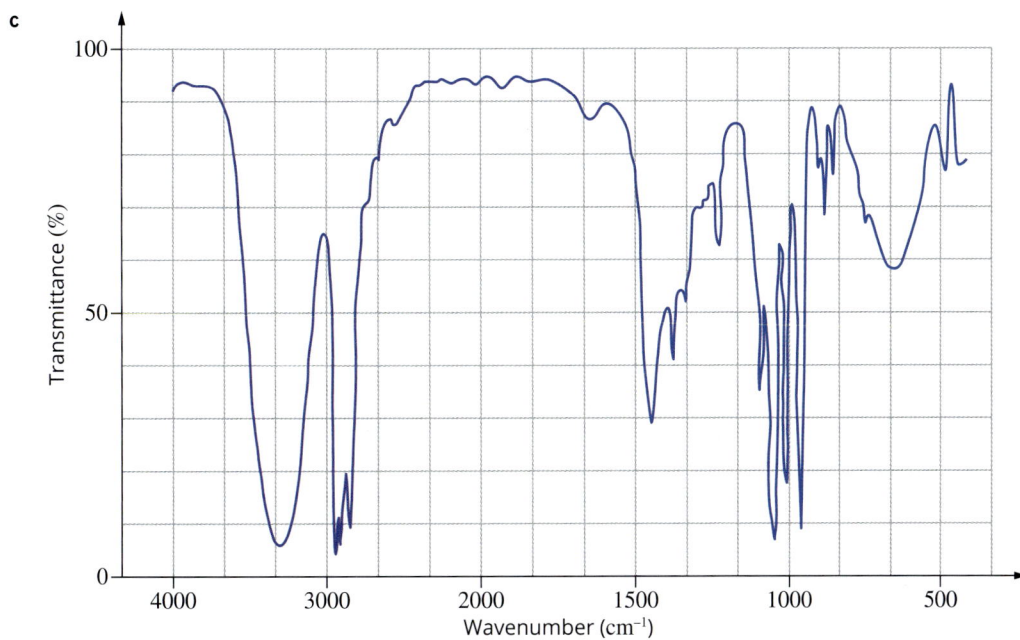

c

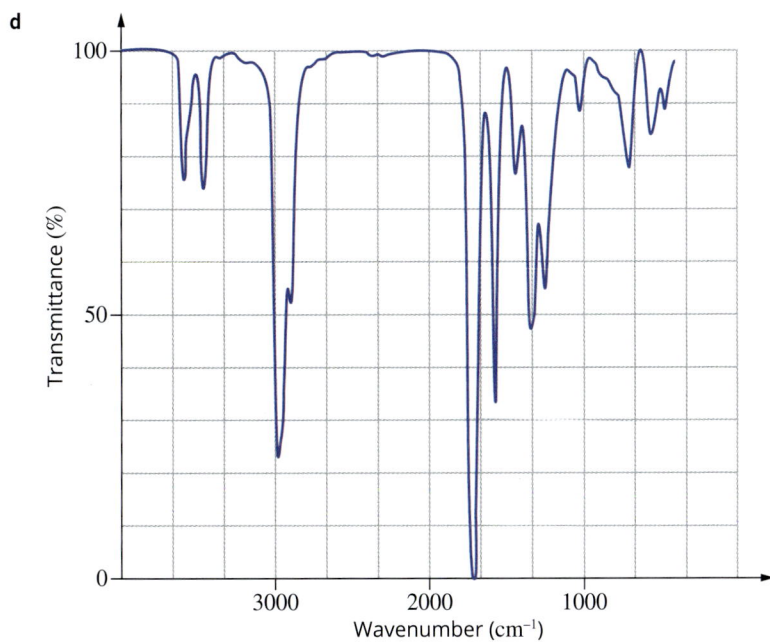

d

16.3 Nuclear magnetic resonance spectroscopy

Nuclear magnetic resonance (NMR) spectroscopy is one of most powerful techniques for determining the structure of complex molecules. NMR spectroscopy is used to distinguish between atoms in a molecule. As you saw in the previous section, IR spectroscopy provides information about which bonds and functional groups are present in a molecule. In combination with IR spectroscopy and other techniques, NMR spectroscopy enables chemists to determine the exact structure of a molecule (Figure 16.3.1).

FIGURE 16.3.1 A research chemist places a sample tube into an NMR spectrometer.

> **i** Atomic number (Z) is the number of protons in a nucleus.
>
> Mass number (A) is the total number of protons and neutrons in a nucleus.

PRINCIPLES OF NUCLEAR MAGNETIC RESONANCE SPECTROSCOPY

NMR spectroscopy uses electromagnetic radiation in the radio frequency range to obtain information about the structure of molecules. The energy of the radio waves is too low to cause electronic, vibrational or rotational transitions.

In order to interact with radio waves, the nuclei of the atoms must have a property called **nuclear spin**. Only nuclei that have an odd atomic number (Z) or an odd mass number (A), such as ^{1}H, ^{13}C, ^{14}N and ^{31}P, have a nuclear spin. The odd number of nuclear particles causes these nuclei to behave like tiny bar magnets.

In the presence of an external magnetic field, nuclei with spin can line up either in the same direction as the field (lower energy) or in the opposite direction (higher energy), as shown in Figure 16.3.2. A nucleus with spin that is not aligned with an external field is in an unstable arrangement.

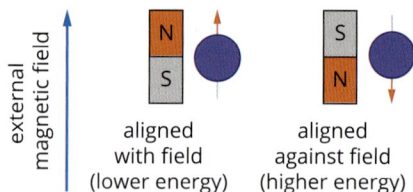

FIGURE 16.3.2 Small magnets and nuclei with spin interact with an external magnetic field.

When nuclei are inside the NMR spectrometer, they are normally in a low-energy state and aligned with a strong magnet. A radio transmitter is used to provide the energy to 'flip' the nuclei into a high-energy state. Over time, the nuclei tend to flip back into a lower-energy spin (Figure 16.3.3). As they do, they release a pulse of energy, which is measured and displayed in graphical form as an **NMR spectrum**.

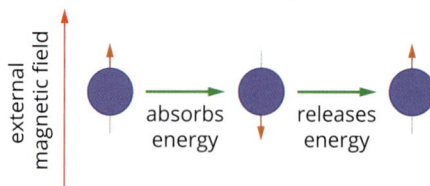

FIGURE 16.3.3 Absorption and release of energy as a nucleus changes spin

The difference in energy between the higher and lower energy spin states depends on the type of nucleus and the chemical environment surrounding the nucleus.

A common type of NMR spectroscopy, called **carbon-13 NMR spectroscopy**, examines the ^{13}C nucleus and is useful in investigating the carbon atoms inside organic molecules. The most common form of NMR spectroscopy is based on the hydrogen-1 (^{1}H) nucleus. This nucleus contains one proton and no neutrons. This type of spectroscopy is usually called **proton NMR** or ^{1}H NMR spectroscopy. It can give information about the structure of any molecule containing hydrogen atoms.

> **i** A hydrogen nucleus is a proton, so chemists using NMR spectroscopy tend to use the words 'hydrogen' and 'proton' interchangeably.

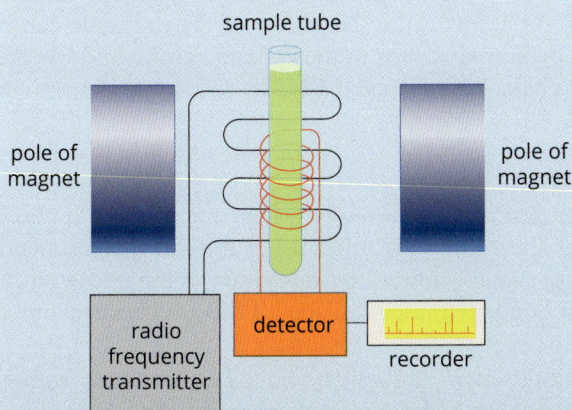
Hydrogen and carbon chemical environments

An NMR spectrum provides information about the number and type of hydrogen and carbon nuclei in an organic compound. Atoms that are in the same chemical environments are called **equivalent** atoms and absorb the same energy and produce a single signal in the NMR spectrum.

A chemical environment consists of the atoms and electrons that surround a specific atom. Inside a molecule, atoms can be said to have the same chemical environment if they are attached in the same way to the same atoms. For example, the simplest organic molecule, methane, contains only one hydrogen environment and one carbon environment and gives only one signal in each of its carbon-13 NMR and proton NMR spectra.

Figure 16.3.5 shows the structures of three organic molecules with their atoms colour-coded to show the different hydrogen and carbon environments.

> **i** The chemical environment of an atom consists of the atoms and electrons that surround it.

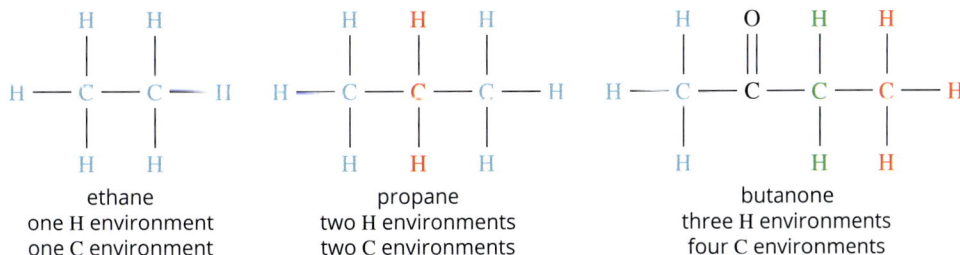

FIGURE 16.3.5 The chemical environments in ethane, propane and butanone. Different colours represent different chemical environments.

The six hydrogen atoms in ethane are in the same environment because each is part of a $-CH_3$ group attached to the other $-CH_3$ group. The two carbon atoms are also in the same environment. As a result, ethane has just one signal in its proton NMR spectrum and one signal in its carbon-13 NMR spectrum.

Propane has two different hydrogen and two different carbon environments. The six hydrogen atoms in the $-CH_3$ groups are all in the same environment, each being part of three hydrogen atoms on a carbon attached to a $-CH_2-$ group. The two hydrogen atoms in $-CH_2-$ make up the second environment, which is different from each of the hydrogen atoms in the $-CH_3$ groups on the ends.

Again, the carbons in the $-CH_3$ groups are equivalent and occupy one environment, but the carbon in the centre occupies a second and different environment. The proton NMR and carbon-13 NMR spectra each show two signals.

Butanone has three different hydrogen environments and four carbon environments. The hydrogen atoms in the two $-CH_3$ groups at either end of the molecule are not equivalent. One group is bonded directly to the carbonyl group, while the other is bonded to the $-CH_2-$ group. The proton NMR spectrum contains three signals. Each of the carbon atoms in the backbone of the molecule can be distinguished from the others by how close it is to the carbonyl group and whether it is on the end or within the chain. The carbon-13 NMR spectrum of butanone contains four different signals.

Chemical shifts

Nuclei emit different frequencies of radio energy when analysed in different spectrometers. To ensure that the results obtained using different experimental conditions are comparable, the signals emitted by nuclei are compared with the signal from a reference compound, tetramethylsilane (TMS). The structure of TMS is shown in Figure 16.3.6.

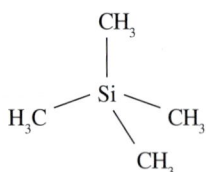

FIGURE 16.3.6 The structural formula of tetramethylsilane (TMS)

Tetramethylsilane is chemically inert and can be added to a sample without causing a chemical reaction. It contains hydrogen atoms, carbon atoms and a silicon atom in a symmetrical arrangement, so it has only one chemical environment in each type of NMR spectroscopy. TMS produces a single peak in both the carbon-13 NMR and proton NMR spectra that is well away from the peaks that are usually of interest.

The difference in energy needed to change spin states in a sample is compared to the energy needed to change spin states in TMS. This energy difference is called the **chemical shift**, and is measured in parts per million (ppm). The chemical shift of TMS is defined as zero. The lowercase Greek letter delta δ (difference) is often used to represent the chemical shift.

The actual magnetic field experienced by the nucleus is not the same as the applied external magnetic field. Electrons around each nucleus also have spin, so they have an associated magnetic field that shields the nucleus from the applied magnetic field. The amount of **nuclear shielding** depends on the other atoms surrounding the nucleus. This in turn affects the amount of energy needed for the nucleus to change its spin.

The energy emitted when the nucleus flips to the lower spin state depends on the amount of nuclear shielding experienced. For example, a carbon atom in a $-CH_2-$ group absorbs at a slightly different frequency than a carbon atom in a $-CH_3$ or $C-OH$ group. Similarly, a hydrogen atom in a $-CH_2-$ group absorbs at a slightly different frequency than a hydrogen atom in a $-CH_3$ or $C-OH$ group. As a consequence, the chemical shift of carbon and hydrogen in each of these groups is different.

CARBON-13 NUCLEAR MAGNETIC RESONANCE SPECTROSCOPY

Carbon-13 is a naturally occurring isotope of carbon that has a nuclear spin. The natural abundance of the carbon-13 isotope is only 1.1%. The most abundant isotope of carbon is carbon-12, which has no spin and is therefore not detected by NMR spectroscopy.

The carbon-13 isotope can be used in NMR spectroscopy to identify different carbon atom environments within a molecule. The chemical shift relative to the TMS reference depends on the chemical environment a carbon atom experiences within a molecule, and ranges from 0 ppm to about 200 ppm (Table 16.3.1).

TABLE 16.3.1 Typical carbon-13 NMR chemical shifts

Type of carbon	Chemical shift (ppm)
$-\overset{\mid}{\underset{\mid}{C}}-\overset{\mid}{\underset{\mid}{C}}-$	5–40
$R-\overset{\mid}{\underset{\mid}{C}}-Cl \text{ or } Br$	10–70
$R-\overset{\mid}{\underset{\parallel}{C}}-\overset{\mid}{\underset{\mid}{C}}-$ (C=O)	20–50
$R-\overset{\mid}{\underset{\mid}{C}}-N\diagdown$	25–60
$-\overset{\mid}{\underset{\mid}{C}}-O-$ alcohols, ethers and esters	50–90
$-C\equiv C-$	75–95
$\diagup^{C}=^{C}\diagdown$	90–150
$R-C\equiv N$	110–125
(benzene ring)	110–160
$R-\overset{\mid}{\underset{\parallel}{C}}-$ (C=O) esters or carboxylic acids	160–185
$R-\overset{\mid}{\underset{\parallel}{C}}-$ (C=O) aldehydes or ketones	190–220

Each carbon environment is represented by a single peak in the spectrum. In the carbon-13 NMR spectrum for chloroethane shown in Figure 16.3.7 on page 484, the two signals represent the two carbon environments.

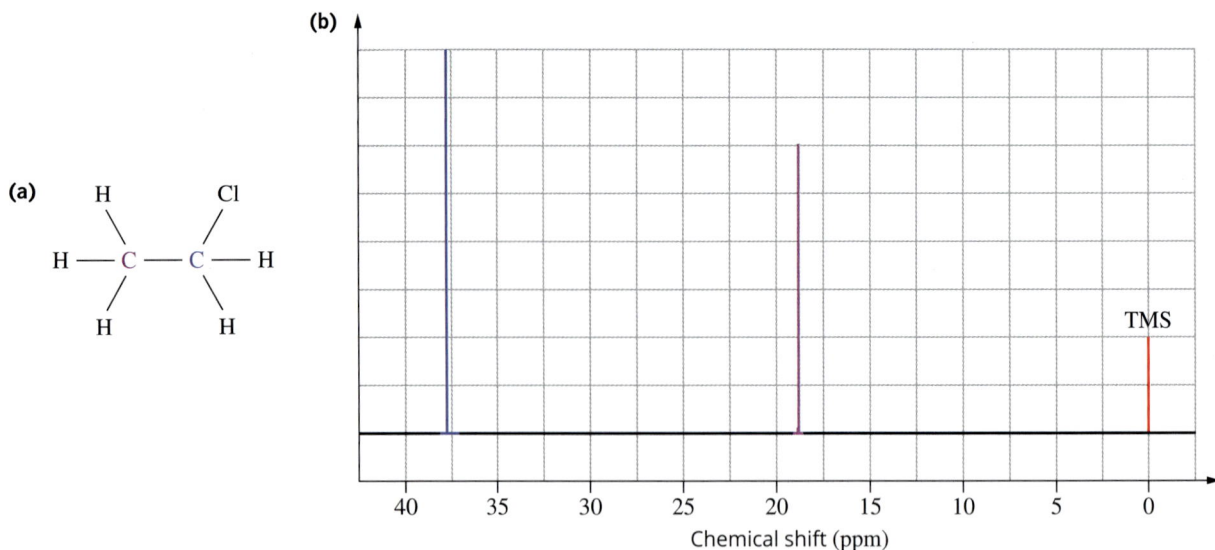

FIGURE 16.3.7 (a) The structure of chloroethane. (b) The carbon-13 NMR spectrum of chloroethane. The colours represent the different carbon environments and their different peaks.

A carbon-13 NMR spectrum provides information about the carbon backbone of an organic molecule.

- The number of peaks indicates the number of different carbon atom environments in the molecule.
- The chemical shift of the peaks helps identify the atoms or group of atoms to which a carbon atom is attached.
- Equivalent atoms generate signals that have the same chemical shift.

INTERPRETATION OF CARBON-13 NUCLEAR MAGNETIC RESONANCE SPECTRA

The structural formula and carbon-13 NMR spectrum of methyl ethanoate (CH_3COOCH_3) are shown in Figure 16.3.8. The spectrum has three peaks, indicating that there are three different carbon environments in the methyl ethanoate molecule. There are no equivalent carbon atoms because the number of peaks in the spectrum is the same as the number of carbon atoms in the formula.

The chemical shifts provide the following information about the atoms or group of atoms to which the carbon atom generating the peak is attached.

- The peak at approximately 170 ppm is generated by the carbon atom in the carbonyl group (C=O).
- The peak at approximately 50 ppm is generated by the carbon atom bonded to an oxygen atom by a single bond in $-O-CH_3$.
- The peak at approximately 20 ppm is generated by the carbon atom in the CH_3 group that is attached to the C=O group.

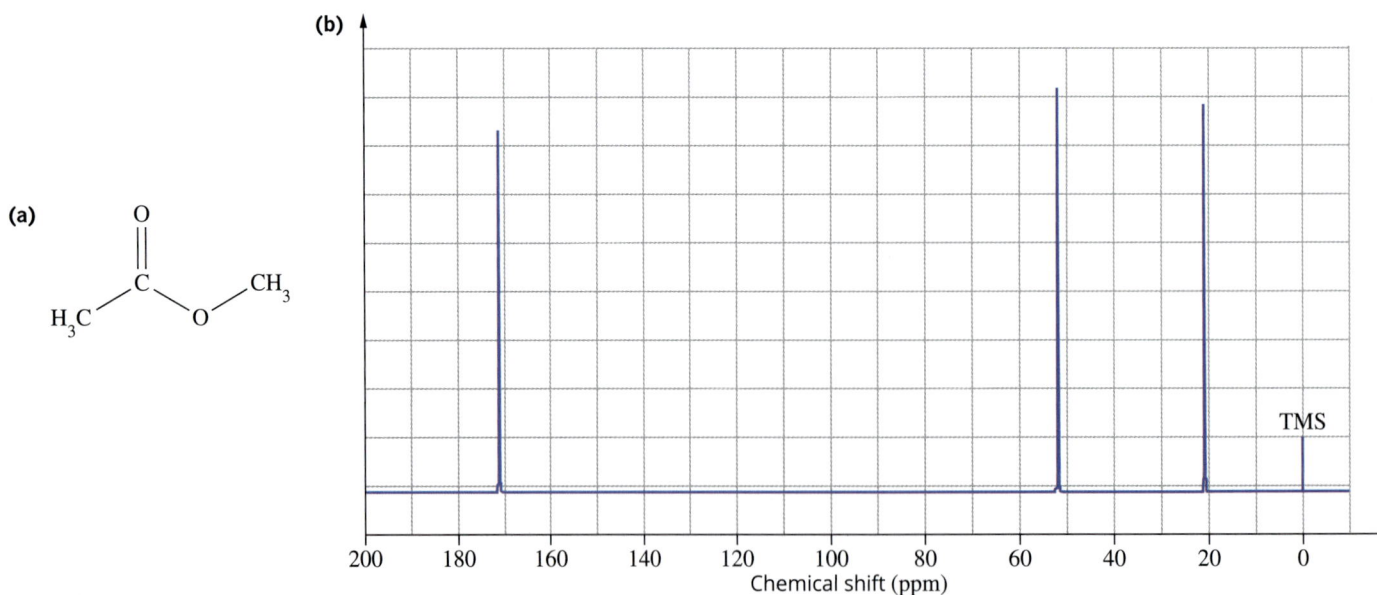

FIGURE 16.3.8 (a) The structural formula and (b) carbon-13 NMR spectrum of methyl ethanoate

Worked example 16.3.1

INTERPRETING A CARBON-13 NUCLEAR MAGNETIC RESONANCE SPECTRUM

The carbon-13 NMR spectrum of an alcohol that has the molecular formula C_3H_8O is shown below. Determine the structure and identity of the alcohol.

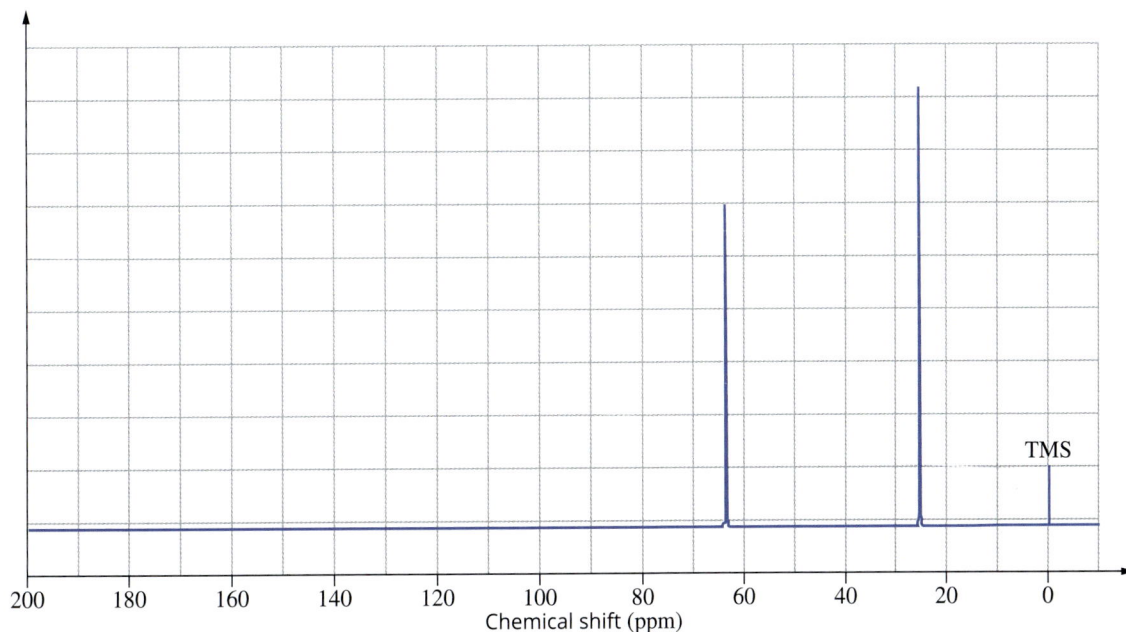

Thinking	Working
What information does the formula provide about the compound?	Two molecules are possible from the formula: propan-1-ol and propan-2-ol.
Identify the number of different carbon environments.	There are two signals so there must be two different carbon environments.
Identify the number of equivalent carbon atoms.	The formula indicates that there are three carbon atoms in a molecule of the compound. The number of peaks indicates that there are two different carbon environments. So there must be two equivalent carbon atoms.
If possible, use the chemical shifts in Table 16.3.1 (page 483) to identify the types of carbon atoms. Remember that the ranges are broad.	The peak at 64 ppm indicates the presence of a carbon atom attached to a hydroxyl group (C–OH). The peak at 25 ppm is generated by the carbon atom in a –CH$_3$ group.
Determine a structure of the compound that is consistent with the information you have gathered. Remember that equivalent carbon atoms generate peaks with the same chemical shift.	The molecular formula of the alcohol is C_3H_8O. The compound is either propan-1-ol or propan-2-ol. The carbon-13 NMR spectrum has two peaks, indicating two unique carbon environments. However, the molecule has three carbon atoms so there must be two carbon atoms that are equivalent. This suggests that there are two identical –CH$_3$ groups in the structure. The structure of the compound consistent with this data is:
Identify the compound.	The compound is propan-2-ol.

Worked example: Try yourself 16.3.1

INTERPRETATING A CARBON-13 NUCLEAR MAGNETIC RESONANCE SPECTRUM

The carbon-13 NMR spectrum of an alcohol that has the molecular formula $C_4H_{10}O$ is shown below. Determine the structure and identity of the alcohol.

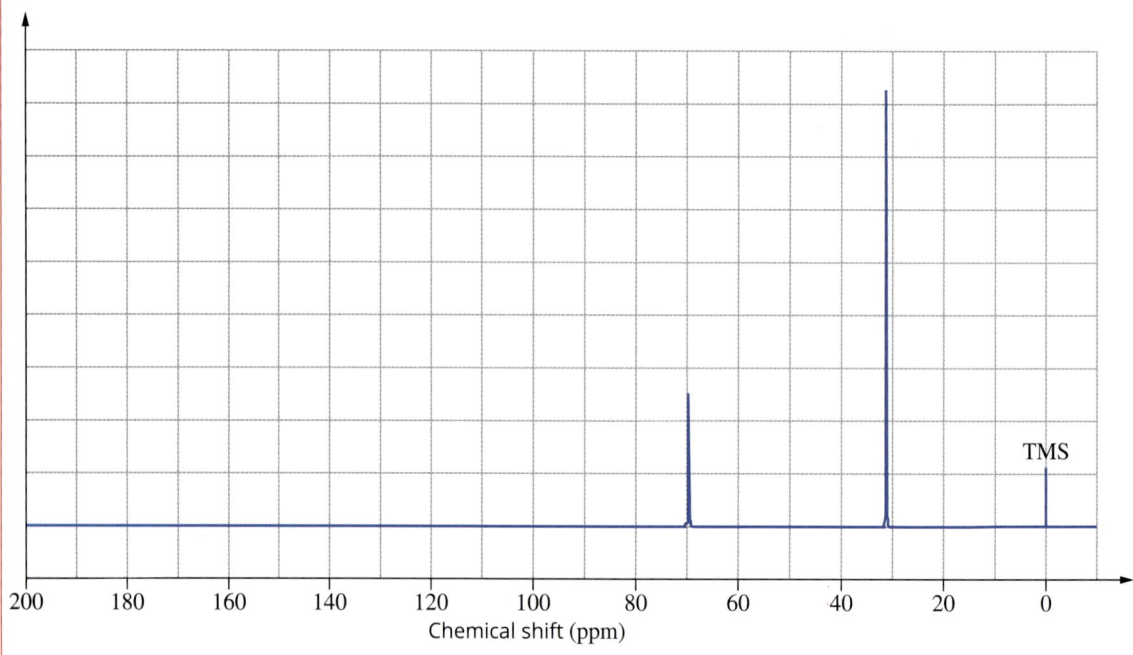

PROTON NUCLEAR MAGNETIC RESONANCE SPECTROSCOPY

> **i** Atoms that are equivalent generate signals that have the same chemical shift.

Proton NMR spectroscopy, also known as ^1H NMR spectroscopy, is used to identify the different hydrogen atoms in a molecule. This involves finding the number of chemically distinct hydrogen environments in the molecule.

The number of signals in a proton NMR spectrum is the same as the number of different hydrogen environments. Hydrogen atoms that are in the same chemical environment have the same chemical shift, so they produce the same signal.

The structural formula and proton NMR spectrum of propanone are shown in Figure 16.3.9. All six hydrogen atoms are in equivalent $-CH_3$ groups, which are bonded to the central carbonyl group. Equivalent protons have the same chemical shift, so the proton NMR spectrum shown in Figure 16.3.9 has only one signal.

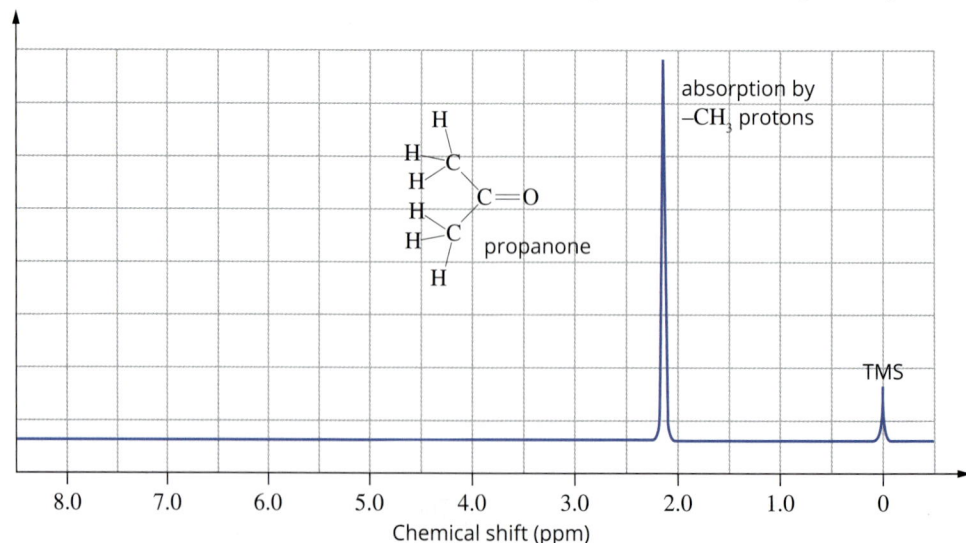

FIGURE 16.3.9 The proton NMR spectrum of propanone

Figure 16.3.10 shows the structural formula and spectrum of dimethoxymethane ($C_3H_8O_2$), which has two signals. The signal with a chemical shift of 4.6 ppm is due to the protons on the central carbon. The signal with a chemical shift of 3.4 ppm is due to the protons in the $-CH_3$ groups, which are equivalent.

The size of the signals is measured by the area under the curve of each signal. The peak area of each signal is proportional to the number of hydrogen atoms in the environment it corresponds with. In the spectrum of dimethoxymethane (Figure 16.3.10) the signals have relative peak areas of one and three, corresponding to the ratio of hydrogen atoms in the two environments in the molecule.

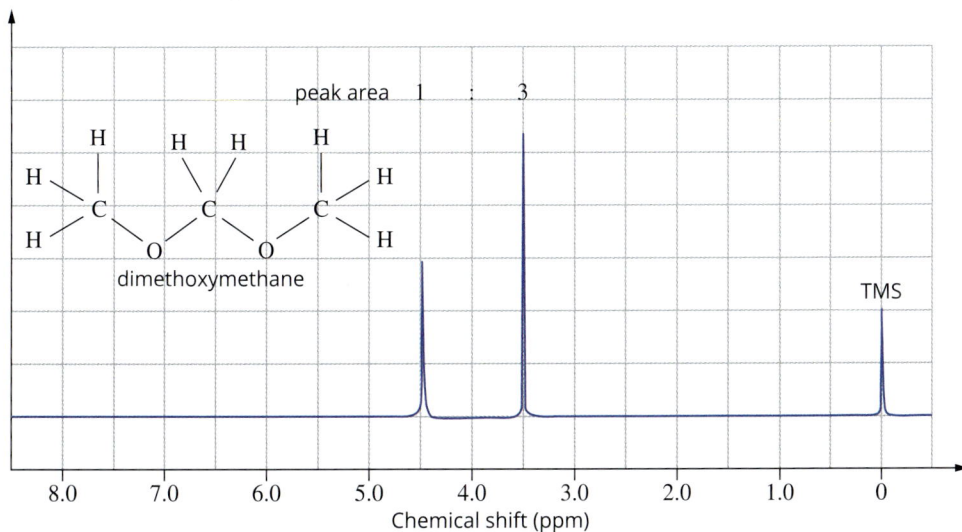

FIGURE 16.3.10 The proton NMR spectrum of dimethoxymethane

Signal splitting

Figure 16.3.11 shows the structural formula and proton NMR spectrum of chloroethane. The hydrogen atoms in the molecule are in two different environments. The signals generated by the different types of hydrogen atoms are shown in matching colours. The relative peak areas indicated above each peak correspond to the number of hydrogen atoms in each environment.

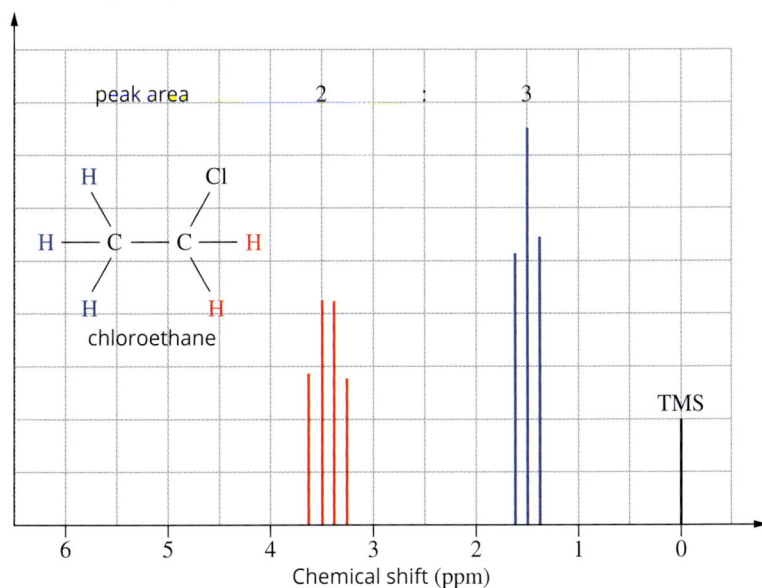

FIGURE 16.3.11 The structural formula and proton NMR spectrum of chloroethane

You will notice that each signal is not a single peak, but a series of close peaks. In high-resolution proton NMR spectra, some signals are seen to split into line (peak) patterns. This is because of the effect of neighbouring hydrogen atoms. The number of lines in a signal is related to the number of hydrogen atoms connected to adjacent atoms by the relationship $n + 1$, where n is the number of hydrogen atoms that are equivalent to each other in neighbouring environments but not equivalent to the hydrogen atom(s) giving rise to the signal. This is called the '$n + 1$ rule'.

An environment is 'neighbouring' if it is up to three bonds away from the hydrogen atoms in question. In the structure of chloroethane, you can see that there are two hydrogen atoms (in red) three bonds away from the hydrogen atoms shown in blue (the $-CH_3$ group). The number of neighbours plus one would be three for this group ($n + 1 = 2 + 1 = 3$), so the signal shows a three-line pattern. The $-CH_2-$ group has three neighbouring protons and gives a signal with a four-line pattern ($n + 1 = 3 + 1 = 4$).

The **splitting pattern** gives important information about which environments are caused by hydrogen atoms close to one another in a molecule. The number of neighbours causes a splitting pattern in a predictable way.

- A hydrogen atom with no neighbours gives a one-line signal (a singlet).
- A $-CH-$ group splits the signal from hydrogen atoms attached to adjacent atoms into two lines (a doublet).
- A $-CH_2-$ group splits the signal from hydrogen atoms attached to adjacent atoms into three lines (a triplet).
- A $-CH_3$ group splits the signal from hydrogen atoms attached to adjacent atoms into four lines (a quartet).

If the neighbouring hydrogen atoms are in an equivalent chemical environment they will not cause splitting of the signal and are not counted as neighbours because they are 'the same'. Also, note that the signal produced by the hydrogen atom in the hydroxyl group of alcohols is not split by hydrogen atoms attached to a neighbouring carbon atom, and does not count as a neighbour. The signal for a hydroxyl group is usually a singlet.

INTERPRETATION OF PROTON NUCLEAR MAGNETIC RESONANCE SPECTRA

A proton NMR spectrum provides a number of pieces of information about the structure of a molecule, including:

- the number of signals, which shows the number of different hydrogen environments
- the relative peak area, which helps to determine the number of hydrogen atoms in each environment
- the splitting of the signals, which provides information about the hydrogen atoms in adjacent environments
- the chemical shift of the signals, which helps to identify the chemical environment in which the hydrogen atoms are located.

By using each piece of this information in turn and considering how the different environments would affect each other, it is often possible to determine the overall structure of a molecule.

Some typical chemical shifts for different types of protons relative to TMS are provided in Table 16.3.2. These can differ slightly in different solvents. Where more than one proton environment is shown in the formula, the shift refers to the protons shown in bold.

TABLE 16.3.2 Typical proton NMR chemical shifts

Type of proton (shown in bold)	Chemical shift (ppm)
R — **CH₃**	0.8–1.0
R — **CH₂** — R	1.2–1.4
RCH = CH — **CH₃**	1.6–1.9
R₃ — **CH**	1.4–1.7
CH₃ — C(=O) — OR or **CH₃** — C(=O) — NHR	2.0
R — C(**CH₃**)(=O)	2.1–2.7
R — **CH₂** — X (X = F, Cl, Br or I)	3.0–4.5
R — **CH₂** — OH, R₂ — **CH** — OH	3.3–4.5
R — C(=O) — NH**CH₂**R	3.2
R — O — **CH₃** or R — O — **CH₂**R	3.3
C₆H₅ — O — C(=O) — **CH₃**	2.3
R — C(=O) — O**CH₂**R	4.1
R — O — **H**	1–6 (varies considerably under different conditions)
R — **NH₂**	1–5
RHC = **CH₂**	4.6–6.0

TABLE 16.3.2 Typical proton NMR chemical shifts (*continued*)

Type of proton (shown in bold)	Chemical shift (ppm)
C₆H₅—**OH** (phenol)	7.0
C₆H₅—**H** (benzene ring H)	7.3
R—C(=O)—N**H**CH₂R	8.1
R—C(=O)—**H**	9–10
R—C(=O)—O—**H**	9–13

CHEMFILE ICT

Magnetic resonance imaging

A form of NMR technology called magnetic resonance imaging (MRI) is used as a tool in medicine to provide a highly detailed picture of anatomical features and diseased tissue without the use of harmful radiation such as X-rays.

The scanner is effectively an NMR machine; the patient takes the place of the sample and is passed into the opening of a huge magnet and radio receiver.

The human body contains a large amount of water, which is an abundant source of protons. Normally, MRI measures the strength of the water signal in each area of the body, creating a detailed three-dimensional map. Bone, fat, muscle and tissues contain different amounts of water, allowing them to be distinguished from one another. Normal, healthy tissue gives a different response than a tumour or diseased tissue. A powerful computer is used to analyse the data and present a coloured image of the patient's body. The red and yellow areas in Figure 16.3.12 show where the brain has atrophied (wasted away) due to a lack of blood flow.

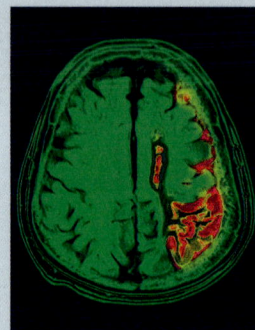

FIGURE 16.3.12 An MRI scan of a human skull, showing a diseased section of the brain in red

Worked example 16.3.2

INTERPRETNG A PROTON NUCLEAR MAGNETIC RESONANCE SPECTRUM

The proton NMR spectrum of a compound with a molecular formula of $C_2H_4Cl_2$ is shown below. Relative peak areas are shown on the spectrum.

Identify this compound using the information provided in the NMR spectrum.

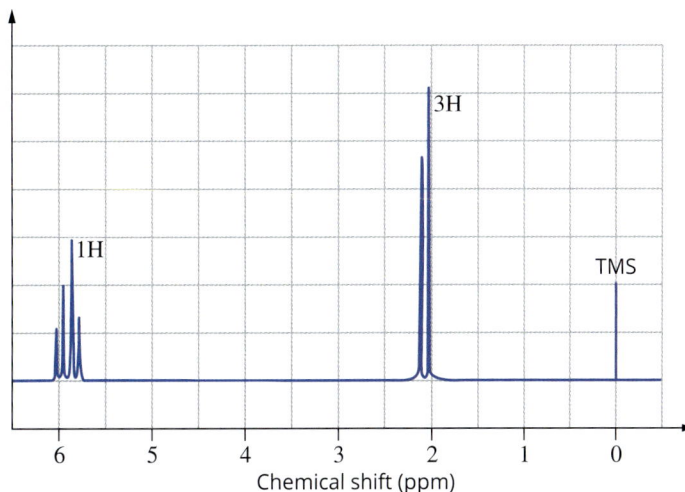

Thinking	Working
What information does the formula provide about the compound?	Two molecules are possible from the formula: either 1,2-dichloroethane or 1,1-dichloroethane.
Summarise the information provided in the NMR spectrum in a table.	<table><tr><th>Chemical shift</th><th>Peak splitting</th><th>Relative peak area</th></tr><tr><td>2.1</td><td>doublet (2-line pattern)</td><td>3</td></tr><tr><td>5.9</td><td>quartet (4-line pattern)</td><td>1</td></tr></table>
Identify the number of different hydrogen environments.	There are two signals so there must be two different hydrogen environments.
If possible, use the chemical shifts in Table 16.3.2 (page 490) to identify the types of protons. Remember the ranges are broad.	The table does not give information about compounds containing two chloro groups, so continue on to the next step.
Use the relative peak area to deduce the number of hydrogen atoms in each environment.	The relative peak areas of the signals at 5.9 ppm and 2.1 ppm are 1:3, so the relative number of hydrogen atoms must be 1:3. The sum of hydrogen atoms in the formula is 4, which means that the peak areas are directly equal to the number of hydrogen atoms in each environment. This suggests that the molecule contains one $-CH-$ group and one $-CH_3$ group.
Use the peak splitting of the signals to identify the types of hydrogen environments.	The signal at 2.1 ppm is a doublet (2-line pattern). The number of lines in the pattern is given by $n + 1$, so this signal must be generated by an environment that has 1 neighbouring hydrogen atom, i.e. a $-CH-$ group. The signal at 5.9 ppm is a quartet (4-line pattern). The number of lines in the pattern is given by $n + 1$, so this signal must be generated by an environment that has 3 neighbouring hydrogen atoms, i.e. a $-CH_3$ group.
Use the information you gathered to identify the compound.	The molecular formula of the compound is $C_2H_4Cl_2$. The compound is either 1,2-dichloroethane or 1,1-dichloroethane. The splitting patterns and peak area indicates that the molecule contains a $-CH_3$ group adjacent to a $-CH-$ group. The molecule must be 1,1-dichlorethane, because its structure fits the evidence from the spectrum.

Worked example: Try yourself 16.3.2

INTERPRETING A PROTON NUCLEAR MAGNETIC RESONANCE SPECTRUM

The proton NMR spectrum of a compound with a molecular formula of $C_2H_3Cl_3$ is shown below. Relative peak areas are shown on the spectrum.

Identify this compound using the information provided in the NMR spectrum.

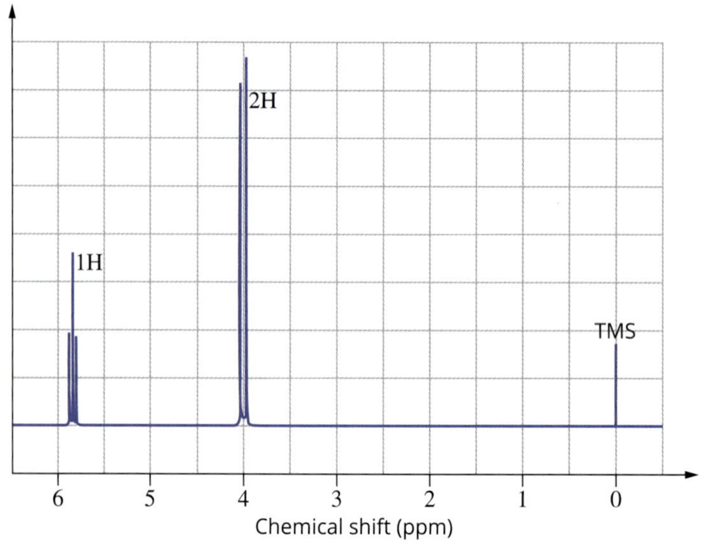

WS 8.6

- -

16.3 Review

SUMMARY

- Atomic nuclei with an odd atomic number (Z) or an odd mass number (A) have nuclear spin.
- When nuclei with spin are placed in a strong magnetic field, they can absorb energy from radio waves and flip into a high-energy spin state. The nuclei emit a signal as they flip back to a low-energy spin state.
- Each signal in a nuclear magnetic resonance (NMR) spectrum corresponds to nuclei in a different chemical environment.
- Chemical shift is characteristic of an atom's environment.
- Carbon-13 (^{13}C) NMR spectroscopy provides information about the number and identity of different carbon atom environments in a molecule.
- The analysis of a carbon-13 NMR spectrum involves studying:
  - the number of signals
  - the chemical shifts of the signals.

- Proton (^1H) NMR spectroscopy provides information about the hydrogen atoms in a molecule.
- The peak area of each signal in a proton NMR spectrum is proportional to the number of hydrogen atoms in the corresponding environment.
- Signals in a proton NMR spectrum may be split into line patterns because of the interaction of hydrogen atoms in neighbouring environments. The number of lines in the splitting pattern indicates the number of hydrogen neighbours by the rule $n + 1$.
- The analysis of a proton NMR spectrum involves the study of the:
  - number of signals
  - relative peak area of each signal
  - chemical shift of the signal
  - splitting pattern.

1 **a** Explain why the carbon atoms in the methyl groups (–CH$_3$) attached to the second carbon atom on the left of the diagram below (circled) are not equivalent to the carbon atom in the methyl group on the right.

 b How many peaks are there in the carbon-13 NMR spectrum of this compound?

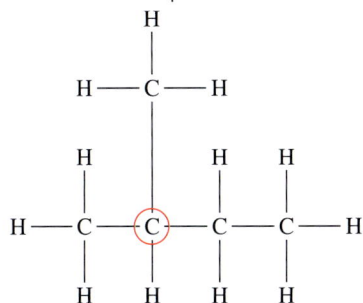

2 The following compounds all have the formula C$_4$H$_9$Cl. The carbon-13 NMR spectrum of which compound only has three peaks?

 A 1-chlorobutane

 B 2-chlorobutane

 C 1-chloro-2-methylpropane

 D 2-chloro-2-methylpropane

3 The molecular formula of both propanal, an aldehyde, and propanone, a ketone, is C$_3$H$_6$O. Describe how you could use carbon-13 NMR spectroscopy to distinguish between propanone and propanal.

4 The carbon-13 NMR spectrum of ethyl ethanoate is shown below.

In the formula for ethyl ethanoate, each carbon atom is identified by a letter. Match the approximate chemical shift of each carbon with the correct identifying letter. The match for the carbon atom labelled A has been completed for you.

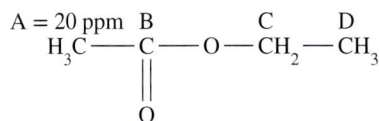

5 Proton NMR spectra give a number of pieces of information about a molecule's structure. What information can be gained from the:

 a number of signals?

 b chemical shift of a signal?

 c relative peak areas?

 d splitting pattern of a signal?

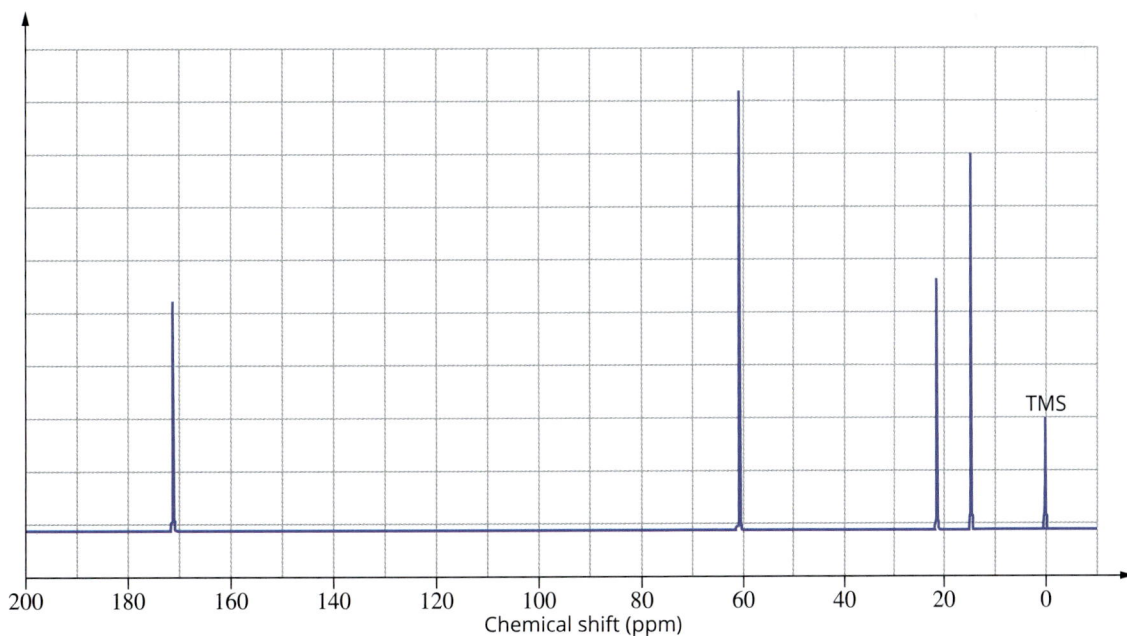

6 Consider the following molecules.

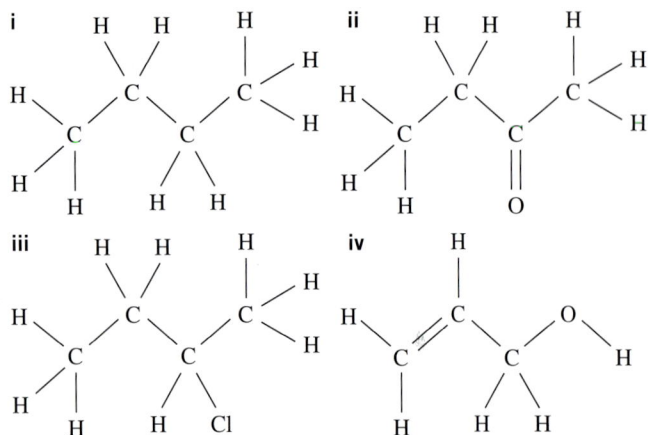

i

ii

iii

iv

a How many different hydrogen environments are in each molecule?

b How many different carbon environments are in each molecule?

c What splitting pattern would you expect to see from the hydrogen environments in molecule **ii**?

d What ratio would you expect to see in the relative peak areas of the signals from the proton NMR spectrum of molecule **i**?

7 The proton NMR spectrum of a compound shows a doublet (two-line pattern) with a chemical shift of 1.8, and a relative peak area of 3. Identify what this environment is likely to be.

8 Ethyl ethanoate is a solvent commonly used in nail polish remover. The proton NMR spectrum and condensed structural formula of ethyl ethanoate are shown in the following figure.

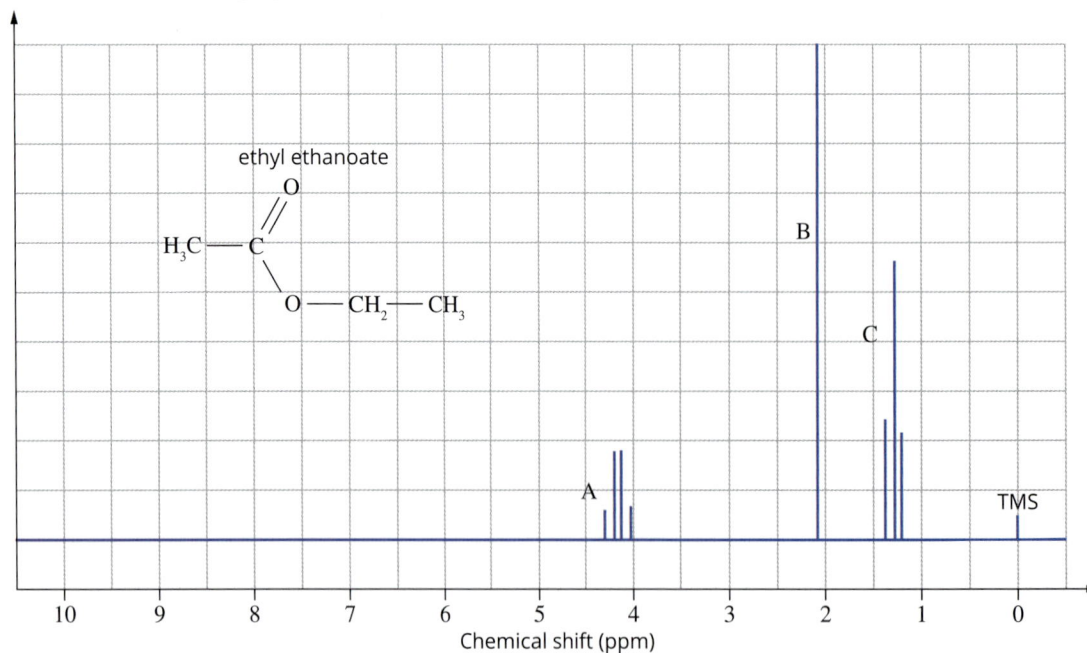

To answer the following questions, you may need to refer to the chemical shift data in Table 16.3.2 (page 490).

a How many hydrogen environments are there in ethyl ethanoate?

b Use the information in Table 16.3.2 to identify the expected chemical shift for the groups present in the ethyl ethanoate molecule.

c What is the relative number of protons in each peak set A, B and C?

d Explain why:

i peak set A is split into a quartet

ii peak set B is a single peak

iii peak set C is a triplet.

e Identify the protons responsible for each peak set and the carbon atoms to which they are bonded.

f How many peaks would you expect in the carbon-13 NMR spectrum of ethyl ethanoate?

16.4 Mass spectrometry

Mass spectrometry is one of the most commonly used analytical tools. It is used to analyse samples of solids, liquids and gases. It is a very sensitive quantitative technique that can detect concentrations in the parts per billion to parts per trillion range.

In Module 1 of this course you studied the use of mass spectrometry in the analysis of isotopes. Mass spectrometry can also be used to study molecules. Each molecule produces a unique mass spectrum, so a molecule can be identified by comparing its mass spectrum with mass spectra held in a database.

GO TO ➤ Year 11 Chapter 3

Mass spectrometry is commonly used to determine the structures of proteins and drugs. It can also detect molecules that are markers for diseases such as cancer. Mass spectrometers have also been used in space exploration to analyse the atmosphere on Mars and on the moons of Saturn. The Mars rover *Curiosity*, shown in Figure 16.4.1, is a robotic laboratory that NASA landed on Mars in 2012. *Curiosity* carries a number of miniaturised analytical instruments, including a mass spectrometer.

Mass spectrometry is often combined with other instrumental techniques, in particular chromatography, for the analysis of mixtures.

FIGURE 16.4.1 An artist's impression of *Curiosity*, a robotic rover, on the surface of Mars

PRINCIPLES OF MASS SPECTROMETRY

A schematic diagram of a **mass spectrometer** is shown in Figure 16.4.2. In a mass spectrometer:

- ions are formed in the ionisation chamber, where the sample is exposed to high voltages
- the ions are separated in a magnetic field on the basis of their mass-to-charge ratio (m/z)
- the number of ions with different m/z values are measured by a detector, and the data is displayed as a **mass spectrum**.

> ℹ A mass spectrometer does not use electromagnetic radiation, unlike the spectroscopic techniques outlined in earlier sections of this chapter. The mass spectrometer gives very accurate information about the mass of positive ions formed in the instrument.

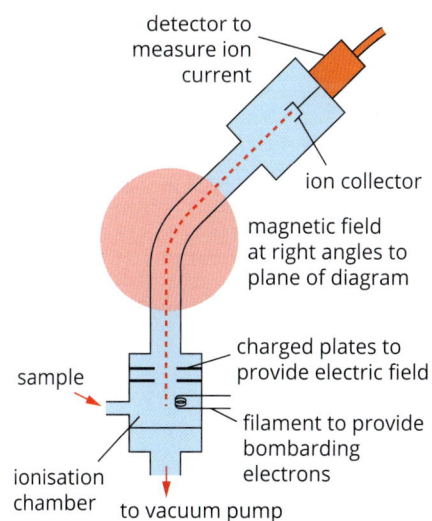

FIGURE 16.4.2 The components of a mass spectrometer

Features of a mass spectrum

A mass spectrum of a sample of pentane is shown in Figure 16.4.3. It is a plot of the abundance, measured as relative intensity, of ions with different mass-to-charge ratios. This spectrum shows the positive ions formed when a sample of pentane was injected into the mass spectrometer.

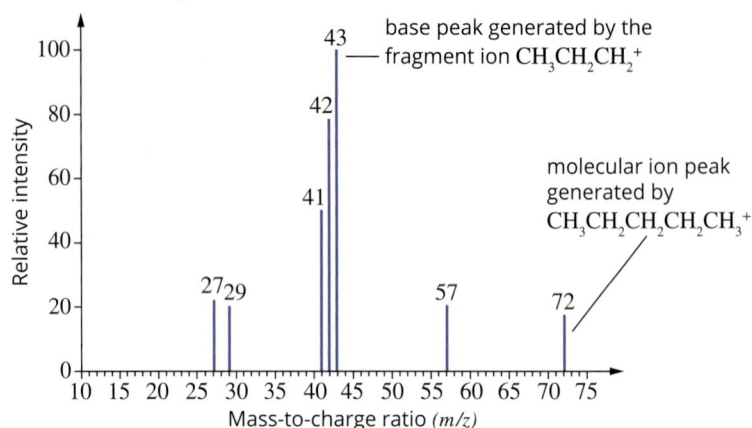

FIGURE 16.4.3 A mass spectrum of pentane ($CH_3CH_2CH_2CH_2CH_3$)

The peak at $m/z = 72$ in pentane's mass spectrum is caused by the **molecular ion**. A molecular ion is formed when the entire molecule loses an electron and becomes positively charged. When ions are singly charged, $z = 1$, so the m/z ratio is the same as the relative molecular mass of the ion. (In most cases the peaks in a mass spectrum are generated by singly charged ions. Mass spectra of ions that have a larger charge are not covered in this course.)

The other peaks in the spectrum, which have smaller m/z values than the molecular ion, represent fragment ions. These are formed when the high-energy electrons in the ionisation chamber cause bonds to break, which then causes the molecule to break up into fragments.

The most intense peak, $m/z = 43$, is called the **base peak** and is produced by the most abundant fragment ion. The base peak is assigned a relative intensity of 100%. The intensity of all the other peaks are measured relative to the base peak. In some spectra the peak with the highest intensity is also the molecular ion. In other spectra the base peak may correspond to a smaller fragment. The relative intensities of the peaks in the spectrum depend on:

- the energy of the ionising electrons
- the ease with which fragments can be formed
- the stability of the fragment ions formed.

Fragmentation

Inside the ionisation chamber, high-energy electrons ionise the sample by knocking an electron off each molecule, producing a positive molecular ion. Because covalent bonds are formed from the sharing of electrons, the removal of electrons can cause the bonds to weaken and break.

The **fragmentation** of the molecule into smaller pieces is represented in the mass spectrum by peaks with m/z smaller than that of the molecular ion. Fragments can be produced by the breaking of almost any bond in the molecular ion. They may be single atoms, small groups of atoms, or large sections of the parent molecule.

The m/z values and formulae of some common fragment ions in mass spectra of organic molecules are listed in Table 16.4.1.

TABLE 16.4.1 Common positive fragment ions

m/z	Formula
15	CH_3^+
17	OH^+
29	$CH_3CH_2^+$, CHO^+
31	CH_3O^+
35 and 37	$^{35}Cl^+$, $^{37}Cl^+$
43	$CH_3CH_2CH_2^+$, CH_3CO^+
45	$COOH^+$
79, 81	$^{79}Br^+$, $^{81}Br^+$

INTERPRETATION OF MASS SPECTRA

The information provided by mass spectrometry can be illustrated by examining the mass spectrum of ethanoic acid (CH_3COOH). Ethanoic acid can be ionised in a mass spectrometer by removing an electron in the following process:

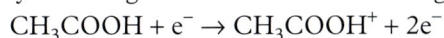

$$CH_3COOH + e^- \rightarrow CH_3COOH^+ + 2e^-$$

The molecular ion, CH_3COOH^+, is unstable and can break into a number of fragment ions, as shown in Figure 16.4.4. The molecular and fragment ions generate peaks in the mass spectrum of ethanoic acid (Figure 16.4.5).

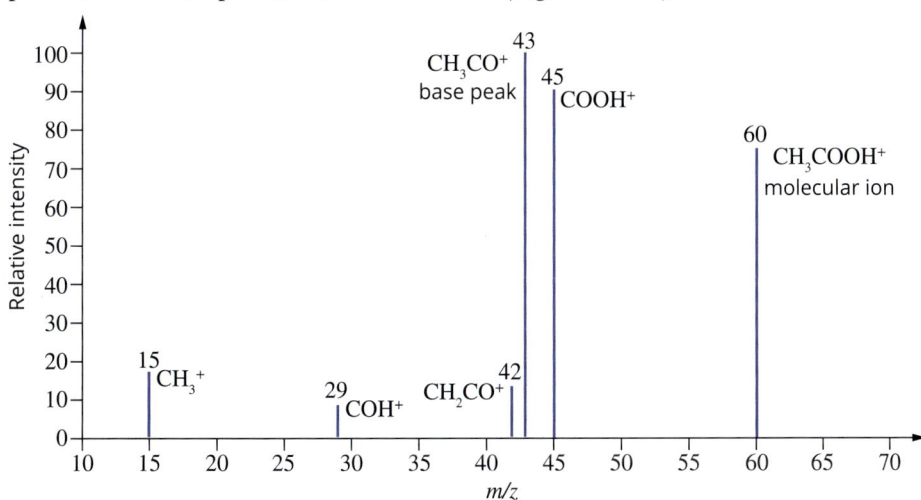

FIGURE 16.4.4 Formation of fragment ions from ethanoic acid

FIGURE 16.4.5 The mass spectrum of ethanoic acid

The mass spectrum of ethanoic acid indicates that the molecular ion has a mass of 60. The mass of the molecular ion is the same as the relative molecular mass of the ethanoic acid molecule. The fragment ions provide information about the structure of the ethanoic acid molecule, as shown in Table 16.4.2.

TABLE 16.4.2 The identities of peaks in ethanoic acid mass spectrum

m/z	Ion identity	How the ion is formed
60	CH_3COOH^+	loss of an electron from the molecule
45	$COOH^+$	loss of CH_3 from the molecular ion
43	CH_3CO^+	loss of OH from the molecular ion
42	CH_2CO^+	loss of H from CH_3CO^+
29	COH^+	loss of an O atom from $COOH^+$
15	CH_3^+	loss of COOH from the molecular ion

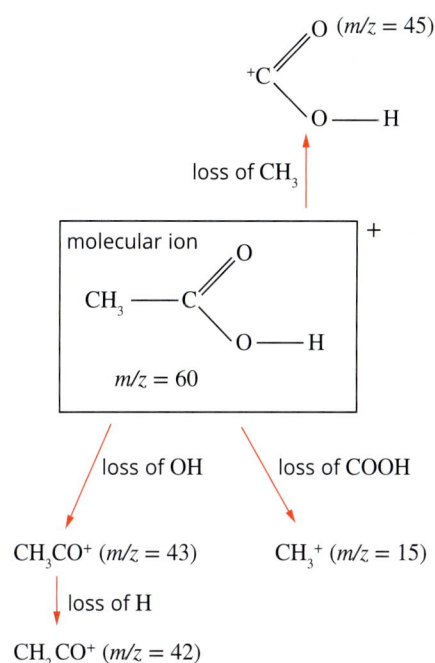

Worked example 16.4.1

DETERMINING THE IDENTITY OF A COMPOUND FROM ITS MOLECULAR ION

The mass spectrum of an unbranched alkane has a molecular ion peak of $m/z = 86$. Determine the molecular formula of the alkane and give its name.

Thinking	Working
The m/z value of the molecular ion is equal to the relative molecular mass of the molecule.	The relative molecular mass of the alkane is 86.
Identify the general formula for the molecule.	The general formula for an alkane is C_nH_{2n+2}.
Use the general formula to set up an equation linking the relative molecular mass M_r to the relative atomic masses A_r of the constituent atoms.	$A_r(C) = 12$ $A_r(H) = 1$ $M_r(C_nH_{2n+2}) = (12 \times n) + 1 \times (2n + 2)$ $= 86$
Solve the equation for n.	$12n + 2n + 2 = 86$ $14n + 2 = 86$ $14n = 84$ $n = 6$
Use the value of n to find the molecular formula and the name.	C_6H_{14}, which is hexane.

Worked example: Try yourself 16.4.1

DETERMINING THE IDENTITY OF A COMPOUND FROM ITS MOLECULAR ION

The mass spectrum of an unbranched alkane has a molecular ion peak at $m/z = 58$. Determine the molecular formula of the alkane and give its name.

Worked example 16.4.1 includes enough information to determine the molecular formula of the unknown compound from the data provided by the mass spectrum. The category or categories of organic compound to which the substance might belong can often be deduced from the molecular formula. Table 16.4.3 shows the general formulae of some different classes of organic compounds.

TABLE 16.4.3 General formulae of different categories of organic compounds

Category	General formula
alkane	C_nH_{2n+2}
alkene	C_nH_{2n}
alkyne	C_nH_{2n-2}
alcohol	$C_nH_{2n+2}O$
haloalkane	$C_nH_{2n+1}X$ (X = F, Cl, Br or I)
aldehyde and ketone	$C_nH_{2n}O$
carboxylic acid and ester	$C_nH_{2n}O_2$
primary amine	$C_nH_{2n+3}N$
primary amide	$C_nH_{2n+1}ON$

Knowledge of the general formula of different classes of organic compounds, together with information derived from IR and NMR spectroscopy, can be used to confirm the presence of particular functional groups, the molecular structure and identity of the compound.

Isotope effects

Most elements exist as mixtures of **isotopes**, as shown in Table 16.4.4. The presence of isotopes leads to the appearance of additional peaks in the mass spectrum of a molecule.

TABLE 16.4.4 Isotopes of some atoms and their percentage abundance

Element	Isotopes	Isotopic mass	Percentage abundance
hydrogen	^1H	1.0	99.98
	^2H	2.0	0.02
carbon	^{12}C	12.0	98.9
	^{13}C	13.0	1.1
oxygen	^{16}O	16.0	99.8
	^{18}O	18.0	0.2
chlorine	^{35}Cl	35.0	75.8
	^{37}Cl	37.0	24.2
bromine	^{79}Br	78.9	50.7
	^{81}Br	81.0	49.3

The amount of ^2H, ^{13}C and ^{18}O in samples is very small, so fragment ions containing these isotopes produce very small peaks in mass spectra and they can be ignored in most cases. However, chlorine and bromine have high proportions of each isotope, so samples that contain them have significant peaks for fragment ions containing each isotope in their mass spectra.

The mass spectrum of chloromethane (CH_3Cl) shows peaks for two molecular ions (Figure 16.4.6).

- The peak at $m/z = 50$ is due to the molecular ion containing ^{35}Cl.
- The peak at $m/z = 52$ is due to the other molecular ion containing ^{37}Cl.

The relative heights of these peaks reflect the relative abundance of the two isotopes.

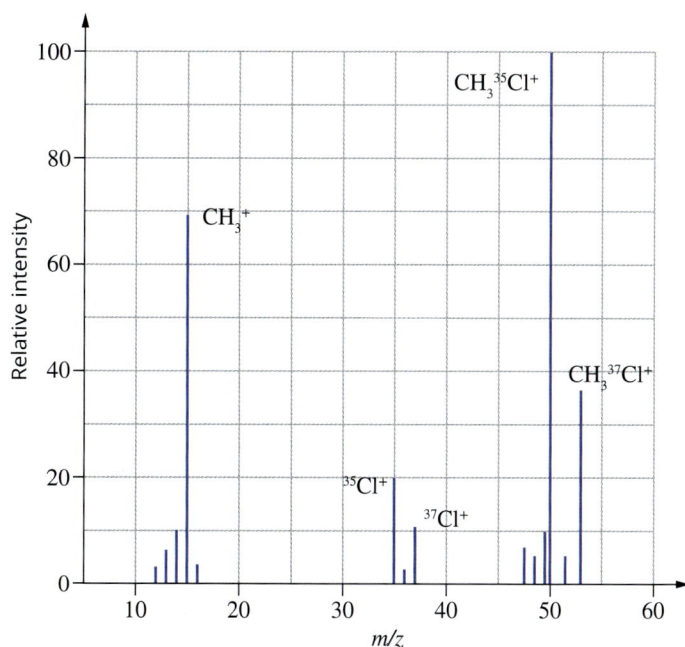

FIGURE 16.4.6 The mass spectrum of chloromethane (CH_3Cl). The two molecular ion peaks are due to the two isotopes of chlorine.

Molecules that have significant proportions of several isotopes can produce complex mass spectra. The mass spectrum of dichloromethane (CH_2Cl_2), a common component of many household products, shows three **molecular ion peaks** (Figure 16.4.7).

- The peak at $m/z = 84$ is due to the molecular ion containing two ^{35}Cl atoms.
- The peak at $m/z = 86$ is due to the molecular ion containing one ^{35}Cl atom and one ^{37}Cl atom.
- The peak at $m/z = 88$ is due to the molecular ion containing two ^{37}Cl atoms.

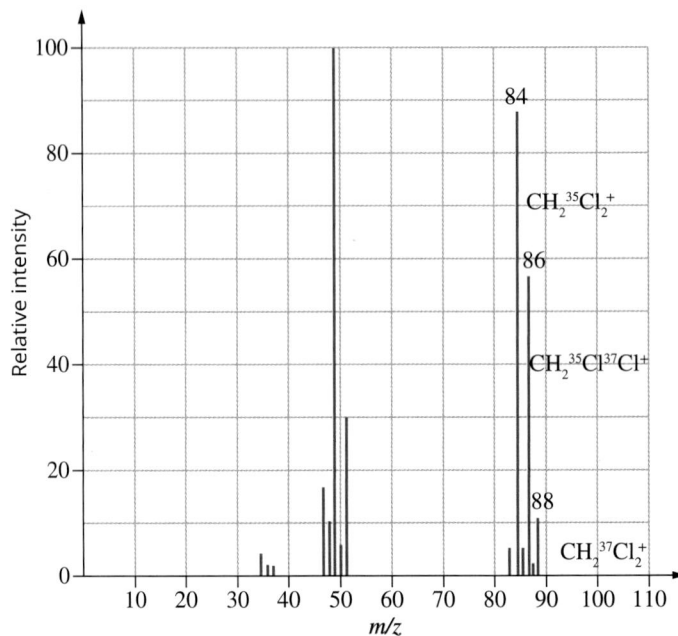

FIGURE 16.4.7 The mass spectrum of dichloromethane (CH_2Cl_2). The three molecular ion peaks are produced by molecular ions with a single isotope of chlorine ($m/z = 84$ and 88) or both isotopes (at $m/z = 86$).

16.4 Review

SUMMARY

- A mass spectrometer measures the mass-to-charge ratio (m/z) of ions.
- The peak that has the highest m/z is usually caused by the entire molecule becoming ionised, and is called the molecular ion peak.
- The molecular ion can break into pieces called fragment ions.
- Fragmentation of a molecule in a mass spectrometer can help to determine its molecular structure.
- Each compound has a unique mass spectrum that can be used to identify it.
- The mass spectrum of a compound containing chlorine or bromine atoms has significant additional peaks because of the high abundances of different isotopes.

KEY QUESTIONS

1 A straight-chain alkane produced the following mass spectrum.

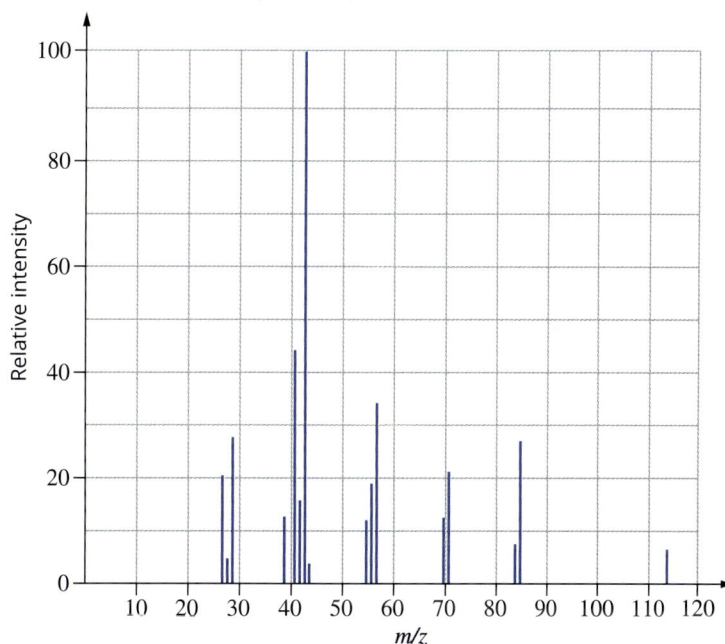

a What is the molar mass of the compound?
b What is the m/z value of the base peak?
c What is the name of the alkane represented?
d What is the formula for the fragment ion with an m/z value of 85?

2 What are the formulae of the molecular ions that would be found in the mass spectrum of 1,1-dibromoethane?

16.4 Review *continued*

3 The mass spectrum of a bromoalkane is shown here.

   a What is the formula of the bromoalkane?

   b Explain why the mass spectrum has two peaks at $m/z = 122$ and $m/z = 124$.

   c Account for the relative heights of these two peaks.

   d Write a possible formula for the ion responsible for the peak at $m/z = 43$.

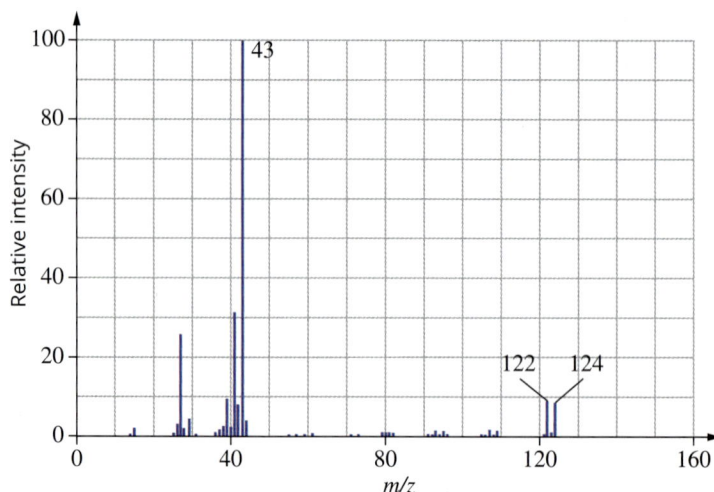

4 Use the following mass spectra to determine the molecular formula of each of the molecules represented by the following mass spectra.

   a a ketone

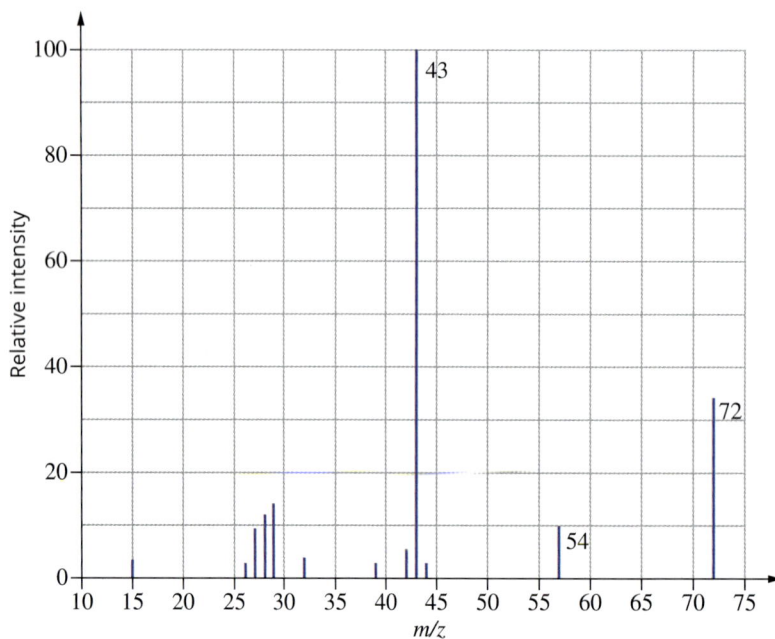

   b an amide.

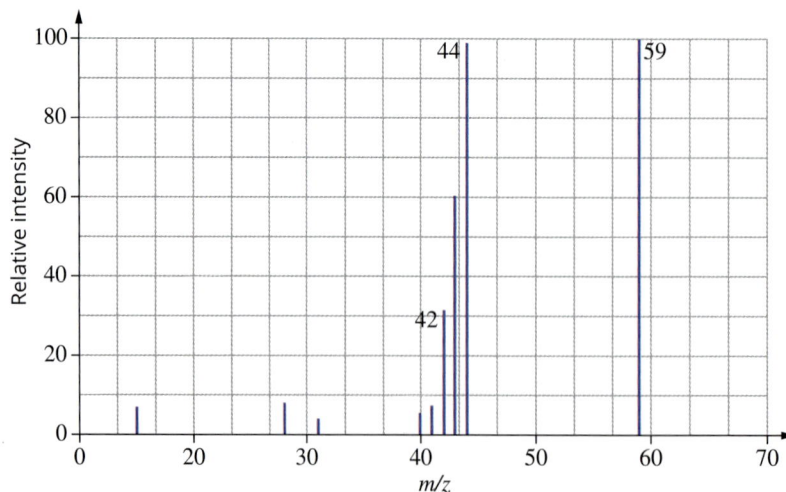

16.5 Determination of molecular structure by spectroscopy

Chemists determine the structure and identity of unknown compounds by employing a range of analytical techniques. Each technique provides a different piece of information about the compound's structure which, when considered together, can identify the substance. The process can be compared to piecing together the pieces of a jigsaw puzzle.

The structures of organic compounds are often determined using a combination of IR spectroscopy, NMR spectroscopy and mass spectrometry. Chemical and physical properties can also provide clues about the identity of a compound.

In this section you will investigate how the structure of an unidentified compound can be determined. In the worked examples and questions, you may need to refer to the IR and NMR information in Tables 16.2.4 (page 473), 16.3.1 (page 483) and 16.3.2 (page 489).

COMBINING ANALYSES TO LEARN MORE

Ethanol will be used as an example of how the results of different types of analysis can be used to identify an unknown organic compound. Ethanol has a molar mass of $46\,g\,mol^{-1}$. The structural formula of ethanol is shown in Figure 16.5.1, and the mass spectrum is shown in Figure 16.5.2. From the spectrum, the following can be determined:

- There is a molecular ion peak at $m/z = 46$, which corresponds to a relative molecular mass of 46.
- The fragment ion peaks are identified on the spectrum and are consistent with the fragmentation of a molecule with the formula CH_3CH_2OH.

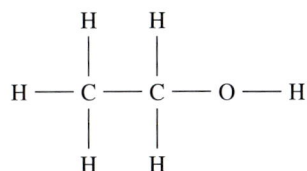

FIGURE 16.5.1 The molecular structure of ethanol

FIGURE 16.5.2 The mass spectrum of ethanol

The infrared spectrum of ethanol (Figure 16.5.3) provides the following information:

- The most prominent feature is the broad absorption band at 3400 cm^{-1} produced by the O–H bond, and confirms the presence of an alcohol hydroxyl group.
- The absorption bands produced by the C–H and C–O bonds are also evident.

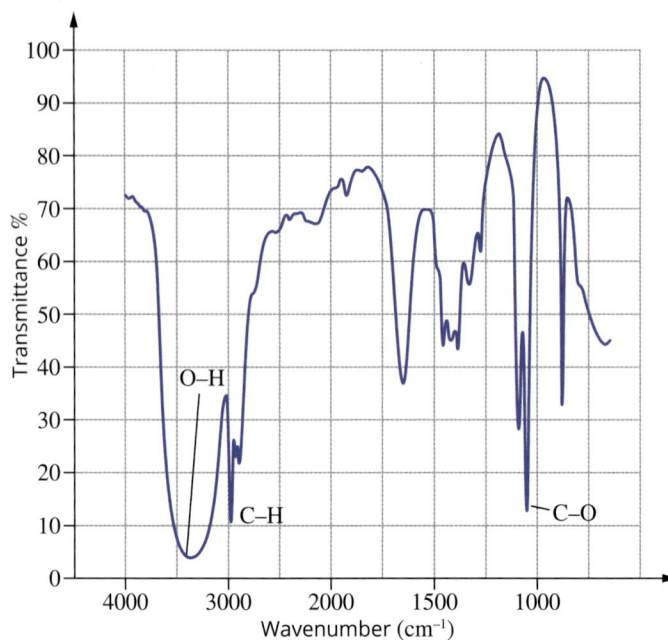

FIGURE 16.5.3 The IR spectrum of liquid ethanol

The carbon-13 NMR spectrum of ethanol shown in Figure 16.5.4 provides the following information:

- There are two signals, meaning that the molecule contains two different carbon environments.
- The signal at 58 ppm corresponds to the signal of a carbon attached to a hydroxyl group, –CH$_2$–OH.
- The signal at 18 ppm is consistent with the signal from a carbon in a methyl group, –CH$_3$.

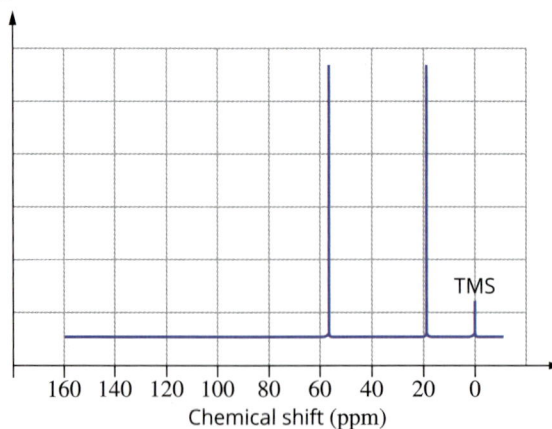

FIGURE 16.5.4 The carbon-13 NMR spectrum of ethanol

The proton NMR spectrum of ethanol is shown in Figure 16.5.5. It provides the following information:

- There are three signals, which means that the molecule contains three different hydrogen environments.
- The signal with a chemical shift of about 3.7 ppm is a four-line pattern or quartet and has a relative peak area of 2. The chemical shift and peak area are consistent with the signal of a $-CH_2-$ group adjacent to a hydroxyl group. The splitting pattern indicates there are three hydrogen atoms in a neighbouring environment. (Remember that a proton on an $-OH$ group does not usually split the signals of adjacent protons.)
- The signal at 1.2 ppm is a triplet (three-line pattern) with a relative peak area of 3. This is consistent with the signal of a $-CH_3$ group adjacent to a $-CH_2-$ group.
- The singlet at 2.6 ppm is consistent with the signal of an alcohol hydroxyl group.

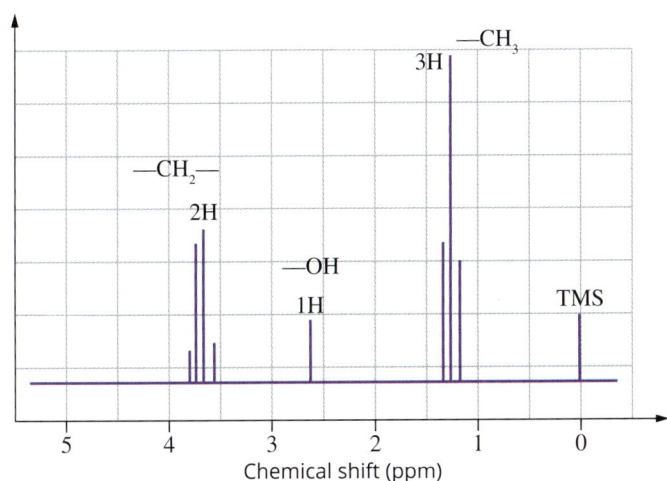

FIGURE 16.5.5 Proton NMR spectrum of ethanol

When each piece of evidence from analysing the different spectra is put together, you can see that the structure must be CH_3CH_2OH. Each of the spectra contains the peaks expected of ethanol, and none of the spectra contains information that is inconsistent with ethanol.

WS
8.7

Worked example 16.5.1

DEDUCING MOLECULAR STRUCTURE FROM SPECTROSCOPIC DATA

A fruity-smelling liquid has an empirical formula of $C_3H_6O_2$. The compound does not react with a solution of sodium hydrogen carbonate. Use this information and the mass, IR and NMR spectra provided to deduce the structure and name of the compound.

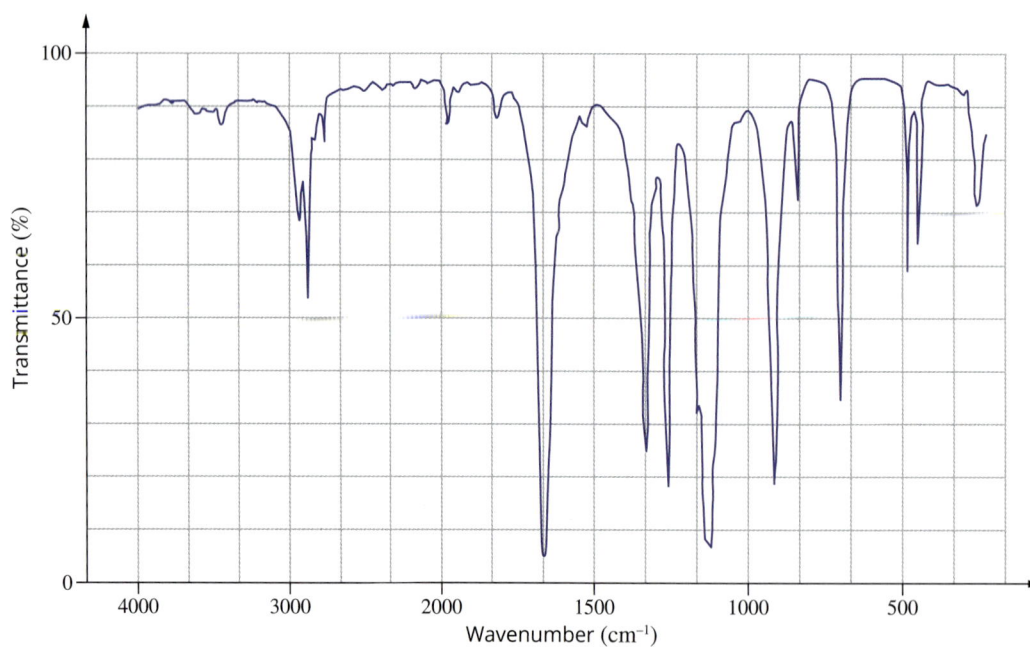

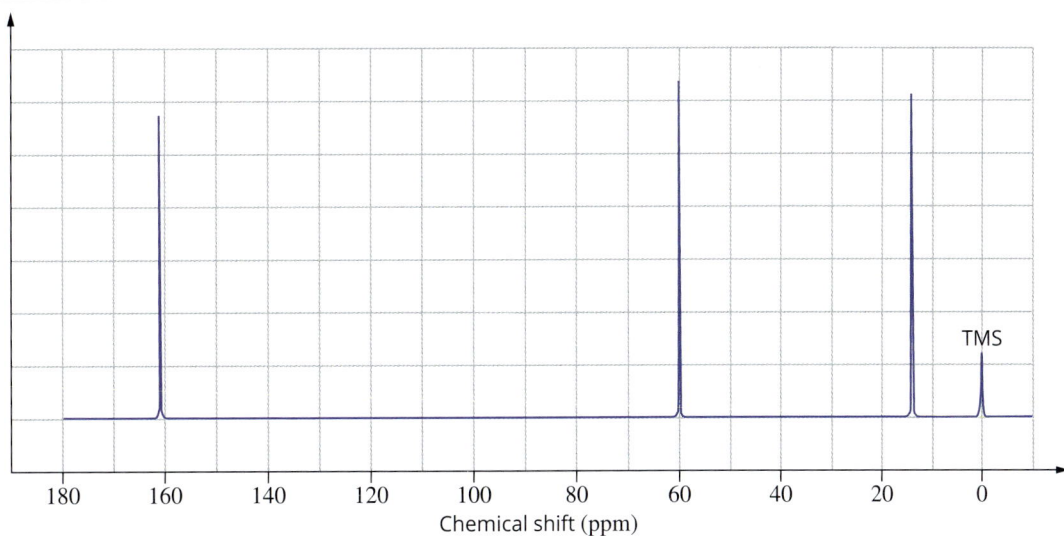

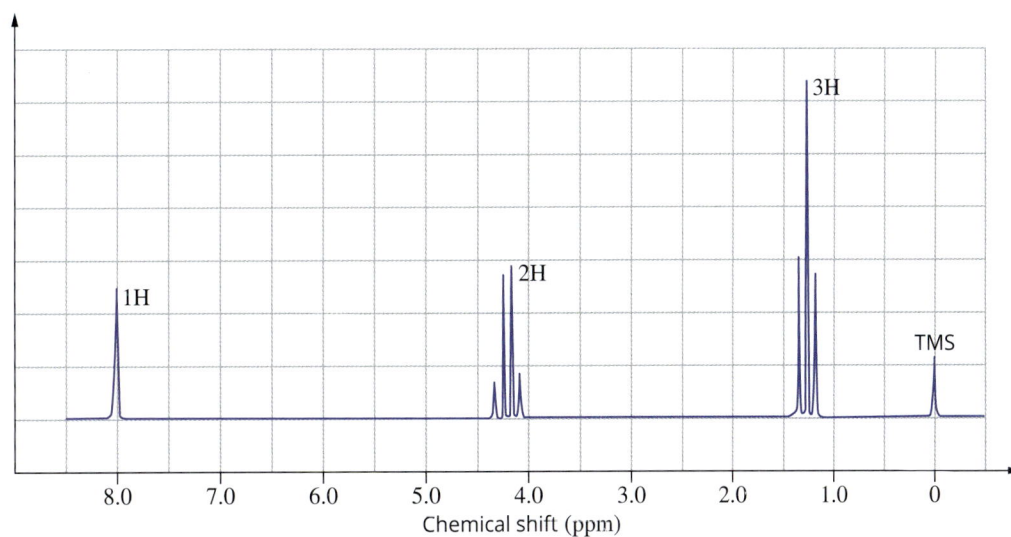

Thinking	Working
Use the mass spectrum to identify the molecular ion, and hence the relative molecular mass. Use this information to determine the molecular formula of the compound.	The peak with the largest mass-to-charge ratio is at $m/z = 74$, so the relative molecular mass is 74. This mass is consistent with the molecular formula of $C_3H_6O_2$.
Use the molecular formula and any physical and chemical data provided to identify the categories of organic compounds to which the substance might belong.	The formula is consistent with that of a carboxylic acid or an ester. The fruity odour and lack of reactivity with a sodium hydrogen carbonate solution suggests that the compound is an ester.
Use the IR spectrum to identify functional groups present in the compound. (Refer to Table 16.2.4 on page 473.)	The IR spectrum shows a strong absorption band at $1700 \, cm^{-1}$, suggesting the presence of a C=O bond, and hence a carbonyl group. The IR spectrum does not contain a strong, broad absorption band in the range of $2500–3500 \, cm^{-1}$, indicating there is no O–H bond in the molecule and that the –COOH functional group found in carboxylic acids is not present. This confirms that the compound is an ester.

Use the carbon-13 NMR spectrum to identify the different carbon environments. (Refer to Table 16.3.1 on page 483.)	There are three signals in the carbon NMR spectrum and so the molecule contains three different carbon environments.
	The number of carbon environments corresponds to the number of carbon atoms in the molecular formula, so each environment represents one carbon atom.
	The signal at 161 ppm is consistent with a carbon in a carbonyl group.
	The signal at 60 ppm is consistent with a carbon attached to an oxygen atom by a single bond.
	The signal at 14 ppm is consistent with a carbon atom in a methyl group ($-CH_3$).
Use the proton NMR spectrum to identify the different hydrogen environments. (Refer to Table 16.3.2, page 489.)	The proton NMR data is summarised in the following table.

Chemical shift (ppm)	Splitting pattern	Relative peak area
1.3	triplet (3-line pattern)	3
4.2	quartet (4-line pattern)	2
8.0	singlet (1-line pattern)	1

The spectrum contains three signals and so there are three different hydrogen environments.

The sum of the relative peak areas is 6, which is consistent with the molecular formula; each unit of peak area corresponds to one hydrogen atom.

The signal at 1.3 ppm is consistent with the signal produced by a $-CH_3$ group with two hydrogen atoms in a neighbouring environment.

The signal at 4.2 ppm is consistent with the signal produced by a $-CH_2-$ group singly bonded to the oxygen of an ester group, with three hydrogen atoms in a neighbouring environment.

The signal at 8.0 ppm is a singlet, indicating that there are no hydrogen atoms attached to adjacent atoms. The chemical shift is quite large and could be consistent with a hydrogen atom attached to a carbonyl group.

Use the data from the spectra to deduce the structure of the compound.	The data provided by the spectra show that:

- the molecular formula of the compound is $C_3H_6O_2$
- the compound has a carbonyl group, but no hydroxyl group so it is not a carboxylic acid
- it is an ester
- the compound has a $-CH_2CH_3$ group attached by a single bond to an oxygen atom
- the compound has a HC=O group.

A structure consistent with this data is:

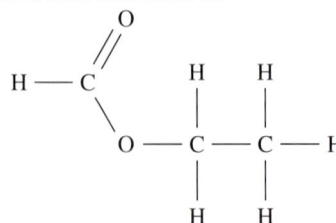

Name the compound.	The compound is ethyl methanoate.

Worked example: Try yourself 16.5.1

DEDUCING MOLECULAR STRUCTURE FROM SPECTROSCOPIC DATA

A liquid with a fruity odour has an empirical formula of C_2H_4O. Chemical tests show that the compound is not an aldehyde or ketone. The chemical does not react with a solution of sodium hydrogen carbonate. Use this information and the mass, IR and NMR spectra provided to deduce the structure and name of the compound.

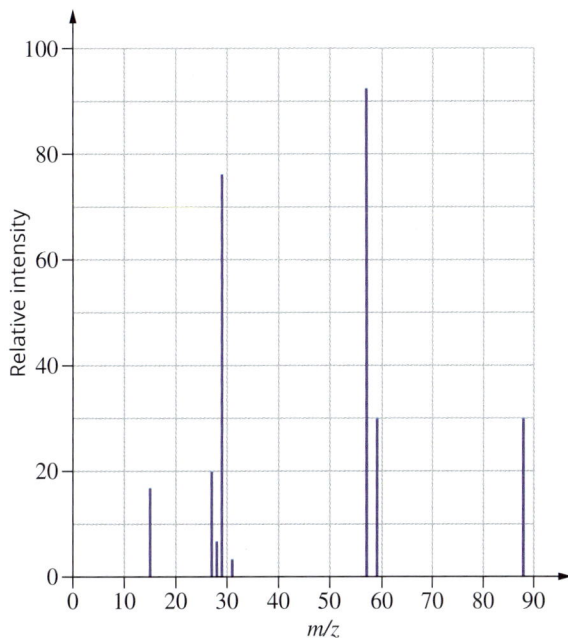

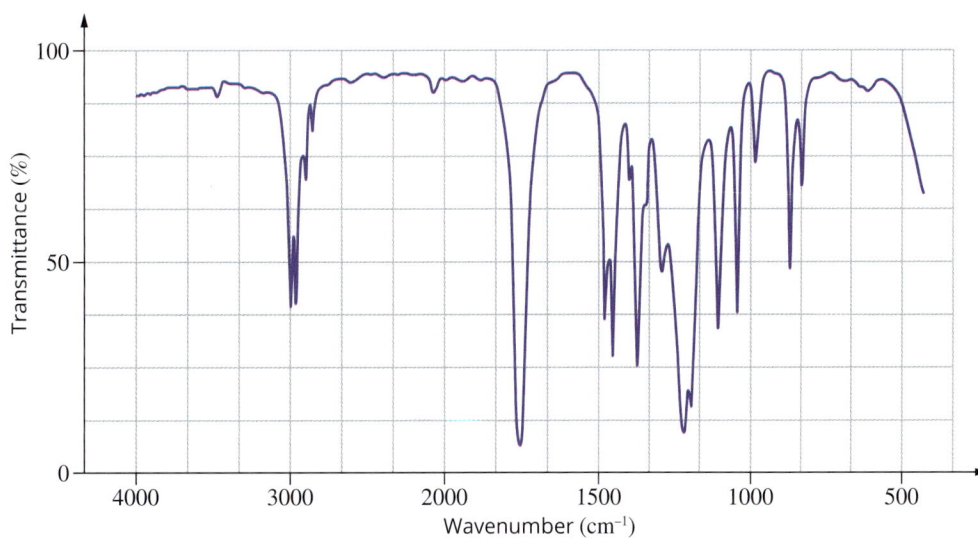

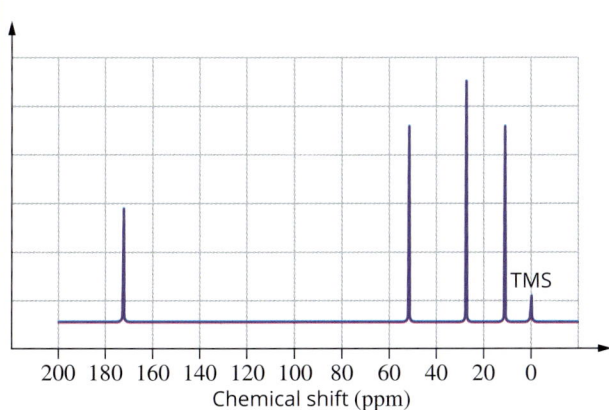

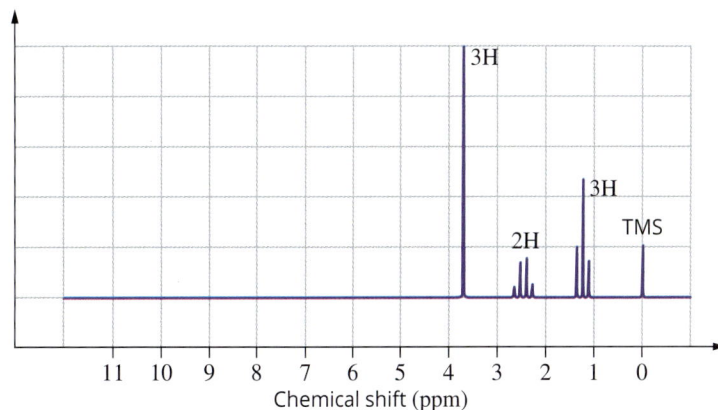

16.5 Review

SUMMARY

- A combination of information derived from mass spectrometry, infrared spectroscopy, carbon-13 NMR spectroscopy and proton NMR spectroscopy can be used to determine the molecular structure of organic compounds.
- The molecular formula of a molecule can be determined from its mass spectrum if its empirical formula is known.

- The infrared spectrum of a compound provides evidence about functional groups present in a molecule.
- The carbon-13 and proton NMR spectra provide detailed information that can be used to determine the connectivity of atoms and overall structure of a molecule.

KEY QUESTIONS

1 Various spectroscopic techniques provide different information about the molecular structure of a compound. Identify the spectroscopic techniques that provide the following information.
   a the functional groups
   b the relative molecular mass
   c the number of different carbon environments
   d the number of different hydrogen environments.

2 The following spectroscopic data was used to identify a compound consisting of C, H and O.

Instrumental technique	Data
IR spectroscopy	very broad absorption band at 3000 cm^{-1}, narrow absorption band at 1750 cm^{-1}
mass spectrometry	molecular ion peak at $m/z = 60$

   a Identify the functional group present in the compound.
   b Determine the identity of the compound.
   c How could carbon-13 NMR and proton NMR spectroscopy be used to confirm the identity of the compound?

3 Use the given molecular structure below to answer the following questions.

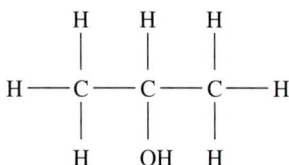

$$H-\overset{\overset{\displaystyle H}{|}}{\underset{\underset{\displaystyle H}{|}}{C}}-\overset{\overset{\displaystyle H}{|}}{\underset{\underset{\displaystyle OH}{|}}{C}}-\overset{\overset{\displaystyle H}{|}}{\underset{\underset{\displaystyle H}{|}}{C}}-H$$

   a Determine the m/z for the molecular ion peak of the mass spectrum of this compound.
   b What is the range of wavenumbers in the IR spectrum for the functional group of this compound?
   c How many peaks are there in the carbon-13 NMR spectrum of this compound?
   d How many peaks are there in the proton NMR spectrum of this compound?

4 The following data was used to identify a compound consisting of C, H and N.

Instrumental technique	Data
IR spectroscopy	broad absorption band at 3400 cm^{-1}
mass spectrometry	molecular ion peak at $m/z = 59$
carbon-13 NMR spectroscopy	3 peaks
proton NMR spectroscopy	4 peaks

   a Identify the functional group present in the compound.
   b Calculate the molecular formula of the compound.
   c What information about the structure of the compound is provided by the NMR data?
   d Determine the condensed structural formula and name of the compound.

5 The molecular ion peak of an alkane has $m/z = 72$. The carbon-13 NMR spectrum shows two peaks and the proton NMR spectrum contains one peak. Identify the alkane.

6 An industrial solvent has the molecular formula C_4H_8O. Use the infrared, proton NMR and carbon-13 NMR spectra to determine the structural formula and name of this molecule. Explain your reasoning.

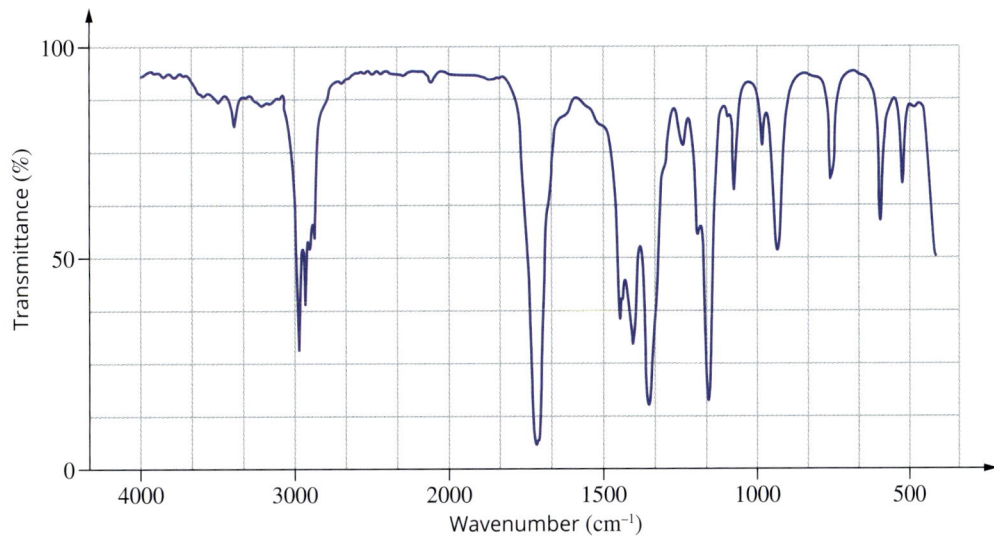

Chemical shift	Peak splitting	Relative peak area
1.0	triplet	3
2.1	singlet	3
2.4	quartet	2

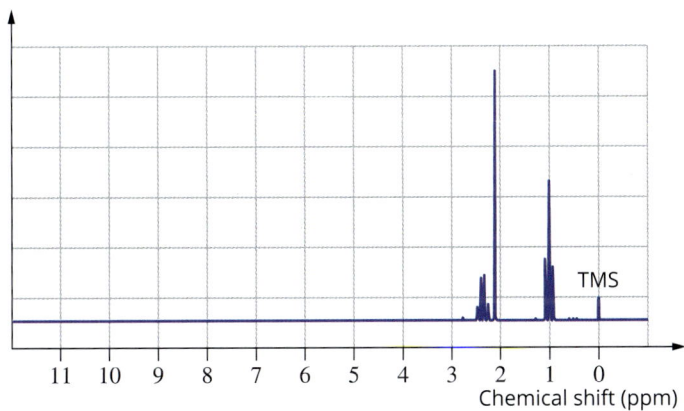

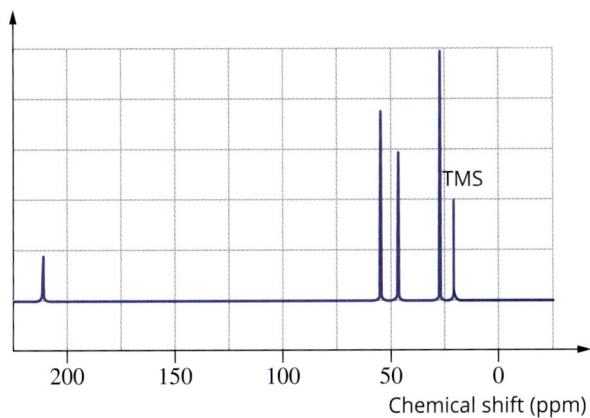

7   An unidentified organic compound composed of 48.6% carbon, 8.2% hydrogen and 43.2% oxygen by mass produced the spectra shown below. Use this information to determine the name of the compound.

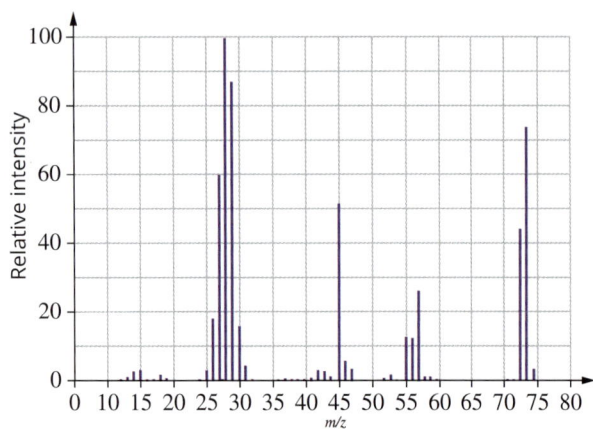

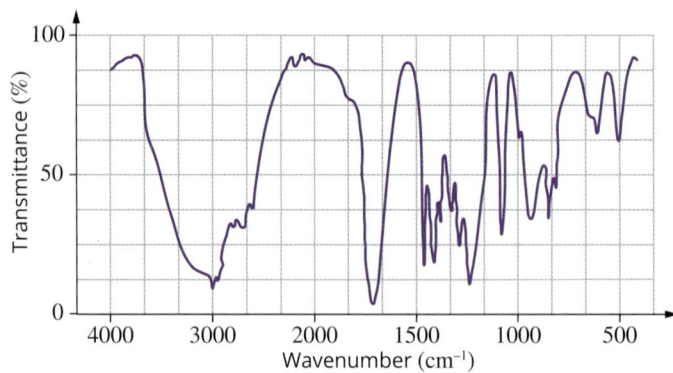

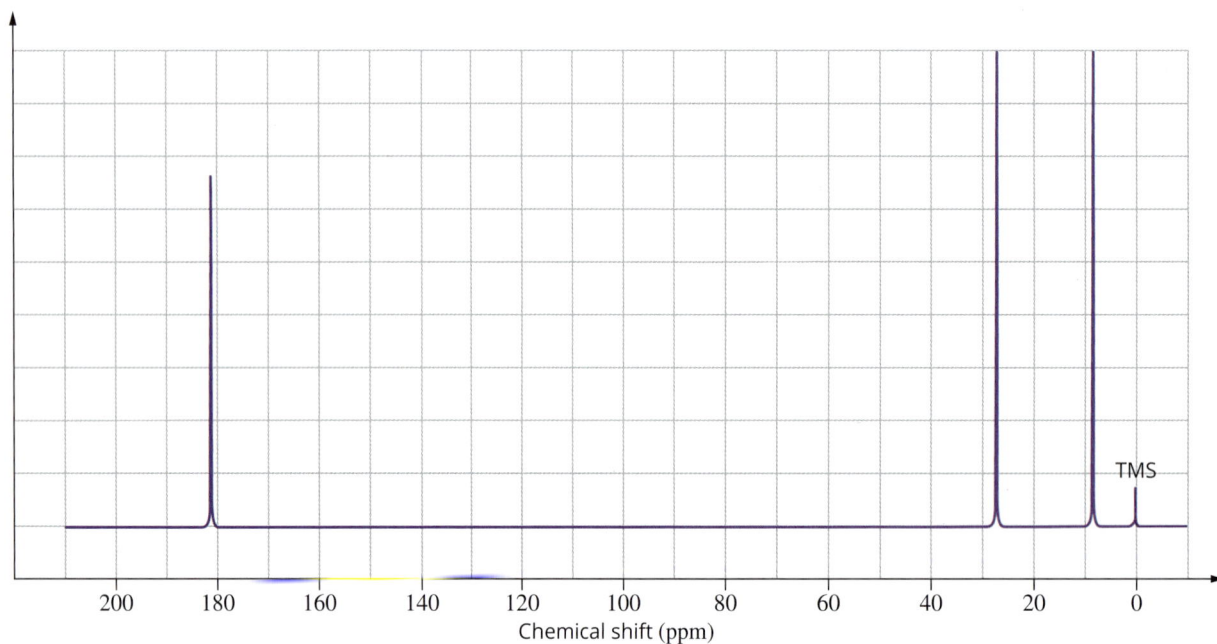

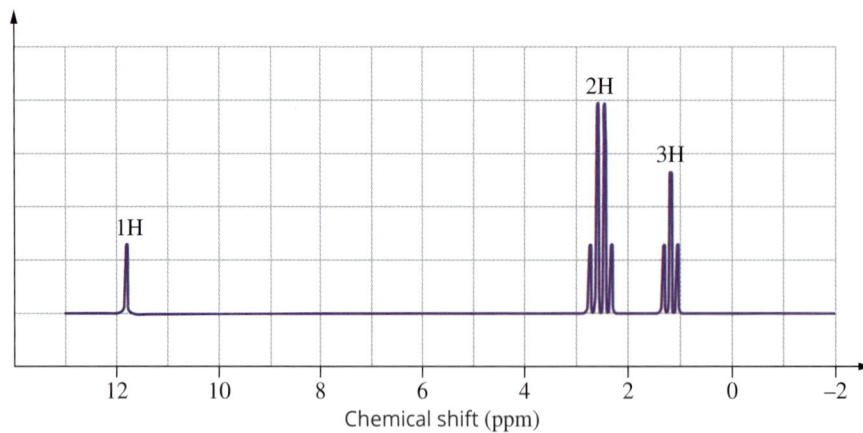

Chapter review

KEY TERMS

absorbance
absorption band
analyte
base peak
calibration curve
carbon-13 NMR
  spectroscopy
chemical shift
dipole

electromagnetic spectrum
equivalent
fingerprint region
fragmentation
functional group
infrared (IR) spectroscopy
isotope
mass spectrometer
mass spectrometry

mass spectrum
molecular ion
molecular ion peak
nuclear magnetic
  resonance (NMR)
  spectroscopy
NMR spectrum
nuclear shielding
nuclear spin

proton NMR spectroscopy
quantitative
splitting pattern
transmittance
vibrational energy level
wavenumber

REVIEW QUESTIONS

1   Describe a chemical test, including expected results, that can be used to test for the presence of the functional groups in:
    a   alkenes
    b   carboxylic acids
    c   alcohols.

2   Outline the limitations of the acidified dichromate test when testing for the presence of alcohols.

3   List the carbon-containing bonds in 2-bromoethanol, in order from the bond that will absorb the lowest-energy infrared radiation to the bond that will absorb the highest-energy infrared radiation.

4   The IR spectra of two liquid samples, A and B, are shown below.

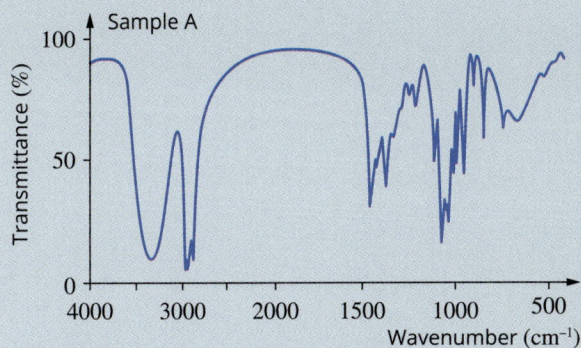

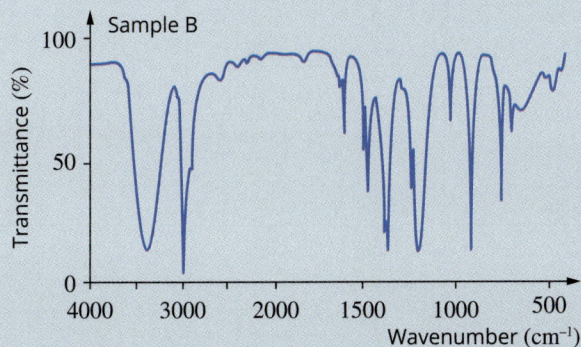

a   Explain how these two spectra confirm that both samples are alcohols.

b   Are these two spectra from the same compound? Explain your answer.

5   What absorption bands in an infrared spectrum are required to indicate the presence of:
    a   a hydroxyl group?
    b   an amide group?
    c   an aldehyde?
    d   a chloroalkane?

6   Explain the use of tetramethylsilane (TMS) in NMR spectroscopy.

7   Ethyl methanoate, methyl ethanoate and propanoic acid are isomers with the formula $C_3H_6O_2$. Match each of these compounds with the following spectra.
    Spectrum A

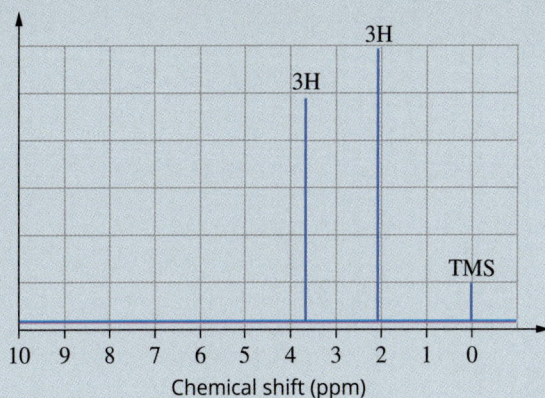

Spectrum B

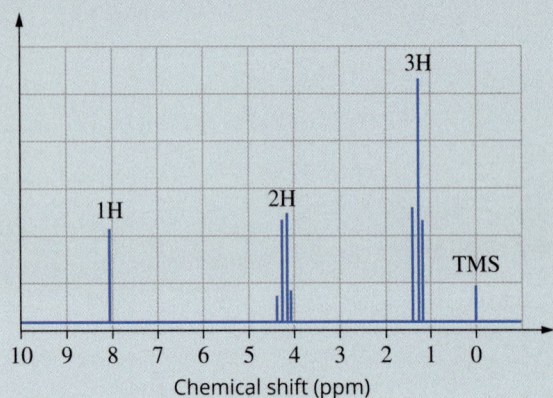

Spectrum C

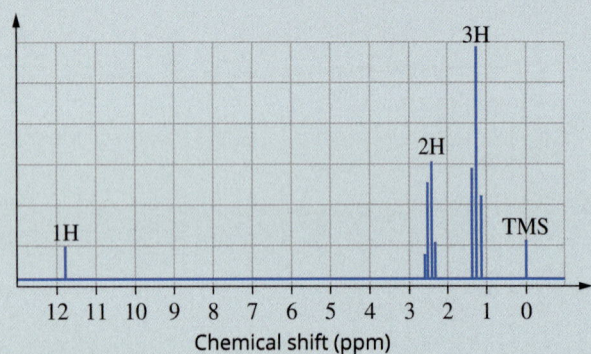

8   A team of chemists isolate a molecule with the molecular formula C_3H_6O. They suspect that the molecule is a ketone because of its chemical properties. Explain how they could use the proton and carbon-13 NMR spectra to determine whether they are correct.

9   Draw a table to predict the expected the number of peaks in carbon-13 NMR and proton NMR spectra of each of the molecules listed below.
    a   propane
    b CH_3CH_2Br
    c $CH_3COOCH_2CH_3$

10 The mass spectrum of an alkane is shown in below.

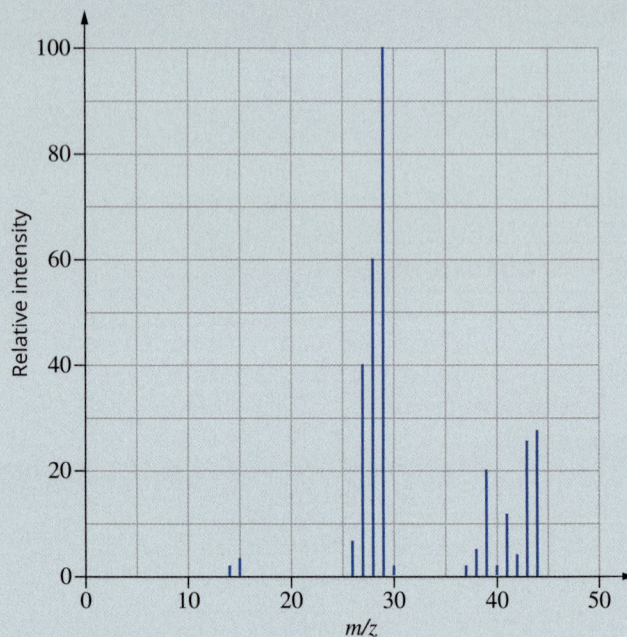

Identify:
    a   the formula of the molecular ion
    b   the ion responsible for the base peak.

11 The mass spectrum of an alkyne is shown below. What is the molecular formula of the alkyne?

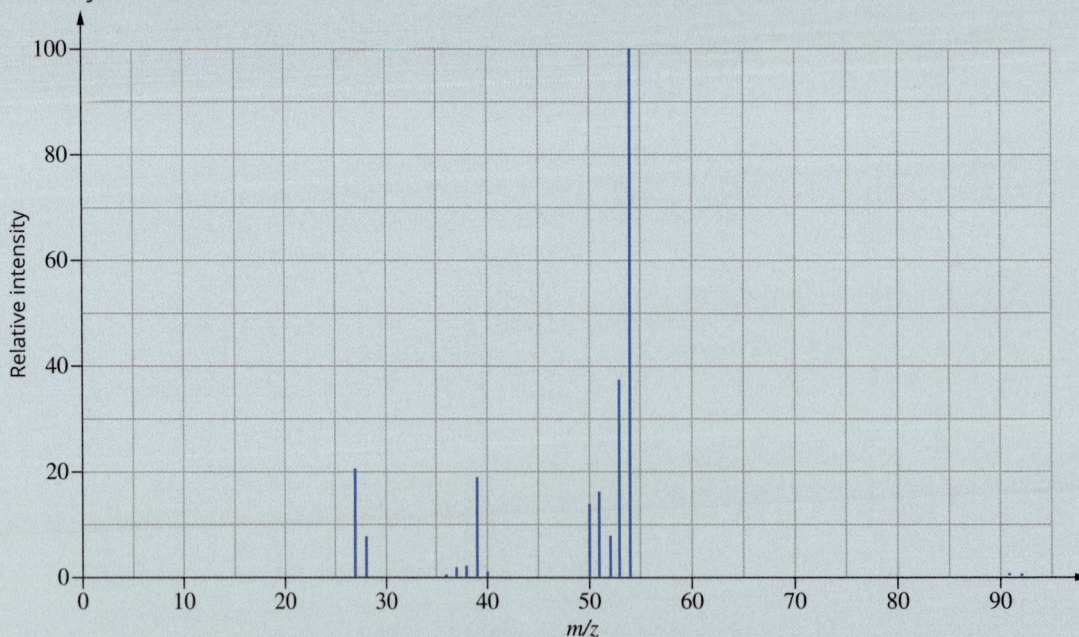

12 A number of compounds with different structures may form molecular ions with the same m/z ratio. Give the molecular formula of a compound that would give an m/z value of 58 if the molecule:

   a is an alkane

   b contains one oxygen atom

   c contains two amine groups.

13 The mass spectrum of a haloalkane with a molecular formula of $C_2H_4Cl_2$ is shown below.

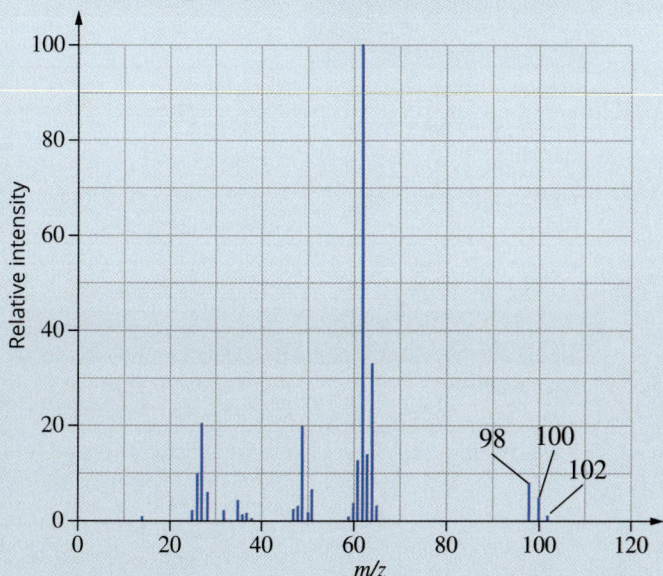

   a Explain why the mass spectrum has peaks with m/z values of:

     i 98

     ii 100

     iii 102.

   b Why is the peak with $m/z = 98$ the largest of these peaks?

   c Determine whether the haloalkane is 1,1-dichloroethane or 1,2-dichloroethane. Explain your answer.

   d Write a possible formula for the ion responsible for the base peak.

14 An unknown compound has a molecular formula C_3H_6O. Its IR spectrum has a strong, sharp absorption band at 1750 cm^{-1}. The carbon-13 NMR has three peaks. The proton NMR spectrum has three sets of peaks: a singlet, a triplet and a quartet. What is the identity of this compound?

15 A hydrocarbon has the empirical formula C_5H_{12}. The m/z of the molecular ion peak is 72. The proton NMR spectrum has a single peak. The carbon-13 NMR has two peaks. What is the identity of this compound?

16 A combination of chemical tests and different instrumental techniques was used to analyse a compound that had an empirical formula of C_2H_4O. The reaction of the compound with a solution of sodium hydrogen carbonate produced a gas which turned limewater milky. The mass, IR, proton NMR and carbon NMR spectra of this compound are shown in the following figures. Details of the proton NMR spectrum are given in the table.

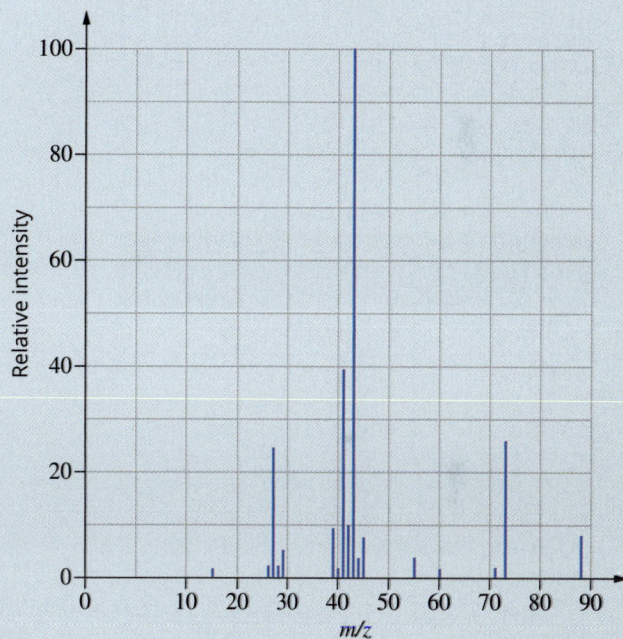

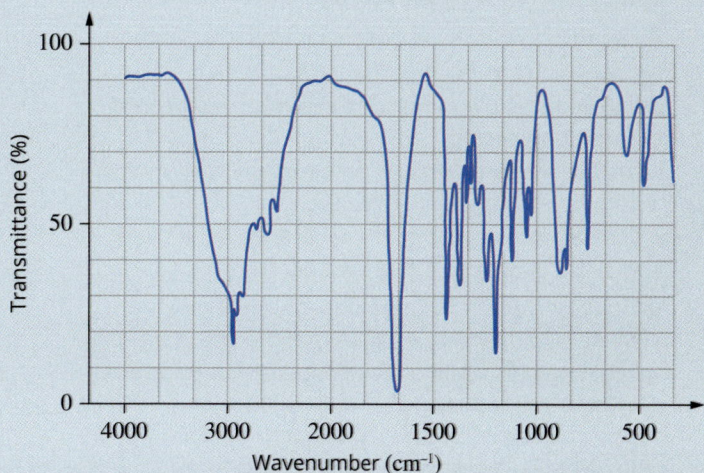

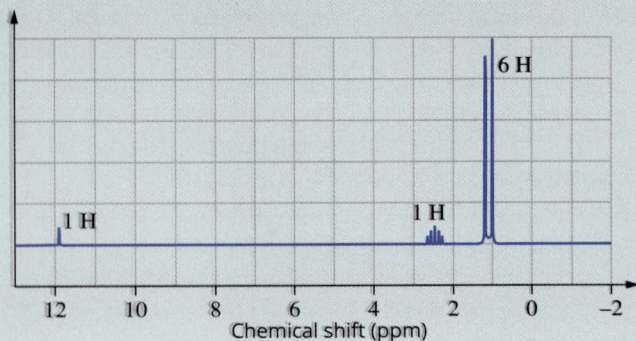

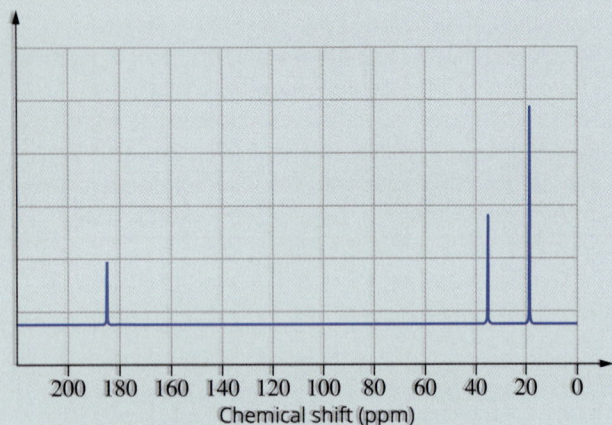

Proton NMR data summary

Chemical shift (ppm)	Peak splitting	Relative peak area
1.1	doublet (2)	6
2.6	septet (7)	1
11.8	singlet (1)	1

What specific information about the compound does each of these spectra provide? Use this information to determine the condensed structural formula and name of the compound.

17 Explain how each of the techniques of NMR spectroscopy, IR spectroscopy and mass spectrometry can be used in the identification of an organic molecule.

18 It is sometimes suggested that proton NMR spectroscopy is the only analytical technique needed for organic molecules.
  a Explain why proton NMR spectroscopy is so useful for analysing organic molecules.
  b What other techniques are needed for a complete analysis of organic molecules?

19 Automatic detectors that use mass spectrometry are often employed by security guards and police officers to search for explosives and illicit drugs. They are powered by a computer that can tell if an illegal substance is present and identify what it is. Explain what the computer should look for in the mass spectrum.

20 A chemist carried out a series of tests to identify the elements present in an unknown organic substance, X. She also carried out some chemical tests to identify the functional groups present in X and used spectroscopic techniques to help her identify the substance. The results of her experiments were recorded in the following table.

Analysis type	Result
Elemental analysis	Only carbon, hydrogen and oxygen were detected.
Chemical analysis	
reaction with bromine water	no reaction
reaction with NaHCO₃ solution	no reaction
reaction with methanoic acid	A compound with a fruity odour was produced.
reaction with acidified dichromate solution	The solution changed colour from orange to green.
Spectroscopic analysis	
mass spectrum	A molecular ion peak at $m/z = 74$ was detected.
IR spectrum	A broad absorption band centred at $3300\,cm^{-1}$ was detected. No absorption band between $1680\,cm^{-1}$ and $1750\,cm^{-1}$ was evident.
carbon-13 NMR	Three peaks were detected.

  a On the basis of the elemental analysis, to which classes of organic compounds could substance X belong? (Limit your answer to the classes of organic compounds that you have studied in this course.)
  b Do the chemical tests indicate the class or classes of organic compounds to which substance X might belong? Justify your answer in terms of an interpretation of the data provided by the chemical tests.
  c From the IR data, what conclusion can you make about the class of compounds to which substance X belongs? Explain your reasoning.
  d Use information obtained from the mass spectrum to determine the molecular formula of substance X.
  e Substance X can be one of several different compounds that have same the same molecular formula as substance X and the same functional group as indicated by the IR data. Draw the condensed structural formulae of these compounds.
  f What information about the structure of substance X is provided by the carbon-13 NMR data?
  g Identify the compound by its systematic name.

21 Reflect on the Inquiry activity on page 462. What did the ball bearings represent? Contrast the ball bearing model with the process in a real mass spectrometer.

Chemical synthesis and design

In this course you have learnt about a range of chemicals and their structures and properties. The chemicals you have studied include metals, pharmaceuticals, polymers, soaps, acids and fuels. These are important raw materials or products that our society relies upon. Most of these chemicals do not occur naturally; they have to be manufactured. This is the job of the chemical industry.

In this chapter you will see an overview of the Australian chemical industry and investigate how the theory you have learnt throughout your chemistry course is vital to the safe manufacture of chemicals in a competitive global environment.

Content

INQUIRY QUESTION

What are the implications for society of chemical synthesis and design?

By the end of this chapter, you will be able to:

- evaluate the factors that need to be considered when designing a chemical synthesis process, including but not limited to:
  - availability of reagents
  - reaction conditions (ACSCH133)
  - yield and purity (ACSCH134)
  - industrial uses (e.g. pharmaceutical, cosmetics, cleaning products, fuels) (ACSCH131)
  - environmental, social and economic issues

Chemistry Stage 6 Syllabus © NSW Education Standards Authority for and on behalf of the Crown in right of the State of NSW, 2017.

17.1 Chemical synthesis and design

Is baking just a chemical reaction?

COLLECT THIS ...

- 125 g butter
- 4 eggs
- 2 cups milk
- 1 cup sugar
- 1 cup desiccated coconut
- ½ cup plain flour

- 2 teaspoons vanilla essence
- baking dish
- balance
- blender, electric beater or wooden spoon
- cream (optional)

DO THIS ...

1 Weigh the baking dish.
2 Add all the ingredients, mixing well.
3 Reweigh the baking dish containing the ingredients.
4 Bake in a moderate oven (180°C) for 1 hour or until brown on top.
5 Reweigh once cooled.
6 Enjoy with cream!
7 Weigh the empty dish.

RECORD THIS ...

Record all mass measurements.
Describe any waste you have created.

REFLECT ON THIS ...

1 If the initial and final masses are different, why could this be?
2 What waste have you created, and how should it be disposed of?
3 What would have happened if you had cooked the mixture at 260°C?
4 Where did your raw materials come from?

SNAPSHOT OF THE AUSTRALIAN CHEMICAL INDUSTRY

The chemical industry is one of the most diverse and broad in its reach across Australian society, environment and industry. The sector can be broadly divided into three categories based on what is produced:

- basic chemicals: industrial gases, fertilisers, synthetic resins, organic chemicals, inorganic chemicals
- speciality chemicals: explosives, paints, polymers, foam products, adhesives, inks, glues, surface cleaners
- consumer chemicals: cosmetics and toiletries, soaps and detergents, pesticides, pharmaceuticals, food.

Figure 17.1.1 shows a crop of canola that has been bioengineered to produce long-chain omega-3 fatty acids. Chemists have confirmed that these fatty acids are the same as those found in fish. As the current global rate of fishing is unsustainable, it is hoped that this Australian development will provide a sustainable alternative source of long chain omega-3 fatty acids.

Chemistry Australia, which represents the Australian chemistry industry, provides the following snapshot of the importance to Australia of our chemical industry:

- It employs over 60 000 skilled workers and is the leading employer of Australia's science, technology, engineering and mathematics capability.
- It includes over 5500 small to large businesses.

> ⓘ Australian chemical industries can be divided into three categories: basic chemicals, specialty chemicals and consumer chemicals.

FIGURE 17.1.1 A canola crop that has been genetically modified to produce long-chain omega-3 fatty acids

- It is our second largest manufacturing sector.
- It delivers over $11.6 billion to Australia's GDP.

About 80% of the industry's output is inputs for other sectors. An example is polymers produced by our chemical industry. Many of these are then used to manufacture components for the construction industry. Every job in the chemical sector creates approximately five more jobs in sectors farther along the supply chain.

Figure 17.1.2 provides a visual representation of the flow-on effect of the chemical industry.

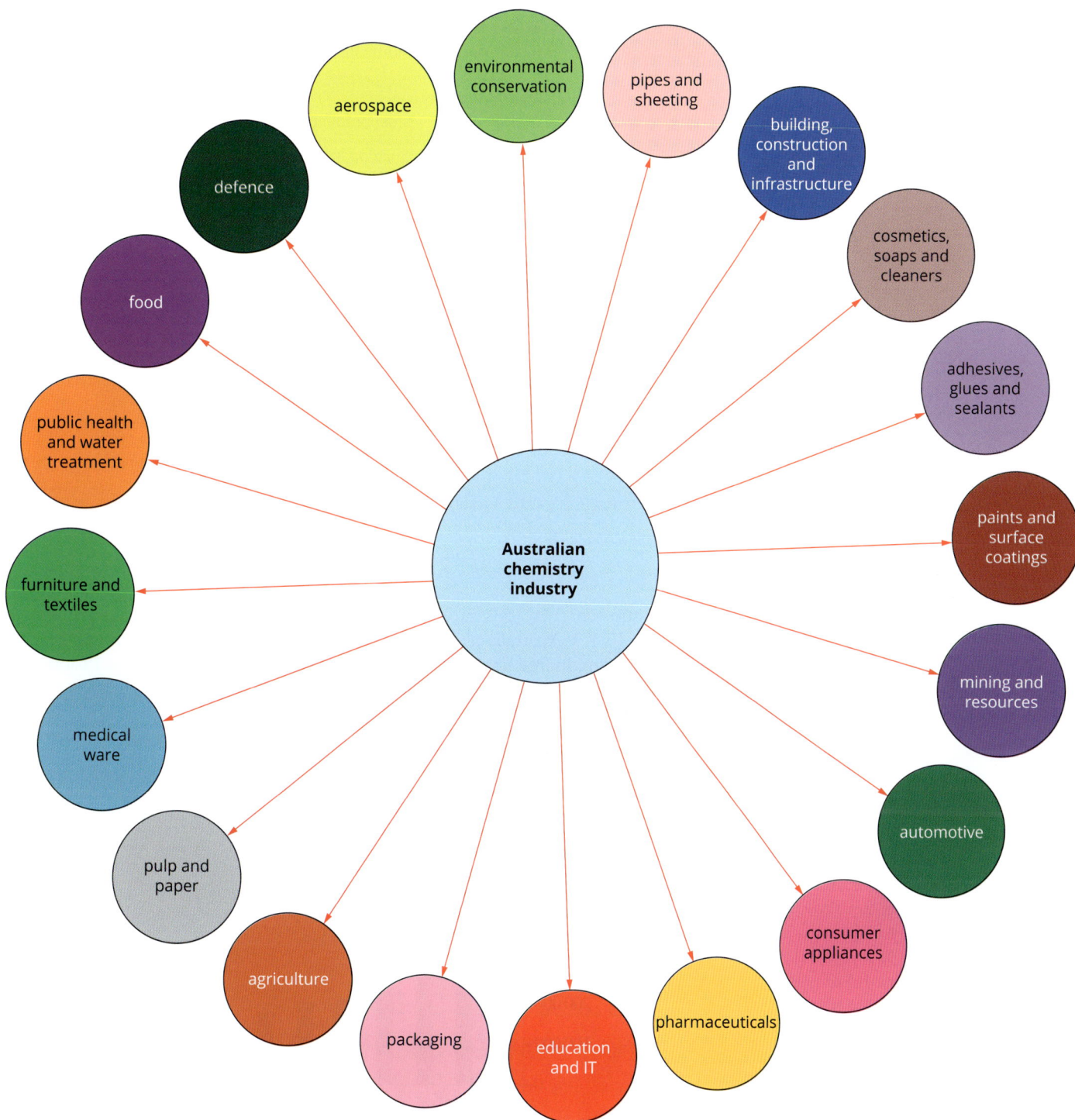

FIGURE 17.1.2 The flow-on effect of the chemical industry on other Australian industries

Table 17.1.1 is a list of some of Australia's largest companies that use or manufacture chemicals as a critical part of their business. Many of these companies will be familiar to you. They are listed in alphabetical order because it would be difficult to rank them in order of profit or production levels, which can vary significantly each year. It is also difficult to discern what proportion of production occurs in Australia, because many of these companies are global organisations.

TABLE 17.1.1 Examples of companies that are involved in the Australian chemical industry

Company	Examples of products
Alcoa	aluminium, alumina
BHP	smelted metals
BlueScope Steel	steel products
Boral	building materials, cement, plaster
Caltex	fuels, lubricants
CSL	biopharmaceuticals
CSR	building materials
DuluxGroup	paints, chemicals
Lion-Nathan	beverages, dairy products, juices
Nufarm	pesticides, herbicides, fungicides
Orica	chemicals, explosives, PVC
Rio Tinto	aluminium, smelted metals
Rosella	sauces, processed foods
SPC Ardmona (Coca-Cola Amatil)	processed foods
Tasmanian Alkaloids	pharmaceuticals
Unilever	soaps and detergents, personal care, food, drinks

The top ten chemicals produced in Australia from petrochemicals are shown in Figure 17.1.3. Australia also produces large volumes of metals such as steel and aluminium, and inorganic chemicals such as sulfuric acid and fertilisers. Production levels can vary significantly with global market prices.

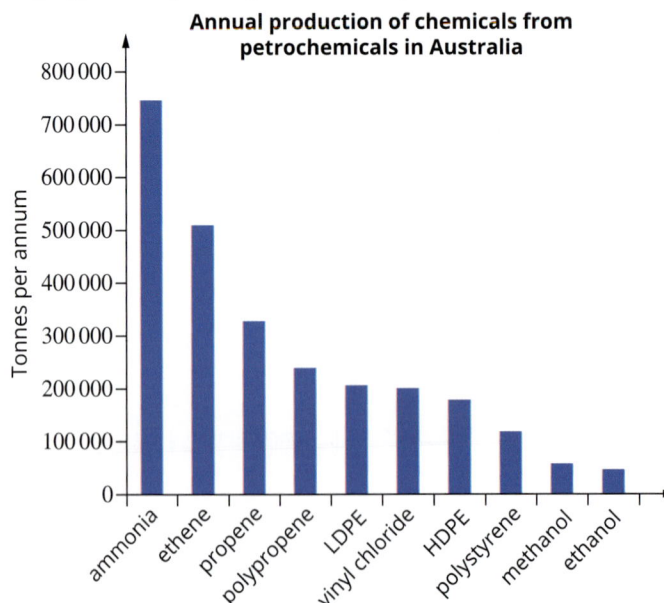

FIGURE 17.1.3 The top 10 chemicals in terms of the amount (tonnes per annum) produced in Australia from petrochemicals

Case study: Qenos

There are many considerations in building a chemical plant. The major considerations are:

- location
- source of raw materials
- product uses
- reaction conditions
- energy supply
- water supply
- transport infrastructure
- commodity price and market
- safety
- emissions and disposal of wastes
- labour force
- ethical considerations.

The infrastructure required can cost over a billion dollars, and the markets are very competitive. Globalisation of industries over recent decades has led to the closure of many plants that were once viable. For example, Australia once had more than five large tyre manufacturing factories and several car manufacturing plants; now there are none. The following case study highlights some of the factors to be considered in planning a viable chemical plant.

Qenos produces ethene, polyethene and other polymers at its production facilities at Botany in NSW and Altona in Victoria (Figure 17.1.4). The company employs over 700 people in these plants. Qenos shares the majority of the Botany Industrial Park (BIP) with two other large companies, Orica Australia and Huntsman Corporation Australia. It is common for chemical manufacturers to form a complex. This allows for sharing of expertise, transport infrastructure, disposal facilities and raw materials. It is also considered more desirable to locate several hazardous industries together than to place them at different locations in populated areas.

Qenos uses ethane as a raw material. The ethane is tapped from the Cooper Basin in outback South Australia and piped nearly 1400 km to Botany. The ethane is passed through what is known as a **cracker**, where it is converted to ethene. This is a one-step process but is not simple. To obtain a viable yield, the following conditions are essential:

- temperatures up to 900°C
- a very short reaction time
- low hydrocarbon concentrations
- rapid cooling of products to prevent their decomposition.

The conditions chosen are not random; they are the result of an understanding of principles of reaction rates and equilibrium systems.

The ethene is purified from other products using fractional distillation. It is then polymerised to various forms of polyethene (Figure 17.1.5).

FIGURE 17.1.4 A section of the large Qenos plant required to produce ethene from ethane

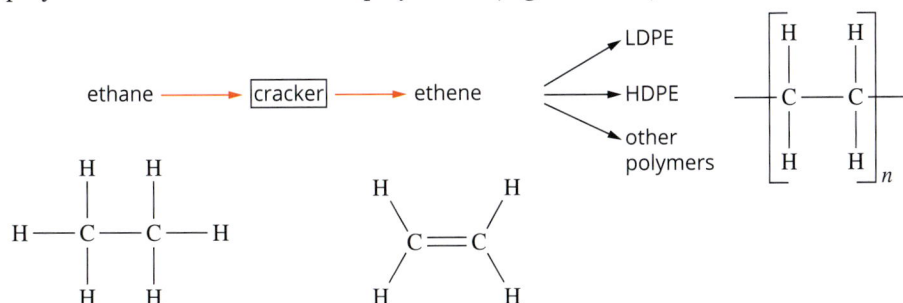

FIGURE 17.1.5 Qenos converts ethane to ethene, then polymerises ethene to polyethene.

Many items that are used in the home, such as clingwrap, drink bottles, micro-irrigation pipes, moulded plastics and telecommunication conduits are made from polymers produced by Qenos. Ethene is also sold to other industries that use it to make other products.

Ethene is a volatile gas stored under high pressure. Qenos has to meet high safety standards to conduct an industry such as this in the vicinity of a major city. Waste needs to be minimised and emissions must be controlled. Many regulations are also in place to ensure a safe environment for the workers on the site.

CHEMICAL SYNTHESIS FACTORS

Location and availability of reagents

Ethane gas is easily transported through pipes. To produce polyethene in NSW, a pipe had to be built from the natural gas fields in South Australia. Qenos was then free to choose a location like Botany because of its access to a port, energy and water supply. For other industries the location of the raw materials determines the location of the plant. The Cassegrain Kalara Tea Tree Oil extraction plant is located on the northern coast of NSW as the climate there suits the growing of tea-tree plantations. It would not be viable to transport trees with such a low oil content to a processing plant in a distant location. It is more practical to extract the oil close to where the trees grow and then transport the extracted oil.

Other examples where the raw material dictates the plant location are:
- Mining at Broken Hill. The concentrations of metals such as lead and zinc are as low as 2–3%. It is not viable to transport the ore to another region if 97–98% of the transported material will end up as waste.
- Dairy and cheese industry factories. Bega and Tilba (Figure 17.1.6) are in the heart of a fertile dairy farming district in south-eastern NSW. It is practical to process the milk close to the source.
- Biofuel plants. These plants use waste agricultural products from sugar and wheat processing plants to produce biodiesel or bioethanol. Plants such as the Manildra facility near Nowra shown in Figure 17.1.7 are located in the cropping districts.
- Coal-fired power stations. These are located near the coal deposits to eliminate transport costs.

The location of raw materials is not the only determinant of plant location. Some other factors that might influence the choice of location are:
- Specialised technology or expertise. The University of Sydney lists companies such as Rio Tinto, Qantas, Elastagen and Sirtex Medical as research partners. It is convenient for the University and for industry to combine on high-tech projects. One of the common areas of combined research is in medical and pharmaceutical research (Figure 17.1.8).
- Port facilities. The steel industry has used Newcastle and Port Kembla for chemical plants as they can ship in high volumes of raw materials and ship out high volumes of exports.
- Remoteness. Lead **smelters** produce significant emissions, including toxic gases such as SO_2. Tailings from the smelter can also lead to high lead content in local soils. It can be an advantage for such plants to be in remote areas where fewer people are impacted.
- Water supply. Facilities such as coal-fired power stations need to be close to an adequate water supply (Figure 17.1.9).
- Where the product is sold. Many of Australia's petrol refineries are located near capital cities because it means overall shorter distances for tranporting the fuel.

FIGURE 17.1.6 The dairy industry usually processes milk near the fertile areas of each state.

FIGURE 17.1.7 A tanker loads bioethanol at Manildra. The plant is located near the wheat processing facility.

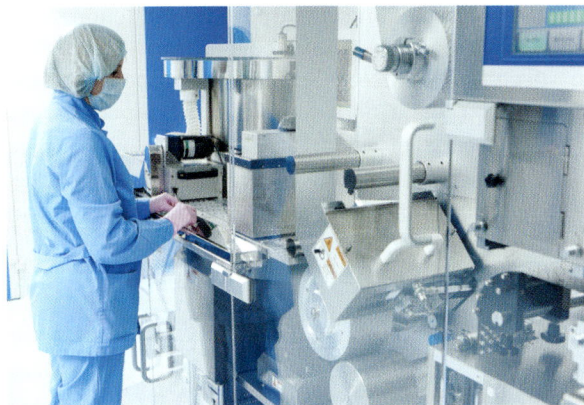

FIGURE 17.1.8 Pharmaceutical manufacturing is a high-tech industry in which research is often shared with tertiary institutions.

FIGURE 17.1.9 Coal-fired power stations need to be located close to a significant water supply.

REACTION CONDITIONS

The chemical industry is highly competitive, so chemical companies do not leave the efficiency of their manufacturing plants to chance. They thoroughly research the optimum conditions for reactions that will lead to the highest conversion rates with the lowest production costs.

Earlier in this chapter you learnt that Qenos converts ethane into ethene. This is a reversible endothermic reaction:

$$C_2H_6(g) \rightleftharpoons C_2H_4(g) + H_2(g)$$

This process does not work at normal temperatures and pressures because the system is at or close to equilibrium. Applying equilibrium principles suggests that the yield will be improved under the following conditions:

- High temperatures (around 900°C) are used. For an endothermic reaction, the value of the equilibrium constant K_{eq} increases with temperature.
- Low pressures are used. The ratio of reactant particles to product particles is 1:2, so low pressure favours the forward reaction.
- A catalyst is used. Although the catalyst does not change the yield it does increase the reaction rate.
- The temperature of the products is cooled rapidly. This prevents further decomposition of the ethene to ethyne or carbon (Figure 17.1.10).

FIGURE 17.1.10 Controlling the conditions in a manufacturing process can have a marked impact on the success of the process.

Similar research is conducted into the optimal production conditions for other chemicals, including foods. For example, cocoa beans are roasted at 130°C for several hours to successfully extract, but not decompose, the cocoa. Chocolate produced from the cocoa has a narrow optimum temperature range; at around 50°C it will flow but not coagulate.

The food chemists in the dairy industry are responsible for the careful control of many processes, ranging from the action of rennin on milk to form cheese to the action of bacteria on milk to form yoghurt. All of these processes need to run at specific temperatures and pH values for optimum production.

Another example of the importance of controlling reaction conditions is the production of ammonia from nitrogen and hydrogen gases:

$$N_2(g) + 3H_2(g) \rightleftharpoons 2NH_3(g)$$

The graphs in Figure 17.1.11 show the variation of yield with temperature and pressure. The graphs illustrate that high pressure will improve the yield of ammonia but high temperature will limit the yield. Chemists use conditions that are a compromise between yield and the cost of production.

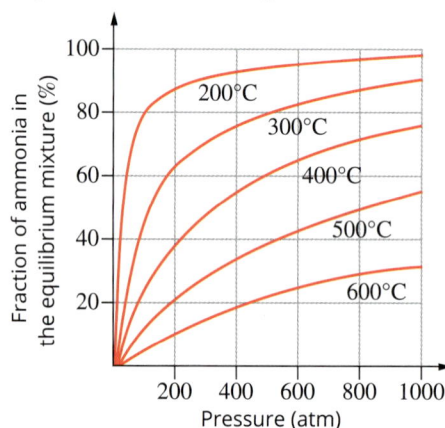

FIGURE 17.1.11 The percentage of ammonia present when a mixture of nitrogen and hydrogen has reached equilibrium

YIELD AND THE CHEMICAL INDUSTRY

Many industrial processes involve a number of steps in order to make the final product. At each step the conversion from reactants to products is usually less than complete. At every step in a reaction pathway the amount of product diminishes. Industrial chemists must consider the efficiency of a reaction pathway and the wastes that are produced (Figure 17.1.12).

In this section, you will learn to perform calculations that can be used to determine the efficiency of processes that involve chemical reactions and help in the development of strategies to minimise waste.

Yield

Theoretical and actual yields

The mass of product that can be formed if all reactants react to produce the product according to the reaction equation is known as the **theoretical yield**. The theoretical yield is calculated using the mole ratios of the equation and assumes 100% conversion of the reactants. However, when reactants are mixed together in the correct mole ratio, the amount of products will not always be exactly as predicted from stoichiometric calculations.

FIGURE 17.1.12 Most chemical reactions carried out in industrial processes are not 100% efficient and so waste chemicals are produced. The reduction or elimination of waste chemicals is a major concern for industrial chemists.

A number of factors can influence the amount of product that will be produced for a given reaction.

- When a reaction reaches equilibrium rather than continuing on to completion, the **actual yield** will be less than the theoretical yield.
- If the reaction rate is slow, the reaction may not proceed to completion in the time available. This will reduce the actual yield so that the theoretical yield is not obtained.
- Loss of reactants and products during transfers between reaction vessels, and in separation and purification stages such as filtration, will result in less product than expected.

> **ℹ** Theoretical yield is the maximum amount of product that can be formed based on stoichiometric calculations using the limiting reactant, and assumes 100% conversion.

Percentage yield

The **percentage yield** compares the actual yield to the theoretical yield. It is a measure of the efficiency of a production process, for the particular conditions and method used for the synthesis. The higher the value of the percentage yield, the greater the degree of conversion from reactants to products for the reaction.

Percentage yield can be calculated using the formula:

$$\text{percentage yield} = \frac{\text{actual yield}}{\text{theoretical yield}} \times \frac{100}{1}$$

Worked example 17.1.1

CALCULATING THE PERCENTAGE YIELD OF A REACTION

30.0 g of propan-2-ol was oxidised to propanone using an acidified solution of $K_2Cr_2O_7$. The propanone that was distilled from the reaction mixture had a mass of 20.0 g. Calculate the percentage yield of this oxidation reaction.

Thinking	Working
Write an equation for the reaction.	$CH_3CHOHCH_3 \xrightarrow{H^+/Cr_2O_7^{2-}} CH_3COCH_3$ In this case it is not necessary to write a full equation. Because a molecule of the organic product has the same number of carbon atoms as the organic reactant, the number of moles of the product is equal to the number of moles of the reactant.
Use the formula $n = \frac{m}{M}$ to determine the amount of reactant.	$n(CH_3CHOHCH_3) = \frac{m}{M}$ $= \frac{30.0}{60.10}$ $= 0.499 \text{ mol}$
Use the mole ratio for the reaction to determine the amount, in mol, of the product that would be made if all of the reactant reacted.	$\text{mole ratio} = \frac{\text{coefficient of } CH_3COCH_3}{\text{coefficient of } CH_3CHOHCH_3} = \frac{1}{1}$ $n(CH_3COCH_3) = n(CH_3CHOHCH_3)$ $= 0.499 \text{ mol}$
Use the formula $m = n \times M$ to determine the mass of the product if all of the reactant reacts. This is the theoretical yield of the product.	$m(CH_3COCH_3) = n \times M$ $= 0.499 \times 58.08$ $= 29.0 \text{ g}$
Calculate the percentage yield for this reaction from the formula: $\text{percentage yield} = \frac{\text{actual yield}}{\text{theoretical yield}} \times \frac{100}{1}$	$\text{percentage yield} = \frac{20.0}{29.0} \times \frac{100}{1}$ $= 69.0\%$

Worked example: Try yourself 17.1.1

CALCULATING THE PERCENTAGE YIELD OF A REACTION

> 80.0 g of propan-1-ol was oxidised to propanoic acid using an acidified solution of $K_2Cr_2O_7$. The propanoic acid obtained at the end of the reaction had a mass of 55.0 g. Calculate the percentage yield of this oxidation reaction.

Percentage yields in multistep syntheses

When a reaction proceeds by a number of steps, the overall percentage yield is reduced at each step. The yield for each step has an effect on the overall yield. A low yield in one of the intermediate reactions can have a significant effect on the amount of final product obtained.

A comparison of the overall percentage yields for different pathways to the same product can be used to determine whether a particular synthetic pathway is the best way to produce an organic compound. Finding the most efficient pathway for the production of a desired chemical is critical, because wasting valuable reactants is poor economic and environmental practice.

Worked example 17.1.2

CALCULATING THE PERCENTAGE YIELD OF A MULTISTEP SYNTHESIS

> Calculate the overall percentage yield for the preparation of C from A if it proceeds by a two-step synthesis:
>
> $$A \rightarrow B \text{ followed by } B \rightarrow C$$
>
> The yield of $A \rightarrow B$ is 80% and the yield of $B \rightarrow C$ is 70%.

Thinking	Working
Calculate the overall yield of C by multiplying the percentage yields together and expressing as a percentage (multiplying by 100).	The overall yield of C is: $\frac{80}{100} \times \frac{70}{100} \times \frac{100}{1}$ = 56%

Worked example: Try yourself 17.1.2

CALCULATING THE PERCENTAGE YIELD OF A MULTISTEP SYNTHESIS

> Calculate the overall percentage yield for the preparation of D from A if it proceeds by a three-step synthesis:
>
> $$A \rightarrow B \text{ followed by } B \rightarrow C \text{ followed by } C \rightarrow D$$
>
> The yield of $A \rightarrow B$ is 90%, the yield of $B \rightarrow C$ is 80% and the yield of $C \rightarrow D$ is 60%.

Atom economy

An important objective for an industrial chemist who is developing a reaction pathway is to use a sequence of chemical reactions that minimises energy consumption, reduces waste and has a low impact on the environment.

One consideration when planning reaction pathways is to maximise **atom economy**.

> ℹ The atom economy for a chemical reaction is a measure of the percentage of the atoms in the reactants that end up in the desired product.

As you can see in Figure 17.1.13, if the atom economy of a reaction is high, then there are few, if any, waste products.

high atom economy

reactants → desired product

lower atom economy

reactants → desired product + waste

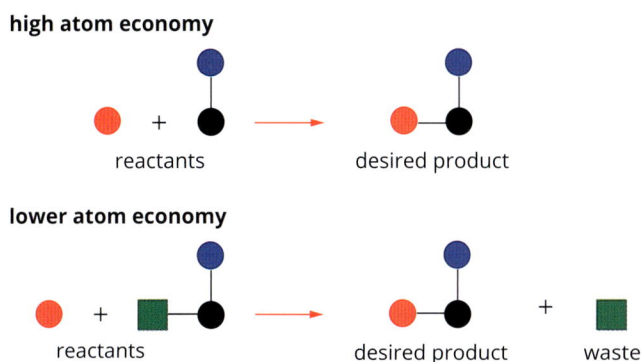

FIGURE 17.1.13 The different symbols represent different atoms or groups of atoms. In a high atom economy reaction, all or most of the atoms in the reactant molecules end up in the desired product molecule.

Calculating the atom economy of a reaction provides a method of accounting for the use of materials in a manufacturing process. It tracks all the atoms in a reaction and calculates the mass of the atoms of reactants actually used to form products as a percentage of the total mass of reactants. From this, the mass of reactant atoms that end up as waste can also be calculated.

Once the balanced equation for a reaction is known, the atom economy can be calculated using the formula:

$$\text{atom economy} = \frac{\text{molar mass of desired product}}{\text{molar mass of all reactants}} \times 100$$

Because the total mass of products is equal to the total mass of reactants, the following formula can also be used:

$$\text{atom economy} = \frac{\text{mass of desired product}}{\text{mass of all reactants}} \times 100$$

Use Worked example 17.1.3 to help you with calculations of atom economy.

Worked example 17.1.3

CALCULATING ATOM ECONOMY

Calculate the atom economy in the production of ethanol from chloroethane. In this process, chloroethane is heated with a solution of sodium hydroxide. The equation for the reaction is:

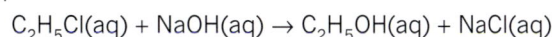

$$C_2H_5Cl(aq) + NaOH(aq) \rightarrow C_2H_5OH(aq) + NaCl(aq)$$

Thinking	Working
Calculate the total molar mass of the reactants.	$M(C_2H_5Cl) + M(NaOH)$ $= [(2 \times 12.01) + (5 \times 1.008) + 35.45] + [22.99 + 16.00 + 1.008]$ $= 104.51\,\text{g mol}^{-1}$
Calculate the molar mass of the required product.	$M(C_2H_5OH) = (2 \times 12.01) + (6 \times 1.008) + 16.00$ $\qquad\qquad = 46.07\,\text{g mol}^{-1}$
Calculate the atom economy for the reaction using the formula: $$\text{atom economy} = \frac{\text{molar mass of desired product}}{\text{molar mass of all reactants}} \times 100$$	$\text{Atom economy} = \frac{46.07}{104.51} \times 100$ $\qquad\qquad = 44.08\%$ In this process 44.08% of the starting materials are converted to the desired product. The remainder of the chemicals used is waste.

Worked example: Try yourself 17.1.3

CALCULATING ATOM ECONOMY

Calculate the percentage atom economy in the formation of 1-iodopropane ($CH_3CH_2CH_2I$) from propan-1-ol. The equation for the reaction is:

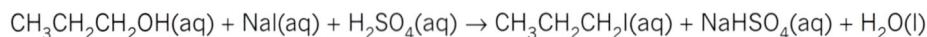

$$CH_3CH_2CH_2OH(aq) + NaI(aq) + H_2SO_4(aq) \rightarrow CH_3CH_2CH_2I(aq) + NaHSO_4(aq) + H_2O(l)$$

FIGURE 17.1.14 Most chemical industries have a quality control department, responsible for ensuring the purity of a product is high and that any labelling of ingredients is accurate.

PURITY AND QUALITY CONTROL

Another important aspect of chemical manufacture is **quality control**. Consumers need to be confident that the product they are purchasing is pure enough to perform as expected. This is easier to explain with some examples.

- Food products. The labels on foods tell you about the nutritional properties of the food. If you are allergic to a particular preservative you need to be confident that the label will accurately tell you what preservatives are in the food (Figure 17.1.14).
- Petrol. Drivers need to be confident that the level of impurities in petrol is very low to prevent damage to the vehicle.
- Laboratory reagents. Impurities in reagents can result in false or misleading results in chemical analyses and investigations. This is especially true for reagents that include molecules required for specific reactions, such as DNA fragments used in gene sequencing.

Qenos needs to test the quality of the raw materials it uses as well as the products it manufactures. Natural gas arriving by pipe is tested for ethane content as well as sulfur content and other impurities. The ethene Qenos sells is tested to ensure that other chemicals produced in this reaction have been successfully removed.

CHEMFILE EU

PAN Pharmaceuticals

In 2003 supermarket and chemist shoppers were surprised to see many health foods and alternative medicines taken off the shelves. The Therapeutic Goods Administration issued a recall of 219 products manufactured and supplied by PAN Pharmaceuticals because of poor quality control (Figure 17.1.15). Several items were found to have grossly misleading labelling, leading to the possibility of severe health issues in consumers. The company collapsed as a result of the controversy.

FIGURE 17.1.15 Pharmaceutical products being cleared from shop shelves after the 2003 recall

ECONOMIC CONSIDERATIONS

Like all industries, chemical companies need to make a profit. To do this, companies seek to minimise expenses and maximise revenue from sales. In a global market it is not always easy to control either of these factors. Figure 17.1.16 shows the severe drops in the world price of iron ore in 2015. Given the high volume of Australian exports of iron ore, this trend was disastrous and almost single-handedly placed Australia in recession. Our agricultural industries face the same fluctuations in export markets when drought or floods strike different competitor's crops.

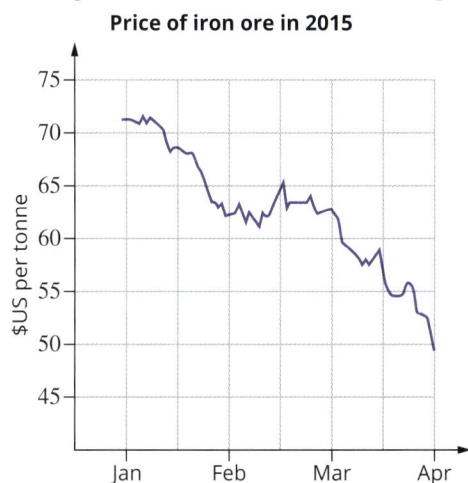

Price of iron ore in 2015

FIGURE 17.1.16 The world price of iron dropped markedly in 2015, causing a fall in profits and taxes paid. Global chemical markets are very competitive.

The demise of the car industry in Australia is another example of the competitive nature of manufacturing markets. Since 2012, Ford, Holden and Toyota have all ceased assembling cars in Australia. Their closures had a flow-on effect to associated industries supplying components such as brake pads, upholstery and specialty polymers to the car makers (Figure 17.1.17).

ENVIRONMENTAL AND SOCIAL CONSIDERATIONS

Chemical industries take in raw materials and convert them to new substances. During this process, waste is often produced. The disposal of waste can be a major problem, especially if it involves toxic materials or gaseous emissions. Chemical industries have a responsibility to minimise the impact of their business on the environment, but they also have to make a profit.

FIGURE 17.1.17 Workers assembling a car at a Toyota plant in Altona, Victoria. Many industries supplying speciality parts for the cars were impacted by the Toyota closure.

CHEMFILE EU

Union Carbide, Bhopal

An accident at the Union Carbide chemical plant in Bhopal, India, serves as a reminder to the world of the dangers associated with chemical processes. In 1984 the pesticide plant accidentally released over 30 tonnes of the toxic gas methyl isocyanate. Over 600 000 people were exposed to the gas, and estimates place the death toll at between 3800 and 16 000. Toxic material remains at the site to this day (Figure 17.1.18) and the area is still classed as contaminated.

Legal proceedings and compensation case have continued in the years since this disaster. Regulations and procedures of chemical plants all over the world were tightened and reviewed after the event.

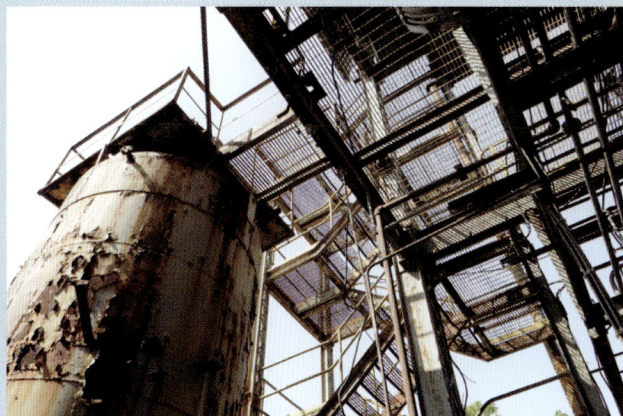

FIGURE 17.1.18 Over thirty years after the Union Carbide disaster, the site remains in a dilapidated and contaminated state.

Energy industry

Open cut or underground coal mines both leave large holes in the ground that need to be dealt with. When the coal is burnt, the main reaction releasing energy is

$$C(s) + O_2(g) \rightarrow CO_2(g)$$

CO_2 is a problem greenhouse gas, especially in the volumes produced by a power station (Figure 17.1.19). As well as CO_2, the combustion of coal also produces particulates such as SO_2, NO and NO_2, which are all problem emissions. State governments are aware that any plans to open new coal-fired power stations will be met with significant opposition.

Fracking

The USA has boosted its energy supplies substantially through the use of **fracking**, a process in which sand, steam or chemicals are used to shake gas free from rock or coal. Significant lobbying groups exist in most Australian states opposing the opening of fracking sites because of concerns they will contaminate watertables (Figure 17.1.20).

Nuclear industry

Australia could make a profit from the sale of uranium to any bidder on the world market. Uranium can be used in nuclear power plants. However, there is potential for the uranium to be used in weapons, so ethical considerations need to be taken into account. Australia sells uranium to countries that have signed the Treaty on the non-Proliferation of Nuclear Weapons, but controversially agreed to sell uranium to India, a non-signatory country, in 2016.

Mining industry

Figure 17.1.21 shows one of the mines at Broken Hill. It is obvious that a mine will have an impact upon the local environment, so the company has a responsibility to restore the area as it progresses. Most companies are aware of this responsibility and direct resources to minimise their impact. As well as a hole in or under the ground, mining companies also have to manage waste and emissions. Figure 17.1.22 shows a laboratory worker testing effluent from a mine.

Zinc and lead ores are often sulfide compounds such as ZnS and PbS. During smelting, the sulfur is converted to SO_2 gas. This is a toxic gas and emissions need to be managed (Figure 17.1.23).

GREEN CHEMISTRY

The laws and treaties that were enacted to reduce global pollution were often aimed at dealing with wastes after they had been generated, and did not address methods to reduce the production of waste.

Green chemistry outlines a set of principles that can be used as a framework to evaluate the environmental impact of a chemical process. It focuses on methods that reduce or eliminate hazardous waste. The green approach is that the best way to minimise waste is not to produce it in the first place. Its ultimate goal is to implement energy-efficient, hazard-free, waste-free, efficient chemical processes without sacrificing their effectiveness. Ideally:

- goods needed by society should be produced by methods that are not harmful to the environment
- fossil fuels, and other non-renewable resources, should be replaced by renewable ones
- goods produced by society should either be recyclable or biodegradable
- the processes used to manufacture the product should produce either no wastes or wastes that are recyclable or biodegradable.

FIGURE 17.1.19 Emissions from coal-fired power stations are fairly obvious. Water from cooling towers is relatively harmless but many other greenhouse gases are emitted in large volumes.

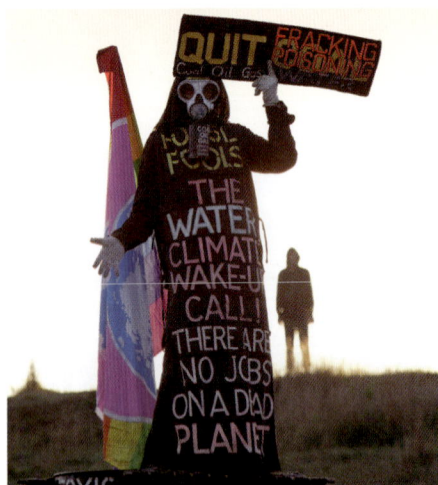

FIGURE 17.1.20 An anti-fracking sign from the Northern Territory. Many people in Australia oppose the use of fracking technology.

FIGURE 17.1.21 One of the mines at Broken Hill

Principles of green chemistry

In their book *Green Chemistry: Theory and Practice*, Paul Anastas and John Warner developed 12 principles of green chemistry to help assess how environmentally benign a chemical reaction or process is. These are listed in Table 17.1.2.

TABLE 17.1.2 The 12 principles of green chemistry

1	Prevent waste	It is better to design chemical processes to prevent waste than to treat waste or clean it up after it is formed.
2	Design safer chemicals and products	Design chemical products to be fully effective, yet have little or no toxicity.
3	Design less hazardous chemical syntheses	Methods should be designed that use and generate substances with little or no toxicity to humans and the environment.
4	Use renewable raw materials	Use starting materials that are derived from renewable resources such as plant material rather than those derived from fossil fuels that will eventually run out.
5	Use catalysts, not stoichiometric reagents	Minimise waste by using catalysts in small amounts that can carry out a single reaction many times. They are preferable to stoichiometric reagents, which are used in excess and work only once.
6	Avoid chemical derivatives	Avoid using blocking or protecting groups or any temporary modifications if possible. Derivatives use additional reagents and generate waste.
7	Maximise atom economy	Design syntheses so that the final product contains the maximum proportion of the starting materials. There should be few, if any, wasted atoms.
8	Use safer solvents and reaction conditions	Avoid using toxic solvents to dissolve reactants or extract products.
9	Increase energy efficiency	Energy requirements should be minimised. Run chemical reactions at room temperature and pressure whenever possible.
10	Design for degradation	Chemical products should be designed to break down into harmless substances after use so that they do not accumulate in the environment.
11	Analyse in real time to prevent pollution	Include continuous monitoring and control during processing to minimise or eliminate the formation of by-products.
12	Minimise the potential for accidents	Design chemicals and their forms (solid, liquid or gas) to minimise the potential for chemical accidents including explosions, fires and releases to the environment.

FIGURE 17.1.22 Liquid and solid waste from mining operations is referred to as tailings. Companies have to contain and manage this waste.

FIGURE 17.1.23 The Mount Isa smelter in North Queensland smelts both copper and lead. The high chimneys help to disperse emissions away from the city itself.

Green chemistry practices have major long-term cost benefits to businesses and reduce long-term damage to the environment.

By switching to **renewable energy sources** and biomaterials, and manufacturing chemicals that degrade into harmless substances, green chemistry can protect the planet from long-term deterioration.

Industry can benefit too from green chemistry considerations, since greater efficiency leads to reduced costs and improved profits. As discussed earlier in this chapter, the atom economy approach is a method of accounting for the use of materials in a manufacturing process.

> ℹ Green chemistry methods have been described as 'preventative medicine for the environment.'
>
> Two commonly used slogans for green chemistry are 'Benign (or harmless in this context) by design' and 'Preventing pollution, sustaining the Earth'.

(a)

(b)

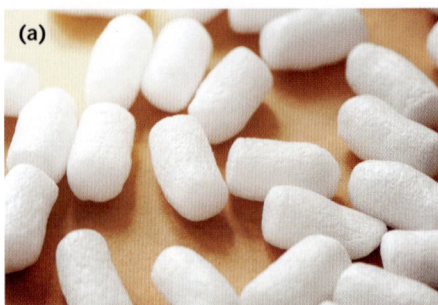

FIGURE 17.1.24 (a) Polystyrene foam pellets. (b) Biodegradable foam pellets made from cornstarch.

Green chemistry in action

Many innovative methods are being implemented by industry to conform to green principles. Two examples are described briefly here.

- Petroleum is the raw material for the manufacture of polystyrene. Polystyrene foam (or expanded polystyrene) is an excellent heat insulator and shock absorber, so it is commonly used in food containers and packaging (Figure 17.1.24a). In the past, polystyrene foam containers used in the takeaway food industry were expanded with chlorofluorocarbons (CFCs), which damage the ozone layer. These CFCs have been replaced by pentane as the expanding gas, and much polystyrene foam has been replaced with cardboard containers. Small puffed pellets made of cornflour, a **renewable resource**, can also be used as a replacement for the expanded polystyrene pellets used in packaging (Figure 17.1.24b).

- Adipic acid is a compound used in large quantities to make nylon and other useful products. The usual way to make adipic acid is from benzene, a known carcinogen. Scientists have found a way, using genetically altered bacteria as catalysts, to make adipic acid from glucose. Glucose, found naturally in plants, is a harmless substance and can be obtained from waste plant material such as stems, corn husks and even fallen leaves.

DS 8.1 WS 8.8 WS 8.9 WS 8.10

17.1 Review

SUMMARY

- The Australian chemical sector is large, employing thousands of skilled workers and producing goods that contribute significantly to the economy. Much of the output from the chemical industry serves as input to other industries.
- Chemical industries can be categorised as producing basic chemicals, speciality chemicals, or consumer chemicals.
- Chemical industries are large and expensive to build, and they operate in very competitive markets. Intensive research needs to be invested in the design and operation of these plants so that they operate safely and remain viable.
- Key considerations for the chemical industry are:
  - sources of raw materials
  - location
  - product uses
  - reaction conditions
  - energy supply
  - water supply
  - transport infrastructure

  - commodity price and market
  - safety
  - emissions and waste disposal
  - labour force
  - ethical considerations.
- The theoretical yield of a chemical reaction is the mass of the product that would be formed if the limiting reactant reacted completely.
- When a reaction proceeds by a number of steps, the overall percentage yield is reduced at each step.
- The overall yield of the product of a multistep reaction is found by multiplying the percentage yields of each step together and expressing as a percentage.
- Green chemistry aims to reduce waste in chemical processes, rather than having to deal with the wastes produced.
- Waste reduction methods include maximising atom economy, using small amounts of effective catalyst, avoiding high temperatures and pressures, and designing products that degrade.

1 Last century Australia had several factories where pharmaceuticals were manufactured. Today many pharmaceuticals, such as aspirin, are no longer made in Australia. Discuss reasons for this change.

2 A company purchases land in Port Kembla to manufacture sulfuric acid, a chemical used in the refining of iron ore. Sulfuric acid can be made from sulfur dioxide gas (SO_2). The SO_2 is converted to sulfur trioxide (SO_3) and then to sulfuric acid.

  a Suggest three reasons that might lead a company to choose Port Kembla for this plant.

  b Discuss the precautions the company might have to consider.

3 Bioethanol is made at Manildra (near Nowra) from waste products of the wheat industry.

  a Give three reasons why this plant is located at Manildra rather than Broken Hill.

  b The production of bioethanol uses waste from the wheat industry. However, there are limitations on the volume of ethanol that can be produced at this plant. What are some of those limitations?

4 Chloroethane can be produced from the reaction between ethane and chlorine gas. The equation is

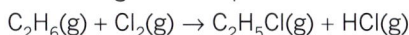

$$C_2H_6(g) + Cl_2(g) \rightarrow C_2H_5Cl(g) + HCl(g)$$

  a Calculate the atom economy for the production of chloroethane.

  b If the mass of chloroethane produced from 4.00 g of ethane is 5.40 g, calculate the percentage yield.

5 Hydrogen gas can be produced from methane in a process known as steam reforming. The equation for the process is:

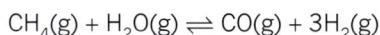

$$CH_4(g) + H_2O(g) \rightleftharpoons CO(g) + 3H_2(g)$$

This is an endothermic reaction that is conducted at low pressures and temperatures of over 1000°C. The catalyst used is nickel metal. The hydrogen gas produced can be used as a fuel or in industries such as ammonia production. The conditions for this reaction are chosen carefully to maximise the yield and efficiency of the reaction. List three of the conditions chosen and explain briefly how the choices are designed to improve the yield.

6 Two different methods produce a particular compound. The first method is much less economical in terms of atom economy. The second method uses a hazardous starting material. List some of the factors you would need to take into account when deciding which method of production should be used.

Chapter review

KEY TERMS

actual yield
atom economy
cracker
fracking

green chemistry
percentage yield
quality control
renewable energy source

renewable resource
smelter
theoretical yield

REVIEW QUESTIONS

1 Which of the following industries is least likely to be located at the source of its raw materials?
   A multivitamin manufacturer
   B ethanol from sugar cane industry
   C copper smelter
   D cheese factory

2 Secondary schools are consumers of chemicals.
   a List five chemicals you have used in your experimental program this year.
   b List one chemical that you have used at school that is also commonly used in your home.
   c List one chemical that you have used that had to be handled with caution.
   d List one example of an experiment where different procedures were required for the disposal of the chemicals used.

3 Many industries install heat exchangers into their plants. As the name suggests, a heat exchanger transfers energy from one section of the plant to another.
   a Explain why heat exchange systems are likely to play an important role in manufacturing.
   b Is a heat exchanger more useful for an exothermic process or an endothermic process? Explain your answer.

4 Australia has been gradually closing its oil refineries despite the fact that we use large volumes of petrol. Give three reasons for these closures.

5 Chemistry Australia states that most products made by the chemical industry are used by other industries. Give two examples of chemicals that are inputs to other sectors of the Australian economy.

6 The graph below shows the price of electricity in NSW from February 2015 to May 2016.

NSW — wholesale electricity prices (percentage change)

a What conclusion can you draw from this graph?
b Suggest two reasons for the trend evident in the graph.
c Explain how the trend shown in this graph impacts upon the Australian chemical industry.
d Will the impact be the same upon each industry? Explain your answer.

7 Proponents of the coal industry suggest that the adoption of 'green-coal' technology will ensure coal remains an important fuel in Australia.

  a What aspects of the use of coal is green technology attempting to address?

  b How does green-coal technology work?

8 The production of sulfuric acid involves the exothermic reversible reaction between SO_2 and O_2. The equation is

$$2SO_2(g) + O_2(g) \rightleftharpoons 2SO_3(g)$$

What does equilibrium theory suggest about each of the following variables in this process?

  a the temperature used

  b the pressure used

  c the ratio of each reactant used

  d the use of a catalyst.

9 Copper smelters produce SO_2 emissions. Chemical plants that produce sulfuric acid are often placed near metal smelters. Explain why this can be a mutually beneficial arrangement.

10 Ethanol can be produced by two different pathways.
Pathway A: $C_2H_4(g) + H_2O(l) \rightarrow C_2H_5OH(aq)$
Pathway B: $CH_3CH_2Cl(g) + KOH(g) \rightarrow$
$$C_2H_5OH(aq) + KCl(aq)$$

  a Which of the two pathways offers the higher atom economy? Explain your answer.

  b These two reactions belong to different categories of organic reactions. What are the two categories?

11 Calculate the percentage yield for the reaction in which 20.0 g of ethanol is oxidised to produce 21.5 g of ethanoic acid according to the equation:

$$C_2H_5OH \xrightarrow{\text{H}^+/\text{Cr}_2\text{O}_7{}^{2-}} CH_3COOH$$

12 Compound D can be synthesised by a reaction pathway that involves a number of intermediate steps. The yield for each step is shown:

$$A \xrightarrow{70\%} B \xrightarrow{50\%} C \xrightarrow{90\%} D$$

  a Determine the overall yield for the preparation of compound D from compound A.

  b How would the overall yield be affected if the yield for B → C was only 10%?

13 Oxirane (also called ethylene oxide) has been manufactured in the past by what was known as the chlorohydrin route, as shown in the figure below.

Reaction 1

$$2CH_2\!\!=\!\!CH_2 + 2Cl_2 + Ca(OH)_2 \longrightarrow 2\underset{H_2C \text{---} CH_2}{\overset{O}{\diagdown\!\diagup}} + CaCl_2 + 2HCl$$

oxirane

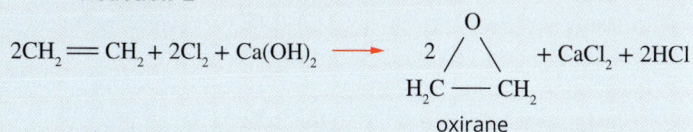

Oxirane is now produced using a catalytic method according to the pathway shown in the figure below.

Reaction 2

$$CH_2\!\!=\!\!CH_2 + \tfrac{1}{2}O_2 \xrightarrow{\text{catalyst}} \underset{H_2C \text{---} CH_2}{\overset{O}{\diagdown\!\diagup}}$$

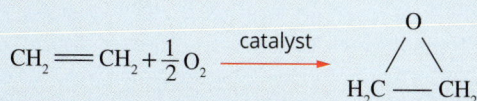

Calculate the atom economy for the preparation of oxirane by both of these reactions.

14 An old method for the manufacture of phenol (C_6H_5OH) from benzene (C_6H_6) used sulfuric acid and sodium hydroxide in several steps. The overall equation is:

$$C_6H_6(l) + H_2SO_4(aq) + 2NaOH(aq) \rightarrow$$
$$C_6H_5OH(aq) + Na_2SO_3(aq) + 2H_2O(l)$$

Calculate the atom economy of this process when phenol is the desired product.

15 When ethanamide is produced by the reaction of ethanoic acid and ammonia, the atom economy is 76.7%. Calculate the total mass of reactants, in kilograms, required to make 2.00 kg of ethanamide.

16 Aspirin can be synthesised by an esterification reaction according to the pathway shown the figure below.

A student reacted a 2.50 g sample of salicylic acid ($M = 138.12 \text{ g mol}^{-1}$) with an excess of ethanoic anhydride, using sulfuric acid as a catalyst. After purification a mass of 2.35 g of pure aspirin ($M = 180.15 \text{ g mol}^{-1}$) was obtained.

  a Calculate the theoretical yield of aspirin for the reaction.

  b Calculate the percentage yield of aspirin for the reaction.

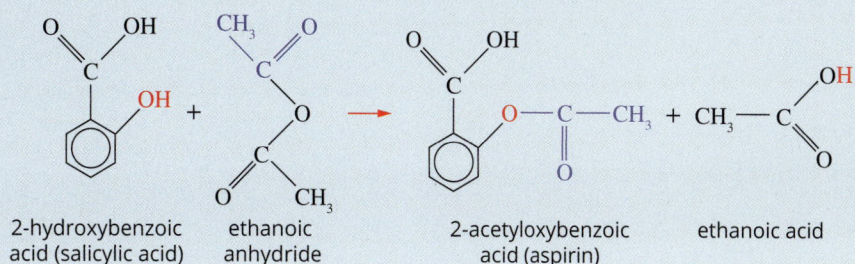

2-hydroxybenzoic acid (salicylic acid)   ethanoic anhydride   2-acetyloxybenzoic acid (aspirin)   ethanoic acid

17 Imagine that an aluminium refinery is proposed for NSW. The plant will receive concentrated Al_2O_3 from Queensland and use electricity to produce aluminium metal.

If this industry is to be located in NSW, several factors would need to be considered when choosing an exact location. For each variable below, comment on the importance of that variable for this proposed industry.

a transport   **b** energy

c emissions   **d** tailings

e work force   **f** economics

g safety.

18 Ammonia and the fertiliser ammonium nitrate (NH_4NO_3) are both manufactured on a very large scale at the Orica plant at Kooragang Island near Newcastle. The plant uses methane gas to produce hydrogen gas. This is then reacted with nitrogen from the air to produce ammonia. The reaction is:

$$N_2(g) + 3H_2(g) \rightleftharpoons 2NH_3(g)$$

This is an exothermic reaction. A different part of the plant produces nitric acid from ammonia, and a third part combines the nitric acid with the ammonia to form ammonium nitrate.

a Sulfur is scrubbed from the incoming methane gas before the methane is reacted. Explain why.

b Explain what conditions are likely to be used to maximise the yield of the production of ammonia from nitrogen and hydrogen.

c What is ammonium nitrate used for?

d The source of raw materials for this site was not a significant factor. Explain why.

e Give three reasons why Kooragang Island might have been chosen for the location of this plant.

f Calculate the atom economy for the production of ammonia from nitrogen and hydrogen.

19 In each of the following cases, explain which of the key ideas of green chemistry is being considered when selecting between the chemical processes:

a a process that uses hexane (C_6H_{14}) as a solvent, one that uses water as a solvent, or one that uses no solvent

b a process that needs to be carried out at 400°C, or one that proceeds at an acceptable rate at 25°C in the presence of a catalyst

c a process that forms a product that needs to be purified, or one in which the product requires no purification

d a process that uses a starting material produced from petroleum, or one that uses ethanol from the fermentation of sugars.

20 Reflect on the Inquiry activity on page 518. Describe how the cooking process is an example and analogy for chemical synthesis.

REVIEW QUESTIONS

Applying chemical ideas

Multiple choice

1 Adding which one of the following substances to copper(II) sulfate solution will not result in the formation of a precipitate?

A $BaCl_2(aq)$

B $NH_4Cl(aq)$

C $Na_2CO_3(aq)$

D $Zn(s)$

2 Excess silver nitrate ($AgNO_3$) is added to a 250.0 mL sample of river water. The precipitate of silver chloride ($AgCl$) was dried and weighed. Its mass was found to be 20.37 g. What is the concentration of chloride ions in the river water?

A $0.142\,gL^{-1}$

B $0.569\,gL^{-1}$

C $20.2\,gL^{-1}$

D $81.5\,gL^{-1}$

The following information relates to Questions 3 and 4. The absorption spectrum of a coloured compound is shown below.

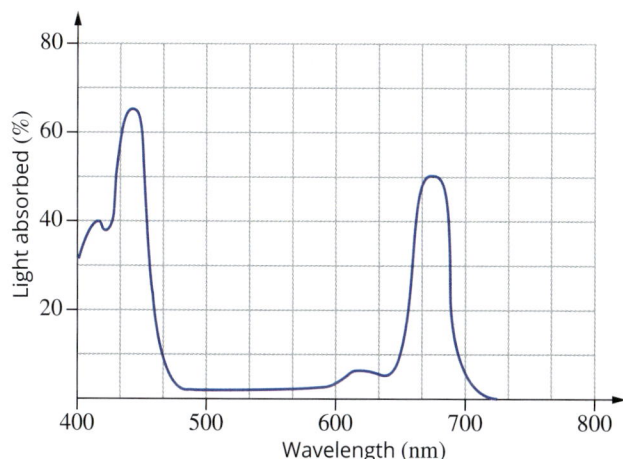

3 What is the best description of the colour of this compound?

A violet

B blue

C green

D orange-red

4 If the concentration of this compound is to be determined by UV–visible spectroscopy, which one of the following wavelengths would be most suitable to use?

A 420 mm

B 460 mm

C 550 mm

D 670 mm

5 Dissolved calcium ions are responsible for the 'hardness' of water. The concentration of calcium ions in a dam was determined by atomic absorption spectroscopy (AAS). Several solutions of known concentration of calcium ions were tested, and the results were plotted as a calibration curve, as shown below.

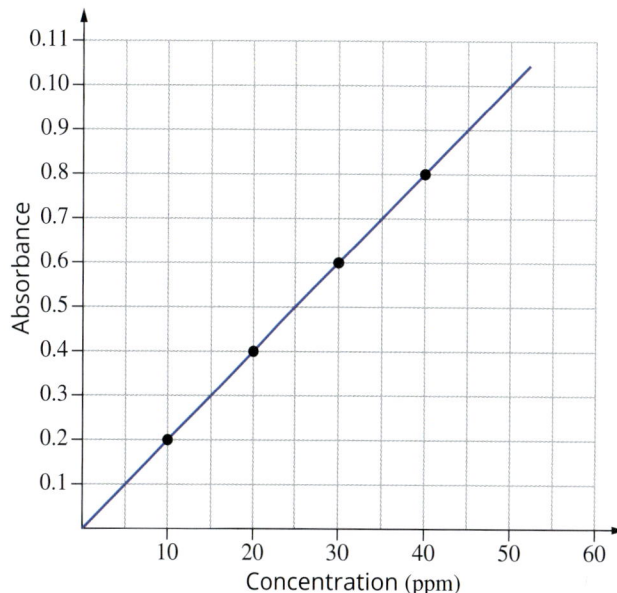

25.0 mL of the dam water was diluted to 100 mL with distilled water. The absorption of the diluted solution, measured under the same conditions as the standards, was 0.3.

What was the approximate concentration of calcium in the dam water?

A 4 ppm

B 16 ppm

C 30 ppm

D 64 ppm

6 Which of the following industrial processes is not likely to add to mineral levels in New South Wales waterways?

A concentrating copper ore at Broken Hill

B extracting tea-tree oil in northern New South Wales

C operating desalination plants

D manufacturing fertiliser near Newcastle

7 Which of the following solids would be the easiest to distinguish in the flame test?

A strontium carbonate

B strontium chloride

C copper chloride

D lithium chloride

8 Which of the following combinations of solutions will form a coloured precipitate when mixed?

A silver nitrate and sodium chloride

B copper(II) nitrate and zinc nitrate

C calcium nitrate and sodium carbonate

D copper(II) sulfate and sodium hydroxide

9 The identity of an ion can be determined by testing whether it forms precipitates and, if it does, by taking note of the colour of the precipitate. Which of the following tests could be used to determine the identity of a cation?

A Add hydrochloric acid, then ammonia.

B Add hydrochloric acid, then sodium hydroxide.

C Add silver nitrate, then nitric acid.

D Add silver nitrate, then either barium chloride or nitric acid.

10 Which of the following ions cannot be identified using complexation reactions?

A Ag^+

B K^+

C Cu^{2+}

D Fe^{3+}

11 Select the correct statement about a conductometric titration.

A An indicator is added to highlight the point at which the electrical conductivity is at a minimum.

B The anions in the titration will have no impact upon the conductivity.

C The conductivity of the solution under the burette increases with each addition but not by the same amount.

D It is not necessary to approach the equivalence point by adding one drop of solution at a time.

12 Which of the following options describes how to prepare a calibration curve to be used with an atomic absorption spectrometer?

A Run a series of unknown concentration solutions through the instrument.

B Draw a straight line from the origin to the absorbance of the unknown solution.

C Test a series of solutions of known, but varying, concentrations.

D Compare the results obtained from more than one spectrometer.

13 Which of the following will not react with acidified potassium dichromate ($K_2Cr_2O_7$)?

A $(CH_3)_3COH$

B $(CH_3)_2CHOH$

C $CH_3CH_2CH_2OH$

D $(CH_3)_3CCH_2OH$

14 Which of the following will not immediately turn red bromine water colourless?

A C_5H_{10}

B CH_2CHCH_3

C C_6H_{14}

D oct-1-ene

15 Which of the following instruments would be the best suited to measure the concentration of copper ions in a solution?

A mass spectrometer

B UV–visible spectrophotometer

C infrared spectrometer

D proton NMR

16 Under analysis by proton NMR spectroscopy, which of the following molecules contains the greatest number of hydrogen environments?

A CH_3CH_2OH

B $CH_3CHClCH_3$

C $CH_3CH_2CH_2CH_3$

D $CH_3CH_2COCH_2CH_3$

17 Hydrogen gas can be produced from the endothermic reaction between ammonia gas and steam. The equation is:

$$2NH_3(g) + 4H_2O(g) \rightleftharpoons 2NO_2(g) + 7H_2(g)$$

What conditions are most likely required to provide a high yield of hydrogen?

A high temperature, high pressure and an excess of ammonia

B high temperature, low pressure and an excess of steam

C low temperature, low pressure and an excess of NO_2

D low temperature, high pressure and an excess of steam

18 Which of the following reactions has an atom economy of 100%?

A substitution of chlorine on methane using chlorine gas

B condensation reaction between ethanol and ethanoic acid

C reaction of chloroethane and ammonia

D addition reaction of ethene and chlorine gas

19 Which statement about propan-1-ol and propan-2-ol is not true?

A The carbon-13 NMR spectrum of propan-1-ol has three peaks, and that of propan-2-ol has two peaks.

B The proton NMR spectrum of propan-1-ol has four peaks, and that of propan-2-ol has three peaks.

C The mass spectra of both will show a peak at a mass-to-charge ratio of 60.

D The fingerprint region of the IR spectra will be identical for both compounds.

20 In the mass spectrum of an organic compound, the signal produced by the unfragmented molecular ion and the signal produced by the most abundant particle correspond respectively to the:

A parent (molecular) ion peak and main ion peak
B main ion peak and base peak
C parent (molecular) ion peak and base peak
D base peak and parent (molecular) ion peak.

Short answer

1 A student wishing to determine the identity of a cation in a solution tests a sample of the solution by adding HCl. A white precipitate forms. The student then tests a second sample of the same solution by adding ammonia. A white precipitate forms again.

a What type of charge do cations have?
b What conclusion can the student draw from the two tests?
c Write a balanced ionic equation for the reaction occurring in the first test.
d Suggest a possible anion that might be present in the solution.

2 The structure around copper ions in a concentrated solution of copper sulfate is shown here.

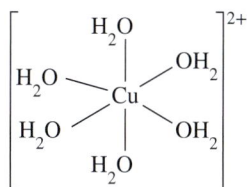

$$\begin{bmatrix} & H_2O & \\ H_2O & & OH_2 \\ & Cu & \\ H_2O & & OH_2 \\ & H_2O & \end{bmatrix}^{2+}$$

a What is the name given to this type of formation?
b Write a chemical formula for this structure.
c Write a balanced chemical equation for its formation.
d Explain what you would observe if this structure was found in an aqueous solution.
e What is the name given to substances, such as water, that are present in these structures?

3 Excess potassium chloride solution is added to a solution containing 3.15 g of lead(II) nitrate. A white precipitate forms.

a Write a balanced chemical equation for the formation of the precipitate.
b Write an ionic equation for the formation of the precipitate.
c For this reaction:
  i name the precipitate
  ii name any spectator ions.
d Assuming there was sufficient potassium chloride to react with all of the lead(II) nitrate:
  i calculate the amount, in mol, of lead(II) nitrate that would react
  ii calculate the mass of precipitate that would form.

4 A solution of lead(II) nitrate is prepared by dissolving 9.80 g of solid lead(II) nitrate in water. The total volume of the solution formed was 50.0 mL.

a Calculate the molar concentration of this solution.
b The lead(II) nitrate solution is diluted by adding 30.0 mL of water. What is the new concentration of the solution?
c The lead(II) nitrate solution is mixed with 50.0 mL of 0.650 mol L^{-1} sodium iodide. A bright yellow precipitate forms.
  i Write an ionic equation for the formation of the precipitate.
  ii Calculate the mass of precipitate that forms.

5 To analyse the iron content of bore water, all of the iron ions in 1.30 L of bore water were first converted to Fe^{3+}(aq) ions by oxidation. These were then reacted with excess OH$^-$ to form a precipitate $Fe(OH)_3$(s). The $Fe(OH)_3$(s) was collected and dried, then heated strongly so that it decomposed to produce Fe_2O_3(s) and water.

a Write an ionic equation for the precipitation of $Fe(OH)_3$(s).
b Write an equation for the production of Fe_2O_3(s) from $Fe(OH)_3$(s).
c The mass of Fe_2O_3(s) obtained was 1.095 g.
  i Calculate the mass of iron in the 1.30 L of water.
  ii Calculate the molar concentration of iron in the water.

6 A solution containing nickel(II) ions is green, so its concentration could be determined using UV–visible spectroscopy.

a Explain how a suitable wavelength is chosen to analyse the solution containing the nickel(II) ions.
b Explain how the concentration of nickel(II) ions in the solution would be experimentally determined.

7 Deep-sea fish can build up high levels of mercury from contaminated water. A 3.0 g sample of fish is ground up and mixed with water. The mixture is made up to 100 mL with water. A sample of the solution is analysed by atomic absorption spectroscopy, giving an absorbance reading of 0.25.
Use the following calibration curve to determine the:

a percentage mass of mercury in the fish
b concentration in ppm of mercury in the fish.

Mercury testing

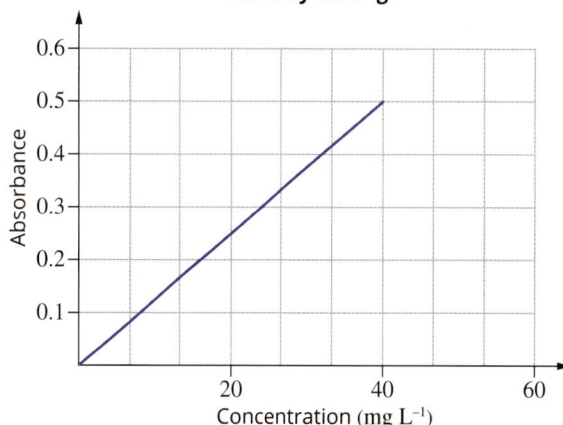

8 Proton NMR spectra of the following three compounds were recorded.

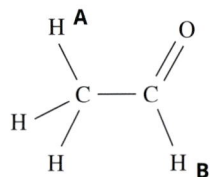

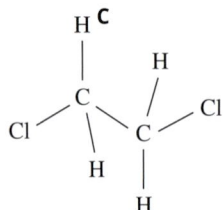

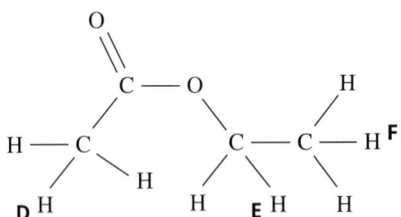

a What type of electromagnetic radiation is absorbed and emitted in NMR spectroscopy?

b What changes in the molecules are associated with this emission and absorption?

c Describe the role of tetramethylsilane (TMS) in NMR spectroscopy.

d The spectra of the three compounds included the following signals. In each case, select the letter labelling the H atoms most likely to be responsible for the signal, and give a brief justification. (You may need to refer to Table 16.3.2 on page 489.)

i quartet at $\delta = 8.5$

ii singlet at $\delta = 2.1$

iii quartet at $\delta = 4.1$

iv singlet at $\delta = 3.7$

v triplet at $\delta = 1.2$

vi doublet at $\delta = 2.2$

9 The following is the structure of the amino acid isoleucine.

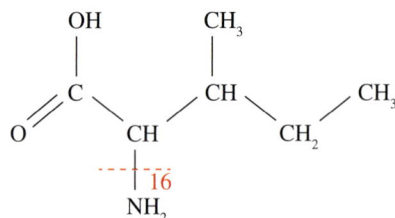

a What is its molecular formula?

b What is its relative molecular mass?

c The mass spectrum of isoleucine includes a signal at $m/z = 16$. The dotted line shows how cleavage might occur to produce the $[NH_2]^+$ fragment that would account for this signal.

For each of the following m/z values from the spectrum of isoleucine, write the formula of the fragment ion likely to be responsible for it and add a dotted line to your diagram to show a simple bond cleavage that could produce this fragment ion.

i $m/z = 15$

ii $m/z = 29$

iii $m/z = 57$

d The base peak in the mass spectrum is at $m/z = 86$.

i What is meant by the 'base peak' in a mass spectrum?

ii Suggest the fragment that has been lost from the molecular ion to produce the ion responsible for the base peak.

10 The structures of propan-2-ol and propanone are shown below. The infrared spectra of these compounds are labelled IR spectrum A and IR spectrum B.

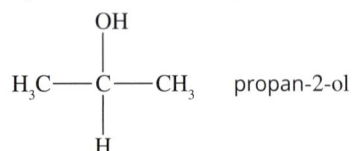

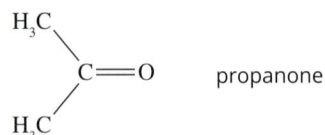

IR spectrum A

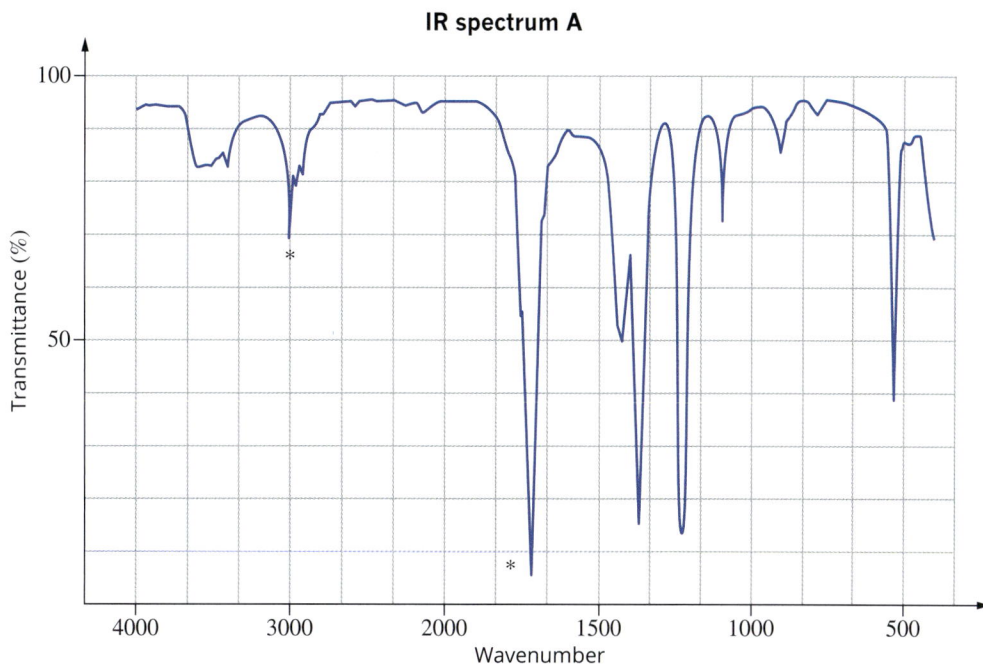

IR spectrum B

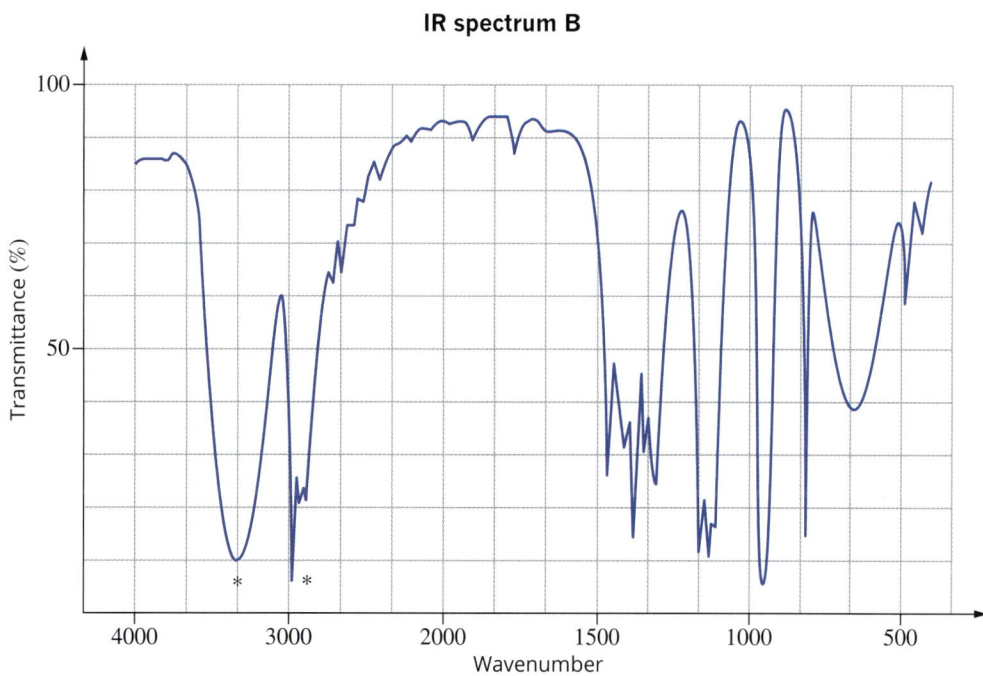

a Identify the bonds that produced the IR absorption marked with an asterisk (*) in each spectrum.

b Determine which spectrum represents which molecule.

c The proton NMR spectrum of propanone is shown below.
Explain why there is only a single peak although there
are six hydrogen atoms in the molecule.

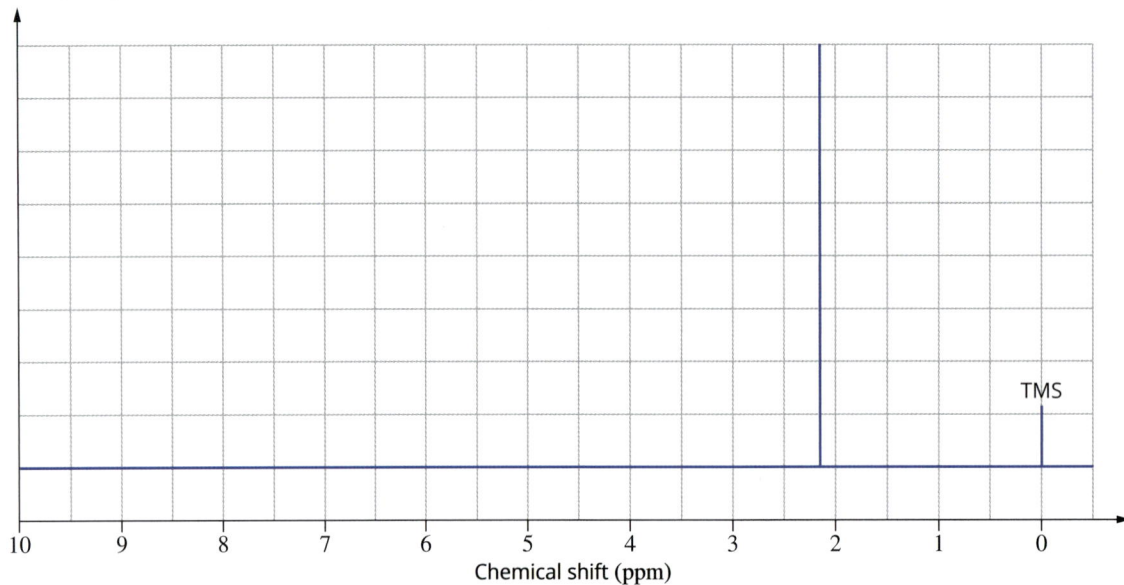

Chemical shift (ppm)

d The carbon-13 NMR spectrum of propanone is shown
below. Explain why there are two peaks although there
are three carbon atoms in the molecule.

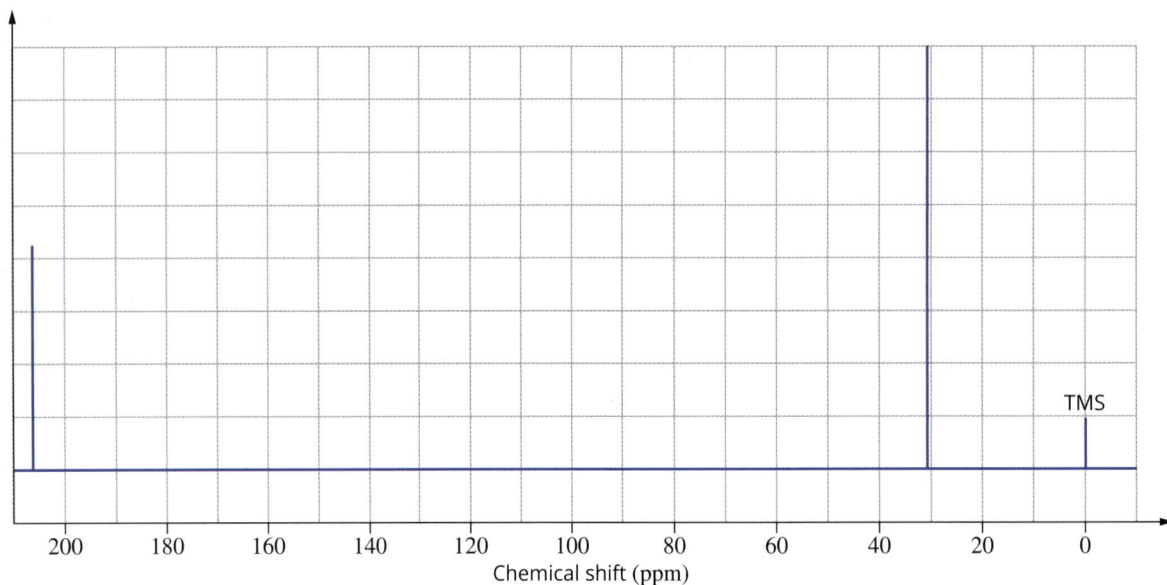

Chemical shift (ppm)

e How many sets of peaks would you expect in proton NMR and carbon-13 NMR spectra of propan-2-ol? Provide an explanation for your answers.

f The mass spectrum of propanone is shown below.

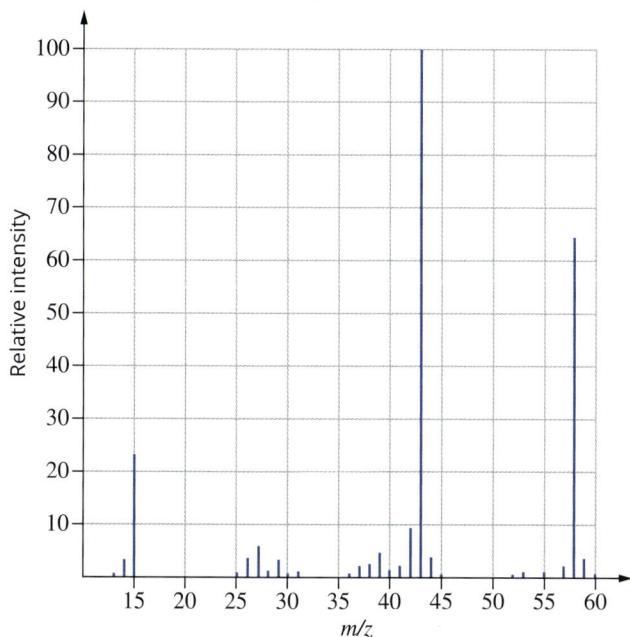

i What is the mass of the molecular ion?

ii What information does this provide about the molecule?

iii Suggest a formula for the fragment ion that produces the peak at $m/z = 43$.

11 A series of tests are conducted on a solution to determine whether it contains Fe^{3+} ions.

a The addition of HCl to the solution does not produce any precipitate. What does this indicate to you about whether Fe^{3+} is present or not? Explain your answer.

b The addition of a small amount of concentrated ammonia produces an orange solution. This is due to the formation of a metal complex between Fe^{3+} and 3 molecules of water and 3 hydroxide ions. Write a chemical formula for this complex.

c Atomic absorption spectroscopy can be used to determine the Fe^{3+} concentration in the solution. Explain carefully how this analysis would be performed.

d KSCN is added to the solution to form a deep red complex, $FeSCN^{2+}$. The concentration of this complex can be determined using UV–visible spectroscopy.

i Write an ionic equation for this reaction.

ii What wavelength of light should be used for this testing?

12 The concentration of a NaBr solution is to be determined by a conductometric titration against silver nitrate solution. A 20.00 mL sample of NaBr is added to a beaker and placed under a burette containing $0.20 \, mol \, L^{-1}$ $AgNO_3$ solution. Electrodes are placed in the beaker to record the electrical conductivity. Nitrate ions are bulky ions that do not affect the electrical conductivity as much as the metal ions.

a Write a balanced chemical equation for the reaction.

b Refer to the equation to explain why the electrical conductivity is decreasing when the first additions of $AgNO_3$ are made from the burette.

c Refer to the equation to explain why the electrical conductivity increases significantly with further additions after the equivalence point has been reached.

d A graph shows the minimum conductivity occurs after 15.00 mL of $AgNO_3$ has been added. Determine the concentration of the NaBr solution.

13 Demand for lithium is growing because of the increased use of rechargeable batteries. Imagine that a deposit of lithium chloride is found near the Darling River in north-western New South Wales. The deposit has an average concentration of 2.5% lithium by mass, which is considered a viable concentration. It is proposed to mine this deposit. Lithium is extracted by electrolysis: the lithium ore is heated to a liquid and an electric current is passed through the solution. A small amount of $CaCl_2$ is added to the molten solution; this serves to significantly lower the melting point of the LiCl.

As part of a feasibility study into this venture, answer the following questions:

a It is likely that the lithium plant will have to be located near the deposit. Why is this?

b This is a remote location. List an advantage of the location being remote, and two disadvantages.

c What advantage is it to the company running the plant if the melting point of the LiCl is lowered by the addition of $CaCl_2$?

d Will the location of the plant cause any issues obtaining the labour force required? Explain your answer.

e List two factors that will influence the economic viability of this plant.

f There are several environmental considerations relevant to the location of this plant. Discuss these considerations.

14 a Molecule A has a molecular formula of C_3H_8O. It reacts with acidified $K_2Cr_2O_7$ to form molecule B. A gas is evolved when molecule B is mixed with $NaHCO_3$ solution.

    i Draw a likely structure for each of these two molecules.

    ii Write a balanced equation for the reaction between molecule B and $NaHCO_3$.

    iii Are there any other possible structures for molecule A? Explain your answer.

  b Bromine is added to a sample of molecule C and the bromine becomes colourless. Molecule C has a straight-chain structure, and its molecular formula is C_4H_8.

    i Draw a possible structure for molecule C.

    ii Draw the molecule that will be formed when molecule C reacts with bromine.

    iii Are there any other possible structures for molecule C? Explain your answer.

  c A small piece of sodium is added to a sample of molecule D with molecular formula CH_4O. A gas is produced. Write a balanced equation for the reaction.

15 The spectra of butanoic acid and ethyl ethanoate are compared using several different instruments.

  a i Draw the structural formula of each substance.

    ii What type of isomerism do molecules of these two substances exhibit?

  b Samples of both substances are analysed in a mass spectrometer.

    i What is the m/z ratio of the molecular ion peak for both substances?

    ii Suggest the m/z ratio for a peak that would be found in the spectra of both substances.

  c Identify the wavenumber range of an absorbance band that would be different in the IR spectra of these two substances. Explain your answer.

  d The NMR spectra of both substances will also differ.

    i How many different environments will each substance have when analysed by proton NMR spectroscopy?

    ii Describe the splitting pattern of the peaks in the proton NMR spectra of both substances.

    iii How many different environments will each substance have when analysed by carbon-13 NMR?

Symbols, units and fundamental constants

TABLE 1 Units and symbols based on the SI system*

Quantity	Symbol for physical quantity	Corresponding SI unit	Symbol for SI unit	Definition of SI unit
Mechanics				
length	l	metre	m	fundamental unit
area	A	square metre	m^2	
volume	V	cubic metre	m^3	
mass	m	kilogram	kg	fundamental unit
density	d	–	$kg\,m^{-3}$	
time	t	second	s	fundamental unit
force	F	newton	N	$kg\,m\,s^{-2}$
pressure	P	pascal	Pa	$N\,m^{-2}$
energy	E	joule	J	Nm
Electricity				
electric current	I	ampere	A	fundamental unit
electric charge	Q	coulomb	C	As
electric potential difference	V	volt	V	$J\,A^{-1}\,s^{-1}$
Nuclear and chemical quantities				
atomic number	Z	–	–	–
neutron number	N	–	–	–
mass number	A	–	–	Z + N
amount of substance	n	mole	mol	fundamental unit
relative atomic mass	A_r	–	–	–
relative molecular mass	M_r	–	–	–
molar mass	M	–	–	$kg\,mol^{-1}$
molar volume	V_m	–	–	$m^3\,mol^{-1}$
concentration	c	–	–	$mol\,m^{-3}$
Thermal quantities				
temperature	T	kelvin	K	fundamental unit
specific heat capacity	c	–	–	$J\,kg^{-1}\,K^{-1}$

*Units listed in red are the arbitrarily defined fundamental units of the SI system.

TABLE 2 SI prefixes, their symbols and values

SI prefix	Symbol	Value
pico	p	10^{-12}
nano	n	10^{-9}
micro	μ	10^{-6}
milli	m	10^{-3}
centi	c	10^{-2}
deci	d	10^{-1}
kilo	k	10^{3}
mega	M	10^{6}
giga	G	10^{9}
tera	T	10^{12}

TABLE 3 Some physical constants

Description	Symbol	Value
Avogadro's constant	N_A	$6.022 \times 10^{23}\,mol^{-1}$
charge of electron	e	$-1.60 \times 10^{-19}\,C$
mass of electron	m_e	$9.109 \times 10^{-31}\,kg$
mass of proton	m_p	$1.673 \times 10^{-27}\,kg$
mass of neutron	m_n	$1.675 \times 10^{-27}\,kg$
gas constant	R	$8.314\,J\,mol^{-1}\,K^{-1}$
ionic product for water	K_w	$1.0 \times 10^{-14}\,mol^2\,L^{-2}$ at 298 K
molar volume of an ideal gas	V_m	
at 273 K, 100 kPa		$22.71\,L\,mol^{-1}$
at 298 K, 100 kPa		$24.79\,L\,mol^{-1}$
specific heat capacity of water	c	$4.18\,J\,g^{-1}\,K^{-1}$
density of water	d	$1.0\,g\,mL^{-1}$ at 298 K

SIGNIFICANT FIGURES

The number of significant figures of a piece of data indicates the precision of a measurement. For example, compare the following sets of data:

- A jogger takes 20 minutes to cover 4 kilometres.
- A sprinter takes 10.21 seconds to cover 100.0 metres.

The sprinter's data has been measured more precisely than that of the jogger. This is indicated by the greater number of significant figures in the second set of data.

Which figures are significant?

A significant figure is a non-zero integer or a zero that follows a non-zero integer.

In the data above:

- the distance '4 kilometres' has one significant figure
- the time '20 minutes' has two significant figures (the zero follows the integer 2)
- the 10.21 seconds and 100.0 metres each have four significant figures.

A zero that comes before any integers, however, is not significant. For example:

- the value 0.0004 has only one significant figure, whereas the value 0.0400 has three significant figures. The zeroes that come before the integer 4 are not significant, whereas those that follow the integer are significant.

Using significant figures

In chemistry you will often need to calculate a value from a set of data. It is important to remember that the final value you calculate is only as precise as your least precise piece of data.

Addition and subtraction

When adding or subtracting values, the answer should have no more digits to the right of the decimal place than the value with the least number of digits to the right of the decimal place.

Example

12.78 mL of water was added to 10.0 mL of water. What is the total volume of water?

12.78 mL + 10.0 mL = 22.78 = 22.8 mL

Because one of the values (10.0 mL) has only one digit to the right of the decimal place, the answer will need to be adjusted so that it too has only one digit to the right of the decimal place.

Multiplication and division

When multiplying and dividing values, the answer should have no more significant figures than the value with the least number of significant figures.

Example

An athlete takes 3.5 minutes to complete four laps of an oval. What is the average time taken for one lap?

Average time = $\frac{3.5}{4}$ = 0.875 = 0.88 minutes

Because the data (3.5 minutes) has only two significant figures, the answer will need to be adjusted to two significant figures so that it has the same degree of precision as the data. (Note: The 'four' is taken to indicate a precise number of laps and so is considered to have as many significant figures as the calculation requires. This applies to values that describe quantities rather than measurements.)

Rounding off

When adjusting the number of significant figures, if the integer after the last significant figure is equal to or greater than 5, then the last significant integer is rounded up. Otherwise, it 'stays the same'.

Statistics

If a calculated statistic such as mean or uncertainty has more significant figures than the data, it is usual practice to round the value to one more significant figure than there is in the data. It is important to note that this is only common practice and not a rule. If in doubt, always abide by the rules detailed above.

For example, for the dataset [4, 5, 6, 6, 7, 7] the mean is 5.833, so this would conventionally be rounded to 5.8.

The uncertainty is 5.833 − 4 = 1.833, so this would be rounded to 1.8.

If you do round multiple values, as in this example, make sure you round to a consistent and appropriate number of significant figures.

STANDARD FORM

A value written in standard form is expressed as a number equal to or greater than 1 and less than 10 multiplied by 10^x, where x is an integer. For example, when written in standard form:

- 360.0 becomes 3.600×10^2
- 0.360 becomes 3.60×10^{-1}
- 0.000456 becomes 4.56×10^{-4}.

Sometimes you will need to use standard form to indicate the precision of a value.

TABLE 1 Table of relative atomic masses*

Element name	Symbol	Atomic number	Relative atomic mass	Element name	Symbol	Atomic number	Relative atomic mass	Element name	Symbol	Atomic number	Relative atomic mass
actinium	Ac	89	–	hafnium	Hf	72	178.49	praseodymium	Pr	59	140.9077
aluminium	Al	13	26.9815	hassium	Hs	108	–	promethium	Pm	61	–
americium	Am	95	–	helium	He	2	4.00260	protactinium	Pa	91	231.0359
antimony	Sb	51	121.76	holmium	Ho	67	164.9303	radium	Ra	88	–
argon	Ar	18	39.948	hydrogen	H	1	1.0080	radon	Rn	86	–
arsenic	As	33	74.9216	indium	In	49	114.82	rhenium	Re	75	186.21
astatine	At	85	–	iodine	I	53	126.9045	rhodium	Rh	45	102.9055
barium	Ba	56	137.33	iridium	Ir	77	192.22	roentgenium	Rg	111	–
berkelium	Bk	97	–	iron	Fe	26	55.845	rubidium	Rb	37	85.468
beryllium	Be	4	9.01218	krypton	Kr	36	83.80	ruthenium	Ru	44	101.07
bismuth	Bi	83	208.9804	lanthanum	La	57	138.9055	rutherfordium	Rf	104	–
bohrium	Bh	107	–	lawrencium	Lr	103	–	samarium	Sm	62	150.4
boron	B	5	10.81	lead	Pb	82	207.2	scandium	Sc	21	44.9559
bromine	Br	35	79.904	lithium	Li	3	6.94	seaborgium	Sg	106	–
cadmium	Cd	48	112.41	livermorium	Lv	116	–	selenium	Se	34	78.97
caesium	Cs	55	132.9055	lutetium	Lu	71	174.967	silicon	Si	14	28.086
calcium	Ca	20	40.08	magnesium	Mg	12	24.305	silver	Ag	47	107.868
californium	Cf	98	–	manganese	Mn	25	54.9380	sodium	Na	11	22.9898
carbon	C	6	12.011	meitnerium	Mt	109	–	strontium	Sr	38	87.62
cerium	Ce	58	140.12	mendelevium	Md	101	–	sulfur	S	16	32.06
chlorine	Cl	17	35.453	mercury	Hg	80	200.59	tantalum	Ta	73	180.9479
chromium	Cr	24	51.996	molybdenum	Mo	42	95.95	technetium	Tc	43	–
cobalt	Co	27	58.9332	moscovium	Mc	115	–	tellurium	Te	52	127.60
copernicium	Cn	112	–	neodymium	Nd	60	144.24	tennessine	Ts	117	–
copper	Cu	29	63.55	neon	Ne	10	20.180	terbium	Tb	65	158.9254
curium	Cm	96	–	neptunium	Np	93	–	thallium	Tl	81	204.384
darmstadtium	Ds	110	–	nickel	Ni	28	58.693	thorium	Th	90	232.038
dubnium	Db	105	–	nihonium	Nh	113	–	thulium	Tm	69	168.9342
dysprosium	Dy	66	162.50	niobium	Nb	41	92.9064	tin	Sn	50	118.71
einsteinium	Es	99	–	nitrogen	N	7	14.0067	titanium	Ti	22	47.87
erbium	Er	68	167.26	nobelium	No	102	–	tungsten	W	74	183.84
europium	Eu	63	151.96	oganesson	Og	118	–	uranium	U	92	238.0289
fermium	Fm	100	–	osmium	Os	76	190.2	vanadium	V	23	50.942
flerovium	Fl	114	–	oxygen	O	8	15.9994	xenon	Xe	54	131.29
fluorine	F	9	18.9984	palladium	Pd	46	106.4	ytterbium	Yb	70	173.05
francium	Fr	87	–	phosphorus	P	15	30.9738	yttrium	Y	39	88.9058
gadolinium	Gd	64	157.25	platinum	Pt	78	195.08	zinc	Zn	30	65.38
gallium	Ga	31	69.72	plutonium	Pu	94	–	zirconium	Zr	40	91.22
germanium	Ge	32	72.63	polonium	Po	84	–				
gold	Au	79	196.9666	potassium	K	19	39.098				

*Based on the atomic mass of $^{12}C = 12$.
The values for relative atomic masses given in the table apply to elements as they exist in nature (without artificial alteration of their isotopic composition) and to natural mixtures that do not include isotopes of radiogenic origin.

Atomic radii and boiling temperatures of selected elements

Legend (per cell): Atomic radius ($\times 10^{-12}$ m) / **Symbol** / Boiling temperature (K)

1	2	3	4	5	6	7	8	9	10	11	12	13	14	15	16	17	18
32 **H** 20																	37 **He** 4
130 **Li** 1615	99 **Be** 2741											84 **B** 4723	75 **C** 5100	71 **N** 77	64 **O** 90	60 **F** 85	62 **Ne** 27
160 **Na** 1156	140 **Mg** 1363											124 **Al** 2792	114 **Si** 3538	109 **P** 554	104 **S** 718	100 **Cl** 239	101 **Ar** 87
200 **K** 1032	174 **Ca** 1757	159 **Sc** 3109	148 **Ti** 3560	144 **V** 3680	130 **Cr** 2944	129 **Mn** 2334	124 **Fe** 3134	118 **Co** 3200	117 **Ni** 3186	122 **Cu** 2833	120 **Zn** 1180	123 **Ga** 2502	120 **Ge** 3106	120 **As** 886	118 **Se** 958	117 **Br** 332	116 **Kr** 120
215 **Rb** 961	190 **Sr** 1650	176 **Y** 3618	164 **Zr** 4679	156 **Nb** 5014	146 **Mo** 4912	138 **Tc** 4535	136 **Ru** 4420	134 **Rh** 3968	130 **Pd** 3236	136 **Ag** 2435	140 **Cd** 1040	142 **In** 2345	140 **Sn** 2875	140 **Sb** 1860	137 **Te** 1261	136 **I** 457	136 **Xe** 165
238 **Cs** 944	206 **Ba** 2118	194 **La** 3737	164 **Hf** 4873	158 **Ta** 5728	150 **W** 5828	141 **Re** 5869	136 **Os** 5281	132 **Ir** 4701	130 **Pt** 4098	130 **Au** 3109	132 **Hg** 630	144 **Tl** 1746	145 **Pb** 2022	150 **Bi** 1837	142 **Po** 1235	148 **At** 640	146 **Rn** 211
242 **Fr** 950	211 **Ra** 1413	201 **Ac** 3473															

Common ions and solubilities of ionic compounds

TABLE 1 Names and formulae of some common positive and negative ions

Positive ions (cations)						Negative ions (anions)			
+1		**+2**		**+3**		**−1**		**−2**	
caesium	Cs^+	barium	Ba^{2+}	aluminium	Al^{3+}	acetate (ethanoate)	CH_3COO^-	carbonate	CO_3^{2-}
copper(I)	Cu^+	cadmium(II)	Cd^{2+}	chromium(III)	Cr^{3+}	bromide	Br^-	chromate	CrO_4^{2-}
gold(I)	Au^+	calcium	Ca^{2+}	gold(III)	Au^{3+}	chloride	Cl^-	dichromate	$Cr_2O_7^{2-}$
lithium	Li^+	cobalt(II)	Co^{2+}	iron(III)	Fe^{3+}	cyanide	CN^-	hydrogen phosphate	HPO_4^{2-}
potassium	K^+	copper(II)	Cu^{2+}			dihydrogen phosphate	$H_2PO_4^-$	oxalate	$C_2O_4^{2-}$
rubidium	Rb^+	iron(II)	Fe^{2+}	**+4**		fluoride	F^-	oxide	O^{2-}
silver	Ag^+	lead(II)	Pb^{2+}	lead(IV)	Pb^{4+}	hydrogen carbonate	HCO_3^-	sulfate	SO_4^{2-}
sodium	Na^+	magnesium	Mg^{2+}	tin(IV)	Sn^{4+}	hydrogen sulfate	HSO_4^-	sulfide	S^{2-}
		manganese(II)	Mn^{2+}			hydrogen sulfide	HS^-	sulfite	SO_3^{2-}
		mercury(II)	Hg^{2+}			hydrogen sulfite	HSO_3^-		
		nickel	Ni^{2+}			hydroxide	OH^-	**−3**	
		strontium	Sr^{2+}			iodide	I^-	nitride	N^{3-}
		tin(II)	Sn^{2+}			nitrate	NO_3^-	phosphate	PO_4^{3-}
		zinc	Zn^{2+}			nitrite	NO_2^-	phosphide	P^{3-}
						permanganate	MnO_4^-		

TABLE 2 Solubility of common ionic compounds in water

Soluble ionic compounds		
Soluble in water (>0.1 mol dissolves per L at 25°C)	**Exceptions: insoluble** (<0.01 mol dissolves per L at 25°C)	**Exceptions: slightly soluble** (0.01–0.1 mol dissolves per L at 25°C)
most chlorides (Cl^-), bromides (Br^-) and iodides (I^-)	$AgCl$, $AgBr$, AgI, PbI_2	$PbCl_2$, $PbBr_2$
all nitrates (NO_3^-)	no exceptions	no exceptions
all ammonium (NH_4^+) salts	no exceptions	no exceptions
all sodium (Na^+) and potassium (K^+) salts	no exceptions	no exceptions
all ethanoates (CH_3COO^-)	no exceptions	no exceptions
most sulfates (SO_4^{2-})	$SrSO_4$, $BaSO_4$, $PbSO_4$	$CaSO_4$, Ag_2SO_4
Insoluble ionic compounds		
Insoluble in water	**Exceptions: soluble**	**Exceptions: slightly soluble**
most hydroxides (OH^-)	$NaOH$, KOH, $Ba(OH)_2$, NH_4OH^*, $AgOH^{**}$	$Ca(OH)_2$, $Sr(OH)_2$
most carbonates (CO_3^{2-})	Na_2CO_3, K_2CO_3, $(NH_4)_2CO_3$	no exceptions
most phosphates (PO_4^{3-})	Na_3PO_4, K_3PO_4, $(NH_4)_3PO_4$	no exceptions
most sulfides (S^{2-})	Na_2S, K_2S, $(NH_4)_2S$	no exceptions

*NH_4OH does not exist in significant amounts in an ammonia solution. Ammonium and hydroxide ions readily combine to form ammonia and water.
**$AgOH$ readily decomposes to form a precipitate of silver oxide and water.

TABLE 1 Bond energies and average bond energies

Single bonds (kJ mol^{-1})							
C–H	414	N–H	391	O–H	463	F–F	159
C–C	346	N–C	286	O–O	144		
C–N	286	N–N	158	O–F	191	Cl–F	255
C–O	358	N–O	214	O–Cl	206	Cl–Cl	242
C–F	492	N–F	278	O–I	201		
C–Cl	324	N–Cl	192			Br–F	249
C–Br	285	N–Br	243	S–H	364	Br–Cl	219
C–I	228			S–F	327	Br–Br	193
C–S	289	H–H	436	S–Cl	271		
		H–F	567	S–Br	218	I–Cl	211
Si–H	323	H–Cl	431	S–S	266	I–Br	178
Si–Si	226	H–Br	366			I–I	151
Si–C	307	H–I	298				
Si–O	466						

Multiple bonds (kJ mol^{-1})							
C=C	614	N=N	470	O=O	498		
C≡C	839	N≡N	945				
C=N	615			S=O	523		
C≡N	890			S=S	429		
C=O	804						

TABLE 2 Standard enthalpies of formation and standard entropies

Substance	Formula	$\Delta H°_f$ (kJ mol^{-1})	$S°$ (J mol^{-1} K^{-1})
ammonia	$NH_3(g)$	−45.9	+192.8
butane	$C_4H_{10}(g)$	−126	+310
carbon dioxide	$CO_2(g)$	−393.5	+213.8
carbon monoxide	$CO(g)$	−110.5	+197.7
ethane	$C_2H_6(g)$	−84.0	+230
ethanol	$C_2H_5OH(l)$	−277.7	+161
ethene	$C_2H_4(g)$	+52.0	+220
ethyne (acetylene)	$C_2H_2(g)$	+228	+201
glucose	$C_6H_{12}O_6(s)$	−1271	+209.2
hydrogen	$H_2(g)$	0	+130.7
hydrogen bromide	$HBr(g)$	−36.3	+198.7
hydrogen chloride	$HCl(g)$	−92.3	+186.9
hydrogen fluoride	$HF(g)$	−273.3	+173.8
hydrogen iodide	$HI(g)$	+26.5	+206.6
methane	$CH_4(g)$	−74.8	+186
nitrogen	$N_2(g)$	0	+191.6
nitrogen dioxide	$NO_2(g)$	+33.1	+240.0
nitrogen monoxide	$NO(g)$	+90.2	+210.8
octane	$C_8H_{18}(l)$	−250.3	+359.8
oxygen	$O_2(g)$	0	+205
propane	$C_3H_8(g)$	−104.6	+270
water(g)	$H_2O(g)$	−241.8	+188.8
water(l)	$H_2O(l)$	−285.8	+70.0

TABLE 3 Enthalpies of combustion*

Substance	Formula	$\Delta H°_c$ (kJ mol^{-1})
butane	$C_4H_{10}(g)$	−2886
carbon (graphite)	$C(s)$	−394
ethane	$C_2H_6(g)$	−1560
ethene	$C_2H_4(g)$	−1411
ethanol	C_2H_5OH	−1367
glucose	$C_6H_{12}O_6(s)$	−2803
hydrogen	$H_2(g)$	−286
methane	$CH_4(g)$	−890
methanol	$CH_3OH(l)$	−725
octane	$C_8H_{18}(l)$	−5450
propane	$C_3H_8(g)$	−2220

*Values are measured at standard state conditions (298 K, 1 bar).

Answers

Chapter 1 Working scientifically

1.1 Questioning and predicting

1 An inquiry question ends with a question mark and guides the investigation. A hypothesis is a cause-and-effect statement that can be tested through an investigation. The purpose is a statement outlining the aim of the investigation.

2 A   **3** qualitative   **4** A   **5** A   **6** C

1.2 Planning investigations

1 **a** valid   **b** reliable   **c** accurate

2 F   **3** C and D   **4** B

5 **a** pH of water   **b** mass of mussel

    c temperature of water, method of pH measurement, equipment used to measure mass, type of mussel

6 • Weigh 10 g of marble chips into a conical flask. Record the mass.
    • Add a plug of cotton wool to the mouth of the conical flask.
    • Tare the balance when the conical flask, marble chips and cotton wool plug are on the balance.
    • Use a measuring cylinder to measure 100 mL of 0.5 mol L^{-1} hydrochloric acid.
    • Remove the cotton wool plug.
    • Immediately add the hydrochloric acid to the conical flask, add the cotton wool plug, and record the mass.

1.3 Conducting investigations

1 in a logbook

2 **a** systematic error   **b** mistake
    c random error   **d** systematic error

3 **a** 17.92, 17.98 and 18.02 mL
    b 17.97 mL   **c** random error

4 **a** systematic error   **b** mistake   **c** random error

1.4 Processing data and information

1 **a** 23   **b** 21   **c** 22

2 **a** 4   **b** the least number possible
    c the least number possible

3 **a** y-axis   **b** x-axis

4 31

5 **a** As the temperature of a solution increases, the solubility of CH_4, O_2 and CO decreases. The solubility of He in solution decreases slightly as the temperature increases from 3°C to 35°C, then is relatively constant.
    b In general, the solubility of gases in solution decreases as the temperature of the solution increases.

6 **a**

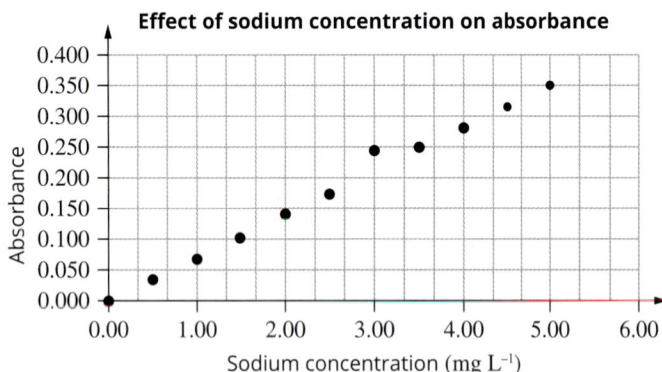

Effect of sodium concentration on absorbance

    b any data point that does not fit an observed pattern or trend
    c data point at 3 mg L^{-1}

d

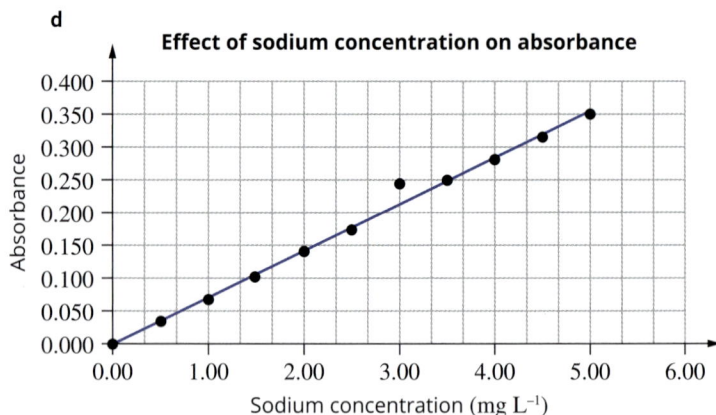

Effect of sodium concentration on absorbance

e 2.17 mg L^{-1}

7 Label x-axis 'Time' with units, include units on y-axis, use consistent scale on x-axis, use scale from 0 to 12 on y-axis, use scatter plot instead of bar graph, include a more descriptive title.

8 **a** least accurate (difficult to estimate the volume to nearest 1 mL)
    b more accurate than beaker (can be estimated to nearest 0.1 mL)
    c most accurate (can be estimated to 2 decimal places)

1.5 Analysing data and information

TY 1.5.1 112 g

1 bar graphs, histograms, pie diagrams

2 Rate was constant between t_0 and t_1; increased instantaneously at t_1, gradually decreased until t_2, then was constant but greater than before t_1.

3 **a** 700 g   **b** 45 g   **c** 66 g

4 qualified authors, published in a reputable peer-reviewed journal, detailed method, valid, reliable, accurate, precise, limitations outlined, assumptions outlined, suggested future improvements or research directions

1.6 Problem solving

1 A

2 The procedure was repeated five times to minimise random errors.

3 Precipitate the sodium ions and then use gravimetric analysis, or use atomic absorption spectroscopy.

4 **a** the equipment set-up, the time required for each step
    b **i** C_2HCl_3 **ii** $C_2H_2ClF_3$ **iii** $C_2HBrClF_3$

1.7 Communicating

1 C   **2** A, B, C

3 **a** 2.35×10^5 **b** 6.55×10^{-7}
    c It allows very large and very small numbers to be expressed easily.

4 Stierwalt, S. (2016). Will salt water quench the world's thirst? *Scientific American, 315*(5).
https://www.scientificamerican.com/article/will-salt-water-quench-the-world-s-thirst

Chapter 1 Review

1 **a** bar graph   **b** line graph
    c scatter graph with trend line   **d** pie diagram

2 B   **3** C   **4** A

5 purpose: a statement outlining the purpose of an investigation
hypothesis: a cause-and-effect statement that can be tested through an investigation
variables: the factors that can change in an investigation

6 **a** dependent   **b** controlled   **c** independent

7 independent variable: source of water
dependent variable: lead concentration
controlled variables: method of lead analysis, sample size, temperature of sample

8 **a** independent variable: type of organic acid
dependent variable: dissociation constant
b independent variable: type of ionic compound
dependent variable is the solubility of substance in water at 50°C
c independent variable: type of alcohol
dependent variable: the property

9 **a** corrosive chemical   **b** toxic chemical
c flammable chemical

10 0.070 50 L

11 **a** mean: the average of a set of data
b mode: the most frequent value in a set of data
c median: the middle value in a set of data

12 16.33 ± 0.55 **13** the mean

14 **a** Student answers will vary. Sample answer: 2 significant figures = 0.032, 3 significant figures = 0.0302, 4 significant figures = 0.030 20, 5 significant figures = 0.030 200
b Report the final calculation to the least number of significant figures used in the calculation.
c Report the final calculation to the least number of decimal places used in the calculation.

15 **a** mistake   **b** random error   **c** systematic error

16 **a** Accuracy is how close a measurement is to the true value. Precision is how close measurements are to each other.
b more than one independent variable changed at a time, inappropriate method used, outliers included in data analysis, insufficient sample size used
c Student answers will vary. Sample answer: The experiment was repeated only three times.

17 **a** reliability   **b** accuracy   **c** validity   **d** precision

18 It gives appropriate credit to others, avoids plagiarism, and enables the reader to obtain further information.

19 **a** Student answers will vary. Sample answer: To investigate the effect of temperature on the pH of water.
b independent variable: water temperature
dependent variable: measured pH
controlled variables: source of water, sample size, method used, calibration technique
c quantitative
d universal indicator, colour chart: low precision
calibrated pH data-logging equipment: high precision
e indirect linear relationship

20 Similarities: credible sources, 2016 year of publication for Stierwelt and Li articles, Stierwelt and Romanok articles use data from the USA, Elmahdi and BOM articles use Australian information, all sources related to water quality
Differences: Stierwalt article information fully summarised but others not; Stiewalt and Li articles have different focuses and conclusions

21 Student answers will vary. Sample answer: Design a valid experiment to test the manufacturer's claim and compare to published findings from a consumer magazine.

22 Student answers will vary. Sample answer: The student would need to propose a hypothesis for the causation and test the hypothesis. This could include investigating whether people who died from entanglement in bedsheets had consumed cheese on the night of their death, the type of cheese, allergies towards cheese, the quantity of cheese consumed, etc.

23 Student answers will vary. Possible answers include checking that: there is a clear inquiry question, hypothesis, purpose and an appropriate risk assessment; variables are clearly defined; appropriate methodology used; answer is accurate, precise, reliable and valid; sources are acknowledged appropriately; strengths and weaknesses are discussed; patterns and trends in data are identified and discussed; appropriate chemical nomenclature and scientific conventions are followed; tables and figures are clearly labelled, relevant and signposted; writing style is appropriate for the intended audience.

24 **a** 132 g $NaNO_3$ per 100 g of water
b 161 g $AgNO_3$ per 100 g of water
c 68 g   **d** 60 g   **e** 100 g

25 It does not show the state of each reactant, reaction conditions, catalysts required, percentage yield of CO_2 in each pathways, rate of reaction, and equilibrium constant for each step.

26 Students answers will vary.

27 Students answers will vary.

28

Measurement	Value	Number of significant figures in measured or calculated value
mass of crucible and lid (g)	41.893	5
mass of crucible, lid and Mg ribbon (g)	42.633	5
mass of crucible, lid and MgO (g)	43.143	5
mass of Mg (g)	0.740	3
mass of MgO (g)	1.250	4
% Mg in MgO	59.2%	3
% O in MgO	40.8%	3

29 **a** $BaCl_2$
b The mass of precipitate was constant after adding 90 mL of $BaCl_2$, so all sulfate ions had precipitated as $BaSO_4$ and the $BaCl_2$ was in excess at the end of the experiment.
c Adding smaller volumes of $BaCl_2$, e.g. 15 mL increment, would help determine more accurately when the $BaCl_2$ would be in excess.

Chapter 2 Static and dynamic equilibrium

2.1 Chemical systems

1 B

2 reversible, energy, matter, rates, remains constant

3 **a** closed   **b** open   **c** closed   **d** open

4 $130 \, kJ \, mol^{-1}$

2.2 Dynamic equilibrium

1 C

2

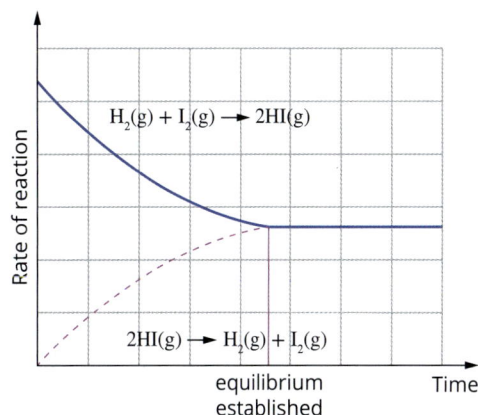

Only reactants are present initially, and they undergo reaction to form the products. As the concentration of the reactants decreases, the rate of this reaction decreases. The upper curve therefore shows the rate of the forward reaction.
The lower curve shows the rate of the reverse reaction. As the number of product particles increases, the rate of the reverse reaction increases. When the rates of the forward and reverse reactions become equal, equilibrium is established.

3 closed, decreases, less, reverse, increases, equal

4 **a** $0.07 \, mol \, L^{-1}$ **b** $0.00 \, mol \, L^{-1}$ **c** $0.03 \, mol \, L^{-1}$
d $0.08 \, mol \, L^{-1}$ **e** 0.04 mol
f There is no change in concentration of NO_2 or N_2O_4. The system is at equilibrium and the forward and reverse reactions are occurring at the same rate.
g 6 s
h The intensity of the brown colour will increase as the concentration of NO_2 increases until equilibrium is reached. The colour of the reaction mixture will then remain constant.

5 B

6 a $-0.55\,\text{kJ mol}^{-1}$ **b** Yes, as ΔG is negative

Chapter 2 Review

1 A   **2** C   **3** D

4 a open; both energy and matter (carbon dioxide and water vapour) are exchanged with the surroundings

  b closed; only energy is exchanged with the surroundings

  c open; both energy and matter is exchanged with the surroundings

  d closed; only energy is exchanged. Temperature changes result in changes in volume, but there is no exchange of matter.

5 a False   **b** True   **c** True   **d** False

6 a Chemical equilibrium is 'dynamic' because both forward and reverse reactions occur at the same rate. An equilibrium develops between water vapour and liquid water when wet clothes are in a sealed bag, with water evaporating as rapidly as water vapour condenses, so the clothes remain wet.

  b When the bag is opened, water vapour escapes and the rate of evaporation exceeds the rate of condensation. The system is not in equilibrium and the clothes dry.

7 iii, iv, ii, i.

8 Equilibrium can occur only in a closed system, so b and f are at equilibrium. In a, c, d and e, the systems are open and so these cannot be at equilibrium.

9 Initially, collisions between SO_2 and O_2 reactant molecules occur frequently, with sufficient molecules having the correct energy and orientation to produce product molecules, SO_3. As more product molecules are formed, they collide with sufficient energy to decompose to the reactant molecules, SO_2 and O_2. The forward and reverse reactions continue to occur, with the rate of the forward reaction decreasing over time and the rate of the reverse reaction increasing over the same time interval. Finally, the rates of the reactions become equal and equilibrium is established.

10 Static equilibrium occurs when the rates of the forward and reverse reactions of a system are equal and almost zero. There is no movement of reactant and product particles in either the forward or reverse direction, e.g. graphite $\rightleftharpoons$ diamond. Dynamic equilibrium occurs when the rate of the forward reaction is equal to the rate of the reverse reaction. The concentrations of the reactants and products do not change over time, but at the atomic level the reactants are continually forming products and the products continually forming reactants, e.g. $2SO_2(g) + O_2(g) \rightleftharpoons 2SO_3(g)$

11 Combustion reactions are irreversible because the products, CO_2 and H_2O, are stable molecules and do not react to re-form the reactants at normal temperatures. Non-equilibrium systems are irreversible, so combustion is considered to be a non-equilibrium system.

12 The entropy of the cards (ΔS_{system}) decreases when they are arranged in order. However, the person is using energy in the process, releasing gaseous CO_2 and H_2O and heat to the atmosphere and the entropy of the surroundings ($\Delta S_{surroundings}$) increases. Overall, $\Delta S_{surroundings}$ is greater than ΔS_{system} and the entropy of the universe increases overall, in accord with the second law of thermodynamics.

13 The deployment of air bags is irreversible, so this system can be considered to be a non-equilibrium system.

14 $-2866\,\text{kJ mol}^{-1}$; $\Delta G°$ is negative, so respiration is spontaneous

15

	Photosynthesis	Room
a	decrease (–)	decrease (–)
b	non-spontaneous (+)	non-spontaneous (+)
c	increases	increases

16 a HR_w is red and R_w^- is green.

  b $R_w^-(aq) + H^+(aq) \rightarrow HR_w(aq)$

  c The R_w^- formed by adding a base can be converted back to HR_w by adding an acid, so it can be described as reversible.

Chapter 3 Calculating an equilibrium constant

3.1 The equilibrium law

TY 3.1.1 $K_{eq} = \dfrac{[SO_3]^2}{[SO_2]^2[O_2]}$ **TY 3.1.2** $K_{eq} = [Pb^{2+}][I^-]^2$

1 $Q = \dfrac{[HCl]^2}{[H_2][Cl_2]}$

2 $Q < K_{eq}$, so the reaction will shift to the right.

3 a a system in which all the species are in the same phase

  b a system in which the species are in different phases

  c $Q = \dfrac{[\text{products}]^{\text{coefficient}}}{[\text{reactants}]^{\text{coefficient}}} = K_{eq}$ at equilibrium

  d It is the ratio of the equilibrium concentrations of the products divided by the equilibrium concentrations of the reactants raised to the power of their coefficients. It is given the symbol K_{eq}. Its value changes with temperature.

4 $K_{eq} = \dfrac{[[Cu(NH_3)_4]^{2+}]}{[Cu^{2+}][NH_3]^4}$

  $Q > K_{eq}$, so the concentration of $Cu(NH_3)_4]^{2+}$ must decrease and the concentration of the reactants must increase in order to reach equilibrium. This will occur if the reaction moves to the left, producing more reactants.

5 a $K_{eq} = [NH_3][H_2S]$ **b** $K_{eq} = [Ag^+][Cl^-]$

  c $K_{eq} = \dfrac{1}{[Ag^+]^2[CO_3^{2-}]}$ **d** $K_{eq} = \dfrac{[H_2O]^2[Cl_2]^2}{[HCl]^4[O_2]}$

3.2 Working with equilibrium constants

1 a $K_{eq} = \dfrac{[NH_3]^2}{[N_2][H_2]^3}$ **b** 0.01

  c $K_{eq} = \dfrac{[N_2]^{\frac{1}{2}}[H_2]^{\frac{3}{2}}}{[NH_3]}$ **d** 10

  e i The value of the equilibrium constant is the reciprocal of the original constant.

    ii The new equilibrium constant is equal to the square root of the original constant.

2 a 0.020   **b** 50

3 a 8.35   **b** 0.767   **c** 1.30   **d** 0.346

4 B

5 a increased   **b** decreased   **c** increased   **d** decreased

3.3 Calculations involving equilibrium

TY 3.3.1 0.694   **TY 3.3.2** $0.17\,\text{mol L}^{-1}$ **TY 3.3.3** 0.0248

1 0.10   **2** 1.1×10^2 **3** $0.127\,\text{mol L}^{-1}$

4 3.3×10^{-2} **5** 2.41×10^{-3}

6 a $0.011\,\text{mol L}^{-1}$ **b** 0.020

  c The value of the reaction quotient is 0.077, which is greater than the equilibrium constant at the same temperature as calculated in part b. Thus the system is not at equilibrium. A net backwards reaction will occur.

Chapter 3 Review

1 B   **2** $K_{eq} = \dfrac{[Fe^{2+}]^2[Sn^{4+}]}{[Fe^{3+}]^2[Sn^{2+}]}$ **3** D

4 a $2NO(g) \rightarrow N_2(g) + O_2(g)$ **b** $S_2(g) + 2H_2(g) \rightarrow 2H_2S(g)$

  c $NO_2(g) \rightarrow \frac{1}{2}N_2O_4(g)$

5 a $K_{eq} = \dfrac{1}{[Cu^{2+}][CO_3^{2-}]}$ **b** $K_{eq} = [Cu^{2+}][CO_3^{2-}]$

  c $K_{eq} = \dfrac{[PCl_5]^4}{[Cl_2]^{10}}$ **d** $K_{eq} = \dfrac{[Cl_2]^{20}}{[PCl_5]^8}$

6 The reaction quotient is the ratio of the concentrations of the products to the concentration of the reactants, with the index of each concentration the same as the coefficient of the substance in the reaction equation. The value of the reaction quotient becomes equal to the equilibrium constant at equilibrium.

7   As Q for the reaction is larger than K_{eq}, the reaction must move to decrease Q. This will happen with a decrease in the concentration of the products. There will be a net backwards reaction, decreasing the concentration of ethyl ethanoate as the mixture reaches equilibrium.

8   a   less than   b $\dfrac{[H_2O]^2[N_2]}{[H_2]^2[NO]^2}$ c   moves to the right

9   a   No. K_{eq} is very small.   b 10^{10}
    c   Yes. K_{eq} is very large (provided the rate is sufficiently fast).

10 a $K_{eq} = \dfrac{[Br_2][Cl_2]}{[BrCl]^2}$
    b   i   5.7   ii   0.031   iii 1.0×10^3 iv   0.18

11 The reaction is not at equilibrium and will shift towards the left to reach equilibrium.

12 0.53   13   3.6   14   0.019

15 a $K_{eq} = \dfrac{[PCl_3][Cl_2]}{[PCl_5]}$ b   0.400
    c $0.80\,\text{mol L}^{-1}$ d $K_{eq} = \dfrac{1}{0.400} = 2.50$

16 0.098   17   557

18 a $[A] = 1.0\,\text{mol L}^{-1}$, $[B] = 0.25\,\text{mol L}^{-1}$, $[D] = 1.5\,\text{mol L}^{-1}$
    b $0.016\,\text{mol L}^{-1}$ c   0.032 mol

19 a   The system is not at equilibrium and will shift to the left, resulting in a net reverse reaction.
    b   The system is not at equilibrium and will shift to the right, resulting in a net forward reaction.

20 a   i   increase   ii   increase   iii   decrease   iv   decrease
    b   enthalpy change was endothermic

21 a closed system

Chapter 4 Factors that affect equilibrium

4.1 Le Châtelier's principle

TY 4.1.1   A net reverse reaction has occurred. The position of equilibrium has shifted to the left.

1   a   net forward reaction   b   net reverse reaction
    c   net forward reaction
2   a   a net forward reaction   b   a net reverse reaction
3   a   net reverse reaction; equilibrium will shift to the left
    b   net forward reaction; equilibrium will shift to the right
4   B

4.2 Further applications of Le Châtelier's principle

TY 4.2.1   The system will shift to the left.
TY 4.2.2   There is a net reverse reaction, with higher concentrations of reactants, CO_2 and H_2, and lower concentrations of products, CH_4 and H_2O.

1   B
2   a   net forward reaction   b   no effect   c   net forward reaction
3   a   Doubling the pressure causes increased frequency of collisions and an increased rate of both the forward and reverse reactions. Since there are more particles on the left side there will be more successful collisions in the forward direction, so a net forward reaction results.
    b   Increasing the pressure causes an increased frequency of collisions and an increased rate of both the forward and reverse reactions. Because there is an equal chance of reactant molecules colliding and forming a product, or product molecules colliding and forming the reactants (2 mol of reactants and 2 mol of products), there is no overall net reaction.
    c   A temperature increase means all reactant and product molecules have more energy and move faster. There will be more frequent collisions and more molecules will have the necessary energy to overcome the activation energy barrier. Hence there will be a net forward reaction.
4   a   decrease   b   increase

Chapter 4 Review

1   a   If an equilibrium system undergoes a change, the system will adjust itself to partially oppose the effect of that change.
    b $A + B \rightarrow C + D$; a net forward reaction occurs. The system can be regarded as partially opposing the change and trying to restore equilibrium.
2   a   Adding a reactant causes a net forward reaction.
    b   Removing a reactant causes a net reverse reaction.
    c   Removing a product causes a net forward reaction.
3   a   More $H_2(g)$ has been added, causing a net forward reaction.
    b   Some $H_2(g)$ could have been removed, lowering the concentration of $H_2(g)$ and causing a net reverse reaction.
4   If Ca^{2+} ions were inefficiently absorbed from food, decreased concentrations of these ions could occur in body fluids. As a consequence, a net forward reaction would occur, resulting in decreased amounts of calcium phosphate in bones.
5   a   increase   b   increase
6   B and D   7   C
8   a   curve A: NO_2; curve B: N_2O_4 b   A
9   D
10 a   i   increase temperature   ii   increase temperature
        iii   decrease temperature
    b   i   cannot cause forward reaction   ii   increase volume
        iii   cannot cause forward reaction
11 a   net reverse reaction   b   net forward reaction
    c   no effect
12 C
13 a   i   net forward reaction   ii   no change
        iii   net forward reaction
    b   i   increase   ii   no change   iii   no change
    c   likely to be large, since the reaction will be almost complete
14 a   Lighter. Le Châtelier's principle: Increasing the system's temperature increases the energy of its substances. The reaction opposes an increase in energy by absorbing energy. Because the reverse reaction is endothermic, this favours a net reverse reaction (K_{eq} will decrease).
        Collision theory: A higher temperature causes all molecules to have more energy and there are more frequent collisions. The temperature increase affects the rate of the endothermic reaction more than the exothermic reaction because a higher proportion of molecules have the necessary energy to overcome the activation energy barrier. So, the net reaction will be the reverse, endothermic reaction.
    b   Lighter. Le Châtelier's principle: An increase in volume causes a decrease in pressure. The system will oppose the change by increasing the pressure, so the equilibrium position moves in the direction of the most particles, producing more NO and O_2.
        Collision theory: Decreased pressure means that collisions will be less frequent. The rate of the reaction involving the smaller number particle (the reverse reaction) will decrease the least. Therefore the equilibrium shifts to the left.
    c   No change. Le Châtelier's principle: The system cannot adjust to oppose the addition of a catalyst. There is therefore no net reaction.
        Collision theory: Adding a catalyst increases the rates of the forward and back reactions equally. There is no net reaction because the change in the frequency of collisions is equal in both directions.
    d   Darker. Le Châtelier's principle: The reaction opposes the change by consuming the added O_2 and shifts toward the right to produce more brown NO_2.
        Collision theory: Adding O_2 increases its concentration and causes the rate of the forward reaction to increase. As O_2 is consumed the rate of the forward reaction decreases and the rate of the reverse reaction increases until a new equilibrium is established. Overall, there is a net forward reaction.
15 a   decrease the temperature   b   decrease the volume
16 a   i   decrease   ii   decrease   iii   increase
        iv   no change   v   no change
    b   i   increase   ii   increase   iii   increase
        iv   increase   v   no change

17 i

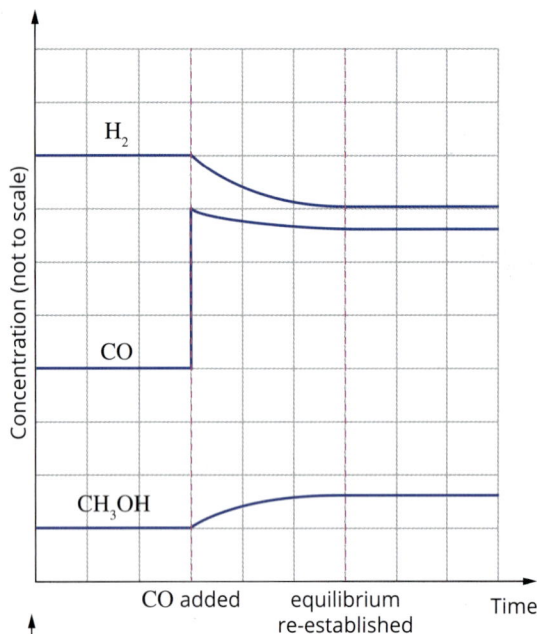

ii

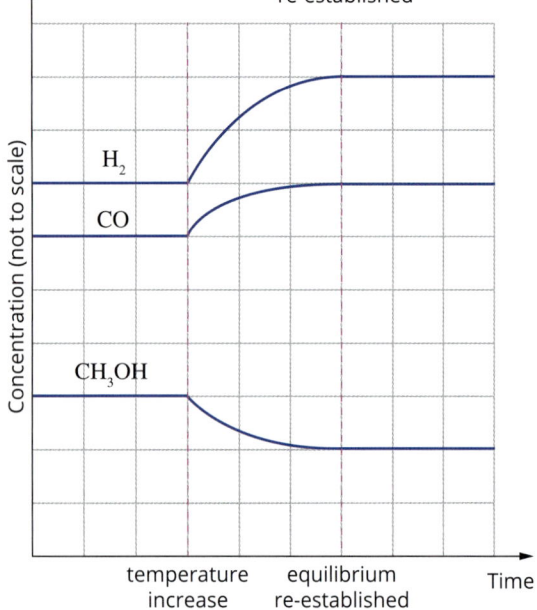

18 a The rates of the forward and reverse reactions are equal and the rate of production of ammonia is constant. The system is at equilibrium. The frequency of effective collisions between N_2 and H_2 molecules is constant.

b The concentrations of all species will increase. The system will adjust to reduce the concentrations overall and will favour the forward reaction. According to collision theory, an increase in concentration causes the frequency of all collisions in both directions to increase. An increase in the rate of production of ammonia is favoured.

c The reactant molecules collide and produce ammonia. As the concentrations of reactant molecules decrease, the rate of production of ammonia decreases. As more ammonia is formed, the reverse reaction increases. After t_2 equilibrium is re-established.

19 a $2SO_3(g) + CO_2(g) \rightleftharpoons CS_2(g) + 4O_2(g)$

b $K_{eq} = \dfrac{[CS_2][O_2]^4}{[SO_3]^2[CO_2]}$

c i 0.11 mol   **ii** 1.6×10^{-3}

d i increase   **ii** increase   **iii** no effect   **iv** decrease

   v no effect

20 a $K_{eq} = \dfrac{[SO_3]^2}{[SO_2]^2[O_2]}$

b 15–20 minutes, 25–30 minutes, 35–40 minutes

c 1.56   **d** 10 minutes   **e** 3.50

f The volume was decreased, which resulted in an increased pressure. Because the value of K_{eq} at 25–30 minutes is larger than at 15–20 minutes and this is an exothermic reaction, a decrease in temperature must also have occurred.

21 When the rates at which water is transferred between the containers become equal, a dynamic equilibrium is established and no further change in water levels occurs.

In part B of the activity, when more water is added to one container, a new equilibrium is formed but the relative amounts of water in the containers is different to that of the first equilibrium.

Chapter 5 Solubility and equilibria

5.1 Process of dissolution of ionic compounds

TY 5.1.1 no precipitate

1 $NaNO_3(s) \xrightarrow{H_2O(l)} Na^+(aq) + NO_3^-(aq)$

$Ca(OH)_2(s) \xrightarrow{H_2O(l)} Ca^{2+}(aq) + 2OH^-(aq)$

2 When potassium bromide, an ionic compound, is added to water, the positive ions attract the partial negative charges on the oxygen atoms in water molecules and the negative ions attract the partial positive charges on the hydrogen atoms in water molecules. This attraction is enough to overcome the attraction between the ions in the lattice, and the ions enter solution.

3 a Na^+/CO_3^{2-} **b** Ca^{2+}/NO_3^- **c** K^+/Br^-

   d Fe^{3+}/SO_4^{2-} **e** Cu^{2+}/Cl^-

4 A, D, E, G, H, J

5 a yes, silver chloride   **b** yes, aluminium hydroxide

   c yes, copper(II) phosphate   **d** no precipitate

   e yes, lead(II) fluoride   **f** no precipitate

5.2 Solubility of ionic compounds and equilibrium

TY 5.2.1 $K_{sp}= [Ag^-]^2[CO_3^{2-}]$ **TY 5.2.2** 5.62×10^{-12}

TY 5.2.3 $2.1 \times 10^{-6}\,mol\,L^{-1}$ **TY 5.2.4** no precipitate

TY 5.2.5 yes, barium sulfate   **TY 5.2.6** $1.1 \times 10^{-12}\,mol\,L^{-1}$

1 a $K_{sp} = [Ca^{2+}][SO_4^{2-}]$ **b** $K_{sp} = [Zn^{2+}][CO_3^{2-}]$

   c $K_{sp} = [Pb^{2+}][I^-]^2$ **d** $K_{sp} = [Fe^{3+}][OH^-]^3$

2 2.2×10^{-19} **3** $5.6 \times 10^{-4}\,mol\,L^{-1}$ **4** yes

5 $1.2 \times 10^{-9}\,mol\,L^{-1}$

6 cycasin, seeds are either are roasted briefly, then leached in water for a short time, or only leached but for a longer time

Chapter 5 Review

1 a dissociation

   b i $Cu^{2+}(aq)$, $NO_3^-(aq)$ **ii** $Zn^{2+}(aq)$, $SO_4^{2-}(aq)$

     iii $NH_4^+(aq)$, $PO_4^{3-}(aq)$

2 a K^+/CO_3^{2-} **b** Pb^{2+}/NO_3^- **c** Na^+/OH^- **d** Na^+/SO_4^{2-}

   e Mg^{2+}/Cl^- **f** Zn^{2+}/NO_3^- **g** K^+/S^{2-} **h** Fe^{3+}/NO_3^-

3 a $Mg(CH_3COO)_2(s) \xrightarrow{H_2O(l)} Mg^{2+}(aq) + 2CH_3COO^-(aq)$

   b $AgNO_3(s) \xrightarrow{H_2O(l)} Ag^+(aq) + NO_3^-(aq)$

   c $KBr(s) \xrightarrow{H_2O(l)} K^+(aq) + Br^-(aq)$

   d $Ba(OH)_2(s) \xrightarrow{H_2O(l)} Ba^{2+}(aq) + 2OH^-(aq)$

   e $Na_3PO_4(s) \xrightarrow{H_2O(l)} 3Na^+(aq) + PO_4^{3-}(aq)$

4 B

5 Magnesium ions have a positive charge, so the partially negatively charged oxygen atoms in the water molecules are attracted to them. The water molecules are arranged around the magnesium ion with their oxygen atoms pointed towards the magnesium ion. Chloride ions have a negative charge, so the partially positively charged hydrogen atoms in the water molecules are attracted to them. The water molecules are arranged around the chloride ion with their hydrogen atoms pointed towards the chloride ion.

6 Student answers will vary.

   a Examples: Na_2CO_3, $(NH_4)_2CO_3$ and K_2CO_3

   b Examples: $CaCO_3$, $MgCO_3$ and Ag_2CO_3

7 Student answers will vary.
  a Examples: Na_2SO_4, K_2SO_4 and $(NH_4)_2SO_4$
  b Examples: $CaSO_4$, $BaSO_4$ and $PbSO_4$

8 55 g

9 **a** silver chloride **b** iron(II) hydroxide
  c lead(II) iodide **d** none

10 **a** **i** magnesium sulfide **ii** barium sulfate
   iii iron(III) hydroxide **iv** silver chloride
  b **i** $Na_2S(aq) + MgI_2(aq) \rightarrow 2NaI(aq) + MgS(s)$
   ii $K_2SO_4(aq) + Ba(NO_3)_2(aq) \rightarrow 2KNO_3(aq) + BaSO_4(s)$
   iii $FeCl_3(aq) + 3NaOH(aq) \rightarrow 3NaCl(aq) + Fe(OH)_3(s)$
   iv $NH_4Cl(aq) + AgCH_3COO(aq) \rightarrow NH_4CH_3COO(aq) + AgCl(s)$
  c **i** $Mg^{2+}(aq) + S^{2-}(aq) \rightarrow MgS(s)$
   ii $Ba^{2+}(aq) + SO_4^{2-}(aq) \rightarrow BaSO_4(s)$
   iii $Fe^{3+}(aq) + 3OH^-(aq) \rightarrow Fe(OH)_3(s)$
   iv $Ag^+(aq) + Cl^-(aq) \rightarrow AgCl(s)$

11 **i** iodine **ii** nitrogen **iii** chlorine **iv** chlorine

12

	$MgSO_4$	KCl	NaOH	$AgNO_3$	$FeBr_2$
$Pb(CH_3COO)_2$	$PbSO_4$	$PbCl_2$ (slightly soluble)	$Pb(OH)_2$	–	$PbBr_2$ (slightly soluble)
K_2CO_3	$MgCO_3$	–	–	Ag_2CO_3	$FeCO_3$
BaI_2	$BaSO_4$	–	–	AgI	–
Na_3PO_4	$Mg_3(PO_4)_2$	–	–	$Ag_3(PO_4)_2$	$Fe_3(PO_4)_2$
NH_4S	MgS	–	–	Ag_2S	FeS

13 D

14 **a** $FeCl_2(s) \rightleftharpoons Fe^{2+}(aq) + 2Cl^-(aq)$
  b $AlOH_3(s) \rightleftharpoons Al^{3+}(aq) + 3OH^-$
  c $Ag_2SO_4(s) \rightleftharpoons 2Ag^+(aq) + SO_4^{2-}(aq)$
  d $Ba_3(PO_4)_2(s) \rightleftharpoons 3Ba^{2+}(aq) + 2PO_4^{3-}(aq)$

15 **a** $K_{sp} = [Pb^{2+}][Cl^-]^2$ **b** $K_{sp} = [Zn^{2+}][OH^-]^2$
  c $K_{sp} = [Ag^+]^2[CrO_4^{2-}]$ **d** $K_{sp} = [Ba^{2+}][SO_4^{2-}]$

16 **a** $BaCO_3$ **b** $Fe(OH)_2$ **c** $PbCl_2$

17 Molar solubility is the number of moles of a solute that will dissolve per litre of water to form a saturated solution.

18 Sodium chloride is very soluble in water, so it can be considered to dissociate completely and only the forward reaction occurs. Silver chloride is only sparingly soluble in water and very little solid dissolves. The ions dissociate into solution at the same rate that others return to the ionic lattice. This is an equilibrium system, so the equation has an equilibrium arrow.

19 The initial concentration of ions is zero. When the salt is added, ions enter the solution. Therefore, the change in concentration is always positive.

20 **a** 6.57×10^{-6} **b** 1.08×10^{-10} **c** 2.6×10^{-12}

21 **a** $4.5 \times 10^{-13}\,mol\,L^{-1}$ **b** $7.31 \times 10^{-7}\,mol\,L^{-1}$
  c $1.44 \times 10^{-2}\,mol\,L^{-1}$

22 Ionic compounds that dissociate to produce different numbers of ions have different relationships to K_{sp}. Because silver cyanide dissociates to form two ions, it has a different relationship to K_{sp} than aluminium hydroxide, which produces four ions in solution.

23 **a** $4.82 \times 10^{-2}\,g$ **b** $3.1 \times 10^{-15}\,g$

24 **a** **i** no precipitate **ii** precipitate will form **iii** no precipitate
  b **i** $3.53 \times 10^{-3}\,g$ **iii** $0.91\,g$

25 **a** precipitate will form **b** no precipitate
  c precipitate will form

26 **a** precipitate will form **b** no precipitate
  c precipitate will form

27 **a** $3.9 \times 10^{-9}\,mol\,L^{-1}$ **b** $3.5 \times 10^{-34}\,mol\,L^{-1}$
  c $7.0 \times 10^{-11}\,mol\,L^{-1}$

28 **a** **i** $9.23 \times 10^{-9}\,mol\,L^{-1}$ **ii** $5.68 \times 10^{-17}\,mol\,L^{-1}$
  b The molar solubility of silver iodide is much less in potassium iodide solution than in pure water, because of the presence of a common ion, I^-. Le Châtelier's principle states that a system at equilibrium will shift its position so as to partially oppose the change. Here, the equilibrium position will shift to the left.

29 One example is the bitter yam. It was picked carefully to avoid damaging the roots, then leached in running water to remove the toxins. Finally, it was roasted before being eaten. Another example is cycad seeds. They are either roasted briefly before leaching in water, or leached for a longer time without roasting.

30 This increases the surface area, exposing more of the seed to the water, and facilitates the removal of the toxin.

31 The Epsom salts ($MgSO_4$) dissociated in water, yielding Mg^{2+} ions. These ions attach to the polar 'head' group of fatty acid molecules found in soaps and detergents and prevent them from lathering via the precipitation of insoluble soap 'scum'.

Module 5 Review

Multiple choice

1 C	**2** D	**3** B	**4** D
5 D	**6** A	**7** B	**8** D
9 B	**10** A	**11** C	**12** B
13 C	**14** C	**15** A	**16** D
17 B	**18** C	**19** A	**20** D

Short answer

1 **a** $CO_2(g) + NO(g) \rightarrow CO(g) + NO_2(g)$
  b $440\,kJ\,mol^{-1}$ **c** $+300\,kJ\,mol^{-1}$ **d** endothermic

2 **a** **i** no **ii** no
  b **i** no, but the rate of the forward reaction is equal to that of the back reaction.
   ii yes
  c yes

3 **a** The forward and reverse reaction rates are equal up until time T.
  b It increases the frequency of collisions between reactant particles so the rate of the forward reaction increases initially and there is a net forward reaction. This will consume the reactant particles (so the forward reaction will slow down) and generate product particles (so the reverse reaction will speed up) until equilibrium is re-established and no further change will occur.
  c **i** adding Y **ii** adding a catalyst
   iii adding an inert gas
  d The particles will be moving with less kinetic energy and hence colliding less frequently. There will be a lower proportion of collisions that meet the activation energy requirement and fewer successful collisions, and a lower rate. This is true for both forward and reverse reactions.
  e There will be a net forward reaction.
  f Exothermic. Lowering the temperature will always induce a shift in the exothermic direction, which in this case must be the forward reaction, since that is the direction of the shift.

4 **a** A: NO_2; B: N_2O_4 **b** $K_{eq} = \frac{[NO_2]^2}{[N_2O_4]}$

  c The final concentration will be unchanged, but it will be reached in less time.

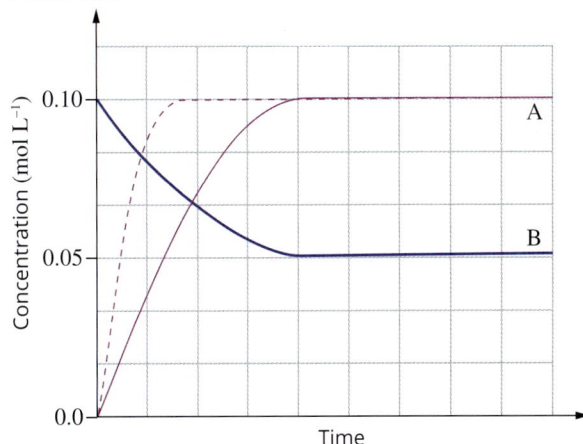

  d 0.20

5 a decreased **b** decreased **c** no change
d decreased **e** increased **f** decreased
g decreased **h** no change **i** no change

6 a Iodine (I_2) has been added, followed by a net forward reaction to re-establish equilibrium.
  b The temperature has been increased, resulting in a net back reaction (because the forward reaction is exothermic).
  c Equilibrium exists when the concentrations are constant (see diagram).
  d Doubling the volume will halve all concentrations but the mixture remains at equilibrium and there is no shift (see diagram).

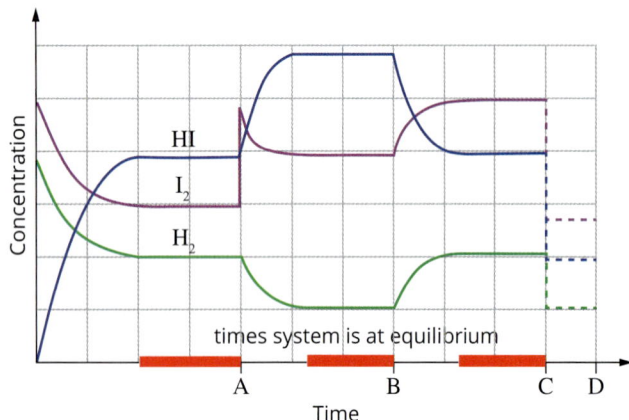

7 a $CH_4(g) + H_2O(g) \rightleftharpoons CO(g) + 3H_2(g)$
  $CO(g) + 2H_2(g) \rightleftharpoons CH_3OH(g)$
  b i They are catalysts.
  ii The yield would be poorer.
  iii High pressure will increase the reaction rate so products form faster. Also, it will favour the forward reaction and increase yield.
  c i Exposure to CO will drive the first reaction to the right. This lowers the concentration of free haemoglobin (Hb_4) which drives the second reaction to the left, removing $Hb_4(O_2)_4$.
  ii High O_2 pressure will drive the second reaction to the right. This lowers the concentration of free haemoglobin (Hb_4) which drives the first reaction to the left, removing $Hb_4(CO)_4$.
  d $CH_3OH(g) + O_2(g) \rightarrow CO(g) + 2H_2O(g)$

8 a $K_{sp} = [Li^+][Br^-]$ **b** $K_{sp} = [Pb^{2+}][I^-]^2$ **c** $K_{sp} = [Ca^{2+}]^3[PO_4^{3-}]^2$

9 a $PbCl_2$ **b** AgI **c** BaS **d** $Ni(OH)_2$

10 a 1.08×10^{-7} **b** precipitate will form

11 a i $CH_4(g) + 2O_2(g) \rightarrow CO_2(g) + 2H_2O(g)$
  ii $CH_4(g) + H_2O(g) \rightarrow CO(g) + 3H_2(g)$
  b i No, as reaction is not reversible.
  ii Yes, as reaction is reversible.
  c i 2 mol **ii** less than
  d i No; it is determined by the amount of methane available.
  ii yes
  e $\Delta G° = -1041\,kJ\,mol^{-1}$

12 a i K_{eq} increases as the forward, exothermic reaction is favoured, resulting in more products when equilibrium is re-established.
  ii It shifts to the right as the forward, exothermic reaction is favoured.
  iii It decreases as the forward reaction is favoured.
  iv It decreases as the forward reaction is favoured.
  b i K_{eq} is unchanged as temperature has not changed.
  ii It shifts to the right as the system partially opposes an increase in pressure by moving in the forward direction as there are fewer product molecules than reactant molecules.
  iii It increases due to the decrease in volume.
  iv It decreases as the forward reaction is favoured.
  c i K_{eq} is unchanged as temperature has not changed.
  ii It shifts to the right, as the system partially opposes the addition of oxygen by moving in the forward direction to remove some oxygen.

  iii It decreases as the forward reaction is favoured.
  iv It decreases as the forward reaction is favoured.

13 a i 0.083 **ii** 144 **iii** 0.29
  b 4.1 mol **c** 0.009

14 a i All ammonium compounds are soluble.
  ii NH_4^+, CO_3^{2-}
  iii $(NH_4)_2CO_3(s) \rightarrow 2NH_4^+(aq) + CO_3^{2-}(aq)$
  b decreases
  c i ionic bonds in ammonium carbonate; hydrogen bonds in water
  ii ion–dipole bonds between ammonium or carbonate ions and water molecules
  d $(NH_4)_2CO_3(aq) + Pb(NO_3)_2(aq) \rightarrow PbCO_3(s) + 2NH_4NO_3(aq)$

15 a 7.0×10^{-8} **b** $1.3 \times 10^{-3}\,mol\,L^{-1}$
  c precipitate will form **d** no precipitate
  e $9.8 \times 10^{-7}\,mol\,L^{-1}$ **f** $Mg(OH)_2$

Chapter 6 Properties of acids and bases

6.1 Introducing acids and bases

1 $HBr(g) + H_2O(l) \rightarrow H_3O^+(aq) + Br^-(aq)$
2 H_2SO_4/HSO_4^- and $H_2NO_3^+/HNO_3$
3 a H_2O **b** H_3O^+ **c** CH_3NH_2
4 a NH_4^+ **b** CH_3COOH **c** $H_2PO_4^-$ **d** HCO_3^- **e** OH^-
5 Brønsted–Lowry acid–base reactions involve the exchange of a proton (H^+ ion).
The acid (HCl) donates the proton to the base.
$HCl(aq) + NaOH(aq) \rightarrow NaCl(aq) + H_2O(l)$
This can be shown more clearly by the ionic equation.
$H^+(aq) + OH^-(aq) \rightarrow H_2O(l)$
6 Acting as an acid, whereby the reactant donates one proton:
  a $HCO_3^-(aq) + H_2O(l) \rightarrow CO_3^{2-}(aq) + H_3O^+(aq)$
  b $HPO_4^{2-}(aq) + H_2O(l) \rightarrow PO_4^{3-}(aq) + H_3O^+(aq)$
  c $HSO_4^-(aq) + H_2O(l) \rightarrow SO_4^{2-}(aq) + H_3O^+(aq)$
  d $H_2O(l) + H_2O(l) \rightarrow OH^-(aq) + H_3O^+(aq)$
Acting as a base, whereby the reactant accepts one proton:
  a $HCO_3^-(aq) + H_2O(l) \rightarrow H_2CO_3(aq) + OH^-(aq)$
  b $HPO_4^{2-}(aq) + H_2O(l) \rightarrow H_2PO_4^-(aq) + OH^-(aq)$
  c $HSO_4^-(aq) + H_2O(l) \rightarrow H_2SO_4(aq) + OH^-(aq)$
  d $H_2O(l) + H_2O(l) \rightarrow H_3O^+(aq) + OH^-(aq)$

6.2 Reactions of acids and bases

TY 6.2.1 37.5 mL **TR 6.2.2** $-53\,kJ\,mol^{-1}$
TY 6.2.3 $2H_3O^+(aq) + Ca(HCO_3)_2(s) \rightarrow Cu^{2+}(aq) + 4H_2O(l) + 2CO_2(g)$
TY 6.2.4 $6H^+(aq) + 2Al(s) \rightarrow 2Al^{3+}(aq) + 3H_2(g)$
1 a i $Mg(s) + 2HNO_3(aq) \rightarrow Mg(NO_3)_2(aq) + H_2(g)$
  ii $Mg(s) + 2H^+(aq) \rightarrow Mg^{2+}(aq) + H_2(g)$
  b i $Ca(s) + H_2SO_4(aq) \rightarrow CaSO_4(aq) + H_2(g)$
  ii $Ca(s) + 2H^+(aq) \rightarrow Ca^{2+}(aq) + H_2(g)$
  c i $Zn(s) + 2HCl(aq) \rightarrow ZnCl_2(aq) + H_2(g)$
  ii $Zn(s) + 2H^+(aq) \rightarrow Zn^{2+}(aq) + H_2(g)$
  d i $2Al(s) + 6CH_3COOH(aq) \rightarrow 2Al(CH_3COO)_3(aq) + 3H_2(g)$
  ii $2Al(s) + 6H^+(aq) \rightarrow 2Al^{3+}(aq) + 3H_2(g)$
2 a magnesium nitrate **b** calcium sulfate
  c zinc chloride **d** aluminium ethanoate
3 a i $Al(OH)_3(s) + 3HF(aq) \rightarrow AlF_3(aq) + 3H_2O(l)$
  ii $Al(OH)_3(s) + 3H^+(aq) \rightarrow Al^{3+}(aq) + 3H_2O(l)$
  b i $Fe(OH)_2(s) + 2HNO_3(aq) \rightarrow Fe(NO_3)_2(aq) + 2H_2O(l)$
  ii $Fe(OH)_2(s) + 2H^+(aq) \rightarrow Fe^{2+}(aq) + 2H_2O(l)$
  c i $ZnCO_3(s) + 2CH_3COOH(aq) \rightarrow Zn(CH_3COO)_2(aq) + CO_2(g) + H_2O(l)$
  ii $ZnCO_3(s) + 2H^+(aq) \rightarrow Zn^{2+}(aq) + CO_2(g) + H_2O(l)$
  d i $Sn(HCO_3)_2(s) + 2HCl(aq) \rightarrow SnCl_2(aq) + 2CO_2(g) + 2H_2O(l)$
  ii $Sn(HCO_3)_2(s) + 2H^+(aq) \rightarrow Sn^{2+}(aq) + 2CO_2(g) + 2H_2O(l)$
4 a $H_2SO_4(aq) + 2NaOH(aq) \rightarrow Na_2SO_4(aq) + 2H_2O(l)$
  b 0.0250 mol **c** 1.4 kJ **d** 0.0250 mol
  e $-55\,kJ\,mol^{-1}$
5 A

Chapter 6 Review

1 **a** NH_4^+ **b** HCl   **c** HCO_3^- **d** H_3O^+
   e CH_3COOH

2 **a** $PO_4^{3-}(aq) + H_2O(l) \rightarrow HPO_4^{2-}(aq) + OH^-(aq)$
   b The $H_2PO_4^-$ accepts a proton from water, and acts as a base:
     $H_2PO_4^-(aq) + H_2O(l) \rightarrow H_3PO_4(aq) + OH^-(aq)$
     The $H_2PO_4^-$ donates a proton to the water, and acts as an acid:
     $H_2PO_4^-(aq) + H_2O(l) \rightarrow HPO_4^{2-}(aq) + H_3O^+(aq)$
   c $H_2S(aq) + H_2O(l) \rightarrow HS^-(aq) + H_3O^+(aq)$

3 **a** Cl^- **b** H_2O **c** OH^- **d** SO_4^{2-}

4 **a** Sulfuric acid (H_2SO_4) is a diprotic acid because each molecule can donate two protons to a base.
     The HSO_4^- ion, however, is amphiprotic because it can act as either an acid or a base, depending on the environment. In water it will undergo both acid and base reactions.
   b A strong acid is one that dissociates completely in solution (e.g. HCl). A weak acid is one that partially dissociates in solution.

5

   donated

6 A and D

7 **a** A diprotic acid can donate two protons.
   b A diprotic acid dissociates in two stages.
     Step 1: $H_2CrO_4(aq) + H_2O(l) \rightarrow HCrO_4^-(aq) + H_3O^+(aq)$
     Step 2: $HCrO_4^-(aq) + H_2O(l) \rightarrow CrO_4^{2-}(aq) + H_3O^+(aq)$

8 The extent of the dissociation decreases progressively from each subsequent stage. This is because it is harder to remove a proton from a negatively charged species (HA^-) than from a neutral species (H_2A).

9 D

10 **a** $Fe(s) + 2HF(aq) \rightarrow FeF_2(aq) + H_2(g)$
   b $HClO_4(aq) + LiOH(aq) \rightarrow LiClO_4(aq) + H_2O(l)$
   c $HNO_3(aq) + KHCO_3(aq) \rightarrow KNO_3(aq) + CO_2(g) + H_2O(l)$
   d $Li_2CO_3(aq) + 2CH_3COOH(aq) \rightarrow 2LiCH_3COO(aq) + CO_2(g) + H_2O(l)$

11 **a** $Fe(s) + 2H^+(aq) \rightarrow Fe^{2+}(aq) + H_2(g)$
   b $H^+(aq) + OH^-(aq) \rightarrow H_2O(l)$
   c $H^+(aq) + HCO_3^-(aq) \rightarrow CO_2(g) + H_2O(l)$
   d $CO_3^{2-}(aq) + 2H^+(aq) \rightarrow CO_2(g) + H_2O(l)$

12 1.5 L

13 **a** $HClO_4(aq) + NaOH(aq) \rightarrow NaClO_4(aq) + H_2O(l)$
   b $-53.9 \, kJ\,mol^{-1}$
   c The reaction may not have been carried out under standard conditions; ΔT of the solution is lower than expected due to poor insulation of the calorimeter.

14 **a** $NaHCO_3(s) + HCl(aq) \rightarrow NaCl(aq) + CO_2(g) + H_2O(l)$
   b A minimum of 2.0 kg of sodium hydrogen carbonate would be required.

15 Spectator ions are ions that are present in the reaction mixture but do not participate in a chemical reaction.

16 **a** **i** A Brønsted–Lowry acid is a proton donor.
     ii A strong base is a substance that dissociates completely in water.
     iii Molarity is a measure of concentration of a solution expressed in $mol\,L^{-1}$.
     iv The conjugate acid of a base contains one more hydrogen ion (proton) than the base.
   b An amphiprotic substance can act as an acid (proton donor) or a base (proton acceptor).
     Acting as an acid: $HCO_3^-(aq) + H_2O(l) \rightarrow CO_3^{2-}(aq) + H_3O^+(aq)$
     Acting as a base: $HCO_3^-(aq) + H_2O(l) \rightarrow H_2CO_3(aq) + OH^-(aq)$

17 **a** HCl/Cl^- and H_2O/OH^-
   b HNO_3/NO_3^- and NH_4^+/NH_3
   c HCO_3^-/CO_3^{2-} and H_3O^+/H_2O

18 As water acts as an amphiprotic substance, it can accept protons. The hydrogen ion in solution readily reacts with water to form the hydronium ion. Writing the hydronium ion in an equation makes it easier to see that a proton transfer has occurred.

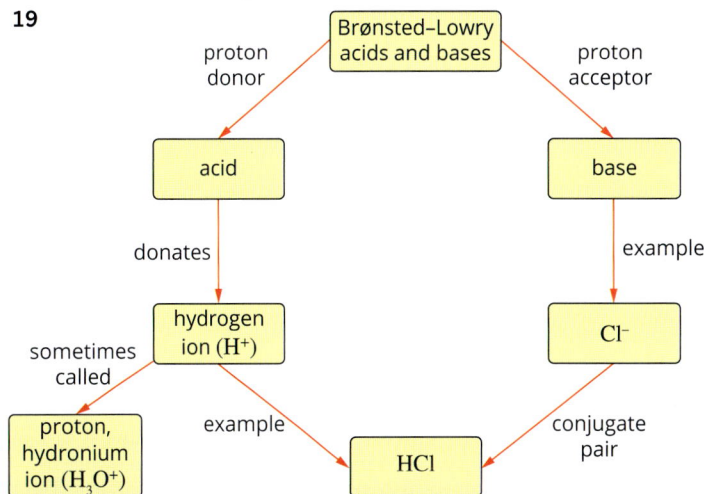

19

20 Acid and metal carbonate reaction; vinegar is an acid (ethanoic acid) and the bicarbonate of soda is a carbonate.

Chapter 7 Using Brønsted–Lowry theory

7.1 Strength of acids and bases

1 **a** $HClO_4(aq) + H_2O(l) \rightarrow H_3O^+(aq) + ClO_4^-(aq)$
   b $HCN(aq) + H_2O(l) \rightleftharpoons H_3O^+(aq) + CN^-(aq)$
   c $CH_3NH_2(aq) + H_2O(l) \rightleftharpoons CH_3NH_3^+(aq) + OH^-(aq)$

2 Stage 1: $H_3AsO_4(aq) + H_2O(l) \rightleftharpoons H_3O^+(aq) + H_2AsO_4^-(aq)$
   Stage 2: $H_2AsO_4^-(aq) + H_2O(l) \rightleftharpoons H_3O^+(aq) + HAsO_4^{2-}(aq)$
   Stage 3: $HAsO_4^{2-}(aq) + H_2O(l) \rightleftharpoons H_3O^+(aq) + AsO_4^{3-}(aq)$

3 A

4 Perchloric acid is a stronger acid than ethanoic acid and dissociates more readily, so more hydronium ions would be present in solution, making it a better conductor of electricity.

7.2 Acidity and basicity of solutions

TY 7.2.1 $1.8 \times 10^{-9} \, mol\,L^{-1}$ **TY 7.2.2** 5.8   **Ty 7.2.3** 12.3
TY 7.2.4 12.25   **TY 7.2.5** $3 \times 10^{-4} \, mol\,L^{-1}$

1 $1 \times 10^{-11} \, mol\,L^{-1}$ **2** $1.8 \times 10^{-6} \, mol\,L^{-1}$ **3** $1.0 \times 10^{-9} \, mol\,L^{-1}$
4 12.0   **5** 11.0   **6** $1 \times 10^{-8} \, mol\,L^{-1}$ **7** 12.699

7.3 Dilution of acids and bases

TY 7.3.1 $1.00 \, mol\,L^{-1}$ **TY 7.3.2** 60.0 mL   **TY 7.3.3** 1.48
TY 7.3.4 11.7

1 $7.5 \times 10^{-2} \, mol\,L^{-1}$ **2** 30 mL   **3** 100 mL
4 2.0   **5** 12.600
6 **a** **i** $0.001 \, mol\,L^{-1}$ **ii** $1 \times 10^{-11} \, mol\,L^{-1}$ **iii** 3.0   **iv** 11.0
   b **i** $0.03 \, mol\,L^{-1}$ **ii** $3 \times 10^{-13} \, mol\,L^{-1}$ **iii** 1.5   **iv** 12.5
   c **i** $1 \times 10^{-12} \, mol\,L^{-1}$ **ii** $0.01 \, mol\,L^{-1}$ **iii** 12.0   **iv** 2.0
   d **i** $3 \times 10^{-5} \, mol\,L^{-1}$ **ii** $3 \times 10^{-10} \, mol\,L^{-1}$ **iii** 4.5   **iv** 9.5
   e **i** $1 \times 10^{-12} \, mol\,L^{-1}$ **ii** $0.01 \, mol\,L^{-1}$ **iii** 12.0   **iv** 2.0

Chapter 7 Review

1 $HClO_4(aq) + H_2O(l) \rightarrow H_3O^+(aq) + ClO_4^-(aq)$
2 $HClO_3(aq) + H_2O(l) \rightleftharpoons H_3O^+(aq) + ClO_3^-(aq)$
3 $NH_3(aq) + H_2O(l) \rightleftharpoons OH^-(aq) + NH_4^+(aq)$
4 $H_2PO_4^-(aq) + H_2O(l) \rightleftharpoons H_3PO_4(aq) + OH^-(aq)$
5 $(CH_3)_2NH(aq) + H_2O(l) \rightleftharpoons (CH_3)_2NH_2^+(aq) + OH^-(aq)$
6 **a** $Ca(OH)_2(aq) \xrightarrow{H_2O(l)} Ca^{2+}(aq) + 2OH^-(aq)$
   b As calcium hydroxide dissociates in water, it releases hydroxide ions, known for their strong basic properties.
7 **a** $1 \times 10^{-11} \, mol\,L^{-1}$ **b** $10^{-9} \, mol\,L^{-1}$
   c $1.8 \times 10^{-6} \, mol\,L^{-1}$ **d** $2.9 \times 10^{-3} \, mol\,L^{-1}$
   e $1.5 \times 10^{-13} \, mol\,L^{-1}$ **f** $4.5 \times 10^{-2} \, mol\,L^{-1}$

8 **a** 11.0   **b** 9   **c** 5.74
   d 2.54   **e** 12.82   **f** 1.35
9 **a** **i** $0.1\,mol\,L^{-1}$ **ii** $1 \times 1^{-13}\,mol\,L^{-1}$
   b **i** $10^{-3}\,mol\,L^{-1}$ **ii** $10^{-11}\,mol\,L^{-1}$
   c **i** $10^{-7}\,mol\,L^{-1}$ **ii** $10^{-7}\,mol\,L^{-1}$
   d **i** $2 \times 10^{-12}\,mol\,L^{-1}$ **ii** $5 \times 10^{-3}\,mol\,L^{-1}$
10 minimium: $3.5 \times 10^{-8}\,mol\,L^{-1}$; maximum: $4.5 \times 10^{-8}\,mol\,L^{-1}$
11 a factor of 100
12 **a** $[H_3O^+] = 0.001\,mol\,L^{-1}$; $[OH^-] = 1 \times 10^{-11}\,mol\,L^{-1}$
   b $[H_3O^+] = 1 \times 10^{-10}\,mol\,L^{-1}$, $[OH^-] = 1 \times 10^{-4}\,mol\,L^{-1}$
   c $[H_3O^+] = 3 \times 10^{-9}\,mol\,L^{-1}$, $[OH^-] = 3 \times 10^{-6}\,mol\,L^{-1}$
   d $[H_3O^+] = 2 \times 10^{-6}\,mol\,L^{-1}$, $[OH^-] = 6 \times 10^{-9}\,mol\,L^{-1}$
   e $[H_3O^+] = 3 \times 10^{-10}\,mol\,L^{-1}$, $[OH^-] = 4 \times 10^{-5}\,mol\,L^{-1}$
   f $[H_3O^+] = 3 \times 10^{-14}\,mol\,L^{-1}$, $[OH^-] = 0.3\,mol\,L^{-1}$
13 $2 \times 10^{-9}\,mol\,L^{-1}$
14 **a** $10^{-2.0}$ or $0.01\,mol\,L^{-1}$ **b** 0.005 mol   **c** 12.0
15 **a** pH = 2.30; pOH = 11.70   **b** pH = 10.30; pOH = 3.70
   c pH = 3.00; pOH = 11.00
16 0.111 L or 111 mL   **17** 990 mL   **18** increase
19 Solution A: weaker base, few freely moving charged particles—ammonia
   Solution B: neutral, no freely moving charged particles—glucose
   Solution C: strong base, many freely moving charged particles—sodium hydroxide
   Solution D: strong acid, many freely moving charged particles—hydrochloric acid
   Solution E: weaker acid, few freely moving charged particles—ethanoic acid
20 **a** $NaOH(s) \xrightarrow{H_2O(l)} Na^+(aq) + OH^-(aq)$
   b Sodium hydroxide is regarded as a strong base because sodium hydroxide completely dissociates within water producing hydroxide ions which are a strong base.
   c $2.4 \times 10^2\,g$
   d **i** 0.42 mL
     ii As it is such a small volume, it would be very difficult to measure out before the dilution. It would be better to dilute the stock solution by, say, a factor of ten, and then from that dilution, further dilute it in subsequent steps.
   e pOH = 1.70
   f pH = 12.30; $[H_3O^+] = 5.0 \times 10^{-13}\,mol\,L^{-1}$
21 Add equal amounts of red cabbage indicator to two test tubes. Then add equal amounts of the strong or weak acid into each test tube. The stronger acid, which contains a higher hydronium ion concentration, could cause the colour of the red cabbage indicator to change to a greater extent than the weak acid.

Chapter 8 Quantitative analysis

8.1 Calculations involving acids and bases

TY 8.1.1 10.0 mL   **TY 8.1.2** **a** H_2SO_4 **b** 0.523 g
1 **a** $H_2SO_4(aq) + 2KOH(aq) \rightarrow K_2SO_4(aq) + 2H_2O(l)$ **b** 15.0 mL
2 **a** $2HNO_3(aq) + Ca(OH)_2(aq) \rightarrow Ca(NO_3)_2(aq) + 2H_2O(l)$
   b $0.133\,mol\,L^{-1}$
3 **a** 0.00200 mol   **b** 0.00160 mol
   c Na_2CO_3 is the limiting reactant and H_2SO_4 is in excess.
   d 0.00040 mol
4 **a** $HNO_3(aq) + KOH(aq) \rightarrow KNO_3(aq) + H_2O(l)$
   b 0.001985 mol   **c** 0.001985 mol   **d** $0.1087\,mol\,L^{-1}$

8.2 Volumetric analysis

1 **a** A and D   **b** B and C
2 $0.2500\,mol\,L^{-1}$ **3** 4.08 g   **4** 25.42 mL
5 **a** A standard solution is a solution of accurately known concentration. A primary standard is a substance used to make a standard solution. It should be readily obtained in a pure form, have a known formula and can be stored without deteriorating or reacting with the atmosphere. It should also be cheap and have a high molar mass.

   b The equivalence point in a titration occurs when the reactants have reacted in the mole ratio shown by the reaction equation. The end point occurs when the indicator changes colour.
   c A burette is a piece of equipment capable of accurately delivering a range of volumes of a liquid (generally up to 50.00 mL). Pipettes usually deliver only a fixed volume of liquid (e.g. 20.00 mL).
   d An aliquot is the volume of liquid delivered from a pipette. A titre is delivered by a burette.

8.3 Titration and conductivity curves

1 **a** strong base added to a strong acid
   b strong base added to a weak acid
   c weak base added to a strong acid
   d weak base added to a weak acid
2 The strong acid will have the lowest intercept with the pH axis. The intercept shown on graphs **a** and **c** is at approximately pH = 1, which represents a monoprotic acid concentration = $0.1\,mol\,L^{-1}$.
3 7
4 Graph **c** represents the titration of a strong acid against a weak base. At the equivalence point, the solution contains the conjugate base of the strong acid and the conjugate acid of the weak base. The conjugate acid of the weak base dissociates to form hydronium ions, thus lowering the pH.
5 Graph **d** is the titration curve of a weak acid and a weak base. There is no rapid change in pH at the equivalence point, making it difficult to accurately determine its exact location on the graph.
6 Graph a: phenolphthalein, methyl orange or bromothymol blue
   Graph b: phenolphthalein, bromothymol blue
   Graph c: methyl orange
7 Graph **a** is the pH curve of the titration of a strong base with a weak acid and indicates that the equivalence point occurred when a titre 20.0 mL of acid has been added. A weak acid was added which reacts to produce a weak base. The weak base dissociates in water causing the pH of the equivalence point to be above 7. Graph **b** is the conductivity curve of a strong acid and a strong base and indicates that a titre of 20.0 mL of base was required to reach the equivalence point. The conductivity initially decreases due to the replacement of H^+ ions with Na^+ ions. Conductivity drops to a minimum when all the H^+ ions have just reacted. Conductivity increases as excess NaOH is added to the mixture.
8 B
9 **a** In a volumetric titration, a change in the colour of an indicator is used to determine the end point. In a conductimetric titration, the end point is determined from the change in conductivity shown on a conductivity graph.
   b Any two of the following situations:
    • the analysis of a coloured solution where the colour change of an indicator cannot easily be detected
    • a turbid or cloudy solution where the colour of the indicator is masked
    • a very dilute solution.

8.4 Calculations in volumetric analysis

TY 8.4.1 $0.108\,mol\,L^{-1}$ **TY 8.4.2** $12.88\,mol\,L^{-1}$
1 $0.770\,mol\,L^{-1}$
2 **a** $CH_3COOH(aq) + NaOH(aq) \rightarrow NaCH_3COO(aq) + H_2O(l)$
   b 0.02145 mol   **c** 0.02145 mol   **d** $0.858\,mol\,L^{-1}$
3 $10.45\,mol\,L^{-1}$
4 **a** $HNO_3(aq) + KOH(aq) \rightarrow KNO_3(aq) + H_2O(l)$
   b 0.02145 mol   **c** 0.02145 mol   **d** $0.858\,mol\,L^{-1}$
   e $54.1\,g\,L^{-1}$
5 $0.735\,mol\,L^{-1}$ **6** $0.658\,mol\,L^{-1}$

8.5 Acid dissociation constants

TY 8.5.1 **a** 7.52   **b** 4.26   **c** 0.055%
TY 8.5.2 1.3×10^{-5}
1 **a** $NH_4^+(aq) + H_2O(l) \rightleftharpoons NH_3(aq) + H_3O^+(aq)$
    $K_a = \dfrac{[NH_3][H_3O^+]}{[NH_4^+H_4^+]}$

b $HCOOH(aq) + H_2O(l) \rightleftharpoons HCOO^-(aq) + H_3O^+(aq)$

$K_a = \dfrac{[HCOO^-][H_3O^+]}{[HCOOH]}$

c $HCN(aq) + H_2O(l) \rightleftharpoons CN^-(aq) + H_3O^+(aq)$

$K_a = \dfrac{[CN^-][H_3O^+]}{[HCN]}$

2 A

3

Acid	Formula	K_a	pK_a
nitrous	HNO_2	7.1×10^{-4}	3.15
methanoic	$HCOOH$	1.8×10^{-4}	3.74
hydrogen cyanide	HCN	6.2×10^{-4}	9.21
hypochlorous acid	$HOCl$	3.0×10^{-4}	7.52

4 **a** 1.44   **b** 3.6%

5 $0.06\,mol\,L^{-1}$

6 pH = 1.73; % dissociation = 4%

7 **a** $NH_3(aq) + H_2O(l) \rightleftharpoons NH_4^+(aq) + OH^-(aq)$

$K_b = \dfrac{[NH_4^+][OH^-]}{[NH_3]}$

b $CH_3COO^-(aq) + H_2O(l) \rightleftharpoons CH_3COOH(aq) + OH^-(aq)$

$K_b = \dfrac{[CH_3COOH][OH^-]}{[CH_3COO^-]}$

c $CN^-(aq) + H_2O(l) \rightleftharpoons HCN(aq) + OH^-(aq)$

$K_b = \dfrac{[HCN][OH^-]}{[CN^-]}$

8.6 Buffers

1 D

2 **a** $NH_4^+(aq) + H_2O(l) \rightleftharpoons NH_3(aq) + H_3O^+(aq)$

b $HPO_4^{2-}(aq) + H_2O(l) \rightleftharpoons H_3O^+(aq) + PO_4^{3-}(aq)$

c $HCO_3^-(aq) + H_2O(l) \rightleftharpoons CO_3^{2-}(aq) + H_3O^+(aq)$

3 **a** basic   **b** basic   **c** basic

4 C

5 **a** The addition of a small amount of HCl to the ethanoic acid buffer system will disturb the equilibrium. As equilibrium is re-established, the added H_3O^+ from HCl reacts with CH_3COO^-. The position of the equilibrium shifts to the left. Because the buffer contains a relatively large amount of CH_3COO^-, most of the added H_3O^+ is consumed and there is a small change in the concentration of H_3O^+.

   b When a small amount of OH^- is added to the buffer system, the OH^- reacts with CH_3COOH. The excess OH^- is consumed without any large change in the concentration of H_3O^+.

6 C

7 **a** $H_2CO_3(aq) + H_2O(l) \rightarrow HCO_3^-(aq) + H_3O^+(aq)$

   b When acid is added, the concentration of H_3O^+ increases and the equilibrium is disturbed. In accordance with Le Châtelier's principle, the position of equilibrium moves to the left to re-establish equilibrium

8 $H_6C_8O_7(aq) + H_2O(l) \rightarrow H_5C_8O_7^-(aq) + H_3O^+(aq)$

Chapter 8 Review

1 C   **2** $0.7999\,mol\,L^{-1}$ **3** 21.2 g

4 0.0150 L or 15.0 mL

5 **a** 0.0200 mol **b** 0.0160 mol **c** K_2CO_3 **d** 0.0060 mol

6 40.0 mL

7 **a** HNO_3 **b** 0.690 g

8 **a** A burette delivers a precise variable volume of solution.

   b A pipette delivers a precise set volume of solution.

   c A standard flask is used to prepare a solution of known concentration.

9 Near the equivalence point, a very small addition of either the acid or the base in the burette can cause a large change in pH. A sharp end point is one where the indicator changes colour with just one additional drop of the solution from the burette. Selecting the indicator based on the expected equivalence point enables for a sharp end point to be seen.

10 **a** $H_2SO_4(aq) + K_2CO_3(aq) \rightarrow K_2SO_4(aq) + H_2O(l) + CO_2(g)$

    b $0.03551\,mol\,L^{-1}$ **c** $0.03148\,mol\,L^{-1}$

11 **a** $2HCl(aq) + Na_2CO_3(aq) \rightarrow 2NaCl(aq) + H_2O(l) + CO_2(g)$

    b $0.05125\,mol\,L^{-1}$ **c** $0.1013\,mol\,L^{-1}$

    d Sulfuric acid is a diprotic acid so only half the volume of is required.

12 **a** $0.04166\,mol\,L^{-1}$ **b** $0.07100\,mol\,L^{-1}$

13 **a** $HOI(aq) + H_2O(l) \rightleftharpoons H_3O^+(aq) + OI^-(aq)$

    b $K_a = \dfrac{[OI^-][H_3O^+]}{[HOI]}$ **c** $1.6 \times 10^{-6}\,mol\,L^{-1}$ **d** 2.6×10^{-11}

14 1.6×10^{-4}

15 **a** 3.70   **b** 4.4%

16 acid, base, less than

    base, acid, greater than

17 0.14

18 CN^- and H_3O^+: $7.9 \times 10^{-6}\,mol\,L^{-1}$; HCN: $0.10\,mol\,L^{-1}$

19 no; pH of HBr = 1.0; pH of HOBr = 4.81

20 **a** K_b: 6.6×10^{-10}, 3.4×10^{-7}

     pK_b: 10.83

    b chlorate (ClO_3^-); it has the highest K_b value or the lowest pK_b value

21 **a** Both solutions contain the same amount of acid since they have the same volume and concentration. The perchloric acid and hypochlorous acid solutions require the same amount, in mol, and consequently volume, of sodium hydroxide to reach the equivalence point.

    b Perchloric acid has a large K_a indicating that it is a strong acid. At the equivalence point the solution contains ClO_4^-, the very weak conjugate base of a strong acid, so the pH at the equivalence point will be 7.

    Hypochlorous acid has a small K_a indicating that it is a weak acid. The solution at the equivalence point contains ClO^-, the conjugate base of a weak acid, which will react with water to form OH^- ions, so pH at the equivalence point will therefore be greater than 7.

22 B, as it contains ethanoate ion and its conjugate acid, ethanoic acid

23 HPO_4^{2-}, left, H_3O^+, small

    $H_2PO_4^-$, H_3O^+

24 $H_2CO_3(aq) + H_2O(l) \rightleftharpoons HCO_3^-(aq) + H_3O^+(aq)$. An increase in the pH of blood indicates a decrease in $[H_3O^+]$. The buffer equilibrium responds by shifting to the right to increase $[H_3O^+]$. Overall, $[H_2CO_3]$ decreases, $[HCO_3^-]$ increases, $[H_3O^+]$ slightly decreases.

25 The buffer can be summarised as

    $H_2CO_3(aq) + H_2O(l) \rightleftharpoons HCO_3^-(aq) + H_3O^+(aq)$.

    Because both species are present, the equation can move to the right or the left depending on the $[H_3O^+(aq)]$. Thus it is a buffer.

26 A

27 **a**

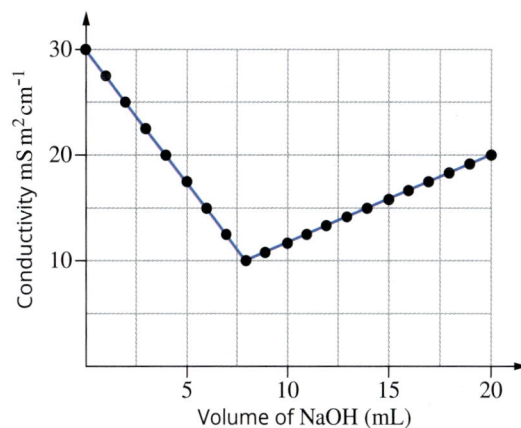

    b $0.4\,mol\,L^{-1}$

    c The conductivity of a solution is determined by the:
- degree of ionisation or dissociation of the electrolyte
- identity of ions
- charge of the ions
- concentration of ions
- mobility of the ions
- temperature of the solution

28 a $0.375\,mol\,L^{-1}$

b As indicated by its pK_a, methanoic acid is a weak acid and is only dissociated to a slight extent, and so has a low conductivity. As NaOH is added, the conductivity increases due to the presence of Na^+ ions and the formation of methanoate ions, $HCOO^-$.

At the equivalence point 25.0 mL of NaOH solution has been added. The solution now only contains Na^+ and $HCOO^-$ ions and the conductivity of the solution is at a minimum.

As more NaOH solution is added, concentration of Na^+ and OH^- ions increases and the conductivity increases sharply.

29 a

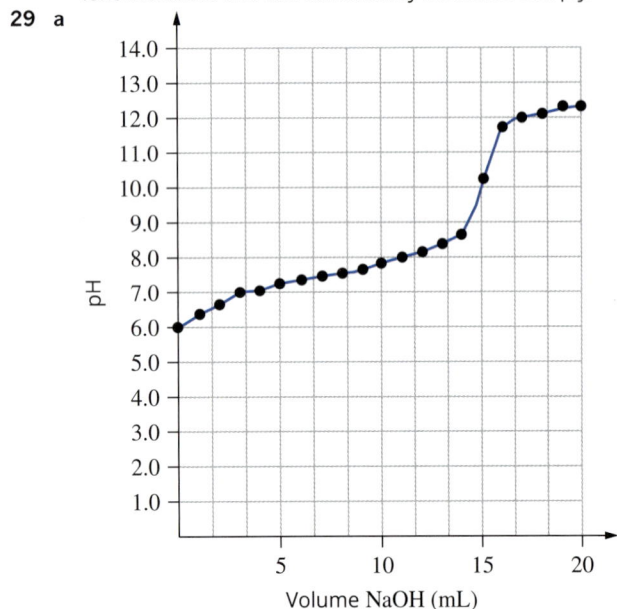

b $0.19\,mol\,L^{-1}$

30 a a strong base added to a weak acid
b a strong acid added toa weak base
c strong base added toa strong acid
d weak base added to a strong acid

31 $0.13\,mol\,L^{-1}$

32 a anhydrous sodium carbonate as it meets the criteria for a primary standard

b Use an analytical balance to weigh Na_2CO_3 in a clean, dry weighing bottle or beaker. Transfer the solid into a volumetric flask using a dry funnel. Wash any solid particles from the bottle or beaker using deionised water. Half fill the volumetric flask with deionised water, stopper and swirl the flask vigorously to dissolve the solid Na_2CO_3. Add deionsied water up to the calibration line on the neck of the volumetric flask. The bottom of the meniscus should be level with the calibration mark. Stopper and shake the flask to ensure an even concentration throughout.

c The final rinse of a burrette and a pipette must be with the acid or base they are to be filled with to avoid dilution of the solution. The volumetric flask and conical flask must only be rinsed with deionised water.

33 Lactic acid $(C_3H_6O_3)$ is a monoprotic acid. It dissociates according to the following equation: $C_3H_6O_3(aq) + H_2O(l) \rightleftharpoons H_3O^+(aq) + C_3H_5O_3^-$ (aq). This causes a rise in $[H_3O^+]$ in the blood, which affects the hydrogen carbonate/bicarbonate buffer and causes the buffer to move to the left side of the equation and absorb the excess H_3O^+.

34 a Carbon dioxide is not removed and the blood pH will fall as concentration of carbon dioxide increases.

b $H_2CO_3(aq) + H_2O(l) \rightleftharpoons HCO_3^-(aq) + H_3O^+(aq)$
The reaction between the basic HCO_3^- and hydronium ions reduces the concentration of H_3O^+.

35 a $H_5C_8O_7^-(aq)$
b $H_6C_8O_7(aq) + H_2O(l) \rightleftharpoons H_5C_8O_7^-(aq) + H_3O^+(aq)$

c Citric acid solution when mixed with approximately equimolar solution of its conjugate base (citrate) will form a buffer with a pH below 7.

d As the hydronium ion concentration rises, the equilibrium is disturbed, so the position of equilibrium moves to the left to re-establish equilibrium. In a more alkaline environment, some of the citric acid molecules will be consumed. This minimises the impact on hydronium ion concentration, so pH is minimally affected.

36 This experiment is a crude form of volumetric analysis. The design of the experiment can be improved to produce a more accurate result by adding the vinegar in smaller portions, such as 1 mL, using an indicator to detect when all the bicarbonate of soda has been consumed, and using a different base to react with the vinegar.

Module 6 Review

Multiple choice

1	C	**2**	A	**3**	B	**4**	A	**5**	B
6	D	**7**	D	**8**	C	**9**	A	**10**	D
11	B	**12**	C	**13**	A	**14**	B	**15**	C
16	D	**17**	A	**18**	A	**19**	C	**20**	B
21	C								

Short answer

1 a $0.313\,mol\,L^{-1}$ **b** $0.313\,mol\,L^{-1}$ **c** $3.2 \times 10^{-14}\,mol\,L^{-1}$
d 13.49 **e** 0.51

2 a $2HCl(aq) + Zn(s) \rightarrow ZnCl_2(aq) + H_2(g)$
b $2HNO_3(aq) + Ca(OH)_2(aq) \rightarrow Ca(NO_3)_2(aq) + 2H_2O(l)$
c $H_2SO_4(aq) + Na_2CO_3(aq) \rightarrow Na_2SO_4(aq) + CO_2(g) + H_2O(l)$
d $Mg(s) + 2HNO_3(aq) \rightarrow Mg(NO_3)_2(aq) + H_2(g)$

3 a A strong acid is an acid that readily donates protons. Alternatively, a strong acid is an acid that completely dissociates in water.
b Student answers will vary. Possible answers include H_2CO_3 or H_2SO_4 or H_3PO_4.
c i $HCO_3^-(aq) + H_2O(l) \rightarrow H_2CO_3(aq) + OH^-(aq)$
ii $HCO_3^-(aq) + H_2O(l) \rightarrow CO_3^{2-}(aq) + H_3O^+(aq)$
d H_3O^+

4 a i 13.00 **ii** 1.000 **iii** −0.014
b 16.8 g

5 a Solution C. It is the only solution with a pH above 7 and sodium hydroxide is a base.
b Solution B. Because it is an acid the pH must be less than 7. A and B are acids (pH less than 7 or turns blue litmus red). B has the higher conductivity and, since they all have the same concentration, B must dissociate the most and so must be the stronger acid.
c The pH of A must be greater than 1.5 but less than 7. It is an acid because it turns blue litmus paper red, but it will have ahigher pH than solution B because it has a lower conductivity.
d i $0.03\,mol\,L^{-1}$ **ii** $3 \times 10^{-11}\,mol\,L^{-1}$

6 a Propanoic acid is a weak acid so it is partially dissociated. The concentration of $H^+(aq)$ ions in a propanoic acid solution will therefore be lower than in solutions of nitric acid or sulfuric acid, both strong acids, of equal concentration. As the concentration of $H^+(aq)$ ions is lowest, the pH of the propanoic acid solution will be highest.
b Sulfuric acid is diprotic. In water, one hydrogen ion is completely donated to water. In addition, there is partial dissociation of the $HSO_4^-(aq)$ ion to release a second hydrogen ion. So the overall concentration of $H^+(aq)$ ions is higher than in a solution of the monoprotic nitric acid of the same concentration, and the pH of the solution will be lower.

7 a $1.0 \times 10^{-10}\,mol\,L^{-1}$ **b** 11.0

8 a $NH_3(aq) + HCl(aq) \rightarrow NH_4Cl(aq)$ or $NH_3(aq) + H^+(aq) \rightarrow NH_4^+(aq)$
b $0.827\,mol\,L^{-1}$ **c** 10.6 g
d yellow at start of titration, orange at equivalence point and pink when excess acid is present

e i the same; the amount, in mole, of ammonia in the flask is unchanged by the addition of water

ii lower; phenolphthalein indicator would change colour before equivalence point is reached

iii higher; the flask would contain some drops of diluted cleaner as well as the 20.00 mL of it measured out, so more HCl would be needed to reach equivalence.

9 a 0.00924 mol

b i 0.462 mol L^{-1} **ii** 54.6 g L^{-1} **iii** 5.46%(w/v)

c The solution was in fact not saturated or it cooled during handling and so the solubility decreased.

10 a i $H_2SO_4(aq) + H_2O(l) \rightarrow HSO_4^-(aq) + H_3O^+(aq)$
$HSO_4^-(aq) + H_2O(l) \rightarrow SO_4^{2-}(aq) + H_3O^+(aq)$

ii $HSO_4^-(aq)$

iii H_2SO_4/HSO_4^- or HSO_4^-/SO_4^{2-} or H_3O^+/H_2O

iv H_2SO_4, SO_4^{2-}, HSO_4^-

b i $H_2SO_4(aq) + Zn(s) \rightarrow ZnSO_4(aq) + H_2(g)$

ii $2H^+(aq) + Zn(s) \rightarrow Zn^{2+}(aq) + H_2(g)$

iii The pH increases as the acid is consumed.

c i $H_2SO_4(aq) + K_2CO_3(s) \rightarrow K_2SO_4(aq) + H_2O(l) + CO_2(g)$

ii $2H^+(aq) + K_2CO_3(s) \rightarrow 2K^+(aq) + H_2O(l) + CO_2(g)$

iii The solid would disappear quickly and a gas would be evolved.

d i $H_2SO_4(aq) + 2LiOH(aq) \rightarrow Li_2SO_4(aq) + 2H_2O(l)$

ii 0.234 mol

11 $\Delta H = 53.5$ kJ mol^{-1}

12 a i NH_4^+ **ii** NH_3

iii NH_4Cl or any other salt containing NH_4^+

b i The equilibrium is disturbed. As equilibrium is re-established, the added H_3O^+ from HCl reacts with NH_3. The position of the equilibrium shifts to the right. Because the buffer contains a relatively large amount of NH_3, most of the added H_3O^+ is consumed and there is a small change in the concentration of H_3O^+.

ii The OH^- reacts with NH_4^+ and the excess OH^- is consumed without any large change in the concentration of H_3O^+.

c $NH_3(aq) + HCl(aq) \rightarrow NH_4^+(aq) + Cl^-(aq)$

d i No, only conjugate acid present.

ii Yes, both weak acid and conjugate base are present.

iii No, only strong acid and conjugate acid present.

13 a i $HCl(aq) + KOH(aq) \rightarrow KCl(aq) + H_2O(l)$

ii As KOH is added, H^+ ions react with OH^- to form water. H^+ ions are very conductive, so the addition of K^+ ions does not compensate for the loss of conductivity.

iii After the equivalence point, there are no further losses of ions from the solution. The conductivity will increase with the extra ions added.

iv 0.15 mol L^{-1}

b 9.4 mL

14 a $HIn(aq) + H_2O(l) \rightarrow H_3O^+(aq) + In^-(aq)$

b i blue

ii The system opposes the added H_3O^+ by moving in the reverse direction, forming more HIn, which will be yellow.

iii The added OH^- reacts with H_3O^+ lowering the H_3O^+ concentration. The system moves in the forward direction to oppose this, forming more In^- which is blue in solution.

c i $K_a = \frac{[H_3O^+][In^-]}{[HIn]}$ **ii** $K_a = \frac{[H_3O^+] \times 1}{1}$, so pH = 7.

Chapter 9 Structure and nomenclature of organic compounds

9.1 Diversity of carbon compounds

1 B

2 a A structural formula is a graphic representation of the molecular structure, showing how the atoms are arranged.

b A condensed structural formula shows the connections in the structure of a molecule without showing single bonds (but double and triple bonds may be shown).

c A saturated organic compound contains all single bonds between carbon atoms.

d An unsaturated organic compound contains one or more double or triple bonds between carbon atoms.

e Position isomers have the same molecular formula but have the functional group on a different carbon in the chain.

3 A and C

4 a 2-methylpropane and butane

b

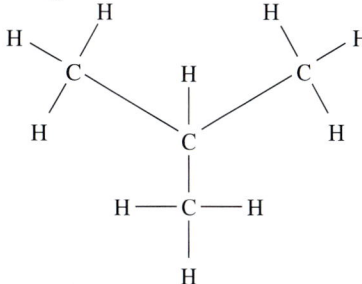

2-methylpropane (C_4H_{10})   butane (C_4H_{10})

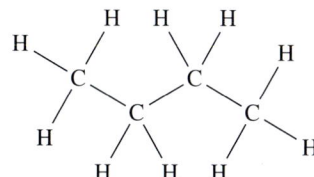

5 The carbon atoms in alkanes have four bonds to other atoms. The angle around between each bond is 109.5° and the geometry around each carbon is tetrahedral. The carbon–carbon bonds are much less than 180° and so the chain is zig-zag shaped.

9.2 Hydrocarbons

TY 9.2.1 3,6-dimethyloctane **TY 9.2.2** 3,4-dimethylhex-2-ene

1 a 3,3-dimethylhex-1-yne **b** 2-methylbut-2-ene

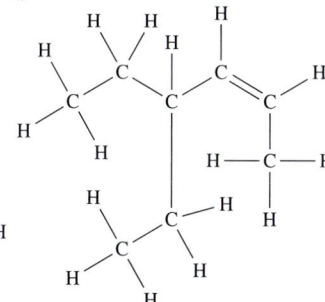

c 4-ethylhex-2-ene

2 a

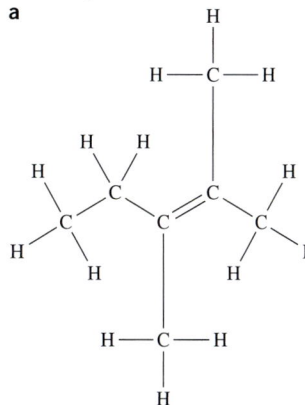

2,3-dimethylpent-2-ene

b

4-ethylhex-2-ene

c

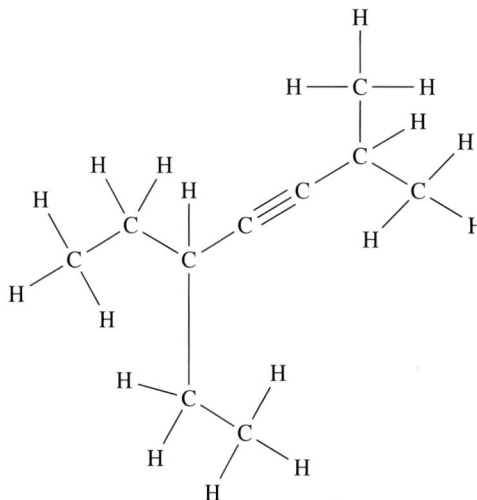

5-ethyl-2-methylhept-3-yne

d

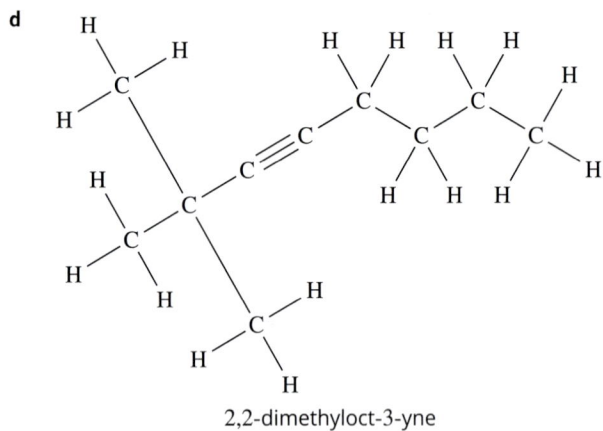

2,2-dimethyloct-3-yne

3 C and D

4 There are five possible isomers.

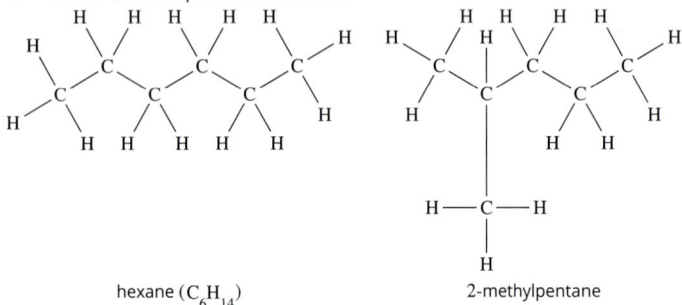

hexane (C_6H_{14})

2-methylpentane

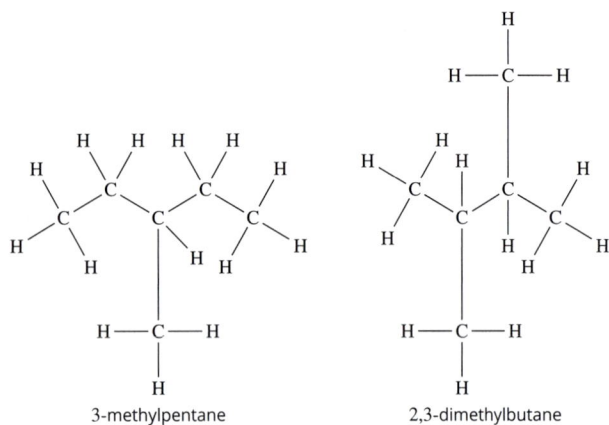

3-methylpentane

2,3-dimethylbutane

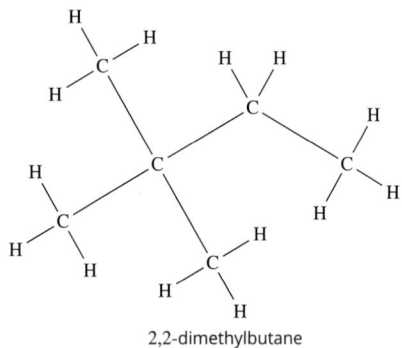

2,2-dimethylbutane

9.3 Functional groups—Part 1

1 3-bromo-2-fluoropentane

2 $CH_3CHIFCHClCH_2CH_2CH_3$

3 2-methylbutan-2-ol

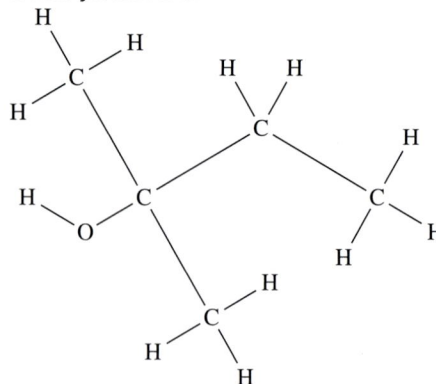

4 **a** 1-bromopropane   **b** 2-chloro-4-methylpentane
   c pentan-1-ol   **d** octan-4-amine

5 Chloroethane has no isomers and so numbers are not needed. In propan-3-amine, the carbons should be numbered from the carbon atom closest to the amino functional group. Thus the amino group is located on the first carbon instead of the third carbon. Hence, the correct name is propan-1-amine.

9.4 Functional groups—Part 2

1 **a** ketone   **b** aldehyde   **c** amide   **d** ester

2 **a** methyl methanoate   **b** methanoic acid
   c propyl butanoate   **d** methyl ethanoate
   e ethyl hexanoate

3 ethanoic acid

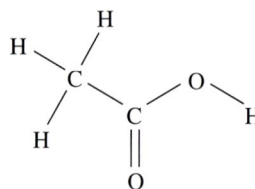

4 **a** propanamide   **b** butanamide
   c propanone   **d** butanal

5 **a**

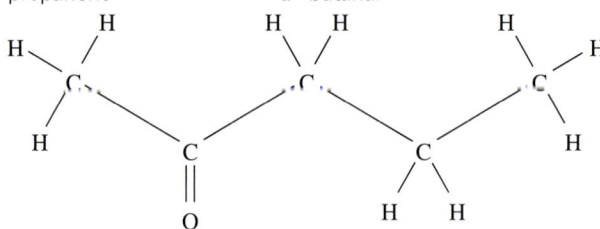

b

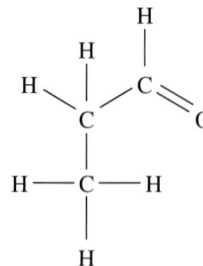

c

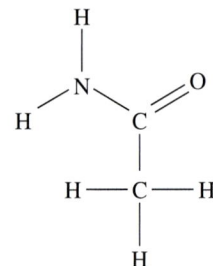

9.5 An overview of IUPAC nomenclature

TY 9.5.1 6-chlorohexan-1-amine

1 **a** –C≡C–
   b

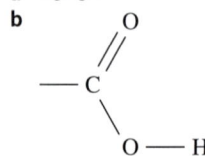

   c

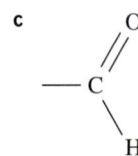

d

O
‖
— C — N — H
        |
        H

e

H
|
— C — O — H
|
H

f

O
‖
— C
   \
    O —

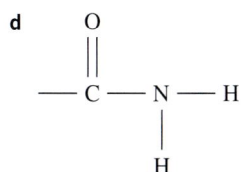

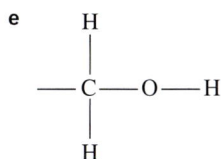

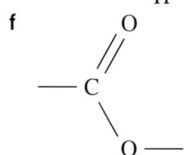

2 **a** 3-hydroxybutanoic acid   **b** 3-methylpentan-2-amine
   c 4-chloro-3-ethylpenan-2-ol   **d** 5-fluoropent-2-yne

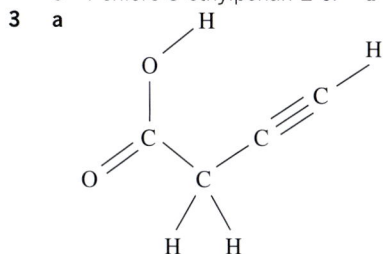

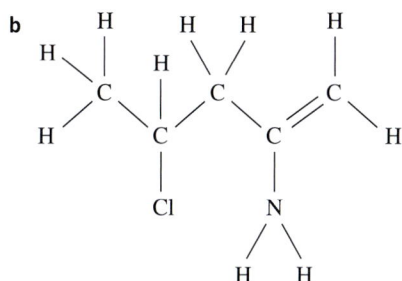

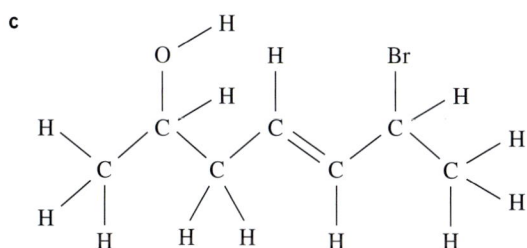

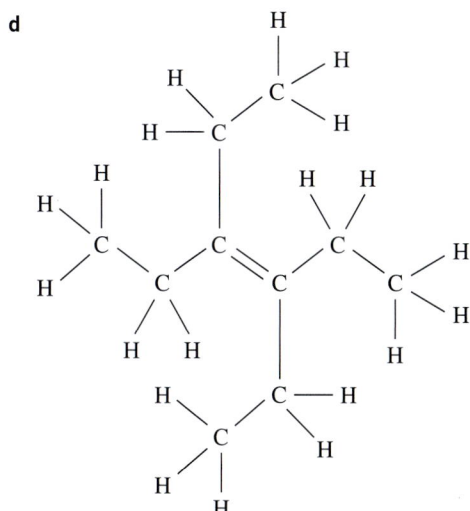

3 **a**

b

c

d

4 **a** **i** $CH_2=CHCH_2NH_2$ **ii** $CH_3CHClCH_2CH_2COOH$
   iii $CH_2=CHCHOHCH_2CH_3$
   b **i** prop-2-en-1-amine   **ii** 4-chloropentanoic acid
   iii pent-1-en-3-ol.

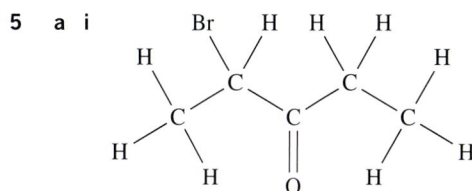

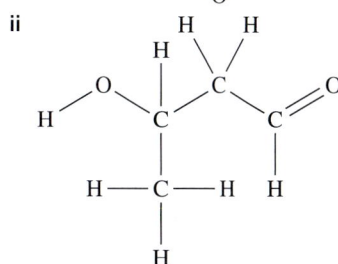

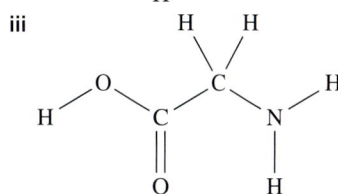

5 **a** **i**

ii

iii

   b **i** 2-chlorobutanamide   **ii** dichlorodifluoromethane
   iii methanal

Chapter 9 Review

1 2-chloropentane

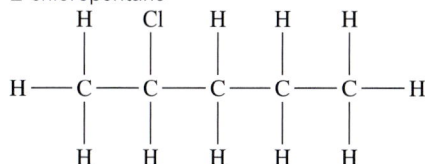

H   Cl H   H   H
| | | | |
H—C—C—C—C—C—H
| | | | |
H   H   H   H   H

3-chloropentane

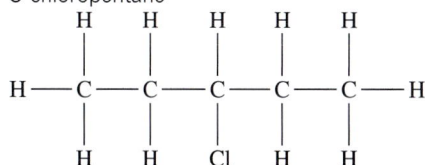

H   H   H   H   H
| | | | |
H—C—C—C—C—C—H
| | | | |
H   H   Cl H   H

2 Chain isomers have different configurations of alkyl groups; position isomers refer to isomers where one or more functional groups are in a different position.

3 Position isomers have the functional group on different carbon atoms; functional group isomers will have different functional groups but maintain a common molecular formula.

4 Position isomers: $CH_2=CHCH_2CH_3$ (but-1-ene) and $CH_3CH=CHCH_3$ (but-2-ene). These are position isomers because the location of the carbon–carbon double bond is different.
Chain isomers: $CH_2=C(CH_3)_2$ (2-methylpropene) and $CH_2=CHCH_2CH_3$ (but-1-ene). These are chain isomers because the longest carbon chain and position of alkyl groups are different.

5 **a** 2,4-dimethylhexane   **b** 4,4-dimethylhex-1-ene
   c ethyl butanoate

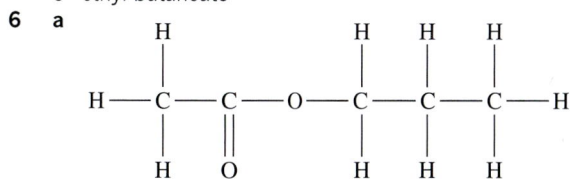

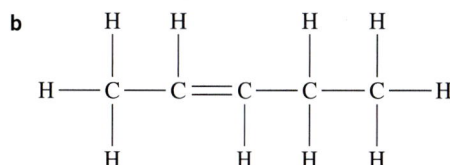

6 **a**

H   H   H   H
| | | |
H—C—C—O—C—C—C—H
| ‖ | | |
H   O   H   H   H

   b

H   H   H   H
| | | |
H—C—C=C—C—C—H
| | | |
H   H   H   H

c

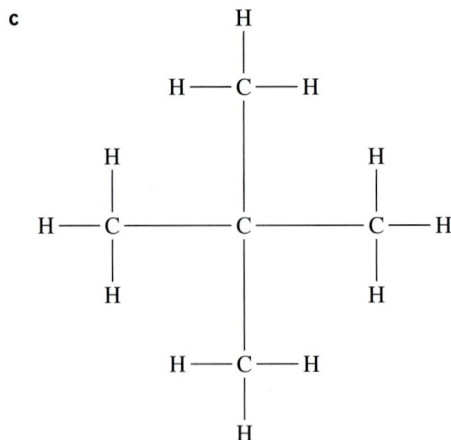

7 **a** C_5H_{12} **b** C_6H_{12} **c** C_4H_6 **d** C_7H_{14}

8 Three: pentane, 2-methylbutane, 2,2-dimethylpropane.

9 If an ethyl group is on the second carbon, the longest chain is 6 carbons long and the correct name would be 2-methylhexane.

10

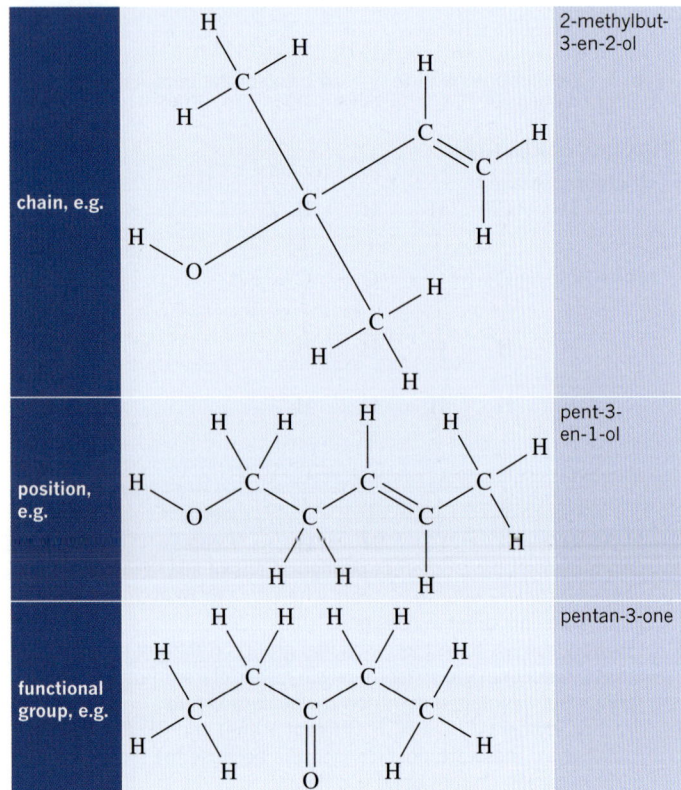

11 **a** nitrogen, hydrogen **b** chlorine
    c oxygen, hydrogen

12 In a primary alcohol, the hydroxyl group is attached to a carbon atom which is attached to one other carbon atom, e.g. propan-1-ol. In a secondary alcohol, the hydroxyl group is attached to a carbon which is attached to two other carbon atoms, e.g. propan-2-ol.

13 **a** 2-aminopropan-1-ol **b** 8-chlorooctan-2-ol
    c 2-iodoheptan-3-amine

14 Aldehyde: terminal carbonyl group. Ketone: secondary carbonyl group. Carboxylic acid: terminal carbonyl with hydroxyl attached to the same carbon. Amide: terminal carbonyl group with amino attached to the same carbon.

15 Carboxyl and amide carbons have three bonds to the carbon atom within the functional group. The carbon atom in these functional groups can only make one more additional bond to connect to a carbon chain and so can never be within a chain.

16 **a** but-3-en-oic acid   **b** 4-aminobutan-2-ol
    c butyl ethanoate   **d** 2-methylhex-3-ene
    e 4-fluorobut-1-yne   **f** 1-bromobut-2-ene

17 **a** heptyl propanoate

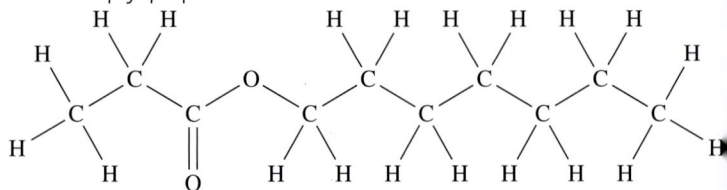

    b 4-iodo-3-methylpent-2-ene

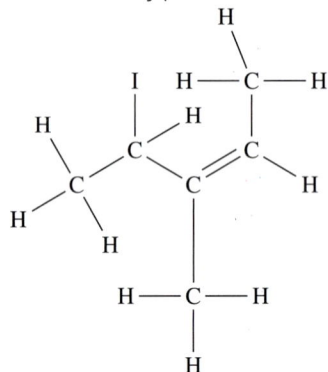

    c oct-4-enoic acid

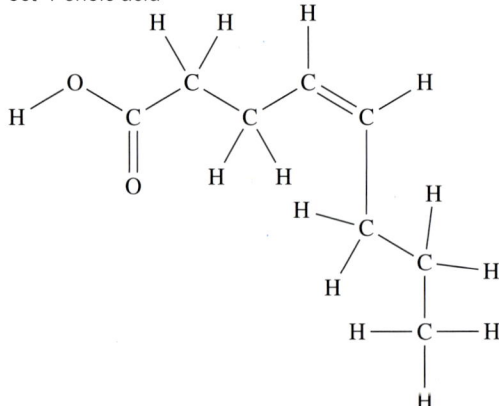

    d 3-methylbutan-1-amine

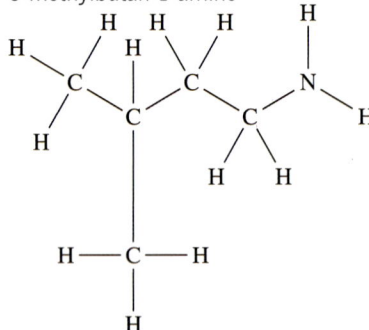

    e 3-hydroxy-2-methylbutanamide

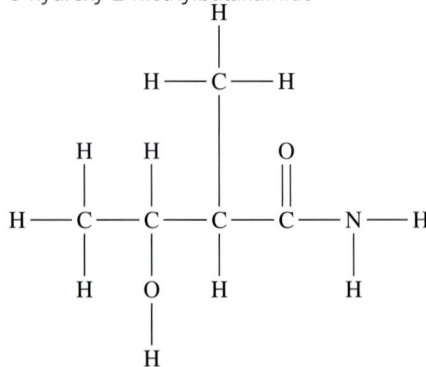

18 a $CH_3CH_2CH=CHCH_2CH_2CH_2CH_3$
b $CH_3OOC(CH_2)_4CH_3$ **c** $CH_2FCH_2CH_2OH$
d $HOCH_2CH_2CH_2COOH$ **e** $H_2NCH_2CH(CH_3)CH(CH_3)CH_2CH_3$

19 a $CH_3CH_2CH_2COCH_3$
b $CH_3CH(CH_3)CH_2CH_2OH$ or $(CH_3)_2CHCH_2CH_2OH$
c $CH_3CH_2CONH_2$ **d** $CH_3CHClCH_2C\equiv CH$
e $CH_3CH_2COOCH_2CH_3$

20 a but-1-ene **b** 2-aminoethan-1-ol
c 3-chloro-hex-1-yne **d** 2-chloro-3-methylpentane
e 4,4-dimethylpent-1-ene **f** 4-bromoheptane

21 a alcohol; heptan-1-ol **b** haloalkane; 4-chloroheptane
c alcohol; hexan-2-ol **d** carboxylic acid; pentanoic acid
e amine; butan-2-amine **f** alkane; 2-methyloctane
g alkene; 2-methylprop-1-ene **h** ketone; propanone
i aldehyde; propanal **j** amide; pentanamide

22 For each formula, more than one structure is possible.
a $C_5H_{11}Cl$, 1-chloropentane

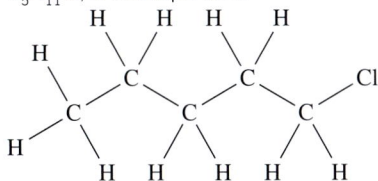

b C_4H_8O, butanone

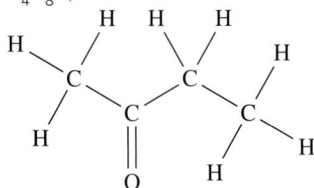

c $C_3H_6O_2$, propanoic acid

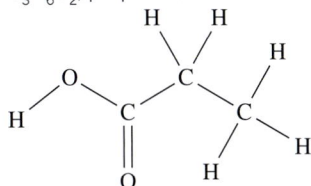

d $C_4H_8O_2$, butanoic acid

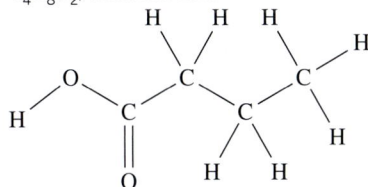

e $C_5H_{13}N$, pentan-1-amine

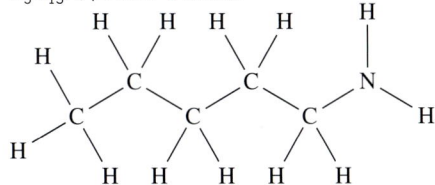

f C_3H_7NO, propanamide

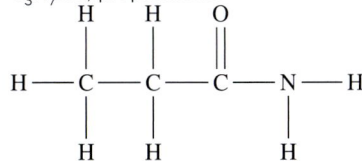

23 Student responses will vary.

Chapter 10 Properties of hydrocarbons and haloalkanes

10.1 Boiling points, melting points and solubilities of organic compounds

1 alkane, dispersion forces, increases, insoluble, weaker, hydrogen bonding

2 $CH_3CH(CH_3)CH_3$, $CH_3CH_2CH_2CH_3$, $CH_3CH_2CH_2CH_2CH_2CH(CH_3)CH_3$, $CH_3CH_2CH_2CH_2CH_2CH_2CH_2CH_3$
Boiling point increases with molecular size. The presence of branching within the molecule will result in a lower boiling point compared to a molecule of similar size with a straight chain structure.

3 CHCH, CH_3CHCH_2, $CH_3CH_2CH_2CH_3$, $CH_3CH_2CH_2CH_2Cl$
Boiling point increases with molecular size, so ethyne, an alkyne, is the smallest molecule and has the lowest boiling point. The only haloalkane in the group, 1-chlorobutane ($CH_3CH_2CH_2CH_2Cl$), has the highest boiling point because the chlorine–carbon bond is polar and creates a dipole–dipole attraction, which is stronger than the dispersion forces experienced by the straight-chained butane. Therefore 1-chlorobutane has a higher boiling point.

4 a miscible **b** miscible **c** immiscible **d** miscible

10.2 Impacts of use of organic substances

1 coal, natural gas and oil
2 Organic chemists have the skills needed to synthesise many modern drugs that are made from small organic molecules.
3 on the Safety Data Sheets (SDS)
4 the Globally Harmonized System of Classification and Labelling of Chemicals

Chapter 10 Review

1 The forces are dispersion forces. These are weak forces of attraction between non-polar molecules, such as hydrocarbons. As the chain length of the hydrocarbon molecule increases, the strength of dispersion forces increases because of greater surface area between molecules.

2

Property	Hydrocarbon
intramolecular bond type	covalent
intermolecular bond type	dispersion forces
melting point, high or low?	low
boiling point, high or low?	low
solubility in water	insoluble
solubility in organic solvents	soluble

3

Name	Formula	Condensed structural formula	Physical state at room temperature
methane	CH_4	CH_4	gas
ethane	C_2H_6	CH_3CH_3	gas
propane	C_3H_8	$CH_3CH_2CH_3$	gas
butane	C_4H_{10}	$CH_3CH_2CH_2CH_3$	gas
pentane	C_5H_{12}	$CH_3CH_2CH_2CH_2CH_3$	liquid
hexane	C_6H_{14}	$CH_3CH_2CH_2CH_2CH_2CH_3$	liquid

4 The addition of a halogen atom introduces polarity, so the carbon–halogen bond allows dipole–dipole attractions to occur. These attractions are stronger than the dispersion forces of hydrocarbons and require more energy to overcome, making the boiling point higher.

5 2-methylpropane and butane have the lowest boiling points because alkanes are non-polar, so dispersion forces are the only intermolecular forces between molecules. Dispersion forces are not as strong as other intermolecular forces, so the boiling points of alkanes are low. Molecules of butane have a greater surface area and can fit more closely together than molecules of 2-methylpropane, forming stronger intermolecular bonds. Hydrogen bonds exist between the propan-1-ol molecules because of the electronegative nature of the oxygen atom. These bonds are stronger than the dispersion forces between 2-methylpropane and butane molecules and the dipole–dipole forces in methyl methanoate molecules.

6 Boiling points of compounds are determined by the strength of the intermolecular forces. Weak dispersion forces are present in all molecules, whether polar or non-polar, so the masses must be similar when making comparisons on the effect of changing functional groups.

7 **a** $CH_3CH(CH_3)CH(CH_3)CH_2CH_2OH$, $CH_3CH(CH_3)$ $CH_2CH_2CH_2CH_2OH$, $CH_3(CH_2)_5CH_2OH$
   b These alkanes are non-polar so they would have greater solubility in octane because octane is a non-polar solvent.

8 Intramolecular bonds: covalent bonds between atoms in octane molecules
   Intermolecular bonds: dispersion forces between the non-polar hydrocarbon molecules of octane

9 Water is a very polar molecule, and the main intermolecular force between the molecules is hydrogen bonding. This force is too strong to be overcome by mixing the water with non-polar molecules such as hydrocarbons.

10 CH_3Cl would be the most soluble in water, as the C–Cl bond is polar so chloromethane molecules are polar, allowing them to form dipole-dipole attractions with water molecules. The other molecules also contain polar C–Cl bonds, but their longer non-polar hydrocarbon chains reduce the solubility of the molecules in water.

11 smog, acid rain, the destruction of natural ecosystems and climate change

12 **a** Oct-1-ene is an alkene and is non-polar. Therefore, it is immiscible in a polar solvent such as water and will not dissolve. It will sit on the surface of the water in a less dense layer.
   b 7-methyloct-1-yne is an alkyne and (like the alkene oct-1-ene) is non-polar. When the two substances are added they will mix together completely.

13 Coal, oil and natural gas are denser than wood, so more energy can be produced per unit of fuel.

14 They use online resources to search for Safety Data Sheets, experimental methods and hazard labels, and to generate risk assessments.

15 **a** Hexane is a clear, colourless, volatile liquid with a petrol-like odour. It is less dense than water.
   b Place hexane in a shallow vessel in an operating fume cupboard and allow the solvent to evaporate.
   c Move the patient to fresh air and keep at rest in a position comfortable for breathing. Get medical advice or attention if they feel unwell.

16 Vegetable oil represents a hydrocarbon. It was chosen because, like hydrocarbons, it is non-polar, less dense than water and insoluble in water.

Chapter 11 Products of reactions involving hydrocarbons

11.1 chemical properties of hydrocarbons

1 $CH_4(g) + Cl_2(g) \xrightarrow{UV\ light} CH_3Cl(g) + HCl(g)$
   $CH_3Cl(g) + Cl_2(g) \xrightarrow{UV\ light} CH_2Cl_2(g) + HCl(g)$
   $CH_2Cl_2(g) + Cl_2(g) \xrightarrow{UV\ light} CHCl_3(g) + HCl(g)$
   $CHCl_3(g) + Cl_2(g) \xrightarrow{UV\ light} CCl_4(g) + HCl(g)$

2 **a** chloroethane **b** 1,2-dichloroethane
   c ethanol **d** ethane

3 **a**
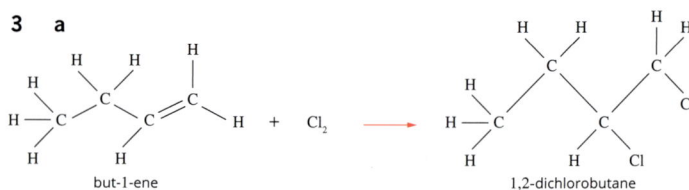
but-1-ene + Cl_2 → 1,2-dichlorobutane

   b

but-2-ene + HBr → 2-bromobutane

4 **a** but-1-ene or but-2-ene
   b 2-methylprop-1-ene
   c pent-3-ene

Chapter 11 Review

1

Reactants	Type of reaction	Product
alkene and hydrogen	addition (hydrogenation)	alkane
alkene and hydrogen bromide	addition	bromoalkane
alkene and water (with a catalyst)	addition (hydration)	alcohol
alkene and bromine	addition	dibromoalkane

2
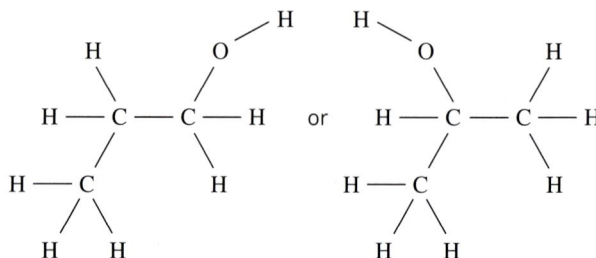

3 **a** $CH_3CH_2CH_2CH_3(l) + Cl_2(g) \xrightarrow{UV\ light} CH_3CH_2CH_2CH_2Cl(l) +$ $HCl(g)$ (other chloroalkane products are possible)
   b $2C_2H_6(g) + 7O_2(g) \rightarrow 4CO_2(g) + 6H_2O(g)$

4 **a** $CH_3CH_2CH_2CH_3(g) + Cl_2(g) \xrightarrow{UV\ light} CH_3CH_2CHClCH_3(g) +$ $HCl(g)$ (other chloroalkane products are possible)
   b $CH_3CH_2CH_2CH_3(l) + 7O_2(g) \rightarrow 5CO_2(g) + 4H_2O(g)$
   c $CH_2CHCH_3(g) + 3O_2(g) \rightarrow 3CO(g) + 3H_2O(g)$

5 React the alkene with hydrogen gas in the presence of a metal catalyst such as nickel.

6 Fluorine would be the most reactive, because reactivity decreases down the halogen group as the electronegativity decreases.

7 Bromine solution. It stays orange/brown in the presence of ethane but becomes colourless when ethene is present.

8 B   **9** C

10
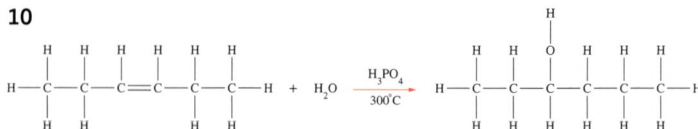

11 **a** but-2-ene
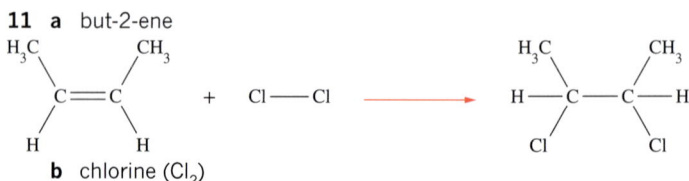
   b chlorine (Cl_2)

12 **a** propane

  b 1-bromopropane and 2-bromopropane

  c 1,2-dibromopropane

13 **a** $2C_8H_{18} + 25O_2 \rightarrow 16CO_2 + 18H_2O$

  b $C_4H_8 + HCl \rightarrow C_4H_9Cl$

  c $C_5H_{10} + Br_2 \rightarrow C_5H_{10}Br_2$

  d $C_5H_{12} + Br_2 \xrightarrow{\text{UV light}} C_5H_{11}Br + HBr$ (other bromoalkane products are possible)

14 C

15 **a** ethanol

  b $C_2H_4(g) + H_2O(g) \xrightarrow[300°C]{H_3PO_4} C_2H_5OH(g)$

16 The vegetable oil is the most spreadable because it is a liquid at room temperature. This is because it contains polyunsaturated molecules, i.e. molecules that contain multiple C=C double bonds. These cause 'kinks' in the molecules, so they are not able to pack closely together and the dispersion forces between molecules are therefore weaker.

  Margarine and dairy blend contain partially hydrogenated vegetable oils, which reduces their degree of unsaturation. This reduces the number of 'kinks' in the molecules, so they are able to pack more closely together. The dispersion forces between molecules are therefore stronger. This causes the oils to turn into a solid fat, which reduces their spreadability.

  Butter is the least spreadable because it contains saturated molecules, which are straight-chained, resulting in strongdispersion forces between molecules.

Chapter 12 Alcohols

12.1 Physical wand chemical properties of alcohols

1 (lowest) $CH_3CHOHCH_3$, $CH_3CH_2CH_2OH$, $CH_3CH_2CH_2CH_2OHCH_3CH_3CH_3$, $CH_3CH_2CH_2CH_2CH_2CH_2CH_2OH$ (highest)

2 The non-polar hexane molecules form stable interactions with the non-polar hydrocarbon chain of propan-1-ol. The attraction between methanol molecules due to hydrogen bonding is too strong to be overcome by the very weak dispersion forces that might occur with the very short hydrocarbon chain of methanol.

3 **a** tertiary **b** secondary **c** secondary

4 **a** $2C_5H_{12}O(g) + 15O_2(g) \rightarrow 10CO_2(g) + 12H_2O(g)$

  b pentan-3-ol, secondary; 2-methylbutan-2-ol, tertiary; pentan-1-ol, primary

  c Pentan-3-ol will be oxidised to pentan-3-one.

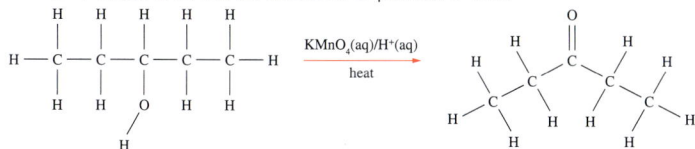

  2-methylbutan-2ol is a tertiary alcohol so will not react under the conditions described.
  Pentan-1-ol will be oxidised to the carboxylic acid.

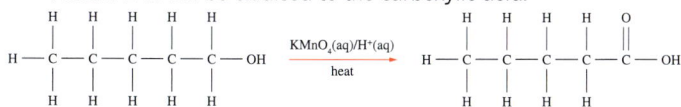

  The propanal will be produced first but because there is no mention of how harsh the reaction conditions are, it is assumed that pentan-1-ol is oxidised completely to propanoic acid

  d 0.0503 mol

5 **a** butan-2-ol **b** pentan-2-ol **c** butan-1-ol

6 **a** $CH_3Cl \xrightarrow{\text{OH}^- \text{ or H}_2\text{O with catalyst}} CH_3OH$

  b $CH_3CH_2CH_2Cl \xrightarrow{\text{OH}^- \text{ or H}_2\text{O with catalyst}} CH_3CH_2CH_2OH$

---

7 Yeast and bacteria do not survive in ethanol concentrations that are greater than about 15%, so the concentration of ethanol must be increased by distilling the mixture.

12.2 Fossil fuels and biofuels

1 A non-renewable fuel cannot be replenished at the rate at which it is consumed. A renewable fuel can be replenished at a rate at which it is consumed.

2 For a fuel to be sustainable, the starting material must be produced at least as quickly as it is consumed, and it must be possible for the environment to absorb or process all of the wastes produced in making and using the fuel.

3 renewable: bioethanol, biogas, biodiesel
  non-renewable: coal, oil, LPG, natural gas, coal seam gas

4 **a** The rate of global energy use is more than can be supplied by wood. Wood has a relatively low energy density and is unsuitable for many portable/transport applications.

  b Using a non-renewable energy source cannot be sustained indefinitely but moderate and careful use now can increase the likelihood that it will meet some needs of future generations.

5 Crude oil consists of a range of hydrocarbons with different boiling temperatures. The applications for each fraction is influenced by its boiling temperature and so fractional distillation is needed to separate them.

6 **a** advantage **b** disadvantage

  c advantage **d** advantage

  e disadvantage

Chapter 12 Review

1 D

2 **a** $CH_3CH(CH_3)CH(CH_3)CH_2CH_2OH$, $CH_3CH(CH_3)CH_2CH_2CH_2CH_2OH$, $CH_3(CH_2)_5CH_2OH$

  b They would have greater solubility in hexane because hexane is a non-polar solvent. The presence of the single polar hydroxyl group would not be enough to overcome the non-polar characteristic of the large hydrocarbon chains.

3 **a** ethanol + sodium bromide

  b pentan-1-ol + hydrogen iodide

  c hexan-2-ol + potassium chloride

4 **a** There are many different fermentation processes and these are caused by many different microorganisms. Most fermentation reactions are catalysed by more than one organism. Different species can produce different products, or different mixtures of products. The reactions depend strongly on temperatures and concentrations.

  b

Advantages of haloalkane reactions	Advantages of fermentation
faster reaction	lower cost
produces a pure product	lower temperature required
produces a higher yield	can be performed by low-skilled operators
	more likely to produce a renewable resource
Disadvantages of haloalkane reactions	**Disadvantages of fermentation**
chloroethane is suspected to cause cancer; other haloalkanes are toxic	slower
haloalkanes are more flammable than ethanol–water mixtures	produces a mixture

5 **a** aldehyde (mild conditions, lower temperatures) or carboxylic acid (higher temperatures, longer reaction times)

  b ketone **c** no reaction

6 **a**

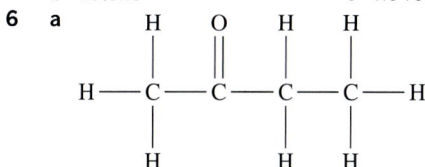

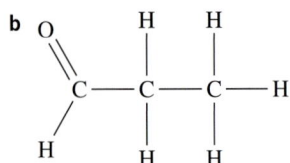

b

c no reaction

7 **a** No reaction between a tertiary alcohol and H^+/MnO_4^-.
b Ethanoic acid is formed if the reaction time is long and the temperature is high.
c The ketone pentan-3-one is formed from a secondary alcohol.
d The aldehyde butanal is formed when the temperature is mild and the product is removed as it is formed.

8 **a** $CH_3CH_4CH_4OH \xrightarrow[\text{or conc acid}]{Al_2O_3} CH_3CH{=}CH_2$
b $CH_3CH_2CH_2CH_2Cl \xrightarrow{OH^-} CH_3CH_2CH_2CH_2OH$
c $CH_3CH_2CH_2OH \xrightarrow{HBr} CH_3CH_3CH_3Br$

9 **a** $2C_5H_{11}OH(l) + 15O_2(g) \rightarrow 10CO_2(g) + 12H_2O(l/g)$
b $2CH_3CHOHCH_3(l) + 9O_2(g) \rightarrow 6CO_2(g) + 8H_2O(l/g)$

10 **a** $-2.52 \times 10^3\,kJ\,mol^{-1}$
b Not all of the energy released was used to heat the water. Some may be used to heat the metal and some may be lost to the surroundings.

11 Apart from the difficulties in daily travel, lack of crude oil and natural gas would make transport of manufactured goods difficult and costly. It would also stop the production of all the products that are derived from crude oil, including plastics, synthetic fibres, dyes, paints, solvents, detergents and pharmaceuticals.

12 D

13 They are separated by fractional distillation. The crude oil is heated and introduced into a fractionating column, which separates the components on the basis of their boiling point.

14 The formation of fossil fuels has occurred over millions of years. They will not be replaced in the foreseeable future.

15 soybean, canola and palm oil

16 C

17 the rate of production of the starting material, the ability of the environment to absorb or convert the waste products from the fuel's use

18 **a** petrol, bioethanol, biogas   **b** B

19 Photosynthesis uses six molecules of carbon dioxide to produce one molecule of glucose:
$6CO_2(g) + 6H_2O(l) \rightarrow C_6H_{12}O_6(aq) + 6O_2(g)$
Fermentation of glucose produces ethanol and two molecules of CO_2:
$C_6H_{12}O_6(aq) \rightarrow 2CO_2(g) + 2CH_3CH_2OH(aq)$
Combustion of ethanol releases heat and four molecules of CO_2:
$2CH_3CH_2OH(l) + 3O_2(g) \rightarrow 3H_2O(g) + 2CO_2(g)$
Therefore, all of the carbon dioxide released into the atmosphere by the fermentation and combustion of ethanol has been taken in by plants in the process of photosynthesis.

20 **a**, **b**, **d**, **e** and **f** are all advantages; **c** is a disadvantage

21 **a** E10 petrol is a mixture of 10% ethanol and 90% conventional petrol.
b It will extend the availability of petrol as a fuel and will allow more of the larger fractions from crude oil to be used as a feedstock for other uses rather than being burnt as a fuel.

22 All of the points are interrelated. Sample answers are given here; many other valid answers are possible.
a Polar ice caps are shrinking, contributing to sea level rise and affecting wildlife that depend on the ice caps. Melting ice adds cold, fresh water to the ocean, which could alter the major ocean currents, resulting in unexpected climate changes, e.g. in western Europe.
b Changed weather patterns may cause more droughts and floods and more intense storms, and may change growth patterns in plants that might lead to both plant and animal extinctions.

c The changed weather patterns can result in crops failing, affecting the economy and driving some people to starvation.
d Some plants and animals that depend on particular weather patterns for propagation or for key parts of their life cycle may become extinct.

23 **a** Biochemical fuels are derived from renewable resources such as plants. Ethene is derived from crude oil, a non-renewable resource.
b the fermentation by yeasts of sugar derived from sugar cane or from grains such as maize

24 Student answers may vary. Examples include China, USA, Russia, India, Japan, Canada, Germany, Brazil, South Korea and France.

25 **a** The cost of electricity could rise if other energy sources are required to replace coal, which is relatively abundant and cheap.
b Biofuels could potentially be carbon neutral—the carbon dioxide produced from the combustion of the fuels is offset by the carbon dioxide absorbed to grow the crops used to make the fuels.

26 Ethanol is insoluble in vegetable oil because the hydrogen bonds between ethanol molecules and the dispersion forces between vegetable oil molecules are stronger than intermolecular forces formed between the molecules of the two different substances.

Chapter 13 Reactions of organic acids and bases

13.1 Physical properties of organic acids and bases

1 $CH_3CH_2CH_2CH_3$, $CH_3CH_2CH_2NH_2$, $CH_3CH_2CH_2OH$, CH_3CH_2COOH, $CH_3CH_2CONH_2$
The strength and extent of hydrogen bonding increases, resulting in stronger intermolecular forces between molecules and a higher boiling point.

2 CH_3NH_2, $CH_3CH_2NH_2$, $CH_3CH_2CH_2NH_2$, $CH_3CH_2CH_2CH_2NH_2$, $CH_3CH_2CH_2CH_2CH_2CH_2NH_2$
Longer-chain amines have stronger dispersion forces between molecules and a higher melting point than shorter-chain amines.

3 octanoic acid, octan-2-one and heptan-1-amine

4 Amides have much more extensive hydrogen bonding than amines.

5 octan-1-ol

13.2 Chemical properties of organic acids and bases

1 **a**

b

c

2 **a** $CH_3(CH_2)_3COOH(aq) + H_2O(l) \rightleftharpoons CH_3(CH_2)_3COO^-(aq) + H_3O^+(aq)$
b $CH_3CH_2CH_2NH_2(aq) + H_2O(l) \rightleftharpoons CH_3CH_2CH_2NH_3^+(aq) + OH^-(aq)$
c no reaction

3
a The molecule needs to be boiled with a strong base.
b $CH_2OHCHOHCH_2OH$ and $CH_3(CH_2)_3CH=CH(CH_2)_2CH=CH(CH_2)_3COO^-$

4 The non-polar hydrocarbon tails of stearate ions are unable to overcome the hydrogen bonding between water molecules. Instead, they are attracted to each other, forming a micelle. This leaves the charged heads of the stearate ions facing the water.

5 It remains surrounded by hydrocarbon tails in a non-polar environment.

13.3 Organic reaction pathways

1
a ethene $\xrightarrow[\text{H}_3\text{PO}_4]{\text{H}_2\text{O}}$ ethanol $\xrightarrow{\text{NH}_3}$ ethanamine

b butane $\xrightarrow[\text{UV}]{\text{Cl}_2}$ 1-chlorobutane $\xrightarrow{\text{OH}^-}$ butan-1-ol

c 1-chloropentane $\xrightarrow{\text{OH}^-}$ pentan-1-ol $\xrightarrow{\text{K}_2\text{Cr}_2\text{O}_7/\text{H}^+}$ pentanoic acid

2
a methane $\xrightarrow[\text{UV}]{\text{Cl}_2}$ chloromethane $\xrightarrow{\text{OH}^-}$ methanol $\xrightarrow{\text{K}_2\text{Cr}_2\text{O}_7/\text{H}^+}$ methanoic acid

b ethene $\xrightarrow[\text{H}_3\text{PO}_4]{\text{H}_2\text{O}}$ ethanol

c Stage 1: propane $\xrightarrow[\text{UV}]{\text{Cl}_2}$ 1-chloropropane $\xrightarrow{\text{OH}^-}$ propan-1-ol
Stage 2: methane $\xrightarrow[\text{UV}]{\text{Cl}_2}$ chloromethane $\xrightarrow{\text{OH}^-}$ methanol $\xrightarrow{\text{H}^+/\text{Cr}_2\text{O}_7^{2-}}$ methanoic acid
Stage 3: propan-1-ol + methanoic acid $\xrightarrow{\text{H}^+}$ 1-propyl methanoate + water

3
a pentan-1-ol
b sodium hydroxide or potassium hydroxide
c pentanoic acid
d acidified potassium dichromate or potassium permanganate and heat
e ammonia

4 Stage 1: butane $\xrightarrow[\text{UV}]{\text{Cl}_2}$ 1-chlorobutane $\xrightarrow{\text{OH}^-}$ butan-1-ol
Stage 2: ethene $\xrightarrow[\text{H}_3\text{PO}_4]{\text{H}_2\text{O}}$ ethanol $\xrightarrow{\text{H}^+/\text{Cr}_2\text{O}_7^{2-}}$ ethanoic acid
Stage 3: ethanoic acid + butan-1-ol $\xrightarrow{\text{H}^+}$ butyl ethanoate + water

Chapter 13 Review

1 For organic molecules that have a similar molar mass, the boiling points are determined by the strength of intermolecular forces between molecules. Dispersion forces are weakest, then dipole–dipole forces; hydrogen bonds are the strongest. Generally, the greater the hydrogen bonding, the higher the boiling point.

2 Boiling points of compounds are determined by the strength of the intermolecular forces. Weak dispersion forces are present in all molecules, whether polar or non-polar, so they must be kept as close to constant as possible when making comparisons on the effect of changing functional groups. Because the strength of dispersion forces increases with molecular size, it is important to select compounds that have a similar molar mass.

3
a CH_3CHO, CH_3COOH, $CH_3(CH_2)_6CHO$, $CH_3(CH_2)_5COOH$
b The molecules with longer hydrocarbon chains, $CH_3(CH_2)_6COH$ and $CH_3(CH_2)_5COOH$, would have greater solubility in hexane because hexane is a non-polar solvent.

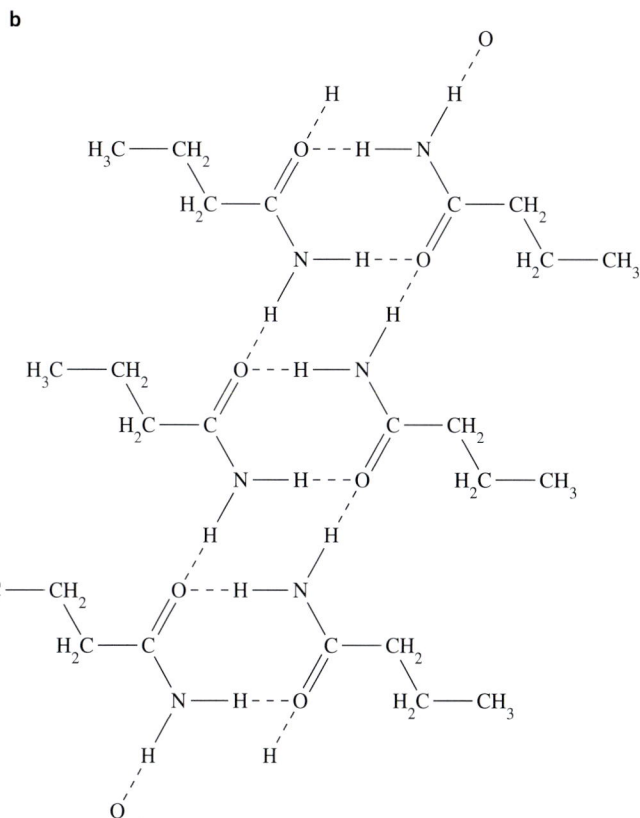

4
a

hydrogen bond

b

c The molecules have more extensive hydrogen bonding.

5 Methyl ethanoate can hydrogen bond with one or more water molecules. The answer shown here has the moleculeforming two hydrogen bonds with water.

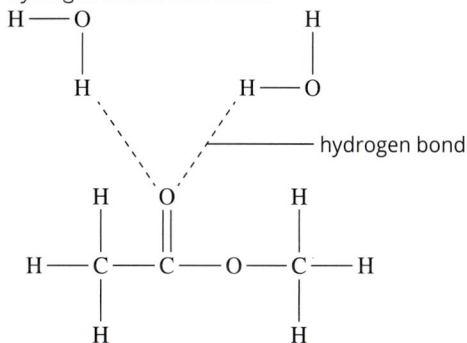

hydrogen bond

6
a $CH_3CH_2COOCH_3 + H_2O$
b $CH_3COO(CH_2)_4CH_3 + H_2O$
c $HCOOCH(CH_3)_2 + H_2O$

7
a ethanol, propanoic acid and a strong acid, such as sulfuric acid, to catalyse the reaction
b propanoic acid and ammonia
c butanoic acid and ammonia
d methanoic acid, methanol, and a strong acid, such as sulfuric acid, to catalyse the reaction

8
a

b

c

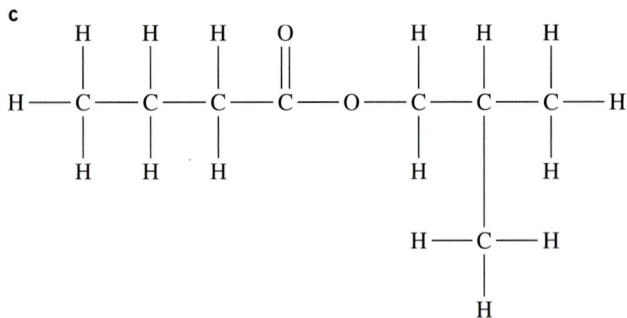

9 **a** $CH_3(CH_2)_3NH_3^+ + OH^-$ **b** does not dissociate in water
10 The electronegative oxygen atom of an amide draws electron density away from the nitrogen atom, reducing its ability to hold a positive charge after accepting a H^+ ion. The nitrogen atom is the most electronegative atom in an amine, so it draws electron density from the rest of the molecule. This extra electron density means that an amine is better at holding the positive charge when it acts as a base and accepts H^+.
11 **a** The hydrocarbon chain is hydrophobic and the COONa section is hydrophilic.
   b the hydrocarbon chain (hydrophobic end) of the molecule
12 Soap molecules are surfactants (surface-active agents). The hydrophobic section of the surfactant molecule adsorbs onto the oil stain and the charged heads of the molecules provide a hydrophilic coating for the oil. Surfactant molecules move between the oil and the fabric to completely surround the oil in a ball-like structure called a micelle and this micelle is carried off into the solution. A solution of oil-containing micelles in water is called an emulsion.
13 **a** 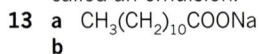 $CH_3(CH_2)_{10}COONa$
   b

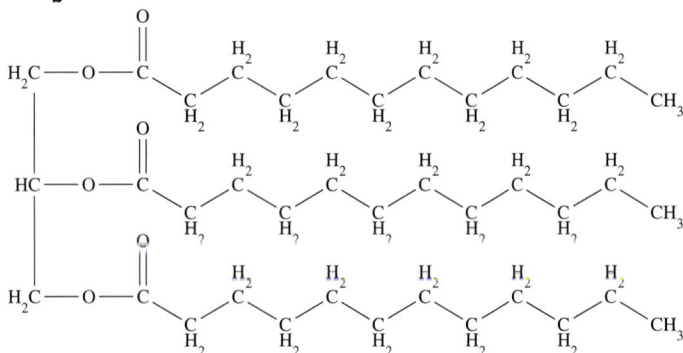

14 C
15 **a** Cl_2 and UV   **b** propan-2-ol
16 **a**

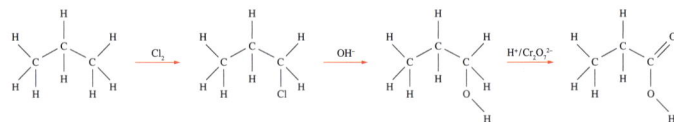

   b

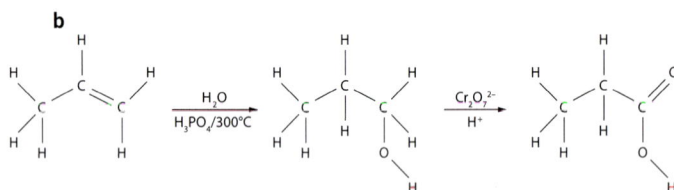

17 **a** Step 1: ethene $\xrightarrow[H_3PO_4]{H_2O}$ ethanol
   Step 2: 1-chloropropane $\xrightarrow{OH^-}$ propan-1-ol $\xrightarrow{H^+/Cr_2O_7^{2-}}$ propanoic acid
   Step 3: ethanol + propanoic acid $\xrightarrow{H_2SO_4}$ ethyl propanoate
   b ethane $\xrightarrow[UV]{Cl_2}$ chloroethane $\xrightarrow{OH^-}$ ethanol $\xrightarrow{H^+/Cr_2O_7^{2-}}$ ethanoic acid $\xrightarrow{ethanol, H_2SO_4}$ ethyl ethanoate

18 **a** **i** $CH_3CH_3 \xrightarrow[UV]{Cl_2} CH_3CH_2Cl$

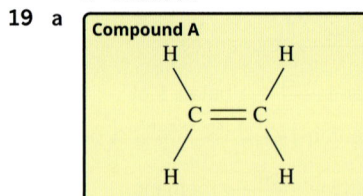

   ii $CH_2CH_2 \xrightarrow[H_3PO_4]{H_2O} CH_3CH_2OH$
   iii $CH_3CH_2Cl \xrightarrow{OH^-} CH_3CH_2OH$
   iv $CH_3CH_2OH \xrightarrow{H^+/Cr_2O_7^{2-}} CH_3COOH$
   b **i** substitution   **ii** addition   **iii** substitution
      iv oxidation
19 **a**

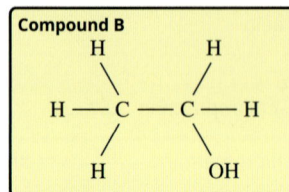
Compound A

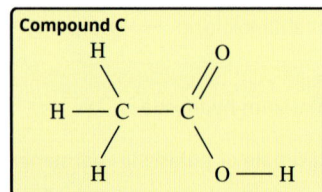
Compound B

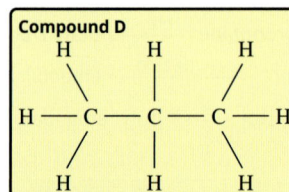
Compound C

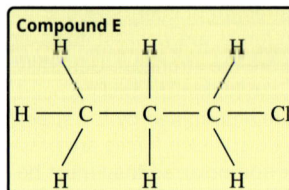
Compound D

Compound E

   b The bromine test for unsaturated hydrocarbons. When aqueous Br_2 is added to A, an addition reaction will occur and the solution will turn from orange to colourless. If aqueous Br_2 is added to D, no reaction will occur and the solution will remain orange.
   c B
20 Bicarbonate of soda reacts with vinegar in an acid and metal carbonate reaction. This reaction produces carbon dioxide gas, which is trapped in the washing detergent.

Chapter 14 Polymers

14.1 Additional polymers

1 C
2 A and D
3 **a** CH_2 **b** CH_2 **c** CH   **d** C_2H_3Cl
4 **a** C_9H_{18} **b** $C_{12}H_{18}Cl_6$ **c** $C_{130}H_{260}$
5 three full units and half a repeating unit at start and end of segment

6 Polymers usually consist of thousands to millions of monomer repeating units.

7 **a** High-density polyethene (HDPE) is made of relatively unbranched chains of polyethene, which can pack more closely together than the branched chains of low-density polyethene (LDPE). HDPE is therefore stronger and slightly less flexible than LDPE. Both HDPE and LDPE are chemically unreactive, waterproof, non-conductors and only slightly permeable to gases.

   b **i** LDPE   **ii** HDPE   **iii** LDPE

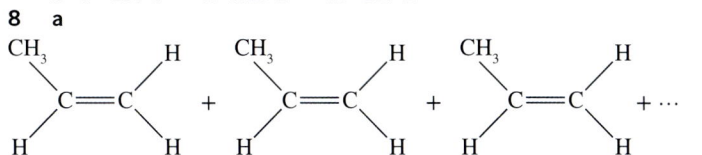

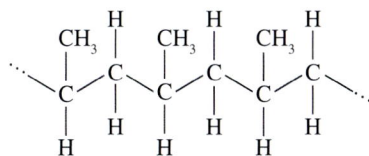

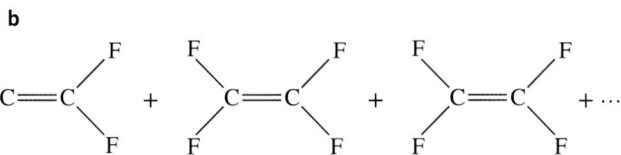

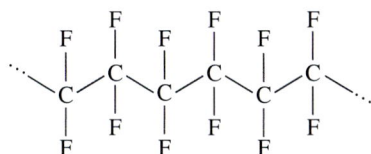

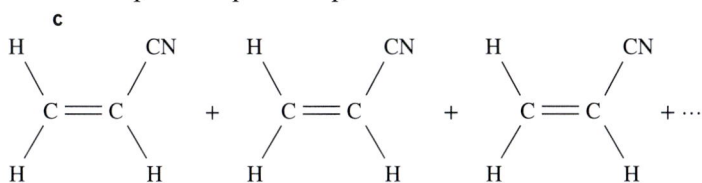

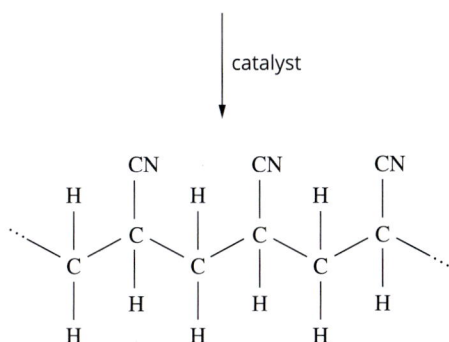

8 **a**

   b

   c

14.2 Condensation polymerisation

1 D

2 **a**

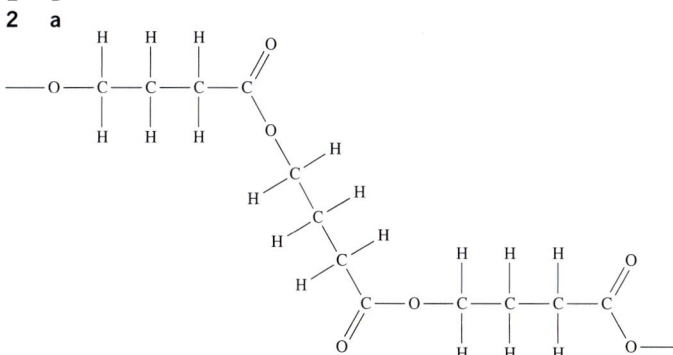

   b water
   c polyester

3 A and D

4 **a**

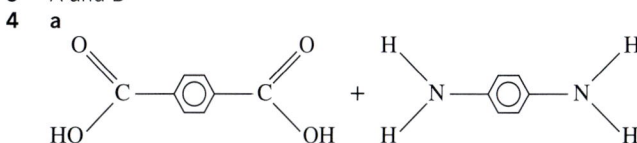

   b be very tough yet relatively light
   c The presence of C=O and –N–H bonds allows for hydrogen bonding between neighbouring polymer chains. The polymer chains will pack together tightly as there are few, if any, side-chains.

5 **a** Both made from monomers, both contain very long polymer molecules.
   b addition polymers: made from monomers that contain carbon–carbon double bonds; large molecules
   condensation polymers: made from monomers that contain a functional group at either end of the molecule; small molecules

6 dispersion forces, dipole–dipole attractions, covalent bonds

7 **a** The polymer used in the handle will have cross-links while the polymer used for the coating will not.
   b relatively high melting point, be durable, non-toxic, low friction
   c high melting point, tough, non-flammable

Chapter 14 Review

1 C

2 **a**

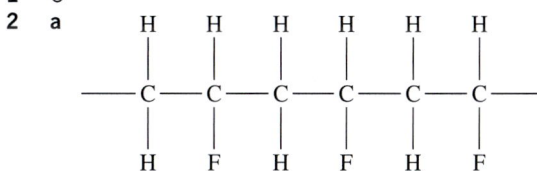

   b The highly electronegative fluorine atoms will cause dipole attractions between neighbouring molecules.

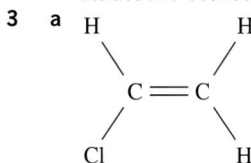

3 **a**

   b 6
   c dipole–dipole attractions

4 **a** small molecule that is able to react to form long chains of repeating units
   b softens when heated, allowing it to be reshaped; this is because the bonds between molecules are broken and the molecules become free to move

c does not melt when heated, but at high temperatures, covalent bonds are broken and the material decomposes or burns; cannot be moulded

d one or more covalent bonds that connect neighbouring polymer chains

e a chemical added to plastics to make them more flexible

5 **a** False **b** False **c** False **d** True

6 A, C and D

7 **a** The ethene molecule has a carbon–carbon double bond.

b

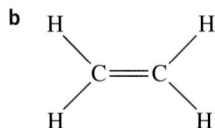

c no; it is a saturated compound

8 **a** Several thousand ethene monomers undergo an addition polymerisation reaction to make one molecule of polyethene.

b Ethene ($CH_2{=}CH_2$) is unsaturated because it contains a carbon–carbon double bond. Polyethene is saturated because it contains only single bonds between carbon atoms.

c It is the simplest whole-number ratio of elements in a compound. The empirical formula of $CH_2{=}CH_2$ is CH_2.

9 **a**

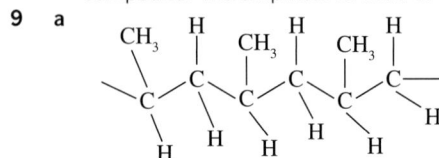

b

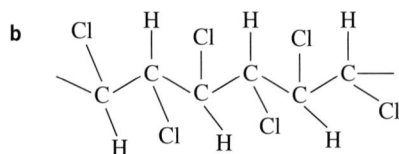

c

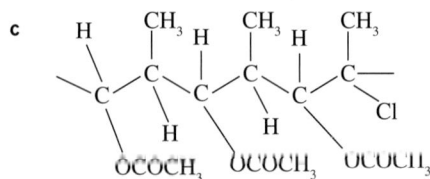

10 **a** weak dispersion forces **b** dipole–dipole attractions
c weak dispersion forces **d** weak dispersion forces
e dipole–dipole attractions

11 –H, –F, –Cl, –C_6H_5, –$NC_{12}H_8$

12 **a** more **b** fewer **c** lower **d** lower **e** less

13 C

14 **a** polyamide **b** polyamide **c** polyester **d** polyester

15

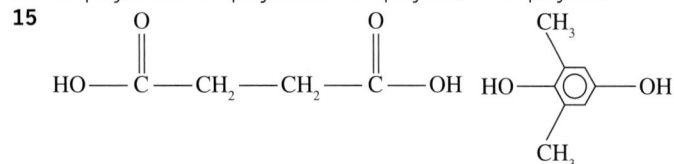

16 **a**

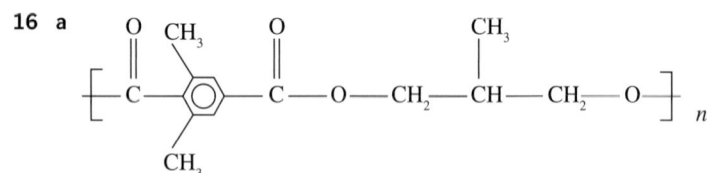

b

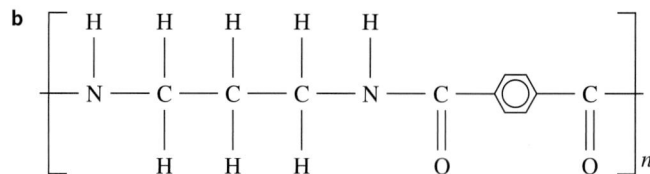

17 **a** amide **b** 99

18

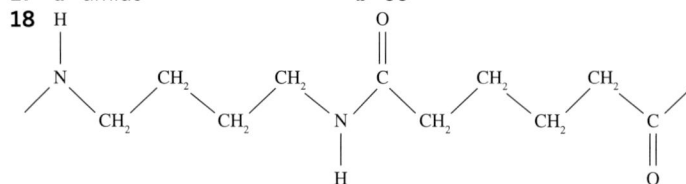

19 **a** **i**

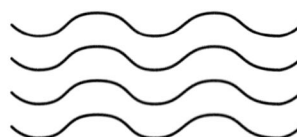

ii

iii

b **i**

polymer easily stretched

ii

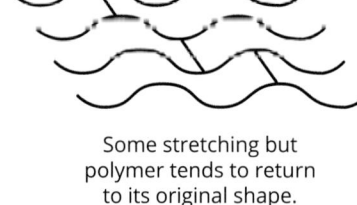

Some stretching but polymer tends to return to its original shape.

iii

no stretching possible

20 Interchain bonds are much stronger in thermosetting polymers.

21 When heated strongly, both the interchain and within-chain bonds break.

22 **a** thermosetting **b** thermoplastic **c** thermosetting
d thermoplastic **e** thermoplastic

23 **a** the polymer used in saucepan handles
b Saucepan handles are much harder and more resistant to the effect of heat than elastic bands and golf balls.

24 The relative molecular mass would have increased. The melting point of the polymer would have increased. The overall strength of interchain forces would have increased. The electrical conductivity of the polymer would have remained the same.

25 A

26 a HCl   **b** 4999   **c** amide

d

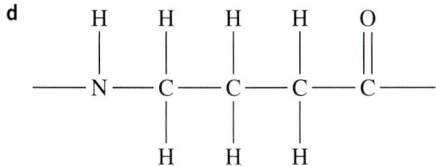

27 No. The monomers used to make polymers are products of the petrochemical industry and at the moment are relatively inexpensive. It would be more costly to produce a polymer from milk. Also, a polymer from milk would have limited applications due to its limited properties. Polymers derived from petrochemicals have a range of useful properties.

Module 7 Review

Multiple choice

1 C	**2** D	**3** B	**4** C
5 B	**6** D	**7** C	**8** A
9 C	**10** C	**11** D	**12** C
13 C	**14** A	**15** C	**16** B
17 C	**18** A	**19** A	**20** B

Short answer

1
a i C_7H_{16} ii e.g. $CH_3CH_2CH_2CH(CH_3)CH_2CH_3$
b i $C_4H_{10}O$ ii e.g. $CH_3CH_2CHOHCH_3$
c i $C_3H_6O_2$ ii e.g. CH_3CH_2COOH
d i $C_5H_{11}OCl$ ii e.g. $CH_2Cl(CH_2)_4OH$
e i C_8H_{16} ii e.g. $CH_3CH_2CHCHCH_2CH(CH_3)_2$
f i $C_6H_{12}O$ ii e.g. $CH_3CH_2CH(CH_3)CH_2CHO$
g i C_8H_{12} ii e.g. $CH_3CCCH_2CH_2CHCHCH_3$
h i $C_6H_{12}O$ ii e.g. $CH_3CHCHCOH(CH_3)_2$
i i $C_4H_7NO_2$ ii e.g. $CH_3COCH_2CONH_2$

2
a

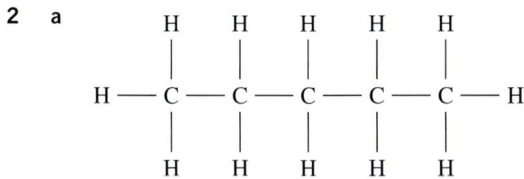

b

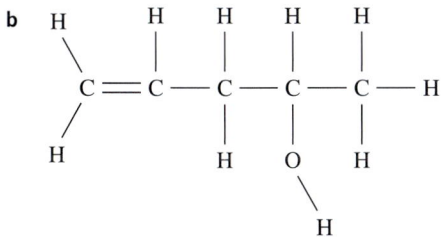

c

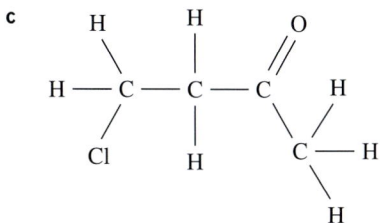

d

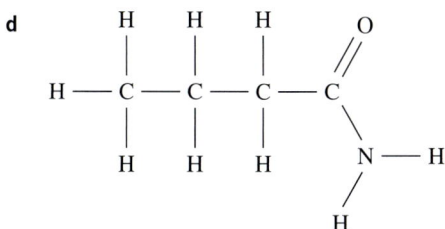

e

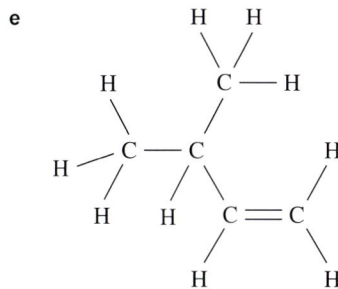

f

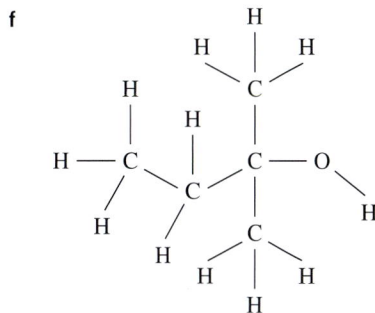

g

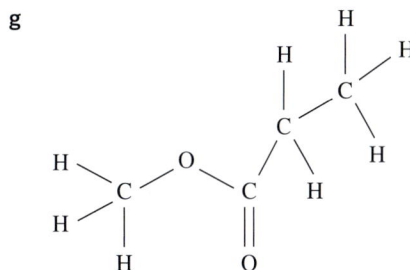

h

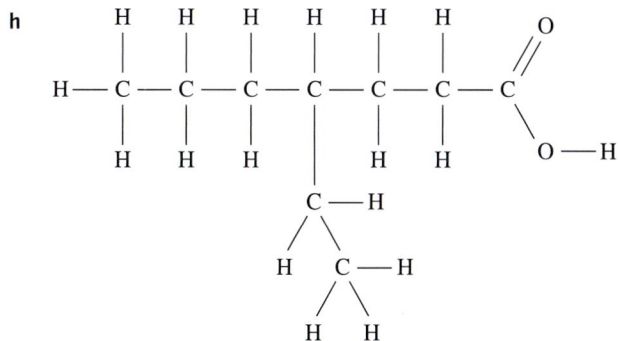

i

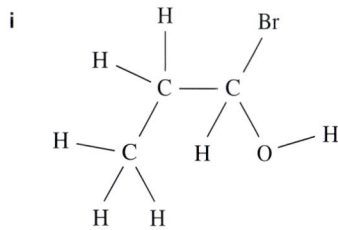

j

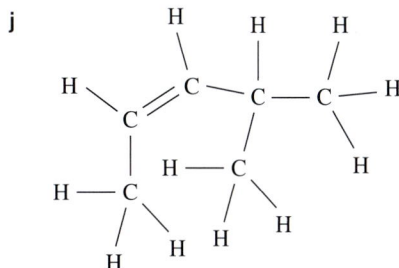

k

H—C—C—C—I (structure with N at top)

l

(structure)

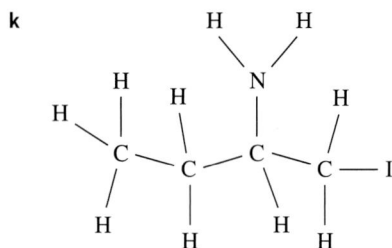

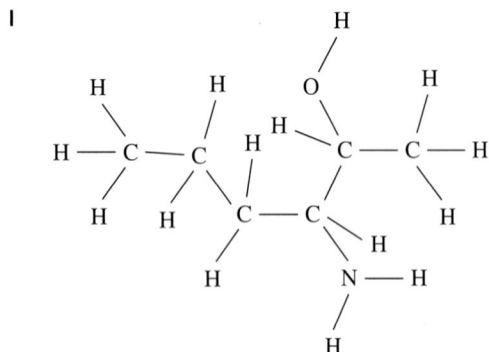

3 **a** acidified dichromate ($H^+/Cr_2O_7^{2-}$) or acidified permanganate (H^+/MnO_4^-), heating with distillation of product
 b heating with hydroxide ions (e.g. KOH, NaOH), or H_2O with catalyst
 c H_2O and acid catalyst (e.g. H_3PO_4 or H_2SO_4)
 d acidified dichromate ($H^+/Cr_2O_7^{2-}$) or acidified permanganate (H^+/MnO_4^-), heating under reflux
 e H_2 and Ni catalyst (other metals sometimes used)

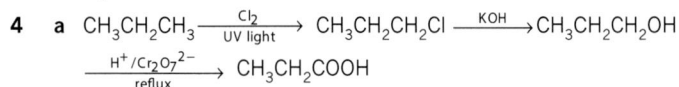

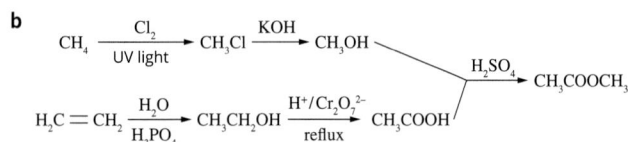

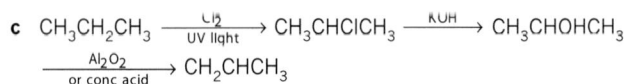

4 **a** $CH_3CH_2CH_3 \xrightarrow[\text{UV light}]{Cl_2} CH_3CH_2CH_2Cl \xrightarrow{KOH} CH_3CH_2CH_2OH$

 $\xrightarrow[\text{reflux}]{H^+/Cr_2O_7^{2-}} CH_3CH_2COOH$

 b

 $CH_4 \xrightarrow[\text{UV light}]{Cl_2} CH_3Cl \xrightarrow{KOH} CH_3OH$

 $H_2C=CH_2 \xrightarrow[\text{H}_3\text{PO}_4]{H_2O} CH_3CH_2OH \xrightarrow[\text{reflux}]{H^+/Cr_2O_7^{2-}} CH_3COOH \xrightarrow{H_2SO_4} CH_3COOCH_3$

 c $CH_3CH_2CH_3 \xrightarrow[\text{UV light}]{Cl_2} CH_3CHClCH_3 \xrightarrow{KOH} CH_3CHOHCH_3$

 $\xrightarrow[\text{or conc acid}]{Al_2O_3} CH_2CHCH_3$

5 **a** $CH_3CH_2COOH + NaHCO_3 \rightarrow NaCH_3CH_2COO + CO_2 + H_2O$
 b $CH_3CH_2CH_2OH + H_2O \rightarrow CH_3CH_2COOH + 4H^+ + 4e^-$
 c $CH_3CH_2COOH + CH_3CH_2OH \rightarrow CH_3CH_2COOCH_2CH_3 + H_2O$
 d $CH_3CH_2COOH + CH_3CH_2NH_2 \rightarrow CH_3CH_2COO^- + CH_3CH_2NH_3^+$
 e $2CH_3CH_2COOH + 7O_2 \rightarrow 6CO_2 + 6H_2O$

6 **a** but-2-yne **b** heptane **c** 2,2,3-trimethylpentane
 d butanoic acid **e** 2-methylpropan-1-ol

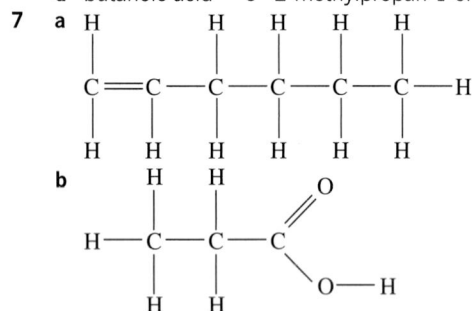

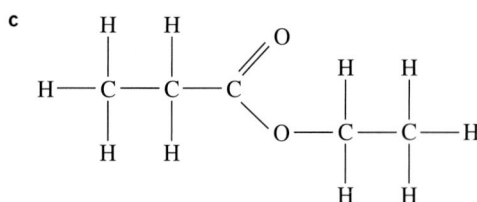

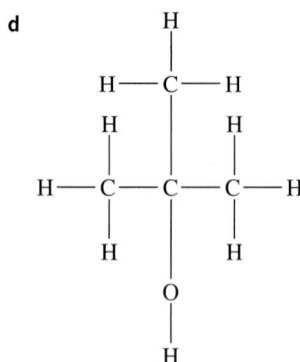

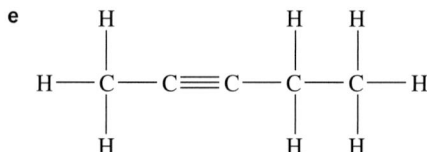

7 **a** (structure)
 b (structure)

c (structure)

d (structure)

e (structure)

8 **a** $CH_3(CH_2)_4COOH$ or $CH_3CH_2CH_2CH_2CH_2COOH$
 b $CH_3C(CH_3)_2CH_2CH(C_2H_5)CH_2CH_2CH_3$ or $(CH_3)_3CCH_2CH(C_2H_5)CH_2CH_2CH_3$
 c $CH_3CHOHCH_2CH_3$
 d $HCCCH_3$
 e $CH_2C(CH_3)CH_2CH(CH_3)CH_2CH_3$

9 **a** (structure)

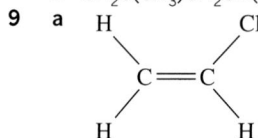

 b **i** It will char and blacken.
  ii Thermosetting polymers have strong cross-links between polymer chains so the layers cannot slide past each other and melt.

10 **a** A monomer is a small molecule that is able to bond with other monomers to form a long-chain molecule called a polymer; e.g. ethene molecules are the monomers that join together to form the polyethene polymer.
 b A thermoplastic polymer is one that softens on heating but becomes hard again when cooled, e.g. polyethene. A thermosetting polymer is one that doesn't soften on gentle heating but will char if heated sufficiently, e.g. melamine.
 c A branched polymer is a linear polymer that has some of the atoms forming branches attached to the polymer backbone, e.g. low density polyethene. Relatively weak intermolecular forces exist between chains. A cross-linked polymer has covalent bonds linking polymer chains, resulting in a rigid polymer that does not soften on heating, e.g. melamine.
 d Crystalline regions occur when atoms in chains are arranged in a regular pattern, thus strengthening the polymer. Non-crystalline regions occur when the atoms in the chain are randomly arranged.

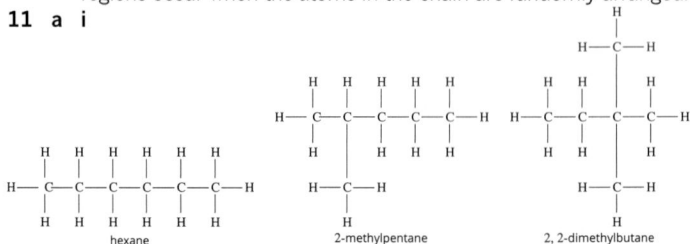

11 **a** **i**

 hexane

 2-methylpentane

 2, 2-dimethylbutane

ii Chain isomers have the same molecular formula but their structures are different due to different branching arrangements; e.g. hexane is straight chained, but 2-methylpentane has a methyl branch at carbon 2.

iii Physical properties such as boiling point will be similar. The presence of the same atoms in the molecules means the properties will be similar but the different molecule shapes will affect the strength of bonding between molecules.

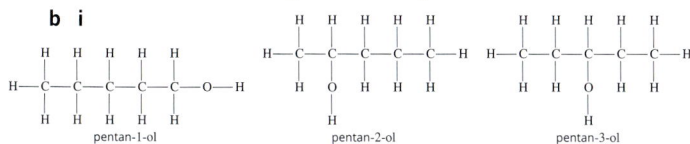

b i

pentan-1-ol   pentan-2-ol   pentan-3-ol

ii Position isomers have the same molecular formula and functional groups but the functional groups are located on different parts of the chain; e.g. pentan-1-ol has a hydroxyl group at carbon 1, but pentan-2-ol has the hydroxyl group at carbon 2.

iii A primary alcohol, such as pentan-1-ol, will form an aldehyde, then a carboxylic acid when reacting with acidified $K_2Cr_2O_7$. The secondary alcohols pentan-2-ol and pentan-3-ol will form a ketone when reacting with acidified $K_2Cr_2O_7$.

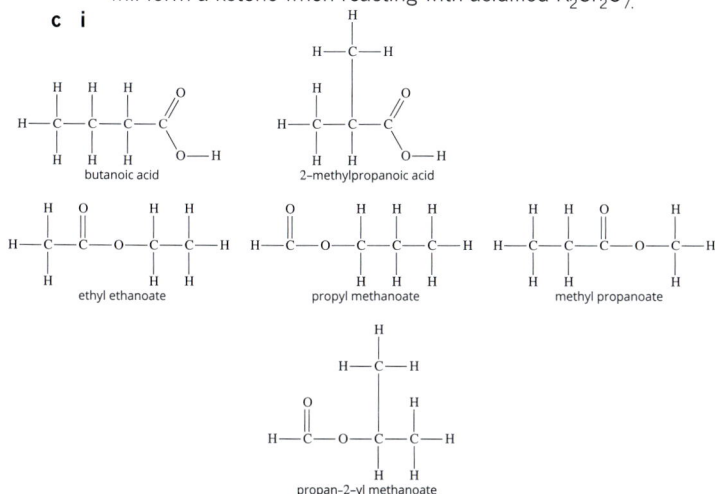

c i

butanoic acid   2-methylpropanoic acid

ethyl ethanoate   propyl methanoate   methyl propanoate

propan-2-yl methanoate

ii same molecular formula but contain different functional groups; e.g. carboxyl and ester

12

Functional groups present	Correct IUPAC name
hydroxyl	heptan-3-ol
carboxyl, fluoro	3-flurobutanoic acid
alkene/alkenyl	pent-2-ene
amino	4-ethylhexan-3-amine
hydroxyl, amino	1-aminopropan-2-ol
hydroxyl, chloro	5-chlorohexan-3-ol
hydroxyl, carboxyl	6-hydroxyoctanoic acid
bromo	2-bromo-3-methylpentane
ester	methyl butanoate

13

	IUPAC name	Condensed structural formula	Reactants and reaction conditions that could be used to form this molecule
a	butanone	$CH_3CH_2COCH_3$	butan-2-ol and acidified $K_2Cr_2O_7$
b	hexanal	$CH_3CH_2CH_2CH_2CH_2CHO$	hexan-1-ol and acidified $K_2Cr_2O_7$
c	propanamide	$CH_3CH_2CONH_2$	propanoic acid and NH_3
d	ethyl methanoate	CH_3CH_2OOCH	ethanol and methanoic acid, H_2SO_4

14
a $CH_3CH_2COOH(l) + H_2O(l) \rightleftharpoons H_3O^+(aq) + CH_3CH_2COO^-(aq)$
b $CH_3CH_2CH_2NH_2(l) + H_2O(l) \rightleftharpoons CH_3CH_2CH_2NH_3^+(aq) + OH^-(aq)$
c $CH_3CH_2COOH(l) + CH_3CH_2CH_2NH_2(l) \rightarrow$
$\qquad CH_3CH_2CONHCH_2CH_2CH_3(l) + H_2O(l)$
d $CH_3CH_2COOH(l) + CH_3CH_2CH_2OH(l) \rightarrow$
$\qquad CH_3CH_2COOCH_2CH_2CH_3(l) + H_2O(l)$
e $CH_3(CH_2)_{17}COOH(aq) + NaOH(aq) \rightarrow NaCH_3(CH_2)_{17}COO(aq) + H_2O(l)$

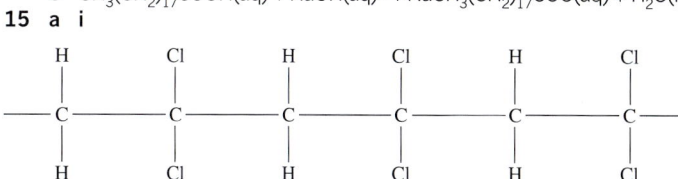

15 a i

ii addition polymerisation
iii The linear version will be harder, more brittle and more crystalline, and have a higher melting point and higher density.
iv There are no crosslinks between the polymer chains, so the polymer melts readily when heated. Once molten it can be remolded into a new product.

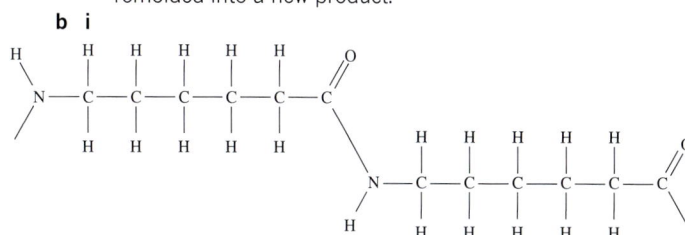

b i

ii condensation polymerisation
iii The presence of nitrogen and oxygen atoms allows hydrogen bonds to form between chains. The forces of attraction between the molecules are relatively high, so the melting point is also relatively high.

Chapter 15 Analysis of inorganic substances

15.1 The source of salts in the environment

1 A
2 a metal with a relatively high density that has a toxic effect on living organisms; e.g. cadmium, lead, chromium, copper and mercury, and the metalloid arsenic
3 by combustion of fuels and wastes (indirect), improper disposal of batteries, natural deposits in the Earth, and leaching from landfill
4 a ammonium nitrate, superphosphate or ammonium sulfate
   b The use of fertilisers leads to run-off into water supplies.
5 a Hard water contains relatively high levels of metal ions.
   b Ca^{2+}, Mg^{2+}
   c It limits the effectiveness of soaps and detergents and it causes deposits to form in kettles and pipes.

15.2 Qualitative techniques for detecting salts

TY 15.2.1 The formation of a white solid indicates Ca^{2+} ions might be present.

TY 15.2.2 Ca^{2+}

1 B
2

Compound	Flame colour
strontium chloride	scarlet
strontium carbonate	scarlet
copper chloride	green
potassium sulfate	lilac
sodium nitrate	yellow

3 a Both barium compounds produce a green flame but the flame from the compound containing sulfate ions is different. Therefore the metal ion is causing the visible flame colour.

  b Not all metals produce a visible flame colour. It can be difficult to distinguish one flame colour from another. The presence of several metal ions will cause confusion.

4 a PbI_2 b $Pb^{2+}(aq) + 2I^-(aq) \rightarrow PbI_2(s)$

5 a $Cu(OH)_2$ (or $[Cu(H_2O)_4(OH)_2]$ if the water molecules are shown)

  b Several metals could produce a precipitate with OH^- ions, but Cu^{2+} is one of the few that will be blue.

  c $Cu^{2+}(aq) + 2OH^-(aq) \rightarrow Cu(OH)_2(s)$

6 a The metal ion is most likely to be Ag^+ or Pb^{2+}.

  b The metal ion is Ag^+.

7 $[CoCl_4]^{2-}$

8 a Fe^{3+} b H_2O

  c The metal ion is positively charged. The water molecules are orientated so that their oxygen atoms, through their lone pairs, form bonds with the metal ion.

15.3 Gravimetric analysis of a salt

TY 15.3.1 1.485 g   **TY 15.3.2** 1.72%   **TY 15.3.3** 0.0321 mol L^{-1}

TY 15.3.4 0.0862 mol L^{-1}

1 C

2 a false   b true   c true

  d true (as long as the precipitate is stable when heated)

  e true   f true   g true

3

Poor practice	Impact
Precipitate is not dried to constant mass.	Mass of the precipitate is too high because of the presence of water.
Precipitate is not washed with deionised water.	Mass of the precipitate is too high because of the presence of impurities.
Precipitate is left on the sides of the flask.	Precipitate is pure but due to sample loss its measured mass is lower than it should be.
Precipitate decomposes when heated.	The composition of the precipitate is not known.

4 a silver nitrate

  b $AgNO_3(aq) + NaCl(aq) \rightarrow AgCl(s) + NaNO_3(aq)$ c 1

5 8.96 g

6 a 0.0200 mol   b 2   c 8.52 g

7 3.38 g

8 a $2KI(aq) + Pb(NO_3)_2(aq) + PbI_2(s) + 2KNO_3(aq)$

  b $n(Pb^{2+}) = 0.5 \times n(K^+)$

  c Because the precipitation of PbI_2 leads to the total number of ions in the solution decreasing.

15.4 Determining salt concentration by colorimetry and UV–visible spectroscopy

TY 15.4.1 8.8 mg mL^{-1}

1 a 0.080 mol L^{-1} solution   b 0.30 mol L^{-1} solution

2 Copper(II) sulfate is blue because it transmits blue light and absorbs light of other frequencies. A colorimeter measures the amount of light absorbed by a sample, so light of a colour other than blue must be used.

3 blue

4 a 0.15 mol L^{-1} Fe^{2+} b 0.60 mol L^{-1}

  c Fe^{2+} ions are oxidised to Fe^{3+} with acidified permanganate (H^+/MnO_4^-) before the addition of KSCN. The reaction of KSCN with Fe^{3+} forms the highly coloured red metal complex $FeSCN^{2+}$. The concentration of the complex can then be determined using spectrophotometry.

5

Solution	Complementary colour
green	purple
purple	green
orange	blue
green–yellow	violet
blue–green	red

6 a

AAS calibration curve for sodium analysis

  b 175 mg L^{-1}

7 Blue is the complementary colour of orange, so a blue filter should be used. Place the sample in a glass or plastic cell and pass light through it. Measure the absorbance at the selected wavelength and determine the concentration from a calibration curve.

8 a 450 nm and 660 nm

  b 660 nm or 450 nm

15.5 Determining concentration by atomic absorption spectroscopy

TY 15.5.1 52 mg L^{-1}

1 electrons, higher, emit, lower

2 A spectrum of the light produced when an element is excited by heat or radiation. It appears as distinct lines characteristic of the element.

3

Component	Description
flame	where the sample is sprayed and light is absorbed
hollow-cathode lamp	produces light with wavelengths that are absorbed by the metal being analysed
computer	converts the amount of light detected into the amount of light absorbed by the sample
monochromator	selects a specific wavelength of light
detector	measures the amount of light

4 C

5 a, b

AAS calibration curve for potassium analysis

  b 4.7 mg L^{-1}

6 a true   b false   c false   d true

  e false

7 The absorbance is directly proportional to the concentration.

Chapter 15 Review

1 **a** Any three of the following: mining, agriculture, sewage treatment and domestic drainage, the burning of fuels containing trace amounts of mercury, leaching from landfill, incorrect disposal of batteries and fluorescent light bulbs.

b by precipitation reactions; e.g. addition of calcium hydroxide will precipitate insoluble heavy metal hydroxides

2 Many possible answers. Some regions are high in limestone (region near Jenolan), some are high in particular minerals; e.g. Broken Hill.

3 **a** AgBr

b $Ag^+(aq) + Br^-(aq) \rightarrow AgBr(s)$

c Other metals ions such as Pb^{2+} will form a precipitate with Br^- ions, but the yellow colour would make Ag^+ highly likely.

4 **a** green

b to vaporise traces of other substances that could lead to a false result

c It would give the flame a green colour, and so interfere with the test.

d Relatively few elements may be analysed in this way and the presence of one element may mask the presence of another. Colours emitted by some elements are similar and difficult to distinguish, and a relatively large amount of sample is needed to give a clear colour.

5 **a** metal complex or complex ion

b Cl^-

c $Cu^{2+}(aq) + 4Cl^-(aq) \rightleftharpoons [CuCl_4]^{2-}(aq)$

d HCl solution could be added to a solution containing copper(II) ions. If Cu^{2+} is present, this complex should form and it is likely to have a green colour.

6 No reaction with Cl^- rules out Pb^{2+} and Ag^+. A white precipitate suggests a main group metal, probably Al^{3+}.

7

Ca(NO₃)₂	Na₃PO₄	Ca₃(PO₄)₂	NaNO₃
27 mol	18 mol	9.0 mol	54 mol
0.72 mol	0.48 mol	0.24 mol	1.44 mol
0.54 mol	0.36 mol	0.18 mol	1.1 mol
1.2 mol	0.80 mol	0.40 mol	2.4 mol

8 **a** lead(II) chloride, lead(II) hydroxide, copper(II) hydroxide

b $Pb(NO_3)_2(aq) + CuCl_2(aq) \rightarrow PbCl_2(s) + Cu(NO_3)_2(aq)$
$Pb^{2+}(aq) + 2Cl^-(aq) \rightarrow PbCl_2(s)$
$Pb(NO_3)_2(aq) + Ba(OH)_2(aq) \rightarrow Pb(OH)_2(s) + Ba(NO_3)_2(aq)$
$Pb^{2+}(aq) + 2OH^-(aq) \rightarrow Pb(OH)_2(s)$
$CuCl_2(aq) + Ba(OH)_2(aq) \rightarrow Cu(OH)_2(s) + BaCl_2(aq)$
$Cu^{2+}(aq) + 2OH^-(aq) \rightarrow Cu(OH)_2(s)$

9 18.4%   **10** 3.07%   **11** 1.2%

12 The experimental errors include: the precipitate was not dried completely, the precipitate was not washed, the presence in the solution of other metal ions that form precipitates.

13 **a** $Ag^+(aq) + Cl^-(aq) \rightarrow AgCl(s)$

b $2Ag^+(aq) + CrO_4^{2-}(aq) \rightarrow Ag_2CrO_4(s)$

c $0.060\,mol\,L^{-1}$

14 **a** $Ba^{2+}(aq) + SO_4^{2-}(aq) \rightarrow BaSO_4(s)$

b The formation of precipitate lowers the concentration of ions in the solution and, hence, conductivity.

c No further precipitate can form, so each time more ions are added the conductivity increases.

d The two lines can be drawn from two readings of conductivity before equivalence point and two after. The value of the equivalence point is the intersection of the two lines.

e $0.23\,mol\,L^{-1}$

15 In order from left to right: light source, coloured filter, sample solution, detector, recorder

16 **a** 700 nm   **b** orange/red region   **c** blue

17

Component	Function
detector	measures the intensity of light
filter	selects a range of wavelengths of light
light source	provides ultraviolet and visible light of all wavelengths
monochromator	allows selection of light of a particular wavelength
sample cell	transparent container that holds the sample
recorder	displays the absorbance measurement

18 **a** $0.10\,mol\,L^{-1}$ **b** 31%

c It is strongly absorbed by a blue solution.

19 **a** false   **b** false   **c** true   **d** false

20 When atoms absorb energy, electrons can to be promoted to various higher energy levels. Electrons can return to the ground state from these excited states by undergoing a number of transitions of different energy. Each transition results in a line of specific energy in the emission spectrum.

21 in the flame of the spectrometer

22 **a** Both involve the absorption of electromagnetic radiation of particular wavelengths characteristic of the substance under investigation. The amount of radiation absorbed is measured by a detector. The amount of light absorbed is proportional to the amount of the light-absorbing substance in the sample.

b In AAS, the sample is sprayed into a flame and light of a particular wavelength is passed through the flame. Atoms of the element being analysed absorb some of the radiation and the amount of light absorbed indicates the amount of the element present in the sample. AAS can be used to detect most metals. In UV–visible spectroscopy, two lights are used to produce radiation covering the visible and UV spectrum. The 'light' is passed through a prism to produce the desired wavelength; for UV analysis a silica sample holder is used. UV spectroscopy can be used to analyse many colourless compounds as well as coloured ones. It can give information about the structure of the substance, and can be used to determine the concentration of ions and molecules, including complex organic substances.

23 **a**

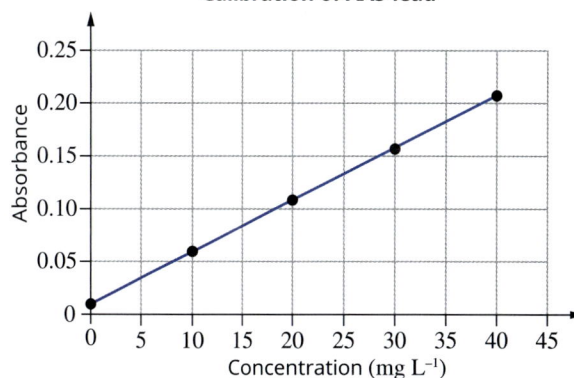

Calibration of AAS-lead

b $26\,mg\,L^{-1}$

24

Technique	Feature
conductometric titration	Conductivity is measured while one solution is added to another.
atomic emission spectroscopy	A sample is injected into a flame.
colorimetry	A filter is used to select a range of wavelengths of visible light.
UV–visible spectrometry	A monochromator selects light of an exact wavelength that is strongly absorbed by the sample.
gravimetric analysis	The mass of a precipitate is used to determine the concentration of a salt.

25 a $Al_2(SO_4)_3(aq) + 3Ba(NO_3)_2(aq) \rightarrow 3BaSO_4(s) + 2Al(NO_3)_3(aq)$
$Na_2SO_4(aq) + Ba(NO_3)_2(aq) \rightarrow BaSO_4(s) + 2NaNO_3(aq)$
  b 0.0161 mol   **c** 0.0121 mol
26 a Fe_2O_3 **b** 4.8 mol
  c No. All compounds containing sodium ions are soluble in water.
27 a green   **b** 1.0
  c The absorbance obtained from a sample needs to be plotted on a calibration curve constructed from a series of standard solutions of the $FeSCN^{2+}$ complex.
  d a hollow-cathode lamp with an iron (Fe) filament
28 a The solution should show no reaction with HCl but should form a blue precipitate with ammonia.
  b The solution should show no reaction with $AgNO_3$ but should form a white precipitate with $BaCl_2$.
  c green
  d a hollow-cathode lamp containing a copper filament
  e $Cu^{2+}(aq) + 2OH^-(aq) \rightarrow Cu(OH)_2(s)$
  f $Cu^{2+}(aq) + 4Cl^-(aq) \rightleftharpoons [CuCl_4]^{2-}(aq)$, or
$[Cu(H_2O)_6]^{2+}(aq) + 4Cl^-(aq) \rightleftharpoons [CuCl_4]^{2-}(aq) + 6H_2O(l)$
29 Student answers will vary. A possible answer is to compare the electrical conductivity of a salt solution and sugar solution to distinguish between salt and sugar. The salt solution will conduct electricity because the salt dissociates in water to release Na^+ and Cl^- ions. When sugar dissolves in water it does not dissociate into ions, so it does not conduct electricity.

Chapter 16 Analysis of organic substances

16.1 Chemical tests for functional groups

1 Test a solution of the compound by adding some solid $NaHCO_3$ to it. The presence of an acid is indicated by the formation of bubbles of CO_2. The presence of CO_2 is confirmed by bubbling the gas through limewater. An indicator will change colour in the presence of an acid. Carboxylic acids react with alcohols, forming esters, which have fruity odours.
2 Add some bromine water to the liquid, which will become colourless as it reacts with the carbon–carbon double bond in alkenes.
3 a A small piece of metallic sodium will react with an alcohol producing hydrogen gas.
  b React the alcohol with a $ZnCl_2$/concentrated HCl mixture. Primary alcohols do not react, secondary alcohols react slowly, and tertiary alcohols react quickly.
4 The bromine test indicates the presence of a carbon–carbon double bond, while the reaction with sodium hydrogen carbonate indicated the presence of the carboxyl functional group (–COOH).

16.2 Infrared spectroscopy

TY 16.2.1 C=O carbonyl group and C–H bonds; propanone (CH_3COCH_3)

1 a vibrational   **b** valence electron movement
  c valence electron movement
2 a microwave   **b** infrared   **c** radio   **d** gamma rays
3 a O–H at 3230–3550 cm^{-1} and C–O at 1000–1300 cm^{-1}
  b N–H at 3300–3500 cm^{-1} and C=O at 1680–1750 cm^{-1}
  c N–H at 3300–3500 cm^{-1}
  d O–H at 2500–3000 cm^{-1}, C=O at 1680–1750 cm^{-1} and C–O at 1000–1300 cm^{-1}
  e C=O at 1680–1750 cm^{-1} and C–O at 1000–1300 cm^{-1}
  f C=O at 1680–1750 cm^{-1}
4 The absorption bands from C–O and C–C bonds are in the fingerprint region below 1400 cm^{-1}. Many molecules contain these bonds in various functional groups, so they give few clues to the structure of a compound. The exact wavenumber of C–O and C–C absorption bands are highly specific to an individual molecule. Along with the rest of the molecule's spectrum. They can be compared to a spectral data base for positive identification.

5 a O–H (acids) at approx. 3000 cm^{-1}, C=O at approx. 1700 cm^{-1}
  b C–H at approx. 2800 cm^{-1}, C=O at approx. 1700 cm^{-1}
  c O–H (alcohols) at approx. 3300 cm^{-1}, C–H at approx. 2800 cm^{-1}
  d N–H (amines) at approx. 3400 cm^{-1}, C–H at approx. 2900 cm^{-1}, C=O at approx. 1700 cm^{-1}

16.3 Nuclear magnetic resonance spectroscopy

TY 16.3.1 2-methylpropan-2-ol   **TY 16.3.2** 1,1,2-trichloroethane

1 a The carbon atoms in the two $-CH_3$ groups attached to the second carbon atom from the left are equivalent since both are bonded to the same $-CH-$ group. The $-CH_3$ group on the right is not equivalent to these as it is attached to the $-CH_2-$ group rather than a $-CH-$ group.
  b four
2 C
3 The carbon-13 NMR spectrum of propanal has three peaks since there are three different carbon environments in the molecule. The carbon-13 NMR spectrum of propanone has two peaks since the carbon atoms in each $-CH_3$ group are equivalent and will generate peaks that have the same chemical shift. The carbon atom in the carbonyl group (C=O) generates the second peak.
4 B: 170 ppm, C: 60 ppm, D 14 ppm
5 a number of non-equivalent hydrogen environments
  b type of hydrogen environment
  c relative number of hydrogen atoms in each hydrogen environment
  d number of hydrogen atoms neighbouring a specific hydrogen environment
6 a i 2   **ii** 3   **iii** 4   **iv** 4
  b i 2   **ii** 4   **iii** 4   **iv** 3
  c triplet (3-line pattern), a quartet (4-line pattern) and a singlet (1-line pattern)
  d 3:2
7 $RCH=CHCH_3$: three hydrogen atoms, one hydrogen atom on a neighbouring atom and a typical chemical shift of 1.6–1.9 ppm
8 a three
  b $-COCH_3$: 2.1–2.7 ppm, $-CH_3$: 0.8–1.0 ppm, $-OCH_2-$: 3.3 ppm
  c A:B:C = 2:3:3
  d Using the $n + 1$ rule:
  • quartet at A indicates that there are three hydrogens attached to an adjacent atom
  • single peak at B indicates that there are no hydrogens attached to the adjacent atom
  • triplet at C indicates that there are two hydrogens attached to the adjacent atom.
  e A = $-CH_2-$ group
B = methyl group of CH_3COO-
C = methyl group of $-CH_2CH_3$
  f four

16.4 Mass spectrometry

TY 16.4.1 C_4H_{10}, butane

1 a 114 g mol^{-1} **b** 43   **c** C_8H_{18}, octane   **d** $C_6H_{13}^+$
2 $C_2H_4{}^{79}Br_2^+$, $C_2H_4{}^{79}Br^{81}Br^+$, $C_2H_4{}^{81}Br_2^+$
3 a The general formula is C_3H_7Br. A possible formula is $CH_3CH_2CH_2Br$.
  b Peak at $m/z = 122$ is due to the ^{79}Br isotope; peak at $m/z = 124$ is due to ^{81}Br isotope.
  c The two isotopes of bromine, ^{79}Br and ^{81}Br, are found in almost equal abundances so the peaks are almost equivalent in height.
  d $CH_3CH_2CH_2^+$
4 a C_4H_8O **b** C_2H_5ONH

16.5 Determination of molecular structure by spectroscopy

TY 16.5.1 methyl propanoate

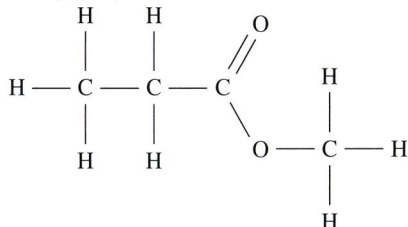

1 a IR spectroscopy   b mass spectrometry
  c carbon-13 NMR spectroscopy   d proton NMR spectroscopy
2 a $-COOH$; compound is a carboxylic acid
  b ethanoic acid (CH_3COOH)
  c There are two carbon environments in CH_3COOH, so the carbon-13 NMR will have two peaks: one corresponding to the carbon in the $-CH_3$ group, the otherto the carbon in the $-COOH$ group. There are also two hydrogen environments, so the proton NMR will also have two peaks: peaks: one corresponding to the hydrogens in the $-CH_3$ group, the other corresponding to the hydrogen in the $-COOH$ group.
3 a $m/z = 60$ b between 3230 and 3550 cm^{-1}
  c two peaks   d three peaks
4 a N–H bond in a primary amine
  b C_3H_9N
  c The three peaks in the carbon-13 NMR represent three different carbon environments. There are no equivalent carbon atoms since there are also three carbon atoms in the formula. The proton NMR spectrum indicates that there are four hydrogen environments.
  d $CH_3CH_2CH_2NH_2$, propan-1-amine
5 2,2-dimethylpropane
6 butanone ($CH_3CH_2COCH_3$)
7 propanoic acid

Chapter 16 Review

1 a Bromine water will become colourless when mixed with an alkene, indicating the presence of a C=C bond.
  b Carboxylic acids react with $NaHCO_3$ solution to form CO_2 gas, which can be detected with limewater. Carboxylic acids contain the $-COOH$ functional group.
  c The $-OH$ functional group in alcohols can be detected using a small piece of metallic sodium, which reacts slowly with alcohols to form bubbles of hydrogen gas.
2 An acidified dichromate solution turns green when added to a primary or secondary alcohol but there is no colour change when it is added to a tertiary alcohol. This means that an acidified dichromate solution can be used to test for primary and secondary alcohols but not for tertiary alcohols. This test does not distinguish between primary and secondary alcohols.
3 C–Br, C–O, C–H
4 a Both spectra contain broad, a strong absorption band at 3300 cm^{-1}, which corresponds to the expected absorbance by alcohol O–H bonds. The spectra do not contain peaks at 1700 cm^{-1} and so they cannot be carboxylic acids.
  b The two spectra have different peaks in the fingerprint region (below 1400 cm^{-1}) and so cannot be for the same molecule.
5 a broad absorption at 3230–3550 cm^{-1}
  b absorption at 3300–3500 cm^{-1} and 1680–1750 cm^{-1}
  c absorption at 1680–1750 cm^{-1}
  d absorption at 700–800 cm^{-1}
6 TMS is used as a reference in NMR spectroscopy. The location of a signal is compared to the TMS signal and called the chemical shift.
7 A: methyl ethanoate
  B: ethyl methanoate
  C: propanoic acid

8 Proton NMR spectra can give an indication of the number of different hydrogen environments. The peak splitting indicates the environments of neighbouring hydrogens. The peak areas provide information about the number of equivalent hydrogen atoms. Carbon-13 NMR spectra give an indication of the number of different carbon environments. Two peaks indicate two different carbon environments.
Because C_3H_6O is a ketone, it must be propanone. All of the hydrogens would be found in a $-CH_3$ bonded to a C=O, so there would be only one peak in the proton NMR spectrum. The chemical shift data from the carbon-13 NMR spectrum would show two peaks for the two carbon environments. One peak would correlate to a chemical shift indicating a $-CH_3$ carbon environment and another would correlate to the C=O carbon environment.

9

Compound	No. of peaks in carbon-13 NMR spectrum	No. of peaks in proton NMR spectrum
propane	2	2
CH_3CH_2Br	2	2
$CH_3COOCH_2CH_3$	4	3

10 a $C_3H_8{}^+$ b $C_2H_5{}^+$
11 C_4H_6
12 a C_4H_{10} b C_3H_6O c $C_2H_6N_2$
13 a i 98 corresponds to the molecular ion made up of two ^{35}Cl isotopes.
    ii 100 corresponds to the molecular ion with one ^{35}Cl and one ^{37}Cl isotope.
    iii 102 corresponds to the molecular ion with two ^{37}Cl isotopes
  b ^{35}Cl is the most abundant isotope, so it has the largest peak.
  c If the haloalkane is 1,1-dichloroethane, it would be reasonable to expect peaks with $m/z = 83$ and $m/z = 15$ due to the fragment ions $CH_3{}^+$ and $CH^{35}Cl_2{}^+$ that areproduced when the molecular ion CH_3CHCl_2 fragments. These peaks are not present, so the haloalkane must be 1,2-dichloroethane.
  d $^{35}ClCH_2CH^+$
14 propanal
15 2,2-dimethylpropane
16 $(CH_3)_2CHCOOH$; 2-methylpropanoic acid
17 NMR spectroscopy is used to identify types of atoms within the molecule and can give information about their chemical environment and connectivity. IR spectroscopy is usually used to identify general functional groups in a molecule but can also be used for positive identification by analysing the fingerprint region compared to a reference. Mass spectrometry gives information about the molecular mass and possible fragments within a molecule, which can lead to confirmation of a suspected structure.
18 a Proton NMR spectroscopy can be used to identify the number and types of hydrogen chemical environments, the relative numbers of hydrogen atoms in each environment and the connectivity of adjacent environments.
  b IR spectroscopy is useful for identifying functional groups. Many molecules have isolated or symmetrical hydrogen environments, which leads to simpler and less informative spectra. Carbon NMR spectroscopy can be used to identify sections of a molecule that contain no hydrogen environments. Mass spectrometry is useful for ensuring that a proposed structure is correct. In many cases mass spectrometry is more powerful for the identification of molecules when the proton NMR spectroscopy is too complex to easily analyse.
19 The computer could look for specific ion peaks that would correspond to the molecular ions of illegal substances. Itcould then confirm the presence of these compounds by identifying the fragment ions of that compound.

20 a carboxylic acids, esters, alcohols, aldehydes and ketones

b The chemical test suggests that the unknown substance is either an aldehyde or a primary or secondary alcohol, because these classes of organic compounds react with an acidified dichromate solution. The reaction of X with methanoic acid suggests that X might be an alcohol. Carboxylic acids react with alcohols to produce esters, which generally have a sweet smell. Since X did not react with bromine water it can be assumed that that there no carbon–carbon double bonds in X. The lack of reaction with $NaHCO_3$ solution indicated that X was not a carboxylic acid.

c The broad absorption centred at $3300\,cm^{-1}$ in the IR spectrum indicates that X is an alcohol. The absence of an absorption between $1680\,cm^{-1}$ and $1750\,cm^{-1}$ generated by substances that have a carbonyl carbon (C=O) indicates that X is not a carboxylic acid, ester, aldehyde or ketone.

d $C_4H_{10}O$

e $CH_3CH_2CH_2CH_2OH$, $(CH_3)_2CHCH_2OH$, $CH_3CH_2CHOHCH_3$, $(CH_3)_3COH$

f The carbon-13 NMR spectrum has three peaks indicating that there are three different carbon environments. The formula for X indicates that a molecule of X has four carbon atoms, one more than the number of distinct carbon environments. Therefore two carbon atoms must have the same environment and be equivalent. Equivalent carbon atoms generate signals that have same chemical shift.

g 2-methylpropan-1-ol

21 The ball bearings represent atoms. The periodic table shows atomic mass, which dictates the behaviour of an atom in a mass spectrometer.

Chapter 17 Chemical synthesis and design

17.1 Chemical synthesis and design

TY 17.1.1 55.8%   **TY 17.1.2** 43%   **TY 17.1.3** 55.18%

1 globalisation, labour and energy can be sourced more cheaply in other countries

2 a Port Kembla offers port facilities for transport and already has a steel industry, so it has technical expertise and a skilled workforce. The short travel time transporting sulfuric acid to the steelworks reduces costs and risks associated with transport.

b Sulfuric acid is extremely corrosive. It has to be stored and transported carefully. Leaks into local waterways would not be tolerated. SO_2 is a toxic gas. Emissions near a city would need to be controlled and limited.

3 a Manildra is close to a wheat-growing area, so the raw materials are readily available. It is also an area where many vehicles that might use bioethanol blends are operating. It would be costly to transport the wheat to Broken Hill and then the bioethanol from Broken Hill.

b Fertile land is required to grow wheat. Australia is a very dry continent with a high percentage of arid land. Farming also requires resources such as fuel and fertiliser. Too high a level of crop growth would lead to more energy being put into the farming than would be provided by the bioethanol. There are also incentives given to grow wheat for food, rather than for biofuel production.

4 a 63.89%   **b** 62.9%

5 High temperature: For endothermic reactions, the yield increases with temperature.
Low pressure: The use of low pressure favours the forward reaction, increasing the yield.
Catalyst: The surface of the nickel acts as a catalyst for this reaction, weakening the bonds in the reactant particles. More product can be produced in a given time if the rate of reaction is increased.

6 Some factors would include:
- the difference between the atom economies of each process
- the degree of hazard of the starting material
- the cost of disposing of or recycling waste materials from the first method
- the cost of managing the hazardous material from the second method
- whether the hazardous material in the second method can be degraded into a benign compound.

Chapter 17 Review

1 A

2 a Student answers will vary. Possible answers include $CuSO_4$, NaCl, CH_4, CO_2, HCl and $CaCO_3$.

b Student answers will vary. Possible answers include NaCl, $NaHCO_3$ or vinegar

c Student answers will vary. Possible answers include acids and bases at high concentrations.

d Student answers will vary. Possible answers include experiments using lead-containing solutions or strong acids.

3 a They save money by lowering energy costs. The energy produced in one part of the plant is transferred to another part instead of using external energy.

b Exothermic. Exothermic reactions release energy.

4 Student answers will vary. Possible answers include cheaper labour overseas, dwindling domestic supplies of oil, dangers of storing petrochemicals in large cities.

5 Student answers will vary. Possible answers include ammonium phosphate, which is used as a fertiliser in agriculture, and steel, which used by the construction industry.

6 a Significant price rises occurred during 2015–2016.

b Coal-fired power stations are approaching the end of their lifespan, costing money to replace; electricity infrastructure is deteriorating.

c Global chemical markets are already very competitive. Increasing electricity prices place further financial pressure on industries. Increased costs reduce profit margins, which makes the Australian chemical industry less competitive.

d The impact will vary with the industry. The amount of energy required for some processes is much greater than for others.

7 a Green-coal technology seeks to improve the efficiency of the production of electricity from coal and to lower the emissions produced.

b The coal is dried and ground before combustion. Sulfur is stripped off before combustion, or the SO_2 gas produced is stripped from the emissions before their release. The CO_2 produced is stored underground rather than released to the atmosphere.

8 a The yield will decrease as the temperature increases.

b An increase in pressure will increase the yield.

c Oxygen in the air is very cheap—an excess of oxygen helps push the reaction forwards.

d The use of a catalyst will not change the yield but equilibrium will be reached faster.

9 It can be difficult for the smelter to dispose of the SO_2 as it is a toxic emission. If it is used in the production of sulfuric acid, it solves the emissions problem and provides an inexpensive raw material for the sulfuric acid. Transport of the SO_2 is also simple.

10 a Pathway A. All atoms in the reactant end up in the product

b Pathway A: addition reaction, pathway B: substitution reaction

11 82.4%

12 a 32%   **b** 6.3%

13 Reaction 1: 32.39%
Reaction 2: 100.0%

14 36.73%   **15** 2.61 kg

16 a 3.26 g   **b** 72.1%

17 a Transport: This industry should be located on the coast near a port so that aluminium oxide can be brought in and aluminium exported.

b Energy: This industry will have high electricity use. Proximity to a cheap or renewable source of electricity would be important.

c Emissions. Emissions will not be high as the ore does not contain sulfur. It will produce CO_2. This is a greenhouse gas but not a danger to surrounding residents.

d Tailings. The plant uses concentrated Al_2O_3 so the volume of tailings will not be high.

e Work force. A large refinery requires access to a large workforce of skilled operators. It would be helpful to be located near a city or large town.

f Economics. The global price of aluminium fluctuates significantly. It is difficult to predict the viability of the plant.

g Safety. This is an industry where care would need to be taken. Large volumes of very hot material are used, as well as large and heavy machinery.

18 a If the sulfur is not removed, toxic SO_2 will be produced during the production of ammonia.

b The reaction is exothermic so a relatively low temperature should be used. High pressure can be used as the number of product particles is less than the number of reactant particles. The removal of ammonia from the reaction will also push the reaction in the forward direction.

c mainly as a fertiliser; can also be used for explosives

d Nitrogen can be obtained from the air, so any site will work. Hydrogen is obtained from methane. Methane would need to be piped or shipped from another state of Australia.

e It is close to a port, has a large population from which to draw a labour force, and is relatively close to conventional power supplies.

f The atom economy will be 100%, because NH_3 is the only product.

19 a safer, or no solvents

b increasing energy efficiency

c atom economy, use of solvents

d use of renewable raw materials

20 • There are reactants and products.
• Energy is required.
• Not all reactant atoms end up in the products.
• The reactants are changed in the reaction.
• There are optimum conditions for the process.
• Waste is created.

Module 8 Review

Multiple choice

1 B	**2** C	**3** C	**4** B
5 D	**6** B	**7** C	**8** D
9 A	**10** B	**11** D	**12** C
13 A	**14** C	**15** B	**16** A
17 B	**18** D	**19** D	**20** C

Short answer

1 a positive   **b** cation is Pb^{2+}

c $Pb^{2+}(aq) + 2Cl^-(aq) \rightarrow PbCl_2(s)$

d a nitrate or an acetate

2 a a complex ion or (transition) metal complex

b $[Cu(H_2O)_6]^{2+}$

c $Cu^{2+}(aq) + 6H_2O(l) \rightarrow [Cu(H_2O)_6]^{2+}(aq)$

d a characteristic blue colour

e ligand

3 a $Pb(NO_3)_2(aq) + 2KCl(aq) \rightarrow PbCl_2(s) + 2KNO_3(aq)$

b $Pb^{2+}(aq) + 2Cl^-(aq) \rightarrow PbCl_2(s)$

c i lead(II) chloride

ii potassium ions and nitrate ions

d i 0.00951 mol   **ii** 2.64 g

4 a 0.592 mol L^{-1} **b** 0.370 mol L^{-1}

c i $Pb^{2+}(aq) + 2I^-(aq) \rightarrow PbI_2(s)$ **ii** 7.51 g

5 a $Fe^{3+}(aq) + 3OH^-(aq) \rightarrow Fe(OH)_3(s)$

b $2Fe(OH)_3(s) \rightarrow Fe_2O_3(s) + 3H_2O(g)$

c i 0.7659 g   **ii** 0.0105 mol L^{-1}

6 a A sample of a solution containing Ni^{2+} ions is scanned in a UV–visible spectrophotometer to determine its absorbance across a range of wavelengths. The wavelength that gives the highest absorbance is chosen.

b Prepare a series of standard solutions containing nickel(II) ions. Measure their absorbance at an appropriate wavelength and plot a calibration curve. Measure the absorbance of the unknown solution and determine its concentration from the calibration curve.

7 a 0.067%   **b** 6.7×10^2 ppm

8 a radiowaves (radio frequencies)

b nuclear magnetic dipoles switching between low and high energy states, corresponding to alignment with the external magnetic field

c It is used as an internal standard for determination of chemical shifts.

d i B. High chemical shift is characteristic of an aldehyde and the quartet results from three adjacent H atoms.

ii D. Singlet suggests no neighbouring H atoms. Chemical shift is consistent with an adjacent C=O group.

iii E. Quartet shows three neighbouring H atoms. Moderately high chemical shift is consistent with an adjacent O atom.

iv C. Singlet because all H atoms in the molecule are equivalent so no splitting is observed. Chemical shift is consistent with an adjacent halogen (Cl) atom.

v F. Triplet suggests two neighbouring H atoms, and low chemical shift is consistent with being either carbon or hydrogen.

vi A. Doublet suggests one neighbouring H atom and chemical shift is consistent with an adjacent C=O group.

9 a $C_6H_{13}NO_2$ **b** 131

c

i CH_3^+ **ii** $C_2H_5^+$ **iii** $C_4H_9^+$

d i The base peak is the strongest signal in the mass spectrum; i.e. the most abundant fragment ion.

ii 131 – 86 = 45 mass units lost, likely to be COOH

10 a Spectrum A: about 3000 cm^{-1} is C–H, about 1700 cm^{-1} is C=O
Spectrum B: about 3000 cm^{-1} is C–H, about 3400 cm^{-1} is O–H (alcohol)

b Spectrum A is propanone; spectrum B is propan-2-ol.

c All six hydrogens are in the same bonding environment and are 'equivalent'.

d The two terminal carbon atoms are in identical environments and hence absorb and emit the same frequency.

e Proton NMR: three peaks, as there are three different H environments (–CH$_3$, –CHOH– and –CHOH–)
Carbon-13 NMR: two peaks, as there are two different C environments (–CH$_3$, –CHOH–)

f i 58

ii It provides the relative molecular mass from which the molecular formula can be deduced.

iii $[CH_3CO]^+$

11 a The lack of a precipitate only indicates that Ag^+ and Pb^{2+} are not present. Fe^{3+} (as well as a number of other cations) could be present.

b $[Fe(H_2O)_3(OH)_3]$

c A hollow-cathode lamp containing iron would need to be used in the spectrometer. A series of standard solutions would need to be prepared and their absorbance measured to produce a calibration curve. The absorbance of the unknown solution could then be tested measured. Use the calibration curve to determine the concentration of Fe^{3+}.

d i $Fe^{3+}(aq) + SCN^-(aq) \rightleftharpoons FeSCN^{2+}(aq)$ **ii** about 480 nm

12 a $NaBr(aq) + AgNO_3(aq) \rightarrow AgBr(s) + NaNO_3(aq)$

b A precipitate of AgBr forms, so the total number of metal ions in the solution decreases, and the electrical conductivity decreases.

c After the equivalence point, no further precipitate will form. All extra metal ions added will increase the total number of metal ions in the solution, increasing the conductivity.

d $0.15\,mol\,L^{-1}$

13 a The deposit is 2.5% lithium, and the remaining 97.5% of other materials will generally be waste materials. It is usually not viable to transport so much waste material along with the lithium-containing ore to another site for processing.

b Advantage: disposal of waste affects fewer people. Disadvantages: transport facilities would need to be developed, as would accommodation and infrastructure.

c Melting ionic solids requires considerable energy. Every drop in the temperature required represents an energy and cost saving.

d There are unlikely to be the skilled workers required at the remote location, and it may be difficult to attract workers to this location.

e the world price of lithium, the price of electricity or the world demand for lithium

f Waste and run-off would need to be prevented from entering the Darling River. The large area where the mine is would need to be revegetated. Emissions from the plant may have to be controlled.

14 a i

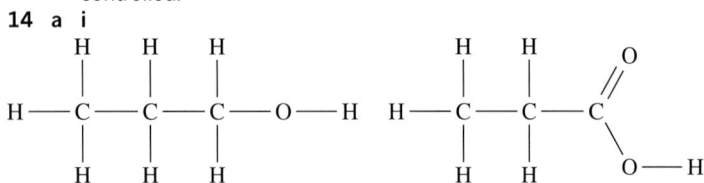

ii $CH_3CH_3COOH(aq) + NaHCO_3(aq) \rightarrow NaCH_3CH_3COO(aq) + CO_2(g) + H_2O(l)$

iii no; a secondary alcohol will not form a carboxylic acid.

b i

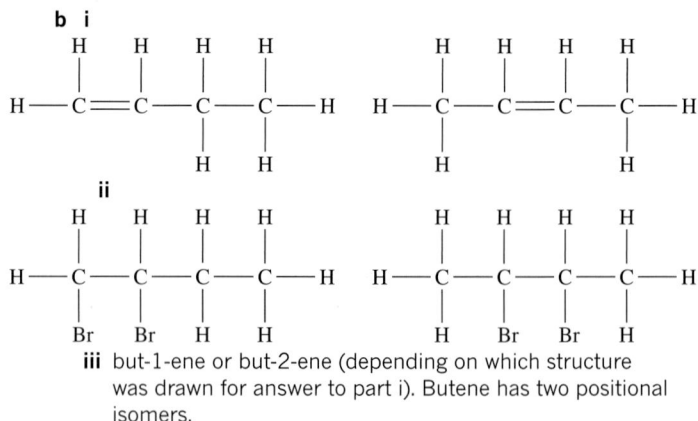

ii

iii but-1-ene or but-2-ene (depending on which structure was drawn for answer to part i). Butene has two positional isomers.

c $2CH_3OH(l) + 2Na(s) \rightarrow 2CH_3ONa(l) + H_2(g)$

15 a i

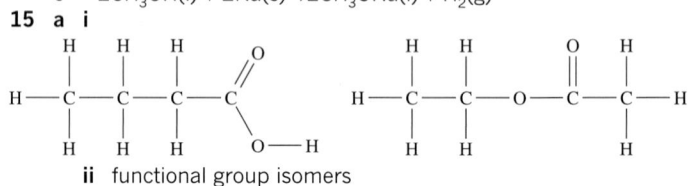

ii functional group isomers

b i 88

ii 29 (other answers are possible)

c Broad band around $2500-3300\,cm^{-1}$. This corresponds to an O–H (acid) bond in butanoic acid but not in ethyl ethanoate.

d i butanoic acid = 4; ethyl ethanoate = 3

ii butanoic acid = triplet, sextet (not exactly symmetrical), triplet and singlet; ethyl ethanoate = triplet, quartet and singlet

iii butanoic acid = 4, ethyl ethanoate = 4

Glossary

A

absorbance A measure of the capacity of a substance to absorb light of a specified wavelength.

absorption band The inverted peaks in an infrared spectrum that represent the frequencies of infrared radiation absorbed by specific bonds.

accuracy How close a measured value of a quantity is to the true or accepted value of the quantity. A measurement that is very close to the accepted value is described as accurate. Compare with *precision*.

acid A substance capable of donating a hydrogen ion (proton).

acid–base reaction A reaction in which one substance, an acid, donates a hydrogen ion (proton) to another substance, a base.

acid–base titration The process of finding the concentration of an acid or base by neutralising the acid or base under investigation with an acid or base of known concentration.

acid dissociation constant The equilibrium constant that is a measure of the dissociation, or strength, of an acid in aqueous solution; symbol K_a. Also known as acidity constant.

acidic buffer solution An aqueous solution in which the concentration of hydronium ions (H_3O^+) is greater than the concentration of hydroxide ions (OH^-). At 25°C, pH < 7.

acidic proton A proton bonded to an electronegative element (oxygen, nitrogen of fluorine) that is donated to a base during an acid–base reaction.

acidic solution An aqueous solution in which the concentration of hydronium ions (H_3O^+) is greater that the concentration of hydroxide ions (OH^-). At 25°C, the pH of an acidic solution is less than 7.

acidity The concentration of H_3O^+ ions in an aqueous solution. Acidity is measured using the pH scale.

acidity constant The equilibrium constant that is a measure of the dissociation, or strength, of an acid in aqueous solution; symbol Ka. Also known as acid dissociation constant.

activation energy The minimum energy required by reactants for a reaction to occur; symbol E_a. This energy is needed to break the bonds between atoms in the reactants, enabling products to form.

actual yield The mass of product actually obtained during a chemical reaction. This will be less than or equal to the theoretical yield.

addition polymer See *addition polymerisation*.

addition polymerisation The formation of a polymer by an addition reaction in which many unsaturated monomers bond together by a rearrangement of C=C double bonds without the loss of any atom or molecule.

addition reaction A reaction in which a molecule binds to an unsaturated hydrocarbon, forming a single carbon–carbon bond. In this process two reactant molecules form one product.

affiliation A connection or association with an organisation.

alcohol An organic compound containing the hydroxyl (–OH) functional group. The names of all alcohols have the suffix '-ol'.

aldehyde A homologous series of organic molecules that contain the carbonyl functional group, C=O, bonded to a hydrogen on one end of the molecule. Aldehydes can be recognised by the presence of a –CHO group at one end of a compound's condensed structural formula.

aliquot A measured volume of liquid delivered by a pipette.

alkali A soluble base, or a solution of a soluble base.

alkane A saturated hydrocarbon with the general formula C_nH_{2n+2}.

alkene An unsaturated hydrocarbon containing one carbon–carbon double bond; general formula C_nH_{2n}.

alkyl group A hydrocarbon group with one less hydrogen atom than an alkane; general formula C_nH_{2n+1}, e.g. methyl $(–CH_3)$.

alkyne An unsaturated hydrocarbon containing one carbon–carbon triple bond; general formula C_nH_{2n-2}.

amide A compound containing the –CONH– functional group. This group forms the link between amino acids in proteins, where it is also called a peptide link.

amide functional group A functional group in which a nitrogen atom is attached to a carbonyl group, with the remaining bonds on the nitrogen taken by hydrogen atoms (in simple or primary amides, $–CONH_2$). alkyl or aryl groups (in secondary or substituted amides, –CONHR), or carbon atoms (in tertiary amides, $–CONC_2$).

amine A homologous series of organic molecules that contain the amino functional group.

amino functional group A functional group consisting of a nitrogen atom covalently bonded to two hydrogen atoms, $–NH_2$.

amorphous region A region in a polymer in which molecules are tangled in a random arrangement.

amphiprotic The ability to act as both an acid (proton donor) and a base (proton acceptor).

analyte The chemical substance that is of interest in a chemical analysis.

anhydrous Containing no water.

aqueous The solution resulting when a chemical species has been dissolved in water. This is shown by writing '(aq)' after the name or symbol of the chemical.

Arrhenius theory The theory proposed by Svante Arrhenius that acids are substances that produce H^+ ions in water and bases are substances that produce OH^- ions in water. The Arrhenius theory can be used for reactions in water.

artesian basin An underground area of porous rock lying above rock that is not permeable to water. Rain seeps into the porous rock and is trapped underground.

atom economy A method of tracking the atoms in a reaction equation to calculate the mass of the atoms of reactants actually used to form products as a percentage of the total mass of the reactants.

atomic absorption spectroscopy (AAS) An analytical method that uses light absorption to measure the concentration of a metal in a sample.

atomic emission spectroscopy (AES) An analytical method that uses the emission of radiation from a heated sample to determine the concentration of a solution.

average titre The average of concordant titres.

B

bar graph A graph in which values or frequencies of data are shown as bars.

base A substance capable of accepting a hydrogen ion (proton).

base dissociation constant The equilibrium constant that is a measure of the dissociation, or strength, of a base in aqueous solution; symbol Kb. Also known as base constant.

base peak The peak in a mass spectrum that has the highest intensity. It is assigned an intensity of 100.

basic buffer solution An aqueous solution in which the concentration of hydronium ions (H_3O^+) is less than the concentration of hydroxide ions (OH^-). At 25°C, pH > 7.

basic solution An aqueous solution in which the concentration of hydronium ions (H_3O^+) is less than the concentration of hydroxide ions (OH^-). For a basic solution at 25°C, pH > 7.

basicity the concentration of OH^- ions in an aqueous solution. Basicity is measured using the pH scale.

Beer–Lambert law The absorbance of light by a substance can be calculated using the formula $A = \varepsilon lc$, where c is the molar concentration in $mol\,L^{-1}$, l is the sample cell width in cm, and ε is the molar absorption coefficient in $cm^{-1}\,mol^{-1}\,L$.

bias Measured values that are consistently in one direction (higher or lower) from the actual value.

biochemical fuel See *biofuel*

biodegradable Capable of being decomposed by bacteria, fungi or other organisms.

biodiesel A fuel derived from plant or animal matter, consisting of long-chain alkyl esters. Biodiesel is typically made by reacting triglycerides with an alcohol.

bioethanol Ethanol produced by fermenting the sugar and starch components of plants using yeast.

biofuel A fuel that can be produced from crops or other organic material. Examples of biofuels are ethanol from the fermentation of sugars, methane from digestion in animals, and biogas from plant and animal wastes.

biogas A mixture of gases produced by the decomposition of organic matter in the absence of oxygen.

bond energy The amount of energy required to break a covalent bond.

bond strength The strength of a covalent bond. In general, higher energy bonds have a greater bond strength.

bore water Water brought to the surface by drilling into an underground water-bearing region of porous rock.

Brønsted–Lowry theory A theory that defines an acid as a proton (hydrogen ion) donor and a base as a proton acceptor. For example, in the reaction $HCl(g) + H_2O(l) \rightarrow H_3O^+(aq) + Cl^-(aq)$, HCl is the proton donor and is therefore an acid, and H_2O is a proton acceptor and is therefore a base.

buffer capacity A measure of the ability of a buffer solution to resist a change in pH when an acid or a base is added.

buffer solution A solution that resists a change in pH when small quantities of an acid or base are added. Buffers are composed of a weak acid and its conjugate weak base, or a weak base and its conjugate weak acid.

burette A graduated glass tube with a tap at one end, used for delivering accurate volumes of liquids.

C

calibration curve A plot of data involving two variables that is used to determine the values for one of the variables.

calorimetry The experimental method by which the heat energy released by the combustion of a fuel or a food, or another chemical reaction such as a neutralisation reaction, is measured.

carbon neutral A process that absorbs the same amount of carbon that it generates. The carbon dioxide absorbed from the atmosphere by a carbon neutral process compensates for the carbon dioxide produced by the process.

carbon-13 NMR spectroscopy A type of nuclear magnetic resonance spectroscopy that investigates the ^{13}C nucleus. It is used to determine the chemical environment of carbon atoms in compounds. Also called carbon NMR and ^{13}C NMR spectroscopy.

carbonyl functional group A functional group that consists of a carbon atom double-bonded to an oxygen atom, $-CO-$. This group is present in aldehydes, ketones, carboxylic acids, amides and esters.

carboxyl functional group A functional group that consists of a hydroxyl group attached to the carbon of a carbonyl group, $-COOH$. This group is present in carboxylic acids.

carboxylic acid A homologous series of organic molecules that contain the carboxyl functional group ($-COOH$).

catalyst A substance that increases the rate of a reaction but is not consumed in the reaction. A catalyst enables the reaction to proceed along a pathway with a lower activation energy.

chain isomer An isomer of an organic molecule resulting from a branching of the hydrocarbon chain.

chemical shift The position of a signal in the nuclear magnetic resonance (NMR) spectrum, relative to the signal produced by the tetramethylsilane (TMS) standard. It is measured in parts per million (ppm).

closed system A system in which only energy is exchanged with the surroundings.

coal seam gas Natural gas trapped by pressure in a coal seam.

collision theory A theoretical model that accounts for the rates of chemical reactions in terms of collisions between particles occurring during a chemical reaction.

colorimeter An instrument that measures the absorbance of a selected colour of light by a sample solution.

colorimetry a technique that measures the absorbance of a selected colour of light by a sample solution.

combustion See *combustion reaction*

combustion reaction A rapid reaction with oxygen accompanied by the release of large amounts of heat; also called burning.

common ion effect a reduction in solubility of a sparingly soluble salt caused by the presence of a common ion

competing equilibria Equilibria that have a common reactant; each equilibrium can be regarded as competing for this reactant. The equilibrium with the larger equilibrium constant has a significant effect on the position of equilibrium of the other reaction.

complementary colours Pairs of colours that are often described as 'opposites'. When combined with each other, these colours 'cancel' each other out to form a greyscale colour such as white or black.

complex ion An ion with a metal ion at its centre and other ions or molecules surrounding it. The anions or molecules surrounding the metal ion are called ligands.

complexation The formation of a complex when ligands surround and bond with a central metal ion.

concentrated See *concentrated solution*

concentrated solution A solution that has a high ratio of solute to solvent.

concentration A measure of how much solute is dissolved in a specified volume of solution; usually measured in $\mu g\,L^{-1}$, $mg\,L^{-1}$ or $g\,L^{-1}$.

concentration fraction The ratio of concentrations of products to reactants in a reversible reaction, as expressed in the equilibrium law. It can also be called the reaction quotient.

concordant titre Referring to a set of titres that are within a narrow range, e.g. a range of 0.10 mL from smallest to largest titre.

condensation polymer A polymer formed by a condensation reaction, involving the elimination of a small molecule (often water) when monomers bond together. The monomers have functional groups at both ends of the molecule.

condensation polymerisation The formation of a polymer by condensation reactions.

condensation reaction A reaction in which two molecules link together by eliminating a small molecule such as water.

condensed structural formula A simple representation of the structural formula of an organic molecule. A condensed structural formula shows the atoms connected to each carbon atom, but not all the bonds, e.g. $CH_3CH_2CH_3$.

conductivity A measure of the ability of a solution to conduct electricity.

conductivity curve A graph showing the change in conductivity during a titration.

conductivity meter An instrument used to measure conductivity.

conductometric titration A titration in which the conductance of the solution is monitored in order to determine the equivalence point.

conjugate acid An acid that contains one more hydrogen ion (proton) than a base, e.g. HCl is the conjugate acid of Cl^-.

conjugate acid–base pair An acid and its conjugate base. The conjugate base contains one less hydrogen ion (proton) than the acid.

conjugate base The conjugate base of an acid contains one less hydrogen ion (proton) than the acid, e.g. Cl^- is the conjugate base of HCl.

continuous variable A quantitative variable that can have any value within a range, e.g. time, pH, concentration.

controlled variable A variable that is kept constant during an investigation.

cracker Apparatus used to convert saturated carbon–carbon bonds to double or triple bonds.

credible Referring to information from an authoritative source such as a peer-reviewed journal or a recognised an expert in the field.

cross-link A covalent bond between different chains of atoms in a polymer or other complex molecule.

crystalline region A region where polymer molecules line up parallel to each other and pack closely together.

D

data analysis The analysis of research findings to look for patterns or trends, usually using mathematical methods.

dehydration reaction a reaction that removes water from the reacting molecule.

dependent variable The variable that is measured or observed to determine the effect of changes in the independent variable.

dilute See *dilute solution*.

dilute solution A solution that has a relatively low ratio of solute to solvent.

dilution factor The ratio of the final volume to the aliquot volume.

dilution The addition of a solvent to a solution to reduce its concentration.

dimer A molecule composed of two identical subunits that may be molecules in their own right, joined by strong intermolecular forces, such as hydrogen bonds.

dipole The separation of positive and negative charges in a molecule.

dipole–dipole attraction An intermolecular force between polar molecules in which the partially positively charged end of one molecule is attracted to the partially negatively charged end of another molecule.

diprotic acid An acid that can dissociate in water to form two H_3O^+ ions.

discrete variable A variable that can have only certain values. Examples are valence number, number of samples, and quantum energy level.

dispersion force The force of attraction between molecules caused by temporary dipoles induced in the molecules. The temporary dipoles are the result of random fluctuations in the electron density.

dissociate Break up.

dissociation The process in which molecules or ionic compounds separate into smaller particles such as atoms or ions. Examples of dissociation include the dissolution of NaCl in water, forming $Na^+(aq)$ and $Cl^-(aq)$ ions, and the reaction of HCl gas with water, forming $H^+(aq)$ and $Cl^-(aq)$.

dissociation constant A measure of the extent of dissociation of a compound, particularly in relation to an acid or base.

distillation The separation of liquids as a result of selective evaporation.

dynamic equilibrium The point in a chemical reaction when the rate of the forward reaction is equal to the rate of the reverse reaction.

E

elastomer A rubbery material, composed of long molecules, that is capable of recovering its original shape after being stretched.

electrical conductivity A measure of the degree to which a specified material or solution conducts electricity. The unit is usually microsiemens per centimetre ($\mu S\,cm^{-1}$).

electromagnetic radiation A form of energy consisting of sinusoidally oscillating electric and magnetic waves at right-angles to each other. It includes visible light, radio waves and X-rays.

electromagnetic spectrum The range of frequencies over which electromagnetic radiation is propagated, from extremely low frequencies of about 1 Hz to above 10^{28} Hz.

electronegative Referring to an atom that can attract electrons in a covalent bond towards itself.

electronic configuration The arrangement of electrons in an atom according to the shell model of the atom, in which electrons are arranged in layers (shells) around the nucleus.

elimination reaction A type of reaction where an atom or atoms are removed from the molecule. An example is a dehydration reaction.

emission spectrum A spectrum produced when an element is excited by heat or radiation. It appears as distinct lines characteristic of the element.

emulsion A suspension of small droplets of one liquid in another.

end point A point in a titration at which the indicator changes colour, usually marking the completion of the reaction.

endothermic A reaction that absorbs energy from the surroundings; ΔH is positive.

energy content The amount of energy per gram or per $100\,g$, or per mole (if a nutrient is a pure substance), that a food or fuel can supply. Units may be $kJ\,g^{-1}$, $kJ/100\,g$ or $kJ\,mol^{-1}$.

energy profile diagram A diagram that shows the potential energy changes during the course of a reaction.

enhanced greenhouse effect An increase in the temperature of Earth's surface because of an increased concentration of greenhouse gases, as a result of human activities.

enthalpy change The difference in the total enthalpy of the products and the total enthalpy of the reactants; symbol ΔH. Also known as heat of reaction.

enthalpy of neutralisation The enthalpy of neutralisation is the change in enthalpy that occurs when an acid and a base undergo a neutralisation reaction to form one mole of water.

entropy A measure of the number of possible arrangements in a thermodynamic system. Rates of the forward and reverse reactions are equal.

equilibrium The point in a chemical reaction when the quantities of reactants and products are constant.

equilibrium constant The value of the concentration fraction when equilibrium is reached; symbol K_{eq}.

equilibrium law An expression for the equilibrium of a chemical reaction. For the reaction:
$aW + bX \rightleftharpoons cY + dZ$ the equilibrium law is
$K_C = \frac{[Y]^c[Z]^d}{[W]^a[X]^b}$, where K_c is a constant at a particular temperature.

equilibrium yield The amount of product obtained when a chemical reaction reaches equilibrium.

equimolar An equal number of moles of subtances.

equivalence point The point in a titration at which the reactants have reacted in their expected mole ratios.

equivalent A term used in NMR spectroscopy to describe atoms that require the same amount of energy to change spin state, and hence have the same chemical shift.

ester A molecule that contains the ester functional group (–COO–), which is made up of a carbonyl group, with another oxygen atom bonded to it. This functional group is not found on the end carbon of a molecule.

ester functional group The functional group that is the result of the reaction between an alcohol and a carboxylic acid. It consists of a carbonyl group bonded to an oxygen atom bonded to another carbon atom, –COO–.

esterification reaction The chemical reaction between an alcohol and a carboxylic acid to form an ester as the main product.

eutrophication A process by which pollution from sources such as chemical fertiliser or sewage cause the over-enrichment of water by nutrients. This causes the overgrowth and decay of plants, de-oxygenation of water and the death of organisms.

excited electron An electron that has absorbed a particular quantity of energy and moved from its ground state to a higher energy level. An atom is said to be excited when an electron is not in the lowest electron energy level possible (i.e. not in the ground state).

exothermic Releasing energy into the surroundings. In an exothermic reaction, ΔH is negative.

expertise Expert knowledge or skills in a field.

extent of reaction The relative amounts of products compared with reactants. The extent of a reaction is indicated by the value of the equilibrium constant.

F

fermentation The breakdown of sugar solutions by the action of enzymes in yeasts, producing ethanol and carbon dioxide. The chemical equation for the fermentation of glucose is:
$C_6H_{12}O_2(aq) \rightarrow 2CH_3CH_2OH(aq) + 2CO_2(g)$

fingerprint region The part of the infrared (IR) spectrum below $1400\,cm^{-1}$ that is unique to a particular molecule.

flame test A test used to detect the presence of or identify elements. The sample is burned and the emission spectrum analysed.

foam A polymer with a very low density because of the inclusion of small gas bubbles.

fossil fuel A hydrocarbon fuel formed by the decomposition of plant and animal material over millions of years. Fossil fuels including coal, oil and natural gas.

fracking The process of injecting sand, water or chemicals at high pressure into coal or rock to release trapped natural gas.

fractional distillation A method of separating a mixture of hydrocarbons, such as crude oil, based on their different boiling points.

fragmentation See *fragmentation pattern*

fragmentation pattern The characteristic graph shape that represents the break-up of a molecular ion into a number of smaller parts in mass spectrometry.

fuel A substance with stored energy that can be released relatively easily to generate heat or power. The stored energy can be in the form of chemical energy (e.g. methane) or nuclear energy (e.g. uranium).

functional group An atom or group of atoms in an organic molecule that largely determine the molecule's properties and reactions, e.g. –OH, –COOH.

functional group isomer An isomer that arises from having different functional groups.

G

Gibbs free energy A measure of the effects of enthalpy and entropy on the rate of a reaction, i.e. whether it is spontaneous or not.

gravimetric analysis A method for determining the amount of solute in a solution, based on the mass of the residue after evaporating the solvent.

green chemistry Principles set out a framework for evaluating the environmental impacts of a chemical process.

greenhouse effect The process by which heat energy radiated from Earth's surface is absorbed and re-radiated by gases in the atmosphere. The greenhouse effect maintains the temperature of the Earth's surface within a range suitable for life.

greenhouse gas A gas that is able to absorb and re-radiate heat radiation. These gases contribute to the greenhouse effect. The main greenhouse gases are carbon dioxide, methane and water vapour.

ground state The state of an atom in which the electrons occupy the lowest possible energy levels.

groundwater Water that lies below the land surface in soil or porous rock.

H

halo functional group A functional group that consists of a halogen atom bonded to the carbon chain. The halo functional groups are named fluoro-, chloro-, bromo- and iodo-.

haloalkane A molecule derived from an alkane, containing at least the one halogen functional group.

halogen An element in Group 17 of the periodic table: fluorine, chlorine, bromine, iodine, astatine and the synthetic element tennessine.

hard water Water with a high metal ion concentration, and thus requiring a lot of soap to obtain a lather or froth.

hardness A measure of the amount of metal ions (mainly calcium and magnesium) in water; the more minerals in the water, the harder the water. This 'hardness' means it is hard to get a lather using soap or detergents, because the metal ions react strongly with the negatively charged ions in soap molecules to form insoluble compounds. This effectively removes soap from the solution, so more soap is needed to achieve a lather.

heat of reaction The exchange of heat between a system and its surroundings during a chemical reaction under constant pressure; symbol ΔH. Also known as enthalpy change.

heavy metal A metal with high density; usually used to describe a metal that poses a threat to health.

heterogeneous See *heterogeneous reaction*

heterogeneous reaction A chemical reaction in which at least two of the species are in different state or phase.

high-density polyethene (HDPE) A form of the polymer polyethene that is formed from polymer chains with very few, short branches. Because of this structure, the polymer chains are packed closely together, making the polymer dense. HDPE can have a percentage crystallinity as high as 95% and has excellent mechanical properties. HDPE is used to make pipes, buckets, and food containers such as milk bottles.

homogeneous See *homogeneous reaction*

homogeneous reaction A chemical reaction in which all the species are in the same state or phase.

homologous series A series of organic compounds in which each member of the group differs from the previous member by a $-CH_2$ unit. Examples are alkanes, alkenes and alcohols.

hydrated An ion surrounded by water molecules. Hydrated ions can be found in aqueous solutions or crystalline solids.

hydration reaction A reaction that involves water as a reactant.

hydrocarbon A compound that contains only carbon and hydrogen atoms. There are four types of hydrocarbons: alkanes, alkenes, alkynes and alkenynes.

hydrogen bond A type of intermolecular, dipole–dipole force where a hydrogen atom is covalently bonded to a highly electronegative atom such as oxygen, nitrogen or fluorine. Because of the disparity of electronegativity values between the atoms involved, the hydrogen develops a partial positive charge and bonds to lone pairs of electrons on neighbouring atoms of oxygen, nitrogen or fluorine.

hydrogen halide Diatomic molecules consisting of a hydrogen atom and a halogen atom joined by a covalent bond. HF, HCl, HBr, HI and HAt are hydrogen halides.

hydrogenation reaction A reaction of alkenes with hydrogen gas to make alkanes. It is a type of addition reaction and it happens in the presence of a catalyst.

hydrolysis A reaction involving the breaking of a bond in a molecule using water as a reactant. Two smaller molecules are usually formed.

hydronium ion The H_3O^+ ion.

hydroxide ion The OH^- ion.

hydroxyl functional group A functional group that consists of an oxygen atom covalently bonded to a hydrogen atom, $-OH$. It is the functional group that defines alcohols.

hypothesis A tentative explanation for an observation that is based on evidence and prior knowledge. A hypothesis must be testable and falsifiable and define a proposed relationship between two variables.

I

ICE table See *reaction table*.

immiscible Unable to mix with or dissolve in another liquid; for example, oil is immiscible in water.

independent variable The variable that is changed in an experiment in order to determine the effect on the dependent variable.

indicator A substance that changes colour when it comes into contact with a solution with a particular pH range. Examples are red and blue litmus paper, phenophthalein, methyl orange and bromothymol blue.

infrared (IR) spectroscopy An analytical technique that uses the infrared part of the electromagnetic spectrum to investigate the vibrational energy of molecular bonds.

inquiry question A specific question that can be answered through an investigation.

insoluble Unable to dissociate in water.

interfacial polymerisation A polymerisation process in which monomers are dissolved in different liquids of different polarities that do not mix. The polymer forms at the interface of the different liquids.

ion–dipole attraction The attraction that forms between dissociated ions and polar water molecules when an ionic solid dissolves in water.

ionic product The mathematical product of the concentration of ions of a sparingly soluble salt present in a solution. Also called the ionisation constant.

ionic product of water The equilibrium constant (symbol K_w) equal to the product of the concentration of hydronium and hydroxide ions in pure water, i.e. $K_w = [H_3O^+][OH^-]$. At 25°C, $K_w = 1.0 \times 10^{-14}$.

ionisation constant of water See *ionic product of water*

ionise The reaction of a molecular substance with a solvent to form ions in solution. When some polar molecules dissolve in water they ionise to form a hydronium ion, e.g.: $HCl(g) + H_2O(l) \rightarrow H_3O^+(aq) + Cl^-(aq)$.

irreversible reaction A reaction in which significant reaction can occur in one direction only.

isomer Molecules that have the same molecular formula but a different arrangement of atoms.

isotope Any one of two or more forms of the same element that contain equal numbers of protons but different numbers of neutrons in their nuclei. For example, ^{12}C and ^{13}C are isotopes of carbon.

IUPAC nomenclature A set of rules for naming organic molecules. It is usually systematic and gives the number of carbon atoms and the location and type of functional groups present.

K

ketone A homologous series of organic molecules that contains the carbonyl functional group (C=O) within the carbon chain.

L

Le Châtelier's principle If an equilibrium system is subjected to a change, the system will adjust itself to partially oppose the effect of the change.

ligand Negative ion or polar molecule that can form bonds with a transition metal ion.

line spectrum See *emission spectrum*.

liquefied petroleum gas A mixture of propane and butane that is separated from natural gas or crude oil. It is stored under pressure to liquefy the propane and butane.

literature review A summary of current published knowledge in a particular area.

low-density polyethene (LDPE) A form of the polymer polyethene that has many short-chain and long-chain branches. This means the polymer chains do not pack together closely in the crystal structure and therefore have weaker intermolecular forces. As a result, LDPE has a lower tensile strength and increased ductility in comparison to other polythene polymers.

M

mass spectrometer An instrument designed to measure the mass-to-charge ratio, m/z, of particles.

mass spectrometry An analytical technique that uses the mass-to-charge ratio (m/z) of atoms, molecules and fragments of molecules to identify substances.

mass spectroscopy See *mass spectrometry*

mass spectrum A graph of data produced from a mass spectrometer which shows the abundance or relative intensity of each particle, and their mass-to-charge, m/z, ratios.

mean The sum of all the values in a data set divided by the number of values in the data set. It is commonly called the average of a set of numbers.

median The middle value of an ordered data set. To calculate the median, arrange the data set in ascending order, then count the number of data values. If the number of values is odd, select the middle value. If the number of values is even, select the two middle values, add them together and divide by 2.

metal complex A central metal atom surrounded by molecules or ions.

micelle A sphere-shaped arrangement of many molecules that has a polar head and a long non-polar chain.

mineral Any naturally occurring inorganic substance that is solid and can be represented by a chemical formula, e.g. quartz.

miscible Liquids that can be mixed in any ratio to form a homogeneous solution. Compare with *immiscible*.

mistake An avoidable error made by a person doing an investigation or experiment.

mode The most frequent value in a data set. Arrange the data set in ascending order, then count the number of each data value.

model A description that scientists use to represent the important features of what they are trying to describe.

molar absorption coefficient A measure of how strongly a substance absorbs light of a particular wavelength. It is given a symbol ε. Also known as *molar absorptivity*.

molar absorptivity See *molar absorption coefficient*

molar solubility the number of moles of a salt that will dissolve per litre of water to form a saturated solution.

molarity The amount of solute, in moles, dissolved in 1 L of solution ($mol\,L^{-1}$).

molecular formula A formula for a compound that gives the actual number and type of atoms present in a molecule. It may be the same as or different from the empirical formula.

molecular ion A whole molecule with an overall positive or negative charge. In this course positively charged molecular ions are investigated.

molecular ion peak A peak in a mass spectrum that is caused by the presence of a whole molecule ion. The peak with the greatest m/z value is likely to be due to the molecular ion in most cases.

monochromator An instrument that transmits a narrow band of wavelengths of light or other radiation.

monomer A small molecule that can react to form long chains of repeating units, called polymers.

monoprotic acid An acid molecule that generates only one hydronium ion when ionised in water.

N

natural gas A fossil fuel composed of a mixture of hydrocarbons that are trapped in the Earth's crust. Natural gas consists mainly of methane (CH_4). It is extracted in gaseous form and then liquefied under pressure for transport and storage.

neutral solution A solution in which the concentration of hydronium ions (H_3O^+) equals the concentration of hydroxide ions (OH^-), so it is neither acidic nor basic. At 25°C a neutral solution has a pH of exactly 7.

neutralisation reaction A reaction in which an acid reacts with a base to form a salt plus water in a solution with a pH of 7.

neutralise To react an acid with a base in stoichiometric proportions to form a solution of a salt and water.

nitrification The oxidation of ammonia or ammonium ion in the soil to nitrate ions

nominal variable A non-numerical variable with categories but no order associated with it.

non-equilibrium system A system that is not at equilibrium and can never reach an equilibrium state. The reactions involving such systems are considered to be irreversible.

non-renewable Referring to resources that cannot be replaced at the rate at which they are used.

non-spontaneous reaction A reaction that would not normally occur without the application of electrical energy. Compare *spontaneous reaction*.

nuclear magnetic resonance (NMR) spectroscopy A technique used to analyse materials using the interaction of the nucleus of particular isotopes, most commonly usually ^1H or ^{13}C, with an external magnetic field and electromagnetic radiation.

nuclear magnetic resonance (NMR) spectrum The representation in graph form of the energy required to change a nucleus from a low energy spin state to a high-energy spin state.

nuclear shielding Modification of the magnetic field experienced by a nucleus in an external magnetic field caused by the magnetic field of surrounding atoms in the molecule.

nuclear spin A property of a nucleus with an odd number of protons or neutrons that causes it to interact with a magnetic field. The nuclear spin can be either with or against an external magnetic field.

O

open system A system that allows matter and energy to be exchanged with the surroundings.

ordinal variable Non-numerical variable that has some sort of order associated with it.

organic molecule A molecule that is based on a hydrocarbon skeleton. Many organic molecules also contain non-metal elements such as oxygen, nitrogen, sulfur and chlorine.

outlier A value that lies well outside the trend line for a set of data.

oxidation reaction a reaction where a chemical species such as a metal atom or a non-metal ion loses electrons.

P

p-function A negative logarithmic function used to determine the strength of a variable or interaction. For example, pH is the measure of acidity of a solution.

parallax error The perceived shift in an object's position when it is viewed from different angles.

parent molecule The alkane from which the name of a molecule is derived.

percentage dissociation A measure of the amount of acid or base that has dissociated in a solution.

percentage uncertainty A measure of the uncertainty of a measurement, compared to the measured value.

percentage yield A measure of the quantity of a product obtained from a chemical process, compared to the maximum amount possible if the reaction were complete, expressed as a percentage.

personal protective equipment (PPE) Equipment such as laboratory coats, gloves and goggles, designed to be worn by an individual for protection against hazards.

persuasion Attempting to convince (someone of) or induce an opinion or outcome.

petrodiesel The most common form of diesel fuel. It is produced from crude oil by fractional distillation. The composition of petrodiesel varies, but is generally around 75% alkanes and 25% aromatic hydrocarbons. The alkanes range from $C_{10}H_{22}$ to $C_{15}H_{32}$.

pH A measure of acidity and the concentration of hydronium ions, in solution. Acidic solutions have a pH value less than 7 at 25°C and bases have a pH value greater than 7 (at 25°C). Mathematically, pH is defined as $pH = -\log_{10}[H_3O^+]$.

pH curve A graph of pH against volume of titrant

pH scale See *pH*

phenomenon Something that occurs and can be observed to have occurred.

phosphate buffer An important buffer system that operates in the internal fluid of all cells that works to stabilise pH.

photosynthesis The chemical process by which oxygen and glucose are produced in plant cells in the presence of light.

pie chart A graph that displays relative proportions of quantities as slices of a 'pie'.

pipette A calibrated glass tube used to transfer very accurate volumes of liquid.

pK_a A measure of the extent of dissociation of an acid; $pK_a = -\log_{10}(K_a)$.

plastic A property of a material that can be reshaped by application of heat and pressure. In society, polymers are often referred to as plastics.

plasticiser Small molecules that soften a plastic by weakening intermolecular attractions between polymer chains.

pOH See *pOH scale*

pOH scale A measure of basicity and the concentration of hydroxide ions in solution. Basic solutions have a pOH value less than 7 at 25°C and acids have a pOH value greater than 7 (at 25°C). Mathematically, pOH is defined as $pOH = -\log_{10}[OH^-]$.

polar Referring to bonds or molecules with a permanent dipole.

polar bond A covalent bond in which the electrons are not shared equally between the two atoms in the bond.

polyamide A condensation polymer formed from the reaction of monomers with amine and carboxyl functional groups

polyester A condensation polymer formed from the reaction of monomers with hydroxyl and carboxyl functional groups

polymer A long-chain molecule that is formed by the reaction of thousands or millions of repeating units (monomers).

polymerisation The process of synthesising a polymer.

polyprotic acid An acid molecule that generates more than one hydronium ion when ionised in water.

position isomer An isomer that arises from having the functional group on a different location on the carbon chain.

position of equilibrium The relative amounts of reactants and products at equilibrium. The position of equilibrium varies depending on the extent of the reaction.

precipitate The solid formed during a reaction in which two or more solutions are mixed.

precipitation reaction A reaction between substances in solution in which one of the products is insoluble.

precision A measure of how close measurements are to each other. Measurements that are very close to each other are said to be precise. Compare with *accuracy*.

primary alcohol An alcohol in which the carbon that is bonded to the –OH group is only attached to one alkyl group.

primary amide An amide that is bonded only to a carbonyl carbon.

primary amine An amine in which the nitrogen atom is bonded to one carbon and two hydrogen atoms.

primary source A source that is a first-hand account derived from original research.

primary standard A substance of known high purity that may be dissolved in a known volume of solvent.

proton acceptor A negatively charged ion that will react with a positively charged hydrogen ion; in Brønsted-Lowry theory this is referred to as a base.

proton donor A substance that gives a proton to a base; in Brønsted-Lowry theory this is referred to as an acid.

proton NMR spectroscopy Also called ^1H NMR spectroscopy. A type of nuclear magnetic resonance spectroscopy that investigates the ^1H nucleus. It is used to determine the chemical environment of hydrogen atoms in compounds and gives information about the environments neighbouring each hydrogen atom.

purpose The aim of an investigation.

Q

qualitative Relating to the characteristics or qualities of a variable, rather than to measured values.

qualitative analysis An analysis to determine the identity of the chemicals present in a substance.

qualitative variable A variable that is measured according to its characteristics or qualities, rather than numerically.

quality control Procedures used to ensure that a product or service conforms to a set of quality criteria.

quantitative Relating to measured values rather than quality.

quantitative analysis An analysis to determine the concentration of the chemicals present in a mixture.

quantitative variable A variable that is measured numerically, rather than by characteristics or qualities.

R

random error An error that is the result of an unknown or unpredictable factor. Unlike systematic errors, random errors have no regular pattern.

rate of reaction The change in concentration of a reactant or product over a period of time (usually one second).

raw data The information and results collected and recorded during an experiment.

reaction pathway A series of chemical reactions that converts reactants into a product in a number of steps.

reaction quotient This is another name for the concentration fraction. It is the ratio of concentrations of products to reactants in a reversible reaction, as expressed in the equilibrium law.

reaction table A tool for solving equilibrium problems, sometimes referred to as an ICE table, where I stands for the initial amounts (or concentrations) for each species in the reaction mixture, C represents the change in the amounts (or concentrations) for each species as the system moves towards equilibrium, and E represents the equilibrium amounts (or concentrations) of each species when the system is in a state of equilibrium.

reliability The consistency of results when an experiment is repeated.

renewable Resources are renewable if they are not finite (e.g. wind power) or can be replenished (e.g. biochemical fuels).

renewable energy source An energy source that is not finite (e.g. wind power) or can be replenished (e.g. biochemical fuels).

renewable resource a resource that is not finite (e.g. wind power) or can be replenished (e.g. biochemical fuels)

reputation How well a person or organisation is known or perceived.

reversible reaction A reaction in which significant reaction can occur in the reverse direction because the products present and can react with each other under suitable conditions.

rhetoric A style of communicating that aims to be persuasive.

S

safety data sheet (SDS) A summary of the risks of using a particular chemical, including measures to be followed to reduce risk.

salinity The amount of salt present in water or soil. Salinity is usually measured in parts per thousand (ppt or ‰), $mg\,L^{-1}$ or $g\,kg^{-1}$.

salt A substance formed from a metal or ammonium cation and an anion. Salts are the products of reactions between acids and bases, metal oxides, carbonates or reactive metals.

saponification A process in which soap is produced by heating a fat or vegetable oil in the presence of an alkali.

saturated (1) Referring to an organic molecule that contains only carbon–carbon single bonds. (2) Referring to a solution that contains the maximum amount of solute that can normally be dissolved at a particular temperature.

saturated solution See *saturated* (definition 2).

scatter plot A graph of bivariate data (data that contains values for two variables) represented as points on a number plane.

second law of thermodynamics A law that states that the total entropy of the universe cannot decrease over time, so that the amount of entropy in the universe is always increasing.

secondary alcohol An alcohol in which the carbon bonded to the –OH group is also bonded to two alkyl groups. The alkyl groups can be the same or different.

secondary source A source that used data or information derived from another source.

self-ionisation An ionisation reaction of pure water in which water behaves as both an acid and a base.

shale gas Natural gas that is trapped in shale rock, usually well below Earth's surface.

side chain The R group in an amino acid molecule.

significant figures The number of digits in a value that indicates its accuracy.

slightly soluble Referring to a salt that will dissociate in water at a rate of $0.1–0.01\,mol\,L^{-1}$.

smelter The process in which a metal ore is heated in order to separate the metal from the other elements in the ore.

solubility A measure of the amount of solute dissolved in a given amount of solvent at a given temperature.

solubility product a measure of the equilibrium solubility of a sparingly soluble salt, equal to the product of the concentration of ions in a saturated solution of a sparingly soluble salt.

solubility table A reference table that can be used to predict the solubility of ionic compounds.

soluble Able to dissociate in water.

solute A substance that dissolves in a solvent. For example, sugar is the solute when it dissolves in water.

solution A homogeneous mixture of a solute dissolved in a solvent.

solvent A substance, usually a liquid, that is able to dissolve a solute to form a solution. Water is the most common solvent.

sparingly soluble Referring to a salt that dissociates to a very small extent in solution.

spectator ion An ion that remains in solution and is unchanged during a reaction. Spectator ions are usually not included in ionic equations.

spectroscopy Chemical analysis methods based on the way that radiation, especially ultraviolet and visible light, interacts with matter.

splitting pattern A multi-peaked signal produced by a proton in a ^1H NMR spectrum when it has hydrogens in neighbouring environments. The number of lines in the pattern is equal to the number of neighbouring hydrogen atoms plus one ($n + 1$).

spontaneous reaction A reaction that does not require an external source of energy. Spontaneous reactions produce energy, unlike non-spontaneous reactions.

standard solution A solution that has an accurately known concentration of solute.

standardised Referring to a solution for which the concentration of solute has been determined accurately, usually by titration with a standard solution.

static equilibrium The state of a chemical system when the rates of the forward and reverse reactions are equal and zero. There is no movement of reactant and product particles in either the forward or reverse direction.

stem name The name that corresponds to the prefix for the longest chain of carbons in the molecule

stoichiometry The calculation of relative amounts of reactants and products used or required in a chemical reaction. Balanced chemical equations give the whole-number ratios of the amounts (in moles) of reactants and products.

strong acid An acid that readily donates a hydrogen ion (proton) to a base.

strong base A base that readily accepts a hydrogen ion (proton) from an acid.

structural formula A formula that represents the three-dimensional arrangement of atoms in a molecule and shows all bonds as well as all atoms.

structural isomers Compounds with the same molecular formula but different structures.

substitution reaction A reaction that involves the replacement of an atom or group of atoms with another atom or group of atoms.

super acid An acid that has acidity greater than the acidity of 100% sulfuric acid.

surfactant A substance consisting of long molecules with one hydrophobic 'tail' and one hydrophilic 'head' that are able to form micelles and modify the surface properties of a liquid. The name is an abbreviation of 'surface-active agent'.

surroundings The rest of the universe around a particular chemical reaction. The chemical reaction is the system. Energy moves between the system and surroundings in exothermic and endothermic reactions.

sustainable Able to support energy and resources into the future without depletion.

system In chemistry, a system is a chemical reaction. A system operates within its surroundings. Energy can move between the two. You always consider energy as being absorbed or released from the perspective of the system. For example, energy is absorbed into the system from the surroundings, or energy is released by the system to the surroundings.

systematic error An error that produces a constant bias in measurement. (Systematic errors are eliminated or minimised through calibration of apparatus and the careful design of a procedure.)

T

tertiary alcohol An alcohol in which the carbon bonded to the –OH group is also bonded to three alkyl groups.

tetrahedral Having the shape of a tetrahedron, in which four points are at equal distances from each other and spread as far apart as possible in three dimensions.

theoretical yield The mass of product that would be formed if the limiting reagent reacted fully.

thermochemical equation A chemical equation that includes the enthalpy change of the reaction, ΔH. For example:
$$2H_2(g) + O_2(g) \rightarrow 2H_2O(g) \quad \Delta H = -572\,kJ\,mol^{-1}$$

thermoplastic A polymer that softens and melts when heated, allowing it to be remoulded or recycled. This is a result of the intermolecular bonds breaking, allowing the molecules to become free to move.

thermosetting A polymer that does not melt when heated. Instead, at high temperatures the covalent bonds are broken and the polymer decomposes or burns. Thermosetting polymers therefore cannot be remoulded into a different shape.

titrant An acidic or basic solution of known concentration used in a titration.

titration The process used to determine the concentration of a reactant where one solution is added from a burette to a known volume of another solution.

titration curve A plot of the volume of titrant added to a solution against the pH of of the solution.

titre The volume of liquid, measured by a burette, used in a titration.

transmittance The ratio of light that passes through a sample compared to the light given off by the source.

trend An observed pattern of data in a particular direction.

trend line A line indicating the general trend of data on a graph. Also known as line of best fit.

triprotic acid An acid molecule that generates three hydronium ions when ionised in water.

U

uncertainty An error associated with measurements made during experimental work.

unsaturated (1) Referring to a hydrocarbon that is composed of molecules with one or more carbon–carbon double or triple bonds. (2) Referring to a solution that contains less solute than is in a saturated solution at the same temperature.

unsaturated solution See *unsaturated* (definition 2).

ultraviolet–visible (UV–visible) spectrometer An analytical device that measures the absorbance of a solution in the UV–visible region of the spectrum. Also known as UV–visible spectrophotometer.

V

valence number The number of valence electrons (electrons in the outer shell) in an atom of an element.

valence shell electron pair repulsion theory (VSEPR) A model used to predict the shape of molecules. The basis of VSEPR is that the valence electron pairs surrounding an atom mutually repel each other, and therefore adopt an arrangement that minimises this repulsion, thus determining the molecular shape.

validity Refers to whether the evidence supports an argument.

variable Any factor that can be controlled, changed and measured in an experiment.

vibrational energy levels Different fixed energies that molecules can have as a result of the bending and stretching of bonds.

volumetric analysis An analysis involving the measurement of volumes, such as titration.

volumetric flask A laboratory flask calibrated to contain a precise volume.

vulcanisation A chemical process for converting natural rubber or related polymers into more durable materials by the addition of sulfur or other cross-linking agents.

W

water cycle The continuous process by which water is circulated throughout the Earth and its atmosphere. Water passes into the atmosphere as water vapour, falls to Earth in liquid or solid form, passes into groundwater, lakes, streams or oceans, and returns to the atmosphere through evaporation.

wavenumber A unit of frequency used in infrared spectroscopy. It is equal to the inverse of the wavelength of the radiation, and is measured in cm^{-1}.

weak acid An acid that is only partly ionised in water.

weak base A base that accepts hydrogen ions (protons) from acids only to a limited extent.

Y

yield The amount of product formed in a chemical reaction.

Z

Ziegler–Natta catalyst A catalyst for addition polymerisation developed by Karl Ziegler and Giulio Natta. The catalyst contains a mixture of titanium chloride ($TiCl_3$) and triethylaluminium ($Al(CH_2CH_5)_3$).

Index

Attributions

Cover image: Dennis Kunkel/Microscopy/Science Photo Library.

The following abbreviations are used in this list: t = top, b = bottom, l = left, r = right, c = centre.

123RF: Radu Razvan Gheorghe, p. 377r; Sergei Gorin, p. 333t; Kjersti Jorgensen, p. 99; kajornyot, p. 298; Logos2012, p. 325c; Luchschen, p. 528l; Dmytrii Minishev, p. 379t; nitr, p. 357; picsfive, p. 53.

AAP: Thiess/PR Handout Image, p. 411b; Dean Lewins, p. 528r; Paul Miller, p. 54tl.

Age Fotostock: Mirco Vacca, p. 271l.

Alamy Stock Photo: a-plus image bank, p. 107b; Robert Brook, p. 524; BSIP SA, p. 490; Lee Dalton/JPL/NASA, p. 495; Jeff J Daly, p. 199; DOE Photo, p. 311l; Genevieve Vallee, p. 531b; Anna Gowthorpe, p. 529c; Greenshoots Communications, p. 339; Mike Greenslade/ VWPics, p. 530c; Hemis, p. 252cbl; Richard Heyes, p. 364; Steffen Hauser, p. 181; Peter Horree, p. 117t; Huntstock, p. 305; Mike Kahn/Green Stock Media, p. 326; RooM the Agency, p. 252tl; Sciencephotos, pp. 145t, 415r; Science History Images, p. 302l; Martin Shields, p. 56; Sueddeutsche Zeitung Photo, p. 61; Melissa Teo, p. 304c.

Auscape International Photo Library: Frank Woerle, p. 201t.

Australian Science Teachers Association: Australian Science Teachers Association 2016, except where indicated otherwise. This work is licensed under a Creative Commons Attribution 3.0 license, p. 307.

Chemistry Australia: p. 519.

Chemistry Education Association: Bob Hogendoorn, p. 195.

Chemlink: Data from "Overview," Chemlink, www.chemlink.com.au/industry.htm, p. 520.

CSIRO Publishing: Reproduced with permission from CSIRO Publishing. The cover from taken from AJC Volume 70, issue 4, www.publish.csiro.au/CH/issue/8366, p. 6.

Government of Western Australia: Department of Primary Industries and Regional Development, Government of Western Australia © 2016, p. 233r.

Fairfax: Based on: 'Iron ore price hammered below $US50 per tonne', Australian Financial Review, afr.com, p. 529t; Rohan Thomson. The Canberra Times., p. 522t.

Flickr: Brisbane City Council. Photo provided by Friends of Sherwood Arboretum Association Inc. Used under CC BY 2.0 License., p. 200tr; Tatiana Gerus. Licensed under CC BY 2.0 License., p. 253.

Fotolia: ALCE, p. 410; Andrea Danti, p. 54tr; Disto89, p. 374t; Dreaming Andy, p. 278; EuToch, p. 380; Freer, p. 375l; Kilala, p. 145b; gmstockstudio, p. 333b; Jeayesy, p. 374c; molekuul.be, p. 376; Nomad_Soul, p. 374b; Popova Olga, p. 375r; Roy Pedersen, p. 272; PhotoSGr, p. 282; pixdesign123, p. 116; siraphol, p. 252cr; Smileus, p. 416t; Syda Productions, p. 427br; tadamichi, p. 27; taddie, p. 427tl; Michael Tewes, p. 276; Bogdan Vasilescu, p. 252br; Maren Winter, p. 343t; thieury, p. 97b.

Getty Images: BanksPhotos, p. 444r; Boyer/Roger Viollet, p. 93; Greg Elms, p. 271r; Cathy Finch, p. 427tr; MacGregor, p. 377l; Diana Mayfield, p. 226; Mitch Reardon, p. 83; John Sanford, p. 450tl; Prof. K Seddon & J.Van Denberg/Queen's University, Belfast, p. 294-5; James L. Stanfield/National Geographic, p. 413; Andrew Unangst, p. 64l; Keith Wood, p. 334.

Manildra Group: p. 338; p. 522b.

Melburnian: Licensed under a CC BY 3.0 license., p. 360.

National Center for Biotechnology Information: PubChem Compound Database; CID=9576780, pubchem.ncbi.nlm.nih.gov/ compound/9576780 (accessed Dec 5, 2017)., p. 33.

Newspix: Jane Ollerenshaw, p. 477.

Pearson Education Ltd: Alice McBroom, pp. 103, 146, 191, 284; Natalie Book, p. 384 (all).

Pharmaceutical Journal: Royal Pharmaceutical Society, p. 358.

Powershop: Based on 'Changing electricity prices in NSW and what that means if you're our customer', https://blog.powershop.com.au/ changing-electricity-prices-nsw-2016/, p. 534.

Qenos Pty Ltd: p. 521.

Rural Industries Research and Development Corporation: Based on Konczak, L., et al. *Health Benefits of Australian Native Foods; An evaluation of health-enhancing compounds,* RIRDC Pub. No. 09/133 © 2009 Rural Industries Research and Development Corporation, Canberra., p. 201b.

Sanders, Robert: Courtesy of Robert Sanders, p. 453.

Science Photo Library: pp. 171c, 171t, 248-9, 398-403, 390b, 416b, 464c; Andrew Lambert Photography, pp. 13l, 13r, 76, 105, 147, 163, 169, 170, 321r, 436, 464t, 468t, 468c; Dr Juerg Alean, p. 450tr; BeautifulChemistry.net, pp. 72-3; Estate of Francis Bello, p. 365; British Antarctic Survey, p. 235b; British Library, p. 124r; Andrew Brookes, pp. 460-1; Dr Jeremy Burgess, pp. 385, 412; Martyn F. Chillmaid, pp. 193, 314l, 314r, 321c, 321l, 383, 411r, 417br, 417l, 417tr, 419, 421, 444l, 463, 464br; Carlos Clarivan, p. 449; Colin Cuthbert, p. 469bl; Jack Dykinga/US Department of Agriculture, p. 469t; Jan Hinsch, p. 235t; Steve Horrell, p. 184-5; Mikkel Juul Jensen, p. 311r; Geoff Kidd, p. 232; Dorling Kindersley/UIG, p. 114l; Dennis Kunkel/Microscopy, p. i; R.E. Litchfield, p. 388t; Middle Temple Library, p. 131b; Cordelia Molloy, p. 81; National Oceanic and Atmospheric Administration (NOAA), pp. 236b, 236t; National Optical Astronomy Observatories, p. 450b; Oxford University Images, p. 480; Alfred Pasieka, p. 113; Paul Rapson, pp. 392, 454; Victor De Schwanberg, p. 261; David Taylor, p. 77; TEK Image, pp. 64r, 469br; Trevor Clifford Photography, p. 302r; Javier Trueba/MSF, pp. 50-1, 55; Uk Crown Copyright of Fera, pp. 404-5, 537-44.

Science Source - Photo Researchers, Inc: Charles D. Winters, p. 128.

Scotch College: Chris Commons, p. 92.

Shutterstock: 540784, pp. 318-9; 612202, p. 337r; Adwo, p. 530b; Africa Studio, p. 198r; AG-Photos, p. 49, 135-40; Albo003, p. 161; Alybaba, p. 200l; Vladimirskaya Anastasia, p. 299; Leonid Andronov, p. 323; Anneka, p. 327; Andrey Armyagov, p. 198l; auremar, p. 115; Andrey Bayda, p. 325bl; Arindambanerjee, p. 529b; David Barber, p. 518; Bildagentur Zoonar GmbH, p. 530t; Brocreative, p. 107t; cobalt88, p. 131t; Coprid, p. 171b; Edith Czech, p. 54bl; dextroza, p. 415l; Hywit Dimyadi, p. 325br; DoubleO, pp. 141, 243-7; Everett Historical, p. 124l; e X p o s e, p. 57; FeyginFoto, p. 381; FiledIMAGE, p. 336b; Nor Gal, p. 532t; Frank Gaertner, p. 304t; Gemenacom, p. 59; Eric Gevaert, p. 337bl; Albina Glisic, p. 336c; Gnohz, p. 337tl; Richard Goldberg, p. 343c; Antonio Guillem, p. 390t; Shawn Hempel, p. 532b; ang intaravichian, p. 114r; isak55, p. 2-3; Jillian Cain Photography, p. 130; Dmitry Kalinovsky, p. 523l; Kamilpetran, p. 523r; Elena Kharichkina, p. 197b; Josipa Kosanovic, p. 121; Olesya Kuznetsova, p. 310; Magnetix, pp. 362b, 362t, 448; michaeljung, p. 41; Teerasak Ladnongkhum, p. 373; Christian Lagerek, p. 517; John Le, p. 411t; Katrina Leigh, p. 427bl; Michal Ludwiczak, pp. 142-3; Magnetix, p. 167; Shane Maritch, p. 252bl; Patrizio Martorana, p. 531t; Mastersky, p. 200br; melissaf84, p. 123; Dmitri Melnik, p. 66; ppart, p. 252clt; prudkov, p. 343b; Stefan Redel, p. 97t. Viktorija Reuta, pp. 15r, 46; royaltystockphoto.com, p. 87; Ivan_Sabo, p. 353; Phil Schlicht, pp. 250-1; sevenke, p. 231; Annette Shaff, p. 296; Smileus, pp. 308-9; Standard Studio, p. 388b; Alexy Stiop, p. 197t; ThamKC, p. 388c; Maria Uspenskaya, pp. 348-9; Andrii Vodolazhskyi, p. 91; wavebreakmedia, p. 117b.

SDBSWeb: sdbs.db.aist.go.jp, National Institute of Advanced Industrial Science and Technology, 27 October 2017., pp. 484-6, 493.

Smithsonian Institution, National Museum of American History: Earl S. Tupper Papers, Archives Center, National Museum of American History, Smithsonian Institution, p. 379b.

Soil Quality Pty Ltd: http://soilquality.org.au/factsheets/soil-acidity, p. 233l.

Vigan, Tyler: Spurious Correlations, tylervigan.com. Data sources: U.S. Department of Agriculture and Centers for Disease Control & Prevention, p. 27.